Chapter Title	Focus Company Used in Main Illustration	Focus Company Logo	Type of Organization
12. Financial and Cost-Volume-Profit Models	Fairfield Blues, Inc.	Fairfield BLUES INC.	Owner of minor league baseball team
13. Cost Management and Decision Making	Bootstrap Industries	Bootstrap INDUSTRIES	Non-profit company providing jobs
14. Making Long-Term Capital Investment Decisions	Rascals, Inc.	Rascals inc.	Book and music retailer
15. Budgeting and Financial Planning	Collegiate Apparel Company	CAC COLLEGIATE APPAREL COMPANY	Small manufacturer of college T-shirts
16. Standard Costing, Variance Analysis, and Kaizen Costing	Koala Camp Gear Company	Koala Camp Gear Company	Manufacturer of camping tents
17. Flexible Budgets, Overhead Cost Management, and Activity-Based Budgeting	Koala Camp Gear Company	Koala Camp Gear Company	Manufacturer of camping tents
18. Organizational Design, Responsibility Accounting, and Evaluation of Divisional Performance	Outback Outfitters, Ltd.	OUTBACK OUTFITTERS	Large retailer of camping equipment and apparel
19. Transfer Pricing	Outback Outfitters, Ltd.	OUTBACK OUTFITTERS	Large retailer of camping equipment and apparel
20. Using Lead and Lag Measures to Communicate, Motivate, and Evaluate	Valley Commercial Bank	Valley COMMERCIAL BANK	Independent, five-branch bank
21. Incentive Systems and Performance Evaluation	Valley Commercial Bank	Valley COMMERCIAL BANK	Independent, five-branch bank

Second Edition

Cost Management

Strategies for Business Decisions

Ronald W. Hilton
Cornell University

Michael W. Maher
University of California, Davis

Frank H. Selto
University of Colorado at Boulder
The University of Melbourne

McGraw-Hill Irwin

Boston Burr Ridge, IL Dubuque, IA Madison, WI New York San Francisco St. Louis
Bangkok Bogotá Caracas Kuala Lumpur Lisbon London Madrid Mexico City
Milan Montreal New Delhi Santiago Seoul Singapore Sydney Taipei Toronto

McGraw-Hill Higher Education
A Division of The ***McGraw-Hill*** *Companies*

COST MANAGEMENT: STRATEGIES FOR BUSINESS DECISIONS
Published by McGraw-Hill/Irwin, a business unit of The McGraw-Hill Companies, Inc., 1221 Avenue of the Americas, New York, NY, 10020.
Some ancillaries, including electronic and print components, may not be available to customers outside the United States.

This book is printed on acid-free paper.

1 2 3 4 5 6 7 8 9 0 WCK/WCK 0 9 8 7 6 5 4 3 2

ISBN 0-07-247434-3

Publisher: *Brent Gordon*
Sponsoring editor: *Steve DeLancey*
Managing developmental editor: *Gail Korosa*
Marketing manager: *Ryan Blankenship*
Senior project manager: *Christine A. Vaughan*
Manager, new book production: *Melonie Salvati*
Coordinator freelance design: *Mary L. Christianson*
Senior producer, Media technology: *David Barrick*
Supplement producer: *Susan Lombardi*
Photo research coordinator: *Judy Kausal*
Photo researcher: *Charlotte Goldman*
Freelance designer: *Design Solutions*
Cover photograph: *© Image Bank*
Typeface: *11/12 Times Roman*
Compositor: *Carlisle Communications, Ltd.*
Printer: *Quebecor World Versailles, Inc.*

Library of Congress Cataloging-in-Publication Data

Hilton, Ronald W.
Cost management : strategies for business decisions / Ronald W. Hilton, Michael W. Maher, Frank H. Selto.—2nd ed.
p. cm.
Includes bibliographical references and index.
ISBN 0-07-247434-3 (alk. paper)
1. Managerial accounting. 2. Cost accounting. I. Maher, Michael, 1946- II. Selto, Frank H. III. Title.
HF5657.4.H548 2003
658.15'52—dc21 2001055801

INTERNATIONAL EDITION ISBN 0-07-115099-4

www.mhhe.com

To my wife, Meg, and to our sons, Tim and Brad.

Ronald W. Hilton

To my family: my wife Miriam, my daughters Krista and Andrea, and my father Bill, who have taught me just about everything worth knowing.

Michael W. Maher

To my parents, Frank and Dorothy Selto, who taught me the value of love, hard work, and integrity. To my wife, Linda, and sons, Michael and Mark, who inspire and support me. To my first accounting teachers, Bill Bruns and Gary Sundem, who surprised me by demonstrating that accounting can be fun, useful, and intellectually challenging and that an academic career can be immensely rewarding. Finally, to my students, who every semester teach me something significant.

Frank H. Selto

About the Authors

Ronald W. Hilton A Professor of Accounting at Cornell University, Professor Hilton teaches in the areas of managerial accounting and cost-management systems. With bachelor's and master's degrees in accounting from The Pennsylvania State University, he received his Ph.D. from The Ohio State University.

A Cornell faculty member since 1977, Professor Hilton also has taught accounting at Ohio State and the University of Florida, where he held the position of Walter J. Matherly Professor of Accounting. Prior to pursuing his doctoral studies, Hilton worked for Peat, Marwick, Mitchell and Company and served as an officer in the United States Air Force.

Professor Hilton is a member of the Institute of Management Accountants and has been active in the American Accounting Association. He has served as associate editor of *The Accounting Review* and as a member of its editorial board. Hilton also has served on the editorial board of *Journal of Management Accounting Research.* He has been a member of the resident faculties of both the Doctoral Consortium and the New Faculty Consortium sponsored by the American Accounting Association.

With wide-ranging research interests, Professor Hilton has published articles in many journals, including the *Journal of Accounting Research, The Accounting Review, Management Science, Decision Sciences, The Journal of Economic Behavior and Organization, Contemporary Accounting Research,* and the *Journal of Mathematical Psychology.* Author of *Managerial Accounting,* he also has published a monograph in the AAA *Studies in Accounting Research* series. He is a co-author of *Budgeting: Profit Planning and Control* and of *Cost Accounting: Concepts and Managerial Applications.* Hilton's current research interests focus on contemporary cost-management systems and international issues in managerial accounting. In recent years, he has toured manufacturing facilities and consulted with practicing managerial accountants in North America, Europe, Asia, and Australia.

Michael W. Maher A Professor of Management at the University of California–Davis, Professor Maher previously taught at the University of Michigan, the University of Chicago, and the University of Washington. He also worked on the audit staff at Arthur Andersen & Co. and was a self-employed financial consultant for small businesses. He received his BBA from Gonzaga University (which named him Distinguished Alumnus in 1989) and his MBA and Ph.D. from the University of Washington, and he earned the CPA from the state of Washington.

Professor Maher was president of the Management Accounting Section of the American Accounting Association and has served on the editorial boards of *The Accounting Review, Accounting Horizons, Journal of Management Accounting Research,* and *Management Accounting.* Co-author of two leading textbooks, *Principles of Accounting* and *Managerial Accounting,* Maher has co-authored several additional books and monographs, including *Internal Controls in U.S. Corporations* and *Management Incentive Compensation Plans,* and published articles in many journals, including *Management Accounting, The Journal of Accountancy, The Accounting Review, Journal of Accounting Research, Financial Executive,* and *The Wall Street Journal.*

For his research on internal controls, Professor Maher was awarded the American Accounting Association's Competitive Manuscript Award and the AICPA Notable Contribution to Literature Award. He also has received the award for the Outstanding Tax Manuscript, and from the students at the University of California's Graduate School of Management, he has received the Annual Outstanding Teacher Award three times and a special award for outstanding service twice. Maher's current research includes studies of the efficacy of online education, health care costs, and corporate corruption.

Frank H. Selto Professor Selto has been on the faculty at the University of Colorado at Boulder since 1985, where he has taught accounting at the undergraduate and graduate levels and served as Division Chair of Accounting and Information Systems. Recently appointed a Research Fellow of the University of Melbourne, Selto has taught at the University of Denver, the University of Colorado at Denver, and the University of Washington. He holds MBA and Ph.D. degrees in accounting from the University of Washington and BS and MS degrees in mechanical engineering from Gonzaga University and the University of Utah, respectively. Prior to earning his MBA and Ph.D. degrees, he worked as a mechanical engineer and served as an officer in the US Army Corps of Engineers.

Active in the American Accounting Association and its Management Accounting Section, Professor Selto was the editor of the Education Research section of *The Accounting Review* and has served on the editorial boards of *The Accounting Review, Journal of Management Accounting Research, Management Accounting Research,* and *Accounting Horizons.* A researcher of management accounting and management control, Selto has published articles in the *Journal of Accounting Research, Accounting, Organizations & Society, Journal of Cost Management* and *Journal of Management Accounting Research,* one of which was recognized as a Notable Contribution to the Management Accounting Literature.

Introduction

We are pleased and excited to offer the second edition of the ground-breaking text, *Cost Management: Strategies for Business Decisions.* The new edition keeps the best features of the first and improves the rest. If you are new to this text, the Preface describes its mission and vision, which the changing world has reinforced. It also describes the text's key features, which we have refined, and each chapter's aims and strengths, which we have improved as well. Those who are returning to *Cost Management* will notice a somewhat different chapter order and several entirely new chapters—all the result of listening to you, who are both our customers and colleagues.

As we write this Preface, the world economy is recovering from the dot-com and high-technology bubble that burst. It seems as if an entire generation of entrepreneurs and investors believed or hoped that stock prices were keyed to revenues or promises of revenues. Millions of dot-com employees and investors were greatly disappointed to learn, after all, that companies must earn revenues and manage the other half of the income equation—costs, of course. Where we once saw free spending on corporate perquisites, we now observe managers carefully examining activities and expenditures to see if they truly add value in excess of their cost. This is what *Cost Management* is all about—adding more value at lower cost. We are convinced that there has never been a better time to sound our message: *Costs do not just happen; they are the result of management decisions.* Neither we nor our students can continue to passively measure costs; we must actively manage costs to deliver more value. We do our students and their (future) employers a disservice if we do not stress and deliver this message in tangible, memorable ways.

Vision and Mission

Steve Jackson—University of Southern Maine

I believe that we need to emphasize the use of accounting information and its use in decision making and start to move away from the accounting coverage from the preparer prospective. This book is moving in that direction.

Cost Management's original, proactive vision is stronger and more clearly presented in the second edition. Its vision is that every resource must be used to provide value or it is wasted. The most valuable contributions from accountants/financial analysts/consultants are analysis, interpretation, communication, and identification of opportunities for improvement. These uses of information are the focus of *Cost Management.*

Our mission (and that of the field of cost management) is to prepare the next generation of financial managers and consultants. These individuals will make decisions that greatly influence the cost structure and performance of organizations. The mission is communicated through presentation and explanation of "best cost-management practices" throughout the text.

Measurement of costs is still important, but accuracy is not as important as relevance and timeliness for key strategic decisions. In fact, most companies have automated their cost-accounting systems, so the actual task of measurement is now less important than the design, interpretation, and identification of opportunities and methods for improving costs and performance.

Development of the Second Edition

The first edition of *Cost Management* began as a concept based on extensive discussions among the authors and editors in 1997. The revision of the second edition began in earnest in the fall of 2000. We are convinced that the market is ready for this cost-management text that is grounded in best practices. Our beliefs are reinforced by the Institute of Management Accountants' 2000 survey of practice, which confirmed its 1997 study that the role of the "management accountant" has evolved dramatically in the past decade. Indeed, most individuals in this role do not identify themselves or their jobs as "accounting." Rather, they are internal "financial analysts" or "business consultants." We know that many progressive teachers of cost and managerial accounting have seen these changes and are ready for a text that supports their efforts to prepare their students for this exciting new set of challenges.

This second edition is the result of nearly three years of teaching experience with the text, feedback from adopters of the first edition, continued observation of the ever-changing world of cost management, and extensive reviews of drafts of new and revised chapters. The primary focus of writing the second edition has been to strengthen the message while improving the readability and accessibility of the innovative presentations of the text. We heard loud and clear that the first edition was greatly appreciated for its innovations but that we should improve the communication and presentation of some topics. Thus, in many ways, writing the second edition was as much work as the first edition because we sought to continue to innovate and improve without losing sight of our vision and mission. Reviewers of the second edition chapters overwhelmingly agree that we have succeeded, and we are pleased to present this revised text to the market.

Leslie Kren—University of Wisconsin (Milwaukee)
I think a lot of excellent work was done on the pedagogy in this text. Great illustrations from practice, thoughtful in-chapter problems. I think it is very well done.

Key Features

The text accomplishes its goals by incorporating five key elements to reinforce learning and retention throughout all chapters:

- Cost-management focus
- Realistic company settings
- Decision-making emphasis
- Best cost-management practices
- Reliable-research findings

Cost-Management Focus

The primary principle of cost management is that costs do not simply happen; they are the results of management decisions. To prevent mistakes and identify opportunities, cost management focuses on the anticipation of the impacts of alternative decisions. *Cost Management* combines value chain, activity-based costing, value-added analyses, activity-based management, and economic value added to build a logical and easily communicated view of the subject. This proactive cost-management perspective motivates all of the book's topics. This approach is not as radical as it might seem. More and more companies are adopting cost management in one way or another, and complementary business curricula (e.g., marketing, management, and operations) have embraced the approach.

Realistic Company Settings

The concepts and applications of each chapter are developed in the context of a focus company, which is closely based on the actual practices and experiences of a real company. Although the focus organizations are not real themselves, they are realistic and motivate students by making their cost-management study more tangible and interesting. The use of focus companies provides an environment in which abstract, conceptual discussions become more practical and communicate the decision-making context of cost management. This focus provides grounded, logical descriptions of the origins of cost-management problems and their solutions. The text has a balance of manufacturing, service, government, mature, and start-up focus companies to demonstrate that cost-management concerns are universally applicable.

Alexander Sannella—Rutgers University
The students absolutely love the "storyteller" pedagogy used with the sample companies.

Masako Darrough—
Baruch College (CUNY)
The discussion on nonprofits adds a real strength to the book.

The focus-company context also shows that strategic, cross-cultural, international, technological, or communication issues really do complicate concepts that at first seem straightforward. However, cost management contributes reliable principles that guide managers toward successful solutions.

Many companies, of all sizes and industries, have embraced team-based decision making. This is having a profound effect on the role of individuals who previously might have had predominantly functional roles and loyalties. Effective cost-management analysts participate in team decision making and understand how to work with individuals from different cultures and functional backgrounds. The text prominently features team decision making with emphases on interaction and communication.

The use of realistic focus companies provides the context in which cost-management is used to identify opportunities and prevent costly mistakes. These companies reflect real-world practices of large, established companies that have been improving their productivity by downsizing, embracing technology, and outsourcing many functions, including finance and accounting. The relatively fewer accountants in large firms must be more entrepreneurial and strategic in outlook. Furthermore, most job growth in the US economy comes from small companies. More dramatically, an entrepreneurial spirit is sweeping former state-controlled economies both in established and developing countries. Many opportunities for cost management exist around the world in small and start-up companies. The text provides numerous applications in smaller companies to illustrate cost management's impact.

CollegePak

CollegePak Company manufactures backpacks sold to college and high school students through college bookstores and other traditional retail outlets. Although the company started by focusing on the college market, which explains the name CollegePak, it has expanded into the high school market and now is considering an entry into the middle school and elementary school markets as well. The company operates a single production facility located in Trenton, New Jersey. CollegePak's market covers all regions of the United States, and the company has recently entered the European market. The family-owned company has been in business for 22 years, and its annual sales are now $4.5 million. CollegePak has been profitable every year since its founding by Gustavo Perez, who turned over the company's reins to his daughter, Maria, four years ago. Both credit the company's success to four factors: a reliable, durable, functional product; a successful marketing approach that focuses directly on the collegiate market; an outstanding group of employees from the top management team to the machine operators' helpers; and a strong commitment to sound cost-management practices. As Gustavo has said more than once, "You can't be successful in business unless you understand what it costs you to make your product. Then you must manage that cost diligently to consistently deliver value to customers at a price they will pay." CollegePak's current president echoes her father's sentiment, adding that "we have an outstanding cost-management team. It has pulled us out of the fire many a time by finding ways to create value at lower cost."

Decision-Making Emphasis

Joyce Berg—
University of Iowa
Chapters include a good coverage of tools used in decision making. Good students will gain a good working knowledge of tools they can use on the job. I actually get the feeling that my students could go into a firm and immediately add value.

Each chapter begins with the feature *Cost-Management Challenges,* which illustrate the chapter content the student must master. The *challenges* engage the student and require the integration of content, and are addressed in integrative discussions at the chapter's end.

Each of the book's focus companies faces critical decisions that motivate its use of cost-management principles. These decisions include how to use scarce capacity, whether to add a new complex line of business, and how to design incentives to motivate employees to take risks and find innovative solutions. Each chapter actively involves the student in this problem solving by posing content applications, called *You're the Decision Maker,* at key points in the chapter. These are neither quizzes nor examples of end-of-chapter problems. Rather, they are integral to the chapter because they extend the text by asking the student to apply the knowledge gained in the chapter to realistic conditions. These are excellent opportunities for students to flex their new cost-management muscles in a nonthreatening environment. They also can be used as the basis of interactive classroom discussions.

Cost-Benefit Analysis of Outsourcing

You're the **Decision Maker 1.5**

Refer to the information in Exhibit 1–6.

a. Explain why some costs and benefits in the analysis are quantified but others are not. How do you think Pursuit.Com measured the quantified costs and benefits?

b. Is it possible that the nonquantified costs or benefits of this decision could be more important than those that are quantified? Explain with an example from Exhibit 1–6.

c. Explain how the personnel, facilities, and support cost savings listed in Exhibit 1–6 might not result in actual cost savings.

d. *Team Focus:* Assume that you are the cost-management analyst assigned to the Pursuit.Com team that will make recommendations about outsourcing the company's accounts receivable process. How can you use the analysis to help the team's analysis and decision making? What problems and information needs should you anticipate?
How can you gather more information?

e. Ethical Considerations: Has Pursuit.Com identified all costs of the outsourcing alternative? If personnel are laid off or dismissed to realize cost savings, does Pursuit.Com have any obligations to those employees? Could the way that Pursuit.Com treats those employees affect retained or future employees? Explain.

(Solutions begin on page 22.)

James Russell Hardin—Pittsburg State University
The "You're the Decision Maker" activities are excellent, allowing the students to practice what has just been covered.

Best Cost-Management Practice

Many cost-management techniques originated in mature manufacturing companies. Thus, it makes sense to discuss these concepts as best practices that can be adapted to other settings. Service, government, and start-up organizations alike have found cost-management techniques to be immensely valuable. Since many developed countries are becoming service economies, extensive focus on cost management in service organizations will be beneficial to students who will find rewarding careers managing or consulting to service companies.

Most cost texts reflect a strong US influence, which is excessive for international audiences and too narrow for the many US students who will work in international companies. Many US-based companies generate more than half of their sales outside the country and work extensively through foreign subsidiaries or partners. The text adds case, survey, and empirical information regarding European, American, and Australasian experiences. *Cost Management in Practice* features demonstrate the applicability of cost management to well-known companies.

Catherine Usoff—Bentley College
I find the approach of the text to be very progressive and highly reflective of what cost accountants (or internal business consultants) will be doing in organizations.

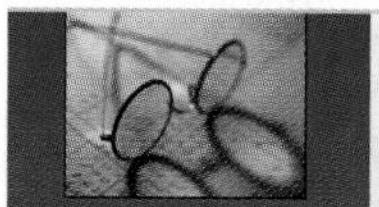

Cost Management in Practice 4.1

Use of Activity-Based Costing

Activity-based costing has maintained a high profile as a cost-management innovation for about two decades. Enough time has passed to assess whether it is a passing fad. Studies of company practices indicate that a large number of manufacturing and service companies, as well as some organizations in the public sector, are using ABC.

Some companies have tried ABC and dropped it. Reasons for this include its implementation cost. In the case of a Hewlett-Packard division that one of the authors studied, management obtained a great deal of information from ABC, restructured the company as a result, and no longer had the problems that ABC had uncovered. ABC had served its purpose and was no longer needed.

A recent survey of practices in the United Kingdom indicated that 37.8 percent of the companies that provided usable responses were using ABC or were considering using it. The study reported these results:

ABC Adoption Status	Number of Companies in Study	Percent of Companies in Study
Currently using it	31	17.5%
Currently considering using it	36	20.3
Considered but rejected it	27	15.3
Had not considered using it	83	46.9
Total	177	100.0%

Although ABC has its roots in manufacturing companies, the study found that the financial services companies surveyed were more likely to use ABC than were manufacturing companies. *Source: J. Innes, F. Mitchell, and D. Sinclair,* "Activity-Based Costing in the U.K.'s Largest Companies." *(Full citations to references are in the Bibliography.)*

Many management problems are communication problems. Accountants and financial analysts must learn to communicate their information, interpretations, and recommendations effectively. Otherwise, their use of cost-management techniques will not add value to organizations. The text stresses the importance of communication within and at the end of each chapter.

Reliable Research Findings

We know that answering the question, What kind of research do you do in accounting? can be difficult. This book is not an overt defense of academic research, but we believe that an effective way to demonstrate the value of research to both academics and cost managers is to include short descriptions of research studies that address important cost-management issues.

Catherine Usoff—Bentley College
The students should have an understanding of the research that is being done and what it can tell us about current business practices.

Cost-management research is an evolving field, and researchers are creating and applying new knowledge daily. This text incorporates cost-management research that has been replicated and applied successfully. These findings are used in examples, and particularly important findings are highlighted in *Research Insights.* Because cost management is a new and evolving field, research has not given us all the answers. Indeed, researchers have not identified all of the important questions. The text, therefore, does not accept all research uncritically and identifies important areas for future research in these features. We believe that this approach makes the inclusion of research more credible and can stimulate some students to regard research favorably in their careers and perhaps cause a few to seek careers in academia.

What Drives Costs?

Most discussions in the professional literature (e.g., journals such as *Strategic Finance, Journal of Cost Management*) focus on how to choose cost drivers for particular businesses. These discussions can be interesting accounts of the challenges that specific companies have faced, but little reliable evidence suggests whether a cost driver used in one company is the same cost driver that should be used in another company. Consequently, cost management analysts might feel the need to "reinvent the wheel" nearly every time they undertake a new activity-based costing project. The few studies of many companies, have found that the volume of outputs, the complexity of operations (e.g., many different types of products), and the nature of customer service activities have a significant effect on costs. *For example see A. M. Novin,* "Applying Overhead: How to Find the Right Bases and Rates," *for a basic approach. See also R. Banker and H. Johnson,* "An Empirical Study of Cost Drivers in the U.S. Airline Industry," *and G. Foster and M. Gupta,* "Manufacturing Overhead Cost Driver Analysis," *for more sophisticated approaches.*

Research Insight 4.1

Strong Pedagogy

Robert Lin—California State University, Hayward
The text has provided excellent pedagogy in all chapters.

To help students learn the principles of cost management and gain an appreciation for its importance in the contemporary business environment, *Cost Management* includes a wide range of pedagogical features.

- *Flexible sequence of chapters written in modular style.* The authors realize that instructors of cost management prefer to cover topics in a course in a widely different order. We have chosen a topical sequence that makes sense to us, but we also have endeavored to write modular chapters to the extent possible. This makes it possible for instructors who wish to cover the topics in a different sequence to do so.
- *Learning objectives.* Each chapter's learning objectives appear at the beginning of the chapter and are repeated in the margin where they are first addressed. Moreover, the learning objectives covered by each end-of-chapter exercise, problem, or case are indicated in the margin next to the assignment item.
- *Cost-Management Challenges.* This feature at the beginning of each chapter is intended to engage the students in mastering the chapter's content.
- *Focus companies.* These realistic organizations provide a framework in which to present comprehensive illustrations to stimulate students' interest in cost-management topics. All of the topics in each chapter are covered in the context of the same focus company. The illustration begins with a company document, such as a memo, report, or email correspondence, which alludes to the issues to be addressed in the chapter. A company logo appears throughout the chapter to tie exhibits and topical coverage to the focus illustration.
- *Photos.* A photograph at the beginning of each chapter depicts an important aspect of the focus company and adds to the realism of the coverage. In

addition, numerous photos from real-world organizations depict operational concepts and cost-management practices. These photos are intended to engage the students and emphasize key points.

- *Spreadsheet exhibits.* Many of the exhibits are Excel spreadsheets used to make students more comfortable with this widely used analytical tool and emphasize its usefulness in the practice of cost management.
- *Key terms.* Key terms are defined in the text when they are introduced, and the definitions are repeated in the margins for easy reference. A list of each chapter's key terms appears at the end of the chapter along with a page reference to the term's definition. The key terms and their definitions also appear in the Glossary at the end of the text.
- *You're the Decision Maker.* These decision scenarios appear throughout each chapter to actively engage the students in the decisions the focus company faces.
- *Cost-management in practice.* This feature highlights the cost-management practices of real-world organizations.
- *Research insight.* This element in each chapter relates relevant and sound research findings to the chapter's topic.

End-of-Chapter Materials

Each chapter ends with approximately 50 items that reinforce and extend the chapter's learning objectives. These include assignments focusing on ethical issues, international dimensions, group work, Internet use, and communication skills. Logos are used to identify these assignments. Types of assignments include the following:

- **Review questions** relate to the main chapter topics. They require short written or verbal responses that can be synthesized directly from the text. Responding to these questions requires a basic mastery of the chapter's learning objectives.

Review Questions

1.1 Review and define each of the chapter's key terms.
1.2 What is the primary objective of cost management?
1.3 What is the concept of the value chain, and why is it important for cost management?
1.4 What is strategic decision making? Give examples of several strategic decisions.
1.5 What are some cost management techniques that help make better management decisions?
1.6 What are cross-functional teams, and why are they important?
1.7 How do companies use benchmarking to make important decisions?
1.8 How does outsourcing affect an organization's value chain?

- **Critical analysis questions** extend the chapter's learning to novel, complex, or ambiguous situations. These questions cannot be answered by rote memorization but require analytical reasoning by analogy or logical extension of chapter materials. They can be used to stimulate small group discussions.

Critical Analysis

2.20 Evaluate this statement: Issues of product costing are irrelevant for service organizations since they cannot build up inventories of services, and all costs for providing services are expensed in the period they are used. Service firms effectively use throughput costing.
2.21 Evaluate this statement: Issues of product costing are unimportant for virtual organizations that outsource their production operations.
2.22 Prepare a diagram that illustrates how the following resources—headquarters, facilities, division managers, information systems personnel—can be considered both direct and indirect in a company that has four operating divisions, each of which provides multiple services.
2.23 Respond to this comment from an economist friend: You cost-management analysts use an overabundance of cost terms to interest on any inventories they maintain. If divisions want to tie up the company's resources in inventory, then they should pay the company at least the interest it could be earning if the treasurer had the same amount of cash.
2.27 Explain how making more products than can be sold in a period can increase the organization's operating income. Is this a sustainable tactic to increase operating income? Would this happen in a service company, or is it an issue only in manufacturing companies? Explain.
2.28 Respond to this comment: Your analysis of last month's financial performance demonstrates that it really doesn't matter whether we use throughput, variable, or absorption costing. All the costs are accounted for; you've just put them in different places. I can't see what real difference this analysis makes. Isn't this just a bean-counting exercise?

Exercises are relatively straightforward repetitions or applications of chapter topics and analyses. Students can solve exercises by directly applying the analyses in each chapter or by obtaining additional information from the library or Internet. Completing exercises requires a basic mastery of each chapter's learning objectives.

Exercises

Exercise 6.21
Customer Profitability
LO1

An Internet search of the key phrase "customer profitability" results in thousands of "hits," many of which are Web sites of companies seeking to sell software or consulting services. Choose a sample of five of these Web-sites and write a memo that evaluates the information they present and how well they present it.

Exercise 6.22
Customer Database
LO1

Building a customer database can be expensive. Free information is available in the United States from the Census Bureau's Web site (*www.census.gov*). Visit this site (particularly the Economic Census link), and prepare a short report describing the type of information available that might be useful to start-up businesses.

Exercise 6.23
Customer Data Warehouse
LO1

Data mining and data warehousing techniques are potential tools to use to analyze customer profitability. Many companies have had disappointing results using them, however, despite great expense and effort in building data warehouses information. Search the internet for information about data mining and warehousing, and write a memo that makes recommendations for guiding a data warehouse project to deliver useful customer profitability information.

Exercise 6.24
Customer Profitability
LO2

Fontinalis Company produces, sells, and distributes two products, Brooks and Redds, to two types of customers, urban and rural. Using the following information, prepare a customer profitability statement:

Fontinalis Product Profitability	Total	Brooks	Redds
Contribution margin ratio	46.7%	40.0%	60.0%
Revenues	$9,000,000	$6,000,000	$3,000,000
Customer sales to:			
Sales of:		Urban	Rural
Brooks	100%	70%	30%
Redds	100%	20%	80%
Operating costs traced to customers	$3,000,000	$2,200,000	$800,000

Problems generally are more challenging than exercises because they either require more sophisticated analyses of specific topics or integrate several related topics. Problems often represent a realistic situation or a professional examination level of difficulty. The ability to solve each chapter's problems means that the student has achieved intermediate-level mastery of the chapter's learning objectives.

Problem 7.72
Cycle Time and Throughput Efficiency
LO 3

Insurance companies spend considerable resources on processing claims (which results in a claim denial or payment to cover a loss). Short, accurate processing is desirable because both customers and the company benefit by resolving claims satisfactorily and by using minimum resources to do so. To improve its insurance claims processing, Global Insurance Company began a pilot project in its Northwest Region claims office to track the time to process each new automobile loss claim during a recent quarter. Processing time begins when a company representative receives a claim and ends when the final settlement is reached. Following are time data related to processing these claims at the company's Northwest Region.

Average 8-Hour Days Spent in

Days to Complete	Percent	Number	Processing by Adjusters	Waiting for Adjusters	Waiting for Information	Revisions and Corrections	Average Cycle Time in Days
0–10	4%	11,520	0.25	3.50	4.10	0.12	7.97
11–20	10	28,800	0.34	8.10	10.10	0.11	18.65
21–30	30	86,400	0.65	9.40	15.20	0.15	25.40
31–40	24	69,120	1.30	9.10	25.60	0.28	36.28
41–50	19	54,720	2.40	11.90	31.40	0.44	46.14
51–60	8	23,040	2.90	12.30	38.20	0.88	54.28
More than 60	5	14,400	3.10	11.50	49.70	2.60	66.90
Total	100%	288,000					

Required

a. Compute the overall average cycle time and throughput efficiency ratio in total and for each stage of processing for automobile loss claims during the quarter. (*Note:* These data can be easily analyzed with a computer spreadsheet.)

b. Comment on the apparent cause(s) of long cycle times and low throughput efficiencies.

c. What recommendation would you make to Global Insurance Company to improve its processing of automobile loss claims?

- **Cases** are conceptually the most challenging chapter-ending materials. They usually are set in real or realistic company settings and show the ambiguous decision-making environment of cost-management practice. Cases, which rarely have a single correct solution, are excellent opportunities for advanced individual or small-group learning, class discussions, and presentations.

Cases

Case 5.51
Reengineering the Accounting Function
(LO 4, 6)

Communication

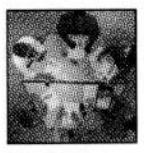
Team

An alternative to using ABM to identify opportunities for process improvement is to use benchmarking information to identify where an organization falls short of competitors and best practices. At 2 percent of sales, Cummins-Engine's overall accounting costs were twice as high as companies with world-class accounting functions, and the company was determined to improve. More detailed benchmarking information revealed that accounts payable costs and payroll costs were four and three times higher, respectively, than best practices. These areas seemed to offer the opportunity for great improvement. Cummins created a cross-functional team to analyze these transaction processes and make recommendations for improvement that would increase the quality of transaction processing and achieve best-practice costs (i.e., cost reductions of 75 percent).

Cummins Engine's top management was fully committed to the project. It provided resources to the project team that enabled it to educate Cummins' finance and operating personnel around the world about the project's methods and objectives. Management also committed to no forced layoffs of personnel whose jobs would be affected by resulting process changes.

In the early part of the project (the "baseline" phase), the team recognized that accounts payable, cash disbursement, and procurement processes should be integrated and located at a single site rather that at 50 sites within the United States alone, and that new software and hardware would be required. The team began with a pilot study, however, so that it could understand the complexities of the project before launching a worldwide implementation. The pilot study allowed the team to identify tangible objectives for the new system that included:

- Electronic data interchange (EDI).
- Linkage between procurement, accounts payable, and cash disbursement.
- Use of client-server technology.
- Outsourcing of non-value-added activities such as check printing.
- Improvement of process quality measures involving statistical quality-control techniques.
- Software compatible with Cummins' data architecture at a competitive price and with a user-friendly graphical interface.

Project implementation was phased in over a three-year period, with inflexible target dates for each phase and continuous communication with affected finance and operating personnel. The workforce in accounts payable was reduced by 80 percent, costs reached best-practice levels, and errors were reduced dramatically. (The workforce reduction occurred through attrition, assigning employees to other areas, and early retirement plans.)

Required

Form small groups to prepare a report that answers the following questions:

a. What are the differences between the activity-based management approach and the benchmarking approach used by Cummins Engine to identify opportunities for process improvement? What are the relative advantages and disadvantages of the benchmarking approach to identifying opportunities?

b. What interests, skills, and knowledge would be required for members of a project team such as the one at Cummins to analyze accounts payable?

c. What are specific steps that Cummins Engine took to ensure the success of the accounts payable project?

d. Does the Cummins project appear to be perfect, or can you recommend improvement(s) and/or identify area(s) of concern if you were to copy this approach at another organization?

[Adapted from T. Compton, L. Hoshower, and W. Draeger. "Reengineering Transaction Processing Systems at Cummins Engine"]

Chapter-by-Chapter Strengths

The following discussions indicate whether the chapter is new or revised from the first edition, include major changes from the first edition, and present highlights of the chapter.

Part 1: Setting the Stage: The Importance of Analyzing and Managing Costs

Chapter 1: Cost Management and Management of the Value Chain

- Chapter 1 is a revision of the first edition's Prologue and Chapter 1. This new chapter economizes on introductory reading without losing the cost-management message.
- Chapter 1 provides essential material that is the foundation for the remainder of the text. The chapter focuses on managing the value chain and describes

relevant cost-management information and techniques with particular focus on using benchmarking and cost-benefit analysis.

- Chapter 1's focus company is a successful telecommunication company, Pursuit.Com, which is facing strong pressure from domestic and international competitors. Among the decisions the company must make is whether to outsource some or all of its accounting services to improve the competitiveness of its primary services and products.
- Pursuit.Com compares its performance to best practices and considers both quantitative and qualitative costs and benefits to make its decisions.

Chapter 2: Product Costing Systems: Concepts and Design Issues

- A new chapter in this edition, Chapter 2 combines elements from several first edition chapters. The rationale for this change is to introduce cost systems and concepts early as well as to simplify presentations and applications in this and subsequent chapters.
- The focus company, CollegePak, provides the opportunity to discuss cost information to support and evaluate its expansion plans. The emphasis is on the clear presentation and explanation of cost terms and uses, which can be confusing for many students. The straightforward setting eliminates unnecessary complexity that is distracting at this point in the text.
- Chapter 2 addresses the meaning of "cost" and the fact that alternative measures of cost could be appropriate for different decisions. This discussion in other texts typically is quite abstract. The focus company provides a tangible application and illustration of the issues, solutions, and implications of alternative measures of cost.

Chapter 3: Cost Accumulation for Job-Shop and Batch Production Operations

- Chapter 3 is a major revision of the content of the first edition's Chapter 6. The rationale for this major content and placement change is twofold. First, we have found that students more naturally grasp the concept of cost accumulation in a straightforward setting. Second, the earlier placement of the material allows subsequent chapters to add complexity to reinforce learning without requiring students to learn both basic concepts and complex applications.
- Glass Creations, the focus company, creates and markets stained glass windows, doors, and artwork and faces strong competition from much larger, mass producers. Glass Creations needs to measure and manage the costs of its jobs to better understand which products create sustainable advantage and value. Its analysis requires choices about cost system design, as well as identification of the attributes of products that customers prefer and are willing to pay for.
- The chapter discusses the use of a product-costing system called *job-order costing* (or *job costing*) designed for organizations, such as Glass Creations, which produce unique products, services, and custom orders. The job-order costing system helps such companies measure the cost of the resources used in the production process for the purpose of helping management to better manage those resources and their costs.

Stacy Kovar—Kansas State University
This has an excellent illustration of how to arrive at activity costs and rates. Failure to cover this material is a significant weakness of other texts.

Part 2: Activity-Based Management

Chapter 4: Activity-Based Costing Systems

- Chapter 4, a revision of the first edition's Chapter 5, simplifies the presentation of ABC but retains the first edition's innovations and message.
- Chapter 4 illustrates the activity basis for measuring and analyzing costs; this costing approach is known as "activity-based costing." ABC measures the costs of

resources used to perform activities and builds the costs of products and services by accumulating the activities performed and their costs. This chapter's strength is the clear but detailed exposition of how to design and use ABC systems.

- The focus company, Precision Molding, Inc., uses five levels of activities to describe its processes and measure its costs. The company faces the major decision of whether to begin a new line of business that could be very profitable but is more complex than its current business. ABC allows the company to accurately estimate the costs of this new business.

Chapter 5: Activity-Based Management

- Chapter 5 is a revision of the first edition's Chapter 10. The second edition moves the presentation of ABM to immediately follow that of ABC to reinforce the importance of using ABC information for more than product costing. Chapter 5 discusses how to use ABC information to make process improvements, meet target cost objectives, and create more value at lower cost.
- The chapter continues with Precision Molding, Inc., as it considers a new product line, which requires process improvements before profitability can be expected.
- By identifying value-added and non-value-added activities (as well as activity costs from Chapter 4), the discussion focuses on how the company can use ABM to find opportunities to improve its processes sufficiently to generate a profit.
- The chapter's unique strength is its ability to build on a thorough explanation of ABC as the basis for a straightforward but powerful application of ABM.

Catherine Usoff—
Bentley College
The process orientation is wonderful and it highlights where cost accountants will be adding value to organizations.

Chapter 6: Managing Customer Profitability

- Chapter 6, a new chapter for the second edition, reflects the increasing importance of managing customer profitability and relations. This approach, which often is activity based, is nearly universal in some industries (e.g., banking), and its application is increasing in nearly every economic and government sector. The placement of the chapter reflects the natural use of ABC and ABM information to manage customer profitability.
- HealthWave, the chapter's focus company, must dramatically improve its profitability or risk being liquidated by its parent company. HealthWave analyzes its major customers to identify those that are profitable and not profitable and seeks ways to improve the profitability of less profitable ones.
- The chapter leads students step-by-step through an entire customer-profitability analysis and uses the information to find opportunities for improvement.

Il-Woon Kim—
University of Akron
Most other books do not emphasize the importance of customer profitability analysis enough.

Chapter 7: Managing Quality and Time to Create Value

- Chapter 7 is a revision of the first edition's Chapter 11 and adds coverage of productivity and capacity measures.
- Through its focus company, the chapter discusses how analysts increasingly measure and interpret nonfinancial indicators of internal performance that complement financial, cost-based measures. The most important of these operational areas of performance are quality, productivity, capacity, and time.
- The focus company, Transformation Customer Services, Inc., competes primarily on the quality of its services and rapid response to customers' service needs. Thus, these areas of performance are particularly important.
- Chapter 7 thoroughly investigates and applies quality, productivity, capacity, and time measures to situations with which our students must gain familiarity.

Gerry Rosson—
Lynchburg College
The material is very easy to read. The discussion of managing quality and JIT was effective.

Part 3: Process Costing and Cost Allocation

Chapter 8: Process-Costing Systems

- Chapter 8 is a revision of the first edition's Chapter 7. It simplifies the discussion and presentation of process-costing analysis.
- The focus company is Spirit Beverages, a sports drink company, an organization that produces similar items in a continuous process. Its use of process costing to measure its costs of production and the efficiency of its processes is easy to understand.

Chapter 9: Joint-Process Costing

- A revision of the first edition's Chapter 8, Chapter 9 streamlines the presentation of joint-cost analysis.
- The focus company represents companies that produce multiple products from common inputs and that must decide which products to sell after joint products appear (split-off) or after further processing. After they determine the appropriate products, they can allocate production costs using one of several acceptable methods.
- National Wood Products, the joint-product focus company, processes timber into multiple products and must decide, based on competitive commodity market prices, which products to sell as is or after further processing. The chapter discusses how companies whose several divisions transfer products to each other and should consider the companywide profitability of their decisions.

Chapter 10: Managing and Allocating Support-Service Costs

Lawrence Klein—Bentley College
Using a not-for-profit entity, a city administrative structure with associated service departments, is an excellent example for this topic; the material is thoroughly discussed and logically developed.

- Chapter 10 is a revision of the first edition's Chapter 9, which simplifies the presentation and discussion of cost-allocation methods.
- The allocation of the costs of support services by organizations to production departments for many legitimate reasons is a chapter focus. Although all cost allocations are arbitrary, they can be useful for promoting organizational goals if done carefully. Thus, the chapter emphasizes that "arbitrary should not mean capricious."
- The City of Rock Creek allocates support services to improve decision making by departments that provide services directly to citizens to regulate the use of support services and recover the costs of services necessary to support the other departments.
- Although service cost allocations might be important in all types of organizations, the chapter demonstrates that they are particularly important in government and service organizations that typically have not used services available in the market.

Part 4: Planning and Decision Making

Chapter 11: Cost Estimation

Paul Hutchinson—University of North Texas
Another major strength was the use of a service firm for illustrating chapter content. Service firms usually do not get emphasized in accounting texts.

- A revision of the first edition's Chapter 12, Chapter 11 improves its presentations and discussions.
- Prior chapters assumed knowledge of cost drivers, and this chapter demonstrates how to identify those drivers and estimate cost relationships using multiple regressions, account analysis, and the engineering method.
- CC Catering, a company developed by entrepreneurial students, uses various cost-estimation methods to estimate five cost drivers tied to the cost hierarchy. The chapter uses their analyses to illustrate how to use this information for cost management, decision making, and planning. The results have a major impact not only on the business but also on the two entrepreneurs' career plans.

- The chapter compares the information requirements of multiple regression, account analysis, and the engineering method, showing that for many applications, multiple regression is the least costly method. The chapter also demonstrates the advantages and disadvantages of alternative cost-estimation methods.

Chapter 12: Financial and Cost-Volume-Profit Models

- This is a new chapter for the second edition; it focuses on the principles and applications of financial modeling. The chapter includes elements from several first-edition chapters related to financial modeling, including simple CVP models and the Theory of Constraints, and adds explicit guidance on building and using spreadsheet models and modeling the effects of uncertainty. This second edition's use of an entire chapter on financial modeling underscores its importance.
- Fairfield Blues, a company that owns a minor league baseball team and a stadium, has built financial models to support its product (baseball games and summer concerts) decision making. This company demonstrates that modeling opportunities and difficulties are not confined to manufacturing companies. Any organization that can identify and quantify its cost and revenue drivers can benefit from financial modeling.
- The company's managers started with a simple CVP model and expanded it to include multiple products, taxes, multiple cost and revenue drivers, and effects of uncertainty. They use these models to reflect expected and possible effects of their decisions about product volumes and attributes.

Alexander Sannella—Rutgers University
This is the best chapter in the book. It is clear, well-written, great examples, etc.

Stacy Kovar—Kansas State University
I love the discussion of spreadsheet models. This makes it possible to incorporate ABC. This chapter improves on other texts in a big way.

Chapter 13: Cost Management and Decision Making

- This is a new chapter that expands on decision-making materials in the first edition's Chapter 12. The new chapter uses an explicit decision-making framework to present consistent approaches to making common business decisions. The chapter uses target costing, decision trees, and cost-benefit analysis to evaluate both quantitative and qualitative information.
- Focus company Bootstrap Industries successfully employs workers whose disabilities make them unemployable in the eyes of most companies. The presentation explores the nonprofit's attempts to meet both qualitative and quantitative goals to succeed while noting that its decision-making environment and tasks are not different from most organizations.
- The chapter presents a common structure for making decisions about new technology, outsourcing, products and services, and pricing special orders.

Chapter 14: Strategic Issues in Making Long-Term Capital Investment Decisions

- Chapter 14 is a revision of the same innovative chapter from the first edition.
- Capital budgeting chapters in most cost-accounting texts focus on the discounted-cash-flow model; however, this chapter recognizes that nearly all students will have already covered DCF in their finance or managerial accounting courses. Therefore, we focus on strategic issues, sources of information, sensitivity analysis, relevance of nonfinancial information, approval process, and follow-up to the decision.
- Rascals, Inc., the focus company for this chapter, is a record and book retailer that is investing in e-commerce in Central Europe. Consequently, it faces numerous interesting strategic issues, information-gathering problems, and risks, that are not faced in routine equipment replacement or simple expansion investments.
- Students who have not covered DCF or who want a refresher will find a straightforward presentation in the chapter Appendix.

Leslie Kren—University of Wisconsin (Milwaukee)
The discussion of the decision issues related to capital investments is much more complete than the typical text.

Chapter 15: Budgeting and Financial Planning

- Chapter 15 is a revision of the same chapter from the first edition that improves and clarifies the presentation.
- The chapter discusses the role of budgeting in the strategic planning process and the development of the master budget. In addition to discussing the steps in preparing a master budget, the chapter provides extensive coverage of sales forecasting, behavioral issues in budgeting, and contemporary topics such as the international aspects of budgeting, e-budgeting, and ethics. The chapter Appendix covers inventory management issues.
- Collegiate Apparel Company, the focus company, is a small manufacturer of t-shirts bearing the names of major colleges in Canada and the United States. Budgeting is critically important in this small but rapidly growing company for planning, resource acquisition, plant expansion, and bank financing.

Neil Wilner—University of North Texas
The book uses a strategic emphasis throughout and this helps to motivate what is often a mundane chapter.

Part 5: Evaluating and Managing Performance: Creating and Managing Value-Added Effort

Chapter 16: Standard Costing, Variance Analysis, and Kaizen Costing

- Chapter 16, a revision of the same chapter of the first edition, improves and clarifies the presentation.
- The chapter covers standard-costing systems, cost-variance analysis, and the cost-reduction process known as *kaizen costing.* Coverage includes the standard-setting process, use of standard costing in nonmanufacturing settings, determination of the significance of variances, behavioral effects of standard costing, impact of information technology, and changing role of standard costing in today's manufacturing environment. The chapter Appendix covers production-mix and yield variances.
- Koala Camp Gear Company, this chapter's focus company, manufactures camping tents. Cost control is crucial in this small manufacturer of high-quality products with a growing international reputation.

Paul Hutchinson—University of North Texas
The authors do an excellent job on basic standard costing.

Chapter 17: Flexible Budgets, Overhead Cost Management, and Activity-Based Budgeting

- Chapter 17 is a revision of the same chapter of the first edition that improves and clarifies the presentation.
- The focus on Koala Camp Gear continues from the preceding chapter. The chapter emphasizes the importance of the company's management of overhead and support-service costs to improve its competitive position in the global market.
- Chapter 17 focuses on the use of flexible budgeting and standard costing in the management and control of overhead costs, as well as the use of activity-based flexible budgets. The chapter emphasizes the interpretation of standard and activity-based flexible budgets, overhead variances, the choice of activity measures, and performance reporting.
- The chapter appendices cover cost-variance proration, backflush costing, and sales variance analysis.

Chapter 18: Organizational Design, Responsibility Accounting, and Evaluation of Divisional Performance

- This chapter, a revision of the first edition's Chapter 19, improves and clarifies the presentation.
- This chapter covers responsibility accounting, performance reporting, and investment center performance measures, which include return on investment, residual income, and economic value added.

- The focus company for this chapter is Outback Outfitters, a large retailer of camping equipment and apparel with both mail-order and store-based retail operations. The company has grown through acquisition; its need of a responsibility accounting system to help manage its ever more diverse operations provides the framework for the presentation.
- The chapter includes extensive coverage of organizational design issues, behavioral effects of responsibility accounting systems, and implementation issues in divisional performance measurement.

Chapter 19: Transfer Pricing

- This chapter, a revision of the first edition's Chapter 20, improves and clarifies the presentation.
- The focus company again is Outback Outfitters, the focus company of the preceding chapter. Outback has acquired Koala Camp Gear Company as its own private-label manufacturer of camping equipment and apparel. Transfer pricing for internal sales between Outback's new manufacturing division and its retail and mail-order divisions is exemplified as management begins to use this process.
- The chapter covers the role and purpose of transfer pricing and explores several approaches to setting transfer prices. It has ample coverage of incentive problems in transfer pricing and the international implications of transfer pricing systems.

Chapter 20: Using Lead and Lag Measures to Communicate, Motivate, and Evaluate

- Chapter 20 is a major revision of the first edition's Chapter 2. Its current placement near the end of the text reflects the summary nature of its presentations and discussions. This chapter and the final Chapter 21 serve as capstone topics for the entire text.
- Valley Commercial Bank, the chapter's focus company, prepares performance measures for its various operations as indicated by responsibility and informativeness of measures. These include nonfinancial and financial measures of performance that are key indicators of the company's strategic success (or failure). The bank combines these key indicators of performance into a performance measurement model, commonly known as the *balanced scorecard.*
- This chapter describes the properties and measures of leading and lagging indicators of performance and the way organizations combine these measures with strategy to implement a balanced scorecard.

Chapter 21: Incentive Systems and Performance Evaluation

- Chapter 21 is a major revision of the same chapter from the first edition. As the last chapter of the text, it truly can serve as a capstone topic because all issues of cost management and performance measurement can be the focus here.
- The chapter continues the experiences of Valley Commercial Bank from the preceding chapter. The bank seeks to use its leading and lagging measures of performance to evaluate performance and create incentives for employees to achieve the bank's strategy.
- The bank's consideration of both theoretical and practical issues of evaluating performance and motivating employees with incentive systems includes performance evaluation approaches such as financial, nonfinancial, narrow, broad, absolute, relative, formula-based, and subjective measures. This situation is used to present incentives including salary; bonuses; current, deferred, and stock awards; and stock options. The chapter also discusses trade-offs among the many alternative features of evaluation and incentive systems.

Ranjani Krishnan—Michigan State University
This is an interesting topic, which is of great current interest to accounting scholars and practitioners. The flow of the materials is good. I like the treatment of agency theory and its implications.

Supplements to the Text

For Instructors

Instructor's Manual (ISBN 0-07-247436-X)—This aid prepared by Roger Doost, Clemson University, includes detailed chapter outlines with teaching tips and suggestions for alternate ways to present the text material.

Solutions Manual (ISBN 0-07-247445-9)—Prepared by the textbook authors and carefully reviewed by outside sources, this manual contains solutions to all assignments from the text.

Solutions Transparencies (ISBN 0-07-247443-2)—Set in large, boldface type for maximum readability, acetates of the solutions are available for lecture use.

Test Bank (ISBN 0-07-247444-0)—The Test Bank prepared by Kathleen Sevigny, Bridgewater State College, and Karen Tabak, Maryville University, offers true/false, multiple choice, and essay questions and extended problems requiring analysis and interpretation.

Brownstone's Diploma—A computerized version of the manual test bank, this test-generator program offers extensive capabilities including random question selection based on learning objectives, type of question, and level of difficulty. It is available on the Instructor Presentation Manager CD-ROM.

Instructor Presentation Manager CD-ROM (ISBN 0-07-247435-1)—This comprehensive multimedia CD contains PowerPoint slides prepared by Richard Rand, Tennessee Tech University, the Solutions Manual, the Instructor's Manual, Check Figures, Exhibits from the Text, Computerized Test Bank, Spreadsheet Assignments, Videos, and much more. With the Presentation CD-ROM, you can customize the supplements to fit your needs for in-class presentations.

Video Library (ISBN 0-07-237617-1)—These short videos developed by Dallas County Community College provide the impetus for lively classroom discussion. The focus is on the preparation, analysis, and use of accounting information for business decision making.

Website (*www.mhhe.com/hms2e*)—The Website features materials for instructors and students, including downloadable supplements, text updates, on-line quizzes, Internet research projects, Excel templates, PowerPoint slides, communication exercises, and CMA review questions. The Website will also include exciting and interactive Focus Sites, which are based on the "You're the Decision Maker" activities within the chapters. Created by co-author, Frank Selto, these six simulated Focus Sites are based on six of the chapter focus companies and include management interviews, cost information on spreadsheets, and have students making decisions based on the information in the text and on the "company site." They reinforce the importance of cost management and the use of focus companies in the chapters. These Websites are designed for both self-study by students and additional assignments by instructors. Full assignment and solution materials are available to adopting instructors.

McGraw-Hill's Knowledge Gateway—The Complete Resource for Teaching Online Courses. McGraw-Hill/Irwin, in partnership with Eduprise, is proud to bring this unique service to instructors. This comprehensive Website contains a wealth of information for any professor interested in teaching online. Level one is available to any instructor browsing our Website. Level two is reserved for McGraw-Hill customers and contains access to free technical and instructional design assistance. For more details, visit *http://mhhe.eduprise.com/home.nsf*.

PageOut—McGraw-Hill's unique point-and-click course Website tool, enabling you to create a full-featured, professional quality course Website without knowing HTML coding. With PageOut you can post your syllabus online, assign McGraw-Hill Online Learning Center or eBook content, add links to important off-site resources, and maintain student results in the online grade book. You can send class announcements, copy your course site to share with colleagues, and upload original files. PageOut is free for every McGraw-Hill/Irwin user and, if you're short on time, we even have a team ready to help you create your site!

For Students

Study Guide (ISBN 0-07-247438-6)—Written by Janice Mereba, North Carolina A&T State University, each chapter includes an overview of the main topics as well as multiple choice, true/false, and short-answer questions tied to the chapter goals.

PowerWeb—Keeping your accounting course timely can be a job in itself, and now McGraw-Hill/Irwin does that job for you. PowerWeb is a site from which you can access all the latest news and developments pertinent to your course without all of the clutter and dead links of a typical online search. Students can visit PowerWeb to take a self-grading quiz or check a daily news feed analyzed by an expert in cost accounting. This powerful tool is packaged free with new copies of the text.

GradeSummit—This is an online diagnostic self-assessment and exam preparation tool for students. As a student answers questions, diagnostic results provide valuable feedback that helps students identify their strengths and weaknesses, enabling them to target their study time more efficiently. It is available as a package with the text for a small fee.

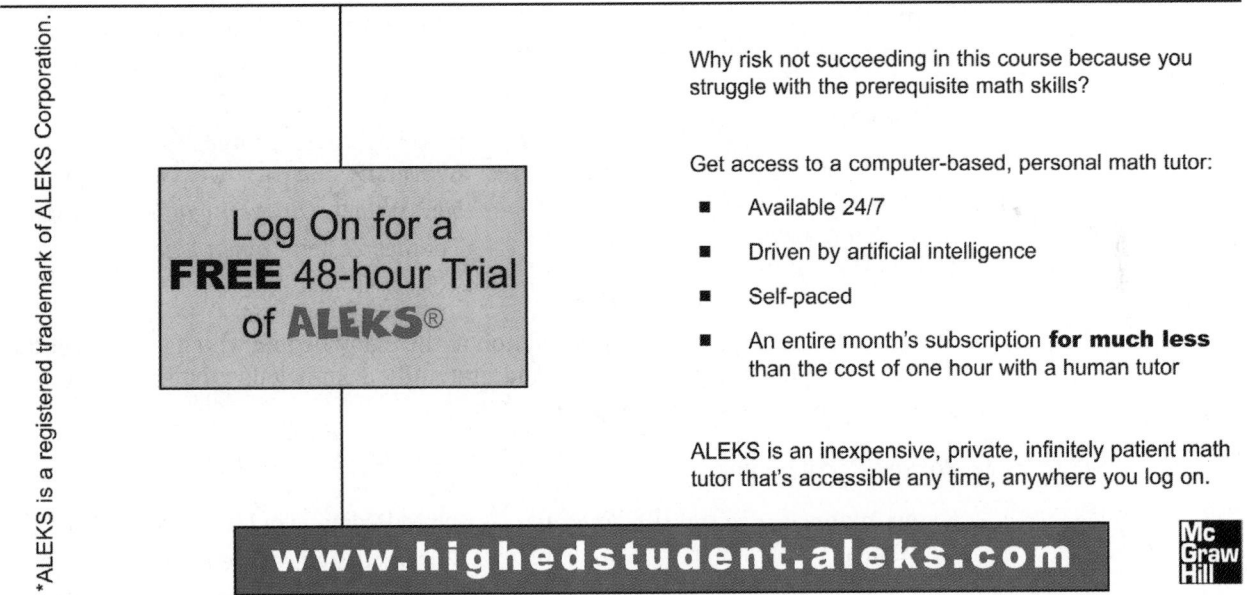

Acknowledgements

We have learned from long experience that the most useful comments challenge our assumptions and expose any weaknesses in our thought or exposition. The many reviewers, editors, and students who challenged us and held us to the highest standards have contributed to the success of this revision. The authors sincerely appreciate the efforts of the many people who have helped to improve this text. Our students continue to challenge us and insist that our text be at least as accessible as we are. Numerous professors in reviews and focus groups have thoroughly reviewed, criticized, and commented on the first and second editions. We have thoroughly digested that invaluable input and feedback, especially when some of it was harsh. In particular, we want to thank the following professors for their help in preparing the second edition.

Penne Ainsworth, *University of Wyoming*
Homer Bates, *University of North Florida*
Joyce Berg, *University of Iowa*
Marv Bouillon, *Iowa State University*
Annhenrie Campbell, *California State University, Stanislaus*
Thomas Clausen, *Kansas State University*
Elizabeth Cole, *Old Dominion University*
John Core, *University of Pennsylvania*
Masako Darrough, *Baruch College*
Leslie Eldenburg, *University of Arizona*
Michael Finch, *University of Maryland*
James Russell Hardin, *Pittsburg State University*
Cynthia Heagy, *University of Houston, Clear Lake*
Paul Hutchison, *University of North Texas*
Steven Jackson, *University of Tennessee, Martin*
Il-Woon Kim, *University of Akron*
Lawrence Klein, *Bentley College*
Stacy Kovar, *Kansas State University*
Leslie Kren, *University of Wisconsin, Milwaukee*
Ranjani Krishnan, *Michigan State University*
Robert Lin, *California State University, Hayward*
Danny Litt, *University of California, Los Angeles*
Jordan Lowe, *University of Nevada, Las Vegas*
Joan Luft, *Michigan State University*
Mary Ellen Oliverio, *Pace University*
David Platt, *University of Texas, Austin*
Peter Poznanski, *Cleveland State University*
Jenice Prather-Kinsey, *University of Missouri*
Gerald Rosson, *Lynchburg College*
Alexander Sannella, *Rutgers University*
Ali Sedaghat, *Loyola College, Maryland*
David Stout, *Villanova University*
Nathan Stuart, *University of Florida*
Catherine Usoff, *Bentley College*
Gloria Vollmers, *University of Maine*
David Wallin, *The Ohio State University*
Sally Widener, *Rice University*
Patrick Wilkie, *George Mason University*
Neil Wilner, *University of North Texas*
Thomas Zeller, *Loyola University, Chicago*

The authors also express their appreciation to the many people who have contributed to the development of this textbook and gratefully acknowledge their valuable constructive criticism and many suggestions.

Survey Participants

Karen Adamson, *Central Washington University*
Neil Adkins, *Marshall University*
Penne Ainsworth, *University of Wyoming*
Henry Anderson, *University of Central Florida*
Rowland Atiase, *University of Texas at Austin*
Jack Bailes, *Oregon State University*
Homer Bates, *University of North Florida*
James Bedingfield, *University of Maryland*
Margaret Boldt, *Murray State University*
Marvin Bouillon, *Iowa State University*
Tom Buckoff, *North Dakota State University*
Dennis Caplan, *Columbia University*
Bill Carter, *University of Virginia*
Gordon Chapman, *Eastern Washington University*
Kim Charland, *Kansas State University*
Al Chen, *North Carolina State University*

Ray Clanton, *University of Central Oklahoma*
Peter Clarke, *University College, Dublin*
Susan Crosson, *Santa Fe Community College*
Larry Ducharme, *University of Washington*
Michael Eames, *Santa Clara University*
Robert Elmore, *Tennessee Tech University*
James Emig, *Villanova University*
Neil Fargher, *University of Oregon*
Len Fertuck, *University of Toronto*
David Franz, *San Francisco State University*
Karen Frey, *Gettysburg College*
Ann Gabriel, *University of Notre Dame*
Jackson Gillespie, *University of Delaware*
Robert Greenberg, *Washington State University*
Dale Grinnell, *University of Vermont*
Daryl Guffey, *East Carolina University*
Rama Guttikonda, *Alabama State University*
Steven Hansen, *University of California, Los Angeles*
James Hardin, *Pittsburg State University*
Ennis Hawkins, *Sam Houston State University*
Leon Hoshower, *Ohio University*
Muhammed Hussein, *University of Connecticut*
Raffi Indjejikian, *University of Michigan*
Phillip Jagolinzer, *University of Southern Maine*
Holly Johnston, *Boston University*
Hussein Kandiel, *SUNY—Plattsburgh*
Robert Kee, *University of Alabama*
David Keys, *Northern Illinois University*
Il-Woon Kim, *University of Akron*
Lawrence Klein, *Bentley University*
Paul Koogler, *Southwest Texas State University*
Leon Korte, *University of South Dakota*
Leslie Kren, *University of Wisconsin–Milwaukee*
Joan Luft, *Michigan State University*
Ron Marshall, *Michigan State University*
Annie McGown, *Texas A&M University*
Kevin McNelis, *New Mexico State University*
Janice Mereba, *Delaware State University*
Bruce Miller, *University of California, Los Angeles*
David Morris, *North Georgia College*
Ann Murphy, *Metro State College—Denver*
Gordon Niemi, *Northwestern Michigan University*
Emeka Nwaeze, *Rutgers University*
Marilyn Okleshen, *Mankato State University*
Richard Ortman, *University of Nebraska at Omaha*
Guy Owings, *Pittsburgh State University*
Janet Papiernik, *Edinboro University of Pennsylvania*
Barbra Peck, *University of Illinois–Chicago*
Claire Purvis, *California State University–San Bernardino*
Olga Quintana, *University of Miami*
Priscilla Reese, *Idaho State University*
Roy Regal, *University of Montana*
Leslie Richeson, *Franklin and Marshall*
Diane Roberts, *University of San Francisco*
Jack Ruhl, *Western Michigan University*
Grant Russell, *University of Waterloo*
Jane Saly, *University of Minnesota*
Henry Schwarzbach, *University of Rhode Island*
Robert Seay, *Murray State University*
Inshik Seol, *University of Massachusetts*
Doug Sharp, *Wichita State University*
Karl Sherman, *Lake Superior State University*
Jeffrey Shields, *Suffolk University*
Frank Shuman, *Utah State University*
Kenneth Sinclair, *Lehigh University*
Mark Soczek, *Washington University*
Lanny Solomon, *University of Missouri–Kansas City*
Parvez Sopariwala, *Grand Valley State University*

Carolyn Stokes, *Francis Marion University*
Cathy Sullivan, *James Madison University*
Paulette Tandy, *University of Nevada–Las Vegas*
Leslie Turner, *Northern Kentucky University*
Michael Ulinski, *Pace University*
Bente Villadsen, *University of Michigan*
David Wallin, *The Ohio State University*
Timothy West, *Iowa State University*
Jackson White, *University of Arkansas*
Tom Zeller, *Loyola University*

Text Reviewers

Penne Ainsworth, *University of Wyoming*
Margaret Boldt, *Murray State University*
Dennis Caplan, *Columbia University*
John Chandler, *University of Illinois*
Kim Charland, *Kansas State University*
Al Chen, *North Carolina State University*
Ray Clanton, *University of Central Oklahoma*
Peter Clarke, *University College, Dublin*
Roger Doost, *Clemson University*
Michael Eames, *Santa Clara University*
James Emig, *Villanova University*
Len Fertuck, *University of Toronto*
David Franz, *San Francisco State University*
Rosalie Hallbauer, *Florida International University*
Holly Johnston, *Boston University*
Suresh Kalagnanam, *University of Saskatchewan*
David Keys, *Northern Illinois University*
Il-Woon Kim, *University of Akron*
Lawrence Klein, *Bentley University*
Les Kren, *University of Wisconsin–Milwaukee*
Joan Luft, *Michigan State University*
Janice Mereba, *Delaware State University*
David Morris, *North Georgia State University*
Ann Murphy, *Metropolitan State College of Denver*
Marilyn Okleshen, *Mankato State University*
Roy Regel, *University of Montana*
Diane Roberts, *University of San Francisco*
Hanno Roberts, *Norwegian School of Management*
Jeff Shields, *Suffolk University*
Frank Shuman, *Utah State University*
Ken Sinclair, *Lehigh University*
Cathy Sullivan, *James Madison University*
Bente Villadsen, *University of Iowa*
David Wallin, *Ohio State University*
Jim Xie, *University of Alberta*
Tom Zeller, *Loyola University*

We acknowledge James Emig (Villanova University), Beth Woods, Catherine Usoff (Bentley College) and Russell Hardin (Pittsburg State University) for their thorough checking of the text for accuracy and completeness. We also acknowledge Lanny Solomon (University of Missouri) for his help with special topics.

The authors acknowledge the Institute of Management Accountants for permission to use problems from the Certified Management Accountant (CMA) examinations. We also acknowledge the American Institute of Certified Public Accountants for permission to use problems from the Uniform CPA Examinations, Questions, and Unofficial Answers.

Finally, the authors express their gratitude to the many fine people at McGraw-Hill/Irwin, who have so professionally guided this book through the development and publication processes. In particular, we acknowledge Steve DeLancey, Gail Korosa, Christine Vaughan, Mary Christianson, Melonie Salvati, Judy Kausal, Dave Barrick, Ryan Blankenship, and Sue Lombardi.

A special acknowledgment goes to JaNoel Lowe for her superb copyediting of the text.

Ronald W. Hilton
Michael W. Maher
Frank H. Selto

Brief Contents

Contents

Microsoft
Sun

PART

I

Setting the Stage

The Importance of Analyzing and Managing Costs

A Look at This Part

The first part describes how cost management supports key elements of modern management decision making. Part I introduces cost management and management of the value chain, cost system design, and measurement of product costs.

A Look Ahead

The second part covers the activity-based approach to cost management. Part II covers activity-based costing, activity-based management, customer profitability, and management of internal processes.

CHAPTER

1

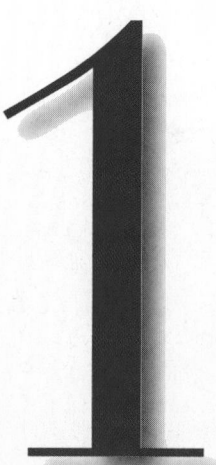

Cost Management and Management of the Value Chain

Finding Opportunity and Leading Change

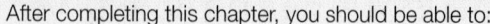

After completing this chapter, you should be able to:

1. Explain how cost management helps organizations meet their strategic goals by proactively managing costs rather than passively measuring costs.
2. Apply benchmarking, cost-benefit, and value-chain analysis to consider and evaluate changes to an organization's value chain.
3. Describe how to effectively implement and manage change.
4. Discuss the Standards for Ethical Conduct for management accountants (Appendix).

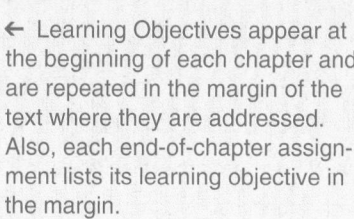

← Learning Objectives appear at the beginning of each chapter and are repeated in the margin of the text where they are addressed. Also, each end-of-chapter assignment lists its learning objective in the margin.

↓ Chapters begin with a company document that introduces the issues to be addressed in the chapter. These focus companies are fictional, but are closely based on actual practices of real companies. A company logo appears throughout the chapter to tie the exhibits and topics to the company.

EMAIL MEMORANDUM

To: Melanie DelVal, Chief Financial Officer
From: Frank Barnes, President and CEO
Subject: Internal Services

Pursuit.Com

Melanie,

At the recent Telecommunication Conference that you had to miss because of your trip to Hong Kong, I attended a session devoted to industry trends. I was surprised to learn that many companies in our industry no longer perform some traditional, internal service functions. They reportedly have reduced costs and maintained quality of service by contracting with external service providers.

Needless to say, Melanie, we need to be sure that our costs are managed carefully. We cannot afford to give away any cost advantages to our competitors. I will send you copies of the analysis presented by US EAST. I think you will find it interesting and provocative.

Please see me early next week to discuss whether we should consider outsourcing some of our service functions.

Hope you had a pleasant trip.

Frank

Cost-Management Challenges

1. **How** do cost-management analysts interact with others and contribute to the formulation of an organization's strategy?
2. **How** do cost-management analysts measure the expected effects of alternative ways to organize resources?
3. **How** do cost-management analysts lead change?

↑ Cost Management Challenges ask you to comprehend and master the chapter's content. Suggested solutions are at the end of the chapter.

EMAIL MEMORANDUM

To: Frank Barnes, President and CEO
From: Melanie DelVal, Chief Financial Officer
Subject: RE: Problems in Customer Billing

Pursuit.Com

Frank,

I know that outsourcing services is a growing trend in many industries, but I have not had a chance to analyze whether this would work for us. We have to be careful to arrange all of our internal resources so that they support our strategic initiatives. We may be able to outsource some services that either do not deal with sensitive information or are routine. I will have a preliminary proposal for you early next week. If you agree, we should be able to gather the right information to support a decision within a month or so.

The trip to Hong Kong (and Sydney) with the Emerging Markets team was great. I believe that we have tremendous opportunities in the Pacific Rim, but we need to consider risks as well. I will brief you later this week at our regular Executive Committee meeting.

Melanie

Identifying Cost-Management Challenges at Pursuit.Com

Pursuit.Com

Pursuit.Com, Inc., a small, high-growth telecommunication company, uses cost management to improve its decision making and performance. The telecommunication industry is evolving rapidly, and competition is fierce among established companies, such as AT&T and Motorola, and more recent entrants, such as Qwest Communications and Level 3 Communications. Companies in this industry (and other technology-based industries) compete on the basis of superior technology, marketing, and cost management. Cost managers must understand their companies' technology and marketing challenges and find opportunities and develop innovative ways to improve quality and cost. These improvements to quality and cost often involve dramatically different ways to organize internal resources and provide support services.

A decade ago, an engineering manager, Frank Barnes, and a marketing director, Jackie Lin, worked for a large, multinational telecommunication company. Barnes and Lin observed that their employer was not providing data-communication products and services that met the needs of small, fast-growing companies. Their employer focused instead on the data-communication needs of large companies.

This two-person team saw a potentially lucrative, unfilled telecommunication market and left to form Pursuit.Com. The company's mission was to provide quick, flexible, and reliable data-communication devices and services to small companies with good growth potential. Its motto, "Your Communication Partner," signaled its focus on providing customized telecommunication products and services to customers. Pursuit.Com's founders realized early the importance of managing costs. One of their first professional hires was an experienced cost manager, Melanie DelVal, who joined the company as chief financial officer (CFO).

Career Perspectives An organization's chief financial officer (CFO) is responsible for managing the financial resources and the financial managers of the firm. CFOs, who increasingly also manage human and information resources, typically are trained in accounting and finance as undergraduates or as graduate students and often are professionally certified (e.g., certified public accountant, certified management accountant, certified financial manager). Several professional organizations that can provide information about financial management careers and certification include the Financial Executives Institute (www.fei.org), American Institute of CPAs (www.aicpa.org), Institute of Management Accountants (United States) (www.imanet.org), Society of Management Accountants (Canada) (www.cma-canada.org), Institute of Chartered Accountants (Australia) (www.icaa.org.au), and Institute of Chartered Management Accountants (Great Britain).

The Institute of Management Accountants (United States) recently completed a study of the current and future work activities and competencies of financial managers, which can be found under "IMA studies". This study indicates that the role of financial managers in many companies is changing to focus on, among other things, customer profitability, process improvement, performance evaluation, and strategic planning. The most important qualities a financial manager needs include a strong work ethic; an understanding of the business; and problem-solving, interpersonal, and listening skills. The modern financial and cost manager is hardly the stereotypical cost accountant but a successful business consultant. The stereotyped cost accountant, complete with green eyeshade and calculator, who records the financial data about events from a distance, is a relic of the past in many companies. It is likely that no one at these companies even has the title "cost accountant." A more common title is "financial analyst" or "business consultant." These titles and the tasks they represent demonstrate a dramatic evolution in accountants' jobs from preparers of reports to proactive managers and consultants. More evidence of the change in the field can be found by reviewing articles in *Emerging Practices in Cost Management,* edited by J. B. Edwards, and by noting the conclusions of the study completed by several PricewaterhouseCoopers employees (T. Walther, H. Johansson, J. Dunleavy, E. Hjelm, *Reinventing the CFO: Moving from Financial Management to Strategic Management*). (Full citations to references are in the Bibliography.)

Pursuit.Com's products include reliable fiber-optic data-communication switches that route incoming and outgoing data to the right servers and users. Pursuit.Com also provides other products (including software solutions to data sharing and communication) and services (consulting on data communication and reporting) to optimize the use of its switches and software. Pursuit.Com currently has more than 200 full-time employees and has doubled its sales from products and services in the past three years. Since data communication needs are growing rapidly, Pursuit.Com believes its market and profitability will grow, too.[1]

Understanding the Organizational Role of Cost Management

LO 1 Explain how cost management helps organizations meet their strategic goals, by proactively managing costs rather than passively measuring assets.

The challenge facing Pursuit.Com is competition coming from nearly anywhere in the world. Its competitors in the telecommunication industry range from small start-up firms with less than 20 employees to giants such as Qwest, NYNEX, and British Telecom. To meet this competition, Pursuit.Com must be constantly aware of its strengths, weaknesses, opportunities, and competitors' threats as it considers which products and services to provide and which markets to serve. Because the company is small, it cannot afford major mistakes in the products and services it provides or in the customers it serves. CFO DelVal and her team of cost-management analysts develop financial and nonfinancial information about alternative opportunities and uses of resources to help Pursuit.Com make decisions consistent with its goal of earning long-term, competitive profits.

Several years ago, Pursuit.Com computerized most of the data-focused, recording work of the cost accountant. The company also redesigned its information system to make data widely available throughout the company. Because of changes in information technology and increased competition, most organizations now need cost-management analysts with broad a knowledge of the business more than they need cost accountants who just measure and report costs. Cost-management analysts transform cost accounting (and other) data into information used to support strategies, improve products, services, and use of resources, and systematically reduce costs. Cost-management analysts are the most reliable sources of information on the impacts of planned and actual management decisions at Pursuit.Com. This reliable information is especially important in a rapidly changing, globally competitive industry such as telecommunication.

Characteristics of Cost-Management Analysts

Melanie DelVal told Pursuit.Com's new cost-management analysts that they were all technically competent, or she would not have hired them. In addition, she selected them on the basis of personal attributes that indicated they could work closely with other employees to help those employees make better decisions. These new analysts also exhibited attributes of openness, awareness, honesty, diligence, and creativity, which are as important to Pursuit.Com as technical accounting, finance, or engineering knowledge.

Cost-management analysts are often trained as accountants, financial analysts, engineers, or consultants, but they can come from any educational or work background. They contribute cost-management attitudes and results to every type of organization, including manufacturing or service, private or government, large or small, mature or start-up. As at Pursuit.Com, cost-management analysts are often members of management teams, constantly on the lookout for ways to improve the use of the organization's

[1] The firm's founders and employees own 90 percent of the corporation's stock. An investment firm that specializes in supporting small high-technology companies owns the other 10 percent. The current owners hope to publicly sell shares of the firm in the next several years to obtain additional capital for the firm and liquidity for the owners.

A jazz combo is a good analogy for a modern cross-functional team. Each player has a primary position but also must adjust to the actions, strengths, and weaknesses of the other members.

resources. These analysts are especially successful because they have broad knowledge about the organization, its services, and the people and markets that it serves. Cost-management analysts must have high ethical standards, which they use in their organizations when they "tell it like it is." These attributes prompt other organization members to trust and use cost-management analysts' reports and recommendations.[2]

Pursuit.Com's Team Focus

Teams are replacing individual decision makers in many organizations, including Pursuit.Com. A few years ago, different people and functions within organizations performed separate parts of cost management but did not communicate effectively with each other. These people usually operated in separate functional roles that often impeded cooperation among functional areas. *Functional roles* usually are narrowly defined jobs that focus on specific types of activities, such as accounting or marketing. Persons who were restricted to functional roles often were most interested in parts of business issues that fit their own expertise. In some companies, people operating in these different functional areas rarely spoke with each other, and their actions did not reflect consistency with organizational goals.

People from different training and backgrounds at Pursuit.Com now come together in small, cross-functional, diverse teams to make many management decisions. They are assigned to specific departments such as accounting, engineering, or marketing, but they spend most of their time and efforts in team activities. Cost management is an integral part of a cross-functional and entrepreneurial approach to management decision making. Accountants who are preparing to become cost-management analysts must be ready to work in cross-functional teams and to seek innovative, entrepreneurial solutions.

---

[2]The Institute of Management Accountants has published standards of ethical conduct, which are discussed in the Appendix to this chapter.

Research Insight 1.1

Research Insights present research findings relevant to the chapter topic.

Team Selection

Selecting the right form of team is crucial to organizational success. Peter Drucker, the eminent management consultant, observes that there are only three types of teams. He uses sports and music analogies to describe them. The first type of team is similar to doubles tennis or a jazz combo. The team is small, and although each player has a primary position, each adjusts to the actions, strengths and weaknesses of the others. This type of team is most likely to create dramatic innovations and is becoming very popular in high-technology firms. The second type of team is similar to a soccer team (football to the world outside the United States) or orchestra. In soccer and orchestras, each player has specific responsibilities, but they all play in unison—moving up and down the field as the flow of the game dictates. The strength of this type of team is its ability to execute plans flexibly, and it is common in larger firms that practice "mass customization"—preparing variations of basic products and services to meet customers' specific needs. The third type of team is the baseball team, on which each player has a fixed position and role and usually plays independently of other players (music from this type of team would not be pleasant listening). The strength of this type of team is its development of individual expertise, but its greatest weakness is its inflexibility. This type of team is disappearing because it has not been capable of responding quickly in today's rapidly changing environment. See P. Drucker, *Managing in a Time of Great Change.* (Full citations to references are in the Bibliography.)

Team Decision Making

Because team-based decision making is so important in modern organizations, occasionally throughout the text we will ask you, the reader, to assume the role of a team member faced with an important decision. We will ask you to consider four important aspects of team decision making: (1) the nature of the decision, (2) the information your team needs, (3) the possible conflicts that could arise within the team and with parties external to the team, and (4) the pros and cons of various team decisions. We include an answer to this issue here. In the rest of the book, however, answers to these decision-making problems appear at the end of each chapter. Often, the Decision Maker features present extensions and additional opportunities for learning. You should consider these Decision Maker features as integral parts of the chapter, not as extra or optional reading.

One of the first team decisions, and perhaps the most important one, is to choose the type of team and its membership for a particular task or decision. Place yourself in the role of Pursuit.Com's top managers who are choosing teams for two different, critically important tasks: (1) developing a new communication service and (2) delivering an existing service to a growing set of customers.

- How would you choose types and members of teams for each of these tasks?

  First, review Research Insight 1.1 and the previous discussion of teams, and then consider the nature of each task. Developing a new service requires innovative thinking and the ability to change directions quickly as opportunities and problems arise. A jazz combo team could be best for this task. Delivering an existing service to changing customers probably can be best accomplished by a soccer team—somewhat larger and designed to move quickly in unison to adapt its "play" to changing conditions.

  Second, consider which employees are best suited to each type of team and task. Successful soccer team members might need a coach who can oversee their work, whereas a jazz team could resent a conductor. Successful small-team members, just like virtuoso jazz musicians, have individual areas of expertise but also are eager to complement and work with each other to develop creative solutions.

  What types of people and what backgrounds would you include in this team? Members of a soccer team to deliver an existing service should be higher in teamwork orientation than in individual aspirations, but creativity and willingness to depart from or adapt standard procedures are still important. Conversely, the jazz combo team to develop a new service can have more creative, individualistic members, but they still need to be committed to finding a team solution that benefits the company as a whole.

(Solutions begin on page 22.)

You're the Decision Maker 1.1

You're the Decision Maker scenarios are used to let you get involved in the decisions faced by the focus company. After you've considered them, suggested solutions are at the end of the chapter.

Cost Management and the Cost-Management Analyst

Cost management is important to organizations because it is more than measuring and reporting product and service costs. It is a *philosophy,* an *attitude,* and a *set of techniques* to create more value at lower cost.

Philosophy. First, cost management is a *philosophy* of improvement because it promotes the idea of continually finding ways to help organizations make the right decisions to create more *customer value* at lower cost.[3] Efficient companies (such as Pursuit.Com) provide products and services that customers want by using the minimum of the organization's scarce resources while continuously seeking to improve value and costs.

Attitude. Second, cost management represents a proactive *attitude* that all of the costs of products or services result from management decisions. In other words, *costs do not just happen.* Therefore, analysts do not simply document decisions and record costs. Instead, they are active partners in making management decisions to develop and improve products and services and reduce costs.

---

[3]Customers demonstrate value by the prices they are willing to pay. Constituents of nonprofit organizations express value by supporting preferred organizations with donations of money, time, and other resources. Constituents of government organizations express value preferences by voting, lobbying, or supporting political candidates.

Exhibit 1–1 Cost Management Support of Management Decisions: A Recipe for System Design Pursuit.Com

Management Decisions	Cost-Management System Element	Cost-Management Technique Pursuit.Com
1. Choose the organization's long-term strategy	Knowledge of the organization, its competitors, and its environment	Analyze relative competitiveness by comparing processes to competitors and best practices
2. Define the organization's scale and scope of operations	Measures of expected efficiency of acquiring and using resources in alternative operations	Analyze current and possible changes in value chain and economic cost drivers
3. Plan and organize the use of resources into efficient operations	Identification of opportunities for improving the value and cost of new or existing products and services	Analyze current business and production processes for efficiency Measure expected out-of-pocket and opportunity costs of decisions
4. Implement plans and organizational change	Leadership of organizational change	Provide leadership for cross-functional teams
5. Evaluate results of plans and changes	Measures and reports of actual outcomes of activities, processes, products, and services	Measure periodic and product flows of costs through business, production, marketing, and distribution processes and activities
6. Motivate and evaluate performance of individuals and subunits	Measures and methods for motivating and evaluating personnel	Develop incentive programs and measure improvement, productivity, quality, cycle time, and customer satisfaction
7. Communicate plans and results to constituents	Communication of the results of cost management activities	Provide frequent and timely communications to match decision making
8. Evaluate success of decision making and making improvements	Differences between actual outcomes and plans or expectations	Explain and interpret differences between actual outcomes and plans

cost-management system *is a set of cost-management techniques that function together to support the organization's goals and activities*

↑ Key Terms are defined in the text and repeated in the margins for easy reference. A list of key terms appears at the end of the chapter with a page reference. The terms also appear in the glossary at the end of the text.

Pursuit.Com

Techniques. Third, cost management is a set of reliable *techniques.* These techniques can be used individually to support a specific decision or together to support the organization's overall management. A set of cost-management techniques that function together to support the organization's goals and activities is called a **cost-management system.**

Cost management supports management's strategic decision making by identifying an organization's comparative strengths and weaknesses and better ways to use, improve, or eliminate them (weaknesses). We present key management decisions made at Pursuit.Com and other organizations in the first column of Exhibit 1–1. The cost-management system elements (second column of Exhibit 1–1) are at the heart of managing any business, non-profit organization, or government unit.[4] Pursuit.Com managers use cost-management information daily. CFO DelVal and her staff reinforce awareness of the cost-management system with periodic seminars and training sessions for all managers.

CFO DelVal recently conducted an orientation for several new employees to describe Pursuit.Com's cost-management system. The system is not the most elaborate or expensive, but it effectively matches information to the types of decisions that managers and other employees must make. Throughout the orientation, DelVal emphasized the techniques, shown in the third column of Exhibit 1–1, that cost-management analysts use to support decision making at Pursuit.Com and the way the techniques work together as a

[4]For example, see R. Cooper and R. Slagmulder, "Strategic Cost Management" T. Freeman "Transforming Cost Management into a Strategic Weapon."

system. Although the system currently works well, DelVal encouraged the new employees to always be alert for deficiencies and to make recommendations for improvement.

In this chapter we introduce the cost-management techniques that Pursuit.Com uses to support the first four types of decisions in Exhibit 1–1. Subsequent chapters cover all of the types of management decisions in detail.

Choosing a Long-Term Strategy at Pursuit.Com

Managers at Pursuit.Com rely on cost-management information to help identify sources of *competitive advantage*—what the organization can do better than others to provide valued products and services now and in the future for which customers are willing to pay higher prices. Identifying its market niche—meeting unique data-communication needs of small, fast-growing, high-technology firms—was a critical strategic decision for Pursuit.Com's founders. Because the company provides telecommunication services more quickly and reliably than competitors, customers are willing to pay premium prices.

Benchmarking: A Cost-Management Technique for Strategic Choice and Improvement

LO 2 Apply benchmarking, cost-benefit, and value-chain analysis to consider and evaluate changes to an organization's value chain.

benchmarking *is a technique for determining an organization's competitive advantage by learning about its own products, services, and operations and comparing them against the best performers*

benchmarks *are important competitive features that form the bases of comparison and exist either inside or outside one's own organization, or in other industries*

Benchmarking is a technique for determining an organization's competitive advantage by learning about its own products, services, and operations and comparing them with the best performers. **Benchmarks,** which are important competitive features that form the bases of comparison, exist either inside or outside the organization, or in other industries. Comparing a company's performance with the best can be a sobering experience, but failing to do so could be the corporate equivalent of hiding its head in the sand. Managers of Xerox Corporation, for example, were shocked to learn how poor its U.S. performance was compared to that of its Fuji-Xerox subsidiary in Japan. This revelation prompted serious reevaluation of the firm's strategy and led to dramatic improvements in its operations.

Benchmarking can identify both the sources of competitive advantage and the threats to those advantages from competitors. Benchmarking can reveal, for example; that although Pursuit.Com's products are far superior to competitors' in function, its product and service costs are higher. If competitors' costs are lower, they can offer customers more value or the same value at lower prices.

Exhibit 1–2 is a benchmarking report on the service costs of accounting procedures at a division of US EAST, which competes in some markets with Pursuit.Com, relative to the best performers in the world.[5] US EAST took steps to dramatically reduce the cost of its accounting functions. As a result of these published findings, Pursuit.Com became interested in whether it could reduce the costs of its accounting services and followed through on what it found. Many improvements come about because managers pay attention to what competitors do (or do not do!).

Column A of Exhibit 1–2 lists various accounting procedures performed, and column B shows the annual costs of these procedures at US EAST. The average cost per transaction for each procedure at US EAST is in column C. Column D presents average costs per transaction for the largest U.S. companies, the FORTUNE 100. Note that US EAST's average costs are comparable to the FORTUNE 100's average costs (e.g., \$15.20 versus \$15.00 for processing an accounts receivable transaction). US EAST's costs, however, are much higher than average costs of companies with the most efficient accounting procedures (only \$4.60 to process an accounts receivable transaction at a company rated best in world—column E).

[5]The critical reader may wonder about the origin of these costs that are so important to management decisions. Analysts measure these costs and fully disclose the assumptions that support the measures. Most of this textbook develops methods for estimating and measuring costs to support management decisions.

Exhibit 1–2

Benchmarking Analysis of Accounting Activities at US EAST

	A	B	C	D	E
1	US EAST Accounting Procedure	Cost per Year (US$ millions)	US EAST Cost per Transaction	FORTUNE 100 Average	Best in World
2	Accounts receivable	$38.4	$15.20	$15.00	$4.60
3	General ledger	1.2	n/a*	n/a*	n/a*
4	Accounts payable	1.5	8.90	7.00	1.80
5	Payroll	1.0	7.30	5.00	1.72
6	Credit and collections	0.9	12.00	16.00	5.60
7	Total	$43.0			

*n/a = not available

Source: Adapted from S. Coburn et al., "Benchmarking with ABCM."

Benchmarking analysis exposes relative cost advantages or disadvantages and poses this question: Should Pursuit.Com be satisfied with costs that compare with the FORTUNE 100's costs, or should it strive to meet the best in the world? Pursuit.Com, for example, seeks competitive advantage by providing customized telecommunication products and services in its market niche. Does that mean Pursuit.Com should invest heavily in accounting services (or other internal processes)? It should do so only if these services are essential to its main source(s) of competitive advantage. Otherwise, Pursuit.Com should seek the least expensive way to provide quality accounting services (and other organization functions), which could be performed by external parties. You should work through You're the Decision Maker 1.2 to see how to use this benchmarking information.

You're the Decision Maker 1.2

Benchmarking Accounts Receivable

Refer to the information in Exhibit 1–2.

a. Approximately how many accounts receivable transactions did US EAST process?

b. How much money could US EAST save annually if it could process accounts receivable transactions as cheaply as the best in world and if the number of transactions remained constant?

c. At the current level of transactions, how much money could US EAST save annually if it turned over its credit and collection activities to an outside collection agency that charged $2 more per transaction than the best in world?

d. What considerations beyond cost savings might be important to a decision to use an outside collection agency? Why?

(Solutions begin on page 22.)

Choosing Pursuit.Com's Scale and Scope of Operations

value chain *is a set of linked operations or processes that begins with obtaining resources and ends with providing products or services that customers value*

An especially useful way to determine the scale and scope of an organization's operations is to understand the concept of the value chain. The **value chain** describes an organization as a set of linked operations or processes that begin with obtaining resources and end with providing products or services that customers value. A **process** is a related set of tasks, manual or automated, that transforms inputs into identifiable outputs. Each part of the value chain describes a type of process that an organization performs, and each process in the chain should focus on improving customer value. Exhibit 1–3 shows a generic value chain. Note that the value chain also shows that managers must decide how to apply the organization's valuable (and scarce) physical and human resources to each linked process.

Exhibit 1–3

Value Chain: Sources of Competitive Advantage

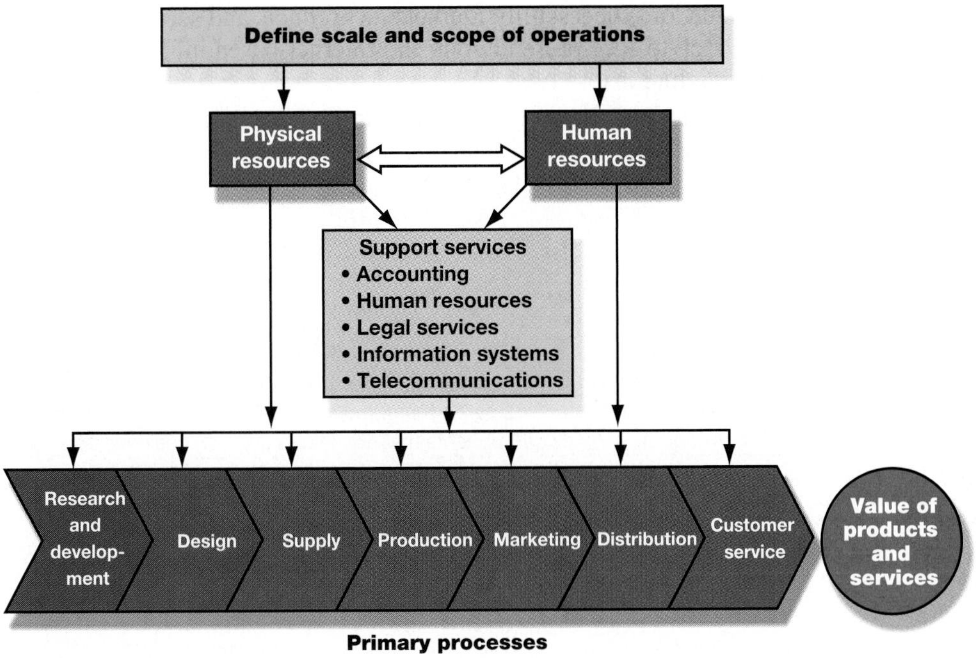

The complete value chain includes the following processes, which are exemplified by Pursuit.Com:

Research and development (R&D). Pursuit.Com has extensive R&D operations to develop new telecommunication switches and software applications.

Design. Pursuit.Com implements its telecommunication developments, in part, by designing innovative fiber-optic switches and software switching and sharing applications.

Supply. Pursuit.Com has strong relations with its external suppliers, who work closely with Pursuit.Com to control the quality and timing of shipment of supplies. Some external suppliers, such as Corporate Express,[6] have become part of Pursuit.Com's **extended value chain,** which encompasses the ways companies obtain their resources and distribute their products and services, possibly using the services of other organizations.

Production. Pursuit.Com assembles its own fiber-optic devices and writes its own software applications.

process *is a related set of tasks, manual or automated, that transforms inputs into identifiable outputs*

extended value chain *encompasses the ways companies obtain their resources and distribute their products and services, possibly using the services of other organizations*

[6] For more about Corporate Express, see case 1.38 in the Cases section of this chapter. Companies such as Saturn, Coca-Cola, Exxon, and Hewlett-Packard save more than $100 per order and tens of millions of dollars per year by outsourcing their supply functions to Corporate Express.

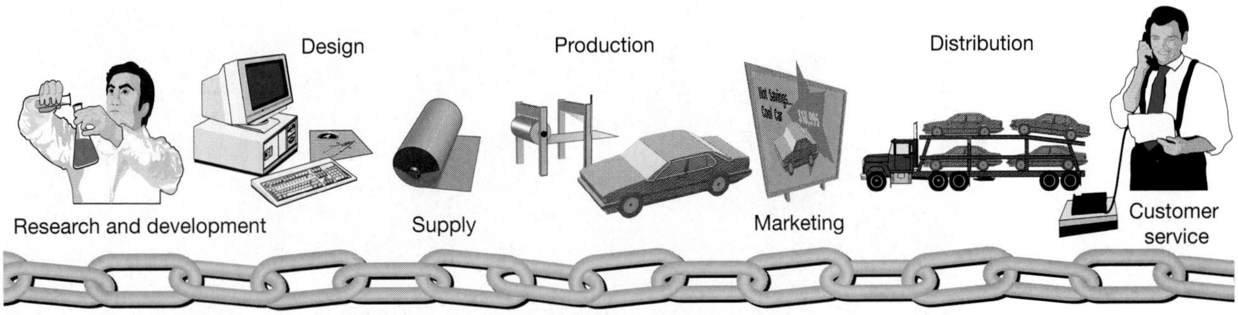

The value chain

Marketing. Pursuit.Com successfully markets its products and services using both traditional, face-to-face presentations and Internet-based information (e.g., Web sites) and solicitations.

Distribution. Pursuit.Com contracts with land-based delivery companies for local and regional deliveries and with air-delivery companies that can deliver products anywhere in the world.

Research Insight 1.2

Outsourcing and the Value Chain

Research on outsourcing components of the value chain has identified several characteristics of firms and their operations that could lead to more outsourcing. Firms are focusing their resources on those parts of the value chain that are most important to their goals and are outsourcing other operations. Some observers predict that, in 10 to 20 years, most firms will have outsourced every part of the value chain except the few key components that are unique and sources of competitive advantage. Information services (information technology, Internet services) and traditional support services (legal, logistics, human resources, payroll, accounting transactions, and tax) are most likely to be outsourced: Companies seeking to reduce costs or gain access to specialized information (information technology, foreign markets) are more likely to outsource parts of the value chain. Because outsourcing can result in loss of control and internal expertise, trust and reliable measurement of outsourcing performance are essential. Providing outsourced services is one of the fastest growing businesses in the world. *Source: S. Widener and F. Selto, "Management Control Systems and Boundaries of the Firm."*

Customer service. Pursuit.Com guarantees the performance of its products and services and moves quickly to resolve customer problems or complaints.

Support services. Some companies would not identify support functions, such as accounting, human resources, legal services, information systems, and telecommunications, as critical parts of the value chain. Therefore, all of these support functions could be candidates for outsourcing. Other companies do define some support functions as sources of their competitive advantage.

Sara Lee contracts with external bakeries to prepare its food products. By outsourcing most of its value chain, Sara Lee can focus on managing its most important competitive advantage—its brand name.

Configuring Pursuit.Com's Value Chain

Managers at Pursuit.Com considered whether the organization should perform all of its value-chain processes and support services itself or outsource some of them. One possibility for Pursuit.Com was to contract with other organizations to provide some of the value-chain processes. In general, an organization can decide, for example, that its competitive advantage is not tax planning or preparing tax returns, so it contracts with an organization of tax professionals to provide tax services.

virtual organizations *maintain only the most important operations of the value chain and outsource everything else*

The Virtual Organization

So-called **virtual organizations** that are now emerging maintain only the most important operations of the value chain and outsource everything else. For example, Sara Lee Corporation has outsourced every part of the value chain except for the management and control of its Sara Lee brand name of pastries and other food items. Sara Lee now contracts with external suppliers, bakeries, and distributors to develop, prepare, and deliver food products to retail stores. Sara Lee previously performed all of these value-chain processes itself but decided that managing only the brand name created competitive advantage. As long as Sara Lee can ensure the quality of its external partners' processes, the company can concentrate on ways to increase the value of its brand without worrying about operational details. *Sources: "Sara Lee: Playing with the Recipe," and R. Reich, "Brand-Name Knowledge."*

Cost Management in Practice 1.1

Actual practices of real-world organizations are presented here.

Value-Chain Analysis of Sara Lee

Refer to Cost Management in Practice 1.1 describing Sara Lee Corporation. Place yourself in the role of someone who is considering founding a virtual organization and wishes to learn from Sara Lee's experiences.

a. Describe Sara Lee's value chain now that it is a virtual organization.

b. What problems might Sara Lee have as a business organization that has outsourced most of its value chain?

c. *Team Focus:* What types of teams do you think Sara Lee should use to manage its outsourced value chain?

(Solutions begin on page 22)

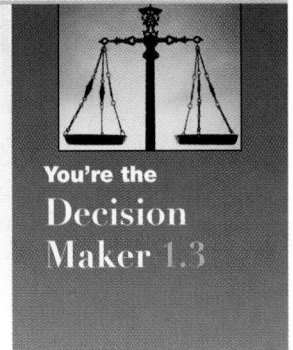

You're the Decision Maker 1.3

Analyzing Alternative Value-Chain Configurations

As an example of managing the value chain, we review the way Pursuit.Com analyzed its accounts receivable process using cost management information. This review illustrates the way cost management analysts carefully prepare information to support strategic decisions.

Pursuit.Com decided that its competitive advantage lies in meeting customers' unique data-communication needs quickly and reliably. Managers acknowledged that accurate and timely information about customers' accounts receivable is important for managing those accounts and Pursuit.Com's cash flow. They also decided, however, that Pursuit.Com was not going to become a major provider of data-communication switches and services by having the best accounts receivable process in the industry. Consequently, CFO DelVal decided to analyze Pursuit.Com's accounts receivable process to see if it could be performed more efficiently.

Formation of a Cost-Management Team

DelVal decided that a small, diverse team should analyze accounts receivable. She assigned Jason Moffit, a new cost-management analyst, to direct it. Also on the team were Ellen Matsumura, an information systems analyst, and Nelson Figueroa, a customer service manager. DelVal reasoned that these three individuals were technically

The development of the Hewlett-Packard Deskjet printer involved teams from manufacturing, accounting, marketing, and finance. By their interaction, the team lowered costs and speeded development, providing H-P a competitive market advantage.

competent and representative of the affected parties. She asked them to develop an innovative solution that accomplished the company's information and customer-relations needs—at a lower cost.

- Moffit understood the accounting transactions and record-keeping necessary to maintain the accuracy of the information. He also understood Pursuit.Com's need to create more customer value at lower cost.
- Matsumura had superior process-analysis skills, although she had only a basic knowledge of accounts receivable processes.
- DelVal added Figueroa to the team because she knew that any solution to reducing the costs of accounts receivable processing must not impair customer relations, and she was counting on him to provide a customer focus to the analysis.

At the team's first meeting, members decided on a plan of action and the required steps of their analysis. Then they divided the duties among themselves and agreed to review each other's work quickly and provide feedback. Finally, they agreed to attend a series of meetings when they could discuss their progress and prepare their recommendations to the CFO. They wanted answers to the following questions:

- What needs to be accomplished by processing accounts receivable?
- How is accounts receivable currently processed, and how much does it cost?
- Do the people who do the work have recommendations for improvement?
- What are the costs and benefits of outsourcing accounts receivable?

Importance of Accounts Receivable Information

Matsumura interviewed several key users of accounts receivable information to determine their needs. CFO DelVal was concerned about the need for accurate information about the

	Customer 1	Customer 2	. . .	Total by Date
Date of credit sale or collection				
January 1, 200x	$	$		$
January 2, 200x	$	$		
. . .				
Total by customer	$	$		Grand total $

Exhibit 1-4

Matrix of Selected Accounts Receivable Information

Pursuit.Com

ages of accounts receivable since these greatly affect her forecasts of cash flows.[7] She also was concerned about the overall collectability of credit sales because she did not want to misstate the magnitude of this important balance sheet account in the company's periodic financial reports. DelVal also wanted to be able to provide customers' credit histories with Pursuit.Com to sales personnel to avoid extending credit to nonpaying customers.

Vice president of marketing and sales, Rory Enright was concerned that aggressive collection efforts could damage customer relations, especially if a customer had paid already. Enright was most concerned about the accuracy of monthly billing statements and current accounts receivable information.

From these interviews, the team determined that the accounts receivable process should provide the following information:

- Each customer's current outstanding credit sales.
- Each customer's pattern of sales and payments on credit sales.
- The overall age distribution of outstanding credit sales.

Matsumura visualized this information as a two-dimensional matrix, shown in Exhibit 1-4, which was the basis for designing an electronic *database* of credit sales information.[8] These data could be sorted, classified, updated, summed by rows or columns, transcribed to billing statements and aging analyses, and communicated readily to customers and salespersons.

The Processing and Costs of Accounts Receivable Information

Next, the team interviewed the individuals whose regular activities involve accounts receivable information. The people interviewed and their descriptions of their involvement with accounts receivable appear in each column of Exhibit 1-5. Note that, except for the accounts receivable clerk, these are individuals whose duties involve more than accounts receivable.

The last row of Exhibit 1-5 shows Moffit's estimates of the amounts of each person's time spent using or processing accounts receivable information. Multiplying this

[7]Budgeting cash flows is covered in more detail in Chapter 15. "Budgeting and Financial Planning." An *aging analysis* typically shows outstanding accounts receivable partitioned by 0–30 days old, 31–60 days old, and so on. In general, older receivables are less likely to be collected.

[8]Note that this matrix represents a traditional sales journal, accounts receivable general ledger account, subsidiary ledger accounts, and part of the cash receipts journal. Of course, these data could be part of a larger sales database with other relevant information, such as invoice numbers, customers' addresses, credit limits, products or services sold, sales terms, and salesperson. The design and use of electronic databases is beyond the scope of this text. The interested reader should consult a current database design text, such as D. Hollander and Cherrington, *Accounting, Information Technology, and Business Solutions.*

Exhibit 1–5 Pursuit.Com's Analysis of the Accounts Receivable Process

	Employees					
	Sales Data Entry Clerk	**Sales Manager**	**Accounting Manager**	**Salespeople (15)**	**Accounts Receivable Clerk**	**Information Systems Technician**
Major tasks related to accounts receivable	• Open morning mail • Record amounts received from customers since previous morning • Prepare daily summary • Send checks and daily payment summary to sales manager • Monthly, prepare billing statements from subsidiary ledgers	• Review checks and daily payment summary • Send checks, daily payment summary to accounting manager • Review prior day's sales summary • Monthly, send updated credit authorizations to salespersons	• Review checks and daily payment summary • Evaluate payments, past-due accounts • Send checks and daily payment summary to accounts receivable clerk • Monthly, review billing statements • Monthly, revise customer credit authorization and limit; send to sales manager	• Approve credit sale after review of customer credit authorization • Prepare sales invoices • Send copies of sales invoices to accounts receivable clerk (and to affected operations) • Respond to customers' complaints about incorrect billing	• Post payments to accounts receivable subsidiary ledger • Total checks and post to cash receipts journal • Send checks to treasurer's office • File daily payment summary • Balance cash received with cash sales invoices • Post cash and sales received to sales and cash receipts journals • Post credit sales to subsidiary ledgers • Prepare and file daily sales summary • Make corrections • Monthly, prepare aging analysis	• Maintain software and hardware • Revise report formats as requested • Monthly, prepare report of volume of accounts receivable transactions
Annual salaries	$23,000	$68,000	$62,000	$750,000	$28,000	$ 48,000
% time on A/R	×0.25	×0.08	×0.10	×0.10	× 1.00	×0.03
Cost estimate	$ 5,750	$ 5,440	$ 6,200	$ 75,000	$28,000	$ 1,440
Grand total						$121,830

percentage by each person's annual salary yields an estimate of the cost of that time. It is important to note, however, that *these cost estimates are not the amounts the company would save* if each individual ceased working with accounts receivable information. Rather, these costs indicate that if the company could redesign jobs to eliminate the need for accounts receivable information, employee time costing approximately $121,830 per year either is not needed or could be used for other purposes. This amount is equivalent to the salaries of two or more people.

Eliminating all use of accounts receivable information is not reasonable because it is indispensable for some decisions and reports. Since most employees who work with accounts receivable are salaried, it also is not reasonable to expect that anyone's pay would be cut to reflect time not spent on accounts receivable information. However, it is reasonable to expect that Pursuit.Com could find a way to provide accounts receivable information more efficiently so that employees could spend more time on operations that create customer value instead of spending time processing paperwork. This is where the cost-management team comes in—it helps realign processes to add more value at lower cost.

For example, the 15 salespeople spend approximately 10 percent of their time filling out invoices and finding credit information on customers. What if that time could be cut in half? Assume that each salesperson generates approximately $3,000,000 per year in sales using 90 percent of that person's available time.[9] If that person can spend 95 percent of the time generating sales, each might generate $3,166,667 in sales annually [$3,000,000 × (0.95/0.90)]. This amounts to a total of $2,500,000 increased sales each year ($166,667 × 15).

The amount of these additional sales, less all of the cost of the additional sales, is the forgone profit, or opportunity cost, caused by inefficient processing of accounts receivable information. **Opportunity cost** is the largest net benefit given up by choosing one action that precludes taking other actions. For example, if Pursuit.Com chooses to continue its current accounts receivable process, it will give up, or forgo, the profits from additional sales that salespeople could generate with the time they spend on accounts receivable activities. Opportunity cost is as real a cost as the salaries paid to the salespeople, even though it would never show explicitly on any accounting statement because it is not the result of an actual transaction.

opportunity cost *is the largest net benefit given up by choosing one action that precludes taking other actions*

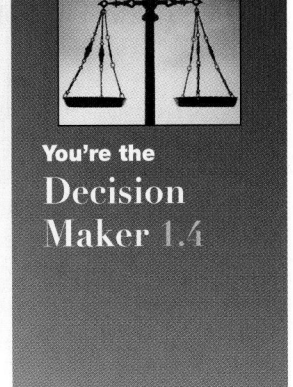

Analysis of Accounts Receivable Processing

Refer to Exhibit 1–5. Assume that you are a member of the team that is reviewing Pursuit.Com's activities.

a. What are possible reasons that the task "correcting mistakes" is part of the job of the accounts receivable clerk? Would it be desirable to eliminate this task? Explain why or why not.

b. Find at least three tasks performed by different people that probably cause delays in communicating important information. How could these delays adversely affect someone's decision making?

c. *Team Focus:* Assume that you have decided to try to eliminate the task "correcting mistakes." Describe how you should approach this change. For example, whom should you involve? What information do you need? What conflicts can you anticipate? What is the best way to communicate your team's recommendations?

(Solutions begin on page 23.)

You're the Decision Maker 1.4

Employee Recommendations for Improving the Internal Processing of Accounts Receivable

The team was surprised by the "avalanche" of suggestions and complaints they received from other employees about Pursuit.Com's accounts receivable process. Clearly, this seemingly innocuous process touched many lives, and nearly everyone

---

[9]Salespeople (and others, too) quite likely spend significant amounts of time on additional tasks that do not create value. For simplicity, assume that this is the only work improvement being considered.

had recommendations for improvements. Employees felt comfortable speaking up because they knew from the company's previous efforts to improve processes that no blame would be assigned and no one would lose his or her job for making suggestions that were implemented. In fact, employees were motivated to make their jobs more productive because they knew that adding more value at lower cost increased their job security and chances for good raises and bonuses.

The most common complaint was that too many people had to "touch" the accounts receivable documents and reports. For example, four different people prepared, reviewed, and processed the daily sales summary. This had some desirable features, since no single person controlled all the accounts receivable information, but the repetitive processing created delays and opportunities for mistakes. "Couldn't this process be streamlined?" employees asked. Another common complaint was from salespeople who believed they were not providing customers with good service because they were unable to easily access current information about customers' accounts. They lamented, "Shouldn't salespeople be able to review this information immediately and work with customers to resolve conflicts—now, not later?" Surprisingly, even the accounts receivable clerk wondered whether there was a way to eliminate most of his work because he was bored with the job and was ready for something more challenging that would add more value to the company. "Does Pursuit.Com really need a full-time accounts receivable clerk? Even though I don't make that much, I could be doing something more valuable to the company than just pushing paper around. Just look at all the manual steps I have to take. Why isn't all this processing done on the computer?" he wondered.

Costs and Benefits of Outsourcing Accounts Receivable

Before recommending any change in the value chain, analysts at Pursuit.Com compare the costs and benefits of the proposed change. Ideas such as outsourcing certain operations might sound reasonable, but if the benefits of outsourcing, typically measured in cost savings or increased profits, do not outweigh the costs, management will likely decide against the change.

cost-benefit analysis *is a method of measuring the effects of proposed improvements by comparing both the costs and benefits of a proposal*

quantitative information *is expressed in dollars or other quantities relating to size, frequency, and so on*

qualitative information *is descriptive and based on characteristics or perceptions, such as relative desirability, rather than quantities*

Cost-benefit analysis is a method to measure the effects of proposed improvements by comparing both the costs and benefits of a proposal. Cost-management analysts at Pursuit.Com always perform cost-benefit analyses to assess whether proposed changes in the value chain are worthwhile. These analysts have found that just going through the process of identifying the types of costs and benefits of a decision is useful cost-benefit analysis, even if precise costs and benefits are not available.

Exhibit 1–6 is Pursuit.Com's analysis of whether to outsource its accounts receivable process. Review this exhibit carefully, particularly the comments in the third column. This exhibit shows the types of information (quantitative and qualitative) that managers use to make important decisions. **Quantitative information** is expressed in dollars or other quantities relating to size, frequency, and so on. **Qualitative information** is descriptive and based on characteristics or perceptions, such as relative desirability, rather than quantities.

The analysis in Exhibit 1–6 compares the costs and benefits of outsourcing accounts receivable processing to Pursuit.Com's current method of internal processing. The company must be concerned with both the *qualitative* and *quantitative* costs and benefits. In some cases (for example, concerns about employee morale and customer perception of service quality), qualitative information can outweigh quantitative information in making a decision. For example, a company might find an opportunity to reduce its costs in the short run, but that violates its long-term mission or strategy. The company must weigh this qualitative factor against the short-run quantitative factor.

Exhibit 1–6 Costs and Benefits of Outsourcing Accounts Receivable Process at Pursuit.Com

Quantitative Information		Qualitative Information
Annual Benefits of Outsourcing Accounts Receivable		**Comments and Assumptions**
1. Personnel cost savings	$ 0	Can save $121,000 by laying off personnel. They can be transferred to other operations, resulting in no cost savings, but benefits may occur if they perform useful activities. This would be true of all alternatives.
2. Facilities cost savings	90,000	Can be saved or used by other operations, net of remodeling costs.
3. Support cost savings	60,000	Can be saved or applied to other operations. Could entail reductions of personnel.
4. Quality of service	—	Is not quantifiable, but service provider guarantees quality of service, which requires vigilance by contract administrators.
Total annual quantifiable benefits	$150,000	
Annual Costs of Outsourcing Accounts Receivable (A/R)		
1. Contracted service	$180,000	At expected volume of transactions. Contract to be renegotiated if volumes exceed expectation by more than 5%.
2. Contract administration	12,000	Requires one part-time contract administrator plus support (service, space, and facilities).
3. Training costs	40,000	Retraining of displaced personnel.
4. Loss of direct contact with customers	—	Not quantifiable, but could result in loss of customer goodwill and loss of customers to competitors.
5. Adverse effects of personnel reductions	—	Not quantifiable, but outsourcing A/R might be seen as first step in outsourcing all accounting operations with adverse effects on employee morale and productivity.
Total quantifiable costs	$232,000	
Net annual quantifiable benefits (costs)	$ (82,000)	

Cost-Benefit Analysis of Outsourcing

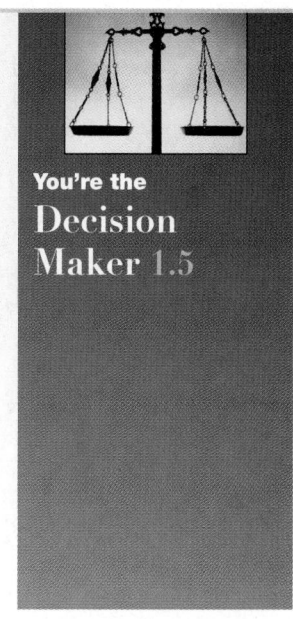

You're the **Decision Maker 1.5**

Refer to the information in Exhibit 1–6.

a. Explain why some costs and benefits in the analysis are quantified but others are not. How do you think Pursuit.Com measured the quantified costs and benefits?

b. Is it possible that the nonquantified costs or benefits of this decision could be more important than those that are quantified? Explain with an example from Exhibit 1–6.

c. Explain how the personnel, facilities, and support cost savings listed in Exhibit 1–6 might not result in actual cost savings.

d. *Team Focus:* Assume that you are the cost-management analyst assigned to the Pursuit.Com team that will make recommendations about outsourcing the company's accounts receivable process. How can you use the analysis to help the team's analysis and decision making? What problems and information needs should you anticipate?
How can you gather more information?

e. Ethical Considerations: Has Pursuit.Com identified all costs of the outsourcing alternative? If personnel are laid off or dismissed to realize cost savings, does Pursuit.Com have any obligations to those employees? Could the way that Pursuit.Com treats those employees affect retained or future employees? Explain.

(Solutions begin on page 23.)

Team Recommendations

The team prepared two alternatives for CFO DelVal's review. The first alternative was to revise the internal processing of accounts receivable. The team estimated the net costs to improve the process was approximately $100,000 per year. The second alternative was to outsource the processing of accounts receivable. A service provider had submitted a bid of $180,000 per year for the next three years to provide the outsourced service, resulting in net costs of $82,000 per year, as shown in Exhibit 1–6. The key trade-off that the team identified was whether the losses of customer contacts and control over sensitive customer information would outweigh the lower cost of the outsourced service. This trade-off was not straightforward, so the team presented both choices to the CFO, who had ultimate responsibility for making the decision.

DelVal ultimately decided to outsource the processing of accounts receivable for the following reasons, which are central to the goals of cost management:

- Pursuit.Com's executive committee always looked for ways to concentrate its resources on its processes that generate competitive advantages, and managing accounts receivable did not generate competitive advantages. Personal contacts with customers are important, but the sales force and customer service representatives can have the most impact.
- Pursuit.Com's employees should provide more value by analyzing and interpreting accounts receivable information rather than by preparing it.
- The annual cost difference between outsourcing or managing accounts receivable internally was not great, but DelVal suspected that the cost and time to develop the internal solution would be much more than the team had estimated.
- The outsourced-service provider was ready to provide customized service with little delay. This even included "real-time" access to sales accounts by salespeople and other Pursuit.Com employees who need customer sales information.
- The outsource provider had an excellent reputation for quality of service, and the service contract guaranteed nondisclosure of company or customer information to any other party.

Implementing Plans and Organizational Change at Pursuit.Com

LO 3 Describe how to effectively implement and manage change.

Pursuit.Com uses an eight-step process that other successful organizations also use to implement plans and change.[10] DelVal used the following steps to manage the decision to outsource the processing of accounts receivable:

1. *Identify a need for change.* Knowing that competitors were changing their management of accounting (and other) services to reduce costs was DelVal's motivation for examining Pursuit.Com's accounts receivable process. In the company's highly competitive industry, all firms are looking for cost advantages.
2. *Create a team to lead and manage the change.* DelVal chose a talented, representative team to analyze the accounts receivable process. This team had access to all of the people and information they would need to complete their analysis.
3. *Create a vision of the change and a strategy for achieving the vision.* Pursuit.Com's strategy is to provide superior telecommunication services and products. Accounting processes, including accounts receivable, must support that strategy, too. Fortunately, this vision was widely shared within Pursuit.Com, so it seemed natural to people who dealt with accounts receivable to question whether their task and process were consistent with the company's overall strategy. Pursuit.Com prepared this analysis for success by the way that

[10]This process is adapted from John P. Kotter, "Why Transformation Efforts Fail."

it had managed previous changes. Affected individuals were involved and rewarded (not laid off or "downsized"!) for helping to make improvements.

4. *Communicate the vision and strategy for change and have the change team be a role model.* Pursuit.Com constantly communicates the vision and strategy of the company ("Your Communication Partner") and encourages input from employees. The analysis team was well suited and trained to gather that input and include it in its analyses and recommendations. Giving credit for others' suggestions increases the chances that they will participate again in the future.
5. *Encourage innovation and remove obstacles to change.* The CFO reserved the right to make final decisions, but she gave control to the analysis team to develop solutions to processing accounts receivable. She chose a small, diverse team that was well suited to generating innovative solutions.
6. *Ensure that short-term achievements are frequent and obvious.* Analyzing accounts receivable is an example of a relatively small effort that could have an obvious impact on the company. Pursuit.Com tried to break up its large problems into smaller ones that teams could analyze and solve in a short amount of time. Managers made sure that the efforts were coordinated and well publicized. Even projects that did not meet their original objectives were treated as successes because the company learned why something did not work. This was valuable information that helped to prevent future failures.
7. *Use successes to create opportunities for improvement in the entire organization.* By focusing on relatively small issues, the company could point to many examples of employees' contributions to significant improvements. This practice made future improvements even more likely and, importantly, encouraged employees to recommend improvements even if they were small.
8. *Reinforce a culture of more improvement, better leadership, and more effective management.* The climate of striving for improvements permeates Pursuit.Com. Employees know that opportunities for improvement always exist and that managers take their recommendations seriously.

Chapter Summary

This first chapter has two purposes. The first purpose is to explain what cost management is, and the second is to illustrate what cost-management analysts do.

Cost management is (1) a *philosophy* of seeking increased customer value at reduced cost, (2) an *attitude* that all costs are caused by management decisions, and (3) a reliable set of *techniques* that increase value and reduce cost. Effective cost management allows managers to make critical decisions that affect the performance and success of the organization. Cost-management analysts need broad knowledge of the organization's activities and the way those activities interact to be able to provide information, interpretations, and analyses of alternative courses of action that managers are contemplating. They also identify opportunities to improve operational efficiency. Important cost management techniques include benchmarking and cost-benefit analysis.

Cost-management analysts are valued members of the management team because they understand how managing the organization's value chain affects cost, quality, and customer value. They also are trusted sources of objective information. Companies use cost-management teams to evaluate alternative uses of resources. This analysis often relies on benchmarking and cost-benefit analysis. Successfully managing change requires an understanding that the way a change is managed will affect the success of not only that change but also of future changes. Successful companies often use a formal process to lead and manage change.

Key Terms

For each term's definition, refer to the indicated page or turn to the glossary at the end of the text.

Benchmarking, 9
Benchmarks, 9
Cost-benefit analysis, 18
Cost-management system, 8
Extended value chain, 11
Opportunity cost, 17
Process, 10
Qualitative information, 18
Quantitative information, 18
Value chain, 10
Virtual organizations, 13

Meeting the Cost Management Challenges

1. How do cost-management analysts interact with others and contribute to the formulation of an organization's strategy?

Cost-management analysts are integral members of cross-functional teams that analyze and manage an organization's operations. Helping choose the right strategy requires that managers understand the available alternatives and their qualitative and quantitative impacts on the future performance of the organization. Cost-management analysts help identify the alternatives and estimate their effects on future performance.

2. How do cost-management analysts measure the expected effects of alternative ways to organize resources?

Cost-management analysts identify quantitative and qualitative effects, which requires understanding how organizations obtain and use resources. Cost-management analysts measure the net quantitative benefits of alternatives (expected benefits less costs). Describing qualitative effects of alternatives can be just as important as measuring quantitative effects since decisions might be greatly influenced by qualitative differences among alternatives. Managers can choose an alternative with low (even negative) net benefits because of expected qualitative effects.

3. How do cost-management analysts lead change?

Cost-management analysts lead by example and by including all affected parties in the planning and implementing of major changes. Applying Kotter's eight-step change process (see pages 20–21) can increase the chances that an organization will effectively implement a planned change.

Solutions to You're the Decision Maker

1.1 Team Decision Making p. 7

Solution is in the body of the chapter.

1.2 Benchmarking Accounts Receivable p. 10

a. Number of transactions = Accounts receivable cost ÷ Cost per transaction
= \$38,400,000 ÷ \$15.20/transaction
= 2,526,316 transactions (rounded up)

b. Cost saving per transaction = US EAST cost − Best-in-world cost
= \$15.20 − \$4.60
= \$10.60/transaction

Annual cost savings = Cost saving per transaction × Number of transactions

Annual cost savings = \$10.60/transaction × 2,526,316
= \$26,778,950

c. Outside collection agency cost = Best in world + \$2.00
= \$5.60 + \$2.00
= \$7.60

Cost saving per transaction = \$12.00 − \$7.60 = \$4.40/transaction

Annual cost savings = Cost saving per transaction × Number of transactions
= \$4.40/transaction × (\$900,000 ÷ \$12/transaction)
= \$330,000

d. These cost savings might appear to be quite large, but cost management analysts at US EAST to consider whether all of the cost indeed would be saved. Other considerations are the quality and reliability of the external provider of the service. In many cases these nonfinancial considerations can be as important as the financial impacts.

1.3 Value-Chain Analysis of Sara Lee p. 13

a. One can speculate that the operations of a truly virtual organization would consist of creating and maintaining an image (or brand) and managing all of the other operations through contracts. Sara Lee's value chain might look like the figure on page 23.

b. Successful control of outsourced operations and enhancement or protection of the image of Sara Lee products depend on substitutes for direct management of operations. These substitutes include contracts, sharing information, long-term relationships with suppliers and distributors, and measuring the performance of the providers of outsourced services. Thus, management is based almost entirely on communications and information, not first-hand observations. If these substitutes for direct management are not accurate, reliable, or timely, one of Sara Lee's partners could do serious harm to its image before top management could intervene. Similarly, if Sara Lee's partners do not communicate changes in the market or with certain customers, the company could miss valuable opportunities to improve its competitive position.

c. Since the organization is virtual, most of the individuals working with Sara Lee are not its employees. The relatively few Sara Lee employees probably would be organized in several different types of teams. Some employees might be organized in small, jazz combo teams to analyze market opportunities and changes and to work with developers of new products. Other teams might be contract administration teams that are more similar to soccer teams—flexible but focused on managing existing contracts.

1.4 Analysis of Accounts Receivable Processing p. 17

a. Errors can result from incorrect entries or incorrectly transcribed entries. Invoice errors also can lead to incorrect payments or reordering and reshipping supplies and delays in filling customers' orders. If eliminating the need to correct these errors is highly desirable because the corrections and delays they cause the consume resources (time, effort, and money) that could be used for more valuable activities.

No human process can be 100 percent error free, however, and cost-management analysts should estimate the costs and benefits of possible improvements to Pursuit.Com's accounts receivable process. A direct electronic link between the company and the customer might improve communications and eliminate most errors. On the other hand, the frequency of errors might be quite low and the impacts of the occasional error small, and eliminating all errors might be prohibitively expensive. Thus, tolerating some errors can be a lower cost option. Often, though, this rather narrow approach to cost-benefit analysis ignores benefits that extend beyond the specific problem at hand. For example, direct electronic links could improve scheduling and coordination of services that might result in even more savings and sales.

b. One example is processing the daily sales summary. As mentioned before, four people sequentially review and use this summary. This probably delays the deposit of payments in the company's bank account by several days. Another example of a delayed task that could cause decision-making problems is the monthly preparation of aging analysis and billing statements. Based on an analysis showing past due accounts, the sales manager might urge salespeople to request payments from customers when, in fact, the customers had paid some time before. This delay also could cause the accounting manager, for example, to downgrade a customer's credit standing even though payment recently had been received. A third example is a salesperson extending credit to a customer who is delinquent on past payments because the salesperson does not have ready access to the current credit standing.

c. Assess the impacts of mistakes: What do they cost the company in lost time and customer goodwill? If these are significant (and they probably are), convincing employees whose work results in mistakes to find ways to eliminate them should be relatively easy—if employees also stand to gain from this improvement. In some cases, employees felt they benefited from perpetuating mistakes because that ensured more work for them. This misguided attitude in most cases reduces job security because customer value is sacrificed. Sometimes tracing mistakes back to a single cause can remedy the problem (this is covered in Chapter 7, "Managing Quality and Time"). Using a modified version of Kotter's eight-step process for managing change probably is a good idea—without overdoing it (see the next section in the chapter).

1.5 Cost-Benefit Analysis of Outsourcing p. 19

a. Not all costs and benefits can be measured easily or with enough accuracy to justify attaching dollar values to them. Some cost-management analysts do believe that people pay attention only to measurable costs and benefits, so they might argue the value of trying to measure all of them. On the other

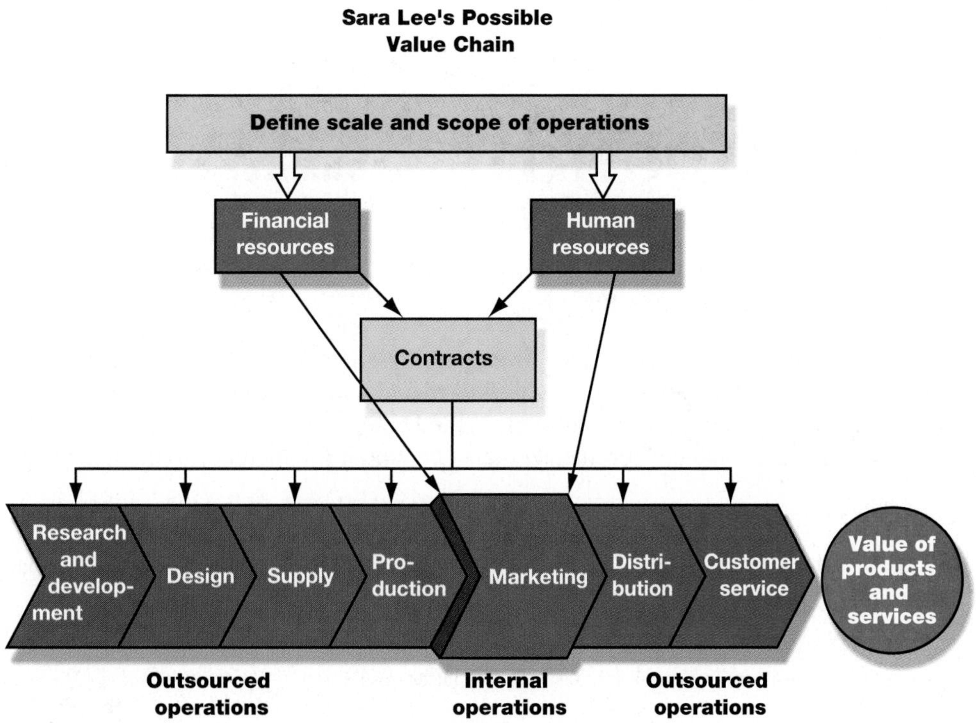

hand, others believe that attaching highly inaccurate dollar figures to some costs or benefits reduces the confidence that managers have in all numbers.

Measures of the future costs and benefits will be somewhat subjective because the future is uncertain, and specific measures depend on assumptions about future changes (organizational structure, market demand, technological change, etc.). Organizations usually rely on accountants, financial analysts, or cost-management analysts to develop these measures. They base their measures on their understanding of the way the organization has acquired and used resources in the past and the way changes will affect the resources needed. They rely on information from their own organization and from sources outside that help them predict the effects of changes. This is a complex topic that is covered in more detail in subsequent chapters of this text.

b. Probably the best decision-making environment exists when cost-management analysts clearly communicate the confidence they have in their measurements and team members discuss the importance of all costs and benefits. Therefore, some nonquantified costs or benefits might be more important than the quantified ones and can lead to proper decisions that contradict the numbers. For example, outsourcing accounts receivable, which includes billing, can result in loss of direct communication with existing customers. Pursuit.Com might lose opportunities to tell customers about new services and changes in existing ones, making them more vulnerable to promotions by competitors. Loss of good customers can outweigh the net benefits of outsourcing accounts receivable.

c. If the resources currently used to process accounts receivable, such as employees and facilities, were used for different purposes, these costs really might not be saved. The cost of processing accounts receivable would decrease, but these saved costs could shift to other operations and not be saved by the company as a whole. Many organizations fail to recognize that shifted costs are not really saved costs.

d. Identifying quantified and nonquantified costs and benefits is a good first step. The next step is to use your preliminary analysis to begin a discussion within the team about the reasonableness of the estimates and whether the nonquantified items are important. Starting with a preliminary analysis usually is better than starting a team meeting with a "blank sheet." On the other hand, you need to be careful since some team members who are less quantitatively inclined might not think to challenge your preliminary figures or ask "what if" questions—these estimates could be treated as the unshakable truth. Although the estimates might be reasonable first guesses, they could be quite inaccurate. All team members need to challenge and ultimately feel comfortable with what the numbers do and do not say.

e. Outsourcing and downsizing decisions often result in costs that the organization might not recognize. If reassigned employees need training, they will not be fully productive for some time. These costs must be considered. Most large organizations have formal "severance" policies that specify the terms of dismissal (e.g., notice, pay, benefits). The organization usually is legally obligated to live up to these terms. Do organizations have ethical obligations that extend beyond their legal obligations? One point of view is that employees joined the organization knowing what its severance policy is. They should not expect more than the policy specifies. In fact, if managers give more, they might be betraying their responsibility to owners and other contributors because they pay the cost of the additional severance benefits, perhaps unknowingly. Another view is that, depending on the economic climate and the availability of jobs, the organization might "owe" loyal employees assistance in finding other employment. A more pragmatic perspective is that the organization can enhance its reputation with potential employees and reduce morale problems with retained employees by treating its dismissed employees generously. Thus, it could be in the organization's (and its owners') best interests to provide more than the contractually agreed-on severance benefits.

Appendix to Chapter One

Institute of Management Accountants: Standards of Ethical Conduct for Management Accountants[11]

LO 4 Discuss the Standards for Ethical Conduct for management accountants (Appendix).

Management accountants have an obligation to the organizations they serve, their profession, the public, and themselves to maintain the highest standards of ethical conduct. In recognition of this obligation, the IMA has promulgated the following standards of ethical conduct[12] for management accountants; adherence to them is integral to achiev-

[11]In the past, management accountants performed many cost-management activities. Although few professionals call themselves management accountants nowadays, the IMA still is the major professional body in the U.S. that promotes cost management.

[12]National Association of Accountants, *Statement No. 1B,* "Statements on Management Accounting: Objectives of Management Accounting". These standards are reprinted with the permission of the Institute of Management Accountants. Also see www.imanet.org.

ing the objectives of management accounting. Management accountants shall not commit acts contrary to these standards, nor shall they condone the commission of such acts by others within their organizations.

Competence. Management accountants have a responsibility to:

- Maintain an appropriate level of professional competence by ongoing development of their knowledge and skills.
- Perform their professional duties in accordance with relevant laws, regulations, and technical standards.
- Prepare complete and clear reports and recommendations after appropriate analyses of relevant and reliable information.

Confidentiality. Management accountants have a responsibility to:

- Refrain from disclosing confidential information acquired in the course of their work except when authorized, unless legally obligated to do so.
- Inform subordinates as appropriate regarding the confidentiality of information acquired in the course of their work and monitor their activities to assure the maintenance of that confidentiality.
- Refrain from using or appearing to use confidential information acquired in the course of their work for unethical or illegal advantage either personally or through third parties.

Integrity. Management accountants have a responsibility to:

- Avoid actual or apparent conflicts of interest and advise all appropriate parties of any potential conflict.
- Refrain from engaging in any activity that would prejudice their ability to carry out their duties ethically.
- Refuse any gift, favor, or hospitality that would influence or would appear to influence their actions.
- Refrain from either actively or passively subverting the attainment of the organization's legitimate and ethical objectives.
- Recognize and communicate professional limitations or other constraints that would preclude responsible judgment or successful performance of an activity.
- Communicate unfavorable as well as favorable information and professional judgments or opinions.
- Refrain from engaging in or supporting any activity that would discredit the profession.

Objectivity. Management accountants have a responsibility to:

- Communicate information fairly and objectively.
- Disclose fully all relevant information that could reasonably be expected to influence an intended user's understanding of the reports, comments, and recommendations presented.

Review Questions

1.1 Review and define each of the chapter's key terms.

1.2 What is the primary objective of cost management?

1.3 What is the concept of the value chain, and why is it important for cost management?

1.4 What is strategic decision making? Give examples of several strategic decisions.

1.5 What are some cost management techniques that help make better management decisions?

1.6 What are cross-functional teams, and why are they important?

1.7 How do companies use benchmarking to make important decisions?

1.8 How does outsourcing affect an organization's value chain?

1.9 What is a virtual organization?

1.10 How do cost-management analysts use cost-benefit analysis to help determine the scope of an organization's operations?

1.11 What is a process?

1.12 How would you measure the cost of a process? Is this always an out-of-pocket cost?

1.13 How do you distinguish between quantitative information and qualitative information?

1.14 What are the eight elements of leading and managing change?

Critical Analysis

1.15 "Cost accounting and cost management really are the same functions and operations." Do you agree or disagree? Explain.

1.16 Peter Drucker, the famous management consultant, has said, "Every three years, an organization should challenge every product, every service, every policy, every distribution channel with the question: If we were not in it already, would we be going into it now?" Why is this question important? How can cost managers help pose and answer this question?

1.17 Assume that you are a vice president of the largest department store in the region. The store president has called you in to give you a challenging assignment: "Though we are the largest store, only 10 percent of the region's residents are our customers. Find out why the other 90 percent are not." Why could this be a critically important assignment? How would you organize a team to find the answers?

1.18 Refer to Exhibit 1–2. How could US EAST determine whether it has a competitive advantage in the processing of accounting transactions? What would it mean to employees of US EAST if it does or does not have an advantage?

1.19 A recent survey by KPMG, one of the world's largest business services firms, determined that 88 percent of other large U.S. companies have outsourced at least some parts of their value chains or support services. One of the most commonly outsourced services is income tax reporting. Assume that you are a cost-management analyst of a large company. How would you determine whether to outsource tax services? How might this trend in outsourcing tax services affect individuals interested in careers in the taxation field?

1.20 "If every manager minimizes the cost of the process he or she supervises, overall costs of the company will decrease." Do you think this would be a wise strategy? Why or why not?

1.21 Some years ago, General Motors installed industrial robots worth billions of dollars in its automobile assembly lines, believing that the robots would increase the efficiency of its manufacturing processes and improve profitability. In fact, General Motors lost many billions of dollars more despite the fact that it was able to make automobiles more quickly using the robots. What reasons can you think of to explain this paradox?

1.22 For many years, department stores prospered because they enhanced the process of shopping, which for many people was a break from the routine of housework and child care and was an opportunity to obtain information about available products and services. What changes have occurred in recent years that might explain the rise in shopping in "virtual stores" via the Internet? What do these changes imply for the retail processes of traditional department stores?

Exercises

↓ Exercises, problems, and cases include the learning objective they cover. Also included is a logo indicating whether the material focuses on ethics, group work, communication skills, or Internet use. A spreadsheet logo indicates that an Excel template is available on the website for that problem.

Exercise 1.23
Characteristics of Successful Cost-Management Analysts
(LO 1)

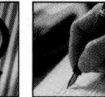

Internet Communication

Review the IMA analysis of management accounting practice (*www.imanet.org*) and prepare a memo or visual presentation (instructor's choice) that explains one of the following:

a. The most important personal attributes of successful financial managers.
b. The most important competencies for entry-level financial managers.
c. The financial management activities that will increase the most in the future.
d. The four quotations from in-person interviews that you find most interesting.

Exercise 1.24
Cost-Management Techniques
(LO 1)

Global

New Zealand recently transformed many of its government agencies into private corporations. This is a difficult process that many developing and former communist and socialist countries have been implementing. Match the following general techniques of cost management with the management decisions in these new corporations that were most likely to be assisted by using the techniques.

Cost Management Technique

a. Learning about how operations work
b. Organizing resources into efficient activities and operations
c. Measuring actual and expected costs of activities, products, and services
d. Identifying profitable products, services, customers, and distribution

Management Decision

____The design of incentive bonuses of up to 12 percent of salary by Electricity Corporations (ECNZ) for middle managers based on meeting difficult profit goals

____The use of seminars called "What If I Owned the Business?" by Television Corporation (TVNZ) to introduce staff to issues of competition

e. Identifying opportunities for improvements in the value of products and services
f. Communicating effectively
g. Motivating and evaluating personnel

____ECNZ's decision to restructure into four major operating divisions: Production, Marketing, Power Transmission, and Construction
____The decision by Coal Corporation (CoalCorp) to evaluate every job currently performed to determine which is essential to the goal of profitability
____TVNZ's new focus on estimating the costs of television programming and production
____The decision by Public Works Corporation (WORKS) to sell its poorly performing Property and Computing Services divisions
____TVNZ's analysis of the programming and advertising practices of its new commercial rival, TV3.

Adapted from B. Spicer et al., *Transforming Government Enterprise.*

Exercise 1.25
Teamwork
(LO 1)

Select the decision-making team that most likely would be best for each of the following operations or decisions. Explain your choices.

Type of Team

a. Individual (no team)
b. Small doubles tennis team whose members have special skills that complement each other's strengths and weaknesses
c. Large soccer team whose members have assignments but work closely together
d. Large swimming team whose members have individual responsibilities and normally do not interact but share in team outcomes

Operation or Decision

____Word processing center of a large university where most of the work is preparing exams, copying articles, and preparing promotional materials
____Development of a new business curriculum to meet specific educational needs
____Design of advertising campaign to counter a rival's new product announcement
____Development of a new video game for Nintendo
____Writing a new cost-management textbook
____Completion of a complex project with a short, rigid deadline
____Completing an application to graduate school
____Competing in a collegiate intramural volleyball league

Exercise 1.26
Management Decision Making
(LO 1)

Review the elements of management decision making in Exhibit 1–1. Assume that you are considering beginning a small business that will sell coffee, espresso, and possibly various other drinks in a university's engineering center. Outline a plan to begin this business. First, for each decision-making element, describe several decisions you must make. Second, try to arrange these decisions in roughly the order you must make them, from the earliest to the latest or ongoing decisions. Third, describe the information you will need to make these decisions.

Exercise 1.27
Strategic Decisions
(LO 1)

Internet

Two of the world's largest soft drink companies are PepsiCo and Coca-Cola. Find their most recent annual reports in either your library or on the Internet (look, for example, at the companies' Websites or the Securities and Exchange Commission's EDGAR site, *www.sec.gov*). From the presidents' letters, identify and list similarities and differences in these two competitors' declared strategies.

Exercise 1.28
Cost-Benefit Analysis
(LO 2)

Quantorus Corporation manufactures disk drives for computers by assembling parts and components from hundreds of suppliers. Cost-management analysts have been analyzing costs to produce disk drives and have determined that a large proportion of the cost is caused by detecting and replacing faulty components received from suppliers. Most faulty components currently cannot be detected until they are assembled into products that then fail performance tests. On the next page are estimated annual costs of three alternative decisions to manage this aspect of operations.

Alternatives for Supply of Disk Drive Components	Cost per Year (US$ thousands)
1. Continue current supply and assembly operations—detect and replace faulty components	$2,331
2. Thoroughly inspect incoming components before they are assembled	$1,708
3. Develop close relationships with a few selected suppliers that will guarantee the performance of all components	$1,387

Required

a. Describe and explain other possible costs and benefits of each alternative.

b. How do you think cost-management analysts might have developed these cost estimates?

c. Which alternative do you recommend? Why?

Exercise 1.29
Benchmarking
(LO 2)

Communication

Find a recent article in a professional magazine, such as *Strategic Finance, Journal of Cost Management,* or *Harvard Business Review,* that describes an actual use of benchmarking.

Required

a. Prepare an outline of the article that identifies the following:
- Reasons for benchmarking at this organization.
- Areas of operations that this organization had benchmarked
- Sources of information for benchmarking at this organization.
- Who maintains and uses the benchmark data at this organization.
- Whether benchmarking was a success, and how "success" was defined and measured.

b. Present your own evaluation of the success of this benchmarking effort.

Exercise 1.30
Value-Chain Analysis
(LO 2)

Match the following operations with appropriate elements of an organization's value chain.

Value-Chain Element	Operation or Decision
a. Research and development	____Dell Computer's replies to customers' questions via email
b. Design	____Electronic ordering link between Container Industries, Inc., and a division of DuPont Corp. that supplies raw plastic pellets to Container Industries
c. Supply	____Purchase by 3-Squared, Inc. of McData Corp. to acquire its data communications technology
d. Production	____Pick up of StorageTek Corp.'s packaged disk drives by United Parcel Service for delivery to customers
e. Marketing	____Development of animation for Yahoo! home pages
f. Distribution	____RCA's outsourcing of the assembly of its portable CD players to a company in Mexico
g. Customer service	____Updating Canterbury New Zealand's electronic Internet catalogue of sport and casual clothing

Exercise 1.31
Cost-Benefit Analysis
(LO 2)

For each of the following decisions, describe what other than out-of-pocket cost information might cause individuals to choose the alternative (excluding advance knowledge of outcomes):

Decision	Out-of-Pocket Cost of the Decision	Out-of-Pocket Cost of Alternative
a. Do not renew contract with external custodial service	$250,000 per year	$300,000 per year
b. Eliminate one-third of the employees at the regional warehouse	$2,200,000 per year	$3,000,000 per year
c. Outsource the manufacture of a key component to the biggest-selling product	$1,600,000 per year	$2,760,000 per year
d. Cut back spending on employee training	$500,000 per year	$1,440,000 per year
e. Replace manually operated machines with computer-controlled machines	$6,500,000 per year	$1,200,000 per year

f. Send a passport and visa application to the nearest Australian consulate by regular return mail	$1.00 per application	$34.00 per application
g. Decline the optional damage coverage on your rental car in Greece	$35 per day	$45 per day
h. Upgrade all personal computers in the office from operating on Microsoft Windows 3.1 to Windows NT	$5,000 per workstation (includes new computer and software)	$400 per workstation (includes increased memory and hard drive)

Problems

Problem 1.32
Benchmarking
(LO 2)

Consider the following data on last year's accounting operations that were obtained by Contaminant Measuring Systems, Inc. (CMS), from an industry trade association that gathers and reports benchmarking data from all members of the association anonymously.

CMS Accounting Operation	CMS Cost per Year	CMS Cost per Transaction	Association Average Cost per Transaction (without CMS)
Accounts receivable	$ 48,300	$18.00	$15.00
General ledger	21,200	6.20	4.80
Accounts payable	32,500	9.30	7.00
Payroll	22,000	7.10	5.20
Credit & collections	8,900	10.25	6.00
Total	$132,900		

Required

a. How many of each type of transaction did CMS perform that year?

b. In nearly every case, the association average cost per transaction was less than CMS's cost. How might other companies operating in the same industry have lower accounting transaction costs?

c. If CMS could process accounts receivable transactions at the association's average cost, how much would it save each year at the same levels of transactions?

d. Security Detection Devices Corporation (SDDC) is a comparably sized competitor of CMS and has the same number of accounting transactions per year as CMS. SDDC, however, processes each accounting transaction for 20 percent less than the association average. What total cost advantage does SDDC have over CMS just in the area of accounting costs per year? What is the importance to CMS of knowing this cost advantage?

e. Why do many companies benchmark their performance against their own industry and the best in the world?

Problem 1.33
Outsourcing
(LO 2)

Core States Oil Company, Inc., is a large oil and gas producer headquartered in Oklahoma. Historically, most of its operations have been in the continental United States. However, in the past decade, Core States expanded its operations to 14 foreign locations where it operates alone or in conjunction with foreign companies or governments. Core States currently maintains a large department of 73 highly trained tax specialists who report to the chief financial officer and assist with planning for the tax impacts of management decisions for domestic and foreign operations. The tax department also prepares its many, complex tax returns. Core States is considering eliminating its internal tax department and outsourcing all of its tax planning and tax return preparation to a large international business services firm. A cost management team has prepared the following preliminary calculations:

Core States Tax Operation (number of personnel)	Cost per Year
Tax-related information systems	
Personnel (12)	$ 721,300
Computer hardware/software	135,600
Tax planning	
Domestic (11.5)	598,700
Foreign (8.5)	606,100
Tax return preparation	
Domestic (24)	1,159,200
Foreign (17)	979,200
Total	$4,200,100

Required

a. What is the most that Core States Oil Company should pay for tax services from an external provider if all but the information systems costs could be saved?

b. What considerations in addition to cost should be important to Core States' decision to outsource its tax services?

c. Evaluate the business services company's offer to provide tax planning and return preparation services for $2.8 million per year. This offer is contingent, however, on Core States' acceptance of another offer from the business services company to improve Core States' tax information systems at a one-time cost of $1.35 million. This improvement should reduce annual costs of the information system by $300,000 per year for the next five years and greatly improve the accuracy and responsiveness of the system. (Ignore the time value of money.)

Problem 1.34
Ethical Issue
(LO 4)

Ethics

Paul Martinez recently joined Toxic, Inc., as assistant controller. Toxic processes chemicals to use in fertilizers. During his first month on the job, Martinez spent most of his time getting better acquainted with those responsible for plant operations. In response to his questions as to the procedure for disposing of chemicals, the plant supervisor responded that Martinez was not involved in the disposal of waste and would be wise to ignore the issue. Of course, this just drove him to investigate the matter further. He soon discovered that Toxic was dumping toxic waste in a nearby public landfill late at night. He also learned that several members of management appeared to be involved in arranging for this dumping. He was unable, however, to determine whether his superior, the controller, was involved. Martinez considered three possible courses of action. He could discuss the matter with the controller, anonymously release the information to the local newspaper, or discuss the situation with an outside member of the board of directors whom he knows personally.

Required

a. Does Martinez have an ethical responsibility to take a course of action? Why or why not?

b. What course of action do you recommend? Why?

[CMA adapted]

Problem 1.35
Costs and Benefits of Internal Orders
(LO 2)

Ante Division is part of a large corporation. It normally sells to outside customers but, on occasion, sells to another division of its corporation. When it sells internally, corporate policy states that the price must be cost plus 20 percent. Ante received an order from Beta Division for 5,000 units. Ante's planned output for the year had been 25,000 units before Beta's order. Ante's capacity is 37,500 units per year. The costs for producing those 25,000 units follow:

	Total	Per Unit
Materials	$ 20,000	$ .80
Labor	100,000	4.00
Other manufacturing costs	100,000	4.00
Total costs	$220,000	$8.80

Based on these data, Ante's controller, who was new to the corporation, calculated that the unit price for Beta's order should be $10.56 ($8.80 × 120 percent). After producing and shipping the 5,000 units, Ante sent Beta an invoice for $52,800. Shortly thereafter, Ante received a note from the buyer at Beta stating that this invoice was not in accordance with company policy. Because Ante would incur the labor and "other" costs regardless of whether it accepted Beta's order, the unit cost should have been only $0.80 to cover Ante's opportunity costs. The price paid would be $0.96 ($0.80 × 120 percent) per unit, and the total payment to Ante should be $4,800.

Required

a. What are the costs and benefits of internally "sourcing" products and services? Which can be quantified and which cannot?

b. If the corporation asked you to review the current inter-company policy, what policy would you recommend? Why? (*Note:* You need not limit yourself to Beta Division's calculation or to current policy.)

Problem 1.36
Cost-Benefit Analysis
(LO 2)

Amanda's Coffee, Inc., operates a small coffee shop in the downtown area. Its profits have been declining, and management is planning to expand and add ice cream to the menu. The annual ice cream sales are expected to increase revenue by $30,000. The cost to purchase ice cream from the manufacturer is $20,000. The present manager will supervise the coffee shop and ice cream shop. Due to expansion, however, the labor costs and utilities would increase by 40 percent. Rent and other costs will increase by 20 percent.

AMANDA'S COFFEE, INC.
Annual Income Statement
Before Expansion

Sales revenue	$38,000
Costs	
Food	15,000
Labor	12,000
Utilities	2,000
Rent	4,000
Other costs	2,000
Manager's salary	6,000
Total costs	$41,000
Operating profit (loss)	$ (3,000)

Required

Should management open the ice cream shop? Show an analysis of the costs and benefits of adding ice cream.

Problem 1.37
Cost-Benefit Analysis
(LO 2)

Change Management Corp. helps companies adapt organizational structures to current industry trends. Recently, one of its officers was approached by a representative of a high-tech research firm that offered a contract to Change Management for some help in reorganizing the company. Change Management reported the following costs and revenues during the past year.

CHANGE MANAGEMENT CORP.
Annual Income Statement

Sales revenue	$1,200,000
Costs	
Labor	570,000
Equipment lease	84,000
Rent	72,000
Supplies	54,000
Officers' salaries	350,000
Other costs	38,000
Total costs	$1,168,000
Operating profit	$ 32,000

If Change Management decides to take the contract to help the company reorganize, it will hire a full-time consultant at $134,000. Equipment lease will increase by 5 percent because it must buy certain computer equipment. Supplies will increase by an estimated 10 percent and other costs by 15 percent. The existing building has space for the new consultant. In addition, management believes that no new officers will be necessary for this work, and officers' salaries will not change.

Required

a. What costs would be incurred as a result of taking the contract?

b. If the contract will pay $150,000 in the first year, should Change Management accept it?

c. What considerations, other than costs, are necessary before making this decision?

Cases

Case 1.38
Analysis of Alternatives
(LO 2)

You have recently been hired as a new financial analyst by Corporate Express, the world's largest supplier of office supplies to large corporations. Corporate Express takes orders from its customers via the Internet, processes those orders with office supply manufacturers, and delivers the supplies to the corporate employees who ordered them. Corporate Express' customers do not need to hire anyone whose job is to order, receive, or distribute supplies, nor do customers need supplies inventories or warehouses. Large customers (such as Coca-Cola and Hewlett-Packard) save millions of dollars per year by outsourcing their office supply tasks to Corporate Express.

The vice president of marketing is concerned that the company's policy to serve only large companies does not fit its strategic goals. The VP of marketing believes it might be worthwhile to offer limited services to small, rapidly growing businesses because they could graduate to the full line of services offered to large companies. As a first step, the VP has asked you to analyze the costs and benefits of serving small and large customers.

You have developed the following information:

Annual Average Data	One Large Company	One Small Company
Number of orders per year	2,000	200
Sales value of supplies per order in dollars	$1,000	$400
Cost of supplies to Corporate Express as a percent of sales	80%	80%
Processing cost per order	$40	$40
Delivery cost per order as a percent of sales	5%	5%
Cost to create and maintain Internet access per customer per year	$2,000	$2,000

Required

a. Compute the annual profit generated from an average large or small company.

b. Would it be worthwhile to add 10 small customers to replace one large customer? Why or why not?

c. If other characteristics of small firms differ from those of large ones, would this change your evaluation? Give an example.

d. Do you recommend that Corporate Express consider this business alternative further?

Case 1.39
Outsourcing
(LO 2)

Many companies use the services of *internal auditors,* who perform various investigative and consulting tasks within organizations, such as reviewing divisional financial statements and making recommendations to improve operating performance (e.g., improving quality and customer service). In the past, this has provided both career paths for professional internal auditors and valuable training for new managers, who benefit from seeing firsthand many of the company's operations. In recent years, however, many companies have begun to outsource their internal auditing services.

Consider this recent discussion between the new chief financial officer (CFO) and the long-time director of internal auditing (DIA) at Jeans 'R Us, a large manufacturer of casual and fashion denim clothing, which has experienced serious declines in profitability.

CFO: We need to look very hard at all of our support services and consider whether we can afford them. We need to talk seriously, because I think that outsourcing internal auditing will save the company millions of dollars. In our current situation, we need to save costs wherever we can.

DIA: I think you are being shortsighted. I believe our staff can provide the best possible service to management because it understands our business. An external provider of internal audit services just will not appreciate the unique aspects of our business and our culture.

CFO: I understand that internal audit has had a long tradition here, but based on our budget constraints, I think we have no choice but to use an outside service. The service provider we are considering has a worldwide staff with wide-ranging expertise that we can utilize. You know that many of our manufacturing plants are foreign operations and require the auditors to be fluent in speaking and writing the local language and to understand the local culture. Furthermore, all of our data communications rely on information technology that changes every year. To keep internal auditing staff with these talents at Jeans 'R Us will just be too costly. And what about all of the travel expenses in the internal audit department?

DIA: I'm sorry, but you don't appreciate that internal audit is a strength of the company that has been built over the years by a trust between the internal auditors and the operational and financial management. You cannot replace that level of trust and understanding with outsourced internal auditors whose only loyalty is to the fee they will collect. Internal audit is a "partner" promoting valuable improvements, and top management has always supported it in that way. If you outsource internal audit, you will change the climate of cooperation and trust and free flow of information that you need. In the long run, you will end up paying a lot more for inferior service. Outsourcing internal audit will be a serious mistake. If you insist on this approach, I will go straight to the board of directors. By the way, you know that internal audit reports to the board each year on whether they can rely on the company's financial statements.

Required

a. Describe the possible costs and benefits of outsourcing internal auditing at Jeans 'R Us.

b. What pressures are motivating the arguments of both the CFO and the DIA?

c. How do you interpret the DIA's last comment?

d. Can you recommend a course of action that might satisfy the CFO, DIA, and board of directors?

Case 1.40
Proactive Role of Cost Management
(LO 1)

Boeing Company is the world's largest manufacturer of commercial jet airplanes. To meet growing demand, Boeing in 1997 decided to more than double its rate of production from approximately 17 to more than 40 planes per month. Boeing reported that this increase in production, which normally would be considered a fortunate turnaround, unfortunately could have cost the airplane manufacturer more than $2.6 billion in 1997–1998 for unnecessary costs. Unexpected delays and disruptions caused these extra costs. Financial analysts on Wall Street predicted that Boeing's production problems would persist for nearly a year (which proved to be true) as the company struggled to "ramp up" its production level. The next day, after the reports from Boeing and analysts, Boeing's common stock declined 7.6 percent, or $4.12 per share.

Required

a. If this event were announced today and Boeing's common stock lost $4.12 per share, approximately how much total (before-tax) wealth would Boeing's common shareholders lose today?

b. Describe Boeing's value chain in general terms.

c. What parts of Boeing's value chain would be affected by doubling its production operations?

d. Explain how Boeing's decision to quickly double its production level actually could reduce its profitability.

e. Cost-management support of management's decision to double output might have saved Boeing and its stockholders a lot of money (and prevented some unflattering publicity). Describe in general terms what support operations you might have anticipated to support Boeing's doubling of production.

Case 1.41
Proactive Role of Cost Management
(LO 1, 2, 3)

Interview with Jamie O'Connell, president, CEO, and cofounder of Datacom, Inc., a leading designer and manufacturer of storage area network (SAN) switching devices.[13]

Author: How did you decide to drop other products and direct Datacom's resources toward the design and manufacture of these behind-the-scenes network switches? This was a major strategic decision, wasn't it?

O'Connell: This was a huge decision. We have staked the future of the company on it, but let's be clear about strategic decision making at Datacom. Before we made this decision, we—and I do mean all of us at Datacom—spent months understanding our strengths and weaknesses, our competitors' strengths and weaknesses, our customers' future needs, our business partners, and the future of data-network technology. *I* did not make this decision, *we* made the decision to focus on these very important, high-value switches.

Author: Is it really possible to involve everyone? Can you trust everyone with the responsibility of this kind of decision?

O'Connell: Yes, yes, and yes. Of course it takes time, but who knows our capabilities and customers better than our own employees? And anyone who won't take responsibility for shaping the future of this company should look for another job. In this competitive and dynamic industry, we need the help and input of everyone. This decision affects every employee, stockholder, business partner, their families, and the community. True, the ultimate decision was up to the board of directors and me, but we could not and did not make this decision in a vacuum. That would have been irresponsible.

Author: Can you talk a bit about the role of cost management personnel and the information that supported this decision?

O'Connell: One of the great strengths of our company is a finance group that understands the company's business and technology. I think that is essential in a technology-driven company of our size. Not only that, they truly understand cost management and how to effectively support our strategic decision making. These are not your typical green eyeshade bean counters. The CFO, in particular, brings what I call the "reality of finance" to our analysis of the future of data-storage technology. Most of us are engineers by background, and we tend to focus on the technology more than the business. We would not have made our decision to focus on fiber-optic switches so confidently and responsibly without the daily use of cost management insight and information. We might not have predicted the future of technology and the market perfectly, but we understood beforehand, as well as we could, our alternatives and their impacts on this company and its stakeholders. This was vital, strategic information. Without it, we might as well be playing the lottery with the company's resources. Current events are proving that we chose correctly, and we are positioned to be worldwide leaders in this rapidly growing market.

Required

a. CEO O'Connell of Datacom, Inc., referred to various elements of making strategic decisions. How can cost-management information support each of these elements?

b. What quantitative and nonquantitative costs and benefits might be relevant to Datacom's strategic decisions?

c. How can organizations choose which processes to perform and which to outsource to business partners?

---

[13]Datacom is the disguised name of a real company, with approximately 200 employees and $200 million sales. SANs are high-capacity, high-speed configurations of data-storage devices, such as disk drives, that are accessible to computer networks through Datacom's fiber-optic switches.

CHAPTER

2

Product Costing Systems: Concepts and Design Issues

After completing this chapter, you should be able to:

1. Explain the role of product costs, period costs, and expenses in financial statements.
2. Prepare an income statement and a schedule of cost of goods manufactured and sold.
3. List the components of manufacturing cost, and diagram their flow through a production process.
4. Explain how unit-level, variable, and fixed costs differ.
5. Distinguish between the costs of resources used and those of resources supplied.
6. Discuss the importance to cost management of understanding opportunity costs, sunk costs, committed costs, direct costs, and indirect costs.
7. Prepare income statements using absorption, variable, and throughput costing.
8. Reconcile income under absorption, variable, and throughput costing.
9. Discuss the advantages and disadvantages of absorption, variable, and throughput costing.

Cost-Management
Challenges

1. **What** are the significant inputs to a production process, and how do cost managers track the flow of costs through the process?
2. **How** can alternative methods to calculate product costs create different incentives?
3. **How** should cost-management analysts measure costs for internal decision making?

EMAIL MEMORANDUM

EMAIL MEMORANDUM

CollegePak

Memorandum

To: Jack Canfield
Director of Cost Management

From: Maria Perez
President

CC: Anne Harrison
Vice President of Manufacturing

Jorge Gonzalez
Vice President of Marketing and Sales

Re: Projections of operating income for the new plant

Jack: The new plant in central Pennsylvania will be on line soon. Since we're focusing on a single product line there in the beginning, I'm requesting that you prepare separate operating income statements for this plant for each of the first three years of operations. That will enable us to see how the new product line is doing.

As you know, we compete effectively by being the low-cost producer of quality backpacks, and we cannot let our cost structure change from what has been successful for us in the past. In particular, we have to watch our committed costs. Our competitors surely will take advantage if our costs increase and we try to raise prices.

Please give these issues some thought, and we'll discuss them at our next Monday morning meeting.

The explosion in technology we are experiencing, coupled with increasing worldwide competition, is forcing organizations to produce high-quality goods and services and to provide outstanding customer service, and to do so either at the lowest possible cost or in a distinctive way that others cannot imitate. Success in this highly competitive environment demands that a company have a highly effective cost-management system. The role that cost management plays in helping organizations to maintain a competitive advantage is to help create more value at lower cost by efficiently managing an organization's value chain of activities, processes, and functions. These are some examples:

- In formulating its strategy, Southwest Airlines' management team considers the cost savings from being a low-cost, no-frills airline and the benefits of partnering with others in the travel industry to increase the value of its no-frills approach.
- The Boeing Company uses cost-management techniques to better understand and control the costs of aircraft production, which includes managing the costs of using many suppliers of outsourced services and products.
- Whirlpool found through its cost-management system that some of its products cost much more and others much less to produce than management previously had realized. These discoveries led to critical decisions about which products to produce, outsource, or drop.
- AT&T uses cost-management information to help management make better decisions about the services it provides. On the basis of this information, it has extended its value chain to include providing products and services for many forms of communication in ways that others cannot easily imitate (e.g., cable access to the Internet).
- Cost management techniques at Hewlett-Packard help its engineers to design products for ease of manufacturability and reduce the development time of new products, which creates a competitive advantage by being first in the market.
- Blue Cross/Blue Shield uses cost-management data to better understand the cost of its services. With this information, the company can make decisions about which services to offer and how to price them.

This list could be many times longer, but as these examples show, cost-management information helps organizations in various ways to be successful in achieving their goals. In each case, these organizations are using cost-management information to identify the activities and processes they can perform better than their competitors and to build competitive advantages.

CollegePak

The email memorandum from CollegePak Company's president to the director of cost management requests operating income statements for a new product line, and discusses CollegePak's cost commitments. These are routine issues for a company's cost-management team. This chapter explores these and other aspects of the vital role of cost management in today's business environment. Before continuing the discussion, however, let's first find out about the chapter's focus company, CollegePak.

CollegePak Company manufactures backpacks sold to college and high school students through college bookstores and other traditional retail outlets. Although the company started by focusing on the college market, which explains the name CollegePak, it has expanded into the high school market and now is considering an entry into the middle school and elementary school markets as well. The company operates a single production facility located in Trenton, New Jersey. CollegePak's market covers all regions of the United States, and the company has recently entered the European market. The family-owned company has been in business for 22 years, and its annual sales are now $4.5 million. CollegePak has been profitable every year since its founding by Gustavo Perez, who turned over the company's reins to his daughter, Maria, four years ago. Both credit the company's success to four factors: a reliable, durable, functional product; a successful marketing approach that focuses directly on the collegiate market; an outstanding group of employees from the top management team to the machine operators'

Exhibit 2–1 CollegePak's Value Chain

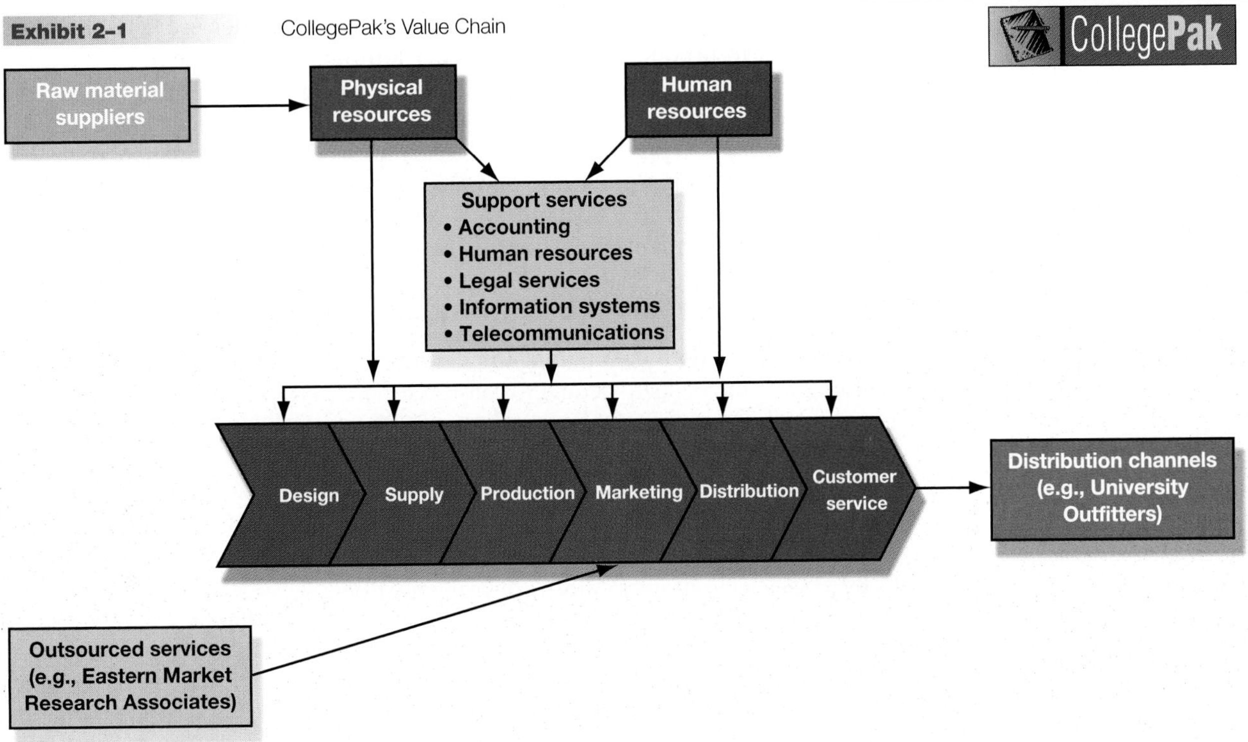

helpers; and a strong commitment to sound cost-management practices. As Gustavo has said more than once, "You can't be successful in business unless you understand what it costs you to make your product. Then you must manage that cost diligently to consistently deliver value to customers at a price they will pay." CollegePak's current president echoes her father's sentiment, adding that "we have an outstanding cost-management team. It has pulled us out of the fire many a time by finding ways to create value at lower cost."

CollegePak's value chain in Exhibit 2–1 depicts its internal processes: product design, purchasing and material handling, production, marketing, distribution, and customer service. Notice, however, that the value chain also shows the *upstream suppliers* on which CollegePak relies for raw materials, energy and various services as well as the *downstream distributors* through which CollegePak sells its backpacks. One service firm in CollegePak's upstream value chain is Eastern Market Research Associates, a consulting company that CollegePak uses for various market-research studies that fall outside the scope of the company's small marketing team's expertise. On the downstream end of the value chain is University Outfitters, one of CollegePak's oldest retail customers. Although a few companies perform nearly all of their value-chain activities, CollegePak, like most companies, has decided to outsource some services to others who can do them more efficiently. Unlike some of its competitors, CollegePak would not outsource its manufacturing processes because design and control of costs and quality are what it does best. Maintaining that aspect of competitive advantage does not just happen, however, and CollegePak must work hard to control costs.

LO 1 Explain the role of product costs, period costs, and expenses in financial statements.

The Meaning of Cost

An important first step in studying cost management is to gain an understanding of the various types of costs incurred by organizations and how they actively manage those costs. At the most basic level, a **cost** can be defined as the sacrifice made, usually measured by the resources given up, to achieve a particular purpose. If we look more carefully, however, we find that the word *cost* can have different meanings depending on the context in which it is used. In addition, cost data classified and recorded in a

cost *is the sacrifice made, usually measured by the resources given up, to achieve a particular purpose*

particular way for one purpose could be inappropriate for another use. For example, the costs incurred to produce gasoline last year are important in measuring British Petroleum's income for the year, but those costs might not be useful in planning the company's refinery operations for the next year if the cost of oil has changed significantly or if the methods to produce gasoline have improved. The important point is that different cost concepts, classifications, and measures are used for different purposes. Understanding these differences enables the cost-management analyst to provide appropriate cost data to the managers who need it.

Product Costs, Period Costs, and Expenses

expense *is defined as the cost incurred when an asset is used up or sold for the purpose of generating revenue*

product cost *is a cost assigned to goods that were either purchased or manufactured for resale*

cost of goods sold *is the expense measured by the cost of the units sold during a specific period of time*

inventoriable cost *is another term for product cost*

period costs *are identified with the time period in which they are incurred rather than with units of purchased or produced goods*

An important issue in both cost management and external financial reporting is the timing with which the costs to acquire assets or services are recognized as expenses. An **expense** is defined as the cost incurred when an asset is used up or sold for the purpose of generating revenue. The terms *product cost* and *period cost* are used to describe the events that cause their conversion into expenses.

A **product cost** is a cost assigned to goods that were either purchased or manufactured for resale; it is used to value the inventory of manufactured goods or merchandise until the goods are sold. In the period of the sale, the product costs are recognized as an expense called **costs of goods sold.** The product cost of merchandise inventory acquired by a retailer or wholesaler for resale consists of the purchase cost of the inventory plus any shipping charges. The product cost of manufactured inventory includes all costs incurred in its manufacture. For example, the labor cost of a production employee at Intel is included as a product cost of the microchips manufactured. Another term for product cost is **inventoriable cost** since product costs are stored as the cost of inventory until the goods are sold. See Exhibit 2–2, which illustrates the relationship between product costs and cost-of-goods-sold expense.

Any cost that is not a product cost is a **period cost.** These costs are identified with the period of time in which they are incurred rather than with units of purchased or produced goods. Period costs are recognized as expenses during the time period in which they are incurred. (Thus, period costs are *not* included in the cost of inventory.) For financial reporting by manufacturing, retail, and service-industry firms, all research and development as well as selling and administrative costs are treated as period costs. As we will see later in this chapter and throughout the text, however, this distinction does not have to be true for internal, cost-management information. Exhibit 2–3 illustrates the nature of period costs.

Costs Reported in Financial Statements

LO 2 Prepare an income statement and a schedule of cost of goods manufactured and sold.

Financial statements provide an important means of communicating about an organization's operations to people both inside and outside of the organization. Internal uses of such information include decision making, planning, and cost management. Creditors, investors, governmental agencies, and other interested parties are external users of financial statements.

Before returning to CollegePak, let's briefly consider the role of costs in the financial statements of service-industry firms and retailers. The reason for this digression is that the financial statements of these types of firm are simpler than those of manufacturing companies such as CollegePak. After discussing these simpler cases, we will examine CollegePak's statements. Two organizations in CollegePak's value chain are a management consulting company, Eastern Market Research Associates (EMRA), and a retailer specializing in merchandise for college students, University Outfitters. CollegePak's management has engaged EMRA to do specialized research on the market for backpacks such as those CollegePak manufactures. This important market-research effort is too specialized and extensive to be accomplished in-house by CollegePak's own marketing personnel, so management has outsourced it to EMRA. On the downstream end of CollegePak's value chain, University Outfitters is one of the oldest distribution channels for its products.

Exhibit 2–2

Product Costs and Cost of Goods Sold

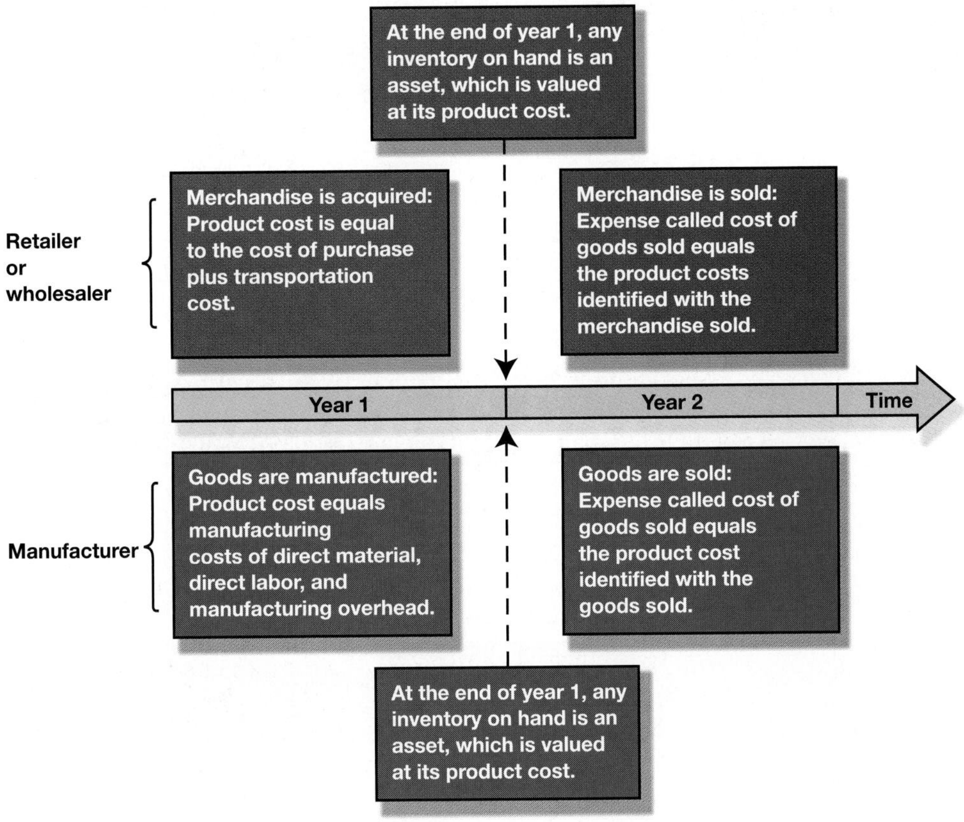

Exhibit 2–3

Period Costs

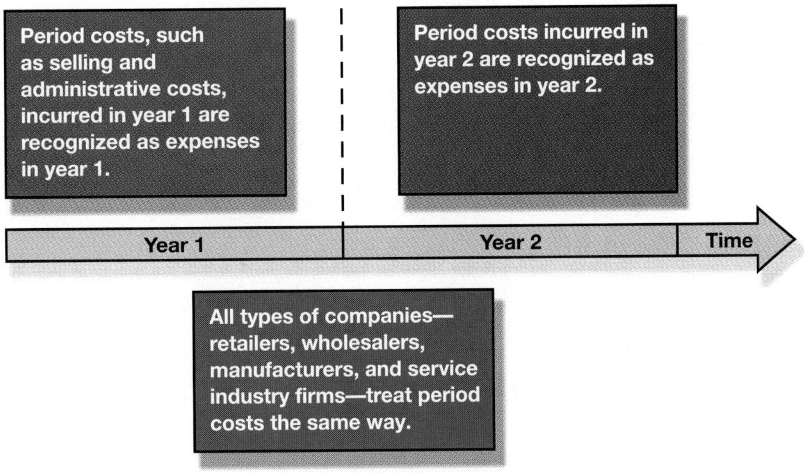

Service Firms

Service firms provide customers a product that is consumed as it is produced. Thus, service firms do not carry inventories of produced goods. For example, management consulting firms provide a variety of services to improve their clients' business processes. Labor costs tend to be the most significant cost category for most service organizations. The costs associated with EMRA are reported in the income statement in Exhibit 2–4. The costs of its services include the cost of billable hours, which are the hours billed to clients, plus other charges. (For example, the cost of billable hours includes the cost of compensation for the consultants who provide the service; the other charges might include the cost of specialized software purchased to meet the client's needs). Costs that are not part of services billable to clients are included in selling and administrative costs.

Exhibit 2–4

Income Statement for a Service Industry Firm

EASTERN MARKET RESEARCH ASSOCIATES
Income Statement
For the Year Ended December 31, 20x2

Sales revenue	$1,000,000
Cost of consulting services sold	600,000
Gross margin	$ 400,000
Selling and administrative expenses	290,000
Operating profit	$ 110,000

Exhibit 2–5

Income Statement and Schedule of Cost of Goods Sold for a Retailer

UNIVERSITY OUTFITTERS
Income Statement
For the Year Ended December 31, 20x2

Sales revenue	$1,000,000
Cost of goods sold	530,000
Gross margin	$ 470,000
Selling and administrative expenses	200,000
Operating profit	$ 270,000

UNIVERSITY OUTFITTERS
Schedule of Cost of Goods Sold
For the Year Ended December 31, 20x2

Beginning inventory		$ 100,000
Cost of goods purchased:		
Merchandise cost	$600,000	
Transportation-in costs	30,000	
Total cost of goods purchased		630,000
Cost of goods available for sale		$ 730,000
Less: Cost of goods in ending inventory		200,000
Cost of goods sold		$ 530,000

Retail Companies

Retail and wholesale companies, including supermarkets, clothing stores, furniture stores, and motorcycle distributors, sell tangible products that can be inventoried. The income statement for these companies includes revenue and cost items such as those for service companies, but it also includes the expense *cost of goods sold* to track the tangible goods they buy and sell.

University Outfitters is a retail company that sells a variety of merchandise typically needed by college students, such as books, paper, sportswear, and CollegePak's backpacks. The company's *income statement* and *schedule of cost of goods sold* are shown in Exhibit 2–5, which illustrates the computation of the cost of goods sold on the income statement; the schedule shows the following information for University Outfitters:

- The $100,000 beginning inventory on January 1, 20x2, represents the cost of the books, paper, apparel, backpacks, and other merchandise on hand at the beginning of the year.
- The company's total cost of goods purchased was $630,000.
- Based on this information, University Outfitters had merchandise costing $730,000 available for sale. This is the cost of the goods that the company *could have sold.*
- At year-end, the company subtracted the value of its merchandise inventory on hand costing $200,000 to arrive at the cost of merchandise sold, $530,000.

Cost management plays an important role in many types of organizations. The financial statements of service-industry firms, retailers, and manufacturing companies use cost information.

The income statement summarizes University Outfitters' operating performance with the following information:

- *Sales revenue.*
- *Cost of goods sold,* which comes from the schedule of cost of goods sold.
- The gross margin (the difference between sales revenue and cost of goods sold) is \$470,000 (\$470,000 = \$1,000,000 sales revenue − \$530,000 cost of goods sold). If you were University Outfitters' general manager, you would know that, on average, every \$1 of sales gave you \$.47 to cover selling and administrative costs and earn a profit.
- *Marketing and administrative costs.*
- *Operating profit.*

The term *costs of goods sold* is intended to be self-descriptive. It includes only the costs to obtain the goods that were sold. It does not include the costs of *selling* them, such as the salaries of the sales personnel, which are selling costs, or the salaries of the top managers, which are administrative costs.

Manufacturing Companies

LO 3 List the components of manufacturing cost, and diagram their flow through a production process.

A manufacturing company such as CollegePak has a more complex income statement than do service or retail companies. Whereas the retailer *purchases* the goods for sale, the manufacturer *makes* them. CollegePak purchases materials (for example, fabric and thread), hires employees to convert the materials into finished products, and then offers the products for sale. These additional activities add to the complexity of CollegePak's cost structure and financial reports. These are the three major categories of manufacturing costs.

direct materials *are resources such as raw materials, parts, and components that one can feasibly observe being used to make a specific product*

- **Direct materials** are resources such as raw materials, parts, and components that one can feasibly observe being used to make a specific product. The term "feasibly observe" means that the cost of observing the use of the resource is less than the benefit of doing so. For example, observing the use of fabric, thread, buckles, and other fasteners that CollegePak uses to make backpacks is easy; therefore, the costs of these resources are all direct material costs. Materials that one cannot feasibly identify with making a specific product (that is, it is too costly to observe the various uses of these resources) are discussed later.

  The seemingly interchangeable use of the terms *raw material* and *direct material* is somewhat confusing. However, there is a difference in their meanings. *Before* material enters the production process, it is called *raw* material. *After* it enters production, it becomes *direct* material. Thus, the cost of raw material *used* in production equals the direct-material cost.

direct labor *is the cost of compensating employees who transform direct materials into a finished product*

- **Direct labor** is the cost of compensating employees who transform direct material into a finished product. The cost of fringe benefits for direct-labor personnel, such as employer-paid health-insurance premiums, workers' compensation, and the employer's pension contribution, are also included in direct-labor cost. These costs are just as much a part of the employees' compensation as are their regular wages, and CollegePak includes them in direct-labor cost. Although conceptually correct, this treatment of fringe benefits is not always used by other companies. Some companies classify all fringe-benefit costs as *manufacturing overhead,* which is defined next.

manufacturing overhead *includes all costs of transforming materials into a finished product other than direct materials and direct labor*

indirect-material *cost relates to materials that either (1) are not a part of the finished product but are necessary to manufacture it or (2) are part of the finished product but are insignificant in cost*

indirect-labor *cost consists of the wages of production employees who do not work directly on the product but are required for the manufacturing facility to operate*

- **Manufacturing overhead** includes all other costs of transforming materials into a finished product, which one cannot feasibly observe being used to make specific products, but are necessary for the production process. Some examples of manufacturing overhead follow.

  Indirect-material cost relates to materials that either (1) are not a part of the finished product but are necessary to manufacture it or (2) are part of the finished product but are insignificant in cost. ("Insignificant in cost" means that the cost of collecting information about the use of these materials exceeds the value of the information collected.) Some examples include lubricants for CollegePak's production machinery and cleaning materials, repair parts, and light bulbs for the production plant.

  Indirect-labor cost consists of the wages of production employees who do not work directly on the product yet are required for the manufacturing facility's operation. These employees include supervisors, maintenance workers, purchasing managers, and material-handling employees. (When labor is only a small part of total manufacturing costs, some companies classify *all* labor as overhead because observing the way labor is used is too costly. Most companies, including CollegePak, do not follow this practice.)

  Manufacturing overhead also includes *other manufacturing costs,* such as depreciation on the factory building and equipment, insurance on the factory building and equipment, heat, light, power, and similar expenses incurred to keep the manufacturing facility operating. In today's manufacturing environment, managing manufacturing overhead costs is becoming more and more important as they comprise an increasing part of companies' cost structures. As a manager at Daimler-Chrysler noted, when you put in a robot to perform an operation that was previously performed by a person, you increase overhead and decrease direct labor. Why does overhead increase in this scenario? If the setup, depreciation, and operating costs of the robotic equipment, as well as the salaries of the technicians who program and maintain it, cannot be tied to specific products, these costs are part of manufacturing overhead. These overhead costs, which sometimes are ignored in decisions to automate processes, can result in total costs that exceed cost savings from replacing direct labor. For example, a major auto manufacturer once automated one of its assembly plants only to find that its total costs were higher than before, and it could not assemble enough additional cars to justify the increased cost.[1]

Support (or **service**) **departments** are an important source of manufacturing overhead costs. These departments do not work directly on a product but are necessary to operate the production process. Support departments include supplier relations, machine maintenance, production scheduling, engineering, purchasing, material handling, and quality assurance. Notice that many of the indirect-labor employees mentioned earlier actually work in a support department. Recall from Chapter 1 that many organizations perceive that the activities of some support departments do not add to their competitive advantages and have outsourced them. The costs of these outsourced activities used for production also should be counted as part of overhead costs.

support (or service) departments *do not work directly on a product but are necessary for the production process to operate*

Other manufacturing overhead costs include overtime premiums and the cost of idle time. An **overtime premium** is the extra hourly compensation paid to an employee who works beyond the time normally allowed by regulation or labor contracts. Suppose, for example, that an employee's regular hourly wage rate is $12 and that he or she receives time and a half ($18) for each overtime hour. The $6 of *additional* compensation per hour is the overtime premium. **Idle time** is time that an employee does not spend productively because of events such as equipment breakdowns or new setups of production runs. Idle time is an unavoidable feature of most manufacturing processes. The costs of employees' overtime premiums and idle time are classified as overhead so that they can be spread across all products rather than being associated with a particular product or batch of products.

overtime premium *is the extra hourly compensation paid to an employee who works beyond the time normally allowed by regulation or labor contracts*

idle time *is time not spent productively by an employee*

Although we use the term *manufacturing overhead* in this book, other synonyms used in practice are *burden, factory overhead, factory expense*, and simply *overhead.*

Prime costs and conversion costs. In manufacturing companies, you are likely to encounter the following two categories of costs: prime and conversion. **Prime costs** are direct costs, namely the costs of direct material and direct labor. **Conversion costs** are the costs incurred to convert direct material into the final product, namely, costs for direct labor and manufacturing overhead.

prime costs *include direct material and direct labor*

conversion costs *include direct labor and manufacturing overhead*

Nonmanufacturing costs. Nonmanufacturing costs include selling and administrative costs, which are not used to produce products. CollegePak incurs **selling costs** to obtain customer orders and provide finished products to customers. These include costs such as sales commissions, sales personnel salaries, and the sales departments' building occupancy costs. CollegePak incurs **administrative costs** to manage the organization and provide staff support, including executive and clerical salaries; costs for legal, computing, and accounting services; and building space for administrative personnel.

selling costs *are the costs of sales personnel, databases, equipment, and facilities devoted to sales activities*

administrative costs *are incurred to manage the organization and provide staff support*

Nonmanufacturing costs are period costs for financial reporting purposes and thus are expensed in the period incurred. For managerial purposes, however, managers often want to see nonmanufacturing costs associated with specific products. For example, managers at PepsiCo assign the cost of advertising and promotion for Diet Pepsi to that specific product so that they can measure its total cost. Chapter 4 discusses activity-based costing, which is a method to observe how most, if not all, costs of the value chain are used to manufacture products (or serve customers and provide services).

Sometimes distinguishing between manufacturing costs and nonmanufacturing costs is conceptually difficult. For example, are the salaries of staff who handle factory

[1] Chapter 5, "Activity-Based Management," covers the redesign of processes to generate more value at lower cost.

payrolls manufacturing or nonmanufacturing costs? What about the rent for offices for the manufacturing vice president? Some of these costs have no clear-cut classification, so companies usually set their own guidelines and follow them consistently.

Stages of Production and the Flow of Costs

raw material *refers to material that has not yet been entered into production*

work in process *refers to partially completed products*

finished goods *are products ready for sale*

cost-accounting systems *measure the usage and cost of resources in production*

Suppose that we are able to tour CollegePak's Trenton production facility. We would encounter the following stages of production:

- We would see **raw material** that has not yet been put into production (e.g., bolts of fabric).
- Next we would find **work in process**, which refers to partially completed products being worked on.
- Finally, somewhere past the end of the production process, perhaps in the shipping area, we would find **finished goods** ready for sale.

Manufacturing organizations use **cost-accounting systems** to measure their use of resources in these three production stages. These systems have three major categories of inventory accounts, one category for each of these three production stages: *raw-material inventory, work-in-process inventory, and finished-goods inventory.*

Each inventory account typically has a beginning inventory amount, additions and withdrawals during the period, and an ending inventory based on what is still on hand at the end of the period. Those costs added to inventory accounts are called *inventoriable costs.*

A simplified version of the production process at CollegePak's Trenton plant reviews how this works. It is a traditional manufacturer that produces products, places them in inventory, and then seeks to sell those products. Exhibit 2–6 shows the stages of production from the receipt of raw material through manufacturing to the storage of finished goods. CollegePak's Raw Material Receiving Work Center receives its fabric. The employees in this department are responsible for checking each order to ensure that it meets quality specifications and that the goods received are those ordered.[2]

When the production process begins, the Cutting Work Center cuts and seals the edges of the fabric pieces needed for the main part of each backpack in the production batch and the various small pieces of fabric used for the front and side pockets on each backpack. Then the Cutting Work Center sends the pieces to the Sewing Work Center, which sews them together to form the backpacks in the production lot. Both the cutting and sewing operations are semiautomated with significant touch (i.e., direct) labor involved.

Next the Sewing Work Center sends the backpacks to the Finishing Work Center, which adds the straps, buckles, snaps, zippers, and the CollegePak label, as well as any other trim items, such as the logo of the college or university where the backpacks will be sold. Then the backpacks transfer to the Quality Assurance Work Center, where they are inspected for fabric, sewing, or other flaws. Note that the partially completed products in the Cutting, Sewing, Finishing, or Quality Assurance Work Centers are part of work in process. The costs associated with any product still in these work centers at the end of an accounting period is included in Work-in-Process Inventory.

After Quality Assurance inspects the backpacks, the products become finished goods inventory. The Finished Goods/Shipping Work Center stores the finished goods, packages them for shipment, and ships them to various retailers, who are CollegePak's customers. The costs of any products that are finished but have not yet been sold to customers are included in the Finished-Goods Inventory account at the end of an accounting period.

[2]Chapter 7, "Managing Quality and Time to Create Value," discusses different production processes that can be more efficient than CollegePak's approach. Chapter 7 also discusses ways that many companies ensure the quality of incoming materials by partnering with suppliers. Effectively, they outsource this value-chain activity to suppliers.

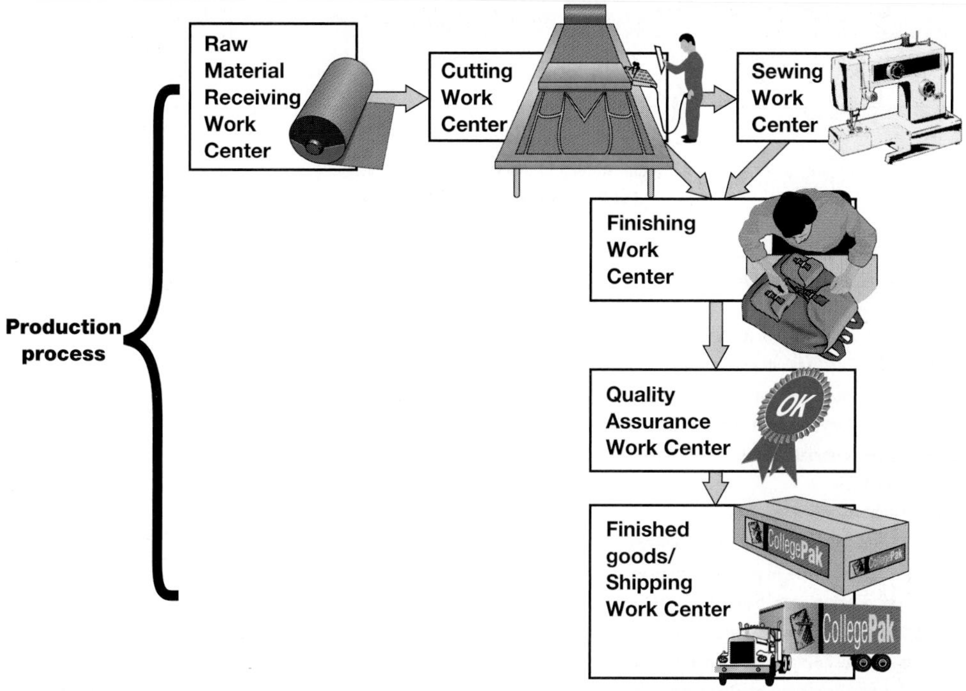

Exhibit 2-6

CollegePak's Production Stages

Exhibit 2-7

Income Statement for a Manufacturer

COLLEGEPAK
Income Statement
For the Year Ended December 31, 20x2

Sales revenue	$4,500,000
Cost of goods sold (see Ex. 2–8)	2,810,000
Gross margin	$1,690,000
Less: Selling and administrative expenses	1,440,000
Operating profit before taxes	$ 250,000

Income Statement and Schedule of Cost of Goods Manufactured and Sold

CollegePak's income statement for the most recent year, shown in Exhibit 2–7, is a typical income statement for a manufacturer. The income statement shows that CollegePak generated sales revenue of $4,500,000, had costs of goods sold of $2,810,000, and incurred selling and administrative expenses of $1,440,000 for the year.

Now let's consider how to derive the cost-of-goods-sold amount on CollegePak's income statement. The cost management group in a manufacturing company usually uses the cost accounting system to provide management with a schedule of cost of goods manufactured and sold, such as the one shown in Exhibit 2–8 for CollegePak. This schedule reflects the costs of the goods manufactured and sold during a *period* of time, and its result, cost of goods sold, is shown on the income statement for that period. Thus, like the income statement, this schedule is prepared for a *period* of time.

Direct material. Let's focus on the amount for direct material on CollegePak's schedule of cost of goods manufactured and sold, lines 7 through 12 in Exhibit 2–8.

- The company's raw-material inventory on hand January 1, $200,000, is added to the $800,000 of raw material purchased during the year. This yields the raw material available for use during the year, $1,000,000.

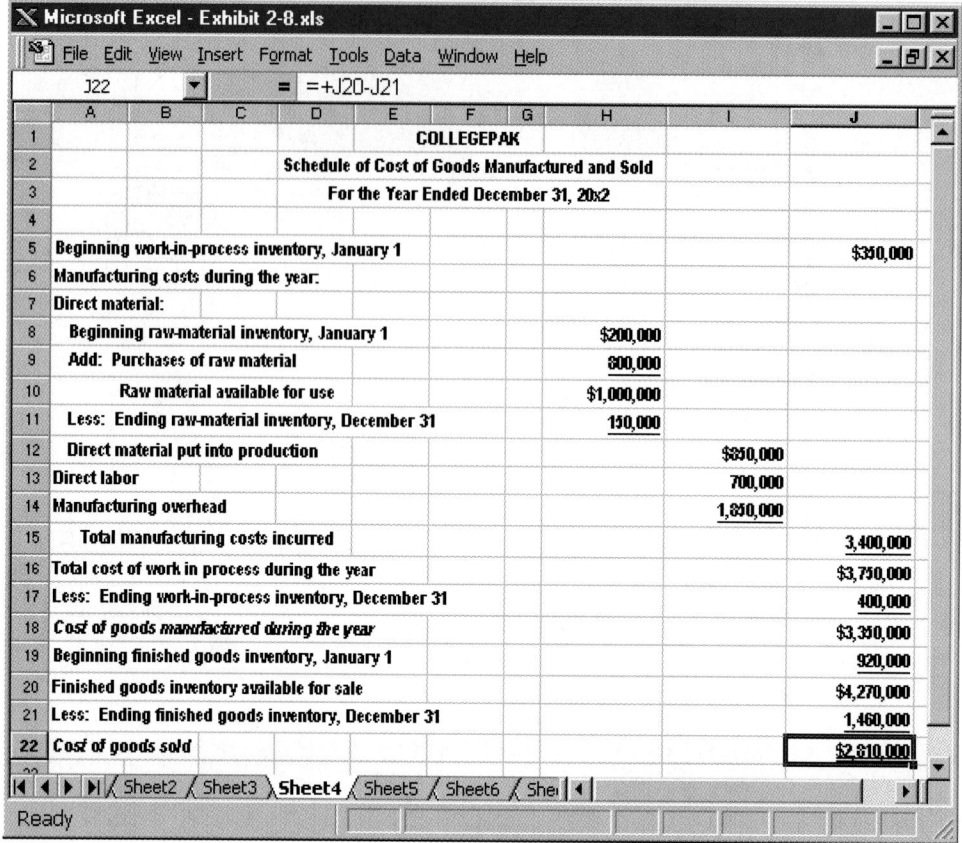

Exhibit 2–8

CollegePak: Schedule of Cost of Goods Manufactured and Sold

Microsoft Excel - Exhibit 2-8.xls

J22 = =+J20-J21

COLLEGEPAK			
Schedule of Cost of Goods Manufactured and Sold			
For the Year Ended December 31, 20x2			
Beginning work-in-process inventory, January 1			$350,000
Manufacturing costs during the year:			
Direct material:			
Beginning raw-material inventory, January 1	$200,000		
Add: Purchases of raw material	800,000		
Raw material available for use	$1,000,000		
Less: Ending raw-material inventory, December 31	150,000		
Direct material put into production		$850,000	
Direct labor		700,000	
Manufacturing overhead		1,850,000	
Total manufacturing costs incurred			3,400,000
Total cost of work in process during the year			$3,750,000
Less: Ending work-in-process inventory, December 31			400,000
Cost of goods manufactured during the year			$3,350,000
Beginning finished goods inventory, January 1			920,000
Finished goods inventory available for sale			$4,270,000
Less: Ending finished goods inventory, December 31			1,460,000
Cost of goods sold			$2,810,000

- Deducting the ending inventory on December 31, $150,000, the cost of direct material put into production during the year was $850,000.

Work in process. Now let's turn our attention to the work in process on CollegePak's schedule of cost of goods manufactured and sold. The Work-in-Process Inventory account had a beginning balance on January 1 of $350,000, as shown in Exhibit 2–8.

- Exhibit 2–8 also shows the following: Costs incurred during the year for direct material were $850,000 (see the calculations given above for direct material); direct-labor cost was $700,000, and manufacturing overhead was $1,850,000. The sum of direct material, direct labor, and manufacturing overhead costs incurred, $3,400,000, is the total manufacturing cost incurred during the year. Managers in production and operations give careful attention to these costs. CollegePak knows that it must manage these costs effectively on a daily basis to be competitive.
- Next we add the beginning work-in-process inventory cost to the total manufacturing cost to obtain the total cost of work in process during the year. This is a measure of the costs of resources purchased in a previous year that have gone into production during the year. Some of these costs were in the work in process inventory on hand at the beginning of the year (the beginning inventory), but CollegePak incurred much of the cost during the current year (the total manufacturing costs).
- At year-end, the cost of the Work-in-Process Inventory account is subtracted to arrive at the cost of goods manufactured during the year. This amount represents the cost of the good backpacks finished during the year.

Finished goods. After inspection, Quality Assurance transfers the good work finished and inspected during the period to the finished-goods storage area before shipment to customers. (Under a just-in-time inventory and production-management system, goods are shipped to customers directly from the production line, so no finished-goods inventory exists. CollegePak maintains a finished goods inventory, however.) The Finished-Goods Inventory account appears as follows on the financial statements:

- Exhibit 2–8 shows that CollegePak had $920,000 of finished goods inventory on hand at the beginning of the year (January 1). From the discussion about work in process, we know that CollegePak completed $3,350,000, which was transferred to finished-goods inventory. Therefore, CollegePak had $4,270,000 of finished-goods inventory available for sale in total.
- Of the $4,270,000 available, CollegePak had $1,460,000 of finished goods still on hand at the end of the year. That means that the cost of goods sold was $2,810,000 ($4,270,000 available − $1,460,000 in ending inventory).

Schedule of cost of goods manufactured and sold. As part of its internal reporting system, CollegePak prepares a schedule of cost of goods manufactured and sold. This report is only for managerial use; it rarely appears in external financial statements. Cost-management analysts typically prepare this schedule to summarize and report manufacturing costs for managers' use. Some companies have experimented with preparing these reports for production employees and supervisors, who in some cases have found them effective communication devices. For example, management at CollegePak might use its schedule of cost of goods manufactured and sold to communicate the magnitude of manufacturing overhead or work-in-process inventory to stimulate creative ideas from employees for more effectively managing these amounts. Most important, CollegePak can use existing production costs as a basis for evaluating changes in its value chain, such as processes that it can decide to retain or outsource. These types of decisions are discussed in detail in later chapters of this text.

Flow of Manufacturing Costs

The following diagram summarizes the types of manufacturing costs and their flow through the manufacturing accounts. The detailed process used to record these cost flows will be covered in detail in Chapter 3, along with some important conceptual issues about cost-system design. Moreover, some of the more controversial issues involved in determining the amounts to be entered into Work-in-Process Inventory as product costs will be explored later in this chapter. For now, let's just note that the basic flow of costs in a manufacturing operation is very simple, as the diagram shows. As we will see, however, determining the *amounts* that flow through the accounts can be far less straightforward.

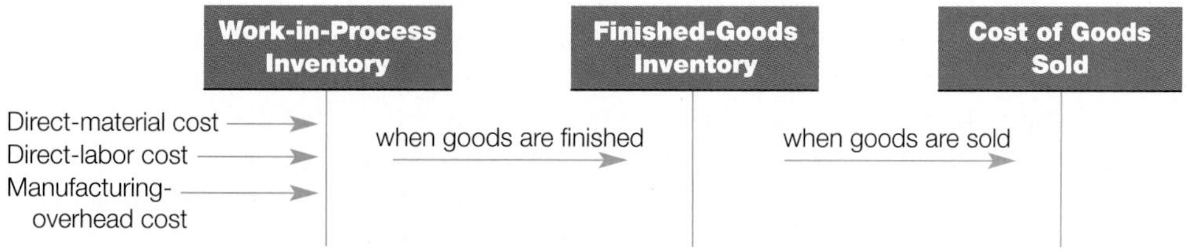

Production Costs in the Service Industry

Firms in the service industry and many nonprofit organizations also engage in production. What distinguishes these organizations from manufacturers is that the producer cannot inventory a service, whereas a manufacturer can store its finished goods. Businesses such as Hyatt Hotels, Allstate Insurance, American Airlines, and the New York Yankees, produce services. Similarly, nonprofit service organizations, such as Habitat for Humanity or New York's Metropolitan Opera, are engaged in service production. Service firms can use the same cost classifications that manufacturing companies do, although this practice is less common. For example, an airline produces air-transportation services. Direct materials for flights include jet fuel and food and beverages. Direct labor for flights is provided by the flight crew. Overhead includes amortization of leased aircraft, depreciation of baggage-handling equipment, and insurance.

Managing the costs of value-chain activities is important in service firms and nonprofit organizations for the same reasons it is in manufacturing firms. These activities can signal opportunities for improvement, can be the basis of competitive advantage, and can create more value for the organization at lower cost. Pricing bank and insurance services, setting enrollment targets in universities, and determining cost reimbursements in hospitals involves cost analysis. As service and nonprofit organizations occupy an ever-increasing role in our economy, applying cost-management methods to their activities assumes ever-greater importance.

Cost-Management Concepts: Different Costs for Different Purposes

An understanding of cost concepts is absolutely critical to cost management. Moreover, different perspectives on costs are important in different managerial situations. In making a decision about flight routes, for example, Air France needs information about the additional costs it would incur if it adds another flight on the Paris-to-New York route. For cost-control purposes, Hertz needs information about both the expected cost of operating its national reservations center and the actual costs incurred in running the center. In deciding whether to expand its operations by adding branches in upper Manhattan, Citibank needs information about the costs and benefits of doing so as well as the costs and benefits of alternative uses for its available resources. The phrase "different costs for different purposes" often is used to convey the notion that different characteristics of costs can be important to understand in a variety of managerial circumstances. This section explores some key cost terms and concepts used in cost management. We use these concepts throughout the book as we explore various issues in contemporary cost-management systems.

Cost Drivers

activity *is any discrete task that an organization undertakes to make or deliver a good or service*

cost driver *is a characteristic of an activity or event that causes costs to be incurred by that activity or event*

One of the most important cost concepts is the way a cost changes in relation to changes in the organization's activity. **Activity** is any discrete task that an organization undertakes to make or deliver a good or service. The number of computers manufactured by Dell, the number of days of patient care provided by the Mayo Clinic, and the number of loans issued by Citibank are all measures of output activity. The activities that cause costs to be incurred are called "cost drivers."

A **cost driver** is a characteristic of an activity or event that causes that activity or event to incur costs. In most organizations, costs respond to widely differing cost drivers. For example, at CollegePak, among the cost drivers for the cost of labor in the Cutting Work Center is the quantity of backpacks manufactured and the number and shapes of the fabric pieces in each backpack. (These are *not* the only cost drivers, but we defer a complete discussion of cost-driver analysis to Chapter 4, where we discuss the cost-management tool *activity-based costing.*) In contrast, the cost of machine setup labor is driven by, among other things, the number of production runs. The cost of material-handling labor is driven by material-related factors such as the quantity and cost of raw material used, the number of parts in various products, and the number of raw-material shipments received. (Again, we defer the discussion of

Exhibit 2–9
Cost Drivers

Cost	Examples of Cost Drivers
Cost of food served at Philadelphia Children's Hospital	Number of days of patient care
Fuel costs at Federal Express	Number of tons of cargo transported; distance flown
Cost of handling insurance claims at State Farm Insurance	Number of claims processed
Cost of material handling at Ford Motor Company	Number of material moves, weight of material handled, type of material handled
Cost of taking customer orders at Microsoft Corporation	Number of customer orders, type of products ordered

other cost drivers to Chapter 4.) Thus, lumping all manufacturing labor costs together and saying that they are driven by the quantity of products manufactured is an oversimplification. In state-of-the-art cost-management systems, cost-management analysts carefully separate various types of costs into different groupings called *cost pools* and identify the most appropriate cost driver for each cost pool.

The cost driver and cost pool concepts are important aspects of many topics discussed in subsequent chapters and are particularly central to Chapter 4, which introduces activity-based costing. The examples in Exhibit 2–9 illustrate the identification of cost drivers in both the manufacturing and service sectors.

Cost Behavior

LO 4 Explain how unit-level, variable, and fixed costs differ.

Any organization produces and distributes its services or products by engaging in various activities. Costs do not just happen; they are the result of decisions about the number and nature of activities that the firm undertakes and the levels of those activities. To be able to make informed decisions, plan operations, and evaluate performance, management must first know which activities cause costs to be incurred and how changes in activity levels affect the various costs incurred by the firm. "Cost behavior" refers to the way in which costs respond to changes in decisions and activity.

Chapter 11 discusses cost behavior and the methods used to estimate costs in considerable detail. At this juncture, however, we need to explore the two most fundamental types of cost behavior before continuing the discussion of how product and service costs are managed.

Fixed versus variable costs. Suppose that company management is contemplating a change in the volume of an activity. Different managers might ask questions such as these:

- *A production manager at Toyota Corporation.* How much will our costs decrease if we cut the volume of production by 1,000 automobiles per month?
- *A manager of Marriott Corporation's campus food service.* How much will our costs increase if we serve 200 more meals per day?
- *The president of your college or university.* How much will costs increase if the number of students enrolled increases by 10 percent?

To answer questions such as these, the managers need to know which costs are **variable costs,** which are the costs of resources used that change in total in direct proportion with the change in the activity volume, and which are **fixed costs** that remain unchanged in total as the activity volume changes. (*Note:* Both variable costs and fixed costs can change, however, if an organization makes changes in *decisions* about which resources to acquire and how to use them in productive processes. Again, we will have more to say about this issue throughout the text.)

variable costs *change in total in direct proportion with a change in the activity volume*

fixed costs *remain unchanged in total as the volume of activity changes*

Exhibit 2–10

CollegePak: Variable Cost Graph

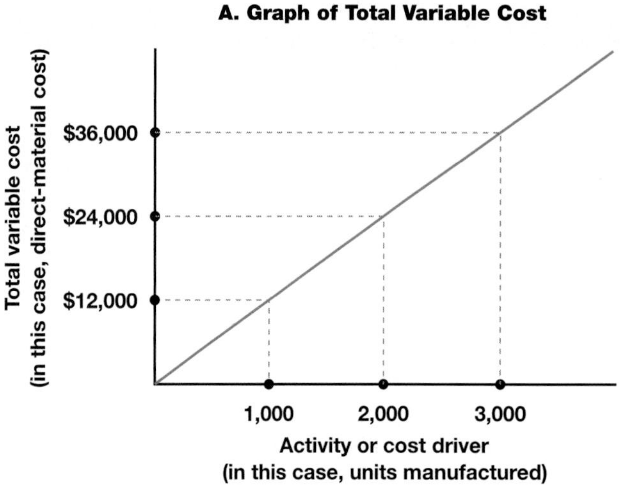

Exhibits 2–10 and 2–11 depict variable cost behavior and fixed cost behavior, respectively. Notice in these exhibits that production volume is on the horizontal axis, and cost (variable or fixed, total and unit, measured in dollars) are on the vertical axis. Exhibit 2–10, which focuses on variable costs, shows CollegePak's total direct-material cost across a range of production activity levels, assuming that direct material costs $12 for each unit manufactured. Total variable costs increase in direct proportion to changes in volume. Thus, if volume doubles, say from 1,000 to 2,000 units, total variable costs also double, but the unit variable cost remains constant at $12.

Exhibit 2–11 depicts CollegePak's fixed manufacturing overhead cost assumed to be $300,000 per year. Notice that total fixed cost in Panel A remains constant at a particular level and does not increase as volume increases. As Panel B shows, however, the fixed cost *per unit* declines as volume increases.

Variable manufacturing costs typically include costs for direct material, various manufacturing overhead items (for example, electricity used to power production equipment), and some types of direct labor. Portions of certain nonmanufacturing costs, such as distribution costs and sales commissions, typically vary with respect to output volume. However, much manufacturing overhead and many nonmanufacturing costs typically are fixed with respect to output volume.

Direct labor traditionally has been considered a variable cost. Today, however, the production process at many firms is very capital intensive. In a setting in which a fixed amount of labor is needed only to keep machines operating, direct labor is probably best considered a fixed cost. (We will explore this issue more later in the chapter.) For a retailer, such as University Outfitters, variable costs include the cost of the merchandise and some selling and administrative costs. All of a retailer's product costs are variable. For manufacturers, a portion of the product cost is fixed. For service organizations, variable costs typically include compensation for some types of direct labor (such as temporary employees) as well as costs for office supplies, photocopying, and printing.

The identification of a cost as fixed or variable is valid only within a specific range of output volume. For example, suppose that the manager of an Outback Steakhouse restaurant in a shopping complex increased its capacity from 150 to 250 seats, requiring an increase in the costs of rent and supervision. Although these costs are usually considered to be fixed, they change when the decision to increase seating capacity moves output activity beyond a specific range. This range within which the *total* fixed costs and *unit* variable costs do not change is called the *relevant range.* The **relevant range** is the range of activity over which the company expects to operate and over which assumed cost patterns are reasonably accurate.

relevant range *is the range of activity over which the company expects to operate and over which assumed cost patterns are reasonably accurate*

Variable Costs and Unit-Level Costs

The term "variable cost" is a traditional term in cost-accounting and cost-management practice. Use of this term *assumes* that we are discussing a cost that varies in

Exhibit 2–11 CollegePak: Fixed Cost Graphs

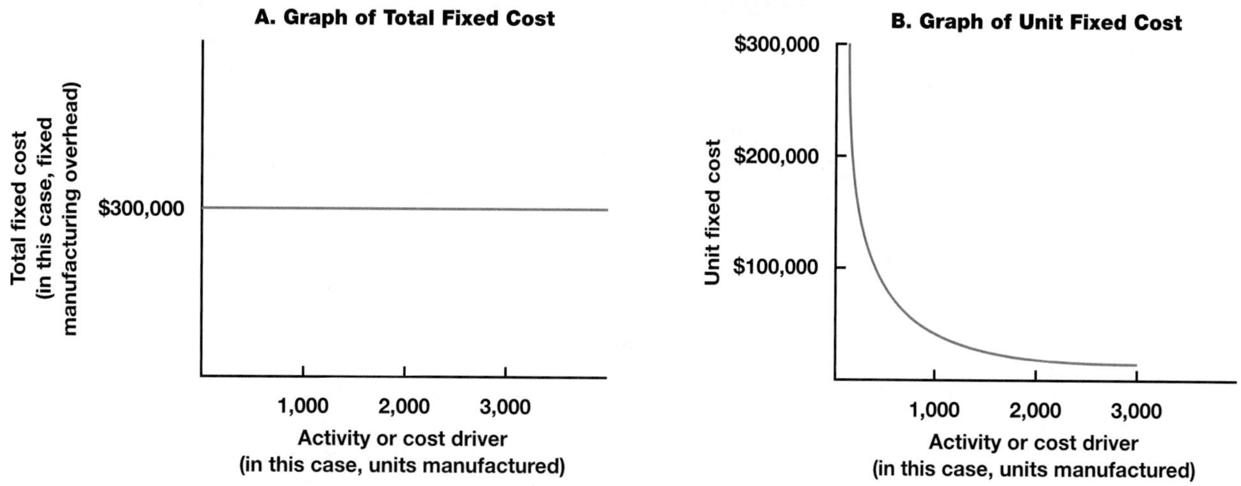

total in direct proportion to output activity, which typically is measured in terms of the number of units of product manufactured or service produced. As contemporary cost-management systems have developed in both theory and practice, however, cost managers have realized the importance of being very careful about using this term because costs can vary in total in relationship to many different cost drivers, not just the number of units produced. For example, consider the cost of setting up a cutting machine at CollegePak's Trenton plant. (Setting up a machine involves making detailed adjustments so that it performs the desired operation.) The machine must be set up for each production run, which typically consists of several hundred backpacks of a particular size and style. Suppose that the production run, or "batch," is for 500 DesignerPaks, one of CollegePak's most popular product lines. The direct-material cost for these backpacks is incurred for every unit because every backpack requires fabric, thread, and various fasteners. Thus, direct-material cost is variable, in the traditional sense, because it varies in total with the number of units produced. The 500 DesignerPaks in this production run require twice as much direct material as 250 DesignerPaks would have required.

What about the cost of setting up the cutting machine? How many times does this need to be done? Of course, it is just once for this 500-unit batch of DesignerPaks. So, *using traditional terminology,* we classify direct material as a variable cost since it varies in total with the number of backpacks manufactured, but we classify the setup cost of the cutting machine as a fixed cost since it remains constant across all 500 DesignerPaks in the batch.

Now think carefully about this. Taking a slightly different perspective, we could say that *both* the direct-material cost and the setup cost are variable costs, but *they are*

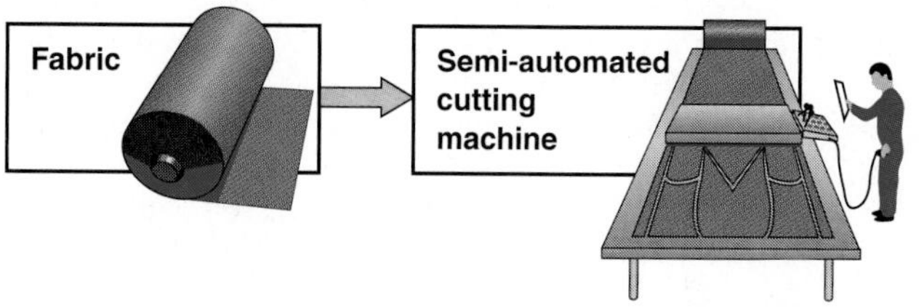

unit-level costs *are incurred for every unit of goods manufactured or service produced*

batch-level costs *are incurred for every batch of goods or services produced*

product-level costs *are incurred for each line of goods or services*

customer-level costs *are incurred for specific customers*

facility- (or) general-operations-level costs *are incurred to maintain the overall facility and infrastructure of the organization*

variable with respect to two different cost drivers. Direct-material cost is variable with respect to the cost driver, number of units produced, which is the traditional meaning for the term "variable cost." The setup cost for the cutting machine also is variable, however, but it is variable *with respect to the number of batches.* It is true that the setup operation does not have to be done for every *unit* produced, but it does have to be done for every *batch* produced.[3]

Now we have identified a terminological problem. What does it mean to say that a particular cost is variable or fixed? The classification of a cost as variable requires us to ask, Variable with respect to what? or, better yet, *Variable with respect to what cost driver(s)?*

Cost hierarchy. Contemporary cost-management systems have overcome this terminological problem with the concept of a *cost hierarchy.* The hierarchy can have many different levels; a relatively simple hierarchy includes the following five types of costs.

1. **Unit-level costs** are incurred for every unit of product manufactured or service produced.
2. **Batch-level costs** are incurred for every batch of product or service produced.
3. **Product-level costs** are incurred for each line of product or service.
4. **Customer-level costs** are incurred for specific customers.
5. **Facility-level** (or **general-operations-level**) **costs** are incurred to maintain the organization's overall facility and infrastructure.

See Exhibit 2–12 for some examples of these types of costs for CollegePak. We will explore and use the concept of a cost hierarchy in much greater detail in Chapter 4, which discusses activity-based costing. For our purposes here, it is sufficient simply to realize that when the term "variable cost" is used, it is crucial to ask the question, Variable with respect to what cost driver? In general, if variable cost is used without any further explanation, it is most likely used in the traditional sense (i.e., variable with respect to the number of units of product or service produced).

[3]For a familiar analogy, suppose that you and your friend decide to make some cookies. You want to make chocolate chip cookies, but your friend is partial to peanut butter. Being the convivial pair that you are, you decide to compromise and make a batch of each. What type of cost do the ingredients represent? Their cost will vary in proportion to the number of cookies of each type that you make. Therefore, their cost is variable with respect to the number of units produced. But what about (the cost of) your time required to clean up the mixer after each batch? This operation needs to be performed only once per batch, so it is variable with respect to the number of batches produced, not the number of cookies produced.

Exhibit 2–12

CollegePak's Cost Hierarchy

CollegePak

Cost Hierarchy	Examples of Costs at Each Level
Unit-level costs	Costs for direct material, such as fabric; electricity to run the production equipment
Batch-level costs	Setup costs for production runs; material-handling costs incurred to deliver batch quantities of raw material to the production area.
Product-level costs	Design costs for a line of backpacks, such as the DesignerPak, which specifies aspects such as size, color, number of pockets
Customer-level costs	Costs to obtain licenses of university logos, which CollegePak sews onto some lines of backpacks
Facility-level costs	Production manager's salary, depreciation on the plant, and insurance on the facility and equipment

The electricity and welding material used by robotic welders represent *unit-level* costs, since these costs are incurred for every unit produced.

Moving materials in batch quantity to the production line is a *batch-level* cost, because it is incurred for each production batch.

Designing a product using this computer-aided design software represents a *product-level* cost.

Special packaging for a particular customer constitutes a *customer-level* cost.

The depreciation and insurance on this refinery represent *facility-level* costs.

Cost of Resources Used versus Resources Supplied

LO 5 Distinguish between the costs of resources used and those of resources supplied.

Another important issue in thinking about variable and fixed costs involves the utilization of productive capacity. An organization's productive capacity is limited by things such as the overall size of the production facilities, the number and speed of production machines, and the size and skills of its work force. The most limiting aspects of the production process are sometimes referred to as production "bottlenecks." (Chapters 4 and 7 provide discussions of the use of productive capacity and production bottlenecks, respectively.)

At CollegePak's Trenton plant, the company employs skilled workers who are highly trained in running the production machinery. Making and selling more or fewer backpacks will use more or fewer resources and will cause the *costs of using* these resources to go up or down. For example, making more backpacks will use more skilled labor; we know this because the use of skilled labor easily can be traced to the additional products manufactured. However, making or selling more or fewer products and services might not cause the costs of *supplying* these resources to go up or down. CollegePak pays skilled employees for *at least* 40 hours per week even if the demand for backpacks is not sufficient to keep them busy for that many hours. Therefore, the costs of *using* skilled employees to make backpacks could vary with the number of products manufactured, but the costs of *supplying* (paying the wages and benefits for) skilled employees would not vary unless CollegePak decides to hire or lay off production workers as the demand requires.

Failing to distinguish between the cost of *supplying* (e.g., spending for) resources and the cost of *using* resources has caused much confusion and controversy among cost managers, accountants, financial analysts, and engineers. We need to be clear about this, and we identify as unit-level costs those costs incurred for resources that are *both supplied and used* to produce units of a product or service. The term "variable cost" will be used in its traditional sense to refer to the cost of a resource whose *use* varies with the number of units of product manufactured or service provided. Note that all unit-level costs are variable costs, but not all variable costs are unit-level costs.

A digression: The pizza business. To focus our thoughts on this issue, let's briefly digress to consider a familiar scenario. Suppose that you have just taken a job at the nearby college pizza shop making pizzas. (You know, the one just down the street where you go with your friends after an exam to celebrate, or before studying for the exam to fortify yourself, or when you should be studying for the exam because, well, eating pizza is more fun than studying.) You work the 8:00 to 10:00 p.m. shift three evenings a week, Monday, Wednesday, and Friday. In addition to the obvious fringe benefit of getting to scarf the occasional slice of pizza with your favorite toppings, you receive a wage of $7 an hour. So each evening that you work, you make $14.

After a brief training session and a little experience, you can make a pizza in 5 minutes. This includes picking up a premeasured lump of pizza dough, patting it out, twirling it ostentatiously over your head a few times, putting it down, covering it with pizza sauce, applying the cheese and other toppings, and tossing it in the oven. (The difference in time required to apply the toppings on a plain cheese pizza or one with "the works" is negligible.) You have one 20-minute break during your 2-hour shift, so on a busy evening, you could make as many as 20 pies (100 minutes available ÷ 5 minutes per pizza).

Now suppose that during the first week of October, you experience very different levels of demand on the three evening shifts. Monday-night football causes a steady demand for pizzas, and you make and sell 20 pies that evening. Wednesday evening is pretty slow, and you make just 10 pies. Friday evening, which normally is very busy, is unusually slow because of a pep rally held that evening before the next day's big game against your school's arch rival, the Fighting Piglets. You make just 1 pie.

Now we must calculate the cost of your labor for a pizza during each of your three shifts. One fairly simple answer is to divide your labor cost per shift by the number of pizzas you made in each shift, as follows:

Shift	Your Labor Cost	Pizzas Made	Cost per Pizza
Monday	$14.00	20	$ .70
Wednesday	14.00	10	1.40
Friday	14.00	1	14.00

Let's stop and think about this. Does this analysis make any sense? Most accountants and managers would argue that it does not make much sense to say that Monday's pizzas cost $.70 each for your labor, Wednesday's cost $1.40 each, and the one you made Friday evening cost $14.00! This result highlights the problem of confusing the cost of a resource *supplied* with the cost of a resource *used.* The cost of your labor *supplied* during each shift was $14.00, but the cost of your labor *used* varied from shift to shift due to widely different demand levels. Many cost managers would argue that the cost of your labor *used* should be computed as shown in the middle column of the following table.

(a) Shift	(b) Cost of Your Labor Supplied (2 hours × $7.00 per hour)	(c) Cost of Your Labor Used ($.70 × number of pizzas made*)	(d) Cost of Your Labor Used per Pizza	(e) Cost of Unused Capacity ($14.00 − cost of labor used)
Monday	$14.00	$14.00 ($.70 × 20)	$.70 ($14.00 ÷ 20)	$ .00
Wednesday	14.00	7.00 ($.70 × 10)	$.70 ($7.00 ÷ 10)	7.00
Friday	14.00	.70 ($.70 × 1)	$.70 ($.70 ÷ 1)	13.30

*$.70 = $14.00 per shift ÷ 20 pizzas, at capacity production.

The moral of the story is that it is very important to distinguish between the cost of resources used and the cost of resources supplied. This distinction can affect the decisions that managers make about the organization's operations. This issue will reappear later in this chapter as we explore some controversial issues in determining product costs.

Committed Costs, Opportunity Costs, and Sunk Costs

LO 6 Discuss the importance to cost management of understanding opportunity costs, sunk costs, committed costs, direct costs, and indirect costs.

For many years, accountants have used the term "fixed costs" for production or non-production costs that do not vary with production or sales volumes, such as costs of salaries, rent, depreciation, and property taxes. However, decisions cause costs—costs do not just happen—and an organization makes many more decisions than just those related to production volume. No resource decisions are irreversible. All future costs, therefore, are variable with respect to some decision, so no future cost really can be fixed. It might be costly to change a resource cost in the future (e.g., renegotiate or nullify a resource contract), but it can be changed.

Committed costs. A better term to use for costs that are not intended to vary with production or sales volume might be **committed costs.** This term reflects the fact that the organization has committed to a certain level and type of resource spending, but it can change that commitment (at some further cost, perhaps). In most organizations, labor cost is a committed cost and cannot be changed easily because of contractual obligations, company policy, or its critical importance. Other committed costs could include lease obligations, licenses, and various taxes. In contrast, "discretionary costs," such as some costs for advertising, remodeling, or charitable giving, could be changed quickly and easily. This is a difference of degree; that is, both committed and discretionary costs can be changed, but changing committed costs is more difficult.

committed costs *are not intended to vary with production or sales volume*

When labor is a committed cost, as for many unionized companies or organizations with strong employment policies, making more or fewer units of product might not affect the cost to supply labor positively or negatively. If this is so, spending for labor resources is not different from spending for other physical capacity resources. In organizations where this is true of other resources as well, the only unit-level cost of products and services that varies proportionately with the number of units produced could be the cost of parts and materials. Under these conditions, the cost to supply all other resources would not vary with the number of units produced.

Opportunity costs. Think for a moment about the cost of your college education. Certainly, the cash outflows for tuition, books, and fees are important costs. We often call these "outlay costs." Cash is not the only resource that many college students sacrifice, however; they also sacrifice their time to get a college education. This sacrifice of time is an **opportunity cost.** Recall from Chapter 1 that an opportunity cost is the forgone benefit that could have been realized from the best alternative use of a resource. For example, many of you gave up jobs to take the time to earn a college degree. The forgone income is part of the cost of getting a college degree and is the forgone benefit that could have been realized from an alternative use of a scarce resource—time. Of course, no one can ever know all opportunities possible at any moment. Hence, some opportunity costs are undoubtedly not considered. Accounting systems typically record outlay costs but not opportunity costs. Unfortunately, managers sometimes incorrectly ignore or downplay opportunity costs in making decisions. One way you can add value to your organization is to remind your managerial colleagues of the opportunity costs that they might have ignored in making decisions.

opportunity cost *is the forgone benefit that could have been realized from the best alternative use of a resource*

Sunk costs. Most organizations have made payments in the past to acquire resources that they now control. These resources include equipment, buildings, and purchased technology or knowledge. Should you consider the costs of these resources when making production decisions? That is, should the past payments for these resources be part of the costs of future products and services? The correct answer is no; past payments for resources are **sunk costs;** they cannot be undone. Just as with any other resource, only the *opportunity cost* of these already acquired resources should be counted as part of the cost of future products and services. If these resources have no alternative use or value (that is, they cannot even be sold to others), how much you paid for them does not matter; their opportunity costs are zero.

sunk costs *are past payments for resources that cannot be changed by any current or future decision*

This fact leads to a common behavioral problem. Managers sometimes have a tendency to consider sunk costs when making a decision although they were incurred in the past and cannot be affected by a current or future decision. In some cases, managers are unwilling to admit that payments for unproductive resources have been wasted, so they continue to value the resources at their book value unless they are required to write these assets down to a lower value. Cost-management personnel can assist their management colleagues in this area by ensuring that they do not inappropriately consider sunk costs when they analyze decision alternatives. (This issue will be addressed more extensively in Chapter 13, which covers cost management and decision making.)

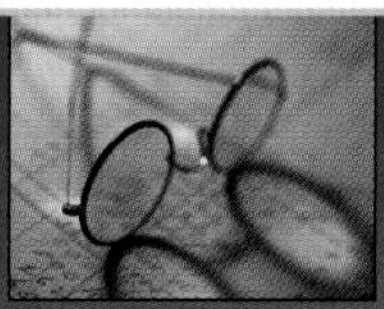

Cost Management in Practice 2.1

Designing Costing Systems That Serve Decision Makers

Progressive cost-management analysts at Borg-Warner Automotive Diversified Transmission Products Corporation anticipated recent trends in designing costing systems that serve decision makers by providing the information they need to improve their products' competitiveness and value. Cost-management analysts first learned what decisions had to be made by their internal customers, corporate managers, and plant managers, whose needs were very different. They learned, for example, that plant managers need specialized information about how processes use resources and how that use can be improved, but not the great amount of detail on past departures from standards that had been provided. Corporate managers who had received the same cost reports as plant managers were overwhelmed by the accumulated detail of all plant-level reports and could not find the information they needed to improve their strategic choices. By working closely with decision makers at both levels, cost-management analysts were able to design effective costing systems and reports. *Source: G. Hanks, M. Freid, and J. Huber,* "Shifting Gears at Borg-Warner." *Also see P. Drucker,* "The Information Executives Truly Need." *(Full citations to references are in the Bibliography.)*

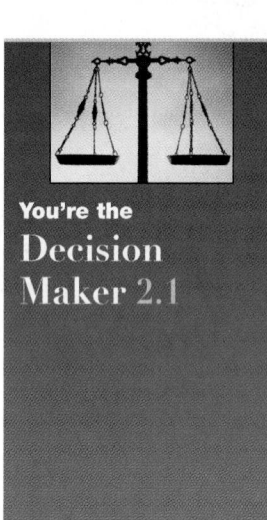

You're the Decision Maker 2.1

Relevant Costs for a Decision

Suppose that CollegePak received a special order for a product it does not usually produce, a special gift bag to be handed out to the delegates at a political convention. Suppose also that CollegePak currently has excess production capacity, and so management is considering the acceptance of the special order.

Production of the special order would require 8,000 yards of the fabric stylex. CollegePak no longer uses this particular type of fabric for any of its current products, but it does have 8,000 yards of it on hand from previous years. The stylex could be sold to a wholesaler for $14,500; its book value is $2.00 per yard. CollegePak could buy new stylex for $2.40 per yard.

The special order also requires 1,000 yards of a fabric called duraban, a material regularly used by CollegePak in its stock products. The current stock of duraban is 8,000 yards, at a book value of $8.10 per yard. If the special order is accepted, CollegePak will be forced to restock Duraban earlier than expected at a predicted cost of $8.70 per yard. Without the special order, the purchasing manager predicts that the price will be $8.30 when the regular restocking takes place. Any order of duraban must be in the amount of 5,000 yards.

a. What is the relevant cost of the stylex for the purpose of analyzing this special-order decision?

b. Discuss each stylex cost figure with regard to its relevance to the decision.

c. What is the relevant cost of the duraban?

d. Discuss each duraban cost figure with regard to its relevance to the decision.

(Solutions begin on page 68.)

Traceability of Resources

Another useful dimension of resources is the ease with which the cost of a resource can be traced to a decision or set of decisions. Cost managers sometimes ask, 'If we make this particular decision, what resources must we obtain or use, and what will they cost?' The acquisition and use of all resources is caused by management decisions, but the ease of tracing the costs of these resources to specific decisions is important for analyzing the cost effects to those decisions of the organization.

Direct costs. Sometimes seeing how specific decisions have caused the acquisition and use of specific resources is easy. These decisions are directly responsible for those resources, and their costs are called the **direct costs** of those decisions. For example, CollegePak's decision to produce a new line of backpacks would cause the use of the materials necessary to make them. Making more backpacks causes the use of more materials. Likewise, the decision to open a sales office in Boston creates the use of specific physical and human resources necessary to staff it. Seldom, however, is tracing *all* resources to *all* decisions easy.

direct costs *of a cost object are traceable to that cost object*

Indirect costs. Resources that are difficult to trace to specific management decisions are the **indirect costs** of those decisions. Other common names for indirect costs are "overhead, common costs," and "burden," although these sometimes convey a derogatory image (e.g., unproductive or unnecessary).

indirect costs *of a cost object are not feasibly traceable to that cost object*

CollegePak hired Jorge Gonzales as vice president of marketing and sales; that hiring decision is directly responsible for recruiting and paying for this human resource. Although Gonzales manages all of CollegePak's sales operations, tracing any of his cost to the decision to open the Boston sales office is not easy. Thus, he could be classified as an indirect resource of the Boston office. CollegePak hired Anne Harrison, vice president of manufacturing, to manage its manufacturing processes, but she does not actually manufacture a single backpack herself. Thus, although she is necessary to support production, CollegePak uses this human resource to indirectly support the manufacture of its products. Thus, Harrison's salary is an indirect cost of manufacturing.

The distinction between direct and indirect costs is not restricted to human resources. For example, CollegePak's administrative team in its Trenton facility manages the company and manufactures its products in the same large building using the same computer network. How much of the building and computer network resources are used for administration? How much is used for manufacturing each backpack? Tracing these resources directly to decisions about either administration or manufacturing, let alone to manufacturing specific products, is not easy. Thus, the costs associated with the building and computer network would be considered an indirect cost for both administration and manufacturing.

To summarize, any cost that can be directly related to a *cost object* is a direct cost of that cost object. A **cost object** is any entity to which a cost is assigned, for example, a decision, a unit of inventory, a department, or a product line. Those costs that cannot be directly related to a cost object are indirect costs. Cost-management analysts use the terms "direct cost" and "indirect cost" much as a nonaccountant might expect, but the fact that a cost might be direct to one cost object and indirect to another could be a source of confusion. For example, the salary of a supervisor in a manufacturing department is a direct cost of that department but an indirect cost of the individual products the department produces. Therefore, when someone refers to a cost as being either direct or indirect, you should immediately ask, Direct or indirect with respect to what cost object? Units produced? A department? A division? (When we use *direct* and *indirect* to describe labor and materials, the cost object is the unit being produced.) See Exhibit 2–13 for several examples of direct and indirect costs.

cost object *is any entity to which a cost is assigned*

Exhibit 2–13

Direct and Indirect Costs

Cost	Classification as Direct or Indirect
Salary of a Harley-Davidson plant manager	Direct cost of the plant; indirect cost of each department in the plant
Advertising for a particular Ramada Inn in Cleveland, Ohio	Direct cost of that hotel; indirect cost of that hotel's Food and Beverage Department
Salary of the U.S. Secretary of the Interior	Direct cost of the Interior Department; indirect cost of Yosemite National Park

Income-Reporting Effects of Alternative Product-Costing Systems

LO 7 Prepare income statements using absorption, variable, and throughput costing.

Operating income is a key measure used to evaluate the performance of both entire companies and segments of them. Managers watch the bottom line as they make the decisions that determine the future of their companies. The product-costing method used, however, can significantly affect a manufacturing company's reported income. This section explores three alternative product-costing methods. It begins by comparing the two traditional methods, absorption costing and variable costing. Then it examines a method that is more recent in origin, throughput costing.

What Costs Should Be Considered Product Costs?

As discussed earlier, the typical product-costing system applies manufacturing overhead, direct material, and direct labor to Work-in-Process Inventory as a product cost. When the manufactured goods are finished, these product costs flow from Work-in-Process Inventory into Finished-Goods Inventory. Finally, during the accounting period when the goods are sold, the product costs flow from Finished-Goods Inventory into Cost of Goods Sold, an expense account. The following diagram summarizes this flow of costs:

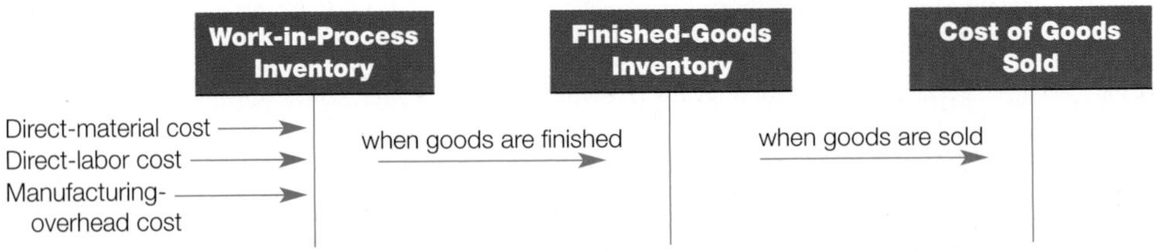

Since the costs of production are stored in inventory accounts until the related goods are sold, these costs are said to be "inventoriable costs." This section addresses whether *all* costs added to the manufacturing inventory accounts in the preceding diagram should be treated properly as product costs or whether *some* of them more properly should be considered period costs.[4]

absorption or **full costing** *applies all manufacturing-overhead costs to (or absorbed by) manufactured goods along with direct-material and direct-labor costs*

variable or **direct costing** *applies only variable manufacturing overhead to manufactured goods as a product cost along with direct material and direct labor costs*

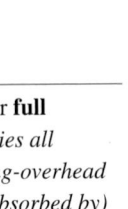

Fixed manufacturing overhead: The key. One type of product-costing system includes direct material, direct labor, and *both* variable and fixed manufacturing overhead in the product costs that flow through the manufacturing accounts. This approach to product costing is **absorption** or **full costing** because *all* manufacturing-overhead costs are applied to (or absorbed by) manufactured goods along with direct-material and direct-labor costs. An alternative approach to product costing is **variable** or **direct costing** in which *only variable* manufacturing overhead is applied to Work-in-Process Inventory as a product cost along with direct-material and direct-labor costs.[5]

See Exhibit 2–14 for a summary of the distinction between absorption and variable costing. Notice that the distinction involves the *timing* at which fixed manufacturing overhead becomes an expense. Eventually, fixed overhead is expensed under both product-costing systems. Variable costing considers fixed overhead a period expense and expenses it *immediately*, as it is incurred. Absorption costing, however, *inventories* fixed overhead with the other product costs (i.e., for direct material, direct labor, and variable overhead) until the accounting period during which the manufactured goods are sold.

Illustration of Absorption and Variable Costing

CollegePak

To illustrate the income effects of absorption and variable costing, we return to the discussion of CollegePak. After several years of success with its Trenton, New Jersey, operations, the company built a new plant in central Pennsylvania. (Recall the email memorandum at

[4] If you wish to review the discussion of product costs and period costs earlier in the chapter, see pages 38 and 39.

[5] Here we use the term "variable cost" in its traditional meaning (i.e., those costs that vary in total in proportion to the volume of output activity). The term "fixed cost" also is used in its traditional sense (i.e., those costs that do not vary in total with respect to the volume of output, within the relevant range).

Exhibit 2–14 Absorption versus Variable Costing

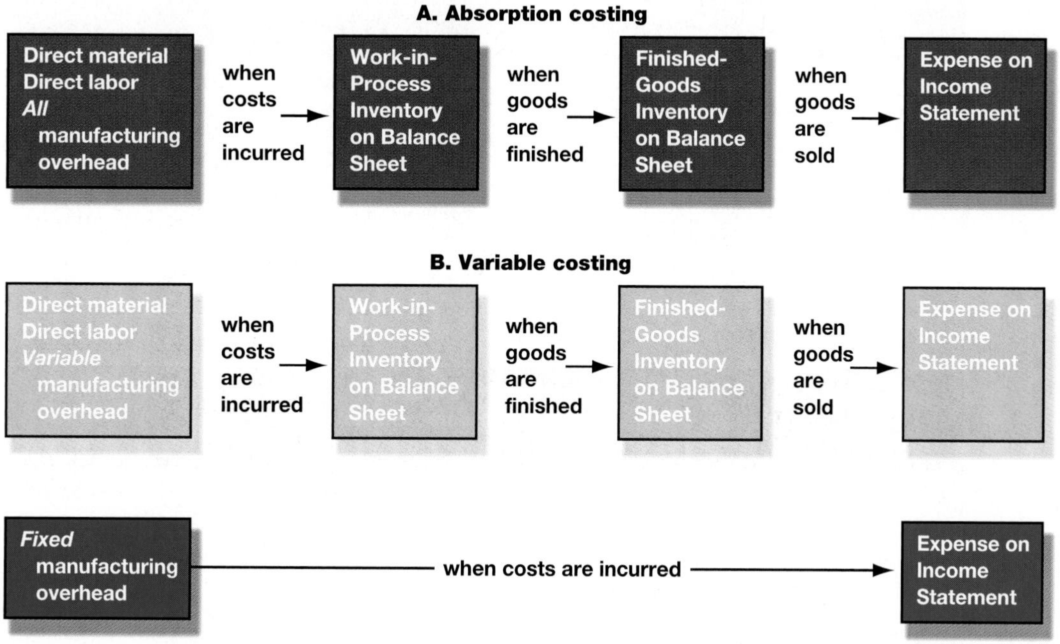

Exhibit 2–15 Basic Data for Illustration: Pennsylvania Plant of CollegePak Company

		Year 1	Year 2	Year 3
Production and inventory data				
Planned production (in units)		25,000	25,000	25,000
Finished-goods inventory (in units), January 1		0	0	7,500
Actual production (in units)		25,000	25,000	25,000
Sales (in units)		25,000	17,500	32,500
Finished-goods inventory (in units), December 31		0	7,500	0
Revenue and cost data, all three years				
Sales price per unit				$48
Manufacturing costs per unit				
Direct material				$12
Direct labor				8
Variable manufacturing overhead				4
Total variable cost per unit				$24
Used only under absorption costing	Fixed manufacturing overhead:			
	Annual fixed overhead / Annual production	$300,000 / 25,000		12
	Total absorption cost per unit			$36
Variable selling and administrative cost per unit				$ 4
Fixed selling and administrative cost per year				$50,000

the beginning of the chapter.) The new plant was built to manufacture a new line of backpacks to be sold under the brand name ScholarPak, and marketed primarily in Europe. CollegePak's president wanted to watch the new product line's performance closely so she asked that separate income statements be generated for the Pennsylvania plant's operations.

See Exhibit 2–15 for cost, production, and sales data for the first three years of the Pennsylvania plant's operations and Exhibit 2–16 for comparative income statements for the first three years using both absorption and variable costing.

Exhibit 2–16

Income Statements under Absorption and Variable Costing

CollegePak

COLLEGEPAK COMPANY
Absorption-Costing Income Statement
Pennsylvania Plant

		Year 1	Year 2	Year 3
	Sales revenue (at $48 per unit)	$1,200,000	$840,000	$1,560,000
1	Less: Cost of goods sold (at absorption cost of $36 per unit)	900,000	630,000	1,170,000
	Gross margin	$ 300,000	$210,000	$ 390,000
	Less: Selling and administrative expenses:			
2 No	Variable (at $4 per unit)	100,000	70,000	130,000
fixed	Fixed	50,000	50,000	50,000
overhead	Operating income	$ 150,000	$ 90,000	$ 210,000

COLLEGEPAK COMPANY
Variable-Costing Income Statement
Pennsylvania Plant

		Year 1	Year 2	Year 3
	Sales revenue (at $48 per unit)	$1,200,000	$840,000	$1,560,000
	Less: Variable expenses:			
1	Variable manufacturing costs (at variable cost of $24 per unit)	600,000	420,000	780,000
	Variable selling and administrative costs (at $4 per unit)	100,000	70,000	130,000
	Contribution margin	$ 500,000	$350,000	$ 650,000
	Less: Fixed expenses:			
2	Fixed manufacturing overhead	300,000	300,000	300,000
	Fixed selling and administrative expenses	50,000	50,000	50,000
	Operating income	$ 150,000	$ 0	$ 300,000

Absorption-Costing Income Statements

Examine the absorption-costing income statement in the upper half of Exhibit 2–16. Two features of these income statements are highlighted in the left-hand margin. First, notice that the cost of goods sold expense for each year is determined by multiplying the year's sales by the absorption-manufacturing cost per unit, $36. Included in the $36 cost per unit is the fixed manufacturing-overhead cost of $12 per unit. Second, notice that on the absorption-costing income statement, the only period expenses are the selling and administrative expenses. There is no deduction of fixed-overhead costs as a lump-sum period expense at the bottom of each income statement. As mentioned, fixed manufacturing-overhead costs are included in cost of goods sold on these absorption-costing income statements.

Variable-Costing Income Statements

Now examine the income statement based on variable costing in the lower half of Exhibit 2–16. Notice that its format and that of the absorption-costing statement are different. The format of the variable-costing statements highlights the separation of variable and fixed costs. The variable-costing statement also highlights an amount called the **contribution margin,** which is defined as sales revenue less all variable costs. The contribution margin, as its name implies, is the amount of sales revenue left *after* covering all variable costs to *contribute* to covering fixed cost and profit. (This contribution-margin concept is discussed extensively in Chapters 12 and 13.)

contribution margin *is the amount of sales revenue remaining, after covering all variable costs, to contribute to covering fixed cost and profit*

Let's focus on the same two aspects of the variable-costing statements that we discussed for the absorption-costing statements. First, the manufacturing expenses sub-

		Year 1	Year 2	Year 3
1	Cost of goods sold under absorption costing	$ 900,000	$ 630,000	$1,170,000
	Variable manufacturing costs under variable costing	600,000	420,000	780,000
	Subtotal	$ 300,000	$ 210,000	$ 390,000
2	Fixed manufacturing overhead as a period expense under variable costing	300,000	300,000	300,000
	Total	$ 0	$ (90,000)	$ 90,000
	Operating income under variable costing	$ 150,000	$ 0	$ 300,000
	Operating income under absorption costing	150,000	90,000	210,000
	Difference in operating income	$ 0	$ (90,000)	$ 90,000

Exhibit 2–17

Reconciliation of Income under Absorption and Variable Costing: Pennsylvania Plant, CollegePak Company

CollegePak

tracted from sales revenue each year include only the variable costs, which amount to $24 per unit. Second, fixed manufacturing overhead is subtracted as a lump-sum period expense at the bottom of each year's income statement.

Reconciliation of Income under Absorption and Variable Costing

LO 8 Reconcile income under absorption, variable, and throughput costing.

Examination of Exhibit 2–16 reveals that the operating income reported under absorption and variable costing is sometimes different. Although it is the same for the two product-costing methods in year 1, it is different in years 2 and 3. Let's figure out why these results occur.

No change in inventory. Year 1 had no change in inventory over the course of the year. Beginning and ending inventories are the same because actual production and sales are the same. Think about the implications of the stable inventory level for the treatment of fixed manufacturing overhead. On the variable-costing statement, the $300,000 of fixed manufacturing overhead incurred during year 1 is an expense in year 1. Absorption costing, however, applies fixed manufacturing overhead to production at the rate of $12 per unit. Since all units produced in year 1 also were sold in year 1, all fixed manufacturing-overhead cost flowed through the inventory accounts into Cost of Goods Sold. Thus, the entire $300,000 of fixed manufacturing overhead is an expense of year 1 under both variable and absorption costing.

The year 1 column of Exhibit 2–17 reconciles that year's income reported under absorption and variable costing. The reconciliation focuses on the two places in the income statements where differences occur for absorption and variable costing. The blue numbers in the left-hand margin of Exhibit 2–17 correspond to the blue numbers in the left-hand margin of the income statement in Exhibit 2–16.

Increase in inventory. In year 2, inventory increased from zero on January 1 to 7,500 units on December 31. The increase in inventory was the result of production exceeding sales. Under variable costing, the $300,000 of fixed overhead cost incurred is an expense of year 2, just as it was in year 1. Under absorption costing, however, only a portion of the year 2 fixed manufacturing overhead is expensed in year 2. Since the fixed overhead is inventoried under absorption costing, some of this cost *remains in inventory* at the end of year 2.

The year 2 column of Exhibit 2–17 reconciles that year's income reported under absorption and variable costing. As before, the reconciliation focuses on the two places in the income statements where differences for absorption and variable costing occur.

Decrease in inventory. In year 3, inventory decreased from 7,500 units to zero. Sales during the year exceeded production. As in years 1 and 2, under variable costing, the $300,000 of fixed manufacturing overhead incurred in year 3 is an expense of year 3.

Under absorption costing, however, *more than* $300,000 of fixed overhead is an expense in year 3 because some of the fixed overhead incurred during the prior year, which was inventoried then, is now an expense of year 3 when the goods are sold.

The year 3 column of Exhibit 2–17 reconciles that year's income using absorption and variable costing. Once again, the blue numbers on the left-hand side of Exhibit 2–17 correspond to those on the left-hand side of the income statement in Exhibit 2–16.

Shortcut to reconciling income. When inventory increases or decreases during the year, reported income differs under absorption and variable costing. This results from the fixed overhead that is inventoried under absorption costing but expensed immediately under variable costing. The following formula can be used to compute the difference in the amount of fixed overhead expensed in a given time period under the two product-costing methods. (An important assumption underlying this formula is that fixed overhead remains the same for the two accounting periods.)

$$\begin{array}{c}\text{Difference in fixed}\\ \text{overhead expensed}\\ \text{under absorption}\\ \text{and variable costing}\end{array} = \begin{array}{c}\text{Change in}\\ \text{inventory}\\ \text{in units}\end{array} \times \begin{array}{c}\text{Fixed-overhead}\\ \text{rate per unit}\end{array}$$

As the following table shows, this difference in the amount of fixed overhead expensed explains the difference in reported income under absorption and variable costing.

Year	Change in Inventory (in units)		Fixed-Overhead Rate		Difference in Fixed Overhead Expensed		Absorption-Costing Income Minus Variable-Costing Income
Year 1	0	×	$12	=	0	=	0
Year 2	7,500 increase	×	12	=	$ 90,000	=	$ 90,000
Year 3	7,500 decrease	×	12	=	(90,000)	=	(90,000)

Length of time period. The discrepancies between absorption-costing and variable-costing income in Exhibit 2–16 occur because of the changes in inventory levels during years 2 and 3. Production and sales commonly differ over the course of a week, month, or year. Therefore, the income measured for those time periods often differs for absorption and variable costing. This discrepancy is likely to be smaller over longer time periods. Over the course of a decade, for example, CollegePak cannot sell much more or less than it produces. Thus, the income amounts under the two product-costing methods, when added together over a lengthy time period, will be approximately equal under absorption and variable costing.

Notice that in Exhibit 2–17 the *total* income over the three-year period is $450,000 under *both* absorption and variable costing. This results from the fact that CollegePak's Pennsylvania plant produced and sold the same total number of units over the three-year period.

Evaluation of Absorption and Variable Costing

LO 9 Discuss the advantages and disadvantages of absorption, variable, and throughput costing.

Some managers find absorption costing to be nonintuitive and confusing and prefer to use variable costing for internal income reporting. Variable costing dovetails much more closely than absorption costing with any operational analyses that require a separation between fixed and variable costs. Later chapters detail these types of analyses; they include such value-chain decisions as adding a production process and outsourcing a service.

Product-cost information. Product costs computed under absorption costing could be more accurate measures of the use of production resources than those computed under variable costing because absorption costs recognize and contain fixed, indirect production costs. However, just as the overall average cost could misstate product costs by allocating indirect production costs, absorption costs could misstate the use of indirect production resources. It is possible that CollegePak's various product lines use indirect production resources to a different degree. Absorption costing also ignores each product line's differential use of nonproduction resources. Thus, absorption costing actually could distort the costs to provide products and services if they represent greatly different levels of support from indirect resources. For example, one product line might need much more design support than another, but allocations unrelated to resource usage obscure this difference.[6]

Pricing decisions. Many managers prefer to use absorption-costing data in cost-based pricing decisions. They argue that fixed manufacturing overhead is a necessary cost incurred in the production process. To exclude this fixed cost from the inventoried cost of a product, as variable costing does, is to understate the product's cost. For this reason, many companies that use cost-based pricing base their prices on absorption-costing data.

Proponents of variable costing argue that a product's variable cost provides a better basis for making the pricing decision. They note that any price above a product's variable cost makes a positive contribution to covering fixed cost and profit.

Unit costs under absorption costing can be misleading for decision making. When fixed costs are allocated to each unit, as they are under absorption costing, the *fixed* costs could appear as though they are *variable.* For example, allocating some of the factory insurance cost to each unit of product results in including insurance as part of the "unit cost" even though the total insurance cost does not increase with the manufacturer of another unit of product. Therefore, cost data that include unitized fixed costs could be misleading if used incorrectly. Later chapters cover this issue in detail.

Cost Management in Practice 2.2

Absorption versus Variable Costing in the Financial Services Industry

American National Bank in Chicago offers a check-processing service for small banks in the area. Small banks accumulate their day's checks and send them to American National, which presents them to the banks on which they are drawn. The major variable costs of this service are those for processing the checks and outside vendor charges, such as the use of the Federal Reserve clearinghouse for checks drawn on certain banks. In addition, fixed indirect costs are added to the variable costs of each product line. The sum of variable and fixed costs are full costs that cover all costs of running the bank, including general and administrative costs.

Several other financial institutions also offer this service. Although American National relies on its excellent reputation for quality service to justify charging a higher price than its competitors, it nevertheless has dropped its prices in recent years to avoid losing customers. At one point, its prices were less than 80 percent of the unit costs charged to the product line. Although it appeared that the bank could not justify continuing to offer the service based on a comparison of prices and full costs, several executives were not convinced that the full absorption-cost numbers developed for monthly financial reporting purposes were appropriate for the decision about whether to drop this service. Consequently, these executives decided to analyze which costs and revenues would change from dropping the service.

Their analysis indicated that few, if any, of the indirect costs allocated to the product line would be saved by dropping this service. Furthermore, some of the processing costs included depreciation and other costs that would not be cash savings if the service were discontinued. Their analysis indicated that the bank could lose several million dollars in contribution to fixed cost and profit by dropping the service. Based on this analysis, the bank decided against dropping the service. *Source: Based on an author's research.*

Definition of an asset. Another controversy about absorption and variable costing hinges on the definition of an asset. An *asset* is a thing of value owned by an organization with future service potential. Under generally accepted accounting principles, assets are valued at their cost. Because fixed costs represent part of the cost of production, advocates of absorption costing argue that inventory (an asset) should be valued at its full (absorption) cost of production. Moreover, they argue that these costs have future service potential since the inventory can be sold in the future to generate sales revenue.

Proponents of variable costing argue that the fixed-cost component of a product's absorption-costing value has no future service potential. Their reasoning is that the fixed

[6]Chapter 4, which covers activity-based costing, addresses this concern about traditional absorption-costing systems.

manufacturing-overhead costs incurred during the current period will not prevent these costs from being incurred again in the next period. Fixed-overhead costs will be incurred every period regardless of production levels. In contrast, the incurrence of variable costs in manufacturing a product allows the firm to avoid incurring these costs again.

To illustrate, let's return to the information detailed in Exhibits 2–15 and 2–16. The Pennsylvania plant produced 7,500 more units in year 2 than it sold. It carried these units in inventory until they were sold. CollegePak will never again have to incur the costs of the direct material, direct labor, and variable overhead incurred in year 2 to produce those particular products, yet it must incur approximately $300,000 of fixed-overhead costs every year although the firm has the 7,500 units from year 2 in inventory.

Use of both costing methods. In the age of computerized accounting systems, it is straightforward for a company to prepare income statements under both absorption and variable costing. Since absorption-costing statements generally are used for external reporting, managers need to review the effects of their decisions on financial reports to outsiders, yet it is difficult to deny the benefit of variable-costing income reporting as a method for dovetailing with operational analyses. Preparation of both absorption-costing and variable-costing data for internal management use is perhaps the best solution to the controversy.

JIT manufacturing environment. Most manufacturing firms now strive to minimize inventories because they do not create value but use valuable resources. As shown in the year 1 example for the Pennslvania plant, when inventories are zero or very small, differences between absorption- and variable-costing operating income also are small.

In a just-in-time inventory and production-management system, companies keep all inventories very low. Since finished-goods inventories are minimal, inventory changes little from period to period. Thus, in a JIT environment, the *income differences* under absorption and variable costing generally are insignificant. Note, however, that absorption- and variable-costing income statements provide different information about the costs incurred in the production process even if net income is not significantly different. In other words, the "bottom line" is not the only important number on an income statement. (Chapter 7 covers the cost-management implications of JIT systems in detail.)

You're the Decision Maker 2.2

Absorption and Variable Costing

Some years after opening its first Pennsylvania plant, CollegePak built another one in Scranton, Pennsylvania, to manufacture another new line of backpacks with the brand name CoolPak, which is sold in the middle school market. Planned production for the most recent year was 10,000 units. The company achieved this production level but sold only 9,000 units. Other data follow:

Direct material	$40,000
Direct labor	20,000
Fixed manufacturing overhead	25,000
Variable manufacturing overhead	12,000
Fixed selling and administrative expenses	30,000
Variable selling and administrative expenses	4,500
Finished-goods inventory, January 1	None

There were no work-in-process inventories at the beginning or end of the year.

a. What would the finished-goods inventory cost be on December 31 for the new product line under the variable-costing method?

b. Which costing method, absorption or variable costing, would show a higher operating income for the new product line for the year? By what amount?

c. Why might a manager deliberately produce more products than the company can sell in a period?

(Solutions begin on page 68.)

Throughput Costing

In recent years, some managers have been advocating *throughput costing* as an alternative to either absorption or variable costing. **Throughput costing** assigns *only* the unit-level *spending* for direct costs as the cost of products or services. Advocates of throughput costing argue that adding any other indirect, past, or committed costs to product cost creates improper incentives to drive down the average cost per unit by making more products than can be used or sold. Since these other costs are committed, making more units with the same level of resource spending arithmetically reduces the average cost per unit and makes the production process appear to be more efficient. Throughput costing avoids that incentive because the cost per unit depends only on unit-level *spending* (e.g., costs of materials), not how many units are made.[7] Using throughput costing means that cost-management analysts must distinguish between (1) spending for resources caused by the decision to produce different levels of products and services and (2) the use of resources that the organization has committed to supply regardless of the level of products and services provided. (Chapter 4 covers this important distinction in the context of activity-based costing.)

throughput costing *assigns only the unit-level spending for direct costs as the cost of products or services*

Suppose that CollegePak's cost-management team decided that only direct materials qualified as a throughput cost. This implies that CollegePak's management has *committed,* at least for the time being, to provide *all* other resources (i.e., direct labor and all manufacturing-support costs included in manufacturing overhead) regardless of how many backpacks CollegePak produces. Throughput costing considers all other indirect, discretionary, committed, or past spending for resources to be operating costs of the period (i.e., *period costs*).[8] Under throughput costing, then, CollegePak's income statements for the three years in our illustration would appear as in Exhibit 2–18. Notice that all costs other than the throughput cost (only direct materials in this illustration) are considered to be operating costs of the period.

A comparison of the reported income under throughput costing (Exhibit 2–18) with the reported income under either variable or absorption costing (Exhibit 2–16) reveals substantial differences in the "bottom line" under the three methods for each year. Proponents of throughput costing argue that this method alone eliminates the incentive to produce excess inventory simply to reduce unit costs by spreading *committed* resource costs (i.e., direct labor and variable- and fixed-manufacturing overhead) across more units. The incentive for such overproduction disappears under throughput costing because all nonthroughput costs (direct labor and manufacturing overhead in our illustration) are expenses of the period regardless of how many units are produced.

Use of Absorption, Variable and Throughput Costing throughout the World

Although absorption costing is required for financial and tax reporting in most parts of the world, many companies (in the range of 30 percent to 50 percent, based on some survey results) operating throughout the world have found it worthwhile to also prepare variable cost information for internal purposes. As yet, throughput costing appears to be too new a concept to have motivated surveys of its use. Nonetheless, variation in practice clearly indicates that cost-management analysts should understand the differences in cost-measurement systems so that they can apply them in appropriate situations and are familiar with them if they move about large, international organizations that use different costing methods in various locations. For example, see C. Drury and M. Tayles, "Product Costing in UK Manufacturing Organisations" and E. Shim and E. Sudit, "How Manufacturers Price Products."

Research Insight 2.1

[7]This statement ignores possible effects of gaining or losing purchase discounts on purchases by changing production levels. These effects usually are small, but they would be considered a benefit or cost of changing purchasing levels.

[8]Note that in some cases, an organization might pay for its labor force or other resources such as energy consumption on an hourly or piece-rate basis, depending on how many units of product it makes. Because these resources are supplied and used on an hourly or piece-rate basis, these would be unit-level costs and, therefore, product costs under throughput costing.

Exhibit 2–18

Income Statements under Throughput Costing

CollegePak

COLLEGEPAK COMPANY
Throughput-Costing Income Statement
Pennsylvania Plant

	Year 1	Year 2	Year 3
Sales revenue (at $48 per unit)	$1,200,000	$840,000	$1,560,000
Less: Cost of goods sold (at throughput cost: direct-material cost)*	300,000	210,000	390,000
Throughput	$ 900,000	$630,000	$1,170,000
Less: Operating costs:			
Direct labor[†]	$ 200,000	$200,000	$ 200,000
Variable manufacturing overhead[‡]	100,000	100,000	100,000
Fixed manufacturing overhead[‡]	300,000	300,000	300,000
Variable selling and administrative costs[§]	100,000	70,000	130,000
Fixed selling and administrative costs[§]	50,000	50,000	50,000
Total operating costs	$ 750,000	$720,000	$ 780,000
Operating income	$ 150,000	$ (90,000)	$ 390,000

* Standard direct-material cost per unit of $12 multiplied by sales volume in units.

[†] Assumes that management has committed to direct labor sufficient to produce the planned annual production volume of 25,000 units; direct-labor cost is *used* at a rate of $8 per unit produced. (See Exhibit 2–15.)

[‡] Assumes management has committed to support resources sufficient to produce the planned annual production volume of 25,000 units; variable-overhead cost is *used* at a rate of $4 per unit produced. Fixed overhead is $300,000 per year. (See Exhibit 2–15.)

[§] Variable selling and administrative costs *used* amount to $4 per unit sold. Fixed selling and administrative costs are $50,000 per year. (See Exhibit 2–15.)

Chapter Summary

Cost management helps an organization's management create more value at lower cost by efficiently managing the organization's value chain of activities, processes, and functions. *Cost-management information* is used in a variety of roles to help organizations be successful in achieving their goals. An important first step in studying cost management is to gain an understanding of the various types of costs that organizations incur and the way that the organizations actively manage those costs. At the most basic level, a *cost* is defined as the sacrifice made, usually measured by the resources given up, to achieve a particular purpose.

Financial statements provide an important means of communication about an organization's operations to people both inside and outside the organization. Internal uses of such information include decision making, planning, and cost management. External uses of financial statements are made by creditors, investors, governmental agencies, and other interested parties. A manufacturing company has a more complex income statement than do service or retail companies. Whereas the retailer purchases goods for sale, the manufacturer makes them. The three major categories of manufacturing costs are direct material, direct labor, and manufacturing overhead, which includes all other costs of transforming materials into a finished product. Cost managers track the flow of production costs using three accounts: *Work-in-Process Inventory, Finished-Goods Inventory,* and *Cost of Goods Sold;* the latter is an expense on the income statement.

An understanding of *cost concepts* is absolutely critical to cost management. Moreover, the ability to view different managerial situations from the appropriate perspective is important. Among the more important cost concepts is *cost behavior*, which refers to the way in which costs respond to changes in decisions and activity. *Variable costs* are the costs of resources used that change in total in direct proportion with a change in volume of activity. Contemporary cost-management systems have expanded the notion of a variable cost with the concept of a cost hierarchy, which more explicitly describes the way in which a cost varies. *Fixed costs* remain unchanged in total as the volume of activity changes. Other important cost concepts include *product and period costs, direct and indirect costs*, and the distinction between the cost of *resources supplied* and *resources used.*

Absorption and variable costing are two alternative product-costing systems, which differ in their treatment of fixed manufacturing overhead. *Absorption (or full) costing* applies fixed overhead to produced goods as a product cost. Therefore, the fixed-overhead cost remains in inventory until the goods are sold. *Variable (or direct) costing* applies fixed overhead as a period cost that is expensed during the period when it is incurred. *Absorption costing* is required for external reporting and tax purposes.

However, variable costing is more consistent with operational decision analyses, which require a separation of fixed and variable costs.

Some accountants and managers advocate *throughput costing,* in which only throughput costs are inventoried as product costs. They argue that throughput costing reduces the incentive for management to produce excess inventory simply for the purpose of spreading committed (nonthroughput) costs across a larger number of units produced.

Key Terms

For each term's definition, refer to the indicated page or turn to the glossary at the end of the text.

absorption (full) costing, 58
activity, 48
administrative costs, 43
batch-level costs, 52
committed costs, 55
contribution margin, 60
conversion costs, 43
cost, 37
cost-accounting system, 44
cost driver, 48
cost object, 57
cost of goods sold, 38
customer-level costs, 52
direct costs, 57
direct labor, 42
direct materials, 42
expense, 38
facility-level (general-operating-level) costs, 52
finished goods, 44
fixed costs, 49
idle time, 43
indirect costs, 57
indirect labor, 42
indirect material, 42
inventoriable costs, 38
manufacturing overhead, 42
opportunity costs, 55
overtime premium, 43
period costs, 38
prime costs, 43
product cost, 38
product-level costs, 52
raw material, 44
relevant range, 50
selling costs, 43
sunk costs, 55
support (or service) departments, 43
throughput costing, 65
unit-level costs, 52
variable (direct) costing, 58
variable costs, 49
work in process, 44

Meeting the Cost Management Challenges

1. **What** are the significant inputs to a production process, and how do cost managers track the flow of costs through the process?

The significant inputs to a production process are direct material, direct labor, and manufacturing overhead. Manufacturing overhead consists of indirect material, indirect labor, and other manufacturing costs, such as utilities and depreciation on the plant and equipment. Cost managers track the flow of costs for these inputs using three accounts: Work-in-Process Inventory, Finished-Goods Inventory, and Cost of Goods Sold. Production costs are entered into Work-in-Process Inventory as they are incurred. When the products are finished, their production costs are transferred from Work-in-Process Inventory to Finished-Goods Inventory. Finally, when the goods are sold, their production costs are transferred from Finished-Goods Inventory to Cost of Goods Sold, which is an expense on the income statement.

2. **How** can alternative methods to calculate product costs create different incentives?

If managers of manufacturing companies are rewarded on the basis of profits (this is very common), the way that product costs are calculated can affect incentives to produce more parts, assemblies, and products than can be sold. Specifically, variable costing and absorption costing add costs of *resources used* to products without considering whether *spending* to supply resources is affected. Levels of spending for some resources might be unaffected by how those resources are used (e.g., salaries or rent). Making more units with the same capacity reduces the average cost of products produced. Since the costs of products are held in inventory until the products are sold, these costs also can be "hidden" in inventory. Under throughput costing, only spending for resources is counted as costs of products, and all other costs are expensed. Average product costs cannot be reduced and profits increased merely by making more products than can be sold. Therefore, proponents argue, throughput costing alone aligns the financial incentives of managers with the objective of using resources wisely.

3. **How** should cost-management analysts measure costs for internal decision making?

Although the previous discussion indicates that the answer should be straightforward (i.e., use throughput costing), this actually is a difficult question to answer outside the context of a specific organization. Most organizations are required to use absorption costing for financial and tax reporting. Therefore, the decision to use a different costing method internally depends on whether the benefits (i.e., making better operating decisions) outweigh the costs of an additional costing system. Although it might seem intuitively obvious that managers should make better decisions using throughput costing, remarkably little reliable research indicates that better decisions really result. The lack of research might be attributed to the newness of throughput costing and the reluctance of organizations that have successfully employed it to give away a source of competitive advantage. It also might be that using absorption costing is beneficial in complex organizations because it ensures that indirect costs are not forgotten in production and pricing decisions. It also could be that the costs of using additional internal information are higher than the benefits. Although improvements in costing practices are always possible and should be explored, asserting that all firms using absorption costing for internal purposes are making a mistake is not necessarily accurate.

Solutions to You're the Decision Maker

2.1 Relevant Costs for a Decision p. 56

a. The relevant cost of the stylex to be used in producing the special order is the $14,500 sales value that the company will forgo if it uses the material. This is an example of an opportunity cost.

b. 1. $14,500 sales value; discussed in (a).

2. $16,000 book value (8,000 yards × $2 per yard); irrelevant since the book value is a sunk cost.

3. $19,200 current purchase cost (8,000 yards × $2.40 per yard); irrelevant since the company will not be buying any stylex.

c. The relevant cost of duraban is calculated as follows:

Cost of replacing the 1,000 yards to be used in the special order (1,000 yards × $8.70)	$ 8,700
Additional cost incurred on the next order of duraban as a result of having to place the order early* [4,000 yards × ($8.70 − $8.30)]	1,600
Total relevant cost	$10,300

*This cost would not be incurred if the special order were not accepted.

d. 1. $64,800 book value (8,000 yards × $8.10 per yard); irrelevant, since it is a sunk cost.

2. Cost of the 1,000 yards to be used in the special order; relevant, as shown in (c).

3. $8.70 price if the next order is placed early; relevant since this is the cost of replacing the used duraban.

4. $8.30 price if the next order is placed on time; relevant because an additional 4,000 yards in the next order will be purchased at a $.40 per yard premium ($8.70 price − $8.30 price).

2.2 Absorption and Variable Costing p. 64

Inventory calculations (units)

Finished-goods inventory, January 1	0 units
Add: Units produced	10,000 units
Deduct: Units sold	9,000 units
Finished-goods inventory, December 31	1,000 units

a. Inventoriable costs under variable costing:

Direct material used	$40,000
Direct labor incurred	20,000
Variable manufacturing overhead	12,000
Total	$72,000

Cost per unit produced = $72,000/10,000 units = $7.20

Ending inventory: 1,000 units × $7.20 per unit = $7,200

b. Difference in reported income: Since *inventory increased* during the year, income reported under absorption costing is $2,500 higher than income reported under variable costing. Calculations follow:

Predetermined fixed-overhead rate

$$= \frac{\text{Fixed manufacturing overhead}}{\text{Planned production}} = \frac{\$25{,}000}{10{,}000 \text{ units}} = \$2.50 \text{ per unit}$$

$$\begin{array}{c}\text{Difference in fixed}\\ \text{overhead expensed under}\\ \text{absorption and variable costing}\end{array} = \begin{pmatrix}\text{Change in}\\ \text{inventory,}\\ \text{in units}\end{pmatrix} \times \begin{pmatrix}\text{Predetermined}\\ \text{fixed-overhead}\\ \text{rate}\end{pmatrix}$$

$$= (1{,}000 \text{ units}) \times (\$2.50 \text{ per unit}) = \$2{,}500$$

c. Some accountants and managers argue that absorption costing gives managers an incentive to produce more units than can be sold in a period. By producing more units, the fixed manufacturing costs, which are treated as product costs under absorption costing, are averaged over a larger number of units. This reduces the product cost per unit reported under absorption costing.

Review Questions

2.1 What is the difference between the meanings of the terms *cost* and *expense*?

2.2 What is the difference between product costs and period costs?

2.3 Is cost of goods sold an expense? Explain.

2.4 What are the three categories of product cost in a manufacturing operation? Describe each element briefly.

2.5 What does the term *variable cost* mean?

2.6 What does the term *fixed cost* mean?

2.7 Distinguish among material resources, conversion resources, and operating resources.

2.8 Distinguish between production and nonproduction resources. Give examples of each.

2.9 Explain the concept of traceability and the way it is used to classify resources as direct or indirect.

2.10 Is a resource always either direct or indirect? Explain.

2.11 What is a unit-level cost? How does it differ from an average cost? How does it differ from a variable cost?

2.12 Define and give an example of each of the following costs:

a. Opportunity cost
b. Outlay cost
c. Product cost
d. Period cost
e. Direct cost
f. Indirect cost

2.13 Is a committed cost the same as a fixed cost? Explain.

2.14 How does throughput costing differ from variable or absorption costing?

2.15 What are the differences among throughput, contribution margin, and gross margin on an income statement?

2.16 Explain how absorption costing can create an incentive to make more products than can be sold.

2.17 Timing is the key in distinguishing between absorption, variable, and throughput costing. Explain this statement.

2.18 When inventory increases, is absorption-costing or variable-costing income higher? Why?

2.19 Do throughput, variable, and absorption costing result in significantly different income measures in a JIT setting? Why?

Critical Analysis

2.20 Evaluate this statement: Issues of product costing are irrelevant for service organizations since they cannot build up inventories of services, and all costs for providing services are expensed in the period they are used. Service firms effectively use throughput costing.

2.21 Evaluate this statement: Issues of product costing are unimportant for virtual organizations that outsource their production operations.

2.22 Prepare a diagram that illustrates how the following resources—headquarters, facilities, division managers, information systems personnel—can be considered both direct and indirect in a company that has four operating divisions, each of which provides multiple services.

2.23 Respond to this comment from an economist friend: You cost-management analysts use an overabundance of cost terms to cover up the fact that you really do not understand opportunity costs. You create jobs for yourselves based on unintelligible jargon. Not that that's a bad thing.

2.24 Respond to this observation: So, there really is no fundamental difference between tracing costs and allocating costs. The only difference is the degree of accuracy with which you want to trace costs.

2.25 A colleague challenges you: What do you mean that there is no such thing as a *fixed cost?* Pick up any microeconomics or cost-accounting book, and you will see the term used all the time. We have lots of fixed costs in our organization, don't we? What about your salary and the depreciation of your computer? Why do you want to replace *fixed cost* with *committed cost?*

2.26 Individually or as a group, prepare written arguments for and against the following proposition. (Be prepared to present your arguments.) The company needs to use absorption costing for financial and tax reporting. We make so many products in so many places that it would be too expensive to develop a separate accounting system based on throughput costing in addition to the system we are required to have. The way to keep divisions from making more than they can sell is to charge them interest on any inventories they maintain. If divisions want to tie up the company's resources in inventory, then they should pay the company at least the interest it could be earning if the treasurer had the same amount of cash.

2.27 Explain how making more products than can be sold in a period can increase the organization's operating income. Is this a sustainable tactic to increase operating income? Would this happen in a service company, or is it an issue only in manufacturing companies? Explain.

2.28 Respond to this comment: Your analysis of last month's financial performance demonstrates that it really doesn't matter whether we use throughput, variable, or absorption costing. All the costs are accounted for; you've just put them in different places. I can't see what real difference this analysis makes. Isn't this just a bean-counting exercise?

2.29 Evaluate this criticism of the financial management of processes: All this emphasis on operating income, regardless of how you measure it, contributes to our continuing, short-term outlook. If we focus only on operating income, managers will do whatever they can to increase that measure, regardless of long-term impacts. This is what is wrong with modern business. We need to look beyond this period's operating income and focus on the long-term.

2.30 A production manager was debating with company management because production had been charged with a large unfavorable fixed-overhead volume variance. The production manager explained: After all, if marketing had lined up sales for these units we wouldn't have been forced to cut production. Marketing should be charged with the volume variance, not production. Do you agree with the production manager? Why or why not?

2.31 The term *direct costing* is a misnomer. *Variable costing* is a better term for this product-costing method. Do you agree or disagree? Why?

2.32 Prime costs are always direct costs, and overhead costs are always indirect. What is your opinion of this statement?

Exercises

Exercise 2.33
Income Statement; Schedule of Cost of Goods Sold
(LO 1, 2)

The following items appeared in the records of Shoreline Products, Inc., for the last year:

Administrative costs	$ 304,000
Depreciation, manufacturing	103,000
Direct labor	482,000
Finished-goods inventory, January 1	160,000
Finished-goods inventory, December 31	147,000
Heat, light, and power	87,000
Marketing costs	272,000
Miscellaneous manufacturing costs	12,000
Plant maintenance and repairs	74,000
Raw-material purchases	313,000
Raw-material inventory, January 1	102,000
Raw-material inventory, December 31	81,000
Sales revenue	2,036,000
Supervisory and indirect labor	127,000
Supplies and indirect materials	14,000

Work-in-process inventory, January 1	135,000
Work-in-process inventory, December 31	142,000

Required

Prepare an income statement with a supporting schedule of cost of goods sold.

Exercise 2.34
Cost Behavior; Current Issues in Cost Management
(LO 4)

Read "Hollywood Rushes to Beat a Strike," *Business Week,* January 8, 2001. The article discusses Sony's plans to begin shooting the sequel to *Men in Black.* According to the article, the movie's star, Will Smith, will reportedly earn a $20 million salary, plus 20 percent of the studio's revenues after the film is released.

Required

What type of cost-behavior pattern does this actor's compensation represent? What other actor compensation arrangement does the article discuss, and what cost-behavior pattern is represented?

Exercise 2.35
Basic Concepts
(LO 1, 4)

Indicate whether each of the following costs incurred in a manufacturing operation are fixed or variable (F or V) and whether they are period costs or product costs (P or R) under absorption costing.

a. Transportation-in costs on materials purchased.
b. Assembly-line workers' wages.
c. Property taxes on office buildings for administrative staff.
d. Salaries of the company's top executives.
e. Overtime pay for assembly workers.
f. Sales commissions.
g. Office rent for sales personnel.
h. Salaries for sales supervisors.
i. Office rental for cost-management staff.
j. Administrative office heat and air conditioning.

Exercise 2.36
Basic Concepts
(LO 1, 3, 4)

Indicate whether each of the following costs incurred in a manufacturing operation is included in prime costs (P), conversion costs (C), or both (B).

a. Factory heating and air conditioning.
b. Production supervisor's salary.
c. Transportation-in costs on materials purchased.
d. Assembly-line worker's salary.
e. Direct material used in production.
f. Indirect material used in production.

Exercise 2.37
Basic Concepts
(LO 1, 4)

Indicate whether each of the following costs incurred in a manufacturing operation is fixed or variable (F or V) and whether it is a period cost or product cost (P or R) under absorption costing.

a. Factory security personnel.
b. Utilities in cost-management analysts' office.
c. Factory heat and air conditioning.
d. Power to operate factory equipment.
e. Depreciation on furniture for company executives.

Exercise 2.38
Statements for a Merchandising Company
(LO 1, 2)

PC, Inc., sells computers. On January 1 of this year, it had a beginning merchandise inventory of $500,000, including transportation-in costs. It purchased $2,600,000 of merchandise, had $260,000 of transportation-in costs, and had marketing and administrative costs of $1,600,000 during the year. The ending inventory of merchandise on December 31 of this year was $300,000, including transportation-in costs. Revenue was $5,000,000 for the year.

Required

Prepare an income statement with a supporting schedule of cost of goods sold.

Exercise 2.39
Statements for a Manufacturing Company
(LO 1,2)

Global

The following balances appeared in the accounts of Nishimoto Machine Tool Company during the current year. (*y* denotes *yen*, the Japanese national currency.)

	January 1	December 31
Raw-material inventory	328,000*y*	366,000*y*
Work-in-process inventory	362,000*y*	354,000*y*
Finished-goods inventory	146,000*y*	150,000*y*

During the year 1,732,000*y* of direct material was used in production, and the year's cost of goods sold was 6,000,000*y*.

Required

Prepare a schedule of cost of goods sold, and fill in the following missing data.

a. Cost of raw material purchased during the year.

b. Cost of goods manufactured during the year.

c. Total manufacturing costs incurred during the year.

Exercise 2.40
Statements for a Manufacturing Company
(LO 1, 2)

The following information appears in Alexis Company's records for last year:

Administrative costs	$ 88,600
Manufacturing building depreciation	54,000
Indirect materials and supplies	12,600
Sales commissions	30,400
Raw-material inventory, January 1	36,800
Direct labor	71,200
Raw-material inventory, December 31	38,000
Finished-goods inventory, January 1	21,800
Finished-goods inventory, December 31	18,000
Raw-material purchases	44,600
Work-in-process inventory, December 31	26,200
Supervisory and indirect labor	28,800
Property taxes, manufacturing plant	16,800
Plant utilities and power	47,000
Work-in-process inventory, January 1	30,800
Sales revenue	420,800

Required

Prepare an income statement with a supporting schedule of cost of goods sold.

Exercise 2.41
Statements for a Manufacturing Company
(LO 1, 2)

The following information appears in Tots' Toy Factory records for last year:

Administrative costs	$21,550
Manufacturing building depreciation	12,500
Indirect materials and supplies	2,150
Sales commissions	7,100
Raw-material inventory, January 1	8,200
Direct labor	16,300
Raw-material inventory, December 31	9,000
Finished-goods inventory, January 1	4,450
Finished-goods inventory, December 31	4,050
Raw-material purchases	10,150
Work-in-process inventory, December 31	5,550
Supervisory and indirect labor	6,200
Property taxes, manufacturing plant	3,700
Plant utilities and power	10,750
Work-in-process inventory, January 1	6,600
Sales revenue	97,200

Required

Prepare an income statement with a supporting schedule of cost of goods sold.

Exercise 2.42
Cost Behavior for Decision Making
(LO 4, 5, 6)

Excalabur Company manufactured 1,000 units of product last year and identified the following costs associated with the manufacturing activity (variable costs are indicated with V, fixed costs with F):

Direct material used (V)	$35,200
Direct labor (V)	66,500
Supervisory salaries (F)	31,100
Indirect materials and supplies (V)	8,000
Plant utilities (other than power to run plant equipment) (F)	9,600
Power to run plant equipment (V)	7,100
Depreciation on plant and equipment (straight-line, time basis) (F)	4,800
Property taxes on building (F)	6,500

Required

Unit variable costs and total fixed costs are expected to remain unchanged next year. Calculate the unit cost and the total cost if 1,400 units are produced next year.

Exercise 2.43
Cost Behavior
(LO 4)

Refer to the information in the preceding exercise.

Required

Construct graphs of total fixed and variable costs.

Exercise 2.44
Variable and Absorption Costing; Comparison of Operating Profit
(LO 7)

Spreadsheet

Marvelous Mustard Company produces a specialty mustard product, which it sells over the Internet for \$21.50 per case. The company produced 120,000 units (cases) and sold 104,000 units last year. There were no beginning inventories or ending work-in-process inventories last year. Manufacturing costs and selling and administrative costs for last year follow:

Direct material	\$780,000
Direct labor	450,000
Manufacturing overhead (unit level; variable)	180,000
Manufacturing overhead (facility level; fixed)	180,000
Selling and administrative (unit level; variable)	140,000
Selling and administrative (facility level; fixed)	120,000

Required

a. Compute the unit product (manufacturing) cost using variable costing.
b. Compute the operating profit using variable costing.
c. Compute the operating profit using absorption costing.

Exercise 2.45
Straightforward Exercise on Absorption versus Variable Costing
(LO 7, 8)

Spreadsheet

California Catsup Company produces catsup, which it sells exclusively to fast-food restaurants in five-gallon containers, which have the following price and variable costs:

Sales price	\$15
Direct material	5
Direct labor	2
Variable overhead	3

Budgeted fixed overhead in 20x0 was \$300,000. Actual production totaled 150,000 five-gallon containers, of which 125,000 were sold. No variances were recorded in 20x0. The company incurred the following selling and administrative expenses.

Fixed	\$50,000 for the year
Variable	\$1 per container sold

Required

a. Compute the standard product cost per container of catsup under (1) absorption costing and (2) variable costing.
b. Prepare income statements for 20x0 using (1) absorption costing and (2) variable costing.
c. Reconcile the income reported under the two methods by listing the two key places where the income statements differ.
d. Reconcile the income reported under the two methods using the shortcut method.

Exercise 2.46
Comparison of Variable and Absorption Costing
(LO 7, 8)

The following questions are based on Piscataway Pickle Corporation, which produces gourmet pickles that sell for \$12 per unit (one jar). Of the 100,000 units produced, 80,000 were sold during year 1; all ending inventory was in finished-goods inventory. The company had no inventory at the beginning of the year.

Direct material (unit-level or variable cost)	\$240,000
Direct labor (unit-level or variable cost)	160,000
Manufacturing overhead (unit-level or variable cost)	80,000
Manufacturing overhead (facility-level or fixed cost)	240,000
Selling and administrative (unit-level or variable cost)	80,000
Selling and administrative (facility-level or fixed cost)	128,000

Required

a. In presenting inventory on the balance sheet at December 31, what is the unit cost under absorption costing?

b. In presenting inventory on a variable-costing balance sheet, what is the unit cost?

c. What is the operating profit using variable costing?

d. What is the operating profit using absorption costing?

e. What is the cost of the ending inventory using absorption costing?

f. What is the cost of the ending inventory under variable costing?

[CPA adapted]

Exercise 2.47
Difference in Income under Absorption and Variable Costing
(LO 7, 8)

Berger Lawn Equipment Company manufactures lawn mowers with a unit variable cost of $200. The mowers sell for $450 each. Budgeted fixed manufacturing overhead for the most recent year was $2,200,000. Planned and actual production for the year were the same.

Required

Under each of the following conditions, state (a) whether income is higher under variable or absorption costing and (b) the amount of the difference in reported income under the two methods. Treat each condition as an independent case.

1. Production	20,000 units
Sales	23,000 units
2. Production	10,000 units
Sales	10,000 units
3. Production	11,000 units
Sales	9,000 units

Exercise 2.48
Throughput Costing
(LO 7)

Spreadsheet

Compute throughput product cost of goods sold, throughput, and operating income from the following data for each month. Note the relationship between variable and indirect conversion costs.

	Month 1	Month 2	Month 3
Beginning inventory, in units	0	0	100
Units produced	500	600	400
Units sold	500	500	500
Sales	$50,000	$50,000	$50,000
Material cost	10,000	10,000	10,000
Direct conversion cost used	12,000	14,400	9,600
Indirect conversion cost	8,000	5,600	10,400
Indirect operating cost	16,000	16,000	16,000

Exercise 2.49
Variable Costing
(LO 8)

Refer to the data in the preceding exercise. Compute variable cost of goods sold, contribution margin, and operating income. Why is operating income different from one month to the next?

Exercise 2.50
Absorption Costing
(LO 8)

Refer to the data in Exercise 2.48. Compute absorption cost of goods sold, gross margin, and operating income. Why is operating income different from one month to the next?

Exercise 2.51
Comparison of Income Amounts under Absorption and Variable Costing
(LO 7, 9)

Communication

Alameda Security Systems, Inc., uses the following unit costs for one of the products it manufactures:

Direct material	$164.00
Direct labor	70.80
Manufacturing overhead (based on planned production of 5,000 units):	
Variable	31.20
Fixed	28.00
Selling and administrative costs (based on 6,500 units sold):	
Variable	20.80
Fixed	14.00

This year, 1,500 units were in beginning finished-goods inventory, 5,000 units were produced, and 6,500 units were sold at $400 per unit. The beginning inventory was valued at $266 per unit using variable costing and at $294 per unit using absorption costing. There was no beginning or ending work-in-process inventory

Required

a. Prepare an income statement for the year using variable costing and a contribution-margin format.

b. Would reported operating profits be more, less, or the same if absorption costing were used? Support your conclusions with an income statement using absorption costing.

Exercise 2.52
Absorption, Variable, and Throughput Costing
(LO 7, 8, 9)

Information taken from Ticonderoga Lumber Company's records for the most recent year is as follows:

Direct material used	$290,000
Direct labor	100,000
Variable manufacturing overhead	50,000
Fixed manufacturing overhead	80,000
Variable selling and administrative costs	40,000
Fixed selling and administrative costs	20,000

Required

a. Assuming that Ticonderoga Lumber Company uses variable costing, compute the inventoriable costs for the year.

b. Compute the year's inventoriable costs using absorption costing.

c. Now assume that the company uses throughput costing and has *committed* to spending for direct labor, variable overhead, and fixed overhead in the amounts given in the problem. Under this scenario, compute the company's inventoriable cost for the year.

[CMA adapted]

Exercise 2.53
Absorption, Variable, and Throughput Costing
(LO 7, 8, 9)

Pensacola Pillow Company's planned production for the year just ended was 10,000 units. This production level was achieved, but it sold only 9,000 units. Other data follow:

Direct material used	$40,000
Direct labor incurred	20,000
Fixed manufacturing overhead	25,000
Variable manufacturing overhead	12,000
Fixed selling and administrative expenses	30,000
Variable selling and administrative expenses	4,500
Finished-goods inventory, January 1	None

There were no work-in-process inventories at the beginning or end of the year.

Required

a. What would be Pensacola Pillow Company's finished-goods inventory cost on December 31 under the variable-costing method?

b. Which costing method, absorption or variable costing, would show a higher operating income for the year? By what amount?

c. Suppose that Pensacola Pillow Company uses throughput costing, and the cost of direct material is its only unit-level cost. What would be the company's finished-goods inventory on December 31?

[CPA adapted]

Exercise 2.54
Internet Search
(LO 7, 9)

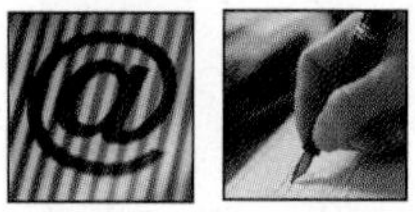

Internet Communication

Search the Internet for at least one example of an actual organization that uses throughput or variable costing (preferably not a university class or consultant's homepage). (*Hint:* Begin by using a search engine to find sites with the key words "variable cost" or "throughput." Prepare a memorandum to your instructor that describes:

a. The organization—its name, industry, size, profitability, strategy, etc.

b. The way that the organization uses variable or throughput costing

c. Any costs or benefits the organization discloses about using variable or throughput costing

Problems

Problem 2.55
Unknown Account Balances
(LO 1, 2, 3)

Each of the following columns is independent and for a different company. Use the data given, which refer to one year for each company, to find the unknown account balances.

	Company		
Account	**1**	**2**	**3**
Raw-material inventory, January 1	$ 24,600	$ 8,000	$ 45,000
Raw-material inventory, December 31	20,000	12,400	(d)
Work-in-process inventory, January 1	11,600	12,560	(e)
Work-in-process inventory, December 31	12,000	12,560	85,200
Finished-goods inventory, January 1	254,200	2,800	334,480
Finished-goods inventory, December 31	(a)	4,600	367,400
Purchases of raw material	262,000	(c)	248,400
Cost of goods manufactured during the year	679,200	58,000	1,518,220
Total manufacturing costs	679,600	58,000	1,526,800
Cost of goods sold	760,000	56,200	(f)
Gross margin	328,000	13,400	1,874,600
Direct labor	173,000	23,200	(g)
Direct material used	(b)	15,000	234,200
Manufacturing overhead	240,000	19,800	430,600
Sales revenue	1,088,000	69,600	3,359,900

Problem 2.56
Impact of a Decision on Income Statements
(LO 4, 5, 6)

You have been appointed manager of an operating division of Micro, Inc., a manufacturer of products using the latest developments in microprocessor technology. Your division manufactures the chip assembly, CH-1. On January 1 of this year, you invested $1 million in automated processing equipment for the chip assembly. At that time, your expected income statement for this year was as follows:

Sales revenue	$1,600,000
Operating costs:	
Variable (cash expenditures)	$ 200,000
Fixed (cash expenditures)	750,000
Equipment depreciation	150,000
Other depreciation	125,000
Total operating costs	$1,225,000
Operating profit (before taxes)	$ 375,000

On November 15 of this year, a sales representative for Hanimoto Machine Company approaches you. Hanimoto wants to rent to your division a new assembly machine that would be installed on December 31 for an annual rental charge of $230,000. The new equipment would enable you to increase your division's annual revenue by 10 percent. The more efficient machine would decrease fixed cash expenditures by 5 percent. You will have to write off the cost of the automated processing equipment this year because it has no salvage value. Equipment depreciation shown on the income statement is for the automated processing equipment.

Your bonus is determined as a percentage of your division's operating profit before taxes. Equipment losses are included in the bonus and operating profit computation.

Ignore taxes and any effects on operations on the day of installation of the new machine. Assume that the data given in your expected income statement are the actual amounts for this year and next year if you keep the current equipment.

Required

a. What is the difference in this year's divisional operating profit if the new machine is rented and installed on December 31 of this year?

b. What would be the effect on next year's divisional operating profit if the new machine is rented and installed on December 31 of this year?

c. Would you rent the new equipment? Why or why not?

Problem 2.57
Schedules of Cost of Goods Manufactured and Sold; Income Statement
(LO 1, 2, 3)

The following data refer to Fresno Fashions Company for the year 20x2:

Sales revenue	$950,000
Work-in-process inventory, December 31	30,000
Work-in-process inventory, January 1	40,000
Selling and administrative expenses	150,000
Income tax expense	90,000
Purchases of raw material	180,000
Raw-material Inventory, December 31	25,000
Raw-material Inventory, January 1	40,000
Direct labor	200,000
Utilities: plant	40,000
Depreciation: plant and equipment	60,000
Finished-goods inventory, December 31	50,000
Finished-goods inventory, January 1	20,000
Indirect material	10,000
Indirect labor	15,000
Other manufacturing overhead	80,000

Required

a. Prepare Fresno Fashions' schedule of cost of goods manufactured for the year.
b. Prepare Fresno Fashions' schedule of cost of goods sold for the year.
c. Prepare Fresno Fashions' income statement for the year.

Problem 2.58
Fixed and Variable Costs; Forecasting
(LO 4)

Charlotte Electronics Corporation incurred the following costs during 20x1. The company sold all of its products manufactured during the year.

Direct material	$3,000,000
Direct labor	2,200,000
Manufacturing overhead:	
Utilities (primarily electricity)	140,000
Depreciation on plant and equipment	230,000
Insurance	160,000
Supervisory salaries	300,000
Property taxes	210,000
Selling costs:	
Advertising	195,000
Sales commissions	90,000
Administrative costs:	
Salaries of top management and staff	372,000
Office supplies	40,000
Depreciation on building and equipment	80,000

During 20x1, the company operated at about half of its capacity due to a slowdown in the economy. Prospects for 20x2 are slightly better. The marketing manager forecasts a 20 percent growth in sales over the 20x1 level.

Required

Categorize each of the preceding costs as most likely variable or fixed. Forecast the 20x2 amount for each cost item.

Problem 2.59
Characteristics of Costs
(LO 4, 6)

The following terms are used to describe various characteristics of costs.

1. *Opportunity cost*
2. *Out-of-pocket cost*
3. *Sunk cost*
4. *Prime cost*
5. *Conversion cost*
6. *Average cost*

Required

Choose one of the terms to characterize each of the following amounts.

a. The management of a high-rise office building using 2,500 square feet of space in the building for its own management functions but could be rented for $250,000.

b. The cost to build an automated assembly line in a factory was $800,000 when the line was installed three years ago.

c. The direct-material and direct-labor cost incurred by a mass customizer such as Gateway Computer to produce its most popular line of laptop computers.

d. The cost of feeding 500 children in a public school cafeteria is $800 per day, or $1.60 per child per day.

e. The cost of merchandise inventory purchased two years ago, which is now obsolete.

f. The cost of direct labor and manufacturing overhead incurred in producing frozen, microwavable pizzas.

g. The $1,000 cost of offering a computer workshop for a group of 20 students, or $50 per student.

Problem 2.60
Variable Costs; Graphical and Tabular Analyses
(LO 4)

Carlson Sheet Metal. Inc. incurs a variable cost of $40 per pound for direct material to produce a special alloy used in manufacturing aircraft.

Required

a. Draw a graph of the firm's direct material cost, showing the total cost at the following production levels: 10,000 pounds, 20,000 pounds, and 30,000 pounds.

b. Prepare a table that shows the unit cost and total cost of direct material at the following production levels: 1 pound, 10 pounds, and 1,000 pounds.

Problem 2.61
Fixed Costs; Graphical and Tabular Analyses
(LO 4)

High Flight Company manufactures a special fabric used to upholster the seats in small aircraft. The company's annual fixed production cost is $100,000.

Required

a. Graph the company's fixed production cost showing the total cost at the following production levels of upholstery fabric: 10,000 yards, 20,000 yards, 30,000 yards, and 40,000 yards.

b. Prepare a table that shows the unit cost and the total cost for the firm's fixed production costs at the following production levels: 1 yard, 10 yards, 10,000 yards, and 40,000 yards.

c. Prepare a graph that shows the unit cost for the company's fixed production cost at the following production levels: 10,000 yards, 20,000 yards, 30,000 yards, and 40,000 yards.

Problem 2.62
Reconstructed Financial Statements
(LO 1, 2, 3)

The following data appeared in Garcia Mesa Company's records on December 31 of last year:

Raw-material inventory, December 31	$ 42,500
Raw-material purchased during the year	180,000
Finished-goods inventory, December 31	45,000
Indirect labor	16,000
Direct labor	200,000
Plant heat, light, and power	18,600
Building depreciation (7/9 is for manufacturing)	40,500
Administrative salaries	25,700
Miscellaneous factory cost	15,950
Selling costs	18,500
Maintenance on factory machines	6,050
Insurance on factory equipment	9,500
Distribution costs	800
Taxes on manufacturing property	6,550
Legal fees on customer complaint	4,100
Direct material used	191,050
Work-in-process inventory, December 31	12,300

On January 1, at the beginning of last year, the Finished-Goods Inventory account had a balance of $40,000, and the Work-in-Process Inventory account had a balance of $12,950. Sales revenue during the year was $812,500.

Required

Prepare a schedule of cost of goods sold and an income statement.

Problem 2.63
Unknown Account Balances
(LO 1, 2, 3)

Each of the following columns is independent and for a different company. Use the data given, which refer to one year for each example, to find the unknown account balances.

	Company		
Account	**1**	**2**	**3**
Raw-material inventory, January 1	(a)	$ 3,500	$ 16,000
Raw-material inventory, December 31	$ 3,600	2,900	14,100
Work-in-process inventory, January 1	2,700	6,720	82,400
Work-in-process inventory, December 31	3,800	3,100	76,730
Finished-goods inventory, January 1	1,900	(d)	17,200
Finished-goods inventory, December 31	300	4,400	28,400
Purchases of raw materials	16,100	12,000	64,200
Cost of goods manufactured during the year	(b)	27,220	313,770
Total manufacturing costs	55,550	23,600	308,100
Cost of goods sold	56,050	27,200	302,570
Gross margin	(c)	16,400	641,280
Direct labor	26,450	3,800	124,700
Direct material used	15,300	(e)	66,100
Manufacturing overhead	13,800	7,200	(g)
Sales revenue	103,300	(f)	943,850

Problem 2.64
Cost Concepts
(LO 3, 4, 5, 6)

The following data pertain to a product manufactured by Eastern Company:

Sales price	$160 per unit
Fixed costs:	
Selling and administrative	$20,000 per period
Manufacturing overhead	$15,000 per period
Variable costs:	
Selling and administrative	$5 per unit
Manufacturing overhead	$30 per unit
Direct labor (manufacturing)	$10 per unit
Direct material (manufacturing)	$40 per unit
Number of units produced and sold during the period	1,000 units

Required

a. How much is the variable *manufacturing cost* per unit?
b. How much is the *variable cost* per unit?
c. How much is the *full absorption cost* per unit?
d. How much is the *prime cost* per unit?
e. How much is the *conversion cost* per unit?
f. How much is the *profit margin* per unit?
g. How much is the *contribution margin* per unit?
h. How much is the *gross margin* per unit?
i. If the number of units increases from 1,000 to 1,100, which is within the relevant range, will the *fixed manufacturing cost* per unit decrease, increase, or stay the same? Why?

Problem 2.65
Cost Concepts
(LO 1, 3)

Item (a) through (e) are based on the following data pertaining to Pacific Company's manufacturing operations:

Inventories	**April 1**	**April 30**
Raw material	$ 9,000	$ 7,500
Work in process	4,500	3,000
Finished goods	13,500	18,000

Additional information for the month of April:

Raw material purchased	$21,000
Direct-labor costs	15,000
Manufacturing overhead	20,000

Required

Calculate the following amounts for the month of April.

a. Prime costs
b. Conversion costs
c. Total manufacturing costs
d. Cost of goods manufactured
e. Cost of goods sold

[CPA adapted]

Problem 2.66
Cost Data for Managerial Purposes
(LO 4, 5, 6)

Communication

Florida Fruits, Inc., agreed to sell 40,000 cases of Fang, a dehydrated fruit drink, to NASA for use on space flights at "cost plus 10 percent." The company operates a manufacturing plant that can produce 120,000 cases per year, but it normally produces 80,000. The costs to produce 80,000 cases are as follows:

	Total	**Per Case**
Direct material	$ 960,000	$12.00
Direct labor	1,520,000	19.00
Supplies and other costs that vary with production	640,000	8.00
Costs that do not vary with production	440,000	5.50
Variable selling costs	160,000	2.00
Administrative costs (all fixed)	160,000	2.00
Total	$3,880,000	$48.50

Based on these data, company management expects to receive $53.35 (that is, $48.50 × 110 percent) per case for those sold on this contract. After completing 10,000 cases, the company sent a bill (invoice) to the government for $533,500 (that is, 10,000 cases at $53.35 per case).

The president of the company received a call from a NASA representative, who stated that the per-case cost should be as follows:

Materials	$12
Labor	19
Supplies and other costs that vary with production	8
Total	$39

Therefore, the price per case should be $42.90 (that is, $39 × 110 percent). NASA ignored selling costs because the contract bypassed the usual sales channels.

Required

What price would you recommend? Why? Write a memo to management explaining your reasoning. (*Note:* You need not limit yourself to the costs selected by the company or by the NASA representative.)

Problem 2.67
Variable-Costing Operating Profit and Reconciliation with Absorption Costing
(LO 7, 8, 9)

Communication

You have been given the following information concerning Orion Company, which manufactures the ever-popular cosmic gismo.

- *Sales:* 10,000 units per year at a price of $46 per unit
- *Production:* 15,000 units in year 1; 5,000 units in year 2
- *Beginning inventory:* None in year 1
- *Variable (unit-level) cost:* $5 per unit

- *Facility-level production costs for the year:* $225,000, all fixed
- *Ending finished-goods inventory in year 1:* One-third of that year's production
- *Annual facility-level selling and administrative costs:* $140,000, all fixed

Required

a. Prepare absorption-costing income statements for year 1, year 2, and the two years taken together.

b. Prepare variable-costing income statements for year 1, year 2, and the two years taken together.

c. Write a short report to management that reconciles absorption-costing operating profit to variable-costing operating profit for year 1 and year 2.

Problem 2.68
Variable-Costing Operating Profit versus Absorption-Costing Operating Profit
(LO 7, 8, 9)

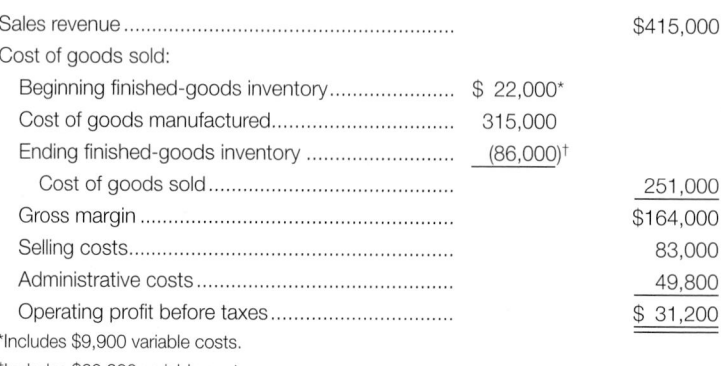

Communication

Lake Superior Fabricating Company (LSFC) employs an absorption-costing system for external reporting and internal management purposes. The latest annual income statement follows:

Sales revenue		$415,000
Cost of goods sold:		
Beginning finished-goods inventory	$ 22,000*	
Cost of goods manufactured	315,000	
Ending finished-goods inventory	(86,000)†	
Cost of goods sold		251,000
Gross margin		$164,000
Selling costs		83,000
Administrative costs		49,800
Operating profit before taxes		$ 31,200

*Includes $9,900 variable costs.
†Includes $60,200 variable costs.

Management is somewhat concerned that although LSFC is showing adequate income, it is short of cash to meet operating costs. The following information has been provided to assist management with its evaluation of the situation:

Schedule of Cost of Goods Manufactured

Direct material:		
Beginning inventory	$ 16,000	
Purchases	62,000	
Ending inventory	(22,000)	$ 56,000
Direct labor		125,100
Manufacturing overhead:		
Variable		39,400
Fixed (including depreciation of $30,000)		94,500
Cost of goods manufactured		$315,000

There are no work-in-process inventories. Management reports that it is pleased that this year's manufacturing costs are 70 percent variable compared to last year's costs when they were only 45 percent variable. Although 80 percent of the selling costs are variable, only 40 percent of the administrative costs are considered variable. The company uses the first-in, first-out (FIFO) inventory method.

Required

a. Prepare a variable-costing income statement for the year.

b. Write a short report to management that explains why the company might be experiencing a cash-flow shortage despite the adequate income shown in its absorption-costing income statement.

Problem 2.69
Absorption and Variable Costing; Incomplete Records
(LO 7, 8, 9)

Communication

On December 31 of last year, a fire destroyed the bulk of the accounting records of Solares Company, a small, one-product manufacturing firm. In addition, the chief accountant mysteriously disappeared. You have the task to reconstruct last year's records. The general manager has said that the accountant had been experimenting with both absorption costing and variable costing.

The records are a mess, but you have gathered the following data for last year:

Sales	$450,000
Actual fixed manufacturing costs incurred	66,000
Actual variable manufacturing costs per unit for last year and for units in beginning finished-goods inventory on January 1 of last year	3
Operating profit, absorption-costing basis	60,000
Notes receivable from chief accountant	14,000
Contribution margin	180,000
Raw-material purchases	175,000
Actual selling and administrative costs (all fixed)	21,000
Gross margin	81,000

The company had no beginning or ending work-in-process inventories. You also learn that the absorption cost per unit in last year's beginning finished-goods inventory is the same as the absorption cost per unit for units produced during the year.

Required

a. Prepare a comparative income statement on an absorption-costing and a variable-costing basis.

b. At a meeting with the board of directors, the following questions were raised:

1. How many units did we sell last year?
2. How many units did we produce last year?
3. What were the unit production costs last year under both absorption and variable costing?

Write a short report responding to these questions.

c. Reconcile the operating profit under variable costing with that under absorption costing, showing the exact source of the difference.

Problem 2.70
Variable versus Absorption Costing; JIT
(LO 7, 8, 9)

Global

Communication

Vancouver Tool Corporation (VTC) manufactures small electric hand tools in Vancouver, British Columbia. The firm uses a standard absorption-costing system for internal reporting purposes; however, the company is considering using variable costing. Data regarding VTC's planned and actual operations for 20x0 follow:

	Planned Activity	Actual Activity
Beginning finished-goods inventory in units	35,000	35,000
Sales in units	140,000	125,000
Production in units	140,000	130,000

	Budgeted Costs		
	Per Unit	**Total**	**Actual Costs**
Direct material	$12.00	$1,680,000	$1,560,000
Direct labor	9.00	1,260,000	1,170,000
Variable manufacturing overhead	4.00	560,000	520,000
Fixed manufacturing overhead	5.00	700,000	715,000
Variable selling expenses	8.00	1,120,000	1,000,000
Fixed selling expenses	7.00	980,000	980,000
Variable administrative expenses	2.00	280,000	250,000
Fixed administrative expenses	3.00	420,000	425,000
Total	$50.00	$7,000,000	$6,620,000

The budget per-unit cost figures were based on VTC producing and selling 140,000 units in 20x0. VTC uses a predetermined overhead rate for applying manufacturing overhead to its product. A total manufacturing-overhead rate of $9 per unit was employed for absorption-costing purposes in 20x0. Any overapplied or underapplied manufacturing overhead is closed to the Cost of Goods Sold account at the end of the year. The 20x0 beginning finished-goods inventory for absorption-costing purposes was valued at the prior year's budgeted unit manufacturing cost, which was the same as the 20x0 budgeted unit manufacturing cost. There are no work-in-process inventories at either the beginning or the end of the year. The planned and actual unit selling price for 20x0 was $70 per unit.

Required

Was VTC's 20x0 income higher under absorption costing or variable costing? Why? Compute the following amounts.

a. The value of VTC's 20x0 ending finished-goods inventory under absorption costing.

b. The value of VTC's 20x0 ending finished-goods inventory under variable costing.

c. The difference between VTC's 20x0 reported income calculated under absorption costing and calculated under variable costing.

d. Suppose that VTC had introduced a JIT production and inventory-management system at the beginning of 20x0.

  1. What would likely be different about the scenario as described in the problem?

  2. Would reported income under variable and absorption costing differ by the magnitude you found in requirement (c)? Explain.

[CMA adapted]

Problem 2.71
Production Costs
(LO 7, 8, 9)

Communication

Integer Peripherals, Inc., manufactures computer data storage devices. Its Colorado division designs and assembles the MicroDrive for laptop computers. You have gathered the following data for the MicroDrive for the recently completed month of February. (All *dollar amounts* are in thousands.)

INTEGER PERIPHERALS, INC.
Summary of Operations
MicroDrive Division

Account Balances	
Inventories (all), Feb. 1	$225
Other assets, Feb. 1	550
Total assets, Feb. 1	$775
Inventories (all), Feb. 28	$290
Other assets, Feb. 28	540
Total assets, Feb. 28	$830

Transactions	
Units produced	12,000
Units sold	10,000
Material purchased	$ 480
Material used	445
Variable manufacturing labor used	200
Indirect production costs:	
Depreciation on manufacturing building and equipment	180
Manufacturing supervisory salaries	50
Manufacturing overhead	525
Sales revenue	2,750
Indirect operating costs	
Selling costs	440
Administrative costs	570

Required

a. Compute the cost of goods sold using each of the following methods.

  1. Throughput costing

  2. Variable costing

  3. Absorption costing

b. Compute contribution to profit, operating expense, and operating income using each costing method.

c. Write a short report to management demonstrating why operating income is different for each costing method.

Problem 2.72
Product Costs; Spreadsheet
(LO 6, 7, 8, 9)

GPS, Inc., has collected the following production information for its two products for a recent year.

	A	B	C	D	E	F	G
1	Models	1500 XS		3000 XL		Total	
2	Quantities produced and sold	12,000		9,000		21,000	
3	Direct costs	Total	Per Unit	Total	Per Unit	Total	Per Unit
4	Direct-material costs	$185,444		$589,740			$36.91
5	Direct conversion costs	45,200		148,500			9.22
6	Direct operating costs	39,600		41,200			3.85
7	Total direct costs	$270,244		$779,440			$50.00*
8	Indirect costs						
9	Indirect conversion costs					$3,568,000	
10	Indirect operating costs					2,789,000	
11	Total indirect costs					$6,357,000	
12	Total costs (direct + indirect)					$7,406,684	

*Rounded

Ethics

GPS, Inc., traces direct material to products produced. Although GPS pays its highly skilled workforce on a salary basis, the company traces direct conversion costs to products produced. GPS also traces direct operating costs, which are composed of 40 percent packaging materials and 60 percent distribution labor, to products sold. Conversion and operating costs in total (direct plus indirect) do not vary with units produced. For financial reporting purposes, GPS allocates indirect conversion costs to products on an equal, per-unit basis. Untraced conversion and operating costs are expensed during the period in which they are incurred.

Required

a. Fill in the highlighted, blank cells (*Hint:* Create a computer spreadsheet to solve this problem. *Another hint:* When you complete the spreadsheet, the highlighted cells should contain formulas that reference appropriate numbers but should not contain any numbers themselves. For example, C4 = B4/B2).

b. Compute the following costs per unit for each product model:

1. Throughput cost
2. Variable cost
3. Absorption cost

c. Compute the effects on product costs in requirement (b) of changing the product mix to 12,000 units of each product produced and sold.

d. Is there anything wrong with this attitude: "The board of directors sets the incentive plan, and I am just playing by the rules. The rules don't say anything about how many units I should produce." If managers are evaluated on annual, externally reported operating profit, as computed in requirement (b3), comment on the ethics of knowingly producing more units than can be sold in a period.

Problem 2.73
Operating Income
(LO 7, 8)

Refer to the preceding problem and the following additional information.

	Model 1500XS	Model 3000XL	Total
Units produced	12,000	9,000	21,000
Units sold	11,000	8,000	19,000
Sales revenue			$8,400,000

Required

a. Compute contribution to profit, operating expense, and operating income using:
   1. Throughput costing
   2. Variable costing
   3. Absorption costing
b. Explain the differences between each pair of operating income measures.

Problem 2.74
Conversion of Variable to Absorption Costing
(LO 7, 8, 9)

Communication

Hathaway Company uses variable costing for internal management purposes and absorption costing for external reporting purposes. Thus, at the end of each year, financial information must be converted from variable costing to absorption costing for external reports. At the end of last year, management anticipated that sales would rise 20 percent this year. Therefore, production was increased from 20,000 units to 24,000 units. However, economic conditions kept sales volume at 20,000 units for both years.

The following data pertain to the two years:

	Last Year	This Year
Sales (units)	20,000	20,000
Beginning inventory (units)	2,000	2,000
Production (units)	20,000	24,000
Ending inventory (units)	2,000	6,000
Unapplied variable overhead	$10,000	$ 8,000
Selling price per unit	$60	$60

Variable cost per unit for both years was composed of the following:

Conversion	$21
Material	9
Total	$30

Indirect costs for each year follow:

Production	$600,000
Selling and administrative	200,000
Total	$800,000

Conversion costs are production costs traced directly to products as resources are used. Untraced indirect cost is expensed during the period. Absorption costing allocates indirect production costs per unit based on an estimated volume of 20,000 units per year.

Required

Use the preceding data to complete the following:

a. Present the income statement for this year based on variable costing for this year.
b. Present the income statement for this year based on absorption costing for this year.
c. Write a short report to management that explains the difference, if any, in the operating profit figures.

[CMA adapted]

Problem 2.75
Comparison of Variable and Absorption Costing: Profit Performance Analysis
(LO 7, 8, 9)

Communication

Tammari Enterprises released the following figures from its records for year 1 and year 2:

	Year 1	Year 2
Sales (units)	250,000	250,000
Production (units)	250,000	344,000
Selling price per unit	$40	$40
Variable manufacturing cost per unit	$24	$24
Annual committed manufacturing cost	$860,000	$860,000
Variable selling and administrative costs per unit sold	$2.40	$2.40
Committed selling and administrative costs	$840,000	$840,000
Beginning inventory	$0	?

Required

a. Prepare income statements for both years using absorption costing.
b. Prepare income statements for both years using variable costing.

c. Comment on the two operating profit figures. Write a brief report explaining why the operating profits are different, if they are.

Problem 2.76
Comparison of Variable and Absorption Costing
(LO 7, 8)

The following questions are based on Larue Corporation, which produces a single product it sells for $12 per unit. Of the 100,000 units produced, 80,000 were sold during year 1; all ending inventory was in finished-goods inventory. Larue had no inventory at the beginning of the year.

Direct material (unit-level cost)	$240,000
Direct labor (unit-level cost)	160,000
Factory overhead (unit-level cost)	80,000
Factory overhead (capacity cost)	240,000
Selling and administrative (unit-level cost)	80,000
Selling and administrative (capacity cost)	128,000

Required

a. In presenting inventory on the balance sheet at December 31, what is the unit cost under absorption costing?

b. In presenting inventory on a variable-costing balance sheet, what is the unit cost?

c. What is the operating profit using variable costing?

d. What is the operating profit using absorption costing?

e. What is the ending inventory (dollar amount) using absorption costing?

f. What is the ending inventory (dollar amount) under variable costing?

[CPA adapted]

Problem 2.77
Throughput Costing, Absorption Costing, and Variable Costing
(LO 7, 8)

Edison Corporation, which uses throughput costing, just completed its first year of operations. Planned and actual production equaled 10,000 units, and sales totaled 9,600 units at $72 per unit. Cost data for the year are as follows:

Direct material (per unit)	$ 12
Conversion cost:	
Direct labor	45,000
Variable manufacturing overhead	65,000
Fixed manufacturing overhead	220,000
Selling and administrative costs:	
Variable (per unit)	8
Fixed	118,000

The company classifies only direct material as a throughput cost.

Required

a. Compute the company's total cost for the year assuming that variable manufacturing costs are driven by the number of units produced and that variable selling and administrative costs are driven by the number of units sold.

b. How much of this cost would be held in year-end inventory under (1) absorption costing, (2) variable costing, and (3) throughput costing?

c. How much of the company's total cost for the year would be included as an expense on the period's income statement under (1) absorption costing, (2) variable costing, and (3) throughput costing?

d. Prepare Edison's throughput-costing income statement.

Cases

Case 2.78
Inventory Turnover
(LO 1)

Ethics

University Bookstore is a profit-making organization that reports to the Student Council. Martha Wailua, a part-time student employee, noticed that the managers at the bookstore seemed unconcerned about the costs of carrying large inventories. For example, several times a year the manager of the general merchandise department (one of six departments) bought large quantities of merchandise (clothing, gift items, etc.) with the university and sports team logos to get quantity discounts. The general merchandise manager also had argued successfully for more warehouse space for the merchandise, for which the bookstore pays rent to the university. Inevitably, several months later, the manager marks down the unsold merchandise to purchase cost or less to make room for the next purchase. This seemed very inefficient to Wailua, and she began to analyze the bookstore's purchases and sales for the past year. She gathered the following data.

Department	Cost of Goods Sold	Average Inventory	Percent of Warehouse Space	Average Number of Days Items Were Purchased in Advance of Sale
New textbooks	$ 5,730,972	$ 840,475	25%	63
Used textbooks	1,258,007	180,600	12	37
Trade books	563,686	370,500	10	86
Supplies	662,560	251,700	8	71
General merchandise	883,251	640,600	25	94
Computers	2,246,600	402,000	20	28
Total store	$11,345,076	$2,685,875	100%	66.3

Required

a. Compute inventory turnover ratios (i.e., cost of goods sold ÷ average inventory) for each department and the bookstore as a whole. What would these ratios tell Wailua about the management of inventories at University Bookstore? Is it reasonable to compare these ratios across departments? Why or why not?

b. A privately owned store in the university commercial area sells licensed (general) merchandise with the university's logo and reported to Wailua that its inventory turnover ratio for the past year was 5.30. Is that a legitimate benchmark for University Bookstore? Why or why not?

c. What are the benefits and costs to the bookstore of its methods for purchasing and inventory?

d. What information would Wailua need to place a dollar figure on all of those costs?

e. Wailua has learned that the manager of the General Merchandise Department is a close personal friend of the bookstore manager and receives incentive prizes from suppliers for ordering large quantities of merchandise. What are her ethical responsibilities?

Case 2.79
"I Enjoy Challenges"; Effect of Changes in Production and Costing Method on Operating Profit
(LO 7, 8, 9)

Communication

(This classic case is based on an actual company's experience.) Brassinni Company uses an actual cost system to apply all production costs to units produced. The plant has a maximum production capacity of 40 million units but produced and sold only 10 million units during year 1. There were no beginning or ending inventories. Brassinni Company's income statement for year 1 follows:

BRASSINNI COMPANY
Income Statement
For the Year Ending December 31, Year 1

Sales (10,000,000 units at $6)		$ 60,000,000
Cost of goods sold:		
Direct (10,000,000 at $2)	$20,000,000	
Indirect	48,000,000	68,000,000
Gross margin		$ (8,000,000)
Selling and administrative costs		10,000,000
Operating profit (loss)		$(18,000,000)

The board of directors is concerned about the $18 million loss. A consultant approached the board with the following offer: "I agree to become president for no fixed salary. But I insist on a year-end bonus of 10 percent of operating profit (before considering the bonus)." The board of directors agreed to these terms and hired the consultant as Brassinni's new president.

The new president promptly stepped up production to an annual rate of 30 million units. Sales for year 2 remained at 10 million units. The resulting Brassinni Company absorption-costing income statement for year 2 follows:

BRASSINNI COMPANY
Income Statement
For the Year Ending December 31, Year 2

Sales (10,000,000 units at $6)		$60,000,000
Cost of goods sold:		
Cost of goods manufactured:		
Direct (30,000,000 at $2)	$ 60,000,000	
Indirect	48,000,000	
Total cost of goods manufactured	$ 108,000,000	
Less: Ending inventory:		
Variable (20,000,000 at $2)	$ 40,000,000	
Indirect (20/30 × $48,000,000)	32,000,000	
Total inventory	$ 72,000,000	
Cost of goods sold		36,000,000
Gross margin		$24,000,000
Selling and administrative costs		10,000,000
Operating profit before bonus		$14,000,000
Bonus		1,400,000
Operating profit after bonus		$12,600,000

The day after the statement was verified, the president took his check for $1,400,000 and resigned to take a job with another corporation. He remarked, "I enjoy challenges. Now that Brassinni Company is in the black, I'd prefer tackling another challenging situation." (His contract with his new employer is similar to the one he had with Brassinni Company.)

Required

a. Write a report to Brassinni's board of directors evaluating the company's year 2 performance.

b. Using variable costing, what would operating profit be for year 1? For year 2? What are the inventory values? (Assume that all selling and administrative costs are committed and unchanged.) Compare those results with the absorption-costing statements.

c. What would year 2's operating profit (loss) be if Brassinni used absorption costing with an indirect manufacturing overhead rate of $4.80 ($48,000,000 indirect manufacturing costs ÷ 10,000,000 estimated unit sales)?

1. Prepare an income statement using absorption costing and the $4.80 indirect cost per unit for year 2.

2. Prepare a table to show how this year 2 income statement differs from the year 2 income statement given in the case (i.e., as originally prepared by the company).

Case 2.80
Absorption and Variable Costing; Import Decisions
(LO 7, 8, 9)

Global

Cotierre imports designer clothing manufactured by subcontractors in Mexico. Clothing is a seasonal product. The goods must be ready for sale prior to the start of the season. Any goods left over at the end of the season usually must be sold at steep discounts. The company prepares a dress design and selects fabrics approximately six months before a given season. It receives these goods and distributes them at the start of the season. Based on past experience, the company estimates that 60 percent of a particular lot of dresses will be unsold at the end of the season and will be marked down to one-half of the initial retail price. Even with the markdown, a substantial number of dresses will remain unsold and will be returned to Cotierre and destroyed. Although a large number of dresses must be discounted or destroyed, the company needs to place a minimum order of 1,000 dresses to have a sufficient selection of styles and sizes to market the design.

Recently, the company placed an order for 1,000 dresses of a particular design for $25,000 plus import duties of $5,000 and a $7 commission for each dress sold at retail, regardless of the price. Return mailing and disposing of each unsold dress cost $3 after the end of the markdown period.

Required

a. Use absorption costing to compute the cost of each dress in this lot of dresses.

b. Suppose that the company sells 30 percent of the dresses in this lot for $75 each during the first accounting period. Using absorption costing, what is the value of the ending inventory? What is the operating profit or loss for the period, assuming no other transactions and that the season has not ended, so that the number of dresses subject to markdown or to be returned is unknown?

c. During the second period, 10 percent of the 1,000 dresses were sold at full price, and 30 percent were sold at the half-price markdown. The remaining dresses were returned and disposed of. Using absorption costing, what is the operating profit or loss for the period, assuming no other transactions?

d. Suggest a method to account for these dresses that would more closely relate revenues and costs.

CHAPTER

3

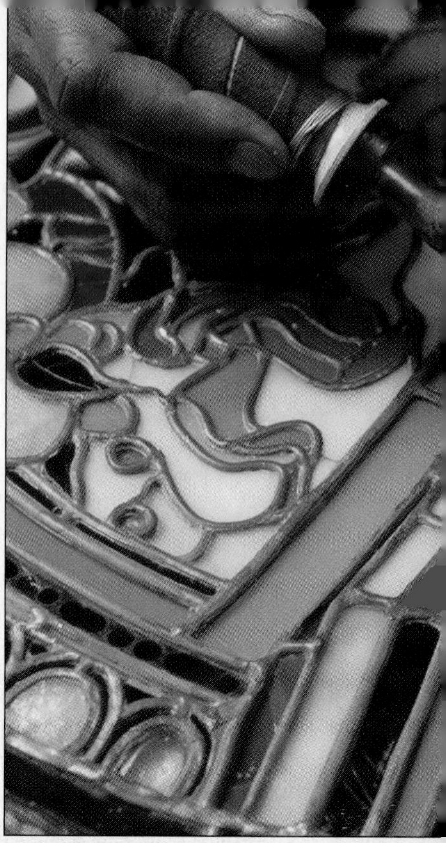

Cost Accumulation for Job-Shop and Batch Production Operations

After completing this chapter, you should be able to:

1. Explain the differences in job-order, process, and operation costing.
2. Explain how costs flow through the manufacturing accounts.
3. Assign costs to production jobs or projects using a job-order costing system.
4. Prepare accounting journal entries to record job costs.
5. Use a predetermined overhead rate to assign indirect resource costs to production jobs.
6. Explain how to measure production costs under actual, normal, and standard costing systems.
7. Discuss the role of job-order costing in service organizations.
8. Understand how companies manage long-term projects and their costs.

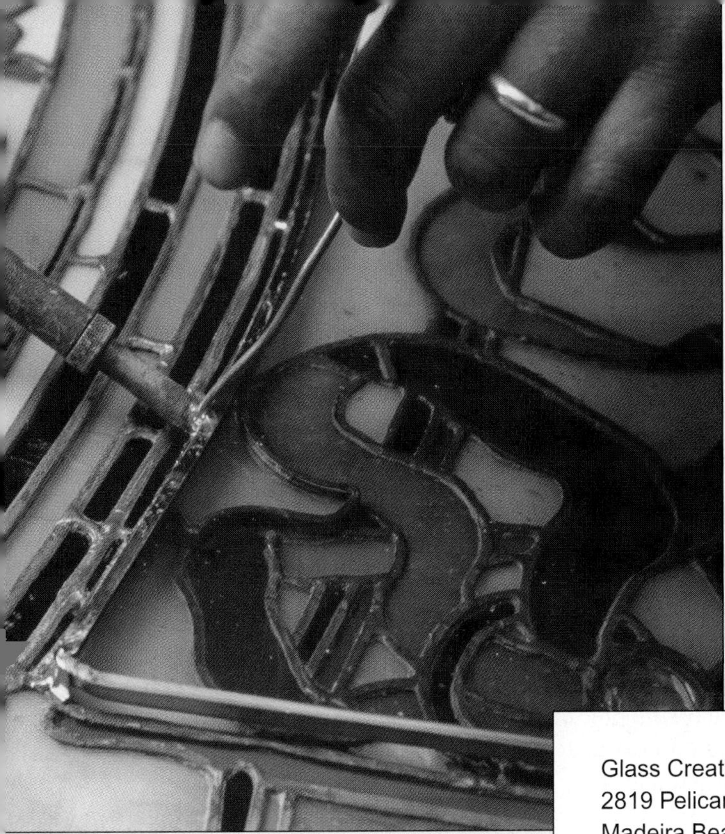

Cost-Management
Challenges

1. **What** factors should a cost-management analyst consider when designing a product-costing system?

2. **What** features should a job-order costing system have, and how can they be developed?

3. **How** can cost-management analysts use job-cost information to support planning and decision-making activities?

Glass Creations
2819 Pelican Drive
Madeira Beach, Florida 33708

January 30

Ms. Grace Riley
Gulf Coast Aquarium
Tampa, Florida

Dear Ms. Riley:

We have completed the estimates for the two stained glass doors you are planning for the aquarium's main entry portico. Our designer has developed sketches for some beautiful stained glass panels for the doors following the guidelines you gave us during our meeting in November. Each door has six stained glass panels, featuring a variety of marine species, from dolphins and whales to starfish and sea horses. The panel designs are, as you requested, very colorful. I think you will be pleased with them.

We have carefully estimated the costs of the doors, which cover the materials, design talent, glass workers' labor, and applied overhead, which is based on the projected labor time required for the job. As per our previous discussions, our price for your nonprofit organization will be cost plus a modest 10 percent profit margin.

I will call you next week to set up a meeting so that we can go over the design sketches and the projected job-cost figures. Naturally, we will be happy to make any modifications that you wish. Thank you for allowing us to make a contribution to your aquarium project.

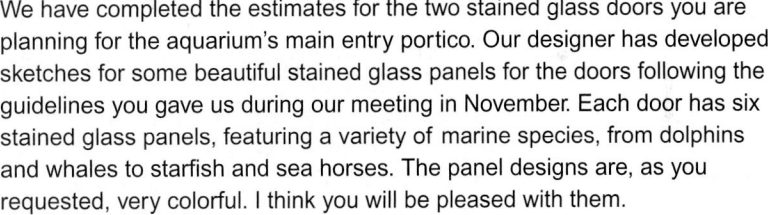

Sincerely,

Jeremiah Jacobson-Wiley

Jeremiah Jacobson-Wiley

Glass Creations creates and markets stained glass windows, doors, and free-standing pieces for private homes, businesses, and other organizations. The small, family-run business is located in Madeira Beach, Florida, a barrier island community on the Gulf Coast in the Tampa/St. Petersburg area. Jeremiah and Anita Jacobson-Wiley, who studied fine arts in college, founded the business 15 years ago. Both are involved in the design and creation of the stained glass pieces. In addition, Glass Creations' employees include one other designer, several highly skilled glass workers, a framing technician, and various office personnel. Tom Nakagawa, a certified management accountant, provides support to the firm in purchasing, production scheduling, accounting, and cost management.

Almost from its inception, Glass Creations has been a successful business, with sales and profit growing, at least modestly, almost every year. The Jacobson-Wileys can now boast the placement of their leaded, glazed, etched, and stained glass creations in almost every state in the United States and several foreign countries. The couple's most famous piece, "Calm Over Calamity," depicts a Native American lad of about 10 years standing calmly only a few feet away from a very menacing grizzly bear. The piece stands some 12 feet high and contains several hundred pieces of stained glass. It was commissioned by a commercial bank in Vancouver, British Columbia, where it is permanently installed in the lobby. As the correspondence on the preceding page indicates, Glass Creations is currently developing the design and cost estimate for two elaborate stained glass doors to be installed in the new Gulf Coast Aquarium.

Glass Creations designs and creates stained glass windows, doors, and other pieces in the firm's Madeira Beach glass studio. Roughly 75 percent of the firm's sales are for single, unique pieces, most of which are commissioned by private homeowners and businesses. They sell for prices ranging from $350 for a simple, relatively small piece, to tens of thousands of dollars for large, complex pieces. Glass Creations has produced stained glass pieces for all types of religious organizations, but the vast majority of its products are secular in nature. The remainder of Glass Creations' products are its windows, which are produced in small batches and sold as stock items at arts festivals, on the firm's Web site, or through catalogues of specialized building materials. Among the firm's stock windows are the pelican window, the blue heron window, and the dolphin window. Each unit in a batch of these types of window uses the same basic design with minor modifications from batch to batch. Moreover, the units within a batch typically are somewhat different because of the different glass colors used.

Although Glass Creations has been profitable throughout its life as a business, its owners recently became concerned because several large window manufacturers have begun to produce glazed, etched, and stained glass windows for private homes. These companies employ more mechanization than Glass Creations' artists use, and they produce stock windows in larger batches, thus driving down the costs. The Jacobson-Wileys are now concerned that these larger competitors might satisfy enough of the consumer demand for stained glass and other artistic windows to adversely affect Glass Creations' business. Although this has not been a problem yet, it is a cause for concern. Anita worries that consumers will not recognize or perhaps fail to properly appreciate the difference between a mass-produced window and one made by a skilled Glass worker in a studio. As Jeremiah recently said, "Anita and I are in this business because we love what we do. It's a really satisfying medium in which to work. But we do have to make a living. We have several employees and lots of bills to pay, not to mention providing for a secure retirement."

The owners must make some important marketing and strategic decisions to thrive in this potentially more competitive environment. For example, they must decide whether Glass Creations should compete with the large window manufacturers for the stock artistic window market or should concentrate on the custom design market? They must also determine how best to use the typically slow months of December and January. Should they aggressively seek more custom design work or use this period to produce stock windows for inventory to be sold later in the spring and summer months when arts festivals are in full swing and the home building industry picks up.

During their first decade as the owners of a small business, the Jacobson-Wileys focused exclusively on the artistic side of their enterprise. They were artists, after all, not businesspeople. However, they became increasingly aware of their problem related to the seemingly total unpredictability of the cost (and, by implication, the profit) on large, custom glass pieces. Sometimes Glass Creations bid too high on a job and lost it. Other times it bid too low and got the job but lost money on it. As Jeremiah said in frustration, "The profit margins on our various jobs were all over the map. We'd just never know what to expect." That frustration, coupled with several lean years of the "starving artist" syndrome, led the owners to hire Nakagawa, a college friend who had majored in business, to support their operations in a number of important business functions. The owners were becoming frustrated by spending too much time ordering materials, making estimates, and so on, and not getting enough time in the studio. They needed Nakagawa to help develop a sound costing system and help manage costs. He installed a simple product-costing system for Glass Creations, which gave the Jacobson-Wileys a much better idea of the costs of their jobs, which in turn helped them make better cost estimates for prospective jobs.

As the Jacobson-Wileys learned, a key element in deciding which products to offer is understanding the company's product costs. For example, Glass Creations has many opportunities to bid on commissioned pieces. Should it bid on every design? How much should it bid on the pieces for which it competes? This chapter explores a cost-accounting system called "job-order costing" (or simply "job costing"), which traces costs in organizations such as Glass Creations. This chapter discusses job-order costing using Glass Creations' business. The methods illustrated apply, however, to all types of organizations—manufacturing, service, nonprofit, and government—for which job-order costing is appropriate.

Choice among Product-Costing Systems

LO 1 Explain the differences in job-order, process, and operation costing.

Cost-management analysts could ask themselves and the managers with whom they work a number of questions regarding the nature of the information needed to support their organization's decision making. Answers to these questions have direct implications for designing a **product-costing system,** which accumulates the costs of a production process and assigns them to the products or services that constitute the organization's output. One question of direct interest for the Jacobson-Wileys to consider for Glass Creations' cost-system design is the following: Are specific costs of each product and product line necessary, or are average costs across products adequate?

product-costing system *accumulates the costs of a production process and assigns them to the products that constitute the organization's output*

As cost-management analysts develop answers to this question a certain type of costing system usually appears to be most appropriate. The most common types of product-costing systems include *job-order costing* and *process costing,* as well as their hybrid, *operation costing.* In addition, other important variations of costing systems can be implemented in conjunction with job-order, process, or operation costing. We address these other cost-system design variations later in this chapter.

Evaluating Major Types of Product-Costing Systems

Job-order costing treats each individual job as the unit of output and assigns costs to it as it uses resources. A job can be a single, unique product, such as Glass Creations' piece "Calm Over Calamity," a custom home, a super tanker, a feature film, or an architectural design. Alternatively, a job can be a relatively small batch of identical or very similar products, such as Glass Creations' dolphin window that is produced in batches of about 20 to 25 units, or batches of printed wedding invitations, high-quality furniture, or heavy construction equipment. Job-order costing creates and maintains separate records or accounts for each job. Job-order costing is appropriate for the following types of production processes.

job-order costing *treats each individual job as the unit of output and assigns costs to each job as resources are used*

- Each unit or batch of products is distinct and clearly distinguishable from other products.

- Each unit is of relatively high value, which makes the benefits of separately assigning production costs worth the cost of doing so.
- Each unit or batch of products is often priced differently, frequently in accordance with a bidding process.
- Each unit or batch of products can feasibly have its direct costs traced.

Glass Creations and other producers of unique jobs can see important benefits of tracing resource costs to each job that justify the expenses of doing so. Job-order costing is useful for the following purposes:

- *Identifying types of jobs* that are likely to be most profitable so that the organization can specify the scope and scale of its operations.
- *Providing data to predict costs of future jobs* so that the organization chooses appropriate jobs on the basis of the resources needed and their expected profitability.
- *Managing the costs of current jobs* to ensure that they stay within expectations and to provide early warning if costs will exceed expectations.
- *Renegotiating job contracts* before introducing any significant changes in jobs that will affect resources, costs, or profits.
- *Reporting actual financial results* of the period's operations to demonstrate the organization's efficiency to external parties such as creditors and stockholders.

Research Insight 3.1

Management of Rising Health Care Costs

Increasing health care costs are a universal concern, but solutions to problems of maintaining quality of care and controlling costs vary. Some countries have implemented large bureaucracies or have turned to managed care to control health care costs. An interesting experiment in New Zealand, which is successfully privatizing many aspects of previously public activities, shows that quality of care and costs can be controlled simply by making physicians both aware of the costs of various care-related activities and accountable for the costs of the resources they use to complete each "job"— the care of a patient. The Independent Practice Association (IPA) of physicians in the Christchurch area has formed a cost-management team to estimate costs of resources used to perform various activities (e.g., medical tests and procedures) and communicate these costs to IPA members. Additionally, the IPA periodically reports costs of resources used per job by its members. The combination of increased awareness and reporting reportedly has reduced health care costs without reducing the quality of care. An important reason for the success of this experiment might be that IPA physicians believe that they are responsible for controlling costs and are willing to do so without the threat of regulatory intervention. *Source: K. Jacobs, "Costing Health Care: A Study of the Introduction of Cost and Budget Reports into a GP Association." (Full citations to references are in the Bibliography.)*

Managers use their knowledge of the cost of past jobs to estimate the costs of prospective jobs. Accurate cost estimates on future jobs help them prepare competitive bids. The Jacobson-Wileys know that if Glass Creations bids too high on a commissioned job, it will not be awarded the job and if the bid is too low, the company could lose money on the job. Artists working on commissioned pieces, construction contractors, and other businesspeople who bid on jobs must have reliable estimates of the costs of prospective jobs to prepare bids that are low enough to win but high enough to make a profit.[1]

Managers compare actual job costs to the estimated (*budgeted*) job costs to help manage them. A contractor once noted that if she did not have job-cost information, she could have experienced huge cost overruns without anticipating it. For example, on one job she estimated the cost of lumber at a certain level. Then a hurricane hit the southeastern United States, causing lumber prices to double. She did not realize that the lumber shipped to the

[1]Economists sometimes refer to the "winner's curse," which means that if you bid low enough to get the job, you could well have bid too low to make a profit.

Commercial aircraft manufacturers usually build planes to order and account for them as jobs for specific customers. Pictured here is the assembly of Boeing's 737-900 jetliner at Boeing's Renton, Washington plant.

job was at the higher posthurricane prices until she got the job cost information. Based on this information, she redesigned the job to use less lumber where it was not essential.

Managers can use job-cost information to renegotiate contracts with customers. Glass Creations has found that jobs often turn out differently than the customer originally specified. Sometimes these changes are inexpensive, and the company does the extra work as part of good customer service. Other times the changes are expensive, and the customer and the firm need to negotiate who will bear their cost. Reliable cost information helps management know (1) whether the changes are expensive or inexpensive and (2) what the changes cost so that the commissioned price or bid can be renegotiated.

To summarize, job-order costing is important for both pricing and cost management. Businesses must be able to estimate costs accurately if they are to be competitive and profitable.

Widespread use of job-order costing. Many companies that produce customized products and services use job-order costing. Examples include Morrison-Knudsen, the worldwide construction company; The Boeing Company, the large commercial airplane manufacturer and defense contractor; Mayo Clinic, the world-renowned hospital where the jobs are "cases"; Universal Studios, the producer of jobs such as the movie *Jurassic Park III;* Accenture and Deloitte-Touche, worldwide business-services firms, whose jobs often are called "clients"; and McGraw-Hill, the publisher of this and other leading textbooks.

Process costing. In contrast, **process costing,** discussed in depth in Chapter 8, treats all units processed during a time period as the output to be costed and does not separate and record costs for each unit produced. The next time you have a bottle of Coke or Pepsi, consider whether the bottler tracked the cost of the specific bottle you are drinking. Not likely! It would be prohibitively costly to do so and without benefit since the bottler would not expect any cost variation among bottles of the same soft drink. Process costing is appropriate for the following types of production processes:

process costing *treats all units processed during a time period as the output to which costs are assigned and does not separate and record costs for each unit produced*

- Units of output that are relatively homogeneous and indistinguishable from one another.
- Individual product units that are typically of relatively low value.
- Individual product units for which it is not feasible to trace direct costs.

Exhibit 3–1

Examples of Job-Order, Operation, and Process Costing

Job-Order Costing	Operation Costing	Process Costing
NASA space shuttle mission	Toyota's automobiles	British Petroleum's gasoline
Universal Studios' *AI: Artificial Intelligence* or *Jurassic Park,* by Steven Spielberg	H & R Block's tax returns	Quaker Oats' oatmeal
A custom home built by American Homes	Woolrich's sweaters	Levi's jeans
Steinway's pianos	Wilson's basketballs	Intel's computer chips
Microsoft's tax return	Dell's computers	Georgia Pacific's lumber
A heart transplant at the Mayo Clinic	Eddie Bauer's shirts	Olympia Stains' paints
Installation of multiple, high-end photocopiers and related business-systems equipment by Xerox in a new office building	Xerox's mid-range photocopiers for light use by small business and individuals	Xerox's photocopier paper

Companies that use continuous processes (such as bottling beverages, manufacturing chemicals, grinding flour, refining oil, and processing credit-card transactions) to produce many identical units of product or service use process costing.

operation costing *is a hybrid of job-order and process costing and is used by companies that produce batches of similar products with significantly different types of material*

Operation costing. Another product costing method is **operation costing.** Also covered in Chapter 8, this method is a hybrid of job-order and process costing used when companies produce large batches of similar products in which significantly different types of materials are used. Examples include shirts made from different fabrics such as cotton and wool and basketballs covered with real or simulated leather. As output becomes more unique and separately identifiable, job costing becomes more appropriate. Conversely, as separate units of output become indistinguishable, process costing is more appropriate. An organization where output falls somewhere between the two extremes might use operation costing.

Some organizations use job-order costing for their unique projects and process costing for their continuous processes. A large homebuilder, such as American Homes, might use process costing for its many standardized homes and job-order costing for its more expensive, semicustom homes. Honeywell, Inc., a high-tech company, uses process costing for most of its furnace thermostats but job-order costing for specialized defense and space contracting work. See Exhibit 3–1 for examples of products and services best suited to job-order costing, operation costing, and process costing.

Basic Cost-Flow Model

LO 2 Explain how costs flow through the manufacturing accounts.

As your previous accounting courses probably discussed, all cost-accounting systems rely on a basic cost-flow model, which is a periodic accounting framework for recording the costs of jobs (or processes). The basic cost-flow model is an inventory model or equation since it measures resources acquired to produce products or services that have not yet been sold. This model applies to all of an organization's physical resources. The basic cost-flow equation follows:

$$\underset{\text{BB}}{\overset{\text{Job cost}}{\textit{beginning balance}}} + \underset{\text{TI}}{\overset{\text{Resource}}{\textit{transfers in}}} - \underset{\text{TO}}{\overset{\text{Resource}}{\textit{transfers out}}} = \underset{\text{EB}}{\overset{\text{Job cost}}{\textit{ending balance}}}$$

Cost Flows and Jobs

The cost-flow model assigns costs of resources used to complete jobs according to the cost-flow equation, as explained here:

- At any time, every active job has a beginning balance (BB) measuring the cost of resources used on the job to date. The beginning balance might be zero if the job so far is only an idea. (Although one could argue that human resources have been used to generate the idea, the beginning balance still is zero.)
- Resources used or transferred in (TI) during a particular time period also are assigned to measure resource usage. The time period for recording costs can be of any length to suit decision-making needs.
- Transfers out (TO) record the accumulated costs of products or services transferred to another process in the organization, completed and stored, or sent to the customer. Transfers out ordinarily are the costs of good products suitable for further processing or sale but also can include the costs of defective products that must be reworked or scrapped. (We defer discussion of costs of defective or scrapped products until Chapter 8).
- The ending balance (EB) for the job is a residual that can be found by the simple algebra of the cost-flow equation:

$$\text{EB} = \text{BB} + \text{TI} - \text{TO}$$

You use this same model when you periodically update your checking account. Alternatively, if you use a debit or ATM card, the bank's system perpetually updates your account balance. Similarly, inventory systems either periodically or perpetually update inventory balances, depending on the need and technology used.

The ending balance, EB, also can be determined by (1) physically observing the number of units of product or service completed and (2) costing them using an appropriate cost-driver rate. If all of the model's components do not balance the cost-flow equation, evidence indicates an unintentional error, wasted resources, or, perhaps, theft or fraud. One of the best features of the basic cost-flow model is its use as a powerful tool for controlling the use of all physical resources. By making the misuse of physical resources difficult, the cost-flow model becomes a *control mechanism,* which is a policy or procedure that helps the organization ensure that its goals and objectives are met. (This topic is discussed in Chapters 18 and 21, which cover responsibility accounting and performance evaluation, respectively.)

Simple cost flow examples. Examine the examples in Exhibit 3–2, and observe how to use the cost-flow equation to solve for the missing inventory element in each column:

Cost-Flow Equation (BB + TI − TO = EB)

B1: $BB + \$8{,}000 - \$11{,}000 = \$16{,}000$
$BB = \$16{,}000 - \$8{,}000 + \$11{,}000$
$BB = \$19{,}000$

C2: $\$4{,}000 + TI - \$61{,}000 = \$3{,}000$
$TI = \$3{,}000 - \$4{,}000 + \$61{,}000$
$TI = \$60{,}000$

D3: $\$5{,}000 + \$8{,}000 - TO = \$7{,}000$
$-TO = \$7{,}000 - \$5{,}000 - \$8{,}000$
$-TO = -\ \$6{,}000$
$TO = \$6{,}000$

E4: $\$3{,}000 + \$55{,}000 - \$48{,}000 = EB$
$EB = \$10{,}000$

Microsoft Excel - Exhibit 3-2

File Edit View Insert Format Tools Data Window Help

E4 = EB = ?

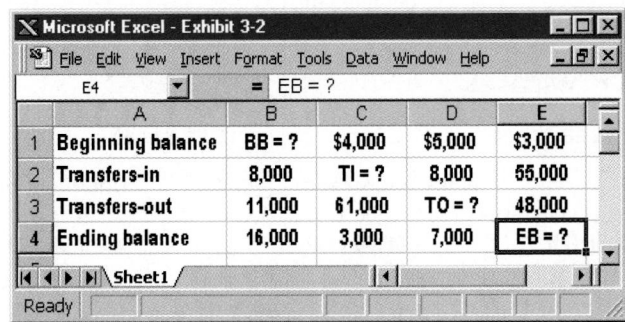

	A	B	C	D	E
1	Beginning balance	BB = ?	$4,000	$5,000	$3,000
2	Transfers-in	8,000	TI = ?	8,000	55,000
3	Transfers-out	11,000	61,000	TO = ?	48,000
4	Ending balance	16,000	3,000	7,000	EB = ?

Sheet1

Ready

Exhibit 3–2

Cost-Flow Examples

We are ready to add a slight complication to the basic cost-flow model by recognizing that most organizations use several types of inventory accounts to manage job costs. Most commonly, these additional accounts include Work-in-Process and Finished-Goods Inventories, which record costs as jobs are in process and when they have been completed, requiring cost flows to be managed and recorded in several related accounts. (Recall the discussion of the inventory accounts in Chapter 2.)

Managing and Using Cost-Flow Information

LO 3 Assign costs to production jobs or products using a job-order costing system.

job-cost record *(or **file, card** or **sheet**) reports the costs of all production-related resources used on the job to date*

Companies such as Glass Creations that use job-order costing employ several accounts (or files) to track the costs of resources used on jobs. These accounts are the sources of data for product costing, estimating costs of future jobs, and financial reporting for both internal and external purposes. The Work-in-Process (WIP) Inventory account collects all costs of resources used on various jobs not yet completed. Each job also has its own job-cost record or subsidiary account. The **job-cost record** (*or* **file, card** or **sheet**) records the costs of all production-related resources used on the job to date.

The total cost in the Work-in-Process account is the sum of the costs in all active (but not completed) jobs, as recorded on their respective job-cost records. Similarly, the Finished-Goods Inventory account collects total costs of all completed jobs not yet sold to customers. The Cost of Goods Sold account records the costs of finished goods (or jobs) that have been sold during a specific period. The basic cost-flow model ties these accounts together as Exhibit 3–3 shows.

Transfers in (TI) to Work-in-Process Inventory include direct-material, direct-labor, and manufacturing-overhead costs. As jobs or products are completed, they and their accumulated costs are transferred out (TO) of the Work-in-Process Inventory account. This cost of completed goods becomes the transfers in (TI) to the next sequential process (if there are sequential production processes) and ultimately, as Exhibit 3–3 shows, to Finished-Goods Inventory. The transfers out of Finished-Goods Inventory become the transfers in to Cost of Goods Sold, which is an expense of the period.

Exhibit 3–3

Product and Cost Flows

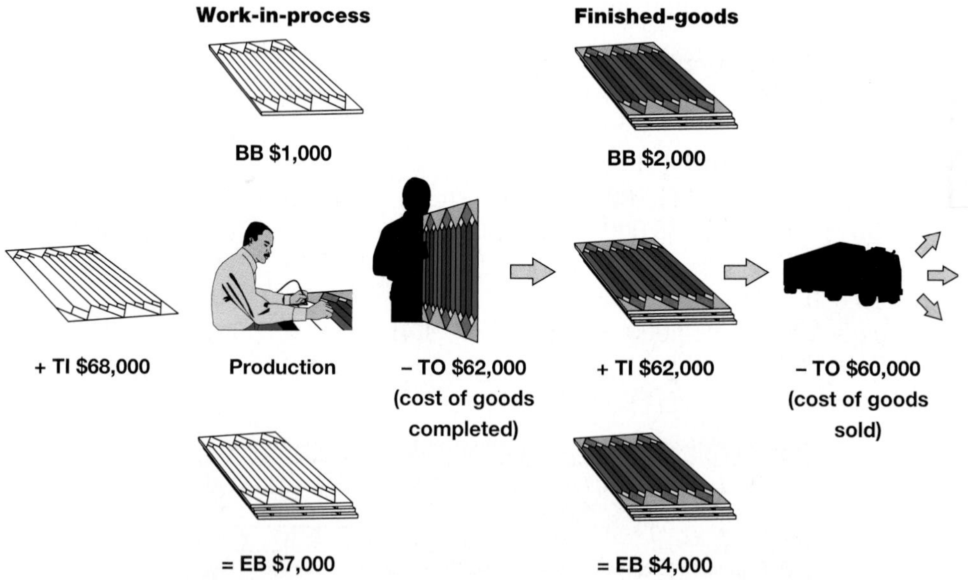

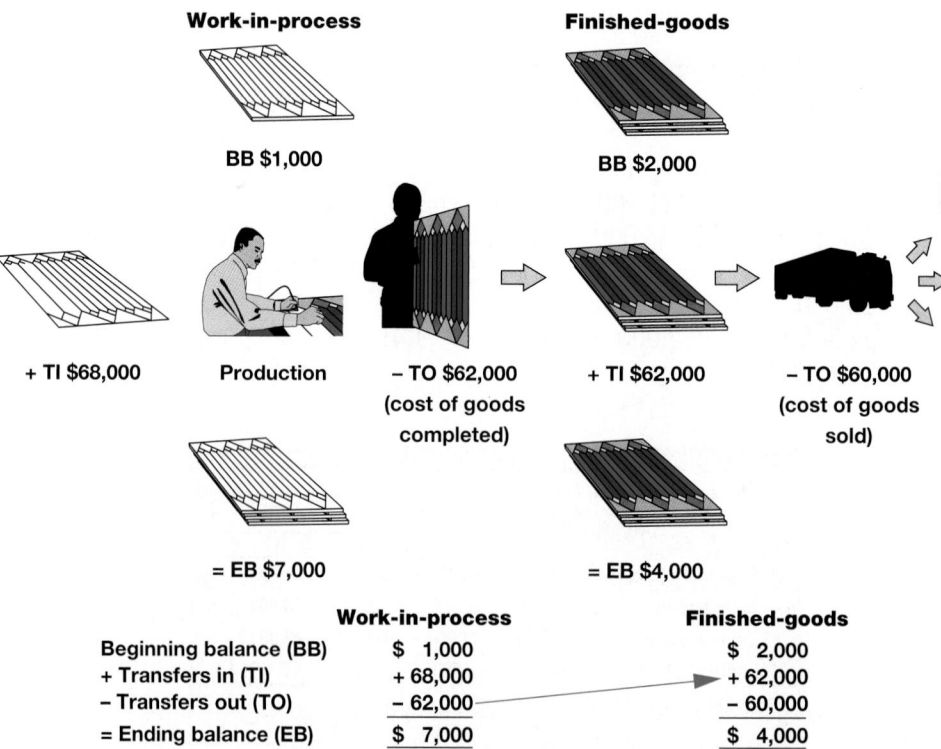

	Work-in-process	Finished-goods
Beginning balance (BB)	$ 1,000	$ 2,000
+ Transfers in (TI)	+ 68,000	+ 62,000
– Transfers out (TO)	– 62,000	– 60,000
= Ending balance (EB)	$ 7,000	$ 4,000

Cost Management in Practice 3.1

Cost Managent for the International Space Station

Costs of jobs and projects could be understated if all levels of resources are not analyzed and assigned in a credible manner as good job-cost systems do. A new, orbiting space station is a high-profile project still proceeding despite revelations that much of the spending has been for higher-level resources that have not resulted in tangible space hardware and may delay the job's completion. The new space station was conceived in 1984 as an international project (involving the United States, Japan, Russia, Canada, and several European countries) to foster space science and travel, but the first piece was not orbited until November 1998 (by a Russian rocket). In the intervening years, the United States alone has spent billions of dollars on support costs that, according to Congressional inquiries, did nothing to directly advance the project. Subsequently, it appears that drastically reducing spending levels on higher-level resources actually resulted in dramatic improvements in job progress. Accounting for all levels of resources consumed by the job could greatly increase its disclosed cost, but some analysts fear that now forcing the project to stay within its planned $27.5 billion budget could lead to cutting corners on safety and performance. Job-order costing information can play a useful role in this situation by enabling program managers to look carefully at the cost of individual components of the space station and then to answer questions as to where to cut costs with minimal deterioration of safety standards or performance.

Sources: Business Week, *"Earth to Congress: Scrap the Space Station," "The Super Collider Is Science. The Space Station Is Pork," and "2002, a Space Odyssey—or Just Pork in the Sky?"*

Building a space station is an exciting job for both astronauts and cost-management analysts.

The Process of Tracking Job-Order Costs

In job-shop or batch-production operations, managers estimate and manage costs by keeping separate cost records for each job. The primary cost document for a job is the "job-cost record" (also called a "job-cost file or sheet"). See Exhibit 3–4 for a printout of the job-cost record for Glass Creations' job P01-20. [This job-numbering scheme denotes that this is the first batch of pelican windows during the current year (P01) and the quantity is 20 units]. Note that this record shows detailed calculations for the direct materials, direct labor, and manufacturing overhead charged to the job and that Nakagawa, Glass Creations' cost analyst, compared the actual costs accumulated for the job with the estimated costs to evaluate employee performance in managing costs. Any significant differences are noted on the job-cost record. The comparison also provides feedback on the accuracy of the cost estimates, which is important for future pricing decisions.

Product-Costing System Design Issues

Three design aspects of Glass Creations' product-costing system are noteworthy at this juncture. First, as noted previously, the company uses *job-order costing.* It is an appropriate method for Glass Creations because the firm's products are relatively heterogeneous, and many of them are custom jobs. Second, Glass Creations uses *absorption costing,* which was explained in detail in Chapter 2. Thus, the manufacturing overhead shown on the job-cost record in Exhibit 3–4 includes both variable and fixed overhead as product costs. Third, Glass Creations uses a *normal costing system,* which assigns actual costs of direct material and direct labor to each production job but *applies* (or allocates) the manufacturing overhead using a *predetermined overhead rate* based on a cost driver. This third design aspect of Glass Creations' product-costing system (i.e., normal costing and the use of a predetermined overhead rate) is explored in more detail later in the chapter. For now, it is important to realize only that these three terms

Exhibit 3–4 Job Cost Record

GLASS CREATIONS

Job number:	P01-20	**Stock number or name of customer:**	PEL-100
Date started:	January 8	**Date finished:**	January 26
Description:	Pelican window—quantity 20	**Job supervisor:**	Brent Dean

Direct Materials			Direct Labor			Manufacturing Overhead		
Date	**Requisition Identifier**	**Cost**	**Date**	**Employee Identifier**	**Cost**	**Date**	**Direct-Labor Hours × Overhead Rate**	**Cost**
Jan 8	P01-20-A	$1,000	Jan 8	D01: 3 @ $21	$ 63	1/31	113 @ 30*	3,390
Jan 13	P01-20-B	400	Jan 12–18	G03: 60 @ $22	1,320			
Total		$1,400	Jan 12–18	G06: 40 @ $22	880			
			Jan 18	F02: 10 @ $15	150			
			Total	Total 113	$2,413			

*Predetermined overhead rate (explained later in chapter)

Total Job Cost

Direct materials	$1,400
Direct labor	2,413
Manufacturing overhead	3,390
Total	$7,203

Transferred to Finished-Goods Inventory

Direct materials	$1,400
Direct labor	2,413
Manufacturing overhead	3,390
Total	$7,203

Cost Comparison

Explain below any differences between estimated job cost and costs accumulated for job: None

(job-order, absorption, and normal costing) describe the type of product-costing system employed by Glass Creations.

Recording Job-Order Costs

Most companies with job-shop or batch-production environments follow the basic job-order costing steps presented in this section. We show the journal entries to record the costs incurred by Glass Creations in January, a typically slow month. Several employees take their vacations then, and during the current year, the studio worked on only three jobs.

In a job-order costing system, Work-in-Process Inventory is a *control account* because it is supported by cost records in the subsidiary ledger. Costs associated with each job are recorded on a job-cost record as shown in Exhibit 3–4. Thus, job-cost records serve as *subsidiary ledgers* to the Work-in-Process Inventory account. This enables management to identify the costs for a particular job by reviewing its job-cost record.

One of Glass Creations' jobs, C12-05, in process on January 1, had been started during December of the preceding year. [The different job number used for custom jobs (C) denotes that this custom job, was started on December 5 (12-05).] After some additional work, it was completed and installed for the customer in January. Glass

Exhibit 3–5

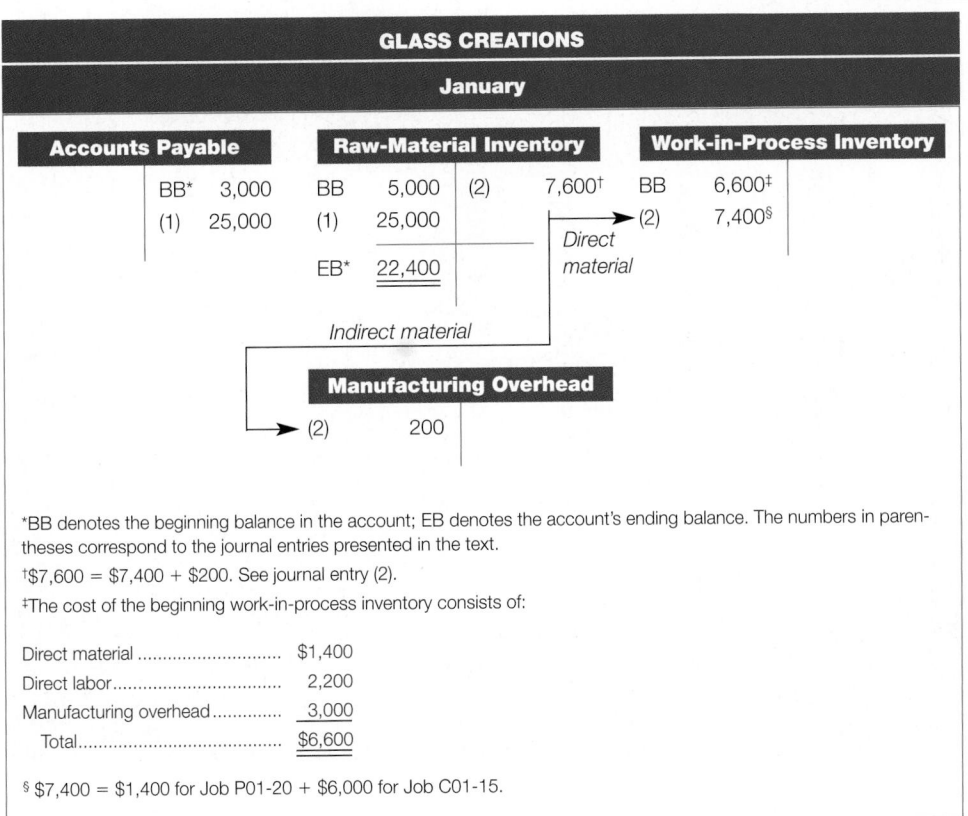

Cost Flows through the Manufacturing Accounts: Direct Material

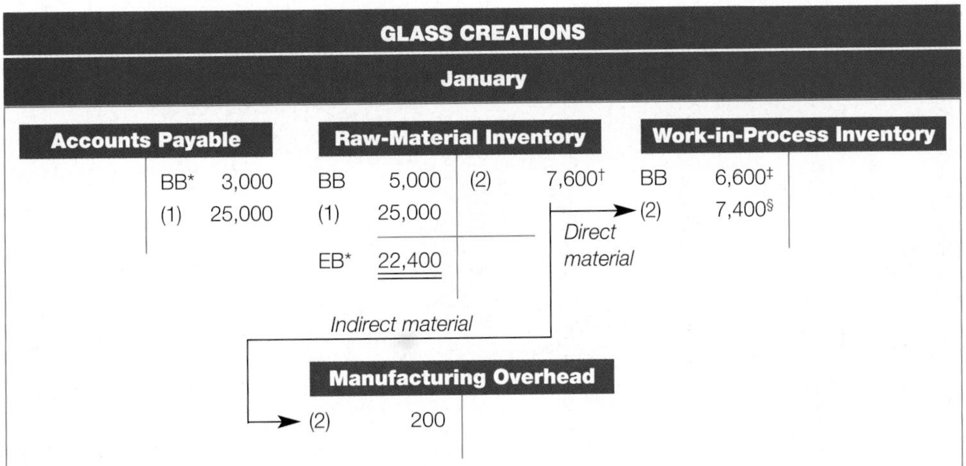

*BB denotes the beginning balance in the account; EB denotes the account's ending balance. The numbers in parentheses correspond to the journal entries presented in the text.

†$7,600 = $7,400 + $200. See journal entry (2).

‡The cost of the beginning work-in-process inventory consists of:

Direct material	$1,400
Direct labor	2,200
Manufacturing overhead	3,000
Total	$6,600

§ $7,400 = $1,400 for Job P01-20 + $6,000 for Job C01-15.

Creations' second job, P01-20, was started on January 8 and moved to finished-goods inventory on January 26. On January 31, it awaited shipment to various customers. Its costs are presented on the job cost record in Exhibit 3–4. The third job, C01-15 (a custom job started on January 15), was still in process on January 31. Therefore, the following is the status for each of these production jobs on January 31.

Job	Status on January 31
C12-05	Sold
P01-20	Finished but not sold
C01-15	In process

Beginning inventories. Exhibit 3–5 shows the beginning balances in the Raw-Material Inventory and Work-in-Process Inventory accounts. Raw-Material Inventory on January 1 was $5,000. Beginning Work-in-Process Inventory on January 1 consisted of only job C12-05, which had incurred the following costs during December of the previous year:

Direct material	$1,400
Direct labor	2,200
Manufacturing overhead applied	3,000
Total	$6,600

So the balance in the Work-in-Process Inventory account on January 1 was $6,600.

Notice the difference between the Raw-Material Inventory, $5,000, that has not yet been entered into production, and the direct-material component of beginning Work-in-Process Inventory, $1,400. The $1,400 amount has already been sent to production.[2]

[2]Recall from Chapter 2 the seemingly interchangeable use of the terms "raw material" and "direct material." As noted, the meaning of these terms is different. *Before* materials are entered into the production process, they are called *raw* materials. *After* they enter production, they become either *direct* materials or *indirect* materials. Thus, the cost of raw material *used* equals the direct-material cost plus the indirect-material cost.

Production of stained glass windows by skilled artists is a painstaking job that entails significant direct labor and support services such as purchasing and material handling for the delicate glass pieces.

These beginning balances are shown in Exhibit 3–5. There was no beginning Finished-Goods Inventory on January 1.

LO 4 Prepare accounting journal entries to record job costs.

Direct material. In January, Glass Creations purchased $25,000 of raw material. This purchase anticipated the Gulf Coast Aquarium job mentioned in the letter at the beginning of the chapter and was made somewhat early to take advantage of an exceptionally favorable price for glass. This purchase was recorded as follows:

(1)	Raw-Material Inventory	25,000	
	Accounts Payable		25,000

material requisition form *is the source document for the transfer of raw material from Raw-Material Inventory to Work-in-Process Inventory and to the job-cost record for the production job*

When raw material is needed for a production job, the job supervisor, one of the owners, or one of the other skilled glass workers requisitions it using a **material requisition form.** This is the source document for the entry transferring the cost of a raw material from Raw-Material Inventory to the Work-in-Process Inventory account and to the job-cost record for the production job. No materials were requisitioned for job C12-05 in January. Job P01-20 had requisitions for raw material totaling $1,400 (see Exhibit 3–4). The journal entry to record this transfer of the cost of raw material follows:

(2a)	Work-in-Process Inventory	1,400	
	Raw-Material Inventory		1,400

To record the requisition of raw material and its entry into production.

Raw material of $6,000 was requisitioned for Job C01-15 and recorded in entry (2b). The raw-material classification is also used for indirect materials and supplies. These costs are not assigned to specific jobs but are charged to the Manufacturing Overhead account. For Glass Creations, the $200 of indirect material requisitioned in January was also recorded in entry (2b), as follows:

(2b)	Work-in-Process Inventory	6,000	
	Manufacturing Overhead	200	
	Raw-Material Inventory		6,200

To record direct-material cost of $6,000 assigned to job C01-15 and indirect material costs of $200 charged to Manufacturing Overhead.

Journal entries (2a) and (2b) are combined into one journal entry (journal entry 2) in Exhibit 3–5. Notice that Exhibit 3–5 also includes the ending raw-material inventory, which can be found as follows:

Beginning inventory	+	Purchases	−	Requisitions	=	Ending inventory
$5,000	+	$25,000	−	$7,600	=	$22,400

Direct labor. Production employees are usually paid an hourly rate and account for their time each day on time records, which now are generally computerized. These records account for the hours spent on each production job during the day. The company's total cost includes the employee's gross pay plus the employer's share of social security and employment taxes, the employer's contribution to pension and insurance plans, and any other benefits that the company pays for the employee. In general, these costs range from 15 to 70 percent of the wage rate, depending on a company's benefit plan. Companies generally add their benefit costs to the wage rate when assigning costs to production jobs.

Glass Creations' cost-management analyst recorded accumulated costs of $22,413 for production employees during January. Of the $22,413 total, $16,413 was attributed to direct-labor costs, including employee benefits and taxes. The $16,413 is charged (debited) to Work-in-Process Inventory and assigned to the specific jobs worked on during the period. Based on the time records, the jobs were charged direct-labor costs as follows: job C12-05, $6,000 in January (for 285 direct-labor hours of differing wage rates); job P01-20, $2,413 (for 113 direct-labor hours) as indicated in the job-cost record in Exhibit 3–4; and job C01-15, $8,000 (for 380 direct-labor hours, also of differing wage rates). Since design costs are easily traceable to specific jobs, they are included in direct labor. Moreover, design costs for existing stock windows are minimal.

The remaining $6,000 (of the $22,413 discussed earlier) is indirect labor and is charged to Manufacturing Overhead. Recall from Chapter 2 that indirect labor is the cost of compensating employees such as supervisory, custodial, maintenance, security, and material-handling personnel, as well as idle time and overtime premiums paid to direct-labor employees. Glass Creations is a small firm, of course, and its employees perform a variety of activities. Sometimes an employee works directly on a specific job (classified as direct labor) and sometimes does work unrelated to any particular job, such as general cleanup of the glass studio (classified as indirect labor). This is typical for small companies.

The following entry records Glass Creations' labor costs in January:

(3)	Work-in-Process Inventory........................	16,413	
	Manufacturing Overhead...........................	6,000	
	Wages Payable		22,413

To record direct-labor costs of $16,413 assigned to production jobs and indirect labor costs of $6,000 charged to Manufacturing Overhead.

The flow of labor costs through the manufacturing accounts is shown in Exhibit 3–6.

Manufacturing overhead. Accounting for manufacturing overhead is less straightforward than for direct labor and direct material. Manufacturing overhead is a heterogeneous pool of indirect costs. These costs are assigned to individual production jobs based on an overhead rate calculated with respect to a cost driver, such as machine or direct-labor hours.[3] We address the process of establishing this overhead rate in the next section. At this point, however, note that Glass Creations' approach to assigning overhead is the simplest such system possible. We will explore *activity-based costing* (ABC), a more elaborate approach, in Chapter 4. As you will see then, the ABC approach provides more accurate cost information but is also more costly to implement and use.

[3]The concept of *cost driver* was introduced and defined in Chapter 2 and will be explored in more depth in Chapter 4.

Exhibit 3–6

Cost Flows through the Manufacturing Accounts: Direct Labor

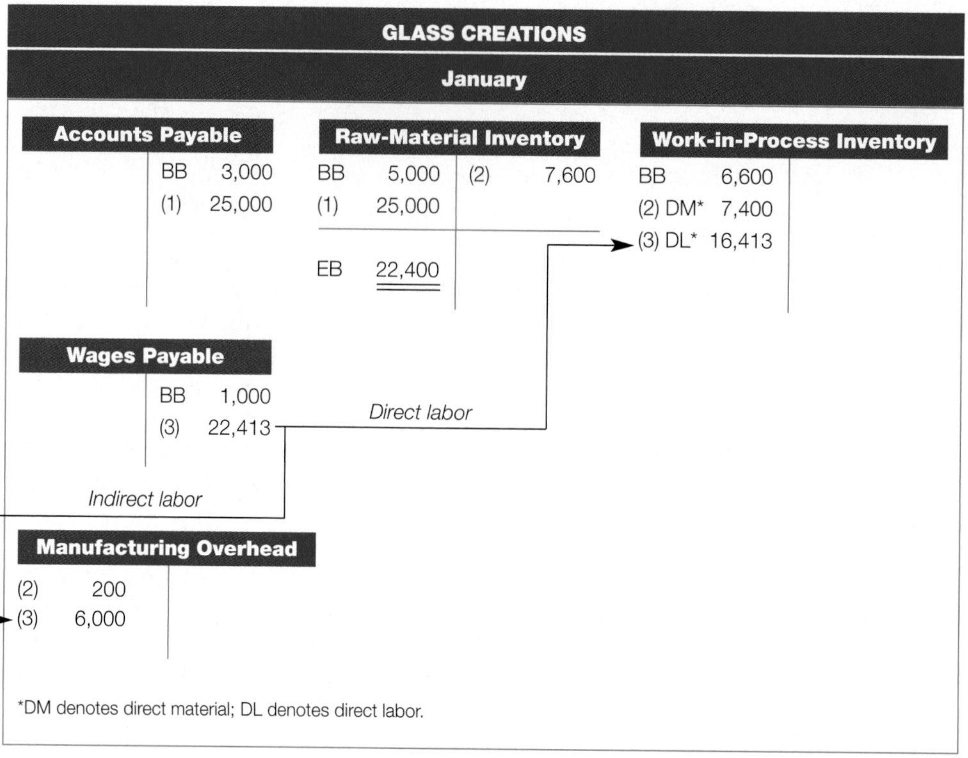

GLASS CREATIONS
January
Accounts Payable
BB 3,000
(1) 25,000
Raw-Material Inventory
BB 5,000
(1) 25,000
(2) 7,600
EB 22,400
Work-in-Process Inventory
BB 6,600
(2) DM* 7,400
(3) DL* 16,413
Wages Payable
BB 1,000
(3) 22,413
Direct labor
Indirect labor
Manufacturing Overhead
(2) 200
(3) 6,000

*DM denotes direct material; DL denotes direct labor.

At Glass Creations, indirect manufacturing costs, including costs such as indirect material, indirect labor, electricity, and insurance, are accumulated in the Manufacturing Overhead account. Glass Creations uses absorption costing, discussed in Chapter 2, so it treats *all* manufacturing overhead (variable and fixed) as a product cost. In large manufacturing companies, each department typically has its own Manufacturing Overhead account so each department manager can be held accountable for that department's overhead costs. This helps top management evaluate how well department managers are managing their overhead and support department costs. Then these departmental overhead accounts are combined into one account, simply called *Manufacturing Overhead.*

In January, Glass Creations charged indirect-material costs of $200 and indirect labor costs of $6,000 to the Manufacturing Overhead account as shown earlier in entries (2) and (3). Utilities and other overhead costs credited to Accounts Payable were $12,000. The $700 portion of prepaid insurance applicable to the period is also included in the actual overhead amount, as is depreciation of $6,000. These items total $18,700 and represent the actual overhead incurred during the period, in addition to indirect material and indirect labor.

The journal entry to record manufacturing overhead follows:

(4)	Manufacturing Overhead	18,700	
	Accounts Payable		12,000
	Prepaid Expenses		700
	Accumulated Depreciation		6,000

To record actual manufacturing overhead costs other than indirect labor and indirect materials.

predetermined overhead rate *is the budgeted manufacturing overhead divided by the budgeted level of the cost driver*

The entry is labeled (4) in the manufacturing account diagram in Exhibit 3–7.

Use of Predetermined Overhead Rates

LO 5 Use a predetermined overhead rate to assign indirect resource costs to production jobs.

Companies have traditionally used predetermined overhead rates to assign manufacturing overhead to individual production jobs. The **predetermined overhead rate** usually is established before the year in which it is to be used and remains the same for the entire year. By using a predetermined overhead rate, a company *normalizes* (i.e.,

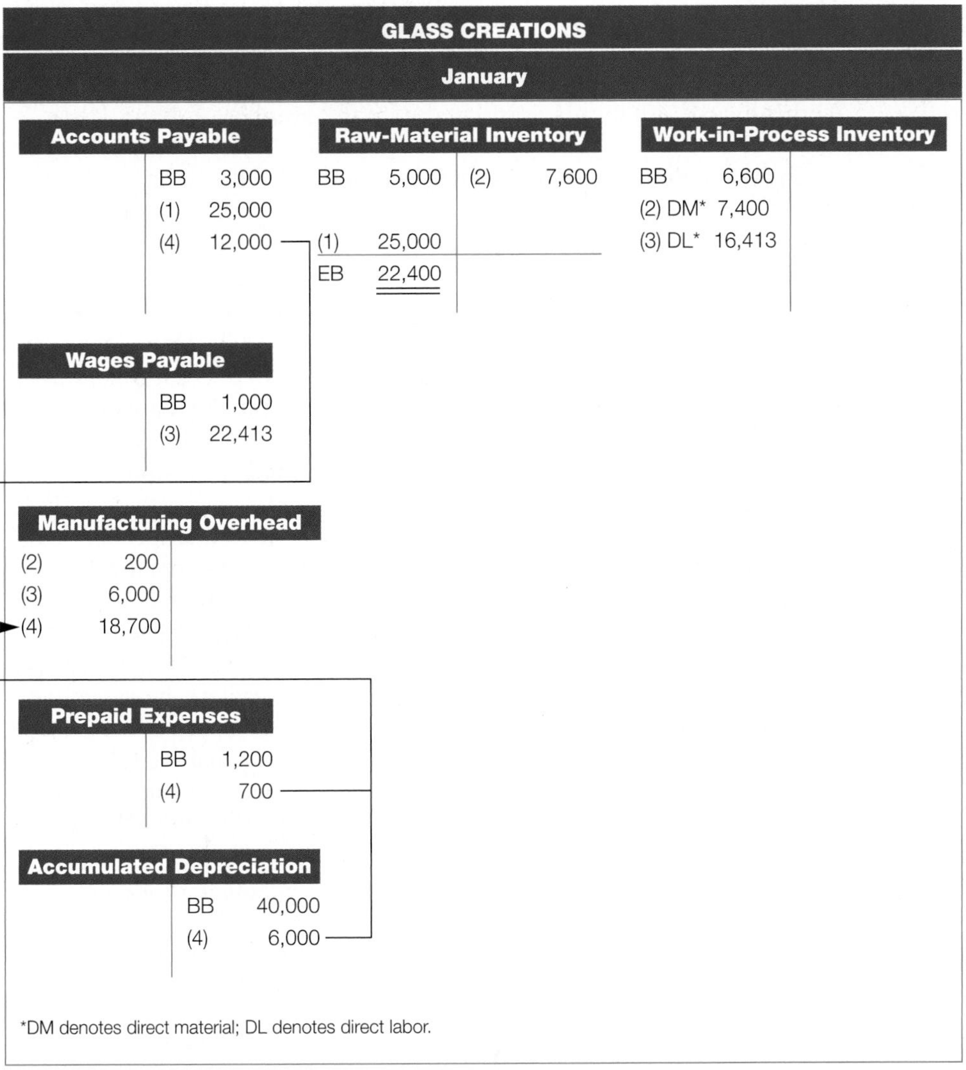
GLASS CREATIONS
January
Accounts Payable
BB 3,000
(1) 25,000
(4) 12,000
Raw-Material Inventory
BB 5,000
(1) 25,000
EB 22,400
(2) 7,600
Work-in-Process Inventory
BB 6,600
(2) DM* 7,400
(3) DL* 16,413
Wages Payable
BB 1,000
(3) 22,413
Manufacturing Overhead
(2) 200
(3) 6,000
(4) 18,700
Prepaid Expenses
BB 1,200
(4) 700
Accumulated Depreciation
BB 40,000
(4) 6,000
*DM denotes direct material; DL denotes direct labor.

Exhibit 3–7

Cost Flows through the Manufacturing Accounts: Manufacturing Overhead

smooths out) overhead applied to various production jobs. Over time, manufacturing overhead costs can be quite erratic. Preventive maintenance costs often are higher in months when activity is low. Utility costs in cold climates are higher in the winter than in the summer; the opposite is true in warm climates. If *actual* overhead costs were assigned to production jobs, more overhead would be assigned in some months than in other months. In addition, a company might not know its actual overhead costs until the end of an accounting period. Management can prepare financial statements and use product cost data for cost-management and decision-making purposes based on a reliable estimate of product costs by using predetermined overhead rates.

Because predetermined overhead rates *normalize* the application of manufacturing overhead to jobs, the resulting product costs are called "normal costs;" this product costing method is the **normal costing system.** Predetermined overhead rates can be established by following a five-step approach.

normal costing system *assigns to production jobs the actual cost of direct material, actual cost of direct labor, and applied manufacturing overhead, which is calculated by multiplying the predetermined overhead rate by the actual amount of the cost driver*

Step 1. *Identify the costs to be included as indirect costs.* Glass Creations has developed a detailed list of cost items included as manufacturing overhead. The total of these costs represents the company's total manufacturing overhead.

Step 2. *Establish the costs for each cost item identified in step 1.* Budgeted (i.e., estimated) annual manufacturing-overhead costs for Glass Creations total $360,000 based on last year's actual manufacturing overhead adjusted for anticipated changes this year. (We discuss the budgeting process in detail in Chapter 15.)

Step 3. *Select the cost driver(s).* Operating personnel at Glass Creations have determined that the number of direct-labor hours is the best cost driver to use for manufacturing overhead costs. That is, manufacturing overhead costs are highly correlated with the number of direct-labor hours used.

Glass Creations uses only a single, volume-related cost driver for its overhead application. Activity-based costing uses multiple cost drivers to assign indirect production costs to products (as well as other cost objects; see Chapter 4). This approach results in much more accurate cost assignments but is also considerably more costly to implement and use.

Step 4. *Estimate the amount of the cost-driver rate.* Glass Creations' practical production capacity, given its artistic talent and size, is estimated to be 12,000 direct-labor hours during the year. ("Practical capacity" refers to the level of activity that can reasonably be expected under normal operating conditions, allowing for scheduled machine maintenance.)

To be most useful for describing resource supply and usage, the quantity estimate of the cost driver should be based on the practical capacity of the firm's resources to perform activities. Manufacturing firms often have more objective data on machine-based process capacities, but their estimates of human-based process capacities can be quite subjective. "Subjective" does not mean random, capricious, or useless, however, but based on sound judgment and experience. These decisions are better than random guesses or making decisions based on no information. Glass Creations' estimates are based on experience, but they still could be the least objective data in this product-costing analysis. This subjectivity is common in many companies, particularly small ones.

Step 5. *Compute the predetermined overhead rate.* This calculation follows:

$$\text{Predetermined overhead rate} = \frac{\text{Budgeted manufacturing overhead for the year}}{\text{Budgeted direct-labor hours for the year}}$$

$$= \frac{\$360{,}000}{12{,}000 \text{ direct-labor hours}} = \$30 \text{ per direct-labor hour}$$

In January, Glass Creations used its predetermined overhead rate to apply manufacturing overhead to individual production jobs as follows:

	Actual Direct-Labor Hours (DLH) Used in January		Predetermined Overhead Rate		Manufacturing Overhead Applied
Job C12-05	285	×	$30 per DLH	=	$ 8,550
Job P01-20..................	113	×	$30 per DLH	=	3,390
Job C01-15	380	×	$30 per DLH	=	11,400
Total	778		$30 per DLH	=	$23,340

Glass Creations' entry to record the application of manufacturing overhead to jobs using the predetermined overhead rate follows. The flow of these applied overhead costs through the manufacturing accounts is illustrated in Exhibit 3–8.

(5)	Work-in-Process Inventory........................	23,340	
	Manufacturing Overhead.......................		23,340
	To record the application of manufacturing overhead to production jobs.		

Limitation of direct labor as a cost driver. In traditional product-costing systems, like the one used by Glass Creations, the most common volume-related cost drivers are direct-labor hours and direct-labor cost. However, there is a trend away from using di-

Exhibit 3–8

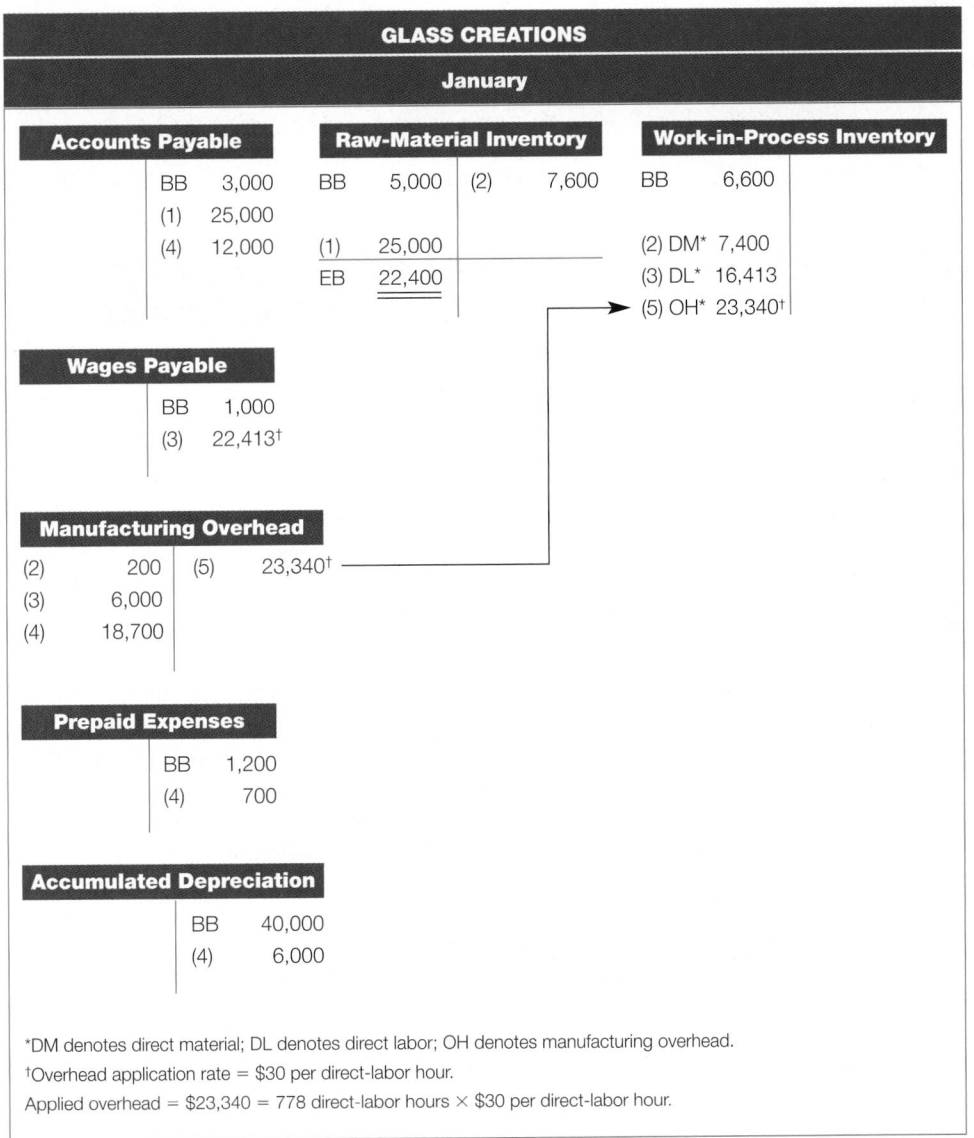

Cost Flows through the Manufacturing Accounts: Actual and Applied Manufacturing Overhead

GLASS CREATIONS

January

Accounts Payable

		BB	3,000
		(1)	25,000
		(4)	12,000

Raw-Material Inventory

BB	5,000	(2)	7,600
(1)	25,000		
EB	22,400		

Work-in-Process Inventory

BB	6,600		
(2) DM*	7,400		
(3) DL*	16,413		
(5) OH*	23,340†		

Wages Payable

		BB	1,000
		(3)	22,413†

Manufacturing Overhead

(2)	200	(5)	23,340†
(3)	6,000		
(4)	18,700		

Prepaid Expenses

		BB	1,200
		(4)	700

Accumulated Depreciation

		BB	40,000
		(4)	6,000

*DM denotes direct material; DL denotes direct labor; OH denotes manufacturing overhead.

†Overhead application rate = $30 per direct-labor hour.

Applied overhead = $23,340 = 778 direct-labor hours × $30 per direct-labor hour.

rect labor as the overhead application base. Many production processes are becoming increasingly automated through the use of robotics and computer-integrated manufacturing systems. Increased automation brings two results. First, manufacturing-overhead costs represent a larger proportion of total production costs. Second, direct labor decreases in importance as a productive input. As direct labor declines in importance as a productive input, it becomes less appropriate as a cost driver. For this reason, many firms have switched to machine hours, process time, or throughput time as cost drivers that better reflect the pattern of overhead cost incurrence. **Throughput** (or **cycle**) **time** is the average time required to convert raw materials into finished goods ready to be shipped to customers. It includes the time required for activities such as material handling, production processing, inspecting, and packaging.

throughput (or **cycle**) **time** *is the average time required to convert raw material into finished goods*

Many companies not only have moved away from direct labor as a cost driver but also have abandoned the idea of using *any* single, volume-related cost driver. Many of them use multiple, departmental predetermined overhead rates. For example, a manufacturer's assembly department might use direct-labor hours as a cost driver, its machining department might use machine hours, and its material-handling department might use pounds of raw material moved. Still other organizations have adopted activity-based costing (ABC), which identifies the key activities they engage in and uses multiple cost drivers associated with these activities. ABC is the topic of Chapter 4.

Exhibit 3–9 Manufacturing Overhead Account

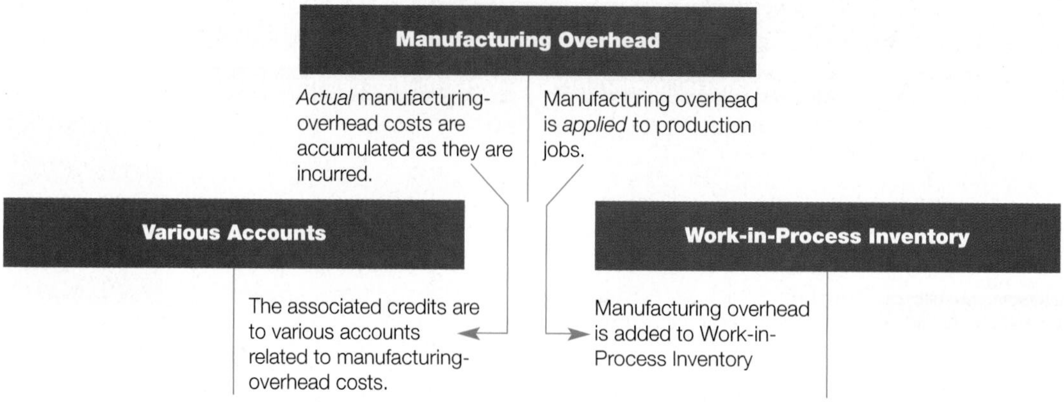

For Glass Creations' simple, labor-intensive production process, direct labor is probably an appropriate cost driver, particularly when viewed from a cost–benefit perspective. The benefits associated with the increased information accuracy from a more elaborate product-costing system would not likely exceed the additional costs to generate the information for a company such as Glass Creations.

Manufacturing overhead account: A summary. Exhibit 3–9 summarizes the accounting procedures used for manufacturing overhead. The left side of the Manufacturing Overhead account accumulates *actual overhead* costs as they are incurred throughout the accounting period. The actual costs incurred for indirect material, indirect labor, factory and equipment depreciation, utilities, property taxes, and insurance are recorded as additions to the left (debit) side of the account.

The right (credit) side of the Manufacturing Overhead account is used to record *overhead applied* to Work-in-Process Inventory.

The left side of the Manufacturing Overhead account accumulates *actual* overhead costs and the right side *applies* overhead costs using the predetermined overhead rate, which is based on *estimated* overhead costs. The estimates used to calculate the predetermined overhead rate generally prove to be incorrect to some degree. Consequently, a nonzero balance (usually relatively small) generally is left in the Manufacturing Overhead account at year-end; its disposition is covered later in the chapter.

Transfers to Finished-Goods Inventory. When jobs are transferred from production to finished goods, an entry is made to transfer the costs of the jobs from the Work-in-Process Inventory account to the Finished-Goods Inventory account. For example, Glass Creations completed jobs C12-05 and P01-20 in January and transferred them to finished-goods inventory. The journal entry is as follows:

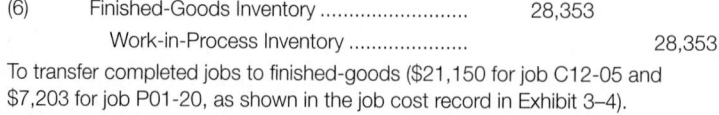

(6)	Finished-Goods Inventory	28,353	
	Work-in-Process Inventory		28,353

To transfer completed jobs to finished-goods ($21,150 for job C12-05 and $7,203 for job P01-20, as shown in the job cost record in Exhibit 3–4).

Notice that the amount transferred includes costs incurred in both the current and previous periods. For example, the transfer for job C12-05 includes $6,600 from beginning Work-in-Process Inventory and $14,550 of costs incurred in January to complete the job ($6,000 of direct labor and $8,550 of applied overhead, which was computed as 285 direct-labor hours to finish the job in January × $30 per direct-labor hour.

Transfers to Cost of Goods Sold. When finished goods are sold, their production cost is transferred from Finished-Goods Inventory to Cost of Goods Sold, which is an expense account. For example, Glass Creations sold job C12-05 in January for a total of $33,000, the commissioned price for this custom job. The profit on this job, $11,850, although enormous relative to the job cost of $21,150, is not far out of line for high-end, commissioned works of art. Nevertheless, this is one of Glass Creations' most profitable jobs ever. The journal entries recording this transaction are as follows:

(7)	Cost of Goods Sold	21,150	
	Finished-Goods Inventory		21,150
	Accounts Receivable	33,000	
	Sales Revenue		33,000

To transfer finished-goods inventory to cost of goods sold and to record the corresponding sales revenue. [Note: Job C12–05 was the only one sold in January.]

Overhead variance. The Manufacturing Overhead account is a temporary account, so it is "closed" at the end of an accounting period. *Closing* an account means that its balance is transferred to some other account, leaving a zero balance in the closed account at the end of the accounting period. You might recall from your study of financial accounting that this is the way that revenue and expense accounts are treated. That is, they are closed to the Income Summary account at the end of the accounting period, which leaves them with a zero balance. Usually this closing process is not performed until the end of the year when the books are closed. For illustrative purposes, however, let's assume that Glass Creations closes its Manufacturing Overhead account each month.

Under normal costing, the *actual* manufacturing overhead (recorded in the left side of the Manufacturing Overhead account) is unlikely to equal the amount of overhead *applied* (based on budgeted overhead and recorded on the right side of the account). The difference between the **applied-overhead** and the **actual overhead** amounts is the **overhead variance.** When actual overhead exceeds applied overhead, we say that overhead was *underapplied,* and the amount of the overhead variance equals **underapplied overhead.** In the opposite case, the variance equals **overapplied overhead.**

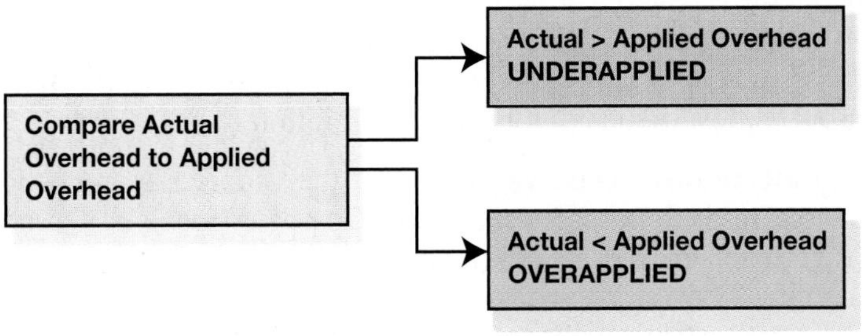

During January, Glass Creations credited $23,340 to Manufacturing Overhead (as *applied* manufacturing overhead, based on the budget), and debited $24,900 to Manufacturing Overhead (*actual* overhead).[4] The $1,560 difference is the *overhead variance,* in this case *underapplied overhead.* We explain the process used to dispose of (i.e., close) this overhead variance later in the chapter.

What does it mean to say that Glass Creations has *underapplied* overhead in January? Recall that it applies overhead at the predetermined rate of $30 per direct-labor hour based on *budgeted* manufacturing overhead and *budgeted* direct-labor hours

applied overhead, *calculated by multiplying the predetermined overhead rate by the actual amount of the cost driver, is the amount of manufacturing overhead assigned to Work-in-Process Inventory as a product cost*

actual overhead *is the amount of manufacturing overhead actually incurred during an accounting period*

overhead variance *is the difference between the actual and the applied manufacturing overhead amounts*

underapplied overhead *refers to actual overhead that exceeds applied overhead*

overapplied overhead *refers to actual overhead that is less than applied overhead*

---

[4]Applied overhead:

$23,340 = 778 direct-labor hours used in January × $30 per direct-labor hour

Actual overhead:

Indirect material	$ 200
Indirect labor	6,000
Insurance	700
Depreciation	6,000
Utilities and other overhead	12,000
Total	$24,900

Exhibit 3–10

Glass Creations: Cost of Jobs Before Prorating the Manufacturing Overhead Variance

Costs of Jobs Before Prorating the Manufacturing Overhead Variance

Job No.	Beginning Inventory, January 1	Direct Material	Direct Labor	Manufacturing Overhead Applied in January	Charged To Job	Status of Job at End of Month
C12-05	$6,600	$ -	$6,000	$8,550	$21,150	Cost of Goods Sold
P01-20		1,400	2,413	3,390	7,203	Finished-Goods Inventory
C01-15		6,000	8,000	11,400	25,400	Work-in-Process Inventory
Total	$6,600	$7,400	$16,413	$23,340	$53,753	

for the year. Since these are *estimates,* they typically are inaccurate, at least to some extent. To say that Glass Creations underapplied overhead in January means that the predetermined rate of $30 per direct-labor hour proved to be too low to apply enough overhead to Work-in-Process Inventory to equal January's actual manufacturing-overhead cost of $24,900. Thus, $24,900 in overhead costs were actually incurred in January, but only $23,340 was applied. Hence, the term "underapplied overhead." In most instances, these underapplied or overapplied amounts tend to be relatively small and, thus, usually do not reflect gross inaccuracies in the predetermined overhead rate.

proration *of the overhead variance assigns proportionate amounts of it to Work-in-Process Inventory, Finished-Goods Inventory, and Cost of Goods Sold*

How to report the manufacturing-overhead variance to management. At year-end, the manufacturing overhead variance is either (1) **prorated** (i.e., allocated) to Work-in-Process Inventory, Finished-Goods Inventory, and Costs of Goods Sold or (2) closed to Cost of Goods Sold. The Excel spreadsheet in Exhibit 3–10 recaps the costs of January's three production jobs before proration.

Method 1: Prorate the overhead variance. If the variance is prorated to Work-in-Process Inventory, Finished-Goods Inventory, and Cost of Goods Sold, the cost of each job is adjusted to approximate its actual cost. The status and cost of each of Glass Creations' jobs before prorating the overhead variance are shown in Exhibit 3–10. The variance is prorated so that each account and job bear a share of the $1,560 manufacturing-overhead variance. This share is proportional to the overhead applied to the account during the month as shown in the Excel spreadsheet in Exhibit 3–11. The following entry prorates the overhead variance and closes the Manufacturing Overhead account at the end of January.

Cost of Goods Sold	571.43	
Finished-Goods Inventory	226.51	
Work-in-Process Inventory	762.06	
Manufacturing Overhead		1,560.00

A small number of firms that are required to do so under the rules specified by the *Cost Accounting Standards Board (CASB)* prorate the overhead variance. This federal agency was chartered by Congress in 1970 to develop cost-accounting standards for large government contractors. Congress discontinued the agency in 1980 and recreated it in 1990. Its standards apply to significant government contracts and have the force of federal law.

Method 2: Close the Overhead Variance to Cost of Goods Sold. Most companies, including Glass Creations, do not prorate the manufacturing-overhead variance to Work-in-Process Inventory, Finished-Goods Inventory, and Cost of Goods Sold, but close the entire variance to Cost of Goods Sold as in the following journal entry:

Exhibit 3–11

Glass Creations: Prorating the Overhead Variance

Microsoft Excel - Exhibit 3-11.xls

H12 = =SUM(H9:H11)

Prorating the Overhead Variance

Job No.	Account	Manufacturing Overhead Applied in January[a]	Percentage of Total Overhead Applied in January[b]		Overhead Variance to be Prorated		Prorated Variance[c]
C12-05	Cost of Goods Sold	$8,550	36.63%	x	$1,560	=	$ 571.43
P01-20	Finished-Goods Inventory	3,390	14.52%	x	1,560	=	226.51
C01-15	Work-in-Process Inventory	11,400	48.85%	x	1,560	=	762.06
Total		$23,340	100.00%				$ 1,560.00

[a]From Exhibit 3-10.

[b]Column C amount / $23,340; rounded. For example, the formula for cell D9 is as follows: C9 / 23,340

[c]Rounded to nearest cent.

Cost of Goods Sold	1,560	
Manufacturing Overhead		1,560

In a company with many types of products and inventories, proration can be complicated. If the amounts to be prorated are immaterial relative to operating income or do not affect managerial decisions, proration might not be necessary. The difference in net income between prorating the variance and assigning it to Cost of Goods Sold is a matter of timing. Any difference between actual and applied overhead eventually is expensed, even if a company prorates. Prorating the overhead variance merely defers expensing the portion allocated to Work-in-Process and Finished-Goods Inventory until the products are sold. For managerial purposes, one must ask how useful it is to revalue work-in-process and finished-goods inventories to their actual cost. A large overhead variance could affect some cost-management, performance-evaluation, pricing, and other decisions, but if the variance is small, proration is probably not worthwhile.

However the variance is disposed of, the key managerial issue is to understand the causes of the difference between actual and applied overhead. Management might need to revise overhead rates, impose new cost-management procedures, or take other action.

Summary of Job-Cost Flows

The flow of all manufacturing costs from purchasing raw materials to selling the finished product appears in Exhibit 3–12. Notice that Glass Creations' schedule of cost of goods manufactured and sold (Exhibit 3–13) presents the data from the manufacturing accounts in Exhibit 3–12. It might be helpful to cross-reference each item in the schedule in Exhibit 3–13 to the accounts in Exhibit 3–12. Exhibit 3–13 also presents Glass Creations' income statement for January.

Selling and Administrative Costs

Selling and administrative costs do not flow through the inventory accounts because they are period costs, not product costs, and are expensed during the period incurred.

Exhibit 3–12 Summary of Job Costs

GLASS CREATIONS

January

Accounts Payable			
		BB	3,000
		(1)	25,000
		(4)	12,000

Raw-Material Inventory			
BB	5,000	(2)	7,600
(1)	25,000		
EB	22,400		

Work-in-Process Inventory			
BB	6,600	(6)	28,353
(2) DM	7,400		
(3) DL	16,413		
(5) OH	23,340		
EB	25,400		

Finished-Goods Inventory			
BB	0	(7)	21,150
(6)	28,353		
EB	7,203		

Wages Payable			
		BB	1,000
		(3)	22,413

Manufacturing Overhead			
(2)	200		
(3)	6,000		
(4)	18,700	(5)	23,340

Cost of Goods Sold			
(7)	21,150		

Prepaid Expenses			
		BB	1,200
		(4)	700

Accumulated Depreciation			
		BB	40,000
		(4)	6,000

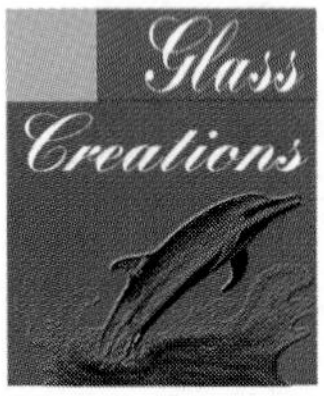

Glass Creations' selling and administrative expenses (all on account) amounted to $8,000 in January. The entry to record these expenses follows:

Selling and Administrative Expenses	8,000	
Accounts Payable		8,000
To record selling and administrative expenses incurred in January.		

Notice that these expenses appear on the income statement in Exhibit 3–13.

Meaning of the Overhead Variance

The $1,560 manufacturing-overhead variance discussed in the preceding section appears in the schedule of cost of goods manufactured and sold in Exhibit 3–13 as underapplied manufacturing overhead. As explained in the preceding section, a common method for disposing of the overhead variance is to close it to Cost of Goods Sold. Glass Creations uses this method, and the result of closing January's underapplied overhead amount of $1,560 is to adjust Cost of Goods Sold upward by $1,560, as shown in Exhibit 3–13.

Why does actual overhead typically differ from applied overhead? Remember that applied overhead is based on a predetermined overhead rate based on budgeted

Exhibit 3–13

Income Statement and Schedule of Cost of Goods Manufactured and Sold

GLASS CREATIONS
Income Statement
For the Month of January

Sales revenue	$33,000
Less: Cost of goods sold (see following schedule)	22,710
Gross margin	$10,290
Less: Selling and administrative expenses	8,000
Operating income	$ 2,290

GLASS CREATIONS
Schedule of Cost of Goods Manufactured and Sold
For the Month of January

Beginning work-in-process inventory, January 1			$ 6,600
Manufacturing costs during the month			
Direct material:			
Beginning raw-material inventory, January 1	$ 5,000		
Add: Purchases	25,000		
Raw material available for use	$30,000		
Less: Ending raw-material inventory, January 31	22,400		
Total raw material used	$ 7,600		
Less: Indirect material used	200		
Direct material entered into production		$ 7,400	
Direct labor		16,413	
Manufacturing overhead applied		23,340	
Total manufacturing costs incurred			47,153
Total cost of work in process			$53,753
Less: Work-in-process inventory, January 31			25,400
Cost of goods manufactured			$28,353
Add: Beginning finished-goods inventory January 1			0
Less: Ending finished-goods inventory, January 31			7,203
Cost of goods sold (unadjusted)			$21,150
Add: Underapplied overhead*			1,560
Cost of goods sold (adjusted for underapplied overhead)			$22,710

*Glass Creations closes underapplied or overapplied overhead to Cost of Goods Sold.

amounts for both manufacturing overhead and the cost driver (in this case, direct-labor hours) using the five-step approach outlined earlier to establish the predetermined rate. Glass Creations *budgeted* $360,000 of total manufacturing overhead costs and 12,000 direct-labor hours. Thus, for every direct-labor hour used, $30 in manufacturing overhead is *applied* to Work-in-Process Inventory. Since this application of overhead is based on budgeted amounts, applied overhead typically does not equal actual overhead during any accounting period (unless, of course, the budgeted amounts happen to be the same as the actual amounts).

Difference between Actual, Normal, and Standard Costing

LO 6 Explain how to measure production costs under actual, normal, and standard costing systems.

Suppose that Glass Creations had used actual overhead costs rather than a predetermined overhead rate to compute job costs. Then management would have waited until the actual overhead costs were known and then assigned them to jobs based on the actual number of direct-labor hours worked. At the end of January, management would know that the actual overhead cost amounted to $24,900 and would assign this cost to jobs based on the actual direct-labor hours (DLH) worked on each job, as follows:

$$\frac{\text{Actual manufacturing overhead costs}}{\text{Actual direct-labor hours used}} = \frac{\$24{,}900}{778 \text{ DLH}} = \$32.01 \text{ per DLH*}$$

*Rounded

actual costing *assigns only actual costs of both direct and indirect resources (i.e., direct material, direct labor, and manufacturing overhead) to products*

standard costing *uses a predetermined (or standard) rate for both direct and indirect costs (i.e., direct material, direct labor, and manufacturing overhead) to assign manufacturing costs to products*

The actual manufacturing overhead applied to each job in January is computed as follows:

	Direct-Labor Hours Used		Actual Overhead Rate		Manufacturing Overhead Applied
Job C12-05	285	×	$32.01	=	$ 9,122.85
Job P01-20	113	×	32.01	=	3,617.13
Job C01-15	380	×	32.01	=	12,163.80
Total	778	×	32.01	=	$ 24,903.78*

*Differs from the actual overhead amount of $24,900 because of rounding error in the $32.01 rate.

Actual costing assigns only the actual costs of both direct and indirect resources (i.e., direct material, direct labor, and manufacturing overhead) to the products. **Standard costing** uses a predetermined (or standard) rate for both direct and indirect costs to assign manufacturing costs to products. (Compare this to the normal-costing approach used by Glass Creations, which uses a predetermined rate for indirect costs only.) The following display compares actual, normal, and standard costing.

	Actual Costing	Normal Costing	Standard Costing
Direct costs	Actual rate × Actual inputs	Actual rate × Actual inputs	Predetermined rate × Standard allowed inputs
Indirect costs	Actual rate × Actual inputs	Predetermined rate × Actual inputs	Predetermined rate × Standard allowed inputs

To summarize, organizations can choose among these three methods for assigning costs to production jobs. They may use *actual costing,* which assigns direct-resource costs to jobs as they are used and assigns the costs of indirect resources when the actual amounts spent on these resources are known, usually at the end of each accounting period. The advantage to actual costing is that the measurement of job costs is accurate. The disadvantage is that the cost information is not timely since it is available only at the end of the accounting period.

When organizations need continuous or interim cost reports or early warning information on the cost status of jobs, they use *standard or normal costing,* which assign indirect resource costs as they are used before the amounts actually spent are known. Thus, standard and normal costing require the use of *estimates* of cost-driver rates.

Normal costing bases cost-driver rates on past spending for indirect resources and could be appropriate when business conditions are relatively stable. However, even under stable conditions, spending for indirect resources can vary from one period to the next. For example, preventive maintenance activities often are higher in months when activity is low. By using average resource spending, a company normalizes the costs of work in different periods. Organizations that use normal costing expect differences between average (i.e., normalized) and actual resource spending to average out over time. Companies engaged in cost-plus contracts often use normal costing, including The Boeing Company and Rockwell International, which use it for their government defense-contract work.

An advantage of the standard costing system, in addition to relatively stable product costs, is that the standard cost provides a benchmark against which the actual production cost can be compared. The resulting variances between actual and standard costs provide valuable cost-management information to use in controlling costs. Many manufacturing companies use standard-costing systems as a cost-management tool. (Chapters 16 and 17 discuss standard costing and cost variance analysis in detail.)

You're the Decision Maker 3.1

Normal Costing and Predetermined Overhead Rates

Suppose that Glass Creations computed its predetermined overhead rate on a quarterly basis instead of annually. The following projections have been made for the year:

	Estimated Manufacturing Overhead	Estimated Direct-Labor Hours	Quarterly Predetermined Overhead Rate
First quarter	$ 50,000	2,000	?
Second quarter	122,500	3,500	?
Third quarter	100,000	4,000	?
Fourth quarter	87,500	2,500	?
Total	$360,000	12,000	

One of Glass Creations' most popular products, the blue heron window, requires the following *direct* inputs:

Direct material	$100 per unit
Direct labor (@$22 per hour)	5 hrs per unit
Direct labor (@$15 per hour)	1 hr per unit

a. Calculate the quarterly predetermined overhead rate for each quarter.

b. Determine the cost of one blue heron window if it is manufactured in February versus October.

c. Suppose that the company's pricing policy calls for a 20 percent markup over cost. Calculate the price to charge for one blue heron window in February versus October.

d. Calculate the predetermined overhead rate if it is calculated annually.

e. Based on your answer to part d, what is the cost per unit if it is manufactured in February? In October?

f. What is the price per heron window if the predetermined overhead rate is calculated annually?

g. What do you recommend to Glass Creations for its product costing system? Quarterly or annual predetermined overhead rates? Explain.

(Solutions begin on page 121.)

Choice of Cost Driver for Overhead Application

Our illustration used direct-labor hours as the cost driver to apply overhead to jobs at Glass Creations. Organizations use a variety of cost drivers to apply overhead to products, including the number of machine hours, the number of direct-labor hours, and the amount of direct-labor cost on each job. The choice of cost drivers for applying overhead is an important and complex topic and is discussed in more detail in Chapter 4.

Job-Order Costing in Service Organizations

LO 7 Discuss the role of job-order costing in service organizations.

Job operations frequently are used in service organizations, such as architectural firms, consulting firms, moving companies, and consulting firms. The job-order costing process is basically the same in both service and manufacturing organizations except that service firms generally use fewer direct materials than manufacturing firms do.

An architectural firm, for example, is very interested in the profitability of each job (referred to as a "client"). Bids to obtain or retain a client typically are based on

Deere and Company carefully tracks the costs of the resources used to manufacture its equipment.

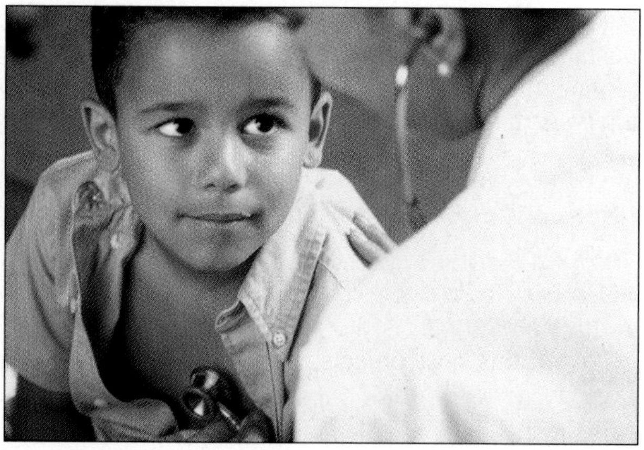

In the health care industry, patient cases are similar to "jobs" in that treatment costs are carefully tracked by patient and by diagnosis.

projected costs estimated using actual results for comparable jobs. Job-order costing, therefore, provides management the information necessary to assess job profitability and to use historical cost data to estimate costs for bidding purposes. (Many firms use an even more sophisticated approach, called *customer profitability analysis* to assess the profitability of each customer or client; see Chapter 6).

Application of Job-Order Costing to the Value Chain

Glass Creations' value chain, shown in Exhibit 3–14, includes its important business functions of design, purchasing and material handling, production, marketing, distribution, and customer service. (The value chain for most manufacturers begins with research and development, but this is not a relevant function for Glass Creations.) Notice that the *design* and *production* components are highlighted to reflect the fact that the design and creation (or production) of stained glass and other artistic glass pieces are the primary functions of Glass Creations. These two functions, above all others, distinguish it from its competitors. Nevertheless, the other functions in the value chain are not completely unimportant. Securing the stained glass and channeled lead strips used to create each piece are important, too. Finding the right sources of supply at the best possible prices is a key element in helping Glass Creations to be profitable. Marketing the studio's windows, doors, and other artistic pieces is important as well. The firm has done limited advertising but doing more is being considered as competition in the business increases. Distribution channels are similarly important for Glass Creations. The studio relies on arts festivals, builders' catalogues, and their own Web site as its primary distribution channels. Customer service is not a major element of Glass Creations' value chain because problems with the studio's glass pieces after they are sold or installed are rare. For most companies, however, this is a key element of the value chain. Think, for example, about your last automobile purchase. Have you been satisfied with the dealership's service department? If not, would that affect your next automobile purchase decision?

Now what, you might ask, does this discussion have to do with job-order costing? The point is that traditional product-costing systems, and job-order costing systems in particular, have tended to emphasize the production component of the value chain to the relative exclusion of the other components. Most of our discussion of Glass Creations' job-order costing system focused on the actual production costs for its stained glass pieces. Little was said about measuring or managing the costs of design, purchasing, marketing, and so forth, yet all of these functions are important contributors to the firm's profitability.

Exhibit 3–14

Glass Creations' Value Chain

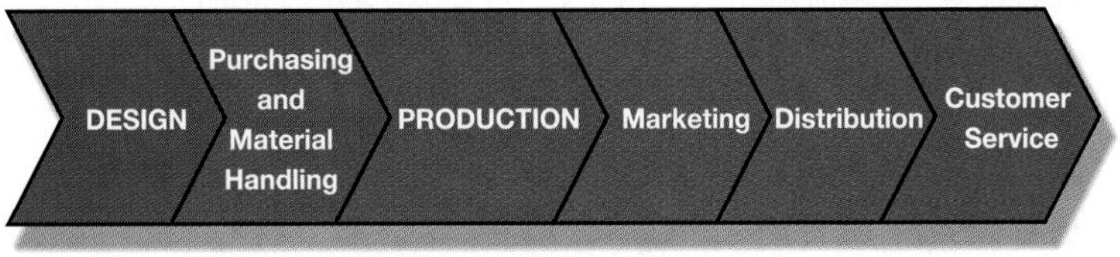

What is needed to overcome this deficiency is a broader focus on *all* of the *activities* in the organization's value chain. Then the costing system can be built on those activities by measuring the costs of the resources they use and associating those costs with various cost objects, including the organization's product or service output. Activity-based costing (covered in Chapter 4) is better suited to this value-chain perspective than are traditional approaches to product costing like Glass Creations' system.

Job and Project Management

LO 8 Understand how companies manage long-term projects and their costs.

Managing jobs and projects requires attention to quality, customer satisfaction, costs, and adherence to schedules. When jobs fall behind schedule or costs become higher than expected, some individuals might be tempted to compromise quality or even to cheat. Neither behavior is usually successful for, in the long run, reputations for quality and honesty generate more opportunities than shortsighted opportunism does. This section discusses the methods for tracking and ensuring successful project management and the aspects of behavior sometimes associated with jobs.

Project Management

Supervision of subcontractors is a critical aspect of project management.

Complex jobs (for example, bridges, shopping centers, and complicated lawsuits) often take months or years to complete and require the work of many different departments, divisions, or subcontractors. These projects, unlike short jobs that can be evaluated relatively quickly (typically within a reporting period), are more difficult to evaluate. Consider the job of painting a small house. The painter might estimate the costs and bid on the job accordingly. A week later, when the job is complete, the painter can compare estimated costs to actual costs and evaluate the job's profitability. In contrast, consider a contractor building a hospital, which will take more than two years to complete. The contractor must find a way not only to bid on the project but also to evaluate it at critical intervals to update and anticipate the cost and timing changes.

Project cost and time budgets. The contractor of a long-term project must first establish a budget of costs to be incurred throughout the project at various stages of completion. The stage of completion usually appears in reports as a percentage of completion for the entire project or as the completion of certain critical steps in the project. Then, as the project progresses, the contractor evaluates two critical areas: (1) the budgeted cost of work completed to date versus the actual cost of work completed to date and (2) the budgeted percentage or stage of completion since the project began versus the actual percentage or stage of completion. The two graphs in Exhibit 3–15 are examples of useful information for evaluating the progress of project costs and schedules.

Exhibit 3–15

Project Percentage of Completion Charts

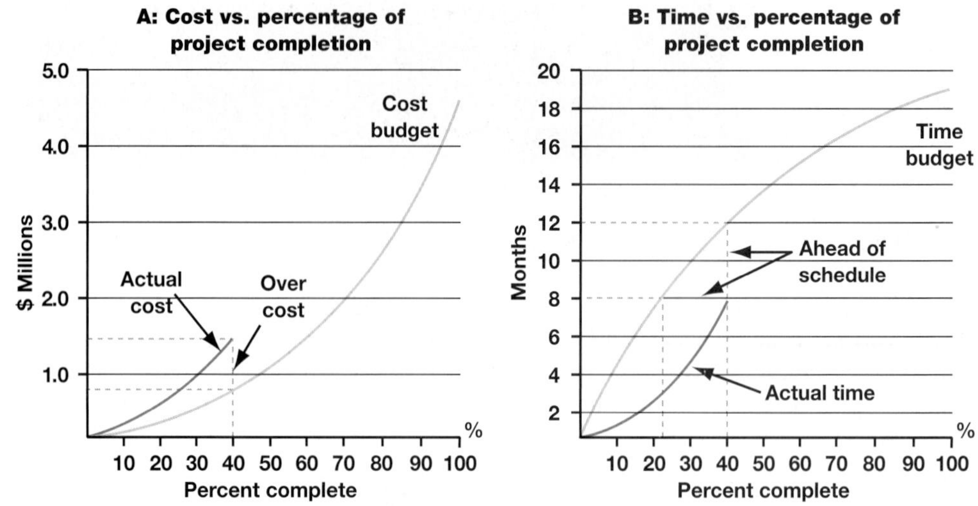

Exhibit 3–15 shows that the project is 40 percent complete (the horizontal axes of panels A and B). The budget line indicates that, for this stage of completion, costs should be $ .9 million, as shown in panel A. The actual cost line indicates, however, that actual costs were $1.4 million. Thus, at the 40 percent stage of completion, the project has a cost overrun of $500,000.

Although we know that cost overruns have occurred, we do not know whether the project is on schedule. Panel B of Exhibit 3–15 shows that the project should be 23 percent complete by month 8. Because the contractor is 40 percent complete by month 8, the project is approximately four months ahead of schedule. The trade-off of earlier completion for a higher cost might be acceptable to the customer. Given the complex nature of projects, however, revising budgeted costs and budgeted percentages or stages of completion throughout the project to reflect these changes might be desirable. (Most major projects require changes due to their inherent uncertainty.) Thus, the graphs in Exhibit 3–15 need updating to reflect revised cost and time budgets to allow managers to evaluate the project by comparing actual results against the revised budget, which reflects current expectations.

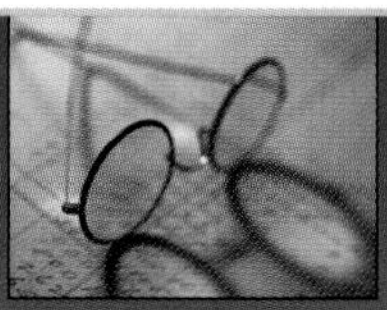

Cost Management in Practice 3.2

Cost Overruns on the Chunnel

Cost overruns and delays of large projects dramatize the difficulties and importance of careful project management. Constructing the 50-kilometer tunnel (also known as the Chunnel) connecting Dover, England, to Calais, France, under the English/French Channel far exceeded the original cost estimates and took many more months to complete than expected. The economic and political ripples from construction delays and cost overruns, which doubled the project's cost to nearly $15 billion, spread throughout England and France. Adversely affected have been:

- *Construction companies,* which lost more than $1 billion on the project because of mistakes and costly changes that were not recovered.
- *Tourist destinations,* such as Euro Disneyland in France, that counted on British tourists who arrived years late.
- *Transportation companies,* such as Virgin Group and Eurostar Ltd., that mobilized resources to profit from the Chunnel but had to finance the resources without incoming revenues while they waited for it to be completed.
- *Stockholders* whose shares plummeted as the Eurotunnel Group lost billions each year under the weight of its immense debt.

Sources: Business Week, *"Curse of the Chunnel," "A Money Pit Called the Chunnel," "Virgin vs. British Airways: The Great Train Rivalry."*

Exhibit 3–16 Gantt Chart for Building a Custom Home

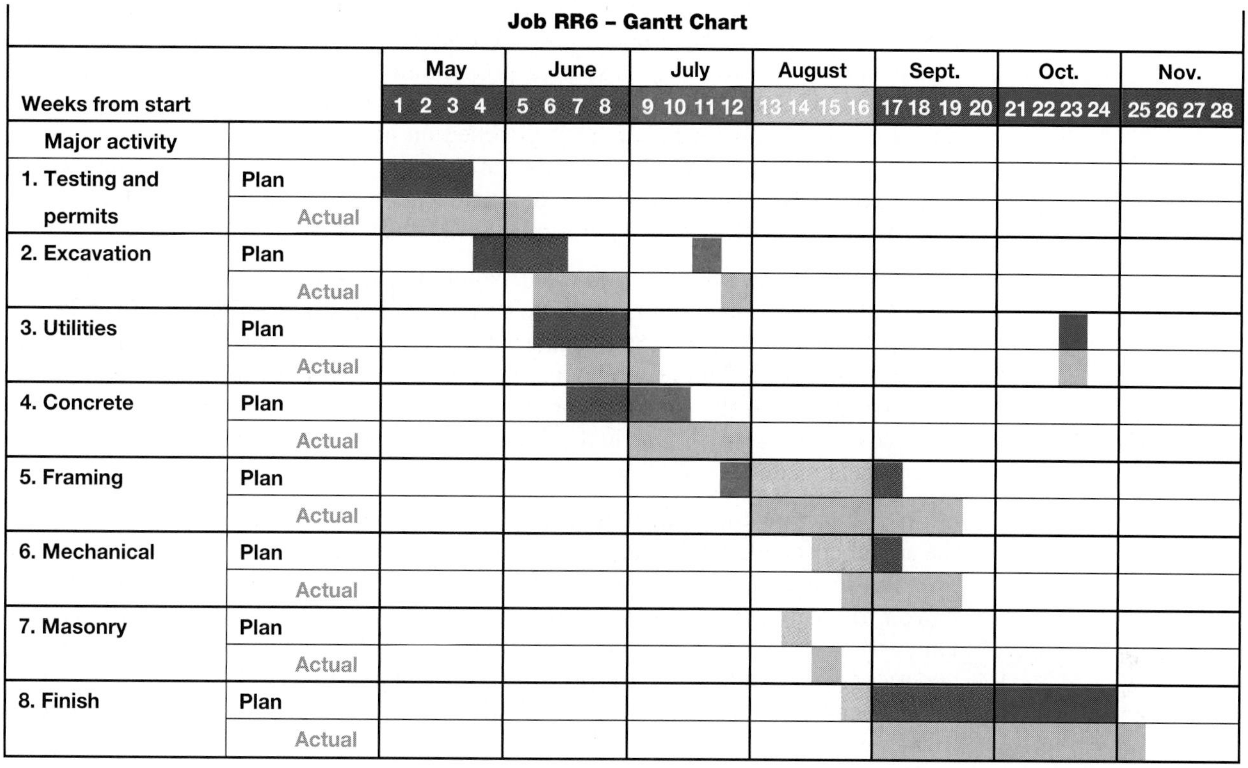

Project scheduling. Many companies engaged in large, complex projects use a project scheduling aid called a **"Gantt chart"** (named after its developer, Henry Gantt), which depicts the timing, sequencing, and overlapping of major project activities. A Gantt chart for building a custom home is shown in Exhibit 3–16; it shows the eight major construction activities (corresponding to the home builder's job-costing system) and reflects planned and actual start-and-finish dates by week for the project's duration. The colored bars describe the original building plan by each activity. For example, the builder planned to start the permitting process in the first week of May and complete that activity by the end of the third week. The actual completion of each activity is shown in the gray bars below the plan. As shown, the permitting activity took two weeks longer than expected, which delayed excavation because it could not commence without the proper permits. Because many building activities are sequential, the permitting delay affected the entire building plan. The chart shows that the project finished only one week later than planned. More important, the builder was able to notify the customer about the delay early and to manage the building process so that only a week was lost. The Gantt chart allowed the builder to visualize what to expect and what to modify over the life of the project soon enough to favorably affect its cost and timing.

Gantt chart *depicts the stages required to complete a project and the sequence in which the stages are to be performed*

Job-Cost and Project Improprieties

Organizations occasionally have been criticized for improprieties in assigning costs to jobs, in some cases resulting in criminal proceedings, ruined careers, large fines, or prison terms. For example, major defense contractors have been caught overstating the cost of their jobs. Several universities have overstated the costs of research projects (which are jobs for costing purposes) to be reimbursed by the government. Improprieties in job costing generally result from one or more of the following actions: misstating the stage of completion, charging costs to the wrong jobs or categories, or simply misrepresenting the cost.

Misstating the stage of completion. Management needs to know the stage of completion of projects to evaluate performance and control costs. If the expenditures on a job are 90 percent of the amount budgeted but the job is only 70 percent complete, management needs to know as soon as possible that the job will require higher costs than estimated. Job supervisors who report the stage of completion of their jobs are in positions to affect managers' decisions based on how realistic the supervisors' estimates are. Some contracts allow for partial payments to contractors based on the percentage of the project's completion. An unethical contractor might overstate the actual percentage of completion to receive unauthorized payments.

Charging costs to the wrong job. To avoid the appearance of cost overruns on a specific job, supervisors sometimes are tempted to encourage employees to charge its costs to other jobs that are not in danger of cost overruns. At a minimum, this practice misleads managers who rely on accurate cost information for pricing, cost control, and other decisions. It also can cheat the organization or people paying for a job on a cost-plus-a-fee basis if the actual job costs based on resource usage do not total as much as claimed.

Misrepresenting the cost of a job. What about the problem of misrepresenting the actual costs of a job? Sometimes managers know a job's correct costs but intentionally deceive a customer to obtain a higher payment. Sometimes deceiving a banker to obtain a larger loan for the job by overstating its expected cost is possible. One way to combat these potential problems is to insist on audits of the job's financial records to avoid such deception. Government auditors generally work on-site at defense contractors, universities, and other organizations that have large government contracts.

Preventing improprieties by understanding contracts. Intentional misrepresentation is not the same as agreeing to a contract that is favorable to your interests. Contracts and agreements for jobs usually result from negotiating and bargaining, and each side strives for favorable terms. Naivete in contracting could be the cause of disappointment (and learning the hard way), but lack of understanding of terms and conditions is not usually grounds to recover damages or nullify contracts.

Especially in the context of job-order costing, it is important for parties who agree to the terms for reimbursement of job costs that the definition of costs and method of tracing them are clearly described. For example, agreeing to reimburse a contractor for simply "the costs of construction" is unwise without clarifying the nature and scope of eligible costs. With that liberal terminology, one would expect the contractor to interpret the costs of construction broadly. This might be acceptable to both parties, but getting a clear agreement before signing is wise. In fact, references to "cost" as a basis for reimbursement, performance, or allocations of profit should be clarified for any contract or agreement. For example, a general partner might sell limited partnerships to others who share the profits of the partnership after the general partner's costs have been covered. Without clarification about what costs are allowed to be charged to the partnership, the general partner could be tempted to allocate as many costs as possible from his or her related activities to it.

Most project contractors have learned over the years that it is far better for the job, the customer, and their reputation if:

- The contractor and the customer clearly agree on what the project's contract covers and what it does not.
- Both parties agree to all changes before the contractor executes them.
- Both parties resolve disputes amicably and without resort to legal proceedings if at all possible.

These stipulations are not always attainable, which is why contractors and sophisticated customers have capable lawyers.

Exhibit 3–17 Excerpt from Cost and Profit Table

	Direct Material		Direct Labor		Manufacturing Overhead		Profit	
Job No.	***Estimate***	**Actual**	***Estimate***	**Actual**	***Estimate***	**Applied**	***Estimate***	**Actual**
C12-05	$1,520	$1,400	$7,900	$8,200	$11,100	$11,550	$12,480	$11,850
P01-20	1,400	1,400	2,413	2,413	3,390	3,390	1,440	Unsold

Use of Job-Order Costing Information for Planning and Decision Making

In Glass Creations' case, Tom Nakagawa used the job-cost information to analyze the relative profitability of two types of jobs, stock and commissioned glass pieces. He made a comprehensive list of every job undertaken in the past five years, the period during which the costing system had been in place. He prepared a cost and profit table, from which two entries are shown in Exhibit 3–17.

The job-costing system gave Glass Creations' owners information allowing them to plan the costs of both types of new work. The job-cost information showed that stock items are less profitable than custom (commissioned) jobs in most cases. Moreover, custom jobs generally are relatively low-risk jobs since a buyer already has commissioned the piece. Unfortunately, not enough commissioned work is available during a typical year to keep the glass studio busy, given its current size and talent staffing.

The Jacobson-Wileys considered using the slow months of December and January to build an inventory of stock windows to sell in the busier spring and summer months. However, Nakagawa's analysis indicated that Glass Creations would be forced to rent space in another building to store the window inventory, to insure it, and to provide security for it. All things considered, it became apparent that building stock windows for inventory was not the best strategy. The owners concluded that the best way to increase their productivity during the slow winter months was to seek to increase their commissioned business by advertising and attending more arts festivals, which are good places to gain exposure for their products. If they are able to increase their commissioned work, they will solve two problems simultaneously. First, they will increase the productivity in the studio in the December–January period. Second, they will reduce their reliance on the stock window business, thereby minimizing the effect of potentially losing that type of business to their new competitors. This evolving strategy would not have been possible without the information provided by Glass Creations' job-order costing system.

Information Technology and Job-Cost Information

Research Insight 3.2

Too much of the information technology (IT) efforts of many organizations could focus on improving the quality of "inside" information (e.g., improved job-cost information). Most IT improvements take advantage of declining computing costs and increasing computing speed to deliver more data to more people, but as Peter Drucker argues, IT specialists are sometimes providing the wrong "data" and ignoring the right "information" for today's competitive environment. To build wealth and value, today's managers need more information about external competitors, changes in markets, and profitable opportunities. The challenge for cost managers and IT specialists is to understand the need for information as well as they currently understand the capability of "technology." *Source: P. Drucker, "The Next Information Revolution."*

Chapter Summary

Cost-management analysts work closely with their management colleagues to design cost-management systems to support their organization's decision making. An important component of a cost-management system is the product-costing system, which accumulates the costs of a production process and assigns them to the products that constitute the organization's output. The most common types of product-costing systems include job-order costing, process costing, and operation costing.

Job-order costing treats each individual job as the unit of output and assigns costs to it as resources are used. A *job* may be a single, unique product or a relatively small batch of identical or very similar products. Job-order costing is useful for identifying types of jobs likely to be most profitable, providing data to predict costs of future jobs, managing the costs of current jobs, renegotiating job contracts, and financial reporting of actual results of the period's operations.

Process costing (see Chapter 8) treats all units processed during a period as its output and does not separate and record costs for each unit produced. *Operation costing* (also covered in Chapter 8) is a hybrid of job-order and process costing used when companies produce batches of similar products with significantly different types of materials.

Companies using job-order costing employ several accounts (or files) to track the costs of resources used on jobs. These accounts are the sources of data for product costing, estimating costs of future jobs, and financial reporting for both internal and external purposes. The Work-in-Process Inventory account collects all costs of resources used on various jobs that have not been completed. Each job also has its own job-cost record on which the costs of all production-related resources used on that job to date are reported.

Companies have traditionally used *predetermined overhead* rates to assign manufacturing overhead to individual production jobs. The predetermined overhead rate is usually established before the year in which it is to be used and remains the same for the entire year. Predetermined overhead rates normalize (i.e., smooth out) the application of manufacturing overhead to jobs. Thus, the resulting product costs are called "normal costs," and this product-costing method is called "normal costing."

The Manufacturing Overhead account records both *actual overhead* and the *overhead applied* to Work-in-Process Inventory. Under normal costing, the actual manufacturing overhead is unlikely to equal the amount of overhead applied, which is based on budgeted overhead. The difference between the actual and the applied manufacturing overhead amounts is the *overhead variance* referred to as *overapplied* or *underapplied overhead.* At year-end, the manufacturing overhead variance is either (1) prorated (i.e., allocated) to Work-in-Process Inventory, Finished-Goods Inventory, and Cost of Goods Sold or (2) closed to Cost of Goods Sold.

Alternatives to *normal costing* include actual costing and standard costing. *Actual costing* assigns only the actual costs of both direct and indirect resources (i.e., direct material, direct labor, and manufacturing overhead) to the products. *Standard costing* uses predetermined (or standard) rates for both direct and indirect costs to assign manufacturing costs to products.

Managing jobs and projects requires attention to quality, customer satisfaction, costs, and adherence to schedules. Among the tools used in project management are *project percentage of completion charts* and *Gantt charts.* Organizations occasionally have been criticized for the following improprieties in assigning costs to jobs: misstating the percentage of completion, charging costs to the wrong job, and misrepresenting the job costs. In the context of job-order costing, parties who agree to the terms for reimbursement of job costs should require the definition and method of tracing of costs to be clearly described before signing a contract.

Job-order costing systems are indispensable for reporting and controlling costs of jobs, particularly when the jobs are numerous and complex. Job-order costing systems also provide valuable information as feedback for decision making and planning future operations.

Key Terms

For each term's definition, refer to the indicated page or turn to the glossary at the end of the text.

actual costing, 112
actual overhead, 107
applied overhead, 107
Gantt chart, 117
job-cost record (or file, card or sheet), 96
job-order costing, 91
material requisition form, 100
normal costing, 103
operation costing, 94
overapplied overhead, 107
overhead variance, 107
predetermined overhead rate, 102
process costing, 93
product-costing system, 91
proration, 108
standard costing, 112
throughput (cycle) time, 105
underapplied overhead, 107

Meeting the Cost Management Challenges

1. What factors should a cost-management analyst consider when designing a product-costing system?

Designers of cost systems must evaluate the trade-offs of the costs of designing and operating the system itself and the expected value of the information it provides. No organization would implement a cost system that measured every resource and activity cost with 100 percent accuracy (if that could be defined), instantaneously, and for every authorized decision maker. Cost-management analysts must design and implement a system that supports the organization's most important decisions well, usually within a development and operating budget. This often means that relatively fewer important decisions are supported by less accurate or timely information. The cost system itself should not consume more resources than the savings to be gained by using it to make better decisions.

2. What features should a job-order costing system have, and how can they be developed?

As jobs become more unique and individually important to the organization, the job-cost system should more precisely trace or assign costs to jobs. The method of measuring job costs also should differ, depending on the relative importance of easily traced, direct job costs versus less easily assigned, indirect costs. The costs of major activities must be assigned using predetermined cost-driver rates, which could be difficult to measure. The complexity of resources, activities, cost-driver rates, and products or services jointly determines the complexity and cost of the job-costing system. Thus, a job-costing system should trace direct costs to jobs and assign indirect costs as accurately as necessary to support management decisions.

3. How can cost-management analysts use job-cost information to support planning and decision-making activities?

Understanding what drives the costs of jobs—the various activities that are performed to design and complete jobs—is critical to planning the use of resources and making decisions about which jobs to seek. This is particularly true when the nature of jobs (i.e., necessary activities to perform them) varies greatly. Job-costing systems should provide information on (a) the completion of past jobs and (b) cost-driver rates. Both types of information should be useful to decision makers who must plan how to organize resources for current jobs and how to bid for future jobs.

Solutions to You're the Decision Maker

3.1 Normal-Costing and Predetermined Overhead Rates p. 113

a.

Quarter	Predetermined Overhead Rate	Calculations
1	$25 per DLH	$ 50,000 ÷ 2,000
2	35 per DLH	$122,500 ÷ 3,500
3	25 per DLH	$100,000 ÷ 4,000
4	35 per DLH	$ 87,500 ÷ 2,500

b.

	February	October
Direct material	$100	$100
Direct labor ($22 × 5) + ($15 × 1)	125	125
Manufacturing overhead:		
6 hrs × $25 per hr.	150	
6 hrs × $35 per hr.		210
Total cost	$375	$435

c.

	February	October
Total cost	$375	$435
Markup (20%)	75	87
Price	$450	$522

d.

$$\text{Predetermined rate} = \frac{\text{annual budgeted manufacturing overhead}}{\text{annual budgeted direct-labor hours}}$$

$$= \$360{,}000/12{,}000$$

$$= \$30 \text{ per direct-labor hour}$$

e.

	February	October
Direct material	$100	$100
Direct labor ($22 × 5) + ($15 × 1)	125	125
Manufacturing overhead (6 hr. × $30)	180	180
Total cost	$405	$405

f.

Total cost	$405
Markup (20%)	81
Price	$486

g. Glass Creations' use of quarterly overhead rates might *undercost* and *underprice* the blue heron window in February and *overcost* and *overprice* it in October. For this reason, the use of a predetermined overhead rate calculated annually rather than quarterly is preferable. This is the essence of normal costing (i.e., smoothing out fluctuations in the overhead rate and reported product costs over a reasonably long period of time, in this case, one year).

Review Questions

3.1 What is a product-costing system and what does it do?

3.2 What are the characteristics of the following three product-costing methods: (a) job-order costing, (b) process costing, and (c) operation costing? Give an example of a product or service that would be accounted for by each method.

3.3 What is each component of the basic cost-flow model? Describe each component.

3.4 Describe the basic cost-flow model as an algebraic equation.

3.5 Distinguish between work-in-process, finished-goods, and cost of goods sold.

3.6 Explain how to measure the costs of a product using normal costing, actual costing, and standard costing.

3.7 How are the events "complete a job," "sell a job," and "end the accounting period" different and how are inventory accounts affected by these events?

3.8 How does job-order costing differ for service organizations and manufacturing organizations?

3.9 How can overhead be over- or underapplied?

3.10 Does it matter how the overhead variance is disposed? Explain.

3.11 Describe several ways in which job costing can be misused.

3.12 Is job-order costing information sufficient to support management decisions? Why or why not?

3.13 What are the characteristics of companies likely to use a job-order costing system?

3.14 Why is the use of direct-labor as a cost driver for manufacturing overhead declining?

3.15 What are the purposes of the following documents: (a) material requisition form, (b) labor time record, and (c) job-cost record.

3.16 Explain the benefits of using a predetermined overhead rate instead of an actual overhead rate.

3.17 Describe one advantage and one disadvantage of prorating overapplied or underapplied overhead.

Critical Analysis

3.18 Would a dentist, an architect, a landscaper, and a lawyer use job-order costing or process costing? Explain.

3.19 An employee of Doughties Foods overstated inventories to make periodic profits higher. Using the basic cost-flow model, explain how overstating inventories could increase profits. If the employee did this a second and a third time, use the basic cost-flow model to show what the effect would be. How could this misrepresentation be detected?

3.20 Interview the manager of a construction company (for example, a company that does house construction, remodeling, landscaping, or street or highway construction) about how it bids on prospective jobs. Does it use cost information from former jobs similar to prospective ones, for example? Does it have a specialist in cost estimation to project the costs of prospective jobs? Write a report to your instructor summarizing the results of your interview.

3.21 Interview the manager of a campus print shop or a print shop in the local area about how the company bids on prospective jobs. Does it use cost information from former jobs similar to prospective ones, for example? Does it have a specialist in cost estimation to project costs of prospective jobs? Write a report to your instructor summarizing the results of your interview.

3.22 A co-worker states, I don't know why we spent so much money on that new job-costing system. I can do everything we need on a simple spreadsheet. If the CFO had listened to me, we could have saved a lot of money. Would it have been desirable to follow your co-worker's advice? Why or why not?

3.23 Your manager tries to persuade you that all of the overhead variance should be charged to Cost of Goods Sold. This is appealing to you since you have hundreds of jobs and many overhead accounts to reconcile, and this is the least fun part of your job. Why should you consider this argument with caution?

3.24 How might job-order costing for a homebuilder be similar to and differ from that used by a consulting firm?

3.25 A government contractor had a contract with NASA, to build a space shuttle. Under this contract, all costs of development and construction are to be reimbursed and the contractor is to be guaranteed a specific profit. At the same time, the contractor had a fixed-fee contract with the U.S. Air Force to build fighter planes, which limited total reimbursement to the contractor to a fixed amount. The Air Force contract had a cost overrun that the contractor transferred to the NASA contract. Explain how this might have been accomplished and why the contractor might have thought it was desirable.

3.26 Motion picture contracts often offer some participants residual profits, which are shares of profits computed after all costs of production have been covered. Sometimes blockbuster movies never pay residual profits because they do not fully recover their costs, which could include up-front payments to movie stars and producers. If you sold your novel to a producer in exchange for residual profits that never materialized, yet the stars and producers made millions of dollars, is there anything wrong or unethical about this?

Exercises

Exercise 3.27
Basic Cost-Flow Model
(LO 2)

A small building-supply company, Cut-Rite Lumber, experienced the following events during the year:

- Incurred $125,000 in selling costs.
- Purchased $400,000 of building material.
- Paid $10,000 for vehicles and transportation resources.
- Incurred $200,000 of general and administrative costs.
- Took a periodic inventory at year-end and learned that building material costing $125,000 was on hand. This compared with a beginning inventory of $150,000 on January 1.
- Determined that sales revenue during the year was $1,000,000.

All costs incurred were added to the appropriate accounts. All sales were for cash.

Required

Give the amounts for the following items in Cut-Rite Lumber's Building-Material Inventory account:

a. Beginning balance (BB).
b. Transfers in (TI).
c. Ending balance (EB).
d. Transfers out (TO).

Exercise 3.28
Basic Cost-Flow Model
(LO 2)

Assume that the following events occurred at a division of American Homes, Inc., a large homebuilder, for the current year.

1. Purchased $180 million in building material.
2. Incurred construction labor costs of $104 million.
3. Determined that general and administrative overhead was $164 million.
4. Transferred 70 percent of the materials purchased to jobs (work) in process.
5. Completed work on 60 percent of the jobs in process. Costs are assigned equally across all work in process.

The inventory accounts have no beginning balances. All costs incurred were debited to the appropriate accounts and credited to Accounts Payable.

Required

Give the amounts for the following items in the Work-in-Process account:

a. Transfers in (TI).
b. Transfers out (TO).
c. Ending balance (EB).

Exercise 3.29
Basic Cost-Flow Model
(LO 2)

Fill in the missing items for the following inventories:

	(A)	(B)	(C)
Beginning balance	$34,000	$ 14,200	$ 78,000
Ending balance	?	12,400	64,000
Transferred in	32,000	?	140,000
Transferred out	38,000	44,000	?

	(D)	(E)	(F)
Beginning balance	$136,000	$ 56,800	$312,000
Ending balance	?	49,600	256,000
Transferred in	128,000	?	560,000
Transferred out	152,000	176,000	?

Exercise 3.30
Basic Cost-Flow Model
(LO 2)

Fill in the missing items for the following inventories:

	(A)	(B)	(C)
Beginning balance	$170,000	$ 71,000	$390,000
Ending balance	?	62,000	320,000
Transferred in	160,000	?	700,000
Transferred out	190,000	220,000	?

	(D)	(E)	(F)
Beginning balance	$ 5,000	$?	$12,000
Ending balance	?	16,000	12,000
Transferred in	75,000	45,000	56,000
Transferred out	79,000	52,000	?

Exercise 3.31
Basic Cost-Flow Model
(LO 2, 3)

The following T-accounts represent data from a division of Tower Design's accounting records. Find the missing amounts represented by the letters. (*Hint:* Rearrange accounts to conform with the flow of costs.)

Cost of Goods Sold	
41,000	

Raw-Material Inventory		
BB	(a)	
Purchases	9,000	TO 10,500
EB	3,750	

Finished-Goods Inventory		
BB	23,000	
	(c)	(d)
EB	(f)	

Work-in-Process Inventory		
BB	3,000	
Material	(b)	
Labor	8,500	
Overhead	(e)	29,300
EB	4,850	

Exercise 3.32
Basic Cost-Flow Model
(LO 2, 3)

The following T-accounts represent data from a division of Bridal Wear Corporation's accounting records. Find the missing amounts represented by the letters. (*Hint:* Rearrange accounts to conform with flow of costs.)

Cost of Goods Sold	
123,000	

Raw-Material Inventory		
BB	(a)	
Purchases	27,000	TO 31,500
EB	11,250	

Finished-Goods Inventory		
BB	69,600	
	(c)	(d)
EB	(f)	

Work-in-Process Inventory		
BB	9,000	
Material	(b)	
Labor	25,500	
Overhead	(e)	87,900
EB	14,550	

Exercise 3.33
Assignment of Costs to Jobs
(LO 2, 3, 4, 5)

Anvil Wild, Inc., is a custom manufacturer of furniture that uses job-order costing. The following transactions to support job 402, for a custom meeting room set—a large table plus 16 chairs—occurred in January:

a. Purchased $10,000 of materials.
b. Issued $500 of supplies from raw-material inventory.
c. Purchased $7,000 of raw material.
d. Paid for the raw material purchased in transaction (a).
e. Issued $8,500 in raw material to the production department.
f. Incurred production labor costs of $12,500, which were credited to Payroll Payable.
g. Paid $23,250 cash for utilities, power, equipment maintenance, and miscellaneous items for the manufacturing plant.
h. Applied overhead on the basis of 185 percent of $8,500 in material costs.
i. Recognized depreciation on manufacturing property, plant, and equipment of $6,250.

Required

Prepare journal entries to record these transactions.

Exercise 3.34
Assignment of Costs to Jobs
(LO 2, 3, 4, 5)

Refer to the data in the preceding exercise. The following balances appeared in the accounts of Anvil Wild for January before closing temporary accounts:

	Beginning	Ending
Material inventory	$18,525	
Work-in-process inventory	4,125	
Finished-goods inventory	20,750	$17,900
Cost of goods sold	32,925	

Required

Prepare T-accounts to show the flow of costs during the period from raw-material inventory purchases through cost of goods sold.

Exercise 3.35
Costs Traced to Jobs
(LO 2, 3, 4, 5)

Partially completed T-accounts and additional information for Triangle Company for the month of March follow:

Raw-Material Inventory

	Debit	Credit
BB	2,000	
	8,000	6,400

Work-in-Process Inventory

	Debit	Credit
BB	4,000	
Labor	6,000	

Finished-Goods Inventory

	Debit	Credit
BB	6,000	
	12,000	8,000

Cost of Goods Sold

Debit	Credit

Manufacturing Overhead

Debit	Credit
5,200	

Additional Information

- Labor wage rate was $24 per hour.
- Overhead is applied at 80 percent of direct-material cost.
- During the month, sales revenue was $18,000, and selling and administrative costs were $3,200.

Required

a. What was the amount of direct material issued to production during March?
b. What was the amount of manufacturing overhead applied to production during March?
c. What was the cost of products completed during March?
d. What was the balance of the Work-in-Process Inventory account at the end of March?
e. What was the manufacturing-overhead variance during March?
f. What was the operating profit for March?

Exercise 3.36
Predetermined Cost-Driver Rate
(LO 3, 5)

Global

Rosita Corporation, located in Buenos Aires, Argentina, manufactures cutlery. Management estimates manufacturing overhead to be 44,000*p* and direct-labor costs to be 80,000*p* for year 1. The actual manufacturing labor costs were 20,000*p* for job 1, 30,000*p* for job 2, and 40,000*p* for job 3 during year 1; the actual manufacturing overhead was 52,000*p*. Manufacturing overhead is applied to jobs on the basis of direct-labor costs using a predetermined rate. (*p* denotes the peso, Argentina's national currency. Several countries use the peso as their monetary unit. On the day this exercise was written, Argentina's peso was worth 1.002 U.S. dollars.)

Required

a. How much manufacturing overhead (in Argentina's peso) was assigned to each job during year 1?
b. What was the manufacturing overhead variance for year 1?

Exercise 3.37
Overhead Application Using a Predetermined Rate
(LO 3, 5)

Paige Printing uses a job-order costing system. The following debits (credits) appeared in the Work-in-Process account for May:

	Description	Debits	Credits
May 1	Balance	$ 5,000	
Entire month	Direct material	30,000	
Entire month	Direct labor	20,000	
Entire month	Factory overhead	16,000	
Entire month	To finished goods		$60,000

Paige Printing applies overhead to production at a predetermined rate of 80 percent based on direct labor cost. Job 75, the only job still in process at the end of May, has been charged with direct labor of $2,500.

Required

What was the amount of direct material charged to job 75?

[CPA adapted]

Exercise 3.38
Overhead Variance Calculation
(LO 3, 5)

Brady Co. uses a predetermined cost-driver rate based on direct-labor hours. For October, Brady's budgeted overhead was $600,000 based on budgeted activity of 100,000 direct-labor hours. Actual overhead amounted to $650,000 with actual direct-labor hours totaling 110,000.

Required

How much was overhead overapplied or underapplied?

[CPA adapted]

Exercise 3.39
Under- or Overapplied Overhead Prorated
(LO 3, 5)

Refer to the information in the preceding exercise. Prorate the overhead variance as follows:

Work-in-process inventory	10%
Finished-goods inventory	25
Cost of goods sold	65

Exercise 3.40
Closing the Overhead Variance
(LO 3, 5)

Refer to the information in exercise 3.38. Prepare an entry to close the overhead variance into cost of goods sold.

Exercise 3.41
Predetermined Overhead Rate
(LO 3, 5)

Kustom-Kraft, Inc., manufactures one product and accounts for costs using a job-order costing system. You have obtained the following information from the corporation's books and records for the year ended December 31, year 1:

- Total manufacturing cost during last year was $500,000 based on actual direct material, actual direct labor, and manufacturing overhead applied on the basis of actual direct-labor dollars.
- Manufacturing overhead was applied to work in process at 75 percent of direct-labor dollars. Applied manufacturing overhead for the year was 33 percent of the total manufacturing cost during the year.

Required

Compute actual direct material, actual direct labor, and applied manufacturing overhead. (*Hint:* The total of these costs is $500,000.)

Exercise 3.42
Job Costs for a Service Organization
(LO 3, 5)

At the beginning of the month, Tiana Corporation had two jobs in process that had the following costs assigned from previous months:

Job No.	Direct Labor	Applied Overhead
X-10	$1,280	?
Y-12	840	?

During the month, jobs X-10 and Y-12 were completed but not billed to customers. The completion costs for X-10 required $1,400 in direct labor. For Y-12, $4,000 in direct labor was used.

During the month, a new job, Z-14, was started but not finished; it was the only new job. Total direct-labor costs for all jobs amounted to $8,240 for the month. Overhead in this company refers to the cost of work that is not directly traced to particular jobs, including copying, printing, and travel costs to meet with clients. Overhead is applied at a rate of 50 percent of direct-labor costs for this and previous periods. Actual overhead for the month was $4,000.

Required

a. What are the costs of jobs X-10 and Y-12 at (1) the beginning of the month and (2) when completed?

b. What is the cost of job Z-14 at the end of the month?

c. How much was the manufacturing overhead variance for the month?

Exercise 3.43
Job Costing in a Service Organization
(LO 3, 7)

For September, Twiddle & Company worked 600 hours for client A and 1,400 hours for client B. Twiddle bills clients at the rate of $140 per hour; labor cost for its audit staff is $70 per hour. The total number of hours worked in September was 2,000, and overhead costs were $20,000. Overhead is applied to clients at $12 per labor hour. In addition, Twiddle had $84,000 in selling and administrative costs. All transactions are on account. All services were billed.

Required

a. Show labor and overhead cost flows through T-accounts.

b. Prepare an income statement for the company for September.

Exercise 3.44
Supply Chain; Job-Order Production Environment
(LO 1)

Global

Read "Boeing Weighs Giving Japan 747 Wing Job," *The Wall Street Journal,* January 2, 2001, by Jeff Cole. The article discusses how executives at Boeing negotiated a contract with Mitsubishi Heavy Industries to manufacture the wings for a line of Boeing's jumbo jets.

Required

What is the role of outsourcing and supply-chain management in a job-order production environment such as an aircraft manufacturer? How would Boeing's job-order costing system account for the costs of the wings manufactured by Mitsubishi?

Exercise 3.45
Job-Order Costing for Feature Film Production; Internet
(LO 1)

Internet

Visit the Web site of a film producer, such as Warner Brothers (*www.warnerbros.com*), MGM (*www.mgm.com*), or Walt Disney Studios (*www.disney.com*).

Required

Read about one of the company's recent (or upcoming) film releases. Then discuss why job-order costing is or is not an appropriate costing method for feature film production.

Problems

Problem 3.46
Cost Flows
(LO 2, 3, 5)

Kansas City Quality Instruments produces sensitive heat-measurement devices in three manufacturing stages: (1) meter assembly, (2) case assembly, and (3) testing. The company has a large backlog of orders and had no beginning inventories because all units in production last year were sold by the end of the year. At the start of this year, the firm received an order for 4,000 devices.

- The company purchased $260,000 of materials on account. Meter assembly used $210,000 of the materials in production, case assembly used $40,000, and testing used $10,000.
- Production labor costs of $640,000 were incurred.
- These costs were assigned as follows: meter assembly, $200,000; case assembly, $350,000; and testing, $90,000. Overhead costs of $1,040,000 were charged to departments based on materials used [($210,000/$260,000) × $1,040,000] to meter assembly, for example).
- Ninety percent of the costs charged to meter assembly were transferred to case assembly during the period; 95 percent of the costs charged to case assembly (including the costs transferred in from meter assembly) were transferred to testing. All costs charged to testing were transferred to finished goods, and all finished units were delivered to the buyer.

Required

Use T-accounts to show the flow of costs for this order.

Problem 3.47
Analysis of Overhead Using a Predetermined Rate
(LO 2, 3, 5)

Eclipse Corporation uses a job-order costing system for its production costs. A predetermined cost-driver rate based on machine hours is used to apply facility-level overhead to individual jobs. An estimate of overhead costs at different volumes was prepared for the current year as follows:

Machine hours	50,000	60,000	70,000
Unit-level overhead costs	$350,000	$420,000	$490,000
Facility-level overhead costs	216,000	216,000	216,000
Total overhead	$566,000	$636,000	$706,000

The expected volume is 60,000 machine hours for the entire year. The following information is for November, when jobs 50 and 51 were completed:

Inventories, November 1	
Raw materials and supplies	$ 10,500
Work in process (job 50)	54,000
Finished goods	112,500
Purchases of raw materials and supplies	
Raw materials	$135,000
Supplies	15,000
Materials and supplies requisitioned for production	
Job 50	$ 45,000
Job 51	37,500
Job 52	25,500
Supplies	6,000
Subtotal	$114,000

Job	Production Machine Hours (MH)	Direct-Labor Hours (DLH)
Job 50	3,500 MH	2,000 DLH
Job 51	3,000 MH	3,000 DLH
Job 52	2,000 MH	3,500 DLH

Labor costs:	
Production labor wages (all hours @ $8)	$ 68,000
Support labor wages (4,000 hours)	17,000
Supervisory salaries	36,000
Subtotal	$121,000
Building occupancy costs (heat, light, depreciation, etc.):	
Factory facilities	$ 6,500
Sales and administrative offices	2,500
Subtotal	$ 9,000
Factory equipment costs:	
Power	$ 4,000
Repairs and maintenance	1,500
Other	2,500
Subtotal	$ 8,000

Required

a. Compute the predetermined cost-driver rate (combined unit and facility) to use to apply overhead to individual jobs during the year.

[*Note:* Without prejudice to your answer to requirement (a), assume that the predetermined cost-driver rate is $9 per machine hour. Use this amount in answering requirements (b) through (e)]

b. Compute the total cost of job 50 when it is finished.

c. Compute the overhead costs applied to job 52 during November.

d. Compute the total amount of overhead applied to jobs during November.

e. Compute the actual factory overhead incurred during November.

f. At the end of the year, Eclipse Corporation had the following account balances:

Overapplied overhead	$ 1,000
Cost of goods sold	980,000
Work-in-process inventory	38,000
Finished-goods inventory	82,000

What is the most common treatment of the overapplied overhead, assuming that it is not material?

[CMA adapted]

Problem 3.48
Job Costing in a Service Organization
(LO 2, 3, 5, 7)

Communication

Cozy Cleaners has five employees and a president, Marty Stuart. Stuart and one of the five employees manage all the marketing and administrative duties. The remaining four employees work directly on operations. Cozy Cleaners has four service departments: dry cleaning, coin washing and drying, special cleaning, and repairs. A time report is marked, and records are kept to monitor the time each employee spends working in each department. When business is slow, there is idle time, which is marked on the time record. (Some idle time is necessary because Cozy Cleaners promises 60-minute service, and it must have reserve labor available to accommodate fluctuating peak demand periods throughout the day and the week.)

Some of the November operating data are as follows:

	Idle Time	Dry Cleaning	Coin Washing and Drying	Special Cleaning	Repairs
Sales revenue		$4,625	$5,250	$2,000	$625
Direct labor (in hours)	25	320	80	125	90
Overhead traceable to departments:					
Cleaning compounds		500	250	400	0
Supplies		125	200	175	140
Electric usage		250	625	100	25
Rent		200	500	90	10

Additional Information

- Each of the four employees working in the operating departments makes $8 per hour.
- The fifth employee, who helps manage marketing and administrative duties, earns $1,500 per month, and Stuart earns $2,000 per month.
- Indirect overhead (i.e., overhead that is not traceable to departments) amounted to $512 and is assigned to departments based on direct-labor hours used. Because of the idle hours, some overhead will not be assigned to a department.
- In addition to salaries paid, marketing costs for such items as advertising and special promotions totaled $400.
- In addition to salaries, other administrative costs were $150.
- All sales transactions are in cash; all other transactions are on account.

Required

Management wants to know whether each department is contributing to the company's profit. Prepare an income statement for November that shows the revenue and cost of services for each department. Write a short report to management about departmental profitability. No inventories were kept.

Problem 3.49
Job Costs in a Service Organization
(LO 2, 3, 5, 7)

Spreadsheet

For the month of May, Midtown Consultants worked 1,000 hours for Nocando Manufacturing, 300 hours for Sails, Inc., and 500 hours for Original John's Restaurants. Midtown Consultants bills clients at $80 an hour; its labor costs are $30 an hour. A total of 2,000 hours were worked in May with 200 hours not billable to clients. Overhead costs of $30,000 were incurred and assigned to clients on the basis of direct-labor hours. Because 200 hours were not billable, some overhead was not assigned to jobs. Midtown Consultants had $20,000 in marketing and administrative costs. All transactions were on account.

Required

a. What are the revenue and cost per client?

b. Prepare an income statement for May.

Problem 3.50
Assignment of Costs Using Predetermined Cost-Driver Rate
(LO 2, 3, 5)

The following transactions occurred at Arrow Space, Inc., a small defense contractor that uses job costing:

a. Purchased $71,600 in raw material on account.

b. Issued $2,000 in supplies (indirect material) from raw-material inventory to the production department.

c. Paid for the raw material purchased in (a).

d. Issued $34,000 in raw material to the production department.

e. Incurred wage costs of $56,000, which were debited to Payroll, a temporary account. Of this amount, $18,000 was withheld for payroll taxes and credited to Payroll Taxes Payable. The remaining $38,000 was paid in cash to the employees. See transactions (f) and (g) for additional information about the Payroll account.

f. Recognized $28,000 in fringe benefit costs, incurred as a result of the wages paid in (e). This $28,000 was debited to Payroll and credited to Fringe Benefits Payable.

g. Analyzed the Payroll account and determined that 40 percent represented production labor; 40 percent manufacturing support (overhead) labor; and 20 percent administrative and marketing costs.

h. Paid for utilities, power, equipment maintenance, and other overhead items for the manufacturing plant totaling $43,200.

i. Recognized depreciation of $21,000 on manufacturing property, plant, and equipment.

j. Applied manufacturing overhead on the basis of 400 percent of *production* labor costs.

Required

Prepare T-accounts to show the flow of costs during the period. The following balances appeared in Arrow Space's accounts before closing temporary accounts:

	Beginning	Ending
Raw-material inventory	$74,100	?
Work-in-process inventory	16,500	?
Finished-goods inventory	83,000	$ 66,400
Cost of goods sold	0	131,700

Problem 3.51
Cost Estimation Using Alternative Cost-Driver Rates
(LO 2, 3, 5)

Refer to the information in the preceding problem. Arrow Space, Inc., has determined that 65 percent of its manufacturing overhead spending is related to jobs' use of material, and 35 percent is related to jobs' use of production labor.

Required

a. Based on information in this problem and the preceding problem, calculate cost-driver rates using actual material cost and production labor costs as possible cost-driver bases.

b. Arrow Space, Inc., is considering bidding on two jobs with the following budgeted characteristics:

Job	A	B
Direct-material cost:	$40,000	$30,000
Production labor cost	20,000	30,000

Estimate the costs of these two jobs using (1) the original cost-driver rate of 300 percent of production labor and (2) the cost-driver rates derived in requirement (a).

c. What are the possible outcomes if bids for the two jobs are based on the original cost-driver rate but resource costs are actually *used* in accordance with the new cost-driver rates?

Problem 3.52
Cost Flows through Accounts
(LO 2, 3, 5)

Communication

You are employed by the consulting group Reengineering Management Consultants, which Leevies Pants, Inc., has asked to help in improving its job-costing system. Leevies employed 20 full-time workers at $8 per hour. Since beginning operations last year, it had priced the various jobs by marking up the sum of direct-labor and direct-material costs by 20 percent. Despite operating at capacity, however, last year's performance was a great disappointment to the managers. In total, 10 jobs were accepted and completed, incurring the following total costs:

Direct material	$103,540
Direct labor	400,000
Manufacturing overhead	104,000

Of the $104,000 manufacturing overhead, 30 percent was unit level and 70 percent was facility level. This year Leevies expects to operate at the same activity level as last year, and overhead costs and the wage rate are not expected to change. For the first quarter of this year, Leevies had just completed two jobs and was beginning the third. The costs incurred follow:

Jobs	Material	Production Labor	Overhead
111	$13,720	$49,000	$13,390
112	9,300	31,240	11,570
113	9,400	19,760	2,160
Total factory overhead	27,120		
Total selling and administrative costs	11,200		

In the first quarter of this year, 40 percent of selling and administrative costs were job level and 60 percent were facility level. Leevies has told you that jobs 111 and 112 were sold for $85,000 and $55,000, respectively. All over- or underapplied overhead for the quarter is expected to be expensed on the income statement.

Required

a. Begin your analysis by presenting in T-accounts the absorption, *actual* manufacturing cost flows for the three jobs in the first quarter of this year.
b. Using last year's costs and direct-labor hours as this year's estimate, calculate predetermined cost-driver rates for unit-level overhead as a percentage of direct-material cost and facility-level overhead as a percentage of direct-labor cost.
c. Present in T-accounts the absorption, *normal* manufacturing cost flows for the three jobs in the first quarter of this year. Use the cost-driver rates derived in requirement (b).
d. Prepare income statements for the first quarter of this year under the following costing systems:
   (1) Absorption, actual.
   (2) Absorption, normal.
e. Prepare a short presentation to demonstrate and explain whether the choice of method in requirement (d) makes a difference.

Problem 3.53
Flow of Costs to Jobs; Journal Entries
(LO 2, 3, 4, 5)

Bright Equipment Company assembles light and sound equipment for installation in various entertainment facilities. An inventory of material and equipment is on hand at all times so that installation could start as quickly as possible. Special equipment has been ordered as required. On September 1, the Materials and Equipment Inventory account had a $48,000 balance. The Work-in-Process Inventory account is maintained to record the costs of installation work not yet complete. There were two such jobs on September 1, with the following costs:

	Wheels and Spokes Country Music Hall Job 46	Stars Theater Job 51
Material and equipment	$32,000	$95,000
Technician labor	6,500	9,700
Overhead (applied)	4,800	14,250

Overhead has been applied at 15 percent of the costs of material and equipment installed. During September, two new installations were begun. Additional work was done on jobs 46 and 51, with the latter completed and billed to Stars Theater. Details on the costs incurred on jobs during September follow:

Job	46	51	55	56
Material and equipment	$3,200	$14,200	$17,000	$6,200
Technician labor (on account)	1,800	1,200	3,100	900

Other Period Events

- Received $25,000 payment on job 55 delivered to the customer.
- Purchased material and equipment for $18,700.
- Billed Stars Theater $175,000 and received payment for $100,000 of that amount.
- Determined that payroll for support personnel totaled $1,300.
- Issued supplies and incidental installation material for current jobs costing $310.
- Recorded overhead and advertising costs for the installation operation as follows (all cash except equipment depreciation):

Property taxes	$1,100
Showroom and storage area rental	1,350
Truck and delivery cost	640
Advertising and promotion campaign	1,200
Electrical inspections	400
Telephone and other miscellaneous	650
Equipment depreciation	900

Required

a. Prepare journal entries to record the flow of costs for the installation operation during September.

b. Calculate the amount of over- or underapplied overhead for the month. This amount is closed to Cost of Goods Sold.

c. Determine inventory balances for Material and Equipment Inventory and Work-in-Process Inventory.

Problem 3.54
Cost-Driver Rates
(LO 2, 3, 5)

Communication

Premier Pasta Company prepares, packages, and distributes six frozen pasta entrees in two different container sizes. It prepares the different pastas and different sizes in large batches. It uses a normal job-order costing system. Manufacturing overhead is assigned to batches by a predetermined rate on the basis of machine hours. The company incurred manufacturing-overhead costs during two recent years (adjusted for changes using current prices and wage rates) as follows:

	Year 1	Year 2
Machine hours worked	1,380,000	1,080,000
Manufacturing-overhead costs incurred:		
Support (indirect) labor	$11,040,000	$ 8,640,000
Employee benefits	4,140,000	3,240,000
Supplies	2,760,000	2,160,000
Power	2,208,000	1,728,000
Heat and light	552,000	552,000
Supervision	2,865,000	2,625,000
Depreciation	7,930,000	7,930,000
Property taxes and insurance	3,005,000	3,005,000
Total manufacturing-overhead costs	$34,500,000	$29,880,000

Premier Pasta expects to operate at a level of 1.15 million machine hours in year 3. Using the data from the two previous years, write a report to management that shows the cost-driver rate used to assign manufacturing overhead to its products. Prepare a memo explaining whether it is advisable for Premier Pasta to use an average cost-driver rate for all jobs.

[CMA adapted]

Problem 3.55
Journal Entries in Job-Order Costing
(LO 2, 3, 4, 5)

Spreadsheet

Pittsburgh Pump Corporation manufactures bilge pumps for small boats. It uses a job-order costing system. Normal costing is used, and manufacturing overhead is applied on the basis of machine hours. Estimated manufacturing overhead for the year is $1,464,000, and management expects that 73,200 machine hours will be used.

Required

a. Calculate the company's predetermined overhead rate for the year.

b. Prepare journal entries to record the following events, which occurred during April.

1. Purchased pump impellers from Marion Corporation for $7,850 on account.
2. Processed requisition from the Gauge Department supervisor for 300 pounds of clear plastic. The material cost $ .60 per pound when it was purchased.
3. Processed the Testing Department's requisition for 300 feet of electrical wire, which is considered an indirect material. The wire cost $ .10 per foot when it was purchased.
4. Paid on electric utility bill of $800 in cash.
5. Incurred direct-labor costs of $75,000 in April.
6. Recorded April's insurance cost of $1,800 for insurance on the cars driven by sales personnel. The policy had been prepaid in March.
7. Purchased metal tubing costing $3,000 on account.
8. Made cash payment of $1,700 on outstanding accounts payable.
9. Incurred indirect-labor costs of $21,000 during April.
10. Recorded depreciation of $7,000 on equipment for April.
11. Finished job G22 during April at a total cost of $1,100.

12. Used 7,000 machine hours during April.
13. Made sales on account for April of $176,000. The April cost of goods sold was $139,000.

Problem 3.56
Missing Data; Cost Flows; Income Statement
(LO 2, 3, 5)

A hysterical I. M. Dunce corners you in the hallway 30 minutes before accounting class. "Help me, help me!" I. M. pleads. "I woke up this morning and discovered that my pet German Shepherds Fifo and Lifo ate my homework, and these shredded pieces are all that I have left!" Being a kind and generous soul, you willingly declare, "There's no need to fear! I'm a real whiz at accounting and will be glad to help you." A relieved I. M. Dunce hands you the following torn homework remnants.

	Page 1
Direct-labor hours used	125
Direct-labor rate per hour	$ 15
Raw material purchased	$ 5,250
Raw material beginning inventory	$ 1,400

	Page 2
Manufacturing overhead (actual = applied)	$ 750
Beginning work-in-process inventory	1,500
Cost of goods manufactured	8,000
Ending finished-goods inventory	3,000

	Page 3
Job remaining in ending work-in-process inventory:	
Direct labor	$ 500
Direct material	1,300
Overhead ($2 per labor hour)	200
Ending work-in-process inventory	$ 2,000
Total revenue	$13,500
Gross margin	4,000
Marketing and administrative costs	
Operating profit	1,000

Required

a. Prepare T-accounts to show the flow of costs and determine each of the following:
   1. Selling and administrative costs.
   2. Cost of goods sold.
   3. Beginning finished-goods inventory.
   4. Direct material used.
   5. Ending raw-material inventory.

b. Prepare an income statement.

Problem 3.57
Job Costs in a Service Company
(LO 2, 3, 5, 7)

On June 1, two jobs were in process at McHale Painters, Inc. Details of the jobs follow:

Job No.	Direct Material	Direct Labor
A-15	$174	$64
A-38	32	84

Material inventory (for example, paint and sandpaper) on June 1 totaled $920, and $116 in material was purchased during the month. Indirect material of $16 was withdrawn from material inventory. On June 1, finished-goods inventory consisted of two jobs: A-07, costing $392, and A-21, costing $158. Both jobs were transferred to Cost of Goods Sold during the month.

Also during June, jobs A-15 and A-38 were completed. To complete job A-15 required an additional $68 in direct labor. The completion costs for job A-38 included $108 in direct material and $200 in direct labor.

Job A-40 was started during the period but was not finished. A total of $314 of direct material was used (excluding the $16 indirect material) during the period, and total direct-labor costs during the month amounted to $408. Manufacturing overhead has been estimated at 150 percent of direct-labor costs, and this relationship has been the same for the past few years.

Required

Compute the costs of jobs A-15 and A-38 and the balances in the June 30 inventory accounts.

Problem 3.58
Missing Data; Cost Flows
(LO 2, 3, 5)

A disastrous fire struck the only manufacturing plant of Badomen Equipment, Inc., on December 1. All work-in-process inventory was destroyed, but a few records were salvaged from the wreckage and the company's headquarters. The insurance company has stated that it will pay the cost of the lost inventory if adequate documentation can be supplied. The insurable value of work-in-process inventory consists of direct material, direct labor, and applied manufacturing overhead.

The following information about the plant appears on the October financial statements:

Raw-material inventory, October 31	$ 49,000
Work-in-process inventory, October 31	86,200
Finished-goods inventory, October 31	32,000
Cost of goods sold through October 31	348,600
Accounts payable (raw material suppliers) on October 31	21,600
Manufacturing overhead through October 31	184,900
Payroll payable on October 31	0
Withholding and other payroll liabilities on October 31	9,700
Manufacturing overhead applied through October 31	179,600

A count of the inventories on hand November 30 shows

Raw-material inventory	$43,000
Work-in-process inventory	?
Finished-goods inventory	37,500

The accounts payable clerk tells you that outstanding bills to suppliers totaled $50,100 and that cash payments of $37,900 were made to them during the month. The payroll clerk informs you that the payroll costs last month for the manufacturing section included $82,400 of which $14,700 was indirect labor.

At the end of November, the following balances were available:

Manufacturing overhead through November 30	$217,000
Cost of goods sold through November 30	396,600

Recall that each month there is only one requisition for indirect material. Among the fragments of paper, you located the following information:

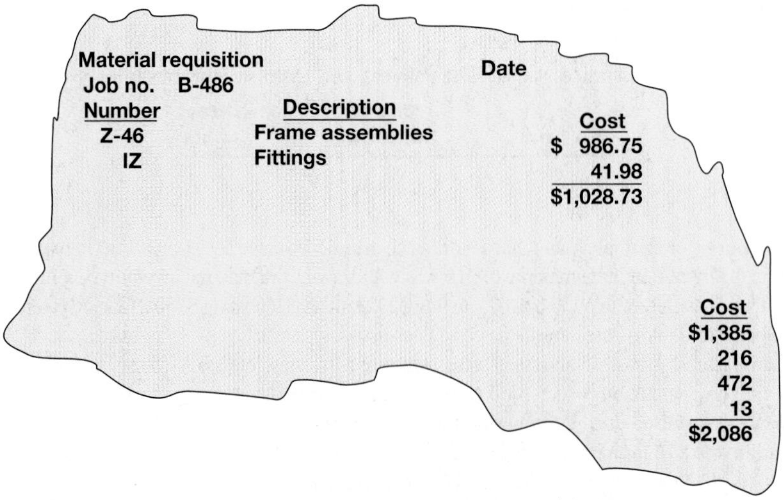

You also learn that the overhead during the month was overapplied by $1,200.

Required

Determine the cost of the work-in-process inventory lost in the disaster.

Problem 3.59
Incomplete Data; Job-Order Costing
(LO 2, 3, 5)

Communication

Pinnelas Printing, Inc., is a rapidly growing company that has not been profitable despite increases in sales. It has hired you as a consultant to find ways to improve the situation. You believe that the problem results from poor cost control and inaccurate cost estimation on jobs. To gather data for your investigation, you turn to the accounting system and find that it is almost nonexistent. However, you piece together the following information for April:

- Production
  1. Completed job 101.
  2. Started and completed job 102.
  3. Started job 103.
- Inventory values:
  1. Work-in-process inventory:

March 31: Job 101	
Direct material	$ 2,000
Labor (960 hours × $10)	9,600
April 30: Job 103	
Direct material	$11,600
Labor (1,040 hours × $10)	10,400

  2. Each job in work-in-process inventory was exactly 50 percent completed as to labor hours; however, all direct material necessary to do the entire job was charged to each job as soon as it was started.
  3. There were no raw-material inventories or finished-goods inventories at either March 31 or April 30.
- Actual manufacturing overhead was $20,000.
- Cost of goods sold (before adjustment for over- or underapplied overhead):

Job 101	
Direct material	$ 2,000
Labor	?
Overhead	?
Total	$30,800
Job 102	
Direct material	?
Labor	?
Overhead	?
Total	?

- Overhead was applied to jobs using a predetermined rate per labor dollar that has been used since the company began operations.
- All raw materials were purchased for cash and charged directly to Work-in-Process Inventory when purchased. Raw material purchased in April amounted to $4,600.
- Direct-labor costs charged to jobs in April totaled $32,000. All labor costs were the same per hour for April for all laborers.

Required

Write a report to management to show the following:

a. The cost elements (direct material, labor, and overhead) of cost of goods sold before adjustment for over- or underapplied overhead for each job sold.

b. The value of each cost element (direct material, labor, and overhead) for each job in work-in-process inventory at April 30.

c. Over- or underapplied overhead for April.

Problem 3.60
Gantt Chart
(LO 8)

Prepare a Gantt chart for the following business plan. Use one week as the incremental time interval.

a. Select a cross-functional planning team, duration two weeks.

b. Hold twice-weekly meetings until the plan is implemented.

c. Identify products or services to meet market needs, consistent with the organization's mission, six weeks, which can begin as soon as the team is assembled.

d. Select team information needs and technology, two weeks; can begin as soon as the team is assembled.

e. Select production technology, two weeks; can begin two weeks before the product or service is finalized.

f. Determine advertising, promotion, and distribution needs and methods, four weeks; can begin two weeks before the product or service is finalized.

g. Set the selling price and allowable (target) product or service cost, one week; can begin when the product or service is finalized.

h. Prepare budgeted sales, cost, and profitability forecasts, two weeks; can begin one week before the product or service is finalized.

i. Design the product or service to meet customer needs, sales price, and allowable cost, six weeks; can begin after sales price and allowable cost are determined.

j. Develop prototype product or service, four weeks; can begin three weeks after beginning design phase.

k. Test market the product or service, four weeks; can begin after the prototype is complete.

l. Present business plan and prototype to executive committee, one week; can begin after test marketing is complete.

Problem 3.61
Gantt Chart
(LO 8)

Prepare a Gantt chart for the following construction project for which you have plans and financing. Use one week as the incremental time interval.

a. Find a suitable location, duration 6 weeks.

b. Hire a construction team, duration 2 weeks; can begin after the site is found.

c. Obtain necessary permits, duration 2 weeks; can begin one week prior to finding the site.

d. Order and receive building materials, 1 week; can begin at any time.

e. Construct building, 8 weeks; can begin after the permits are obtained.

f. Add actual activities after learning that finding the site will take 7 weeks and permits will take 3 weeks.

Problem 3.62
Job Costing and Ethics
(LO 6, 7)

Ethics

Suzie Garcia, an accountant for a consulting firm, had just received the monthly cost reports for the two jobs she supervises: one for Arrow Space, Inc., and one for the US government. She immediately called her boss after reading the figures for the Arrow Space job.

"We're going to be way over budget on the Arrow Space contract," she informed her boss. "The job is only about three-fourths complete, but we've spent all the money that we had budgeted for the entire job."

"You'd better watch these job costs more carefully in the future," her boss advised. "Meanwhile, charge the rest of the costs needed to complete the Arrow Space job to the government job. The government won't notice the extra costs. Besides, we get reimbursed for costs on the government job, so we won't lose any money because of this problem you have with the Arrow Space contract."

Required

a. What should Garcia do?

b. Does it matter that Garcia's company is reimbursed for costs on the US government contract? Explain.

Case

Case 3.63
Motion Picture Project Accounting
(LO 1, 7)

Hollywood accounting can be every bit as creative as a good movie script. At least, that is what some lawyers and journalists seem to be telling us. According to news reports, the hit movie *Forrest Gump,* which won "best picture" honors at the Academy Awards, claimed a worldwide theatrical gross of $661 million in the first 18 months after its release. That amount excludes videocassette and soundtrack revenues, nor does it include licensing fees on Forrest Gump products such as wristwatches, ping-pong paddles, and shrimp cookbooks. Yet, according to Paramount Studios, the film project lost $62 million on a box office gross of $382 million during its first year.

Forrest Gump is one of a string of hit movies to report a loss. Other losers include *Batman, Rain Man, Dick Tracy, Ghostbusters, Alien, On Golden Pond, Fatal Attraction,* and *Coming to America.* Each of these motion pictures grossed well over $100 million, but in each case, costs were reportedly higher than revenues.

How can the studios be losing so much money on their most successful projects? Sometimes what is referred to as a loss is not really a loss at all. Typically, profits are calculated based on contracts between the studios and the film's "net profit participants." In a typical net profit participation contract, "profit" is gross studio revenues after deducting:

- "Negative costs"—production costs and payments to "gross participants" (who receive a percentage of gross studio revenues).
- Studio overhead (some of which is allocated to the film as a percentage of the gross revenue).
- Promotion and distribution costs.
- Advertising overhead (which is computed as a percentage of promotion and distribution costs).
- A distribution fee paid directly to the studio.
- Interest on the unrecovered costs (losses), whether or not the film was financed with debt.

The net profit participation contract is not the same as profit or loss for the motion picture, which is accounted for as a project or job. Net profit participation is a contract for compensation between the studio and certain individuals.

Winston Groom, the author of *Forrest Gump,* retained an attorney to obtain a share of the profits from the film, although Paramount reported a loss. Groom was paid $350,000 for the movie rights to the book and is entitled to 3 percent of the film's net profits. Paramount says it expects *Forrest Gump* to eventually show a profit and has advanced Groom $250,000 against his net profit participation.

At issue in the lawsuit is the way the studios calculate net profit. Critics argue that some of the costs (such as the distribution fee), are not really costs at all; instead, they are studio profits disguised as costs. Overhead allocations, such as studio overhead and advertising overhead, are based on arbitrary allocations, which, some have argued, are much higher than the actual overhead costs that are assignable to the film. In addition, whether the net profit participants should lose compensation because of cost overruns is questionable; they are largely under the control of the director, the stars, and the studio.

Will Paramount ever report a profit for *Forrest Gump?* That depends on how you define "profit" and whose perspective you take. Actor Tom Hanks and director Robert Zemeckis have already made more than $20 million each, including a share of the gross. But from the point of view of the net profit participants (e.g., Winston Groom), the film might never show a profit.

Required

Examine the net profit participant statement of profit and loss on page 138.

a. What amount of box office gross revenues is required before *Forrest Gump* earns a profit according to the net profit participation contract?

b. What amount of box office gross revenues is required before *Forrest Gump* earns a profit for Paramount?

c. Is Paramount's calculation of net profit fair to the net profit participants?

Net Profit Participant Statement of Profit and Loss
Forrest Gump
During Its First Year of Release (in millions)

Box office gross revenues		$382
Less: Amount retained by movie theaters (50%)		191
Studio's gross revenues		$191
Less: Negative costs:		
Production costs	$66.8	
Gross profit participation (director, actors, 16% of studio gross revenues)	30.6	
Studio's overhead (15% of negative costs)	14.6	
Promotion and distribution costs	67.2	
Advertising overhead (10% of promotion and distribution cost)	6.7	
Distribution fee (32% of studio gross revenue)	61.1	
Total operating costs	$ 247	
Operating profit (loss)		(56)
Less: Financing costs (3% above prime on operating loss, assume amount is fixed)		6
Net profit (loss) for distribution to net profit participants		$ (62)

[Adapted from "Forrest Gump—Accountant," a case by G. Pfeiffer, R. Capettini, and G. Whittenburg.]

PART

II

Activity-Based Management

A Look Back

Part I introduced cost management. It discussed managing the value chain, cost system design, and measuring product costs.

A Look at This Part

Part II builds cost management tools to help understand production processes. The topics in this part are recent innovations in the field of cost management. Chapter 4 discusses activity-based costing. Chapter 5 discusses activity-based management. Chapter 6 discusses customer profitability analysis. Chapter 7 discusses the management of quality and time to create value.

A Look Ahead

Part III discusses process costing and cost allocation.

CHAPTER

4

Activity-Based Costing Systems

After completing this chapter you should be able to:

1. Describe how traditional costing could lead to undercosting and overcosting products.
2. Discuss the four steps used in an activity-based costing system.
3. Identify five different levels of resources and activities used in production processes.
4. Estimate the cost of activities and calculate a cost-driver rate.
5. Assign activity costs to goods and services.
6. Analyze the profitability of products and customers.
7. Apply activity-based costing to service and merchandising companies.
8. Distinguish between ABC unit-level costing and ABC full costing of goods and services (Appendix).

Cost-Management Challenges

1. **How** did activity-based cost information help PMI, Inc.?
2. **What** data and knowledge are necessary to support the development of activity-based information?
3. **Is** activity-based information always better than traditional costing information?

PMI Precision Molding, Inc.

The following is the transcript of a recent conference call between Grant Peterson, North American vice president of logistics for MegaBurger Corporation, and the executive staff of Precision Molding, Inc. (PMI). MegaBurger Corporation is one of the world's largest fast-food restaurant chains. PMI is a small company that specializes in plastic-injection molding. Melody Fairchild, president and chief executive officer of PMI, responds to his comments and questions.

Peterson, MegaBurger: Good morning, Melody. Thank you for getting your staff together on such short notice.

Fairchild, PMI: My pleasure. Let me introduce you to the rest of the team. Chad Norris is vice president of manufacturing, Alex Lewis is chief financial officer, and Michael Chia is our vice president of logistics.

Peterson, MegaBurger: Hello, all. Thanks for joining us. Let me outline what we are proposing. We need someone to supply promotional novelty toys, such as action figures and movie tie-ins, to one of our regions, and we believe PMI can do the job. You have a good reputation for quality products, ethical business practices, and community service. PMI is the type of company with which we like to be associated.

We want you and our current supplier in the region to submit bids for this business. Quite frankly, we've been disappointed with our current supplier's business practices, and we're prepared to offer you the business if you show that PMI can supply a quality product with on-time delivery and at a reasonable price.

Fairchild, PMI: Grant, our record for quality and on-time delivery is superb. I believe you've already checked with our current customers to verify that. We're confident that we can exceed your expectations. Before we submit a bid to you, we need to know details about products and distribution to fully evaluate this opportunity.

Peterson, MegaBurger: Melody, you should be receiving a fax with product and delivery specifications. This includes our expected sales and distribution, and, as you know, this is very sensitive information. Before we send this, I must have your agreement that this information stays within PMI.

Fairchild, PMI: Agreed. When do you need our response?

Peterson, MegaBurger: We need your bid within 90 days. I'll be out of the country for the next few weeks, so please contact my assistant if you need more information. Any questions now?

Fairchild, PMI: No, this is clear. We just received your fax. If we have any questions about it, I'll be in touch. Have a safe trip.

PMI Background

"What an opportunity! Can we win this business? Can we profitably supply novelty toys to MegaBurger? I don't know at this time, but we'd better figure it out!" Fairchild exclaimed to her executive team as she hung up the phone.

The small novelty toys are more complex than any product PMI has made. MegaBurger also has very high expectations for quality and on-time deliveries. Winning this bid could mean a large increase in PMI's sales and create future opportunities to partner with MegaBurger, which is a global giant. Fairchild was eager to expand PMI's customer base because she believed the company was too dependent on just two customers. However, she knew that if PMI did not evaluate this opportunity realistically, the company could suffer large losses on the MegaBurger business. Such a mistake could mean disaster for the company's employees and stockholders.

PMI's Competitive Situation

PMI, Inc., founded in 1981, had become one of the dominant manufacturers of plastic, injection-molded products in its geographical region. It emphasized consistent quality, quick order turnaround, reliable distribution, and reasonable prices, with a high level of service. PMI outsourced certain parts of its value chain to suppliers and machine shops that have been reliable business partners since the early 1980s. CEO Fairchild believes that decisions such as selective outsourcing have allowed the company to focus on its primary competitive advantages, which are careful design, quality production, and a high level of customer service.

Until recently, PMI had very little competition, in part because of its long-term contracts with a national discount retail company and an international company that produces products for baby care (such as baby carriers and strollers).

PMI was a small company that, although profitable, could ill afford to make mistakes by doing unprofitable work. PMI's management knew that it must accurately measure the costs of its current processes and apply those costs to current and future products. To prepare its bid for the MegaBurger business, PMI had to have good estimates of the costs to produce the novelty toys. Management needed accurate cost information so it could propose a product price that would ensure the business's profitability. Companies that submit low-price bids to prospective customers often find to their dismay that they have won an unprofitable bid because the prices that they charged were below their costs.

PMI's Products and Processes

We need some background information. PMI's current plastic products range from relatively simple items, such as reusable 1 and 4 liter beverage containers for a national discount retail chain, to complex products, such as plastic baby carriers and strollers. The simple beverage containers require blowing liquefied plastic into a mold, sometimes combining it with different colors for different types of drinks (e.g., green for ginger ale). The more complicated baby-care products, which are under exclusive contract for an international firm, have multiple, complex parts that require complicated molds and precise control over colors, injection pressures, and temperatures. PMI's ability to make these complex products attracted MegaBurger's attention.

The company purchases small plastic pellets that are heated to make liquid plastic, which is put through a process known as "injection molding" that molds the plastic into the desired shapes. See Exhibit 4–1 for the steps involved in the production process:

- Purge or clean the system before each production run to prevent contamination by dirt or leftover plastic and color.
- Set up the machine to ensure that order data are recorded properly and that machine settings are correct for the product.
- Begin the production run to verify production data and ensure that the machine is operating properly; then start the full-scale operation of the run.
- Perform the actual production run.
- Remove products from the mold and visually inspect them to ensure that they meet visual quality standards.
- Recycle defective products to reduce waste and prevent defective products from reaching customers.
- Place good products in inventory in preparation for delivery to customers.
- End the production run so that the machinery and work area are left in a safe, clean condition.

PMI's Costing-System Options

PMI could use a simple cost system, such as the ones discussed in Chapter 3, or a more complex cost system, such as the one discussed in this chapter. In choosing among alternative cost systems, PMI managers must assess the costs and benefits of their choice. The simpler system requires less effort and time but provides less accurate cost estimates. The more complex system requires more effort and time but provides more accurate cost estimates. In general, company managers will weigh the benefits of more accurate cost estimates against the time and effort required to obtain them.

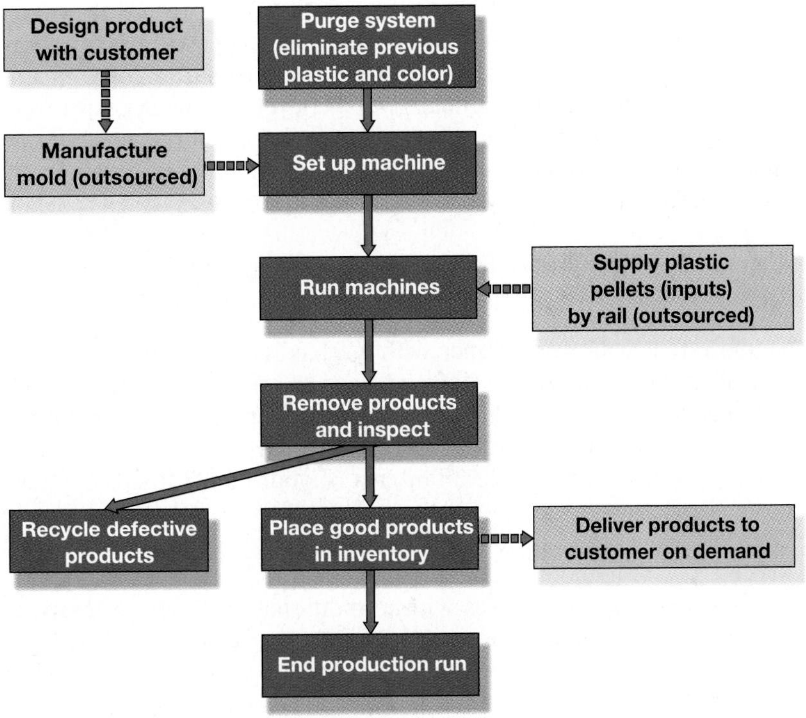

Exhibit 4–1
Injection-Molding Process at PMI

PMI's Costing-System Team

CEO Fairchild knew that reliable cost-management information would be critically important to PMI as it prepared the bid for the MegaBurger business. Accordingly, she asked her chief financial officer (CFO), Alex Lewis, to form the best team possible to prepare the bid for MegaBurger. He already had three top-notch employees in mind. These included a recently hired finance employee, who had just received her MBA with top honors, and a production supervisor with 20 years of experience in the industry, mostly with other companies. The final team member was an employee who worked in product design and did a good deal of consulting with customers who had several years of experience with the company. Lewis realized that the team also would need information from other company employees in all areas, including human resources and information technology, although these people would not be part of the formal team.

The team formed by Lewis discussed different costing-system alternatives with the company's accounting personnel. The team's goal was to find an accounting system to measure the costs of existing products as accurately as possible. The team planned to use this information to estimate the costs of the novelty toys to produce for MegaBurger. Team members knew that MegaBurger's novelty toys would require many of the same activities already being used for existing PMI products. Thus, members believed that using historical data and adjusting these data for differences, such as differences in the costs of materials, would be appropriate for estimating the costs of the MegaBurger toys.

Traditional Costing System

The traditional cost system that many companies use does not trace indirect costs, such as supervisors' salaries and utilities, directly to the product. Instead, using a traditional cost system, companies allocate indirect costs to the product using an allocation base such as direct-labor hours or machine hours. We discussed this type of cost system in Chapter 3.

The advantage of a traditional cost system is its simplicity. However, the saying "you get what you pay for," is appropriate here. The resulting cost data are typically not as accurate as those that more complex and expensive cost systems provide.

Nevertheless, a traditional cost system can be sufficient to meet managers' cost-information requirements, particularly if the level of indirect costs is relatively low compared to direct costs and if the accuracy of cost information is not critical to the company's success. Managers of organizations using a traditional cost system might decide that the costs to implement a more complex cost system are higher than its potential benefits.

Undercosting and Overcosting Products: Cost of Dinner Example

LO 1 Describe how traditional costing could lead to undercosting and overcosting products.

Suppose that you go to dinner with a friend to celebrate the end of finals week at school. You order an entrée ($8) and a cup of specialty coffee ($3). Your friend orders an appetizer ($6), a salad ($5), an entrée ($10), and dessert with coffee ($8). You agree to split the bill at the end of the evening, which means each of you will pay $20 (excluding the tip!). Is this $20 a fair cost of your meal? It is not; your meal was overcosted because you simply took an average of the entire cost of the two dinners. If you were to track the cost of your meal more precisely, your cost would be $11 ($3 + $8), and the cost to your friend would be $29.

A similar problem arises with a traditional cost system. Many companies have found that this system tends to assign costs to products based on an arbitrarily developed average rather than the actual resource usage. As a result, products that are more complex to build and consume more resources (for example, more inspections, machine setups, materials, etc.) are not necessarily assigned their fair share of costs. Instead, many of these complex products' costs could be unfairly assigned to simpler products. Thus, the complex products are undercosted, and the simple products are overcosted. Note the similarity of this problem and the shared dinner bill. Using a simple average of the total meal cost overcosted your simple meal and undercosted your friend's more complex meal.

Refining a Traditional Costing System

Clearly, the traditional costing system has a number of weaknesses, including the problem of undercosting and overcosting products as mentioned. A refined costing system allows for more accurate costing of goods and services. Three key points should be made with respect to refining a traditional costing system.

1. Trace as many costs directly to the good or service as possible, as long as the cost of doing so does not outweigh the benefit. For example, when you and your friend split the dinner tab, you could easily have traced all costs to each of you, thereby resulting in a more accurate assignment of costs.
2. Categorize indirect costs, which are not easily traced to the product, into cost pools. **Cost pools** are groups of individual cost items; costs with similar cost drivers or allocation bases are grouped together. Ideally, match the costs with allocation bases or cost drivers that have a cause-and-effect relationship with the cost. For example, group together all indirect costs driven by machine usage, such as those for machine maintenance and the energy to run the machines.

   Continue this categorization until all indirect costs have been appropriately grouped into pools. Most companies do not allocate some of the administrative costs of running the business to products because these costs are peripheral to the company's production activity.

cost pools *are groups or categories of individual cost items*

3. Use **cost allocation** to assign indirect costs to products. Select an appropriate cost-allocation base for each cost pool established in item 2. Ideally, the allocation base has a causal relationship to the cost pool, so if a particular cost pool has costs driven by machine usage, the amount of time the machine is used (e.g., minutes or hours) is an appropriate cost-allocation base.

cost allocation *assigns indirect costs to products or organizational units (e.g., departments)*

Activity-Based Costing System

LO 2 Discuss the four steps used in an activity-based costing system.

Activity-based costing is a commonly used approach to improve a traditional costing system. **Activity-based costing**, or **ABC**, is a costing method that first assigns costs to activities and then to goods and services based on how much each good or service uses the activities. As defined in Chapter 2, an *activity* is any discrete task that an organization undertakes to make or deliver a good or service. To reduce the cost of goods and services, managers must modify the activities required to produce the goods and services.

activity-based costing (ABC) *is a costing method that first assigns costs to activities and then to goods and services based on how much each good or service uses the activities.*

An increasing number of companies around the world are using ABC systems. To name a few, American Airlines, Hewlett-Packard, Daimler-Chrysler, and the United States Postal Service use or have used it. As noted in Cost Management in Practice 4.1, a survey of 177 companies in the United Kingdom indicated that 37.8 percent of the companies surveyed were using or considering using ABC. Results from this study and similar ones in developed economies around the world indicate that ABC is not a passing fad. A majority of companies still use traditional costing methods such as those discussed in Chapter 3, but the use of ABC appears to be increasing.

Note that ABC is used to establish product costs primarily for decision-making purposes, such as whether to continue offering a product, not for inventory valuation for external reporting.

Cost Management in Practice 4.1

Use of Activity-Based Costing

Activity-based costing has maintained a high profile as a cost-management innovation for about two decades. Enough time has passed to assess whether it is a passing fad. Studies of company practices indicate that a large number of manufacturing and service companies, as well as some organizations in the public sector, are using ABC.

Some companies have tried ABC and dropped it. Reasons for this include its implementation cost. In the case of a Hewlett-Packard division that one of the authors studied, management obtained a great deal of information from ABC, restructured activities as a result, and no longer had the problems that ABC had uncovered. ABC had served its purpose and was no longer needed.

A recent survey of practices in the United Kingdom indicated that 37.8 percent of the companies that provided usable responses were using ABC or were considering using it. The study reported these results:

ABC Adoption Status	Number of Companies in Study	Percent of Companies in Study
Currently using it	31	17.5%
Currently considering using it	36	20.3
Considered but rejected it	27	15.3
Had not considered using it	83	46.9
Total	177	100.0%

Although ABC has its roots in manufacturing companies, the study found that the financial services companies surveyed were more likely to use ABC than were manufacturing companies. *Source: J. Innes, F. Mitchell, and D. Sinclair,* "Activity-Based Costing in the U.K.'s Largest Companies." *(Full citations to references are in the Bibliography.)*

Four steps are used to determine the cost of goods and services using ABC. The following briefly summarizes those four steps. Much of this chapter is devoted to discussing them in detail.

An **activity dictionary** *is a list of activities performed by an organization to produce its products*

Step 1: *Identify and classify the activities related to the company's products.* Activities in all areas of the value chain (product design, production, marketing, distribution, etc.) must be included. People identify the activities that a company performs to produce a product and prepare a list called an **activity dictionary** of these activities. The activity dictionary can be obtained in a number of different ways, including interviews with the employees who perform the activities. As activities are identified, they are classified as unit level, batch level, product level, customer level, or facility level. We discuss these classifications shortly.

Step 2: *Estimate the cost of activities identified in step 1.* Estimate the costs of specific activities that cause costs. These costs are for both *human resources,* such as employee labor for production and machine maintenance, and *physical resources,* such as the cost of machinery and building occupancy. Information must include employee data from personnel interviews and financial data from the accounting department. Then calculate the total cost of each activity.

Step 3: *Calculate a cost-driver rate for each activity.* The activity cost data from step 2 is used to calculate a cost-driver rate that the company can use for assigning activity costs to goods and services. This rate should use a base that has some causal link to the cost. For example, costs of running a production machine are likely caused by the number of hours it is run. Thus, choosing a rate for this activity based on machine hours is wise.

Step 4: *Assign activity costs to products.* The cost-driver rates prepared in step 3 are used to assign activity costs to goods and services. For example, if a particular product uses 1.5 machine hours in production and the rate from step 3 is $50 per hour, the product is assigned $75 based on its machine usage.

Upon completing these four steps, a company can calculate the costs to provide existing goods and services, which can be used to better understand the profitability of each. The activity-based costing data also could be used to estimate the cost of future products.

After discussing the costing-system alternatives, PMI's team decided to use an activity-based costing (ABC) system and at this point became known as the "ABC team," which we shall use in this chapter. First, the team would use ABC to identify the cost of existing products and then it would adjust this cost information as necessary to estimate the cost to produce the MegaBurger products.

Step 1: Identify and Classify Activities Related to Products

Bakery Example

LO 3 Identify five different levels of resources and activities used in production processes.

How would you identify the activities performed to produce goods and services? Imagine for the moment that you own a bakery that makes and sells a variety of cookies. You simply list all activities required to make them. The major categories of activities include purchasing the materials, mixing the dough, forming the cookies, baking, performing quality control through taste tests, and packaging or displaying the cookies. (Performing quality control should be one of the more desirable activities.) Your activity list might have many details. For example, the baking activity might include subactivities such as warming the oven, watching the cookies to prevent burning, washing the pans, and cleaning the oven.

Five-Level Hierarchy of Resources and Activities

unit-level resources and activities *are acquired and performed specifically for individual units of product or service*

batch-level resources and activities *are acquired and performed to make a group, or batch, of similar products*

Analyzing all resources and activities needed to produce and support a company's products and services is made easier by recognizing that these resources and activities support different levels of the company, which are described here. Examples are based on the bakery business.

1. **Unit-level resources and activities.** These are resources acquired and activities performed specifically for individual units of product or service. *Unit resources* could include materials, parts, and components and perhaps labor and energy resources if they are acquired for each unit of output. *Unit activities* could include work efforts that transform the resources into individual products and services. Unit-level resources and activities are directly traceable to units of output.

   In our bakery example, the materials (e.g., dough, chocolate chips) for cookies are unit-level resources because each cookie produced requires them. At PMI, the materials used to make products were part of the unit-level resources.

Bakery workers inspect the quality of batches of product.

2. **Batch-level resources and activities.** These are the resources acquired and the activities performed to make a group, or batch, of similar products. *Batch activities* usually include the work

performed to set up the production machinery to produce a certain batch (i.e., group) of products or to test quality control for a batch of product. Batch-level resources include the expenditure of labor to set up and test machines. Batch-level resources and activities are directly traceable to certain batches but are indirect to the individual units produced.

We return to the bakery example. Mixing the cookie dough for each batch of cookies, placing the batch in the oven, and testing for quality control when the batch comes out of the oven (or even before it goes into the oven) are included in this category because these are required to make a batch of cookies but are indirect activities of one particular cookie.

product-level resources and activities *are acquired and performed to produce and sell a specific good or service*

3. **Product-level resources and activities.** These are the resources acquired and the activities performed to produce and sell a specific good or service. *Product resources* could include specialized equipment, software, and personnel that would not be needed except to provide that particular product. *Product activities* could include the design or advertisement of a particular product. Product-level resources and activities are directly traceable to specific goods or services but are indirectly related to batches or individual units produced.

   Assume that our bakery produces several different types of cookies (peanut butter, chocolate chip, etc.). Developing or purchasing the recipe for each type of cookie is in this category since a recipe is required for each cookie type (product) produced. Furthermore, if a special mixing machine were required for a particular type of cookie (e.g., cream-filled bran cookies), the cost of that particular mixing machine is a product-level resource.

customer-level resources and activities *are acquired and performed to serve specific customers*

4. **Customer-level resources and activities.** These are the resources acquired and the activities performed to serve specific customers. *Customer resources* could include specialized equipment, software, and personnel dedicated to serving specific customers. *Customer activities* could include consulting with customers and making special distribution arrangements for specific customer requirements (e.g., using an air-freight service instead of normal ground service because of a particular customer's needs).

   Suppose that a customer at our bakery asked us to produce 1,000 cookies in the shape of its company logo for which we had to design a special mold. The special mold is a customer-level resource because only this customer requires it.

facility-level resources and activities *are acquired and performed to provide the general capacity to produce goods and services*

5. **Facility-level resources and activities.** These are the resources acquired and the activities performed to provide the general capacity to produce goods and services. *Facility resources* could include land, buildings, and, in some cases, the labor force, which some companies maintain without laying people off despite changes in products, customers, batches, and units of output. *Facility activities* could include the activities of plant or store managers, research and development, and companywide advertising versus product-specific advertising.

   Facility-level resources and activities are directly related to the scale, scope, and location of operations but are indirectly related to customers, products, batches, or individual units produced. The cost of the space leased by our bakery is in this category.

   Ford Motor Company's advertising of the Ford Explorer is in the product-level category. If Ford sponsors a public television program to promote the company's brand name, however, this advertising is in the facility-level category.

Classification Objectives

The objectives of classifying resources and activities into the five categories are to create (1) accurate descriptions of how the organization performs its work and (2) the ability to trace the cost of resources acquired and activities performed to goods and services produced.

Methods for Identifying and Classifying Activities

Organizations generate their activity lists in a variety of ways, including these:

Top-down approach. Some organizations use ABC teams of people at the middle-management level or above. The primary advantage to this top-down approach is that generating the activity dictionary is quick and inexpensive. A large consumer products company used this approach to develop activity dictionaries for many of its operations.[1] FirstData Corporation uses a variation of this approach by slightly modifying a predefined (or boiler plate) activity dictionary based on years of experience with each business unit's processes.[2]

Interview or participative approach. This approach relies on the inclusion of operating employees on the team and/or interviews with them. For example, PMI's ABC team would interview production personnel to identify and understand the activities involved to produce the product. This approach is likely to generate a more accurate activity dictionary than is the top-down approach because individuals doing the work actually provide the information.

One danger associated with the interview or participative approach, however, is that employees might not disclose their activities truthfully if they are concerned about the possible effects of giving higher-level management specific information about what they actually do. Another danger is that employees might not recall their work processes accurately.

Recycling approach. Reusing documentation of processes developed for other purposes is possible. (That is, "Don't reinvent the wheel.") Many companies, for example, have sought and achieved ISO 9000 certification, which requires thorough documentation of their processes.[3] Recycling this documentation into an activity dictionary can be relatively straightforward.

PMI's Activity List

We now return to PMI to describe how the ABC team performed step 1 of the ABC process, identifying and classifying activities related to the company's products.

The ABC team decided to start to establish a list of its activities using the recycling approach because the company had recently identified activities in the production process while preparing for ISO 9000 certification. The team rejected the top-down approach not only because information was already available but also because team members believed that input from all levels of the organization (including production personnel) was needed.

See Exhibit 4–2 for the information for ISO 9000 certification used to list PMI's activities. The ABC team organized this list according to the categories just discussed (unit, batch, etc.). Exhibit 4–2 includes only major categories of PMI's total list to keep the list short; note that Exhibit 4–2 refers to "detailed subactivities omitted" in several places).

The first digit in the left column of the activity list or dictionary in Exhibit 4–2 is the most general activity (e.g., 1.), and the third digit represents the most detailed activity shown. Everything listed under activity 1 refers to unit-level activities and

---

[1] F. Selto, "Implementing Activity-Based Management." (Full citations to references are in the Bibliography.)

[2] D. Carlson and S. M. Young, "Activity-Based Total Quality Management at American Express." (At the time of the article, the majority owner of FirstData Corp. was American Express. It has since become an independent entity.) Brian Higgins of FirstData Corp., an early developer of activity analysis, believes that approximately 200 to 300 activities are sufficient to describe all of the processes of medium-size (less than 1,000 employees) organizations.

[3] The International Organization of Standardization (ISO) based in Geneva administers ISO 9000 certification of companies who either desire or are required by customers to certify the quality of their processes. Many books, articles, and Internet sites are devoted to this certification. Go to *www.isonet.com.*

Exhibit 4–2

PMI, Inc., Activity and Resource List

PMI

Activity/Resource	
Number	**Description**
1.	**Unit Level**
1.1	Acquire and use materials for containers
1.1.1	Medium-grade plastic pellets
1.1.2	Colors
1.2	Acquire and use materials for baby-care products
1.2.1	High-grade plastic pellets
1.2.2	Fasteners
1.2.3	Colors
2.	**Batch Level**
2.1	Set up manually controlled injection-molding machines
2.1.1	Set up manually controlled injection-molding machines (detailed subactivities omitted)
2.1.2	Perform quality control of batches of product produced on manually controlled machines
2.2	Set up computer-controlled injection-molding machines
2.2.1	Set up computer-controlled injection-molding machine (detailed subactivities omitted)
2.2.2	Perform quality control of batches of product produced on computer-controlled machines
3.	**Product Level**
3.1	Design and manufacture molds (outsourced)
3.2	Use manually controlled injection-molding machines
3.2.1	Machine depreciation
3.2.2	Machine maintenance
3.2.3	Machine operation—labor
3.3	Use computer-controlled injection-molding machines (detailed subactivities omitted)
4.	**Customer Level**
4.1	Consult with customers
4.2	Provide warehousing for customers
5.	**Facility Level**
5.1	Manage workers
5.2	Use main building
5.2.1	Lease building
5.2.2	Use utilities
5.2.3	Maintain building

resources; everything listed under activity 2 refers to batch-level activities and resources, and so forth for activities 3 through 5. Activity/Resource 1.2.2 refers to the materials fasteners, part of activity 1.2, acquire and use materials for baby-care products, which are part of activity 1, "unit-level" activities.

As you will note, the activity is actually the *acquisition* of the material and its *use* in producing the product. At PMI, the activities' acquisition and use of the materials to produce the product can be stated in the amount paid for the materials, the cost of inspecting and storing them, and other costs related to acquiring them and getting them ready to be used in the production process.

In interviewing production workers, PMI's ABC team asked a question such as, What do you do to prepare to produce a batch of beverage containers? A production-line employee might respond, "I set these dials and insert these colors every time we start a new batch of beverage containers."

Developing the Activity List

Refer to Exhibit 4–2 and the preceding discussion. Put yourself in the role as a member of the ABC team preparing PMI's list of activities.

a. If you were developing PMI's activity list, would you regard the list in Exhibit 4–2 as complete (not considering the subactivities omitted)? Do certain types of activities seem to be missing? Explain.

b. Suppose that people are reluctant to acknowledge that they perform some types of unproductive activities. How should a company's management deal with this problem?

(Solutions begin on page 164.)

You're the Decision Maker 4.1

Step 2: Estimate the Cost of Activities

LO 4 Estimate the cost of activities and calculate a cost-driver rate.

PMI

The next step in the ABC process is to estimate the cost of the activities identified in step 1. PMI's ABC team proceeded by asking all employees to indicate how much time they spent on each activity in an average week and then identified the physical resources that supported various activities.

PMI's Use of the Employee Activity Data Sheet

The employee activity data sheet completed by Margaret Smythe appears as Exhibit 4–3. Before completing this activity data sheet, Smythe indicated which detailed activities from the list in Exhibit 4–2 that she performed. Using the data Smythe provided, the ABC team customized a blank sheet for her by filling in her department, name, title, and the list of activities she had identified. It emailed the customized sheet to Smythe, who added her estimates of the number of hours per typical week that she spent on each activity. After adding this information, she emailed the sheet back to the team, which computed the cost of her time on activities (multiplying Smythe's hours by the hourly salary and benefits; $30 per hour). The ABC team collected data from all of PMI's employees or from the employees' supervisors in the same way.

Checking Employee Activity Data Sheets

Consider the activity data sheet in Exhibit 4–3. Assume the role of a cost analyst who is reviewing such forms that describe how others typically spend their work time.

One worker's activity data sheet showed she worked 80 hours per week. When asked how this was possible on a sustained basis, she replied, "Well, I don't really put in that many hours, but I work twice as efficiently as everyone else in my area. I want to be sure that you realize how much work I'm getting done for the same number of hours. It would take two people to replace me." How would you accommodate this information in your activity analysis?

(Solutions begin on page 164.)

You're the Decision Maker 4.2

Exhibit 4–3

Employee Activity Data Sheet

PMI

Name Margaret Smythe

Title Supervisor

Wages and benefits per hour $30

Activity Number	Activity Description	Hours per Week	Cost
2.2.1	Set up computer-controlled machine	20	$ 600
2.2.2	Perform quality control of batches of product produced on computer-controlled machines	6	180
4.1	Consult with customers	8	240
5.1	Manage workers	6	180
	Total hours	40	$1,200

Activity Data Sheet Combined with Accounting Information

For each activity, the ABC team combined the information collected from employees with data from the accounting and other records. For example, for the activity "provide warehousing for customers" (4.2), the team collected data about the costs to lease warehouse space and insure the products in the warehouse, and about employee time spent performing warehousing activities (e.g., moving products from place to place).

Step 3: Calculate a Cost-Driver Rate for the Activity

Cost-Driver Rates: Bakery Example

A **cost driver** *is a characteristic of an activity or event that causes costs to be incurred by that activity or event*

cost-driver base *is the base used to trace or assign costs to activities*

cost-driver rate *is the estimated cost of resource consumption per unit of cost-driver base for each activity*

The **cost-driver rate** is the estimated cost of resource consumption per unit of the cost-driver for each activity. A **cost driver** is a characteristic of an activity or event that causes costs to be incurred by that activity or event.[4]

Using the bakery as an example, what drives (or causes) the cost of performing maintenance on the mixing machines? An appropriate cost-driver base might be the number of batches produced (the more batches produced, the more maintenance costs incurred). This rate is calculated by dividing the activity cost by the estimated level of activity in the cost-driver base. For example, if the bakery spends $4,800 per year on activities related to maintaining the mixing machine and produces 400 batches of cookies each year, the cost-driver rate is $12 per batch.

An appropriate cost-driver base should:

- Logically have a cause-and-effect relationship with the activity and its costs.
- Be measurable.
- Predict or explain the activity's use of resources with reasonable accuracy.
- Be based on the resource's practical capacity to support activities.

Practical Capacity Note

This last point requires some explanation. Imagine that a warehouse has 1,000 square feet of capacity for storage. If its cost is $1,000, the cost-driver rate is $1 per square foot ($1,000 ÷ 1,000 square feet).

Now suppose that only 800 square feet of the warehouse is used to store product A with the remaining 200 (1000 − 800) square feet unused. Analysts should assign $800 ($1 per square foot × 800 square feet) to Product A and $200 ($1 per square foot × 200 square feet) to "unused capacity." (Recall our discussion in Chapter 2 that distinguished between resources used—the 800 square feet in this example—and unused capacity—the 200 square feet in this example.) The total resources supplied equal 1,000 square feet, but the cost of only the 800 square feet used by product A should be assigned to it.

Assignment of Cost-Driver Rates to PMI's Activities

PMI's ABC team gathered the activity-cost information from all staff as described previously. Then the team decided to use the cost drivers shown in Exhibit 4–4. To simplify the presentation, we condense the activity list in Exhibit 4–2 according to common cost drivers as shown in Exhibit 4–4. This allows us to work with fewer categories of activities in assigning costs to goods and services for product-costing purposes. For

[4]Often in the ABC literature, authors refer to "cost drivers" when they mean the bases used to trace or assign costs. We use the term "cost drivers" to mean the decisions managers make about the structure and use of resources that drive costs. This is consistent with the economics and strategy literature that gave birth to ABC. See M. Porter, *Competitive Advantage.* To avoid confusion with the economic basis for ABC, we use the term "cost-driver base" to mean the base used to trace or assign costs. Another term for the base used to trace costs is "activity base."

example, the unit-level for materials for baby-care products condenses the individual items—high-grade plastic, fasteners, and colors—into one category that we call "materials for baby-care products."

What Drives Costs?

Most discussions in the professional literature (e.g., journals such as *Strategic Finance, Journal of Cost Management*) focus on how to choose cost drivers for particular businesses. These discussions can be interesting accounts of the challenges that specific companies have faced, but little reliable evidence suggests whether a cost driver used in one company is the same cost driver that should be used in another company. Consequently, cost management analysts might feel the need to "reinvent the wheel" nearly every time they undertake a new activity-based costing project. The few studies of many companies, have found that the volume of outputs, the complexity of operations (e.g., many different types of products), and the nature of customer service activities have a significant effect on costs. *For example see A. M. Novin,* "Applying Overhead: How to Find the Right Bases and Rates," *for a basic approach. See also R. Banker and H. Johnson,* "An Empirical Study of Cost Drivers in the U.S. Airline Industry," *and G. Foster and M. Gupta,* "Manufacturing Overhead Cost Driver Analysis," *for more sophisticated approaches.*

Research Insight 4.1

Exhibit 4–4

Activity List and Cost-Driver Bases

PMI

Activities Resources		Cost-Driver Bases
1.	**Unit Level**	
1.1	Acquire and use materials for containers	Number of units of beverage containers produced
1.2	Acquire and use materials for baby-care products	Number of units of baby-care products produced
2.	**Batch Level**	
2.1	Set up manually controlled machines	Number of batches of beverage containers
2.1.1	Do the set up	
2.1.2	Perform quality control of batches of products produced on manually controlled machines	
2.2	Set up computer-controlled machines	Number of batches of baby-care products
3.	**Product Level**	
3.1	Design and manufacture molds (outsourced)	Number of molds required for each product type
3.2	Use manually controlled machines	Number of different product types (i.e., containers)
3.3	Use computer-controlled machines	Number of different product types (i.e., baby-care products)
4.	**Customer Level**	
4.1	Consult with customers	Number of consultations
4.2	Provide warehousing for customers	Number of cubic feet
5.	**Facility Level**	
5.1	Manage workers	Amount of salaries and benefits of production workers
5.2	Use main building	Number of square feet of each product's usage

The following explains the cost driver for the five cost-driver rates in Exhibit 4–4.

1. *Unit level.* The cost of materials to make both types of products is driven by the number of units produced. In effect, the materials costs vary with the volume of output.

2. *Batch level.* Batches are groups of the same units. For example, a batch of baby-care products could be 100 identical baby seats; a batch of containers could be 1,000 green 1 liter ginger ale bottles with particular lettering. Each batch of units requires the machines to be set up according to design specifications, just as building a house requires following the architect's design specifications. The costs of setting up the machines and of performing quality-control inspections on batches are driven by the number of batches produced. Nearly all of PMI's batch-level costs are labor costs.
3. *Product level.* Activity 3.1, design and manufacture molds, refers to the molds used in machines to shape the liquefied plastic as desired. This activity comprises designing and making the molds and remaking them to satisfy changing customer requirements. PMI outsources this activity to a company that specializes in these activities for plastic products. The outside company owns the mold and leases it to PMI.

   The cost of activities 3.2 and 3.3 are the depreciation, maintenance, and operating costs from using the machines. These operating costs include costs for energy, the labor to operate the manually controlled machines, and a small amount of labor to maintain both the manually controlled and computer-controlled machines.
4. *Customer level.* Activity 4.1, consult with customers, refers to customer consultations about orders, changes in orders, and complaints. The cost of these consultations is composed almost entirely of labor costs. Activity 4.2, provide warehousing for customers, refers to leasing the warehouse space and using personnel to move items in and out of it and to provide its security.
5. *Facility level.* Activity 5.1 refers to the management of production workers and activity 5.2 to the use of the main factory building to produce either containers or baby-care products. Occupancy costs include the lease of the building space, the cost of heating and lighting it, insurance and taxes on it and its contents, and maintenance.

See Exhibit 4–5 for the information the ABC team used to compute the predetermined cost-driver rates. Note that the numbers are calculated for a typical month. The ABC team wanted to derive cost-driver rates that would be generally useful and not affected by large variations in a particular month (e.g., utilities costs). Many companies develop cost-driver rates for a typical or "average" month.

The method that the ABC team used to calculate cost-driver rates is the same method used to develop predetermined overhead rates that you learned in Chapter 3. By using these predetermined rates, the ABC team saved the time and effort of computing cost-driver rates for every month. The predetermined cost-driver rates computed for a typical month might not be exactly the same as those for a specific month, say October, but they are likely to be very close to the actual rates. Many companies are willing to sacrifice a little accuracy to avoid computing actual cost-driver rates every month. (Most

Customers provide feedback about various types of car seats for infants.

Exhibit 4–5 Computing Predetermined Cost-Driver Rates for a Typical Month

(A)	(B)	(C)	(D)	(E)
Activity/Resource	**Cost-Driver Base**	**Activity Cost**	**Activity Volume**	**Predetermined Cost Driver Rate (C) ÷ (D)**
1. Unit Level				
1.1 Acquire and use materials for containers	Units of beverage containers produced	$40,000	1,000,000 units	$.04 per unit
1.2 Acquire and use materials for baby-care products	Units of baby-care products produced	$80,000	8,000 units	$10 per unit
2. Batch Level				
2.1 Set up manually controlled machines	Number of batches of beverage containers	$3,000	10 batches	$300 per batch
2.2 Set up computer-controlled machines	Number of batches of baby-care products	$12,000	20 batches	$600 per batch
3. Product Level				
3.1 Design and manufacture molds	Number of molds required for each product type	$5,000	5 molds	$1,000 per mold
3.2 Use manually controlled machines	Product type (i.e., containers)	$15,000	1 product type	$15,000 for containers per month
3.3 Use computer-controlled machines	Product type (i.e., baby-care products)	$40,000	1 product type	$40,000 for baby-care products per month
4. Customer Level				
4.1 Consult with customers	Number of consultations	$4,000	40 consultations	$100 per consultation
4.2 Provide warehousing for customers	Number of cubic feet	$2,000	10,000 cubic feet	$.20 per cubic foot
5. Facility-Level				
5.1 Manage workers	Salaries and benefits of production workers	$3,000	$15,000 production labor costs	20% of production labor cost
5.2 Use main building	Square feet of each product's usage	$48,000	16,000 sq. ft.	$3 per sq. ft.

Sources of information in this exhibit:

Column (A) activities are from Exhibits 4–2 and 4–4.

Column (B) cost-driver bases are from Exhibit 4–4.

Column (C), the total costs in a typical month for each activity, was developed by the ABC team from reviewing accounting records, interviewing operating personnel, and collecting employee activity data sheets such as that in Exhibit 4–3.

Column (D), the activity volume for each cost-driver base, was developed by the ABC team from interviewing operating personnel and reviewing various records.

Column (E), the predetermined cost-driver rate, is, as indicated, Column (C) divided by Column (D) and is the cost per unit of activity for each cost-driver base.

companies compute predetermined rates once or twice per year.) PMI's CFO Lewis was willing to give up a little accuracy to save time and effort by computing predetermined rates just once a year instead of every month.

Few companies assign *all* of their costs to products. For example, companies generally do not assign the chief executive's salary or other administrative costs to products. An allocation of such costs to products is likely arbitrary and does not reflect a particular product's use of resources. As is common practice, PMI's ABC team did not assign administration costs to the products.

Furthermore, PMI appropriately did not assign the cost of unused capacity to products. Unused main building capacity and employee time paid for but not used in production was not charged to products.

You're the
Decision
Maker 4.3

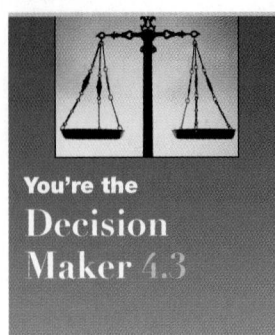

Using Cost-Driver Rates

Review Exhibit 4–5 and the preceding discussion.

a. Does the cost-driver rate for activity 1.1 have the same meaning as the one for activity 2.1? Explain.

b. Suppose that you are PMI's CEO and decide to stop providing warehousing services for customers. Would PMI really save the $2,000 per month for activity 4.2? Why or why not?

c. What other factors would you consider in deciding whether to stop providing warehousing services?

(Solutions begin on page 164.)

Before discussing step 4, we should note that many companies stop at this point and use the information obtained from steps 1 through 3 to identify their cost activities. These companies then focus on the more costly activities and modify processes to reduce or eliminate them. PMI used step 4 in the ABC process, however, to assign activity costs to products.

Step 4: Assign Activity Costs to Products

Bakery Example

LO 5 Assign activity costs to goods and services.

Recall the bakery example in which we established a cost-driver rate for maintenance of the mixing machine. This rate is used to assign mixing-machine maintenance costs to batches of cookies at a rate of $12 per batch. If the bakery makes 10 batches of chocolate chip cookies in a month, it assigns $120 to chocolate chip cookies for mixing-machine maintenance for that month.

PMI Example

See Exhibit 4–6 for the way that PMI's ABC team determined the cost of products for the month of October. Exhibit 4–6 applies the *cost-driver rates for a typical month* from Exhibit 4–5 to the *actual cost-driver volumes* for October.

Column (A) of Exhibit 4–6 shows the activities that we have been discussing. Column (B) shows the cost-driver rate that is related to a particular activity. We derived these rates in Exhibit 4–5. We have omitted listing the cost drivers for each activity to simplify the presentation. Recall that we present these cost drivers in Exhibit 4–5 if you want to review them.

Column (C) presents the actual cost-driver volumes for the month of October. Note that these differ somewhat from the typical month volumes shown in Exhibit 4–5. Columns (D) and (E) present the product costs for each of the two products—containers and baby care products. Columns (D) and (E) show the total ABC costs for October computed using predetermined cost-driver rates and actual cost-driver volumes for October. The unit costs for the two products are computed using the total ABC costs for the month and the monthly production volumes from the top of Column (C):

Containers **$85,200 ÷ 1,200,000 units = $.071 per unit**

Baby-Care Products **$151,000 ÷ 7,000 units = $21.57 per unit**

Note the term "costs traced to products" where the amounts in Exhibit 4–6 are totaled. The ABC team appropriately excluded from the exhibit amounts of certain costs, including particular administrative costs of running the company that were not directly related to production (e.g., the salaries of the CEO and CFO) and the cost of unused parts of the main building because that space was not used to produce either product.

Exhibit 4–6 Assigning Costs to Products for the Month of October

(A)	(B)	(C)	(D)	(E)
			Cost of Products [column (B) × column (C)]	
Activity/Resource	**Predetermined Cost-Driver Rate (from Exhibit 4–5)**	**Actual Activity Volume in October**	**Containers**	**Baby Care**
1. Unit Level				
1.1 Acquire and use materials for containers	$.04 per unit	1,200,000 units	$48,000	NA
1.2 Acquire and use materials for baby-care products	$10 per unit	7,000 units	NA	$70,000
2. Batch Level				
2.1 Set up manually controlled machines	$300 per batch	12 batches	$3,600	NA
2.2 Set up computer-controlled machines	$600 per batch	16 batches	NA	$9,600
3. Product Level				
3.1 Design and manufacture of molds				
Containers	$1,000 per mold	1 mold	$ 1,000	NA
Baby-care products	$1,000 per mold	4 molds	NA	$ 4,000
3.2 Use manually controlled machines	$15,000 for product type	1 product type	$15,000	NA
3.3 Use computer-controlled machines	$40,000 for product type	1 product type	NA	$40,000
4. Customer Level				
4.1 Consult with customers				
Containers	$100 per consultation	2 consultations	$ 200	NA
Baby-care products	$100 per consultation	40 consultations	NA	$ 4,000
4.2 Provide warehousing for customers				
Containers	$.20 per cu. ft.	8,000 cu. ft.	$ 1,600	NA
Baby-care products	$.20 per cu. ft.	2,000 cu. ft.	NA	$ 400
5. Facility Level				
5.1 Manage workers				
Containers	20% of the production labor costs	$ 4,000	$ 800	NA
Baby-care products	20% of the production labor costs	$10,000	NA	$ 2,000
5.2 Use main building				
Containers	$3 per sq. ft.	5,000 sq. ft.	$15,000	
Baby-care products	$3 per sq. ft.	7,000 sq. ft.	NA	$21,000
Total costs traced to products in October, by product type			$85,200	$151,000
Total costs traced to products in October			$236,200	
ABC costs per unit (total ABC costs ÷ product volume (1,200,000 containers and 7,000 units of baby-care products)			$85,200 ÷ 1,200,000 = $.071 per unit	$151,000 ÷ 7,000 units = $21.57 per unit

Sources of information in this exhibit:

Column (A) activities are from Exhibits 4–2, 4–4, and 4–5.

Column (B) cost-driver rates are from Exhibit 4–5.

Column (C), the actual cost-driver volume for the month of October, was collected by the ABC team by interviewing operating personnel and from company records. The cost-driver volume in October is a bit different from that in a "typical" month, which is to be expected in ABC analyses.

Columns (D) and (E), the cost of each product, was computed by multiplying the cost-driver rate in column (B) by the actual cost-driver volume in October in column (C). Column (D) and column (E) show the product cost for containers and baby-care products, respectively.

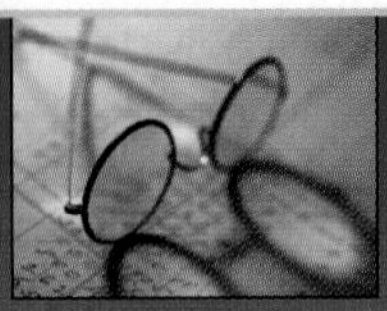

Cost Management in Practice 4.2

How to Successfully Implement Activity-Based Costing

A division of Intensil Communications that is a major U.S. semiconductor manufacturer, implemented a wide-ranging ABC system. The objectives of its ABC system were (1) to improve product costing and (2) use ABC analysis in its internal decision-making and performance evaluations. Reportedly, its system exceeded these objectives. Additional benefits included the use of ABC information to support process improvement and promote cross-functional teamwork that has carried over into other important projects. On the basis of this extensive implementation, Intensil Semiconductor recommends that ABC will succeed if the following are present:

- Objectives are clear and tangible.
- Top management supports ABC.
- Cross-functional team members have strong project management skills.
- The team learns from other companies' experience.
- Communication is regular and honest.
- Sufficient time is allowed to gather and analyze data.

Source: Authors' research.

Product and Customer Profitability

LO 6 Analyze the profitability of products and customers.

The information presented in Exhibit 4–6 is important in measuring both product and customer profitability. It is central to managing products and customers and deciding whether to drop either products or customers.

Product Profitability

PMI

See Exhibit 4–7 for a profitability report for PMI's two products sold during October. Assume that the average selling price for containers and baby-care products was $.10 and $22.00 per unit, respectively. The costs traced to products in Exhibit 4–7 come from Exhibit 4–6. For example, the product-level costs in Exhibit 4–7 are the sum of the product-level costs in Exhibit 4–6 ($16,000 for containers in Exhibit 4–7 = $1,000 + $15,000 for product-level costs in Exhibit 4–6).

Note that the "costs not traced to products" at the bottom of Exhibit 4–7 are the general and administrative costs and unused main building space mentioned earlier that the ABC team did not trace to products.

PMI's management was pleased with the ABC team's work but was disappointed with the results for October. CEO Fairchild stated, "The good news is that we are in the black; the bad news is that we are *barely* in the black. Our operating income was only $5,400 on total revenue of $274,000—a return on sales of about 2 percent. The industry

Exhibit 4–7

ABC Profitability Reports for October

PMI

	Containers	Baby Care	Total
Revenues:			
Containers (1,200,000 × $.10)	$120,000		$120,000
Baby-care products (7,000 × $22.00)		$154,000	154,000
Total revenue			$274,000
Costs traced to products (from Exhibit 4–6):			
Unit level	$ 48,000	$ 70,000	$118,000
Batch level	3,600	9,600	13,200
Product level	16,000	44,000	60,000
Customer level	1,800	4,400	6,200
Facility level	15,800	23,000	38,800
Total costs traced to products	$ 85,200	$151,000	$236,200
Revenues minus costs traced to products	$ 34,800	$3,000	37,800
Costs not traced to products			32,400
Operating income			$ 5,400

Exhibit 4–8

Profitability Reports Comparing Activity-Based Costing to Traditional Costing

PMI

	(A)	(B)	(C)	(D)
	Containers		Baby-Care Products	
	Traditional	ABC	Traditional	ABC
Revenues	$120,000	$120,000	$154,000	$154,000
Costs traced to products:				
Materials*	48,000	48,000	70,000	70,000
Labor and overhead†	48,000	37,200	70,000	81,000
Revenues minus costs traced to products	$ 24,000	$ 34,800	$ 14,000	$ 3,000

Note: These costs exclude costs not traced to products.

*These are the unit-level costs for materials reported in Exhibit 4–7.

†The traditional labor and overhead are simply assumed to be 100 percent of materials costs. The activity-based costing labor and overhead costs are the sums of the batch-level, product-level, customer-level, and facility-level costs traced to products as reported in Exhibit 4–7. Do not assume that the *total* labor and overhead costs assigned to products are the same for the ABC and traditional cost systems because the two systems have such different approaches to assigning costs.

average is about 10 percent return on sales, so we are lagging our peers. Clearly, we have work to do to improve those operating income numbers."

Lewis added, "The ABC team's work has enabled us to pinpoint some of the problems. Look at the baby-care products. Revenue minus costs traced to products is only $3,000 *before considering costs that have not been traced to products.* The container business looks good to me, but we are in trouble with baby-care products. They require complex machinery and frequent quality-control checks, which are costly."

Fairchild commented, "I've been reading literature on activity-based costing, which states that highly complex business often turns out to be more costly than people thought and low-complexity business turns out to be less expensive. We seem to have that situation here. The low-complexity container business is clearly profitable, but the more complex baby-care products business is marginal, *at best!* I'm pleased that we are learning about this now before we are in real financial trouble."

As this conversation suggested, the ABC results surprised management. Before developing the ABC information, the company had assumed that all labor and overhead traceable to products were 100 percent of each product's materials costs. The information comparing the traditional and ABC results in Exhibit 4–8 was a real eye-opener for PMI's management. See the exhibit for the results of the traditional costing approach in columns (A) and (C), and the ABC amounts in columns (B) and (D).

Armed with this information, Fairchild decided to meet with Elizabeth Forney, vice president of marketing to discuss the problem. Forney indicated that the $22 market price per unit was relatively low for the baby-care products and was expected to increase within the next six months. Fairchild and Forney decided to keep producing baby-care products and to monitor the relation between their selling price and costs over the next several months.

Customer Profitability

Analyzing the costs of activities to serve specific customers is called **customer costing.** Combining customer costing with revenues earned from customers is called **customer profitability analysis.**[5] The same activity-based information used to analyze products can be used to measure major customers' contributions to profit.

Some companies are surprised to learn that 10 to 20 percent of their customers generate 80 to 90 percent of their total profit and that some customers actually cause losses (see the discussion in Chapter 6). Some customers require so much service (placing many small orders, for example) that the cost of resources used to serve them

customer costing *analyzes the costs of activities devoted to serving specific customers at each level*

customer profitability analysis *identifies the costs and benefits of serving specific customers or customer types to improve an organization's overall profitability*

[5] Chapter 6 discusses customer profitability analysis in more detail.

(including order processing, setups, and shipping) exceeds the revenue they provide. Customer profitability analysis identifies the most profitable customers so that the company can ensure that they remain customers. Knowing which customers are unprofitable also allows the company either to work with them to reduce the costs they cause or to decide not to continue serving them.

In PMI's case, since beverage containers and baby-care products are sold to separate, individual customers, Exhibit 4–7 can also be used as a customer profitability report. It shows that the customer purchasing containers generates a higher level of profitability than the customer purchasing baby-care products.

Estimation of Costs of New Products Using ABC

Activity-based costing information for existing products can be helpful for estimating the costs of new products if the activities used to make these new products are similar to those used to make the existing ones.

MegaBurger Novelty Toy Decision

PMI

The team at PMI compiled the cost data using ABC and then met with Fairchild to discuss the results. She first asked whether the Megaburger business would be profitable.

To answer Fairchild's questions, Lewis and his team matched MegaBurger's product specifications to the activity list and cost drivers for existing products (Exhibits 4–5 and 4–6). The team then decided that producing novelty toys would be similar to making complex baby-care products with several notable exceptions:

- PMI must use a higher grade of plastic and more colors although smaller amounts of both per unit.
- The product molds for the toys must be more precise. A small error or blemish would be very noticeable in such a small product that children (and collectors) look at very carefully.
- PMI would have more consultations with customers.
- MegaBurger expects its toy suppliers to warehouse the products and ship them directly to its restaurants on demand. This is similar to the baby-care company's requirements except that the MegaBurger project requires complex inventory controls and distribution to many locations. PMI would have to lease additional warehouse space to meet MegaBurger's needs.
- More production space is required. Some space could be obtained in an adjacent building, but the remainder could be obtained from the presently unused space.

PMI's application of the cost information from activity-based costing to assess the product profitability of one of MegaBurger's products is shown in Exhibit 4–9. PMI's ABC team started with the cost-driver rates for the baby-care product in Column B and then adjusted those rates to reflect what it thought the cost-driver rates should be for the MegaBurger product (Column C). Column D presents the adjusted cost-driver rates. Column E shows the cost-driver volume expected for 20,000 units per month. (Each "unit" contains eight novelty toys.) Column F shows each activity's expected cost. Work through this exhibit to see how PMI adjusted its activity-based cost information for existing products (column B) to obtain estimated costs of the new product (column F).

PMI's analysis indicated that the estimated revenues on the MegaBurger job would exceed estimated costs by $18,600 per month as shown at the bottom of Column G. On the basis of the analysis reported in Exhibit 4–9, Fairchild decided that the company had the knowledge and technical capability to be a reliable supplier for MegaBurger. Based on the team's analysis, PMI was able to keep its existing products and still submit a successful and profitable bid to MegaBurger. Fairchild, Lewis, and the ABC team were all excited about the prospect of landing a big contract with MegaBurger.

Exhibit 4–9 Application of ABC Cost Information to Estimate New Product Costs

PMI

Microsoft Excel - Exhibit 4-91.xls

File Edit View Insert Format Tools Data Window Help

92% Arial 10

A2 = Estimating the Monthly Costs of a Proposed Megaburger Product

Estimating the Monthly Costs of a Proposed Megaburger Product

Assumed production: 20,000 units in a month.

A	B	C	D	E	F	G
Activities	**Cost-Driver Rates for Existing Baby-Care Products (from Exhibit 4-5)**	**Adjust-ments to Increase Rates**	**Adjusted Cost-Driver Rates (Column B x Column C)**	**Monthly Level of Activity***	**Estimated Monthly Costs**	**Estimated Monthly Revenues**
Unit-level						
Acquire and use materials	$10 per unit	120%	$12 per unit	20,000 units	$240,000	
Batch-level						
Set up and quality control for computer-controlled injection molding machines	$600 per batch	None	$600 per batch	10 batches	6,000	
Product-level						
Design and manufacture of molds	$1,000 per mold	200%	$2,000 per mold	2 molds	4,000	
Use equipment in production	$40,000 for product type	None	$40,000	1 product	40,000	
Customer-level						
Consult customers	$100 per consultation	200%	$200 per consultation	40 consultations	8,000	
Provide additional warehousing	$.20 per cubic foot	150%	$0.30 per cubic foot	10,000 cubic feet	3,000	
Facility-level						
Manage workers	20% of production labor costs	200%	40% of production labor costs	$6,000 production labor costs	2,400	
Use main building	$3 per square foot	None	$3 per square foot	6,000 square feet	18,000	
Total monthly costs					$321,400	
Monthly revenue per MegaBurger contract ($17 per unit x 20,000 units)						$340,000
Excess of revenues over ABC costs, per month						$18,600

*Assumed monthly activity for the proposed product.

Sheet1 / Sheet2 / Sheet3

Ready NUM

Making Product Decisions

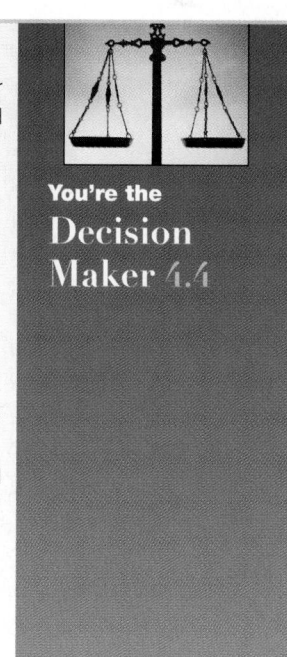

You're the Decision Maker 4.4

Consider the information in Exhibit 4–6. Assume the role of an analyst who will recommend whether to produce a new product line. Assume that PMI obtains sufficient additional capacity to offer a third product line that has the following characteristics per month:

- Uses the same amount of medium-grade plastic and colors per unit as beverage containers and requires two molds.
- Is made on a new injection-molding machine that costs $20,000 per month to use.
- Produces 100,000 units in 15 batches each month.
- Ships products to customers directly from production (no warehousing). However, 2,000 square feet of space for production are needed at a cost of $3 per square foot.
- Provides three customer consultations per month.
- Incurs production labor costs of $4,500. The cost-driver rate for the activity manage workers is 20 percent of production labor costs.

Any cost items not specifically listed are the same per month as for the beverage containers reported in Exhibit 4–6.

a. Estimate the costs of this product using activity-based costing.

b. What additional information would you need before deciding whether to recommend this product?

(Solutions begin on page 164.)

Activity-Based Costing in Service and Merchandising Companies

LO 7 Apply activity-based costing to service and merchandising companies.

Many service and merchandising companies also have benefited from using an ABC system. For example, the United States Postal Service used ABC to decide whether to use debit cards, credit cards, checks, cash, or a combination as payment for postal transactions. ABC results indicated that for the same transaction size, debit cards were slightly less costly and credit cards were only slightly more costly than cash. The Postal Service's customers can use debit and credit cards as well as cash partly as a result of its analysis using ABC.

Service and merchandising organizations (including nonprofit and governmental organizations) implement ABC as described earlier in this chapter; no changes are necessary. Any organization—manufacturing, merchandising, or service—must follow these four steps presented earlier in the chapter and briefly reviewed here for a service organization.

Step 1: *Identify and classify the activities related to the company's products.* A bank can identify activities such as processing ATM transactions, processing car loans, opening customer checking accounts, and maintaining investment accounts. As activities are identified, they are classified as unit-level, batch-level, product-level, customer-level, or facility-level activities.

Step 2: *Estimate the cost of activities identified in step 1.* A bank could estimate the cost of employee time spent processing ATM transactions and ATM machine maintenance costs to the activity processing ATM transactions.

Step 3: *Calculate a cost-driver rate for each activity.* With the activity cost data from step 2, the bank then can calculate a cost-driver rate that will allow the company to assign activity costs to goods and services. This rate's base should have some causal link to the cost. For example, the cost associated with running an ATM machine is likely caused by the number of transactions it processes. Thus, the rate for this activity could be based on the number of transactions.

Step 4: *Assign activity costs to products.* The bank then uses the cost-driver rates identified in step 3 to assign activity costs to goods and services. For example, if a particular customer uses an ATM machine eight times a month and the rate per ATM transaction from step 3 is \$0.50, \$4.00 in costs are assigned to the customer (\$.50 × 8).

Costs and Benefits of Using Activity-Based Costing

This chapter's discussion of activity-based costing implies that implementing it adds value to an organization. This is likely to be true for companies that have complex production processes producing many different products or services in highly competitive markets. This is the reason that companies such as Hewlett-Packard, Daimler-Chrysler, and IBM implemented ABC.

We should remember, however, that implementing ABC is costly. Costs include those to develop and implement the system, to provide additional record-keeping, to change the computer system, and to hire consultants. Therefore, managers must choose carefully when to implement an ABC system. Several "red flags" indicate problems with an organization's costing system and the likely need to refine it. Some of these problem are as follow:

- Indirect costs are significant in proportion to direct costs and are allocated to goods and services using one or two cost pools (and therefore one or two cost-driver rates).
- Goods and services are complex and require many different processes and inputs.

- Standard high-volume goods and services show losses or small profits while complex low-volume goods and services show significant profits.
- Different departments within the company believe that the costs identified for producing goods and providing services (as calculated by accounting) are not accurate and often are misleading.
- The company loses bids it thought were priced relatively low and wins those it thought were priced relatively high.
- The company has not changed its costing system in spite of major changes it has made to its operations.

Although all companies should not implement an ABC system, a firm that experiences several of these problems should seriously consider adopting it.

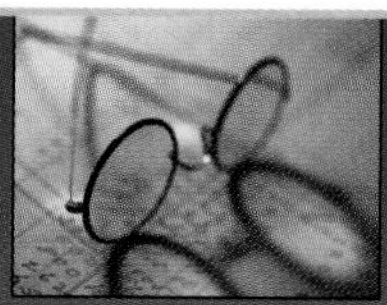

Cost Management in Practice 4.3

Why Companies Use ABC

PMI used ABC to help estimate the costs of a new product. The following list reflects the results of several surveys of practice in the United States, the United Kingdom, and Canada to determine why companies choose ABC.

1. *Cost reduction.* ABC measures how much activities cost. Management can use this information to identify activities that are costly and then take steps to reduce their costs by changing the production process or outsourcing those activities.
2. *Product pricing and decisions of whether to continue producing a product or keeping a particular customer.* ABC implementers generally believe that ABC provides more accurate cost information than conventional costing does. Management can use this information to negotiate price increases with customers or to drop unprofitable products.
3. *Budgeting and performance measurement.* As noted in item 2, ABC implementers generally believe that ABC provides more accurate cost information than conventional costing does. Management can use more accurate cost information to improve budgets and measures of department and division performance. *Sources: J. Innes, F. Mitchell, and D. Sinclair,* "Activity-Based Costing in the U.K." *and research by the authors.*

Chapter Summary

The theme of this book is that managers' decisions drive an organization's costs. To manage costs, managers and employees must understand how those decisions affect the efficiency of work being accomplished. Activity-based costing traces the costs of resources to activities, which are the basic elements of an organization's work. By learning what activities the organization uses to produce goods and services, managers can trace the organization's costs to the products via the activities performed. We trace these costs using these steps:

1. Identify and classify the activities related to the company's products.
2. Estimate the cost of the activities identified in step 1.
3. Calculate a cost-driver rate for each activity.
4. Assign activity costs to products.

ABC can provide data related to a company's processes. These data can be used in various ways to benefit the company. It can identify expensive and inefficient processes that could have been unnoticed in the past. The company can then change these processes to make them more efficient, often reducing their costs and increasing customer satisfaction. ABC data also can be used to establish more accurate cost information for goods and services.

Key Terms

For each term's definition, refer to the indicated page or turn to the glossary at the end of the text.

ABC full costing*, 165
ABC unit costing*, 165
activity-based costing (ABC), 145
activity list (activity dictionary), 146
batch-level resources and activities, 147

*Terms appear in the chapter Appendix.

Meeting the Cost Management Challenges

1. How did activity-based cost information help PMI, Inc.?

Activity-based cost information provides more accurate information about the costs of existing products, which PMI's management used to decide whether to continue supplying particular products (e.g., the baby-care products). (See Exhibits 4–6 and 4–7.) The ABC information showed that the traditional costing system was "undercosting" baby-care products and "overcosting" beverage containers. (See Exhibit 4–8.) The ABC information also helped PMI estimate the cost of the new products for the MegaBurger contract, which would use most of the same activities (at different cost-driver rates, however) as do existing baby-care products. (See Exhibit 4–9.)

2. What data and knowledge are necessary to support the development of activity-based information?

An organization needs the following data: (1) a list of its activities categorized according to the five levels (unit, batch, product, customer, and facility), (2) the cost of each of its activities, (3) the costs per unit of activity (cost-driver rates), and (4) the costs of goods and services (after assigning activity costs to them).

3. Is activity-based information always better than traditional costing information?

It is not. Organizations must determine whether the decision-making value of ABC information exceeds the costs to develop and maintain it. For example, organizations whose goods and services use resources in relatively similar ways might have activity-based costs similar to those obtained by using traditional costing approaches. In this case, the decision-making value would be unaffected by more complex (and costly) ABC estimates of costs. However, activity-based information can be used to support decisions about process improvements. Any organization faced with competition based on price could benefit from process improvements that increase customer value while reducing process costs. This important use of activity-based information is one of the topics of Chapter 5.

Solutions to You're the Decision Maker

4.1 Developing the Activity List p. 151

a. Aside from a reasonable level of detail (which is missing for many types of activities), the list includes few activities that might indicate process inefficiencies. For example, employees could have idle time when machines need repair or during a break in production (due to excess capacity). All employees are not likely to be productively employed every hour for which they are paid. While they might be uneasy about admitting unplanned breaks and idle time, they should realize that these activities exist in most organizations. Including them in the activity list improves the analysis of the organization's work.

b. To answer the question, management or high-level staff might estimate how much time and resources are spent on the omitted activities. This a questionable practice, however, because of its top-down nature. Upper-level managers or staff are unlikely to be able to identify these problem areas with much precision, and a blanket assumption that they exist throughout the organization could do more harm to employee relations than good. It is preferable for individuals who do the actual work to identify these unproductive activities and help the organization to minimize them. As noted in part (a), employees might not want to recognize them because they might be "blamed" for the unproductivity. The organization should promote honesty by not assigning blame but by encouraging and rewarding employees to identify and fix problems. Many firms do this by implementing a "suggestions for improvement program."

4.2 Checking Employee Activity Data Sheets p. 151

Recognizing that the productivity of employees differs is a problem for activity analysis, which implicitly assumes that all hours of effort are applied equally effectively. This employee is making a statement about the organization's lack of recognition for her productivity (if her statement is true) or for the lack of effort other employees in her department exert. If this situation is widespread in the organization, it may indicate serious problems (hiring, evaluation, and incentive) to be addressed before activity analysis can be effective.

4.3 Using Cost-Driver Rates p.156

a. The cost-driver rates have different meanings. The cost-driver rate for activity 1.1 is a unit-level activity for the acquisition and use of materials and, therefore, is easily traced to each unit of product 1. However, the cost-driver rate for activity 2.1 is a batch-level activity not easily traced to particular units but more easily traced to batches of product.

b. PMI might save this amount but only if eliminating the activity really eliminates the need for the resource (i.e., the warehouse).

c. Although eliminating this service could save money, it also could result in losing a customer. If so, then eliminating it could lose benefits that are far greater than the costs that would be saved.

4.4 Making Product Decisions p. 161

a.

Activity Level	Activity Volume	Cost-Driver Rate	Total Cost
Unit—Materials	100,000 units	$ .04	$ 4,000
Batch	15	300	4,500
Product—Molds	2	1,000	2,000
Product—Equipment	1 product	20,000	20,000
Customer—Consultations	3	100	300
Facility—Employee management	Production labor costs are $4,500	20%	900
Facility—Use building	2,000 sq. ft.	$3 per sq. ft.	6,000
Total costs			$37,700

b. The selling price and additional information regarding whether PMI is at practical capacity for all levels of resources prior to making this new product could be helpful. If it is not, PMI might devote unused resource capacity to this new product. For example, PMI could have unused building space to use for the new product. If that were the case, PMI would not have to spend as much as indicated by the costs computed in part (a).

Appendix to Chapter Four

Unit-Level ABC Costing

LO 8 Distinguish between ABC unit-level costing, and ABC full costing of goods and services.

This chapter discussed **ABC full costing** that assigns most, if not all, activity-related costs to specific product lines and then uses this information to calculate the cost per unit for each product. Exhibit 4–6 reports the results of assigning costs to production using ABC full-costing.

An alternative to this approach is **ABC unit-level costing.** It identifies as "unit costs" only those that are clearly and certainly driven by producing units of the goods or services. Exhibit 4–10 shows how ABC unit-level costs are computed using the data in Exhibit 4–6.

ABC full costing *assigns as many costs to products as possible*

ABC unit costing *assigns only the costs of unit-level resources to products*

Cost management analysts have different opinions about the choice between ABC unit-level costing and ABC full costing. We have presented both ideas here so that you will be able to understand their differences when making management decisions.

Note that in Exhibit 4–10 only the unit-level costs—materials—are assigned to units. All other resources, called "higher-level resources," are not assigned. These higher-level resources are batch-level, product-level, customer-level, and facility-level resources. Higher-level resources are tied to higher-level activities but not to unit-level activities in this example.

The concept of ABC unit-level costing is to assign only the costs clearly and certainly driven by specific units to these units. Materials used to make products certainly qualify for this assignment.

Exhibit 4–10

ABC Unit-Level Costing Report

	Containers	Baby-Care Products
Units produced	1,200,000	7,000
Unit-level resources: Materials	$48,000	$70,000
Cost per unit ($48,000 ÷ 1,200,000 units; $70,000 ÷ 7,000 units)	$0.04	$10.00
Higher-level resources: Sum of resources used for batch-level, product-level, customer-level, and facility-level activities*	$37,200	$81,000

*These amounts are the totals of the batch-level, product-level, customer-level, and facility-level amounts presented in Exhibit 4–6.

Cost Differences

The following compares ABC unit-level costing and ABC full costing:

	Containers	Baby-Care Products
ABC unit-level costing cost per unit (Ex. 4–10)	$.04 per unit	$10.00 per unit
ABC full costing per unit (bottom of Ex. 4–6)	$.071 per unit	$21.57 per unit

The per-unit cost for each product using each method differs dramatically because they are based on different concepts. The full-costing approach says, in effect, that a firm has costs because it produces units; therefore, all costs related to the production (and sale) of the units should be assigned to units.

The unit-costing approach says, however, that resources supplied for higher-level activities, such as batch-level and product-level activities, are not caused by the production and sale of each unit. Therefore, these higher-level resources should not be applied to the unit level.

Review Questions

4.1 Review and define each of the chapter's key terms.

4.2 What factors should managers assess in choosing among alternative costing systems?

4.3 How are indirect costs allocated to products using traditional costing systems?

4.4 What are the three key points with respect to refining a traditional costing system?

4.5 What is the ideal relation between allocation bases (cost drivers) and costs?

a. Simple

b. Cause and effect

c. Complex

d. What top management wants

4.6 Why do few companies allocate the general and administrative costs of the business to products?

4.7 Is it true that activity-based costing first assigns costs to products and then to activities?

4.8 Fill in the missing words: An activity is any discrete ____ that an organization ____ to make or deliver a ____ or service.

4.9 Organizations that use or have used activity-based costing include the following:

a. United States Postal Service.

b. American Airlines.

c. Hewlett-Packard.

d. All of the above.

e. b and c of the above.

4.10 Briefly describe the four steps in measuring the costs of goods and services.

4.11 Briefly describe the five levels of resources and activities.

4.12 Fill in the blanks. An activity list (or dictionary) is a ____ of ____ performed by an organization to produce its product.

4.13 Describe how to calculate the cost of an activity.

4.14 Why is employee participation in identifying activities important?

4.15 Describe how to calculate the activity-based cost of a product.

4.16 Why would organizations compute cost-driver rates for a "typical" month instead of for each month of the year?

4.17 "I work for an airline. ABC is irrelevant to my company because we do not manufacture things." Discuss the validity of this statement.

4.18 What "red flags" indicate that companies have problems with their costing systems?

4.19 Is there any fundamental difference in applying ABC to goods versus services? Explain.

4.20 What conditions are necessary for using activity-based costs of existing services for estimating costs of new services to be valid?

Critical Analysis

4.21 Explain why overcosting and undercosting products occur with traditional costing systems.

4.22 Why might a company adopt activity-based costing then stop using it, but consider that its adoption had been a success?

4.23 In developing an activity list, why might employees not want to reveal realistic information about time spent on their activities?

4.24 What criteria should management use to decide whether to assign general and administrative costs to products?

4.25 Refer to Cost Management in Practice 4.2. Why is each of the following important to the success of activity-based costing:

a. Top management's support.

b. Other companies' successes and failures with it.

c. Sufficient time to gather and analyze the data.

4.26 Professor John Shank has said that the use of contribution margins to select products is "a snare, a trap, and a delusion" because a firm will never drop a product that has a positive contribution margin for fear of losing even a small amount of profit.[6] Explain the meaning of this argument. How might the use of activity-based costing (unit level or full cost) improve the product selection process?

4.27 It has been suggested[7] that ABC should be used to measure the costs of "people-intensive" processes but not "machine-intensive" processes. People-intensive processes have adaptable resources, employee-paced work flows, and salary-oriented costs. Examples include engineering and customer service. Machine-intensive processes have machine-paced work flows, depreciation-oriented costs, and employee tasks that depend on technology. Examples include automated painting and robotic assembly. Contrast how ABC and throughput costing treat these types of processes. Make an argument either for or against this proposition.

4.28 Some believe that universities are among the organizations most resistant to change. However, some universities are beginning to analyze the profitability of their major departments and colleges by applying ABC concepts. Develop an exhibit similar to Exhibit 4–4 that shows major university activities and resources (without numbers, of course). How difficult would it be to trace university resource costs to these activities?

4.29 Evaluate this comment: "Historical costs are only the starting point for predicting future costs. . . . Many types of costs, such as inventory, book value of equipment, and allocation of fixed [higher-level resource] costs are not relevant for decision making.'[8]

4.30 One implication of ABC systems could be that using fewer cost-driver bases reduces consumption of resources, which reduces costs. Therefore, this logic continues, managers should seek to reduce the number of cost-driver bases used. A prominent critic of ABC has stated that activity-based prescriptions for improved competitiveness usually entail steps that lead to doing less of what should not be done in the first place. "[F]ocus on reducing variation and lead time in the work itself, and costs will take care of themselves . . . get busy with the improvement process."[9] Can these views be reconciled? Explain.

Exercises

Exercise 4.31
Cost-Driver Identification
(LO 2)

Place the following activities involved in a university's admission process in chronological order and match each to its most likely cost driver. (Cost-driver bases may be used more than once.)

Activities	Possible Cost-Driver Bases
1. Processing applications	a. Number of acceptances
2. Enrolling students	b. Number of applications
3. Receiving applications	c. Number of inquiries
4. Receiving and responding to student inquiries	
5. Accepting students	

Exercise 4.32
Cost-Driver Identification
(LO 2)

Volkswagen Canada developed ABC costs of the wheel-building process at one of its plants.[10] The process involves melting aluminum, pouring the melted aluminum into molds (casting), testing, finishing/polishing, painting, and packaging wheels.

Required

Match each activity with its most likely cost-driver base. (Cost-driver bases may be used more than once.)

Activities	Possible Cost-Driver Bases
1. Melting aluminum	a. Number of wheels
2. Casting aluminum	b. Number of setups
3. X-ray testing	c. Number of casting hours
4. Drilling bolt holes	d. Number of kilograms melted
5. Finishing surfaces	
6. Chrome plating	
7. Painting	
8. Packaging	
9. Setting up machines	
10. Shipping	

[6] Quoted in R. Kee, "Integrating Activity-Based Costing with the Theory of Constraints to Enhance Production-Related Decision Making."

[7] R. Campbell, P. Brewer, and T. Mills, "Designing an Information System Using Activity-Based Costing and the Theory of Constraints."

[8] L. Boyd, "Cost Information: The Use of Cost Information for Making Operating Decisions."

[9] H. T. Johnson, "It's Time to Stop Overselling Activity-Based Concepts: Start Focusing on Total Customer Satisfaction Instead."

[10] Adapted from J. Gurowka, "ABC, ABM, and the Volkswagen Saga."

Exercise 4.33
Different Levels of Activities and Resources
(LO 3)

Match each of the following resources and activities with the most likely activity level.

Resource and Description	Activity Level
1. Production management—salaries and support for managers	a. Unit
2. Marketing research—salaries and support for marketing research to identify new product opportunities	b. Batch
3. Labor—hourly as needed to meet production levels	c. Product
4. Setup labor—set up equipment and software for production runs	d. Customer
5. Utilities—electrical power for operating computing equipment used by setup workers	e. Facility
6. Legal department—salaries and facilities to support legal staff who prepare contracts for each customer	
7. Equipment—equipment specifically designed to produce one product line	
8. Materials—purchased for product manufacturing	
9. Supplies—purchased to support customer-service representatives	
10. Software—programs to control computerized equipment; revised for each batch of product	

Exercise 4.34
Different Levels of Activities and Resources
(LO 3)

Match each of the following activities and resources with the most likely activity level for a social services agency.

Resources and Activities	Activity Level
1. Case workers—personnel who interview and service clients by type of service (child, homeless, and elderly citizen)	a. Unit
2. Supplies—materials for office personnel	b. Product
3. Library—regulations, research, and court documents to support child, homeless, and elderly citizen services	c. Facility
4. Information technology—desktop and mobile computing equipment and personnel to develop and maintain information system	
5. Management—salaries and support for administrators	
6. Building—offices of employees	
7. Automobiles—transportation for caseworkers to meet clients	
8. Utilities—building's electrical power, natural gas, phone, and sanitation services	

Exercise 4.35
Different Activity and Resource Levels
(LO 3)

Match each of the following activities to the most likely activity level for a bank. Suggest a feasible cost-driver base for each, and explain why you think that your chosen cost-driver bases are feasible.

Activity	Activity Level
1. Sales calls—existing commercial customers	a. Unit
2. Sales calls—new commercial customers	b. Batch
3. Commercial loan negotiation	c. Product
4. Commercial loan review	d. Customer
5. Customer file maintenance	e. Facility
6. Community involvement	
7. Employee relations	
8. Commercial loan customer service	
9. Consumer loan customer service	
10. Consumer loan review	
11. Consumer deposit/withdrawal processing	
12. Commercial deposit/withdrawal processing	
13. Advertising particular products	

Exercise 4.36
Activity-Based versus Traditional Costing
(LO 1, 4, 5, 6)

Audio Corporation produces two types of compact discs, standard and high grade. The standard discs are designed for durability rather than accurate sound reproduction. The company only recently began producing the higher-quality, high-grade model to enter the lucrative music-recording market. Since the introduction of the new product, profits have steadily declined. Management believes that the accounting system might not be accurately allocating costs to products, particularly since sales of the new product have been increasing.

Communication

Management has asked you to investigate the cost allocation problem. You find that manufacturing overhead is currently assigned to products based on the direct-labor costs in the products. For your investigation, you have data from last year. Last year's manufacturing overhead was $220,000 based on the production of 320,000 standard units and 100,000 high-grade units. Direct-labor and direct-material costs were as follows:

	Standard	High Grade	Total
Direct labor	$174,000	$ 66,000	$240,000
Direct material	125,000	114,000	239,000

Management believes that overhead costs are caused by three cost drivers. The cost drivers and their costs for last year were as follows:

		Activity Level		
Cost Driver	**Costs Assigned**	**Standard**	**High Grade**	**Total**
Number of production runs	$100,000	40	10	50
Quality tests performed	90,000	12	18	30
Shipping orders processed	30,000	100	50	150
Total overhead	$220,000			

Required

a. How much of the overhead will be assigned to each product if these three cost drivers are used to allocate overhead? What is the total cost per unit produced for each product?

b. How much of the overhead was assigned to each product if direct-labor cost had been used to allocate overhead? What is the total cost per unit produced for each product?

c. How might the results from using activity-based costing in requirement (a) help management understand Audio's declining profits?

Exercise 4.37
Activity-Based Costing in a Service Environment
(LO 4, 5, 6, 7)

Communication

Green Garden Care, Inc., is a lawn and garden care service. It originally specialized in serving small residential clients but recently started contracting for work on office building grounds. Since Glenn Greenthumb (owner) believes that commercial lawn care is more profitable, he is considering dropping residential services altogether.

Five field employees worked a total of 20,000 hours last year, 13,000 on residential jobs and 7,000 on commercial jobs. Wages amounted to $9 per hour for all work done. Materials are included in overhead. All overhead is allocated on the basis of labor-hours worked, which also is the basis for customer charges. Glenn can charge $22 per hour for residential work but only $19 per hour for commercial work.

Required

a. If overhead for the year was $62,000, what were the profits of commercial and residential service using labor-hours as the allocation base?

b. Overhead consists of costs of transportation, equipment use, and supplies, which can be traced to the following activities:

			Activity Level	
Activity	**Cost Driver**	**Cost**	**Commercial**	**Residential**
Transportation	Number of clients serviced	$ 8,000	15	45
Equipment use	Equipment hours	18,000	3,500	2,100
Supplies	Area serviced in square yards	36,000	130,000	70,000
Total overhead		$62,000		

Recalculate profits for commercial and residential services based on these activity bases.

c. What recommendations do you have for management regarding the profitability of these two types of services?

Exercise 4.38
Activity-Based Costing versus Traditional Costing
(LO 1, 4, 5, 6)

Communication

Travel Gadgets Corporation manufactures travel clocks and watches. It currently allocates overhead costs using direct-labor hours, but the controller has recommended an activity-based costing system using the following data:

			Activity Level	
Activity	**Cost Driver**	**Cost**	**Travel Clocks**	**Watches**
Production setup	Number of setups	$50,000	10	15
Materials handling and requisition	Number of parts	15,000	18	36
Packaging and shipping	Number of units shipped	30,000	45,000	75,000
Total overhead		$95,000		

Required

a. Compute the amount of overhead to be allocated to each product under activity-based costing.

b. Compute the amount of overhead to be allocated to each product using direct-labor hours as the allocation base. Assume that the number of direct-labor hours required to assemble each unit is 0.5 per travel clock and 1.0 per watch and that 45,000 travel clocks and 75,000 watches were produced.

c. Should the company follow the controller's recommendations?

Exercise 4.39
Activity-Based Costing versus Traditional Costing
(LO 3, 4, 5, 6, 7)

Communication

Spreadsheet

Jack Chapman & Associates provides consulting and tax preparation services to its clients. It charges a $100 fee per hour for each service. The firm's revenues and costs for the year are shown in the following income statement:

	Tax	**Consulting**	**Total**
Revenue	$130,000	$270,000	$400,000
Expenses:			
Secretarial support	______	______	80,000
Supplies	______	______	72,000
Computer costs, etc	______	______	40,000
Profit	______	______	$208,000

The firm uses ABC and the following cost drivers:

		Activity Level	
Overhead Cost	**Cost Driver**	**Tax Preparation**	**Consulting**
Secretarial support	Number of clients	72	48
Supplies	Transactions with clients	200	300
Computer costs	Computer hours	1,000	600

Required

a. Complete the income statement using activity-based costing and the firm's three cost drivers.

b. Recompute the income statement using direct-labor hours as the only allocation base: 1,300 hours for tax; 2,700 hours for consulting.

c. How might the firm's decisions be altered if it were to allocate all overhead costs using direct-labor hours?

d. Under what circumstances would the labor-based allocation and activity-based costing (using the three cost drivers) result in similar profit results?

Problems

Problem 4.40
Comparison of Traditional Costing and Activity-Based Costing: Service Organization
(LO 1, 7)

Assume that you manage a business that provides services to both state government agencies and private organizations. Contracts for both groups are awarded on the basis of competitive bids. Your contracts with government agencies provide for reimbursement of costs plus a set percentage markup above cost for negotiated levels of service. Your contracts with private organizations are based on fees for levels of service. The relative profitability of the two types of contracts based on average cost information using hypothetical numbers follows:

Ethics

Costs and Revenues	**Government Contract**	**Private Contract**	**Total**
Costs	$2,000	$2,000	$4,000
Revenues:			
Cost × 140%	2,800	NA	2,800
Negotiated fee	NA	3,000	3,000
Profit	$ 800	$1,000	$1,800

You recently completed an ABC analysis that indicates that government contracts are much less costly than estimated previously:

Costs and Revenues	**Government Contract**	**Private Contract**	**Total**
ABC costs	$1,000	$3,000	$4,000
Revenues			
Cost × 140%	1,400	NA	1,400
Negotiated fee	NA	3,000	3,000
Profit	$ 400	$ 0	$ 400

Required

If you used the preceding ABC analysis for contracting, overall profitability would be much less. How should you use this information?

Problem 4.41
Product Profitability Computation: Traditional versus Activity-Based Costing
(LO 1, 4, 5)

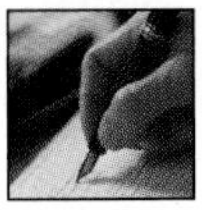
Communication

Import Glass & Crystal Company manufactures three types of glassware: unleaded glass, low-lead crystal, and high-lead crystal. Glass quality increases with higher lead content, which allows for more detailed cutting and etching. Unleaded glass production is highly automated, but cutting and etching crystal products require a varying degree of labor, depending on the pattern's intricacy. Import Glass & Crystal applies all indirect costs according to a predetermined rate based on direct-labor hours. A consultant recently suggested that the company switch to an activity-based costing system and prepared the following cost estimates for year 5 for the recommended cost drivers:

Activity	**Recommended Cost Driver**	**Estimated Costs**	**Estimated Cost-Driver Units**
Order processing	Number of orders	$ 15,000	100 orders
Production setup	Number of production runs	60,000	50 runs
Material handling	Number of pounds of materials used	100,000	80,000 pounds
Machine depreciation and maintenance	Number of machine hours	80,000	8,000 hours
Quality control	Number of inspections	20,000	30 inspections
Packing	Number of units	40,000	320,000 units
Total estimated overhead		$315,000	

In addition, management estimated 5,000 direct-labor hours for year 5.

Assume that the following activities occurred in January of year 5:

	Unleaded Glass	**Low-Lead Crystal**	**High-Lead Crystal**
Number of units produced	20,000	8,000	3,000
Direct-material costs	$13,000	$8,000	$5,000
Direct-labor hours	150	150	200
Number of orders	4	3	2
Number of production runs	1	1	2
Number of pounds of material used	5,000	2,000	1,000
Number of machine hours	580	140	80
Number of inspections	1	1	1
Number of units shipped	20,000	8,000	3,000

Actual direct-labor costs were $15 per hour.

Required

a. (1) Compute a predetermined overhead rate for year 5 for each cost driver using the estimated costs and estimated cost-driver units prepared by the consultant. (2) Also compute a predetermined overhead rate for year 5 using direct-labor hours as the allocation base.

b. Compute the production costs for each product for January using direct-labor hours as the allocation base and the predetermined overhead rate computed in requirement (a,2).

c. Compute the production costs for each product for January using the cost drivers recommended by the consultant and the predetermined rates computed in requirement (a,1). (*Note:* Do not assume that total overhead applied to products in January will be the same for activity-based costing as it was for the labor-hour-based allocation.)

d. Management has seen your numbers and wants to know how you account for the discrepancy between the product costs using direct-labor hours as the allocation base and the product costs using activity-based costing. Write a brief response to management.

Problem 4.42
Product Cost Computation: Traditional versus Activity-Based Costing
(LO 1, 4, 5)

Communication

Shades Company makes three types of sunglasses; Nerds, Stars, and Fashions. Shades presently applies overhead using a predetermined rate based on direct-labor hours. A group of company employees recommended that Shades switch to activity-based costing and identified the following activities, cost drivers, estimated costs, and estimated cost-driver units for year 2 for each activity center.

Activity	Recommended Cost Driver	Estimated Costs	Estimated Cost-Driver Units
Production setup	Number of production runs	$ 60,000	100 runs
Order processing	Number of orders	100,000	200 orders
Material handling	Number of pounds of material	40,000	8,000 pounds
Equipment depreciation and maintenance	Number of machine hours	120,000	10,000 hours
Quality management	Number of inspections	100,000	40 inspections
Packing and shipping	Number of units shipped	80,000	20,000 units
		$500,000	

In addition, management estimated 2,000 direct-labor hours for year 2.

Assume that the following activities occurred in February of year 2:

	Nerds	Stars	Fashions
Number of units produced	1,000	500	400
Direct material costs	$4,000	$2,500	$2,000
Direct-labor hours	100	120	110
Number of orders	8	8	4
Number of production runs	2	4	8
Number of pounds of material	400	200	200
Number of machine hours	500	300	300
Number of inspections	2	2	2
Number of units shipped	1,000	500	300

Direct-labor costs were $20 per hour.

Required

a. (1) Compute a predetermined overhead rate for year 2 for each cost driver recommended by the employees. (2) Also compute a predetermined overhead rate using direct-labor hours as the allocation base.

b. Compute the production costs for each product for February using direct-labor hours as the allocation base and the predetermined rate computed in requirement (a,2).

c. Compute the production costs for each product for February using the cost drivers recommended by the employees and the predetermined rates computed in requirement (a,1). (*Note:* Do not assume that total overhead applied to products in February will be the same for activity-based costing as it was for the labor-hour-based allocation.)

d. Management has seen your numbers and wants to know how you account for the discrepancy between the product costs using direct-labor hours as the allocation base and the product costs using activity-based costing. Write a brief response to management.

Problem 4.43
Product Profitability Computation: Traditional versus Activity-Based Costing
(LO 1, 4, 5, 6)

Cannonball Corporation manufactures three bicycle models: racing, mountain, and children's. The racing model, the Aerolight, is made of a titanium-aluminum alloy. The mountain bike, the Summit, is made of aluminum. The steel-framed children's bike is the Spinner. Because of the different materials used, production processes differ significantly among models in terms of machine types and time requirements.

Once parts have been produced, however, assembly time per unit required for each bike type is similar. For this reason. Cannonball allocates overhead on the basis of machine hours. Last year, the company produced 1,000 Aerolights, 2,000 Summits, and 5,000 Spinners and had the following revenues and expenses:

CANNONBALL CORPORATION
Income Statement

	Aerolight	Summit	Spinner	Total
Sales	$380,000	$560,000	$475,000	$1,415,000
Direct costs:				
Direct material	150,000	240,000	200,000	590,000
Direct labor	14,400	24,000	54,000	92,400
Variable overhead:				
Machine setup	______	______	______	26,000
Order processing	______	______	______	64,000
Warehousing costs	______	______	______	93,000
Energy to run machines	______	______	______	42,000
Shipping	______	______	______	36,000
Contribution margin	______	______	______	471,600
Fixed overhead:				
Plant administration				88,000
Other fixed overhead				140,000
Gross profit				$ 243,600

Cannonball's CFO hired a consultant to recommend cost allocation bases. The consultant recommended the following:

		Activity Level		
Activity	**Cost Driver**	**Aerolight**	**Summit**	**Spinner**
1. Machine setup	Number of production runs	22	34	44
2. Sales-order processing	Number of sales orders received	400	600	600
3. Warehousing costs	Number of units held in inventory	200	200	400
4. Energy	Number of machine hours	10,000	16,000	24,000
5. Shipping	Number of units shipped	1,000	4,000	10,000

The consultant found no basis for allocating the plant administration and other fixed overhead costs and recommended that they not be allocated to products.

Required

a. Using machine hours to allocate production overhead, complete the income statement for Cannonball Company. (See activity 4 for machine hours.) Do not attempt to allocate plant administration or other fixed overhead.

b. Complete the income statement using the bases recommended by the consultant.

c. How might ABC help Cannonball's management make better decisions?

d. After hearing the consultant's recommendations, the CFO decided to adopt ABC but expressed concern about not allocating some overhead (plant administration and other fixed overhead) to the products. In the CFO's view, "Products have to bear a fair share of all overhead or we won't be covering all of our costs." How would you respond to this comment?

Problem 4.44
Benefits of Activity-Based Costing
(LO 1, 6)

Communication

Many companies recognize that their cost systems are inadequate for today's global market. Managers in companies selling multiple products are making important product decisions based on distorted cost information, because many cost systems are designed to focus on inventory valuation.

Required

If management should decide to implement an ABC system, what benefits should it expect?

[CMA adapted]

Problem 4.45
Benefits of Activity-Based Costing
(LO 1, 5)

Communication

Sparkle Manufacturing has just completed a major change in its method to inspect its product. Previously, 10 inspectors examined the product after each major process. The salaries of these inspectors were charged as direct labor to the operation or job. To improve efficiency, Sparkle's production manager recently bought a computerized quality-control system consisting of a microcomputer, 15 video cameras, peripheral hardware, and software. The cameras are placed at key points in the production process, take pictures of the product, and compare these pictures with a known "good" image supplied by a quality-control engineer. This new system allows Sparkle to replace the 10 quality control inspectors with only two quality-control engineers.

The company president is concerned. She was told that the production process is now more efficient, yet she notices a large increase in the factory overhead rate. The computation of the rate before and after automation follows:

	Before	**After**
Estimated overhead	$1,900,000	$2,100,000
Estimated direct labor	$1,000,000	$ 700,000
Predetermined overhead rate	190%	300%

Required

Prepare a report that states how an ABC system might benefit Sparkle Manufacturing and alleviate the president's concern.

[CMA adapted]

Problem 4.46
Cost-Driver Rate Computation and Cost Assignment to Services: Missing Information
(LO 4, 5, 7)

The ABC team at Sky Enterprises, a surveillance company, is attempting to complete a table similar to the one in Exhibit 4–6 except that it is for just one product, Sky Spi. The team has pieced together the following data:

Unit-level actual activity (hours of surveillance) is unknown; predetermined cost-driver rate is $10,000 per unit; total unit cost assigned to the product in November is $14,000,000.

Batch-level activity is 2 (satellite launches); cost of batches assigned to the product is $5,000,000 (predetermined cost driver rate is unknown).

Product-level activity is 1 product; predetermined cost-driver rate is $1,000,000.

Customer-level activity is 100 customers; predetermined cost-driver rate is $50,000 per customer.

Facility-level activity is 50,000 square feet; predetermined cost-driver rate is $500 per square foot.

Required

Prepare a table similar to Exhibit 4–6. You must provide missing data. Label the table column headings as follows: Activity/Resource, Predetermined Cost-Driver Rate, Actual Activity Volume: November, and Cost of Sky Spi: November. All activity levels are for the month of November.

Problem 4.47
Cost-Driver Rate Computation and Cost Assignment to Services: Missing Information
(LO 4, 5, 7)

The ABC team at Spear, Inc., a concert-planning company, is attempting to complete a table similar to the one in Exhibit 4–6 except that it is for just one product, Brit Ni. The team has pieced together the following data:

Unit-level actual activity (number of concerts times number of band members) is 120; predetermined cost-driver rate is unknown; total unit cost assigned to the product in March is $480,000.

Batch-level activity is 12 concerts ("batches" of music); cost of batches assigned to the product is $600,000 (predetermined cost driver rate is unknown).

Product-level activity is 1 product; predetermined cost-driver rate is $100,000.

Customer-level activity (number of consultations with customers) is unknown; predetermined cost-driver rate is $500 per consultation; total customer-level cost assigned to the product in March is $25,000.

Facility-level activity is 5,000 hours of management and high-level staff support; cost of management and staff support assigned to the product in March is $400,000 (predetermined cost-driver rate is unknown).

Required

Prepare a table similar to Exhibit 4–6. You must provide the missing data. Label the table column headings as follows: Activity/Resource, Predetermined Cost-Driver Rate; Actual Activity Volume: March, Cost of Brit Ni: March. All activity levels are for the month of March.

Problem 4.48
Cost-Driver Rate and Computation Cost Assignment to Services: Missing Information
(LO 4, 5, 7)

The ABC team at Social Services is attempting to complete a table similar to the one in Exhibit 4–6 except that it is for just one product, Consultation Sessions. The team has pieced together the following data:

Unit-level activity is 10,000 hours; predetermined cost-driver rate is $50 per hour.

There are no batch-level activities.

Product-level activity is 1 product; predetermined cost-driver rate is $100,000.

Customer-level activity is 4,000 clients; predetermined cost driver rate is $100 per client.

Facility-level activity is 1,000 square feet; total facility cost assigned to the product in January is $3,000. (Predetermined cost-driver rate is unknown.)

Required

Prepare a table similar to Exhibit 4–6. You must provide the missing data. Label the table column headings as follows: Activity/Resource, Predetermined Cost-Driver Rate, Actual Activity Volume: January, Cost of Consultation Sessions: January. All activity levels are for the month of January.

Problem 4.49
Product Profitability
(LO 1, 2, 4, 5, 6)

An ABC team at Minnesota Munchies, a health food company, identified these data for a typical month:

Activity/Resource	Cost-Driver Base	Activity Cost in a Typical Month	Activity Volume in a Typical Month
1. Unit Level			
1.1 Acquire and use material for Product A	Number of units produced	$ 60,000	1,000,000 units
1.2 Acquire and use direct labor for Product A	Number of direct-labor hours worked	20,000	2,000 direct-labor hours
1.3 Acquire and use material for Product B	Number of units produced	80,000	800,000 units
1.4 Acquire and use direct labor for Product B	Number of direct-labor hours worked	30,000	2,000 direct-labor hours
2. Batch Level			
2.1 Quality control	Number of batches	30,000	100 batches
3. Product Level			
3.1 Provide product-level advertising	Number of promotions	100,000	100 promotions
3.2 Provide product-level records	Number of products	20,000	2 products
4. Customer Level			
4.1 Take customer product orders	Number of customer orders	40,000	2,000 customer orders
4.2 Deal with customer complaints	Number of complaints	20,000	1,000 complaints
5. Facility Level			
5.1 Supervise direct labor	Amount of direct-labor costs	10,000	$50,000 for activities 1.2 and 1.4 (supervision costs = 20% of direct labor costs.)
5.2 Use main building	Number of square feet	40,000	10,000 square feet

Minnesota Munchies' management wants you to compute the total cost and unit cost of each product for the month of July, which had the following level of activities:

	Product A	Product B
1.1 and 1.3 Material	800,000 units	900,000 units
1.2 and 1.4 Direct labor	1,600 hours	2,100 hours
2.1 Quality control—batches	50 batches	40 batches
3.1 Advertising projects—promotions	50 promotions	40 promotions

	Product A	Product B
3.2 Products recorded	1 product	1 product
4.1 Customer orders	800 customer orders	900 customer orders
4.2 Customer complaints	600 complaints	300 complaints
5.1 Direct-labor supervision	$16,000	$31,500
5.2 Main building use	6,000 sq. ft.	3,000 sq. ft.

Required

a. Compute the cost-driver rate for each cost-driver base.

b. Use ABC to compute the cost of each of the two products given the activity level for the month of July. Compute both the total cost and unit cost for each product for the month of July.

c. Assume that the company's traditional costing system had assigned overhead costs at a rate of $0.10 per unit of output plus $20.00 per direct-labor hour. Overhead costs are the sum of the batch-level, product-level, customer-level, and facility-level costs. Using this traditional costing approach, compute the cost of each product (including material and direct-labor costs) given the activity level for the month of July. Compute both the total cost and unit cost for each product for the month of July.

d. Do the unit costs of the two products computed under ABC and traditional costing systems differ significantly? If so, what causes the differences?

Problem 4.50
Information Misreported: Traditional versus Activity-Based Costing
(LO 1, 2, 4, 5, 6)

Refer to problem 4.49. You have just discovered that the product manager of product A has been less than honest in reporting the number of direct-labor hours used. In checking the payroll records, you discover that 2,000 direct-labor hours ($20,000 direct-labor costs) actually were used in July to produce Product A, not 1,600 hours as the product manager reported.

Required

a. Using this new information, recompute the total and unit costs for product A for July using both the activity-based and traditional costing systems.

b. Does this new information significantly affect the cost numbers using either traditional or ABC systems?

c. Does this new information affect the cost computations for product B using either the activity-based or traditional costing systems?

d. Why might the product manager of product A have understated the number of direct-labor hours used to produce it?

Problem 4.51
Unit-Based and ABC Full-Costing Comparison (Appendix)
(LO 8)

Communication

Refer to problem 4.49. Management of Minnesota Munchies wants to compare the unit-based cost of each product to its full cost.

Required

a. Compute the total costs of each product for the month of July using the unit-based cost approach described in the chapter Appendix.

b. Repeat requirement (a), but compute the unit cost of each product [divide your results in requirement (a) by the number of units produced in July].

c. Write a brief memo that explains the differences in results between this problem and problem 4.49.

Problem 4.52
Product Profitability in a Service Organization
(LO 1, 2, 4, 5, 6, 7)

An ABC team at Happy Surgeries, an outpatient surgery center that performs 25 different types of surgeries, identified the data shown below for a typical month (excluding costs of surgeons and anesthesiologists). The ABC team learned that surgeries are not performed in batches, so there are no batch level activities or resources.

Activity/Resource	Cost-Driver Base	Activity Cost in a Typical Month	Activity Volume in a Typical Month
1. Unit Level			
1.1 Acquire and use medical supplies	Number of surgeries	$80,000	2,000
1.2 Acquire and use surgical nursing staff	Number of hours of surgery	180,000	2,400

Activity/Resource	Cost-Driver Base	Activity Cost in a Typical Month	Activity Volume in a Typical Month
1.3 Clean operating room and set up for surgeries	Number of surgeries	$100,000	2,000
1.4 Provide recovery room care	Number of hours of patient time in recovery room	120,000	4,000
2. Product Level			
2.1 Maintain information for each type of surgery performed	Number of types of surgeries performed	40,000	20
2.2 Provide special equipment for eye surgeries	Number of types of eye surgery	50,000	1
2.3 Provide hip and knee replacement parts	Number of hip and knee replacements	400,000	50
3. Customer Level			
3.1 Conduct presurgery visit with patient	Number of presurgery patient visits	80,000	4,000
3.2 Make postsurgery calls to patients	Number of calls	30,000	6,000
3.3 Do patients' postsurgery visits	Number of postsurgery visits	50,000	1,000
4. Facility Level			
4.1 Provide supervision	Cost amount of activities 1.2, 1.3, and 1.4	60,000	$400,000 for activities 1.2, 1.3, and 1.4 (Supervision costs = 15% of the costs of activities 1.2, 1.3 and 1.4.)
4.2 Use operating rooms	Number of hours of use	720,000	2,400
4.3 Use recovery rooms	Number of patient hours in recovery room	200,000	4,000

Happy Surgery's management wants you to compute the total cost and unit cost of two of their 25 different products, eye surgery and hip replacement, for the month of March. The activity levels for the month of March follow:

	Eye Surgery	Hip Replacement
1.1 Use medical supplies	50 surgeries	20 surgeries
1.2 Use surgical nursing staff	80 hours of surgery	50 hours of surgery
1.3 Clean operating room and set up for surgeries	50 surgeries	20 surgeries
1.4 Provide recovery room care	100 hours of patient time in the recovery room	80 hours of patient time in the recovery room
2.1 Maintain information for each type of surgery performed	1 type of surgery	1 type of surgery
2.2 Provide special equipment for eye surgeries	1 type of eye surgery	NA
2.3 Provide parts for hip and knee replacement	NA	20 parts (1 per surgery)
3.1 Conduct presurgery visit with patient	80 visits	40 visits
3.2 Make postsurgery calls	120 calls	60 calls
3.3 Do patients' postsurgery visits	50 visits	25 visits
4.1 Supervision	See cost of activities 1.2, 1.3, and 1.4.	See cost of activities 1.2, 1.3, and 1.4.
4.2 Use of operating rooms	80 hours	50 hours
4.3 Use of recovery rooms	100 hours	80 hours

Required

a. Compute the cost-driver rate for each cost-driver base.

b. Using ABC, compute the cost of each product, eye surgery and hip replacement, given the activity level for the month of March. Compute both the total cost and unit cost for each product for the month of March.

c. Assume that the company's traditional costing system had assigned product-level, customer-level, and facility-level costs to surgeries amounting to $815 per surgery. Using this traditional costing approach, compute the cost of eye surgery and hip replacement given the activity level for the month of March. Be sure to add unit-level costs to the $815 per surgery. Compute both the total cost and unit cost for each product for the month of March.

d. Comparing the ABC and traditional costing systems, do the unit costs of the two products differ significantly? If so, what causes the differences?

Problem 4.53
Information Misreported: Traditional versus Activity-Based Costing
(LO 1, 2, 4, 5, 6, 7)

Refer to problem 4.52. You have just discovered an error in data reporting for eye surgeries. The number of eye surgeries during March was 60, not 50. The extra eye surgeries had been misclassified as colonoscopies.

Required

a. Using this new information, recompute the total and unit costs for eye surgeries in March using both ABC and traditional costing systems.

b. Does this new information significantly affect the cost numbers using either traditional costing or ABC systems?

c. Does this new information affect the cost computations for hip replacement surgeries using either ABC or traditional costing systems?

Problem 4.54
Comparison of Unit-Based and ABC Full Costing (Appendix)
(LO 8)

Communication

Refer to problem 4.52. Management of Happy Surgeries wants to compare the unit-based cost of eye surgery and hip replacement to its full cost.

Required

a. Compute the total costs of each product for the month of March using the unit-based cost approach described in the chapter Appendix.

b. Repeat requirement (a) but compute the unit cost of eye surgery and hip replacement [divide your results in requirement (a) by the number of units produced in March].

c. Write a brief memo that explains the differences in results between this problem and problem 4.52.

Problem 4.55
Product Profitability in a Merchandising Company: Traditional versus Activity-Based Costing
(LO 1, 2, 4, 5, 6, 7)

An ABC team at Sporti Gus, a sporting goods store, identified the following data. These amounts exclude the cost of the merchandise itself.

Activity/Resource	Cost-Driver Base	Activity Cost in a Typical Month	Activity Volume in a Typical Month
1. Unit Level			
1.1 Sell goods	Units sold	$23,000	10,000
2. Batch Level			
2.1 Process purchases	Number of purchase orders	6,000	200
3. Product Level			
3.1 Provide product-level advertising	Number of promotions	30,000	200
3.2 Provide product-inventory record-keeping	Number of products	3,000	600
4. Customer Level			
4.1 Accept customer returns	Number of returns	12,000	800

Activity/Resource	Cost-Driver Base	Activity Cost in a Typical Month	Activity Volume in a Typical Month
5. Facility Level			
5.1 Supervise sales personnel	Cost of sales personnel	4,000	$23,000 for activity 1.1 (supervision costs = 17.39% of activity 1.1 costs.)
5.2 Use building	Square feet of shelf space used by merchandise	32,000	8,000

Sporti Gus' management wants you to compute the total cost and unit cost of two products for the month of June, which had the following level of activities:

	Tennis Rackets	Fishing Rods
1.1 Units sold	20	10
2.1 Process purchases	0.25 (1 of 4 items purchased in one purchase order)	1.5 (part of three separate purchase orders)
3.1 Provide product-level advertising	2 promotions	4.5 promotions (part of 12 promotions)
3.2 Provide product-inventory record-keeping	1 product	1 product
4.1 Accept customer returns	6 returns	2 returns
5.1 Supervise sales personnel	See your computations for activity 1.1	See your computations for activity 1.1
5.2 Use building	80 sq. ft.	60 sq.ft.

Required

a. Compute the cost-driver rates for each cost-driver base.

b. Using ABC, compute the cost of each product given the activity level for the month of June. Compute both the total cost and unit cost for each product for the month of June.

c. Assume that the company's traditional costing system had assigned the batch-level, product-level, customer-level, and facility-level costs at a rate of $8.70 per unit sold. Using this traditional costing approach, compute the cost of each product given the activity level for the month of June. Be sure to add the unit-level costs to the $8.70 per unit sold. Compute both the total cost and unit cost for each product for the month of June.

d. Comparing ABC and traditional costing systems, do the unit costs of the two products differ significantly? If so, what causes the differences?

Problem 4.56
Information Misreported: Traditional versus Activity-Based Costing
(LO 1, 2, 4, 5, 6, 7)

Refer to problem 4.55. You have just discovered an error in counting the sales of fishing rods. Sporti Gus actually sold only 8 fishing rods, not 10 (the other two sales were actually rifles).

Required

a. Using this new information, recompute the total and unit costs for fishing rods for June using both the ABC and traditional costing systems.

b. Does this new information significantly affect the cost numbers using either traditional costing or ABC systems?

c. Does this new information affect the cost computations for tennis rackets using either the activity-based or traditional costing systems?

Problem 4.57
Activity Analysis
(LO 2, 3, 4)

Boulder Assembly, Inc., is an outsourcing assembler for local manufacturers. The following data are for a one-week period for the assembly of circuit boards used by two different computer manufacturers (A and B):

- Material costs used and supplied for 3,500 units of board A produced and shipped, $40,000; 2,000 units of board B produced and shipped, $40,000.

Spreadsheet

- Batch setup labor cost used for five batches of board A, $1,000; two batches of board B, $600.
- Batch setup materials used and supplied for seven batches, $4,200.
- Labor supplied (a unit-level cost) for production of both boards, $14,000; usage based on number of manually assembled parts: eight parts for each board A, 16 parts for each board B.
- Facility-level equipment for both products, $25,000, allocated 60 percent to Product A and 40 percent to Product B.
- Packaging and shipping provided on a per-unit basis, $10,500 shipping, $7,000 for materials, and $14,000 for labor.
- Custodial and security service (facility-level cost) for the manufacturing area, $3,000 allocated 50 percent to Product A and 50 percent to Product B.

Required

Prepare an exhibit similar to Exhibit 4–5 using the preceding information.

Problem 4.58
Profitability Analysis
(LO 5, 6)

Refer to problem 4.57.

Required

a. Compute the total and per-unit costs using a format similar to the one in Exhibit 4–6.

b. Boulder Assembly receives a sales price of $30 each for board A and $30 each for board B. Prepare a profitability report similar to the one in Exhibit 4–7. Should Boulder Assembly discontinue either product? Why or why not?

Problem 4.59
Activity Analysis in a Service Organization
(LO 2, 3, 4, 7)

Marketing solutions is a regional provider of telemarketing surveys and sales. (Yes, they are the ones who call you at dinner time!) The basic unit of service is a completed survey or sales call. Assume that all telemarketing labor is paid hourly. Supervisory labor is salaried. The following are data from a recent month:

- Hourly telemarketing labor to complete 22,000 surveys and 90,000 calls, $176,000; completed surveys take 8 minutes each; sales calls 3 minutes each.
- Long-distance phone charges for 10 percent of surveys, $7,000.
- Preparation of scripts for surveys, $5,000, and sales pitches for calls, $4,000.
- Training telemarketing labor to conduct surveys, $13,200.
- Automated dialing equipment that serves all calls, $10,000.
- Occupancy costs, $12,000.
- Two supervisors, $9,600.
- Human Resources Department, $5,200.

Allocate automated dialing equipment, occupancy costs, supervisors, and human resources costs 50 percent to surveys and 50% to telemarketing calls.

Required

Prepare a table similar to the one in Exhibit 4–6 using the preceding data.

Problem 4.60
Profitability Analysis
(LO 5, 6, 7)

Refer to the previous problem.

Required

a. Compute the total per-unit costs as these costs were computed in Exhibit 4–6.

b. Marketing Solutions is paid $5 per completed survey and $2 per completed sales call. Prepare a profitability report similar to the one in Exhibit 4–7. Should Marketing Solutions discontinue either service? Why or why not?

Problem 4.61
Research Report
(LO 1–7)

Internet Communication

Search your library or the Internet for a recent article on an organization's experiences using activity-based costing.

Required

Prepare a short report that includes:

a. A description of the organization (economic sector, size, international scope, etc.).

b. The reasons the organization used ABC.

c. The operations that were the focus of the analysis.

d. The impact(s) of ABC on organizational performance.

Problem 4.62
International Issues
(LO 1–7)

Global

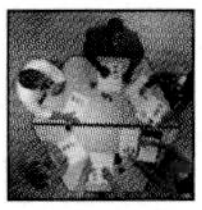
Team

ABC in its modern form was developed largely in the United Kingdom and United States. As a result, ABC might reflect certain cultural norms about business management that are common to these countries but are not worldwide practice. At least one article has contrasted US and French approaches to business that could account for relatively fewer applications of ABC in France than in either the United States or United Kingdom. These factors allegedly include the language, opening of the European Union, preexistence of a complex French full-cost method, management style, class and corporate barriers, and contractual basis for performance evaluation in the United States versus importance of honor and rank in France.

Required

As an individual or (ideally, an internationally diverse) group project, evaluate how these factors could affect the adoption of ABC. If internationally diverse group members are available, contrast US/UK characteristics with those of another country.

Cases

Case 4.63
Activity-Based Costing in Health Care
(LO 1–7)

Communication

Insurance companies and the federal government are restricting reimbursements to health care facilities and causing these facilities to seek cost reductions and more accurate tracing of costs without reducing the quality of care. Marian Rodriguez, the administrator of Community Hospital, is exploring whether ABC can be applied to her hospital's operations. She is meeting with your consulting team to seek your advice and to determine whether to hire you to lead an ABC pilot project that, if successful, could be extended to the rest of the hospital.

> Marian: "I'm not too sure whether ABC is right for our situation, but I believe I should explore it at least. I think ABC is primarily for manufacturing companies, but there might be legitimate parallels between a hospital and a factory."
>
> You: (Provide a brief response to these concerns that might encourage Marian to hire you.)
>
> Marian: "That seems reasonable, though I'm not sure that we want to tell our board of directors and the general public that Community Hospital will be run like a factory. That's not the image we want to project. Nonetheless, I think we should proceed. I suggest that you analyze a typical nursing station and show me what analyses you can produce from an ABC perspective."

You work with nursing staff and the administrator's office to gather the following information:

Nursing Activity	Personnel	Annual Cost
Providing supervision	1	$ 70,000
Delivering nursing care	5	250,000
Cleaning, changing linens and garments	3	60,000
Total annual costs		$380,000
Total patient days (one patient in the hospital for one full day)		2,000
Average nursing cost per patient day		$190

All patients receive approximately the same level of cleaning and changing linens and garments, but the level of nursing care varies. Nursing staff suggested that patient days should be weighted by the level of care required. Using this input, you categorized the patients served by this nursing station in the past year as follows. Weights approximate the intensity of care needed.

Nursing Care Level	Number of Patients	Patient Days	Weight	Weighted Patient Days
Level 1 (needs typical nursing care)	300	600	1	600
Level 2 (needs more than typical nursing care but not intensive care)	300	900	2	1,800
Level 3 (needs most intensive nursing care)	100	500	4	2,000
Totals	700	2,000		4,400

Required

Prepare a report in memorandum form that explains the following:

a. The objective of your ABC analysis.
b. The reason that the average cost per patient day is misleading.
c. The sources of your data and the feasibility of collecting them in the future.
d. The confidence you have in that data to support your analysis and conclusions.
e. The method of tracing operating costs of the nursing station to its activities.
f. The calculations of activity costs per unit and examples of nursing station costs of different patients.
g. The implications of your analysis for managing Community Hospital's nursing stations.

Case 4.64
Choice of Cost System
(LO 1–7)

Huge Company's tooling business unit (TBU) manufactures metal and carbon-fiber parts for the company's major products. TBU's principal focus in recent years has been to schedule its resources properly, but its manager is concerned that the current method of costing the unit's work is causing other business units to send it work that does not use TBU's strengths to the company's overall advantage. TBU computes a combined labor and overhead cost per labor hour and charges each job based on the number of labor hours used. This labor-based charge is added to materials cost to calculate the total job cost.

TBU works for internal customers exclusively, and there is no consideration to allow it to seek outside work. Other business units are allowed to use external suppliers, however, and are encouraged but not required to use TBU, which has 19 work centers, each of which uses computer-controlled machines and processes.

TBU uses two basic types of machines: (1) 6 multi-axis (M) machines, which allow complex parts to be rotated in multiple directions while being completed without removing the part and (2) 13 single-axis (S) machines, which are used for parts that do not have to be rotated more than once to be completed. The M machines were just purchased to replace 6 (S) machines. They are three times as expensive to operate as (S) machines. Each machine is considered a work center and is available 6,000 hours (three shifts) per year.

TBU's employees are highly skilled and are among Huge Company's highest paid hourly workers. They are qualified to work on either type of machine and any type of job. As a practical matter, employees tend to work on machines and jobs that interest them most, but TBU management encourages workers to diversify their efforts. TBU employees are available 2,000 hours per year.

Stainless steel (SS) and aluminum (A) parts are machined from metal stock. Carbon fiber (CF) parts are made by laminating carbon fiber and plastic resins. Carbon-fiber materials are much more expensive and require more labor.

Last year's labor cost and overhead (which includes the costs of management and equipment but excludes materials costs) follow:

Labor (1,000 employees)	$ 90,000,000
Overhead	
Equipment (19 work centers)	190,000,000*
Management and engineering	20,000,000
Total	$300,000,000

*Based on 19 (S) machines.

The following are the data for and characteristics of five representative jobs:

Job	Equipment	Machine Hours	Materials Type	Weight (kg)	Materials Cost	Labor Hours
1	M	7.50	SS	300	$ 30,000	22.50
2	S	10.00	CF	200	100,000	160.00
3	M	8.75	A	350	28,000	21.00
4	S	12.50	A	500	40,000	120.00
5	S	5.00	SS	200	20,000	60.00

Required

a. Compute the costs of each job using the current cost system.

b. Recommend an alternative cost system that recognizes additional differences among jobs.

c. Recompute the job costs using your alternative cost system.

d. Explain differences in decision making at TBU.

e. Identify TBU's internal customers that might be influenced by the use of the alternative cost system.

CHAPTER

5

Activity-Based Management

After completing this chapter, you should be able to:

1. Understand the key steps of an activity-based management system.

2. Demonstrate how to use activity-based costing for target costing.

3. Identify and measure the costs of activities that add value or do not add value in organizations.

4. Use the elements of an activity-based management system to help identify opportunities for process improvements.

5. Evaluate capacity utilization by identifying resources supplied and resources used.

6. Understand methods of and problems related to implementing activity-based costing and management.

Cost-Management Challenges

1. **Is** implementing activity-based costing enough to improve efficiency? Can cost management analysts measure costs more accurately using it and, by doing so, ensure that the organization will meet its efficiency goals?

2. **Do** the numbers "speak for themselves"? Does the cost management analyst's responsibility end with making recommendations for improvements?

3. **How** do you know that activity-based cost-management methods are worthwhile?

PMI Precision Molding, Inc.

The scene is a meeting of the executive committee of Precision Molding, Inc. (PMI), including Melody Fairchild, chief executive officer; Chad Norris, vice president of manufacturing; Alex Lewis, chief financial officer; Michael Chia, vice president of logistics; and Elizabeth Forney, vice president of marketing. The meeting occurred one year after PMI began supplying MegaBurger Corporation with promotional plastic toys. MegaBurger is one of the world's largest fast-food chains, and PMI is a leading supplier of plastic products in its geographical region.

PMI will bid to supply promotional items for MegaBurger for another year. If PMI fails in the bidding process or fails to execute the bid profitably, the company would experience a significant setback in reputation and profitability.

Fairchild (CEO): We need to decide whether to continue supplying toys to MegaBurger. Our business with it was somewhat profitable last year but not at the level we would like. We must increase our income on the MegaBurger business, or continuing it is simply not worth our effort.

Norris (Manufacturing): I've looked at MegaBurger's plans and specifications very closely. These toys and action figures are rather complicated. We've already shown that we're capable of meeting MegaBurger's quality standards, but we need to work closely with our production personnel to make the process more efficient to reduce costs.

Lewis (CFO): We can't make an adequate profit using the current production processes. I can't promise at this point that we'll identify and make enough improvements in our production processes to increase income. My gut feeling is that we can do it, but *everyone* will have to work hard.

Chia (Logistics): Our suppliers indicate no problem in supplying us the materials for these products when we need them. They're eager to continue working with us given the significance of the business. I see no reason not to continue producing the products for MegaBurger.

Forney (Marketing): As you know, this industry is a small world. Given our success with MegaBurger last year, a dozen other companies have invited us to consider bidding on their business. The reputation of being a MegaBurger supplier is already creating new business opportunities for us.

Fairchild (CEO): I agree with Elizabeth that the potential for new business is terrific, but let's focus on MegaBurger for now. I'm hearing a consensus that we should continue with the MegaBurger business.

Alex, I want you to work closely with the ABC team that we established last year when we first considered bidding for the MegaBurger job. That team should recommend improvements in the production processes necessary to reduce costs. I want you to work closely with Chad and Michael to be sure that you fully consider all costs and any necessary improvements in both production and distribution.

Thanks for your input, and good luck to all of us. Alex, let me know your plans for proceeding by tomorrow morning.

Importance of Activity-Based Information to PMI's Success

LO 1 Understand the key steps of an activity-based management system.

We return to our focus company of Chapter 4, Precision Molding, Inc. (PMI). This manufacturer of plastic containers and baby-care products supplied plastic promotional novelty toys to all MegaBurger restaurants in the region last year. The products, although small, are more complex than PMI's other products, and MegaBurger has very high expectations for quality and on-time deliveries. Delivering these products successfully last year resulted in a large increase in sales and the near certainty of continued business with MegaBurger. Although PMI met MegaBurger's quality standards and on-time delivery expectations, PMI has not found MegaBurger's business to be sufficiently profitable.

To continue doing business with MegaBurger, PMI must increase its income; to do that, it must refine its processes. On the basis of the ABC team's analysis, the firm decided that it had the knowledge and technical capability to meet the company's profit goals with respect to the MegaBurger business.

As described in Chapter 4, *activity-based costing (ABC)* focuses on (1) understanding the way resources are used in current processes and (2) accurately measuring product costs using those processes. By itself, however, ABC does not result in the process improvements that might be necessary to achieve desired efficiency. Thus, ABC stops short of being a comprehensive cost-management system. This chapter continues to develop questions raised in Chapter 4 concerning how to build a cost-management system that increases the understanding of the uses of resources and that promotes process improvements. To illustrate these concepts, we discuss how PMI is able to submit a successful and profitable bid to MegaBurger for another year by using activity-based management for its existing processes.

activity-based management (ABM) *is used by management to evaluate the costs and values of process activities to identify opportunities for improved efficiency*

Activity-based management (ABM) evaluates the costs and values of process activities to identify opportunities to improve efficiency. ABM combines activity-based costing analysis and value-added analysis to make process improvements that improve customer value and reduce wasted resources.[1] ABM uses and builds on basic ABC analysis. Recall the four ABC steps discussed in Chapter 4:

Step 1. Identify and classify the activities related to the company's products.
Step 2. Estimate the cost of activities identified in step 1.
Step 3. Calculate a cost-driver rate for the activity.
Step 4. Assign activity costs to products.

ABM takes ABC a step further to include these steps:

- Identify activities as value added or non-value added.
- Score each activity as high or low value added as perceived by the customer.
- Identify opportunities to enhance value-added activities and to reduce or eliminate non-value-added activities.

Activity-Based Costing: Foundation of Process Improvement

Chapter 4 describes how PMI followed the four ABC steps to estimate the cost of the products to be produced for MegaBurger. It used this information to submit a successful bid for last year's business with MegaBurger. To obtain the needed information, CEO Fairchild asked CFO Lewis to create a cross-functional team to evaluate the MegaBurger offer. The team first matched MegaBurger's product and service specifications to the activities and cost-driver rates derived from PMI's activity analysis of its

[1] ABM is a popular business approach to process redesign. Other process redesign business approaches include quality function deployment (QFD), which focuses on improving quality, and business process reengineering (BPR), which generally seeks radical changes to processes. Many believe that ABM is superior to QFD because it focuses on the concept of customer-based value, which is broader than quality. ABM has proved to be more enduring than BPR, probably because ABM embraces continuous improvement rather than BPR's radical change, which sounds more exciting but has proven more difficult to design and to implement. Engineering approaches to process redesign, which could be applied to business processes, often involve computer modeling and simulation of activities that can be described mathematically.

Exhibit 5–1 Application of ABC Cost Information to Estimate New Product Costs

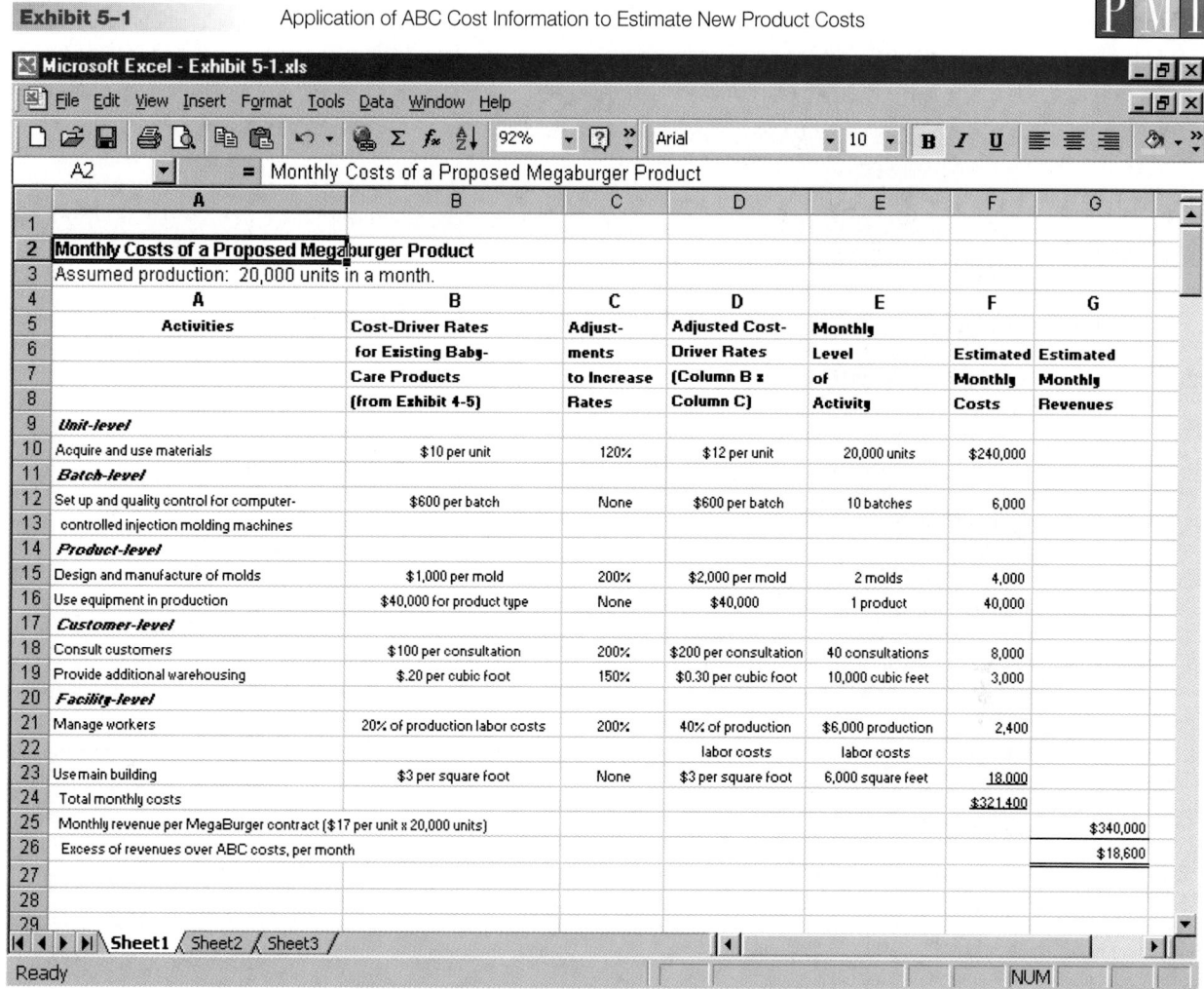

PMI

Microsoft Excel - Exhibit 5-1.xls

A2 = Monthly Costs of a Proposed Megaburger Product

Monthly Costs of a Proposed Megaburger Product

Assumed production: 20,000 units in a month.

A	B	C	D	E	F	G
Activities	**Cost-Driver Rates for Existing Baby-Care Products (from Exhibit 4-5)**	**Adjust-ments to Increase Rates**	**Adjusted Cost-Driver Rates (Column B x Column C)**	**Monthly Level of Activity**	**Estimated Monthly Costs**	**Estimated Monthly Revenues**
Unit-level						
Acquire and use materials	$10 per unit	120%	$12 per unit	20,000 units	$240,000	
Batch-level						
Set up and quality control for computer-controlled injection molding machines	$600 per batch	None	$600 per batch	10 batches	6,000	
Product-level						
Design and manufacture of molds	$1,000 per mold	200%	$2,000 per mold	2 molds	4,000	
Use equipment in production	$40,000 for product type	None	$40,000	1 product	40,000	
Customer-level						
Consult customers	$100 per consultation	200%	$200 per consultation	40 consultations	8,000	
Provide additional warehousing	$.20 per cubic foot	150%	$0.30 per cubic foot	10,000 cubic feet	3,000	
Facility-level						
Manage workers	20% of production labor costs	200%	40% of production labor costs	$6,000 production labor costs	2,400	
Use main building	$3 per square foot	None	$3 per square foot	6,000 square feet	18,000	
Total monthly costs					$321,400	
Monthly revenue per MegaBurger contract ($17 per unit x 20,000 units)						$340,000
Excess of revenues over ABC costs, per month						$18,600

Sheet1 / Sheet2 / Sheet3

Ready NUM

current products. These activities and cost-driver rates are shown in columns A and B of Exhibit 5–1, which is reproduced from Exhibit 4–9 in Chapter 4.

Based on a review of MegaBurger's specifications, the ABC team determined that producing the toys would be similar to making complex baby-care products with several adjustments to improve product quality. Column C of Exhibit 5–1 indicates the adjustments necessary to accurately estimate the cost to produce the MegaBurger products as calculated in columns D, E, and F.

The data in Exhibit 5–1 came from the previous year before PMI actually produced any products for MegaBurger. After producing the MegaBurger products for a year, the ABC team had the new task of considering those results and confirming that the estimates had been accurate. However, the team also realized that process improvements had to be made to enable the company to continue doing business with MegaBurger.

Combination of ABC and Target Costing

LO 2 Demonstrate how to use activity-based costing for target costing.

At this point, PMI's goal was to modify the information obtained last year after considering the firm's first-year results with MegaBurger and as a starting point to decide whether to continue producing toys for it. Revenues from sales to MegaBurger are relatively easy to forecast because of the nature of the contract.

PMI will estimate the toys' **target cost,** which is the highest cost of a good or service that meets both customer needs and company profit goals. The preliminary analysis shown in Exhibit 5–2 indicates that costs to produce toys for MegaBurger are too high to justify their continuation.

target cost *is the highest cost of a good or service that meets both customer needs and company profit goals*

Exhibit 5–2 Target-Costing Analysis of Megaburger Promotional Toys

PMI

Microsoft Excel

File Edit View Insert Format Tools Data Window Help

A1 = Exhibit 5-2

Exhibit 5-2.xls

	A	B	C
1	Exhibit 5-2		
2	**Target Cost Reduction**		
3			
4	***Target cost calculation***		
5	Expected monthly revenue per MegaBurger contract (for 20,000 units)	$340,000	
6	Less required return on sales (20% of revenue)	(68,000)	
7	Target cost per month	$272,000	
8			
9		**Total estimated**	
10		**cost (from**	
11	***Currently feasible costs per month***	**Exhibit 5-1)**	
12	***Unit-level resources and activities***		
13	Acquire and use materials	$240,000	
14	***Batch-level resources and activities***		
15	Set up and quality control-- Computer controlled equipment	6,000	
16	***Product-level resources and activities***		
17	Design and manufacture of molds	4,000	
18	Use computer controlled equipment	40,000	
19	***Customer-level resources and activities***		
20	Consult customers	8,000	
21	Provide additional warehousing	3,000	
22	***Facility-level resources and activities***		
23	Manage workers	2,400	
24	Use building space	18,000	
25	***Total feasible costs per month***	$321,400	
26			
27	Monthly cost reduction target: $321,400 - $272,000	$49,400	
28	Percent cost reduction target (B27/B25)	15.4%	
29			
30			

Ready NUM

The sales price and order quantity shown at the top of column B of Exhibit 5–2 are based on MegaBurger's stated requirements discussed in Chapter 4 (price = $17 per unit, sales quantity = 20,000 units per month, each "unit" is a package of 8 novelty toys). PMI's management set a 20 percent return on sales (ROS) target for the MegaBurger business. This ROS might seem high, but recall that the product margins must cover PMI's administrative and other costs that have not been assigned to each product. Subtracting the required ROS from the expected monthly revenue gives a target cost of $272,000 per month, as shown near the top of column B in Exhibit 5–2. With monthly revenue of $340,000 and monthly costs of $272,000, PMI will generate a monthly product margin of $68,000.[2] (See computations at the top of column B in Exhibit 5–2.)

The ABC team used cost-driver base and rate information (from Exhibit 5–1) to compute the monthly costs for each level of resources and activities (see rows 13 through 25). The total cost—$321,400—shown in B25 is the currently feasible cost per month *without* improving the efficiency of PMI's production processes. A **currently feasible cost** is the cost of all current operations necessary to produce and deliver a product.

currently feasible cost *is the cost of all current operations necessary to produce and deliver a product*

Subtracting the monthly total target cost of $272,000 (B7) from the currently feasible cost of $321,400 (B25) gives the cost reduction target of $49,400 (B27) for the month; which would represent an average cost reduction of 15.4 percent. The ABC team believed that 15.4 percent would be difficult to achieve. Expressing discouragement, some team members thought PMI should forgo the MegaBurger business. Others regarded the findings in Exhibit 5–2 as tangible evidence that PMI needed to

[2] The team was given these figures.

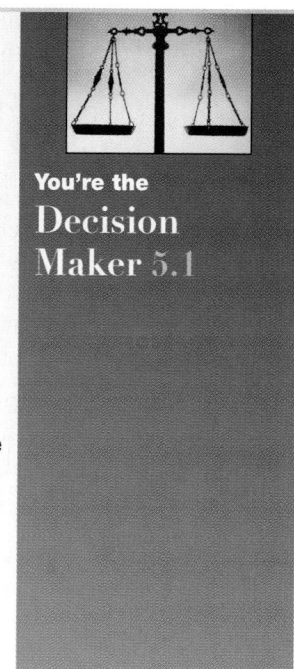

Using Target Costing

You're the
Decision Maker 5.1

Review Exhibits 5–1 and 5–2.

a. Two ways for PMI to reduce costs are to seek a higher price from MegaBurger or accept a lower return on sales (ROS). What total revenue (sales-dollar) amount would justify the business without reducing costs or reducing the 20 percent return on sales? Alternatively, what (lower) return on sales would justify the business without reducing costs or increasing the total revenue? Would you recommend either of these alternatives? Why or why not?

b. Many cost-driver rates of the target-costing analysis in Exhibit 5–2 are taken directly from the original ABC analysis of existing products. Several cost-driver rates are notably different, however, to reflect the team's expectations of differences in the products. Do you think it is advisable to directly apply cost-driver rates from the experience of making existing products to new products? Why or why not?

c. *Team Focus.* Assume that you are PMI's customer-service manager and a member of its cross-functional team analyzing the MegaBurger toy cost information. If costs must be reduced to make PMI's profit goal feasible, does it make sense to recommend that all areas of the company find ways to reduce costs by 15.4 percent? Why or why not? As an alternative, does it make more sense to focus cost-reduction efforts on the largest costs?*

(Solutions begin on page 204.)

*This is the so-called Willie Sutton rule of cost reduction. Willie Sutton was a notorious bank robber, who after capture was asked why he robbed banks. He replied, "Because that's where the money is."

improve its processes to become more efficient. After much discussion, the team presented the cost reduction target to PMI's top management as an objective for the company to achieve by redesigning its production processes.

Importance of Customer-Perceived Value

LO 3 Identify and measure the costs of activities that add value or do not add value in organizations.

Value-added activities enhance the value of products and services in the eyes of the customer while meeting its own goals. Note that customers could be either internal or external to the organization, but the ultimate test of customer value is external customer's perception. **Non-value-added activities** do not contribute to customer-perceived value. Eliminating these activities by redesigning processes would not reduce customer value.

value-added activities *enhance the value of products and services in the eyes of the organization's customers while meeting its own goals*

non-value-added activities *do not contribute to customer-perceived value*

PMI must improve processes to reduce costs. An appropriate place to start is to identify activities as value added or non-value added. The company's goal is to eliminate non-value-added activities while making value-added activities more efficient.

Eliminating Non-Value-Added Activities: Competitive Necessity

In a competitive environment, an organization should waste as few resources on non-value-added activities as possible because competitors are continuously striving to create more customer value at lower cost. For example, many banks recently eliminated most levels of approval for consumer and commercial loans because the multiple approval layers almost never affected the decision of granting the loans. The multiple approvals merely used scarce resources and delayed final approval, and the delays greatly annoyed customers. Those loan approval levels represented non-value-added activities because neither customers nor the bank realized value from them. By substituting information technology for multiple levels of manual assessments of loan applications, some banks now are able to advertise nearly instant loan decisions. These businesses seek to attract customers from less efficient banks by offering more value through faster loan decisions at lower cost because their process needs fewer approval levels.

Even in a less competitive environment, organizations have incentives to reduce non-value-added activities because they could apply the freed-up resources to value-added activities or distribute them to their employees and owners. Unless individuals in the organization derive benefits from the non-value-added activities, such as extra on-the-job perquisites, the organization might be better off using the resources for value-added activities. Organizations without non-value-added activities should be better able to compete than organizations that have allowed wasteful practices to become part of their culture.

Competition can appear unexpectedly. An environment that is currently not competitive could become competitive quickly if, for example, competitors are able to copy superior products or technology or provide substitutes for them. RCA and other US television manufacturers, for example, virtually lost their hold on the US market in the face of effective, international competition from Japanese companies such as Sony and Hitachi, which offered lower-priced, higher-quality TVs. Some countries could and have rewritten regulations that guaranteed a market for some products and services to encourage competition and lower costs for citizens. Deregulation of many industries in the United States and elsewhere has been very difficult for firms that were not prepared to compete.

Sources of non-value-added activities. All organizations have some non-value-added activities that can be reduced or eliminated. These are the most likely sources of the non-value-added activities:

- Producing to build up inventory.
- Waiting for processing.
- Spending time and effort to move products from place to place.
- Transporting workers to work sites.
- Producing defective products.

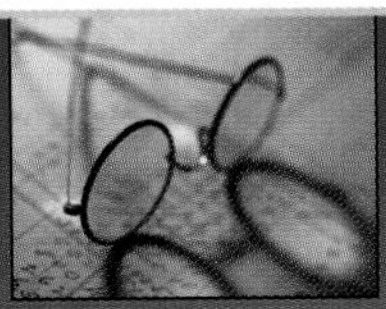

Cost Management in Practice 5.1

Importance of Identifying Non-Value-Added Activities in Deregulated Industries

Many current or former state-owned enterprises in developing economies have faced difficult transitions in recent years because they were unprepared for a sudden exposure to global competition, which punishes firms with wasteful practices. For example, New Zealand deregulated many of its utilities and exposed formerly state-owned enterprises, such as its electric utility and television-broadcasting company, to direct competition. Researchers have documented the innovative but sometimes wrenching changes made by these newly privatized companies as they faced domestic and international competition from which they had been shielded for decades. In most cases, the organizations changed capital and organizational structures, employment relations, productive processes, performance evaluations, cost-management systems, and organizational attitudes and cultures (all key cost drivers) to eliminate non-value-added activities. *Source: B. Spicer, D. Emanuel, and M. Powell,* "Transforming Government Enterprises: Managing Radical Change in Deregulated Environments." *(Full citations to references are in the Bibliography.)*

Identifying Value-Added Activities

The test for whether an activity adds customer value is met by answering two questions:

1. Would an external customer encourage the organization to do more of that activity?
2. Would the organization be more likely to reach its goal by performing that activity?

If both answers are yes, the activity adds value. If either answer is no, the activity adds no value and consumes scarce resources, perhaps unnecessarily. Answering these two questions also leads to two related questions:

1. How should an organization measure its value-added activities?
2. Who should be responsible for performing the measurement activity?

How should an organization measure its value-added activities? The value-added/non-value-added dichotomy is important, but it could be too restrictive. Some activities, such as delivering service on time, obviously add value, and the organization would benefit from enhancing those activities. Other activities, such as rewrite faulty software code or rework faulty products, obviously add no value because they should not have to be performed, and customers would not willingly pay for them. Although it might not be possible to entirely eliminate non-value-added activities such as these, organizations should identify them to truthfully portray the current state of processes and to motivate employees to eliminate or reduce these activities.

The large number of assemblies awaiting processing is a sign of inefficient processes that generate excess inventory.

Other activities, which could be necessary because of current technology, policy, or regulatory requirements, might lie between these extremes, and identifying them as one extreme or the other could lead management to make incorrect decisions about whether to enhance or eliminate them. For example, customers probably do not care whether an organization spends its resources to file its periodic tax returns. This process obviously is necessary but customers would not rate it as highly value-added. Most would agree, however, that eliminating this process altogether would be a mistake.

Many companies identify the value of their activities on a scale from 1 to 5 or 1 to 10 with the higher end representing added value. The narrower the scale, the more likely the organization is to misclassify an activity because the categories might not fit well. The wider scale, however, could make distinguishing levels of value more difficult for individuals. Although practices vary, a five-point scale could provide the right amount of detail for measuring levels of value added in most cases. On a five-point scale, an activity that is necessary but does not add value from the customer's perspective could be rated 3 while obviously value-added or non-value-added activities would be rated as a 5 or 1, respectively.

Who should perform the measurement activity? Ideally, someone who is objective and knowledgeable about what customers value and what the organization must do to meet its goals should measure value. It is unlikely, however, that one person could measure value reliably and without bias—intentional or not. It might not be possible for even a group or team to do so without input from others, such as internal and external customers. The reasons are numerous:

1. *Everyone's knowledge is limited.* For example, the sales manager might believe he or she knows what customers want and are willing to pay for, but customers are diverse, and their preferences could change over time. Asking a single customer might not generate representative answers. Furthermore, external customers might not communicate their desires directly to the company; they just might shop elsewhere if they are not satisfied.

   Another possibility is that customers could have different values, and the organization would have to decide whether to satisfy only one or both types of customer. Some level of market research and knowledge is essential to understanding what customers value. This reinforces the benefit of using cross-functional teams.
2. *Everyone's responses are potentially biased.* The warehouse supervisor could argue that inventory management and warehousing are crucial to ensuring customer value. This might be due, in part, to the fact that providing and managing product inventories is part of the business routine. Because some current jobs involve managing inventory and the warehouse, the supervisor might be unwilling to jeopardize those jobs even though he or she is responsible to the management and stockholders. Thus, the supervisor could be tempted to provide misleading information that would protect employees' jobs.

> Alternatively, an upwardly mobile supervisor might tell cost managers what he or she thinks they want to hear: that jobs can be cut without harming processes. Although inventory and warehouse operations could seem necessary because of current processes, they are non-value-added activities unless they are performed at the request of customers.

At any rate, the customer could care very little whether the company even has an inventory. Instead, the customer just wants the product on time and with the expected quality.

In practice, cost management analysts or market researchers measure value-added activities using anything from a single person's beliefs to sophisticated surveys of internal and external customers. If the organization cannot justify expending many resources to measure its activities, the benefits of doing so might not be expected to be significant. If that is the case, the organization could be better off using its resources on more beneficial activities.

Performing PMI's Value-Added Analysis

PMI used a different cross-functional team headed by the director of marketing research to measure value-added activities using small groups of internal and external customers. It used a five-point scale (5 = highest value, 1 = lowest value). Other teams, including the ABC team working on the MegaBurger bid, used this team's output to evaluate and improve existing processes.

A partial list and valuation of PMI's activities appears in Exhibit 5–3 for manually controlled injection molding for a typical month. This list formed the basis of the ABM analysis. The complete value-added analysis measures the costs and value of the activities in all parts of the organization's value chain. Although this can be a formidable task, it could be necessary if departments or processes depend on each other. That is, improving a process in one area might not be possible without considering its ties to other processes and areas. For example, improving the processing of customer orders could require changes in several functional areas such as marketing, engineering, and accounting and in multiple production and distribution processes. Thus, a piecemeal approach to ABM that does not consider process interactions might not be feasible or successful if attempted.

Notice that PMI is using a large proportion of its resources on low-valued activities. If PMI could save these resources or redirect them to high-valued activities, it could either reduce its costs or greatly increase its effectiveness in generating customer value.

Looking at one activity within Exhibit 5–3, we can begin to see how this information might help PMI. Activity 2.1.6.5, move completed order to warehouse, is rated 2 on the customer value scale, indicating that this activity has little, if any, value as perceived by the customer. PMI can review this process to find a way to eliminate, or at least minimize, it. For example, perhaps the completed order immediately could be shipped to Megaburger rather than stored in a warehouse. PMI should review all activities that add little or no value (scores 1, 2, and 3) to find ways to minimize or eliminate them.

Tasks Required by Activity-Based Management

Activity-based management uses the information derived from activity and value-added analyses to identify opportunities for process improvements. The twin objectives of ABM are, first, to identify non-value-added activities to eliminate or at least reduce them and, second, to identify value-added activities to enhance them. The next ABM stage is to actually redesign processes to eliminate wasteful spending on non-value-added activities.

An organization is unlikely to simply eliminate wasteful activities without redesigning entire processes. This is similar to making across-the-board cost cuts, which reduce both value-added and non-value-added activities, without changing the required work. If the organization can eliminate non-value-added activities by redesigning processes, the resources that these activities waste could either be saved to reduce spending or applied to value-added activities to increase their effectiveness. Thus, simply eliminating non-value-added activities could create short-term benefits, and redesigning processes to eliminate the need for such activities can generate long-term benefits.

Exhibit 5–3 PMI's Activity List: Set up and Quality Control for Manually Controlled Machines for a Typical Month

		ABC Data			Value-Added Data
A	B	C	D	E	F
Activity	Activity Description	Subactivity Cost	Subactivity Cost	Activity Cost	Customer Value
2.1	Set up manually controlled machines			$3,000	
2.1.1	Set manually controlled injection-molding machine dials		$ 200		3
2.1.2	Perform quality control of batches produced on manually controlled machines		200		3
2.1.3	Observe start of production run		100		5
2.1.4	Remove pieces and inspect		300		3
2.1.5	Recycle defective pieces		100		1
2.1.6	Place good pieces in inventory		2,000		
2.1.6.1	Trim excess plastic	$500			1
2.1.6.2	Place trimmings in recycle bags	400			1
2.1.6.3	Place good piece in bin or box	200			3
2.1.6.4	Log out completed order	200			3
2.1.6.5	Move completed order to warehouse	500			2
2.1.6.6	Register completed order in inventory	200			2
2.1.7	End production run		100		3

Detailed Activity Analysis

As an example of ABM, refer to Exhibit 5–3. The first activity level shown is the overall set up and quality control check of the manually controlled machines (activity 2.1). The next level is a subactivity, 2.1.1, set manually controlled injection-molding machine dials. Further down the list of activities is another level of subactivities in the shaded area of Exhibit 5–3 (activities 2.1.6.1 through 2.1.6.6).

Sorting activities by cost and value. The most direct use of the information presented in Exhibit 5–3 is simply to sort the activities by value and by cost. These rankings can clearly identify opportunities for improvement. Summing the costs of an activity, for example, 2.1, by adding the cost of all the activities rated from 1 to 5 as shown in column F of Exhibit 5–3 yields the summary information shown in Exhibit 5–4.

This table indicates that activities rated 3 and lower consume about 97 percent of the resources. PMI's cost management analysts need to find out why these activities that consume so many resources are generating so little value for customers. A competitor that could eliminate these low-value-added activities would have a cost advantage over PMI, particularly if PMI's other production processes also consume so many resources but generate so little value.

This process seems to have great room for improvement. For example, if PMI could eliminate activities rated 1 by redesigning the process, its cost would decline by 33.3 percent.

Not surprisingly, analysis of PMI's other processes yielded similar information, which identified many opportunities for process improvement to increase the profitability of current products, including the MegaBurger novelty toys.

Exhibit 5–4

Comparisons of Activity Values and Costs: PMI's Activity 2.1: Set Up Manually Controlled Machines

PMI

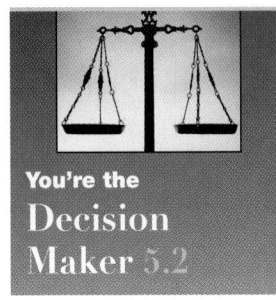

Customer Value	Sum of Activity Cost	Percentage
5 (highest value)	$ 100	3.3%
4	0	0.0
3	1,200	40.0
2	700	23.3
1 (lowest value)	1,000	33.3
Total	$3,000	100.0%

Data come from Exhibit 5–3.

You're the **Decision Maker 5.2**

Using Value-Added Analysis

Review Exhibit 5–3.

a. Based on the information in Exhibit 5–3 for PMI, where would you start to evaluate potential improvements for existing activities?

b. Which three activities would you recommend eliminating and why?

(Solutions begin on page 204.)

Identification of Process-Improvement Opportunities

LO 4 Use the elements of an activity-based management system to help identify opportunities for process improvements.

From the analysis just discussed, the production team learned that the company was spending a large proportion of cost on low-valued activities. Team members closely observed several activities, among them the subactivity, place good pieces in inventory, which had no activities valued above "3," to find precisely where they could make improvements. The results of the analysis of this activity appears in Exhibit 5–5, which has time data before and after improvements.

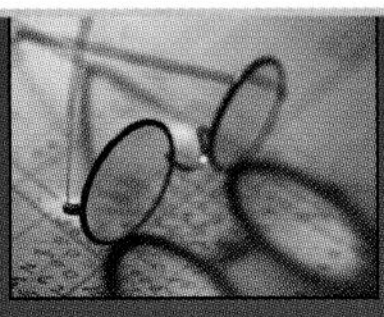

Cost Management in Practice 5.2

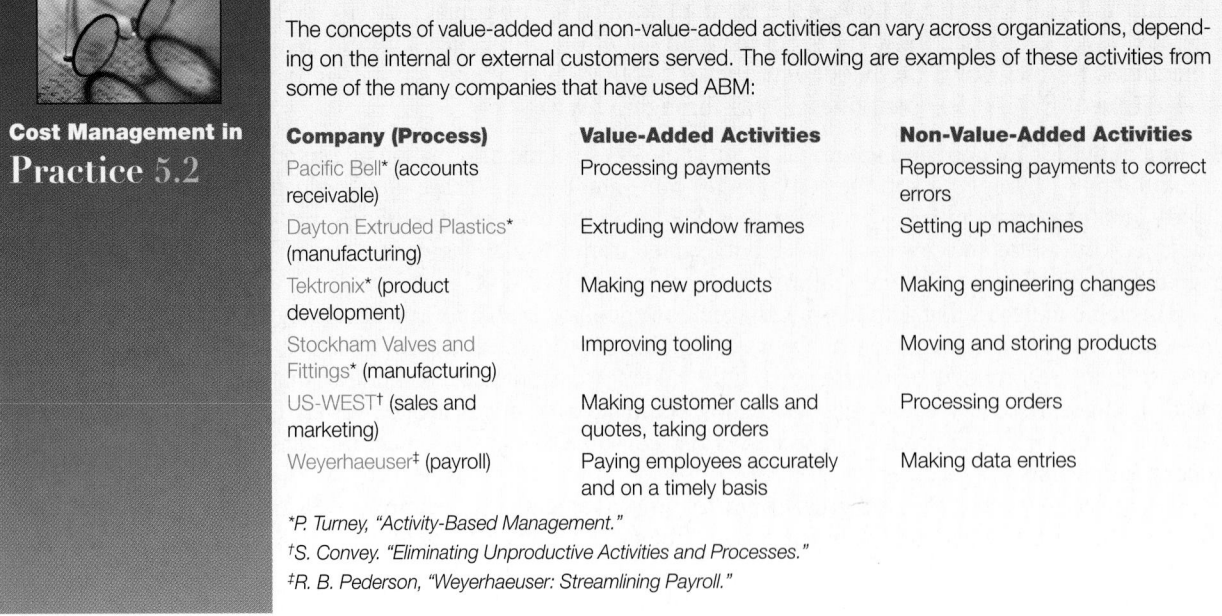

Examples of Value-added and Non-value-added Activities

The concepts of value-added and non-value-added activities can vary across organizations, depending on the internal or external customers served. The following are examples of these activities from some of the many companies that have used ABM:

Company (Process)	Value-Added Activities	Non-Value-Added Activities
Pacific Bell* (accounts receivable)	Processing payments	Reprocessing payments to correct errors
Dayton Extruded Plastics* (manufacturing)	Extruding window frames	Setting up machines
Tektronix* (product development)	Making new products	Making engineering changes
Stockham Valves and Fittings* (manufacturing)	Improving tooling	Moving and storing products
US-WEST† (sales and marketing)	Making customer calls and quotes, taking orders	Processing orders
Weyerhaeuser‡ (payroll)	Paying employees accurately and on a timely basis	Making data entries

*P. Turney, "Activity-Based Management."

†S. Convey. "Eliminating Unproductive Activities and Processes."

‡R. B. Pederson, "Weyerhaeuser: Streamlining Payroll."

Exhibit 5–5

Value-Added Analysis of Injection-Molding Process: Place Good Pieces in Inventory

PMI

Sub-Activity	Before process improvements Elapsed Time: 100 unit order	After process improvements Elapsed Time: 100 unit order
Trim excess plastic	83 min.	———
Place trimmings in recycle bags	60 min.	———
Place good piece in bin or box	25 min.	25 min.
Log out completed order	30 min.	15.1 min.
Move completed order to warehouse	60 min.	30 min.
Register completed order in inventory	28 min.	12.1 min.
Total elapsed time	**286 min.**	**82.2 min.**

Asking the Question, Why?

Anyone who has been around four-year-old children knows that they often repeatedly ask adults the question, Why? This is a rational process of exploration that adults have rediscovered in seeking to find why the performance of non-value-added activities persists in organizations. Asking why often enough (some believe that asking it five times in sequence almost always is enough) most likely will identify the root cause of performing the activity. Identifying and changing that root cause almost always eliminates the need for a non-value-added activity and often leads to additional benefits because of linkages among processes.

In consultation with the mold supplier, the production team asked why employees needed to trim excess plastic from molded products. These reasons were identified:

1. The product's appearance and function require the removal of the excess.
2. Under high-injection pressure, plastic leaks from the edges of the mold.
3. High pressure is required to mold the products properly.
4. The design of the molds permits leakage.
5. The molds are based on old designs.

Bar-coding systems reduce non-value-added recording time.

The company could rework or replace old molds with improved designs to eliminate the need to trim the excess plastic and recycle excess trim. This would reduce the labor time by 143 minutes and prevent loss of good material, which had been given to the recycler in exchange for its removal.

The team also examined record-keeping activities and persuaded Norris, the vice

bar-coding systems *create a unique bar code for each order and allow companies to mark and track all orders electronically*

president of manufacturing, to install a **bar-coding system** that creates a unique bar code for each order and allows the company to mark and track all orders electronically. This benefited the entire company by eliminating non-value-added record-keeping activities and the need to correct recording errors.

PMI expected the bar-coding system to create resource savings for virtually all its orders. As a result of this and similar analyses, production teams were able to reduce the time of several processes dramatically while increasing product quality and customer service. PMI was able to offer more customer value while consuming fewer resources and to transfer that knowledge to the production of MegaBurger toys.

Identifying the Cost of Saved Resources

Operators of injection-molding machines at PMI, on average, earn $10 per hour (including benefits). Before process improvements, the cost of the activity, place good pieces in inventory for a 100-unit baby-care order was:

$$(286 \text{ minutes} \div 60 \text{ minutes per hour}) \times \$10 \text{ per hour} = \$47.67$$

After process improvements, the cost of this activity was reduced to

$$(82.2 \text{ minutes} \div 60 \text{ minutes per hour}) \times \$10 \text{ per hour} = \$13.70$$

This represents a savings of $33.97 (= $47.67 − $13.70) for every 100-unit order. The savings is 71.3 percent ($33.97 ÷ $47.67).

Capacity Utilization

LO 5 Evaluate capacity utilization by identifying resources supplied and resources used.

resources supplied *refers to the capacity that the organization makes available for use*

resources used *refers to the resources actually used by productive purposes*

unused capacity *is the difference between the resources supplied and the resources used. Unused capacity is the amount of capacity that the organization has supplied that is not being used for productive purposes*

Organizations acquire resources to provide the capacity to produce a certain level of products or services. **Resources supplied** refers to the capacity that the organization makes available for use; their cost is measured by totaling the cost of all resources provided, whether used or not. However, most companies provide more resources than the process uses. **Resources used** refers to the resources actually used by the productive purposes.

In general, ABC estimates the cost of resources used for an activity by multiplying the cost-driver rate (step 3 of ABC) by the cost-driver volume (step 4 of ABC). Financial statements show resources supplied. The difference between the resources supplied and the resources used is **unused capacity.**

To demonstrate this idea of resources used, resources supplied, and unused capacity, imagine that you have rented a storage unit for $100 per month. Your possessions take up 60 percent of the space in the storage unit. Resources supplied for storage total $100 per month, but the resource used are only 60 percent of the space. Therefore, we assign the cost of "resources used" to storage as $60 per month. We assign $40 ($100 resources supplied − $60 resources used) to "unused capacity," representing the 40 percent of the free space in the storage unit.

The reason for assigning only $60 to the activity, storing my possessions, is that they require only 60 percent of the space times the $100 rental charge. Because the resources supplied, or space provided, exceeds what you need, you have unused storage capacity. You could use this unused storage capacity to store more belongings, or you could sublease it to a friend (perhaps for more than the $40 that the unused capacity costs you).

The difference between resources used and resources supplied applies to any resource: peoples' time, equipment, and space, to name a few. Most employees have time when they do not have to serve customers, care for patients, or perform work activities. For example, PMI's production department that makes baby-care products has seven employees who collectively provide labor resources totaling 280 hours per week (*resources supplied*). On average, however, they utilize only 250.5 hours (*resources used*), and the remaining 29.5 hours are unassigned (*unused capacity*) that are available for use, just as the unused space in your storage unit is available for use.

Differences between resource supplied and resource usage generally occur because managers have committed to supply a certain level of resources before using them. Knowing the difference between resources used and supplied helps managers to identify unused capacity, which helps them reduce it or use it in creative ways. Perhaps PMI's production workers could utilize the 29.5 hours of unassigned time to perform other productive functions, such as providing additional workforce training or designing improved factory floor layouts.

Activity-Based Reporting of Unused Resources

Notice that conventional management reports do not typically distinguish between resources used and resources supplied. Instead, cost-management reports (for internal reporting) generally focus on the *resources used,* or costs, of activities. (An example of resource use is the cost of the storage unit used.) Financial accounting reports (for external reporting) generally focus on the *resources supplied* to various parts of the organization. (An example of resource supply is the lease payment for the entire storage unit whether it is used or not.)

Information about both resource used and resource supplied is useful to managers. See Exhibit 5–6 for a reporting format that combines information about resource use

Exhibit 5–6

Donovan Company: ABM Income Statement (January)

A	B Resources Used	C Unused Capacity	D Resources Supplied
Sales			$ 360,000
Unit-level activity costs:			
Materials	$ 60,000	$ 0	$ 60,000
Energy	20,000	0	20,000
Short-term labor	7,000	1,000	8,000
Outside contracts	12,000	0	12,000
	$ 99,000	$ 1,000	$ 100,000
Batch-level activity costs:			
Setups	$ 28,000	$ 12,000	$ 40,000
Purchasing	18,000	2,000	20,000
	$ 46,000	$ 14,000	$ 60,000
Product-level activity costs:			
Parts management	$ 12,000	$ 2,000	$ 14,000
Marketing	28,000	2,000	30,000
Engineering	10,000	2,000	12,000
	$ 50,000	$ 6,000	$ 56,000
Customer-level activity costs:			
Customer service	$ 4,000	$ 4,000	$ 8,000
Facility-level activity costs:			
Long-term labor	$ 10,000	$ 4,000	$ 14,000
Depreciation (buildings)	24,000	16,000	40,000
Administrative	20,000	6,000	26,000
	$ 54,000	$ 26,000	$ 80,000
Total costs	$ 253,000	$ 51,000	$ 304,000
Operating profit			$ 56,000

and resource supply for Donovan Company. Note that column A categorizes costs into the cost hierarchies discussed in Chapter 4. Managers can see the amount of costs in each hierarchy and find ways to manage those resources effectively to reduce costs. For example, managers see that batch-level activities use $46,000 of resources (column B). If managers cut the number of batches in half, they might reduce the use of resources from $46,000 to $23,000.

The report shows managers the unused portion of the resources for each type of cost, perhaps the most important information provided. Consider setup costs as an example. Assume that the cost driver is hours of setup and the cost driver rate is $200 per hour. Based on the information in the income statement, $40,000 was spent on setups (column D). That represents 200 hours of setup capacity ($40,000 ÷ $200 per setup hour). However, the company used only 140 hours ($28,000 resources used ÷ $200 cost driver rate) during the month. The report shows managers that $12,000 (or 60 hours) of unused setup resources is available.

All other things equal, managers could have used perhaps as many as 60 additional hours of setup in January without increasing expenditures. In reality, managers know that some unused resources are a good thing. Having some unstructured time for ad hoc training, leisure, or thinking about ways to improve work and the work environment can boost morale and productivity.

Notice that some costs have more unused resources than others. The unit-related activity costs show little or no unused resources. These costs vary proportionately with output and often have little or no unused resources. Short-term labor, for example, is the cost of piecework labor or temporary help employed on an "as-needed" basis. In a college, a part-time lecturer hired for only one class is an example of short-term labor. Many of us have worked as short-term laborers during the summer in resorts, on farms, fighting forest fires, in retail stores, or providing delivery services.

Facility-related costs have unused resources unless the company operates at full capacity. Long-term labor resources are the costs of employing people who are not laid off during temporary fluctuations in production. In colleges, permanent faculty and staff are examples of long-term labor.

Implementation of Activity-Based Costing and Management

LO 6 Understand methods of and problems related to implementing activity-based costing and management.

Activity-based costing and activity-based management offer feasible ways to evaluate and improve process efficiency, and their benefits could well exceed their costs. Remember that ABC focuses on developing improved product or service costs given current processes. ABM, however, involves identifying opportunities for improving processes. Thus, although not all organizations might need improved product or service costs, most could benefit from process improvements.

Some ABC critics have faulted it for generating, in some cases, product costs that are not significantly different from traditional, functional costs. They argue, therefore, that ABC is too expensive for the benefits it offers. These same critics, however, usually do not consider the benefits of taking ABC to ABM and making significant process improvements. Some ABM advocates argue that ABC product costs are merely a by-product of ABM and process improvement efforts, which can be much more important to the organization's long-term success than knowing current product costs accurately. Activity-based techniques are conceptually appealing, but they are not trivial to implement.

Observers of ABC and ABM implementation have identified a number of factors that appear to influence whether it will be successful or unsuccessful. Research in this area is ongoing, so we must stress that this discussion is preliminary. It appears that not all companies that have considered ABC or ABM have implemented them fully or successfully. Some firms have tried ABC and apparently have found that the cost exceeded the expected benefits.

Research Insight 5.1

Comparison of Resource Use and Resource Supply in a Health Care Organization

In a study conducted in an outpatient surgery center of a large Midwestern US hospital, the researchers compared the effect of a new anesthetic on the resources supplied and resources used to care for patients in the surgery center's recovery rooms. Compared to standard anesthetics, this relatively new drug, Diprivan, enabled patients to wake up faster after surgery and have fewer side effects. The pharmaceutical company producing Diprivan claimed that switching to it could reduce the cost of recovery-room nurses (the resource used) by 33 percent because patients would spend 33 percent less time in the recovery room. The study's research supported the company's claim that *resources used* would decrease by 33 percent. However, the researchers found that the effect of switching to Diprivan would likely not decrease *resources supplied* by 33 percent.

Nurses were hired in shifts of one, four, or eight hours at the hospital. Reducing a patient's time from 60 minutes in the recovery room, for example, to 40 minutes reduced the use of the recovery room's nursing time by 20 minutes (33 percent); however, if the nurse were hired for an eight-hour shift, the hospital still paid the nurse for the full eight hours even if the patient went home early. In the end, the researchers concluded that the *resources supplied*—the amounts paid to recovery room nurses—would decrease in the range of 10 to 20 percent. Therefore, switching to Diprivan would decrease the resources used (i.e., the cost of recovery-room nursing time) by 33 percent but would decrease resources supplied (i.e., amounts spent to pay recovery-room nurses) by only 10–20 percent. Because the decrease in resources used was greater than the decrease in resources supplied, the hospital would have increased its unused capacity in recovery room nursing time. This unused capacity would be available for other uses, such as improving patient care. *Source: M. W. Maher and M. L. Marais,* "A Field Study on the Limitations of Activity-Based Costing When Resources Are Provided on a Joint and Indivisible Basis." *For related articles, see R. Cooper and R. S. Kaplan,* "Activity-Based Systems: Measuring the Costs of Resource Usage"; *and E. Noreen,* "Conditions under Which Activity-Based Costing Systems Provide Relevant Costs."

Should All Organizations Adopt ABC and ABM?

It seems intuitive that companies facing the most price competition are most eager to consider ABC as a way to improve their cost measurement and to identify the most profitable products. Likewise, firms that produce many different, complex products from common facilities might obtain more benefits from ABC than firms that have simpler processes and product offerings.

It might be no coincidence that modern ABC applications began in manufacturing firms facing new, intense competition from foreign firms in industries such as electronics, equipment, and automobile manufacturing. These industries also have pioneered ABM as a way to improve processes and profitability. As service and regulated firms have been exposed to more competition, they also have considered both ABC and ABM as solutions. Many recent applications have been in the service departments (purchasing, finance, administration, and distribution) of manufacturing firms. Financial service, pharmaceutical, and government contracting firms also report using activity-based methods.

Although not all firms have adopted or will adopt ABC or ABM, and some have backed away from it, these methods appear to have had a lasting impact on cost-management practices, particularly in multiproduct firms facing intense price competition.

Can You Be Sure That ABC and ABM Will Be Successful?

Determinants of successful ABC or ABM implementations are less obvious, perhaps, and research continues on this important issue. One thing seems clear: Spending significant effort on planning the project before the first item of data is collected is crucial. Most of the success of ABC or ABM could be attributed to good planning. Although planning does not guarantee success, the six Ps of planning have been validated in many ABC/ABM contexts: prior planning prevents particularly poor performance. Planning issues to consider include these:

- Intended scope of the ABC/ABM project.
- Resources necessary to plan and implement the project.
- Resistance to change.
- Information to be gathered.
- Analysis team's responsibility for information analysis and decision making.

Each of these issues is discussed in more detail.

Intended scope of the ABC/ABM project. An early decision regarding ABC or ABM implementation centers on whether the project is intended to be a problem-solving tool used by cost management analysts or a more ambitious, organizationwide system. In either case, most observers agree that a small pilot project, which has a high chance for success, is the proper way to introduce ABC or ABM to an organization.

pilot project *is a limited-scope project intended to be a small-scale model of a larger, possibly systemwide, project*

A **pilot project** is a limited-scope project intended to be a small-scale model of a larger, possibly systemwide, project. A general-use, or systemwide, project that has not been pilot tested has little hope of succeeding because the organization's complexities will overwhelm the learning and development that must take place first.

Translating the technical requirements of ABC and ABM into a feasible project for an actual organization should be done on a small scale first. Management must also anticipate the linkages across departments, groups, and processes as well as the data-gathering and reporting requirements of the full-scale implementation. For example, PMI created data-input worksheets with the same format for all teams and departments so the worksheets could be collected and combined electronically with minimum effort and chance for data-entry errors.

Resources necessary. Virtually all observers of activity-based methods agree that any ABC or ABM project is a significant undertaking that requires sufficient management commitment, personnel and time, and technology resources.

These workers at Union Carbide's factory in Taft, Louisiana, tore up their old process map, created a new one, and found savings worth more than $20 million. Production people often provide the best suggestions for process improvements.

Management commitment. Unless management is committed to the effort and, more important, to implementing the pilot project recommendations, ABC or ABM is unlikely to have a significant impact on the organization. Gaining this commitment might mean that management analysts must educate top managers to appreciate the benefits and costs of the approach. Since top managers have seen many management fads come and go, they could be skeptical.

The challenge for cost management analysts is to communicate clearly and effectively what ABC/ABM can and cannot be expected to do. Overselling ABC or ABM as the cure for all of an organization's business problems is sure to lead to disappointment. These techniques can be valuable diagnostic and decision-making aids, but they do not replace careful decision making.

Personnel and time. Knowledgeable observers estimate that significant ABC/ABM projects require a three- to four-person, cross-functional team and at least four to six months of full-time effort. Unless the ABC/ABM project is intended only as a demonstration or for a very small company, it most likely cannot be completed successfully by one or two people on a part-time basis. Starving the project for time limits the team to considering only a few activities and might require it to take planning and data-analysis shortcuts that will lessen the confidence in its recommendations.

Technology resources. Personal computer spreadsheets (as used throughout this book) are appropriate for applications in small companies, but they are difficult to use as systems for large organizations. If the intent is to develop an ABC/ABM system, most consultants argue that it is most efficient to begin with existing commercial software rather than develop in-house software that will be difficult to create and maintain. Consultants might be biased in this regard because, after all, selling their services and products is their business. Furthermore, some survey evidence indicates that successful ABC implementation does not depend on using either commercial software or consultants.

Resistance to change. ABC and ABM analyses often indicate the opportunity and need for dramatic changes in organizations. Believing that everyone in the organization will agree with the need for the analyses or the recommendations that follow to revise processes is a mistake. Fear, distrust, and cynicism, which should be expected when jobs are affected, could motivate some of this resistance.

Preventing resistance. Progressive organizations prevent or minimize resistance to change by (1) education and training, (2) widespread sponsorship and participation, and (3) incentives to encourage and reward change. Therefore, advance work is necessary to prepare personnel at all of the organization's levels for the analysis and changes that probably will result. It seems obvious, for example, that gaining affected employees' full participation will be difficult if they believe that ABC/ABM places their jobs in jeopardy (i.e., identifies them as non-value-added personnel). One recommended, bottom-up approach is to educate employees about the competitive necessity of ABC/ABM, give them a voice and influence in the analysis, and assure them that they will have meaningful jobs in the redesigned organization. Otherwise, it might be more effective to plan a top-down approach, using a team or a consultant to devise the solution and impose it on the organization.

In some organizations, employees might be suspicious of the advertised benefits of ABM because management could have implemented different initiatives that were unsuccessful or appeared to have adverse effects on the employees. Employees in these organizations might regard ABM as just the latest management fad and, if they resist long enough, the company will replace it with yet another attempt to change processes. In this situation, a pilot project that demonstrates objectively to suspicious employees what ABM can be expected to do might be imperative.

Effects of culture. Although this practice is somewhat controversial, some authors also recommend that companies with culturally diverse employees be especially sensitive to differences in various cultures, particularly with regard to the roles of individuals versus groups in promoting and accepting changes such as ABC and ABM. US and UK companies, in particular, have often been criticized for assuming that their management approaches will translate naturally to other cultures (perhaps because they have so much foreign investment in developing countries). For example, a bottom-up approach might not work at all in a culture in which employees regard criticizing existing processes as disloyal to the company. It might be more effective for international companies to encourage local solutions that might differ in approach from the most effective ones in the United States or Great Britain. There is much to learn about implementing ABC and ABM in international companies and those with employees from different cultures.[3]

Information to be gathered. ABC and ABM require information not normally available from an organization's information systems. Usually observation, interview, or survey of the organization's employees provide this information. An organization can use any of these methods, but unless the information about resources, activities, and uses of resources is reasonably accurate (e.g., reliable and unbiased), the analyses and recommendations based on the information will not be valid guides for changing processes. It is important to realize that perfect accuracy is neither attainable nor desirable since the costs to obtain perfect information are prohibitive. Nonetheless, concerns about obtaining accurate activity and resource information lead many organizations to hire either consultants or experienced employees to conduct this part of the analysis.

The approach that PMI used to obtain activity and resource use information (described in Chapter 4) is modeled on the experience of several large, successful companies (FirstData Corporation, Procter & Gamble, and SyBase Corporation). PMI used existing documentation (e.g., ISO 9000 information) to prepare the master activity list and surveyed and interviewed employees to measure the uses of resources to perform activities. This information probably was not perfectly accurate, but the CFO stated that he would rather be "approximately correct" (using reasonable ABC information) than "100 percent wrong" (using guesses or financial accounting information, which were the alternatives).

A complication related to gathering reliable information in any organization occurs when the jobs that must change the most are middle-management and staff support. Employees in these positions could be the most resistant to changes that require them to give up power and control. For example, one of PMI's recommendations, which is common at other companies, was that teams should be able to perform minor repairs and adjustments to equipment without having to wait for an engineer or technician. At first, this was resisted by staff personnel who feared they would first train employees to make the repairs and adjustments and then would watch their own jobs disappear. PMI overcame their resistance by redesigning staff jobs to focus more on improving designs and preventing equipment problems than on correcting designs and problems.

Analysis team's responsibility for information analysis and decision making. Although top managers ultimately have the responsibility for authorizing and effecting major changes, the study team is best prepared to analyze the data and make recommendations for several reasons. First, the team is intimately familiar with the data, its strengths, and its weaknesses. Second, empowering and requiring the team to make recommendations gives them control and accountability for the entire project and motivates them to gather and analyze the data carefully and consider a wide range of opportunities for change.

Whether the team should make its recommendations directly to top management depends on the organization's culture and needs. In some organizations, it could be important for the team to solicit and receive input from many individuals and departments

---

[3] For example, see P. Brewer, "National Culture and Activity-Based Costing Systems." (Full citations to references are in the Bibliography.)

before it issues its final recommendations to management. This allows the team to obtain even more information and to "float trial balloons" to gauge the effectiveness of its proposals. In other organizations, however, top management might need to impose major changes and be more involved in developing recommendations for change.

PMI's Decision to Keep MegaBurger as a Customer

PMI

From our earlier discussion, it is clear that PMI decided to implement ABC and ABM. The ABC analysis performed in Chapter 4 provided an estimate of future product costs based on PMI's current processes. PMI's ABC team realized that although the first year's business with MegaBurger was profitable, the profits did not meet the company's target return on sales of 20 percent. Several weeks after the initial meeting regarding the MegaBurger contract, PMI's executive committee met to decide whether to bid on a second year's contract. The following is a transcript from this meeting with Fairchild (CEO), Lewis (CFO and team leader), Norris (VP of Manufacturing), Chia (VP of Logistics), and Forney (VP of Marketing).

> **Fairchild:** Hello, everybody. I know we are concerned about hitting the 20 percent target on the MegaBurger business. What is our plan of attack?
>
> **Lewis:** Our team has done a tremendous amount of work to identify areas for potential cost savings. Its target-cost analysis shows that a 15.4 percent decrease in costs is necessary to meet the 20 percent return on sales target. The team believes that this is attainable. One example of potential savings is in our injection-molding process. We can redesign the molds currently used to reduce the need for trimming products as they come out of the mold.
>
> **Norris:** Our manufacturing employees believe many processes can be improved in addition to the molds just mentioned by Alex. The manufacturing department is now offering a cash bonus to all employees who make a suggestion for a process improvement that is ultimately implemented. Not surprisingly, we have been flooded with ideas, many of which will reduce costs substantially.
>
> **Chia:** Based on this information, I believe we have the capability to reach the 20 percent target. Let's move forward with MegaBurger.
>
> **Fairchild:** I agree. Good work everyone! Based on your efforts, I think we can look forward to working with MegaBurger for another year and to hitting our target of 20 percent return on sales.

Chapter Summary

ABC provides important information about the uses of resources given current processes but stops short of identifying opportunities for decreasing costs and increasing value. Activity-based management (ABM) uses ABC information and perceived customer values, to improve the organization's efficiency and consequently create more value at lower cost. Organizations should redesign processes to reduce or eliminate activities that add no value and either save those resources or reapply them to value-added activities. Implementing ABM (and ABC) could be difficult, but prior planning is essential to doing so effectively. Factors to be considered include the project's scope, necessary resources, resistance to change, information to be gathered, and the analysis team's responsibilities for information analysis and decision making.

Key Terms

For each term's definition, refer to the indicated page or turn to the glossary at the end of the text.

Meeting the Cost-Management Challenges

1. Is implementing activity-based costing enough to improve efficiency? Can cost management analysts measure costs more accurately using it and, by doing so, ensure that the organization will meet its efficiency goals?

Activity-based costing (ABC) usually is not enough for most organizations with inefficient processes. Measuring costs accurately with ABC allows organizations to understand their cost drivers and their processes's consumption of scarce resources. Knowing what drives costs allows employees to manage cost drivers to reduce costs. Cost is only part of the efficiency picture, however; employees also must know which activities drive value as perceived by the customer. Minimizing something that customers value would likely not improve profitability. Therefore, ABC is a valuable first step, but improving efficiency and profitability also requires knowing the drivers of value. Activity-based management considers both cost and value and, therefore, is a more comprehensive guide to cost management.

2. Do the numbers "speak for themselves"? Does the cost management analyst's responsibility end with making recommendations for improvements?

Numbers rarely speak for themselves and typically require analysis and interpretation. Thus, it is just as important for cost management analysts to measure costs as it is for them to communicate the meaning of the cost data. Cost management analysts also need to communicate the reliability of their measurements and the implications of possible errors in the data. In addition, making recommendations for improvement is important, but leading and implementing the required changes is even more important. Many good ideas never get beyond the idea stage because no one takes the lead to implement them.

3. How do you know that activity-based cost-management methods are worthwhile?

Perhaps one can never know for sure, but that is not unique to evaluating ABC or ABM. The effectiveness of any management technique or action is uncertain; that is the reason organizations need managers who can exercise professional judgment. Otherwise, all decisions could be programmed and left to mathematical decision rules. Cost management analysts can evaluate the prospective value of ABC and ABM on the basis of:

- Prior personal experience or the experience of others in similar situations.
- Recommendations of trusted internal or external consultants.
- Results of a small, controlled pilot test in which the cost management analyst has evaluated processes before, during, and after applying ABC and ABM. The "before" conditions provide the basis of comparing cost, time, quality, and so on. The "during" observations yield knowledge of information needs, communication and implementation difficulties, and successful procedures. The "after" conditions permit an objective evaluation of improvements in areas such as cost and quality that could be expected in more complete implementations.

Solutions to You're the Decision Maker

5.1 Using Target Costing p. 189

a. The required higher price must yield a 20 percent return on sales (ROS) given the currently feasible cost. This new total revenue can be computed as follows (solving for "revenue"):

$$\text{Revenue} - (\text{ROS\%} \times \text{Revenue}) = \text{Currently feasible cost}$$

Inputting the known data:

$$\text{Revenue} - (0.20 \times \text{Revenue}) = \$321{,}400 \text{ (from Exhibit 5–2)}$$
$$0.80 \times \text{Revenue} = \$321{,}400$$
$$\text{Revenue} = \$321{,}400/0.80$$
$$\text{Revenue} = \$401{,}750$$

Thus, the total annual revenue of $401,750 is required to make 20 percent ROS given the currently feasible cost of $321,400. At 20,000 units per month, this equates to a $20.09 sales price per unit (versus the previous $17.00 sales price per unit in the original proposal).

If the alternative is to accept a lower ROS at MegaBurger's stated price, the equation is the same but solves for a different variable (ROS). The revenue of $340,000 appears in the information in Exhibit 5–2.

$$\text{Revenue} - (\text{ROS} \times \text{Revenue}) = \text{Currently feasible cost}$$

Inputting the known data, and solving for ROS:

$$\$340{,}000 - (\text{ROS} \times \$340{,}000) = \$321{,}400$$
$$-(\text{ROS} \times \$340{,}000) = \$321{,}400 - \$340{,}000$$
$$(\text{ROS} \times \$340{,}000) = -\$321{,}400 + \$340{,}000$$
$$\text{ROS} = (\$340{,}000 - \$321{,}400) \div \$340{,}000$$
$$\text{ROS} = 0.055 = 5.5\%$$

MegaBurger is not likely to agree to paying a higher price for the product since it can choose from many suppliers. Accepting a lower ROS could be feasible in the short run to get the business, but if PMI really believes that a 20 percent return on sales is appropriate, it should agree to a lower ROS only if it can be sure that it can improve processes sufficiently and quickly to get a 20 percent ROS.

b. If products are sufficiently similar and will use similar processes, the cost-driver rates probably can be used at least as starting points for estimating the costs of new products. PMI's ABC team apparently compared the attributes of the new product with those of existing products and modified cost-driver rates as necessary. An organization should not blindly apply cost-driver rates from current products and processes, but they can provide a valid basis.

c. Managers might argue in favor of equal percentage, across-the-board cuts to "share the pain equitably." This approach is not likely to benefit the entire organization because it ignores the causes of waste—non-value-added activities—which might occur anywhere in the organization and disproportionately in some areas. Scrutinizing only the highest-cost activities for opportunities to cut costs could be expedient but also could allow waste to persist in many smaller activities. Ideally, PMI should identify and try to reduce all non-value-added activities. In practice, many organizations undertake these cost-cutting exercises in times of crisis or short-lived opportunity and believe they cannot afford the time necessary to thoroughly investigate all processes. Thus, they tend to attack the highest-cost processes first. One wonders why organizations do not conduct these analyses without the motivation and time pressure of a crisis.

5.2 Using Value-Added Analysis p. 194

a. A number of different approaches can be used. PMI could first look at activities with a cost above a certain dollar amount (for example, all items above $300) and then select the items that customers ranked as lowest values, or it could start with high-cost activities first, regardless of scores.

Most companies start with the high-cost activities first, thinking that the highest potential for cost savings is within these activities. Even if the customer value-added ranking is relatively high (that is, customers perceive an activity as value added), there might be room for making the process more efficient.

b. Answers will vary, depending on the approach used [see solution to part (a)]. If PMI starts with the lowest value scores first, regardless of the cost, the three activities (recycle defective pieces: $100; trim excess plastic: $500; place trimmings in recycle bags: $400) rated 1 are prime candidates for elimination.

Since value scores of 1 and 2 represent activities that add little (if any) value as perceived by the customer, PMI could start by examining the highest cost activities first within these value scores (trim excess plastic: $500 and move completed order to warehouse: $500).

Regardless of the proposed approach, PMI should remember that the goal is to minimize or eliminate all non-value-added activities and to make all value-added activities as efficient as possible.

Review Questions

5.1 What do ABC and ABM have in common, and how do they differ?

5.2 How can ABC and target costing be used together to motivate ABM?

5.3 What are alternatives to reducing process costs to meet target costs?

5.4 What are the advantages and disadvantages of using knowledge about current processes to evaluate future processes?

5.5 What are examples of value-added and non-value-added activities?

5.6 What is the relationship between non-value-added activities and waste?

5.7 Does eliminating non-value-added activities necessarily eliminate waste?

5.8 What are the questions to ask to determine whether an activity adds customer value?

5.9 How do organizations reduce spending by eliminating non-value-added activities? Is spending reduction the only result of eliminating non-value-added activities?

5.10 What is the difference between a pilot project and a systemwide project?

5.11 Why might individuals resist ABM?

5.12 Must ABM information be 100 percent accurate to be useful? Explain.

Critical Analysis

5.13 Is it fair to assume that all individuals in an organization welcome the opportunity to improve processes by eliminating non-value-added activities? Explain.

5.14 "The cost of repairing all these defective products is killing us. We should hire more highly qualified employees who won't make so many mistakes and who can figure out how to improve our processes so that mistakes are less likely." Write a memo explaining the trade-offs involved with this recommendation.

5.15 You have been hired as a consultant to improve a hospital's patient admission process. Assume that you could describe this process using 100 small activities or 10 broader activities. How would you decide how many activities to use?

5.16 "Come on, be serious. Some of these activities that you have identified as non-value-added just cannot be eliminated. We have to send monthly reports to corporate headquarters, and we need to file tax return information quarterly. This ABM analysis doesn't seem to work in the real world." Respond to this comment.

5.17 According to several writers, corporate America whacked away at labor costs throughout the 1980s. Corporations tamed unions and laid off millions of hourly workers, yet multitudes of US companies still cannot compete with their international rivals, and large operations such as AT&T, General Motors, and Du Pont are going through new rounds of restructuring. Why is competitiveness still so elusive for large US corporations? Prepare a written answer to this question.

5.18 Eastman Kodak Co. expected to save thousands of dollars a year when it laid off Maryellen Ford in a companywide downsizing. Within weeks, however, it was paying more for the same work. A local contractor that gets much of its work from Kodak snapped up Ms. Ford, a computer-aided designer and 17-year Kodak veteran. "I took the project I was working on and finished it here," she says. Instead of paying her $15 per hour plus benefits, Kodak now pays the contractor $65 per hour, and Ms. Ford earns $20 an hour (but gets no benefits). A Kodak spokesman acknowledges that the photography and imaging company has to outsource work during peak periods and adds, "There are a lot of challenges facing the company. People throughout the company are working a lot harder, but I'm not hearing that they're demoralized." He also says that by reducing staff, Kodak has saved money in computer equipment and workspace.[4] Explain what probably took place at Kodak. How would you determine whether Kodak has improved its efficiency by downsizing?

5.19 Explain the following comment: "Cost cutting has become the holy grail of corporate management, but what helps the financial statement up front can end up hurting it down the road."[5]

5.20 Connecticut Mutual Life Insurance offered a lucrative buyout plan to its 1,675 workers. About 900—more than twice the anticipated number—accepted forcing it to fill 400 vacated positions. Senior employees were the ones who left, and the company brought in new entrants at the lower end of the wage scale. The company estimates it will save $10.4 million per year.[6] What are the trade-offs and implications associated with this decision to restructure the workforce?

5.21 Your boss sent the following e-mail this morning: "Today I am announcing a 10 percent reduction in spending in every department, effective immediately. We must improve profitability, and this is the quickest way to improve the bottom line. I assure you that every department will share the pain equally. I am not asking anyone to work harder, but all of us will have to work smarter." Explain why the announced across-the-board cuts in resource spending might not improve but actually worsen profitability. How would this situation differ, if at all, in a governmental agency?

Exercises

Exercise 5.22
Activity Analysis
(LO 1)

Listed here are four activities that some students undertake to prepare for an exam.

1. Gather study materials.
2. Organize study materials.
3. Organize support materials.
4. Study.

Required

Create at least two subactivities for each of the four activities and assign a value score of 1 to 5 (5 having the highest value) to each subactivity.

Exercise 5.23
Steps in Activity-Based Costing and Activity-Based Management
(LO 1)

Label the following steps as appropriate for ABC and for ABM. List them in the proper order starting with the ABC activities.

a. Calculate a cost-driver rate.
b. Score each activity as adding high or low value as perceived by the customer.
c. Assign activity costs to goods and services.
d. Identify opportunities to enhance value-added activities and to reduce or eliminate non-value-added activities.
e. Identify and classify the activities related to the company's goods and services.
f. Identify activities as value added or non-value added.
g. Estimate the cost of activities.

Exercise 5.24
ABC and ABM Steps
(LO 1)

Describe the four steps of ABC and the three additional steps of ABM.

Exercise 5.25
Activity Analysis
(LO 1)

Loomis Distribution Company (LDC) is a distributor of soft drinks. It receives products from beverage manufacturers (e.g., Coca Cola) and ships them to retail outlets (e.g., convenience stores and supermarkets).

Required

The following activities and subactivities of LDC's warehousing process (the receiving and shipping of goods) are *not* in logical order. Arrange them into a numbered, logical sequence (e.g., 1.0, 1.1, . . . , 2.0, 2.1, . . .)

[4] For additional discussion of ABC/ABM implementation issues, see F. Selto, "Implementing Activity-based Management, and M. Shields and M. McEwen, "Implementing Activity-based Costing Systems Successfully."

[5] "Call it Dumbsizing: Why Some Companies Regret Cost-Cutting," *The Wall Street Journal.*

[6] Ibid.

Warehousing Activity	Warehousing Subactivity	Annual Time (hours)
Store beverages	Physically store products	1,400
Receive beverages	Identify where to locate product	700
Pack, mark, and prepare	Update inventory records when product received	200
customer orders for shipping	Unload vehicle	1,200
Ship customer orders	Check products for damage	500
	Return damaged products to supplier	300
	Compare products to purchase order	400
	Return incorrect products to supplier	300
	Package and label products by customer order	400
	Place orders on loading dock for shipment	300
	Load vehicle	1,400
	Prepare invoice and notification of shipment	500
	Retrieve products from storage	1,500
	Update inventory records when product shipped out	500

Exercise 5.26
Value-Added Analysis
(LO 3)

Consider the activities and subactivities in Exercise 5.25.

Required

Form small groups to rate each activity on a value-added scale from 1 to 5, with 5 being the most highly valued from an external customer's perspective.

Exercise 5.27
Value-Added Analysis
(LO 3)

Continue the analysis in Exercise 5.26. The hours spent on various activities are for a five-person warehousing team. Each team member earns on average $16 per hour (including benefits).

Required

What is the cost of each activity?

Exercise 5.28
Activity-Based Management
(LO 4)

Continue Exercise 5.27.

Required

Calculate subtotals for each value-added score (1, 2, 3, 4, and 5). If the company could eliminate low-valued activities (by your definition), how much cost could it save?

Exercise 5.29
Activity Analysis
(LO 1)

Michigan Insurance, Inc. (MII), an insurer of small businesses, has a claims-processing department that receives, processes, and refers casualty and property loss claims to insurance adjusters for resolution. Approximately half of the claims arrive by standard mail; the other half are phoned in by policyholders.

Required

The following activities and subactivities of MII's claims process are *not* in a logical order. Arrange them into a numbered, logical sequence or process (e.g., 1.0, 1.1, . . ., 2.0, 2.1, . . .).

Claims-Processing Activity	Claims-Processing Subactivity	Annual Time (hours)
Receive claims	Take phone call	1,000
Check information	Open mail	700
Analyze claim	Sort mail by claim type	200
Forward claim to adjuster	Refer phone call by claim type	800
	Verify completeness of information on written claim	900
	Compare coverage in policy to casualty or loss claim	800
	Log in claim	500
	Verify accuracy of policy information on written claim	1,000

(continued on next page)

Return incorrect claims to policyholders	400
Review incorrect claims with policyholders	500
File multiple copies of claims	1,400
Send claim and policy copy to adjuster	400
Package copy of claim and policy for shipment to adjuster	500
Log out claim	500

Exercise 5.30
Value-Added Analysis
(LO 3)

Consider the activities and subactivities in Exercise 5.29.

Required

Form small groups to rate each activity on a value-added scale from 1 to 5, with 5 being the most highly valued from an external customer's perspective.

Exercise 5.31
Value-Added Analysis
(LO 3)

Continue the analysis in Exercise 5.30. The hours spent on various activities are for a five-person claims-processing team. Each team member earns on average $20 per hour (including benefits).

Required

What is the cost of each activity?

Exercise 5.32
Activity-Based Management
(LO 4)

Continue Exercise 5.31.

Required

Calculate subtotals for each value-added score (1, 2, 3, 4, and 5). If the company could eliminate low-valued activities (by your definition), how much could it save?

Exercise 5.33
Identify Opportunities for Process Improvement
(LO 4)

Identify a non-value-added activity in your workplace or school.

Required

a. Identify the root cause of performing the non-value-added activity.

b. Does identifying the root cause suggest a way to eliminate the non-value-added activity?

c. What complications can you anticipate in making this change?

Exercise 5.34
Target Costing
(LO 2)

Review the information in Exhibit 5–2 for PMI. Assume that the sales price of $17 per unit remains the same but that the total units to be sold each month increases to 21,000 (from the original proposal of 20,000 units). (Assume that the only costs that will change are the costs driven by unit-level activities.)

Required

How much will this impact the monthly cost-reduction target

a. In dollars?

b. As a percent of currently feasible costs?

Exercise 5.35
Target Costing
(LO 2)

Review the information in Exhibit 5–2 for PMI. Assume that the total number of units to be sold each month remains the same but that the sales price increases to $18 per unit (from the original sales price of $17 per unit).

Required

How much will this impact the monthly cost-reduction target

a. In dollars?

b. As a percent of currently feasible costs?

Exercise 5.36
Target Costing
(LO 2)

Review the information in Exhibit 5–2 for PMI. After further discussion, PMI's management is willing to lower the required return on sales (ROS) to 16 percent (from the original 20 percent).

Required

How much will this impact the monthly cost-reduction target

a. In dollars?

b. As a percent of currently feasible costs?

Exercise 5.37
Resources Supplied versus Resources Used
(LO 5)

Information about two activities for Systems Integration, Inc. follows:

Resources Supplied		Resources Used: Cost-Driver Rate	Resources Used: Cost-Driver Volume
Energy	$7,300	$12 per machine hour	500 machine hours used
Marketing	5,500	20 per sales call	200 sales calls made

Required

Compute the unused capacity for each activity.

Exercise 5.38
Resources Supplied versus Resources Used
(LO 5)

Information about two activities for Quality Printing, which produces brochures, follows:

Resources Supplied		Resources Used: Cost-Driver Rate	Resources Used: Cost-Driver Volume
Machine setups	$10,000	$200 per run	30 runs
Administrative	3,500	300 per job	10 jobs

Required

Compute the unused capacity for each activity.

Exercise 5.39
Resources Supplied versus Resources Used
(LO 5)

Communication

Selected information about several activities for Tahoe Sportswear Products follows:

Resources Supplied		Resources Used: Cost-Driver Rate	Resources Used: Cost-Driver Volume
Material	$50,000	$ 5	10,000
Energy	7,000	15	400
Setups	3,500	50	60
Purchasing	3,000	40	60
Customer service	3,200	50	60
Long-term labor	12,000	40	250
Administrative	24,000	50	400

Required

a. Compute the unused capacity for each activity.

b. Write a short report stating why managers should know the difference between resources used and resources supplied. Give examples of how managers could use the preceding information on resources used and resources supplied.

Problems

Problem 5.40
Activity-Based Costing and Activity-Based Management
(LO 6)

Communication

Robert Lutz, when president and chief operating officer at the former Chrysler (now Daimler-Chrysler), was determined to replace the company's old cost-management system with one that could report costs by process and could separate value-added from non-value-added activities. After reading an article about activity-based costing and activity-based management, Lutz decided this was the system for his company. As Chrysler introduced ABC/ABM, many employees at various levels resisted. The new system represented a threat by changing the existing power structure and revealing inefficient processes hidden by the old cost-management system.

Required

a. Write a short report explaining why you think the Chrysler employees opposed ABC/ABM.

b. Recommend steps to take to mitigate the resistance of employees to the new cost-management system.

Problem 5.41
Activity-Based Costing and Target Costing
(LO 2)

Refer to the information in and format of Exhibit 5–2. PMI is considering producing one product similar to the MegaBurger novelty toys but for another customer. It will ship the product to the customer immediately upon completion. The estimates for this new product follow. Assume that PMI can add capacity as needed at costs comparable to those in Exhibit 5–2. PMI requires a 20 percent return on sales for new business.

Number of units per month	18,000
Sales price per unit	$18.00
Product life	3 years
1. Unit-level costs	
1.1 Acquire and use materials	18,000 units per month; $12.00 per unit
2. Batch-level costs	
2.1 Set up manually controlled machines	10 batches per month; $600 per batch
3. Product-level costs	
3.1 Design and manufacture molds	2 molds for the 1 product (to last 3 years); $4,000 per mold per month
3.2 Use manually controlled injection-molding machines	$40,000 per month
4. Customer-level costs	
4.1 Consult with customers	20 consultations per month, $200 each
4.2 Provide warehousing for customers	None
5. Facility-level costs	
5.1 Manage workers	$3,000 per month
5.2 Use building space	$15,000 per month

Required

a. Calculate the dollar and percentage target-cost reduction for the three-year life of the new product.

b. As the manager responsible for making the decision, would you recommend that the company produce this product? Explain.

Problem 5.42
Activity-Based and Target Costing
(LO 2)

Refer to the information and format of Exhibit 5–2. PMI is considering producing one product similar to the MegaBurger novelty toys but for another customer. It will ship the product to the customer immediately upon completion. The estimates for this new product follow. Assume that PMI's cost of capital recently increased significantly, resulting in a return on sales requirement of 30 percent for all new business.

Number of units per month	24,000
Sales price per unit	$16.00
Product life	3 years
1. Unit-level costs	
1.1 Acquire and use materials	24,000 units per month; $11 per unit
2. Batch-level costs	
2.1 Set up manually controlled machines	10 batches per month; $600 per batch
3. Product-level costs	
3.1 Design and manufacture molds	2 molds for the 1 product (to last 3 years); $3,000 per mold per month
3.2 Use manually controlled injection-molding machines	$40,000 per month
4. Customer-level costs	
4.1 Consult with customer	20 consultations per month; $300 per consultation
4.2 Provide warehousing for customer	$0.30 per cubic foot per month; 8,000 cubic feet
5. Facility-level costs	
5.1 Manage workers	30% of production labor costs; production labor costs are $8,000 per month
5.2 Use building space	$24,000 per month

Required

a. Calculate the dollar and percentage target-cost reduction for the three-year life of the new product.

b. As the manager responsible for making the decision, would you recommend that PMI produce this product? Explain.

Problem 5.43
Activity-Based and Target Costing
(LO 2)

Refer to the information in and format of Exhibit 5–2. PMI is considering producing one product that is similar to the MegaBurger novelty toys but for another customer. This product will be larger and more complex than the MegaBurger products, and it will be sold in retail toy stores throughout the world. The product will be shipped to the customer immediately upon completion. The estimates for this new product follow. PMI's cost of capital recently increased significantly, resulting in a return on sales requirement of 25 percent for all new business.

Number of units per month	15,000
Sales price per unit	$19.00
Product life	3 years
1. Unit-level costs	
1.1. Acquire and use materials	15,000 units per month; $9 per unit
2. Batch-level costs	
2.1. Set up and quality control for manually controlled machines	10 batches per month; $800 per batch
3. Product-level costs	
3.1. Design and manufacture molds	2 molds for the 1 product (to last 3 years); $3,000 per mold per month
3.2. Use manually controlled injection-molding machines	$40,000 per month
4. Customer-level costs	
4.1 Consult with customer	10 consultations per month; $150 per consultation
4.2 Provide warehousing for customer	None
5. Facility-level costs	
5.1 Manage workers	$2,000 per month
5.2 Use building space	$15,000 per month

Required

a. Calculate the dollar and percentage target-cost reduction for the three-year life of the new product.

b. As the manager responsible for making the decision, would you recommend that the company produce this new product for its customer? Explain.

Problem 5.44
Value-Added Analysis
(LO 3, 4)

Communication

Spreadsheet

You have been hired as a consultant for Whoopee, a company that designs Web sites. Whoopee has asked for your advice in assessing customers' perceptions of the value of its products. You collect the following information about Whoopee's design of a Web site for a small co-op grocery store.

Number	Activity Description	Cost	Value (5 = highest value)
1	**Marketing and design**		
1.1	Prepare contract with the customer (the grocery store)	$ 5,000	4
1.2	Perform marketing research for customer	8,000	5
1.3	Whoopee purchases hardware, software, and infrastructure for the customer's site	6,000	4
1.4	Program and construct site	10,000	5
1.5	Whoopee performs payroll services, personnel administration, and other management functions for itself	16,000	2
1.6	Whoopee provides office space for its workers	6,000	1

Required

a. Explain the sources of the customer values. Do you agree with all of the customer values? Why or why not?

b. Create a table similar to Exhibit 5–4 for these activities, and prepare a memo to Whoopee's management summarizing your results.

Problem 5.45
Value-Added Analysis
(LO 3, 4)

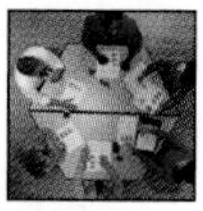

Team

Team focus. Consider two types of restaurants, (1) a favorite place for students to go in the evening and (2) a place to have a meeting.

Required

a. Identify the activities to prepare a meal, serve a customer, and clean up after the meal has been served.

b. For each activity you list in requirement (a), assign a value from 1 (= no value to you as a customer) to 5 (= essential to you as a customer). For example, does your team consider it important to be greeted when you arrive, be provided clean tablecloths, and be served a salad versus serving yourself at a salad bar?

Problem 5.46
Value-Added Analysis
(LO 3, 4)

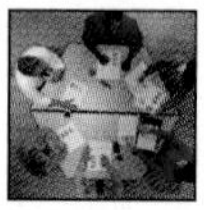

Team

Consider two types of health care organizations, (1) a campus health care center where you will be treated for influenza and (2) a hospital where you will have major surgery.

Required

Form small groups to respond to the following items.

a. Identify the activities to serve a patient and clean up after the patient has been discharged.

b. For each activity you list in requirement (a), assign a value from 1 (= no value to you as a customer) to 5 (= essential to you as a customer). For example, does your team consider it important to be provided with valet parking, to be provided with a nicely decorated waiting room, or to be admitted quickly after you arrive?

Problem 5.47
Activity-Based Management and Process Improvements
(LO 1, 4)

 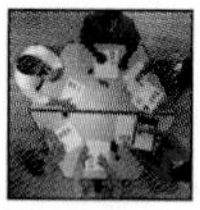

Communication Team

Now that local phone service in the United States is open to competition, some telephone service providers have begun purchasing individual phone services at a discount from the traditional phone companies and reselling them to customers who have been denied service because of poor credit. (College students represent a large group of customers of the resold services.)

Cindy Hodge is considering starting such a nontraditional phone service company in Houston, Texas. The current competitive price in the area is $35 per month, and she currently generates a 20 percent (pretax) return on sales in her other businesses. She expects a turnover of 10% per month (10% of customers will leave to be replaced by an equal number of new customers). She has estimated the following activities as necessary to operate the business for an estimated 1,000 customers.

Activity	Cost
Advertising and promotion	$ 400 per month
Bill collecting	960 per month
Service installation	45 per new customer
Credit analysis	25 per new customer
Phone service purchase from Southwestern Bell	17 per customer per month
Building occupancy	1,000 per month
Equipment utilization	300 per month
Invoicing and billing	3 per customer per month
Business planning and analysis	1,600 per month

Required

Form small groups to respond to the following items.

a. Is this proposed business expected to meet Hodge's financial goal of achieving a 20 percent return on sales? What, if any, cost reductions are necessary?

b. Prepare a short presentation outlining process improvements you would recommend to make the business more profitable.

[Adapted from C. Palmer, "Dial Tones for Deadbeats," *Forbes*.]

Problem 5.48
ABM and Process Improvements
(LO 1, 4)

Communication

Recruiting a medical technologist for a hospital laboratory is a multistep process that includes the following activities.

Recruitment Activity	Personnel	Hourly Rate	Hours Spent	Recruitment Cost
Review need to retain position	HR director	$40	4	$ 160
Revise job description as needed	HR analyst	15	8	120
Assess labor trends and compensation	HR director	40	8	320
Prepare and post job advertisement	HR analyst	15	8	120
Screen applications, verify credentials	HR analyst	15	12	180
Schedule personal interviews	HR analyst	15	6	90
Conduct personal interviews	Lab director	60	12	720
	HR director	40	6	240
Select finalist and make offer	Lab director	60	2	120
	HR director	40	1	40
Process new employee paperwork	HR analyst	15	4	60
Pay relocation expenses for new employee as needed				1,000
Provide orientation and training for new employee	HR analyst	15	4	60
	Lab director	60	2	120
	Technician	30	40	1,200
Total recruitment cost				$4,550

*HR refers to the Human Resources Department.

Required

a. If the hospital did not need to replace a medical technician, would it save these recruitment costs? Explain.

b. The laboratory customers are physicians who request tests and patients who are tested. Which of these recruitment activities would customers regard as value-added or non-value-added? What is the ratio of the cost of non-value-added to value-added activities?

c. Write a report recommending improvements to increase the human resources department's proportion of value-added activities.

[Adapted from R. Stiles and S. Mick. "What Is the Cost of Controlling Quality? Activity-based Accounting Offers an Answer."]

Problem 5.49
ABM Income Statement
(LO 5)

Communication

Spreadsheet

Gavin Corporation manufactures automobile parts. Information regarding its resources for the month of March follows:

	Resources Used	Resources Supplied
Parts management	$ 3,000	$ 3,500
Energy	5,000	5,000
Quality Inspections	4,500	5,000
Long-term labor	2,500	3,500
Short-term labor	2,000	2,400
Setups	7,000	10,000
Materials	15,000	15,000
Depreciation	6,000	10,000
Marketing	7,000	7,500
Customer service	1,000	2,000
Administrative services	5,000	7,000

In addition, Gavin spent $2,500 on 10 engineering changes with a cost driver of $250 per change and $3,000 on four outside contracts with a cost-driver rate of $750 per contract. There was no unused capacity for these two activities. Sales for March were $100,000.

Required

a. Prepare an activity-based income statement (similar to Exhibit 5–6).

b. Write a short report explaining why the ABM income statement provides better information to managers than a traditional income statement. Use Gavin Corporation information in your discussion.

Problem 5.50
Activity-Based Management Income Statement
(LO 5)

Communication

Rio Vista Manufacturing, Inc., manufactures speedboats and canoes. Information regarding its resources for the month of August follows:

	Resources Used	Resources Supplied
Marketing	$28,000	$30,000
Depreciation	24,000	40,000
Outside contracts	12,000	12,000
Materials	60,000	60,000
Setups	14,000	20,000
Energy	20,000	21,000
Parts management	15,000	16,000
Engineering changes	10,000	12,000
Short-term labor	7,000	7,000
Long-term labor	10,000	14,000
Administrative services	20,000	26,000

In addition, Rio Vista spent $22,000 on 800 quality inspections with a cost-driver rate of $25 per inspection and $8,000 on 200 customer service calls with a cost-driver rate of $30 per service call. Sales for August were $350,000.

Required

a. Prepare an activity-based income statement (similar to Exhibit 5–6).

b. Write a short report explaining why the ABM income statement provides better information to managers than a traditional income statement. Use information for Rio Vista in your discussion.

Cases

Case 5.51
Reengineering the Accounting Function
(LO 4, 6)

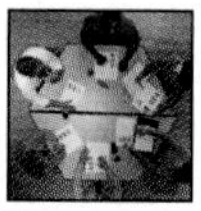

Communication Team

An alternative to using ABM to identify opportunities for process improvement is to use benchmarking information to identify where an organization falls short of competitors and best practices. At 2 percent of sales, Cummins Engine's overall accounting costs were twice as high as companies with world-class accounting functions, and the company was determined to improve. More detailed benchmarking information revealed that accounts payable costs and payroll costs were four and three times higher, respectively, than best practices. These areas seemed to offer the opportunity for great improvement. Cummins created a cross-functional team to analyze these transaction processes and make recommendations for improvement that would increase the quality of transaction processing and achieve best-practice costs (i.e., cost reductions of 75 percent).

Cummins Engine's top management was fully committed to the project. It provided resources to the project team that enabled it to educate Cummins' finance and operating personnel around the world about the project's methods and objectives. Management also committed to no forced layoffs of personnel whose jobs would be affected by resulting process changes.

In the early part of the project (the "baseline" phase), the team recognized that accounts payable, cash disbursement, and procurement processes should be integrated and located at a single site rather than at 50 sites within the United States alone, and that new software and hardware would be required. The team began with a pilot study, however, so that it could understand the complexities of the project before launching a worldwide implementation. The pilot study allowed the team to identify tangible objectives for the new system that included:

- Electronic data interchange (EDI).
- Linkage between procurement, accounts payable, and cash disbursement.
- Use of client-server technology.
- Outsourcing of non-value-added activities such as check printing.
- Improvement of process quality measures involving statistical quality-control techniques.
- Software compatible with Cummins' data architecture at a competitive price and with a user-friendly graphical interface.

Project implementation was phased in over a three-year period, with inflexible target dates for each phase and continuous communication with affected finance and operating personnel. The workforce in accounts payable was reduced by 80 percent, costs reached best-practice levels, and errors were reduced dramatically. (The workforce reduction occurred through attrition, assigning employees to other areas, and early retirement plans.)

Required

Form small groups to prepare a report that answers the following questions:

a. What are the differences between the activity-based management approach and the benchmarking approach used by Cummins Engine to identify opportunities for process improvement? What are the relative advantages and disadvantages of the benchmarking approach to identifying opportunities?

b. What interests, skills, and knowledge would be required for members of a project team such as the one at Cummins to analyze accounts payable?

c. What are specific steps that Cummins Engine took to ensure the success of the accounts payable project?

d. Does the Cummins project appear to be perfect, or can you recommend improvement(s) and/or identify area(s) of concern if you were to copy this approach at another organization?

[Adapted from T. Compton, L. Hoshower, and W. Draeger. "Reengineering Transaction Processing Systems at Cummins Engine"]

Case 5.52
Effects of Changing Cost Drivers
(LO 1)

Communication

TransGlobe Airways (TGA) is an embattled US airline fighting to gain market share from its much larger, traditional competitors, such as United Airlines, Delta, and American-Airlines, as well as successful discount airlines such as Southwest Airlines. TGA's current share of the US market is approximately 5 percent. The executive vice president of marketing, Jack Moore, believes that TGA must improve its customer satisfaction before it can improve its competitiveness. Surveys of TGA's customers indicate that they are most dissatisfied with these areas:

- In-flight meal quality.
- Attitudes of ticket counter and in-flight personnel.
- Storage space for carry-on luggage.
- Legroom in the economy sections of TGA's airplanes.
- Charges for movies and drinks on long flights.
- First-class seating availability for frequent fliers who want to upgrade from economy.

In an executive committee meeting, Moore insists that TGA must begin immediately to retrain personnel to interact well with customers, offer better meals and free movies, and begin remodeling planes to increase first-class seating, legroom in economy, and storage space for carry-on luggage. He is confident that these measures will increase market share dramatically and lead to future profitability.

You are a cost management analyst with TGA whom the chief financial officer invited to attend this executive committee meeting and then asked to prepare estimates of the impacts of making changes to TGA's structural cost drivers. You recall a recent *Wall Street Journal* article that indicated that the most important reasons business travelers choose one airline over another are ticket prices and flight schedules.

Required

a. Prepare a brief, narrative analysis of the possible impacts of these structural changes on customer satisfaction, market share, and profitability.

b. Make alternative recommendations for improving TGA's profitability.

Case 5.53
Activity-Based Management in a University
(LO 6)

"ASP Business Plan Estimates 60 FTE to be Eliminated in Consolidations" trumpeted the headline in the *Silver & Gold Record,* the university's faculty and staff newsletter. Administrators scrambled to justify the $35 million project and reassure worried staff who faced the loss of 60 full-time equivalent (FTE) jobs. Faculty scoffed at yet another administrative boondoggle that would siphon scarce funds from the university's academic mission. Staff council leaders vowed to protect their colleagues who might be affected by the Administrative Streamlining Project (ASP). It has pitted faculty, staff, and administrators against each other as the university struggles to improve its administrative operations. The irony is that nearly everyone agrees that the university's administrative processes are outmoded and inefficient and that the accounting

Communication

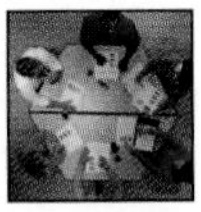
Team

Ethics

system is nearly useless as a management tool, but there is little agreement about how to proceed. Some question the basic premise of the change, however, that the university should become more like a business. A distinguished professor of comparative literature argued against the university's mimicking the business world's addiction to management fads:

> *Let us not ask the university to transform itself overnight in response to the latest fads and fashions of the business world. Let us not encourage an easy experimental attitude toward our structure, aims, and ends. Let our reply to our critics be this: Relax the drive to create a world of conformity, but instead, sit back and enjoy the differences.*

ASP is charged "with improving the University's human resources and financial management business practices by simplifying work, increasing information access, minimizing future administrative costs, and implementing enabling technologies." ASP is expected to be "the first step in a continuous improvement program by providing tools and education that will enable the University to continually change how it does business."

ASP proposes to consolidate the purchasing, accounts payable, payroll, and human resources functions for all of the University's four campuses into two central areas: (1) benefits/payroll and (2) procurement. The expected costs of ASP over its three-year implementation follow:

University personnel to manage and implement ASP	\$11.74 million
PricewaterhouseCoopers, consultants	9.02 million
PeopleSoft software (human resources and finance)	4.32 million
Hardware and networks	3.79 million
Training costs for ASP staff, system staff, and users	2.03 million
Operating expenses	1.75 million
Contingencies	2.28 million
Total implementation cost	\$34.93 million

The ASP plan predicts the following annual savings after implementation:

Elimination of redundant positions (60 FTE)	\$2.63 million
Elimination of "shadow" personnel and budgeting systems	3.34 million
Reduction of data-entry requirements	1.13 million
Elimination of system reconciliation	0.26 million
Total annual savings	\$7.36 million

Members of the University's staff council stood up for their colleagues who face being displaced from their current jobs as a result of ASP. The staff council reminded University officials that staff within the state personnel system have retention rights and can "bump" others from similar positions in the University based on seniority. University officials, including the president, have stressed that layoffs will be a last resort to deal with job reductions and that positions will be eliminated through attrition or reassignment to new jobs. The staff council noted that the ASP budget does not contain any money for retraining staff whom ASP would displace. The ASP director admitted as much but noted that the University had been informed that it needs to set aside money for retraining.

ASP has not identified which jobs to eliminate. Its director recognized the need to "adopt an appropriate strategy for consolidating the campus functions. We could bring up the system, get the offices running, and then consolidate them, or we could consolidate and then bring up the system." One staff council member heatedly announced the doubt that ASP could make the right decisions on which jobs to eliminate: "The ASP committee is all administrators, but ASP affects staff on every side. You need to get opinions from the people actually doing the work. Administrators often don't know what staff do."

Required

Form small groups to prepare a presentation that responds to the following items:

a. Does the ASP objective seem consistent with the University's goals?

b. Why might ASP's objective (not considering its methods) be controversial within the University?

c. What ethical and management responsibilities does the administration have for the University's constituents?

d. Discuss your confidence in the reliability of the cost and savings estimates. How critical are these estimates to the project's implementation and success in meeting its objective?

e. Critique the apparent method being used to implement ASP. Is this implementation approach likely to be successful? Explain.

f. Make recommendations to the University president and the ASP director for improving the implementation process.

[Adapted from *Silver & Gold Record,* March 12, 1998.]

Case 5.54
Banking Processes
(LO 4)

Communication

Ogden Bank has been in the consumer-lending business for more than 100 years. Competitors recently have taken a considerable portion of its market share. In addition, its remaining customers have complained that the bank's loan-approval process is too slow and that finding out the status of a loan application is difficult. The traditional procedure for consumer loan approval is summarized here:

- A loan applicant picks up a standard loan application at the bank, completes it, and mails it to the bank. A mail clerk delivers applications along with regular mail.
- The loan application is delivered to a loan-processing clerk, who logs it in, attaches a routing/status form to the front page, and files it in a folder of outstanding loan applications. At the end of the day or when the folder is full, the clerk delivers the contents to a credit analyst.
- The credit analyst enters data from the application into a computer program, records the results on the status form, and sends the application through interoffice mail to a consumer-lending specialist.
- The consumer-lending specialist approves or rejects the loan application and customizes the loan if necessary according to the particular applicant's needs. From here, all applications go to a pricing specialist via interoffice mail.
- The pricing specialist determines the appropriate interest rate to charge approved applicants by using a computer program written for this purpose. The rate is recorded on the status form of approved applications, which are forwarded to another clerical group.
- These clerks prepare letters informing applicants of the bank's decisions along with a note stating the loan terms of approved applications.
- After the legal department reviews all of this material, clerks mail the bank's decision to the applicants along with a promissory note to be signed and returned to those who are approved.

This process takes four weeks on average, during which time applicants could find alternative financing but could almost never determine the status of their application with Ogden Bank. The bank has engaged you to analyze its loan approval process and make recommendations for improvement.

Required

a. Prepare a brief memo explaining how Ogden Bank could benefit from using ABM and what steps and resources would be necessary to successfully implement it.

b. Suggest and explain at least three ways that Ogden Bank could reduce the cycle time of its loan-application process.

c. Suggest and explain at least three ways that Ogden Bank could improve its communication, internally and externally, about its processes and possible process changes.

[CMA adapted]

CHAPTER

6

Managing Customer Profitability

After completing this chapter, you should be able to:

1. Explain the value of analyzing customer profitability according to major customer types.
2. Organize and prepare customer profitability analyses and reports using activity-based analysis.
3. Identify alternative actions and recommend improvements for overall and customer profitability based on analyzing customer-related activities.

Cost-Management
Challenges

1. **How** can you determine in advance whether investments of time, effort, and information systems to prepare customer profitability information are worthwhile?

2. **How** can customer profitability analysis be more relevant for service and governmental organizations than for others?

3. **How** do you evaluate the trade-offs among the desires for relevant, accurate, and timely information?

4. **How** can cost-management analysts help an organization plan and execute changes in operations to deliver more customer value at lower cost?

5. **How** can you determine whether operational changes in customer service have been beneficial or harmful?

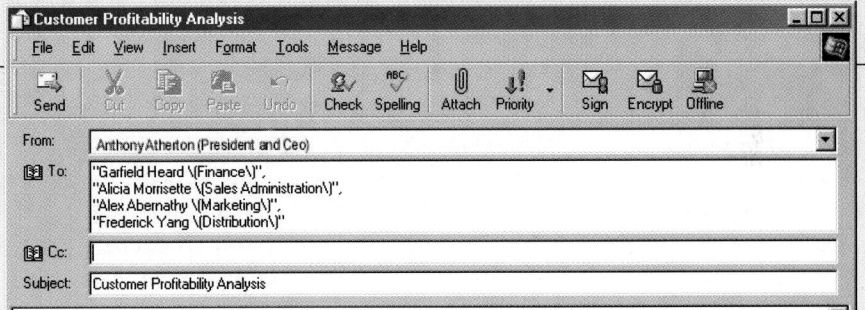

Customer Profitability Analysis

File Edit View Insert Format Tools Message Help

Send Cut Copy Paste Undo Check Spelling Attach Priority Sign Encrypt Offline

From: Anthony Atherton (President and Ceo)

To: "Garfield Heard \(Finance\)",
"Alicia Morrisette \(Sales Administration\)",
"Alex Abernathy \(Marketing\)",
"Frederick Yang \(Distribution\)"

Cc:

Subject: Customer Profitability Analysis

Dear Gar, Ali, Alex, and Fred,

As you know, the effects of our recent acquisition by London Pharmaceuticals continue to ripple through HealthWave. The best is yet to come, in my opinion. The purpose of this email is to formalise my request that you form a cost-management team to thoroughly analyse our customer profitability. I cannot stress the urgency of this request enough. I have reason to believe that our jobs and the future of HealthWave as an organization depend on this analysis.

We need to submit next year's budget to the corporate office in London in six months. That budget needs to clearly and convincingly explain how we will attain corporate's tough return-on-sales goals for next year and the following five years. I am convinced that our traditional product orientation obscures opportunities to improve our profitability. I also am convinced that we must focus on our customers to ensure both their satisfaction, which we always have done, and our profitability, which we need to improve. We need to understand who our customers are, what they want, and what they are willing to pay for. Furthermore, we need to understand which of our resources we apply to customers and whether all of our customers are profitable to us.

Thus, your first step is to analyse our customers and measure their profitability. I am calling the first meeting 9:00 a.m. on Monday morning. Please clear your calendars for most of the day. I will attend the first meeting to underscore the importance of this project and to help set deliverables, but you will carry on as a team thereafter.

Thank you for your willingness to undertake this important task.

Tony

HealthWave, Ltd.

HealthWave, Ltd., is a wholesale-drug company headquartered in Auckland, New Zealand, with manufacturing, marketing, and sales operations throughout Australia and New Zealand (ANZ). A large UK firm, London Pharmaceuticals, recently purchased HealthWave from its stockholders with cash and an exchange of stock. HealthWave was an attractive acquisition because of its strong brand image, customer loyalty, ANZwide customer base, and skilled marketing and sales personnel.[1]

The London parent, however, has notified Anthony Atherton, HealthWave's CEO, that it expects a rapid increase in profitability. Its short-run objective for HealthWave is to increase the company's *return on sales* (ROS), which is operating income divided by sales, from its current 7.3 percent to 10 percent within a year. Furthermore, London expects steady improvement to at least 15 percent ROS within five years. London Pharmaceuticals regards this as a difficult but attainable objective, but at this point, HealthWave is certain only that it will be difficult.[2]

HealthWave's Products

HealthWave's three major product lines are nonprescription drugs, supplements, and herbal remedies. Nonprescription drugs include nonprescription headache, cold, and flu remedies such as aspirin, antihistamines, and cough syrup. Supplements include vitamin and mineral supplements, such as multivitamins, vitamin C, and zinc capsules. Herbal remedies include herbal products such as echinacea, spirulina, and St. John's wort. Profitability depends on maintaining the company's brand name, successful advertising, promotions, and customer service.

CEO Atherton formed a small, cross-functional cost-management team of talented and motivated people from the finance, sales, marketing, and distribution departments who tend to think "outside the box." He believed that their different perspectives and personalities were the right balance of individual talent and team orientation to find innovative and successful solutions to the company's profitability problem. Many jobs, including his perhaps, were at stake.

HealthWave's Customers

LO 1 Explain the value of analyzing customer profitability, according to major customer type.

HealthWave has three primary customer types: pharmacies, groceries, and herbal therapists. It serves pharmacies and groceries through sales representatives and herbal therapists through catalogue and mail-order sales. HealthWave currently has no e-commerce or Internet sales activities but recognizes the need to consider implementing them. HealthWave believes that competition based on customer service is changing, but its traditional focus on product profitability obscures changes in customer preferences.

Importance of Customer Profitability

customer-profitability analysis *identifies the costs and benefits of serving specific customers or customer types to improve an organization's overall profitability*

Customer-profitability analysis is an approach to cost management that identifies the costs and benefits of serving specific customers or customer types to improve an

[1] Also important was the unregulated nature of the ANZ market for over-the-counter medicines and herbal remedies in contrast to the European Union (EU) market where London Pharmaceuticals conducts most of its business. Most countries in the EU market classify over-the-counter and nonfood herbal products as medicines and strictly regulate their distribution and pricing. Similar to the situation in the United States, the ANZ area permits the sale of these nonprescription products, which include most of HealthWave's products. As a result, HealthWave can introduce new products quickly at relatively low cost unlike prescription drug companies, which must submit their new products to lengthy and often costly trials and reviews. On the other hand, HealthWave's profit margins are lower than those of prescription drug companies because patents or regulations do not protect its products.

[2] The analysis in this chapter is informed by the Naturix-Bowen Case Study, The Boston Consulting Group. (Full citations to references are in the Bibliography.)

organization's overall profitability. It is a relatively new but increasingly popular cost-management tool, which has two primary objectives:

- Measure customer profitability.
- Identify effective and ineffective customer-related activities.

Measurement of Customer Profitability

The first objective of customer profitability analysis is to measure the profitability of existing customers or customer types. Most organizations measure profitability according to organizational boundaries (e.g., regions) or product line. These profit measures facilitate management of production-oriented operations. Operating profits, however, usually do not focus on sales or customer-service activities, which can constitute the majority of general and administrative operating costs.

Many organizations seek to increase market share and customer satisfaction without understanding the costs of doing so. Some organizations incur significant costs to satisfy customers but often do not know whether these efforts result in revenues that exceed their costs. Customer-profitability analysis seeks to perform cost-benefit analyses to identify profitable and unprofitable customers. This information helps the organization to ensure that it retains its profitable customers. It can either drop unprofitable customers or find ways to serve them profitably.

Some studies have found that only 20 percent of a company's customers contribute to profits; the remaining 80 percent generate losses. See Exhibit 6–1 for an example of customer profitability analysis that reflects the historical experience of many organizations that are just beginning to use this technique. The chart shows that a small percentage of customers generated significant profits and the majority generated small profits or significant losses. In this example, the top seven customers (20 percent of 34 total customers) contribute 155 percent of the total profit and half of the customers generate losses! The top 7 customers generate more than 100 percent of the profits because serving each at its levels of sales is much cheaper than serving the other 27 customers. This implies that this company is better off serving less than half of its customers.

Profit from top 7 customers	$ 381,147
Total company profit	245,941
Profit from top 7 customers	155.0%

Exhibit 6–1

Pareto Chart of Customer Profitability

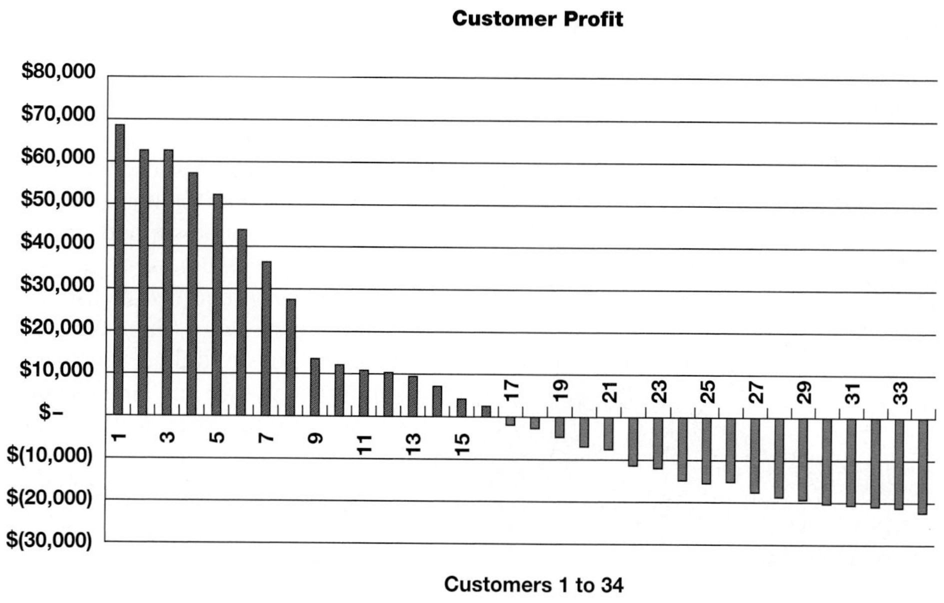

Qualitative considerations. The quantitative factors of customer profitability are important, but companies should not fail to consider, qualitative reasons for retaining marginal or even unprofitable customers, including these:

- Status of being a supplier to a leading company, which can lead to referrals to similar ones.
- Potential for a loss customer to become profitable by serving it more efficiently.
- Use of a loss customer for entry into a new and profitable market by learning how to serve this market.
- Opportunity to receive transfers of knowledge from innovative but unprofitable companies about their cutting-edge needs or product applications.
- Ability to economize on customer-service activities for customers that partner with the organization or share processes with it.

Similarly, a company might *decline* to serve some profitable customers whose business practices or goals are inconsistent with its own. For example, many organizations decline to serve customers with poor environmental or human rights records. Conversely, companies might choose to serve unprofitable customers who promote goals they wish to support.

Identification of Effective and Ineffective Customer-Related Activities

The second objective of performing customer profitability analysis is to identify effective and ineffective customer-related activities. This analysis provides the information that organizations can use to decide which activities to enhance or eliminate that will increase total profitability, decrease or eliminate customer dissatisfaction, and clarify its view of what customers value and will pay for. Enhancing customer activities include simplifying cumbersome order processes, consolidating many small orders into fewer large ones, and teaching customers to minimize costs by eliminating numerous changes to their orders.

Many successful companies, such as Dell, Nike, Hewlett-Packard, Microsoft, General Electric, Federal Express, Marks & Spencer, Thomas Cook Travel, Standard Life Assurance, Bank of America, and Canadian Imperial Bank of Commerce (CIBC), regularly use customer profitability analysis to manage customer relations activities. CIBC, for example, computes the profitability of each of its more than 24 million accounts every month to identify those that are exceptionally profitable or unprofitable. It uses this information to support decisions to add or drop customers or activities. This effort clearly requires intense use of information technology (large companies can spend millions of dollars for customer profitability analysis), and an understanding of the activities that drive customer profitability.

Many organizations also use activity-based costing approaches to measure the effectiveness of resources in serving customers,[3] as discussed in Chapters 4 and 5. Just as ABC can reveal product profitability, customer-profitability analysis can identify profitable or unprofitable customers. This information allows organizations to take appropriate actions to increase their profitability.

Organizations that seek to implement customer profitability analysis must understand its customer-related cost and revenue drivers (see Chapters 4 and 11). Successful organizations recognize that sales-incentive systems, which traditionally have been based on revenue or product contribution margin, must encourage sales activities directed to profitable customers. (Chapter 21 covers incentive systems.)

HealthWave's Traditional Profitability Analysis by Product Line

HealthWave's financial accounting system prepares financial reports by major product line in contribution margin format, which reflects the company's historical product focus.[4] According to Exhibit 6–2, nonprescription products have the highest contribution margin ratio (48 percent), and herbal remedies have the lowest (31 percent). Furthermore, for the recently completed year, the ROS for nonprescription drugs (16.7 percent) exceeds the 10 percent target, but that for supplements and herbal remedy products does not [6.6 and (3.9) percent, respectively]. This ROS comparison could be misleading because it allocates general sales, and administrative costs on the basis of relative sales, a common practice. Only HealthWave's R&D costs are clearly traced to product lines, which also is common because R&D projects often are organized by product line. This traditional profit view is computationally correct but not particularly helpful for identifying opportunities for improving customer-related activities.

Let's measure the magnitude of HealthWave's overall profitability problem, which is independent of the way it traces or allocates costs to products because revenues must exceed total costs by a sufficient amount to meet the profitability goal. The new parent company assigned the profit objective of a 10 percent ROS for the first year after the acquisition. For now, assume that the next year's product-sales

[3] For example, M. Smith and S. Dikoli, "Customer Profitability Analysis: An Activity-Based Costing Approach."

[4] Contribution margin (sales revenue less variable costs) is covered in Chapter 2.

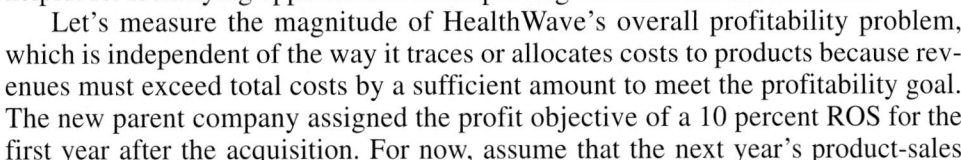

Exhibit 6–2 HealthWave's Product-Line Profitability (NZ$)

	Total	Nonprescription	Supplements	Herbal Remedies
Revenue	$91,000,000	$26,900,000	$44,260,000	$19,840,000
Variable cost of goods sold (CGS)	54,676,200	13,988,000	26,998,600	13,689,600
Contribution margin	$36,323,800	$12,912,000	$17,261,400	$ 6,150,400
Contribution margin ratio (Contribution margin ÷ Revenue)	39.9%	48%	39%	31%
Operating expenses:				
Research and development (R&D)	1,200,000	—	480,000	720,000
General, Sales and administrative (GS&A)*	28,475,296	8,417,423	13,849,633	6,208,240
Total operating expenses	$29,675,296	$ 8,417,423	$14,329,633	$ 6,928,240
Operating income	$ 6,648,504	$ 4,494,577	$ 2,931,767	$ (777,840)
Return on sales	7.3%	16.7%	6.6%	(3.9%)

*Allocated on relative sales

Exhibit 6–3

HealthWave's Cost Reduction Target (NZ$)

Target return on sales	10%
Current sales revenue (Exhibit 6–2)	$91,000,000
Target profit (0.10 × $91,000,000)	9,100,000
Target cost	$81,900,000
Current costs (CGS + R&D + GS&A from Exhibit 6–2)	84,351,500
Target cost reduction	$ 2,451,500

prices, costs, volume, and mix will remain the same. Exhibit 6–3 uses a target-profit approach,[5] applying information from the Total column of Exhibit 6–2. At the same level of sales (NZ$91,000,000), HealthWave must achieve a cost reduction of NZ$2,451,500 to meet this 10 percent goal. (Exhibit 6–3). If sales do not increase with the same level of resource use (one of several possible solutions to the problem), profit improvement must come from reducing costs, many of which are related to customer service.

The next objective of customer-profitability analysis is to identify customer-related actions that can improve the organization's overall profitability. To do so, the cost-management team gathered more information about HealthWave's customers and the services provided to them.

Unlike HealthWave, some organizations tailor their products and services to fit specific customer needs. These organizations might incorporate aspects of job-order costing (Chapter 3) to refine their customer profitability analysis to reflect the customization of production and customer services. Recognizing the "lumpiness" of batch- and product-level costs often is important to this analysis. HealthWave's products are not customized, so production costs are unrelated to customer type. Its service costs, however, are related to customer type.

[5] Target profit and cost analyses are described in more detail in Chapter 13. Briefly, the method computes a target profit based on required return on sales, which yields a target cost (Revenues − Target profit = Target cost). Comparing target cost to current cost results in a cost reduction target.

Research Insight 6.1

Customer Satisfaction and Profitability

An economic perspective of customer service predicts that if service is valued but freely offered, customers will demand more of it than they are willing to pay for. Many commercial firms attest that they are "customer focused" and seek to delight, not merely satisfy, customers. If their actions match their claims, can they do so profitably? In fact, maximizing customer satisfaction can be a recipe for unprofitable operations. On the other hand, some organizations identify more efficient ways to provide services, thus keeping customer satisfaction high and service costs low.

Interest in the drivers of customer profitability, particularly whether customer satisfaction leads to profitability, has stimulated considerable academic research that seeks objective evidence of a link between customer satisfaction and profitability. The evidence currently is mixed but leans toward the conclusion that, as with all economic endeavors, profits show a positive relation with but decreasing marginal returns from increases in customer satisfaction. As one study put it, "The customer is always right, but is it always worth it?" *For a partial list of relevant studies see E. W. Anderson, C. Fornell, and D. R. Lehmann,* "Customer Satisfaction, Market Share and Profitability. Findings from Sweden", *R. D. Banker, G. Potter, and D. Srinivasan,* "An Empirical Investigation of an Incentive Plan That Includes Nonfinancial Performance Measures"; *G. Foster, M. Gupta, and L. Sjoblom,* "Customer Profitability Analysis: Challenges and New Directions"; *G. Foster and M. Gupta,* "The Customer Profitability Implications of Customer Satisfaction"; *C. D. Ittner and D. F. Larcker,* "Measuring the Impact of Quality Initiatives on Firm Financial Performance"; *C. D. Ittner and D. F. Larcker,* "Are Non-Financial Measures Leading Indicators of Financial Performance? An Analysis of Customer Satisfaction"; *E. R. Nelson et al.,* "Do Patient Perceptions of Quality Relate to Hospital Financial Performance?"; *A. T. Rucci, S. P. Kim, and R. T. Quinn,* "The Employee-Customer-Profit Chain at Sears"; *and R. T. Rust and A. J. Zahorik,* "Customer Satisfaction, Customer Retention, and Market Share." *(Full citations to references are in the Bibliography.)*

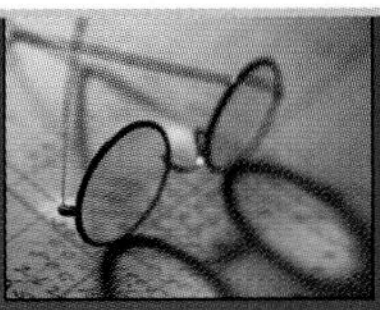

Cost Management in
Practice 6.1

Determinants of Service Quality

An increasing number of companies have made a deliberate decision to give some customers skimpy service because they believe that is all the business of these customers is worth. Information technology, particularly Internet-based commerce, permits the capture of detailed customer-related information to use for performing customer analyses and tailoring activities to customers. Furthermore, companies are using this information to segment their customers into an "A-list," which frequently buys premium products and services and are treated like royalty. "B-list" customers, which tend to shop based on price and convenience, receive impersonal, inflexible automated service or are expected to serve themselves.

These discriminating companies rarely acknowledge that low-profit or unprofitable customers receive minimal service (if any), but when they do, they argue that premium customers' spending justifies the royal treatment. For example, the calls from Charles Schwab's top-rated Signature clients, which have large asset accounts and trade frequently, are answered within a few seconds, but those from less valued customers might not be answered for 10 minutes or more. Similarly, after estimating that answering phone calls from investors costs $13 per call, Fidelity Investments now directs high-cost "serial" callers to its Web site or automated phone system for self-service.

Some critics argue that these customer-segmenting practices resemble invisible "redlining," a controversial form of customer discrimination some laws prohibit. Some companies clearly are using customer profitability analysis to discriminate among customers, but others, such as Capital One Financial Corp and Walker Digital, are letting customers pay for their desired level of service by choosing among alternative products priced according to service levels. This approach increases customers' choices, which is the opposite of discrimination. *Source: D. Brady,* "Why Service Stinks."

Customer Sales Analysis

LO 2 Organize and prepare customer profitability analyses and reports using activity-based costing.

At its first meeting, the HealthWave cost-management team agreed to provide the CEO and executive staff for each customer an analysis of profitability including sales patterns and the customer-related activities. The team recognized the importance of structuring these analyses so that the company could develop more precise information in the future without reinventing the entire exercise. The team decided that it would:

- Use existing information systems whenever feasible to generate customer-related revenues and costs.
- Obtain information from the most recent year to use as a baseline for predictions about future changes.
- Sample voluminous information (e.g., annual deliveries or orders) carefully.
- Use activity-based techniques (see Chapters 4 and 5) to analyze activities not reported by existing information systems.
- Focus on areas of customer-related activities most likely to yield large cost savings.

An obvious step in HealthWave's customer profitability analysis is to identify its customers and the activities the company performs to serve them. Like most organizations, HealthWave has up-to-date customer lists and can use its accounting, sales, and distribution records to calculate customer-level sales, which are an important part of the profit equation. Because these same records enable few organizations, including HealthWave, to identify the way they use resources to serve customers, however, these companies must conduct additional investigations and revise their information systems to consistently provide cost information.

HealthWave Customer Profile

customer profile *categorizes individual or types of customers according to the major activities or factors that drive revenues and costs*

A **customer profile** categorizes individual or types of customers according to the major activities or factors that drive revenues and costs. For example, a bank might profile its customers by maintained account balances, number of transactions, types of services used, and risk, all of which can affect the bank's revenues and cost to serve customers. Presently, HealthWave does not sell to the general public but to three major customer

Exhibit 6–4

HealthWave Customers by Type

	Number of Separate Customer Accounts
Pharmacy customers	11,000
Independent grocery customers	1,500
Major grocery chain customers	4
Herbal therapists	800

types: pharmacies, groceries, and herbal therapists. These categories reflect HealthWave's major revenue and cost drivers. Its pharmacy, grocery, and herbal therapy customers are located throughout Australia and New Zealand. Grocery customers include approximately 1,500 independent grocers and 15,000 grocers served by four major grocery chain accounts. See Exhibit 6–4 for current customer-profile information.

Analysis of Customer Sales Patterns

Because HealthWave's accounting system did not easily yield estimates of customer-level revenues by product line, the system had to be programmed to produce the information shown in Exhibit 6–5. The team wanted to sort product-line revenues (reproduced in the top section of Exhibit 6–5 from Exhibit 6–2) by customer type (pharmacy, grocery, and herbal therapist). Analysis of a carefully selected, *representative sample* of last year's sales and distribution (shipping) data traced product sales to each customer type, as shown in the second section of Exhibit 6–5. For example, last year 78 percent of all *nonprescription drugs* were sold to pharmacies, 22 percent to grocery stores, and none to herbal therapists. Applying estimated percentages of product-line sales provides a way to identify last year's customer-level revenues (row 9, Exhibit 6–5; see also the spreadsheet formula bar). Calculations for pharmacy customers follow (NZ\$000). You should verify revenues traced to grocery customers and herbal therapists.

$$\text{Pharmacy revenue} = ([78.0\%] \times \text{Nonprescription revenue}) + ([8.0\%] \times \text{Supplements revenue}) + ([5.0\%] \times \text{Herbal remedy revenue})$$

$$\text{Pharmacy revenue} = (.78 \times \$26{,}900{,}000) + (.08 \times \$44{,}260{,}000) + (.05 \times \$19{,}840{,}000) = \underline{\underline{\$25{,}514{,}800}}$$

Using last year's average contribution margin ratios by product line permitted a similar calculation for cost of goods sold (CGS) for each customer type (row 10, Exhibit 6–5). CGS calculations follow for pharmacy customers (NZ\$000). You also should verify CGS traced to grocery and herbal therapist customers.

$$\text{Pharmacy CGS} = ([78.0\%] \times \text{Nonprescription revenue}) \times [52.0\%]\ \text{CGS ratio} + ([8.0\%] \times \text{Supplements revenue}) \times [61.0\%]\ \text{CGS ratio} + ([5.0\%] \times \text{Herbal remedy revenue}) \times [69.0\%]\ \text{CGS ratio}$$

$$\text{Pharmacy CGS} = (.78 \times \$26{,}900{,}000) \times .52 + (.08 \times \$44{,}260{,}000) \times .61 + (.05 \times \$19{,}840{,}000) \times .69 = \underline{\underline{\$13{,}755{,}000}}$$

Because pharmacies purchase most of the nonprescription drugs (the most profitable product line in Exhibit 6–2), they have the highest contribution margin ratio (46.1 percent, C12 of Exhibit 6–5). We might expect that pharmacies are the most profitable customers and that herbal therapists are the least profitable. Herbal therapists purchase the most herbal remedy products and have the lowest contribution margin ratio of all customers (33 percent, E12 of Exhibit 6–5). These facts might suggest that herbal therapists are less desirable customers; however, this conclusion is premature because Exhibit 6–5 traced only *manufacturing* costs to customers. To complete the analysis, we must analyze how HealthWave incurs costs to serve customers.

Exhibit 6–5 HealthWave Sales by Product Line and Customer (NZ$)

Microsoft Excel - HealthWave

C9 = =C2*C6+D2*C7+E2*C8

	A	B	C	D	E
1	**Product sales (Exhibit 6-2)**	**Total**	**Non-Prescription**	**Supplements**	**Herbal Remedies**
2	Product-line revenue	$ 91,000,000	$ 26,900,000	$ 44,260,000	$ 19,840,000
3	Contribution margin ratio		48.0%	39.0%	31.0%
4	Cost of goods sold ratio		52.0%	61.0%	69.0%
5	**Traced product sales to:**	**Total**	**Pharmacy**	**Grocery**	**Herbal therapists**
6	Sales of: Non-prescription drugs	100.0%	78.0%	22.0%	0.0%
7	Supplements	100.0%	8.0%	83.0%	9.0%
8	Herbal Remedies	100.0%	5.0%	34.0%	61.0%
9	**Traced customer revenues (C9=C2*C6+D2*C7+E2*C8)**	**$ 91,000,000**	**$ 25,514,800**	**$ 49,399,400**	**$ 16,085,800**
10	**Cost of goods sold (C10=C2*C6*C4+D2*C7*D4+E2*C8*E4)**	**$ 54,676,200**	**$ 13,755,008**	**$ 30,140,662**	**$ 10,780,530**
11	Contribution margin (C11=C9-C10)	$ 36,323,800	$ 11,759,792	$ 19,258,738	$ 5,305,270
12	Contribution margin ratio (C12=C11/C9)	39.9%	46.1%	39.0%	33.0%
13					

Exhibit 6-5 / Exhibit 6-6 / Basic analysis / Common size / Pareto charts /

Ready

Sales and Administrative Cost Analysis

Many sales and administrative costs directly serve customers rather than support manufacturing. Furthermore, not all customers necessarily demand services in direct proportion to their level of sales, as the traditional profit calculations in Exhibit 6–2 imply. Additional analysis of sales and administrative costs will complete HealthWave's customer profitability analysis, which culminates in Exhibit 6–11 and appears at the end of the next section on p. 235. This analysis also will enable HealthWave's cost-management analysis team to provide information useful for managing and improving customer profitability.[6]

We now discuss the way that the cost-management analysis team analyzed other customer-related costs, including these:

- Selling costs
- Marketing costs
- Ordering costs
- Distribution costs
- General and administrative costs

Customer Selling Costs

Selling costs include the costs of all personnel, databases, equipment, and facilities devoted to supporting sales activities. HealthWave's selling resources include salespeople, telephone-order operators, and the sales administration staff personnel. Like many sales-oriented organizations, HealthWave's sales personnel were rewarded in part for the amount of sales revenue they generated. This reward system created an incentive to increase sales, which normally is good, but sales-only rewards do not recognize the costs to make these sales. Thus, sales personnel work to increase sales, but the increased revenues could be less than the costs to do so. HealthWave's customer profitability team began by sorting through the direct benefits and costs of selling activities (see Exhibit 6–6).

Benefits and costs of direct sales. HealthWave organized its selling activities to independent groceries and pharmacies into six sales regions centered in the cities of Auckland, Adelaide, Brisbane, Melbourne, Perth, and Sydney. A separate group of its

[6] Readers not interested in the details of this analysis may skip to page 235, which concludes this detailed analysis of sales and administrative costs.

Exhibit 6–6

HealthWave's Analysis of Annual Selling Resources and Activities (NZ$)

Microsoft Excel - HealthWave

D7 = =D3*D4+D5*D6

	A	B	C	D	E
1	**Selling and ordering resources (NZ$)**	**Total**	**Pharmacy**	**Grocery**	**Herbal Therapists**
2	Sales areas		6	6	
3	Sales representatives		45	25	NA
4	Average salary/yr		$ 55,000	$ 42,000	
5	Major account managers		0	4	NA
6	Average salary/yr		0	$ 200,000	
7	**Sales personnel costs (D7=D3*D4+D5*D6)**	**$ 4,325,000**	**$ 2,475,000**	**$ 1,850,000**	NA
8	Total orders per year		200,000	40,000	6,000
9	Sample percent by sales personnel		80%	15%	0%
10	Sample percent by telephone sales orders		20%	85%	100%
11	total		100%	100%	100%
12	Estimated telephone orders (D12=D10*D8)	80,000	40,000	34,000	6,000
13	Estimated percent telephone orders (effort) by customer (D13=D12/SUM(C12:E12))		50.0%	42.5%	7.5%
14	**Estimated telephone ordering costs and effort (D14=B14*D13)**	**$ 130,000**	**$ 65,000**	**$ 55,250**	**$ 9,750**
15	Estimated percent sales administration effort		25%	62%	13%
16	**Estimated sales administration cost (D16=B16*D15)**	**$ 480,000**	**$ 120,000**	**$ 297,600**	**$ 62,400**
17	Total selling and ordering costs (B7+B14+B16)	$ 4,935,000			
18					

Exhibit 6-5 | Exhibit 6-6 | Basic analysis | Common size | Par

Ready

salespeople works in each sales area to call on and take orders from the pharmacies and independent grocers. A high-level account executive rather than salespeople serves each of the four major grocery chains. The team easily traced the use of these dedicated resources (row 7 in Exhibit 6–6) to pharmacy and all grocery customers by multiplying the number of sales representatives and account managers (if any) by their average annual salaries. For example, the calculation of sales personnel cost traced to grocery customers follows:

Grocery sales personnel cost = (25 sales reps × \$42,000) + (4 major acct executives × \$200,000) = NZ\$1,850,000

Interviews with independent pharmacy and grocery customers indicated that they greatly valued the sales personnels' knowledge of HealthWave's products and its customers' needs. They also valued the personal attention accorded by the sales force. The very few complaints had to do with the difficulty of placing orders via telephone rather than through salespeople or account executives.

Benefits and costs of telephone-based ordering. Customers viewed HealthWave's telephone-based ordering system to be slow and difficult to access. They noted that competitive suppliers were introducing more convenient Internet-based or direct ordering systems that enable customers to easily place orders without the "clunkiness" of dealing with telephone operators. The team noted this as an issue for future consideration.

The accounting system could easily report telephone sales costs (cell B14 in Exhibit 6–6), but tracing these resources to each customer type was more difficult because the telephone sales order staff takes *all* herbal therapy customer orders as well as those placed by some pharmacy and grocery customers. The team decided to measure the telephone ordering effort by using the percentage of orders processed for each customer type. The large number of annual orders required the team to select a *random sample* of orders from each customer type to determine this information (rows 9 and 10 of Exhibit 6–6). The team multiplied these percentages (row 10) by the total number of orders from each customer type (row 8) to estimate the total number of telephone orders placed by customer type. This measures telephone ordering effort. The team then used the estimated percentage of telephone orders (row 13) to estimate the cost of telephone sales to apply to each customer type (row 14). For example, the team determined telephone ordering costs for grocery customers follows:

$$\text{Grocery telephone ordering cost} = 42.5\% \text{ of telephone orders} \times \$130{,}000 = \underline{\underline{\$55{,}250}}$$

Benefits and costs of sales administration. A sales administration staff also supports all sales activities (row 16 in Exhibit 6–6) by maintaining customer, product, and sales-order databases and the schedules and call records of salespeople. The staff also manages advertising placement, coordination of sales promotions, and distribution center activities in each sales area. Sales administration also coordinates the logistics among manufacturing facilities and the six sales regions. [Many organizations, however, have separate departments (and resources) to manage and provide the logistics and ordering activities.]

Because timeliness of information was paramount, the team decided to learn the way that sale administration staff support customers by interviewing most staff members. From these interviews the team estimated the percentages of service to each of the three customer types (row 15 of Exhibit 6–6) and then calculated the costs of serving each type of customer (row 16), as follows:

$$\text{Grocery sales administration cost} = 62\% \text{ effort} \times \$480{,}000 = \underline{\underline{\$297{,}600}}$$

If this process later indicates costs that are disproportionate to sales, the team will focus on this area of customer service.[7] Given the time constraint, however, this was the team's method of using ABC techniques.

Customer Profitability

You're the **Decision Maker 6.1**

The effort and cost percentages in Exhibit 6–6 represent the data that support customer profitability analysis. Clearly, these data are not precise, could contain errors, and might not be actually relevant to decisions about *future* customer profitability.

a. Verify the estimated costs of sales personnel, telephone sales orders, and sales administration costs in Exhibit 6–6.

b. Evaluate the team's decisions concerning its methods of obtaining data for sales costs.

c. What is the average cost of processing a telephone sales order? Is this cost amount useful? Explain.

d. Because salespeople also take orders, should the analysis also consider the costs of the orders they take?

(Solutions begin on page 243.)

Customer Marketing Costs

Marketing costs include the costs of personnel, databases, equipment, and facilities dedicated to providing market research, marketing strategy, and marketing plans. HealthWave has a marketing department to address its marketing needs in the six sales areas. This department designs advertising and promotion materials and campaigns and provides training and information support for sales personnel. It also responds to customer needs forwarded from salespeople and major account executives. The results of the examination of marketing resources and activities are reported in Exhibit 6–7.

marketing costs *include the costs of personnel, databases, equipment, and facilities dedicated to providing market research, marketing strategy, and marketing plans*

Similar to the analysis of sales and administration, the cost management team interviewed marketing management staff members to estimate the percentage of their efforts devoted to each customer type (item 1 in Exhibit 6–7). Marketing personnel believed that the diversity of pharmacy customers and products might require spending relatively more time with this sector.

[7] Actually, observing or recording these support activities over a longer time period might generate accurate and detailed information that supports the reengineering of these activities (see Chapter 5).

Exhibit 6–7 HealthWave's Marketing Activities (NZ$)

Marketing Activities	Total	Pharmacy	Grocery	Herbal Therapist
1. Marketing management	100%	55%	35%	10%
Marketing management cost	$ 360,000	$ 198,000	$ 126,000	$ 36,000
2. Promotions and incentives	100%	44%	56%	0%
Promotion and incentive cost	$ 2,250,000	$ 990,000	$ 1,260,000	$ 0
3. Advertising	100%	50%	50%	0%
Advertising cost	$ 2,400,000	$ 1,200,000	$ 1,200,000	$ 0
4. Catalogue development	100%	0%	0%	100%
Catalogue development cost	$ 250,000	$ 0	$ 0	250,000
Total marketing costs	$ 5,260,000	$ 2,388,000	$ 2,586,000	$286,000

Promotion, advertising, and catalogue costs are committed to support marketing strategies. Using the past year's costs as baselines for its analysis, the team used carefully selected samples of product incentives and promotions to estimate the percentage of these marketing resources used by pharmacy and grocery customers (item 2 in Exhibit 6–7). The team noted that catalogue promotions had not been used in past years. The past year's advertising appeared to equally split between pharmacy and grocery customers (item 3 in Exhibit 6–7). The company's catalogue, which serves herbal therapists but neither pharmacy nor grocery customers, currently is not advertised. All development and mailing costs related to it are attributed to herbal therapists (item 4 in Exhibit 6–7). Sample pharmacy calculations follow. You should duplicate the calculations for other items in Exhibit 6–7.

Pharmacy marketing management cost = 55% effort × $360,000 = $198,000

Pharmacy promotions cost = 44% promotions × $2,250,000 = $990,000

Pharmacy advertising cost = 50% effort × $2,400,000 = $1,200,000

FedEx sorts and consolidates packages at central locations to efficiently distribute shipments to widely dispersed customers.

Customer Distribution Costs

Distribution costs include the costs of packing, shipping, and delivering products or services to customers. HealthWave distributes products to customers using a company-owned, maintained, and operated fleet of trucks serving pharmacy and grocery customers and a private delivery service, PackageXpress serving herbal therapists. See Exhibit 6–8 for the results of the analysis of distribution resources and activities.

distribution costs *include the costs of packing, shipping, and delivering products or services to customers*

Benefits and costs of distribution by company truck fleet. HealthWave operates distribution centers in each of its six sales regions. These centers allow the company to stock and deliver products to reflect regional sales differences. Because the centers are near customers, the company can respond quickly to customers' special orders. Interviews with independent pharmacy, grocery, and major account customers confirmed that they value HealthWave's shipping flexibility. Said one, "We know that HealthWave will respond to our emergencies quickly and accurately, and we really appreciate that they respond eagerly and cheerfully. The other suppliers act like they are doing us a huge favor, and they seem to resent the inconvenience. HealthWave understands customer satisfaction and service."

On average, company trucks deliver shipments twice per month to pharmacies and independent grocers. Numerous small customers believed that this frequency was not necessary at all times during the year. Only several times a year did they need frequent shipments (e.g., at the beginning of the flu and allergy seasons), which probably should be weekly. The truck fleet delivers weekly shipments to the distribution centers operated by the four major grocery accounts in each of the six sales regions.

HealthWave has always considered the costs of the fleet as an operating cost of its customer-oriented business and has never charged explicitly for it, even for special orders or emergencies. The cost-management team intended to measure distribution activity by volume of product delivered multiplied by distance traveled for each customer, but the time constraints of the analysis precluded this detailed analysis. Instead, the team used the delivery schedule, the number of deliveries, and then assigned truck-distribution costs on the basis of the percentage of deliveries to each customer type (item 1 of Exhibit 6–8).

Exhibit 6–8 HealthWave's Distribution Resources and Activities (rounded to nearest NZ$100)

Distribution Resources	Total	Pharmacy	Grocery	Herbal Therapist
Major customer accounts	4	0	4	0
Independent customers	12,500	11,000	1,500	0
Sales/distribution regions	6	0	6	0
Deliveries per major customer account per year	52	0	52	0
Percent by company truck		0	100%	0
Deliveries per independent customer per year	52	26	26	0
Percent by company truck		100%	100%	0%
Deliveries by company truck	326,248	286,000	40,248	0
1. Analysis of truck distribution costs				
Percent of total deliveries by company truck	100%	87.66%	12.34%	0.0%
Company truck distribution cost (rounded)	**$ 8,080,000**	**$ 7,083,200**	**$ 996,800**	**NA**
2. Analysis of outsourced distribution costs				
Percent deliveries by PackageXpress		0%	0%	100%
PackageXpress cost as % of revenue		12%	12%	12%
Customer revenues (Ex. 6–5)		$25,514,800	$ 49,399,400	$ 16,085,800
Outsourced distribution cost	**1,930,300**	**0**	**0**	**1,930,300**
Total distribution costs	$10,010,300			

Example distribution cost calculations in Exhibit 6–8 for grocery and pharmacy customers follow.

Grocery truck deliveries = (4 major accts × 6 sales regions × 52 weekly deliveries × 100% by truck) + (26 biweekly deliveries × 1,500 independents × 100% by truck) = 40,248 deliveries

Pharmacy truck distribution cost = 100% by truck × 87.663% total deliveries × \$8,080,000 = \$7,083,200 (rounded)

Benefits and costs of distribution by PackageXpress. The growth of HealthWave's catalogue business indicated a number of years ago that using the company's own fleet of trucks and drivers to deliver small shipments to widely scattered herbal therapists was prohibitively costly. Outsourcing herbal therapists' deliveries to PackageXpress greatly reduced the cost and increased the reliability and speed of sales deliveries to herbal therapists, whose only concerns were that deliveries were quick and reliable. Herbal therapists interviewed by the team expressed complete satisfaction with the cost, which they paid, and quality of this service.

HealthWave's contract with PackageXpress was based on a daily pickup of small, prepackaged shipments from HealthWave's regional distribution centers and no more than two-day delivery to herbal therapists within each sales region. The cost of this outsourced service to HealthWave is based on a negotiated fee to reserve the service availability and a fee based on weight and volume of shipments. The costs (and shipping fees charged to customers) have averaged 12 percent of the sales value of a shipment, which the team believed was a reasonable estimate for this analysis (item 2 in Exhibit 6–8).

Herbal therapist courier distribution cost = 100% by courier × 12% of revenue × \$16,085,800 = \$1,930,300 (rounded)

Customer General and Administration Costs

All operating costs must be covered by customer sales, and the remaining costs to be assigned to customers are research and development (R&D) and general and administrative costs. Exhibits 6–9 and 6–10 show the analyses of these other costs.

Costs and benefits of R&D. R&D costs are committed annual costs driven by desired new product development goals. R&D projects almost always can be assigned to one of the three product groups. Although these costs are intended to generate future sales, the team chose the very conservative approach of allocating R&D costs to products by the year of spending. This decision resulted in no R&D cost assigned to nonprescription drugs, \$480,000 to supplements, and \$720,000 to herbal remedies. Furthermore, the team assigned these R&D costs to customers based on the percentage of product sales of each category last year (from Exhibit 6–5); see Exhibit 6–9.

Exhibit 6–9 HealthWave's R&D Costs (NZ\$)

Analysis of R&D Costs	Total	Nonprescription	Supplements	Herbal Remedies
R&D projects traced to products	100%	0%	40%	60%
R&D costs traced to products	\$ 1,200,000	0	\$ 480,000	\$720,000
		Pharmacy	**Grocery**	**Herbal Therapist**
Sales of Nonprescription drugs (Ex. 6–5)	100.0%	78.0%	22.0%	0.0%
Supplements	100.0	8.0	83.0	9.0
Herbal remedies	100.0	5.0	34.0	61.0
R&D costs traced to customers	**\$1,200,000**	**\$74,400**	**\$ 643,200**	**\$482,400**

The R&D cost calculation for pharmacy customers follows. You should verify similar calculations in Exhibit 6–9 for grocery customers and herbal therapists.

Pharmacy R&D cost = ($0 R&D cost × 78% nonprescription sales) + ($480,000 R&D cost × 8% supplements sales) + ($720,000 R&D cost × 5% herbal remedy sales) = $74,400

Costs and benefits of general and administration activities. Presumably, all activities of a profit-seeking organization such as HealthWave are (or should be) performed to facilitate or support sales to customers. Because many general and administrative functions and activities are several steps removed from customer-related activities, tracing costs of these functions to customers is usually difficult.

When it was more than a month into its work, the team began its analysis of general and administrative costs—perhaps the most difficult cost to trace to customers because of their diverse activities (e.g., from human resources to tax compliance). Although team members realized that they did not have adequate time to conduct even a limited activity analysis of general administration activities, they believed that these costs (more than $8 million) were too high to ignore. The team therefore took a different approach to these costs; it asked the vice presidents of finance, marketing, and manufacturing[8] to estimate the percentage of general and administrative efforts used to support each customer type. The vice presidents found even this difficult to do and estimated that their percentage of general and administration effort spent was: 30 percent for manufacturing, 50 percent for customer activities, and 20 percent for general business activities (see Exhibit 6–10).

The team then decided to allocate the estimated manufacturing support cost based on the percentage of the cost of goods sold to each customer type (from Exhibit 6–5) and both customer and general and administration support costs based on the percentage of customer sales (also from Exhibit 6–5). Example calculations for pharmacy customers follow:

Pharmacy administrative costs = (Customer service + General and admin. support costs) × Percentage of sales + Manufacturing support costs × Percentage of CGS
= $5,789,000 × .2804 + $2,481,000 × .2516
= $1,623,100 + $624,200 = $2,247,300 (rounded)

[8] Note that the vice president of finance managed human resources and information systems as well as finance. The manufacturing vice president managed manufacturing, supplier relations, and logistics. The vice president of marketing managed marketing, sales, and customer service.

Exhibit 6–10 HealthWave's General and Administration Costs (rounded to nearest NZ$100)

HealthWave INC.

Major Company Activities	Total	Manufacturing	Customer Service and General Administration	
Admin. efforts traced to activities	100%	30%	70%	
Admin. costs traced to activities	$ 8,270,000	$ 2,481,000	$ 5,789,000	
		Pharmacy	**Grocery**	**Herbal Therapist**
Analysis of customer service and general and administration support costs:				
Customer revenues (Ex. 6–5)	$91,000,000	$25,514,800	$49,399,400	$16,085,800
Customer revenues (rounded percentage)	100.00%	28.04%	54.29%	17.68%
Customer service and general and admin. cost	$ 5,789,000	$ 1,623,100	$ 3,142,600	$ 1,023,300
Analysis of manufacturing support costs:				
Customer cost of goods sold (Ex. 6–5)	$54,676,200	$13,755,000	$30,140,700	$10,780,500
Cost of goods sold (rounded percentage)	100.00%	25.16%	55.13%	19.72%
Manufacturing support activity cost	$ 2,481,000	$ 624,200	$ 1,367,600	$ 489,200
Total general and admin. costs traced to customers	**$ 8,270,000**	**$ 2,247,300**	**$ 4,510,200**	**$ 1,512,500**

You're the **Decision Maker 6.2**

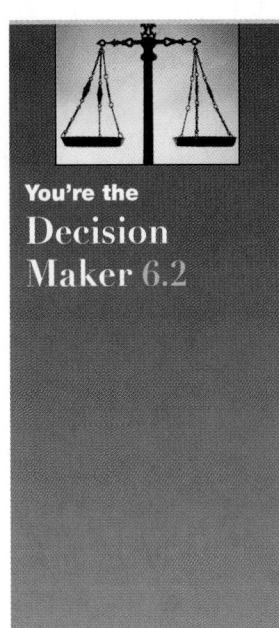

Trade-offs between Accuracy and Timeliness

In its analysis of customer profitability, the team clearly made trade-offs between the accuracy and the timeliness of cost-management information.

a. How might the diversity or complexity of pharmacy customers cause marketing managers to spend relatively more time serving this customer sector? Is it possible to test whether marketing managers actually spend more time serving pharmacy customers? If so, how?

b. What types of resources does HealthWave probably devote to its truck fleet? What costs and benefits should the company consider before deciding whether to retain the fleet or outsource all distribution?

c. The company fleet's costs are relatively high, and the team used an expedient activity base, the number of deliveries, to assign fleet distribution costs to customers. What possible inaccuracies might using this measure create? How might you assess whether the inaccuracies are relevant to the analysis?

d. The team decided to assign general and administrative costs related to customer service based on customer sales percentages. Do you think this was a justifiable assumption? What do you, as a member of the team, recommend knowing that the team was running out of time and concerned about completing the analysis on time?

(Solutions begin on page 243.)

Customer Profitability Analysis

HealthWave INC.

Conducting the type of analyses discussed for HealthWave results in a view of an organization's profitability by customer type that often generates information that differs from that previously available. HealthWave's historic product and functional orientation obscured the costs of selling to and serving customers, assuming that all customers were "average." For most organizations, however, this might not be true (recall Exhibit 6–1).

See Exhibits 6–11 and 6–12 for the cost-management analysis team's computations of HealthWave's customer profitability. Exhibit 6–11 combines all customer-oriented analyses into an income statement format, and Exhibit 6–12 displays customer profitability graphically. Exhibit 6–11 begins with customer-level revenues and cost of goods sold (Exhibit 6–5) and then adds customer-level selling costs (Exhibit 6–6), marketing costs (Exhibit 6–7), distribution costs (Exhibit 6–8), R&D costs (Exhibit 6–9), and general and administration costs (Exhibit 6–10). This "roll up" of the components of customer profitability results in the calculations of customer-level operating income and return on sales figures (bottom of Exhibit 6–11). Note that the total revenues, operating costs, and operating income are the same as in Exhibit 6–2, but the customer profitability analysis has sorted these income items by customer type.

Assuming that the cost-management analysis team's methods and estimates are reasonable, each type of customer clearly does not contribute equally to the company's overall profit. In particular, grocery customers already appear to exceed the long-term target return on sales (16.8% > 15%), whereas herbal therapists and especially pharmacy customers fail to meet even the short-term goal [6.4% and (0.6%) < 10%]. Although herbal therapists are profitable, pharmacy customers generate a significant loss that itself is in excess of the target cost reduction (or profit enhancement) for the first year. This was surprising information to the HealthWave team. Although it believes that a recommendation to drop pharmacy customers just to meet the first-year target was inappropriate at the time, it could present the customer-profitability information in Exhibits 6–11 and 6–12 to help HealthWave identify areas for profit improvement previously that had not been apparent.

Exhibit 6-11 HealthWave's Customer Profitability Statement

Customer Profitability	Total	Pharmacy	Grocery	Herbal Therapist
Revenue (Ex. 6–5)	$91,000,000	$25,514,800	$49,399,400	$16,085,800
Variable CGS	54,676,200	13,755,008	30,140,662	10,780,530
Contribution margin	$36,323,800	$11,759,792	$19,258,738	$ 5,305,270
Contribution margin ratio	39.9%	46.1%	39.0%	33.0%
Operating costs:				
Selling (Ex. 6–6):				
Sales personnel	$ 4,325,000	$ 2,475,000	$ 1,850,000	0
Telephone order system	130,000	65,000	55,250	$ 9,750
Sales administration	480,000	120,000	297,600	62,400
Total selling cost	$ 4,935,000	$ 2,660,000	$ 2,202,850	$ 72,150
Marketing (Ex. 6–7):				
Marketing management	360,000	198,000	126,000	36,000
Promotions and incentives	2,250,000	990,000	1,260,000	0
Advertising	2,400,000	1,200,000	1,200,000	0
Catalogue development	250,000	0	0	250,000
Total marketing cost	$ 5,260,000	$ 2,388,000	$ 2,586,000	$ 286,000
Distribution (Ex. 6–8):				
Company trucks	8,080,000	7,083,201	996,799	0
Courier service	1,930,296	0	0	1,930,296
Total distribution cost	$10,010,296	$ 7,083,201	$996,799	$ 1,930,296
Other operating costs:				
R&D (Ex. 6–9)	1,200,000	74,400	643,200	482,400
General and administrative support (Ex. 6–10)	8,270,000	2,247,284	4,510,232	1,512,484
Total operating cost	$29,675,296	$14,452,885	$10,939,081	$ 4,283,330
Operating income	$ 6,648,504	$ (2,693,093)	$ 8,319,657	$ 1,021,940
Return on sales	7.3%	(10.6%)	16.8%	6.4%

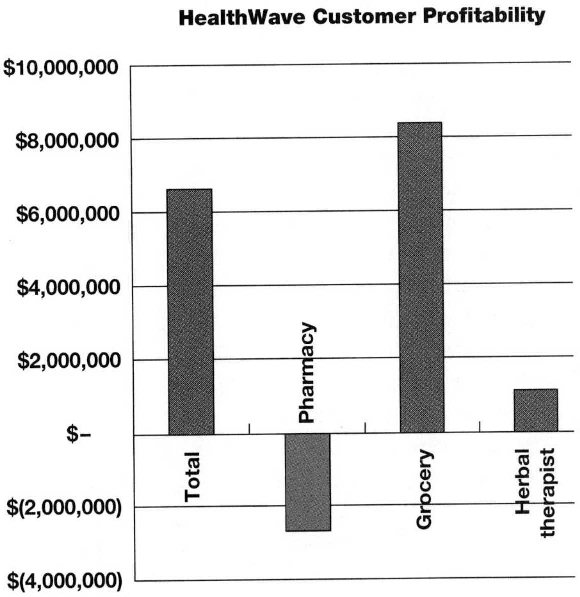

Exhibit 6-12

HealthWave's Customer Profitability Chart

Identification of Alternative Actions and Choice of Appropriate One

Common-Size Profit Statements

LO 3 Identify alternative actions and recommend improvements for overall and customer profitability based on analyzing customer-related activities.

common-size statements *express items as percentages of revenue*

The absolute dollar amounts in Exhibit 6–11 indicate the profit or loss generated by customer type. As mentioned previously, some companies that are information-technology intensive can produce this information for every single customer; its most common use, however, is to identify which customers to encourage and which to drop or discourage (see Cost Management in Practice 6–1). Organizations also can use the information to identify opportunities to transform customer losses into customer profits. To highlight these opportunities, recasting the absolute dollar cost and profit amounts as percentages of revenues can be useful. Financial statements that express items as percentages of revenue are called **common-size statements.**

Dividing the amount in each column in Exhibit 6–11 by its sales revenue reveals each amount as a percentage of revenue. See Exhibit 6–13 for those amounts that indicate the percentage to achieve customer sales for each customer type. Review this exhibit and look for exceptionally large or small percentages of sales across the three types of customers.

Several amounts in Exhibit 6–13 are presented in bold. Look first at the Pharmacy column in the exhibit. Working from the bottom of Exhibit 6–13, the first exceptional figure is the (10.6 percent) return on sales (ROS) for pharmacy customers, which we knew but now see must be related to the much higher relative operating costs estimated for pharmacy customers despite their higher contribution margin ratio. Operating costs for the pharmacy customer type are 56.7 percent of sales but average only 22.1 to 26.6 percent of sales than other customer types provide. Contributing to this much higher cost rate are higher distribution costs (27.8 percent of pharmacy sales compared to only 2 and 12 percent of sales for others) and selling costs (10.4 percent of sales

Exhibit 6–13

HealthWave's Common-Size Customer Profitability Statement

	Percentage (rounded)			
	Total	**Pharmacy**	**Grocery**	**Herbal Therapist**
Revenue (Ex. 6–5)	100.0%*	100.0%	100.0%	100.0%
CGS (Ex. 6–5)	60.1	53.9	61.0	67.0
Contribution margin	39.9%	46.1%	39.0%	33.0%
Operating costs:				
Selling (Ex. 6–6):				
Major grocery chain accounts	0.9	0.0	1.6	0.0
Independents	3.9	**9.7**	2.1	0.0
Telephone order system	0.1	0.3	0.1	0.1
Administration	0.5	0.5	0.6	0.4
Total selling costs	5.4%	**10.4%**	4.5%	**0.5%**
Marketing (Ex. 6–7):				
Marketing management	0.4	0.8	0.3	0.2
Incentives and promotions	2.5	3.9	2.6	0.0
Advertising	2.6	4.7	2.4	0.0
Catalogue development	0.3	0.0	0.0	1.6
Total marketing costs	5.8%	9.4%	5.2%	**1.8%**
Distribution (Ex. 6–8):				
Company truck	8.9	**27.8**	2.0	0.0
Courier service	2.1	0.0	0.0	12.0
Total distribution costs	11.0%	**27.8%**	**2.0%**	12.0%
Other operating costs (Ex. 6–9):				
R&D costs	1.3	0.3	1.3	3.0
General and admin. costs	9.1	8.8	9.1	9.4
Total operating costs	32.6%	**56.7%**	22.1%	26.6%
Operating income	7.3%	**(10.6%)**	16.8%	6.4%

*Calculations use data from Exhibit 6–11.

compared to only 4.5 and 0.5 percent for others). HealthWave apparently serves its grocery and herbal therapists much more efficiently than its pharmacy customers. Can it solve the pharmacy customer-service problem?

Aided by the analysis of the information in Exhibit 6–13, the cost-management team identified four alternative courses of action to improve customer profitability and began to analyze the profit impact of each. The alternatives were:

- Continue the status quo; do nothing.
- Drop pharmacy customers.
- Increase the efficiency of serving pharmacy customers.
- Decrease operating activity costs for all customers.

Continue the Status Quo; Do Nothing

The team did not seriously consider recommending that HealthWave do nothing. Accepting the status quo surely would result in the failure to meet London Pharmaceutical's ROS targets. Furthermore, because competitors most likely also were looking closely at their customer-service operations, keeping the status quo surely would result in erosion of customer satisfaction and loyalty and increased losses. Understanding the implications of keeping the status quo was important motivation for seriously considering its alternatives. Because it was so close to the problem, the team was motivated and knew it must communicate that motivation when recommending changes to HealthWave management and employees. Keeping the status quo was untenable because choosing not to change would mean certain failure.

Drop Pharmacy Customers

A quick review of Exhibit 6–11 *implies* that dropping pharmacy customers also would eliminate the $2,695,600 loss attributed to this customer type. Eliminating this loss appears to provide more than the $2,451,500 cost reduction or profit enhancement needed to meet the target return on sales (see Exhibit 6–3). Certainly, HealthWave must ensure the secrecy of its investigation of whether it can save nearly $2.7 million by dropping pharmacy customers, or pharmacy customers might bolt to other suppliers.

The most certain outcome of dropping pharmacy customers is the loss of $11,759,800 in contribution margin from this customer type (see Exhibit 6–11). To avoid the estimated loss from pharmacy customers, however, HealthWave also has to save at least $14,455,400 in operating costs that have been assigned to this customer type. To properly address this issue, the team must use one of the major ABC principles presented in Chapter 4: Estimates of activity-based costs reflect the *uses* of resources, not necessarily the *acquisition* or *spending* for resources. Some customer-service costs are driven by unit-level or customer-level activities. Presumably, eliminating the customer activities and the capacity to provide them can save these costs, but facility-level decisions and activities drive other costs (e.g., general and administration costs), which do not depend directly on unit- or customer-level activities.

HealthWave faces the difficult decision about whether to drop its unprofitable pharmacy customers. An alternative is to increase the efficiency of serving them.

Let's assume that the team's estimates of customer-related operating costs are reasonably accurate measures of the costs of *using* customer-related resources. Does eliminating those pharmacy customer–related activities also eliminate the *spending* for the capacity to perform those activities? Furthermore, does eliminating pharmacy customers have adverse effects on the sale of goods or provision of services to other customers? The team really needs answers to these questions before correctly measuring the profit impact of dropping pharmacy customers. See the results of Exhibit 6–14 for the team's additional analysis, which focused on these elements related to pharmacy customers:

- Selling costs.
- Marketing costs.
- Distribution costs.
- Other costs.
- Elimination effects on other customers.

1. *Pharmacy-customer selling costs.* The costs to sell to independent pharmacies ($2,475,000, or 9.7 percent of sales) are much higher than those for the other customer types. The four major grocery accounts serve most grocery customers efficiently as a small telephone sales-order system does for herbal therapists. HealthWave's pharmacy customers, on the other hand, tend to be widely dispersed and have no major buying groups. Thus, serving them requires a relatively large dedicated sales force, which HealthWave can eliminate if it drops pharmacy customers, saving $2,475,000 annually.

   By dropping pharmacy customers, the team estimated that HealthWave could reduce its telephone sales-order system by one operator, saving $30,000 annually. Similarly, reducing sales and administration capacity by two employees reduces these costs, saving $65,000 annually. The team estimated that HealthWave would spend approximately 10 percent of the personnel cost savings on counseling and "outplacement" for terminated employees if they could be shifted to other areas. Thus, 90 percent of the cost savings probably could be realized in the short run. The team estimated no reductions in physical facilities or equipment related to sales and administration. Total annual selling cost savings were estimated to be:

   Selling cost savings = .90 × ($2,475,000 + 30,000 + 65,000) = $2,313,000

2. *Pharmacy-customer marketing costs.* The vice president of marketing confirmed that dropping pharmacy customers would reduce the need for marketing management capacity by one manager and two support staff, saving $110,000 annually, net of outplacement costs. Without pharmacy customers, HealthWave would have no need to offer pharmacy incentives and provide advertising, saving $2,190,000 annually. Total annual marketing cost savings will be:

   Marketing cost savings = $110,000 + 2,190,000 = $2,300,000

3. *Pharmacy-customer distribution costs.* Most of the cost of HealthWave's truck fleet supports deliveries to pharmacy customers. Some fleet costs (e.g., the maintenance facility) cannot be reduced proportionately by fewer deliveries without pharmacy customers. Furthermore, an unknown percentage of fleet trips delivers to both pharmacy and independent grocery customers. Thus, HealthWave cannot reduce its fleet capacity by the full amount eliminated and maintain its desired level of service to independent grocery customers. Nonetheless, the team estimated that dropping pharmacy customers would save approximately 80 percent of the pharmacy-related distribution costs after outplacement and other shutdown costs, saving approximately $5,667,000 in the first year:

   Distribution cost savings = .80 × ($7,083,200) = $5,667,000 (rounded)

4. *Other Pharmacy-customer costs.* R&D costs are committed based on desired future product development. Although dropping pharmacy customers reduces the need for the *volume* of future products, the team was reluctant to recommend reducing

Lost Revenue and Saved Cost	Drop Pharmacy Customers
Lost revenue	$(25,514,800)
Saved CGS	13,755,000
Lost contribution margin	$(11,759,800)
Saved operating costs (see text):	
Selling and administration (net of outplacement costs)	2,313,000
Marketing	2,300,000
Distribution	5,667,000
General and administration	1,700,000
Total operating cost savings	$ 11,980,000
Increase in Profit (Cost savings − Lost revenue)	$ 220,200
Total sales without pharmacy ($91,000,000 − $25,514,800)	$ 65,485,200
Total profit without pharmacy ($6,648,500 + 220,200)	6,868,700
Revised return on sales (first year)	10.5%

Exhibit 6–14

Profit Effects of Dropping Pharmacy Customers (rounded NZ$; see Exhibit 6–11)

R&D efforts because of the adverse impact on future revenues. The team believed that HealthWave could reduce general and administrative and customer-service support costs related to pharmacy customers, estimating cost savings of approximately $1,700,000 in the first year (including outplacement costs) by reducing general and administrative capacity. Note that overall, general and administration cost at 9.1 percent of sales is the largest single cost category after cost of goods sold; a close look might identify even more cost-saving opportunities.

General and administration cost savings = $1,700,000

5. *Elimination effects on other customers.* The team anticipated other effects of dropping pharmacy customers, none of which could not be quantified easily. Dropping pharmacy customers might adversely affect manufacturing efficiency, particularly related to nonprescription drugs, 78 percent of which are sold to pharmacy customers. This might reduce grocery-customer contribution margins or make HealthWave products less competitive. Other adverse effects included remaining employee morale which might decline and the loss of beneficial crossover product advertising and promotions. For example, product advertising and promotions that benefit the pharmacy customer segment sometimes also benefit grocery segment customers. On the other hand, marketing and administration efforts could focus more on grocery and herbal therapists and provide them more efficient service without the distraction of pharmacy customers.

Review the team's summary analysis of dropping pharmacy customers in Exhibit 6–14, which indicates that dropping pharmacy customers increases profitability by $220,200. Overall return on sales then increases to 10.5 percent for the first year. Although dropping pharmacy customers results in a loss of their contribution margin, the estimated cost savings and increase in profits are sufficient to increase the return on the reduced level of sales to more than the first-year 10 percent target. According to this analysis (and ignoring qualitative considerations), HealthWave would become a smaller but more profitable company without pharmacy customers. However, does this position it to meet the greater challenge of reaching future ROS targets?

Increase the Efficiency of Serving Pharmacy Customers

An alternative to dropping pharmacy customers is to improve the efficiency of serving them. The most prominent amounts in Exhibits 6–13 and 6–14 reflect distribution costs to pharmacy customers. The team had discovered that one reason for the higher percentage cost of pharmacy distribution is the greater dispersion of its customers (recall that four major association accounts served all but the 1,500 grocery customers efficiently). Herbal therapists were similarly dispersed, but through a contract with PackageXpress, the cost of shipping to them was only 12 percent of sales. Could HealthWave achieve the ROS target by eliminating the truck fleet serving pharmacy customers and totally outsourcing distribution? The team had to keep this very sensitive alternative secret to prevent other employees from learning about it prematurely.

See Exhibit 6–15 for the analysis of HealthWave's replacement of its fleet serving pharmacy customers with outsourced delivery at costs similar to those of its existing contract with PackageXpress (12 percent of sales value). Without considering other service improvements, the estimated distribution-cost savings [$2,605,200 = $5,667,000 − (.12 × 25,514,800)], when added to previous profits, would boost the revised profits sufficiently to meet the first-year target ROS (10.2% > 10%).

Although the effects on HealthWave affected personnel would be negative, outsourcing distribution was the team's preferred alternative. Unlike completely dropping pharmacy customers, outsourcing distribution to this customer type promised less disruption to customers and retained more future market opportunities.

Increasing the efficiency of sales activities to pharmacy customers, which currently cost $2,475,000 (9.7 percent of sales), is another likely source of profit improvement. The team did not believe that selling to pharmacy customers easily could be as efficient as selling to either grocery or herbal therapists, but it suspected that improving sales activities to pharmacies might result in additional cost savings. Because this could require complicated organizational changes at HealthWave *and* for pharmacy customers, HealthWave would not realize these savings quickly. Furthermore, the team believed that improvements in activities supporting all customers might be necessary to meet long-term profit targets.

Exhibit 6–15

Profit Effects of Outsourcing Pharmacy Deliveries (rounded NZ$)

Pharmacy Distribution Cost Savings:	
Pharmacy truck-fleet cost (Ex. 6–14)	$ 5,667,000
Outsourced delivery based on cost of pharmacy sales (.12 × 25,514,800)	3,061,800
Cost savings	$ 2,605,200
Effect on Profits:	
Total sales (Ex. 6–11)	$91,000,000
Revised profit with cost savings (6,648,500 + 2,605,200)	$ 9,253,700
Revised return on sales	10.2%

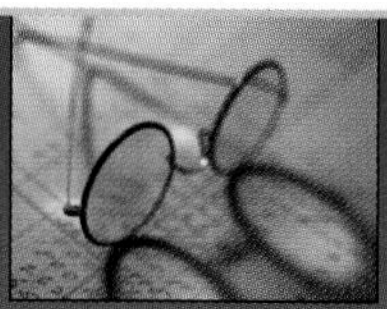

Cost Management in Practice 6.2

Complications of Customer Service

In June 1999, Sun Microsystems, provider of Internet servers and software, learned an invaluable lesson in managing customer profitability. Sun's president received a call from the CEO of eBay (the online auction company) stating that eBay's Web site had been down for 22 hours because of a bug in its very expensive Sun server. Sun's costly crash-effort to revive the site revealed extensive problems related to eBay's installation and use of the server, which Sun had assumed were the customer's responsibilities. After this incident, Sun realized that the occurrence of these problems was imminent worldwide. Most of its dot-com customers were struggling with the complexities of installing and operating large Internet servers, and they expected a trouble-free, plug-and-play server. Their inattention to managing servers was sure to lead to outraged customers. Recognizing that the out-of-pocket costs and damaged reputation from these problems could be devastating to Sun, it quickly identified 14 important customer-related issues, placed a vice president in charge of managing each one, and dramatically overhauled its customer-sales and service activities to internalize and minimize the costs to prevent costly customer emergencies similar to the size that eBay had experienced. *Source: Peter Burrows.* "Sun's Bid to Rule the Web."

Total sales	$91,000,000
Long-term ROS target	15%
Target profit	13,650,000
Total revenue at last year's sales level	$91,000,000
Variable CGS of last year's sales	54,676,200
Contribution margin	$36,323,800
Operating costs after possible distribution savings (29,675,300 − 2,605,200)	27,070,100
Operating income	$ 9,253,700
Target profit improvement required ($13,650,000 − 9,253,700)	4,396,300
Improvement as a percent of operating costs ($4,396,300 ÷ $27,070,100)	16.2%

Exhibit 6–16

HealthWave's Long-Term Profit Target (rounded NZ$)

Decrease Operating Activity Costs for All Customers

Either of the two alternatives that focused on keeping pharmacy customers is likely to achieve profit improvements that would meet the first-year target. However, the team knew that its responsibilities included making recommendations to position HealthWave to meet its long-term profit targets. Assume that HealthWave chooses to increase the efficiency of servicing pharmacy customers by outsourcing distribution rather than to drop them. At last year's sales level of $91,000,000 plus cost savings from outsourcing pharmacy distribution, the company must improve profits by another $4,396,300 to meet the 15 percent long-term ROS target (see Exhibit 6–16). To achieve this profit improvement by decreasing operating activity costs would require a 16.2 percent reduction ($4,396,300 ÷ 27,070,100) within five years.

The team realized that saving this amount from any single activity (e.g., cutting general and administrative costs by more than half) was unlikely. It expected that some profit increase would be achieved by sales growth without proportionate cost increases and HealthWave would apply activity-based management methods (see Chapter 5) on a companywide basis to reduce costs efficiently. Some selling, ordering, and logistics activities were undoubtedly not value added and should be eliminated or improved. Perhaps moving many customer-related activities to the Internet would be cost effective and benefit relations with all customers, although converting HealthWave to e-commerce would be a major undertaking. Making more significant profit improvements promised to be a time-consuming and politically difficult task, but the team resolved to persevere. The company's future depended upon it, and the team already had made a significant start. CEO Atherton and the executive committee decided to seriously explore outsourcing pharmacy deliveries and to move aggressively to increase sales to profitable customers and to improve the efficiencies of other customer services to meet long-run profit targets. As of this writing, the company is on track to meet its goals.

Chapter Summary

HealthWave's cost-management team studied the company's customer profitability by identifying quantitative and qualitative costs and benefits associated with all major resources and activities dedicated to serving customers. Other organizations might find different opportunities for improving customer profitability; some organizations might quantify more or fewer of these factors that affect customer and overall profitability. Nevertheless, the general form of HealthWave's analysis is applicable to most organizations. These profitability analyses might include these elements:

- Obtain top management support for the analysis and implementing difficult action choices it recommends.
- Develop tangible objectives for the analysis (e.g., Exhibit 6–3).

- Obtain top management support to access the information needed to trace activities and resources to customers.
- Build customer profiles and trace sales to customers (e.g., Exhibits 6–4 and 6–5).
- Trace product selling, marketing, and distribution activities and resources to customers (e.g., Exhibits 6–5, 6–6, 6–7, and 6–8).
- Trace other resources to customers (Exhibits 6–9 and 6–10).
- Measure customer profitability (Exhibits 6–11, 6–12, and 6–13).
- Identify and measure the impact of alternative actions to improve customer profitability (Exhibits 6–14 and 6–15).
- Position the organization to continually improve long-term customer profitability.

Key Terms

For each term's definition, refer to the indicated page or turn to the glossary at the end of the text.

Common-size statements, 236
Customer profile, 225
Customer-profitability analysis, 220
Distribution costs, 231
Marketing costs, 229

Meeting the Cost Management Challenges

1. **How** can you determine in advance whether investments of time, effort, and information systems to prepare customer profitability information are worthwhile?

Other than relying on others' experience or consultants' assurances, determining the value of an investment in information to support customer profitability analysis is difficult. Many organizations approach customer profitability analysis by analyzing a segment of their operations first. This cautious approach allows them to assess the costs and benefits of obtaining information without investing in a full analysis, which can be very costly (millions of dollars for large organizations!).

2. **How** can customer profitability analysis be more relevant for service and governmental organizations than for others?

Various organizations employ different types of resources for different customer-service strategies at various costs. However, all types and sizes of organizations potentially can benefit from better understanding how they use scarce resources to serve different customers and customer types. Because service and government organizations use most of their resources to provide services (or they should), customer profitability analysis can be more important to their success than to other types of companies.

3. **How** do you evaluate the trade-offs among the desires for relevant, accurate, and timely information?

Few, if any, organizations have enough time and resources to obtain the information they really want to support their important decisions. Because traditional, product-line profitability information is largely irrelevant for customer profitability analysis, some declare it to be completely irrelevant and inaccurate for that purpose. Trade-offs between relevance, accuracy, and timeliness almost always are necessary. The trade-off might be between (1) information that is only 50 percent accurate but 100 percent timely and relevant versus (2) information that is 100 percent irrelevant and inaccurate but completely timely and relevant. Analysts need to find trade-offs with which they feel comfortable given the importance of the decisions they are supporting. At a minimum, they must fully document and support the information they develop and use so that they and others can understand its limitations and make informed decisions about revising it.

4. **How** can cost-management analysts help an organization plan and execute changes in operations to deliver more customer value at lower cost?

Leading change is an important part of cost-management analysis. Significant resistance and opposition often accompany significant change; this is just human nature. Cost-management analysts should pay careful attention to the recommendations for leading change described in Chapter 1. Although there are no guarantees for seamless change, understanding the nature of change and the natural resistance to it and following a clear plan to lead it increases its chance of success.

5. **How** can you determine whether operational changes in customer service have been beneficial or harmful?

Another common human trait is unwillingness to reevaluate changes or investments that have been made. Often changes have been so difficult to implement that their lack of success is very disappointing and tends to reflect badly on those that led the change. Reevaluations or "postaudits" of an implemented change offer invaluable learning opportunities that should be part of every organization's culture. One strategy to ensure that postaudits occur is to enforce a policy requiring every major decision that involves a customer service change to include a scheduled postaudit.

Solutions to You're the Decision Maker

6.1 Customer Profitability p. 229

a. Costs rounded to the nearest $100.

	Pharmacy	Grocery	Herbal Therapist
Sales personnel cost	45 × $55,000 = $2,475,000	25 × $42,000 + 4 × $200,000 = $1,850,000	NA
Telephone sales order effort	.50 = 40,000 ÷ 80,000	.425 = 55,250 ÷ 80,000	.075 = 6,000 ÷ 80,000
Telephone sales order cost	.50 × $130,000 = $65,000	.425 × $130,000 = $55,250	.075 × $130,000 = $9,750
Sales administration cost	.25 × $480,000 = $120,000	.62 × $480,000 = $297,600	.13 × $480,000 = $62,400

b. The team's decision to calculate and assign costs of *sales personnel costs* seems straightforward, assuming that the costs reflect efforts. For example, no carryover in sales effort for grocery and pharmacy salespeople seems to exist. Assignment of *telephone sales order costs* apparently is accurate, but note that the number of orders reflects the volume of orders but not the complexity of each. A telephone order from one of the large grocery chain accounts is likely to be more complex and require more resources than one from an herbal therapist. Failure to consider complexity could lead to overestimates of the telephone sales order costs to serve customers with simple orders. Interviews with sales administration personnel are the basis of the assignment of *sales administration costs*. Time did not permit a formal observation of the use of these resources, which might have been more accurate. The failure to adjust Exhibit 6–6 or other exhibit for expected changes in cost, technology, organization, or service level is acceptable at this level of analysis.

c. The average cost for an operator to take an order placed by telephone is $1.625 ($130,000 ÷ 80,000), but this does not consider other related quantitative costs (e.g., the complexity of the order) or the qualitative factor of when the order was processed (during a slow or busy time), each of which could affect the cost of taking such orders. If the average cost does not consider these elements, it is less useful.

d. If the only analysis objective is to trace costs by type of customer, separate identification of the cost of salespersons taking orders is not necessary.

6.2 Trade-offs between Accuracy and Timeliness p. 234

a. Many people believe that the diversity and complexity of serving a customer are the most important cost drivers. HealthWave needs to identify what *marketing managers mean* by diversity or complexity. How do more complex customers use marketing managers' time? Is designing or administering marketing programs for pharmacies more complex than for groceries? Is communicating with pharmacies more difficult? Why? How? Perhaps dealing with the four major grocery accounts makes marketing management much simpler for grocery customer type. Observations of how marketing management staff spends its time on randomly selected days can test this proposition.

b. The direct resources devoted to the fleet include the purchase and maintenance of the trucks, fuel, and garage and office facilities as well as the salaries, including benefits, of the drivers, dispatchers, and mechanics. Indirect resources likely include a percentage of marketing management, sales and administration, and general and administrative efforts. Before deciding whether to retain the fleet, HealthWave should consider the qualitative factors of the values of its flexible response to customer orders supplied by the fleet and the company identity provided by its logo on the trucks as well as the disruption caused by terminating employees and liquidating assets.

c. Distribution capacity is a matter of ability to do work or to carry weight (or volume) some distance. Doing so within some time period also is a factor because of the opportunity cost of delivery time. Assigning costs based only on the number of deliveries does not consider the distance of the deliveries or the weight of the shipments. The team's measure of distribution activity treats all as being the same. To the extent that the delivery work performed for different customers is diverse, the team's expedient measure misstates distribution costs across customers. You might assess whether the inaccuracies are relevant by obtaining information to determine whether many smaller deliveries over longer distances (serving pharmacy customers) consume more fleet resources than fewer larger ones over shorter distances (serving grocery customers).

d. Assigning general and administrative costs based on relative sales revenue certainly could be justified, but anyone reviewing the team's work would want assurance that this very large cost ($8,270,000) had been assigned accurately or at least in a way that does not materially affect any decisions based on the information. The team assigned marketing management costs more heavily to pharmacy customers based on interviews with marketing managers, which did not yield precise information, setting a disturbing precedent. You might ask the company's CEO for another week or so to refine estimates of assigned general and administrative costs. In this case, the trade-off of accuracy versus timeliness might tilt toward more accuracy.

Review Questions

6.1 Review and define each of the chapter's key terms.

6.2 How are product-line and customer profitability measures similar and different based on the discussions in this chapter.

6.3 Explain the point made by Exhibit 6–1.

6.4 List typical objectives of customer profitability analysis.

6.5 List and describe each major type of customer-related resource and the activities that drive their use, as illustrated by the analysis of HealthWave.

6.6 Describe the trade-offs analysts often must make when gathering and evaluating information about customer-related resources, activities, and costs.

6.7 Describe how customer profitability analysis can be related to ABC and ABM.

6.8 Describe typical qualitative factors to consider when evaluating alternatives to improve customer profitability.

6.9 Describe several types of improvements that an organization could make to increase its customer profitability.

6.10 How might you apply the recommendations in Chapter 1 for leading change when implementing customer-profitability improvements?

Critical Analysis

6.11 "There's no such thing as product profitability, only customer profitability." Discuss.

6.12 An Internet search of the key phrase "customer profitability" will result in thousands of "hits," many of which are Web sites of companies seeking to sell software or consulting services. If you were looking for assistance in designing and implementing customer profitability analysis, how could you discriminate among these competing sites?

6.13 Professor Johnson argues that ABC techniques have been oversold. Rather than focusing on reducing costs of production or serving customers, he argues, firms should strive to improve customer satisfaction because doing so will increase profitability more than cost cutting will.[9] Critically evaluate this argument.

6.14 A recent article lauded a major e-commerce supplier for its extraordinary commitments to product and service innovation and customer service. The article argued that these commitments are paying off by citing as proof higher than average contribution margins and growth in sales over the past three years. Evaluate this evidence of a payoff from R&D and customer service expenditures.[10]

6.15 Many financial services companies regularly offer credit cards to college students who have a low income and no credit history. On the face of it, this practice seems contrary to that used by many banks, such as Bank of America, to segment credit-card customers by income, risk, services, and profitability. Why do you think companies make these offers to college students?

6.16 Federal Express reportedly segments customers into "good," "bad," and "ugly" categories.[11] It gives good customers, who spend much and demand little service or marketing, preferential treatment; charges bad customers, who spend little but are expensive to serve, higher shipping charges; and it discourages ugly customers, who spend little with poor prospects of increases, from using its services. Is this practice of segmenting and differential pricing evidence of illegal price discrimination by FedEx? Explain.

6.17 Deregulation of telecommunication in the United States has brought increased competition among long-distance telephone service providers, such as AT&T, Sprint, and MCI-Worldcom. Initially, these companies offered up to $50 to customers to switch to their service, but these offers now are rare. How do you explain this change in marketing and promotion?

6.18 A business publication reported across-the-board declines in customer satisfaction in the airline, banking, retailing, hotel, and telecommunication industries, yet most companies in these industries were profitable. How do you explain this apparent mismatch of customer satisfaction and profitability?

6.19 At your company's monthly marketing strategy meeting, the director of customer satisfaction happily reports that 80 percent of customers are at least "satisfied" and half of those are "delighted" with the company's products and services. This is good news because delighted customers are much more likely to be repeat customers. The director argues that with effort, it is possible to reach a customer satisfaction level of 90 percent by focusing on the 20 percent who are dissatisfied. Furthermore, a 50 percent overall delighted rating is within reach. Everyone turns to you for approval to attempt to achieve these higher goals. What is your response?

6.20 "Investing in customer profitability analysis will cost millions—and that's just to get started. I just can't justify that level of spending when our bottom line is so thin." "I challenge that expense-only thinking. The nature of business is spending money to make money. How else are we going to spend money that is more value added?" Referee this argument and develop criteria to judge whether to begin a major customer profitability analysis project.

---

[9] H. T. Johnson, "It's Time to Stop Overselling Activity-Based Concepts." Also see the rejoinder by R. S. Kaplan, "In Defense of Activity-Based Cost Management."

[10] P. Burrows, "Sun's Bid to Rule the Web."

[11] P. C. Judge, "Do You Know Who Your Most Profitable Customers Are?"

Exercises

Exercise 6.21
Customer Profitability
(LO1)

An Internet search of the key phrase "customer profitability" results in thousands of "hits," many of which are Web sites of companies seeking to sell software or consulting services. Choose a sample of five of these Web-sites and write a memo that evaluates the information they present and how well they present it.

Exercise 6.22
Customer Database
(LO1)

Building a customer database can be expensive. Free information is available in the United States from the Census Bureau's Web site (*www.census.gov*). Visit this site (particularly the Economic Census link), and prepare a short report describing the type of information available that might be useful to start-up businesses.

Exercise 6.23
Customer Data Warehouse
(LO1)

Data mining and data warehousing techniques are potential tools to use to analyze customer profitability. Many companies have had disappointing results using them, however, despite great expense and effort in building data warehouses. Search the internet for information about data mining and warehousing, and write a memo that makes recommendations for guiding a data warehouse project to deliver useful customer profitability information.

Exercise 6.24
Customer Profitability
(LO2)

Fontinalis Company produces, sells, and distributes two products, Brooks and Redds, to two types of customers, urban and rural. Using the following information, prepare a customer profitability statement:

Fontinalis Product Profitability	**Total**	**Brooks**	**Redds**
Contribution margin ratio	46.7%	40.0%	60.0%
Revenues	$9,000,000	$6,000,000	$3,000,000
Customer sales to:			
Sales of:		Urban	Rural
Brooks	100%	70%	30%
Redds	100%	20%	80%
Operating costs traced to customers	$3,000,000	$2,200,000	$800,000

Exercise 6.25
Return on Customer Sales
(LO2)

Refer to Exercise 6.24. Fontinalis desires to increase its return on sales to 25 percent. What amount of profit enhancement is required to meet this profitability target at the same level of sales?

Exercise 6.26
Customer Profitability
(LO2)
Spreadsheet

FramCo sells two automotive products, windshield wipers and floor mats, to two types of customers, grocery and auto parts stores. Using the following information, prepare a customer profitability statement:

FramCo Product Profitability	**Total**	**Windshield Wipers**	**Floor Mats**
Contribution margin ratio	64.5%	70.0%	60.0%
Revenues	$11,000,000	$5,000,000	$6,000,000
Customer sales to		Grocery	Auto Parts
Sales of:			
Windshield wipers	100%	50%	50%
Floor mats	100	20	80
Operating costs traced to customers	$ 4,500,000	$2,200,000	$2,300,000

Exercise 6.27
Return on Customer Sales
(LO2)

Refer to Exercise 6.26. FramCo desires to increase its return on sales to 30 percent. What amount of profit enhancement is required to meet this profitability target at the same level of sales?

Exercise 6.28
Customer Profitability
(LO2)

Creekside Research Services (CRS) conducts personnel background checks and supplier reliability research for banks and manufacturers. Using the following information, prepare a customer profitability statement:

CRS Service Profitability	**Total**	**Personnel Checks**	**Supplier Reliability**
Contribution margin ratio	61.8%	65.0%	60.0%
Revenues	$11,000,000	$4,000,000	$7,000,000
Customer sales to		Banks	Manufacturers
Sales of:			
Personnel checks	100%	75%	25%
Supplier reliability	100	20	80
Operating costs traced to customers	$5,500,000	$1,400,000	$4,100,000

Exercise 6.29
Return on Customer Sales
(LO2)

Refer to Exercise 6.28. CRS desires to increase its return on sales to 20 percent. What amount of profit enhancement is required to meet this profitability target at the same level of sales?

Exercise 6.30
Customer-Level Costs
(LO2)

Centennial Shipping (CS) wishes to trace its distribution costs to each of its four customer types, A, B, C, and D. CS delivers some shipments itself and outsources the delivery of others. Use the following information to estimate distribution costs per customer:

CS Customer Profitability	**Total**	**A**	**B**	**C**	**D**
Shipments per year	121,400	40,000	16,600	57,000	7,800
Delivered by CS		80%	90%	25%	80%
Outsourced delivery		20%	10%	75%	20%
CS distribution costs	$6,700,000				
Outsourced shipment costs	120,000				
Total distribution costs	$6,820,000				

Exercise 6.31
Customer-Level Costs
(LO2)

Outrageous Promotions (OP) is interested in to tracing its promotion design costs to each of its three major customer types, groceries, drug stores, and discount stores. OP designs some promotions itself and outsources the other designs. Use the following information to estimate promotion design costs per customer:

OP Customer Profitability	**Total**	**Groceries**	**Drug Stores**	**Discount Stores**
Promotions per year	212	60	52	100
Designed by OP		85%	82%	95%
Outsourced design		15%	18%	5%
OP design costs	$ 112,000			
Outsourced design costs	27,000			
Total design costs by customer	$ 139,000			

Exercise 6.32
Customer-Level Costs
(LO2)

Castle Music seeks to trace its marketing costs to each of its two major customer types, record clubs and retail stores. It employs salespeople in all major world markets to serve retail stores. Account executives serve each of eight major record clubs in Europe and North America. In addition, a staff and a facility support marketing and promotions to all customers. Use the following information to trace marketing costs to customers:

Castle Music Marketing Cost Information and Effort	**Total**	**Record Clubs**	**Retail Stores**
Major account managers	8	8	0
Sales representatives	150	0	150
Average salary/year		$200,000	$32,000
Marketing staff support	100%	30%	70%
Marketing staff cost	$480,000		

Problems

Problem 6.33
Customer-Level Costs
(LO2)

FirstCredit, Inc. (FCI) wishes to trace its service costs to each customer type, rated A, B, or C. A customers are believed to be the most profitable, Bs might become profitable, but Cs are unprofitable. FCI offers commercial loans, consumer loans, and credit cards. Its customer representatives sell services and manage customer accounts. In addition, a staff and a facility support marketing, promotions, and transactions for all customers at an annual cost of $400,000. Use the following additional information to trace service costs to customers:

FCI Service Cost Information	**Total**	**A**	**B**	**C**
Number of customers	3,500	1,000	2,000	500
Customer representatives	22	10	10	2
Average salary/year		$50,000	$40,000	$30,000
Support service staff effort	100%	60%	30%	10%
Support service staff cost	$400,000			

Problem 6.34
Customer Profitability
(LO 2, 3)

Beaujolais Financial Group (BFG) segments its customers into premium members, who purchase extensive services, and standard members, who purchase minimal services. It offers premium members a 10 percent discount on the total package of services purchased but requires standard members to pay full price. BFG devotes one full-time customer representative per 100 premium members and one per 1,000 standard members. Customer representatives receive salaries and a bonus of 1 percent of customer revenue. BFG estimates that it spends twice as much on total promotions for premium members to encourage their loyalty. General and administrative cost, which is *not* traced to customers, is $2,400,000 per year. Use this additional information to complete the following requirements:

Customer Service Resources	Total	Premium	Standard
Number of customers	125,000	45,000	80,000
Average sales salary/year		$35,000	$35,000
Promotion costs	$2,000,000		
Average revenue per customer (before discount)		$440	$50

Required

a. Estimate BFG's customer and overall profitability.

b. Critique BFG's customer service policies and measurements.

Problem 6.35
Customer Profitability
(LO 2, 3)

Communication

Spreadsheet

Lightwave Manufacturing Assembly, Inc., provides outsourced manufacturing assembly for electronic products companies. It currently has two major customers, MBI and TS, for which Lightwave assembles and delivers products on a just-in-time basis. Lightwave incurs annual warehousing and delivery costs solely to serve its customers. Half of annual general and administrative cost is related to processing and managing customer orders; the remainder is not traced to customers. Use this additional information to complete the following requirements:

Customer and Administrative Resources	Total	MBI	TS
Annual number of orders	3,200	1,200	2,000
Average direct cost per order		$5,000	$2,000
Order price markup		60%	60%
Average deliveries per order		5	10
Warehousing costs per year	$1,000,000		
Delivery costs per year	3,100,000		
General administrative costs	2,400,000		

Required

a. Estimate Lightwave's customer and overall profitability.

b. Write a short memo that critiques Lightwave's customer service policies and measurements.

Problem 6.36
Customer Profitability
(LO 2, 3)

Bow House Architectural, Ltd. (BHA), produces commercial and residential architectural designs for national and regional construction firms. It submits designs in competitive bidding and considers the costs of unsuccessful designs as a cost of sales. Marketing efforts have focused on increasing sales of specific designs, but administrative efforts have focused on customer relations. Use this information to complete the following requirements:

Design Activities	Total	Residential	Commercial
Designs submitted	2,700	2,500	200
Designs sold	2,100	2,000	100
Average direct cost per design (all)		$4,000	$25,000
Average markup		100%	150%
Marketing effort	100%	20%	80%
Marketing cost	$2,400,000		

Customer Activities and Resources	Total	Regional	National
Traced sales of			
Residential designs	100%	60%	40%
Commercial designs	100	20	80
Administrative effort	100	60	40
Administrative cost	$3,000,000		

Required

a. Estimate BHA's customer profitability for regional and national customers.

b. Even if national design customers are less profitable than regional design customers why might BHA continue to seek them?

Problem 6.37
Customer Profitability
(LO 2, 3)

Communication

Concrete Constructors Corp. (CCC) is a subcontractor that specializes in installing concrete curbs, gutters, and driveways for commercial and residential development projects. It serves two types of customers, custom home builders and large general contractors. CCC obtains work from the general contractors via a competitive bidding process; its success rate has been 50 percent. It has long-term relationships with several custom home builders, and bidding with them has been 92 percent successful. Use this information to complete the following requirements. You must make judgments of how to assign bidding costs and whether to assign general and administrative costs.

Annual Activities and Resources	Total	Custom Home Builders	General Contractors
Bids submitted—residential	32	22	10
Bids submitted—commercial	13	3	10
Successful bids—residential	24	20	4
Successful bids—commercial	9	3	6
Success rate		92%	50%
Average direct cost of residential job		$10,500	$410,000
Average direct cost of commercial job		$45,000	$250,000
Average markup over cost		100%	50%
Contract management cost	$800,000		
Contract management effort	100%	20%	80%
General administration cost	$410,000		
Bidding cost	$630,000		

Required

a. Estimate CCC's customer profitability.

b. Do you have any reservations about the accuracy of this analysis? If so, discuss them.

Problem 6.38
Customer Profile
(LO 2)

Team

Frederick Squab Brokerage (FSB) offers online securities trading and other services, such as financial planning and portfolio management. It is considering following the lead of competitors that segment their customers and focus marketing efforts. FSB believes that its customers can be segmented by the equally important attributes of account balance, trading frequency, and purchase of other services. These represent major uses of resources to serve customers and drivers of revenue. Following are the data from a random sample of 30 FSB customers.[12]

Random Sample of Customers

Customer	Account Balance	Trades/Yr	Other Services
1	$29,396	135	0
2	85,679	30	1
3	11,027	41	6
4	50,512	31	0
5	20,960	164	13
6	17,674	13	11
7	18,026	10	3
8	32,546	49	11
9	13,738	172	4
10	4,370	20	2
11	42,881	135	1

[12]Note that for some companies, it is feasible to generate these data for millions of customers; sampling can be more efficient, especially in a textbook! (*Hint* to the instructor: The linked problems 6.38–6.41 are easier to answer if data are provided to students electronically.)

Random Sample of Customers

Customer	Account Balance	Trades/Yr	Other Services
12	23,988	38	8
13	35,950	24	6
14	26,398	12	0
15	28,470	11	19
16	42,749	92	0
17	604	14	1
18	54,789	120	2
19	86,367	171	17
20	22,192	3	1
21	17,517	40	8
22	72,023	171	3
23	23,609	52	5
24	25,076	8	1
25	65,984	59	16
26	50,003	107	4
27	897	6	0
28	3,455	47	10
29	51,743	138	9
30	31,791	30	3

Complete the following in small groups.

Required

a. Use this information to develop numerical scores for each customer attribute by classifying customers into no more than four categories within each attribute (e.g., scoring = 1, 2, 3, or 4). (*Hint:* Enter the data into a spreadsheet, such as Excel, and then plot each customer attribute and look for "natural" cutoffs for categories. *Note:* This is somewhat subjective but critically important to this type of analysis.)

b. Add individual attribute scores to obtain overall scores. Use overall scores to segment customers into no more than three categories (A = best, B = middle, and C = worst). You must judge where to make cutoffs here, too.

c. Express any concerns you have about this classification. How can you improve it or validate it?

Problem 6.39
Customer Activities and Revenues
(LO 2)

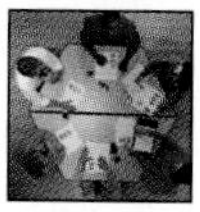

Team

Refer to the data and results of Problem 6.38. In small groups, complete the following.

Required

a. For each customer type (A, B, and C), estimate for the entire customer population the percentage of each type, average account balance, average number of trades, and average number of other services purchased. (*Hint:* This is easily done with Excel's Pivot Table function wizard [look under the Data menu].)

b. FSB charges customers for other services based on the extent and quality of services used. Interest on account balances and trading fees are the same for each customer type. Fill in the following table and estimate FSB's customer-level revenues

Customer Revenue Data	A	B	C
Customer sample percentages	?	?	?
Customer population (1,000,000)	?	?	?
Average account balance	?	?	?
Average annual trades	?	?	?
Average other services	?	?	?
Account revenue (spread)	2%	2%	2%
Trading fee per trade	$ 3	$ 3	$ 3
Other fees per service	$200	$100	$50

Problem 6.40
Customer Costs and Profitability
(LO 2)

Refer to the data and results of Problems 6.38 and 6.39. In small groups, complete the following.

Team

Required

a. Use this additional information to estimate FSB's uses of resources to manage each customer service. Intensity of service means, for example, that FSB uses three times as many service resources to provide "other" services for A customers than for C customers.

Customer Cost Data	A	B	C
Intensity of service per unit of service:			
Account management per account	1	1	1
Trading management per trade	1	1	1
Other services management per service	3	2	1
General and administrative	3	2	1
Service costs:			
Account management	$250,000,000		
Trading management	310,000,000		
Other services management	440,000,000		
General and administrative	360,000,000		

b. Estimate overall and customer profitability.

Problem 6.41
Customer-Level Improvements
(LO 3)

Team Communication

Refer to Problems 6.38–6.40. FSB has identified two alternatives to improve its overall profitability:

1. Drop unprofitable customers; although this will lose those customers' margins, it will save 15 percent of overall committed management costs.
2. Change fees to induce unprofitable customers to either leave or become more profitable and induce more customers to increase their revenue-generating activities. Marketing research indicates changes in the percentage of types of customers as follows. Other customer characteristics, service intensities, and costs remain unchanged.

Customer Revenue Data	Total	A	B	C
Customer sample	100.0%	45.0%	50.0%	5.0%
Account revenue (spread)	NA	1.5%	2.0%	3.0%
Trading fee per trade	NA	$2.50	$3.00	$4.00
Other fees per service	NA	$180.00	$120.00	$150.00

In small groups, complete the requirements.

Required

a. Measure the profit impact of each alternative.

b. Prepare a report that makes and evaluates recommendations for profit improvement.

Cases

Case 6.42
Customer Profitability
(LO 1, 2, 3)

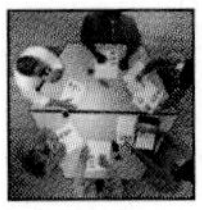

Team Communication

FirstBank of Rock Creek recently spent $400,000 to develop and implement a customer profitability analysis system that calculates the monthly profitability of each of its 40,000 customers.[13] This system also maintains extensive customer-level information about banking and demographic history. FirstBank offers the following services to its customers. (Note: Many customers use multiple services.)

Service	Average Annual Profit per Account
Checking account	$ 50
Savings account	40
Safety deposit	20
Certificate of deposit account	300
Consumer loan	400
Home equity line of credit	500

[13] Adapted from Peter Carroll and Madhu Tadikonda, "Customer Profitability: Irrelevant for Decisions?"; Claire Green, "Profitability Measurement for Small-Business Banking: A Strategic View"; and Gautam Bose and Erick Haskell, "Keeping the Ones with the 'Right Stuff.'"

FirstBank plans to use its customer profitability information to identify opportunities to market and cross-sell other services, such as home equity lines of credit, to checking and savings account customers. In small groups, prepare a report or presentation that answers the requirements.

Required

a. Explain what information you want from the customer profitability analysis system to identify checking and savings account customers most likely to be interested in other banking services.

b. Consider the following two checking-account customers with nearly equal and above average profitability. Does selling a home equity loan to each have equal expected profitability? Explain.

Annual Customer Information	Ms. Smith	Mr. Jones
Profit from checking account	$ 76	$ 76
Average checking account balance	$14,000	$900
Number of checks written	230	60
Number of ATM transactions	24	36
Number of returned checks	0	8
Overdraft fees paid	0	8

Case 6.43
Customer Profitability
(LO 2, 3)

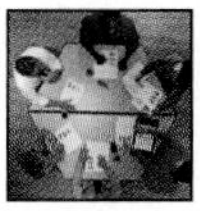
Team

Communication

Corporate Express, the world's largest supplier of office supplies to major corporations, recently hired you as a new financial analyst. Refer to Case 1.38 (page 31) for information about Corporate Express. The company takes orders from its customers' employees via the Internet, processes them with office supply manufacturers, and delivers the supplies to the employees who ordered them. Its customers do not need to hire anyone to order, receive, or distribute supplies. Customers also do not need supplies inventories or warehouses. Large customers (like Coca-Cola and Hewlett Packard) save millions of dollars per year by outsourcing their office supply tasks to Corporate Express.

The vice president of marketing believes it is worthwhile to offer limited services to small, rapidly growing businesses because they could graduate to the full line of services offered to large companies. After analyzing the profitability of serving small and large customers, you have developed the following information for typical customers:

Annual Data	Representative Large Company (500 firms)
Average number of orders per year	2,000
Average sales value of supplies per order	$600
Average cost of supplies to Corporate Express as a percentage of sales	80%
Average processing cost per order	$40
Average delivery cost per order as a percentage of sales	5%
Average cost to maintain Internet access per customer per year	$2,000
Marketing management, average hours per customer	100
Marketing management, total annual cost (25 employees, 2,000 hours per year)	$ 1,250,000
Advertising and promotion, total annual cost	$ 2,000,000
Maintaining electronic catalogue, total annual cost	$ 4,000,000
General and administrative support, total annual cost	$28,000,000

You believe that small companies will place one-tenth as many orders per year as a large company and the amount of an average order will be approximately $500. Marketing management time is discretionary, but you estimate that 25 hours per year should be sufficient to manage a small company account. You are unsure how to trace advertising and promotion, electronic catalogue, and general and administrative costs but suggest allocating advertising and promotion on a per customer basis. Individually or in small groups, prepare a visual and verbal presentation that explains the required items.

Required

a. Compute the annual profit generated from an average large and small company.

b. If your analysis is correct, is it a worthwhile use of scarce capacity to add 10 small customers rather than one large customer? Why or why not?

c. Can you recommend possible ways to make small-customer business attractive to Corporate Express?

d. What improvements in tracing costs do you recommend?

CHAPTER 7

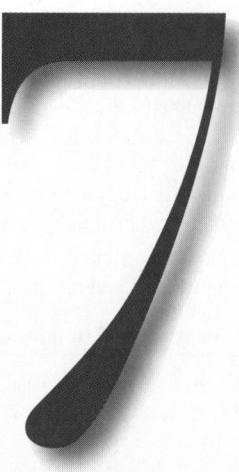

Managing Quality and Time to Create Value

After completing this chapter, you should be able to:

1. Evaluate the similarities and differences of total quality management and return-on-quality approaches to managing quality.
2. Measure and analyze the dimensions of quality with commonly used diagrams, charts, and reports.
3. Understand and explain the importance of managing process time.
4. Measure and manage productivity and capacity.
5. Evaluate how just-in-time methods create benefits by combining management of quality, time, productivity, and capacity.
6. Understand how to construct and use control charts (Appendix).

Cost-Management Challenges

1. **Managing** quality seems to be a general management task, so what can cost-management analysts provide to improve this important activity?

2. **Is** there a conflict between meeting quality and time goals, or do these goals reinforce each other?

3. **How** should cost-management analysts choose among all available quality and time-management tools?

Dedication to quality and customer response time overcomes skeptical bankers

Transformation Customer Services, Inc.

Fast-growing firm sets the pace in the customer service industry

By Harley Earl, Business Correspondent. Dissociated Press

Chicago: The concept of the company was revolutionary—some thought it audacious. The first loan officer to review Chicago-based TCSI's (Transformation Customer Services, Inc.) embryonic business proposal was less than diplomatic. Rhonda Cooper, the company's dynamic CEO, remembers his exact words as, "That is just about the craziest idea I have ever heard. There is no way that I would authorize lending you what you ask, even with your personal assets as collateral. I strongly believe that this is a flawed business concept. First of all, I cannot believe that any business would outsource its customer service representatives—its frontline with the customer—to anyone. Second, if they were to outsource customer service, why would they use you? You have no track record. You don't know their business, their customers, or their competitors. And that raises a third concern—what if you do know their competitors? How could any business be sure that sensitive customer information would not leak to the competition? I'm sorry, but you have come to the wrong place, Ms. Cooper. Have you considered a fast-food franchise?"

"I almost punched him out," a laughing Ms. Cooper recalls, still visibly affected by the banker's lack of vision.

Although that initial refusal hurt deeply, Cooper took away the message that her company would have to clearly communicate and demonstrate to providers of capital and potential service partners that TCSI would and could provide the highest quality service.

Ten years after that shaky start, Cooper's company provides services to many large and mid-sized companies in the US, Europe, and the Pacific Rim. TCSI has been one of the fastest growing service companies on the NASDAQ-AMEX exchange. Depending on the vagaries of the market, TCSI's common stock currently is worth nearly US$1 billion. Not bad for a startup that began in a renovated school annex with two employees, one phone line, and two personal computers.

TCSI now provides customized customer service programs that include providing presale and new product information, enrolling customers in client programs, providing 24-hour technical and help desk support, resolving customer complaints, and conducting customer satisfaction surveys. These services are provided via telephone and Internet connections and depend on the skillful design and use of customer and product databases. To protect critical customer information, TCSI creates organization and information barriers to prevent either employees or information from going to competitors.

To assure its clients that TCSI will provide high-quality service and stay ahead of the increasing competition in this growing industry, TCSI hires and trains capable employees to understand the client's business, industry, and customers. TCSI's employees are so well trained that a client's customer who calls with a question or complaint cannot tell that he or she is talking to an outsourced service provider. If you call the customer service telephone number listed on your microwave oven's warranty card, for example, chances are you are talking to an employee of TCSI, not an employee of the oven's manufacturer. But TCSI is sure that you will not mind or care because you will receive excellent service.

TCSI employees and managers are relentless in their pursuit and maintenance of quality because a slip in quality of service could give competitors the opening they are looking for. "We have no intention of losing any of our valued clients to competitors or our competitive edge based on quality and customer response time," pledges Cooper. "We religiously measure and manage the quality of our personnel, processes, and services because we know that people pay attention to what gets measured and evaluated."

With a keen sense of irony, Cooper recently signed a contract to provide a full range of customer services for Nationwide Bank, a large bank holding company that recently bought the bank that had refused to loan her start-up capital 10 years ago. "I noticed that my original, would-be banker is no longer with the bank. Too bad, I would have liked to ask him how I could help him improve his customer service."

Transformation Customer Services, Inc.

This chapter discusses the methods and measures that TCSI and other companies concerned about product and service quality use to stay ahead of the competition. The chapter describes eight important cost-management tools: histograms, control charts, run charts, cause-and-effect diagrams, scatter diagrams, flowcharts, Pareto charts, and cost-of-quality reports. They are presented as useful tools for monitoring process quality, time, productivity, and capacity and for preventing mistakes in meeting customer needs. The chapter also discusses the way that just-in-time methods combine concerns for managing quality, time, productivity, and capacity.

Many organizations use measures of quality, time, productivity, and capacity as (1) predictors of financial performance (Chapter 11), (2) measures for managing by the theory of constraints (Chapter 12), (3) elements of comprehensive performance measurement systems, such as the balanced scorecard (Chapter 20), and (4) bases for performance-based incentives (Chapter 21). The measurement details presented in this chapter are very important to the later chapters that discuss these uses of the measures.

Importance of Quality

You undoubtedly have experienced poor-quality service or defective merchandise and, as a result, might have decided never to deal with that particular organization again. As a result of poor quality, the company lost you as a customer, which concerns organizations and motivates them to provide quality products and services. Many chief financial officers (CFOs) believe that most important changes in their companies' strategies in recent years have been to improve customer satisfaction and product quality. In today's globally competitive environment, improving quality is clearly a high priority for all organizations. TCSI's chief financial officer, Martin Freeman, agrees that the company's unmatched service quality and rapid response to customers' needs (plus competitive pricing) are the primary reasons for the company's success.

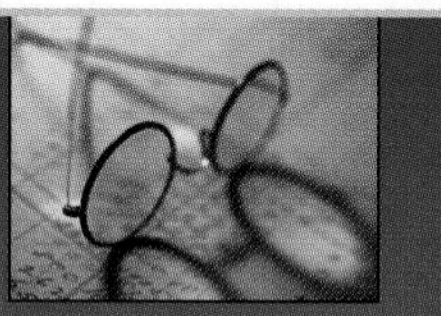

Cost Management in Practice 7.1

Effects of Quality

The effects of quality, good or bad, on the fortunes of companies are not limited to any economic sector or region. Silicon Graphics Inc., the computer company behind the dinosaurs of *Jurassic Park,* did not pay attention to the quality of its lower-end products and missed lucrative Internet opportunities taken over by high-quality, low-cost personal computers. The Warsaw (Poland) Marriott Hotel, in contrast, quickly recognized the importance of quality service in Poland's newly opened market and, by stressing quality in its hiring and training activities, is now rated by guests as among the top five in the international chain.

The Alexander Doll Co. has managed to keep top customers, such as FAO Schwartz, Disney, and Saks, and to grow, even in its high-cost New York location. "Our costs are offset by the benefits of producing here. Number one is that we are on hand every day to oversee and control the quality of the product. We can respond quickly to customers' needs," explained CEO Patricia Lewis. European winemakers, long used to world leadership, lost significant market share to North and South American and Australian competitors that offered higher-quality wine at lower prices. European wine prices crashed in the 1990s as consumers worldwide reacted to their uneven quality. Some European winemakers took extended visits to American and Australian wineries to learn how to improve the quality of their products. The result of increased quality has been a resurgence of French and Italian wine sales. *Sources: R. D. Hof,* "The Sad Saga of Silicon Graphics"; *P. Simpson,* "As Workers Turn into Risk-Takers . . . One Plant Really Turns on the Steam"; *I. J. Dugan,* "If They Can Make it There . . . ." *(Full citations to references are in the Bibliography.)*

Costs of Improving Quality

LO 1 Evaluate the similarities and differences of total quality management and return-on-quality approaches to managing quality.

Should organizations try to improve their quality—at any cost? In the 1980s, that seemed to be the prevailing belief. However, there are now two somewhat competing approaches to improving product and service quality:

1. Total quality management, which originated in the 1980s.
2. Return on quality, a traditional view of quality that is reemerging.

Total Quality Management (TQM)

The Alexander Doll Company competes successfully on the basis of product quality and customer service despite high costs.

Although this is a bit of a simplification, the **total quality management (TQM)** view holds that improvements in quality, as defined by customers, always result in improved organizational performance because improving quality improves efficiency as problems are identified and eliminated. Furthermore, the quest for improved quality is never finished. TQM advocates, inspired by W. Edwards Deming, argue that customers seek the highest-quality products and services and are willing to pay a premium for them.[1] Thus, TQM advocates have claimed that "quality is free" or, more precisely, that improving quality more than pays its own way by creating higher profits. The TQM perspective assumes that quality can and should always be improved, with exceeding customers' quality expectations being the goal. Since customers define quality, customer satisfaction and product or service quality are closely linked. Quite naturally, adopters of TQM assume that increased customer satisfaction and product and service quality are the lead indicators of improved profits.

total quality management (TQM) *is the view that improvements in quality, as defined by customers, will always result in improved organizational performance because improving quality will improve efficiency as problems are identified and eliminated*

Return on Quality (ROQ)

The **return-on-quality (ROQ)** view assumes a trade-off exists between the costs and benefits of improving quality. Although ROQ advocates believe quality is extremely important, they argue that the highest profits are obtained at an **optimum quality level** of products and services, which maximizes profits rather than quality.[2] The optimum quality level almost always is lower than the **maximum quality level,** which is total delight of the customer or zero defects, depending on one's definition of quality. **Total delight** occurs when a customer receives a product or service that far exceeds his or her expectations of quality. A **defect** is an attribute (tangible or intangible) that falls short of customer expectations. According to the ROQ view, at some point, the cost of improving quality must exceed the benefits of increased revenues. In other words, the ROQ approach argues that there can be too much quality, too few defects, and too much customer satisfaction because costs of improved quality could increase at a higher rate than revenues. Even if the ROQ approach is more profitable, however, it might not be the basis of an effective marketing campaign. Furthermore, ROQ might lead to complacency with current levels of quality, whereas TQM is relentless in its search for continuous improvement.

Exhibit 7–1 contrasts the TQM and ROQ views of quality. As the top graph shows, the TQM view implicitly assumes that the maximum profit is achieved at the maximum quality level because total revenues from increasing quality always should grow faster than total costs. ROQ, on the other hand, assumes that less-than-maximum quality maximizes profits. Regardless of the approach, the difference between

return on quality (ROQ) *is the view that assumes there is a trade-off between the costs and benefits of improving quality*

optimum quality level *of products and services maximizes profits rather than quality*

maximum quality level *is total delight of the customer or zero defects, depending on one's definition of quality*

total delight *occurs when a customer receives a product or service that far exceeds his or her expectations of quality*

defect *is an attribute (tangible or intangible) that falls short of customer expectations*

[1]See W. E. Deming, *Automobile Magazine,* "A Seminal Thinker Takes a Detailed Look at the Quality." (Full citations to references are in the Bibliography.)

[2]See R. Rust, A. Zahorik, and T. Keiningham, "Return on Quality (ROQ): Making Service Financially Accountable." ROQ also is similar to the notion of "reasonable assurance" in auditing—it might be uneconomical to detect all defects in financial reporting.

Exhibit 7–1

TQM versus ROQ Views of Quality

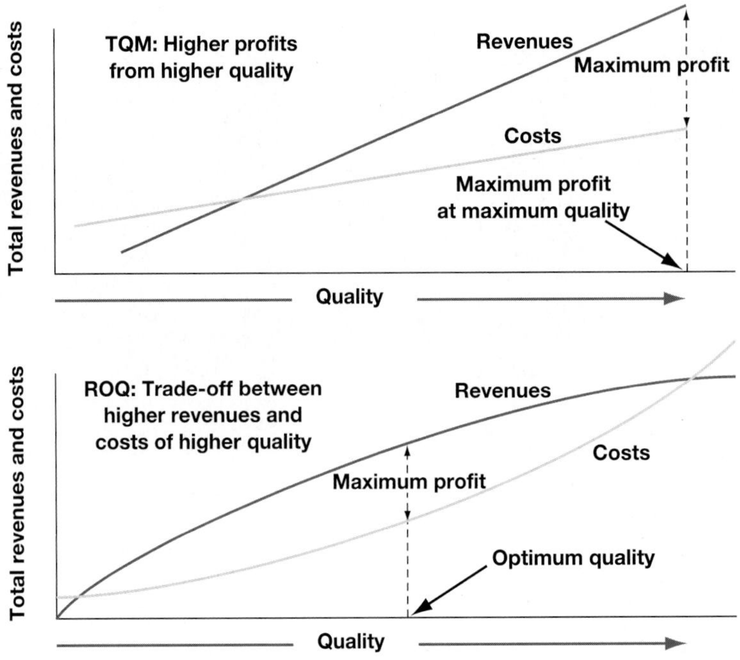

total revenues and total costs represents profit. The bottom graph shows that ROQ assumes that the total revenue and total cost lines converge at high levels of quality and even may cross, reducing profits. Accordingly, beyond the ROQ optimum level of quality, profits actually decline. Note that the TQM revenue and cost lines in Exhibit 7–1 might not be straight lines, but the difference between them is assumed to increase with increases in quality.

Comparison of the Views of Quality

The ROQ view of quality for many years was the traditional view, but the TQM movement eclipsed it in the 1980s as quality became a primary source of global competitive advantage. The ROQ view of quality and customer satisfaction has regained prominence in recent years as many companies have achieved parity in quality and in response to observing the fate of some winners of prestigious quality awards. A number of companies that have strenuously and successfully improved quality and received prizes for their efforts have seen profits drop alarmingly, and some have been forced to declare bankruptcy. Improved quality might not have been the root cause of financial decline in these companies, but ROQ advocates point out that improved quality, indicated by quality awards, did not prevent failure in these companies and does not guarantee success in other companies.

Conflict between TQM and ROQ

At the extremes of the two views, TQM and ROQ do conflict because ROQ's "optimum" quality is usually less than TQM's "maximum" quality. Martin Freeman, CFO at TCSI, prefers a middle position:

> TCSI believes strongly in providing high-quality customer service and uses TQM tools to measure quality. But that does not mean TCSI would bankrupt the company to do *everything* service partners or their customers might want. If service partners are willing to pay for higher-quality service, the company will do its best to provide it, knowing that our competitors will be trying to do the same. On the other hand, we do not take out the calculator every time we consider a quality issue. Since quality service is our whole business, sometimes TCSI decides to increase quality to meet its goals and competition. TCSI pays attention to the numbers but also relies on judgment in the final analysis.

Research Insight 7.1

Return on Quality

The TQM vs. ROQ debate could be characterized as a difference in assumptions about the behavior of *marginal revenues* (the revenue earned from additional sales of products or services) and *marginal costs* from additional increases in quality. TQM argues that marginal revenues will exceed marginal costs, but ROQ argues that, like other economic activities, at some point the marginal cost of increasing quality will exceed the marginal revenues earned. Chris Ittner and David Larcker used survey data to find that a quality-oriented strategy and management participation in quality management were associated with higher performance in a sample of North American, German, and Japanese auto and computer manufacturers. The bottom-line question for organizations and researchers is, Do firms that manage for higher quality *sustain* higher profits? This is an exceedingly difficult question to answer because a short-term increase in profits might not be sustained in the long term as competitors react with their own quality-related initiatives. Some financial research supports this concern. One study found that many companies, once rated as excellent for quality, experienced below-average stock price returns just a few years later, whereas once low-quality firms improved. This indicates that gains from quality must be sustained by continued efforts to outdo the competition; otherwise, competitors quickly catch up.

Additionally, profits could be affected by many influences that are contemporaneous with quality efforts, such as other value-chain activities to develop new products, advertise, and reconfigure supplier and distributor relations. Recently the U.S. National Science Foundation and American Society for Quality Control started a $9 million three-year study to develop reliable information about the extent and impact of quality improvements in US companies. *Sources: C. Ittner and D. Larcker,* "Quality Strategy, Strategic Control Systems, and Organizational Performance"; *and* "Researching the Nitty-Gritty of Quality Control"; *M. Clayman,* "Excellence Revisited." *(Full citations to references are in the Bibliography)*

Dimensions of Quality

Like many competitive organizations, TCSI pursues **customer-focused quality,** which is a broad focus on meeting or exceeding customer expectations rather than a focus on only one of the dimensions of quality (as discussed later). TCSI measures its quality on two generally accepted **quality dimensions:** (1) *product* or *service attributes* and (2) *customer service* before and after the sale. TCSI believes that, to succeed in measuring and managing quality, it must understand customers' expectations on these two dimensions of quality.

customer-focused quality *is a broad focus on meeting or exceeding customer expectations*

quality dimensions *are (1) product or service attributes and (2) customer service before and after the sale*

Product and Service Attributes

A product's or service's **attributes** refer to its tangible and intangible features. **Tangible features,** in general, include performance, adherence to specifications, and functionality. Tangible features of TCSI's services include the following:

- Promptness of responses to customer inquiries.
- Accuracy of responses.
- Resolution of customer inquiries.
- Other criteria specific to each client.

Intangible features of products and services include reputation, taste, appearance, style, and appeal, which could be as important as tangible features to some customers. TCSI relies on its reputation for providing quality services as a major selling point to potential clients and a major factor in retaining current clients.

attributes *of a product or service are its tangible and intangible features*

tangible features *include performance, adherence to specifications, and functionality*

intangible features *of products and services include reputation, taste, appearance, style, and appeal*

Customer Service before and after the Sale

Customers' perceptions of service before and after the sale influence whether they will become new customers and remain repeat customers. Customer service features include (among other activities):

- Provision of presale information.
- Proper treatment of customers by salespeople.

- On-time delivery to the customer after the product or service is ordered.
- Follow-up with customers after the sale.
- Timeliness and accuracy of resolution of questions and complaints.
- Warranty and repair services.

How Organizations Measure Quality

LO 2 Measure and analyze the dimensions of quality with commonly used diagrams, charts, and reports.

Determining customers' expectations and providing superior service are possible only if organizations are able to measure quality and provide helpful feedback to their members. To ensure that TCSI meets or exceeds customers' quality expectations on the two quality dimensions, the company first uses measures that indicate clients' and their customers' evaluations of service quality. Second, to measure the quality the company has delivered, TCSI also measures the satisfaction of clients and their customers with its services. TCSI uses measures similar to those used by other service and manufacturing companies that manage quality carefully.

How does TCSI know whether its quality is either sufficient or a problem? First, the company needs to identify indicators of customer-defined quality. If indicators show that the quality of products and services is deteriorating, the warning could, in turn, trigger an investigation to determine the cause so that the problem can be corrected before it becomes too large. Second, the company needs diagnostic information to suggest what the problem is and, perhaps, a way to solve it. We discuss each of these in turn.

Indicators of Quality

Organizations usually can measure tangible features of *products,* such as dimensions and functional performance, in time to correct faulty or substandard products before exposing them to customers. If the tangible features are important to customers, organizations can use these measures of the features as lead indicators of quality while manufacturing the product and before shipment.

lead indicators *are measures that signal future outcomes of later operations*

Measuring tangible features of *services* in time to prevent problems is difficult because the service is not complete until the customer receives it. Therefore, service organizations often measure what they believe are **lead indicators** of service features, which are measures that signal future outcomes of later operations. These include the capabilities of the personnel and technology that will provide the service.

Intangible features of products and services, such as appearance and appeal, generally occur after the customer receives the product or service. Measures of intangible features reflect customers' personal evaluations and must be obtained indirectly or by surveying current or potential customers.

Customer service features, such as treatment by salespeople and on-time delivery, are similar to intangible product or service features because they must be measured after the customer has had contact with the organization.

Variation causes poor quality. Quality experts believe that variation in process outcomes is a primary source of poor quality. Variability increases the chance for product and service attributes to disappoint customers. Most lead indicators of quality measure some form of variation in product or service attributes. For example, one of the attributes of TCSI's services that the company monitors is average length of time to resolve a customer complaint. TCSI believes that an optimum length of time exists; taking too much time frustrates the customer, but spending too little time increases the chance that the company will not understand and, therefore, will not react properly to the customer's true complaint.

Employees at TCSI (and other organizations) use several tools to measure lead indicators of quality, including histograms, run charts, and control charts.

histogram *is a chart that displays the* frequency distribution *of an attribute's measures—its range and degree of concentration around an average attribute value*

Histograms. A **histogram** is a chart that displays the *frequency distribution* of an attribute's measures—its range and degree of concentration around an average attribute value. A wider range, with less concentration, means more variation and increased like-

Exhibit 7–2 Histograms of Customer-Response Times, before and after Process Improvements

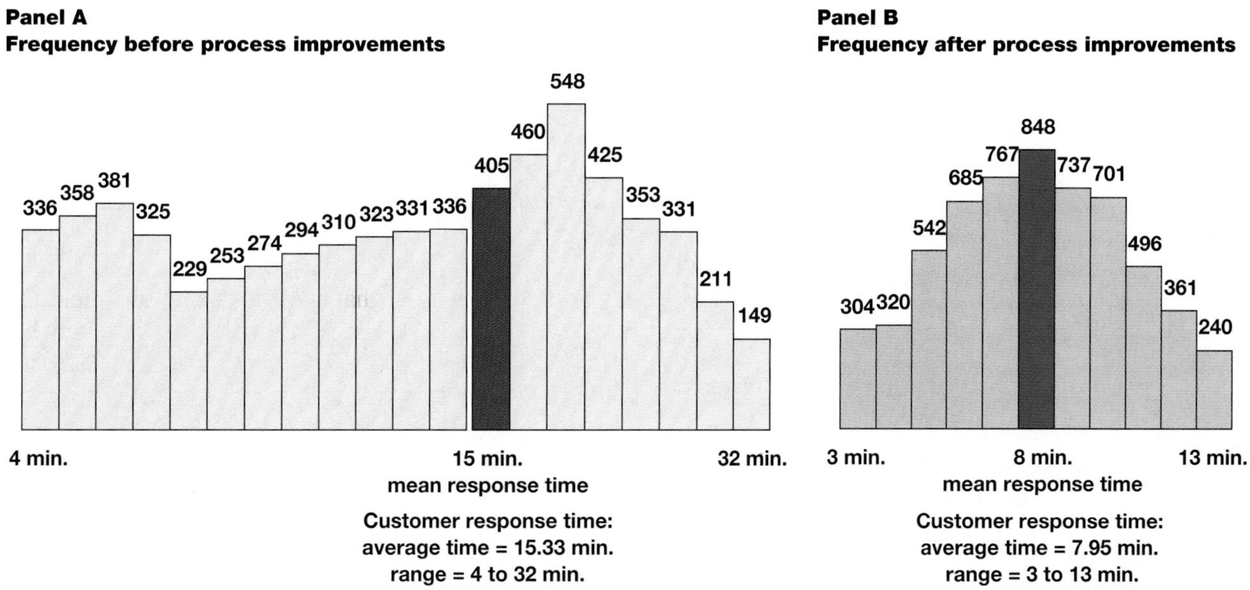

Transformation Customer Services,Inc.

lihood that the customer received poor-quality service. Conversely, a narrower range, with tighter concentration, improves the likelihood that customers received good or high-quality service.

Exhibit 7–2 contrasts histograms of response times before and after improvements to TCSI's complaint resolution process. We discuss how cost-management analysts diagnosed the problem and worked with cross-functional teams to make improvements later. Panel A of Exhibit 7–2 shows the range and concentration of response times during a week before improvements. Some variation is expected because not all complaints are the same. However, in response to customer satisfaction surveys, TCSI decided that response times varied too much, which led it to revise the process. Panel B reflects the effects of process improvements and shows a much tighter concentration (and lower average) of response times during a week after process improvements.

Because the distribution of response times is much tighter and centered around a lower average response time after process improvements, customers who call TCSI are more likely to have their problems resolved quickly and to be more satisfied with TCSI's service.

a **run chart** *shows trends in variation in product or service attributes over time by reflecting measures of important quality features taken at defined points in time*

a **control chart** *describes variation in product or service attributes over time by measuring important quality features but additionally compares them to maximum- and minimum-desired levels*

upper and lower control limits *are maximum- and minimum-desired levels of product or service features*

Run and control charts. A **run chart** shows trends in variation in product or service attributes over time by reflecting measures of important quality features taken at defined points in time. Employees use run charts to identify persistent trends in important attributes that are adverse or beneficial to quality. Panel A of Exhibit 7–3 shows that TCSI's weekly, average customer-response time appears to be permanently lower after the company introduced process improvements in week 7. This chart reinforces the value of the decision to improve processes and provides some justification for more of the same effort.

A **control chart,** panel B in Exhibit 7–3, also describes variation in product or service attributes over time by measuring important quality features but additionally compares them to maximum- and minimum-desired levels, called **upper** and **lower control limits.** A low level of variation in attributes is desirable, but deviations that fall either above the upper control limit or below the lower control limit are unacceptable defects because the product or service will not perform reliably or customers will be disappointed by worse-than-expected intangible features.[3] Cost-management analysts

[3]The chapter Appendix presents a brief overview of some technical details regarding the construction and use of control charts.

Exhibit 7–3 Run and Control Charts of Average Customer Response Time

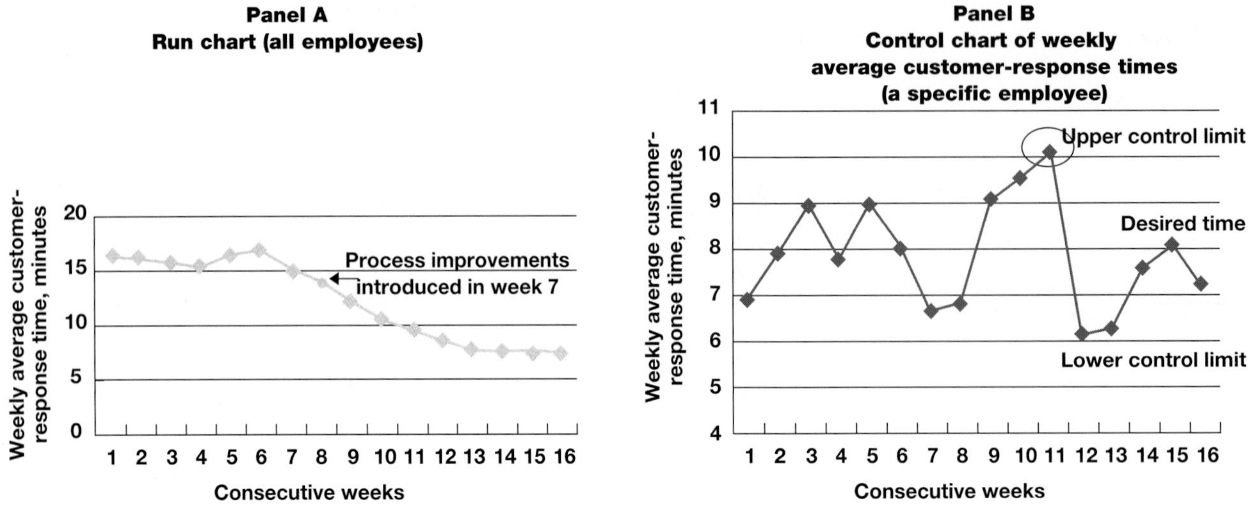

Transformation Customer Services, Inc.

usually prepare and analyze periodic charts such as those in Exhibit 7–3, but many organizations give individuals or teams direct responsibility for measuring product and service attributes as they perform their work so that they can detect any defects immediately and correct them before further processing or shipping them to customers.

Organizations use summary control charts to distinguish between acceptable variations in quality and variations in performance that require further investigation. For example, TCSI evaluates each customer representative's average response time on a weekly basis. Employees whose average response times stray out of the acceptable region receive counseling or additional training.[4] Employees whose performance is exceptionally good receive recognition for their work.

The control chart of one employee's weekly average response times (panel B of Exhibit 7–3) was within the control limits except during week 11 when the average time exceeded the upper control limit. The chart also shows that this employee's average times were trending toward the upper control limit during weeks 9 and 10. Although the average response time in week 9 does not look unusual by itself, the even higher time in week 10 signals a possible upward trend. Some organizations might intervene at this time even though the control limits have not been violated. By week 11, the employee had exceeded the upper limit, and the supervisor counseled the employee.

During counseling, the supervisor and employee discovered that the employee had become concerned about the reliability of the information supporting the new process improvements and was double-checking to be sure to give customers the right information. Upon investigation, the supervisor learned that the client had changed model numbers on several products but had not changed underlying product designs or information. This change, which had not been communicated to TCSI, was the cause of confusion. When customers called with problems, their products' model numbers did not match the documentation available to TCSI's employees. The succeeding weeks 12 and 13 show that the employee probably overcorrected and was tending toward the lower control limit before stabilizing (apparently) near the desired time.

---

[4]If that seems excessive, consider MBNA America, Inc., the large credit-card issuer, which began years ago to evaluate each of its employees on 14 service-attribute measures every day. MBNA believes that such attention to detail is important to maintaining customer satisfaction and retaining customers. There is difference of opinion on how much service employees should be monitored—too little could allow unacceptable service, too much could make the workplace too intrusive and lead to high turnover of skilled employees.

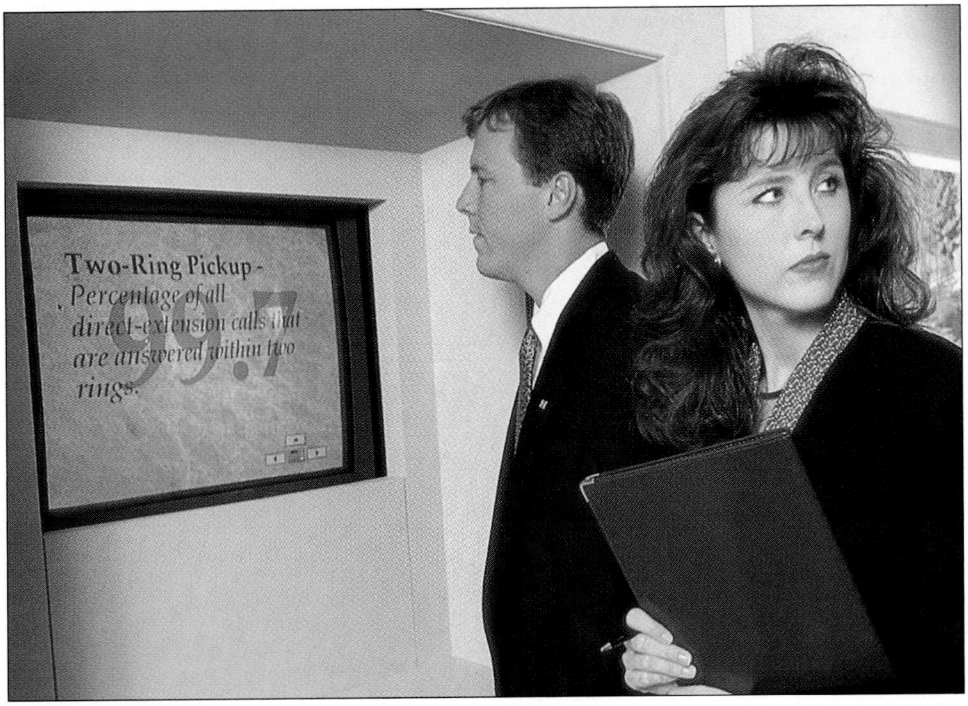

MBNA, the credit-card company, developed 14 different attribute measures of performance. For example, customer address changes must be processed within one day; telephones must be answered within two rings. State-of-the-art technology allows MBNA to monitor performance on a continuous basis. At any given moment, it is possible to obtain a performance measurement that shows, for example, that employees are achieving "two-ring pick-up" 99.7 percent of the time.

Diagnostic Information

Lead indicator information identifies potential quality problems but usually does not diagnose their causes. Cost management analysts, often with team members from production and customer service, use a number of tools, including cause-and-effect diagrams, scatter diagrams, flow charts, and Pareto charts, to diagnose the causes of problems and to identify possible solutions.

Cause-and-effect diagrams. **Cause-and-effect analysis** involves formulating diagnostic signals that identify potential causes of product or service defects. It first defines the defect, for example, *excessive customer response time,* and then the causes that could contribute to the problem. The potential causes of these problems in customer-response time can be deficiencies in:

cause-and-effect analysis *involves formulating diagnostic signals that identify potential causes of product or service defects*

- Human resources (e.g., inadequate training or staffing).
- Physical resources (e.g., insufficient capacity or availability).
- Procedures (e.g., inadequate or out of date).
- Information technology (e.g., unavailable or incorrect information).
- Communication (e.g., failure to communicate changes in procedures or objectives).

These causes often can be identified by asking the question, Why?, until the root cause of the problem is identified. As the causes are identified, the organization can develop and implement corrective measures.

TCSI's customers informed the company through customer satisfaction surveys that they were dissatisfied with both the length and variability of the time required to get a satisfactory response to their inquiries. TCSI was able to identify and correct causes of the problem by asking involved employees why response times were so long and variable. TCSI used a "fishbone," or Ishikawa, cause-and-effect diagram to analyze this problem.[5] Exhibit 7–4 shows the information developed by a team of customer-service employees

[5]Professor Kaoru Ishikawa of Tokyo University was the person most responsible for expanding the use of this analysis in Japan in the 1960s.

Exhibit 7–4

Cause-and-Effect Diagram

Transformation Customer Services, Inc.

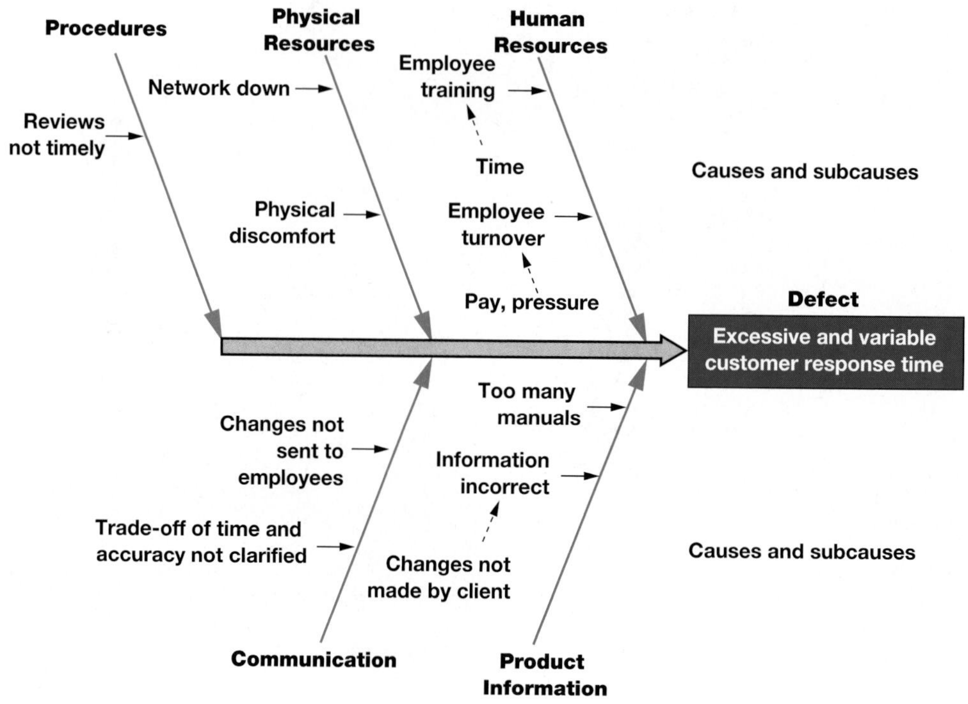

that answers the question. The defect, on the right of the diagram, was due to a number of related causes and subcauses, which are shown as "bones" on the diagram. For example, one of the causes identified by asking, Why?, was employee mistakes (Human Resources on the diagram). A second question—Why did employees make mistakes?—yielded two causes: employee training and employee turnover. A third—Why weren't employees properly trained?—yielded the cause (too little) time. A fourth—Why was employee turnover so high?—yielded the causes (too little) pay, (too much) pressure. TCSI researched each major bone of the diagram similarly to find causes of the defect.

Combining all information in Exhibit 7–4, the team determined that the most important root cause of the problem was complex product information that changed faster than employees could be trained to become familiar with it. TCSI's solution was to develop a centrally maintained, "intelligent" service database that allowed customer representatives to quickly diagnose and correct callers' service problems. TCSI's clients became responsible for entering changed and new product information directly into the database so the information that TCSI employees work with is always current.

The high cost of developing and maintaining this artificial-intelligence tool is justified by the large reduction in the time necessary to serve customers. In addition, the tool reduced stress and conflict in the workplace as well as employee turnover and discomfort. TCSI was able to find and develop a sophisticated information technology solution to its customer-response time problem. Furthermore, the company believed that this solution generated a positive return on quality (ROQ); that is, the benefits of increased sales from improved quality exceeded the costs of improving quality.

scatter diagram *is a plot of two measures that could be related*

Scatter diagrams. Cost management analysts often use a **scatter diagram,** which is a plot of two measures that could be related, to diagnose the cause and effect between outcomes and the activities that might drive them. That is, changes in a value-added or non-value-added activity could cause or be associated with changes in a quality measure. Scatter diagrams are useful for diagnosing whether a suspected cause of a quality problem is really responsible. If plotted points hug a diagonal line, quality and other measures are more likely related. Knowing which of the two variables causes the other suggests a solution for the problem: change the cause to eliminate the problem. As panel A of Exhibit 7–5 shows, the quality measure, customer-response time, appears to be closely related to one suspected cause, frequency of incorrect information. Panel A indicates that as frequency of

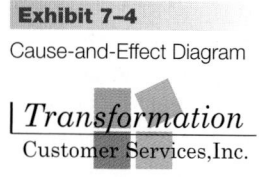

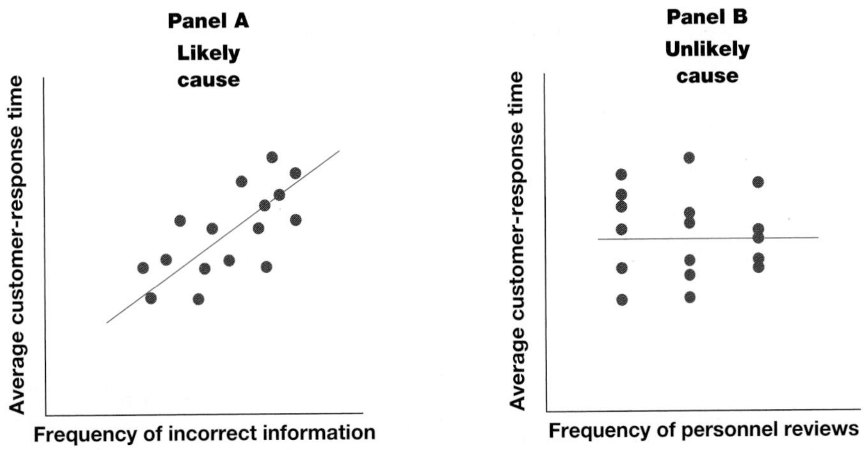

Exhibit 7–5
Scatter Diagrams

Transformation Customer Services, Inc.

incorrect information increases, so does customer-response time. Thus, a reduction in the number of times TCSI's representatives received incorrect information resulted in a reduction in its customer-response time. Panel B, however, does not reflect any discernable relationship between customer-response time and another suspected cause of the problem, frequency of personnel reviews. The frequency of personnel reviews does not appear to affect customer-response time, which indicates that TCSI does not need to devote more resources to conducting frequent personnel reviews to reduce customer-response time. TCSI could have other reasons for frequent reviews, however.

A drawback to relying on scatter diagrams to diagnose causes of quality problems is that the organization must have sufficient reliable information on both quality measures and suspected causes. If sufficient data are not available, as is sometimes the case when processes or quality management efforts are new, the other diagnostic methods we discuss could be more helpful for identifying causes of quality problems.

Flowcharts. A **flowchart** reflects cause-and-effect and sequential linkages among process activities. Knowing which activities cause or precede others in producing a product or offering a service can help diagnose where quality problems arise. Cost-management analysts also might prepare flowcharts to support systems analysis and auditing activities. The flowchart of the actual (not the ideal) customer-response process shown in Exhibit 7–6 helped the TCSI cost-management team discover that the root cause of excessive customer-response time resulted from working with incorrect product information provided by the client. Comparing the actual process to an ideal process can highlight where improvements can be made. Identifying and eliminating non-value-added activities in processes often improves not only the efficiency of the process but also the quality of the product or service.

flowchart *reflects cause-and-effect and sequential linkages among process activities*

Pareto charts. A **Pareto chart** (named after the Italian economist Wilfredo Pareto) prioritizes the causes of problems or defects as bars of varying height, in order of frequency or size. Pareto charts help analysis teams focus on the causes that could offer the greatest potential for improvement. Focusing on correcting the most frequent causes of quality problems, identified by Pareto charts, could show analysis teams where to focus initial efforts to make the most improvement in quality. Exhibit 7–7 is a Pareto chart for the causes of excessive customer-response time at TCSI before process improvements. This chart confirmed what customer representatives had told the analysis team: incorrect client information was responsible for most delays. Nonetheless, the Pareto chart identified other common causes of delays that TCSI also could correct, such as incorrect customer information and insufficient employee training.

Pareto chart *prioritizes the causes of problems or defects as bars of varying height, in order of frequency or size*

Organizations need both lead indicator and diagnostic information about activities to identify problems that require attention. However, most diagnostic information is expensive to collect, so cost management analysts might rely on lead indicators to signal the need to collect diagnostic information.

Exhibit 7–6

Customer Response (to phone call) Activities Flowchart

Transformation Customer Services, Inc.

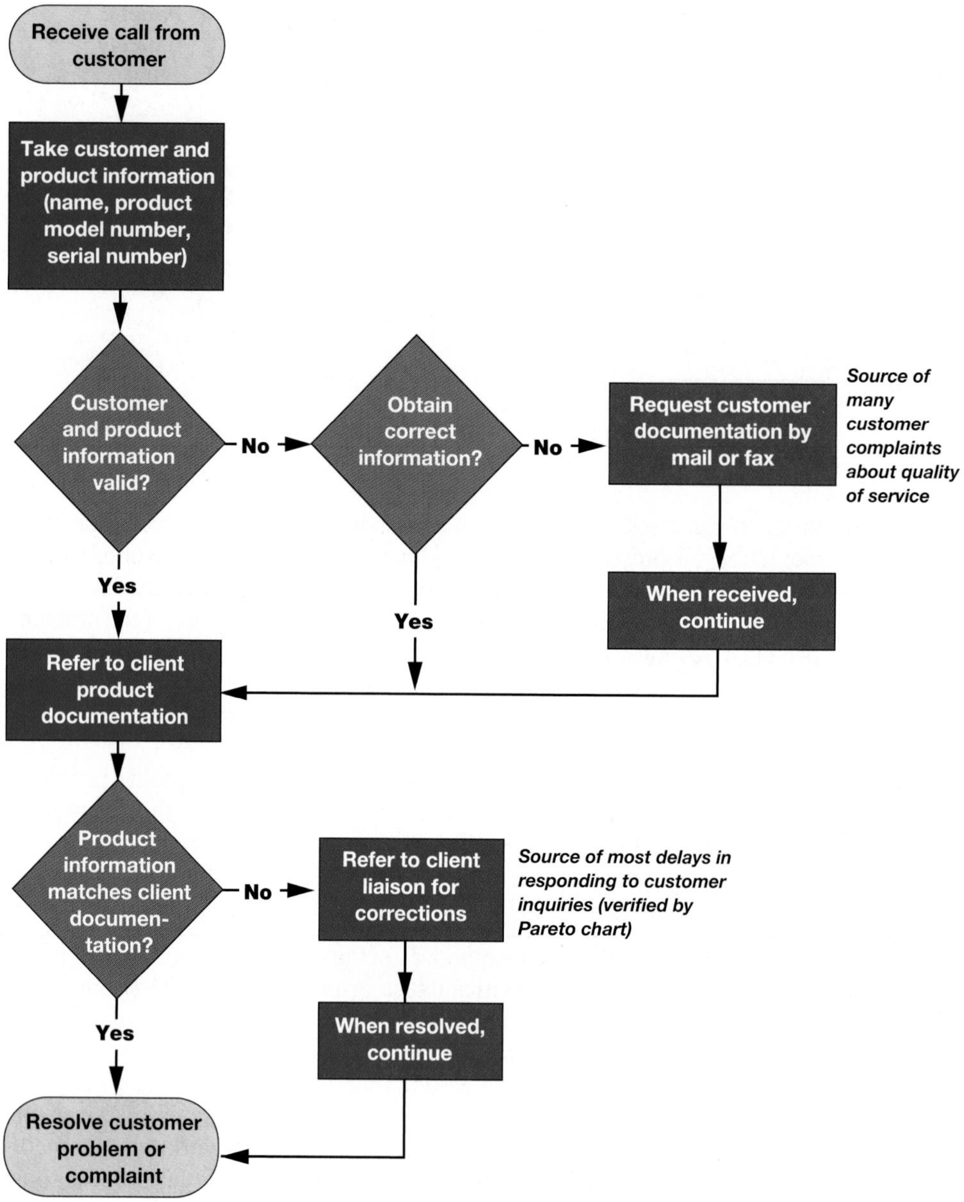
Receive call from customer
Take customer and product information (name, product model number, serial number)
Customer and product information valid?
No
Obtain correct information?
No
Request customer documentation by mail or fax
Source of many customer complaints about quality of service
When received, continue
Yes
Yes
Refer to client product documentation
Product information matches client documen-tation?
No
Refer to client liaison for corrections
Source of most delays in responding to customer inquiries (verified by Pareto chart)
When resolved, continue
Yes
Resolve customer problem or complaint

[Note: This last step has multiple activities depending on the nature of problem or complaint, but a customer representative has authority to resolve most issues.]

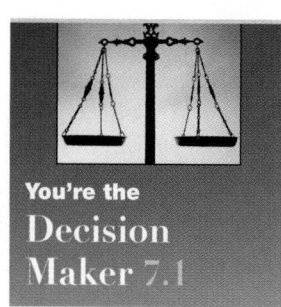

You're the Decision Maker 7.1

Using Diagnostic Quality Information

a. Do you think it is reasonable to delegate the responsibility for diagnosing quality problems to individuals in the departments where quality problems occur?

b. Would it always be better to use a cross-functional team (e.g., across departments or functions) to diagnose quality problems?

(Solutions begin on page 283.)

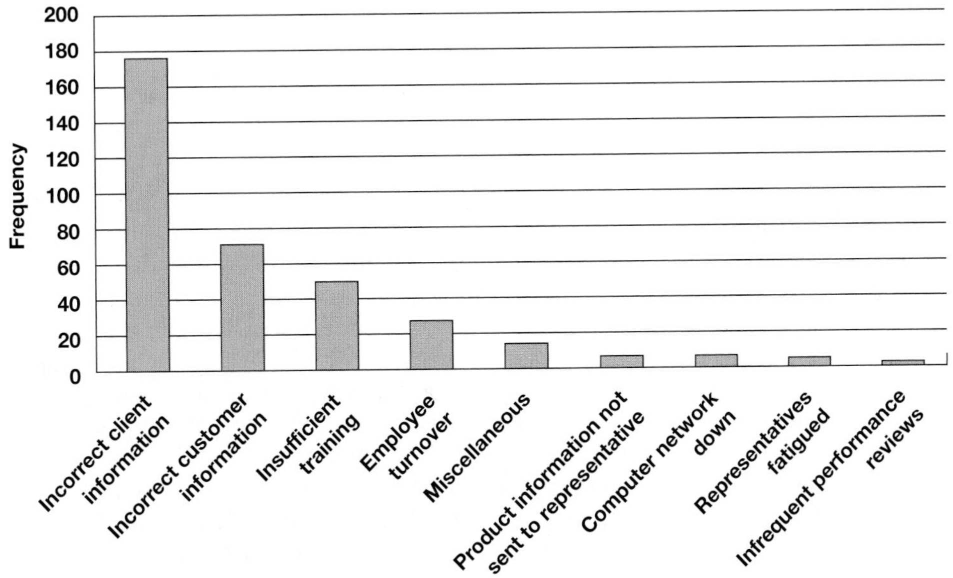

Exhibit 7-7

Pareto Chart

Transformation Customer Services, Inc.

Customer Satisfaction

In addition to measuring lead indicators of tangible and intangible product and service features, many organizations also measure **customer satisfaction,** which is the degree to which expectations of product attributes, customer service, and *price* have been or are expected to be met. Thus, measures of customer satisfaction can be used both as lead indicators of future sales and diagnostic tools to discover causes of unexpectedly low or high sales.

customer satisfaction *is the degree to which expectations of attributes, customer service, and* price *have been or are expected to be met*

The most common methods of measuring customer satisfaction are phone or mail surveys on which companies ask current or potential customers to rate attributes of products or services and customer service on a multiple-point scale.[6] Many organizations outsource the actual measurement of customer satisfaction to benefit from both survey firms' expertise and the ability to generate more valid measures. TCSI market researchers, however, conduct their own customer satisfaction surveys because TCSI believes this an of areas of its expertise. Other common measurement tools are to (1) ask focus groups of customers to evaluate real or proposed products or services and (2) use phantom, or unknown, shoppers, who really are employed by the agency evaluating the product or service and who report their experiences.

As an example of survey questions that TCSI asks clients and their customers, consider how clients and customers rate the *accuracy* of the customer services they have received from TCSI. Was it:

______ Much better than expected?
______ About as expected?
______ Worse than expected?

By asking similar questions about all attributes of its services, TCSI is able to identify its strengths and problem areas as well as what clients and their customers really want. TCSI also uses customer satisfaction ratings to evaluate the performance of its employees and business units. Many organizations believe that strong links exist between meeting quality goals, customer satisfaction, and the organization's goals (e.g., profitability). These

6 Survey research is difficult and requires expertise to do well. Firms use 3- to 10-point scales, but using a 3-point scale might be most effective in identifying attributes that have "delighted," merely "satisfied," or "disappointed" customers. See for example, *www.vanderbilt.edu/CSM/roqpaper.html* and *www.pmresearch.com/information/articles/surveyawry.html*.

organizations might reinforce the importance of these linkages by tying customer satisfaction ratings to incentives for employees. Tying incentives to lead indicators of performance is covered in Chapter 21.

Trade-offs between Quality and Price

Market forces set competitive prices. Customers expect product or service attributes and customer service based on what is available at a comparable price from other sources. Customers buy the product or service that provides them the preferred mix of attributes, customer service, and price. If two products provide the same mix, for example, the customer most likely chooses the product with the lower price. Likewise, if an organization offers superior product attributes or customer service, it might be able to charge higher prices and/or increase its market share. Thus, trade-offs always are made among the various dimensions of a product's quality and its price. Decisions about the dimensions of quality are important cost and revenue drivers for any organization.

Costs of products and services are lead indicators of an organization's ability to meet market prices or offer competitive bid prices. Therefore, organizations that manage quality and the quality/price trade-off also could monitor costs and lead indicators of costs (e.g., changes in cost drivers) closely.

Identifying Costs of Quality

cost of quality (COQ) *is the cost of activities to* control quality *and costs of activities to correct failure to control quality*

As part of their efforts to manage quality drivers, organizations can measure the **costs of quality (COQ)**, which are the costs of activities to *control quality* and the costs of activities to correct *failure to control quality.* Costs to control quality are associated with lead indicators of imminent quality problems, and costs to correct failures could be lead indicators of future decreased sales.

COQ could be most valuable as a communication tool to inform employees at all levels of the magnitude and general sources of quality problems. Most organizations seek to spend most of their quality-improvement efforts on activities controlling quality rather than correcting quality failures. These organizations usually also have low total costs of quality. Organizations that spend most of their efforts on activities to correct quality failures usually have serious quality problems and excessive costs of quality.[7]

Controlling Quality

The two general activities to control quality are prevention activities and appraisal activities.

prevention *activities seek to prevent defects in the products or services being produced*

Prevention. **Prevention** activities seek to prevent defects in the products or services being produced and include the following:

- *Supplier certification.* Using only materials suppliers that can guarantee high quality.
- *Product design for manufacturability.* Designing products that can be made without defects.
- *Quality training.* Training employees to improve quality.
- *Quality evaluations.* Measuring or evaluating employees on their quality capabilities and performance to indicate or motivate improvements.
- *Process improvement.* Evaluating and improving processes to remove causes of defects.

[7]For examples of COQ reporting, see S. Brinkman and M. Appelbaum, "The Quality Cost Report: It's Alive and Well at Gilroy Foods"; L. Carr, "Quality: Cost of Quality—Making It Work"; and S. Kalagnanam and E. M. Matsumura, "Quality: Costs of Quality in an Order Entry Department."

TQM advocates argue that the most efficient use of quality resources is on prevention activities. Preventing defects, they argue, is the only value-added quality activity and the most profitable way to control quality. ROQ advocates agree that preventing defects is effective but also argue that preventing *all* defects could be prohibitively expensive. Some non-value-added quality activities in conjunction with activities that prevent defects could yield the most profitable level of quality.

Appraisal. **Appraisal** activities (also called *detection* or *inspection* activities) inspect inputs and attributes of individual units of product or service to detect whether they conform to specifications or customer expectations and include the following:

appraisal *activities (also called* detection *or* inspection *activities) inspect inputs and attributes of individual units of product or service to detect whether they conform to specifications or customer expectations*

- *Inspecting materials.* Inspecting production materials upon delivery.
- *Inspecting machines.* Ensuring that machines are operating properly within specifications.
- *Inspecting processes.* Manually inspecting the production process.
- *Performing automated inspection.* Using equipment to monitor the production process.
- *Employing statistical process control.* Using employees to inspect every unit for defects as they complete their productive activities (e.g., using control charts).
- *Sampling at end of process.* Inspecting the attributes of a sample of finished products to ensure quality.
- *Testing at end of process.* Testing the performance of all or a sample of finished products under the same or simulated conditions experienced by customers.
- *Field testing.* Testing products in use at customer sites.

Appraisal activities usually are recognized as non-value-added because customers do not pay for inspection—they pay for a high-quality product. Quality experts believe that appraisal activities can be avoided by placing more emphasis on preventing defects. To TQM advocates, an ideal process by design produces zero defects. ROQ advocates, as you can imagine, argue that this ideal process can, in fact, be unprofitable and that some small number of defects is optimal. Therefore, if preventing all defects is not feasible, some testing or appraisal is necessary. The earlier that testing can find defects, however, the lower the cost of defects is likely to be.

This TRW plant in Marshall, Illinois, manufactures air bag crash sensors. Workers become their own inspectors and are personally responsible for the quality of their outputs, an important component in total quality management.

Failing to Control Quality

Failing to control quality causes internal failure and external failure activities. Organizations universally regard these as non-value-added activities.

internal failure *activities are required to correct defective processes, products, and services that are detected before delivering them to customers*

Internal failure. **Internal failure** activities are required to correct defective processes, products, and services that are detected before delivering them to customers. These include the following:

- *Disposing of scrap.* Recycling or dumping materials wasted in the production process.
- *Performing rework.* Correcting defects before the product or service is sold.
- *Reinspecting/Retesting.* Performing quality control testing after rework.
- *Delaying processes.* Reducing throughput because defective items are processed by scarce resources and must be scrapped or reworked—loss of irreplaceable scarce time.

Internal failures are non-value-added activities that can be quite costly—especially from lost processing time. Although this last internal failure activity can be the most costly, it is the most difficult to measure because it can affect future sales.

external failure *activities are required when defective products or services are detected after being delivered to customers*

External failure. **External failure** activities are required to correct defective products or services after they have been delivered to customers. They include:

- *Warranty repairs.* Repairing defective products.
- *Field replacements.* Replacing defective products at the customer's site.
- *Product liability settlements.* Responding to liabilities resulting from product failure.
- *Customer-complaint resolution.* Replacing products or services or adjusting billing to accommodate legitimate customer concerns about products or services received.
- *Restoration of reputation.* Engaging in marketing activities to improve the company's image tarnished from poor product quality.
- *Lost sales.* opportunity costs from decreases in sales resulting from poor-quality products (current and potential customers will go to competitors).

External failure activities could be the most costly because of their effects on the organization's reputation. Although the out-of-pocket costs of these activities can be large, they can be small compared to the opportunity costs of future sales. Because external failure costs have such harmful potential, TQM advocates argue that nearly every activity that would prevent an external failure is cost effective. This argument is difficult to refute because the opportunity costs of forgone sales can be very high but are difficult to measure objectively.

Measuring Costs of Quality

Organizations that use ABC and ABM have the activity-based information necessary to compile cost-of-quality information. The only additional step beyond ABM, discussed in Chapter 5, is classifying activities according to the cost-of-quality category, as described earlier. This requires judgment, and cost management analysts usually work with production personnel to make these classifications. Simply sorting the activity-cost data by cost-of-quality classification yields the cost of the quality measures. Without ABC information, an organization can find preparing COQ measures difficult because traditional accounting systems collect data by organizational function, not by COQ category. Therefore, measuring COQ requires additional analysis, which some organizations find too costly. An added benefit, then, of ABC is ease of measuring COQ.

Not surprisingly, organizations find a high correspondence between the costs of value-added activities and prevention activities and between the costs of non-value-added activities and activities devoted to inspection, internal failure, and external failure. Therefore, enhancing prevention activities should increase value while decreasing or eliminating the need for inspection, internal failure, and external failure activities, which should decrease wasted resources used on non-value-added activities.

Reporting Costs of Quality

Organizations usually sort costs of quality by quality activity and express them as a percentage of sales. Some companies with serious quality problems might spend as much as 30 to 40 percent of sales on quality activities. Companies with excellent quality might spend much less than 10 percent of sales, and most of that cost is for prevention activities.

An example of a quarterly COQ report prepared by cost management analysts for one of TCSI's business units appears in Exhibit 7–8. This report indicates that TCSI spent the most on prevention activities (e.g., value-added quality training and process evaluations). As is typical in companies with excellent quality, this was the largest amount spent on any of the four quality activity categories. More than half of the business unit's cost of quality was on non-value-added activities, as shown in Exhibit 7–9. CFO Freeman instructed the business unit manager to find ways to reverse that percentage while increasing quality of service.

TCSI believes that COQ information is not sufficient by itself to manage quality since it does not measure the quality of services delivered to customers or their satisfaction with services received. However, Freeman uses the COQ information prepared by his staff as one indication of the company's success in managing quality. He looks to see that COQ is less than 10 percent of sales in total and that most of the quality activities are for preventing mistakes, not correcting those that could have been avoided. Note that TCSI does not explicitly measure the opportunity cost of lost business; it uses qualitative measures of forgone sales from customer satisfaction surveys and measures of customer retention (repeat sales).

Exhibit 7–8

Cost-of-Quality Report
First Quarter

Transformation Customer Services, Inc.

	Amounts		Percent of Sales
Sales		$1,765,000	100%
Prevention activities:			
Training	$32,829		
Process evaluation	21,886	$ 54,715	3.10%
Appraisal activities:			
Performance measurement	24,092		
Performance reviews	10,325	34,417	1.95%
Internal failure activities:			
Wasted time	3,883		
Revision of incorrect information	15,532	19,415	1.10%
External failure activities:			
Redoing customer service	6,142		
Resolving complaints with TCSI service	9,213	15,355	0.87%
Total costs of quality		$ 123,902	7.02%

Exhibit 7–9

Relative Proportions of Quality Costs at TCSI

Transformation Customer Services, Inc.

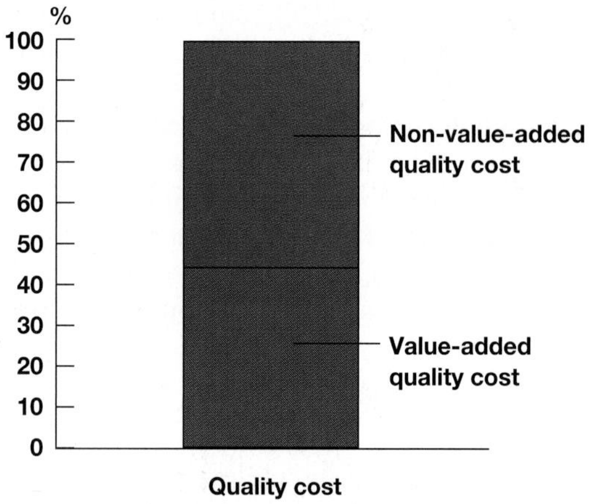

You're the Decision Maker 7.2

Evaluating the Cost of Quality

Some accountants ask this question about COQ: Are we really making a difference, or is COQ just another report? Evaluate these claims about the value of COQ.

a. COQ allows the organization to focus on the reduction or elimination of non-value-added costs of quality.

b. COQ is a better measure of performance than traditional operating income because costs of quality are not buried in FIFO cost of sales.

c. COQ provides a target (e.g., 4 percent of sales for total COQ) that really measures the progress of quality improvements in concrete terms. *Adapted from S. Brinkman and M. Appelbaum,* "The Quality Cost Report: It's Alive and Well at Gilroy Foods."

(Solutions begin on page 283.)

Quality Awards and Certificates

Malcolm Baldrige Quality Award, *created by the U.S. Congress in 1987, recognizes U.S. firms with outstanding records of quality improvement and quality management*

Deming Prize, *created in Japan by the Japanese Union of Scientists and Engineers, is awarded to companies around the world that excel in quality improvement*

ISO 9000 *is a set of international standards for quality management*

Quality has become so important to success that currently many prestigious, internationally recognized awards are given to companies for quality by nearly every country and many professional organizations. For example, the **Malcolm Baldrige Quality Award,** created by the United States Congress in 1987, recognizes US firms with outstanding records of quality improvement and quality management.[8] The **Deming Prize,** created in Japan by the Japanese Union of Scientists and Engineers long before the Baldrige Quality Award, is awarded to companies around the world that excel in quality improvement.[9]

The International Organization for Standardization, based in Europe, has developed international standards for quality management called **ISO 9000.** The ISO standards first gained popularity in Europe but are now global guidelines for the design, development, production, final inspection and testing, installation, and servicing of products, processes, and services. To be certified, a company must document its quality systems and pass a rigorous third-party audit of its manufacturing and customer-service processes.[10]

Organizations proudly display their quality awards and certificates as evidence of their commitment to product and service quality. Many organizations have adopted Baldrige or Deming prize criteria as their internal quality management guidelines even if they do not seek to win a prize for their efforts. TCSI, for example, has adopted criteria from both the

[8]See the Web site *www.quality.nist.gov* for details and recent winners.

[9]The Web site *www.deming.org/TO/demingprizeTO.html* describes the prize. Recent winners include Fuji Photo Optical Co. (*www.fujinon.co.jp*) and Lucent Technologies (*www.lucent.com*).

[10]A Web search on the keywords "ISO 9000" will overwhelm you with millions of "hits." View the ISO homepage at *www.iso.ch/welcome.html.*

Baldrige and Deming awards and has obtained ISO 9000 certification. The company does not plan to apply for any awards, however, because CEO Cooper and CFO Freeman believe that the prizes themselves are unnecessary to the company's success and that the lengthy application and evaluation processes would distract the growing business. Freeman would rather spend his time managing TCSI's quality than applying for quality prizes.

Importance of Managing Time in a Competitive Environment

LO 3 Understand and explain the importance of managing process time.

TCSI and other successful organizations realize that competitive markets continuously demand shorter:

- New product and service development time.
- Customer response time.
- Cycle time.

Accordingly, TCSI focuses on improving the three dimensions of time in all of its business units. This requires that all major business unit activities have time-measurement objectives. Improvements in response time can require simplifying and shortening work processes and almost always require improvements in quality. Poor quality, which requires inspection, testing, and rework, is a major cause of the excessive use of time. Eliminating the causes of poor quality, therefore, can shorten process time dramatically. Just-in-time management approaches simultaneously manage quality and time. Furthermore, some argue that quality and time are inextricably linked.

New Product (or Service) Development Time

New product (or **service**) **development time** is the period between the first consideration of a product and its initial sale to the customer. Firms that respond quickly to customer needs for new products and services can develop an advantage over competitors. For example, Honda identified US consumers' need for fuel-efficient cars, and its early development of them gave Honda a competitive advantage for several years. Likewise, TCSI was one of the first companies to recognize the market's need for outsourced customer services and continues to try to anticipate new market opportunities.

new product (or **service**) **development time** *is the period between the first consideration of a product and its initial sale to the customer*

Many organizations similar to TCSI shorten new product development time by assigning development responsibilities to cross-functional teams who have target-cost and development-time objectives and access to sophisticated design tools.[11] These teams are free from the many layers of approval and bureaucracy that can stifle creativity and extend development time unnecessarily in large organizations. Ensuring that the teams do not have the distractions of other major duties helps. Benchmarking development times in other business units or organizations can be an effective way to motivate and monitor new product development.

Customer-Response Time and Cycle Time

Customer-response time is the amount of time between a customer's placing an order for a product or requesting service and delivering the product or service to the customer. The shorter the response time, the more competitive the company is on this dimension. The components of customer-response time appear in Exhibit 7–10. Improvements can be possible in all components. For example, many companies have reduced order-receipt time by incorporating electronic ordering (via wide area networks or the Internet). Electronic ordering also reduces chances for human errors in the ordering process. Organizations minimize order-waiting time by scheduling bottleneck resources carefully and by keeping some reserve capacity for unexpected but valuable orders. Companies also minimize order-delivery time by using overnight delivery services or, in the case of

customer-response time *is the amount of time between a customer's placing an order for a product or requesting service and the delivery of the product or service to the customer*

[11] See for example, C. Ittner and D. Larcker, "Product Development Cycle Time and Organizational Performance."

Exhibit 7–10

Customer-Response Time

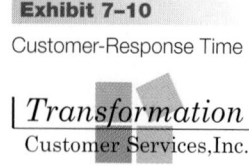

Transformation
Customer Services, Inc.

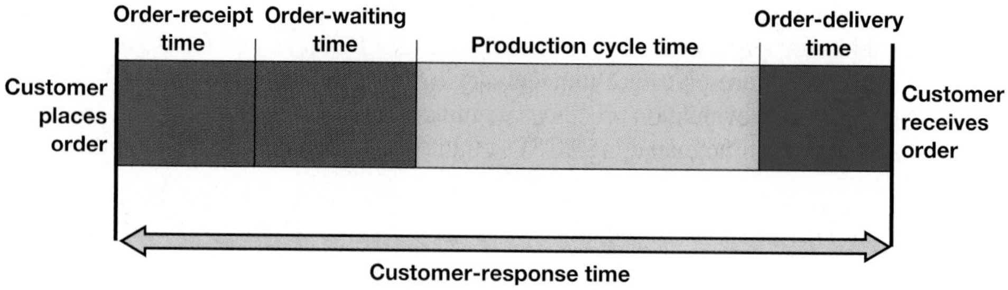

services, delivering them electronically. Most dramatic improvements in customer-response time could be made possible by eliminating non-value-added and poor-quality related activities in **production cycle time** which is the elapsed time between starting and finishing a production process, including any time to correct mistakes.

production cycle time *is the elapsed time between starting and finishing a production process, including time to correct mistakes*

Costs of Time

The old adage, "Time is money," has never been more true. Longer process times mean both higher out-of-pocket costs for human and physical resources and higher costs of forgone opportunities. In fact, time can be the scarcest resource of all. Individuals and organizations with good ideas can always obtain more money, but adding capacity and capability without improving processes and quality can perpetuate inefficiencies that reduce competitiveness. Attractive alternatives can be ignored because of insufficient time to analyze opportunities.

Some manufacturing companies allocate overhead costs to business units and products using cycle time as the cost-driver base although this allocation approach might not accurately measure the use of support resources or the opportunity costs of wasted time, it does get employees' attention. If evaluations and incentives are based on costs or profits, allocations based on cycle time also should motivate employees to improve processes to reduce cycle time. These organizations can use only costs or profits as the basis for performance evaluation since measured profits are improved with cycle time reductions, and cycle time can be reduced and revenues maintained or increased only by improving quality. Since some measures are lead indicators of quality, however, relying only on current profits to motivate employees could lead to myopic behavior, such as ignoring the future effects of current actions. Some organizations rely on multiple, nonfinancial measures (e.g., the balanced scorecard) that are lead indicators of future profits to motivate employees to improve all areas of performance, not just current profits.

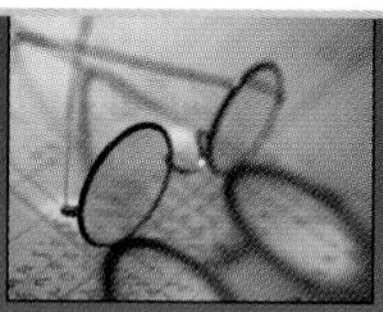

Cost Management in Practice 7.2

Benefits of Managing Time

Many organizations report dramatic improvements in performance as a result of focusing on time management. For example, St. Joseph's Hospital near Atlanta redesigned its health care processes to reduce postsurgery hospital stays. As a result, quality of care increased, costs declined as much as one third for some procedures, and patients were more satisfied and healthier. The bottom line was that the hospital's profits rose 67 percent in one year.

Opel, the German subsidiary of General Motors, reduced non-value-added movement of parts and excess inventories and installed JIT parts delivery and a spirit of continuous improvement. One vital key was hiring and training workers who can work in creative, responsible teams. As these time- and quality-based methods have spread throughout the company, Opel has become one of the few European carmakers poised to compete effectively in Europe after import restrictions on Japanese cars expired in 1999. GM hopes that the lessons learned at Opel, which apparently were not learned during its joint ventures with Japanese carmakers, can be applied to its US operations.

Reductions in communication time and increases in reliability have enabled alliances among individuals and companies to create virtual corporations that are able to locate and employ human capital just in time and to bring new products and services to market much faster than traditional companies. Information sharing and monitoring also are replacing traditional structures and controls. *Sources: P. Burrows,* "Health Care: The Quest for Quality"; *P. Magnuson,* "GM's German Lessons"; *and K. Miller,* "The Virtual Corporation."

Management of Process Productivity and Efficiency

LO 4 Measure and manage productivity and capacity.

Process efficiency—the ability to transform inputs into throughput at the lowest cost—depends on having all employees work toward a common goal. **Throughput** is the amount of goods and services produced and delivered to customers during a period of time measured in dollar terms or physical measures. Managers need to know how well they are managing the organization's processes and activities. Employees can help identify inefficient or wasteful processes and activities to make improvements that meet customers' needs at lower cost.

throughput *is the amount of goods and services produced and delivered to customers during a period of time measured in dollar terms or physical measures*

production processes *directly result in the production of products or services provided to external customers*

business processes *support or enable production processes*

Organizations manage two types of processes: production and business. **Production processes** directly result in the production of products or services provided to external customers. Examples of production processes include Boeing's machining aluminum stock into airplane parts, DataPlay's manufacturing miniature hard drives for MP3 music players, and TCSI's providing outsourced customer services. **Business processes** support or enable production processes; examples include the materials-ordering processes that Boeing uses to ensure that the correct aluminum stock is on hand at just the right time for machining. TCSI's process for taking customer orders is a business process, as is developing information systems to support its customer-service representatives.

Measures of the efficiency of both production and business processes are lead indicators of eventual financial performance. If these measures show that efficiency is declining, employees can intervene to take corrective actions before financial performance is adversely affected. By benchmarking measures of process efficiency against those of more efficient organizations, capable employees also can identify and act on opportunities to improve.

Common measures of efficiency of both production and business processes include, in addition to quality:

- Productivity
- Cycle time
- Throughput time ratio

Exhibit 7–11 shows that measures of throughput and production cycle time are summary measures of efficiency, affected by quality and productivity. A low cycle time—from receipt of an order of a unit of existing product (or service) to its packaging and shipment (delivery) to the customer—and high throughput are possible only if processes are productive, and processes are productive only if they are of high quality.

Measuring Productivity

productivity *is the ratio of outcomes of a process divided by the amount of resources necessary to complete the process*

total factor productivity *is the value of goods and services divided by the total cost of providing them*

Many possible measures exist to determine productivity. **Productivity** is the ratio of the outcomes of a process divided by the amount of resources necessary to complete the process. The broadest measure of productivity is **total factor productivity**, which is the value of goods and services (measured as sales revenue, e.g., in US$) divided by the total cost to provide them. This diagnostic tool is especially useful when benchmarked against that of competitors. For example, as shown in Exhibit 7–12, TCSI compared its total factor productivity for a recent year to that of its competitors in the industry by

Exhibit 7–11

Relations among Process Efficiency Measures

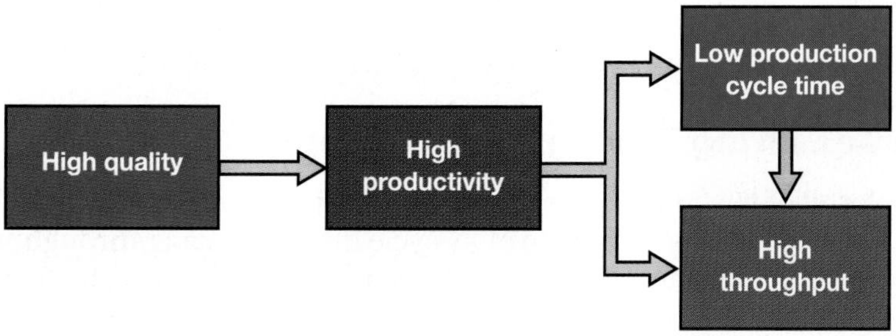

Exhibit 7–12 Competitors' Total Factor Productivity

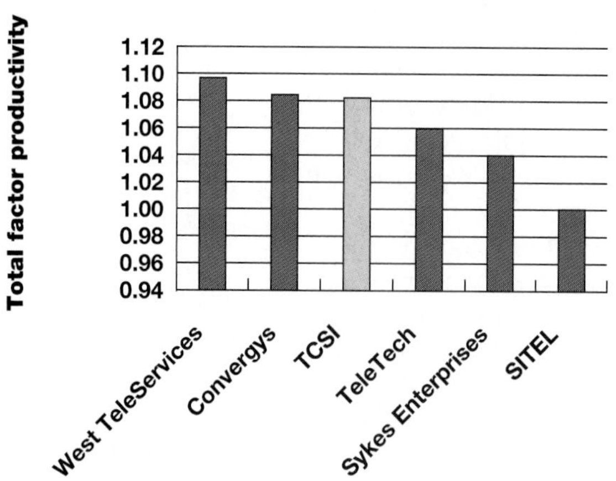

Exhibit 7–13 Trend of Sales per Employee

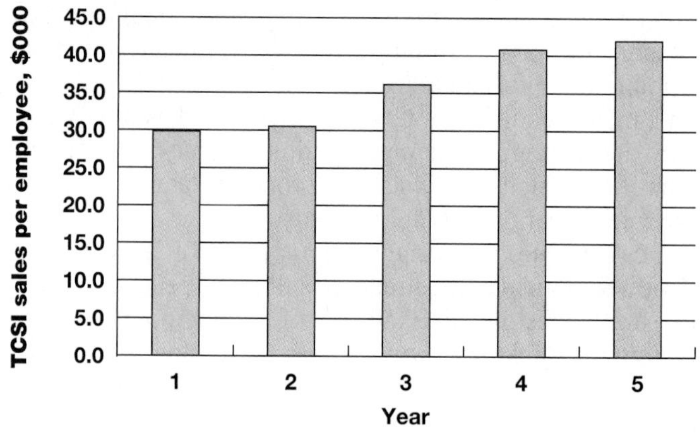

Transformation Customer Services, Inc.

dividing each company's total sales by its total operating expenses. This type of information is freely available at Hoover's Online (*www.hoovers.com*). TCSI's total factor productivity is not the highest in the industry, and the company encourages employees to analyze all business and productive processes for ways to create more value at lower cost. Many employee suggestions for improvement (discussed earlier) focus on ways to reduce waste and improve the use of scarce resources.

More specific productivity measures compare outcomes valued by customers to the scarcest or most valuable resources used to achieve those outcomes, for example, sales revenue per employee. Last year, TCSI's sales revenue was $42,700 per employee. Is this good or bad? Productivity measures are meaningful only when compared over time or benchmarked against those of competitors. The historical trend of TCSI's sales revenue per employee shown in Exhibit 7–13 is increasing, which reflects improving sales productivity.

Measuring Cycle Time

Cycle time at TCSI includes the time elapsed from the start of a customer service call to its end. This definition of cycle time captures all processes that TCSI controls to deliver what customers expect: a quality service response in the shortest possible time.

In nearly all cases, customers and suppliers prefer short cycle times, which require a higher-quality product and fewer resources consumed by it. Therefore, low cycle times mean that organizations are delivering more customer value at lower cost, which is not possible without high quality and productive processes.

average cycle time *equals total processing time for all units divided by good units produced*

throughput efficiency *is the relation of throughput achieved to resources used*

throughput time ratio *is the ratio of time spent adding customer value to products and services divided by total cycle time (also known as the "ratio of work content to lead time")*

Many companies use **average cycle time,** which equals total processing time for all units divided by good units produced, as a summary measure of process efficiency. To be most useful, average cycle time should include the average time necessary to complete and deliver all good units and dispose of units that have to be reworked or scrapped because of defects, which is non-value-added time.

One of TCSI's competitors brags that its service cycle time is as low as TCSI's, but TCSI has learned that this competitor counts only the average time to complete service calls with no mistakes or return calls. TCSI believes that this practice unfairly understates true average cycle time and hides quality problems.

Measuring Throughput Efficiency

Not all of the time a service or product spends in process is productive; that is, value is not added to it every minute of its cycle time. Managing **throughput efficiency,** which relates throughput achieved to the resources used, usually involves finding opportunities to reduce non-value added cycle time. The **throughput time ratio** measures

Microsoft Excel - TCSI

File Edit View Insert Format Tools Data Window Help

A14 =

	A	B	C
1	**Process data**		
2	Good service calls completed	1,500,000	service calls
3	Time adding value	195,000	
4	Time not adding value	180,000	hours
5			
6	**Process analysis**		
7	Total processing time (B3+B4)	375,000	hours
8	Average cycle time (B7/B2)	15	minutes
9	Throughput time ratio (B3/B7)	0.52	

TCSI / **Exhibit 7-14** / Sheet3

Ready

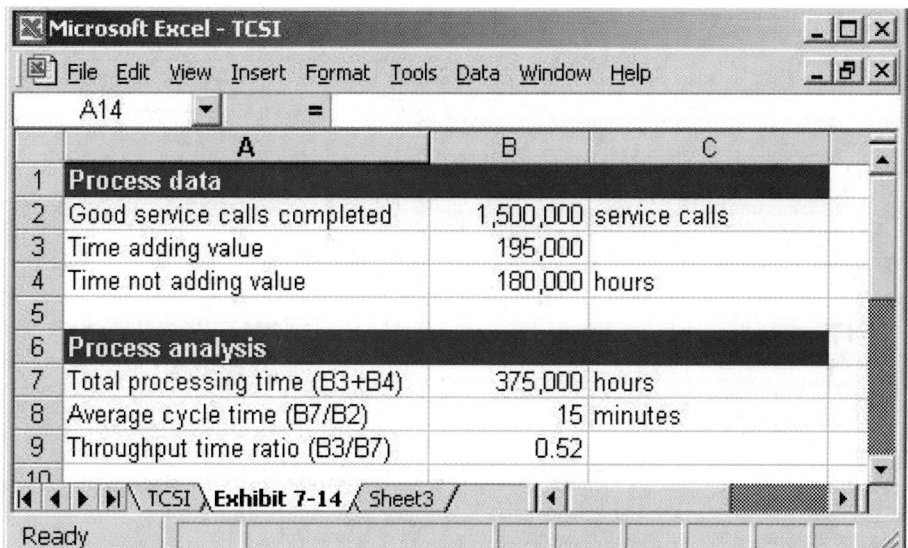

Exhibit 7–14

Analysis of Throughput Time

Transformation
Customer Services, Inc.

throughput efficiency by comparing the time from adding value to the total cycle time, which includes the time spent on both adding value and waiting for processing.

Throughput time ratio = Value-added time ÷ Total processing time

The highest possible value of this ratio is 1.00 or 100 percent, a theoretical ideal. Nonetheless, the closer an organization comes to a 100 percent throughput ratio, the more efficient its processes are, and the more quickly it can fill customers' orders. In some organizations, only 5 percent (or less) of its product or service cycle time is spent adding value; at least 95 percent of the time is wasted by waiting for processing or correcting mistakes. Efficient companies have achieved throughput time ratios of more than 50 percent by eliminating unnecessary delays and defects.

TCSI computes its throughput time ratio for service calls each week. See Exhibit 7–14 for a spreadsheet with data from a recent week. Value-adding time (cell B3: column B, row 3) includes receiving customers' calls, researching problems, giving advice, and ensuring that problems have been resolved. Time spent without adding customer value (B4) includes the time customers spend waiting on hold and for information as well as reworking defective or incomplete advice—activities that use scarce resources without creating anything for which customers are willing to pay. The average cycle time (B8) is the total processing time (B7) divided by the good service calls completed (units produced) that time period (B2). A defective service call requires one or more return calls by the customer to resolve a problem. The throughput time ratio (B9) is the time spent adding value (B3) divided by total processing time (B7). Higher ratios (over time or across competitors) indicate better uses of the scarcest resource of all—time.

Managing Process Capacity

Process capacity is a measure of a process's *ability* to transform resources into valued products and services, usually expressed as a rate of processing inputs or generating outputs per time period. For example, the commuting capacity of a highway could be expressed in terms of the number of commuter vehicles entering the city per hour. Using this definition, one might incorrectly conclude that widening the highway or increasing its speed limit would increase the commuting capacity vehicle in the city. This logic is flawed, however, because the perspective of capacity is too narrow. The capacity of the *entire* commuting process—or the manufacturing or service process—must be considered. Therefore, widening or increasing a highway's speed limit without providing for additional destination *parking* would not increase commuting capacity;

process capacity *is a measure of a process's* ability *to transform resources into valued products and services*

Exhibit 7–15
Measures of Capacity

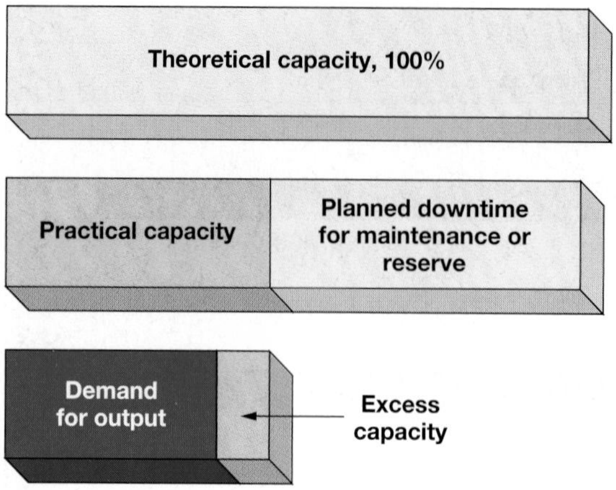

instead of waiting on the highway, commuters will be looking for parking places. A process- or systemwide perspective is necessary to manage capacity.

Measuring Capacity

theoretical capacity *of a process is the maximum possible rate of transformation of inputs into outputs if the process were fully used, with no downtime or unused capacity*

Three common measures—theoretical, practical, and excess capacity—influence how organizations manage process capacity. The **theoretical capacity** of a process is the maximum possible rate of transformation of inputs into outputs if the process were fully used, with no downtime or unused capacity. Most organizations, however, operate processes at less than theoretical capacity (e.g., at 80 percent of theoretical capacity) for a number of reasons, including the following:

- Planned downtime usually is necessary for scheduled maintenance or improvements to equipment and procedures.
- Unplanned downtime caused by breakdowns in equipment or delays in supply of inputs can make it impossible to operate at theoretical capacity.
- Some capacity can be reserved for unforeseen needs and the ability to be flexible.
- Demand for the output of the process might be less than the theoretical capacity.

practical capacity *of a process is its* theoretical capacity *less planned downtime for scheduled maintenance or improvements*

excess (or **unused**) **capacity** *is the amount (if any) by which practical capacity exceeds the demand for the output of the process*

The **practical capacity** of a process is its *theoretical capacity* less planned downtime for scheduled maintenance or improvements. **Excess** (or **unused**) **capacity** is the amount (if any) by which practical capacity exceeds the demand for the output of the process. Note that organizations sometimes allow processes to operate in excess of practical capacity (i.e., at negative excess capacity) to meet urgent needs. In the long run, however, skipping maintenance and planned improvements will lead to breakdowns and reduced capacity. Exhibit 7–15 shows relationships between measures of capacity for a process with theoretical and practical capacities in excess of demand. Chapter 12, "Financial Modeling," discusses managing processes when demand exceeds capacity. Persistent excess capacity indicates wasted resources; negative excess capacity can indicate lost opportunities.

Managing Quality + Time + Productivity + Capacity = JIT

LO 5 Evaluate how just-in-time methods create benefits by combining management of quality, productivity, and capacity.

just-in-time (JIT) *process to purchase, make, and deliver services and products just when needed*

inventory carrying costs *are costs of receiving, handling, storing, insuring, and becoming obsolete*

The objective of **just-in-time (JIT)** processes is to purchase, make, and deliver services and products just when needed. Organizations that use JIT find that it not only reduces, or potentially eliminates, **inventory carrying costs,** which are costs of receiving, handling, storing, insuring, and becoming obsolete, but also requires high-quality processes. Defective products are incompatible with JIT because in theory no inventory is in reserve to keep production processes operating. Thus, defects trigger investigations of processes to eliminate their causes. Without wasteful efforts needed to correct defects, JIT processes also have short cycle times. The JIT philosophy—avoiding waste and non-value-added activities—is closely linked to activity-based management.[12] Thus, service organizations also apply JIT.

Think of JIT and the quality requirements for a course report. Suppose that you begin it just soon enough to complete it before it is due. If all goes as planned, you

[12]Surveys show that manufacturing firms report improvements in cycle time and quality as a result of adopting JIT, particularly those that use batch and continuous flow processes (e.g., R. White, "An Empirical Assessment of JIT in U.S. Manufacturers," and M. Youssef, "Measuring the Intensity Level of JIT Activities and Its Impact on Quality").

will finish printing the report just before class and hand it in on time. Fine—if all goes well.

Suppose, however, that your personal computer crashes while you are writing the report. This presents a major problem for you because you attempted to apply the JIT philosophy with a defective machine in your production process. Use of JIT forces you to think through all of the things that could go wrong and to correct them in advance of your report. If you use JIT to prepare course reports, you need to be sure that everything involved is reliable: your machine (or a backup), your transportation to deliver the product (your report), and your access to other resources, such as the library or the Internet. In short, to apply JIT, you cannot allow unreliable activities or defective resources in your process.[13]

JIT Manufacturing

Service-based companies such as TCSI are ideally situated to implement the JIT philosophy because they can focus on improving quality and eliminating waste without the encumbrances of physical plants, inventories, and entrenched production processes. Manufacturing companies, however, also can gain from applying the JIT philosophy to their management of physical resources. For example, manufacturers should realize that customers do not care whether the manufacturer maintains inventories or has the largest, most efficient forklifts to move parts and materials from one manufacturing activity to the next. As far as customers are concerned, these are non-value-added activities that only waste resources and increase costs. Nor are customers interested in paying for the manufacturer to fix defective products. They prefer defect-free products, and if a competitor offers defect-free products at a lower cost, the customer has an obvious reason to buy elsewhere. Concerns for eliminating the waste caused by non-value-added activities and unnecessary defects converge in the solution offered by JIT manufacturing. We now compare the filling of the same order by a traditional manufacturer and a JIT manufacturer.

Traditional "push" manufacturing. A traditional manufacturer begins the manufacturing cycle by forecasting total orders for a time period, say a month. Considering beginning and ending inventory levels yields the required production level. Based on the forecasted level of production and materials inventories, the manufacturer orders materials and then schedules production at each defined activity of the process. Thus, forecasting and scheduling activities push production through the process. For example, a traditional manufacturer of personal computers does the following:

- Forecasts sales (by model) well in advance of the start of production to accommodate purchasing and production lead times.
- Orders all components (circuit boards, disk drives, DVD or CD-ROM drives, processor chips, and so on).
- Prepares a production schedule and gives orders to all functional groups (motherboard assembly, storage device assembly, final assembly, etc.) to assemble the required number of parts, components, and computers.
- Upon receiving a customer order, ships products from finished goods inventory if the product is available, or if the product is not available, either places it on backorder status to be filled as soon as possible or expedites a special order.

Why is this approach to manufacturing possibly inefficient? First, it is driven by sales forecasting, which can be an inaccurate guide to production scheduling. Employees in every functional activity are motivated to meet production schedules regardless of overall sales. If sales are less than forecasted, the company invests too

[13] General Motors experienced this vulnerability when a labor strike affected its plants throughout North America that depended on timely shipments of assemblies. See N. Templin, "GM Walkout Hits Production at Mexican Sites," and G. Burkins and F. R. Bleakley, "UAW Strike Hits GM 'Just in Time' to Cripple Firm."

much in unused parts and unsold finished goods inventory, which consumes resources unnecessarily and can result in obsolete inventories. If sales are more than forecasted, the company must either backorder its sales, which could result in dissatisfied customers and lost sales, or rush orders for parts and expedite production beyond what was planned, which could greatly increase costs. Thus, pushing production through the company motivates adherence to production schedules and inhibits flexibility, regardless of the impact on throughput—the result of sales to customers.

Second, the traditional manufacturer usually does not balance the timing of receiving materials and of all production activities with capacity. Not considering capacity can result in a temporary, wasteful buildup of inventories if this is merely a matter of timing, or a permanent buildup of inventories if managers are covering their quality problems by ordering too many materials or overproducing. Thus, push production also can reduce the motivation to improve quality and can reinforce the motivation to overuse capacity.

JIT "pull" manufacturing. Although a JIT manufacturer also uses long-term sales forecasting to determine its scale of operations and capacity, JIT production is "pulled" through the process by customer orders rather than pushed by a master production schedule. For example, consider how Dell Computer Corporation or Gateway pulls an order through its production process in a sequence almost the reverse of that of the traditional manufacturer:

- A customer places an order for a computer with specific features.
- The sales order triggers a production order.
- The production order triggers the ordering and assembly of individual components, which are started immediately and designated for the specific order.
- The requirements for components trigger orders to suppliers, which ship parts immediately.
- The customer receives the ordered computer approximately one week later.

A traditional manufacturer could be just as flexible to customer orders by forecasting sales perfectly, which is not possible, or by investing in large enough inventories to avoid all backorders, which could be prohibitively costly. Obviously, the JIT approach is flexible to customer needs and requires lower inventory levels than traditional methods—only as much as is necessary to process each order. JIT production is not trivial to design, implement, or manage, however.

Dell Computer assembles its products just in time to fill customer orders quickly, thus eliminating wasted effort and time. Dell's inventories are minimized because customer orders pull computers through its assembly processes.

Role of cost management. The cost-management analyst can fill a valuable role by measuring the costs of excess inventories and costs of quality that traditional push production methods encourage. Often these costs have the most impact when they are benchmarked against more efficient competitors. Revealing these cost disadvantages could induce companies to consider adopting a JIT production approach. Consider the summary information in Exhibits 7–16 and 7–17 that contrast the production performance of two relatively

Exhibit 7-16 Inventory Management at Three Computer Manufacturers

Manufacturer Production Method	Dell Computer Corp. JIT	Compaq Computer Corp. Traditional	IBM Traditional
Qualitative and quantitative data from recent Form 10-K filed with the Securities and Exchange Commission	"The Company's build-to-order manufacturing process is designed to allow the Company to quickly produce customized computer systems and to achieve rapid inventory turnover and reduced inventory levels, which lessens the Company's exposure to the risk of declining inventory values. This flexible manufacturing process also allows the Company to incorporate new technologies or components into its product offerings quickly."	"In managing production, we must forecast customer demand for our products. Should we underestimate the supplies needed to meet demand, we could be unable to meet customer demand. Should we overestimate the supplies needed to meet customer demand, cash and profitability could be adversely affected."	"The company's businesses are characterized by rapid technological changes and corresponding shifts in customer demand, resulting in unpredictable product transitions and shortened life cycles. . . . In addition, from time to time the company may experience difficulties or delays in the development, production or marketing of new products and services."
Sales revenue	$12,327,000,000	$24,584,000,000	$78,508,000,000
No. of employees	16,000	32,656	269,465
Sales per employee	$770,437 per employee	$752,817 per employee	$291,347 per employee
Cost of goods sold	$9,605,000,000	$17,833,000,000	$47,899,000,000
Inventories (year-end)	$233,000,000	$1,570,000,000	$5,139,000,000
Inventory turnover*	41.2 times per year	11.3 times per year	9.3 times per year

*IBM's sales and cost of goods sold also include large sales of software and services, which lead to overstatement of IBM's inventory turnover ratio, which might be roughly half the calculated amount.

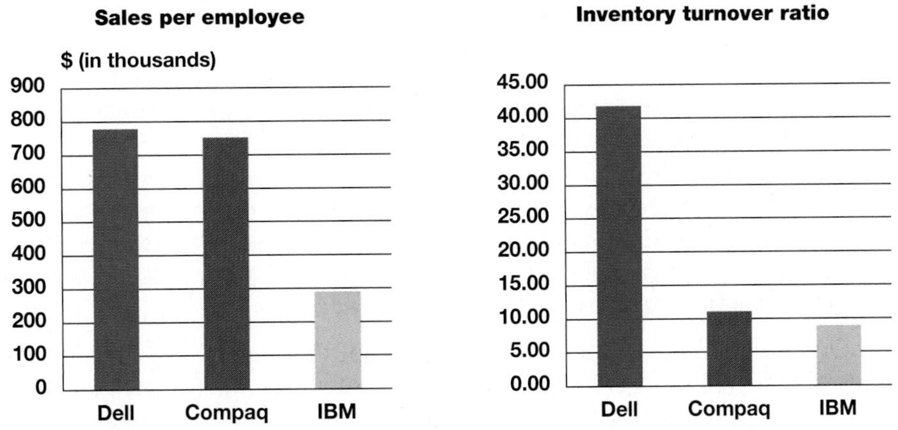

Exhibit 7-17
Comparative Sales and Production Performance

traditional computer manufacturers (Compaq Computer Corp. and IBM) with a more efficient competitor (Dell Computer Corporation), which openly states that it has competitive advantages because of its flexible, JIT manufacturing approach.

Observe that Dell's and Compaq's employees generate comparable sales revenue per employee (and more than twice as much as IBM's), which indicates that Dell and Compaq use human resources with equal effectiveness. However, Dell manages its costs more effectively; it has a much lower inventory level and a much higher inventory turnover ratio, reflecting more efficient production processes than either competitor. How does that benefit Dell? Assuming comparable inventory levels year-round (we should use *average* inventory levels) and a cost of capital of 8 percent (approximately the long-term stock market return), Dell enjoys *at least* a $106,960,000 annual opportunity-cost advantage over Compaq [0.08 × ($1,570,000,000 − $233,000,000)], from its management of its inventories alone.[14]

JIT Success Factors

How is the JIT manufacturer able to reliably produce and deliver its products? Manufacturers that apply JIT find that the following six factors are essential. Furthermore, all of them appear to be necessary; an organization probably cannot implement JIT successfully without implementing *all* of its components, at least to some degree.

1. *Commitment to quality.* All employees must be involved in the quality process. Defects cause delays and require buffer inventories. Employees must be able and motivated to take preventive actions. However, if defects occur, the sooner employees can detect a defect, the sooner they can correct it, minimizing lost time and resources.
2. *Creation of flexible capacity or predictable orders.* Short setup times and the ability to customize products is necessary to respond to unique orders. Mass-production can benefit from JIT if producers are able to stabilize orders through advance or long-term purchase agreements.
3. *Achievement of reliable supplier relations.* Suppliers must be reliable, providing on-time deliveries of high-quality materials. Unreliable suppliers necessitate buffer inventories. Developing strong supplier relationships often means reducing the number of suppliers, which also results in savings in support services that manage suppliers and orders.
4. *Development of smooth production flow.* Unbalanced production leads to delays at bottlenecks and the need for excess buffer inventories. Organizing production activities to respond to individual orders can mean configuring activities into "cells" that focus on completing a unique order rather than linear assembly lines best suited to producing large batches of identical items.
5. *Maintenance of a well-trained, motivated, flexible workforce.* In a production cell environment, workers must be well trained and cross-trained to use various machines and work on different areas of their production cell. Furthermore, they must be able and motivated to correct problems as they occur to keep the production process operating.
6. *Achievement and improvement of short cycle and customer-response times.* Short customer-response times enable companies to respond quickly to customer needs. Eliminating non-value-added time and activities results in shorter cycle times. For example, unnecessary paperwork or travel and movement of parts and assemblies waste time.

Organizations could benefit from JIT even if they cannot implement its components perfectly. In many areas of the world, for example, instantaneous resupply of materials is not possible, so many nearly JIT companies maintain some inventories. They still benefit from applying JIT principles to eliminate waste in other activities even though they still have inventories.

The cost-management analyst also fills a valuable role in JIT manufacturing organizations by identifying other areas for improvement and by monitoring perform-

[14]Note that this figure does not include the cost savings from the reduced costs of storing, insuring, becoming obsolete, and so on associated with maintaining smaller inventories. Nor does it reflect possibly higher costs of special supplier relationships and more frequent deliveries of materials. The former costs can be quite large, but the latter costs are probably small given these large companies' purchasing power. Smaller companies can experience somewhat higher costs of supplier relationships using JIT that could be offset by other cost savings.

ance in the preceding six components of JIT production using the same type of lead-indicator and diagnostic tools useful for managing quality. For example, measuring and reporting defects, causes of defects, cycle times, and employee capabilities support the management of both quality and time.

Research Insight 7.2

Benefits of JIT

Verifying average economic benefits derived from adopting JIT is just as difficult as establishing consistent evidence on the benefits of improving quality (see Research Insight 7.1) for many of the same reasons. The great majority of self-reports (e.g., Cost Management in Practice 7.2) are the apparent successes. Firms would be reluctant to disclose that they had failed at JIT. Even firms that successfully adopt JIT could be simultaneously involved in other improvement efforts. Furthermore, they might adopt JIT because of competitive necessity and might not expect to get ahead of the competition, but only to stay even. A recent study using financial statement data demonstrates how difficult it is to isolate the effects of a single organizational factor such as JIT. The study did find that firms declaring that they had adopted JIT—though we do not know whether they adopted some or all of its components and how widely they adopted JIT—on average had significantly higher inventory turnover ratios afterward than did comparable firms that apparently did not adopt JIT. This confirms that JIT has a beneficial effect on the use of scarce resources.* However, this effect apparently did not extend to improvements in return on assets (ROA) because all firms in the study on average experienced declines in ROA. The study attributes this finding to general economic conditions. However, JIT firms, especially those that serve many customers, had a lower decline in ROA than did non-JIT firms, which suggests that some JIT firms were better insulated from adverse economic conditions. The bottom line is that, although the logic of JIT is compelling, we cannot be sure that adopting JIT results in improved profitability for all firms. More research is necessary to isolate contemporaneous and complementary effects. Some research on JIT processes indicates that firms do not and should not adopt management techniques in isolation, and it could be that the way firms bundle JIT with other techniques determines organizational performance.

Sources: R. Balakrishnan, T. Linsmeier, and M. Venkatachalam, "Financial Benefits from JIT Adoption: Effects of Customer Concentration and Cost Structure"; *F. Selto, C. Renner, and S. M. Young,* "Assessing the Organizational Fit of a JIT Manufacturing System."

*This finding is supported by some studies, such as that by T. Billesbach and R. Hayen, "Long-Term Impact of Just-in-Time on Inventory Performance Measures," but not supported by others, such as that by S. Procter, "The Extent of JIT Manufacturing in the UK: Evidence from Aggregate Economic Data," which could not find evidence of average improvements in inventory turnover ratios that could be attributed to JIT.

Chapter Summary

TCSI and other companies have been successful because they understand the informational and organizational requirements for managing quality, time productivity, and capacity. These requirements include:[15]

1. *Employee responsibility and authority.* Employees, not just managers, should collect and use information to get feedback and solve problems. Information should be bottom up in the organization, not just top down. Traditional accounting reports are based on data collected and aggregated by accountants, who present reports to managers, who then typically send some of the information down to the workers. These reports can be meaningful to accountants and managers but not necessarily to other employees, who might not see the impacts of their actions on aggregated performance.
2. *Lead indicator and diagnostic information.* Cost management information should be more detailed and focused on activities than that produced by traditional accounting systems. Instead of reporting just the cost of defects, for example, the information system should also report the types and causes of defects.

[15] Adapted from Chris Ittner and David Larcker, "Total Quality Management and the Choice of Information and Reward Systems."

3. *Problem-solving information.* The information should include problem-solving information such as that coming from quality control charts, not just financial reports. Financial reports would indicate a decline in revenues, for example, but not its causes. Control charts, however, could show an increase in customer complaints as a likely cause of the revenue decline. To carry this a step further, other charts could indicate the cause of increased customer complaints.
4. *Timely information.* The information should be available quickly (for example, daily or "real time") so workers can get quick feedback. Frequent information accelerates identifying and correcting problems. Traditional accounting systems often report weekly or monthly, which does not allow a quick response to problems.
5. *Appropriate evaluations and rewards.* Evaluations and rewards should be based on performing activities that lead to high quality and customer satisfaction in addition to financial measures of performance, which usually lag quality performance. This reflects that you get what you reward.

Key Terms

For each term's definition, refer to the indicated page or turn to the glossary at the end of the text.

Appraisal (also called *detection* or *inspection*), 267
Attributes, 257
Average cycle time, 274
Business processes, 273
Cause-and-effect analysis, 261
Control chart, 259
Costs of quality (COQ), 266
Customer-focused quality, 257
Customer-response time, 271
Customer satisfaction, 265
Defect, 255
Deming Prize, 270
Excess (or unused) capacity, 276
External failure, 268
Flowchart, 263
Histogram, 258
Intangible features, 257
Internal failure, 268
Inventory carrying costs, 276
ISO 9000, 270
Just-in-time (JIT), 276
Lead indicators, 258
Lower control limit, 259
Malcolm Baldrige Quality Award, 270
Maximum quality level, 255
New product (or service) development time, 271
Optimum quality level, 255
Pareto chart, 263
Practical capacity, 276
Prevention, 266
Process capacity, 275
Production cycle time, 272
Production processes, 273
Productivity, 273
Quality dimensions, 257
Return on quality (ROQ), 255
Run*, 286
Run chart, 259
Scatter diagram, 262
Statistical control chart*, 284
Tangible features, 257
Theoretical capacity, 276
Throughput, 273
Throughput efficiency, 274
Throughput time ratio, 274
Total delight, 255
Total factor productivity, 273
Total quality management (TQM), 255
Upper control limit, 259

*In the chapter appendix

Meeting the Cost Management Challenges

1. Managing quality seems to be a general management task, so what can cost-management analysts provide to improve this important activity?

In our competitive economy, all members of organizations (private and government) need to be concerned about quality. There are several practical issues of managing and improving quality that can benefit from cost-management information. For example, some organizations have found it difficult to convince employees that they have a quality problem and that they therefore need to change practices and processes to improve quality. Cost-management analysts can demonstrate the magnitude of quality problems by benchmarking their organization's quality against internal quality goals and competitors' quality performance. They also can use the cost-of-quality report to identify and demonstrate any imbalance between costs of controlling or failing to control quality. Furthermore, because cost-management analysts can measure these effects of quality, they can have a strong and lasting impression on employees who now can see tangible evidence of the effects of quality and formulate clear quality goals. Reliable cost-management information can greatly reinforce an attitude of improving quality.

2. Is there a conflict between meeting quality and time goals, or do these goals reinforce each other?

If one were to look at each of these performance dimensions separately, they could conflict. For example, under the pressure to meet tight on-time delivery objectives, employees might cut corners on quality processes. Meeting the delivery schedule might achieve some short-term benefit, but at the cost of worsened customer satisfaction or external failure costs. This is a mistake that some companies have made in the past, but most organizations now realize that time and quality objectives can reinforce each other if companies pursue and reward them simultaneously. Mutual reinforcement is why JIT methods can be so successful—reducing process time is not possible without improvements in quality, and improving quality reduces process time by reducing testing, rework, and so on. Thus, it usually is shortsighted to try to improve process time without also improving quality, and vice versa.

3. **How** should cost-management analysts choose among all available quality and time-management tools?

There is no shortage of measures, charts, diagrams, and reports that cost-management analysts can use to study and communicate quality and time performance. Furthermore, there are many ways to present the information: text, tables, graphs, pictures, black and white, full color, and so on. Preparing too much quality and time information could be as mistaken as preparing too little. Individuals can process only so much information, and an *overload* of it can obscure or reduce the impact of any single piece of information. In other words, if presented with too much information, people just might "tune out" and put it all in the "circular file." Therefore, *cost-management analysts should find the most important quality and time information for the decisions facing their employees and the most salient way to communicate it.* Both are necessary.

For example, defects in certain product features could be the most important measures of quality in a particular situation. Cost-management analysts measure these accurately and in a timely manner but might try to communicate the information via computer spreadsheets filled to the margins with numbers. Since almost no one has the time to find the most important numbers to them among the mass of numbers presented, the quality message is lost. Although many people comprehend graphical information more easily than tabular data, no amount of effort spent on preparing fancy, full-color charts could make up for presenting the wrong quality or time data. To find the right combination of information and communication medium, cost-management analysts must first communicate with decision makers who will use the information by *listening to* what they need and by *seeking feedback* from them about the usefulness of cost-management information.

Solutions to You're the Decision Maker

7.1 Using Diagnostic Quality Information, p. 264

a. Diagnosing and improving quality cannot be divorced from the authority and responsibilities given to individuals and the way they are evaluated. In an ideal organization, individuals or groups would be able to objectively and thoroughly evaluate the causes of quality problems and act to eliminate them. Furthermore, they would be able to understand how their actions either to improve or not improve quality performance affect the rest of the organization. This is not always the case.

b. A cross-functional team can be better able to diagnose and correct quality problems than either individuals or a functional team. Both of these parties "might not see the forest for the trees" or, because of narrow evaluation criteria (e.g., this period's profits), might have incentives to hide rather than correct quality problems.

7.2 Evaluating the Cost of Quality, p. 270

a. COQ can be a valuable communication device by identifying the magnitude and types of quality problems. If this report is visible and regarded as reliable, it is hard to ignore, for example, the very high costs of activities to correct internal and external failures. COQ does not, by itself, suggest ways to eliminate these activities, but it does make their impact on profits clear.

b. Profits are still an important goal of profit-seeking organizations, so profit reports cannot be ignored. However, costs of quality are buried in costs of sales and general overhead. Furthermore, if a company uses FIFO, it is possible that current costs of quality are hidden in inventories and will not affect profits until future periods. It is probably incorrect to say that COQ is "better" than traditional profits since they measure different areas of performance. It is likely that COQ does add useful information about how the organization consumes resources, perhaps unnecessarily, to perpetuate quality problems.

c. Any numbers that become performance objectives have the appearance of being "concrete" or "hard" numbers. Some even believe that the true COQ objective is for total quality costs to be zero. What should the COQ objective be? ROQ advocates would say that some level of COQ is optimal and that it can be driven too low. Perhaps the most defensible approach is to avoid hard COQ objectives since COQ is a result of quality activities, not a measure of quality itself. One should recognize that high levels of COQ are indicative of quality problems and that competition will require improvements—but this should already be known. Quality improvements come from understanding what customers want and meeting or exceeding their expectations.

Appendix to Chapter Seven

Construction and Use of Control Charts

LO 6 Understand how to construct and use control charts (Appendix).

Control charts display measures of important product or service attributes for individual items or for a sample of items to disclose attribute measures and variation in the production process. Organizations use control charts for several purposes, including process control, assurance sampling, and inspection activities. In most cases, control charts provide multiple benefits such as (1) causing employees to directly monitor the quality of their work, (2) detecting defects quickly and at the source, and (3) providing a common, objective means of communicating the quality of a process or product.

Statistical Control

A **statistical control chart** *displays customer response times against the historical mean and historical variation*

Organizations could base control charts on historical data of attributes achieved or on desired levels of the attributes. For example, historically, one of TCSI's customer service representative's response process times have averaged 7.95 minutes over the past 16 weeks, as appears in Exhibit 7–18. Using this historical performance, TCSI could prepare a **statistical control chart,** which displays attributes, for example, customer-response times, against the historical parameters of the *mean* (7.95 minutes) and *variation.*[16] Variation usually is displayed as an interval based on the historical *range* of outcomes (high to low) or 2 or 3 *standard deviations* above and below the mean (e.g., between 10.70 and 5.19 minutes). Some experts recommend basing variation on range because it is easier to both compute for small samples and explain to employees than standard deviation. Because using the range to set the allowable interval requires access to special tables (available in all texts on quality control), we show intervals using standard deviation.

Target Control

Alternatively, TCSI could prepare a control chart based on specified or target levels of product attributes. For example, suppose that market and customer service research reveals that properly responding to a customer inquiry should take 7.5 minutes and that variation of plus or minus 2.0 minutes is within the range of acceptable service. In an ideal situation, the natural variation of a process is less than specified or target levels, but many quality problems result from natural process variation exceeding the target variation. Redesigning a process to reduce its natural variation can be more economical than imposing stricter target control levels that result in many defects, causing high levels of internal and external failure.

A control chart based on target-attribute parameters might classify a different set of outcomes as defects than would a statistical control chart. Exhibit 7–19 shows two sets of controls, statistical in blue and target in red. The horizontal lines in the middle of the chart reflect either the statistical (blue) or target (red) value of the attribute. The upper lines of the chart reflect the statistical (blue) or target (red) upper control limits (UCL). To give speedy customer service, customer-response times should not exceed the appropriate UCL level. The lower lines reflect the statistical (blue) or target (red) lower control limits (LCL). To fully consider the customer's inquiry, customer-response time should not fall below the appropriate LCL.[17]

The circled observations identify customer-response times that exceed or fall below *target* control limits. The statistical control limits, in contrast, do not identify any violations of control limits. Whether to use the tighter target limits rather than the looser statistical limits depends on the organization's estimates of the relative costs of:

- Intervening when a violation is detected (correctly or incorrectly) using tight limits. These costs include finding and correcting causes of defects, rework, delays, and even lost sales.
- Not intervening when a violation (from the customer's perspective) occurs but is not detected using loose limits. These costs include internal and external failures, which could be large.

---

[16]This form of control chart is called an $\bar{X}$ (X-bar) chart, since it is based on the historical mean, or *X*-bar. Many other forms of control chart are based on other statistical descriptions of historical or target attributes.

[17]Note that control limits do not have to be symmetrical. For example, an organization might believe that the consequences of exceeding an upper limit are worse than falling below a lower limit (or vice versa) and could set the UCL closer to the mean and the LCL farther from the mean (or vice versa).

Exhibit 7–18

Weekly Average Customer-Response Time

Transformation Customer Services, Inc.

Week	Average Response Time
1	6.89
2	7.89
3	9.60
4	7.77
5	9.70
6	8.07
7	6.62
8	6.84
9	9.13
10	9.63
11	10.13
12	5.45
13	6.29
14	7.79
15	8.12
16	7.26
Statistical Control Parameters	
Overall mean	7.95 min.
Standard deviation (SD)	1.378 min.
2 SDs	2.755 min.
UCL = Mean + 2 SD	10.70 min.
LCL = Mean − 2 SD	5.19 min.
Target Control Parameters	
Target mean	7.50 min.
Target deviation	2.00 min.
UCL = Mean + 2.00	9.50 min.
LCL = Mean − 2.00	5.50 min.

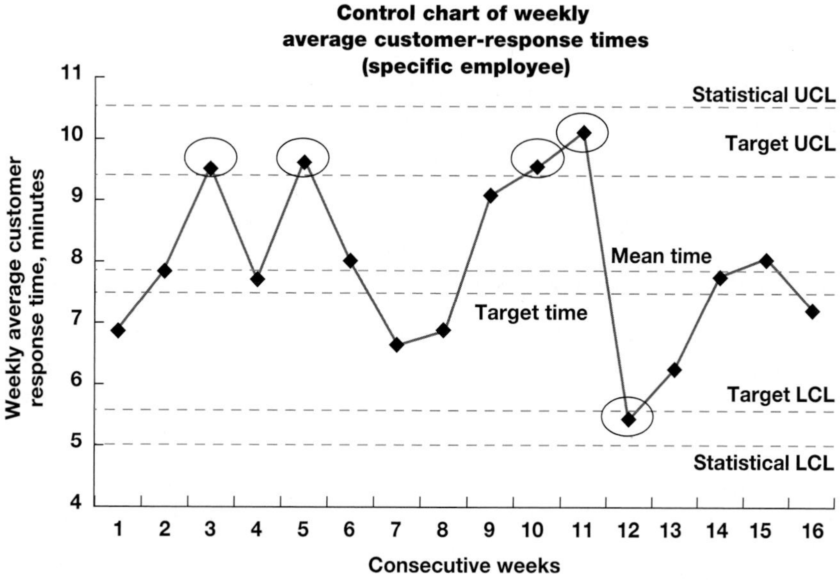

Exhibit 7–19

Control Chart of Weekly Average Customer-Response Times (specific employee)

Auditors face the same situation when deciding to perform additional auditing tests based on results of sampling transactions. For example, does a low level of confirmed account balances signal an out-of-control accounting system, or is this a chance occurrence? Considering the costs of making errors, auditors want to be able to assure users of the financial statements (and themselves!) that the financial statements fairly present the organization's status and performance.

Patterns of Variation

run *is sequential values above or below the mean or values sequentially increasing or decreasing*

A process can be out of control (exhibiting undesirable variation) even if attribute measures do not violate control limits. Attribute measures could exhibit runs, cycles, extreme jumps, or concentrations at control limits, which can signal the need for intervention or opportunities for improvement. Based on an approximately 1 percent statistical probability of a **run** (sequential values above or below the mean or values sequentially increasing or decreasing) occurring by chance, a statistically out-of-control process can be identified using the following rules of thumb:[18]

- *Seven successive values* on the same side of the mean or target.
- *Four or more successive values* outside 1 standard deviation from the mean or target.
- *Two or more successive values* outside 2 standard deviations from the mean or target.

Causes of runs include the following:

- Worker fatigue.
- Wear and deterioration of tools and equipment.
- Changes in environmental conditions.
- Accumulation of waste, scrap, and excess parts that cause congestion.
- Learning and improved use of resources.

The following can cause cyclical behavior:

- Recurring conditions (night/day, heat/cold).
- Rotation of employees, equipment, or suppliers.
- Rotation of testing and inspection.
- Periodic maintenance or training.

Causes of extreme jumps include these:

- Changes in tools, equipment, or setups.
- Change of employees.
- Changes or errors in testing or reporting procedures.

The following can cause values concentrated near control limits:

- Major differences in the quality of resources (human and physical).
- Mistakenly plotting outcomes from different processes on the same chart.

Benefits of Control Charts

Cost management analysts, industrial engineers, quality control specialists, managers, and employees in all types of organizations throughout the world have found that control charts are simple, versatile, and inexpensive tools for managing the quality of their

[18]A 1 percent chance can be too stringent; that is, the costs of not detecting an actual run can be high relative to the costs of intervening. Setting a less stringent criterion, say 5 or 10 percent, leads to fewer consecutive observations signaling a run.

products and services. If these charts are based on sound statistical evidence and compelling market research, control charts are reliable guides for controlling processes, preventing defects, and measuring quality performance.

Review Questions

7.1 Review and define each of the chapter's key terms.

7.2 Why is managing quality important?

7.3 Why is managing time important?

7.4 Why do advocates of TQM expect to earn higher profits?

7.5 What are the similarities and differences between TQM and ROQ?

7.6 What are the two dimensions of quality?

7.7 What is the major difference between tangible and intangible product features that affects management of quality?

7.8 How are process and product variations lead indicators of quality?

7.9 How do lead indicators of quality differ from diagnostic information about quality?

7.10 How does customer satisfaction differ from quality?

7.11 Is cost of quality a lead indicator or diagnostic information? Explain.

7.12 How do organizations make trade-offs among the four types of quality activities?

7.13 Is COQ more consistent with TQM or ROQ? Explain.

7.14 How are managing quality and managing time related?

7.15 Is JIT possible without high-quality processes? Explain.

7.16 What are some useful indicators of productivity? How are they measured?

7.17 What is cycle time? How is it measured?

7.18 What is throughput efficiency? How is it measured?

7.19 Explain the concept of process capacity. Use an example from the chapter to describe the capacity of a specific process.

7.20 What is the difference between theoretical and practical capacity? Why might an organization choose to operate processes at practical capacity rather than at theoretical capacity?

Critical Analysis

7.21 An engineer argues, "Quality means the product will perform faultlessly." A marketing manager retorts, "No, quality is whatever the customer says it is." Are these views conflicting? Explain.

7.22 You are discussing the importance of quality with a colleague. She says, "High quality may have been an important part of business competition in the 1980s and 1990s when quality varied across companies. Now, increasing quality is much less important than decreasing new product development time." Evaluate this comment.

7.23 In 1990, Wallace Co. won the Malcolm Baldrige Quality Award. Two years later this small oil company filed for bankruptcy. Explain how this could have happened.

7.24 Contrast these statements. Federal Express: "We're trying to isolate quality improvements that just don't add any value . . . to the customer." Hewlett-Packard: "Asking what quality is worth is like asking what my left lung is worth."

7.25 Consider your school's course-registration process. Why would goals to improve cycle time require improvements in quality?

7.26 In its marketing activities, United Airlines stresses the importance of on-time flight departures and dealing with customer complaints. Qantas Airlines stresses its safety record and in-flight service. Are both airlines concerned with quality? Explain.

7.27 Allegiance Insurance Company sends a questionnaire to policyholders that have filed a claim. The questionnaire asks them whether they are satisfied with the way the claim has been handled. What useful information does Allegiance Insurance obtain?

7.28 Why did students (in the 1960s) demand to evaluate university courses?

7.29 United Parcel Service (UPS) (*www.ups.com*) assumed that on-time delivery was the most important feature of its service and stressed (literally) its importance to UPS employees. UPS managers were confused as to why the company was not gaining market share even though customers rated the company's on-time delivery very high. Explain this apparently contrary result.

7.30 Motorola (*www.motorola.com*) has employed its Six Sigma approach to managing quality since 1987. ("Six Sigma" refers to the probability of a defect occurring based on the area under a normal probability curve that is 6 standard deviations from the mean. This probability is .0000002 percent, or only 2 defects, per million events.) The company use these six steps:

- Identify the product you create or the service you provide.
- Identify the customer(s) for your product or service and determine what they consider important.
- Identify what you need to satisfy the customer.
- Define the process for doing the work.
- Mistake-proof the process and eliminate wasted effort.
- Ensure continuous improvement by measuring, analyzing, and controlling the improved process.

Is Motorola's approach to quality more closely aligned with TQM or ROQ? Explain.

7.31 Consider the book in front of you. What are its tangible and intangible features? Are any more important than others?

Can you rate these features according to a three-point scale? Is each feature:

1 = Much better than expected?

0 = About as expected?

−1 = Worse than expected?

Should the publisher and authors of the book be interested in your ratings?

7.32 What are the similarities and differences between TQM, ROQ, and COQ? Can an organization employ all three approaches to managing quality? Explain.

7.33 Allegheny Industries' top executives are evaluated on the basis of annual profits and earnings per share. Middle managers are evaluated on the basis of cycle time and product quality. Are these evaluations consistent? Does it matter? Explain.

7.34 The chapter mentioned that a competitor of TCSI measures cycle time for only the products that pass through its processes without defects. Do you think this is necessarily a bad practice? What incentives might motivate such a practice?

7.35 Is it possible for a company to increase the throughput efficiency of one process to the point where an additional increase could reduce the company's overall profitability? If so, give an example.

7.36 Respond to this comment: "I think the way you have measured practical capacity is just an excuse to keep from trying to use our processes more efficiently. We should be trying to get as close to theoretical capacity as possible. Isn't that what is meant by 'continuous improvement'? Otherwise, aren't we wasting resources?"

7.37 Find a newspaper or magazine article about a recent transportation project (e.g., widening or adding a highway). Critically evaluate this project from a system-wide viewpoint, as discussed on p. 275.

Exercises

Exercise 7.38
Standards of Quality
(LO 1)

Internet

How do the Baldrige Quality Award (*www.quality.nist.gov*), the Deming Prize (*www.deming.org/TO/demingprizeTO.html*), and ISO 9000 (*www.iso.ch/welcome.html*) differ?

Exercise 7.39
Costs of Quality
(LO 2)

ZZK Industries manufactures zippers. The following table presents its financial information for one year:

Sales	**$450,000**
Material inspection	$ 6,500
Scrap	8,500
Employee training	13,000
Returned goods	3,000
Finished goods inspection	15,000
Processing customer complaints	8,000

Required

a. Classify these items into prevention, appraisal, internal failure, or external failure costs.

b. Prepare a cost-of-quality report for the year.

Exercise 7.40
Quality According to the Customer
(LO 1)

What are the most important customer-quality attributes for each of the following products or services?

a. Tuxedo for a bridegroom.

b. Microwave oven.

c. Accounting course at a university.

d. Cruise on a Princess ship.

e. Frozen dinner.

f. Tax return prepared by a professional.

Exercise 7.41
Quality According to the Customer
(LO 1)

What are the most important attributes of each of the following products or services?

a. Personal computer.

b. Television programming.

c. Meals in a fine restaurant.

d. Student study guides for an accounting text.

e. In-line skates.

f. Legal representation in traffic court.

Exercise 7.42
Quality According to the Customer
(LO 1)

What is the most important customer *quality trade-off* for each of the following products and services?

a. Personal computer.

b. Portable compact disc player.

c. Checking account.

d. Taxi ride through New York.

e. Personal clothing.

Exercise 7.43
Costs of Quality
(LO 2)

Spreadsheet

Vedral Industries manufactures computer printers. The following represents financial information for two years:

	Year 1	Year 2
Sales	$2,450,000	$2,200,000
Costs:		
Process inspection	16,500	18,800
Scrap	18,500	19,300
Quality training	198,000	130,000
Warranty repairs	43,000	48,000
Testing equipment	70,000	70,000
Customer complaints	28,000	34,000
Rework	170,000	185,000
Preventive maintenance	135,000	95,000
Materials inspection	65,000	48,000
Field testing	94,000	124,000

Required

a. Classify these items into costs of prevention, appraisal, internal failure, or external failure activities.

b. Calculate the ratio of the prevention, appraisal, internal failure, and external failure costs to sales for year 1 and year 2.

c. Construct a cost-of-quality report for year 1 and year 2.

Exercise 7.44
Costs of Quality
(LO 2)

Owenborrogh Corporation manufactures air conditioners. The following represents its financial information for two years.

	Year 1	Year 2
Sales	$1,960,000	$1,760,000
Costs:		
Process inspection	13,200	15,000
Scrap	14,800	15,500
Quality training	158,000	105,000
Warranty repairs	34,000	38,000
Testing equipment	56,000	56,000
Customer complaints	22,500	27,200
Rework	136,000	148,000
Preventive maintenance	108,000	76,000
Materials inspection	52,000	38,000
Field testing	75,000	99,000

Required

a. Classify these items into costs of prevention, appraisal, internal failure, or external failure activities.

b. Calculate the ratio of the prevention, appraisal, internal failure, and external failure costs to sales for year 1 and year 2.

c. Construct a cost-of-quality report for year 1 and year 2.

Exercise 7.45
Costs of Quality
(LO 2)

Ramirez Corporation manufactures refrigerators. The following represents its financial information for two years.

	Year 1	Year 2
Sales	$3,920,000	$3,520,000
Costs:		
Process inspection	26,400	30,000
Scrap	28,800	30,100
Quality training	305,000	220,000

	Year 1	Year 2
Warranty repairs	70,000	75,000
Testing equipment	115,000	115,000
Customer complaints	44,500	54,200
Rework	272,000	195,000
Preventive maintenance	220,000	152,000
Materials inspection	105,000	75,000
Field testing	150,000	200,000

Required

a. Classify these items into costs of prevention, appraisal, internal failure, or external failure activities.

b. Calculate the ratio of the prevention, appraisal, internal failure, and external failure costs to sales for year 1 and year 2.

c. Construct a cost-of-quality report for year 1 and year 2.

Exercise 7.46
Cost of Quality
(LO 2)

The following are selected operating costs for Watson Products for last month.

Warranty claims	$ 476
Design engineering	600
Supplier evaluations	450
Lost contribution margins due to poor quality	300
Quality training	500
Rework	725
Equipment maintenance	1,154
Product testing	786
Product repair	695

Required

What is Watsons' total prevention and appraisal cost for last month?

[CMA adapted]

Exercise 7.47
Quality and Time Control (Appendix)
(LO 2, 6)

S
Spreadsheet

Prepare a run chart from the following, sequential weekly cycle-time data from the manufacture of computer tape storage devices. Use the historical mean of cycle time and a 2 standard-deviation upper and lower control limit. What does this chart indicate?

Week	Average Cycle Time in Hours
1	133.4
2	158.8
3	121.9
4	120.3
5	125.8
6	133.1
7	140.7
8	122.8
9	135.7
10	165.3
11	128.1
12	103.3
13	102.5
14	101.4
15	118.9
16	127.8
17	132.2
18	135.5

Exercise 7.48
Quality and Time Control
(LO 2, 6)

Prepare a quality control chart from the following sequential, monthly cycle-time data from the manufacture of computer library devices. The desired level of performance is 140. The upper control limit is 160, and the lower control limit is 120. What does this chart indicate?

Month	Average Cycle Time in Hours
January	124.0
February	175.0
March	147.5
April	97.0
May	153.2
June	132.0
July	228.0
August	152.0
September	172.0
October	112.0
November	138.0

Exercise 7.49
Quality Control
(LO 2, 6)

Prepare a quality control chart from the following sequential, weekly test data from the manufacture of computer tape storage devices. The desired level of performance is 1.5. The upper control limit is 2.1, and the lower control limit is 1.2. What does this chart indicate?

Week	Average Test Performance
36	1.7
37	1.7
38	1.7
39	1.6
40	1.6
41	2.2
42	1.4
43	1.4
44	2.0
45	2.1
46	1.2

Exercise 7.50
Quality Control (Appendix)
(LO 6)

Prepare a quality control chart from the following sequential, weekly cycle-time data from the manufacture of computer-tape storage devices. Use the historical mean cycle time and a 2 standard-deviation upper and lower control limit. What does this chart indicate?

Week	Average Cycle Time
35	55
36	33
37	93
38	82
39	49
40	73
41	88
42	45
43	69
44	36
45	101
46	107
47	89
48	74
49	64
50	55
51	52
52	57

Exercise 7.51
Quality Control
(LO 2)

Prepare a Pareto chart using the following data on causes of adjustments to domestic and foreign customers' billings during the month of January. What does this chart indicate?

Causes of Defects	Frequency
Correction of incorrect prior adjustments	10
Miscellaneous	30
Product did not perform	12
Product prices disputed	115
Product returned	15
Product shipped by wrong priority	70
Product shipped to wrong location	30
Shipments to foreign locations	64
Wrong product shipped	20

Exercise 7.52
Quality Control
(LO 2)

Communication

Prepare a Pareto chart using the following data on causes of defects during a week's manufacture of electronic circuit boards.

Causes of Defects	Frequency
Faulty board	6
Improper sequence of components	17
Incoming components	148
Incomplete solder	29
Mounting machine alignment	64
Operator error	23
Testing error	11

Prepare a short presentation that explains what this chart indicates.

Exercise 7.53
Quality versus Cost
(LO 1)

Communication

Canadian Seltzers has discovered a problem involving its mix of flavor to seltzer water that costs the company $3,000 in waste and $2,500 in lost business per period. There are two alternative solutions. The first is to lease a new mix regulator at a cost of $4,000 per period, which would save $2,000 in waste and $2,000 in lost business. The second alternative is to hire an additional employee to manually monitor the existing regulator at a cost of $2,500 per period, saving $1,500 in waste and $1,800 in lost business per period.

Required

Prepare a memo that evaluates the two alternatives. Which alternative should Canadian choose?

Exercise 7.54
Quality versus Cost
(LO 1)

Communication

Hillman Industries has discovered a problem involving the mix of limestone in its dry concrete mix that costs the company $5,000 in waste and $3,500 in lost business per period. There are two alternative solutions. The first is to lease a new mix regulator at a cost of $3,500 per period, which would save $3,500 in waste and $2,000 in lost business. The second alternative is to hire an additional employee to manually monitor the existing regulator at a cost of $3,000 per period, saving $2,500 in waste and $2,000 in lost business per period.

Required

Prepare a memo that evaluates the two alternatives. Which alternative should Hillman choose?

Exercise 7.55
Quality versus Cost
(LO 1)

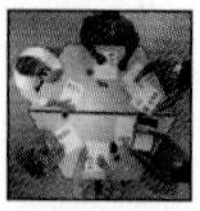

Team

Carlson Corporation has discovered a problem involving welding its bicycle frames that costs the company $3,000 in waste and $1,500 in lost business per period. There are two alternative solutions. The first is to lease a new automated welder at a cost of $3,500 per period, which would save $1,500 in waste and $1,000 in lost business. The second alternative is to hire an additional employee to manually weld the frames at a cost of $3,000 per period, which would save $2,500 in waste and $1,000 in lost business per period.

Required

Form small groups and prepare an analysis of the two alternatives. Which alternative should Carlson choose?

Exercise 7.56
Managing Time
(LO 3)

Internet

Search the Internet for an example of a company that provides outsourced services or manufacturing activities on a just-in-time basis. As a potential customer of that outsource provider, how would you evaluate whether to outsource your services or manufacturing activities to that company? How would you evaluate whether this outsourcing arrangement is beneficial to you?

Exercise 7.57
Managing Time
(LO 3)

Internet Communication

Search your library or the Internet for a research study that investigates the costs and/or benefits of adopting JIT or other time-based process-management methods. Prepare a one-page summary that describes the study's objective, its source(s) of data, and its conclusion. Prepare two questions that, if you could, you would pose to the author(s) about the study.

Exercise 7.58
Productivity
(LO 5)

Using the following information, compute the productivity measures indicated by question marks. What appears to have happened in year 5 relative to previous years?

	Year 5	Year 4	Year 3	Year 2	Year 1
Number of employees	22,230	24,400	24,100	22,000	21,800
Sales revenue ($ millions)	$2,843	$2,796	$2,669	$2,318	$1,993
Operating income ($ millions)	$468	$475	$530	$436	$303
Sales per employee	?	?	?	?	?
Total factor productivity	?	?	?	?	?

Exercise 7.59
Cycle Time
(LO 5)

From the following information, compute the average cycle time per unit of product or service and the throughput efficiencies for each month.

	January	February	March	April
Units completed	100	83	24	70
Processing time	145.3	145.3	170.4	158.4
Waiting time	2,579.5	2,477.8	1,782.7	1,525.7

Exercise 7.60
Capacity and Cycle Time
(LO 5)

Use the following data to supply information now represented by question marks. Practical capacities are 80 percent of theoretical capacities.

	A	B	C	D
Number of 40-hour shifts per week	2	3	1	2
Number of identical assembly lines	3	?	4	5
Available hours per week	?	600	?	?
Average cycle time per unit	3.5 hrs	9.5 hrs	?	?
Throughput time ratio	30%	?	40%	15%
Value-adding cycle time	?	1.9 hrs	?	?
Theoretical capacity in units	?	?	200	?
Practical capacity in units	?	?	?	1,600

Exercise 7.61
Capacity and Cycle Time
LO 5

Use the following data to supply information now represented by question marks. Practical capacities are 80 percent of theoretical capacities.

	A	B	C	D
Number of 40-hour shifts per week	1	2	2	3
Number of identical assembly lines	4	?	7	5
Available hours per week	?	400	?	?
Average cycle time per unit	6.5 hrs	11.5 hrs	?	?
Throughput time ratio	50%	?	25%	15%
Value-adding cycle time	?	1.9 hrs	?	?
Theoretical capacity in units	?	?	700	?
Practical capacity in units	?	?	?	160

Problems

Problem 7.62
Just-in-Time Process
(LO 5)

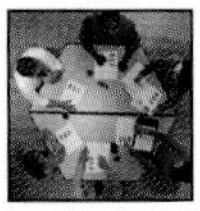

Communication Team

Individually or as a group with your classmates, interview the manager of a retail (or wholesale) store such as a music store, an automobile parts store, or the parts department of an appliance dealership. Ask the manager how items are ordered to replace those sold. For example, does he or she order based on observing inventory levels or place an order each time a customer buys an item? Does the manager appear to use just-in-time inventory? Write a brief report to your instructor summarizing the results of your interview.

Problem 7.63
Total Quality Management
(LO 1)

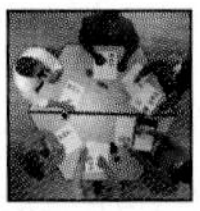

Communication Team

Individually or as a group with your classmates, interview the manager of a fast-food restaurant. Ask the manager how quality of service is measured and used to evaluate his or her performance. Write a brief report to your instructor summarizing the results of your interview.

Problem 7.64
Identification of Quality Control Problems
(LO 2)

Communication Team

Individually or as a group with your classmates, observe an organization of your choice—wholesale, retail, or service. Prepare a short report illustrating examples of lead-indicator and diagnostic signals the organization uses or could use. How could it use quality management tools such as control charts, Pareto charts, and cause-and-effect analysis?

Problem 7.65
Quality and Time Control
(LO 2, 3)

Prepare a flowchart of the following medical appointment process at a Navy medical center.

Prepare appointment book.

Open appointment book.

Is the appointment on shore or aboard ship?

If aboard ship, tell patient to call xxx-xxxx by 1500 hours (3 P.M.) to make own appointment for next working day.

If on shore, issue next available appointment to patient.

Remind patient to call 24 hours in advance to confirm appointment.

Did patient call 24 hours in advance?

If no, cancel appointment and give appointment to new patient.

If yes, give patient confirmation number.

    If yes, does patient show up for appointment?

        If yes, mark appointment book "patient showed."

        If no, mark appointment book "failure: Patient did not show."

            If no, place standby patient in appointment.

            If no, issue failure report to commanding officer.

Required

a. What is a defect in this process?

b. What does this flowchart indicate about possible sources of defects?

c. Can you recommend changes in the process to reduce defects?

Problem 7.66
Quality Control
(LO 2, 6)

Norsk Ferries operates daily round-trip voyages between Seattle and Vancouver using a fleet of three ferries, the *Sea Quill,* the *Neptune,* and the *Orcas.* The budgeted amount of fuel for each round trip is the average fuel usage, which over the last 12 months has been 150 gallons. Norsk has set the upper control limit at 180 gallons and the lower control limit at 130 gallons. The operations manager received the following report for round-trip fuel usage by the three ferries for the period:

	Number of Gallons per Round-Trip		
Trip	***Sea Quill***	***Neptune***	***Orcas***
1	156	155	146
2	141	141	156
3	146	144	167
4	152	161	156
5	156	138	183
6	161	170	177
7	167	149	189
8	186	159	171
9	173	152	176
10	179	140	185

Required

a. Create quality control charts for round-trip fuel usage for each of the three ferries for the period. What inferences can you draw from them?

b. Some managers propose that Norsk present its quality control charts in monetary terms rather than in physical amount (gallons) terms. What are the advantages and disadvantages of using monetary fuel costs rather than gallons in the quality control charts?

Problem 7.67
Inventory Management
(LO 5)

Communication

Consider the following annual information about three companies in the same manufacturing industry.

Company	A	B	C
Production method	JIT	JIT	Traditional
Sales revenue	$327,000,000	$584,000,000	$8,508,000,000
No. of employees	1,600	3,600	29,500
Cost of goods sold	$245,000,000	$414,000,000	$5,191,000,000
Inventories (average)	$ 5,700,000	$ 13,500,000	$ 763,000,000

Required

a. Compare the three companies' uses of human and inventory resources.

b. Assuming a 10 percent cost of capital, what are the relative cost advantages of the most efficient user of inventories relative to the others?

c. Assume that you are a cost-management analyst employed by the least efficient user of inventories. At the request of the company CEO, prepare a short report that analyzes the relative cost advantages and outlines the types of costs and benefits that your company should expect by adopting JIT production.

Problem 7.68
Qualitative Evaluation of JIT
(LO 5)

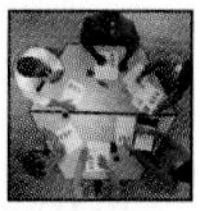

Communication Team

Toyota is credited with refining the practice of JIT. In Japan, it benefits greatly by having most of its suppliers in close proximity because suppliers are able to provide parts and materials almost instantaneously. A Fortune 500 manufacturing company in the center of the United States, which is separated by long distances from most suppliers, instituted JIT practices within local operations but found it necessary to maintain a large, computerized, central warehouse.

Required

Form small groups to consider the following:

a. How could this company benefit from JIT even though it must maintain a costly inventory warehouse? Describe several examples of benefits this company could experience from its application of JIT.

b. Prepare a short presentation that outlines a method for this company to determine whether the benefits from JIT outweigh the costs.

Problem 7.69
Quantitative and Qualitative Evaluation of JIT
(LO 5)

Your manufacturing company is considering adopting JIT production. You have gathered the following annual data, which you believe are relevant to the decision. For this analysis, ignore any initial investment costs necessary to start JIT.

- Average inventory will decline by \$1,200,000, from \$1,500,000 to \$300,000
- Current inventory handling, receiving, storing, and insuring costs are 12 percent of average inventory value plus \$200,000. The committed portion will decline by \$90,000 by transferring three employees to other work. Employee turnover in this area is approximately one-third per year. If any of these employees leaves the company, they will not be replaced.
- Annual costs of quality should change as follows:
  - Prevention (additional training, improved supplier relations)—increase by \$250,000
  - Inspection (employee time and testing equipment)—increase by \$160,000
  - Internal failure (rework, delays)—decrease by \$280,000
  - External failure (lost sales, warranty claims)—decrease by \$210,000.
- Tooling and setup costs will increase by \$140,000 per year
- Opportunity cost of capital tied up in inventory is 10 percent per year

Required

a. What is your estimate of the net annual quantifiable cost or benefit from your company's adopting JIT?

b. What qualitative factors should you consider before deciding this JIT issue?

Problem 7.70
Productivity and External Benchmarks
(LO 4)

Communication Internet

You are a newly hired cost manager for United Airlines (UAL) and are beginning to analyze its competitive position. You believe a good place to begin is to compare UAL's and other airlines' total factor productivity.

Required

a. Gather the most recently available, annual information for the US domestic airline industry similar to that used to prepare Exhibit 7–12 (total factor productivity). Look for the information in your library or on the Internet (for example, search *www.hoovers.com* using the keyword "airline"). Prepare a chart for the US domestic airline industry similar to Exhibit 7–12. (*Note:* This requirement can be completed more easily using spreadsheet software than by hand.)

b. Write a short memo to your CFO describing UAL's relative total factor productivity in the industry.

Problem 7.71
Productivity and Internal Benchmarks
(LO 4)

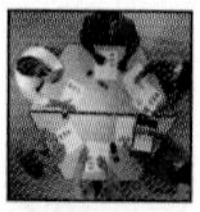

Communication Team

As part of a cost-management analysis team at United Airlines (UAL), you are analyzing its changes in productivity over time. A common measure of airline productivity is the passenger load factor, which is the number of revenue passenger miles (1 ticketed seat flown 1 mile) divided by the number of available seat miles (1 seat mile = 1 seat flown × 1 mile). For example, one flight of a Boeing 737 with 126 seats from Denver to Washington, D.C., a distance of 1,464 miles, generates 184,464 (126 × 1,464) available seat miles. If the flight carries 117 paying passengers, it generates 171,288 (117 × 1,464) revenue passenger miles. This single passenger load factor is 92.8 per cent (171,288 ÷ 184,464, or 117 ÷ 126). You have gathered the following operating data (in millions except for aircraft and employees). (*Note:* This type of data is available from many companies' annual reports. These data can be analyzed with spreadsheet software.)

Selected Operating Data	1999	1998	1997	1996	1995
Revenue passengers	87	87	84	82	79
Revenue passenger miles	125,465	124,609	121,426	116,697	111,811
Available seat miles	176,686	174,008	169,110	162,843	158,569
Number of aircraft	594	577	575	564	558
Number of employees	96,000	91,000	90,000	86,000	81,000

Required

a. Compute and graph UAL's passenger load factor for the years 1993 to 1997. Prepare a group comment on what this analysis says about UAL's productivity over time.

b. Prepare a group analysis of whether these additional data offer any more insights about UAL's productivity over time.

Problem 7.72
Cycle Time and Throughput Efficiency
(LO 3)

Insurance companies spend considerable resources on processing claims (which results in a claim denial or payment to cover a loss). Short, accurate processing is desirable because both customers and the company benefit by resolving claims satisfactorily and by using minimum resources to do so. To improve its insurance claims processing, Global Insurance Company began a pilot project in its Northwest Region claims office to track the time to process each new automobile loss claim during a recent quarter. Processing time begins when a company representative receives a claim and ends when the final settlement is reached. Following are time data related to processing these claims at the company's Northwest Region.

			Average 8-Hour Days Spent in				
Days to Complete	Percent	Number	Processing by Adjusters	Waiting for Adjusters	Waiting for Information	Revisions and Corrections	Average Cycle Time in Days
0–10	4%	11,520	0.25	3.50	4.10	0.12	7.97
11–20	10	28,800	0.34	8.10	10.10	0.11	18.65
21–30	30	86,400	0.65	9.40	15.20	0.15	25.40
31–40	24	69,120	1.30	9.10	25.60	0.28	36.28
41–50	19	54,720	2.40	11.90	31.40	0.44	46.14
51–60	8	23,040	2.90	12.30	38.20	0.88	54.28
More than 60	5	14,400	3.10	11.50	49.70	2.60	66.90
Total	100%	288,000					

Required

a. Compute the overall average cycle time and throughput efficiency ratio in total and for each stage of processing for automobile loss claims during the quarter. (*Note:* These data can be easily analyzed with a computer spreadsheet.)

b. Comment on the apparent cause(s) of long cycle times and low throughput efficiencies.

c. What recommendation would you make to Global Insurance Company to improve its processing of automobile loss claims?

Problem 7.73
Cycle Time and Quality
(LO 3)

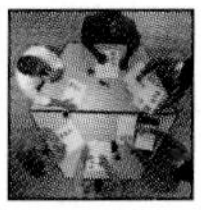

Communication Team

You are concerned that your company is understating its cycle time and throughput efficiency by measuring the cycle time for only those products completed without any defects. Products that are reworked or scrapped (because they cannot be made serviceable) are accounted for separately and removed from cycle time statistics. To understand the impact of this practice, you have decided to track the production of a typical product, Model DAD4700, over the course of four months. Sixteen different workgroups (each composed of approximately 7 to 10 employees) work on different stages of the product (and similar products). Three workgroups of 8 employees each do nothing but analyze and rework defective products (of all types) after the regular workgroups have completed them. You have gathered the following data on the DAD4700 over the past four months. (*Note:* These data can be more easily analyzed with spreadsheet software than by hand.)

Regular Workgroups	January	February	March	April
Units completed without rework	198	134	117	189
Assembly time for good units	1,809.70	1,293.60	1,105.60	1,714.20
Total cycle time for good units	4,994.70	4,791.05	3,397.06	2,891.13

Regular Workgroups	January	February	March	April
Units reworked successfully	10	8	5	13
Units scrapped	1	0	2	0
Rework time for all reworked units	57.20	43.20	54.60	48.60
Total rework cycle time	161.30	153.00	186.40	158.40

Required

a. Compute the average cycle time per unit and the throughput efficiency for good units produced by regular workgroups for each month and overall.

b. Compute the total cycle time and the throughput efficiency for units reworked successfully by rework workgroups for each month and overall. (*Hint:* Recall that these defective units were completed by regular workgroups first; an assumption is necessary.)

c. Compute the cycle times and the throughput efficiencies for each month for good and reworked products combined.

d. Prepare a group comment on the practice of computing separate cycle times and throughput efficiencies for good and reworked products.

e. What is your group's opinion about having separate workgroups perform all rework of defective products?

Problem 7.74
Capacity Management
(LO 4)

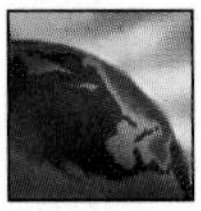
Global

Communication

Rob Barkell, CFO of Monarch Electrical Corp., has asked you to estimate the benefits of changing the company's current production process to a design based on published data from a British electrical manufacturer. The British firm reported the following data for one of its circuit breaker assemblies. You have comparable information about the production of your Monarch's similar products (fourth column).

Production Item	Old British Circuit Breaker Process	New British Circuit Breaker Process	Monarch's Current Process
Average cost of parts and materials inventory	£24,300	£18,000	$110,000
Average cost of orders in process	£12,000	£375	$90,000
Cycle time per unit	20 hr.	35 min.	23 hr.
Number of employees	21	16	33
Production floor area	109 m.²	30 m.²	1,000 ft.²
Output in units per day	330	345	420
Value-adding cycle time percentage	2%	63%	3%

Required

a. If Monarch copied the British firm's approach to managing its processes, what percentage of improvement in each production item could it expect? What new levels of each item could Monarch expect?

b. Is there a relationship between average work-in-process inventory and cycle time? Explain.

c. Monarch Electrical has a goal to earn a 20 percent before-tax return on all its resources. In other words, a resource costing $1,000 per year should earn $200 of profit annually before taxes. Prepare a memo to Barkell explaining that money tied up in inventory cannot be earning that return, so the 20 percent profit that is not earned is an opportunity cost of inventory. What is the opportunity cost of Monarch's inventory for this single product under current conditions? What is the dollar benefit of achieving reduced inventories by adopting the new production approach?

[Adapted from R. C. Barker, "Production Systems without MRP: A Lean Time-Based Design."]

Problem 7.75
Manufacturing Process Improvements
(LO 4)

Southern Cross Electrical, located in the state of Victoria, Australia, recently implemented changes to improve its manufacturing operations. Following are average process statistics before and after changes to one of the company's processes.

Item	Previous Process	Current Process	Percentage Change
Cost of orders in process	$ 5,568	$ 1,377	(75.3%)
Cycle time per unit	16 hr.	2 hr.	(87.5)
Labor time per unit	4.45 min.	3.4 min.	(23.6)
Distance traveled in meters through the process	11.75 m.	5.5 m.	(53.2)
Floor area in meters used	36 sq. m.	12 sq. m.	(66.7)

Required

a. Explain how each of these changes could improve Southern Cross Electrical's profitability.

b. What are possible nonfinancial impacts of the process changes?

c. What decisions would Southern Cross Electrical's managers have to make for the company to benefit financially from these process improvements?

Cases

Case 7.76
Quality Improvement
(LO 1)

Team

Billington Corporation makes bicycle frames in two processes, tube cutting and welding. The tube-cutting and welding processes have a practical capacity of 150,000 and 100,000 units per year, respectively. Committed costs of quality activities follow:

Design of product and process costs	$220,000
Inspection and testing costs	85,000

The demand is very strong. Billington can sell all output it can produce at $180 per frame. It begins producing only 100,000 units in the tube-cutting department because of the capacity constraint on the welding process; any defective units it produces are scrapped. Of the 100,000 units started at the tube-cutting department, 1,000 units (1 percent) normally are scrapped. (Scrap is detected at the end of the tube-cutting operation.) Full costs, based on total manufacturing costs incurred through the tube-cutting operation, equal $105 per unit:

Direct materials (variable per unit)	$ 88
Direct manufacturing, setup, and materials handling labor	7
Equipment, rent, and other overhead (fixed for the year)	10
Full cost per unit	$105

The tube-cutting department sends its good units to the welding department. Unit-level manufacturing costs at the welding department are $43.50 per unit. Welders are very highly trained, and the welding department has no scrap. Therefore, Billington's total sales quantity equals the tube-cutting department's output. Billington's designers are considering several alternative improvements to reduce scrap in the tube-cutting department.

Alternative 1: Leaving the process unchanged but starting enough units in the tube-cutting department so that the welding department can operate at practical capacity.

Alternative 2: Using a different type of tubing that is more resistant to damage and would reduce scrap by 80 percent. It would increase the unit-level costs per unit in the tube-cutting department by $10 but would reduce costs in the welding department by $5.

Alternative 3: Spending an additional amount on training to reduce scrap in the tube-cutting process.

Required

Form small groups to respond to each of the following items:

a. Which alternative—1 or 2—is more attractive financially?

b. How much would the company be willing to spend on training and how much would scrap have to be reduced to make alternative 3 as attractive as either alternative 1 or 2?

c. What other qualitative factors should Billington consider in making the decision?

Case 7.77
Quality Management
(LO 1)

Communication

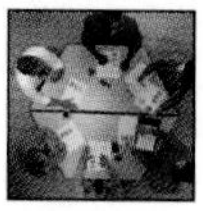
Team

MBNA Corporation is one of the most successful banks in the world and is second in size in the United States only to Citicorp. Like traditional banks, MBNA takes deposits and makes loans, but it has no branch banks, no commercial loans, and only a small number of checking accounts. MBNA specializes in making loans to individuals through a credit card. Credit cards are commodities, but MBNA differentiates itself by the way it attracts and retains the highest-quality customers.

Each of MBNA's 14.4 million customers on average carries an account balance that is more than $1,000 (45 percent) higher than the industry average, has average transactions that are $45 (47 percent) higher than the industry average, and has a loan default loss that is 40 percent lower than the industry average. Its customer retention rate is 97 percent, compared to the industry average of 89 percent.

One of the largest credit-card issuers in the world, MBNA states that through the use of advanced information technology, "We can control every aspect of our customer relationships and ensure consistency and quality in the delivery of our products. In 1997, MBNA's systems efficiently handled 12.5 billion online transactions, 120 million customer payments, 17 million requests for credit cards, and 192 million customer statements and letters." MBNA monitors 70 quality measures daily and evaluates its employees on 14 of them daily.

Required

In small groups or individually, respond to the following items:

a. How does MBNA Corporation define quality?

b. Examine MBNA's homepage and describe how the company attracts its customers.

c. What are the advantages and disadvantages of controlling variation and quality of services as closely as MBNA does?

d. Prepare a written evaluation of whether MBNA's approach to managing quality is desirable in all organizations.

[Adapted from the company's Web site, *www.mbnainternational.com* and various articles from *Business Week*.]

Case 7.78
Analysis of Development Time in the Automobile Industry
(LO 3)

Global

An analysis of the process of developing a new model automobile identified six major development activities, which together define a new model's product development lead time.

1. *Concept generation*—conducting marketing research and combining it with technical possibilities into a product concept to meet future market needs.
2. *Product planning*—translating the concept into product design, styling, and target costs.
3. *Advanced engineering*—conducting basic research to extend technical possibilities.
4. *Product engineering*—developing parts, components, and detailed, feasible designs.
5. *Process engineering*—translating product designs into manufacturing processes.
6. *Pilot run*—testing the manufacturability of the product and process performance.

The study also revealed significant differences in both the average overall product development lead time and the individual activities for high-volume automobile manufacturers in three major regions: the United States, Europe, and Japan. These differences appear in the following comparative Gantt charts which show average time before the start of product sales for each major development activity.

Required

a. Describe the overall and specific development lead-time differences among the three types of manufacturers. What appear to be the most important differences in development lead time?

b. How can shorter development lead times result in competitive advantages for Japanese producers?

c. What factors other than lead time do you think are important for successful development of new products?

d. Explain how you would begin to analyze a typical US product development process with the objective of significantly reducing development lead time.

[Adapted from: K. Clark and T. Fujimoto, *Product Development Performance: Strategy, Organization, and Management in the World Auto Industry*.]

a. U.S. new product development lead time

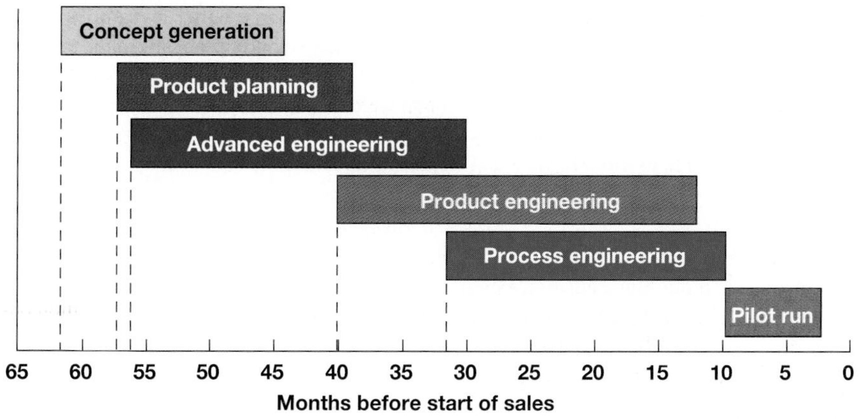

b. European new product development lead time

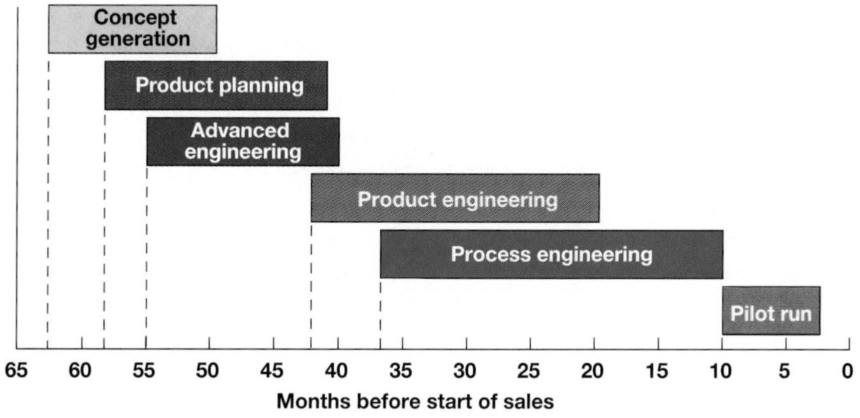

c. Japanese new product development lead time

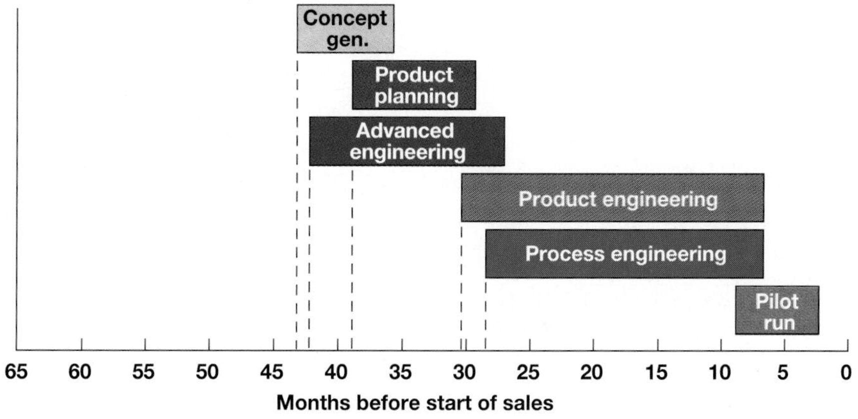

Case 7.79
Qualitative and Quantitative Evaluation of JIT production Costs and Benefits
(LO 5)

You are an analyst employed by a manufacturer that has traditionally produced large batches of identical items based on long-range sales forecasts. The company has maintained large buffer inventories to accommodate unforeseen fluctuations in demand and seemingly inevitable quality problems in the production process, which would result in significant rework and production delays without buffer inventory. Other members of the industry are adopting JIT production methods that are expensive to implement but are much more flexible and require fewer inventories to support production and sales. Your company is beginning to lose market share to its more flexible and efficient competitors.

Required

a. Is the decision for the company to follow its competitors and adopt JIT production something that top management should make and announce to the company as a competitive necessity?

b. Assume that you have been appointed as the leader of a team that will analyze the costs and benefits of adopting JIT and make a recommendation to top management. What type of team do you prefer, and who should be its members?

c. Given the following representative data, what is your estimate of the net annual quantifiable cost or benefit from your company's adopting JIT? Use the format of Exhibit 1–3 of Chapter 1. (For this analysis, ignore any initial investment costs necessary to start JIT, although they can be quite large and must be considered for any final decision.)

- Average inventory will decline by $500,000, from $800,000 to $300,000.
- Current inventory carrying costs are estimated to be 15 percent of average inventory value plus $100,000. The variable portion will decline to 12 percent, and the committed portion used will decline to $60,000 by transferring an employee to other work.
- Costs of quality should change as follows:
- *Prevention* (additional training, improved supplier relations)—increase by $120,000.
- *Inspection* (employee time and testing equipment)—increase by $90,000.
- *Internal failure* (rework, delays)—decrease by $156,000.
- *External failure* (lost sales, warranty claims)—decrease by $185,000.
- Tooling and setup costs will increase by $80,000 per year.
- Opportunity cost of capital tied up in inventory is 10 percent per year.

d. What qualitative factors should you, your team, and your company consider before deciding the JIT issue?

PART

III

Process Costing and Cost Allocation

A Look Back

Part II discusses cost management tools to help understand production processes.

A Look at This Part

Part III discusses several tried and true cost accounting and management techniques. Chapter 8 discusses process costing. Chapter 9 discusses cost determination and management in joint processes. Chapter 10 discusses the allocation of support department costs to production departments.

A Look Ahead

The next part discusses methods of developing and using cost information for decision making.

CHAPTER

8

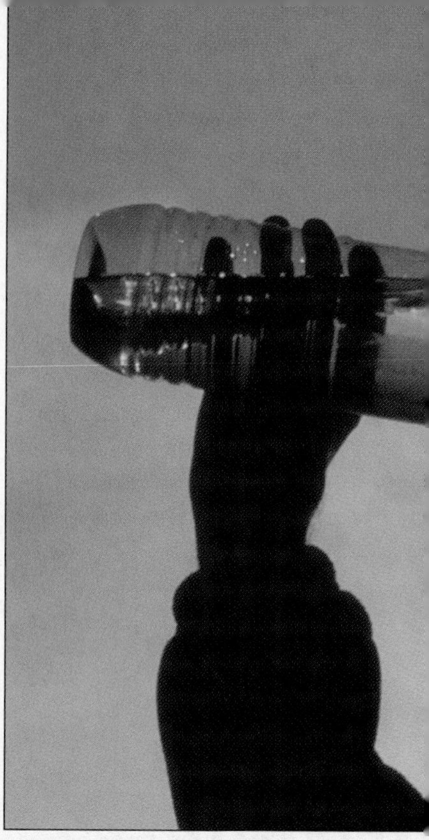

Process-Costing Systems

After completing this chapter, you should be able to:

1. Recognize organizations that should use process costing and those that should use job costing.
2. Explain why process-costing information is useful.
3. Use the five-step costing method to assign process costs to products.
4. Assign process costs to products using weighted-average costing.
5. Account for costs transferred between processes.
6. Analyze and manage "normal" and "abnormal" spoilage.
7. Assign process costs to products using first-in, first-out (FIFO) costing (Appendix A).
8. Compare and contrast the results from weighted-average and FIFO costing (Appendix A).
9. Compare and contrast operation costing with job costing and process costing (Appendix B).

Cost-Management Challenges

1. **How** should Spirit Beverages measure the costs of products, services, and operations?
2. **How** should organizations recognize and measure the costs of spoilage and waste?
3. (Appendix A) **What** is the advantage of first-in, first-out (FIFO) process costing over weighted-average process costing?

Fernando Martinez, the newly hired chief financial officer of Spirit Beverages, sent the following e-mail message to the company's other three senior executives, Sara Engle, chief executive officer; Nasreen Khan, vice president of operations; and Jay Zhou, vice president of marketing.

SPIRIT Beverages

Date: Thurs 17 April 20x3 14:38:39
To: Engle, Khan, Zhou
From: FM
Subject: Plans for developing a financial system

By now you have seen the poor results in last quarter's financial statements. I hope to develop a sound financial system within the next 60 days that will provide us the information needed to turn the situation around. Clearly, you all have done what is necessary to develop a quality product and a strong market. It's my task to improve cost management.

I would like to set a meeting at 10:00 (A.M.) on Friday, 25 April, to outline my plans. My initial thought is that we need to develop a good process-costing information system that fits our type of production process and will tell us our product costs. Knowing our product costs will help us to set prices, particularly for special deals and promotions, and to find ways to reduce costs. Once that basic process-costing system is in place, we can ascertain whether we need to go further, for example, to develop an activity-based costing system. As part of the initial process-costing system, we will get a better handle on whether spoilage in the production process is adding significantly to our costs. I suspect that it is.

Spirit Beverages, Inc., makes a sport drink Spirit, a fortified soft drink that competes with Snapple, Gatorade, and Amino, among others. Spirit Beverages is a closely held company managed by three people who had been college roommates. The company got off to a good start because of good marketing and a quality product, but its financial management system was virtually nonexistent. After three years of successful market growth, the company still had not made a profit. ("You'd think we were a dot.com," complained Sara Engle, one of the founders.) Rather than sell out to a big corporation, the three founders decided to bring in some financial talent, namely, a former consultant with Deloitte & Touche, Fernando Martinez, to try to turn success in marketing into profitable operations.

Introduction to Process Costing

LO 1 Recognize organizations that should use process costing and those that should use job costing.

Chapter 2 discussed issues in designing product-costing systems, and Chapter 3 dealt with product costing in organizations that produce jobs. This chapter focuses on process-costing methods.

As defined in Chapter 3, *process costing* treats all units processed during a time period as the output to be costed and does not separate and record costs for each unit produced. Organizations that produce products in a continuous-flow use process costing including Coca-Cola (cola concentrate), Sherwin-Williams (paint), Royal Dutch Shell (petrochemicals), and Kellogg (cereal).

Job shops record costs for specific jobs. In continuous-flow production, costs are first recorded for each department and then are assigned to the units (for example, gallons of cola concentrate) passing through the department. We show this distinction between job costing and process costing in Exhibit 8–1; note that at the bottom for

Exhibit 8–1 Comparison of Job and Process Costing

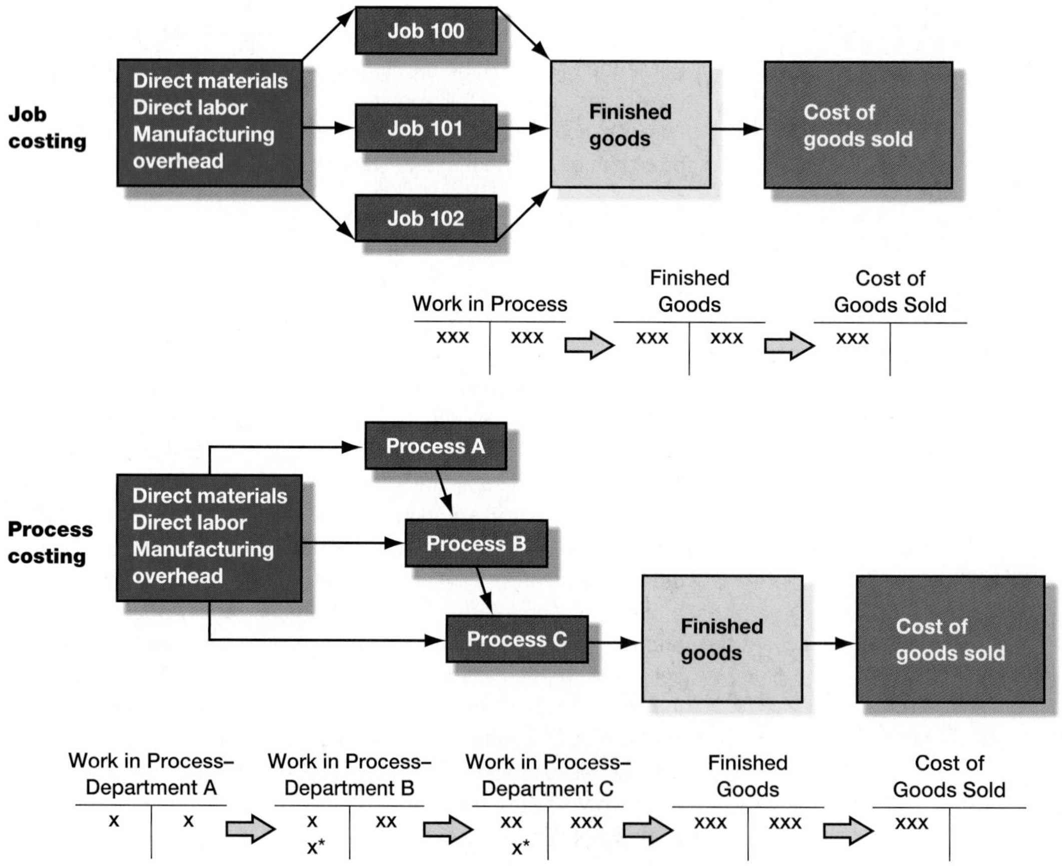

*Direct materials, labor and manufacturing overhead added in production in the department.

process costing, costs are added to the product as it passes through each department. (Although the illustration shows the product passing through each department sequentially, some products might skip departments in practice. In some cases, products could even recycle back through departments if the work was not done right the first time.)

Manufacturing CDs is an example of a continuous process.

Importance of Process Cost Information

LO 2 Explain why process-costing information is useful.

Process costing is vitally important to companies in many ways.[1] The costs assigned to products are commonly used to help set prices, particularly in periods of severe competition or economic downturn. Product costs also are used to identify which products appear to be too costly and need to be redesigned or dropped. Costs assigned to products often are used to determine inventory value for financial reporting. Managers can use product costs to evaluate the efficiency of production operations.

Assignment of Costs to Products

LO 3 Use the five-step costing method to assign process costs to products.

We discuss process costing using five examples, starting from the simplest situation and building to a more complex, realistic one. These examples are adaptable to all possible process-costing situations. These examples use just two categories of resource costs, direct materials and conversion costs, to keep the examples as simple as possible. Recall from Chapter 2 that *direct materials* are resources such as raw materials, parts, and components that one can feasibly observe being made into a specific product and that *conversion costs* include direct labor and manufacturing overhead. Conversion costs can apply to all levels of the cost hierarchy. For example, temporary labor is typically a unit-level conversion cost, and machine setup is an example of a batch-level conversion cost.

To present the five-step costing method to assign process costs to products, we use a number of examples, going from a simple scenario to more complex ones.

Example 1: Department with No Beginning or Ending WIP Inventory

We begin with a simple scenario: no beginning or ending work-in-process (WIP) inventory. This is common for companies that successfully use just-in-time production. Some companies schedule production so that they will have no inventory at the end of a day because work in process could deteriorate or spoil. (Consider a fast-food restaurant leaving partially completed hamburgers, french fries, and milkshakes overnight.)

Spirit Beverages produces a sports drink that it sells to retail stores (such as convenience stores and grocery stores). During October, the Blending Department, which

SPIRIT Beverages

[1] For examples of cost management in process companies, see "Targeting Costs in Process and Service Industries." (Full citations to references are in the Bibliography.)

had no beginning inventory, started 8,000 units (one "unit" is one four-pack of bottles). The following were the plant's manufacturing costs for October:

Direct materials	$16,000
Conversion costs	5,600
Total costs to be assigned	$21,600

All units placed into production in October were completed at the end of the month. The unit cost of goods completed is $2.70 (= $21,600 ÷ 8,000). Broken into components, manufacturing unit costs are as follows:

Direct materials ($16,000 ÷ 8,000)	$2.00
Conversion costs ($5,600 ÷ 8,000)	.70
Manufacturing unit cost of a completed unit	$2.70

As shown, process-costing systems do not track costs for each individual unit. Instead, they average the period's costs over its production. Consequently, managers should realize that if they have experienced large cost increases (or decreases) during the month, the average unit costs probably are out of line with the unit costs they face at the end of the month. In cases where costs changed a lot and quickly, managers should insist on weekly or even daily computations of unit costs.

Example 2: Department with Ending WIP Inventory

The facts for the second scenario are the same as for the first one except that at the end of October, only 6,000 of the 8,000 units started had been completed and transferred out of production. These 6,000 units were either sold or are in the finished goods warehouse at the end of October. All direct materials had been added to each of the 2,000 units still in process at the end of the month, but on average only 20 percent of the conversion costs had been incurred for the 2,000 units in ending WIP inventory. At the end of October, how should the Blending Department calculate the cost of (1) the 6,000 completed units and (2) the 2,000 units still in WIP inventory and not yet completed?

We assign costs to ending WIP inventory and to units completed (transferred out of WIP inventory) in five steps. These steps follow:

1. Summarize the flow of physical units.
2. Compute the equivalent number of units produced.
3. Summarize the total costs to be accounted for; these are the sums of the costs in beginning inventory and the costs incurred in the department during the period.
4. Compute costs per equivalent unit.
5. Assign costs to goods transferred out (completed) and to ending WIP inventory (not completed).

Step 1

For *step 1,* summarize the flow of physical units, using the basic cost-flow model to help account for units:

Beginning inventory + Transfers in − Transfers out = Ending inventory

This example has no beginning inventory. Transfers in (or units started) total 8,000 units and transfers out (to finished goods) total 6,000 units. Thus, ending WIP inventory is 2,000 units (= 0 units of beginning inventory + 8,000 units started − 6,000 units transferred out).

equivalent units
represent the amount of work actually performed on products not yet complete translated to the work required to complete an equal number of whole units

Step 2

Step 2 requires us to understand the concept of **equivalent units,** which represent the amount of work actually performed on products not yet complete translated to the work required to complete an equal number of whole units. This concept is one of the keys to

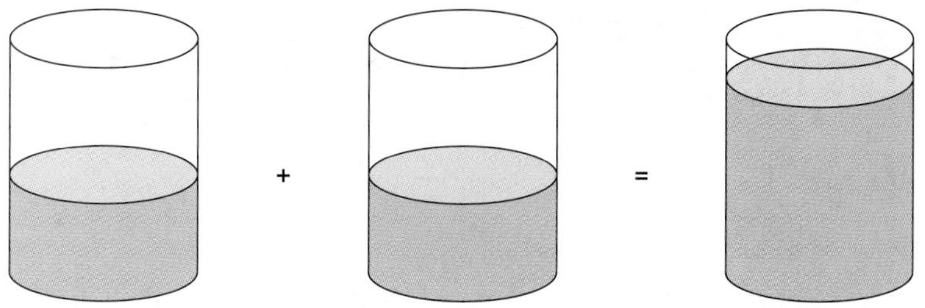

1/2 unit + 1/2 unit = 1 equivalent unit

Exhibit 8–2
Equivalent Unit Concept

Exhibit 8–3
Equivalent Units

Flow of Units	(Step 1) Physical Units	(Step 2) Equivalent Units: Direct Materials	(Step 2) Equivalent Units: Conversion Costs
Units to be accounted for:			
Beginning work-in-process inventory	0		
Units started this period	8,000		
Total units to be accounted for	8,000		
Units accounted for:			
Completed and transferred out	6,000	6,000	6,000
In ending work-in-process inventory	2,000	2,000	400*
Total units accounted for	8,000	8,000	6,400

*2,000 units × 0.20 complete.

process costing. According to this concept, if two units were started at the beginning of a month and each was 50 percent finished at the end of the month, the work performed would be considered equivalent to the work performed to complete one whole unit. Thus, for process-costing purposes, the two half-finished units equal one equivalent unit. The equivalent unit concept is shown in Exhibit 8–2 using two half-full glasses of water.

Many organizations use the equivalent unit (EU) concept. For example, university administrators often count the number of students in a department in terms of *full-time equivalents.* Two half-time students are considered to be one full-time equivalent.

Now we perform step 2 for Spirit Beverages. All direct materials have been added to each unit still in process, and only 20 percent of conversion costs have been incurred. The following describes this situation:

- EU for direct materials totaled 8,000.
- EU for conversion costs totaled 6,400 units [6,000 completed and transferred to finished goods + 400 remaining in work in process (= 2,000 × .20 complete for conversion costs)].

Exhibit 8–3 summarizes steps 1 and 2 for Spirit Beverages.

Note that direct materials just happen to be 100 percent complete with respect to ending WIP inventory in this example. In reality, direct materials might be added throughout the production process and therefore be partially complete for ending WIP inventory. If so, materials are treated the way the conversion costs are treated in this example.

Steps 3, 4, and 5

Steps 3, 4, and *5* provide managers the key cost information that appears in Exhibit 8–4 for Spirit Beverages.

- Step 3 summarizes the costs to be accounted for. It shows no beginning WIP inventory. Current period costs are separated into direct materials and conversion costs.

Exhibit 8–4
Production Costs

Flow of Costs	Total	Direct Materials	Conversion Costs
Costs to be accounted for (Step 3):			
Costs in beginning work-in-process inventory	0	0	0
Current period costs	$21,600	$16,000	$5,600
Total costs to be accounted for	**$21,600**	**$16,000**	**$5,600**
Costs per equivalent unit (Step 4)		$ 2*	$0.875†
Costs accounted for (Step 5):			
Costs assigned to units transferred out	$17,250	$12,000‡	$5,250§
Cost of ending inventory	4,350	4,000#	350**
Total costs accounted for	**$21,600**	**$16,000**	**$5,600**

*$2 = $16,000 ÷ 8,000 EU from Exhibit 8–3.
†$.875 = $5,600 ÷ 6,400 EU from Exhibit 8–3.
‡$12,000 = $2 × 6,000 EU from Exhibit 8–3.
§$5,250 = $.875 × 6,000 EU from Exhibit 8–3.
#$4,000 = $2 × 2,000 EU from Exhibit 8–3.
**$350 = $.875 × 400 EU from Exhibit 8–3.

- Step 4 shows that total current period costs are divided by equivalent units to determine costs per equivalent unit. These unit costs are useful for managers in making pricing and other decisions such as whether to keep or drop products.
- Step 5 shows costs assigned to units completed and transferred out and to units in ending WIP inventory. This information helps managers know how much money is tied up in inventory at the end of the period.

Now that you have learned how to account for costs in a process-costing system under two relatively simple scenarios—one with no beginning or ending WIP inventory, and the other with ending WIP inventory but no beginning WIP inventory—we now discuss the more complex task of accounting for costs when both beginning *and* ending WIP inventory exists.

Example 3: Department with Beginning and Ending WIP Inventory

LO 4 Assign process costs to products using weighted-average costing.

weighted-average costing *is an inventory method that for product-costing purposes combines costs and equivalent units of a period with the costs and the equivalent units in beginning inventory*

Companies generally use one of two process-costing methods to assign costs to inventories when they have beginning inventory: first-in, first-out (FIFO) or weighted-average. You probably have heard these terms before in other accounting classes. The basic idea here is the same as those you learned there.

Weighted-average costing combines the costs in beginning inventory with costs incurred during the period to compute unit costs. Many regard the weighted-average method as easier to learn and apply in practice, so we discuss it first. We present FIFO costing in Appendix A.

To illustrate accounting for process costing using weighted-average costing, let's use the Spirit Beverages example but change some facts, which are shown in panel A of Exhibit 8–5. It also shows a diagram of unit flows for the Blending Department for the month of December. These are the facts:

- The department had 2,000 units in beginning WIP inventory, which it finished during the month.
- Of the 12,000 units started in December, 8,000 were finished; the remaining partially completed 4,000 units were left in ending WIP inventory.

For weighted-average costing, we do not have to know which of the finished units were from beginning inventory and which were started and finished in the current period. This saves considerable time and effort both in textbook problems and in real-world applications.

Exhibit 8–5

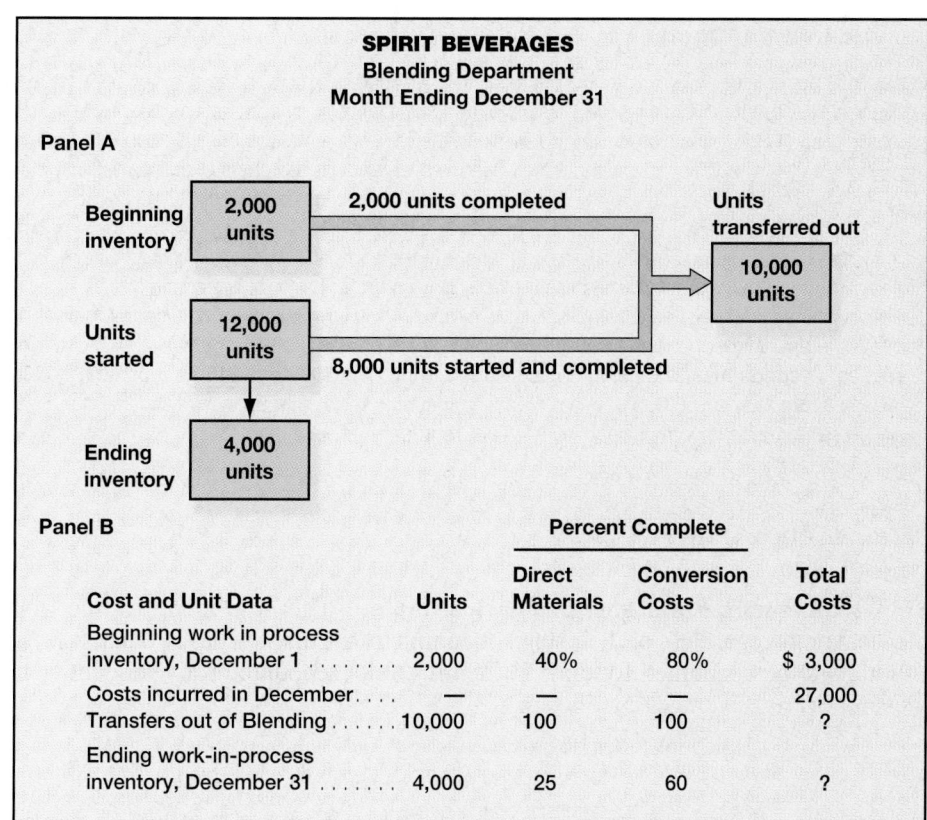

Data for Blending Operation

SPIRIT BEVERAGES
Blending Department
Month Ending December 31

Panel A

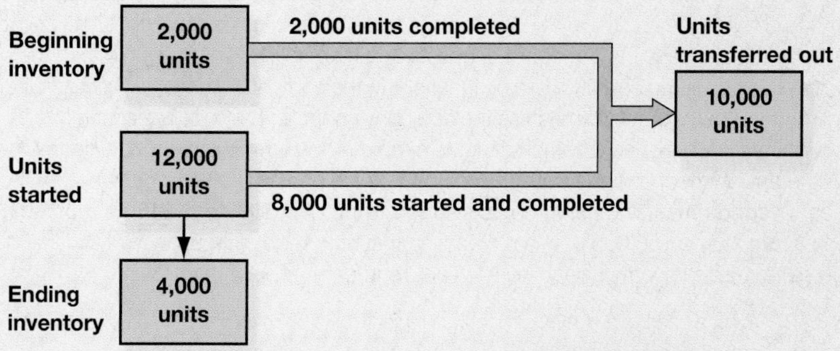

Panel B

		Percent Complete		
Cost and Unit Data	**Units**	**Direct Materials**	**Conversion Costs**	**Total Costs**
Beginning work in process inventory, December 1	2,000	40%	80%	$ 3,000
Costs incurred in December. . . .	—	—	—	27,000
Transfers out of Blending	10,000	100	100	?
Ending work-in-process inventory, December 31	4,000	25	60	?

Panel B of Exhibit 8–5 shows total costs as follows:

Beginning inventory	$ 3,000
Costs incurred in December	27,000

Therefore, the Blending Department manager has $30,000 to account for in December (= $3,000 in beginning inventory + $27,000 in costs incurred during December).

The problem is how much of the $30,000 should be assigned to the 10,000 units transferred out and how much to the partially complete 4,000 units in the Blending Department's ending WIP inventory on December 31.

The Basic Idea: Applying the Basic Cost-Flow Model

The basic cost-flow model provides the underlying framework for solving how much of the cost incurred in the period should be assigned to units transferred out and to ending inventory.

$$\text{Beginning balance } (BB) + \text{Transfers in } (TI) - \text{Transfers out } (TO) = \text{Ending balance } (EB)$$

The basic cost-flow model can also be stated as follows:

$$BB + TI = TO + EB$$

We know that *BB* equals $3,000 and *TI* equals $27,000. By following the five-step process outlined earlier in this chapter, we can determine how much of these costs should be assigned to units transferred out and how much to units in ending inventory.

Five Key Steps

Because this example is more complex than those earlier in the chapter, we discuss the five-step process in detail here.

Research Insight 8.1

Environmental Costs

Chemical, paper, steel, oil, and other companies that produce in continuous processes often have significant environmental costs. Researchers have found that while such companies generally keep good records of such visible costs as fees for permits and the cost of maintaining pollution control equipment, they do not identify additional costs that are buried in overhead. Researchers of companies in the steel industry have found the additional "hidden" costs to be 10 times as much as the visible costs.* A controller in a small company that had pre-tax accounting income of $840,000 estimated the company's environmental costs to be $50,000. Upon further study, the company found the direct and indirect costs totaled $1,000,000, 20 times as much as the company controller had initially estimated.#

Accurate estimates of environmental costs enable managers to make good decisions that both benefit the environment and the bottom line. In the case of the small company noted above, an investment in environmental improvements seemed to be unprofitable when the most that could be saved appeared to be $50,000 per year. Realizing that hundreds of thousands of dollars could potentially be saved made it worthwhile to invest in environmental improvements.

*Joshi, S., R. Krishnan and L. Lave, "Estimating the Hidden Costs of Environmental Regulation." (Full citations to references are in the Bibliography.)

T. Kunes, "A Green and Lean Workplace?"

Step 1: Summarize the flow of physical units. This step identifies the flow of physical units regardless of their stage of completion. This step has two parts: (1) identify units to be accounted for and (2) identify units accounted for. We identify these units for Spirit Beverages as follows:

Step 1a.	Units to be accounted for:	
	Units in beginning WIP inventory	2,000
	Units started this period	12,000
	Total units to be accounted for	14,000
Step 1b.	Units accounted for:	
	Units transferred out	10,000
	Units in ending WIP inventory	4,000
		14,000

Step 1 indicates that we must account for the costs of 14,000 units, of which 2,000 were in beginning inventory and 12,000 were started during December. Of those 14,000 units, 10,000 were transferred out and 4,000 remained in ending inventory at December 31. The following summarizes the flow of physical units in terms of the basic cost-flow model:

From 1a				From 1b		
BB	+	*TI*	=	*TO*	+	*EB*
2,000	+	12,000	=	10,000	+	4,000

Step 2: Compute the equivalent units produced. Some people find step 2 to be the most difficult part of process costing. We intend to make it as straightforward as possible.

Because Spirit Beverages' WIP inventories are at different stages of completion for direct materials and conversion costs, equivalent units must be calculated separately for direct materials and for conversion costs. Units transferred out are 100 percent completed (or they would not have been transferred out). Stages of completion for direct materials and conversion costs in ending inventory are given in panel B of Exhibit 8–5: Ending WIP inventory is 25 percent complete with respect to direct materials and 60 percent complete with respect to conversion costs.

Thus, equivalent units of work completed in December are computed as follows:

	Direct Materials	Conversion Costs
Units transferred out	10,000	10,000
Units in ending WIP inventory:		
Materials (4,000 × .25)	1,000	
Conversion costs (4,000 × .60)		2,400
Total equivalent units	11,000	12,400

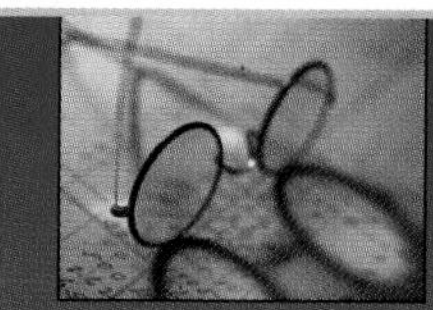

Cost Management in Practice 8.1

Equivalent Units and the SEC

You might wonder who provides these degrees of completion that are so essential to computing equivalent units. Ideally, someone who is objective and honest should prepare these estimates so they are not over- or underestimated to suit the decision maker's purpose. For example, since these figures are used to derive the outcomes of a process, someone could have a motivation to overestimate the degrees of completion to keep costs in inventory, thereby increasing income. Or a decision maker might wish to underestimate the degrees of completion to charge more to cost of goods completed and sold, thereby decreasing income and taxes.

The Securities and Exchange Commission (SEC) investigated Rynco Scientific Corporation, a manufacturer of contact lenses, concerning the way it computed equivalent units of production. According to the SEC, Rynco made errors in calculating the equivalent units of production that led to materially overstated ending inventory and understated losses. As a result of the SEC's investigation, Rynco agreed to hire an accounting firm to conduct a thorough study of its financial statements for a five-year period, and it agreed to restate its financial statements to conform to generally accepted accounting principles. *Source: Authors' research of U.S. Securities and Exchange Commission files.*

Note that these numbers indicate the equivalent number of units *completed* during the month. In general, it is possible that almost all work was done in previous periods, but the finishing touches were applied this period. These numbers do not tell managers how much work was done in the period, but they do tell them the equivalent work *completed.* Of course, *we* know from the facts in this particular example that most of the work was done in December. However, the equivalent units of work completed based on the weighted-average method would not have told the manager how much of the work equivalently completed in December was actually done in December compared to how much was done in November (or previous months). This lack of information about production in December would be a problem for a manager who wants information about worker productivity.

Step 3: Summarize the total costs to be accounted for. Step 3 is easy. The total costs to be accounted for are those in beginning inventory plus those incurred during the period as shown in panel B of Exhibit 8–5. Assume that total costs are separated into direct materials and conversion costs as follows:

	Total Costs	Direct Materials	Conversion Costs
Costs to be accounted for:			
Costs in beginning WIP inventory	$ 3,000	$ 2,000	$1,000
Current period costs	27,000	20,000	7,000
Total costs to be accounted for	$30,000	$22,000	$8,000

This information indicates that $30,000 must be assigned either to products transferred out of the department or to ending WIP inventory.

Step 4: Compute costs per equivalent unit. Step 4 calculates costs per equivalent unit for direct materials (total costs = $22,000; equivalent units = 11,000) and conversion costs (total costs = $8,000; equivalent units = 12,400). The calculation is straightforward; simply divide total costs to be accounted for by the number of equivalent units for each cost category as shown:

	Direct Materials	Conversion Costs
Total costs to be accounted for (from step 3)	$22,000	$ 8,000
Number of equivalent units (from step 2)	11,000	12,400
Cost per equivalent unit	$ 2.00	$.64516

This cost information helps managers make pricing and other decisions.

Exhibit 8-6

Cost Flows: Weighted Average

SPIRIT BEVERAGES
Blending Department
For the Month Ending December 31

Work-in-Process Inventory—Blending

Beginning inventory	3,000	Costs transferred out	?
Current period costs	27,000		
Ending inventory	?		

Finished-Goods Inventory or Next Department in Work in Process

?	

Work-in-Process Inventory—Blending

Beginning inventory	3,000	Costs transferred out	26,452
Current period costs	27,000		
Ending inventory	3,548		

Finished-Goods Inventory or Next Department in Work in Process

26,452	

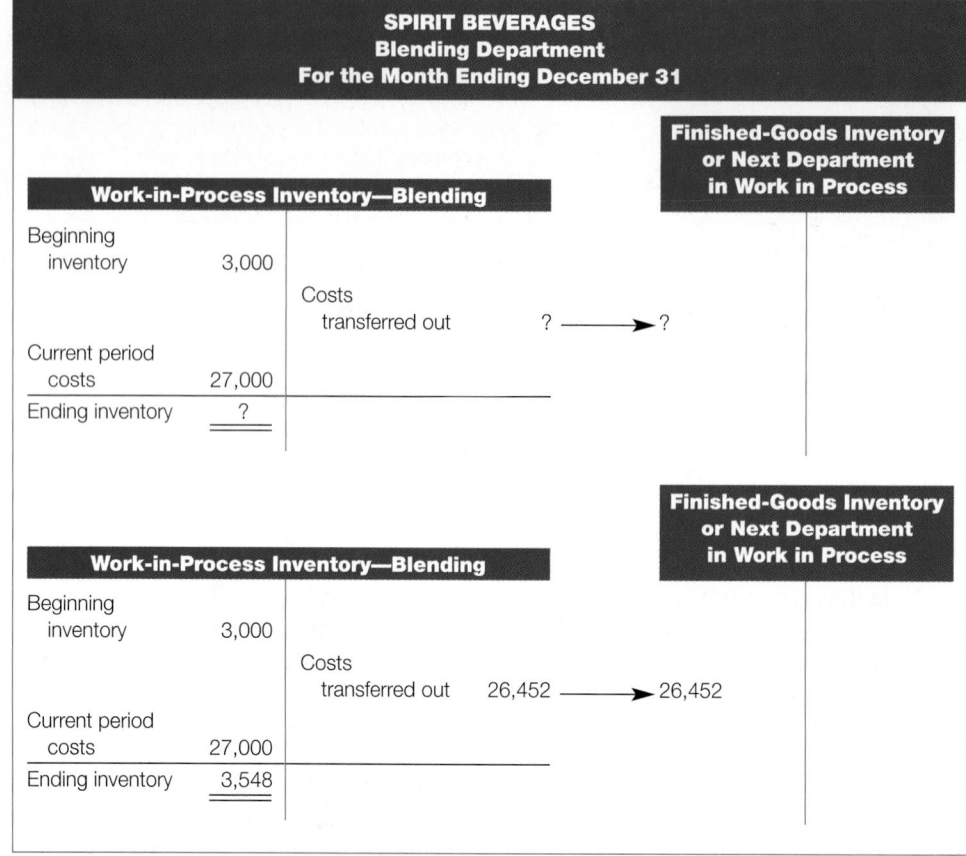

Step 5: Assign costs to goods transferred out and to ending inventory. Now we have the data and computations needed to perform step 5 to complete the task: Assign the costs to be accounted for to goods transferred out and those in ending WIP inventory. To perform step 5, we multiply the cost per equivalent unit (computed in step 4) by the number of equivalent units in ending WIP inventory and transferred out for the period shown in step 2.

Costs accounted for as follows:

Transferred out:	
Direct materials (10,000 units × $2)	$20,000
Conversion costs (10,000 units × $.64516)	6,452
Total transferred out	$26,452
Ending work in process, December 31:	
Direct materials (1,000 EU × $2)	$ 2,000
Conversion costs (2,400 EU × $.64516)	1,548
Total work in process	$ 3,548
Total costs accounted for	$30,000

How to check your work. Note the following equality:

Total costs to be accounted for = Total costs accounted for
[Step 3] [Step 5]

This equality must hold in every case (note that rounding can cause small discrepancies). Costs accounted for must equal costs to be accounted for because of the principle of the basic cost-flow model:

$$BB + TI = TO + EB$$

Costs to be accounted for represent the left side of the equation, $BB + TI$. The costs accounted for represent the right side of the equation, $TO + EB$.

Exhibit 8–7

Production Cost Report: Weighted Average

SPIRIT BEVERAGES
Blending Department
For the Month Ending December 31

		(Section 2) Equivalent Units	
Flow of Units	**(Section 1) Physical Units**	**Direct Materials**	**Conversion Costs**
Units to be accounted for:			
Beginning WIP inventory	2,000		
Units started this period	12,000		
Total units to be accounted for	**14,000**		
Units to be accounted for:			
Completed and transferred out	10,000	10,000	10,000
In ending WIP inventory	4,000	1,000*	2,400†
Total units accounted for	**14,000**	**11,000**	**12,400**
		Costs (Sections 3 through 5)	
Flow of Costs	**Total**	**Direct Materials**	**Conversion Costs**
Costs to be accounted for (Section 3):			
Costs in beginning WIP inventory	$ 3,000	$ 2,000	$ 1,000
Current period costs	27,000	20,000	7,000
Total costs to be accounted for	**$30,000**	**$22,000**	**$ 8,000**
Costs per equivalent unit (Section 4)		**$ 2.00‡**	**$.64516§**
Costs accounted for (Section 5):			
Costs assigned to units transferred out	$26,452	$20,000#	$ 6,452**
Cost of ending WIP inventory	3,548	2,000††	1,548‡‡
Total costs accounted for	**$30,000**	**$22,000**	**$ 8,000**

*Ending inventory is 25 percent complete. 1,000 EU = .25 × 4,000 units.
†Ending inventory is 60 percent complete. 2,400 EU = .60 × 4,000 units.
‡$2.00 = $22,000 ÷ 11,000 EU
§$.64516 = $8,000 ÷ 12,400 EU
#$20,000 = 10,000 EU × $2 per EU
**$6,452 = 10,000 EU × $0.64516 per EU
††$2,000 = 1,000 EU × $2 per EU
‡‡$1,548 = 2,400 EU × $.64516 per EU

How this looks in T-accounts. Although the computations do not require T-accounts, you might find that understanding the big picture is easier if you see how costs flow through T-accounts. Exhibit 8–6 shows the flow of costs through the WIP Inventory T-account for the Blending Department. The top panel shows the T-account at the end of December after the costs incurred during the month were known but before completing the five steps to assign costs to ending inventory and transfers out. The bottom panel shows the T-account after completing step 5.

Managerial Use of the Production Cost Report

production cost reports *summarize production and cost results for a period*

The **production cost report** summarizes the production and cost results for a period. Managers find it an important document for monitoring their flow. Using this report, managers can determine whether inventory levels are getting too high, costs are not low enough, or the number of units produced is too low.

Exhibit 8–7 presents a production cost report for the Blending Department of Spirit Beverages for December. Although it might look complex, you will soon see that this report simply includes the five steps for assigning costs to goods transferred out and to ending WIP inventory described earlier. To help relate the production cost report to those five steps, we present the report in five sections, each of which corresponds to a step.

Sections 1 and 2: Managing the Physical Flow of Units

Sections 1 and 2 of the production cost report correspond to steps 1 and 2 discussed above on pages 312 to 313. Section 1 summarizes the flow of physical units and shows 14,000 units to be accounted for, 10,000 as transfers out and 4,000 in ending inventory. Section 2 shows the equivalent number of units for direct materials and conversion costs separated into equivalent units transferred out and equivalent units remaining in WIP inventory.

Sections 3, 4, and 5: Managing Costs

Sections 3, 4, and 5 provide information about costs. Corresponding to step 3, section 3 shows the costs to be accounted for, \$3,000 in beginning inventory and \$27,000 incurred during December. Section 4 shows how we computed the cost per equivalent unit for direct materials (\$2.00) and conversion costs (\$.64516). Finally, section 5 shows the cost assignment performed in step 5 for direct materials and conversion costs. (Note that some rounding is inevitable. Do not be concerned if your numbers differ from ours by a few dollars.)

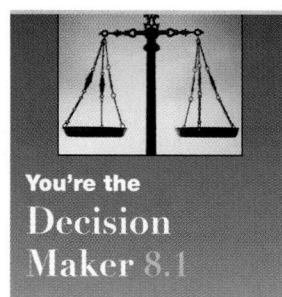

You're the Decision Maker 8.1

Production Cost Report

Review Exhibit 8–7 and the preceding discussion.

a. Why does Spirit Beverages use process costing rather than job costing?

b. Why does the production cost report have separate columns for direct materials and conversion costs? Why not combine the data into one column to simplify the report?

(Solutions begin on page 324.)

Example 4: Department with Costs Transferred in from Prior Departments

Accounting for Transferred-In Costs

LO 5 Account for costs transferred between processes.

prior department costs *are manufacturing costs incurred in another department and transferred to a subsequent department in the manufacturing process*

Our discussion so far has assumed a single department. Products usually pass through a series of departments, however. As they pass from one department to another, their costs must follow.

The costs of units transferred out of one department and into another are called **prior department costs** or *transferred-in costs;* they are the manufacturing costs incurred in another department and transferred to a subsequent department in the manufacturing process. The costs of processing cereal at Kellogg is a prior department cost to its Packaging Department. Equivalent whole units are 100 percent complete in terms of prior department costs, so cost computations for prior department costs are relatively easy.

Let's go back to Spirit Beverages and change the assumptions to allow for prior department costs. Assume that the Blending Department's beginning WIP inventory came from another department. In this example, all facts remain the same as in the previous one except that we include additional costs from the prior department under a new column, Prior Department's Costs. This column includes the prior department's costs of \$5,000 associated with beginning WIP inventory and current costs of \$52,000 (for goods transferred in from the prior department during the month). All other costs and physical units remain the same as in our original example. The following data summary presents the new information in bold.

SPIRIT BEVERAGES
Blending Department
For the Month Ending December 31

	Units	Prior Department's Costs	Blending Department's Costs: Direct Materials	Blending Department's Costs: Conversion Costs
Physical flow:				
Beginning inventory	2,000	**100% complete**	40% complete	80% complete
Ending inventory	4,000	**100% complete**	25% complete	60% complete
Units started **(transferred in)**	12,000	**100% complete**		
Started and completed	8,000	**100% complete**	100% complete	100% complete
Costs incurred:				
Beginning inventory		**$ 5,000**	$ 2,000	$ 1,000
Current costs		**52,000**	20,000	7,000

Exhibit 8–8 is a production cost report that summarizes these data. If you compare this report with the one in Exhibit 8–7, you'll see that Exhibit 8–8 is less complex than it looks. Notice that Exhibit 8–8 simply has the new column Prior Department to account for the goods transferred in from a prior department.

Responsibility for Costs Transferred in from Prior Departments

An important issue for performance evaluation is whether a department manager should be held accountable for all costs charged to the department. This usually is not the case; a department and its people are usually evaluated on the basis of costs that the department adds relative to the good output it produces. A prior department's costs are often excluded when comparing actual department costs with a standard or budget. We discuss this point more extensively in later chapters on performance evaluation, but we mention it here to emphasize that different information is needed for different purposes. Assigning costs to units for inventory valuation requires that the costs of all prior departments be included in the present department product cost calculations. However, assigning costs to departments for performance evaluation usually requires that costs from prior departments be excluded from the present department's costs.

Example 5: Department with Spoilage Costs

LO 6 Analyze and manage "normal" and "abnormal" spoilage.

If you have ever worked on a project that you discarded and then started on a new one, you understand the concept of *spoilage.* From your experience, you understand that spoilage, whether a discarded term paper, meal, or college application, is costly. Sometimes it is a necessary part of doing the job right. Doing something that did not turn out right can be part of the learning experience. If you have learned to play a sport, to dance, or to play a musical instrument, you know that no matter how much instruction you get, at some point you just have to go out and learn from your mistakes.

spoilage *represents goods that are damaged, do not meet specifications, or are otherwise not suitable for further processing or sale as good output*

Spoilage is the term used to describe goods that are damaged, do not meet specifications, or are otherwise not suitable for further processing or sale as good output. By measuring the costs of spoilage and the costs to reduce it (such as the costs to train employees, to use higher-quality materials, and to repair faulty equipment), managers are able to make informed decisions to improve quality and reduce costs.

Managers face these key problems concerning spoilage:

- Identifying whether it exists.
- Determining whether it can be eliminated, and if so, how. For example, spoilage can often be reduced by spending more time training employees.
- Deciding whether eliminating it is worthwhile. For example, is eliminating spoilage worth the cost of employee training?

Exhibit 8–8

Production Cost Report with Prior Department Costs: Weighted Average

SPIRIT BEVERAGES
Blending Department
For the Month Ending December 31

Flow of Units	**(Section 1) Physical Units**	**(Section 2) Equivalent Units: Prior Department**	**Direct Materials**	**Conversion Costs**
Units to be accounted for:				
Beginning WIP inventory	2,000			
Units started this period	12,000			
Total units to be accounted for	**14,000**			
Units accounted for:				
Completed and transferred out	10,000	10,000	10,000	10,000
In ending WIP inventory	4,000	4,000*	1,000†	2,400‡
Total units accounted for	**14,000**	**14,000**	**11,000**	**12,400**

Flow of Costs	**Total**	**Costs (Sections 3 through 5): Prior Department**	**Direct Materials**	**Conversion Costs**
Costs to be accounted for (Section 3):				
Costs in beginning WIP inventory	$ 8,000	$ 5,000	$ 2,000	$ 1,000
Current period costs	79,000	52,000	20,000	7,000
Total costs to be accounted for	**$87,000**	**$ 57,000**	**$22,000**	**$ 8,000**
Costs per equivalent unit (Section 4)		**$4.07143§**	**$ 2.00#**	**$.64516****
Costs accounted for (Section 5):				
Costs assigned to units transferred out	$67,166	$ 40,714††	$20,000‡‡	$ 6,452§§
Cost of ending WIP inventory	19,834	16,286##	2,000**	1,548†††
Total costs accounted for	**$87,000**	**$ 57,000**	**$22,000**	**$ 8,000**

*Ending inventory is 100 percent complete. 4,000 EU = 1.0 × 4,000 units

†Ending inventory is 25 percent complete. 1,000 EU = .25 × 4,000 units.

‡Ending inventory is 60 percent complete. 2,400 EU = .60 × 4,000 units.

§$4.07143 = $57,000 ÷ 14,000 EU

#$2.00 = $22,000 ÷ 11,000 EU

**$.64516 = $8,000 ÷ 12,400 EU

††$40,714 = 10,000 EU × $4.07143 per EU

‡‡$20,000 = 10,000 EU × $2 per EU

§§$6,452 = 10,000 EU × $.64516 per EU

##$16,286 = 4,000 EU × $4.07143

**$2,000 = 1,000 EU × $2 per EU

†††$1,548 = 2,400 EU × $.64516 per EU

lost units *are goods that evaporate or otherwise disappear during a production process*

normal spoilage *is a result of the regular operation of the production process*

abnormal spoilage *is due to reasons other than the usual course of operations of a process*

Normal versus Abnormal Spoilage: Is Spoilage Ever Normal?

Lost units are goods that evaporate or otherwise disappear during a production process. **Normal spoilage** is a result of the regular operation of the production process (see the left half of Exhibit 8–9). Some managers might not consider this to be normal spoilage, however, and strive to eliminate all spoilage. **Abnormal spoilage,** which results from other than the usual course of operations of a process, occurs if units are lost for unusual or abnormal reasons (see the right half of Exhibit 8–9). The debit for abnormal spoilage in the journal entry is made to an account such as Abnormal Spoilage, which writes off the costs as an expense for the period.

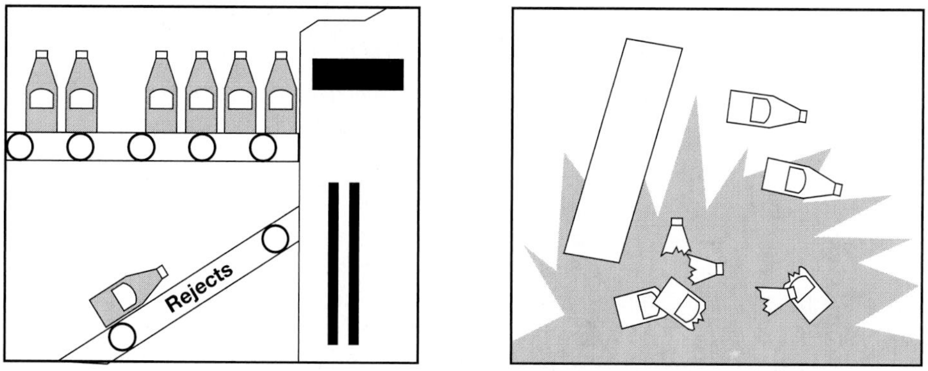

Exhibit 8–9

Normal versus Abnormal Spoilage

In the left half, some bottled soft drinks are rejected because the bottling process did not sufficiently fill the bottles. Although not desirable, the company considers this "normal" spoilage. In the right half, an accident has created "abnormal" spoilage.

To illustrate the accounting for abnormal spoilage, assume that the managers of a Coca-Cola bottling plant discovered that it had received a shipment of defective plastic bottles. These bottles, which had already been filled with soft drink, had to be destroyed at a cost of $8,000. Thus, $8,000 must be taken out of the Work-in-Process Inventory account and charged to the expense account Abnormal Spoilage. Abnormal spoilage is an expense for the period and appears on the income statement. Managers watch the Abnormal Spoilage account closely to identify causes of spoilage and to prevent it from occurring in the future.

Companies that have a zero defect policy might treat *all* spoilage as abnormal. They probably would not consider the left half of Exhibit 8–9 to be normal. Cost Management in Practice 8.2, "Process Costing and Waste at Louisiana Pacific," discusses how and why the company changed its attitude toward "normal" waste.

Here's an example of abnormal spoilage. In 1999 some Belgium children got sick after drinking Coca-Cola made from a bad batch of carbon dioxide. Coke was removed from the shelves and destroyed.

Cost Management in Practice 8.2

Process Costing and Waste at Louisiana Pacific

Louisiana Pacific, one of the largest wood products firms, has operations throughout the Western Hemisphere. The company uses process costing for most of its many processes and is vitally concerned with the costs of its outputs, which include waste that it must treat before disposing of it. At one time, costs of waste disposal were not considered to be material and were counted as normal costs of products. However, higher costs caused by environmental concerns and regulations have motivated Louisiana Pacific to monitor costs of waste from its processes and to find ways to reduce those costs.

Its Chetwynd, British Columbia, mill, for example, utilizes a state-of-the-art mechanical pulping process and a zero-effluent discharge system to produce pulp for use in its paper processes or for sale to other paper manufacturers. Its Samoa, California, mill produces bleached and unbleached kraft pulp by a chlorine-free process, thereby eliminating environmentally dangerous dioxins. Louisiana Pacific decided to sell its Ketchikan, Alaska, Pulp Company subsidiary when the combination of low pulp prices, restricted access to raw timber, and greatly increased costs of reducing and treating its process waste made the plant unprofitable. *Source: Louisiana Pacific Form 10-K, 1997.*

Accounting for Spoilage Costs

Let's go back to example 3 for Spirit Beverages and recall the facts. It had beginning and ending WIP inventory for the month of December but no transfers in from other departments. It had 2,000 units in beginning WIP inventory, which were finished during the month of December. Of the 12,000 units that were started in December, 8,000 were finished, and the remaining 4,000 were left in ending WIP inventory. Total costs to be accounted for were calculated in Exhibit 8–7 and are repeated here.

	Total Costs	Direct Materials	Conversion Costs
Costs to be accounted for:			
Costs in beginning WIP inventory	$ 3,000	$ 2,000	$1,000
Current period costs	$27,000	$20,000	$7,000
Total costs to be accounted for	$30,000	$22,000	$8,000

Now we change the facts slightly; assume that of the 12,000 units started in December, 8,000 were finished, 3,500 were left in ending WIP inventory, and 500 were lost to spoilage. As in example 3, ending WIP inventory is 25 percent complete with respect to direct materials and 60 percent complete with respect to conversion costs.

To determine the cost of spoiled units, we must allocate all costs (beginning WIP inventory and current period costs) to Finished-Goods Inventory, Spoilage, and Ending WIP Inventory accounts. We learn that production people detect spoilage after 50 percent of conversion costs and 20 percent of materials costs have been applied.

Once again, we can use the five-step process (as displayed formally in a production cost report) to allocate costs. Exhibit 8–10 shows a production cost report for this example including spoilage. Note that the only difference between this report and a report without spoilage (Exhibit 8–7) is that equivalent units are calculated for spoiled units in steps 1 and 2, and costs are allocated to spoiled units in step 5.

Exhibit 8–10 indicates that spoiled goods cost $362 for the month of December. In general, the earlier spoilage can be detected in the process, the less costly it is to the company. If spoilage cannot be prevented, it should be detected as early as possible.

The $362 in spoilage costs is typically charged to an expense account when it is transferred out of WIP Inventory. The account most often used is Cost of Goods Sold. However, some companies prorate spoilage costs over inventory accounts (WIP and Finished Goods) and the Cost of Goods Sold based on their respective account balances. As mentioned earlier, if the company deems the spoilage to be abnormal, it should use the expense account, Abnormal Spoilage.

Exhibit 8–10

Production Cost Report with Spoilage: Weighted Average

SPIRIT BEVERAGES
Blending Department
For the Month Ending December 31

Flow of Units	**(Section 1) Physical Units**	**(Section 2) Equivalent Units** Direct Materials	Conversion Costs
Units to be accounted for:			
Beginning WIP inventory	2,000		
Units started this period	12,000		
Total units to account for	**14,000**		
Units accounted for:			
Good units completed and transferred out	10,000	10,000	10,000
Spoiled units transferred out	500	100[‡]	250[§]
Units in ending WIP inventory	3,500	875[*]	2,100[†]
Total units accounted for	**14,000**	**10,975**	**12,350**

Costs (Sections 3 through 5)

Flow of Costs	**Total**	**Direct Materials**	**Conversion Costs**
Costs to be accounted for (Section 3):			
Costs in beginning WIP inventory	$ 3,000	$ 2,000	$ 1,000
Current period costs	27,000	20,000	7,000
Total costs to be accounted for	**$30,000**	**$ 22,000**	**$ 8,000**
Costs per equivalent unit (Section 4)		**$2.00456**[#]	**$.64777**[**]
Costs accounted for good units (Section 5):			
Costs assigned to good units transferred out	$26,524	$ 20,046[††]	$ 6,478[‡‡]
Costs assigned to spoiled goods	362	200[***]	162[†††]
Cost of ending WIP inventory	3,114	1,754[§§]	1,360[##]
Total costs accounted for	**$30,000**	**$ 22,000**	**$ 8,000**

[‡]100 EU = .20 × 500 units.
[§]250 EU = .50 × 500 units.
[*]Ending inventory is 25 percent complete. 875 EU = .25 × 3,500 units.
[†]Ending inventory is 60 percent complete. 2,100 EU = .60 × 3,500 units.
[#]$2.00456 = $22,000 ÷ 10,975 EU
[**]$.64777 = $8,000 ÷ 12,350 EU
[††]$20,046 = 10,000 EU × $2.00456 per EU
[‡‡]$6,478 = 10,000 EU × $.64777 per EU
[***]$200 = 100 EU × $2.00456 per EU
[†††]$162 = 250 EU × $.64777 per EU
[§§]$1,754 = 875 EU × $2.00456 per EU
[##]$1,360 = 2,100 EU × $.64777 per EU

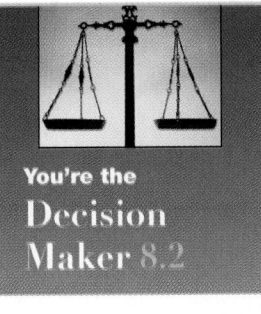

You're the Decision Maker 8.2

Analyzing Process Costs

Review Exhibit 8–10 and the preceding discussion.

a. Which parts of the production cost report do you think hold the most information about what the company needs to do to improve efficiency (and therefore, profitability)?

b. As a manager, what would you focus on to improve the profitability of Spirit Beverages?

(Solutions begin on page 324.)

Analysis of Spirit Beverages' Costs

At the beginning of the chapter, we saw that Fernando Martinez, the newly hired chief financial officer of Spirit Beverages, wanted to develop a good process costing information system that would provide product cost information. This chapter has described the system that Martinez developed. Martinez was pleased to see that the spoilage costs were low compared to his expectations—only $362 in the Blending Department for December compared to total costs of $30,000, according to Exhibit 8–10. Also, Martinez was pleased to see that the conversion costs per unit in the Blending Department were only $.6477 per unit. Most other companies in the industry experienced blending conversion costs in the range of $0.65 to $.80 per unit.

Martinez was appalled at the direct materials costs, however. The cost, $2.00456 per Exhibit 8–10, was considerably higher than other companies in the industry who had direct materials costs ranging from $1.60 – $1.90 per unit. The cost information developed from the process costing system did not tell Martinez that he had to reduce product costs, but it told him to look into the causes of high direct materials costs.

Choice between Job and Process Costing

Job costing collects costs for each unit produced. For example, a print shop collects costs for each order, a defense contractor collects costs for each contract, and a custom home builder collects costs for each house. Process costing accumulates costs in a department for an accounting period (for example, a month) and then spreads them evenly, or averages them, over all units produced that month. Process costing assumes that each unit produced is relatively uniform. Of course, process costing does not provide as much information as job costing because it does not record the cost of each unit produced. The choice of process- versus job-costing systems involves comparing the costs and benefits of each system. The production process being utilized is also a major factor in choosing a cost system.

Consider a housebuilder. Job costing accumulates costs for each house. It is not sufficient simply to record the amount of total lumber delivered to several houses, but records of the amount subsequently returned from each house must be kept. If laborers work on several houses, they must track their time spent on each house. Process costing, however, simply requires recording the total costs incurred on all jobs. For the home builder, process costing records the average cost of all houses built. A custom home builder probably uses job costing. A developer might consider each development a job but use process costing for each house within each development.

Custom home builders generally use job costing to keep track of the costs of each house because each house is typically unique. Builders of tract houses might use process costing if all houses are the same.

Under process costing, the actual cost incurred for a particular unit is not reported. If all units are homogeneous, this loss of information is most likely minimal. It probably is not important for Intel to know whether the cost of the 10,001st microprocessor chip is different from that of the 10,002nd, particularly if the unit cost is calculated primarily to value inventory for external financial reporting. Cost control and performance evaluation take place by department, not by unit produced, in process systems. For companies such as Intel that make homogeneous units, the additional benefits of job costing do not justify the additional record-keeping costs.

What if record-keeping costs were equal under job and process systems for the units in a product line? Then we would say that a job system is better because it provides all data that a process system does, and more. As a general rule, however, a job system is usually more costly than a process system. Thus, managers and accountants must decide whether knowing the actual cost of each unit, which is available in a job-costing system, is enough to justify additional record-keeping costs. Companies producing relatively large, heterogeneous items usually can justify the additional costs for the additional benefits of job costing.

Chapter Summary

Process costing is used when it is not possible or practical to identify costs with specific lots or batches of product. A process-costing system accumulates costs for each production department but does not maintain separate records of costs for each unit produced. When comparing job and process costing, companies generally find that job costing provides more data but has higher record-keeping costs. Managers and accountants must decide whether the additional data available under job costing justify these higher costs. For companies that produce relatively homogeneous units in a continuous process, cost-benefit analysis generally favors process costing.

The two most common process costing methods are weighted-average costing and first-in, first-out (FIFO) costing (discussed in Appendix A). The weighted-average method makes no distinction between beginning inventory and current period costs. As a result, its computations are simpler than those obtained using FIFO costing.

Process costing assigns costs to ending WIP inventory and units completed using five steps:

Step 1: Summarize the flow of physical units.
Step 2: Compute the equivalent number of units produced.
Step 3: Summarize the total costs to be accounted for.
Step 4: Compute costs per equivalent unit.
Step 5: Assign costs to goods transferred out (completed and to ending inventory and to spoiled units, if applicable).

Key Terms

For each term's definition, refer to the indicated page or turn to the glossary at the end of the text.

abnormal spoilage, 318
equivalent units, 308
first-in, first-out (FIFO) costing*, 324
lost units, 318
normal spoilage, 318
operation†, 331
prior department costs, 316
production cost reports, 315
spoilage, 317
weighted-average costing, 310

*Term appears in Appendix A.
†Term appears in Appendix B.

Meeting the Cost Management Challenges

1. How should Spirit Beverages measure the costs of products, services, and operations?

With numerous, undifferentiated outputs, attempting to measure the costs of individual items of output generally is not cost effective. In this case, organizations such as Spirit Beverages usually use process costing, which allows them to average costs across all units produced during a specific time period. An organization might operate numerous processes, however, each of which could have separate cost accounts so that employees can monitor and report cost information. If some individual processes are relatively unimportant, maintaining separate process accounts might not be necessary. In concept, process costing could be performed at the activity level, but organizations usually organize activities into processes or condensed activities. Within processes, organizations determine what number and types of cost categories to manage. The most common categories are materials and conversion costs, but organizations could use as many different material and conversion cost categories as they believe are necessary to generate the information they need and can justify.

2. **How** should organizations recognize and measure the costs of spoilage and waste?

Nearly every process results in some outputs not fit for further processing or delivery to customers. All processes also generate waste from defective units that cannot be reworked or recycled to inefficient use of resources. Because competitive and regulatory (e.g., environmental) pressures are increasing for most organizations, it is advisable to measure spoilage and waste costs separately from costs of producing good output. High spoilage and waste costs indicate inefficient processes that do or could result in competitive disadvantages. Assuming that these costs can be computed reliably (this could be a problem with environmental waste costs), it is better to know the magnitude of the spoilage and waste problem so that it can be attacked in a cost-effective manner than to bury the cost in the costs of good output. These costs should be reported separately but internally to the organization (unless required by external parties).

3. **(Appendix A) What** is the advantage of first-in, first-out (FIFO) process costing over weighted-average process costing?

FIFO separates the costs associated with products produced in a previous period from those produced in the current period. Weighted-average, on the other hand, mixes the costs of previous periods (which are in beginning WIP inventory) with current period production costs. FIFO gives managers more accurate information about current period costs.

Solutions to You're the Decision Maker

8.1 Production Cost Report p. 316

a. Job costing is used to track costs for each unit (or job) produced and for products that are somewhat unique, such as custom homes and landscaping projects. It is not cost effective to track costs for high-volume homogeneous products such as Spirit Beverage's sports drink. Instead, costs are tracked by process and an average cost is determined at the end of the period.

b. Equivalent units and costs are calculated separately for direct materials and conversion costs because ending WIP inventory is typically at different stages of completion for each of these categories. Notice that ending WIP inventory for Spirit Beverages is 25 percent complete with respect to direct materials (i.e., 25 percent of the direct materials needed have been used) and 60 percent complete with respect to conversion costs (i.e., 60 percent of the activities required for conversion costs have been completed). The use of two separate columns in the production cost report allows us to more accurately calculate the costs per equivalent units and assign costs to units transferred out and in ending WIP inventory.

8.2 Analyzing Process Costs p. 321

a. Reviewing costs related to spoiled units is important. Although the costs assigned to spoiled units are not substantial at this point, the company wants to prevent them from increasing in the future and would likely compare them to those of prior periods to review trends. Ending WIP inventory increased from 2,000 units last month to 3,500 units this month. Minimizing inventory levels is an effective way to reduce inventory costs; inventory can be monitored by reviewing this report. Finally, comparing the costs per equivalent unit for direct materials and conversion costs this month with prior months can help to evaluate the efficiency of production operations.

b. Several areas of improvement can help Spirit Beverages increase profitability. It can reduce ending WIP inventory levels, which minimizes inventory handling and storage costs (rent, labor, insurance, etc.). Direct materials represent approximately 73 percent of all costs to be accounted for. Perhaps the company could negotiate a lower materials price with the current supplier or find a different supplier. The number of spoiled units, although not extremely high, should be reviewed, and processes modified to achieve lower spoilage rates.

Appendix A to Chapter Eight

Cost Assignment to Products Using First-In, First-Out Costing

LO 7 Assign process costs to products using first-in, first-out (FIFO) costing.

first-in, first-out (FIFO) costing *is an inventory method that identifies the first units completed as the first ones sold or transferred out*

A disadvantage of weighted-average costing is that it mixes current period costs with the costs of products in beginning inventory, making it impossible for managers to know how much it costs to make a product during the *current period.* **First-in, first-out (FIFO) costing** is an inventory method that identifies the first units completed as the first ones sold or transferred out. FIFO costing separates current period costs from those in beginning inventory and transfers out the costs in beginning inventory in a lump sum (assuming that the units in beginning inventory were completed during the current period) rather than mingling them with current period costs.

FIFO gives managers more accurate information about the work done in the current period. Managers benefit from this separation of current period costs from those in beginning inventory because they can identify and manage current period costs.

If the production process is a FIFO process, the inventory numbers are more likely to reflect reality under FIFO costing than under weighted-average costing because the units in ending inventory are likely to have been produced in the current period. FIFO costing assigns current period costs to those units, but weighted-average costing mixes current and prior period costs in assigning a value to ending inventory.

Example 3: Department with Beginning and Ending WIP Inventory: FIFO

To illustrate accounting for process costing using FIFO, we use the data from example 3 for Spirit Beverages, which assumes beginning and ending WIP inventory (but no transfers in or spoilage). This allows for a comparison of FIFO and weighted-average costing and identification of the resulting differences. Recall the following facts:

		Costs	
	Units	**Direct Materials**	**Conversion Costs**
Beginning WIP inventory	2,000	$2,000	$1,000
Started this period	12,000	20,000	7,000
Transferred out	10,000	?	?
Ending WIP inventory	4,000	?	?

Remember that Panel B of Exhibit 8–5 indicates that *beginning* WIP inventory is 40 percent complete for direct materials and 80 percent complete for conversion costs. *Ending* WIP inventory is 25 percent complete for direct materials and 60 percent complete for conversion costs.

Five key steps. The same five steps are used with FIFO costing as with the weighted-average costing approach and are displayed formally in a production cost report. Similarities and differences within each step are noted in the following discussion.

Step 1: Summarize the flow of physical units. This step identifies the flow of physical units regardless of their stage of completion and is the same for both FIFO and weighted-average costing. Section 1 of the production cost report in Exhibit 8–11 summarizes the flow of physical units, showing 14,000 units to be accounted for, 10,000 as transfers out of the Blending Department, and 4,000 units remaining in ending inventory.

Step 2: Compute the equivalent number of units produced. FIFO costing and weighted-average costing compute equivalent units differently. Recall that FIFO costing separates what was in beginning inventory from what occurs this period. The FIFO equivalent unit computation is confined only to what was produced this period. Under FIFO, we compute equivalent units in three parts for both direct materials and conversion costs:

1. Equivalent units to complete beginning WIP inventory.
2. Equivalent units of goods started and completed during the current period.
3. Equivalent units of goods started during the period and still in ending WIP inventory.

Spirit Beverages had 2,000 units in beginning inventory that were 40 percent complete for direct materials and 80 percent complete for conversion costs at the beginning of the period. Completing the beginning inventory required 1,200 equivalent units for direct materials [$(1.00 - .40) \times 2{,}000$ units], and 400 equivalent units for conversion costs [$(1.00 - .80) \times 2{,}000$ units].

The units started and completed can be derived by examining the physical flow of units. Because 12,000 units were started and 4,000 of them remain in ending inventory,

Exhibit 8–11

Production Cost Report: FIFO

Spirit Beverages
Blending Department
For the Month Ending December 31

Flow of Units	(Section 1) Physical Units	(Section 2) Equivalent Units: Direct Materials	(Section 2) Equivalent Units: Conversion Costs
Units to be accounted for:			
Beginning WIP inventory	2,000		
Units started this period	12,000		
Total units to be accounted for	**14,000**		
Units accounted for:			
Units completed and transferred out			
Beginning WIP inventory	2,000	1,200*	400†
Started and completed currently	8,000	8,000	8,000
Total	10,000	9,200	8,400
Units in ending WIP inventory	4,000	1,000‡	2,400§
Total units accounted for	**14,000**	**10,200**	**10,800**

Costs (Sections 3 through 5)

Flow of Costs	Total	Direct Materials	Conversion Costs
Costs to be accounted for (Section 3):			
Costs in beginning WIP inventory	$ 3,000	$ 2,000	$ 1,000
Current period costs	27,000	20,000	7,000
Total costs to be accounted for	**$30,000**	**$ 22,000**	**$ 8,000**
Costs per equivalent unit (Section 4)		**1.96078#**	**.64815****
Costs accounted for (Section 5)			
Costs assigned to units transferred out:			
Costs from beginning WIP inventory	$ 3,000	$ 2,000	$ 1,000
Current costs added to complete beginning WIP inventory	2,612	2,353††	259‡‡
Total costs from beginning WIP inventory	5,612	4,353	1,259
Current costs of units started and completed	20,871	15,686§§	5,185##
Total costs transferred out	26,483	20,039	6,444
Cost of ending WIP inventory	3,517	1,961***	1,556†††
Total costs accounted for	**$30,000**	**$ 22,000**	**$ 8,000**

*1,200 = 60% × 2,000. 60 percent of costs must be added to complete beginning WIP inventory.

†400 = 20% × 2,000. 20 percent of costs must be added to complete beginning WIP inventory.

‡Ending WIP inventory for direct materials is 25 percent complete.

§Ending WIP inventory for conversion costs is 60 percent complete.

#$1.96078 = $20,000 ÷ 10,200 EU

**$.64815 = $7,000 ÷ 10,800 EU

††$2,353 = 1,200 EU × $1.96078 per EU

‡‡$259 = 400 EU × $.64815 per EU

§§$15,686 = 8,000 EU × $1.96078 per EU

##$5,185 = 8,000 EU × $.64815 per EU

***$1,961 = 1,000 EU × $1.96078 per EU

†††$1,556 = 2,400 EU × $.64815 per EU

according to the FIFO method, the remaining 8,000 were completed. Thus, 8,000 units were started and completed. Another way to get the same result is to observe that of the 10,000 units completed during December, 2,000 came from beginning inventory (according to the FIFO method), so the remaining 8,000 units completed must have been started during December.

Either way one views the physical flow, the department started and completed 8,000 units. Because these 8,000 units were 100 percent complete when transferred out of the department, the units started and completed represent 8,000 equivalent units produced during the current period for both direct materials and conversion costs.

Finally, we determine the number of equivalent units of production in ending inventory.[2] Ending inventory of 4,000 units is 25 percent complete with respect to direct materials and 60 percent complete for conversion costs. Thus, ending WIP inventory has 1,000 equivalent units (.25 × 4,000) for direct materials and 2,400 equivalent units (.60 × 4,000) for conversion costs. These equivalent unit results appear in section 2 of the production cost report in Exhibit 8–11.

Note that the number of equivalent units under FIFO is less than or equal to the number under the weighted-average method because the FIFO computations refer to this period's production only. Weighted-average equivalent units consider all units in the department, whether produced in this period or a previous period. (If the department has no beginning inventory, the weighted-average and FIFO equivalent units are equal.)

Step 3: Summarize the total costs to be accounted for. The total costs to be accounted for under FIFO costing are the same as under weighted-average costing. Whatever our assumption about cost flows, we must account for *all* costs in the department (those in beginning inventory plus those incurred during the period). For Spirit Beverages, these costs are as follows:

	Total Costs	Direct Materials	Conversion Costs
Costs to be accounted for:			
Costs in beginning WIP inventory	$ 3,000	$ 2,000	$1,000
Current period costs	27,000	20,000	7,000
Total costs to be accounted for	$30,000	$22,000	$8,000

These costs are shown in section 3 of the production cost report in Exhibit 8–11.

Step 4: Compute costs per equivalent unit. Under FIFO, the costs per equivalent unit are confined to the costs incurred this period, $27,000, and the equivalent units produced this period, which were computed in step 2 (10,200 for direct materials and 10,800 for conversion costs). In formula form,

$$\text{Cost per equivalent unit} = \text{Current period costs} \div \text{Equivalent units of production this period}$$

Note that only current period costs are included in the numerator. The FIFO method excludes the beginning WIP costs from the cost per equivalent unit calculation. Instead, beginning WIP inventory is assumed to be completed during the period and transferred out to finished goods.

For Spirit Beverages, the cost per equivalent unit under FIFO is calculated here.

Direct Materials

$$\begin{aligned}\text{Cost per equivalent unit} &= \$20{,}000 \div 10{,}200 \text{ equivalent units}\\ &= \$1.96078 \text{ per equivalent unit}\end{aligned}$$

Conversion Costs

$$\begin{aligned}\text{Cost per equivalent unit} &= \$7{,}000 \div 10{,}800 \text{ equivalent units}\\ &= \$.64815 \text{ per equivalent unit}\end{aligned}$$

The cost per equivalent unit appears in section 4 of the production cost report.

[2]For our examples, units in ending inventory come from the current period production. Although it is unlikely, you could encounter cases in practice with inventory levels so high relative to current period production that some of the beginning inventory is still in ending inventory. In that case, you should keep separate the costs and units in ending inventory that come from beginning inventory. Having separated those costs and units, you can perform the computations described in the text for the current period costs.

Exhibit 8–12

Cost Flows: FIFO

SPIRIT BEVERAGES
Blending Department
For the Month Ending December 31

Work-in-Process Inventory—Blending				Finished-Goods Inventory or Next Department in Work in Process
Beginning inventory	3,000	Costs transferred out	?	→ ?
Current period costs	27,000			
Ending inventory	?			

Work-in-Process Inventory—Blending				Finished-Goods Inventory or Next Department in Work in Process
Beginning inventory	3,000	Beginning inventory costs transferred out	3,000	→ 26,483
Current period costs	27,000	Current period costs transferred out	23,483	
Ending inventory	3,517			

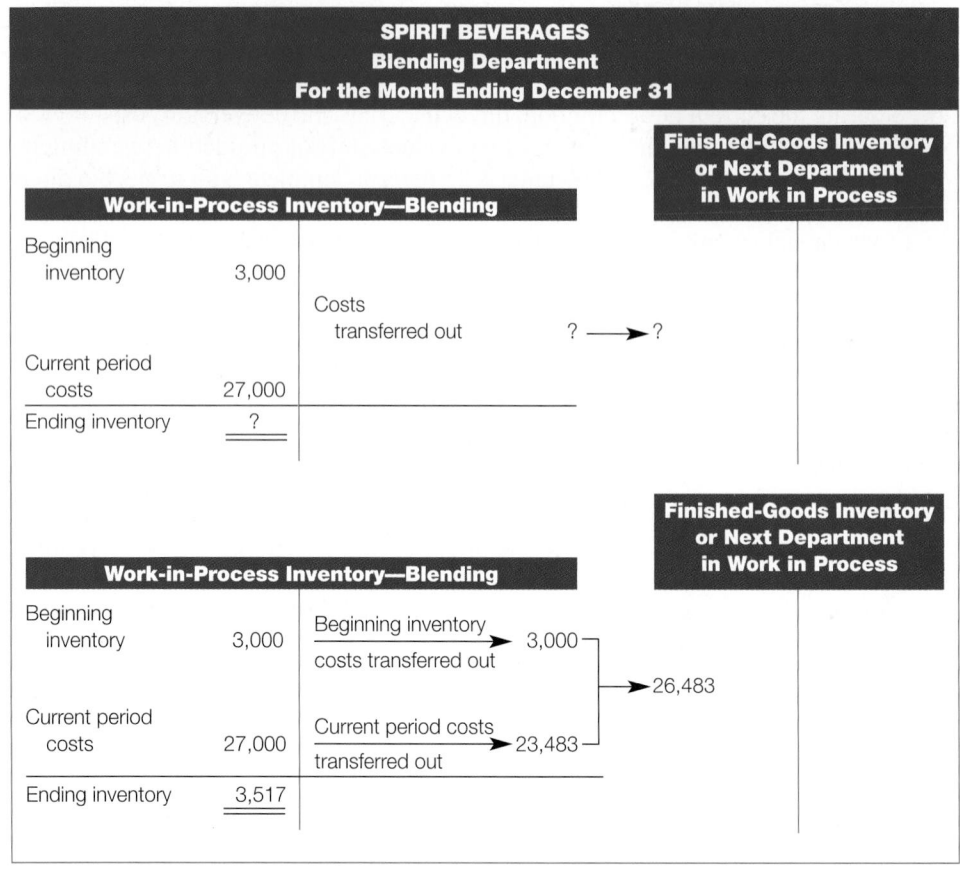

Step 5: Assign costs to goods transferred out and to ending WIP inventory. The cost of goods transferred out has the following components:

Costs in beginning WIP inventory (at beginning of period)	$ 3,000
Costs to complete beginning inventory	2,612
Cost of the 8,000 units started and completed this period	20,871
Cost of ending WIP inventory	3,517
Total costs accounted for	$30,000

These results appear in section 5 of the production cost report. Note that the costs to be accounted for in section 3, $30,000, equal the costs accounted for in section 5, $30,000.

Flow of costs through T-accounts. Exhibit 8–12 shows the flow of costs through the WIP Inventory T-account for the Blending Department using FIFO. The top section shows the T-accounts as they appear before computing cost of goods transferred out and ending WIP inventory amounts. (Note the question marks, which indicate unknown amounts.) After making the computations shown in the production cost report in Exhibit 8–11, we complete the T-accounts as shown in the bottom section of Illustration Exhibit 8–12. It is helpful to use T-accounts to keep the big picture in mind when working on detailed computations such as those reported in Exhibit 8–11.

LO 8 Compare and contrast the results from weighted-average and FIFO costing.

Advantages and disadvantages of FIFO and weighted-average costing. Weighted-average costing does not separate beginning inventory from current period activity. Unit costs are a weighted average of the two, whereas under FIFO costing, unit costs are based on current period activity only. FIFO is typically advantageous when the number of units in beginning WIP inventory is large relative to the number of units started during the period. If this is not the case, beginning WIP inventory has little influence on the average unit cost using the weighted-average approach.

Exhibit 8–13

Comparison of Weighted-Average and FIFO Costing

	Weighted-Average (from Exhibit 8–7)	FIFO (from Exhibit 8–11)
Equivalent unit costs:		
Direct materials	$ 2.00	$1.96078
Conversion costs	.64516	.64815
Cost of goods transferred out	26,452	26,483
Ending WIP inventory	3,548	3,517

Exhibit 8–14

Summary of Steps for Assigning Process Costs to Units

Step 1: Summarize the flow of physical units.

Step 2: Compute the number of equivalent units produced for direct materials and conversion costs.

Weighted average: EU produced = Units transferred out + EU in ending WIP inventory

FIFO: EU produced = EU to complete beginning WIP inventory + Units started and finished during the period + EU in ending WIP inventory

Step 3: Summarize the total costs to be accounted for.

Total costs to be accounted for = Costs in beginning WIP inventory + Costs incurred this period

Step 4: Compute costs per equivalent unit.

Weighted average

$$\text{Weighted-average unit cost} = \frac{\text{Costs in beginning WIP inventory} + \text{Current period costs}}{\text{Units tranferred out} + \text{EU in ending WIP inventory}}$$

FIFO

$$\text{Unit cost of current period work} = \frac{\text{Current period costs}}{\text{EU of current work done}}$$

Step 5: Assign costs to goods transferred out and to ending WIP inventory.

Weighted average: Using weighted average, the cost of goods transferred out equals the total units transferred out times the weighted-average unit cost computed in step 4.

Using weighted average, the cost of goods in ending WIP inventory equals the equivalent units in ending WIP inventory times the weighted-average unit cost computed in step 4.

FIFO: Using FIFO, the cost of goods transferred out equals the sum of the following three items:

a. The costs already in beginning WIP inventory at the beginning of the period.

b. The current period cost to complete beginning WIP inventory, which equals the equivalent units to complete beginning WIP inventory from step 2 times the current period unit cost computed for FIFO in step 4.

c. The costs to start and complete units, calculated by multiplying the number of units started and finished from step 2 times the cost per equivalent unit computed for FIFO in step 4.

Using FIFO, the cost of goods in ending WIP inventory equals the equivalent units in ending WIP inventory from step 2 times the cost per equivalent unit computed for FIFO in step 4.

Exhibit 8–13 compares the equivalent unit costs including direct materials conversion costs, cost of goods transferred out, and ending WIP inventory values under the two methods for Spirit Beverages. Although either weighted-average or FIFO costing is acceptable for assigning costs to inventories and cost of goods sold for external reporting, the weighted-average method has been criticized for masking current period costs. Thus, the unit costs reported for December using weighted-average costing are based not only on December's costs but also on the costs of previous periods that were in December's beginning inventory. For a company such as Phillips Petroleum, which experiences changing crude oil prices, managers' decisions require knowledge of current period costs. If computational and record-keeping costs are about the same under both FIFO and weighted average, FIFO costing is generally preferred.

Exhibit 8–14 summarizes the steps for assigning costs to units in process costing using FIFO and weighted-average costing. Notice how the steps correspond to the production cost report that management uses to monitor production unit and cost flows.

Example 4: Department with Costs Transferred in from Prior Departments: FIFO

Recall that example 4 in the chapter included goods transferred from a prior department. Exhibit 8–15 is a FIFO cost of production report using the data from example 4.

Exhibit 8–15

Production Cost Report with Prior Department Costs: FIFO

SPIRIT BEVERAGES
Blending Department
For the Month Ending December 31

		(Section 2) Equivalent Units		
Flow of Production Units	**(Section 1) Physical Units***	**Prior Department Costs**	**Materials***	**Conversion Costs***
Units to account for:				
Beginning work in process inventory....	2,000			
Units started this period	12,000			
Total units to account for....................	**14,000**			
Units accounted for:				
Units completed and transferred out:				
From beginning inventory	2,000	0†	1,200†	400†
Started and completed, currently	8,000	8,000	8,000	8,000
Units in ending WIP inventory..............	4,000	4,000	1,000	2,400
Total units accounted for....................	**14,000**	**12,000**	**10,200**	**10,800**

Flow of Costs	**Total Costs**	**Prior Department Costs**	**Materials***	**Conversion Costs***
Costs to be accounted for (Section 3):				
Costs in beginning WIP inventory.........	$ 8,000	$ 5,000	$ 2,000	$1,000
Current period costs	79,000	52,000	20,000	7,000
Total costs to be accounted for	**$87,000**	**$57,000**	**$ 22,000**	**$8,000**
Cost per equivalent unit (Section 4):				
Prior department costs ($52,000 ÷ 12,000)		$ 4.33333		
Materials ($20,000 ÷ 10,200)			$1.96078	
Conversion costs ($7,000 ÷ 10,800)				$.64815
Costs to be accounted for (Section 5):				
Costs assigned to units transferred out:				
Costs from beginning WIP inventory....	$ 8,000	$ 5,000	$ 2,000	$1,000
Current costs added to complete beginning WIP inventory:				
Prior department costs	0	0		
Materials......................................	2,353		2,353	
Conversion costs..........................	259			259
Total costs to complete beginning inventory	2,612			
Costs of units started and completed:				
Prior department costs (8,000 × $4.33333)	34,667	34,667		
Materials	15,686		15,686	
Conversion costs	5,185			5,185
Total costs of units started and completed.........................	55,538			
Total costs transferred out	66,150			

Exhibit 8–15 continued on next page

Costs assigned to ending WIP inventory:				
Prior department costs (4,000 × $4.33333)	17,333	17,333		
Materials	1,961		1,961	
Conversion costs	1,556			1,556
Total cost of ending WIP inventory	20,850			
Total costs accounted for	**$87,000**	**$57,000**	**$22,000**	**$8,000**

*See Exhibit 8–11 for calculations.

†EU required to complete beginning inventory.

Exhibit 8–15

Production Cost Report with Prior Department Costs: FIFO *(concluded)*

This concludes our discussion of FIFO process costing.

Appendix B to Chapter Eight

Operation Costing

LO 9 Compare and contrast operation costing with job costing and process costing.

Recall from Chapter 3 that *operation costing* is a hybrid of job-order and process costing and is used when companies produce batches of similar products with significantly different types of material (see Exhibit 8–16). It is used for the manufacture of goods that have some common characteristics plus some individual characteristics. An **operation** is a standardized method of making a product that is repeatedly performed. For example, an automobile assembly plant makes several models on the same assembly line. Each model has seat covers installed; installing them is an operation.

operation *is a standardized method of making a product that is repeatedly performed*

A company using operation costing typically uses different materials for products that pass through the same operation. Some automobiles have leather seats, others cloth seats. Whether the material is leather or cloth, the car passes through the same seat cover installation operation.

Companies such as Nike (shoes) and Volvo (automobiles) use operation costing. Van Heusen, a shirt maker, has a cutting operation and a stitching operation for each shirt, although the materials (cotton, wool, polyester) for each type of shirt can differ.

Product Costing in Operations

The key difference between operation costing, job costing, and process costing is that direct materials for each work order or batch passing through a particular operation are different although conversion costs (direct labor and manufacturing overhead) are the same.

For example, assume that Yahonzi Motorcycle Company makes two models of motorcycles, Jets and Sharks. The Shark has a larger engine and generally more costly direct materials than the Jet. Exhibit 8–17 shows the flow of products through departments (assume that each department has one operation). Note that Jets pass through only the first two departments where operations are identical for both types of motorcycles but Sharks pass through all three departments. Direct materials costs are added

Job Costing	Operation Costing	Process Costing
Job shops making customized products	Operations: Separate materials for each batch; common operations	Mass production in continuous processes

Exhibit 8–16

Comparison of Three Costing Methods

Exhibit 8–17
Overview of Operation Costing

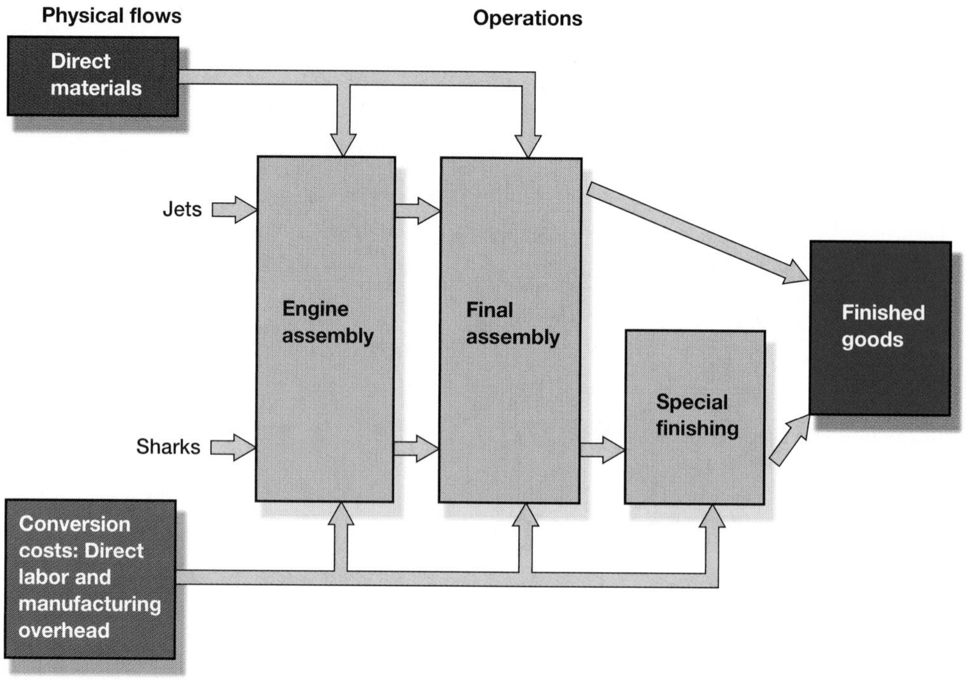

to both models in Engine Assembly and Final Assembly, but none are added to Jets in Special Finishing. Conversion costs are added to Jets in the first two departments and to Sharks in all three departments. In principle, direct materials costs could be added in any operation. In this example, the direct materials costs per unit are higher for Sharks.

Illustration of Operation Costing

Assume that Yahonzi Motorcycle Company management gave the following production work order for the month of March. Each work order is also called a *batch.*

YAHONZI MOTORCYCLE COMPANY

	Work Order 101	Work Order 102
Number and model of motorcycles	1,000 Sharks	2,000 Jets
Direct materials:		
Engine parts	$150,000	$200,000
Motorcycle parts, other than engines	200,000	300,000
Conversion costs (direct labor and manufacturing overhead):		
Engine assembly	50,000	100,000
Final assembly	100,000	200,000
Special finishing	50,000	
Total costs	$550,000	$800,000

Note that the materials costs per unit are higher for Sharks than for Jets but the conversion costs per unit are the same for the two operations that both models pass through. For example, engine assembly conversion costs are $50 per motorcycle for both models ($50,000 ÷ 1,000 units for Sharks; $100,000 ÷ 2,000 units for Jets).

Exhibit 8–18 shows the flow of these costs through T-accounts to Finished Goods Inventory. In practice, direct labor and manufacturing overhead could be combined as they were in a Japanese motorcycle company that one of the authors studied. Direct labor and manufacturing overhead could be charged separately to production as well. In

Exhibit 8–18 Cost Flows through T-Accounts for Operation Costing

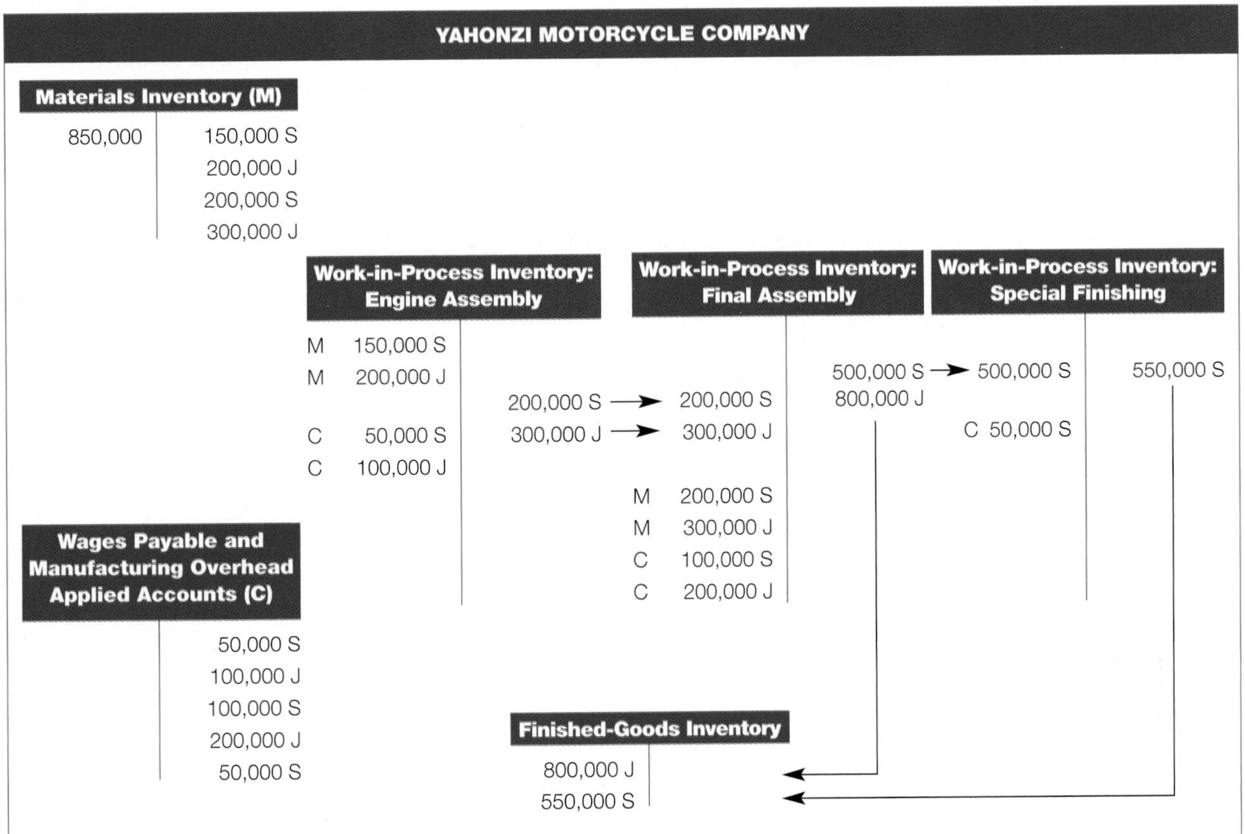

S = Sharks.
J = Jets.
M = Direct materials, credit to Materials Inventory.
C = Conversion costs, credit to Wages Payable and Manufacturing Overhead Applied Accounts.

many companies, direct labor is such a small portion of the total product cost that the accountants classify direct labor as part of manufacturing overhead. For example, in numerous high-tech companies, such as Hewlett-Packard, direct labor is less than 5 percent of total manufacturing costs in many operations.

Comparison of Job Costing, Process Costing, and Operation Costing

We have now discussed how to account for product costs in three types of organizations: job shops, such as construction companies, that use job costing; organizations with continuous flow processing, such as soft drink syrup manufacturers, that use process costing; and companies with operations, such as automobile manufacturers, that use operation costing. Operation costing combines the aspect of job costing that assigns materials separately to jobs (also called *work orders* or *batches* in operation costing) with the aspect of process costing that assigns conversion costs equally to each operation. Thus, in our motorcycle example, Sharks and Jets had different per-unit materials costs but the same operations costs per unit for the two operations that both models passed through.

In practice, you are likely to encounter elements of all three production methods. You also will find that every company has its own unique costing method that does not precisely fit any textbook description. Having studied these three basic costing methods will enable you to learn the variations on the methods presented here.

Review Questions

8.1 Why are equivalent units computed for process costing?

8.2 A manufacturing company has records of its current activity in WIP inventory and its ending WIP inventory; however, the record of its beginning inventory has been lost. What data are needed to compute the beginning inventory? Express your answer in equation form.

8.3 (Appendix A) If costs change from one period to another, why do costs that are transferred out of one department under FIFO costing include units with two different costs?

8.4 (Appendix A) What is the distinction in equivalent units under the FIFO method and under the weighted-average method?

8.5 It has been said that costs of a prior department behave similarly to costs of direct materials. Under what conditions are the costs similar? Why are they accounted for separately?

8.6 Assume that the number of units transferred out of a department is unknown. What is the formula to solve for units transferred out using the basic cost-flow model?

8.7 How does process costing treat spoiled units?

8.8 How are spoilage costs similar to underapplied overhead?

8.9 (Appendix A) What are the relative costs and benefits of weighted-average versus FIFO process costing?

8.10 (Appendix B) How is operation costing similar to, and different from, both job costing and process costing?

Critical Analysis

8.11 Management of a company that manufactures cereal is trying to decide whether to install a job or a process-costing system. The manufacturing vice president has stated that job costing gives the company the best control because it makes possible the assignment of costs to specific lots of goods. The controller, however, has stated that job costing requires too much record keeping. Would a process-costing system meet the manufacturing vice president's control objectives? Explain.

8.12 (Appendix A) A new member of the controller's staff in your company, a large producer of paper products, has just completed a report that urges the company to adopt the last-in, first-out (LIFO) method of process costing. The controller is concerned about the recommendation because the cost records are maintained on a FIFO basis. Indeed, the controller has not even heard of using LIFO for process-cost accounting. Form small groups to prepare a report addressing the following:

a. Would it be possible to use LIFO for process costing? What are the key issues? Would using it be desirable?

b. In your library or on the Internet (company home pages or the SEC's EDGAR database), obtain information on inventory policies of four paper manufacturers (e.g., Mead Corporation, Weyerhaeuser, Westvaco, Simpson Paper). Describe how firms in this industry account for their process costs.

8.13 (Appendix A) Under which of the following conditions will the first-in, first-out (FIFO) method of process costing produce the same cost of goods manufactured as the weighted-average method?

a. When goods produced are homogeneous.

b. When there is no beginning inventory.

c. When beginning and ending inventories are each 50 percent complete.

d. None of these.

[CPA adapted]

8.14 An error was made in computing the percentage of completion of the ending WIP inventory for the current year. The error resulted in assigning a *lower percentage of completion* to each component of the inventory than actually was the case. Assume that there was no beginning inventory. What is the effect of this error on

a. The computation of total equivalent units? (understate or overstate?)

b. The computation of costs per equivalent unit? (understate or overstate?)

c. Costs assigned to cost of goods transferred out for the period? (understate or overstate?)

[CPA adapted]

8.15 In computing the cost per equivalent unit, the weighted-average method considers

a. Current costs only.

b. Current costs plus costs in beginning WIP inventory.

c. Current costs plus cost of ending WIP inventory.

d. Current costs less costs in beginning WIP inventory.

[CPA adapted]

8.16 (Appendix A) When using the FIFO method of process costing, total equivalent units produced for a given period equal the number of units

a. Started and completed during the period plus the number of units in beginning WIP plus the number of units in ending WIP.

b. In beginning WIP plus the number of units started during the period plus the number of units remaining in ending WIP times the percentage of work necessary to complete the items.

c. In beginning WIP times the percentage of work necessary to complete the items plus the number of units started and completed during the period plus the number of units started this period and remaining in ending WIP times the percentage of work necessary to complete the items.

d. Transferred out during the period plus the number of units remaining in ending WIP times the percentage of work necessary to complete the items.

e. None of these.

[CPA adapted]

8.17 One of your process supervisors said to you, "Well, you have to break eggs to make an omelet," as a reason for considering the period's spoilage as a normal cost of production. Is spoilage a normal cost of production? If so, why report it separately?

8.18 Explain how the concept of "normal spoilage" could impede quality improvements in processes. If you do not distinguish between normal and abnormal spoilage, how would you identify "unacceptable" spoilage?

8.19 Explain how an individual could manipulate reported earnings by misstating degrees of completion of ending WIP. Would it be easy to continue this manipulation for subsequent periods? Explain.

Exercises

Exercise 8.20
Equivalent Units Computation, Weighted-Average Method
(LO 4)

Sarah & Sally's Ice Cream Company shows the following information concerning its work in process:

1. Beginning inventory, 4,000 partially complete units.
2. Transferred out, 9,000 units.
3. Ending inventory (materials, 10 percent complete; conversion costs, 20 percent complete).
4. Started this month, 12,000 units.

Required

a. Compute the number of equivalent units for materials using the weighted-average method.
b. Compute the number of equivalent units for conversion costs using the weighted-average method.

Exercise 8.21
(Appendix A) Equivalent Units Computation, FIFO Method
(LO 7)

Refer to the data in Exercise 8.20. Assume that beginning inventory is 20 percent complete with respect to materials and 15 percent complete with respect to conversion costs.

Required

a. Compute the number of equivalent units for materials using FIFO.
b. Compute the number of equivalent units for conversion costs using FIFO.

Exercise 8.22
Equivalent Units Computed, Weighted-Average Method
(LO 4)

Generic Colas, Inc. shows the following information concerning the WIP at its plant:

1. Beginning inventory, partially complete.
2. Transferred out, 30,000 units.
3. Ending inventory, 10,000 units (materials, 20 percent complete; conversion costs, 10 percent complete).
4. Started this month, 35,000 units.

Required

a. Compute the number of equivalent units for materials using the weighted-average method.
b. Compute the number of equivalent units for conversion costs using the weighted-average method.

Exercise 8.23
(Appendix A) Equivalent Units Computed, FIFO Method
(LO 7)

Refer to the data in Exercise 8.22. Assume that beginning inventory is 55 percent complete with respect to materials and 70 percent complete with respect to conversion costs.

Required

a. Compute the number of equivalent units for materials using the FIFO method.
b. Compute the number of equivalent units for conversion costs using the FIFO method.

Exercise 8.24
Equivalent Units Computed, Weighted-Average Method
(LO 4)

Mikee's Cereal Company adds materials at the beginning of the process in Department A. The following information pertains to Department A's work in process during April:

	Units
Work in process, April 1 (60% complete as to conversion costs)	6,000
Started in April	50,000
Completed	40,000
Work in process, April 30 (40% complete as to conversion costs)	16,000

Required

a. Compute the number of equivalent units for materials using the weighted-average method.
b. Compute the number of equivalent units for conversion costs using the weighted-average method.

[CPA adapted]

Exercise 8.25
(Appendix A) Equivalent Units Computed, FIFO Method
(LO 7)

Alyssa Co. has a process-costing system using the FIFO cost-flow method. All materials are introduced at the beginning of the process in Department 1. The following information is available for the month of January:

	Units
Work in process, January 1 (40% complete as to conversion costs)	250
Started in January	1,000
Transferred to Department 2 during January	1,050
Work in process, January 31 (70% complete as to conversion costs)	200

Required

Compute the number of equivalent units of production for materials and conversion costs for the month of January?

[CPA adapted]

Exercise 8.26
Cost per Equivalent Unit Computed, Weighted-Average Method
(LO 4)

The following information pertains to Rubicon Co.'s plant for the month of May:

	Number of Units	Cost of Materials
Beginning work in process	60,000	$13,200
Started in May	160,000	35,200
Units completed	170,000	
Ending work in process	50,000	

All materials are added at the beginning of the process.

Required

Using the weighted-average method, compute the cost per equivalent unit for materials.

[CPA adapted]

Exercise 8.27
(Appendix A) Equivalent Units Computed, FIFO Method
(LO 7)

Department A is the first stage of Kwan Company's production cycle. The following information is available for conversion costs for the month of April:

	Units
Beginning work in process (60% complete)	40,000
Started in April	680,000
Completed in April and transferred to Department B	640,000
Ending work in process (20% complete)	80,000

Required

Using the FIFO method, compute the number of equivalent units for the conversion costs.

[CPA adapted]

Exercise 8.28
Cost per Equivalent Unit (with Spoilage) Weighted-Average Method
(LO 4, 6)

Assume that a Pepsi-Cola bottling plant uses the weighted-average method to account for its WIP inventories. The accounting records show the following information for a particular day:

Beginning WIP inventory:	
Direct materials	$ 488
Conversion costs	136
Current period costs in work in process:	
Direct materials	$5,720
Conversion costs	3,322

Quantity information is obtained from the manufacturing records and includes the following (each unit equals 24 cans of Pepsi-Cola):

Beginning inventory	150 units (partially complete)
Current period units started	1,000 units
Ending inventory	300 units
Percentage of completion:	
Direct materials	40%
Conversion costs	20%
Spoilage	100 units
Percentage of completion:	
Direct materials	100%
Conversion costs	100%

Required

Compute the cost per equivalent unit for direct materials and conversion costs.

Exercise 8.29
Cost Assignment to Units Transferred Out, Spoilage, and Ending Inventory, Weighted-Average Method
(LO 4, 6)

Refer to the data in Exercise 8.28.

Required

Compute the cost of good units completed and transferred out, spoilage, and ending inventory using the weighted-average method.

Exercise 8.30
Cost per Equivalent Unit (with Spoilage) Computed, Weighted-Average Method
(LO 4, 6)

Green Chemicals had beginning WIP inventory of $124,160 on October 1. Of this amount, $50,820 was the cost of direct materials, and $73,340 was for conversion costs. The 8,000 units in the beginning inventory were 30 percent complete with respect to both direct materials and conversion costs.

During October, 17,000 units were transferred out, 500 were spoiled, and 4,500 remained in the ending inventory. Spoiled units were 100 percent complete with respect to materials and 50 percent complete with respect to conversion costs. The units in the ending WIP inventory were 80 percent complete with respect to direct materials and 40 percent complete with respect to conversion costs. Costs incurred during the period amounted to $390,600 for direct materials and $504,640 for conversion costs.

Required

Compute the cost per equivalent unit for direct materials and for conversion costs using the weighted-average method.

Exercise 8.31
Cost Assignment to Units Transferred Out, Spoilage, and Ending Inventory, Weighted-Average Method
(LO 4, 6)

Refer to the data in Exercise 8.30.

Required

Compute the costs of good units completed and transferred out, spoilage, and ending inventory using the weighted-average method.

Exercise 8.32
(Appendix B) Assign Costs to Products—Operation Costing
(LO 9)

The Beefy Bicycle Company makes three types of bicycles—mountain bikes, touring bikes, and racing bikes. The company had the following work orders for the month of September:

Customer	Order Quantity	Order Revenue
Wheelright	40 racing bikes, 40 mountain bikes	$90,000
Jmart Stores	100 mountain bikes, 80 touring bikes	80,000
Bikes "R We	10 racing bikes, 100 mountain bikes	80,000

Direct materials costs for bikes are as follows:

Touring bikes	$200 per unit
Racing bikes	800 per unit
Mountain bikes	300 per unit

Conversion costs incurred in Work-in-Process—Basic Assembly = $100 per unit for all three types of bikes.

Conversion costs incurred in Work-in-Process—Special Assembly = $200 per unit for racing bikes and $40 per bike for mountain bikes. Touring bikes require no special assembly.

Required

a. Compute the product costs for September for each of the three types of bicycles.

b. Show the flow of costs through T-accounts. Assume that all products are transferred to Finished Goods when completed, and then to Cost of Goods Sold when sold. All products in this exercise were sold in September. Use two work-in-process accounts: Work-in-Process—Basic Assembly and Work-in-Process—Special Assembly.

c. Taking into account the revenue from each customer's order and the direct materials and conversion costs required to produce the products for each order, compute customer profits for each order.

Exercise 8.33
(Appendix B) Assign Costs to Products—Operation Costing
(LO 9)

The Loafin' Leather Company makes three types of leather coats—the Brando, the Tori, and the J. Dean. The company had the following work orders for the month of January:

Customer	Order Quantity
N. Beach	30 units of the Tori and 50 units of the Brando
Hoardstrum	100 units of the Brando and 80 units of the Tori
Gop	100 units of the Brando, 30 units of the Tori, and 60 units of the J. Dean

Direct materials costs for leather coats are as follows:

The Brando	$200 per unit
The Tori	300 per unit
The J. Dean	500 per unit

Conversion costs incurred in Work-in-Process—Basic Assembly = $100 per unit for all three types of coats.

Conversion costs incurred in Work-in-Process—Special Finishing = $50 per unit for the Tori and $40 per unit for the J. Dean. The Brando coat requires no special finishing.

Required

a. Compute the product costs for January for each of the three types of coats.

b. Show the flow of costs through T-accounts. Assume that all products are transferred to Finished Goods when completed, and then to Cost of Goods Sold when sold. All products in this exercise were sold in January. Use two work-in-process accounts: Work-in-Process—Basic Assembly and Work-in-Process—Special Finishing.

Problems

Problem 8.34
Production Cost Report (Beginning and Ending WIP Inventory), Weighted-Average Method
(LO 3, 4)

The following data are available for Ebbit Company for the month of February:

	Units	Percentage Complete	Costs
Beginning WIP inventory, February	22,000		
Direct materials		75%	$4,200
Conversion costs		70	2,450
Units started in February	12,000		
Costs incurred in February:			
Direct materials			17,000
Conversion costs			16,800
Ending WIP inventory	6,000		
Direct materials		80	
Conversion costs		60	

Required

Use weighted-average process costing to

a. Prepare a production cost report.

b. Show the flow of costs through the WIP Inventory T-account.

Problem 8.35
(Appendix A) Production Cost Report (Beginning and Ending WIP Inventory), FIFO Method
(LO 3, 7, 8)

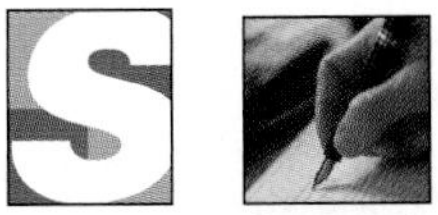

Spreadsheet Communication

Refer to the data in Problem 8.34.

Required

Use FIFO process costing to

a. Prepare a production cost report.

b. Show the flow of costs through the WIP Inventory T-account.

c. Prepare a short memo to Ebbit Company's CFO explaining whether you believe FIFO costing is better than weighted-average costing for the company.

Problem 8.36
Production Cost Report (Beginning and Ending WIP Inventory), Weighted-Average Method
(LO 3, 4)

The following data are available for Travis Company for the month of July:

	Units	Percentage Complete	Costs
Beginning WIP inventory, July	15,000		
Direct materials		60%	$ 8,800
Conversion costs		70	6,500
Units started in July	20,000		
Costs incurred in July:			
Direct materials			13,500
Conversion costs			12,300
Ending WIP inventory....................	5,000		
Direct materials		70	
Conversion costs		80	

Required

Use weighted-average process costing to

a. Prepare a production cost report.

b. Show the flow of costs through the WIP Inventory T-account.

Problem 8.37
Production Cost Report (Beginning and Ending WIP Inventory), Weighted-Average Method
(LO 3, 4)

The following data are available for Needles Production Company for the month of December:

	Units	Percentage Complete	Costs
Beginning WIP inventory, December	20,000		
Direct materials		80%	$20,000
Conversion costs		90	45,000
Units started in December.......................	50,000		
Costs incurred in December:			
Direct materials			27,000
Conversion costs			36,000
Ending WIP inventory.............................	25,000		
Direct materials		30	
Conversion costs		40	

Required

Use weighted-average process costing to

a. Prepare a production cost report.

b. Show the flow of costs through the WIP Inventory T-account.

Problem 8.38
(Appendix A) Production Cost Report (Beginning and Ending WIP Inventory) FIFO Method
(LO 3, 7, 8)

Communication

Refer to the data in Problem 8.37.

Required

Use FIFO process costing to

a. Prepare a production cost report.

b. Show the flow of costs through the WIP Inventory T-account.

c. Prepare a short memo to Needles Production Company's CFO explaining whether you believe FIFO process costing would be worthwhile for the company.

Problem 8.39
Production Cost Report (Prior Department Process Costs), Weighted Average Method
(LO 3, 4, 5)

Recycle Industries of Toronto recycles galvanized steel from automobile bodies in two processes: shredding and degalvanizing. It processes galvanized steel auto bodies in the shredding process and sends the shredded steel to the newly developed degalvanizing process which removes zinc by electrolysis. Zinc, which has a relatively high value, is the principal product of the process. The company transferred 6,000 metric tons of steel to the degalvanizing process this month. Neither process had any spoilage.

Because the galvanized steel is homogeneous and shredded in a continuous process, the company uses a process-costing accounting system to assign costs to it. The following information is available for the degalvanizing process during the last year:

RECYCLE INDUSTRIES, INC.
Degalvanizing Process Last Year

			Degalvanizing Process	
	Units	**Shredding Process Costs**	**Direct Materials**	**Conversion Costs ($Canadian)**
Physical flow (metric tons):				
Beginning inventory	1,000	100% complete	60% complete	75% complete
Ending inventory	2,700	100% complete	80% complete	45% complete
Transferred in	6,000	100% complete		
Costs incurred ($ Canadian):				
Beginning inventory		$ 7,100,000	$ 600,000	$ 420,000
Current costs		43,200,000	2,500,000	6,475,000

Required

a. Prepare a production cost report using weighted-average costing.

b. Show the flow of costs through the WIP Inventory T-account using weighted-average costing.

Problem 8.40
Production Cost Report (Prior Department Process Costs), Weighted Average Method
(LO 3, 4, 5)

Costa Corporation manufactures a child's car seat produced in three separate departments: Molding, Assembling, and Finishing. It uses the weighted-average process-costing method to account for costs of production. The following information was obtained for the Assembling Department for the month of June.

	Amount	**Percentage Complete**
WIP, June 1 (1,000 units):		
Prior department costs transferred in from the Molding Department	$32,000	100%
Costs added by the Assembling Department:		
Direct materials	$20,000	100
Direct labor	7,200	60
Manufacturing overhead	5,500	50
	$32,700	
Total WIP, June 1	$64,700	

During the month of June, the Molding Department transferred into the Assembling Department 5,000 units at a prior department cost of $160,000. The Assembling Department added the following $150,000 of costs:

Direct materials	$ 96,000
Conversion labor	36,000
Manufacturing overhead	18,000
	$150,000

The Assembling Department completed and transferred out 4,000 units to the Finishing Department. At June 30, 2,000 units were still in WIP. The degree of completion of WIP at June 30 was as follows:

Direct materials	90%
Direct labor	70
Manufacturing overhead	35

Required

a. Prepare a production cost report using weighted-average costing.

b. Management wants to decrease the costs of manufacturing the car seat. In particular, it has set the following per-unit targets for this product in the Assembling Department: materials, $20; labor, $10; and manufacturing overhead, $4.50. Has the Assembling Department achieved management's cost targets?

[CPA adapted]

Problem 8.41
Production Cost Report (with Spoilage), Weighted-Average Method
(LO 3, 4, 6)

Creative Paints makes an environmentally sound paint. The following data are available for the month of April:

	Units	Percentage Complete	Costs
Beginning WIP inventory, April	11,000		
Direct materials		75%	$ 3,200
Conversion costs		70	1,450
Units started in April	6,000		
Costs incurred in April:			
Direct materials			16,000
Conversion costs			15,800
Ending WIP inventory	3,000		
Direct materials		80	
Conversion costs		60	
Spoilage	200		
Direct materials		100	
Conversion costs		100	

Required

a. Prepare a production cost report using weighted-average costing.

b. Show the flow of costs through the WIP Inventory T-account.

Problem 8.42
Production Cost Report (with Spoilage), Weighted Average Method
(LO 3, 4, 6)

Outdoors Production, Inc., produces a sealant for wood decks. The following data are available for the month of April:

	Units	Percentage Complete	Costs
Beginning WIP inventory, April	13,000		
Direct materials		70%	$ 6,500
Conversion costs		60	12,000
Units started in April	17,000		
Costs incurred in April:			
Direct materials			16,000
Conversion costs			15,800

Ending WIP inventory	6,000	
Direct materials		60
Conversion costs		55
Spoilage	1,500	
Direct materials		75
Conversion costs		60

Required

a. Prepare a production cost report using weighted-average costing.

b. Show the flow of costs through the WIP Inventory T-account.

Problem 8.43
Equivalent Units Computed, Weighted Average
(LO 3)

Spreadsheet

Required

Answer each of the following questions regarding independent situations.

a. The following information is available for April:

	Units
Work in process, April 1 (40% complete)	25,000
Started in April	120,000
Work in process, April 30 (30% complete)	12,500

Materials are added at the beginning of the process. Using the weighted-average costing method, what are the equivalent units of production for the month of April for materials? For conversion costs?

b. Second Department is the second stage of Hurley Company's production cycle. On May 1, beginning work in process contained 50,000 units, which were 80 percent complete as to conversion costs. During May, 320,000 units were transferred in from the first stage of the production cycle. On May 31, ending WIP in the Second Department contained 40,000 units, which were 90 percent complete as to conversion costs. Materials are added at the end of the process in the Second Department. Using the weighted-average costing method, how many equivalent units were produced on May 31 in the Second Department for materials and conversion costs?

[CPA adapted]

Cases

Case 8.44
Public Policy and Process Costs
(LO 2, 3, 4)

Global

Team

In 1994, President Bill Clinton denied a request from forest-products executives to lift the ban on timber sales from federal lands in the US Northwest. Historically, timber from US federal lands had been sold at below-market prices to provide local economic support. "For communities affected by federal timber, the outlook is dismal," observed an industry consultant in Oregon. In a related development, the British Columbia, Canada, government in 1996 began implementing its Forest Practices Code, which has strict standards for logging activities and reforestation responsibilities. These developments have unfavorably affected a number of US wood and paper products companies that had relied heavily on timber sales from US and BC public lands. They have experienced higher material costs and have had access to lower volumes of timber. Other companies, however, have benefited from the price increases caused by the ban on federal timber sales and increased restrictions on logging in British Columbia because they have either large private timberland elsewhere or long-term supply contracts with private timber owners.

Longview Fibre Co. of Longview, Washington, was one of the companies adversely affected by these developments. For several years after the imposition of these restrictions, the company suffered higher material costs for most of its products. Since Longview Fibre was at a disadvantage compared to its competitors with unaffected sources of material, the company set a goal to significantly reduce its conversion costs. Following are the data that the company disclosed in one of its 1998 quarterly reports for each of its major product lines: timber products (logs and lumber), paper and paperboard, and container-board products (packaging).

LONGVIEW FIBRE CO
Consolidated Statement of Income (Unaudited)
For Six Months Ended April 30, 1998

Net sales:	
Timber products	$ 79,045,000
Paper and paperboard	92,433,000
Container-board products	190,677,000
	362,155,000
Cost of products sold (all products)	329,748,000
Gross profit	$ 32,407,000
Selling, administrative, and general expenses	32,313,000
Operating profit	$ 94,000
Operating profit (loss) by product:	
Timber products	$ 37,309,000
Paper and paperboard	(11,842,000)
Container-board products	(25,373,000)
	$ 94,000

	April 30, 1998	October 31, 1997
Inventories:		
Finished goods	$ 25,445,000	$24,832,000
Work in process	19,220,000	13,868,000
Raw materials and supplies	48,192,000	45,802,000
	$ 92,857,000	$84,502,000

	Sales Quantity
Six months ended April 30, 1998:	
Timber products, thousands of board feet	144,000,000
Paper and paperboard, tons	177,000,000
Container-board products, tons	255,000,000

Required

Work in small groups to develop solutions to the following requirements and then be prepared to present them to the class.

a. Reconstruct the elements of the basic cost-flow model ($BI + TI - TO = EI$) for Finished Goods and Work-in-Process Inventories. (*Hint:* Work backward from cost of goods sold.)

b. Compute the average process cost per unit sold of each of the three product lines. [*Hint:* Work backward from operating profit (loss) for each product.] Assume that selling, general, and administrative costs were assigned to product lines on the basis of relative revenue.

c. Average process costs per unit sold during the comparable period in 1997 follow:

Average Cost per Unit Sold	1997
Timber products, per thousand board feet	$230.47
Paper and paperboard, per ton	502.01
Container-board products, per ton	789.59

Compare the 1997 costs to the 1998 costs computed in part (b). During the 1998 period, the company's costs increased as follows: raw timber, 8 percent; wood chips used to make paper, 36 percent; and container board, 12 percent. From these data, does it appear that the company achieved its goal of reducing conversion costs? Describe a likely scenario that explains the company's changes in costs and 1998 profit performance.

[Adapted from "Splinters Everywhere," and Longview Fibre Co., Form 10-Q, April 30, 1998]

Case 8.45
Choosing Between Job and Process Costing
(LO 1)

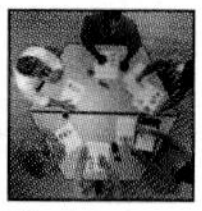

Communication Team

Many companies use process costing for some products and job costing for others. The authors of a study of costing methods described a particular medium-sized manufacturing company as using process costing for its products sold to commercial customers and job costing for products sold to the government.[3] For the government products, each job represented a separate contract with the government, so the company's accountants carefully kept track of which costs should be assigned to each contract. For the commercial products, the company's managers appeared to believe that the averaging of costs across products was sufficient for decision-making and cost control.

Required

Working in groups, identify several companies that would likely have both government and commercial (i.e., non-government) customers. Then identify which of these companies would likely use job costing for its products sold to the government. Write a brief report that explains why these companies would use job costing for products sold to the government.

Case 8.46
Spoilage Costs, Weighted-Average Method
(LO 3, 4, 6)

Anderson Company is a mature firm that manufactures a variety of high-quality sports clothing for college and high school football programs throughout the country. During the last year, the company's profits declined. Anderson has been using cost information that was developed two years ago. To determine the causes for weakened earnings performance, Anderson's controller, Bill Rolland, has asked Amy Kimball, senior cost analyst, to investigate product costing at one of the company's largest plants in Lincoln, Nebraska.

The Lincoln plant manufactures insulated warm-up jackets in a continuous, one-department process. The process first involves the basic assembly of materials packet 1 (liner, shell, hood, pocket linings, zippers), which consumes 70 percent of the conversion costs. At this point, partially complete jackets are inspected. Jackets that pass this inspection are finished with materials packet 2 (embroidered logos, numbers, and players' names). After the finishing process, the jackets are inspected again. Conversion costs are applied uniformly through the process, and the Lincoln plant uses the weighted-average process-costing method. Typical jackets cost $75 to produce and, based on desired return on sales, sell for $125 each in the competitive sports apparel market.

The following information for the most recent month was available to Kimball:

Units in beginning WIP inventory	560 jackets
Conversion costs	$4,506, 25% complete
Materials packet 1	$12,500
Units started	7,600 jackets
Units fully completed	6,600 jackets
Spoilage at first inspection	460 jackets
Spoilage at second inspection	200 jackets
Current costs applied during the month:	
Conversion costs	$278,400
Materials packet 1	$252,700
Materials packet 2	$74,120
Units in ending WIP inventory	900 jackets
Conversion costs	50% complete

[3]K. A. Timian and M. Fleming, "Toward Diversified Cost Accounting Systems."

Required

a. The Lincoln plant manager indicates to Kimball that all but 160 of the spoiled jackets at the first inspection point should be regarded as normal spoilage, and Rolland concurs. Discuss the accounting and management implications of separating spoilage into normal and abnormal spoilage.

b. Prepare a production cost report that analyzes the most recent month's process costs.

c. Given your analysis in requirement (b), what sales price is necessary to generate the desired return on sales? Alternatively, what total process-cost reduction is necessary to maintain the current sales price? What is your recommendation?

[CMA adapted]

CHAPTER

9

Joint-Process Costing

After completing this chapter, you should be able to:

1. Use cost-management information to increase the profits from using scarce resources of joint-production processes.
2. Use cost-management data in the sell-or-process-further decision.
3. Explain why organizations allocate joint costs.
4. Understand how to use the net-realizable-value and physical-measures joint-cost-allocation methods.
5. Know how to account for by-products.
6. Understand how to use the relative sales value at split-off and constant gross margin percentage methods of cost allocation (Appendix).

Cost-Management

Challenges

1. **How** do cost-management analysts anticipate and resolve potential conflicts between joint-product and process decision making and external reporting?

2. **If** joint-cost allocations are arbitrary, does that mean they are meaningless?

National

WOOD PRODUCTS

Address by Malcolm Fries, president and CEO of National Wood Products, Inc., to the company's management team. The setting is National Wood Products' annual, preliminary budget meeting where the company's top staff and division managers planned operations for the coming year. (National Wood Products, Inc., is a fictional company based on information from a number of wood-products firms, including Boise Cascade, International Paper, Longview Fibre, Louisiana Pacific, Pope & Talbot, WestVaco, and Weyerhaeuser.) National Wood Products has three major product lines: lumber, paper pulp, and paperboard (for packaging). The three products come from a standard source—softwood trees such as fir, hemlock, and pine. National Wood Products' customers are companies that use lumber (e.g., U.S. Homes), convert pulp into paper (e.g., Hammermill Paper), or produce packaging from paperboard (e.g., Quaker Oats). All of National Wood Products' customers can buy their lumber, pulp, or paperboard on the open, international market from the cheapest source.

"It looks like we are in for a rough year, and we have to be absolutely sure that we understand our costs and our capabilities. Each of us must make every decision count. We can't afford to waste any of our capacity on products that don't generate the most profit. In particular, we must produce more innovative products, such as specialty lumber, which takes advantage of our ability to dry "green" lumber. I don't need to tell you that the Board and industry analysts are watching us closely. We have to make smart, tough decisions. Let's get to work."

Joint Product Processes

National
WOOD PRODUCTS

joint process *simultaneously converts a common input into several outputs*

joint products *are the products that jointly result from processing a common input*

split-off point *is the point at which joint products appear in the production process*

final product *is one that is ready for sale without further processing*

intermediate product *is a product that might require further processing before it is salable to the ultimate consumer*

joint costs *are costs to operate joint processes, including the disposal of waste*

Many companies that use natural resources face the problem of how to use cost information to manage processes that can produce different products but, perhaps, without the urgency faced by National Wood Products. As does NWP, companies such as Weyerhaeuser (wood), Shell Oil (petroleum and chemicals), Phelps Dodge (minerals), and ConAgra (meat) face the challenge of making informed decisions about these processes using cost information. A **joint process,** simultaneously converts a common input into several outcomes. For example, processing timber results *jointly* in lumber of various grades plus wood chips and sawdust that can be converted into paper pulp. Pulp can be sold or processed further into paperboard. As another example, processing crude oil can result *jointly* in gasoline of various grades, kerosene, jet fuel, asphalt, and/or petrochemicals. The products that jointly result from processing a common input are called **joint products.**

The Importance of Split Off

The point at which joint products appear in the production process is called the **split-off point.** For example, literally, at the point of a saw blade, lumber appears. In refining oil, the split-off point occurs in a "cracking" process, which produces various petroleum products simultaneously. At split off, several types of products appear. A **final product** is one that is ready for sale without further processing. For example, National Wood Products sells specialty and standard lumber as final products. An **intermediate product** is a product that might require further processing before it is salable to the ultimate consumer, either by the producer or by another processor. Thus, an intermediate product might be a final product for one company (the producer) and input for another company that will process it further.

Costs to operate joint processes, including the disposal of waste, are called **joint costs.** Depending on the technology used, joint processes primarily use resources at the batch and facility levels. In most cases, companies set up the joint process to accommodate a specific type of input or to produce a specific type of output in a batch. Thus, an oil refiner might set up the refinery (a large, facility-level resource) to process a batch of crude oil of a particular grade and to produce specific petroleum products. National Wood Products sets up its sawmills to process logs and produce specific types and grades of lumber.

The split-off point is where multiple outputs appear.

In practice, assigning joint costs to the various products for financial reporting and measuring product profitability involves a somewhat arbitrary cost *allocation* based on the quantities of outputs or the relative sales value of the joint products. Therefore, the sequence of decisions involved in the *management of joint processes requires, first, deciding which products to produce and, second, determining how to allocate joint-process costs.*

We now describe National Wood Products' joint-process decision making and costing and the importance of these managerial processes to the firm's profitability. Note that the decisions and methods described in this chapter are applicable to all joint processes.

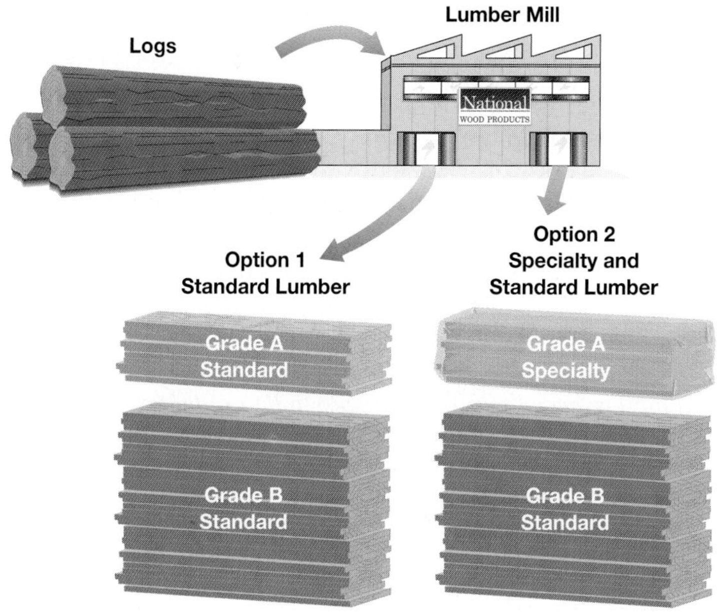

Exhibit 9–1

Measures of Process Capacity

One Input—More Than One Output

At National Wood Products' Georgia mill, raw timber (logs) is the common input to produce the following products:

1. Grade A Standard lumber, which is high quality with minor or no imperfections,
2. Grade B Standard lumber, which has imperfections but is acceptable for jobs that use rough lumber, and
3. Grade A Specialty lumber which is made by further processing Grade A Standard lumber by drying to eliminate the tendency of 'green' lumber to warp.

Note that each log produces both Grade A and Grade B lumber. Management decides whether to process Grade A from Standard to Specialty with the drying process.

Exhibit 9–1 depicts the two alternatives that management can choose: (1) produce Grade A Standard and Grade B Standard or (2) produce Grade A Specialty and Grade B Standard.[1] The cost of the lumber and the cost of processing (e.g., sawing) up to the split-off point are joint costs. This split-off point is where the log has been sawed into lumber. Some of that lumber is Grade A and the rest is Grade B.

The Decision Challenge: Which Joint Products to Produce

LO 1 Use cost-management information to increase the profits from using scarce resources of joint-production processes.

The usual objective governing the production of joint products is to maximize profits, which clearly is an important objective for National Wood Products. In some situations, such as joint ventures among various parties that use the outputs of a process, contracts can specify the products to produce and the amounts.

[1] In practice, many more options for converting logs are available. Furthermore, in computer-controlled sawmills, each log can be evaluated and sawed to maximize the profit from alternative products based on current product prices.

Estimation of Profits from Joint Products

Using its best estimates of sales prices and production costs, National Wood Products makes decisions regarding how to use its mill capacity by going through these steps:

1. *Identify alternative sets and quantities of final products possible from the joint process.* From joint processing of logs, National Wood Products considers two sets of products, Grade A and Grade B Standard lumber—as final products.
2. *Forecast the sales price of each final product.* National Wood Products closely watches regional and international market prices and drivers of demand and prices, such as housing starts and monthly timber harvests reported by the Forest Products Association, an industry trade group. The company also seeks to establish long-term customer relationships and contracts to ensure predictable sales and prices.
3. *Estimate the costs (if any) required to further process joint products into salable products.* To produce Grade A Specialty lumber, National Wood Products incurs additional processing costs for drying the lumber.
4. *Choose the set of products with the overall maximum profit.*

Exhibit 9–2 shows the data to support joint-product decision making at National Wood Products' Georgia sawmill. The top line of Exhibit 9–2 shows the mill's monthly capacity to be 4,700 MBF (1,000 board feet with 1 board foot of lumber as a piece of lumber 1 foot square by 1 inch thick).

Just below the mill capacity is the forecasted sales prices of each of the three types of lumber. Below that are the alternative production quantities. National Wood Products can produce and sell either option 1 (all standard lumber) or option 2 (part specialty and part standard lumber). Option 2 was developed in response to the address by Malcolm Fries (president and CEO of National Wood Products) reported at the beginning of this chapter. Recall that he asked company employees to develop new product ideas. Plant employees at the company's Georgia plant developed the Grade A Specialty lumber as a new product.

Next are the joint costs to produce a total of 4,000 MBF for either option 1 or option 2. These joint costs, which total $1,400,000, include the cost of both obtaining the logs and cutting them into lumber. At this split-off point, the Georgia plant would have

Exhibit 9–2

National Wood Products, Inc., Georgia Mill

Mill capacity per month*	4,700 MBF†
Forecasted sales prices:	
Grade A Standard	$600 per MBF
Grade B Standard	$400 per MBF
Grade A Specialty	$900 per MBF
Alternative production quantities:	
Option 1:	
Grade A Standard	1,000 MBF
Grade B Standard	3,000 MBF
Option 2:	
Grade A Specialty	1,000 MBF
Grade B Standard	3,000 MBF
Joint costs to produce 4,000 MBF of Grade A and Grade B Standard lumber	$1,400,000 per month
Additional costs to convert Grade A Standard to Grade A Specialty ($100 per MBF)	$100,000 per month

*Information is for a typical month.

†The abbreviation MBF refers to 1,000 board feet. One board foot is equivalent to a piece of lumber that is 1 foot square by 1 inch thick. MBF is a typical measure of volume in the US lumber industry. The international standard measure of lumber volume is cubic meters: 1 MBF = 2.4 cubic meters.

Exhibit 9–3

Diagram of Revenue and Costs

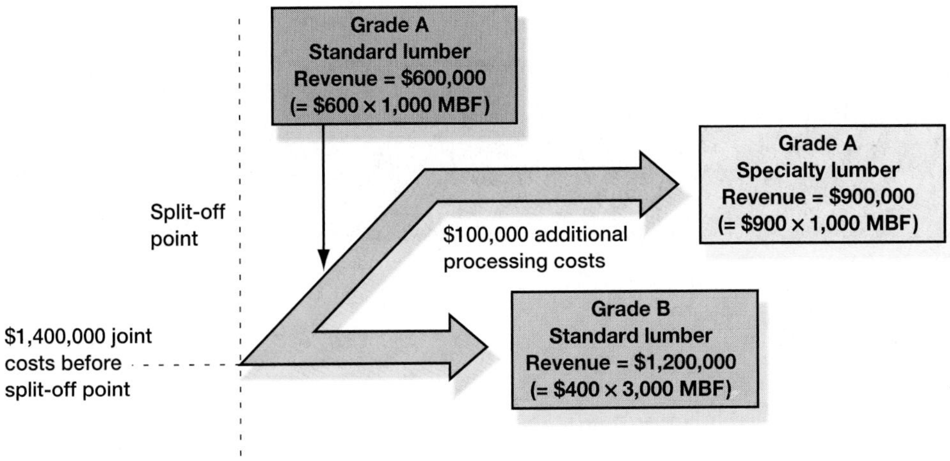

produced 1,000 MBF of Grade A Standard and 3,000 MBF of Grade B Standard lumber. To convert Grade A Standard lumber into Grade A Specialty lumber requires an additional cost of $100,000 to dry 1,000 MBF of Grade A Standard lumber.

Exhibit 9–3 diagrams the production process, showing the costs and revenues of the process and products. Exhibits 9–2 and 9–3 present important information referred to throughout the chapter. Be sure that you understand it before you continue.

You're the Decision Maker 9.1

Operate or Shut Down the Process?

The practical capacity of the Georgia mill is based on running one shift per day five days a week because of limited access to timber in that region. Negotiations to gain access to timber on Native American reservation land to replace reduced timber from U.S. federal land have not progressed satisfactorily (from the company's perspective).

a. A member of the corporate controller's staff has observed that the per-unit cost of lumber from the Georgia mill is higher than at mills running two shifts per day for six days a week. He suggests that the company should consider closing the Georgia mill because other mills are more efficient. Is there a sound basis for this recommendation? Explain.

b. As a member of the Georgia mill management team, how would you respond to the recommendation to close your mill? Consider both local and companywide issues.

(Solutions begin on page 363.)

Decision to Sell Products at Split Off or Process Them Further

LO 2 Use cost-management data in the sell-or-process-further decision.

Many companies have opportunities to sell partly processed products at various production stages. The management team must decide whether selling the output at an intermediate stage or processing it further is more profitable. In such a "sell-or-process-further" decision, the relevant economic data to consider are (1) the potential additional revenue after further processing and (2) the additional costs to process further.

Profit Maximization of Joint-Product Processes

net realizable value (NRV) *is the measure of a product's contribution to profit after the split-off point and is computed as sales revenue minus additional processing costs*

The **net realizable value (NRV)** is the measure of a product's contribution to profit after the split-off point and is computed as sales revenue minus additional processing costs. Computing the NRV of each set of products provides a comparison of each product's sales revenue to costs incurred *after* split off. It is important to note that any *allocation* of the mill's $1,400,000 joint-process costs among products is irrelevant to product decisions. Joint-process costs incurred *prior* to the split-off point are not affected by the decision to sell or process further after the split-off point. Only the revenues from selling or processing beyond the split-off point and any expenditures for additional processing are the relevant

Exhibit 9–4 Georgia Mill: Analysis of Alternatives for a Typical Month

	A Quantity*	B Price per Unit	C Revenue (Column A × Column B)	D Additional Processing Costs	E Net Realizable Value of the split-off point (Column C – Column D)
Option 1: Produce Standard lumber:					
NRV, Grade A Standard lumber...............	1,000	$600	$ 600,000	$ 0	$ 600,000
NRV, Grade B Standard lumber	3,000	400	1,200,000	0	1,200,000
Total net realizable value for Option 1..........					$1,800,000
Option 2: Produce Grade B Standard and Grade A Specialty lumber:					
NRV, Grade A Specialty lumber...............	1,000	$900	$ 900,000	$100,000	$ 800,000
NRV, Grade B Standard lumber	3,000	400	1,200,000	0	1,200,000
Total net realizable value for option 2					$2,000,000

Recommendation: Choose option 2 because it has the higher net realizable value.

*Quantity is expressed in thousand board feet (MBF). 1 unit = 1,000 board feet. One board foot of lumber is equivalent to 1 square foot of lumber that is 1 inch thick.

factors, regardless of the way the company allocates joint costs. It is ultimately necessary to measure whether the total NRV of the most profitable set of products exceeds the joint-process cost but only after selecting the best set of products.

Profit Analysis of Option 1: Grade A Standard Lumber

National WOOD PRODUCTS

The profit analysis of the Georgia mill decision is in Exhibit 9–4. Expected quantities, prices, and further processing costs after the split off are based on the information of products from Exhibit 9–2. The exhibit shows that the total NRV for option 1 equals $1,800,000.

Profit Analysis of Option 2: Grade A Specialty Lumber and Grade B Standard Lumber

According to data in Exhibit 9–4, the total NRV of option 2 is $2,000,000, which is composed of the $800,000 NRV of Grade A Specialty lumber plus the $1,200,000 Grade B Standard lumber. Note that the additional processing of Grade A lumber to convert it from Standard to Specialty lumber cost $100,000 but added $300,000 to revenues from Grade A lumber.

Most Profitable Products

An analysis of Exhibit 9–4 indicates that the most profitable decision is to produce Grade A Specialty and Grade B Standard lumber (option 2). The NRV of this combination exceeds the NRV of option 1. Furthermore, the NRV of $2,000,000 per month for option 2 exceeds the joint-processing cost of $1,400,000 per month (from Exhibit 9–2), so the mill can operate profitably (assuming that general and administrative costs do not exceed $600,000, the difference between the best NRV and the joint-process cost).

Providing this type of accurate cost analysis is one of the most important contributions of cost-management analysts in organizations that use joint-production processes, but it is not their only contribution, as we see in the next section.

Testing the Validity of the Analysis

Refer to Exhibits 9–2 and 9–4.

The analysis in Exhibit 9–4 is based on the company's best estimates of quantities, revenues, and costs, but actual amounts could differ. You have been asked to determine whether the recommendations could differ if these figures have errors.

a. Which figures in Exhibits 9–2 and 9–4 probably are most subject to error? Why?

b. Describe the concept of *materiality* in the context of the analysis in Exhibit 9–4.

c. Sensitivity analysis is a method of systematically testing whether a decision would change by changing one key figure in the analysis at a time and observing the change in expected outcomes. It is a way of asking "what-if" questions about changes in figures and measuring the effects. For example, *what if* economic troubles in Asia reduce the price for specialty lumber to $650 per MBF? Is the decision to produce lumber option 2 *sensitive* to this change in price?

d. What advice regarding the analysis would you give to managers of the Georgia mill to help them in their product planning for the year?

(Solutions begin on page 363.)

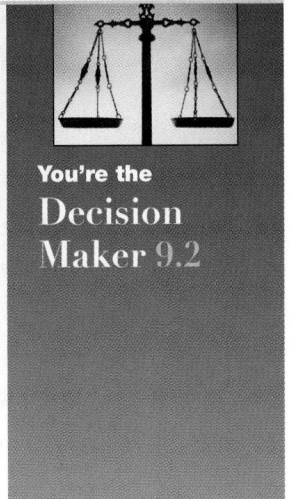

You're the Decision Maker 9.2

Reasons for Allocating Joint Costs

None of the preceding analyses involved allocating any of the $1,400,000 joint cost to any product, but most companies allocate these costs. Why should cost-management analysts be overly concerned with allocating joint costs when such allocations appear to be completely arbitrary? Organizations allocate joint costs for many reasons, including measuring performance, estimating casualty losses, determining and responding to regulatory rates, and specifying and resolving contractual interests and obligations. Manufacturing companies are required to use joint-cost allocations for financial and tax reporting to value inventories and cost of goods sold. For example, valuing inventories and measuring reported income for specialty and standard lumber at National Wood Products' Georgia mill requires the allocation of joint-process costs to both products.

Realize that although there is no precise way to trace joint-process costs to joint products (as activity-based costing seeks to do in other production processes, for example), the results of allocating joint costs in different ways can be very important to management decision making. The following examples demonstrate that, although joint costs might be inexact, they should not be randomly determined. Cost-management analysts need to consider the decision-making implications of seemingly arbitrary joint-cost allocations.

Measuring Performance

Joint-cost allocations can serve as measures of some departmental or division costs when executive performance is evaluated. Many companies compensate executives and other employees, at least partly, on the basis of departmental or divisional earnings for the year, which could be based on allocated joint costs. For example, if one division at National Wood Products is responsible for selling specialty lumber and another is responsible for selling standard lumber, the cost of processing logs could be allocated partly to the specialty lumber division and partly to the standard lumber division.[2] Both divisions have an interest in the way the costs are allocated because of the impacts on

[2]Note also that if one division is in a higher income tax bracket than the other, the company might be motivated to use a joint-costing method that allocates as much cost to the division in the higher bracket as possible to increase its cost of goods sold and reduce its reported income. It is even possible that tax implications could change product choices. This issue is related to transfer pricing, covered in Chapter 19.

divisional profits. The company as a whole, however, must ensure that the divisions work together as a team to maximize overall profits.

Using any cost allocation as a performance measure raises the issue of fairness and could affect the use of resources or provide the incentive to manipulate the performance measure. Managers who are downstream from joint processes and are evaluated in part on the basis of allocated joint costs might feel that cost allocations are not fair since they cannot control the joint costs. An adverse effect of cost allocation occurs if managers mistakenly regard average joint costs per unit as unit-level or marginal costs and make improper product or service decisions based on this mistaken interpretation.

Estimating Casualty Losses

Joint-cost allocations can be useful in valuing inventory for insurance purposes. Should a casualty loss occur, the insurance company and the insured party must agree on the value of the lost goods. For example, suppose that a portion of the specialty lumber at National Wood Products was destroyed in a fire. From National Wood Product's perspective, the cost of the lumber destroyed should include a portion of the joint costs.

Determining and Responding to Regulated Rates

When companies are subject to rate (price) regulation, the allocation of joint costs can be a significant factor in the way regulators determine rates. Thus, the manner of allocating and using joint costs can be important cost drivers in utilities that depend on joint-cost allocations for pricing or reimbursement. The importance of joint-cost allocations continues in many industries, including telecommunications (see Cost Management in Practice 9.1). In some countries, however, utility rates have been partially or completely deregulated, so costs based in part on the allocation of the joint costs to produce energy or gas are becoming less important.

Specifying and Resolving Contractual Interests and Obligations

Many contracts involve parties with potentially conflicting interests. For example, neither the insurance company nor the insured party wishes to pay any more or receive any less than is fair. Both buyers and sellers of contracted products or services are affected by pricing terms in the contract, and neither wishes to give the other an unfair advantage. Often prices for goods and services exchanged among contracting parties are based on costs, including allocated joint costs. Any cost-allocation method contains an element of arbitrariness or inexactness, although activity-based costing (discussed in Chapter 4) attempts to more accurately assign costs to products. Thus, specifying how to allocate costs in advance is advisable.

When joint costs are involved among contracting parties, a great potential for conflict exists because every joint-cost allocation is discretionary. By the nature of joint processes, determining exactly how much of joint process resources is used by any of the resulting joint products is impossible. Joint-cost allocation methods must be clearly stated in contracts before they are implemented. In that sense, the choice of the joint-cost allocation method is not arbitrary but is an integral part of the contract. To leave the definition of the joint-cost or other cost-allocation method ambiguous in a contract when the interests of either party can be affected is to invite dispute. On the other hand, cost-management analysts, by estimating the effects of joint-cost allocations and clearly spelling out how to allocate joint costs, contribute to informed negotiations and a smoothly functioning contractual arrangement.

Joint-cost Allocations and the Telecommunications Industry

Cost Management in Practice 9.1

Anyone interested in exploiting his or her understanding of joint-cost allocations should look for work in the telecommunication industry! Telecommunication companies provide services to the public and to other companies in the industry, in part by selling access to their communication capacity. A large portion of telecommunication capacity is a facility-level resource that is analogous to a joint process, which is impossible to trace to any particular use of the resource. For example, customers or competing companies use network facilities to originate or terminate long-distance or local calls.

In the United States, federal and state governments have regulated charges among telecommunication companies to encourage competition and universal access to telecommunication for citizens. Although *interstate* access rates are regulated by the Telecommunication Act of 1996, federal courts have ruled that regulating *intrastate* access rates is up to individual states. Because access rates are based to a large degree on allocations of joint-capacity costs, numerous disputes have occurred among telecommunication companies competing for access to customers within specific states.

Joint-cost allocations of network costs, for example, were at the heart of a complaint by telecommunication giant AT&T against Ameritech in the State of Ohio regarding appropriate intrastate telephone access rates charged by Ameritech. Because Ameritech owns the capacity (e.g., lines and networks) that other carriers must use in Ohio, overcharging (e.g., misuse of joint costing) allegedly allowed the local Ameritech company to squeeze out competition by allocating higher costs to competitors' use of capacity than to its own customers. MCI joined the fray charging that Ameritech was exploiting its monopoly position by charging competitors too much for the monthly and per-minute costs of access, which contain large amounts of allocated joint costs of Ameritech's operations. MCI recommended a joint-cost-based charge that would save its customers approximately $65 million per month (and make MCI more competitive with Ameritech). One company's strategic joint-cost allocation had become another's cost of doing business. *Source: "The First Report and Order Re Local Competition," FCC Common Carrier Docket 96–98, Part Two. Deposition by Mr. Dennis L. Ricca (MCI, Inc.) for the Ohio Public Utilities Commission. United States Court of Appeals for the Eighth Circuit Opinion No. 96-3321. (Full citations to references are in the Bibliography.)*

Joint-Cost Implications in Contracts

Although properly described and implemented joint-cost allocations can be beneficial, as discussed, managers' lack of awareness of the discretionary nature of joint-cost allocation makes good business for lawyers and litigation support consultants who know something about accounting. In many cases, people or companies became involved in disputes because they did not consider the implications of joint costs in written or oral contracts. Disputes often arise over the application of the word *cost* in cost-sharing agreements. Consider these examples:

- *Example 1.* Two companies, Tulsa Oil and Buffalo Energy, entered a joint venture to drill for oil and natural gas. Tulsa Oil wanted the oil from the well; Buffalo Energy wanted the natural gas. The costs of exploration, drilling, pumping, and separating oil from natural gas are the joint costs shared by the two companies. Neither company would find the venture profitable alone, but, by sharing the costs, both companies find it profitable.

  After 10 years without dispute, worldwide natural gas prices dropped substantially because of new discoveries and increased distribution of natural gas from Russia and neighboring countries. Buffalo Energy wanted out of the joint venture because selling natural gas from this venture was no longer profitable. Tulsa Oil wanted Buffalo Energy to continue sharing the costs of pumping and separating natural gas and oil, so it did not want Buffalo Energy to back out. Buffalo Energy ceased operations and stopped paying the costs of the joint venture: legal war broke out!
- *Example 2.* Consider the State of Alaska's North Slope dispute with British Petroleum and Exxon Mobil over the joint costs of gas-processing plants. The oil companies paid the State of Alaska royalties amounting to one-eighth of the value of oil pumped off the North Slope. However, the oil companies reduced the royalty payment by a portion of joint costs incurred by certain

Joint ventures in oil and gas refining often require an allocation of joint costs to each of the business partners.

gas-processing plants. These plants pumped a common input from underground and processed it into three joint products, two of which were then mostly pumped back into the ground because processing them further was not profitable. The single, retained joint product was oil.

How much of the joint cost of the gas-processing plant should be allocated to the oil. The oil companies wanted to allocate as much joint cost as possible to the oil to reduce their royalty payment to the state. Conversely, the state wanted to allocate as much as possible to the joint products that were pumped back into the ground.

After years of discussion and tens of millions of dollars of legal expense, the case was settled out of court just before going to trial. The resulting allocation was a compromise between the parties to the lawsuit.

Write contracts carefully. Those of you who become lawyers or litigation consultants are likely to work on legal cases involving joint costs because of their inherent arbitrariness. Legal cases involving oil and gas companies alone have hundreds of millions of dollars at stake. Accountants and cost-management analysts have an opportunity and a professional obligation to provide input to their organizations' contracts involving joint or indirect cost allocations. To minimize the incidence of such disputes, you should carefully word contracts to define the meaning, measurement, allocation, and sharing of *costs* and anticipate as many future events as possible that could affect the amount and measurement of costs. Although no contract can completely specify every contingency, above all avoid ambiguous phrases such as "share the costs of processing," which without careful elaboration invite trouble.

Joint Cost-Allocation Methods

LO 4 Understand how to use the net-realizable-value and physical-measures joint-cost-allocation methods.

The two major methods of allocating joint costs are (1) the net realizable value method and (2) the physical-measures method. Other methods, such as the sales value at split off and gross margin, are used much less frequently; they are discussed briefly in the chapter appendix.

Distinguishing between Main and By-Products

main product *is a joint output that generates a significant portion of the net realizable value from the process*

by-product *is the output from a joint-production process that is minor in quantity and/or NRV when compared to the main products*

In practice, companies distinguish between main products and by-products before allocating joint costs because, by convention, joint costs are allocated only to main products. A **main product** is a joint output that generates a significant portion of the net realizable value (NRV) from the process. A **by-product** on the other hand, is the output from a joint-production process that is minor in quantity and/or NRV when compared to the main products. Kerosene, for example, is a by-product of gasoline production. You may have seen advertisements for carpet and cloth mill ends at bargain prices, which often are by-products of textile production. *By-products do not receive allocations of joint costs.* Suppose that as a by-product of cutting the bark off of logs, the Georgia mill also produces wood chips. Assume also that the NRV from the wood chips is considerably less than the NRV from either of the other two products. Therefore, National Wood Products considers the wood chips to be a by-product of lumber production.

Using the Net Realizable Value Method

The **net realizable value (NRV) method** allocates joint costs based on the net realizable value (NRV) of each *main product* at the split-off point. If the main products are to be sold at the split-off point without further processing, the market values or sales prices at split-off are used for this allocation base. If further processing is required, the NRV at the split-off point is computed by deducting those added processing costs from sales value. (If the added processing has not yet been done, then the added processing costs would be estimated.) Using the NRV method, joint costs are allocated to the main products in proportion to their NRVs at the split-off point.

net realizable value (NRV) method *allocates joint costs based on the NRV of each main product at the split-off point*

From the previous analysis, assume that National Wood Products chose to produce Option 2; Grade A Specialty lumber and Grade B Standard lumber. The joint cost up to the split-off point is $1,400,000. Using the NRV method, this $1,400,000 joint cost is allocated based on the relative net realizable values of Grade A Specialty and Grade B Standard lumber. According to Exhibit 9–4, the net realizable value of Grade A Specialty lumber was $800,000, or 40% of the total net realizable value of $2,000,000 for the option (.40 = $800,000 ÷ $2,000,000). The net realizable value of Grade B Standard lumber was $1,200,000, or 60% of the total net realizable value of $2,000,000 for the option (.60 = $1,200,000 ÷ $2,000,000).

Exhibit 9–5 shows the allocation of the $1,400,000 joint cost to each of the two products. Based on the net realizable values, 40% of the $1,400,000 joint cost is allocated to Grade A Specialty lumber and 60% is allocated to Grade B Standard lumber.

Exhibit 9–6 shows the equality of the gross margin percents, calculated as the relation between the gross margins and the NRVs at split-off. This equality is an important feature of the NRV method; namely, that it maintains the relative profitability of the products. Neither the Grade A Specialty nor the Grade B Standard lumber is advantaged or disadvantaged by the NRV method.

We have presented a typical method for allocating joint costs using the economic values of joint products. The Appendix to this chapter presents two alternative methods using economic values.

Using the Physical-Measures Method

The **physical-measures (or quantities) method** is a joint-cost allocation based on the relative volume, weight, energy content, or other physical measure of each joint product at the split-off point. Companies might prefer the physical-measures method when

The physical-measures (or quantities) method *is a joint-cost allocation based on the relative volume, weight, energy content, or other physical measure of each joint product at the split-off point*

Exhibit 9–5

Joint Cost Allocations—NRV Method

National
WOOD PRODUCTS

	Grade A Specialty Lumber	Grade B Standard Lumber	Total
Sales revenue	$900,000	$1,200,000	$2,100,000
Less further processing costs	100,000	0	100,000
Net realizable value	$800,000	$1,200,000	$2,000,000
Proportionate share of net realizable value	40%	60%	100%
Allocated joint process costs	$560,000	$ 840,000	$1,400,000

Computations

Proportional share of NRV:	
Grade A Specialty lumber	40% = $800,000 ÷ $2,000,000
Grade B Standard lumber	60% = $1,200,000 ÷ $2,000,000
	100%
Allocations of joint costs:	
To Grade A Specialty lumber	$ 560,000 = 40% × $1,400,000
To Grade B Standard lumber	$ 840,000 = 60% × $1,400,000
	$1,400,000

Exhibit 9–6

Gross margins: Net Realizable Value Method

National WOOD PRODUCTS

	Grade A Specialty Lumber	Grade B Standard Lumber	Total
Sales revenues	$900,000	$1,200,000	$2,100,000
Less additional processing costs to point of marketability	100,000	0	100,000
NRV at split-off point	800,000	1,200,000	2,000,000
Allocation of joint costs:			
.40 × $1,400,000	560,000		1,400,000
.60 × $1,400,000		840,000	
Gross margin	$240,000	$ 360,000	$ 600,000
Gross margin as a percent of NRV at split-off point*	30%	30%	30%

*30% = 240,000 ÷ $800,000; $360,000 ÷ $1,200,000; $600,000 ÷ $2,000,000

Exhibit 9–7

Joint Cost Allocations: Physical-Measures Method

National WOOD PRODUCTS

	Grade A Specialty Lumber	Grade B Standard Lumber	Total
Quantity produced (MBF)	1,000	3,000	4,000
Proportionate share of physical quantity	25%	75%	100%
	(1,000 MBF ÷ 4,000 MBF)	(3,000 MBF ÷ 4,000 MBF)	
Allocated joint process costs	$350,000	$1,050,000	$1,400,000
	(25% × $1,400,000)	(75% × $1,400,000)	

the prices of their output products are highly volatile or unpredictable. This method is sometimes used when significant processing occurs between the split-off point and the first sales opportunity, or when the market does not set product prices. The latter situation could arise when regulators set prices in regulated pricing situations or in cost-based contract situations, for example.

Many oil- and gas-producing companies allocate joint costs on the basis of the products' energy equivalents (BTU content). They use this method because the products are typically measured in different physical units (e.g., natural gas by thousands of cubic feet, oil by barrels), although oil and natural gas often are produced simultaneously from the same well.

Allocations. We return to the National Wood Products company example. The company produces lumber according to option 2—1,000 MBF of Grade A Specialty lumber and 3,000 MBF of Grade B Standard lumber. Using the physical measures method, cost-management analysts allocate 25% (1,000 ÷ 4,000 total MBF) of the joint process costs to Grade A Specialty lumber and 75% (3,000 ÷ 4,000 total MBF) of the joint process costs to Grade B Standard lumber. Exhibit 9–7 shows the allocation of the $1,400,000 joint process cost to each of the two products; $350,000 (25% × $1,400,000) to Grade A Specialty and $1,050,000 (75% × $1,400,000) to Grade B Standard lumber.

Gross margins. The physical measures method does not allocate costs proportional to economic values, so the gross margins of joint products is not equal, as in the NRV method. Exhibit 9–8 shows that, in this example, Grade A Specialty lumber has a relatively high gross margin compared to Grade B Standard lumber. That is because the physical measures method allocates a relatively low proportion of joint costs to Grade A Specialty lumber.

It is wise not to rely too much on joint product margins or profits for decision making because such margin or profit computations are affected by the methods used to allo-

Gross Margins: Physical-Measures Method	Grade A Specialty Lumber	Grade B Standard Lumber	Total
Sales revenue	$900,000	$1,200,000	$2,100,000
Cost of goods sold			
Joint-cost allocations	$350,000	$1,050,000	$1,400,000
Further processing costs	100,000	0	100,000
Total cost of goods sold	$450,000	$1,050,000	$1,500,000
Gross margins: Physical-measures method	$450,000	$ 150,000	$ 600,000

Exhibit 9-8

Gross Margins: Physical-Measures Method

cate joint costs. Clearly, if it were in the interest of a manager to make Grade A Specialty lumber appear profitable, then that manager would use the physical measures method of joint cost allocation. On the other hand, if a manager were interested in making Grade B Standard lumber appear to be as profitable as Grade A Specialty lumber, then that manager would use the NRV method. Of course, the combined profits of the two products would be the same whatever joint cost allocation method is used. But the relative profitability of joint products can be affected by which cost allocation method is used.

Research Insight 9.1

Preference for Joint-Costing Methods

In practice, companies in similar industries allocate joint costs in a variety of ways, as a study of joint costing in the chemical and petrochemical industries in the United Kingdom indicates. The following table, which summarizes the study results, shows a variety in the preference for the method used. Accountants and managers might prefer different allocation methods in different situations. Alternatively, this variation in preference could reflect the inherently arbitrary nature of joint-cost allocation.

The study shows that some companies did not allocate joint costs at all. Many companies in the study used the net realizable value method, but even more companies used the physical-measures method. We can speculate that the physical-measures method seemed more objective and is more easily used than the NRV method.

Joint-Cost Allocations in Practice

	No Allocation	Net Realizable Value Method	Physical-Measures Method	Other Methods
Oil refining	7	0	0	2
Petrochemicals	1	5	4	0
Coal chemicals	0	1	6	4
Inorganic chemicals	1	2	2	3
Other companies in the chemicals industry	0	3	28	3
Total	9	11	40	12

Source: K. Slater and C. Wootton, A Study of Joint and By-Product Costing in the U.K.

Choosing among Joint-Cost Allocation Methods

The "jointness" of joint-production processes makes the separation of the portion of joint costs attributable to one product from another impossible on a cause-and-effect basis. As a result, allocating joint costs might be somewhat arbitrary. Since nearly any desired joint-cost allocation can be achieved by carefully choosing the method, it is important:

- Not to base product or service production decisions on gross margins (i.e., after joint-cost allocations) unless the choice is in response to regulatory opportunities. (e.g., cost reimbursement from a governmental agency)

- To choose, when allowed, the joint-cost allocation method that maximizes regulated profits or cost reimbursements.
- To clearly define the way to allocate joint costs in contractual agreements among parties that share outputs and costs of joint processes. On the other hand, if contracts do not specify how to allocate joint costs, the party responsible for assigning costs to various products and parties can be expected to use the method that is personally most advantageous. As noted earlier, this lack of specificity can cause contentious negotiations beforehand or expensive litigation afterward.

Basics of Accounting for By-Products

LO 5 Know how to account for by-products.

By-products are by definition relatively minor products; hence, the method used to account for them is not likely to have a major effect on decisions or the financial statements for either internal or external reporting. Some companies make by-product accounting as easy as possible by simply expensing the by-products' separable (additional processing) costs in the period that they are incurred and then recording the total revenue from the by-products when they are sold.

Using this method, the accountants do not have to keep an inventory of the cost to process by-products or compute their net realizable value. Although this simple approach technically violates the matching principle—revenues and expenses should be matched in the same accounting period—this practice is acceptable if the amounts involved are immaterial.

Methods. Two typical methods of accounting for by-products that are sold at split-off are to (1) consider the by-product's NRV as "other revenue" or (2) deduct the by-product's NRV from the costs of main products. To understand these methods, assume that the Georgia mill chose lumber option 2 but sold wood chips at split off. Assume that, after selecting this option, the mill would have sold 1,500 metric tons of wood chips for $72,400 after additional processing (cleaning and drying) of $10,000, giving an NRV of $62,400.

Method 1: Treat the by-product's NRV as other revenue. Treating by-product NRV as other revenue is the simpler method. Since the by-product NRVs are small and the effects on income are immaterial, many companies use this approach. The by-product NRV is simply counted as other revenue, as shown:

Sales revenue	
Main products (Exhibit 9–6)	$2,100,000
Other revenue, by-products	62,400
Total revenue	$2,162,400
Cost of main products sold (Exhibit 9–6, $1,400,000 joint costs + $100,000 additional processing costs)	1,500,000
Gross margin	$ 662,400

Method 2: Deduct the NRV obtained from the sale of the by-products from the cost of the main products. This method can be slightly more complicated *if all main products produced are not sold* in the period that they are produced. The effect on gross margin is the same as Method 1, however, if all main products have been sold, as shown here:

Sales revenue (Exhibit 9–6)	$2,100,000
Cost of goods sold	
Cost of main products sold (Exhibit 9–6, $1,400,000 joint costs + $100,000 additional processing costs)	1,500,000
Less NRV of by-products	(62,400)
Adjusted cost of goods sold	1,437,600
Gross margin	$ 662,400

If all main products produced in the period have *not* been sold, the NRV of by-products should be prorated to the main product inventories and the cost of goods sold. These adjustments would be in proportion to the NRVs or physical measure of main products in those accounts, depending on the method used to allocate joint costs.[3] As one possibility, assume that at the end of the month, all Grade A Specialty lumber had been sold, but all Grade B Standard lumber was still in finished goods. The adjustments to the main product account costs based on the physical-measures method follow:

	Grade A Specialty Lumber	Grade B Standard Lumber	Total
Physical quantity	1,000 MBF	3,000 MBF	4,000 MBF
Proportionate share of quantity	25%	75%	100%
Allocation of by-product NRV	$15,600	$46,800	$62,400
	(.25 × $62,400)	(.75 × $62,400)	

Disposal of Scrap and Waste

Our discussion so far has assumed that the by-product output has a positive net realizable value; that is, its sales value exceeds the costs of further processing. If an output's NRV is negative, it is usually considered scrap or waste and is disposed of legally at minimum cost. Keep in mind, however, that the cost of disposing of scrap or waste can be considerable, particularly if the disposal is harmful to the environment. The cost is usually estimated and counted as part of joint-processing costs (or manufacturing overhead in other processes) and allocated to products as part of joint costing. If scrap and waste are not disposed of properly, the company, its employees, and its directors can be subject to severe penalties.

Many companies have transformed waste into profitable products.

In some cases, environmental regulations that discourage or prohibit dumping scrap or waste have motivated the creation of new products that can be sold profitably (or at lower cost than disposal). For example, years ago, lumber mills burned sawdust and tree bark or dumped it in rivers and landfills. Environmental regulations now prohibit these practices. In response, lumber companies asked, Why not process chips and sawdust into paper pulp and use bark for landscaping and mulch products? Alternatively, why not burn scrap to generate power for other operations? Thus, new sources of raw materials were created from what had been scrap and waste.

Another example to consider, according to the Recyclers' World (*www.recycle.net*), is the growth in recent years

[3]Another complication can arise under either method of accounting for by-products if the cost of processing them occurs in one period but they are not sold until the next period. In such a case, revenues might be recognized at the time of production, but companies could find it necessary to keep an inventory of the by-product processing costs in an Additional By-Product Cost account until the by-products themselves have been sold and cash has been received.

of the active industry to recycle scrap tires, which often sit in large, unsightly, and dangerous piles.[4] These tires have become the raw materials for many new products, including electricity produced by incinerating tires to pavement materials for hiking trails, streets, and highways produced by shredding tires.

[4]Piles of tires can catch fire from lightning strikes, support breeding of disease-carrying mosquitoes, and leach toxic chemicals into water supplies. Every automobile tire sold in most countries carries a fee that subsidizes proper disposal.

Chapter Summary

Joint processes simultaneously produce multiple outputs. Selling or processing these outputs further depends on the net realizable values (sales less further processing costs) of joint products. Product decisions should not be made, if at all possible, based on joint-cost allocations, which arise from the need to assign joint-process costs to two or more products manufactured from a common input. The usual objective of joint-cost allocation is to measure costs of the inputs for financial or contractual reporting. There is no exact way to trace joint costs to products, so arbitrary allocations might be necessary. On the other hand, joint-cost allocations might prove useful or strategically sound in some industries or situations where prices or revenues depend on discretionary choice of the allocation method. The two methods of joint-cost allocation distribute joint costs based on net realizable value (or *estimated* net realizable value) or the physical-measures method. Accounting for by-products seeks to accurately record transactions but at minimum effort and cost.

Key Terms

For each term's definition, refer to the indicated page or turn to the glossary at the end of the text.

by-product, 356
constant gross margin percentage method,* 364
final product, 348
intermediate product, 348
joint costs, 348
joint process, 348
joint products, 348
main product, 356
net realizable value (NRV), 351
net realizable value (NRV) method, 357
physical-measures (or quantities) method, 357
relative sales value at split-off method,* 364
split-off point, 348

*Term appears in chapter Appendix.

Meeting the Cost Management Challenges

1. How do cost-management analysts anticipate and resolve potential conflicts between joint-product and process decision making and external reporting?

In some situations, joint-product decision making should be kept entirely separate from external reporting, such as when an organization sells its products in competitive markets and when joint-process costs are irrelevant to performance evaluations. Thus, measures of cost and profit for internal decision making should be more like throughput costing than absorption costing. That is, costs should reflect resource spending after the split off, and joint-process costs should be included in operating expenses. This should prevent managers from treating joint costs per unit as if they were unit-level costs and should enable them to make profit-maximizing decisions.

Separating joint-product decisions and costing when joint costs are integral parts of evaluations, contracts, and regulated prices is complicated and undesirable. Cost-management analysts must be especially sure that users of cost information, which includes joint-cost allocations, understand the meaning of this information for this more complex costing environment. When contracts are involved, all definitions (costs, sharing, allocation, reimbursement, etc.) must be clearly defined and agreed on in advance.

2. If joint-cost allocations are arbitrary, does that mean they are meaningless?

If joint-costs allocations truly are arbitrary [Webster's: not governed by principle, depending on whim, capricious], they can be dangerous if they are used as if they are based on causation (e.g., cost-driver bases) or deliberate intent. Managers who inappropriately rely on joint-cost information to make product decisions could be misled because joint costs do not behave like unit-level costs. Likewise, arbitrary, ill-defined joint-cost allocations in contracts are subject to dispute if one or more parties to the contract see an advantage to challenging another's interpretation. Therefore, joint-cost allocations can be arbitrary.

However, the word *arbitrary* has another meaning that is more benign and constructive [Webster's: left to discretion, not fixed by statute]. This meaning acknowledges that no joint-cost allocation method is based on higher (e.g., cost-driver) principles. Careful definition of terms and applications can guide certain types of decision making and cooperative ventures. Clearly, many firms, joint ventures, and industries rely on joint-cost allocations that are deliberate and not capricious. It is doubtful that these individuals and firms are being arbitrary in the pejorative sense but use their discretion to develop useful joint-cost mechanisms for sharing costs, profits, and efforts. Without these "arbitrary" arrangements, many business relationships might not proceed. There is a valuable role in these situations for cost-management analysts who understand how to craft useful joint-cost allocations.

Solutions to You're the Decision Maker

9.1 Operate or Shut Down the Process? p. 351

a. High facility-level costs and low levels of production mean high average costs. In the long run, average costs must be surpassed by enough profit to justify the capital investment in the Georgia mill. The company should analyze and improve the mill's constraints on production (bottlenecks), which can be either internal or external. For example, the Georgia mill might have insufficient milling capacity (human or physical capital) to operate on a scale large enough to be more profitable. Alternatively, the mill's location could mean that the area does not have a sufficiently large market to support its capacity. Apparently, however, shortages of inputs (timber) are causing the mill to operate only one shift per day when other mills operate two or more shifts per day. Assuming that the mill is operating below capacity and there is ample opportunity to sell increased mill output profitably, the company needs to consider obtaining more input for the mill or putting the resources to a better use. This could mean closing the Georgia mill.

b. Let's assume that you prefer to continue working at the Georgia mill because of the good working conditions. You are, however, aware of the responsibility to external shareholders and creditors, and you have no intention of misleading your superiors. Your response to the possible closing of the mill should be factual and complete. Consideration of all the costs and benefits would include not only the mill's direct operating costs but also the opportunity costs of lost sales, lost goodwill, and lost skilled personnel. Other costs to consider are the costs of closing the mill, retraining employees for other jobs in the company, and offering severance packages to employees who are dismissed. You might be able to identify how the company could work with potential suppliers of timber to achieve mutual benefits—a fair price for timber, environmentally sensitive removal of timber, replanting trees, and regional income from mill employment and local purchases.

9.2 Testing the Validity of the Analysis p. 353

a. The Georgia mill's products are commodities whose sales prices are set in very competitive markets. Thus, the revenue half of the data is subject to external forces that the company cannot control or forecast with complete accuracy. It is not unusual for some commodity prices to vary by 20 percent or more from year to year, depending on economic conditions. In contrast, production quantities—given timber quality and availability—are probably quite reliable estimates. Joint process and further processing costs also are likely to be known with confidence.

b. *Materiality* means the amount a figure must differ from what is expected before a decision maker would change his or her decision (e.g., the difference between the two alternatives, which is $200,000). The Georgia mill's product decision is based on the expected net realizable values of alternative product mixes. A material difference in any of the elements of NRV—sales and further processing costs—would cause the mill's managers to select a different lumber mix.

c. If the sales price for specialty lumber (only) drops as indicated, the product decision changes completely. Such a decline in price makes producing Grade A Standard lumber the more profitable option.

d. Managers who do not understand sensitivity analysis sometimes accept an initial analysis without asking sufficient "what-if" questions. Cost-management analysts should feel an obligation to subject important product analyses to thorough sensitivity analysis to determine which parameters are most material to product decisions. The sensitivity analysis at least should compute the effects of parameters at extreme values ("best-case" and "worst-case" levels) and most likely values—at first one at a time. Combining the worst-case or best-case values of each parameter results in the worst-case or best-case "scenarios." You should advise managers about which parameters are most sensitive so that they can take steps to minimize adverse effects. These actions include gaining more precise measures of parameters or negotiating long-term sales or supplier contracts to lock in quantities, prices, and costs.

Appendix to Chapter Nine

Other Economic Value Methods

The chapter discussed the typical net realizable value (NRV) method for allocating joint costs. This appendix presents two other methods also based on the economic values of joint outputs: (1) the relative sales value at split-off method and (2) the constant gross margin percentage method.

Relative Sales Value at Split-Off Method

relative sales value at split-off method *allocates joint costs based on the relative sales values of the joint products at their split-off point*

The **relative sales value at split-off method** allocates joint costs based on the relative sales values of the joint products at their split-off point. This method does not consider additional processing costs after the split-off point. Recall that the revenues at the split-off point for National Wood Products' Georgia mill before additional processing were as follows:

Grade A lumber	$ 600,000
Grade B lumber	1,200,000

National WOOD PRODUCTS

Given these values, one-third [$600,000 ÷ ($600,000 + $1,200,000)] of the joint costs would be allocated to Grade A lumber and two-thirds would be allocated to Grade B lumber. The allocated joint costs would be:

To Grade A lumber	.33 × $1,400,000 = $466,667
To Grade B lumber	.67 × $1,400,000 = $933,333

Note that the relative sales value method does not require knowing whether grade A lumber will be processed into specialty lumber because it allocates joint costs based on *relative* values at the split-off point *before* any additional processing.

Constant Gross Margin Percentage Method

constant gross margin percentage method *allocates joint costs to products in a way that the gross margin percentages as a percent of revenue are the same for each joint product*

Another method of joint-cost allocation that is based on the economic values of joint products is the **constant gross margin percentage method.** It allocates joint costs to products in a way that the gross margin percentages as a percent of revenue are the same for each joint product. Three steps are required to use this method:

1. Compute the total gross margin percentage.
2. Use the total gross margin percentage calculated in step 1 to calculate the gross margin for each product (total gross margin percentage × sales value).
3. Deduct the additional processing costs from the total costs to calculate joint costs allocated to each product.

Using the data from the National Wood Products example, we can calculate the allocation of joint costs using the constant gross margin percentage method. Panel A of Exhibit 9–9 shows the data provided and the calculation of the total gross margin per-

Exhibit 9–9

Joint Costs Allocated Using the Constant Gross Margin Percentage Method

National WOOD PRODUCTS

Panel A	Grade A Specialty Lumber	Grade B Standard Lumber	Total
Sales value	$ 900,000	$1,200,000	$2,100,000
Joint costs (step 3)	?	?	1,400,000
Additional processing costs	100,000	0	100,000
Gross margin (step 2)	?	?	$ 600,000
Gross margin percentage (step 1)	28.57143	28.57143	28.57143
Panel B			
Sales value	$ 900,000	$1,200,000	$2,100,000
Joint costs (step 3)*	542,857	857,143	1,400,000
Additional processing costs	100,000	0	100,000
Gross margin (step 2)†	$ 257,143	$ 342,857	$ 600,000
Gross margin percentage (step 1)	28.57143	28.57143	28.57143

*$542,857 =$900,000 – $100,000 – $257,143, etc.

†$257,143 = .2857143 × $900,000 sales value, etc.

centages (step 1). Panel A also indicates the amounts that remain to be calculated (denoted with a question mark). Panel B of Exhibit 9–9 shows the calculation of the gross margin dollar amount for each product (step 2). Once the gross margin dollar amount has been calculated for each product, we can solve for the joint costs to be allocated to each product (step 3), which also is shown in panel B of Exhibit 9–9.

The constant gross margin percentage method is based on the same principle as the NRV method, except for one small difference. The NRV method results in gross margin percentages that are equal as a percent of the *net realizable values* of each joint product, whereas the constant gross margin method requires that gross margin percentages be equal as a percent of the *revenues* of each joint product.

Review Questions

9.1 What are the definitions of the key terms in this chapter?

9.2 What is the nature of a joint-production process?

9.3 How do joint products, intermediate products, and final products differ?

9.4 What are the similarities and differences between joint costs and indirect costs?

9.5 What are the steps to follow to make decisions about producing products from joint processes?

9.6 What could cause a difference between sales revenue and net realizable value?

9.7 What is the objective of joint-cost allocation?

9.8 Why might some accountants express a preference for the net realizable value method of joint-cost allocation over the physical-measures method?

9.9 When might a physical-measures method for allocation he preferred?

9.10 What is the basic difference between the allocation of joint costs to joint products and to by-products?

9.11 What is the condition under which an item should be treated as a by-product rather than as a joint product?

9.12 Why are joint costs irrelevant in the sell-or-process-further decision? What costs are important?

9.13 Under what conditions could the method of joint-cost allocation be important to product or service decisions?

9.14 How do joint products, by-products, and scrap differ?

Critical Analysis

9.15 The chapter indicated that joint costing is used to value inventory and report earnings. Explain at least two other situations when the method of joint-cost allocation could have an impact on decision making.

9.16 How is joint-cost allocation like prorating underapplied overhead?

9.17 Company A and Company B are negotiating the construction and operation of a plant that will produce joint products X and Y and by-product W, which has a positive net realizable value. Company A will use all of product X and operate the plant. Company B argues that it needs only 80 percent of product Y that will be produced. Company A has no use for the excess product Y, but a market for it exists. Prepare a written memo outlining the principles you recommend the companies use to negotiate the sharing of the plant's costs of production.

9.18 Bonzo Oil Co. and Crusty Petroleum, Inc., are entering a joint venture to construct and operate an oil refinery in a foreign country. This refinery will process crude oil in a joint process that results in multiple products, such as gasoline, jet fuel, asphalt, and petrochemicals that require further processing. The companies have determined to jointly create a corporation to operate the refinery and share its outputs and costs fairly. The joint venture will pay a royalty fee to the host country for each barrel of crude oil processed and will charge the costs of operations to Bonzo and Crusty. Ignore taxation, political issues, and technical processing considerations (all of which, by the way, are material).

Form small groups to design a costing system to allocate the costs of *receiving* crude oil, *refining* the crude oil, and *distributing* the products from the refinery that is both fair and informative to Bonzo and Crusty. Be prepared to present proposals in an open forum.

9.19 (continuation of 9.18) A year later, Bonzo Oil experienced a 25 percent decline in the sales of its products and no longer accepts its full shipments of the refinery outputs. Accordingly, Bonzo seeks to renegotiate the agreement based on the joint-costing system prepared previously. Form small groups, half representing Bonzo and half representing Crusty. Considering only your company's interests, prepare proposals to modify the joint-costing agreement. If possible, choose two representative groups to openly resolve their differences and develop a modified agreement.

9.20 Assume that your company operates a joint-production process that generates three main products and one by-product. If you allocate joint costs only for financial reporting, would you ever care whether you use the NRV or the physical-measures method? Explain.

9.21 Top management has decided that your division, which operates a joint-production process, no longer provides a competitive return and should be shut down and all assets liquidated. Prepare an outline of the costs and benefits (to all affected parties) of the decision to shut down and liquidate your division.

9.22 Respond to this comment: "Because joint-cost allocations are arbitrary, there is no rational argument for allocating joint costs except for complying with financial or tax reporting requirements."

9.23 Explain how production decisions based on expected gross margin per unit can be erroneous. Under what conditions could making production decisions this way be an acceptable practice?

9.24 Refer to Exhibit 9–4 as an example of the analysis of alternatives. Assume that changes in some figures cause the relative profitability of products to switch (e.g., a change in the price of Grade A Specialty from $900 to $650 per MBF). What do you recommend for (1) creating the framework (or *model*) for this analysis and (2) communicating the results of the analysis to decision makers?

Exercises

Exercise 9.25
Joint Costing
(LO 1, 3)

Search the Internet for a company that either uses joint costing or provides joint-cost consulting services. Prepare a short presentation that explains (a) the nature of the organization (industry, products, services), (b) how it uses joint costing, and (c) how important you believe joint costs are to its decision making.

Exercise 9.26
Sell or Process Further
(LO 2)

Durango Company processes Chemical DX-1 through a joint-production process. The costs to process one batch of DX-1 are $100,000 for materials and $200,000 for conversion costs. This processing results in two outputs, Laudinium and Tranquil, that sell for a total of $500,000. The sales revenue from Laudinium amounts to $400,000 of the total. Joint-product Tranquil can be processed further and sold for $200,000 as T-Prime. Further processing costs for T-Prime are estimated to be $80,000 for the batch's production.

Required

Which products should Durango produce and sell?

Exercise 9.27
Sell or Process Further
(LO 2)

Glaxxo Mining Corporation operates an ore-processing plant. A typical batch of ore run through the plant yields three refined products: lead, copper, and manganese. At the split-off point, the intermediate products cannot be sold without further processing. The lead from a typical batch sells for $20,000 after incurring additional processing costs of $6,000. The copper is sold for $40,000 after additional processing costs of $5,000. The manganese yield sells for $30,000 but requires additional processing costs of $9,000. The cost of processing the raw ore, including its purchase, is $50,000 per batch.

Required

Which products should Glaxxo produce and sell?

Exercise 9.28
Net Realizable Value Method
(LO 4)

Refer to Exercise 9.26.

Required

Using the net realizable value method, assign joint costs to Durango's final products.

Exercise 9.29
Physical-Measures Method
(LO 4)

Refer to Exercise 9.26. Assume that one batch of DX-1 produces 400 units of Laudinium and 100 units of T-Prime (after additional processing).

Required

Using the physical measures method, assign joint costs to final products.

Exercise 9.30
Relative Sales Value at Split Off and Constant Gross Margin Methods (Appendix)
(LO 6)

Refer to Exercise 9.26.

Required

Allocate the joint costs using (1) the relative sales value at split off and (2) the constant gross margin percentage methods described in the chapter Appendix.

Exercise 9.31
Estimated Net Realizable Value Method
(LO 4)

Refer to Exercise 9.27.

Required

Use the net realizable value method to allocate Glaxxo's joint-processing costs.

Exercise 9.32
Net Realizable Value Method to Solve for Unknowns
(LO 4)

Galway Products, Inc., manufactures Leprechauns and Shamrocks from a joint process using the raw material Green. In a recent month, Galway produced 4,000 Leprechauns having a sales value after the split-off point of $21,000. In the same month, it produced 2,000 Shamrocks having a sales value after split off of $14,000. The portion of the total joint product costs allocated to Leprechauns using the net realizable value method was $12,000.

Required

Compute the total joint-product costs before allocation.

[CPA adapted]

Exercise 9.33
Net Realizable Value Method
(LO 1, 4)

Communication

Prepare a presentation that explains the following features of the net realizable value method.

a. Decision-making implications.

b. Steps to follow for allocating joint costs.

c. Major differences with the physical-quantities method.

Exercise 9.34
Comparison of Methods
(LO 4)

Each of these following situations should be considered independently of the others.

Required

a. Hanks Company manufactures products C and R from a joint process. The total joint costs are $120,000. The net realizable value at split off was $140,000 for 8,000 units of product C and $60,000 for 2,000 units of product R. Assuming that total joint costs are allocated using the net realizable value method, what were the joint costs allocated to product C?

b. Roberts Company manufactures products A and B from a joint process, which also yields a by-product, X. Roberts accounts for the revenues from its by-product sales as other revenue. Additional information follows:

	A	B	X	Total
Units produced	9,000	15,000	6,000	30,000
Joint costs	?	?	?	$117,000
Sales value at split off	$100,000	$100,000	$100,000	$300,000

Assuming that joint-product costs are allocated using the net realizable value method, what was the joint cost allocated to product B?

c. Damon Corp. manufactures products W, X, Y, and Z from a joint process. Additional information follows:

Product	Units Produced	Sales Value at Split Off	Further Processing Costs	Sales Values after Further Processing
W	7,000	$ 70,000	$ 7,500	$ 90,000
X	5,000	60,000	6,000	70,000
Y	4,000	40,000	4,000	50,000
Z	4,000	30,000	3,500	32,000
	20,000	$200,000	$21,000	$242,000

Assuming that total joint costs of $80,000 were allocated using the net realizable value method, what joint costs were allocated to each product?

[CPA adapted]

Exercise 9.35
Comparison of Methods
(LO 4)

The following questions are based on Paris Company, which manufactures products X, Y, and Z from a joint process. Joint-process costs were $80,000. Additional information is provided:

			If Processed Further	
Product	**Units Produced**	**Sales Value at Split Off**	**Sales Values**	**Additional Costs**
X	12,000	$80,000	$110,000	$18,000
Y	10,000	70,000	90,000	14,000
Z	8,000	50,000	60,000	12,000

Required

a. Assuming that joint-product costs are allocated using the physical-measures (units produced) method, what were the total costs of product X (including $18,000 if processed further)?

b. Assuming that joint-product costs are allocated using the net realizable value method, what were the total costs of product Y (including the $14,000 if processed further)?

[CPA adapted]

Exercise 9.36
Relative Sales Value at Split off and Constant Gross Margin Percentage Methods (Appendix)
(LO 6)

Refer to Exercise 9.35.

Required

Allocate the joint costs using (1) the relative sales value at split-off method and (2) the constant gross margin percentage method described in the chapter Appendix.

Exercise 9.37
Physical-Measures Method with By-Product
(LO 4)

Friendly Fertilizer Corporation uses organic materials to produce fertilizers for home gardens. Through its production processes, the company manufactures Nitro, a high nitrogen fertilizer, and Phospho, a high phosphorus fertilizer. A by-product of the process is methane, which is used to generate power for the company's operations. The fertilizers are sold either in bulk to nurseries or in individual packages to home gardeners. The company allocates the costs on the basis of the physical-measures method.

Last month, 275,000 units of input were processed at a total cost of $180,000. The output of the process consisted of 50,000 units of Nitro, 75,000 units of Phospho, and 150,000 units of methane. The by-product methane would have cost $4,000 had it been purchased from the local gas utility. This is considered to be its net realizable value, which is deducted from the joint processing costs of the main products.

Required

What share of the joint costs should be assigned to each main product using the physical-measures method?

Exercise 9.38
By-Products
(LO 4)

Leather Products, Inc., processes cowhide to produce three outputs (leather, suede, dog chews). Leather and suede are considered main products, and dog chews are a by-product. During a recent month, the following events occurred:

- Produced and sold 200 units of leather and 100 units of suede. Produced 25 units of dog chews.
- Recorded $140,000 sales revenue from leather and suede. The cost of sales before accounting for the by-product was $72,000.
- Incurred $100 to process the 25 units of dog chews to completion. These costs are charged as they are incurred against any by-product sales. (None of the by-products were in inventory at the end of the period.)
- Received $450 in revenue from the sale of the 25 units of dog chews.

Required

Prepare an analysis showing the sales revenue, other income, cost of goods sold, other relevant data, and gross margins that would be reported for each of the two methods of by-product accounting described in the text.

Exercise 9.39
By-Products
(LO 4)

The following questions are based on Seinfeld Corporation, which manufactures a product that gives rise to the by-product Castanza. The only cost associated with Castanza is the additional processing cost of $1 for each unit. Seinfeld accounts for Castanza sales first by deducting its separable costs from such sales and then by deducting this net amount from the cost of sales of the major product. (This is Method 2 discussed in the text.) This year, 2,400 units of Castanza were produced; all were sold at $5 each.

Required

a. Sales revenue and cost of goods sold from the main product were $400,000 and $200,000, respectively, for the year. What was the gross margin after considering the by-product sales and costs?

b. If Seinfeld changes its method of accounting for Castanza sales by showing the net amount as other revenue, what would its gross margin be? Explain.

c. If Seinfeld changes its method of accounting as indicated in requirement (b), what are the effects of the change on the company's profits?

[CPA adapted]

Problems

Problem 9.40
Sell or Process Further
(LO 1, 2)

Communication

Charlotte Sawmill, Inc., operates a sawmill facility. The company accounts for the bark chips that result from the primary sawing operation as a by-product. It sells the chips to another company at a price of $24 per hundred cubic feet. Normally, sales revenue from this bark is $1,800,000 per month. The customer loads and transports the bark at no cost to Charlotte.

As an alternative, the company can rent equipment that will process the chips and bag them for sale as decorative garden mulch. Approximately 30 percent of the bark will be graded "large" and will sell for $64 per hundred cubic feet. About 60 percent will be graded "medium" and will sell for $32 per hundred cubic feet. The remainder will be sold as mulch for $8 per hundred cubic feet.

Costs of the equipment to process and bag the chips and the personnel to operate the equipment total $1,040,000 per month, regardless of the amount of bark processed.

Required

Assuming a typical month, prepare a memo to Charlotte's management that demonstrates whether the company should sell the bark for $24 per hundred cubic feet or process it further.

Problem 9.41
Sell or Process Further
(LO 1, 2)

Spreadsheet

Ferguson Corp. uses a joint process that costs $160,000 for inputs and processing per batch. Processing one batch results in the following joint outputs:

Product	Quantity	Sales Price at Split Off	Further Processing	Sales Price after Further Processing
X	1,000,000 liters	$.09 per liter	NA	NA
Y	500,000 liters	$.05 per liter	$20,000	$.10 per liter
Z	100,000 liters	NA	1,500	.02 per liter

Ferguson Corp. allocates joint costs on the basis of volume (liters) of output.

Required

a. What is the first decision that Ferguson's management should make?

b. Prepare a spreadsheet that analyzes the profitability of Ferguson's options.

c. Compute the product costs for each main product in total and per unit for each option presented in requirement **b**.

d. How can your spreadsheet be used to demonstrate the effect of changes in sales prices or costs on Ferguson's decision to sell Product Y at split-off or process it further?

Problem 9.42
Net Realizable Value Method
(LO 4, 5)

Spreadsheet

Crusty Confections Company purchases cocoa beans and processes them into cocoa butter, a powder, and shells. The standard yield from processing each 100-pound sack of cocoa beans is 20 pounds of butter, 45 pounds of powder, and 35 pounds of shells. The powder can be sold for $.90 per pound and the butter for $1.10 per pound at the split-off point. The shells are disposed of at a cost of $2.00 per batch of 35 pounds of shells.

The cost of the cocoa beans is $15 per hundred pounds. Conversion resources to process each 100 pounds of beans up to the split-off point cost $37.

Required

Compute the joint cost allocated to cocoa butter and cocoa powder produced from 100 pounds of cocoa beans using the net realizable value method.

Problem 9.43
Physical-Measures Method
(LO 4)

Refer to Problem 9.42.

Required

Use the physical-measures method to allocate joint costs.

Problem 9.44
Sell or Process Further
(LO 4)

Refer to Problem 9.42. Assume that the cocoa butter could be sold either at split off or after additional processing. The additional processing costs $.15 per pound, at which point the butter can be sold for $1.60 per pound.

Required

a. Should cocoa butter be sold at split off or processed further?

b. Assuming cocoa butter is processed further, allocate the joint costs using the net realizable value method.

Problem 9.45
Sell or Process Further
(LO 4, 5)

Spreadsheet

Refer to Problems 9.42 and 9.44. In addition to possibly processing cocoa butter further, assume that the cocoa shells could be processed further at a cost of $3.00 per batch of 35 pounds and sold for $.05 per pound as garden mulch.

Required

a. Prepare a diagram that describes the possible sets of products and by-products.

b. Allocate the joint costs to the main products using the net realizable value method.

Problem 9.46
Net Realizable Value and Effects of Processing Further
(LO 2, 4)

Communication

IMAC Company produces three products by a joint-production process. Raw materials are put into production in process A, and three products appear at the end of this process. Product X is immediately sold at the split-off point, with no further processing. Products Y and Z require further processing before they are sold. Product Y is processed in process B, and product Z is processed in process C. The company uses the (estimated) net realizable value method of allocating joint-production costs. Following is a summary of costs and other data for the quarter ended September 30.

No inventories were on hand at the beginning of the quarter or on July 1. No raw materials were on hand at September 30. All the units on hand at the end of the quarter were fully complete as to processing.

Products	**X**	**Y**	**Z**
Pounds sold	40,000	118,000	140,000
Pounds on hand at September 30	100,000	0	80,000
Sales revenues	$ 30,000	$177,000	$274,400
Processes	**A**	**B**	**C**
Raw material cost	$112,000	$ 0	$ 0
Direct labor cost	48,000	80,900	191,750
Manufacturing overhead	20,000	21,100	73,250

Required

a. Assume that the entire output of product X could be processed further at an additional cost of $3 per pound and then sold for $5 per pound. What is the effect on operating profits if all product X output for the quarter had been processed and sold rather than all being sold at the split-off point?

b. Write a memo to management indicating whether the company should process product X further and why.

c. Determine the following amounts for each product: (1) net realizable value used for allocating joint costs, (2) joint costs allocated to each of the three products, (3) cost of goods sold, and (4) finished goods inventory costs, September 30.

Problem 9.47
Finding Missing Data: Net Realizable Value
(LO 4)

Air Extracts, Inc., manufactures nitrogen, oxygen, and hydrogen from a joint process. Data on the process are as follows:

Product	**Nitrogen**	**Oxygen**	**Hydrogen**	**Total**
Units produced	8,000	4,000	2,000	14,000
Joint costs	$30,000*	$ (a)	$ (b)	$ 60,000
Sales value at split off	(c)	(d)	15,000	100,000

*This amount is the portion of the total joint cost of $60,000 that had been allocated to nitrogen.

The company uses the net realizable value method of joint-cost allocation.

Required

Determine the values for the lettered spaces.

[CPA adapted]

Problem 9.48
Joint-Cost Allocations with By-Product
(LO 4, 5)

Communication

Exotic Aroma Company buys bulk flowers and processes them into perfumes in a two-stage process. Its highest-grade perfume, Seduction, and a residue that is processed into a medium-grade perfume, Romance, come from a certain mix of petals. In July, the company used 25,000 pounds of petals. The first stage is a joint process that reduces the petals to Seduction and the residue. This first stage had the following costs:

- $100,000 direct materials
- $200,000 conversion

The additional costs of producing Romance in the second (pressing) stage were as follows:

- $44,000 direct materials
- $180,000 conversion

For July, total production yielded 2,000 ounces of Seduction and 8,400 ounces of Romance. There was no beginning inventory on July 1, nor were there uncompleted units.

Packaging costs incurred for each product as completed were $120,000 for Seduction and $308,000 for Romance. The sales price per ounce is $180 for Seduction and $70 for Romance.

Required

a. Allocate joint costs using the net realizable value method. (Packaging and additional processing costs must be subtracted from revenue to compute net realizable values.)

b. Allocate the joint costs using the physical-measures method.

c. Management is concerned about the large disparity in allocation amounts using the physical-measures method versus the NRV method. Management has asked you to explain why this discrepancy occurred. Write a memo to management explaining it.

d. Assume that Exotic Aroma can sell the squeezed petals from the reduction process to greenhouses for fertilizer. In July, it sold 12,000 pounds of squeezed petals that were left over for $1.50 per pound. The squeezed petals are a by-product of reduction. Assume that the net realizable value of by-products reduces the joint costs of main products. Answer requirements (a) and (b) using this new information.

Problem 9.49
Joint Costing in a Process Costing Context: Net Realizable Value Method
(LO 4, 5)

Greek Company produces three products: Alpha, Beta, and Gamma. Alpha and Gamma are main products; Beta is a by-product of Alpha. Information on the past month's production processes follows:

- In process 1, 110,000 units of the raw material Rho are processed at a total cost of $290,000. After processing in process 1, 60 percent of the units are transferred to process 2, and 40 percent of the units (now unprocessed Gamma) are transferred to process 3.
- In process 2, the materials received from process 1 are processed at an additional cost of $76,000. Seventy percent of the units become Alpha and are transferred to process 4. The remaining 30 percent emerge as Beta and are sold at $4.20 per unit after additional processing. The additional processing costs to make Beta salable are $16,200.
- In process 3, Gamma is processed at an additional cost of $330,000. A normal loss of units of Gamma occurs in this process. The loss equals 10 percent of the units processed. The remaining good output is then sold for $24 per unit.
- In process 4, Alpha is processed at an additional cost of $32,960. After this processing, it can be sold for $10 per unit.

Required

a. Prepare a diagram to display Greek Company's revenues, costs, products, and processes.

b. Prepare a schedule showing the allocation of the $290,000 joint cost between Alpha and Gamma using the net realizable value approach. The net realizable value of by-products reduces the joint costs of the related main product. (Method 2 in the text)

[CPA adapted]

Problem 9.50
Maximum Input Price: Net Realizable Value Method
(LO 1, 2)

Communication

Harrison Corporation produces two joint products from its manufacturing operation. Product J sells for $41.50 per unit, and product M sells for $12 per unit at the split-off point. In a typical month, 38,000 units are processed; 30,000 units become product M and 8,000 units become product J after an additional $56,250 of processing costs are incurred.

The joint process has only unit-level costs. In a typical month, the conversion costs of the joint products amount to $114,075. Materials prices are volatile, and if they are too high, the company stops production. Harrison requires a minimum 20 percent return on sales.

Required

Management has asked you to determine the maximum price that the company should pay for the materials.

a. Calculate the maximum price that Harrison should pay for the materials.

b. Write a brief memo to management explaining how you arrived at your answer in requirement (a).

Problem 9.51
Effect of By-Product versus Joint Cost Accounting
(LO 4, 5)

Communication

AMPHIB Corporation processes input Leonardo into three outputs: Michaelangelo, Raphael, and Donatello. At the split-off point, Michaelangelo results in 60 percent of the net realizable value, Raphael results in 30 percent, and Donatello accounts for the balance. The joint costs total $365,500. If Donatello is accounted for as a by-product, its net realizable value at split off of $37,600 is credited to the joint manufacturing costs.

Required

a. What are the allocated joint costs for the three outputs
   (1) If Donatello is accounted for as a main product?
   (2) If Donatello is accounted for as a by-product?

b. Management does not understand why no joint costs are allocated to Donatello when it is accounted for as a by-product. Write a brief memo explaining this.

Problem 9.52
Joint Cost Allocation and Product Profitability
(LO 1, 2, 4)

Silicon Materials, Inc., processes silicon crystals into purified wafers and chips. Silicon crystals cost $60,000 per batch. The process involves slicing the crystals, which produces 45,000 wafers with a market value of $20,000 and 15,000 chips with a market value of $140,000. The cost of operating the heat process is $65,600.

Required

a. If the costs of the crystal and the heat process are allocated on the basis of units of output, what cost would be assigned to each product?

b. If the costs of the crystal and the heat process are allocated on the basis of the net realizable value, what cost is assigned to each product?

c. How much profit or loss does the purified wafers product provide using the data in this problem and your analysis in requirement (a)? Is it really possible to determine which product is more profitable? Explain why or why not.

Problem 9.53
Joint-Cost Allocation and Product Profitability
(LO 1, 2, 4)

Whitehall Corp. produces chemicals used in the cleaning industry. During the previous month, it incurred $300,000 of joint costs in producing 60,000 units of AM-12 and 40,000 units of BM-36. Whitehall allocates joint costs based on the number of units produced. Currently, AM-12 is sold at split off for $3.50 per unit. Flank Corp. has approached Whitehall to purchase all of the AM-12 monthly production after further processing, which will cost Whitehall $90,000 per month.

Required

a. What is the minimum sales price Whitehall should charge Flank for AM-12 after further processing?

b. Assume that Whitehall has agreed to sell AM-12 to Flank after further processing for $5.50 per unit. During the first month, Whitehall delivered 50,000 units to Flank and had 10,000 units remaining in inventory at the end of the month. What is the operating profit generated by sales of AM-12 during the first month, and what is the cost of processed AM-12 still in inventory at the end of the month?

[CMA adapted]

Cases

Case 9.54
Joint-Product Decision Making and Joint-Cost Allocation in a Risky Venture
(LO 1, 2, 3, 4)

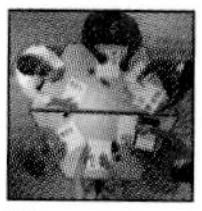
Team

Ethics

In 1979, Honda imported the first automobile into the United States with a galvanized (zinc-coated) body. By 1987 nearly all automobile manufacturers in the world used galvanized metal to extend the life of vehicles. At the same time, the use of galvanized metal for appliances and structural applications, for example, increased.

Through obsolescence and recycling, a rapidly increasing amount of galvanized scrap exists. The zinc coating on this galvanized scrap causes pollution problems due to zinc contamination when the scrap is melted to produce new iron or steel. In conjunction with the University of California–Berkeley, Metal Recovery Technologies, Inc. (MRTI), is improving its doubly patented electrolytic process to strip pure zinc from galvanized scrap. The process originally was developed in 1991 with support from the Argonne National Laboratory and the US Department of Energy. MRTI's process uses much less energy than other methods; produces two pure joint products, zinc and highest-quality, reusable ("black") steel; and prevents environmental damage from zinc and waste resulting from other methods.

The government and the company estimate that using this process to dezinc 5 million tons of galvanized scrap (the amount recycled in the United States each year) could

- Save 50 trillion BTUs of energy.
- Save $140 million in raw materials for US iron and steel companies.
- Save $100 million in foreign exchange spending by reducing the need for zinc imports.
- Eliminate toxic zinc from waste streams.

In 1998 MRTI listed its stock on the Berlin Stock Exchange and received financing of $3 million from Geneva-based Zinc Investments, Inc. With the proceeds of stock sales and the Swiss financing, MRTI revamped its East Chicago, Indiana, plant to reach a commercial scale of 120,000 tons of galvanized scrap per year, which would result in expected revenues of $23 million per year (at 1998 prices) beginning in the year 1999. Clouding the future is the development-stage company's financial performance, which at December 31, 1997, included a net loss of $622,500, current assets of $61,619, and current liabilities of $7,295,282. MRTI's independent auditors raised questions about the company's ability to continue as a going concern, which could affect its ability to raise additional capital.

MRTI expects the following annual costs of operations for the commercialized process:

Material cost (galvanized steel scrap and sodium hydroxide)	$ 6,600,000
Conversion cost (labor, power, depreciation, and amortization)	12,500,000
General and administrative cost	1,800,000

The commercialized process, if successful, would separate and recover 100 percent of the steel and zinc from the galvanized scrap and regenerate the sodium hydroxide in the electrolytic solution. The typical proportion of steel and zinc in galvanized steel is 98 percent steel and 2 percent zinc. The 1998 per-ton market prices for black steel and recovered zinc were $170 and $1,200, respectively.

Required

Prepare group responses to each of the following items for presentation.

a. If MRTI is successful in commercializing its electrolytic process, would the company be profitable?

b. Market prices for nonprecious metals can fluctuate 20 percent per year. Would MRTI be profitable if the prices of the scrap it uses and of the metals it produces decline by 20 percent?

c. Using the original data in the case, compare the profitability of the two joint products using the net realizable value and physical-measures methods.

d. Under what conditions would MRTI have an incentive to use one method or the other to measure product profitability? What ethical responsibilities do MRTI's managers and auditors face?

[Adapted from "A Power-Pinching Way to Recycle Rust-Proof Steel"; and Recyclers' World (*www.recycle.net*).]

Case 9.55
Joint Products from Recycling
(LO 1, 2, 4)

The weight of used tires in Europe was expected to reach 2.5 million tons by the end of 1999. Anne Forteza of IDE Environment argued that more intense retreading and recycling must replace the currently widespread practice of sending used tires to landfills. She estimated that approximately one-half of used tires is retreadable, but the balance is sent to landfills (36 percent), left on vehicles in scrap yards (30 percent), exported for incineration in the United States (8 percent), incinerated for power (22 percent), or incinerated for disposal

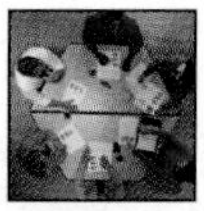
Team

Communication

Global

(4 percent). Aside from power generation, the treatment of most nonretreadable tires is a waste of primary materials, an expensive disposal option, and a source of environmental pollution. Recently passed legislation in France requires alternative, environmentally sound solutions to dumping used tires. Costs of dumping used tires in landfills currently are US$220 per ton (2,000 pounds) and are expected to rise dramatically in France and elsewhere if other European countries adopt similar legislation.

The Alpha Recyclage Project (ARP) was launched in France to demonstrate an economical and environmental treatment of nonretreadable tires. ARP will take large numbers of used tires at no cost if they contain the usual mix of retreadable tires (50 percent), sort them, sell suitable tires to retreaders for US$2 per tire, and treat the rest. ARP uses a cryogenic method to transform the waste tires into primary materials (30 percent fiber, 20 percent steel, and 50 percent reusable rubber pellets). The cryogenic method, which uses liquid nitrogen, is more expensive than mechanical grinding (the other currently feasible method) but is cleaner and results in a higher quality of rubber pellet.

Following are data regarding ARP's annual operations.

Weight of tires collected (average of 20 pounds per tire)	30,000 tons
Sold to retreaders @ US$2 each	15,000 tons
Sorting costs (retreadable vs. recyclable)	$ 100,000
Cryogenic joint-process costs of recycled tires	$ 4,500,000
General and administrative costs	$ 1,900,000
Market price for scrap steel	$ 90 per ton
Market price for scrap fiber	$300 per ton
Market price for scrap rubber pellets	$ 45 per ton

Required

Prepare group responses to the following items for presentation.

a. Is the ARP's process a viable process for disposing of used tires? Why or why not?

b. ARP must report results of operations to the National Council of Car Professions (NCPA), which is sponsoring the project. ARP intends to report revenues and costs by major product.

Prepare an objective and factual report that shows the results of annual operation and explains them in a manner to persuade NCPA to continue to sponsor the project.

[Adapted from "Tire Recycling in Europe," and "Synopsis of Scrap Rubber Reclamation in Canada." *Recycled Rubber Association (www.recycle.net/recycle/assn/narra).*]

Case 9.56
Effect of Cost Allocation on Pricing and Make-versus-Buy Decisions
(LO 1, 2, 4)

Ag-Coop is a large farm cooperative with a number of agriculture-related manufacturing and service divisions. As a cooperative, it pays no federal income taxes. It operates a fertilizer plant, which processes and mixes petrochemical compounds into three brands of agricultural fertilizer: Greenup, Maintane, and Winterizer. The three brands differ with respect to selling price and the proportional content of basic chemicals.

The Fertilizer Manufacturing Division transfers the completed product to the cooperative's Retail Sales Division at a price based on the cost of each type of fertilizer plus a markup. The Manufacturing Division is completely automated so that the only costs it incurs are for the petrochemical inputs plus automated conversion, which is committed for the coming period. The primary feedstock costs $1.50 per kilogram. Each 1,000 kilograms of feedstock can produce either of the following mixtures of fertilizer.

Output Schedules (in kilograms)	A	B
Greenup	500	600
Maintane	300	100
Winterizer	200	300

Production is limited to the monthly capacity of the dehydrator at 750,000 kilowatt-hours. The different chemical makeup of each brand of fertilizer requires different dehydrator use as follows:

Product	Kilowatt-Hour Usage per Kilogram
Greenup	32
Maintane	20
Winterizer	40

Monthly conversion costs are $81,250. The company is producing according to output schedule A. Joint-production costs including conversion are allocated to each product on the basis of weight.

The fertilizer is packed into 50-kilogram bags for sale in the cooperative's retail stores. The Manufacturing Division charges the retail stores its cost plus a markup. The sales price for each product charged by the cooperative's Retail Sales Division is as follows:

	Sales Price per Kilogram
Greenup	$10.50
Maintane	9.00
Winterizer	10.40

Selling expenses are 20 percent of the sales price.

The manager of the Retail Sales Division has complained that the prices charged are excessive and that she would prefer to purchase from another supplier. The Manufacturing Division manager argues that the processing mix was determined based on a careful analysis of the costs of each product compared to the prices charged by the Retail Sales Division.

Required

a. Assume that joint-production costs including conversion are allocated to each product on the basis of weight. What is the cost per pound of each product including conversion costs and the feedstock cost of $1.50 per pound, given the current production schedule?

b. Assume that joint-production costs including conversion are allocated to each product on the basis of net realizable value if it is sold through the cooperative's Retail Sales Division. What is the allocated cost per pound of each product, given the current production schedule?

c. Assume that joint-production costs including conversion are allocated to each product on the basis of weight. Which of the two production schedules, A or B, produces the higher operating profit to the firm as a whole?

d. Would your answer to requirement (c) be different if joint-production costs including committed overhead were allocated to each product on the basis of net realizable value? Explain.

e. Can you recommend an approach to product planning that considers the organization's overall profitability and avoids the divisional controversy? What are the costs and benefits of your recommended approach?

CHAPTER

10

Managing and Allocating Support-Service Costs

After completing this chapter, you should be able to:

1. Explain the importance of managing support-service costs and the reason these costs are allocated.
2. Understand how to choose cost pools and to separate the cost of resources supplied from the cost of resources used.
3. Understand how to choose appropriate allocation bases.
4. Allocate support-service department costs using the direct and step methods.
5. Evaluate the consequences of alternative cost allocations.
6. Allocate support-service department costs using the reciprocal method (Appendix).

City of Rock Creek

The scene is a meeting of Director of Finance Cindy Tukami and her budget staff who, under the guidance of the city manager, are responsible for preparing the draft of the City of Rock Creek's budget for the next fiscal year. After it is approved by the city council, Tukami and her staff administer the budget. She had just presented the draft of next year's budget to an open city council meeting the week before, and it had been a long, debate-filled meeting. The city's operating funds are not keeping pace with growing demands for services, and the city must make difficult trade-offs. The days since the meeting had been filled with angry phone calls and letters from citizens who felt the city was using the proposed budget to take funds away from valued programs to support the city's bureaucracy. The writers and the callers were not about to let that happen.

"At times I think this budget process is hopelessly complex, and no matter what we do, someone is going to raise a ruckus," Tukami observed. "Who would think that something as ordinary as *cost allocations* would cause so many citizens to pack city council meetings, write angry letters to the editor of the local paper, and make us feel like public enemies rather than public servants?

"I know what we are doing is right, but we need to communicate better the whys and hows of what we are doing for the citizens of Rock Creek. They need to understand that we are trying to run an efficient city government, but even a lean government has staff and facilities that need to be paid for somehow.

"I thought our proposal for using an activity-based approach to allocating costs would be so obviously better than what we have been doing that we would get praise, not condemnation. I half-expected to get a medal," she chuckled ruefully.

Tukami was highly qualified for the technical aspects of her job, having her undergraduate degree in accounting from a good university and passing the CPA and CMA exams on the first try. But she was learning a difficult lesson in the art and politics of budgeting. Although a city's budget negotiations might be more open than most, cost-allocation issues can cause friction in nearly every organization—public or private, for-profit or nonprofit. In any organization, managing the process of cost allocation can be just as important as the allocations themselves.

Cost-Management Challenges

1. **Cost** allocations are arbitrary. Does this mean that the way you decide to allocate costs is of no consequence to you or your organization?

2. **Choosing** a cost-allocation approach is always a judgment that is based on an evaluation of trade-offs. How can you be best prepared to evaluate the trade-offs and provide leadership if dramatic changes are needed?

3. **Some** cost-allocation approaches appear to be quite complex. How should you educate other managers to understand the complexities of the cost-allocation process?

Service-Cost Challenge

The goal of every organization should be to achieve the objectives that prompted its creation. Commercial firms are created to provide goods and services and earn at least a competitive profit. Nonprofit hospitals are created to provide superior health care for the community and at least cover their costs of operation. Cities are incorporated to provide essential services to their citizens within budgetary limits. Achieving these goals requires using scarce resources and making complex trade-offs among competing uses. Making these resource trade-offs requires reliable quantitative and qualitative cost-management information about relative costs and benefits of alternatives.

As discussed in earlier chapters, every organization must make cost-driver decisions that determine how to use its resources for productive processes that provide products and services directly to customers, clients, or citizens. The organization decides whether to perform all of the productive processes itself or to outsource some or part of them. In addition, organizations must decide how to support their productive processes, for example, by providing accounting, human resources, and legal support services. These support services could be provided by the organization's internal departments, or by outsourcing them to external providers.

Internal or Outsourced Support Services?

Some might argue that support services are a necessary part of every organization. But are they? Some organizations are outsourcing many of their internal support services. Companies commonly outsource traditional accounting functions such as payroll and accounts payable that require routine, straightforward procedures. Many companies also outsource their human resources, legal, tax, and internal auditing functions. Outsourcing has become a popular way to "right size" or "downsize" organizations. As a result, organizations that provide such services have become some of the fastest-growing industries in developed economies.

Whether to outsource any support service depends on the consideration of a combination of many quantitative and qualitative factors. Cost-management analysts most often are the professionals who prepare and analyze the information to support outsourcing decisions. This information includes the knowledge base required to perform a service, the sensitivity of information needed to perform a service, the relative costs of a service, and the difficulty in finding, managing, and keeping reliable, high-quality service providers.

Knowledge base. Complex or unique organizations might have distinct procedures and cultures that external service providers could have difficulty understanding and supporting. On the other hand, some support-service expertise could be too specialized for the organization to maintain itself. Consider, for example, the management of information technology in foreign countries. Organizations might see advantages to outsourcing these knowledge-based services to external service providers who have specialized expertise in these foreign countries and can provide benefits from economies of scale.

Sensitive information. Some organizations compete on the basis of their knowledge of technology or complex market and political situations. These firms would be reluctant to outsource support services, such as internal auditing, that would allow outsiders to obtain their strategically important knowledge.

Relative costs. Many organizations see the outsourcing of support services as a means to increase budget flexibility and reduce current and long-term costs (health care and pension costs, too). This puts great pressure on internal service departments either to provide comparable services at lower cost or to disappear.

Reliable service providers. A less expensive outsourced service is not cost effective if its reliability and quality are low and adversely affect the organization's ability to meet its objectives. For example, many large firms have outsourced their customer-service departments to other companies (e.g., Teletech *www.teletech.com*). Customer service is a very sensitive function that, if poorly performed, can drive away customers and damage the company's reputation. A damaged reputation can be very difficult to repair.

Management of Internal Support-Service Costs

LO 1 Explain the importance of managing support-service costs and the reason these costs are allocated.

Customers accept products only if their value meets or exceeds the prices that they are charged. This provides a strong discipline to the organization's use of resources for producing products. But internal support-service departments function without such external discipline. How does the organization manage its support-service costs? There are several cost-based, management approaches, two of which are discussed here.[1]

- *Charge internal customers nothing for support services and recover the costs of the services from general revenues.* The advantage to this approach is that it is simple and inexpensive to operate because there is no need either to measure or charge for support-service costs. Its disadvantage is that as long as internal customers perceive *any* positive value from free services, they may demand more without regard to the service costs to the organization. Thus, internal support-service departments could grow dramatically but inefficiently in response to high internal demand. There is no obvious signal to organization managers that they are using resources inefficiently to provide support services that few customers would want if they had to pay for them.
- *Charge the costs of support services provided to using departments and possibly recover the costs from these internal customers.* Because of problems with the first approach, most organizations use cost allocation—a systematic method of assigning the costs of resources to a department, product, or service when directly tracing costs is not possible—to charge support-service costs to internal customers. Many organizations also recover those costs from users in the form of actual payments or transfers of funds on the basis of the allocations. A user department or internal customer would accept support services only if the value of those services meets or exceeds their cost to the department. If user departments are required to utilize internal services, they might control spending for support services by demonstrating that the organization is spending too much for those services.

This second approach also has disadvantages. First, cost allocations are, by nature, arbitrary; they are, at best, *discretionary* and might not measure the uses of resources accurately. Second, if internal customers are required to use internal services, they might spend valuable time negotiating and lobbying over fair prices, which could be an inefficient process.

Poorly designed cost allocations can be the subject of disputes among departments and their constituents. Furthermore, cost allocations can create incentives to use or not use the services inappropriately if the allocated costs are not closely associated with the actual consumption of resources. This leads cost-management analysts to explore the use of activity-based costing (ABC) approaches to cost allocation, which are based on cause-and-effect relationships between support services provided and support-service resources used. Although careful ABC cost allocations can reflect the causes and effects better than other approaches can, they can be far from uncontroversial, as Tukami was learning.

The issues of efficiency, fairness, and team building within private and public organizations are analogous to, although not as socially wrenching as, those that

---

[1]This discussion is similar to portions of Chapter 19, Transfer Pricing, which also considers charging market or negotiated prices for internally exchanged products or services.

Exhibit 10–1

City of Rock Creek Organization Chart

City of Rock Creek

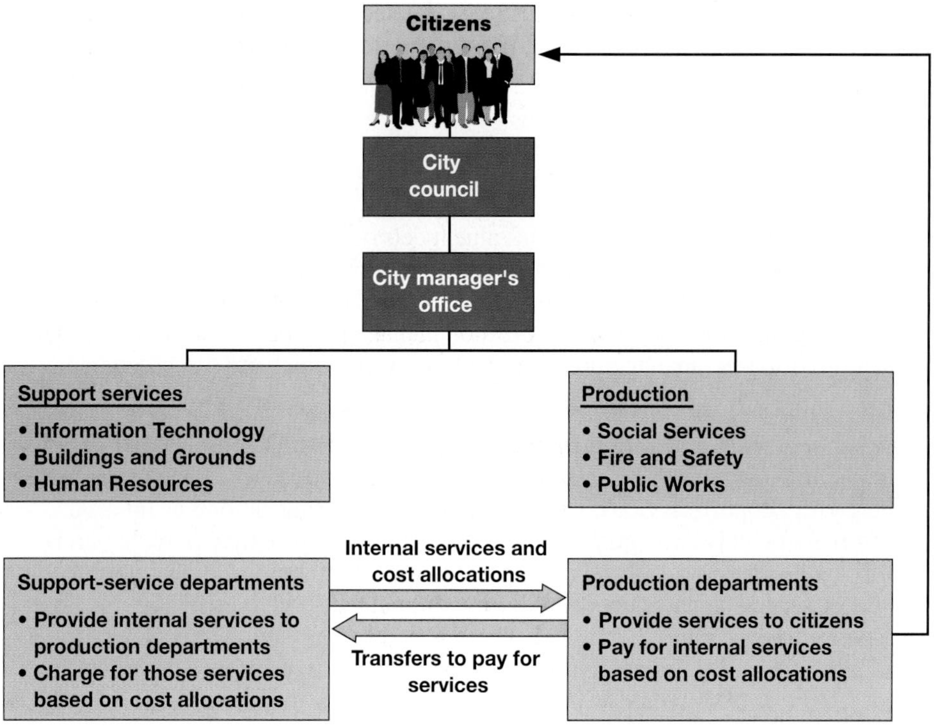

centrally-managed countries recently faced. These countries, such as the People's Republic of China, relied on cost allocations in the past and are now experimenting with market mechanisms to measure the values of goods and services and to allocate resources. These countries are finding not only that market mechanisms are more efficient because they do not require a large bureaucracy of central planners (although they do require enforcement of contracts) but also that market solutions are challenging cultural concepts of fairness and cooperation.

Distinguishing between Support-Services and Production Departments

City of Rock Creek

Tukami's staff had prepared the budget draft after coordinating the spending requests of all the city's departments. The city's organizational chart appears in Exhibit 10–1. This chart separates the two types of departments, production and support services.[2] The **production (or line) departments** provide services directly to the public, for example, public works provides water, sewer, and flood control. The **support-service departments (or indirect departments)** provide support services to each other and to the production departments. Note that the Human Resources department is considered a support service because it provides services to other city departments. Fire and Safety, however, is a production department because it provides a product to citizens. (Note that products can be goods or services. For a city, products are services.)

production (or **line**) **departments** *provide goods and services directly to external customers*

support-service (or **indirect) departments** *provide support services to each other and to the production departments*

The City of Rock Creek actually has more departments than those shown here. The examples become unnecessarily complex and difficult to follow if we include all of the

[2]In commercial firms, these types of departments might be called *direct* or *line departments* (or *divisions*) versus *support, indirect,* or *service departments* (or *divisions*).

Exhibit 10–2

City of Rock Creek: Costs for a Typical Month

City of Rock Creek

Department	Cost*
Production department:	
P1. Social Services	$ 500,000
P2. Fire and Safety	270,000
P3. Public Works	185,000
Total production department costs	$ 955,000
Support-service department:	
S1. Information Technology	$ 36,000
S2. Buildings and Grounds	84,000
S3. Human Resources	25,000
Total support-service department costs	$ 145,000
Total costs	$1,100,000

*The amounts shown are costs (i.e., resources used), not expenditures (i.e., resources supplied).

City's departments. You will learn just as much from this simple example without incurring the pain of struggling with a complex example.

Deciding Who Pays for Internal Support-Service Costs

Many production departments are supported by funds specifically designated for those purposes. For example, sales and property tax revenues, which citizens voted for, support the city library, parks, and recreation departments. These are analogous to the sales revenues that commercial organizations earn from selling products and services.

support-service costs *are the costs of resources supplied by an organization to provide support services*

Support-service costs are the costs of the resources supplied by an organization to provide the support services. These costs include the costs of personnel and the equipment, facilities, and supplies these personnel need to provide the types and levels of support services that the organization desires. In a typical month, the City of Rock Creek spends $145,000 on support services (Exhibit 10–2).

In the City of Rock Creek, as in many private and public organizations, cost allocations measure the charges from support-service departments to production departments. As Tukami learned, making these transfers is not simply a technical or mechanical process, particularly if there is a change in the allocation method, which alters the amounts that production departments pay to support-service departments.

Reasons for Allocating Service Costs

Decision Making and Cost Allocations

Allocating costs to activities unavoidably is done on a somewhat arbitrary basis. Some critics of cost allocation interpret the word *arbitrary* to mean "unfounded" or "without justification." They argue, perhaps correctly, that this type of cost allocation can result in misleading information that causes poor decisions and, therefore, should be avoided. It is going too far, however, to argue that making decisions about support services, products, or direct services should never depend in *any* way on cost allocations.

As we discussed in earlier chapters, the cost-management issue is whether employees make better decisions with or without "deliberate, well-designed" cost allocations that reflect the use of resources.

The City of Rock Creek recognizes that cost allocations are somewhat arbitrary but, like many organizations, has established cost-allocation principles intended to generate useful information for city employees and citizens:

City of Rock Creek

> The city shall employ a cost-allocation system to identify the cost to provide services to the public and recover certain costs incurred by various departments in providing support services to other city departments. The system shall accomplish the following objectives:
>
> **a.** Equitable allocation of service costs to users.
> **b.** Provision of incentives for service providers to deliver products and services efficiently and effectively.
> **c.** Provision of a stable cost-allocation system to facilitate the organization's budgeting for charges and revenues.
> **d.** Promotion of customer confidence in and acceptance of the accuracy, reasonableness, and fairness of the charges they incur.

The city believes that these cost-allocation principles will create the atmosphere of a simulated market for services in which internal customers—those who use the internal services—will negotiate (or demand!) support-service cost allocations that are reasonable measures of the worth of those services. Thus, the allocation of service costs is especially important in nonmarket situations prevalent in both government and private organizations that have internal support-service departments.

You're the Decision Maker 10.1

Principles of Cost Allocation

a. Do you think it is a good idea for organizations to formally express principles of cost allocation? Would it be any more important in a public organization such as a municipality than in a private firm?

b. You are the manager of the Social Services Department (a production department with a budget of approximately $500,000 per month). How might you react if you found out that the Information Technology Department (a support-service department with a budget of approximately $36,000 per month) was increasing its budget by 50 percent over the next year?

c. Take the position of the city manager who is responsible for both support-service and production departments. Which of the four principles of cost allocation identified do you think is most important? How would you resolve disputes over cost allocations?

(Solutions begin on page 401.)

Other Uses of Cost Allocations

Organizations might have cost-allocation requirements from both internal and external parties.

Required reporting. Tax regulations and external financial reporting require allocating manufacturing overhead to the units produced. This overhead often includes allocations of corporate or home-office expenses. Depreciation of long-term assets, which allocates the original cost of an asset over time periods, also is required. Many higher-level costs are allocated to products and services for regulatory purposes in public utilities.

Cost-based contracts. Some organizations work on a cost-basis or cost-plus basis. The federal government sometimes reimburses defense contractors for work done on a cost-plus (a profit) basis. Government agencies, foundations, and private industry reimburse universities for research on a cost-plus (an overhead-rate) basis. The US government, for example, partially reimburses cities and counties for training personnel who administer federal Medicaid programs. Obtaining complete and proper levels of reimbursement requires allocating all allowed costs to the government contract, research work, or training activity.

This Information Technology Department is a support-service department in a company.

Behavior influence. Managers often allocate costs to influence behavior. As mentioned, if costs of services are free to internal customers, you can expect the customers to demand these services as long as they perceive any benefit from them. Under this condition, you also can expect the size of service departments to attempt to grow almost without bounds to meet the demand for their services. On the other hand, allocating service costs to other departments for services provided gives managers of these other departments incentives to control their use of support services. For example, allocating the costs of the Information Technology Department to other city departments based on services provided causes those other department managers to request information technology service only when they believe that the service is worth at least as much as it will cost their departments to obtain it.

Research Insight 10.1

Corporate Cost Allocation

An executive of Kmart, the retail giant, reported during an interview that "allocating corporate headquarters' costs to stores makes each store manager aware that these costs exist and must be covered by the individual stores for the company as a whole to be profitable." Surveys of corporate cost allocation found that the great majority of companies reported allocating common headquarters' costs to divisions. The studies indicated that a primary managerial reason for cost allocation was to give division managers incentives to generate sufficient division profits to cover all corporate costs. *Sources: G. W. Dean, M. P. Moye, and P. J. Blayney,* Overhead Cost Allocation and Performance Evaluation Practices of Australian Manufacturers; *and J. M. Fremgren and S. S. Liao,* The Allocation of Corporate Indirect Costs. *(Full citations to references are in the Bibliography.)*

Cost-Management Implications for Internal Support Services

In the remainder of this chapter, we assume that in response to cost-management information about relative costs and benefits, the organization has decided both to provide internal support services using facility-level resources and allocate the costs of those resources to internal customers. These are important managerial decisions that can affect the organization's efficiency and ability to meet its goals. Once made, these decisions require implementation by cost-management analysts who use a systematic method to allocate support-service costs that also reinforces the organization's goals. We now consider alternative methods for allocating support-service costs.

Cost Allocation from Support-Service Departments to Internal Customers

As mentioned earlier, all cost allocations are at least somewhat arbitrary and cannot precisely link resource spending and resource use. For example, suppose that an organization allocates its human resources department spending (e.g., salaries, depreciation, and utilities) to internal customers proportionately based on the number of total full-time equivalent (FTE) employees in each department. What if a large department with mostly long-time employees needs less service from the human resources department than a smaller department that is hiring and training new employees and consumes much of the service department's time? If costs are allocated based on FTE, the larger department with established employees will be allocated a large share of the human resources department costs even though it uses little of that support-service resource. Likewise, the smaller department will pay only a small share of the cost even though it uses much of the resource. Is this cost allocation based on FTE fair? Will it cause unnecessary disputes? Does it motivate department managers to use human resources services properly? Does it result in the proper level and quality of human resource support services?

Allocating costs on the basis of FTE is easy because the necessary data are readily available. The allocations that result, however, might not accurately reflect the use of resources. But is it cost effective to obtain more accurate information that would allow cost allocations to more closely match the use of support services? Determining the proper basis for cost allocation can be very important, but this is not the only consideration to implementing a cost-allocation method that effectively supports the organization's goals. The process of allocating service costs systematically follows several steps, each of which can affect the success of cost allocations. The steps, which are explained in detail in subsequent sections, follow:

1. Identify the costs to be allocated to internal customers.
2. Choose the appropriate cost-allocation base(s) and rate(s).
3. Select and use a cost-allocation method.
4. Determine whether the cost allocations achieve the desired results; if they do not, begin the process again.

Step 1: Identify the Costs to Be Allocated to Internal Customers

LO 2 Understand how to choose cost pools and separate the cost of resources supplied from the cost of resources used.

Typically, organizations separate support-service costs by department into separate *cost pools,* which are the budgeted or actual spending amounts for distinct sets of resources, as the City of Rock Creek has done. Using multiple cost pools facilitates the management of the different types of support services and should allow more accurate cost allocations to internal customers than using only one cost pool. As shown earlier, Rock Creek uses three support-service cost pools—Information Technology, Buildings and Grounds, and Human Resources—which correspond to the city's organizational structure and management responsibilities.

Support-service use. Organizations might implement multiple cost pools when the *uses* of the service resources have both facility- and unit-level components. For example, suppose that the Information Technology Department leases computer equipment and hires personnel based on the projected demand for services plus reserve capacity. Thus, these computing resources (acquired by facility-level spending) provide two types of services to the city's internal customers: (1) the reserve of capacity available and (2) the current use of capacity. Rock Creek could establish separate cost pools for each type of service.

Deciding how many cost pools to use involves another cost-benefit evaluation. If the organization designs cost pools carefully, using more cost pools should result in cost allocations that match resource use better than using fewer cost pools. This is effectively the message of activity-based costing, which provides better information about the use of service resources, resulting in better management decisions about support-service type, quantity, source, and payment. However, designing and maintaining a complex cost-allocation system with many cost pools can, itself, be very costly. Organizations would not willingly implement a complex cost-allocation system unless the benefits from its better decisions justify the costs required to set up and maintain the system.

Telecommunications and Cost Allocations

The Telecommunications Act of 1996 restructured the US telecommunications industry. Prior to the act, the Federal Communications Commission (FCC) required telecommunication firms to perform very complex cost allocations designed to inhibit subsidizing unprofitable interstate services by allocating their costs to profitable services that were covered by favorable, regulated charge rates. The use of the logic of economics, however, once earnings regulation has been eliminated, avoids the need for the complex cost allocations because an unregulated firm has no incentive to subsidize unprofitable business. Bell Atlantic (now Verizon) made this persuasive theoretical argument before the FCC. This argument could be complicated, however, by *intrastate* regulations, which in the United States still depend on cost allocations. Deregulation and privatization of state-owned or socialized enterprises are having significant effects on cost-allocation practices around the world. *Sources: authors' research and Barry Spicer, David Emmanuel, and Michael Powell,* Transforming Government Enterprises.

Cost Management in Practice 10.1

For the purposes of this chapter, we assume that the City of Rock Creek maintains only three support-service cost pools, one for each support-service department. This level of complexity is sufficient to illustrate the methods and problems of cost allocation.

Costs of resources used separated from the costs of resources supplied. The purpose of cost allocation is to allocate support-service department costs to user departments based on some measure of the user departments' use of resources. As discussed in Chapter 5, the *use* of resources is not necessarily the same as the *supply* of resources. For example, you might spend $100 per month to acquire storage capacity for your belongings but use only 40 percent of the space. In that case, we distinguish between resources supplied (or money spent) of $100 per month, resources used of $40 per month (.40 × $100) and unused capacity of $60 per month ($100 resources supplied − $40 resources used).

Before allocating support-service department costs to user departments, we must first separate resources supplied from resources used. *Only resources used should be allocated to user departments* because users should be charged what they use, not how much money the support-service department spent.

In preparation for either an ABC or a traditional cost allocation, Tukami and her staff began by separating support-service department costs (resources used) from spending (resources supplied), with the following results:

Department	Resources Used	Resources Supplied	Unused Capacity
Information Technology	$36,000	$48,000	$12,000
Buildings and Grounds	84,000	90,000	6,000
Human Resources	25,000	27,000	2,000

Note that Tukami and her staff allocated to user departments only the amounts listed in the Resources Used column. The unused capacity information was included in various reports and was considered during budget negotiations. For example, the relatively large unused capacity in Information Technology existed because some user departments had outsourced these needs to outside companies or had hired information technology specialists to work in their own departments. These user departments no longer required Information Technology Department services. The unused capacity existed because the manager of the Information Technology Department had not fired people when other departments stopped using the department's services.

Step 2: Choose the Appropriate Cost-Allocation Base(s) and Rate(s)

LO 3 Understand how to choose appropriate allocation bases.

cost allocation bases *are factors used to assign indirect costs to cost objects*

Each cost pool should have its own appropriate cost-allocation base. **Cost allocation bases** are factors that cost management analysts use to assign indirect costs to cost objects. Ideally, a cost-allocation base reflects cause-and-effect relationships between resource spending and use, but determining these cause-and-effect relationships could be difficult or costly. In other words, finding a cost-allocation base that approximates cause-and-effect relationships is justified if the benefits from improved decisions exceed the costs of finding and using the base.

Recall that if an organization is able to accurately measure cause-and-effect relationships, it can *precisely trace* costs rather than *approximately allocate* them. If it cannot identify causal relationships between resource spending and use but still desires to allocate costs, it must use a less accurate cost-allocation base. The more closely the allocation base reflects a link between resource spending and use, the more useful allocated costs are likely to be for planning, decision making, and influencing behavior.[3]

Activity-based costing approach. Applying the techniques of ABC (Chapter 4) is an effective way to generate accurate cost-allocation bases, which, to be consistent with Chapter 4, we call *cost-driver bases* to indicate their ABC origins. To summarize, this involves the following:

1. Identifying and measuring the *activities* demanded by internal customers that require support-service spending (e.g., hiring and training new employees) to obtain *cost-driver bases.*
2. Measuring each support-service department's resource spending by level (unit, batch, product, customer, facility).
3. Dividing support-service resource spending by appropriate cost-driver bases to derive *cost-driver rates.*

Using one of the cost-allocation methods discussed later, the organization could allocate support-service costs to internal customers by charging the cost-driver rate for each unit of activity, for example, $X for each new employee hired and trained.

Cindy Tukami applied ABC to measure cost-driver bases and, in her analysis, discovered that:

- Several of the support-service departments needed more capacity to offer expected levels of service.
- Several of the production departments had been greatly undercharged for the services they received, and several others had been overcharged.

These are common outcomes of changing to an ABC approach. Tukami was able to solve the technical problems of ABC, but her political problem in Rock Creek was that she chose to implement an ABC approach that seemed to her to be an obvious improvement without considering others' reactions.[4]

Many organizations have implemented an ABC approach to allocate service-department costs, and most have reported political as well as technical problems. Recall that organizations often design cost allocations explicitly to influence behavior, and individuals often resist unexplained changes. Therefore, successful cost-management analysts anticipate that changing cost-allocation bases might induce changes in behavior that also provoke complaints. We advise cost-management analysts to consider a way to effect change in organizations, even for something as mundane as changing cost allocations. We discuss Tukami's cost-driver base problems in more detail after discussing cost-allocation methods.

[3]The important topic of cost estimation, which examines methods for measuring relationships between costs and activities, is the subject of Chapter 11, so we will not delve into this topic at this point.

[4]Tukami's City of Rock Creek analysis was nearly identical to the analyses presented in Chapter 4, so we do not discuss its technical details.

Use of ABC to Measure Costs

The use of ABC to measure the costs of internal services is increasing. One of the earliest (and best documented) reports was from Weyerhaeuser, the international wood products firm (*www.weyerhaeuser.com*). Weyerhaeuser has developed a comprehensive cost-allocation system based on major activities demanded of its internal service divisions. As the product divisions use internal services, they are charged according to a reasonably simple but thorough set of cost-driver rates. These rates regulate demand for services and, since internal customers have a voice in setting the rates, force the internal service departments to provide high-quality, efficient services. *Source: H. Thomas Johnson and Dennis Loewe,* "How Weyerhaeuser Manages Corporate Overhead Costs."

Cost Management in Practice 10.2

Allocation of support-service department costs. Many organizations have found ABC too costly—either politically or financially—to implement or even consider. They have implemented simpler but probably less accurate approaches to choosing allocation bases and allocation rates. These organizations generally classify support-service costs and choose cost-allocation bases as Exhibit 10–3 shows for labor, equipment, occupancy, and other related costs.

Choice of reasonable and justifiable allocation bases. If an ABC analysis is not possible or justified on a cost-benefit basis, the organization should choose allocation bases that at least seem reasonable and justifiable to internal customers. For example, prior to Tukami's ABC analysis, all support-service department costs were allocated using the following cost-allocation bases. Although these cost-allocation bases seem reasonable, the support-service departments provide a number of services that might not be related to these limited bases. This realization motivated Tukami to apply ABC.

Support-Service Department	
Information Technology	Number of computers, including network servers
Buildings and Grounds	Number of square feet in building
Human Resources	Number of newly hired employees (within one year)

Exhibit 10–3

Traditional Cost-Allocation Bases for Support-Service Costs

	Support-Service Cost	Typical Cost-Allocation Base
Labor related	Supervision	Number of employees, payroll dollars, or labor hours
	Personnel services	Number of employees
Equipment and technology related	Insurance on equipment	Value of equipment
	Taxes on equipment	Value of equipment
	Equipment depreciation	Hours of use or value of equipment
	Equipment maintenance	Number of machines or hours of use
Occupancy related	Building rental	Space occupied
	Building insurance	Space occupied
	Heat and air conditioning	Space or volume occupied
	Concession rental	Space occupied or desirability of location
	Interior building maintenance	Space occupied
Other service related	Materials handling	Quantity or value of materials
	Laundry	Weight of laundry processed
	Billing and accounting	Number of documents
	Indirect materials	Value of direct materials
	Dietary	Number of meals

Rock Creek's allocation bases. The (non-ABC) cost-allocation base amounts expected for each department appear in Exhibit 10–4. We use the data in this exhibit to demonstrate different cost-allocation methods as discussed in Step 3.

Step 3: Select and Use a Cost-Allocation Method

LO 4 Allocate support-service department costs using the direct and step methods.

This section describes two methods that allocate support-service costs: (1) the direct method and (2) the step method. These are the most commonly used methods by both private and public organizations. A third method, the reciprocal method, is more accurate than the two more common methods but is rarely used at this time. Because the reciprocal method could be used more in the future as cost-management analysts and their managers gain familiarity with it, we present it in the chapter Appendix.

We illustrate each method using Rock Creek's expected spending and allocation bases from Exhibit 10–4.

direct method *of cost allocation charges the costs of support-service departments to internal customers without making allocations among support-service departments*

City of Rock Creek

Direct method. The **direct method** of cost allocation charges the costs of support-service departments to internal customers *without making allocations among support-service departments.* All support-service cost allocations go *directly* to production departments.

Application of the direct method to Rock Creek. Exhibit 10–5 describes the allocation of costs using the direct method for the City of Rock Creek. The direct method involves no allocations among the three support-service departments themselves. Thus, it ignores any support-service department relation to any other support-service department.

Allocation of Information Technology Department costs. Tukami and her staff allocated the $36,000 monthly costs of the Information Technology Department based on the number of computers in the production departments. The Public Works, Human Resources, and Buildings and Grounds Departments had outsourced information technology to an outside company, so the Information Technology Department provided support services to only two production departments, Social Services, which had 28 computers and Fire and Safety which had 112 computers.

Using the direct method, the Information Technology Department costs are allocated 20 percent (28 ÷ 140) to Social Services because it had 28 of the 140 total computers and 80 percent (112 ÷ 140) to Fire and Safety which had 112 of them. (See Exhibit 10–4 for a summary of the percentages of Information Technology services used.) The allocation of costs are as follows:

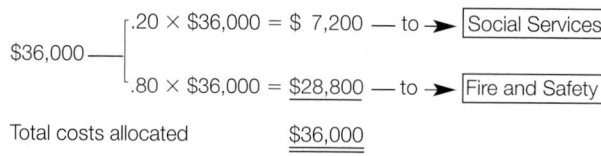

$36,000	.20 × $36,000 =	$ 7,200	— to → Social Services
	.80 × $36,000 =	$28,800	— to → Fire and Safety
Total costs allocated		$36,000	

Allocation of Buildings and Grounds Department costs. Tukami and her staff allocated the $84,000 monthly costs of the Buildings and Grounds Department based on the number of square feet of building space used. (For purposes of this calculation, "building space" included parking areas, walkways, and other outdoor spaces immediately adjacent to buildings.) Because most of Buildings and Grounds' work was for repairs and maintenance, the size of the space was a relevant allocation base. Unlike Information Technology, Buildings and Grounds provided support services to all production departments and to the two other support-service departments, Information Technology and Human Resources.

Exhibit 10-4

Uses of Support-Service in Department Services

City of **Rock Creek**

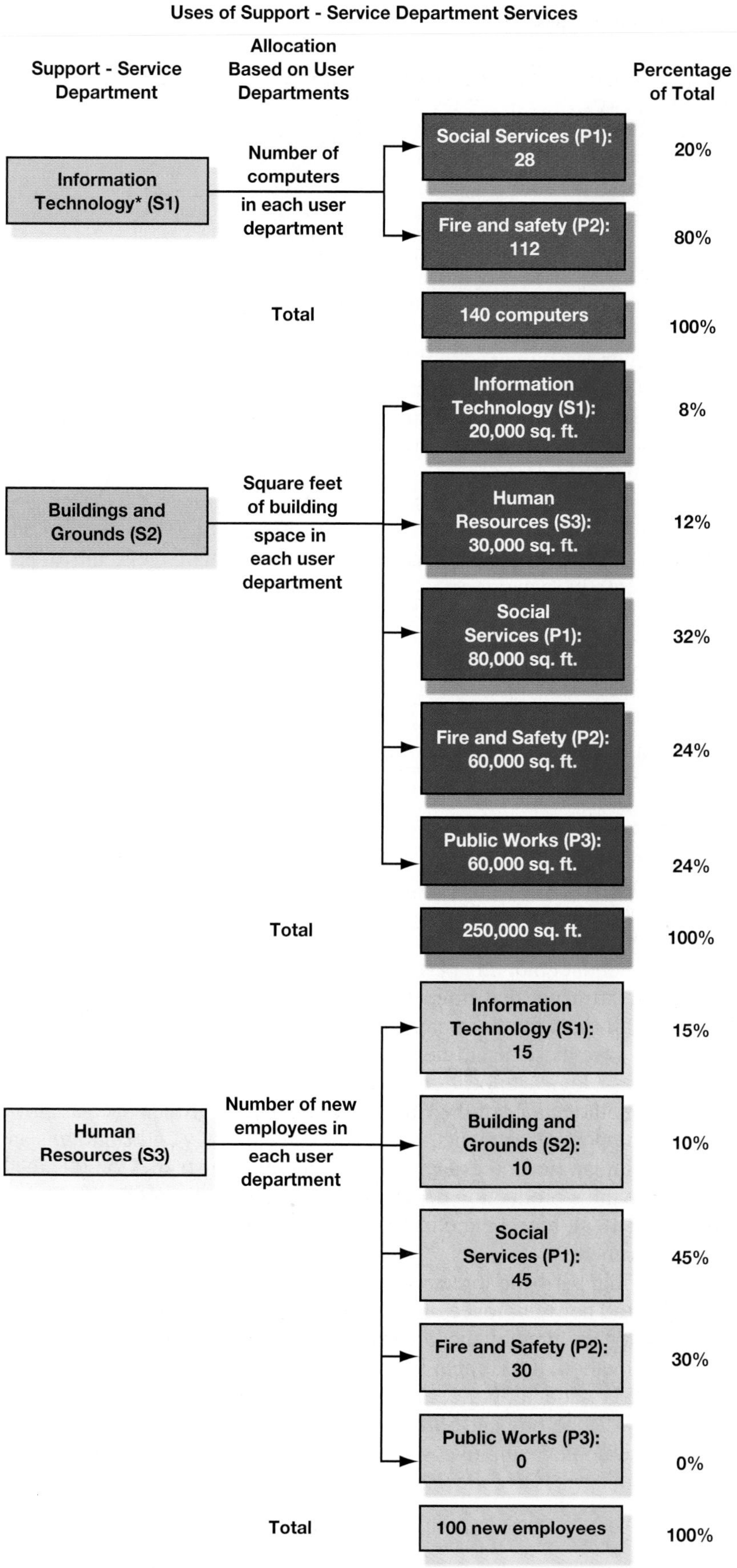

*The information Technology Department provides services to only two departments, Social Services and Fire and Safety. The other three departments—Buildings and Grounds, Human Resources, and Public Works—obtain information technology from outside companies.

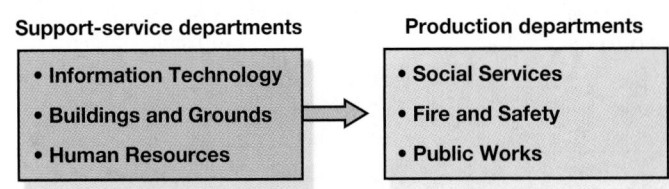

Exhibit 10–5

Allocation of Rock Creek's Support-Service Costs Using the Direct Method

City of Rock Creek

Support-service departments
- **Information Technology**
- **Buildings and Grounds**
- **Human Resources**

⇒

Production departments
- **Social Services**
- **Fire and Safety**
- **Public Works**

Using the direct method of cost allocation, *none* of the Buildings and Grounds Department's costs are allocated to the other support-service departments, Information Technology and Human Resources. *All* of the Buildings and Grounds Department's monthly costs of $84,000 are allocated directly to the three production departments.

Note in Exhibit 10–4 that the five departments use a total of 250,000 square feet. Eliminating the two support-service departments leaves 200,000 square feet used by the three production departments.

Using the direct method, the Buildings and Grounds Department's costs are allocated 40 percent to Social Services (80,000 of the 200,000 square feet for the three production departments), 30 percent to Fire and Safety (60,000 square feet), and 30 percent to Public Works (60,000 square feet). The allocation of costs would be as follows:

$84,000	.40 × $84,000 =	$33,600	— to → Social Services
	.30 × $84,000 =	$25,200	— to → Fire and Safety
	.30 × $84,000 =	$25,200	— to → Public Works
Total costs allocated		$84,000	

Allocation of Human Resources Department costs. Tukami and her staff allocated the $25,000 monthly Human Resources costs based on the number of new employees whom the production departments hired. The City of Rock Creek used new employees, defined as full-time or part-time employees hired within the last year, as the allocation base because most of Human Resources' costs were to advertise positions, hire and train employees, and conduct monthly performance reviews during a probation period following hiring. Departments that hired numerous employees consumed much of Human Resources' staff time. Furthermore, allocating costs to user departments based on "new employees" gave these departments incentives to reduce employee turnover. So new employees was a logical allocation base.

Using the direct method, *none* of the Human Resources Department's costs are allocated to the other support departments, Information Technology and Buildings and Grounds. *All* of the Human Resources Department's monthly costs of $25,000 are allocated directly to the three production departments. The percentage of services used, as reported in Exhibit 10–4, must be modified to eliminate the allocation bases for the support-service departments.

Note that in Exhibit 10–4 the three production and two support-service departments had a total of 100 new employees. Eliminating the two support-service departments leaves 75 employees hired by the three production departments.

Using the direct method, the Human Resources Department's costs are allocated 60 percent (= 45÷75) to Social Services because it had 45 of the 75 new employees and 40 percent (= 30÷75) to Fire and Safety because it had 30 of the 75 new employees. Public Works had no new employees, so it was allocated no Human Resources' costs. The allocation of costs is as follows:

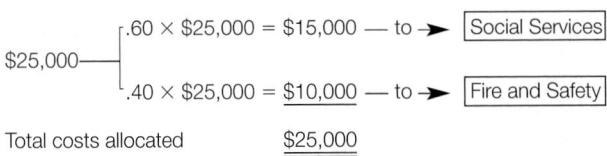

$25,000	.60 × $25,000 =	$15,000	— to → Social Services
	.40 × $25,000 =	$10,000	— to → Fire and Safety
Total costs allocated		$25,000	

The direct method allocates support-service department costs based *only* on the relative amount of the cost-allocation base in each production department.

Because support costs are allocated directly, the order of allocation—which support cost is allocated first, second, and so on—does not affect the amounts allocated. We begin with the Information Technology Department, but we could have begun as easily with any of the others with the same results.

Summary of direct-method results. We summarize the results of the direct method of support-service cost allocation for the City of Rock Creek in Exhibit 10–6. Panel A shows the percentages used in the cost allocation, and Panel B shows the costs allocated to the three production departments. The total charge to each production department for support services appears in columns (D) through (F) of Panel B. These figures are the proposed transfers from each production department to support-service departments and, if approved, would allow support-service departments to recover their costs.

Allocations of service costs in other organizations might not cause actual transfers of funds, but the cost allocations would be added to user departments' total overhead costs.

Limitations of the direct method. Some people have criticized the direct method because it ignores the services that one support-service department provides to another.

Exhibit 10–6 Cost Allocations: Direct Method

City of Rock Creek

Panel A: Percentage of Support-Service Department Cost Allocated to User Departments Based on Text Discussion

		User (Production) Departments		
Support-Service Department	**Support-Service Department Costs**	**Social Services**	**Fire and Safety**	**Public Works**
Information Technology (S1)	$36,000	20%	80%	0%
Buildings and Grounds (S2)	84,000	40	30	30
Human Resources (S3)	25,000	60	40	0

Panel B: Direct Method of Cost Allocation

	Allocations from Support-Service Departments			Allocations to User (Production) Departments		
	(A) Information Technology	**(B) Buildings and Grounds**	**(C) Human Resources**	**(D) Social Services**	**(E) Fire and Safety**	**(F) Public Works**
Department costs before any interdepartment allocations (Exhibit 10–2)	$ 36,000	$ 84,000	$ 25,000	$500,000	$270,000	$185,000
Allocation of Information Technology; 20%, 80%, 0%*	(36,000)	NA†	NA†	7,200	28,800	0
Allocation of Buildings and Grounds; 40%, 30%, 30%*	NA†	(84,000)	NA†	33,600	25,200	25,200
Allocation of Human Resources; 60%, 40%, 0%*	NA†	NA†	(25,000)	15,000	10,000	0
Total department costs after allocations	$ 0	$ 0	$ 0	$555,800	$334,000	$210,200

*These percentages refer to the allocation percentages from Panel A. For example, 20% of Information Technology costs are allocated to Social Services (20% × $36,000 = $7,200).

†NA = not applicable. By definition for the direct method, once costs are allocated from a support-service department, no costs are allocated back to it.

For example, Rock Creek's Human Resources Department hires and trains employees for other support-service departments as well as for production departments. If production departments are not vigilant, support-service departments could overserve each other and pass the costs to the production departments in the form of higher cost allocations. The step method of allocating support-service department costs attempts to remedy this problem by recognizing that support-service departments in fact render services to each other and use the organization's resources to do so.

step method *of cost allocation allocates costs first from the support-service department with the largest proportion of its total allocation base in other support-service departments to other support-service or production departments and then allocates costs from less general support-service departments*

Step method. The **step method** of cost allocation, unlike the direct method, recognizes that some support-service departments provide services to other support services as well as to production departments. Step method allocations usually begin from the service department with the largest proportion of its total allocation base (excluding its own) in other service departments. This is the most *general* service department. For example, Rock Creek's Human Resources Department provides the most services to the other support-services departments. Therefore, it is Rock Creek's most general service department. Using the step method, Rock Creek allocates Human Resources Department costs to all other departments first before allocating any other support-service costs.

Once the organization makes an allocation from a support-service department, no subsequent allocations are made back to that department. Thus, allocations from support-service departments are made in only one direction: from more general support services to less general support services and production departments.

Application of the step method to Rock Creek. We show the flow of Rock Creek's support-service costs using the step method in Exhibit 10–7. We have ordered the support-service departments (top to bottom) from the most to least general. The step method allocates more general support-service department costs to less general support-service department costs. The most general support-service department is Human Resources because it allocates more of its costs to other support-service departments than does either of the other two support-service departments. To see that Human Resources is the most general support-service department, recall the following uses of services among support-service departments (Exhibit 10–4):

City of Rock Creek

- Information Technology provided no services to other support-service departments.
- Of its total services used, Buildings and Grounds provided 8 percent to Information Technology and 12 percent to Human Resources. Thus, the other two support-services departments used 20 percent of the Building and Grounds services.
- Of its total services used, Human Resources provided 15 percent to Information Technology and 10 percent to Buildings and Grounds. Thus, the other two support-services departments used 25 percent of the Human Resources' services.

Based on the fact that Human Resources provided relatively more of its services to other support-service departments than did either Information Technology or Buildings and Grounds, the other two support-service departments, it comes in first and allocates its costs to other departments first. Buildings and Grounds comes in second with 20 percent of its resources used by other support-service departments. The order of allocation for the step method is as follows:

Step Order	Support-Service Department
1	Human Resources
2	Buildings and Grounds
3	Information Technology

Allocation of Human Resources Department costs. Using the step method, Tukami and her staff first allocate the Human Resources costs of $25,000 to all other departments. The percentages used in the allocation appear in panel A of Exhibit 10–7; they are simply the percentages of resources used (based on number of new employees in each department) presented in Exhibit 10–4.

Exhibit 10–7 Cost Allocations: Step Method

City of Rock Creek

Panel A: Percentages of Support-Service Department Cost Allocated to User Departments Based on Text Discussion

Support-Service Department	Support-Service Department Cost	User Departments					
		Human Resources	Buildings and Grounds	Information Technology	Social Services	Fire and Safety	Public Works
Human Resources	$25,000	(100)%*	10%	15%	45%	30%	0%
Buildings and Grounds†	84,000	NA‡	(100)	9%	37	27	27
Information Technology	36,000	NA	NA	(100)	20	80	0

Panel B: Step Method of Cost Allocation

	Support-Service Departments			Production Departments		
	Human Resources	Buildings and Grounds	Information Technology	Social Services	Fire and Safety	Public Works
Department costs before any interdepartment allocations	$ 25,000	$ 84,000	$ 36,000	$500,000	$270,000	$185,000
Allocation of Human Resources**	(25,000)	2,500	3,750	11,250	7,500	0
Allocation of Buildings and Grounds	NA‡	(86,500)	7,785	32,005	23,355	23,355
Allocation of Information Technology	NA	NA	(47,535)	9,507	38,028	0
Total department costs after allocations	$ 0	$ 0	$ 0	$552,762	$338,883	$208,355

*(100) means that 100 percent of the support-service department costs are being allocated to other departments.

†For ease of presentation, we have rounded the percentages, with the percentage allocated to Social Services rounded up to 37%.

‡NA indicates "not applicable" because once costs have been allocated from a support-service department, no costs are allocated back to that support-service department.

**To derive cost allocations, multiply the percentages in Panel A by the support-service departmental costs before any interdepartmental allocations. For example, the allocation of $2,500 from Human Resources to Buildings and Grounds equals 10% from Panel A times $25,000 Human Resources costs before any interdepartmental allocations.

The step method of allocation differs from the direct method by allocating costs to support-service and production departments whereas the direct method allocates costs directly to the production departments. Of course, Human Resources does not allocate any costs to itself. (We recommend that you take a minute to compare panel A of Exhibit 10–7 with panel A of Exhibit 10–6 to see how the direct and step methods differ.)

Using the step method, Tukami and her staff allocated the Human Resources costs as follows. Note that, according to Exhibit 10–4, Public Works had no new employees, so it was allocated no Human Resources costs. The allocation of costs to the other departments follows:

$25,000	.15 × $25,000 = $ 3,750 — to →	Information Technology
	.10 × $25,000 = $ 2,500 — to →	Buildings and Grounds
	.45 × $25,000 = $11,250 — to →	Social Services
	.30 × $25,000 = $ 7,500 — to →	Fire and Safety
Total costs allocated	$25,000	

We show this allocation in panel B of Exhibit 10–7.

After a support-service department's costs have been allocated to other departments, the step method allocates no other support-service department's costs back to itself. Therefore, having allocated Human Resource's costs to other departments, no costs are allocated back to it. (Later, we discuss a method that does allocate costs back and forth among support-service departments.)

Allocation of Buildings and Grounds Department costs. Buildings and Grounds is second in the step method order, so its costs are allocated next. Having already allocated Human Resources' costs to other departments, its use of Building and Grounds resources are not considered in the Buildings and Grounds' allocation. Therefore, based on the number of building square feet for other departments but Human Resources (and Buildings and Grounds, itself, of course), Tukami and her staff calculated the following percentages of resource usage based on the data in Exhibit 10–4:

User Department	Square Feet of Building Space by User Department	Percentage of the Total
Information Technology	20,000 sq. ft.	9% (= 20,000/220,000)
Social Services	80,000 sq. ft.	37
Fire and Safety	60,000 sq. ft.	27
Public Works	60,000 sq. ft.	27
Totals	220,000 sq. ft.	100%

These percentages appear in panel A of Exhibit 10–7. For ease of presentation, we have rounded the percentages, for example, the percentage allocated to Social Services is rounded up to 37 percent. If you do not use these rounded numbers, you will get slightly different cost allocations.

Recall that Building and Grounds' cost of resources used was $84,000 before allocating costs from any other support-service department. Tukami and her staff have already allocated $2,500 from Human Resources to Buildings and Grounds, so the Buildings and Grounds cost to be allocated equals $86,500, which is the total of $84,000 of Buildings and Grounds' own costs plus the $2,500 allocated to it from Human Resources.

Using the preceding percentages, the $86,500 is allocated as follows:

$86,500
- .09 × $86,500 = $ 7,785 — to → Information Technology
- .37 × $86,500 = $32,005 — to → Social Services
- .27 × $86,500 = $23,355 — to → Fire and Safety
- .27 × $86,500 = $23,355 — to → Public Works

Total costs allocated $86,500

Allocation of Information Technology Department costs. Finally, we allocate the Information Technology Department costs. Because the other two support-service departments' costs have already been allocated to other departments, no costs are allocated back to them. Therefore, Information Technology costs are allocated only to the production departments. (The City of Rock Creek's Information Technology Department charges nothing to the other support-service departments. Recall that the principle in the step method is that after a support-service department's costs have been allocated to other departments, no costs are allocated back to it.)

Information Technology costs are allocated based on the number of computers in the departments that it services. Information Technology services only Social Services and Fire and Safety (with 28 and 112 computers, respectively). Tukami and her staff calculated the following resource usage percentages based on the data in Exhibit 10–4. These percentages appear in Panel A of Exhibit 10–7.

User Department	Number of Computers	Percentage of the Total
Social Services	28 computers	20%
Fire and Safety	112 computers	80
Totals	140 computers	100%

Recall that Information Technology's costs were $36,000 before receiving allocation from any other support-service department. Tukami and her staff had already allocated $3,750 from Human Resources plus $7,785 from Buildings and Grounds to Information Technology. This leaves $47,535 ($36,000 + $3,750 + $7,785) to allocate.

Using the preceding percentages, the $47,535 is allocated as follows: See panel B of Exhibit 10–7 for this allocation.

$47,535	.20 × $47,535 =	$ 9,507	— to → Social Services
	.80 × $47,535 =	$38,028	— to → Fire and Safety
Total costs allocated		$47,535	

At this point, all support-service department costs have been allocated to production departments, and the cost-allocation process is complete.

Exhibit 10–8 compares step-method allocations with direct-method allocations. The differences in allocations do not seem large in absolute or relative terms, but some of the larger differences could represent adding or eliminating specific services. For example, if Rock Creek used the step method, Social Services would be charged $3,038 less per month for support services. Even this relatively modest cost-allocation difference could cause controversy when budgets are tight.

Limitations of the step method. The step method might result in more reasonable allocations than the direct method because it recognizes that some service departments also use other service departments. The direct method ignores services among support-service departments. The step method is not necessarily better than the direct method, however. An organization that already uses the direct method could find switching methods uneconomical, particularly if the differences in cost allocations for the methods are small.

The City of Rock Creek uses the direct method because it is simpler. Other organizations also use the direct method because of its comparative simplicity. However, external parties require some organizations, such as many hospitals, to use the step method for cost reimbursement.

The step method does go part way in recognizing that support-service departments can benefit from using the resources of other support-service departments. However, as demonstrated, this use is recognized in only one direction. In fact, all of Rock Creek's support-service departments actually use services from each other. This means that they use **reciprocal services,** which are services provided among multiple support-service departments. If its support-service departments had relatively more reciprocal

reciprocal services *are services provided among multiple support-service departments*

Exhibit 10–8

Comparison of Allocations Using the Direct and Step Methods

City of Rock Creek

Allocations to	Direct Method (Exhibit 10–6)	Step Method (Exhibit 10–7)	Differences Direct – Step
Social Services	$ 55,800	$ 52,762	$ 3,038
Fire and Safety	64,000	68,883	(4,883)
Public Works	25,200	23,355	1,845
Total allocated from support-service departments	$145,000	$145,000	$ 0

services, the city should consider using the *reciprocal method* of cost allocation to explicitly recognize reciprocal services. This method is defined and described in the Appendix to this chapter.

Tukami's accurate but politically incorrect ABC approach. Tukami proposed to continue using the direct method for allocating support-service costs.[5] However, she created a controversy when she unveiled cost allocations based on ABC cost-driver bases that reflect activities expected to be performed in the support-service departments for each production department. This was a radical departure from the simpler but less accurate cost-allocation bases that the city traditionally had used. Given the cost-management stance of this book, her approach seems appropriate. Tukami realized, however, that even ABC approaches cannot establish perfect causality.

The city manager and city council understood the inaccuracies and apparent inequities in the current allocation system and asked Tukami to study alternative cost-allocation bases for future years. They recommended that she present a new proposal for any changes well in advance of preparing the next budget so that the city could respond to comments from all affected departments and citizens.

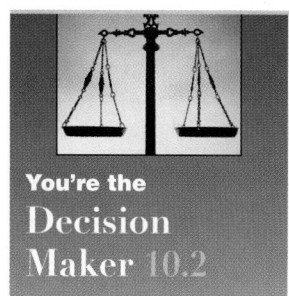

You're the Decision Maker 10.2

Implementation of Changes in Cost-Allocation Approaches

Assume that Cindy Tukami has appointed you to head a team to review her ABC approach and develop a proposal to present to the city council no more than six months from now (with care, this can be a career-enhancing assignment). Develop a plan for preparing this proposal, including recommendations for team membership, division of duties, and an outline of the proposal.

(Solutions begin on page 401.)

Step 4: Determine Whether the Cost Allocations Achieve the Desired Results

LO 5 Evaluate the consequences of alternative cost allocations.

What is the most effective way for an organization to choose the method to allocate support-service costs? Discussions (or arguments) about the "best" approach to allocating support costs can waste valuable time and create dissension and lack of cooperation among departments. Clumsy implementation of new cost allocations is bound to create distrust because affected departments will suspect that the motive is to "steal" funds or profits. This could discredit the finance (or other responsible) department and cause relations among departments to worsen.

On the other hand, negotiations about cost allocations could increase information flow and cooperation if the negotiation process is open and all parties have an opportunity to participate and influence its outcome. An open evaluation of cost-allocation approaches would consider accuracy, effects on departments, and relation of costs and benefits.

Cost-allocation accuracy. One way to determine the best way to allocate costs is to examine how accurately each approach reflects the use of support-service resource costs by departments receiving these services. The direct method does not consider any interactions among service departments, whereas the step method considers some, and the reciprocal method is more thorough in this respect; see the chapter Appendix. Likewise, ABC cost-driver bases better reflect cause-and-effect relations between resource spending and use than do traditional cost-allocation bases.

---

[5] She also considered ABC-step and ABC-reciprocal approaches, but for economy of discussion we do not discuss these.

Conceptually, combining ABC cost-driver bases and the reciprocal method should be the most accurate cost-allocation approach. Likewise, the combination of the direct method and traditional cost-allocation bases could be the least accurate reflection of resource spending, use, and provision of services. Other combinations lie somewhere between those extremes. Technical superiority or accuracy alone might influence the choice of approach. Accuracy, however, is only one consideration in choosing the appropriate approach for allocating support-service costs.

Cost-allocation effects. Another way to compare cost-allocation approaches is to examine the effects of alternative distributions of cost allocations to production (and support-service) departments, as shown in Exhibit 10–8. Cost allocations can have unintended behavioral effects. For example, consider the effects on department managers' performance evaluations that depend on their control of departmental costs.

Effects of distributions of costs. Both direct and step methods allocate the same total support-service cost for the City of Rock Creek, $145,000. Any differences between methods are in the amounts allocated to particular production departments. If the differences are large, alternative cost allocations could affect performance evaluations, decision making, and contracts.

Effects on performance evaluation. If performance evaluations of department managers are based on their abilities to provide services and control costs, which cost-allocation method, direct or step, would they prefer? For example, consider Exhibit 10–8. Social Services and Public Works departments would prefer the step method, but Fire and Safety would prefer the direct method because of the effects on departmental costs.

Effects on decision making. Cost-management analysts should consider the effects of cost-allocation differences on decision making in the affected departments. For example, the step method charges the Social Services Department $3,038 per month less than does the traditional direct method. Since this approximates the monthly cost of a counselor, the department head might regard this difference as important.

Except for the effects of the amounts of support-service costs allocated to production departments, the cost-driver or cost-allocation base itself could influence departmental decision making. For example, if Rock Creek allocates Human Resources Department costs on the basis of new employees, other department managers could perceive that they can reduce their costs (and transfers of funds to support services) by reducing the employee turnover. However, they *should* do this only if the benefits of reducing turnover exceeds the costs. This reasoning also applies to the use of other support services.

Effects on cost-plus contracts. As noted earlier, many organizations sell products on a cost-plus basis in which the "plus" is a profit. Defense contractors, for example, traditionally have sold products to national governments on a cost-plus basis. Government agencies traditionally have reimbursed hospitals and nursing homes on a cost-plus basis for particular types of patients.

Cost-plus contracts give incentives to the supplier of the good or service to seek as much reimbursement as possible and, therefore, to allocate as much cost as possible to the product for which reimbursement is possible. For example, McLaren Construction Co. has contracts with both companies and the City of Rock Creek. For simplicity, assume that McLaren is deciding how to allocate $120,000 of support-service cost between two major contracts, Company A and City of Rock Creek. This $120,000 is a facility-level cost that cannot be directly traced to either contract. McLaren sells commercial jobs at a price set in the market, but the contract with Rock Creek was negotiated for cost plus a fixed profit. Thus, every dollar of overhead that can be allocated to the Rock Creek contract results in an additional dollar of revenue in cost reimbursement.

Suppose that McLaren is choosing between labor hours and construction-equipment hours as the two possible allocation bases. The relative use of labor hours and construction-equipment hours follows:

	Contract	
Possible Allocation Base	**Company A**	**Rock Creek**
Percentage of labor hours used	30%	70%
Percentage of construction-equipment hours used	60	40

Naturally, McLaren prefers to allocate the $120,000 using labor hours because it could seek $84,000 (.70 × $120,000) reimbursement from Rock Creek using labor hours but only $48,000 (.40 × $120,000) from the city using construction-equipment hours. McLaren would be $36,000 ($84,000 − $48,000) better off if it could use labor hours as the allocation base. Of course, Rock Creek would prefer construction-equipment hours for similar reasons. If the Rock Creek contract does not specify how costs should be allocated, McLaren ethically can choose the most advantageous approach.

Since the support-service costs cannot easily be directly attributed to a contract, allocation debates abound in cost-plus contracting. In such cases, specifying in the contract precisely how to define costs and how to make allocations is crucial. Thus, contracts and policies governing cost reimbursement try to clearly specify which costs and cost allocations are allowable.[6]

Cost-allocation costs and benefits. A third consideration in the evolution of cost allocations is the relation of the costs and the benefits of setting up, administering, and maintaining the cost-allocation system. Cost-management analysts must realize that complex cost-allocation systems are not only difficult and costly to design but also are costly to maintain. For example, organizations that implement an ABC approach often find that the ABC information indicates where processes can be greatly improved (this is the topic of Chapter 5). Thus, after cost-management analysts lead and implement process improvements, they might recognize that the previous cost-driver base information is obsolete and requires revision. This can be a continual process of improvement, which is costly but justified if decisions and organizational performance also continue to improve.

If decisions or meeting organizational goals are unaffected by cost allocation type or improvements in the cost allocation used, however, it would be difficult to justify implementing a complex, expensive cost-allocation system. An unchanged or traditional direct approach could be quite adequate in this situation.

Finding the right allocation. Since no absolutely precise allocation of support-service costs exists, an organization could experiment to find the right one. For example, administrators of a large university observed that its faculty and staff were using the university's Wide Area Telephone Service (WATS) so much that the lines were seldom free during the day. WATS allowed the university unlimited toll-free service within the United States. The monthly cost of the service was $10,000, which was fixed at this level for an agreed-upon overall volume of calls. The variable cost per call was zero.

University administrators learned that the average use on the WATS line was 50,000 minutes per month, so they allocated the $10,000 monthly charge to callers (that is, departments) at a rate of 20 cents per minute ($10,000 ÷ 50,000 minutes).

[6]For example, reimbursement by the US federal government to other governmental bodies is covered by a lengthy, detailed document titled OMB Circular A-87. You can find information about these rules by searching on the Web for "Circular A-87" and "Cost Accounting Standards." Reimbursement to government contractors is covered by cost accounting standards.

After being charged for each use of WATS, department heads discouraged their faculty and staff from using it. Hence, the number of WATS minutes used dropped to 25,000 per month. The university increased the rate to 40 cents per minute ($10,000 ÷ 25,000). This decline in use and increase in charge continued until the internal cost allocation per minute exceeded the normal long-distance rates, and the use of WATS dropped almost to zero. The university's total telephone bill increased dramatically because it was paying for both the WATS monthly cost and normal long-distance charges.

University administrators subsequently compromised by charging a nominal fee of 10 cents per minute for WATS calls. According to the university's chief financial officer, "The 10 cents per minute charge made us aware that there was a cost to the WATS service, albeit a fixed cost per month. The charge was sufficiently low, however, so as not to discourage bona fide use of WATS."[7]

Some ethical issues that cost allocations present. The inherent arbitrariness of cost allocation means that usually no clear-cut way to allocate costs exists. This arbitrariness can lead to difficult ethical choices for those responsible for allocating the costs. Consider again the allocation of costs in cost-plus contracts. We have seen cases in which the contracts specified *manufacturing* cost plus a profit, yet the contractor added advertising, general and administrative, and similar costs to manufacturing overhead. This appears to be a violation of the contract terms, but the contractor argued that *full* manufacturing cost should include the allocations of these other costs.

Many lawsuits involving contract and tax disputes have arisen because people have allocated costs in inappropriate ways or contracts have been ambiguous. For example, a fast-growing county was sued by building contractors who argued that the total revenues collected by the county for building permits exceeded the costs to operate the county building department. Thus, the builders argued, the excess revenues amounted to an unfair tax on builders that the county used illegally to fund other programs and services. The county counterargued that permit revenues did not exceed the sum of both direct building department costs and costs allocated from county support services. After years of arguments and court appearances, the judge requested the opinions of outside experts on a reasonable cost-allocation approach and mediated the dispute.

Ethical Cost Allocations

Research Insight 10.2

Professor Mark Wolfson analyzes a classic example of the effects of ambiguous or unethical cost allocations in organizations structured as partnerships. General partners are responsible for conducting the work of the partnership, such as real estate development or oil and gas exploration, for the benefit of limited partners who share in the profits of the partnership. General managers also, however, can allocate their management costs to different partnerships that they manage to maximize their profits but perhaps at the expense of some limited partners. Wolfson finds that limited partners are willing to pay more to participate in partnerships managed by general partners with reputations for ethical cost allocations (and other practices). Therefore, general partners with reputations for ethical cost allocations earned higher returns, while less ethical general partners earned less. *Source: Mark Wolfson,* "Empirical Evidence of Incentive Problems and Their Mitigation in Oil and Gas Tax Shelter Programs."

---

[7]This example is based on Jerold L. Zimmerman, "The Costs and Benefits of Cost Allocations." The solution to this problem is not necessarily a charge of zero. According to Zimmerman, the correct cost to charge users is "the cost imposed by forcing others who want to use the WATS line to either wait or place a regular call . . . this cost varies between zero (if no one is delayed) to, at most, the cost of a regular toll call if a user cannot use the WATS line" (p. 510). The necessary procedure to implement such a costing system is very difficult and costly. Zimmerman suggests that predetermined cost allocations could be a simplified way to approximate the results of the more complicated, theoretically correct system.

Chapter Summary

Allocating service costs should reflect a cause-and-effect relationship between spending for support services and the services provided to internal customers. That is, cost allocations should measure the costs of support services provided. Tracing support-service spending directly to internal customers is usually difficult. Many organizations use reasonable, although not completely accurate, cost allocations based on allocation bases that reasonably describe the use of service resources.

The most common methods of allocating service costs are the direct and step methods. A currently less common method is the reciprocal-cost method (see the Appendix). Cost allocation is not a purely technical exercise since allocations can have both intended and unintended consequences. Therefore, choosing how to allocate costs should not be based solely on technical merits (e.g., recognizing reciprocal services). The way to allocate service costs depends more on the behavior of the departments and divisions that receive the allocations.

Key Terms

For each term's definition, refer to the indicated page or turn to the glossary at the end of the text.

cost-allocation bases, 386
direct method, 388
production (or line) departments, 380
reciprocal method*, 403
reciprocal services, 395
support-service costs, 381
step method, 392
support-service (or indirect) departments, 380

*Term appears in the chapter Appendix.

Meeting the Cost-Management Challenges

1. **Cost** allocations are arbitrary. Does this mean that the way you decide to allocate costs is of no consequence to you or your organization?

Some people use the word "arbitrary" to mean "capricious" or "without justification." If cost allocations in an organization truly are unrelated to either the use of resources or influencing desired behavior, it is difficult to justify any effort devoted to cost allocation. We think that the alternative definition meaning "discretionary" is more than a semantic difference; it reflects the deliberate intent to use cost allocations to achieve some goal. These include the legitimate purposes of managing support-service resources effectively, improved decision making, proper external reporting, faithfully executing of cost-based contracts, and influencing employee behavior. We do not mean to imply, however, that organizations can achieve these outcomes only by allocating costs. Employees might make some decisions better without cost-allocation information, (e.g., production or product-line decisions). We do mean that cost allocations, when considered necessary, should be made carefully and with an awareness of their effects and limitations.

2. **Choosing** a cost-allocation approach is always a judgment that is based on an evaluation of trade-offs. How can you be best prepared to evaluate the trade-offs and provide leadership if dramatic changes are needed?

Knowing the trade-offs you are likely to encounter and the limits to analysis is a good first step. The various trade-offs center around the value of more accurate cost-allocation information versus the cost of improved information. The most accurate cost allocations closely reflect the cause and effect between the desired or actual spending for resources and their use. We must realize, however, that we can never establish this causality with certainty and without measurement error. Therefore, cost-management analysts must judge how close is good enough because we can expect that, consistent with the law of diminishing marginal returns, making further improvements in accuracy costs increasingly more. At some point, the costs of more improvement will exceed the benefits. Armed with this realization, the next step is to identify the benefits and costs of cost allocation—generally and specifically, quantitatively and qualitatively. You might want to review the discussion of cost-benefit analysis in Chapter 1.

Benefits of more accurate cost allocations include better control and use of support services leading, for example, to better service levels, better operations, and less waste of resources. The costs of improved cost allocations include out-of-pocket and opportunity costs of information analysis and upkeep as well as the education of those who are affected by the allocations. Quantifying all of these costs and benefits could be difficult, which is why judgment is necessary: to compare quantitative and qualitative information.

Education and communication are extremely important factors that determine the success of planned changes. If the decisions, evaluations, or behavior of individuals or departments is affected by cost allocations simply to announce a more accurate approach to cost allocation is foolish. The numbers almost never "speak for themselves." In real organizations where budgets and evaluations based on cost allocations matter, any unexplained or unjustified changes in cost allocations can provoke surprise, anger, and unproductive dissension. It is more effective to plan and execute these changes carefully so that affected parties understand why the change is necessary and how the change will affect them. You might want to review the steps for leading change in Chapter 1.

3. **Some** cost-allocation approaches appear to be quite complex. How should you educate other managers to understand the complexities of the cost-allocation process?

In this chapter we have first introduced the importance of cost allocations. Second, we illustrate the methods with simple examples and diagrams. We also contrast the effects of alternative methods so that it is clear that the distributions of costs can differ for each method. If we were addressing only users of cost-allocation information such as managers or executives, we would go no further in explaining how complex the methods become when applied to real organizations. They need to understand that the methods can differ and that you are fully aware of how to implement them. They do not need a great deal of detail, however. We have given you detailed applications because we believe that cost-management analysts need to know more than a simple example. You need to realize that applying cost-allocation methods is conceptually no different from analyzing the simple examples, but implementing them in real situations requires a careful, systematic approach to ensure accuracy and completeness.

Solutions to You're the Decision Maker

10.1 Principles of Cost Allocation p. 382

a. Principles of cost allocation become more important as cost allocations become a larger part of an organization's total costs. Obviously, if most support services are outsourced, cost-allocation principles seem unnecessary. In this case, market transactions take the place of bureaucratic rules and principles. On the other hand, if most support services are internal and production departments bear the costs of those services via cost allocations, it is in the organization's interest to have clear cost-allocation principles and policies. Otherwise, managers will spend unproductive time mediating disputes over cost allocations.

Cost allocations might be more prevalent in public institutions because they seldom obtain or provide services through open markets (although this is changing throughout the world). Furthermore, since public organizations usually exist to provide goods and services that are not available via market transactions, monetary measures of their values are unavailable. Thus, cost allocations might be the predominant quantitative measures of services.

b. As the manager of a production department, you know that spending for support services can affect your department. First, you probably agree that information technology is important, but you might express surprise that you were not informed about this decision, which should have been discussed openly and fully as a major decision. Next, because departments like yours will pay for this increased support-service spending, you might wonder what services your department can expect in return. By challenging the budget increase, you are providing a control on support-service spending, but you also might wonder aloud whether your department might be better off if it could outsource information technology services. Furthermore, you might express concern about the unplanned effects on your budget and whether the city expects your department to reduce its spending to pay for increased support services, to increase fees charged to citizens, or to seek increased funding from tax revenues or state and federal grants. You also could express concern about whether the support-service departments are more concerned with their budgets than with providing reasonable charges for fair services to others. Note that these concerns are similar to those you would have as a department or division manager in a private corporation; sales from departments such as yours must cover spending for internal services.

c. As city manager, you must be concerned with the efficiency with which the city provides services to its citizens. That means ensuring that the city provides the type, quality, and quantity of services that citizens want and need within its budget and according to appropriate laws and regulations. Perhaps the most important principle is *provision of incentives for service providers to deliver products and services efficiently and effectively* because adhering to this principle will ensure that scarce city resources are supplied and used appropriately.

10.2 Implementation of Changes in Cost-Allocation Approaches p. 396

Before Tukami presents the proposal in six months, the finance department must repair the damage to the credibility of ABC as an approach that is consistent with the city's principles of cost allocation. One possible approach follows:

Steps for Leading Change	Possible ABC Plan
• Identify a need for change.	• Review Tukami's analyses to verify that previous cost allocations violate the city's cost-allocation principles and that ABC could improve cost allocations in significant ways.
• Create a team to lead and manage the change.	• Expand the team to include representatives from some of the support-service and production departments, taking care to add skilled, articulate team members but not so many that the team becomes too large to be efficient.
• Create a vision of the change and a strategy for achieving the vision.	• Stress the importance of city efficiency in all departments and that management decisions drive costs. Stress that both accurate cost allocations and process improvements are necessary to meet growing service expectations and the public's desire for lower taxes. Prepare a description of the benefits of an ABC approach, including: • Understanding how decisions affect how work is accomplished. • Learning what activities the organization uses to produce products and services. • Choosing the most profitable uses of scarce capacity. • Measuring the consumption of the organization's resources. • Guiding process improvements. • Steps in the analysis, adapted from Chapter 4, are to: 1. Identify and classify the activities related to services. 2. Estimate the cost of activities identified in step 1. 3. Calculate a cost-driver rate for each activity. 4. Assign activity costs to services.
• Communicate the vision and strategy for change and have the change team be a role model.	• Meet with all department managers to describe the need and proposal for revising cost allocations. Do not be defensive but be prepared to accept criticism and suggestions for improvement. • Have a similar meeting with the city manager and council.
• Encourage innovation and remove obstacles to change.	• Obtain approval from city and department managers to allow the team to develop best solutions.
• Ensure that short-term achievements are frequent and obvious.	• Consider beginning with a pilot project in one support-service department to demonstrate the approach and "work out the bugs."
• Use successes to create opportunities for improvement in the entire organization.	• Communicate the benefits of improvements and indicate how new knowledge about ABC approach can benefit the entire city management.
• Reinforce a culture of more improvement, better leadership, and more effective management.	• Apply the approach throughout the organization and let departments have continuing input to use and improve ABC information.

Appendix to Chapter Ten

Reciprocal Method

LO 6 Allocate support-service department costs using the reciprocal method.

The step and direct methods omit the costs of support services consumed by one service department that were provided by other service departments. The reciprocal method of cost allocation addresses a technical limitation of the step method by making a reciprocal cost allocation when support-service departments provide reciprocal services, that is, they provide services to each other. The **reciprocal method** recognizes and allocates costs of all services provided by any support-service department, including those provided to other support-service departments. If allocation bases are reasonable, this method is the most accurate approach because it reflects the actual process by which services are exchanged among the organization's departments.

reciprocal method *recognizes and allocates costs of all services provided by any support-service department, including those provided to other support-service departments*

The reciprocal method expresses the total costs of each service and production department in equation form:[8]

$$\text{Total departmental costs} = \text{Direct costs of the department} + \text{Service costs to be allocated to the department}$$

This creates one equation for each department in which the unknown element is the total departmental cost. This set of equations (one equation for each unknown total department cost) is then solved simultaneously using matrix algebra.[9] As we shall demonstrate, solving all of the equations simultaneously accounts for all support-service department allocations, including reciprocal services provided by support-service departments to each other. This algebraic approach is also known as the *simultaneous solution method* because it solves a system of equations simultaneously.

For example, assume that the direct overhead costs of the departments at the City of Rock Creek are as follows:

Information Technology (S1)	$ 36,000
Buildings and Grounds (S2)	84,000
Human Resources (S3)	25,000
Social Services (P1)	500,000
Fire and Safety (P2)	270,000
Public Works (P3)	185,000

Using the information in Exhibit 10–4, the total costs of the Social Services Department (P1) is expressed as follows:

$$\text{Total costs} = \text{Direct costs} + \text{Allocated costs}$$
$$P1 = \$500{,}000 + .20\ S1 + .32\ S2 + .45\ S3$$

Similar equations are constructed for each of the other production departments:

$$P2 = \$270{,}000 + .80\ S1 + .24\ S2 + .30\ S3$$
$$P3 = \$185{,}000 + .00\ S1 + .24\ S2 + .00\ S3$$

And for the service departments, the equations are

$$S1 = \$36{,}000 + .08\ S2 + .15\ S3$$
$$S2 = \$84{,}000 + .00\ S1 + .10\ S3$$
$$S3 = \$25{,}000 + .00\ S1 + .12\ S2$$

Now we have a set of equations that expresses the total cost of each department as a function of direct costs and allocated costs.

With the cost relationships written in equation form, the solution now can be found easily using the matrix invert function of a spreadsheet, such as Excel®. The matrix invert function uses inverse matrices, which are generally used to solve systems of mathematical equations involving several variables.

---

[8]The reciprocal method could include all costs of the department, including costs of production in the production departments. In our example, production departments do not provide any services. We are interested only in allocating support-service costs, so we can ignore production costs without affecting the allocation results.

[9]The reader will recall from algebra class that solving two equations with two unknowns by algebraic substitution is relatively straightforward. However, using matrix algebra is preferred with more than two unknowns and equations.

Setting the Equations in Matrix Form

When using matrix algebra to solve simultaneous equations, all coefficients need to be stated in the same terms. For instance,

$$\text{Total costs P1} = \$500{,}000 + .20\ \text{S1} + .32\ \text{S2} + .45\ \text{S3}$$

should be restated as

$$\text{Total costs P1} = 1.00\ \text{P1(direct costs)} + .20\ \text{S1} + .32\ \text{S2} + .45\ \text{S3}$$

This process allows the information to be entered into a matrix on a spreadsheet, such as the one described next.

The following is based on using Excel to solve reciprocal-method cost allocations. The commands are shown in "quotes."

Step 1: Set up the parameter section. The top section of Exhibit 10–9 (on page 405), titled Services, is the parameter section of the spreadsheet. This is the section on which the rest of the spreadsheet is calculated. It includes the matrix into which the percentage of services used and the amount of costs to be allocated will be entered.

Notice that all support-service and production departments are included in both the Performed By and Used By categories regardless whether they perform services for other departments. This creates a matrix with an equal number of rows and columns (remember that a matrix must have an equal number of rows and columns). The percentage of each department's use of another department's services and the amount of costs to be allocated to the user department are entered in the corresponding position.

For example, using the equation S1 = 1.00 S1(direct costs) + .08 S2 + .15 S3, we enter the amount of S2 services used by S1, 0.08, in cell C8; the amount of S3 services used by S1, 0.15, in cell D8; and (1.00) in cell B8 because all of S1 services were used by other departments. We entered 0.00 in cells E8, F8, and G8 because S1 used none of the production departments' services. Using the equation P1 = 1.00 P1(direct costs) + .20 S1 + .32 S2 + .45 S3, we enter .20 in cell B11, .32 in cell C11, .45 in cell D11, and 1.00 in cell E11 (because P1 used all of its own direct costs incurred), and 0.00 in F11 and G11.

The totals presented in row 14 represent the amount of costs remaining in each department after allocation. As you can see, the service departments retain none of their costs but allocate all of them to production departments when finished, but the production departments retain all of their costs. The costs to be allocated, entered in row 18, are entered under the department that incurred them.

Step 2: Set up the inverse matrix. The middle section of Exhibit 10–9 Inverse Matrix, displays the output of the inverse matrix function of the spreadsheet. The output in this section is the same size as the parameter matrix and can be style formatted. Computer spreadsheets have commands that can be used to invert matrices (e.g., MINVERSE in Excel®).

The inverse matrix presents the percentage allocation of each department's costs to other departments. The negative percentages represent a service department's direct costs allocated to/from other service departments. They are negative because they will be reallocated to production departments.

You will notice that for departments S2 and S3, the total of the negative percentages is more than 100 because of the reciprocal nature of the allocations. The service departments allocate costs to other service departments, which are allocated back to them, bringing service departments' total costs to more than their direct costs. Therefore, there will be allocations out of the service departments in excess of 100 percent of their direct costs.

Step 3: Set up the cost allocation table. The bottom section of Exhibit 10–9, Cost Allocation, presents the actual dollar amount of allocation to each department based on the inverse matrix and each department's direct costs. The amount calculated in each

Exhibit 10-9

Reciprocal Method Spreadsheet

City of **Rock Creek**

	A	B	C	D	E	F	G	H
1								
2			*City of* **Rock Creek**					
3								
4	**Services**							
5		**Performed by:**						
6		**S1**	**S2**	**S3**	**P1**	**P2**	**P3**	
7	**Used by:**							
8	S1	(1.00)	0.08	0.15	0.00	0.00	0.00	
9	S2	0.00	(1.00)	0.10	0.00	0.00	0.00	
10	S3	0.00	0.12	(1.00)	0.00	0.00	0.00	
11	P1	0.20	0.32	0.45	1.00	0.00	0.00	
12	P2	0.80	0.24	0.30	0.00	1.00	0.00	
13	P3	0.00	0.24	0.00	0.00	0.00	1.00	
14		0.00	0.00	0.00	1.00	1.00	1.00	
15								
16								
17	**Costs to Be Allocated:**							
18		$36,000	$84,000	$25,000	$0	$0	$0	
19								
20								
21								
22	**Inverse Matrix**							
23		**S1**	**S2**	**S3**	**P1**	**P2**	**P3**	
24	S1	(1.00)	(0.099)	(0.16)	0.00	0.00	0.00	
25	S2	0.00	(1.012)	(0.101)	0.00	0.00	0.00	
26	S3	0.00	(0.121)	(1.012)	0.00	0.00	0.00	
27	P1	0.20	0.398	0.52	1.00	0.00	0.00	
28	P2	0.80	0.359	0.456	0.00	1.00	0.00	
29	P3	0.00	0.243	0.024	0.00	0.00	1.00	
30								
31	**Cost Allocation**							**Total**
32		**From:**						**Allocated to Production**
33		**S1**	**S2**	**S3**	**P1**	**P2**	**P3**	**Departments**
34	**To:**							
35	S1	$(36,000)	$(8,332)	$(3,998)	$0	$0	$0	
36	S2	$0	(85,020)	(2,530)	0	0	0	
37	S3	$0	(10,202)	(25,304)	0	0	0	
38	P1	$7,200	$33,464	$12,996	0	0	0	$53,660
39	P2	$28,800	$30,131	$11,397	0	0	0	$70,328
40	P3	$0	$20,405	$607	0	0	0	$21,012
41								$145,000
42								

Exhibit 10–10

Comparing Direct, Step, and Reciprocal Cost Allocations

City of Rock Creek

Allocations to	Direct Method (Exhibit 10–6)	Step Method (Exhibit 10–8)	Reciprocal Method (Exhibit 10–9)
Social Services	$ 55,800	$ 52,762	$ 53,660
Fire and Safety	64,000	68,883	70,328
Public Works	25,200	23,355	21,012
Total allocated from support-service departments	$145,000	$145,000	$145,000

cell is the percentage in the corresponding inverse matrix cell multiplied by the direct cost in the same column. For instance, the cost allocated out of S1 $(36,000) equals the percentage allocated out of S1 represented in the inverse matrix (1.00) multiplied by S1 direct costs $36,000. Note that the percentages shown in the Inverse Matrix section are rounded for presentation purposes. However, unrounded numbers are used to calculate the cost allocations. Thus, when checking the math, notice that several amounts in the Cost Allocation section have rounding discrepancies.

The totals on the right of the bottom panel of the table show the total costs allocated to each department. Again, the totals for the service departments are negative because they do not remain in the department but are allocated out to the production departments. If you add these negative totals, you will find that they total more than the total service-department costs because some amounts are included twice. For example, the total cost of S1 (the sum of all amounts shown on line 35) includes the allocated costs from S2 and S3 plus all of the S1 direct costs, even though some of the direct costs are allocated to S2 and S3.

Department P1 was allocated $7,200 from S1 plus $33,464 from S2 plus $12,996 allocated from S3 for a total allocation of $53,660 from support-service departments.

Comparative cost allocations using the direct, step, and reciprocal methods appear in Exhibit 10–10. The allocations that result from the step and reciprocal methods are similar. If the City of Rock Creek wished to use a method that recognizes services among support-service departments, the finance department probably should use the reciprocal method since it is technically superior and actually easier to use since spreadsheets do most of the arithmetic. The reciprocal method could be more difficult to explain, however (some peoples' eyes glaze over on hearing the words "matrix" or "simultaneous equations").

Some organizations use the direct method if allocations are not dramatically different just because it is easier to explain to managers and internal customers than other methods. Cost-management analysts, however, should consider all issues raised at the end of this chapter regarding the choice among alternative cost-allocation approaches.

Review Questions

10.1 What factors would you consider when deciding whether to outsource a particular support service?

10.2 What are some costs of the cost-allocation process itself?

10.3 What are some benefits of cost allocation?

10.4 How should a manager decide whether to allocate costs?

10.5 What are some management uses of information based on allocated costs?

10.6 What are four broad categories of common costs and a typical basis for the allocation of costs in each category?

10.7 What are the similarities and differences of allocating service costs for the direct method and the step method (and the reciprocal method, if studied)?

10.8 What criterion should be used to determine the order of allocation from support-service departments when using the step method? Explain why.

Critical Analysis

10.9 Three students share a house. Having better things to do than clean house, they hire someone to come in and clean once each week. How should they share the costs of the housekeeper? One simple solution is to share the cost equally. Suppose, however, that one student's bedroom is twice as large as each of the other students' bedrooms. The second student has a small bedroom and uses the house only four days per week. The third student uses the house all week, has a small bedroom, and is generally acknowledged to be the cleanest of the three. Sharing the cost equally is simple, but is it fair? Form groups of three. Each should take the role of one of the roommates. Using the techniques of the chapter, develop a reasonable way to share housekeeping costs.

10.10 Respond to this comment: "Outsourcing is based on a market economy and, therefore, is the most efficient way to obtain a service."

10.11 Consider the following conversation between a self-styled cost-allocation expert and Joe, the manager of a diner.

Expert: Joe, you said you put in these peanuts because some people ask for them, but do you realize what this rack of peanuts is costing you?

Joe: It's not going to cost! It's going to be a profit. Sure, I had to pay $100 for a fancy rack to hold the bags, but the peanuts cost 24 cents a bag, and I sell 'em for 40 cents. Suppose I sell 50 bags a week to start. It'll take 12 1/2 weeks to cover the cost of the rack. After that I have a clear profit of 16 cents a bag. The more I sell, the more I make.

Expert: That is an antiquated and completely unrealistic approach, Joe. Fortunately, modern accounting procedures permit a more accurate picture that reveals the complexities involved.

Joe: Huh?

Expert: To be precise, those peanuts must be integrated into your entire operation and be allocated their appropriate share of business overhead. They must share a proportion of your expenditures for rent, heat, light, equipment depreciation, decorating, salaries for your waitresses, cook . . .

Joe: The cook? What's he got to do with the peanuts? He doesn't even know I have them.

Expert: Look, Joe, the cook is in the kitchen, the kitchen prepares the food, the food is what brings people in here, and the people ask to buy peanuts. That's why you must charge a portion of the cook's wages, as well as a part of your own salary, to peanut sales. This sheet contains a carefully calculated cost analysis, which indicates that the peanut operation should pay exactly $2,278 per year toward these general overhead costs.

Joe: The peanuts? $2,278 a year for overhead? Nuts! The peanuts salesman said I'd make money—put 'em on the end of the counter, he said, and get 16 cents a bag profit.

Expert [with a sniff]: He's not an accountant. Do you actually know what the portion of the counter occupied by the peanut rack is worth to you?

Joe: Nothing. No stool there, just a dead spot at the end.

Expert: The modern cost picture permits no dead spots. Your counter contains 60 square feet, and your counter business grosses $60,000 a year. Consequently, the square foot of space occupied by the peanut rack is worth $1,000 per year. Since you have taken that area away from general counter use, you must charge the value of the space to the occupant.

Joe: [eagerly] Look! I have a better idea. Why don't I just throw the nuts out—put them in a trash can?

Expert: Can you afford it?

Joe: Sure. All I have is about 50 bags of peanuts—cost about 12 bucks—so I lose $100 on the rack, but I'm out of this nutsy business and no more grief.

Expert: [shaking head] Joe, it isn't quite that simple. You are in the peanut business! The minute you throw those peanuts out, you are adding $2,278 of annual overhead to the rest of your operation. Joe—be realistic—can you afford to do that?

Joe [completely crushed]: It's unbelievable! Last week I was making money. Now I'm in trouble—just because I believed 50 bags of peanuts a week is easy.

Expert [with raised eyebrow]: That is the object of modern cost studies, Joe—to dispel those false illusions.

Form small groups and develop a solution to Joe's problem.

10.12 If support-service cost allocations are arbitrary and potentially misleading, should we assume that managers are foolish for using information about which services to provide based on allocated service costs?

10.13 One critic of cost allocation noted, "You can avoid the problem of arbitrary cost allocations by simply not allocating any higher-level resource service costs to lower-level uses of resources." Prepare a memo outlining the costs and benefits of this approach.

10.14 Explain how cost allocation in an organization could be both a technical and a political exercise.

10.15 (Appendix) What argument(s) could be given in support of the reciprocal method as the preferred method for allocating the costs of service departments?

10.16 Under what conditions are the results from using the direct method of allocations the same as those from the step method? Why?

10.17 Consider a company with two producing departments and one service department. The service department allocates its costs to the producing departments on the basis of the number of employees in each department. If the costs in the service department are fixed by policy for the coming period, what effect would the (unexpected) addition of employees in one production department have on the service costs allocated to the other? Comment on the reasonableness of the situation.

10.18 Prepare a short presentation to explain and comment on this argument: "Cost allocation can never provide an incentive to reduce service costs unless the amount allocated is tied to some controllable driver. Awareness of the service cost serves no purpose if the driver is not controllable."

10.19 The manager of an operating department just received a cost report and has made the following comment with respect to the costs allocated from one of the service departments: "This charge to my division does not seem right. The service center installed equipment with more capacity than our division requires. We seem to be allocated more costs in periods when other departments use less service capacity. We are paying for excess capacity of other departments when other departments cut their usage levels." Explain how this result occurred and how to solve this manager's problem.

Exercises

Exercise 10.20
Alternative Allocation Bases
(LO 3)

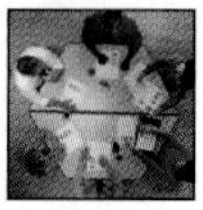

Team

The Klingons and the Romulans own two adjacent tracts of land. Each tract has a surface area of 4,000 acres. During a recent shoot-out between the families, crude oil came bubbling to the surface where a phaser blast entered the ground. A petroleum geologist determined that an underground rock formation that extended under both tracts of land contained a substantial amount of oil. The formation was estimated at 800,000 acre feet of volume, of which 600,000 acre feet were under the Romulans' tract of land.

The Klingons and the Romulans received an offer to buy the mineral rights for $8.5 million provided that they can agree on how much of the purchase price should be allocated to each family.

Required

Form two groups to develop a solution to the allocation problem.

a. As a Klingon, what basis would you recommend for allocating the purchase price? What arguments would you use to support your claim?

b. As a Romulan, what basis would you recommend for allocating the purchase price? What arguments would you use to support your claim?

c. Come together to find a joint solution to the allocation problem (not involving the use of phasers).

Exercise 10.21
Alternative Service-Cost Allocation Bases
(LO 3)

Cytotech Company has a TV station and a radio station that share the common costs of the company's AP wire service, which is $200,000 a year. You have the following information about the AP wire and the two stations:

Station	Wire Service Hours Used This Period	Hours of News Broadcasts
TV	300	100
Radio	450	460

Required

a. What is the AP wire service cost charged to each station if wire service hours are used as an allocation base?

b. What is the AP wire service cost charged to each station using hours of news broadcast as an allocation base?

c. Which method allocates more costs to TV? Which method allocates more costs to radio? When and why would this matter?

Exercise 10.22
Alternative Allocation Bases
(LO 3)

Communication

WARP Enterprises operates a 120,000 square-foot supermarket. Each department in the store is charged a share of the cost of the building. The following information concerning two of the departments in the store is available.

Department	Meat	Dry Goods
Sales revenues	$250,000	$300,000
Cost of goods sold	85,000	90,000
Salaries and other direct expenses	55,000	70,000
Allocated administrative expenses	25,000	27,500
Operating profit before building occupancy costs	$ 85,000	$112,500
Area occupied (square feet)	10,000	30,000

Other departments use the other 80,000 square feet. The total building occupancy costs are $800,000 per year.

Required

a. If area occupied is the basis for allocating building occupancy costs, what is the operating profit or loss for each of these two departments?

b. Would you allocate based on something other than square feet if you learned that the dry goods department is located in a back corner of the store? Explain.

Exercise 10.23
Alternative Service-Cost Allocation Bases
(LO 3)

Quality Credit Company produces two styles of credit reports, standard and executive. The difference between the two is in the amount of background checking and data collection. The executive report uses more skilled personnel because additional interviews and analyses are performed. The relevant figures for the previous year follow.

Allocation Base	Standard Report	Executive Report
Data purchased	$20,000	$30,000
Research hours	12,000	18,000
Interview hours	1,000	4,000
Number of reports	8,000	2,000

The company must allocate $1,600,000 in support-service costs to these two product lines.

Required

For each of the four potential allocation bases, determine the amount of support-service cost allocated to each type of report.

Exercise 10.24
Alternative Allocation Bases
(LO 3)

Communication

Refer to your calculations for exercise 10.23. Your supervisor wants to know the costs to prepare a standard report and an executive report, including the cost of data, labor (which costs $40 per hour), and support services.

Required

a. Prepare four different answers to the question, "How much does it cost to produce?" for each type of report.

b. Prepare a memo explaining to your supervisor why there are four different cost numbers for each report. Also indicate whether total costs are the same for Quality Credit Company regardless of the overhead allocation base used.

c. What do you recommend?

Exercise 10.25
Cost Allocations: Direct Method
(LO 4)

Spreadsheet

Acme Corporation has two production departments, P1 and P2, and two support-service departments, S1 and S2. Direct costs for each department and the percentage of service costs used by the various departments for the month of May are as follows:

		Percentage of Services Used By			
Department	**Direct Costs**	**S1**	**S2**	**P1**	**P2**
S1	$ 80,000		60%	20%	20%
S2	100,000	20%		50%	30%
P1	160,000				
P2	140,000				

Required

Compute the allocation of support-service department costs to producing departments using the direct method.

Exercise 10.26
Service Department Costs Allocated First to Production Departments and Then to Jobs
(LO 4)

Refer to the facts in exercise 10.25. Assume that both P1 and P2 work on just two jobs, 10 and 11, during the month of May. Costs are allocated to jobs based on the number of labor hours in P1 and of machine hours in P2. The labor and machine hours worked in each department are as follows:

		P1	P2
Job 10	Labor hours	80	10
	Machine hours	10	20
Job 11	Labor hours	10	10
	Machine hours	10	90

Required

How much of the support-service department costs allocated to P1 and P2 in the direct method should be allocated to job 10? How much to job 11?

Exercise 10.27
Cost Allocation: Direct Method
(LO 4)

Custom Tailors, Inc., has two service departments (maintenance and general factory administration) and two production departments (cutting and assembly). Management has decided to allocate maintenance costs on the basis of the size of the area in each department and general factory administration costs on the basis of the number of labor hours worked by the employees in each of their respective departments.

The following data appear in the company records for the current period:

	General Factory Administration	Maintenance	Cutting	Assembly
Area occupied (square feet)	1,000	—	1,000	3,000
Labor hours	—	100	100	400
Direct labor costs (operating departments only)	—	—	$3,000	$8,000
Service department direct costs	$20,000	$48,000	—	—

Required

Use the direct method to allocate the service department costs to the production departments.

Exercise 10.28
Cost Allocation: Step Method
(LO 4)

Spreadsheet

Refer to the data for Acme Corporation (exercise 10.25).

Required

Use the step method to allocate the service costs, using:

a. The order of allocation starting with S1.

b. The allocations made in the reverse order (starting with S2).

Exercise 10.29
Cost Allocation: Step Method
(LO 4)

Refer to the data for Custom Tailors, Inc., in exercise 10.27.

Required

Allocate the service department costs using the step method, starting with the maintenance department. How does using this method affect the allocation of costs compared to using the direct method?

Exercise 10.30
Cost Allocation Comparisons
(LO 5)

Refer to the data for Acme Corporation (exercises 10.25 and 10.28).

Required

Compare the results of the direct and step methods. Which method is better?

Exercise 10.31
Cost Allocation: Reciprocal Method (Appendix)
(LO 6)

During the past month, the following costs were incurred in the three production departments and two service departments in the East Bay Company:

P1	$120,000
P2	312,500
P3	390,000
S1	67,000
S2	59,500

The use of services by other departments follows:

	Percentages Used by Internal Customers				
Service Departments	**S1**	**S2**	**P1**	**P2**	**P3**
S1	—	40%	30%	20%	10%
S2	10%	—	20	15	55

Required

Allocate service-department costs to P1, P2, and P3 using the reciprocal method, and present the total costs of P1, P2, and P3 after this allocation.

Exercise 10.32
Cost Allocation: Reciprocal Method (Appendix)
(LO 6)

Refer to the data for Custom Tailors, Inc., in exercise 10.27.

Required

Allocate the service-department costs using the reciprocal method.

Exercise 10.33
Evaluation of Cost-Allocation Methods (Appendix)
(LO 5)

Refer to exercises 10.27, 10.29, and 10.32 (Custom Tailors, Inc.).

Required

a. Which cost-allocation method do you think is best?
b. How much would it be worth to the company to use the best method compared to the worst of the three methods? (Numbers are not required in this answer.)

Exercise 10.34
Explain Differences in Cost-Allocation Methods
(LO 5)

Communication Team

Form small groups and prepare a short visual presentation that Tukami could use to explain the advantages and disadvantages of using traditional cost-allocation bases and ABC cost-driver bases for allocating support-service costs at Rock Creek (in the chapter example).

Problems

Problem 10.35
Service Cost Allocation: Direct Method
(LO 4)

Dual Division Corporation allocates service costs to its Uno and Duo Divisions. During the past month, it incurred the following service costs:

Computing services	$254,000
Human resources	615,000
Custodial services	104,000

The following information concerning various activity measures and service uses by each of the divisions is available:

	Uno	Duo
Area occupied	15,000 sq. ft.	40,000 sq. ft.
Payroll	$380,000	$170,000
Computer time	200 hr.	140 hr.
Computer storage	25 gigabytes	35 gigabytes
Equipment value	$175,000	$220,000
Operating profit, before allocations	$439,000	$522,000

Required

Allocate the service costs to the two divisions using the direct method and the most appropriate of these allocation bases. For computing services, use computer time only.

Problem 10.36
Cost Allocation: Direct Method
(LO 4)

T. Schurt & Company manufactures and sells T-shirts for advertising and promotional purposes. The company has two manufacturing operations, shirtmaking and printing. When the company receives an order for T-shirts, the shirtmaking department obtains the materials and colors requested and has the shirts made in the desired mix of sizes. It sends the completed shirts to the printing department where the custom labels or designs are prepared and silk-screened onto the shirts.

To support the manufacturing activity, the company has a building that houses the two manufacturing departments as well as the sales department, payroll department, and the design and patterns staff. To aid in cost control, the company accumulates the costs of these support functions in separate service departments: (1) building occupancy, (2) human resources, and (3) design and patterns.

During the current period, the direct costs incurred by each department are as follows:

Shirtmaking (P1)	$210,000
Printing (P2)	140,000
Sales (P3)	80,000
Building occupancy (S1)	45,000
Human resources (S2)	20,000
Design and patterns (S3)	10,000

Building occupancy costs are allocated on the basis of the number of square feet of each department. Human resources costs are allocated on the basis of the number of full-time equivalent employees. The design and pattern costs are charged to departments on the basis of the number of designs requested by each department. For the current period, the following table summarizes the usage of services by other service cost centers and other departments:

	S1	S2	S3	P1	P2	P3
Building occupancy (S1) (square feet)	—	8,100	3,900	27,000	36,000	6,000
Human resources (S2) (employees)	3	—	6	30	15	6
Design and patterns (S3) (designs)	—	—	—	15	40	5

Required

Using the direct method for service cost allocations, what are the total costs in each of the three "producing" departments?

Problem 10.37
Cost Allocation: Step Method
(LO 4)

Refer to the facts for problem 10.36.

Required

Compute the cost allocations and total costs in each production department using the step method. Which service costs should be allocated first? Second?

Problem 10.38
Effects of Alternative Cost-Allocation Methods
(LO 4, 5)

Communication

M&P Tool, Inc., has three service departments that support the production area. Outlined here is the budgeted support-service spending by department for the coming year.

Support-Service Departments	Budgeted Spending	Number of Employees
Receiving	$25,000	2
Repair	35,000	2
Tool	10,000	1
Production Departments		
Assembly		25
Bolting		12

The repair department supports the most support-service departments, followed by the tool department. Service costs are allocated to departments based on the number of employees.

Required

a. Using the direct method of cost allocation, determine the amounts of support-service cost that will be allocated to each department.

b. Using the step method of cost allocation, determine the amounts of support-service cost that will be allocated to each department.

c. Do you believe that the method of cost allocation would matter to the support-service departments? To the production departments? Why?

[CMA adapted]

Problem 10.39
Choice of Appropriate Allocation Base
(LO 3)

Communication

SemiTech Corporation's memory chip division manufactures two types of computer memory chips: The RAM-A chip is a commonly used chip for personal computer systems, and the RAM-B chip is used for specialized scientific applications. Unit-level materials costs for the RAM-A chip are 25 cents per unit and for the RAM-B are $1.12 per unit. The division's annual output is 32 million chips. Labor costs in the division total $625,000. Manufacturing overhead is composed of $1.2 million of corporate service cost allocated to the division on the basis of labor costs and $1.2 million of divisional overhead (supervision, materials handling and security, utilities, equipment costs and depreciation, etc.).

The company's assembly process is highly automated. As a result, the primary function for direct labor is to set up a production run and to check equipment settings on a periodic basis. Yesterday the equipment was set up to run 1,600 RAM-B units. When that run was completed, equipment settings were changed, and 200,000 RAM-A units were produced. Part of the daily cost report follows:

	RAM-A	**RAM-B**
Units produced	200,000	1,600
Unit-level materials used	$ 25,000	$1,896
Labor used	$ 2,000	$1,200

Required

a. Recommend how to allocate the memory chip division's overhead (allocated and divisional) to the division's two products. What should influence your choice of allocation bases?

b. For yesterday's production run, what is the total manufacturing cost per unit for RAM-A and RAM-B using your recommended approach?

c. Compare your result in requirement (b) with another approach using a different cost-allocation base(s). Explain the source of the difference between full costs per unit for each product.

Problem 10.40
Step Method with Three Service Departments
(LO 1, 4)

Crash Test Corporation refurbishes automobiles. It operates two production departments, mechanical repair and body work, and has three service departments for its plant: building occupancy, human resources, and equipment maintenance. Management is concerned that the costs of its service departments are getting too high. In particular, management would like to keep the costs of service departments under $500 per unit on average. You have been asked to allocate budgeted service department costs to the two production departments and compute the expected unit costs.

The company decided that building occupancy costs should be allocated on the basis of the number of square feet used by each production and service department. Human resources costs are allocated on the basis of the number of employees; equipment maintenance costs are allocated on the basis of the dollar value of the equipment in each department. The use of each basis by all departments during the current period follows:

	Used By				
Allocation Base	**Building Occupancy**	**Human Resources**	**Equipment Maintenance**	**Mechanical Repair**	**Body Work**
Building area, sq. ft.	5,000	15,000	10,000	180,000	45,000
Employees	9	5	6	35	50
Equipment value	$ 12,000	$240,000	$ 35,000	$ 624,000	$324,000
Budgeted departmental costs	$360,000	$500,000	$264,000	$1,350,000	$965,000

Required

a. Using the step method, determine the allocated costs and the total costs in each of the two producing departments. The allocation order is (1) building occupancy, (2) human resources, and (3) equipment maintenance.

b. Assume that 1,000 units were processed in each of the two producing departments during the current period. Did the company meet management's standards of keeping service department costs below $500 per unit?

Problem 10.41
Cost Allocation: Direct Method
(LO 4)

Pete's Delicious Foods has a commissary that supplies food and other products to its restaurants. Its two support-service departments, purchasing (S1) and general administration (S2), support two direct-service departments, food products (P1) and supplies (P2). As an internal auditor, you are checking the company's procedures for cost allocation. You find the following cost-allocation results for June:

Costs Allocated to P1	Costs Allocated to P2
$40,000 from S1 ? from S2	$22,500 from S2 ? from S1

Total costs for the two support-service departments are $100,000. S2's services are provided as follows:

20 percent to S1
50 percent to P1
30 percent to P2

The direct method of allocating costs is used.

Required

a. What are the total support-service department costs (S1 + S2) allocated to P2?

b. Complete the following:

	To	
From	**P1**	**P2**
S1	$40,000	?
S2	?	$22,500

c. What were the proportions of S1's costs allocated to P1 and P2?

Problem 10.42
Cost Allocation: Step Method with Analysis and Decision Making
(LO 1, 4, 5)

Communication

Chemical Products Corporation is reviewing its operations to determine what additional energy-saving projects it might implement. The company's Utah plant has three service departments and two production departments. This plant has its own electric-generating facilities powered by natural gas wells that the company owns and that are located on the same property as the plant. The service departments are natural gas, electricity generation, and general administration. A summary of the use of services by other service departments as well as by the two production departments at the plant follows:

	Services Provided To				
Services From	**Natural Gas (S1)**	**Electricity Generation (S2)**	**General Administration (S3)**	**Fertilizer (P1)**	**Additives (P2)**
Natural gas	—	40%	—	10%	50%
Electricity generation	10%	—	15%	45	30
General administration.......	10%	15%	—	40	35
Departmental costs	$70,000	$110,000	$48,000	$600,000	$440,000

The company currently allocates the costs of service departments to production departments using the step method. The local power company indicates it would charge $160,000 per year for the electricity now being generated by the company internally. Management rejected switching to the public utility on the grounds that its rates would cost more than the $110,000 cost of the present company-owned system.

Required

a. Prepare for management an analysis of the costs of the company's own electric-generating operations. (Use the step method.) The order of allocation is S1, S2, and S3. Should Chemical Products Corp. purchase or continue to make its own electricity?

b. Indicate how your analysis would change if the company could realize $58,000 per year from the sale of the natural gas now used for electric generating. (Assume no selling costs.)

Problem 10.43
Cost-Allocation: Reciprocal Method (Appendix)
(LO 5)

Refer to problem 10.42 and the data for Chemical Products Corporation.

Required

a. Using the reciprocal method, compute the costs of electricity generation and the costs allocated to production.

b. Explain the differences in costs for the two methods, step and reciprocal.

Problem 10.44
Cost Allocation and Decision Making
(LO 1, LO 4)

Communication

Parker Company's promotion department is responsible for designing and developing all marketing campaign materials and related literature, pamphlets, and brochures. Management is reviewing the effectiveness of the promotion department to determine whether its services could be acquired more economically from an outside promotion agency. Management has received a summary of the promotion department's costs for the most recent year:

PROMOTION DEPARTMENT
Costs for the Year Ended November 30

Department costs	$128,750
Charges from other departments	33,460
Allocated share of general administrative overhead	22,125
Total costs	$184,335

Department costs can be traced directly to promotion department activities such as staff and clerical salaries, including related employee benefits, supplies, and so on. Charges from other departments represent the costs of services that other departments of Parker provide at the promotion department's request. The company has developed a system to charge for such interdepartmental uses of services. For instance, the in-house printing department charges the promotion department for the promotional literature printed. All services provided to the promotion department by other Parker departments are included in the charges from other departments. General and administrative overhead includes costs such as executive salaries and benefits, depreciation, heat, insurance, and property taxes. These costs are allocated to each department in proportion to the number of its employees.

Required

Prepare a report or visual presentation that explains the usefulness of the cost figures as presented for the promotion department as a basis to compare with a bid from an outside agency to provide the same type of activities that Parker's promotion department now provides.

[CMA adapted]

Problem 10.45
Service Department Cost Allocation: Direct and Step Methods
(LO 4)

Doxolby Manufacturing Company has three support-service departments (general factory administration, factory maintenance, and factory cafeteria), and two production departments (fabrication and assembly). A summary of costs and other data for each department prior to allocation of service-department costs for the year ended June 30 follows:

	General Factory Admin.	Factory Maintenance	Factory Cafeteria	Fabrication	Assembly
Direct materials	0	$ 65,000	$ 91,000	$3,130,000	$ 950,000
Direct labor	$ 90,000	82,100	87,000	1,950,000	2,050,000
Manufacturing overhead	70,000	56,100	62,000	1,650,000	1,850,000
Total	$160,000	$203,200	$240,000	$6,730,000	$4,850,000
Direct labor hours	31,000	27,000	42,000	562,500	437,500
Number of employees	12	8	20	280	200
Square footage occupied	1,750	2,000	4,800	88,000	72,000

The costs of the service departments are allocated on the following bases: general factory administration department, direct labor hours; factory maintenance department, square feet occupied; and factory cafeteria, number of employees.

Required

Round all final calculations to the nearest dollar.

a. Assume that Doxolby elects to distribute service department costs to production departments using the direct method. Compute the amount of factory maintenance department costs allocated to the fabrication department.

b. Assume the same method of allocation as in requirement (a). Compute the amount of general factory administration department costs allocated to the assembly department.

c. Assuming that Doxolby elects to distribute service department costs to other departments and using the step method (starting with factory cafeteria and then factory maintenance), compute the amount of factory cafeteria department costs allocated to the factory maintenance department.

d. Assume the method of allocation as in requirement (c). Compute the amount of factory maintenance department costs allocated to factory cafeteria.

[CPA adapted]

Problem 10.46
Cost Allocations: Comparison of Single and Multiple Cost Pools
(LO 2)

Communication

SkyBlue Airlines operates a centralized computer center for the data-processing needs of its reservations, scheduling, maintenance, and accounting divisions. Costs associated with use of the computer are charged to the individual departments on the basis of time usage. Due to recent increased competition in the airline industry, the company has decided that it is necessary to more accurately allocate its costs to price its services competitively and profitably. During the current period, the use of data-processing services and the storage capacity required for each of the divisions was as follows (in thousands of seconds for time usage and in gigabytes for storage capacity):

Division	Time Usage	Storage Capacity
Reservations	2,500	1,500
Scheduling	1,700	600
Maintenance	6,300	210
Accounting	5,000	190

During this period, the cost of the computer center amounted to $7,050,000 for time usage and $5,000,000 for storage-related costs.

Required

a. Determine the computer service cost allocations to each division; you may round all decimals to three places. Use:

(1) A single cost pool and rate based on time used.

(2) Two cost pools and rates based on time used and capacity used.

b. Write an email memo to management (your instructor) explaining whether to use one or two cost pools and why.

Problem 10.47
Cost Allocation for Travel Reimbursement
(LO 4, 5)

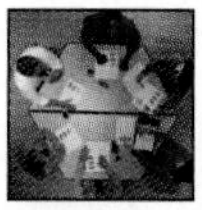

Team

Ethics

Communication

Your company has a travel policy that reimburses employees for the "ordinary and necessary" costs of business travel. Employees often mix a business trip with pleasure either by extending the time at the destination or traveling from the business destination to a nearby resort or other personal destination. When this happens, an allocation must be made between the business and personal portions of the trip. However, the travel policy is unclear on the allocation method to use.

Consider this example. An employee obtained a first-class ticket for $2,640 and traveled the following itinerary:

From	To	Mileage	One-Way Regular Fare	Purpose
Washington, D.C.	Salt Lake City	1,839	$1,400	Business
Salt Lake City	Los Angeles	590	600	Personal
Los Angeles	Washington, D.C.	2,288	1,600	Return

Required

a. Form small groups to compute the business portion of the airfare and state the basis for the indicated allocation that is appropriate according to each of the following independent scenarios:

(1) Based on the maximum reimbursement for the employee.

(2) Based on the minimum cost to the company.

b. Prepare a short presentation to management explaining the method that you think should be used and why. What ethical issues do you perceive and how should they be resolved? You do not have to restrict your recommendation to either of the methods in requirement (a).

Problem 10.48
Cost Allocation for Rate-Making Purposes
(LO 4, 5)

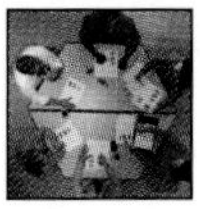
Team

Ethics

Allied Insurance Company asked the regulatory board for permission to increase the premiums of its insurance operations. Insurance premium rates in the jurisdiction in which Allied operates are designed to cover the operating costs and insurance claims. As a part of Allied's expenses, its agents earn commissions based on premium revenues. Premium revenues also are used to pay claims and to invest in securities.

Administrative expenses include the costs to manage the company's investments and investment services (e.g., retirement annuities). All administrative costs are charged against premium revenue. Allied claims that its insurance operations "just broke even" last year and that a rate increase is necessary. The following income statement (in millions) was submitted to support Allied's request:

Insurance income:	
Premium revenue	$300
Operating costs:	
Claims	205
Administrative	55
Sales commissions	40
Total operating costs	$300
Insurance profit (loss)	0
Investment income	35
Profits after Investment income	$ 35

Further investigation reveals that approximately 20 percent of the sales commissions might be considered related to investment activities. In addition, the investment division uses 30 percent of the support services. The state insurance commission (which sets insurance rates) believes that Allied's insurance activities should earn about 5 percent on its premium revenues.

Required

Form separate groups to prepare responses to the following:

a. If you were a consumer group, how would you present Allied's income statement? (For example, how would you allocate administrative costs and sales commissions to the insurance income and investment income categories?) What ethical issues do you perceive as a consumer?

b. If you were Allied's management, what arguments would you present in support of the cost allocations included in the income statement presented in the problem? What ethical issues do you perceive as management?

c. Meet as opposing groups to resolve the allocation issue with the instructor acting as the mediator.

Cases

Case 10.49
University Instructional Cost Study
(LO 1, 5)

Communication

Universities seek to understand their costs of offering services, which include the broad categories of instruction, research, and public service. The largest resource cost is for faculty and staff salaries, which are college or departmental-level expenditures and, in the short run, do not vary with respect to instructional activities. Since university faculty provide most of the university's services, measuring the costs of the three types of service requires the allocation of faculty salaries. Likewise, expenditures for physical plant and libraries support all three types of service, which requires allocations of these costs.

The method and allocation bases used can affect a university's internal decisions about funding staffing in different colleges and departments and, for public and state universities, can affect decisions by state legislatures and governing boards for appropriations and tuition levels.

Many difficulties exist in developing these cost allocations, including these:

- Different sources of funding could restrict the use of funds. For example, nonstate-supported funds might specify that the funds be used to support research activities only.
- Faculty might teach classes in multiple disciplines.
- Faculty might have different assignments with respect to teaching, research, and public service.
- Different levels of classes (undergraduate, graduate, professional) might require different faculty and support resources.
- General administrative and library resources at the university, campus, college, and department levels provide support for all three types of services.

The Office of Planning and Analysis (OPA) of the University of Minnesota conducted an extensive analysis of the costs of instruction at each of the university's five campuses. One objective of the analysis was to measure the cost of instruction per full-year-equivalent (FYE) student in each department, college, and campus. A FYE student is the equivalent of one student taking a normal course load (30 semester credit hours) for a full academic year. The OPA followed these procedures for determining the instructional costs per FYE student:

1. *Allocations of departmental resource costs.* Courses and FYE students taught were assigned by department according to course designation (e.g., accounting courses and FYE students taught in those courses were assigned to the accounting department). Instructors and their salaries were matched with courses taught. Faculty salaries (whole or part) were assigned to departments according to the designation of classes. Salaries were added to departmental administrative costs and allocated to FYE students by dividing total departmental costs by total FYE students taught.
2. *Allocations of support-service costs.* Administrative and support-service costs at the university, campus, and college levels were allocated on the basis of departmental budgets before allocations using the step method. Graduate school administrative costs were allocated using the direct method on the basis of the number of graduate-level credit hours taught. Library costs were allocated directly to research, instruction, and public service based on historical percentages. Other service costs are allocated directly on the basis of FYE student enrollment. These departmental allocations also were divided by total number of FYE students taught.

A summary of results from the most recent OPA analysis at the college level follows:

Comparative Costs of Instruction, University of Minnesota

Campus	College	FYE Student	Departmental Cost per FYE Student	Allocated Cost per FYE Student	Total Cost per FYE Student
Twin Cities	Architecture	381	$ 6,914	$3,449	$10,363
	Biology	1,252	7,006	3,219	10,225
	Education	3,312	4,765	2,916	7,681
	Human ecology	892	5,996	3,325	9,321
	Liberal arts	12,480	4,883	2,621	7,504
	Natural resources	293	4,748	2,689	7,437
	Agriculture	1,185	5,870	3,685	9,555
	Business	2,175	9,059	3,191	12,250
	Dentistry	627	12,129	8,330	20,459
	General college	699	8,303	3,562	11,865
	Public affairs	193	12,501	3,980	16,481
	Engineering	6,627	7,702	3,392	11,094
	Law	801	9,365	2,567	11,932
	Medicine	4,063	15,554	4,422	19,976
	Nursing	368	10,198	4,665	14,863
	Pharmacy	377	15,328	5,040	20,368
	Public health	632	8,441	4,127	12,568
	ROTC	22	12,314	3,300	15,614
	Veterinary	545	14,859	4,991	19,850
	Total Twin Cities	36,924	7,646	3,325	10,971
Duluth	Achievement ctr	39	3,918	2,610	6,528
	Human services	1,107	4,198	2,804	7,002
	Liberal arts	2,071	3,046	2,466	5,512
	Science & engineering	1,970	4,780	2,284	7,064
	Medicine	212	22,944	6,964	29,908
	Business & economics	668	5,268	2,920	8,188
	Fine arts	611	4,498	2,673	7,171
	Total Duluth	6,678	4,740	2,836	7,576
Morris	Academic affairs	1,861	3,663	4,016	7,679
Crookston	Academic affairs	1,043	3,540	4,393	7,934

Required

a. Critique the allocation methods used by OPA to measure cost per FYE student at the college level.

b. A Minnesota state legislator at a recent budget hearing argued, "It is clear that the state could save significant funds by transferring programs from the Twin Cities campus to the Duluth campus. For example, every student in a business program that we transfer from the Twin Cities campus to Duluth would save the state $4,062. And every student in an engineering program that we transfer to Duluth would save nearly $4,030 per student. People are tired of paying high taxes to support inefficient programs. We need to be sure that taxpayers get the most for their money." What are the pros and cons of this argument?

c. How could the OPA figures be used to support higher-education decision making? In what ways are the figures presented either helpful or misleading?

[Adapted from the University of Minnesota's Instructional Cost Study]

Case 10.50
Federal Highway Cost-Allocation Study
(LO 1, 2, 4, 5)

Communication

The US Department of Transportation completed an extensive study of costs and uses of the federal highway system, the Federal Highway Cost Allocation Study (HCAS). This study led to recommendations for significant changes in user fees paid by private citizens (e.g., in fuel taxes) and commercial enterprises (e.g., licenses and fuel taxes paid by highway transportation companies). The costs of highway usage include their construction and repair due to traffic and weather damage. In a major departure from previous studies (most recently in 1982), the HCAS recommended including environmental impacts, safety, congestion, and noise caused by the federal highway system in the costs to be shared by highway users. Federal highway spending, not including mass transit, environmental impacts, and so on, amounted to approximately $27,102,000,000 for the year 2000.

Vehicle miles traveled (VMT) on federal highways in 2000 continued to be dominated by private automobile traffic as shown:

Passenger Vehicles	VMT Total (millions)	Percentage	Number of Vehicles	Percentage
Autos	1,818,461	67.5%	167,697,897	70.0%
Pickups/Vans	669,198	24.8	63,259,330	26.4
Buses	7,397	0.3	754,509	0.3
Single-unit trucks	83,100	3.1	5,970,431	2.5
Combination trucks	115,689	4.3	1,971,435	0.8
Total	2,693,845	100%	239,653,602	100%

Required

a. Compute highway spending costs per vehicle (by type) by allocating year 2000 highway spending on the basis of (1) the number of vehicles and (2) the vehicle miles traveled (VMT). Would inequities be created by either of these allocations? Explain.

b. The federal HCAS recommended the following cost pools and allocation bases for the year 2000 costs:

Cost Pool*	Amount	Allocation Base
New construction and pavement replacement	$19.161 billion	VMTs weighted by passenger car equivalents (PCE)†
Bridge construction and replacement	3.757 billion	VMT
Highway enhancements	4.184 billion	VMT weighted by PCE
Mass transit	5.787 billion	VMT

*Not included in the previous total obligations.

†A passenger car equivalent (PCE) measures each type of vehicle's effects on highways compared to an automobile, pickup, or van. On average, a bus has a PCE of 4.0, a single-unit truck has a PCE of 5.4, and a combination truck has a PCE of 10.6. One mile driven by a bus, for example, has 4 times the effect as an automobile, pickup, or van.

Allocate year 2000 highway costs to the types of vehicles using these cost pools and allocation bases. Compare them to allocations based on VMT alone.

c. The HCAS indicated that user fees for many vehicles did not match highway impacts. For example, the following classes of vehicles were over- or undercharged in 2000 using fees developed in 1997:

Vehicle	Over- Underpayment
Automobiles	$5.6 billion
Combination trucks	(5.8) billion

As a member of the HCAS, write a memo to head of the Department of Transportation outlining recommended changes in user fees and anticipating the difficulties that the department might face by implementing your changes. Also include your evaluation of the feasibility of including environmental and other costs, which have been estimated by a subcommittee of HCAS to be $406 billion in the year 2000, in user fees. More than half of that amount is estimated to be caused by automobiles.

[Adapted from a Federal Highway Cost Allocation Study.]

Case 10.51
WeCare Hospital: Cost-Allocation, Step Method
(LO 4, 5)

The annual costs of hospital care under the Medicare program exceed $20 billion per year. In the Medicare legislation, the US Congress mandated that reimbursement to hospitals be limited to the costs of treating Medicare patients. Ideally, neither non-Medicare patients nor hospitals would bear the costs of Medicare patients, nor would the government bear costs of non-Medicare patients. Given the large sums involved, it is not surprising that cost-reimbursement specialists, computer programs, publications, and other products and services provide hospital administrators the assistance needed to obtain an appropriate reimbursement for Medicare patient services.

Hospital departments can be divided into two categories: (1) revenue producing and (2) nonrevenue producing. This classification is simple but useful. The traditional accounting concepts associated with "service department cost allocation," while appropriate to this context, lead to a great deal of confusion in terminology since all of the hospital's departments are considered to be rendering services.

Costs of revenue-producing departments are charged to Medicare and non-Medicare patients on the basis of actual use of the departments. These costs are relatively simple to apportion. Costs of nonrevenue-producing departments are somewhat more difficult to apportion. The approach to finding the appropriate distribution of these costs begins with the establishment of a reasonable basis for allocating nonrevenue-producing department costs to revenue-producing departments. Statistical measures of the relationships between departments must be ascertained. The cost-allocation bases listed in Exhibit 10–11 were established as acceptable for cost-reimbursement purposes. The regulated order of allocation must be used for Medicare reimbursement.

A hospital then can use either the reciprocal method or the step method to solve the cost-allocation problem. If it uses the step method, the order of departments for allocation is the same as that by which the departments are listed in Exhibit 10–11. Thus, depreciation and maintenance, buildings, is allocated before depreciation, movable equipment. Cost centers must be established for each of these nonrevenue-producing costs that are relevant to a particular hospital's operations.

In the past year, WeCare Hospital reported the following departmental costs:

Nonrevenue producing:	
Laundry and linen	$ 250,000
Depreciation and maintenance, buildings	830,000
Employee health and welfare	375,000
Maintenance of personnel	210,000
Central supply	745,000
Revenue producing:	
Operating room	1,450,000
Radiology	160,000
Laboratory	125,000
Patient rooms	2,800,000

Percentage usage of one department's services by another department follows:

From	To Nonrevenue Producing: Laundry and Linen	Depreciation and Maintenance, Buildings	Employee Health and Welfare	Maintenance of Personnel	Central Supply
Laundry and linen	—	5%	10%	—	—
Depreciation and maintenance, buildings	10%	—	—	10%	—
Employee health and welfare	15	—	—	5%	3%
Maintenance of personnel	—	—	—	—	12%
Central supply	10	—	—	8%	—

From	To Revenue Producing: Operating Rooms	Radiology	Laboratory	Patient Rooms
Laundry and linen	30%	10%	5%	40%
Depreciation and maintenance, buildings	5	2	2	71
Employee health and welfare	25	5	4	43
Maintenance of personnel	36	10	8	34
Central supply	9	4	3	66

The percentage usage of revenue-producing department services by Medicare and other patients follows:

	Medicare	Other
Operating rooms	25%	75%
Radiology	20	80
Laboratory	28	72
Patient rooms	36	64

Required

What is the amount of the reimbursement claim for Medicare services, using the step method of allocation? Use this order of allocation: (1) Depreciation and maintenance, buildings (2) employee health and welfare, (3) laundry and linen, (4) maintenance of personnel, and (5) central supply.

Exhibit 10–11

Bases for Allocating Nonrevenue-Producing Department Costs to Revenue-Producing Departments

Nonrevenue Cost Center	Basis for Allocation
Depreciation and maintenance, buildings	Square feet in each department
Depreciation, movable equipment	Dollar value of equipment in each department
Employee health and welfare	Gross salaries in each department
Administrative and general	Accumulated costs by department
Maintenance and repairs	Square feet in each department
Operation of plant	Square feet in each department
Laundry and linen	Pounds used in each department
Housekeeping	Hours of service to each department
Dietary	Meals served in each department
Maintenance of personnel	Number of departmental employees
Nursing administration	Hours of supervision in each department
Central supply	Costs of requisitions processed
Pharmacy	Costs of drug orders processed
Medical records	Hours worked for each department
Social service	Hours worked for each department
Nursing school	Assigned time by department
Intern/resident service	Assigned time by department

PART IV

Planning and Decision Making

A Look Back

The preceding part discussed process costing and cost allocation.

A Look at This Part

Part IV includes methods of developing and using cost information for decision making. Chapter 11 describes cost estimation methods. Chapter 12 shows how to develop financial and cost-volume-profit models. Chapter 13 discusses the use of cost information in short-term decision-making. Chapter 14 discusses strategic issues in making capital-investment decisions. Chapter 15 covers financial planning and the development of budgets.

A Look Ahead

Part V discusses methods of measuring performance.

CHAPTER

11

Cost Estimation

After completing this chapter, you should be able to:

1. State the reasons that companies estimate the relationship between costs and cost drivers.
2. Graph the following basic cost patterns: variable, fixed, step (semifixed), semivariable, and learning curve.
3. Compare the advantages and disadvantages of simple and multiple regression for cost estimation purposes.
4. Present advantages and disadvantages of account analysis compared to multiple regression for cost estimation.
5. Explain what is gained from using the engineering method compared to using regression and account analysis. Explain why the engineering method is likely to be more costly than regression and account analysis.
6. Identify potential statistical problems with regression analysis (Appendix).

Cost-Management Challenges

1. **Why** should CC Catering estimate costs?

2. **What** cost patterns do the (a) food, (b) cellular telephone, and (c) delivery labor costs at CC Catering follow?

3. **After** doing the multiple regression analysis, what additional information did Leah Cohen require to estimate costs using account analysis?

4. **What** are the advantages to using the engineering method at CC Catering?

5. **Based** on information from the cost estimates and considering CC Catering's new strategy, will the company be successful in the future?

6. **Should** Cohen and Chun give up CC Catering and take jobs in consulting?

EMAIL MEMORANDUM

To: LMCohen@xxxxxx.com

From: JTChun@xxxxxx.com

Re: Future of CC Catering (and us)

C.C. Catering

Hi Leah:

I hope you enjoyed your trip to New Mexico while I was stuck doing the end-of-semester cleanup. It was quiet while you were gone, which gave me a chance to do some serious thinking about our future. I did some quick calculations that indicate we will not be profitable this year; close, but not quite. I am disappointed. I thought we would be in the black this year because of our solid revenue growth.

I think it's time to do some serious analysis of our costs. We should start by identifying cost drivers and estimating cost-driver rates. Do you remember that grouchy old Professor Maier who taught us that cost-driver rates indicate how activities consume costs? We need to know that information to manage our costs better. Also, we need better cost information to make some decisions that I've been thinking about. But more on that when we're both in the office.

Welcome back!

Jessie

[C.C. Catering]

After getting food poisoning from eating catered food at a luncheon for business honor students at their university, Jessie Chun and Leah Cohen decided to start their own company, a catering service, called CC Catering. With their contacts around the university and those of their families, who were heavily involved in community activities, Chun and Cohen believed that they could attract plenty of customers. Starting in the spring of their junior year in college, CC Catering provided Chun and Cohen with good part-time work. In fact, CC Catering eventually provided them with enough opportunity and fun that they turned down offers from several public accounting firms and industry to work full-time in the catering service. Three years later, revenues continue to grow, but Chun and Cohen are disappointed in the lack of profits.

CC Catering provides packaged sandwiches and salads in clear plastic containers (box lunches). The company provides food to numerous official university functions (e.g., administrative meetings), executive education and extension programs, university field trips, and business meetings in town.

Chun and Cohen take a small monthly management salary of $500 each, in addition to paying themselves $15 per hour for each hour worked to obtain customers, prepare meals, deliver meals, and perform other nonmanagement aspects of the operations. At present, both Chun and Cohen own minivans for delivering meals. The company reimburses them at $.30 per mile for deliveries. At the end of each fiscal year (June 30), they decide how much of the operating profit to put back into the business and share the rest 50-50. So far, that calculation has not been done because CC Catering has had no operating profit.

Chun and Cohen decide that it is now time to turn from growing their business to focusing on managing costs and creating profits. In addition, they face an opportunity to subcontract the meal preparation part of the business, and they are considering a strategic change in the business that would emphasize bigger jobs as their core business.

They begin a process of estimating costs for three purposes:

1. *Cost management.* What are the opportunities for reducing costs without reducing value to customers?
2. *Decision making.* How can they change pricing policy to discourage particular customers and attract others? Should they subcontract the meal preparation part of the business?
3. *Strategic planning.* Is there a better customer mix and market niche than they currently have?

Cost Estimation

cost estimation *is the process of estimating the relationship between costs and the cost drivers that cause those costs*

Cost estimation is the process of estimating the relationship between costs and the cost drivers that cause those costs. For example, suppose you are trying to reduce your own personal transportation costs (that is, you are a personal cost-management analyst). You normally drive your car 15,000 miles per year, including commuting. If you use public transportation for commuting, you could reduce the annual mileage to 10,000 miles. How much would you save in automobile costs if you reduced driving by 5,000 miles per year?

The answer to that question is not easy because, as you know, some costs are related to the number of miles driven and others are not. Licensing costs are probably not related to the activity—miles driven—whereas fuel costs are. Repairs and depreciation costs are related to miles driven, but perhaps not proportionately.

Costs Do Not Just Happen

As we have emphasized in this book, costs do not just happen; they are caused by activities. The challenge for cost-management analysts is to identify the activities that cause costs, to estimate the relationship between costs and their causes, and to manage the activities that cause those costs, as shown in Exhibit 11–1. This chapter deals with

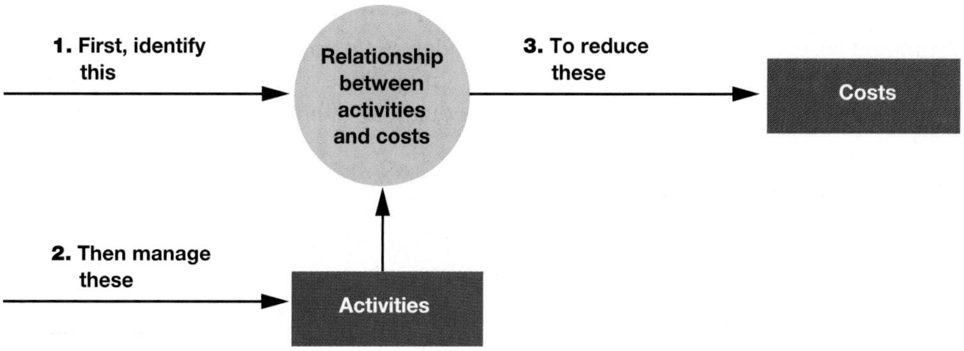

Exhibit 11–1
Estimating the Relationship between Activities and Costs

the middle part of the process shown in Exhibit 11–1, the relationship between activities and costs.

Reasons for Estimating Costs

Organizations estimate costs primarily for three reasons:

LO 1 State the reasons that companies estimate the relationship between costs and cost drivers.

1. To manage costs.
2. To make decisions.
3. To plan and set standards.

Cost Management

As discussed in previous chapters, companies must manage costs to be successful. Many companies have gone out of business because they did not manage costs. Many factories have shut down because managers did not manage costs effectively. Some counties and cities have faced bankruptcy because of poor cost management.

For CC Catering, estimating the relationship between costs and activities will help Chun and Cohen understand how to make the production process more efficient. If they find, for example, that the costs of delivering and setting up each catering job are high, then they should focus on ways to reduce delivery and setup costs. If such costs are not significant, then they should turn their attention to better opportunities for cost management.

Decision Making

In deciding among alternative actions, managers must know the costs that each alternative is likely to incur. These are examples of typical questions that require cost estimates for decision making:

- University of Illinois administrators ask: "What will happen to total costs if we expand the student health center?" Decision: If estimated total costs do not increase much, the university expands the health center.
- Managers at Accenture ask: "How much will it cost to perform the Department of Motor Vehicles information systems job?" Decision: If the cost of the job plus an adequate margin is below the price that Accenture can charge, then it does the job.
- Managers of Tower Records ask: "How much will it cost for us to make CD racks compared to the cost of buying them?" Decision: If it costs Tower Records less to buy the racks than to make them, then it buys them.
- CC Catering currently prepares the meals that it sells. Chun and Cohen are considering outsourcing meal preparation to a local sandwich shop. To decide whether to outsource meal preparation, they should know the cost of preparing meals to compare with a meal preparation bid from the sandwich shop.

These are just a few of the numerous decisions that require the knowledge of the estimated costs of the alternatives being considered. Of course, cost comparison is not the only basis for decision making, but it is a major one—*the* major one in many instances. We discuss decision making in more detail in Chapters 12 and 13.

Planning and Standard Setting

In planning an organization's future, managers specify the activities that they expect people in the organization to perform. Cost estimation assigns a cost to those activities. By knowing the costs of activities, managers know how much cost the organization will likely incur, which is helpful for preparing pro forma financial statements and estimating cash flows. Cost estimation also helps set standards for employee performance by estimating what the costs should be for performing particular activities.

At CC Catering, Chun and Cohen have estimated the costs of meal preparation to set standards. They use these standards to evaluate the performance of undergraduate students hired to help prepare meals. The main reason to consider outsourcing the meal preparation is that their best workers have graduated and taken jobs in public accounting and industry, leaving Chun and Cohen wondering what will happen to costs when they hire and train several new employees.

A Simple World: One Cost Driver and Fixed/Variable Cost Behavior

LO 2 Graph the following basic cost patterns: variable, fixed, step (semifixed), semivariable, and learning curve.

The two key issues in estimating the relationship between costs and activities are (1) the number of cost drivers and (2) the cost behavior. The first issue, the number of cost drivers, refers to the number of factors that analysts believe cause costs. Analysts use only one cost driver in the simplest world. Our discussion of activity-based costing in previous chapters in this book assumes a more complex world with multiple cost drivers. In a Hewlett-Packard plant in Germany, for example, analysts used more than 100 cost drivers in their cost estimation.

The simplest cost behavior pattern is the breakdown of costs into fixed and variable components. You are already familiar with the term *variable costs.* You know that total variable costs change proportionately with total activity. The simple world of one cost driver assumes that costs separate simply into fixed and variable components, and costs increase linearly with the cost driver. In this simple world, analysts estimate the following cost equation:

$$TC = F + VX$$

where

TC = total costs
F = fixed costs that do not vary with the cost driver
V = variable costs per cost driver unit = cost driver rate
X = the number of cost driver units

Exhibit 11–2 depicts this simple relationship when the cost driver is miles driven for an automobile and the amounts are the monthly costs that we estimate for a particular automobile.

This simple cost breakdown into fixed and variable components misses other important types of cost behavior that we discuss later in the chapter. It also ignores the impact of other cost drivers on costs, as you know from our discussion of activity-based costing. Nevertheless, this simple model can be useful and can satisfy a cost-benefit test better than a more complex, albeit more accurate, cost model.

For example, suppose a company contemplates launching a new product for which managers have not fully worked out the product's specifications. The simple model could give managers a rough idea of whether it is worthwhile to proceed with more detailed

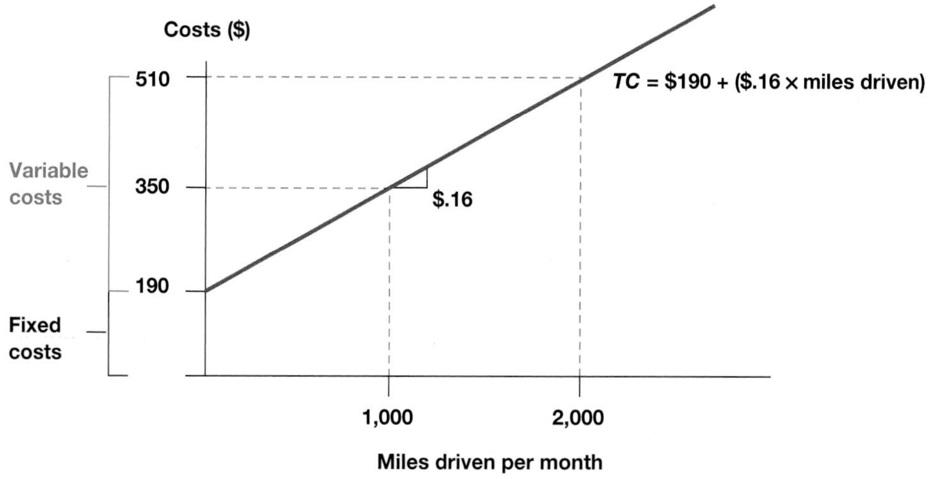

Exhibit 11–2
Simple Model: Automobile Costs

specifications. For companies with simple operations, the simple model can capture the relationship between costs and activities rather well. The manager of a taxicab company could find it sufficient to estimate the variable cost per mile driven, for example, or a retail store that pays commissions instead of salaries might find that more than 90 percent of its costs either vary proportionately with dollar sales or are purely fixed costs.

This chapter discusses estimating costs for both simple and complex environments. That way you will be armed for whatever situation you encounter.

A More Complex World: Multiple Cost Drivers and Complex Cost Behavior

Cost-Benefit Test

A more complex world has multiple cost drivers and more complex cost behavior than the simple world just described. As a manager or analyst, you choose how complex to make the cost estimation model. No "generally accepted rules" dictate how simple or complex to make the model, but good business sense says that you should apply a cost-benefit test to the choice of model complexity. Because you probably will not know what the costs and benefits of a particular cost estimation model are until you have estimated them, you are stuck with the task of attempting cost-benefit analysis before you have a good idea of either the costs or the benefits. This is a common problem in business and should not daunt you. You will avoid serious cost-benefit errors if you avoid estimating complex models when they provide little benefit over simple models. Also, you should estimate complex models when much is to be gained over estimating simple models. Avoid complexity for the sake of complexity and simplicity for the sake of simplicity. Common sense and experience should guide you.

Step Costs

Costs follow all sorts of patterns in the real world. Unlike the simple model presented previously, many costs increase in steps and in curvilinear patterns as activity levels increase.[1]

Step costs appear as shown in Exhibit 11–3. A **step cost,** also called a **semifixed cost,** is a cost that increases in steps as the amount of the cost-driver volume in-

step costs (semifixed costs) *increase in steps as the amount of the cost-driver volume increases*

[1]For example, E. Noreen and N. Soderstrom, "Are Overhead Costs Strictly Proportional to Activity? Evidence from Hospital Service Departments," found that department overhead costs in a large sample of hospitals are not proportional to the activities in the departments. Their results imply that at least some overhead costs increase in steps and that at least some overhead costs are curvilinear. (Full citations to references are in the Bibliography.)

Exhibit 11–3

Step Costs: Costs of Delivery Labor

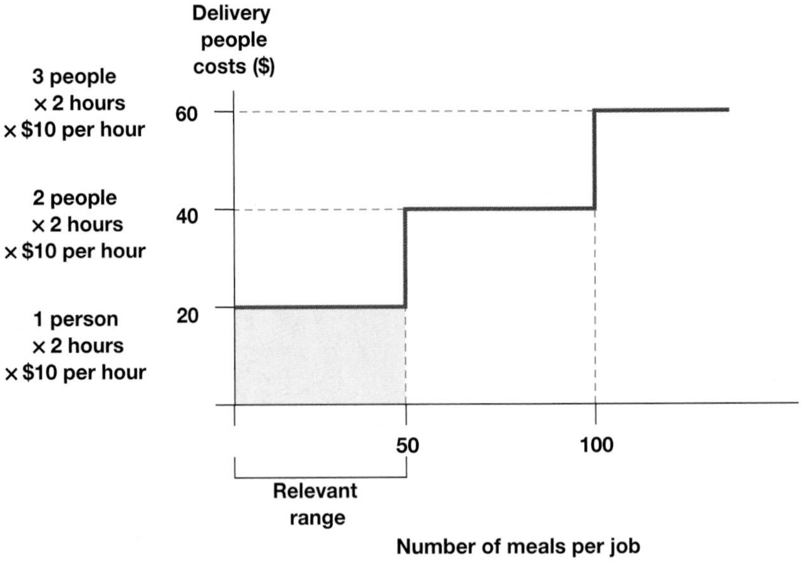

Food servers can serve more than one person, so an increase in the number of customers increases the number of food servers in steps.

creases. Many labor costs are step costs. In Exhibit 11–3, the costs are for delivery people for CC Catering. One delivery person can handle the delivery, setup, and cleanup for 50 meals in the two-hour period. In this example, the step increments are the number of delivery people for each two-hour food delivery period. The cost driver is the number of meals. If the number of meals to be delivered is less than 50, the company hires one delivery person for a two-hour period. If the number of meals is in the 51–100 range for a particular job, management increases the number of delivery people to two, and so forth as Exhibit 11–3 shows.

Step costs are common when people are hired in time increments, such as hourly, daily, or monthly. Examples include nurses in hospital departments where the number of nurses increases in steps as the number of patients increase; waiters and waitresses in restaurants; service personnel at rental car counters; and teachers at universities. In our experience, managers often ignore these steps, assuming that the step costs are either purely fixed or variable. Research shows, however, that managers make erroneous decisions by treating step costs as variable costs.[2]

Relevant range. Managers also rely on the concept of relevant range to deal with step costs. Recall from Chapter 2 that the *relevant range* is the range over which the company expects to operate. Within this range, managers assume particular cost behavior patterns that are reasonably accurate. Such patterns would not necessarily be ac-

[2]See M. W. Maher and M. L. Marais. "A Field Study on the Limitations of Activity-Based Costing When Resources Are Provided on a Joint and Indivisible Basis."

curate outside of the relevant range, however. For example, assume that CC Catering does not usually deliver more than 50 meals per job. Management could assume that 1 to 50 meals per job constitutes the relevant range, as shown in Exhibit 11–3. As long as a delivery person is needed at all, food delivery labor is a fixed cost. However, if the number of meals for a job increases to 75—outside the relevant range—then the assumption that food delivery labor is fixed and, therefore, does not vary with volume is no longer valid.

Semivariable Costs

Costs may also be **semivariable,** which means they have both a fixed and variable component. Many utilities offer products (e.g., electricity, water) for a fixed cost up to a particular volume after which they charge per unit. Exhibit 11–4 shows the semivariable cost for CC Catering's cellular telephone plan that charges $40 per month for up to 600 minutes per month of airtime and then charges $.10 per minute for each minute used over 600.

Semivariable costs *have both a fixed and a variable component*

Nonlinear Cost Behavior

The cost behavior patterns presented so far have been straight lines or sections of straight lines. Costs can also be curved. At CC Catering, for example, food costs are variable. Suppose the company receives a discount based on the volume of bread it buys, with the discount increasing as the volume purchased increases. Line A in Exhibit 11–5 represents variable costs that decrease per unit as volume per period increases.

Line B represents variable costs that increase per unit as volume per period increases. An example of such a cost is the cost of energy in steel plants. If volume of steel production is low, companies use the most energy-efficient methods to produce steel. As volume per period increases, companies find it necessary to use less energy-efficient methods. Consequently, energy is a variable cost whose rate increases as the volume of steel production per period increases.

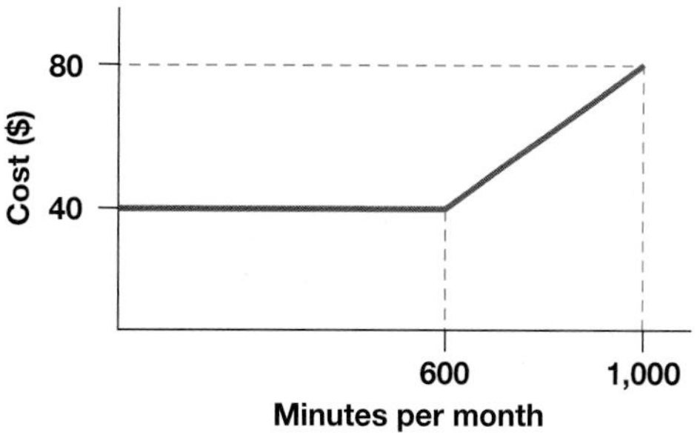

Exhibit 11–4
Semivariable Costs: Cellular Telephone

C.C. Catering

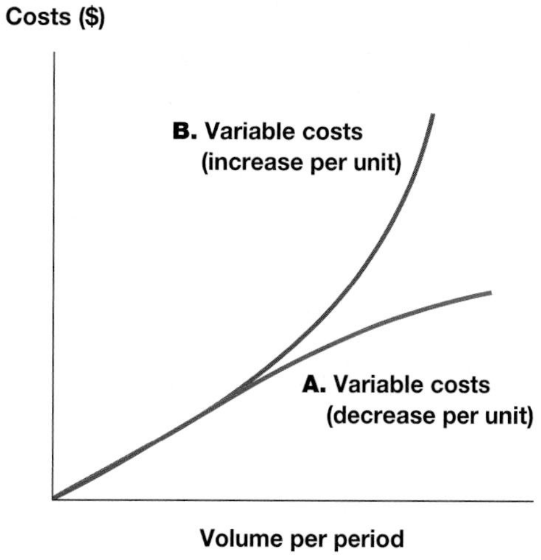

Exhibit 11–5
Variable Cost Behavior

C.C. Catering

Learning Curve

A particular type of nonlinear cost behavior relates to the time required to learn to do a job. You may recall the first time that you used a spreadsheet program on a computer. While you might have been slow at first, your efficiency improved as you gained more experience. In practice, experience—or learning—obviously affects direct labor costs; therefore, it affects costs related to direct labor. For example, if the amount of labor required to do a job decreases because of the learning effect, the supervision of the labor to do the job also decreases.

The **learning phenomenon,** which is a systematic relationship between the amount of experience in performing a task and the time required to perform it, often occurs when companies introduce new production methods, make new products (either goods or services), or hire new employees. For example, the effect of learning on the cost of aircraft

learning phenomenon *is a systematic relationship between the amount of experience in performing a task and the time required to perform it*

manufacturing is well known. Manufacturers of products for the aerospace industry, such as General Electric and Boeing, write contracts that recognize the effect of learning by establishing a lower cost for the second item of an order than for the first, a lower cost for the third than for the second, and so forth.

The idea embodied in the learning phenomenon is that the greater the cumulative cost-driver activity, the greater the experience. The greater the experience, the lower the average number of labor hours required. That is, the average time for a new purchasing agent to prepare 10 purchase orders (the cost-driver volume), for example, is less than the average time per unit to prepare the first 2 purchase orders because the purchasing agent learned how to become more efficient in preparing purchase orders 3 through 10.

Many companies have found a systematic mathematical relation within the learning phenomenon, which is expressed by the following equation:

$$Y = aX^b$$

where

Y = average number of labor hours required for X units of cost-driver volume
a = number of labor hours required for the first cost-driver unit
X = cumulative number of cost-driver units
b = index of learning equal to the log of the learning rate divided by the log of 2. For example, an 80 percent cumulative learning rate is common in practice. For an 80 percent cumulative learning rate, $b = -.322 = \log(.80)/\log(2)$

learning curve *is the mathematical or graphic representation of the systematic relationship between the amount of experience in performing a task and the time required to perform it*

The **learning curve** is the mathematical or graphic representation of the systematic relationship between the amount of experience in performing a task and the time required to perform it. Assume that a company finds an 80 percent cumulative learning rate for producing Product A. This means that the average unit time required to prepare two units is 80 percent of the time required for one; the average unit time for four units is 80 percent of the average time required per unit for two units, and the average time required per unit for eight units is 80 percent of the average time for four units.

Suppose we apply an 80 percent cumulative learning rate to CC Catering for a new employee who is preparing meals. The number of labor minutes for this new meal-preparation employee at CC Catering appears in Exhibit 11–6. Assume the new employee prepares the first meal, one unit, in 1.25 direct labor minutes. Using the 80 percent cumulative learning rate, the *average* time per meal for two meals is estimated to be 1.00 minute

Exhibit 11–6
Labor Minutes at CC Catering

	Number of Labor Minutes	
X	Per Meal—Average (Y)*	Total Time
1	1.25 minutes	1.25 minutes
2	1.00 (80% × 1.25)	2.00†
3	.878	2.634†
4	.80 (80% × 1.00)	3.20
. . .	. . .	. . .
8	.64 (80% × .80)	5.12

*Computations for Y using formula with logarithm.
$Y_2 = 1.25 \times (2^{-.322}) = 1.00$
$Y_3 = 1.25 \times (3^{-.322}) = .878$
$Y_4 = 1.25 \times (4^{-.322}) = .80$
$Y_8 = 1.25 \times (8^{-.322}) = .64$
†2.00 = 2 units × 1.00 minute, 2.634 = 3 units × .878 minute, and so on.

Exhibit 11-7 Labor Minutes and Quantity Produced

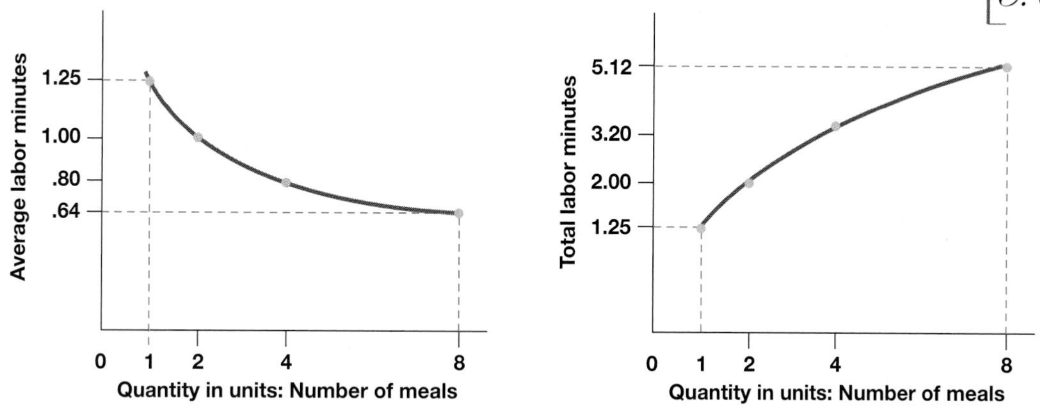

(.80 learning rate × 1.25 minutes). If the average time per meal for two meals is one minute per meal, then the total time for both units (i.e., meals) must be 2.00 minutes.

Four meals would take an average of .80 minutes each (.80 learning rate × 1.00 minutes), or a total of 3.20 minutes according to the 80 percent cumulative learning curve. This means that a total of 1.20 minutes must be expended to produce the third and fourth meals. (1.20 minutes equals 3.20 minutes in total for four meals − 2.00 minutes in total for the first two meals.) As the labor minutes change, so do the costs affected by labor minutes.

Exhibit 11–7 presents the learning curve for meal preparation for a new employee at CC Catering. The curvilinear nature of the relationship between activity volume (i.e., meals prepared) and labor minutes shows large initial learning effects that become increasingly smaller as employees learn how to prepare meals more efficiently.

The function

$$Y = aX^b$$

is curvilinear, as shown in Exhibit 11–7. The function is linear when expressed in log form because

$$\log Y = \log a + b \log X$$

The function is linear when plotted on log-log paper as shown in Exhibit 11–8. A good approximation of the average labor hours required for X units can be obtained from a plot on log-log paper.

Applications to cost management. The learning phenomenon applies to time; thus, it could affect any costs that are a function of time. The phenomenon affects most professional activities such as consulting, legal, medical, and engineering work, as well as any overhead costs related to labor time.

When estimating costs, decision makers should consider the potential impact of learning. The learning phenomenon can affect costs used in cost management, decision making, and performance evaluation. Failing to recognize learning effects can have some unexpected consequences, as shown in the following examples.

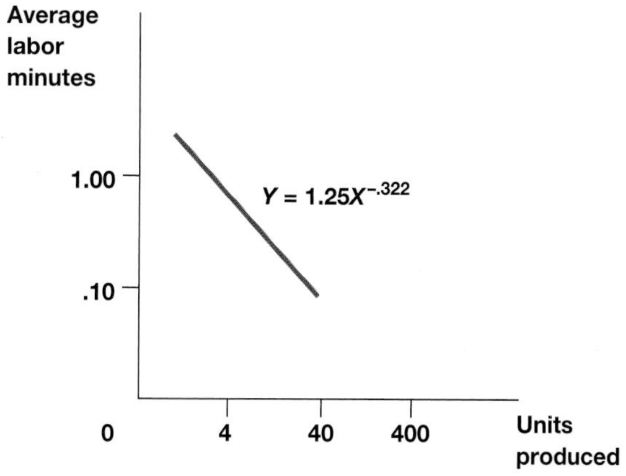

Exhibit 11-8
Labor Minutes and Quantity Produced—Log-Log Relationship

Decision making. Assume that General Electric Company

was considering the production of a new navigational device for NASA. NASA indicates it will pay $500,000 per unit for the device. General Electric engineers and cost managers estimate the cost to General Electric to produce the first four units of the device to be $600,000 per unit. At first, General Electric decided not to produce it because the unit cost exceeded the unit price. NASA assured General Electric that it would order 40 units of the device. After considering the learning phenomenon for the device, General Electric realized that the average cost per unit would drop to $400,000 for 40 units. For four units, the device was unprofitable. For 40 units, it was profitable because of the learning effect.

Performance evaluation. Elite University (not its real name) has developed labor time and cost standards for some of its clerical activities that are subject to the learning curve phenomenon. Management observed that time spent on these activities systematically exceeded the standard. Upon investigating the problem, management found high personnel turnover, which meant that the activities were performed by inexperienced people. As a result, the university never experienced the expected benefits of the learning curve. After making changes in personnel policy, the university reduced turnover and staffed the jobs with more experienced people. The time spent on clerical activities no longer exceeded standards.

You're the Decision Maker 11.1

Using Learning Curves in Marketing Products

Assume that you work in marketing in a company that makes customized products for restaurants and catering companies such as CC Catering. Jessie Chun has asked you to quote a price for four small refrigerated containers with wheels that CC Catering would use to carry meals from the kitchen to the customers' setup locations. Your company would make these containers to CC Catering's specifications. Your production manager tells you that it would cost $1,333 to manufacture the first container. You know that Chun probably would not pay more than $1,000 per container. If Chun will only pay $1,000 per unit, and the manufactured cost is $1,333 per unit, it seems hopeless to make the sale and still have a reasonable margin.

There is a glimmer of hope, however. You recall from discussions with your colleagues in the industrial engineering department that your company has a lot of experience with products like this container. Based on that experience, the engineers have estimated a 75 percent cumulative learning curve for such products. You wonder whether production could get the *average* manufactured cost below $1,000 per container for four containers. Furthermore, perhaps you could sell 8 containers or even 16 containers to CC Catering if the price were low enough per container.

You start with the following chart:

Cumulative Number of Units Produced	Average Manufacturing Cost per Unit	Total Manufacturing Costs
1	$1,333	$1,333
2	?	?
4	?	?
8	?	?
16	?	?

a. Complete the chart by filling in the cost amounts for volumes of 2, 4, 8, and 16 units. What is the average cost per unit for 4 units? For 8 units? For 16 units?

b. Can you sell the containers for $1,000 per unit and have a margin of 20 percent of revenues on the deal? [Assume the desired margin = (Revenues − Manufacturing costs) ÷ Revenues].

c. *Team Focus:* Who should be on the team that decides whether to make and sell containers to CC Catering?

(Solutions begin on page 455.)

Cost-Estimation Methods

We now turn to the specific methods of cost estimation. Recall that CC Catering has grown to a level where Chun and Cohen want to measure costs for cost-management, decision-making, and planning purposes. We discuss three methods commonly used in practice:

1. Statistical methods (using regression analysis).
2. Account analysis.
3. Engineering estimates.

Results are likely to differ from method to method. Consequently, organizations often apply more than one approach to be able to compare and verify results. Managers and analysts who bear ultimate responsibility for all cost estimates frequently apply their own best judgment as a final step in the estimation process. Estimation methods, therefore, should be seen as ways to help management to arrive at the best estimates possible—not as the final answer themselves. The weaknesses of cost-estimation methods as well as their strengths require attention.

Statistical Cost Estimation Using Regression Analysis

LO 3 Compare the advantages and disadvantages of simple and multiple regression for cost estimation purposes.

This section discusses the use of regression analysis to estimate the relationship between costs and cost drivers. **Regression analysis** is a statistical method used to create an equation relating independent (or *X*) variables to dependent (or *Y*) variables. Regression analysis uses data from the past to estimate relationships between costs, which are the dependent variables, and activities, that are the independent variables and will be valid in the future. In particular, this technique will enable you to estimate the cost-driver rates that were given in examples in previous chapters.

The most important step in obtaining regression estimates for cost estimation is to establish the existence of a logical relationship between cost drivers and the cost to be estimated. These cost drivers are *X* terms or independent variables of a regression equation. **Independent variables** are the cost drivers that the analyst believes cause, or at least are correlated with, the dependent variable, costs. The cost to be estimated is the dependent variable, or the *Y* term. **Dependent variables** are caused by, or at least correlated with, independent variables. The distinction between dependent and independent variables should make sense because costs do not just happen, they *depend* on cost drivers. We refer to the *Y* term as *TC* because the *Y* variable is always some measure of total cost (*TC*) in our analyses. Depending on the context, *TC* can refer to the total costs of the organization, total overhead costs of the organization, or some other measure of total cost.

regression analysis *is a statistical method used to create an equation relating independent (or* X*) variables to dependent (or* Y*) variables*

independent variables *are the cost drivers that the analyst believes cause, or at least are correlated with, the dependent variable, costs*

dependent variables *are caused by, or at least correlated with, independent variables*

Regression analysis generates an equation or, visually, a line that best fits a set of data points. In addition, regression techniques provide information that helps a manager to ascertain how well the estimated regression equation describes the relationship between costs and cost drivers.

Many moderately priced handheld calculators have regression capabilities. Computer spreadsheets such as Microsoft® Excel and Lotus 1-2-3® have regression capabilities. More powerful statistical packages such as Minitab, SAS, and SPSS are designed to run regressions. We leave descriptions of the computational details to statistics courses. Instead, we deal here with regression from the standpoint of accountants and managers who must use and interpret regression estimates. (The Appendix to this chapter discusses some of the more technical considerations that might interest users of such programs.)

Existence of a Logical Relationship between Costs and Their Drivers

The first, and perhaps most important, task is to identify the cost drivers. If the relationship between costs and cost drivers has followed a particular pattern in the past, and if that pattern is expected to continue in the future, it is reasonable to use data from the past to estimate cost-driver rates. However, if the past relationship is no longer valid, then it is necessary to adjust the cost-driver rates to reflect reality.

Over time, the cost-activity relationship could change for several reasons. Technological innovation, change in product characteristics, and change in input prices could make the past data inappropriate for estimating the future. This is particularly a problem for many high-tech companies and companies that have products with short life cycles.

Data about the past are useful in companies that have stable production processes and products that do not change. United Airlines and American Airlines, for example, have used regression analysis to estimate the costs of various activities in flying airplanes. Because flight operations have not changed dramatically over the past several years, managers at these airlines considered the use of past data to be appropriate.

Flight operations analysts use data about past passenger travel to predict future passenger travel.

Although the use of past data for future cost estimation has limitations, in many cases it works quite well. Using past data is relatively inexpensive for analysts and managers because data are available in the records. Cost estimations based on past data show past relationships between costs and activities. Past relationships between costs and cost drivers can be a meaningful starting point for estimating the future relationship between costs and activities as long as decision makers recognize the limitations of using past data.

Relevant range of activity. As discussed earlier in this chapter, the limits within which a cost projection are valid is the relevant range for that estimate. For example, if CC Catering has been producing between 1,000 and 4,000 meals per month, the relevant range of its cost estimates are valid between 1,000 and 4,000 meals. If CC Catering expects to produce between, say, 8,000 and 10,000 meals per month in the future, the cost estimates obtained from data for 1,000 to 4,000 meals might not be valid. We say that producing outside the 1,000 to 4,000 meal range is *outside the relevant range.*

Think of the problem of walking in winter on a lake that is frozen over. You have experience that the ice is thick enough to hold you between shoreline and 10 feet out from shoreline. That is the relevant range. When you get farther than 10 feet from shoreline, you are no longer in the relevant range. Your estimates of the relationship between your weight and the ice thickness could no longer be accurate. In a similar way, managers might still use the cost estimates even though the company is operating outside the relevant range, but managers should be aware that they may be "walking on thin ice."

Simple Model for Regression Analysis

Earlier in this chapter, we discussed the simple model with one cost driver. This model is a useful way to get a basic understanding about how to apply regression analysis to cost management. Later we shall discuss a more complex and realistic model.

As noted earlier in this chapter, in a simple world with one cost driver and costs divided simply into fixed and variable components, analysts estimate the following cost equation:

$$TC = F + VX$$

where

TC = total costs
F = fixed costs that do not vary with the cost driver
V = variable costs per unit for the cost driver
X = the independent variable, or cost driver

The regression model is called **simple regression** because it has only one independent variable.

simple regression *is a type of statistical analysis in which the regression equation has only one independent variable*

Although regression programs accept any data for the Y and X terms, entering numbers that have no logical relationship will give you misleading estimates. The following are some logical relationships between costs and cost drivers:

Costs (dependent variables)	Cost Drivers (independent variables)
Costs to operate an automobile	Number of miles driven
Costs to teach students	Number of students taught
Costs to operate CC Catering	Number of meals sold

As you can see, picking logical cost-activity relationships does not require rocket science, just common sense.

Application to CC Catering

Using simple regression, Cohen attempted to find the relationship between the number of meals sold and costs. In particular, she wanted Exhibit 11-9, panel B to estimate the variable cost per meal. From the company's records, she collected the data that appear in panel A of Exhibit 11–9. Those data, which are simply total costs of operating the company each month and the number of meals sold each month for the past 16 months, were readily available in the company's records. It took only about 30 minutes to get the data from the records and input them into Microsoft® Excel.

Cohen's results appear in panel B of Exhibit 11–9. For cost-estimation purposes, when reading the output of a regression program, understand that the intercept term, \$2,619, is an estimate of fixed costs. Of course, it should be used with caution because the intercept at zero activity is outside the relevant range of observations. The coefficient of the X term (in this example, \$2.77 per meal) is an estimate of the variable cost per meal. Visually, this is the slope of the cost line shown in panel C of Exhibit 11–9. The coefficients are often labeled b on the program output.

The cost estimation equation based on this regression result is:

$$\text{Total costs} = \text{Intercept} + (b \times \text{Units of activity})$$

For CC Catering, the cost estimate is:

$$\text{Total costs} = \$2{,}619 + (\$2.77 \times \text{Number of meals})$$

The number \$2.77 estimates the variable cost per meal, assuming that the only cost driver is meals sold. Cohen later made more precise estimates using more cost drivers in the model. Nevertheless, her simple model provides enough information for a discussion of the basic application of regression analysis. It also may be useful as a first approximation of the company's cost-activity relations.

Cohen plotted the data in a scattergraph, which appears in Panel C of Exhibit 11–9. A **scattergraph** plots past costs against past cost-driver levels and visually indicates differences in the relationship between costs and activity at different activity levels. It

scattergraph *plots costs against activity levels*

Exhibit 11-9

Simple Regression Results for CC Catering

C.C. Catering

Panel A
Input data from the company's records

Month*	Total Costs	Units (meals)
Jan, previous year	$ 6,720	1,280
Feb	7,260	1,810
Mar	7,270	1,620
Apr	11,060	2,830
May	12,580	3,630
Jun	8,660	2,610
Jul	8,580	2,460
Aug	9,550	2,640
Sep	13,050	3,620
Oct	11,060	2,840
Nov	7,320	1,820
Dec	7,370	1,650
Jan, current year	6,790	1,260
Feb	7,480	1,850
Mar	6,990	1,710
Apr	11,400	2,940

Panel B
The regression output from Microsoft Excel appears as follows:

$$y = 2.7684x + 2618.7$$

We have reformatted and rounded these numbers to give the following cost equation:

Total costs = $2,619 + $2.77 meals

The R-square of the regression is:

$$R^2 = .93$$

Panel C
Scattergraph

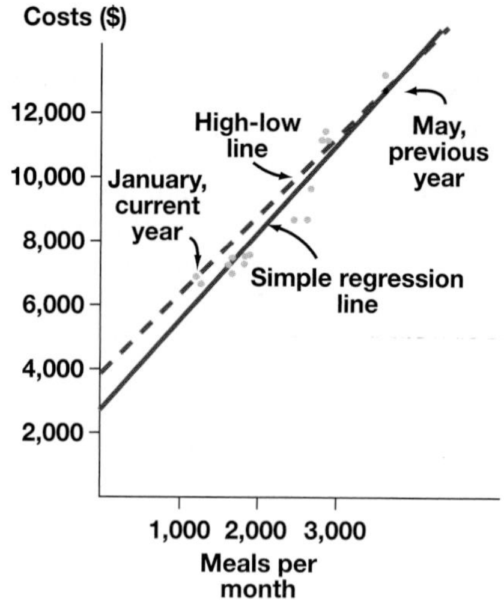

*Cohen obtained the monthly data from the records starting with January of the previous year and continuing through April of the current year.

can reveal the presence of curvilinear relationships between costs, and it can show any data that appear to be unusual. Unusual data often warrant further investigation to look for errors.

high-low method
estimates a cost function using only the costs and the level of cost-driver activity from the highest and lowest levels of cost-driver activity

We have plotted two lines on the scattergraph: one is the regression line, the other is a line connecting the costs at the highest and lowest cost-driver levels. The latter line is based on the **high-low method,** which estimates a cost function using only the costs and level of cost-driver activity from the highest and lowest levels of cost-driver activity. The high-low method is a simple "back of the envelope" way to get estimates of the slope and intercept of a straight line using just two points of data. Using the high-low method, one can either draw a straight line between the two highest and lowest points to the *Y* axis or compute the slope and intercept mathematically using the formula for a straight line.

The high-low method has generally been replaced by the use of spreadsheets and regression analysis. Nevertheless, some people still use it, and it occasionally appears on professional examinations such as the CPA exam. We explain it here so you will not be caught unaware if you hear or read the term "high-low method." However, we regard it as inferior to the regression method because it uses only two data points.

The following explains how to compute the cost function using the data from CC Catering. First, compute the slope of the straight line between the highest and lowest cost-driver level (i.e., number of meals) at CC Catering:

Slope = (Cost at highest number of meals − Cost at lowest number of meals)/(Highest number of meals − Lowest number of meals)

= ($12,580 in May, previous year − $6,790 in January, current year)/(3,630 meals in May, previous year − 1,260 meals in January, current year)

= $2.44 per meal

This compares with the estimate of $2.77 (rounded) per meal in the regression results in panel B of Exhibit 11–9.

Second, compute the intercept by starting with the total cost at either the highest or lowest cost-driver level and then subtracting the estimated total variable cost at that activity:

Intercept = Total cost at highest cost-driver level − (Variable cost per unit × Highest cost-driver level)

or

Intercept = Total cost at lowest cost-driver level − (Variable cost per unit × Lowest cost-driver level)

Using the highest cost-driver level, which is 3,630 meals sold in the previous May at a total cost of $12,580, subtract the total variable costs as follows:

Intercept = $12,580 − ($2.44 × 3,630 meals sold)
= $3,723

Therefore, the high-low cost equation is:

Total costs = $3,723 + ($2.44 × Number of meals)

Comparing these high-low estimates to the estimated intercept in the regression results shown in Exhibit 11–9 of $2,619 (rounded) indicates that the estimated fixed costs are higher (and estimated variable costs per unit are lower) using the high-low method. We have more confidence in the regression results because regression incorporates all input data in the analysis whereas the high-low method incorporates only two points in the analysis.

Panel B of Exhibit 11–9 shows the R-square of the regression. The **R-square** (R^2) is the proportion of the variation in the dependent variable (total costs in our case) explained by the *X* or independent variable (the number of meals in our case). The R-square varies from .00 to 1.00. The number .00 indicates no relationship and 1.00 indicates a perfect relationship between the independent variable and the dependent variable. The R-square indicates how much variation in the dependent variable the independent variable explains. For CC Catering, Exhibit 11–9 shows the R-square to be .93, meaning that the variation in the activity—the number of meals—explains 93 percent of the variation in total costs.

R-square (R^2) *is the proportion of the variation in the dependent variable explained by the X, or independent variables*

Use of the Results

As noted at the beginning of this chapter, Chun and Cohen wish to use cost estimates for cost management, decision making, and planning. Starting with cost management, they want to estimate the cost of activities to identify which activities are costly. Costly activities get attention, but one must first know which ones are costly. The simple regression results shown in Exhibit 11–9 are not much help for cost management. After seeing the results, Chun turned to Cohen and said, "Well, we have an estimate of the variable cost per meal, but I don't see how we can use that information to become more efficient."

Cohen agreed, "Right, you are. This result just gives us a ballpark estimate of the variable cost of each meal without any of the detail that we need to manage costs. Still, it's comforting to know the variable cost estimate isn't more than we charge for meals. Then we would be in big trouble."

Cohen and Chun could use the cost estimate for decision making. They are considering outsourcing meal preparation to a local sandwich shop. To decide whether to do so, they want to know the cost of preparing meals to compare with a meal preparation bid from the sandwich shop. Unfortunately, the simple regression's estimate of variable costs did not indicate the cost of meal preparation.

Despite the limitations noted here, the simple regression estimate could be informative for particular decisions and for planning. Suppose that CC Catering plans to sell 30,000 meals next year at an average price of $4.00 per meal. Cohen and Chun would like to know how much profit the company would make.

The revenue estimate is $120,000 ($4.00 × 30,000 meals). The total cost estimates are based on the regression equation shown in panel B of Exhibit 11–9. Recall that the cost estimate is for the number of meals in one month. To convert the estimated fixed costs from months to years, multiply the intercept by 12. This estimates fixed costs as $31,428 (12 × $2,619). Therefore, the estimated costs for the year for 30,000 meals are:

$$\begin{aligned}\text{Estimated total costs} &= \$31{,}428 + (\$2.77 \times 30{,}000 \text{ meals})\\ &= \$114{,}528\end{aligned}$$

Cohen and Chun believe that the past is a reasonable prediction of the future with one exception—inflation. After thinking about increases in the cost of food, labor, energy, and other costs between the time periods in which the costs in the regression analysis were incurred and next year, they decide to add 6 percent to the estimate of total costs to account for inflation. Their new cost estimate is (rounded to the nearest dollar):

$$\begin{aligned}\text{Estimated total costs} &= \$114{,}528 \times 1.06\\ &= \$121{,}400\end{aligned}$$

Therefore, they expect to show a profit (loss) of

$$\begin{aligned}\text{Operating profit (loss)} &= \text{Total revenue} - \text{Total costs}\\ &= \$120{,}000 - \$121{,}400\\ &= \$(1{,}400)\end{aligned}$$

Cohen and Chun use this information in their personal planning and in thinking about getting a loan to remodel their space. With good job prospects in industry and public accounting, they also ask themselves whether it is worthwhile to continue this company. Cohen asks, "Should we close up shop and get a 'paid' job?" Chun responds that, despite the projected loss, the business provides them with some personal income from the $15 per hour wage and $500 per month management "salary" (both amounts are included in the preceding cost figures). Nevertheless, they would like to find ways to be more efficient and increase profits. To do that, they know they will have to perform activity-based management, which will require a more sophisticated cost analysis than they have done so far.

Use of Multiple Regression Analysis to Estimate Cost Drivers for Activity-Based Management and Decision Making

multiple regression *is a regression equation with more than one independent variable*

Multiple regression is a regression equation with more than one independent variable. Using multiple regression analyses, company analysts learn more about cost behavior than they do from simple regression. Furthermore, multiple regression has potentially greater explanatory power; that is, more of the variation in the dependent variable (total costs) can be explained by including more independent variables (cost drivers). Multiple regression requires more data, which can be time consuming, as we shall soon see for CC Catering.

Research Insight 11.1

Manufacturing Overhead Cost Drivers

Based on a study of 31 manufacturing plants in three industries—electronics, automobile components, and machinery—researchers used regression analysis to identify manufacturing overhead cost drivers. Their approach treated manufacturing overhead cost as the dependent variable and various cost drivers as the independent variables. Each plant was a separate data point, so there were 31 observations in total. The researchers' model had an adjusted R^2 of .78, indicating that the variation in the cost-driver activity levels explained 78 percent of the variation in manufacturing overhead costs.

Many accountants and managers believe that simple volume-based overhead cost drivers, such as machine hours and labor hours, do not fully capture the causes of overhead costs. They argue that other factors, such as the complexity of the production process, also cause overhead costs; consequently, activity-based costing is superior to traditional volume-based overhead allocation methods. These researchers found a strong relationship between overhead costs and both volume- and complexity-based cost drivers.

The researchers also found that plants implementing new manufacturing methods, namely, just-in-time production, total quality management, and the use of work teams for problem solving on the shop floor, had lower overhead costs than those that had not implemented these new manufacturing methods, all other things being equal. This result is particularly important as to whether improved quality increases or decreases costs. *Source: R. J. Banker, G. Potter, and R. G. Schroeder, "An Empirical Analysis of Manufacturing Overhead Cost Drivers." (Full citations to references are in the Bibliography.)*

The first step in performing multiple regression is to identify the activities that are logical cost drivers. As noted earlier in this chapter, some organizations use many cost drivers. Analysts face a cost-benefit trade-off in choosing the number of cost drivers. More cost drivers require more data but probably provide better information. For example, as shown in Research Insight 11.1, researchers using multiple regression found that, for the companies studied, the volume of output and the complexity of operations increased costs, whereas introducing total quality management and other quality improvements reduced costs. These insights would be impossible to obtain from simple regression results.

Generally, we find diminishing marginal returns by using too many cost drivers. At some point, the additional information from the additional cost driver is not worth the effort required to get the data. Furthermore, because of the phenomenon known as *information overload,* decision makers sometimes have trouble processing large amounts of data. Therefore, a limited number of cost drivers can prove to be an advantage by reducing the amount of information to consider.

After thinking carefully about CC Catering's production processes, its cost hierarchy, and the data that she could get from the company's records, Cohen decided to use the following cost drivers:

- *Unit-level: Units.* A unit is a meal sold. The cost related to meals sold includes materials such as the plastic meal containers and the food in each meal. Unit costs also include labor required to prepare meals. (All meals prepared are sold.)
- *Batch-level: Jobs (or batches).* If CC Catering takes an order for, say, 30 meals to be delivered to the dean of students' conference room for a lunch meeting; that order is one job. If the dean of students placed such an order six times in a month, CC Catering counts that as six different jobs.
- *Product-level: New products.* CC Catering sometimes changes its menu, deletes existing meals, and adds new ones. For example, suppose the company adds a Thai noodle salad to its menu. It would incur the costs to experiment with various ingredients, develop a recipe that workers could easily follow in preparing the meal, and revise its menus and advertising copy.
- *Customer-level: New customers.* CC Catering conducts marketing to attract new customers. Once signed on, the company performs a credit check on the new

customer, sets up billing files, and obtains delivery instructions for its drivers. Cohen decided that the activity—obtaining new customers—creates costs that should be estimated.

As an aside, take a minute to note that these cost drivers line up well with the cost hierarchy. That is, CC Catering has unit-level costs driven by the number of meals sold, batch-level costs driven by the number of jobs, product-related costs driven by number of new products introduced, and customer-related costs driven by the number of new customers each month.

Question: Why has CC Catering not included a cost driver for facility-level costs? Answer: There was only one facility throughout this time period, so there would be no variance in that particular independent variable. Estimated facility-related costs are in the intercept of the regression equation.[3]

The cost drivers that you choose in practice might or might not line up well with the cost hierarchy, depending on the nature of the organization. For example, a service company such as Starbucks might not use a cost driver for number of customers. Starbuck's customer-related costs from selling a drink are captured in the cost of selling that drink. So, cost drivers such as the number of units of a particular drink sold include customer-related costs. However, a utility company could have substantial customer-related costs because it collects information about usage, prepares bills, collects and deposits payments received, and maintains account records for each customer. Although each organization is different (which is fortunate, or we would all be quite bored), a good place to start identifying cost drivers is to ask what drives the costs in the following five cost hierarchy levels: unit-level costs, batch-level costs, product-level costs, customer-level costs, and facility-level costs.

This Starbucks employee weighs beans for a customer. The employee's salary would be included in unit-level costs.

Application to CC Catering

When estimating the costs for each cost driver, cost managers must collect total cost information for each time period, for example, total costs for each month. They also must collect information about the level of activity of each cost driver for each time period. To estimate the costs for each of its four cost drivers, CC Catering must collect the information shown in Exhibit 11–10. For the first month studied, which is January of the previous year, CC's records show one facility and the following costs and activities:

- Total costs of operations—$6,720.
- Meals—1,280.
- Different catering jobs—30.
- New products introduced—2.
- New customers—6.

[3]The intercept could include estimated costs of other omitted cost drivers, also. For simplicity, we consider the intercept to be an estimate of only facility-level costs.

Exhibit 11–10

Multiple Regression Results for CC Catering

C.C. Catering

Panel A
Input Data from the Company's Records

		Cost Driver Volume			
Month	**Costs**	**Units (meals)**	**Jobs**	**New Products**	**New Customers**
Jan, previous year	$ 6,720	1,280	30	2	6
Feb	7,260	1,810	28	2	4
Mar	7,270	1,620	34	2	7
Apr	11,060	2,830	51	0	18
May	12,580	3,630	63	0	16
Jun	8,660	2,610	32	4	1
Jul	8,580	2,460	34	3	3
Aug	9,550	2,640	36	2	6
Sep	13,050	3,620	61	0	18
Oct	11,060	2,840	54	0	16
Nov	7,320	1,820	29	2	6
Dec	7,370	1,650	32	2	10
Jan, current year	6,790	1,260	31	2	5
Feb	7,480	1,850	27	2	5
Mar	6,990	1,710	35	0	8
Apr	11,400	2,940	48	0	16

Panel B
Regression Results

We have reformatted and rounded numbers from the regression output to give the following cost function:

$$\text{Total costs} = \$2{,}177 + \$1.91 \text{ meals} + \$28.18 \text{ jobs} + \$160.03 \text{ new products} + \$119.58 \text{ new customers}$$

Adjusted $R^2 = .98$

Interpretation: Estimated facility costs per month are $2,177. Each meal is expected to cost $1.91 holding all other variables constant, each job is expected to cost $28.18 holding all other variables constant, and so forth.

Example: Assume that, for one month, CC Catering sells 2,000 meals, has 50 jobs, develops 2 new products, and adds 10 new customers. What are the company's estimated costs for the month? The answer shown in the following computations = $8,922 (rounded).

Cost Driver	Volume	Rate	Total Costs
Facility	1	$2,177.00	$2,177.00
Meals	2,000	1.91	3,820.00
Jobs	50	28.18	1,409.00
New products	2	160.03	320.06
New customers	10	119.58	1,195.80
Total costs for the month			8,921.86

Cohen obtained this information from the records for each month for 16 months beginning in January of the previous year and entered it into a regression software package (e.g., Microsoft Excel or Minitab). The input data for the multiple regression appear in panel A of Exhibit 11–10. Comparing Exhibits 11–9 and 11–10, we see that the additional data required for the multiple regression approach were number of jobs, number of new products, and number of new customers. The total costs per month and number of meals per month already had been collected for the simple regression.

The results for the multiple regression appear in panel B of Exhibit 11–10. Note that the *adjusted* R-square replaces the R-square that we showed for the simple regression.

The adjusted R-square serves the same purpose as the R-square discussed in the section on simple regression, but it is computed to consider the number of independent variables in the regression. Most analysts use the adjusted R-square, not the R-square, to judge the quality of a multiple regression. At 0.98, the adjusted R-square for CC Catering is quite high, indicating that the independent variables in the multiple regression do well in explaining the CC Catering's variation in total costs.

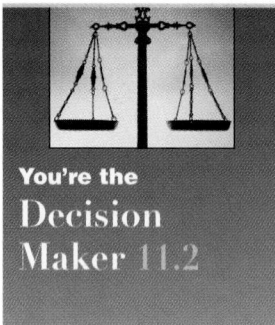

Later in this chapter, we discuss how CC Catering used the multiple regression results. For now, we recommend that you answer the self-study questions in You're the Decision Maker 11.2 to understand how to estimate costs using multiple regression results.

You're the Decision Maker 11.2

Using Regression

a. What are the strengths and weaknesses of simple compared to multiple regression for cost estimation at CC Catering?

b. Assume that CC Catering expects to have the following levels of cost-driver activity in December of the current year: 1,800 meals, 30 jobs, 2 new products, and 12 new customers. Using the results of the multiple regression in Exhibit 11–10, compute CC Catering's expected costs for December. For ease of analysis, assume that inflation is not a factor and that the regression results for the past are valid for projecting costs in December.

(Solutions begin on page 455.)

A Cautionary Note about Using Regression

Regression analysis may have an aura of scientific analysis about it. In fact, it is only as good as the quality of the data and the thought process that goes into developing the model. We recommend that users of regression (1) fully understand the methodology and its limitations, (2) specify the hypothesized relationship between costs and cost drivers with great care, and (3) know the limitations of the data being used. If users do their part in these three areas, regression can be a powerful tool.

Account Analysis Method

LO 4 Present advantages and disadvantages of account analysis compared to multiple regression for cost estimation.

account analysis *is the cost-estimation method based on the past costs associated with each cost driver*

Using the regression method, we let the software do most of the work for us, namely, to find the relationship between each of the independent variables and costs. For regression analysis, the data requirements were (1) total costs each month and (2) total cost-driver volume each month for each of the cost drivers—for example, number of units and number of jobs.

The **account analysis** method is the cost-estimation method based on the past costs associated with each cost driver. Account analysis requires more data because we must separate total costs into cost categories that tie to the cost drivers. For CC Catering, for example, the cost accounts would be analyzed (hence, the name "account analysis") for the past 16 months by dividing total monthly costs into the following categories related to the four cost drivers plus a fifth category for facility-sustaining costs:

1. Unit costs
2. Job costs
3. New-product costs
4. New-customer costs
5. Facility costs

(Recall that in the regression analysis, we did not have a specific cost driver for the facilities. Because the company has just one facility, we assumed the intercept of the regression was the estimated facility cost.)

Exhibit 11–11 Account Analysis for CC Catering

	A	B	C	D	E	F	G	H	I	J	K
1				Costs					Cost Driver Volume		
2		Total Monthly Costs	Units (meals)	Jobs	New Prod.	New Cust.	Facilities	Units (meals)	Jobs	New Prod.	New. Cust.
3	Jan, previous year	$ 6,720	$ 2,442	$ 940	$ 330	$ 734	$ 2,274	1,280	30	2	6
4	Feb	7,260	3,449	884	320	496	2,111	1,810	28	2	4
5	Mar	7,270	3,088	1,052	365	853	1,912	1,620	34	2	7
6	Apr	11,060	5,387	1,528	—	2,162	1,983	2,830	51	0	18
7	May	12,580	6,907	1,864	—	1,924	1,885	3,630	63	0	16
8	Jun	8,660	4,969	996	630	139	1,926	2,610	32	4	1
9	Jul	8,580	4,684	1,052	480	377	1,987	2,460	34	3	3
10	Aug	9,550	5,026	1,108	330	734	2,352	2,640	36	2	6
11	Sep	13,050	6,888	1,808	—	2,162	2,192	3,620	61	0	18
12	Oct	11,060	5,406	1,612	—	1,924	2,118	2,840	54	0	16
13	Nov	7,320	3,468	912	340	734	1,866	1,820	29	2	6
14	Dec	7,370	3,145	996	330	1,210	1,689	1,650	32	2	10
15	Jan, current year	6,790	2,404	968	350	615	2,453	1,260	31	2	5
16	Feb	7,480	3,525	856	320	615	2,164	1,850	27	2	5
17	Mar	6,990	3,259	1,080	—	972	1,679	1,710	35	0	8
18	Apr	11,400	5,596	1,444	—	1,924	2,436	2,940	48	0	16
19		$143,140	$69,643	$19,100	$3,795	$17,575	$33,027	36,570	625	23	145
20											
21	Cost-driver rates*		$1.90	$30.56	$165.00	$121.21	$2,064.19				
22	*Computations for cost driver rates:										
23	Unit costs:		$ 1.90		= $69,643÷36,570 meals			= C19÷H19.			
24	Job costs:		$ 30.56		= $19,100÷625 jobs			= D19÷I19.			
25	New-product costs:		$ 165.00		= $3,795÷23 new products			= E19÷J19.			
26	New-customer costs:		$ 121.21		= $17,575÷145 new customers			= F19÷K19.			
27	Facility costs:		$2,064.19 per month		= $33,027÷16 months of observations.						

Exhibit 11–11 shows the division of total costs into categories for each of the 16 months that CC Catering is analyzing. To obtain the amounts shown in Exhibit 11–11, someone who understands the company's costs must analyze each detailed cost account to categorize it into one of the preceding five categories. With five cost drivers, this task is not too difficult. If a company has, say, 100 cost drivers, the task is daunting.

Good news for those of you who will use account analysis is that information system designers can make your work easier by coding accounts to match the cost drivers. For example, assume that CC Catering uses 50 accounts to track costs. Each of those accounts is assigned to one of the five cost drivers. After that has been done, information systems designers can assign a code, say 1 to 5, for each account. That way, when a cost is recorded in an account, it is automatically assigned to a cost driver.

For example, suppose that the monthly electric bill is recorded with the following entry:

Dr. *248* Electric Expense	88	
Cr. *50* Accounts Payable		88

The numbers in italics are the account codes for the two accounts. Assume that the account Electric Expense is assigned the number 5 to designate it as a facility account. Then instead of 248, the Electric Expense account is 248-5. All account numbers with a 5 after the "-" are classified as a facility cost account. At the end of the month, analysts simply sum the costs in accounts designated "-5" to obtain the total facilities costs for the month. Analysts then sum the costs in accounts designated by "-1" to get the total unit costs, sum the costs in the accounts designated "-2" to obtain the total job costs, and so on for new-product and new-customer costs.

Exhibit 11–11 shows total costs for each month (column B), the breakdown of costs into the four cost-driver categories plus facilities costs (columns C through G), and the cost-driver volume for the four cost drivers (columns H through K). The information in columns C through G is new for the account analysis. The other data in the exhibit were also prepared for the multiple regression analysis. This should give you a feel for the amount of additional data required for account analysis compared to regression analysis.

The cost driver rates from account analysis appear in line 21 of columns C through G. Please examine the computations at the bottom of Exhibit 11–11 to see how to derive the cost driver rates. Those amounts (e.g., $1.90 for the unit cost driver in C21) represent the account analysis version of the multiple regression results shown in panel B of Exhibit 11–10. Later we discuss how CC Catering used these results. For now, we recommend that you answer the self-study questions in You're the Decision Maker 11.3 to see how to apply the account analysis results.

You're the Decision Maker 11.3

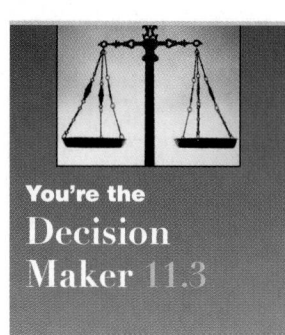

Using Account Analysis

a. Assuming that Leah Cohen had already performed multiple regression, what additional data did she require to perform account analysis?

b. Assume that CC Catering expects to have the following levels of cost-driver activity in December of the current year: 1,800 meals, 30 jobs, 2 new products, and 12 new customers. Using the results of the account analysis in Exhibit 11–11, compute CC Catering's expected costs for December. For ease of analysis, assume that inflation is not a factor and that the account analysis results for the past are valid for projecting costs in December.

(Solutions begin on page 455.)

Choice between Regression and Account Analysis

If faced with the prospects of choosing between regression and account analysis, we usually recommend doing the regression analysis first. Then ask what additional costs would be incurred and what additional benefits might result from obtaining additional information, if any, under account analysis.

Account analysis can provide two benefits. First, it allows decision makers to have a comparison with the regression results. Normally, some differences in cost-driver rates result using two different cost estimation methods. If the cost-driver rates are quite different, however, the analyst should find the source of the difference. This search might reveal data-entry, model-specification, or other problems. This exercise can be a challenging and interesting detective project.

Second, by obtaining the more detailed breakdown of cost data from account analysis, analysts might spot trends or errors or get insights about cost behavior. The more experience you have, the more insights you will develop about cost behavior from looking at detailed cost data.

Neither account analysis nor regression is inherently more accurate. Both have limitations; both have advantages. Account analysis is more expensive than regression because it requires a more detailed breakdown of costs. Consequently, account analysis must provide more information than regression to justify its additional expense.

Data Problems

As we previously mentioned, whether using regression or account analysis, the results are only as good as the data used. Collecting appropriate data is complicated by the following problems:

- *Missing data.* Misplaced source documents or the failure to record a transaction can result in missing data.
- *Outliers.* Observations of extreme cost-activity relationships might unduly affect cost estimates. For example, a hurricane affected operations in a Florida company one August, resulting in high overhead due to one-time costs.
- *Allocated and discretionary costs.* Fixed costs are often allocated on a volume basis, resulting in costs that might appear to be variable. Discretionary costs also might be budgeted so that they appear variable (e.g., advertising expense budgeted as a percentage of revenue).
- *Inflation.* During periods of inflation, historical cost data do not accurately reflect future cost estimates.
- *Mismatched time periods.* The time periods for the dependent and independent variables might not match (e.g., running a machine in February and receiving and recording the energy bill in March).

Managers should be aware of problems in the data. No substitute exists for using experience to understand how costs and cost drivers are related.

Engineering Method

LO 5 Explain what is gained from using the engineering method compared to using regression and account analysis. Explain why the engineering method is likely to be more costly than regression and account analysis.

Statistical methods and account analyses rely on data from the past. By contrast, the engineering method works with the present and future. Analysts make **engineering estimates** of costs, first by measuring the work involved in the activities that go into a product and then by assigning a cost to each of those activities. Analysts prepare a detailed step-by-step analysis of each activity required to make a product, together with the costs involved.

engineering estimates *are cost estimates based on measuring and pricing the work involved in the activities that go into a product*

Analysts can usually obtain engineering estimates of the materials required for each unit of production from drawings and product specification records. Employees in the company's accounting and purchasing departments have data on the cost of materials that analysts can use to price the materials required to make a product. Analysts can perform time-and-motion studies or review labor time records to ascertain the time required to perform each step. Labor records also provide typical wage rates for various jobs. Coupling those wage rates plus benefits with the time required to perform activities gives the estimated labor cost.

Other costs are estimated similarly. For example, analysts can estimate the size and cost of a building based on area construction costs and space requirements. They can estimate the necessary number of supervisors and support personnel based on a direct labor-time estimate.

The engineering approach has an advantage over other cost estimation methods because it details each step required to perform an operation. This permits benchmarking. Another advantage to this approach is that it does not require data from prior activities in the organization. Hence, it can be used to estimate costs for totally new activities.

The engineering approach can identify non-value-added activities. For example, if an engineering estimate indicates that 80,000 square feet of floor area are required for an assembly process but the company has been using 125,000 square feet, managers could find it beneficial to rearrange the plant to make floor space available for other uses. Or, if an engineering estimate indicates that the optimal production run is 1,000 units per setup but the company has been running only 100 units per setup, the managers might change production scheduling to get the optimal production run length.

A difficulty with the engineering approach is that it can be quite expensive to use because it analyzes each activity. Another consideration is that engineering estimates are often based on optimal conditions. Therefore, when evaluating performance, bidding on a contract, planning expected costs, or estimating costs for any other purpose, it is wise to consider that the actual work conditions will often be less than optimal.

To use the engineering method for CC Catering, Chun estimated the following costs.

Unit Costs

To estimate unit costs, Chun started with the materials required for a typical meal: a turkey sandwich, one apple, two oatmeal cookies, one piece of candy, one plastic container, and miscellaneous items such as napkins and plastic utensils. She considered waste; for example, she figured that 1 of 10 apples and 5 percent of turkey and bread would be wasted and that 1 of 40 plastic containers would be defective or ruined during production, and so forth. To estimate labor costs, she timed Cohen in preparing meals under ideal conditions. That was her estimate of the shortest time required to prepare meals. She also timed untrained workers to estimate the longest time for meal preparation. Considering these data, using her experience with the learning effects, and estimating how far along the learning curve the average workers were, she estimated labor time per meal. She multiplied that by the sum of the average wage rate, payroll taxes, and benefits per hour to obtain the preparation cost per meal. To make her analysis comparable to Cohen's work with multiple regression and account analysis, she used input prices that were in effect on average over the previous 16 months. Based on this work, she estimated the cost per meal to be $1.88.

Job Costs

Job costs were mostly labor costs. Preparing a job included taking the order, shopping for food, instructing the meal preparation crew, delivering the meals to the customer's location, overseeing serving, and cleaning up. Some of these costs required cost allocation. For example, one of the employees did a shopping trip for four jobs. In this case, she allocated the costs equally to each job—one-fourth of the time and one-fourth of the mileage to each job. She estimated job costs to average $35.50 per job, considering the fact that job costs would be less for jobs having 50 or fewer meals and more for jobs having 51 to 100 meals, as we discussed in the section on step costs earlier in this chapter.

New-Product Costs

New-product costs included labor to develop and test new meals for the menu, materials used to prepare new meals for testing (including those that were rejected), supervision and labor time to teach the meal preparation crew to prepare new meals, and the costs to print new menus. Chun's estimate of new product costs was $168 per new product.

New-Customer Costs

New-customer costs included the costs of advertising time spent in marketing the company's products, time spent talking to prospective customers, and time spent in setting up a new customer's account in CC Catering's computer system. Chun estimated new customer costs to be $122 per new customer.

Exhibit 11–12 CC Catering: Comparing the Estimated Cost-Driver Rates

C.C. Catering

	Unit Rate (per meal)	Job Rate (per job)	New-Product Rate (per new product)	New-Customer Rate (per new customer)	Facility Rate (per month)
Multiple regression (from Exhibit 11–10)	$1.91	$28.18	$160.03	$119.58	$2,177
Account analysis (from Exhibit 11–11)	1.90	30.56	165.00	121.21	2,064
Engineering (from discussion in the text)	1.88	35.50	168.00	122.00	2,210

Facility Costs

In estimating facility costs, Chun included the base salary that she and Cohen received, rent on the facilities, utilities, and other administrative costs. She estimated these costs to be $2,210 per month.

Comparison of the Estimates

When they were finished, Cohen and Chun compared the costs from each of the three estimation methods, which appear in Exhibit 11–12. Cohen remarked that the three methods gave remarkably similar cost estimates. "Doing all three methods gives us a lot of confidence in our estimates. If we had found quite different cost estimates for any of these cost drivers, then we would have to find the differences, and maybe scrap the entire analysis," she said.

Chun noted, "The regression analyses were the easiest but gave us the least insight. Account analysis enabled us to look at the patterns of costs as they appear in the records. I think the engineering approach was most useful because it required me to work through exactly how the company gets customers, takes orders, prepares meals, and so forth. I learned how we can do some things better from that process. For example, I think we could take advantage of the learning effects by training our people more at the beginning and by finding ways to cut down on employee turnover."

Use of the Results

Cohen and Chun found the cost estimates to be generally useful and, in some cases, surprising. For example, they were surprised to see the cost per job was so low. Chun commented, "I thought the cost of taking the order, getting the food, setting up to prepare the meals, delivering the meals to the customer's location, and cleaning up afterward would be higher. I was prepared to charge a setup price to cover those costs and discourage small customers, but I see that I was wrong."

Cohen replied, "I agree, but I think we should consider a small setup charge in the future to cover the job costs. We should lower our price per meal a little—say by $.40 per meal to $3.60. That should make us even more competitive with Marriott and Saga if we try to get bigger jobs."

"Also, I think we should focus on reducing the unit cost per meal. I think our cramped space is keeping us from being more efficient in putting the meals together, not to mention that it creates a less-than-friendly work environment. We should look for better deals on quality food, too. Perhaps we can beat the local Safeway's, Farmer's Market, and Food Co-op prices," Chun added.

This discussion gives you a sense of the impact of the cost estimation results on CC Catering. Cohen and Chun also used the results to sharpen both their strategic business planning and their personal career planning.

Meals Sold

Recall that plans had been to sell 30,000 meals next year for $4 per meal. Cohen and Chun decided to experiment with their new idea of reducing the price to $3.60 per meal which, after some market research, they decided could increase the number of meals sold from the expected 30,000 (at a price of $4 per meal) to 35,000 meals. They expected to reduce costs per meal by reducing the preparation time and by shopping wisely to take advantage of discounts on food and supplies. They knew that inflation would drive up the cost of food and supplies. Considering all of this, they estimated the cost per meal to be $1.80 per meal on average over the next 12 months.

Jobs

Chun and Cohen expected the number of jobs to be about the same as the number over the previous 12 months because they expected to lose some smaller jobs but gain some larger ones. They estimated the number of jobs to be 500 over the next 12 months. All things considered, they hoped to reduce labor time on deliveries but knew they would be giving wage increases; they estimated the cost-driver rate to be $29.88 per job.

New Products

They estimated 20 new products over the next 12 months. They expected the cost per new product to be $170 (rounded to the nearest dollar).

New Customers

With the new pricing policy and an emphasis on developing customers who order more meals per job, they expected continued growth in their customer base. They expected approximately 120 new customers over the next 12 months. They estimated the average cost per new customer to be $127 (rounded to the nearest dollar).

Facilities

Considering inflation and the amortization of the cost of developing new workspace, they estimated the facilities cost to be $31,000 per year.

Taking all of this into account, Cohen and Chun developed the cost estimates for the next 12 months as shown in Exhibit 11–13.

Exhibit 11–13

CC Catering:
Cost Estimates

C.C. Catering

A Cost Driver	B Cost-Driver Volume*	C Cost per Cost-Driver Unit*	D Total Costs for Next 12 Months; Columns B × C
Meals sold	35,000	$ 1.80	$ 63,000
Jobs	500	29.88	14,940
New products	20	170	3,400
New customers	120	127	15,240
Facility and other			31,000
Total for the year			$127,580

*Data given in text.

Under this scenario, they expect to show a profit (loss) of:

$$\begin{aligned}\text{Operating profit (loss)} &= \text{Total revenue} - \text{Total costs}\\ &= (\$3.60 \times 35{,}000) - \$127{,}580\\ &= \$126{,}000 - \$127{,}580\\ &= \$(1{,}580)\end{aligned}$$

Although the estimates show a small loss for the next 12 months, Cohen and Chun were convinced that their strategy to lower pricing, reduce meal preparation costs, and improve the customer mix to focus on customers who order more meals per job would pay off in the long run.

After seeing these results, Chun pointed out that both women had been offered lucrative jobs in consulting. "Are we crazy to keep doing this catering business?" she asked.

"Maybe," Cohen replied. "We certainly aren't in it for the money. But I'm having a lot of fun, and I figure we can always get a job if this thing goes under. I say we stick with CC Catering for at least a few more years."

"I agree," said Chun.

The Outsourcing Decision

[C. C. Catering]

At the beginning of this chapter, we noted that Cohen and Chun considered outsourcing by subcontracting the meal preparation to a local sandwich shop. The sandwich shop would purchase the food and prepare the meals, thus eliminating some of the costs for the job cost driver and nearly all of the costs for the meals cost driver. The sandwich shop offered to do this work for $2.50 per meal.

Initially, Cohen and Chun thought the opportunity to outsource to be a good deal because they thought the cost per meal to be around $3. After going through the cost estimation exercise described in this chapter, however, they decided not to subcontract meal preparation to the sandwich shop. "We would save only $1.80 per meal at the unit level, and we would lose control over product quality," said Chun.

Cohen disagreed, "You haven't considered administrative opportunity costs of hiring and training food preparation people. Subcontracting meal preparation would free us to spend more time on marketing. Also, we could cut back on our rent and utilities because we would not need as much space." They agreed not to subcontract meal preparation at this time but to reconsider it in the future.

Costs and Benefits of Product Variety

Cohen and Chun also wondered about the costs and benefits of product variety. Companies with much product variety generally generate more revenue. However, research has shown that increasing product variety increases costs, even if volume does not increase. That is, product variety in itself is a cost driver. Chun commented, "I am intrigued by an article I found while doing a library search for publications on cost behavior. [See Research Insight 11.2.] According to the authors, carrying a wide range of products, or product variety, is known to affect costs. On the other hand, marketing studies show that increasing product variety increases revenues. What is not clear is whether the additional revenue from increasing product variety is enough to cover the related increase in costs."

"How does that apply to us?" Cohen asked.

"While we've had a lot of fun developing new meals and expanding our menu, we know from our cost estimation exercise that the cost of developing a new product is at least $150, maybe more. Do we gain enough additional revenue to justify those costs? The answer in the article that I read was no. I wonder what it would be for us," Chun asked.

Cohen laughed, "I think you are really hooked on cost estimation. I just hope I can get you back in the trenches for food prep."

Research
Insight 11.2

Product Variety and Costs

Several studies have shown that cost drivers other than volume affect total costs.* These studies indicate that the greater the variety of products carried by a company, the higher the company's costs, all things being equal. However, greater variety of products can also increase revenue. Some of the reasons are that customers prefer one-stop shopping and are more likely to make impulse purchases if there are more products from which to choose. The question is whether the additional revenues from maintaining a broad product line justify the additional costs. That is, would a company have greater profits with a narrower product line implying lower costs and lower revenues? Or would it be better off with a broader product line implying higher costs and higher revenues?

Professors Ittner, Larcker, and Randall studied the question of whether it was profitable to maintain a broader product line after considering both the costs and revenues implied by a broader product line in a company that produces outdoor packs (e.g., bicycle packs).† They found that greater product variety increased the company's costs, a result consistent with studies of other companies. They found that greater product variety increased the company's revenues, also. Taking into account both increased revenues and increased costs, they found, "the revenue gains from higher sales volumes and broader product lines were offset by increased costs . . . on average, the firm offered greater product variety than optimal."‡ In short, the company could have been more profitable if it had offered less product variety. Of course, these findings are limited by the data available to the researchers and do not consider future benefits that might accrue to the company in the future from having a broad product line today (e.g., dominance of the market might drive out competition). *Sources: *For example, see S. W. Anderson, "Measuring the Impact of Product Mix Heterogeneity on Manufacturing Overhead Cost; R. D. Banker, G. Potter, and R. G. Schroeder, "An Empirical Analysis of Manufacturing Overhead Cost Drivers"; and C. D. Ittner, D. F. Larcker, and T. Randall, "The Activity-Based Cost Hierarchy, Production Policies and Firm Profitability."*

†Ittner, Larcker, and Randall, "The Activity-Based Cost Hierarchy," pp. 143–162.

‡Ibid., p. 159.

Ethical Issues

[C.C. Catering]

Cost estimation results depend on the selection of cost drivers and on the data that are input. Analysts can manipulate the results by choosing particular cost drivers and by choosing particular data on which to do the estimates.

For an example of the effect of cost-driver selection, recall the simple and multiple regressions performed for CC Catering.

Simple regression: Total costs = \$2,619 + \$2.77 meals
Multiple regression: Total costs = \$2,177 + \$1.91 meals + \$28.18 jobs . . .

In the simple regression, the cost-driver rate per meal is \$2.77, whereas it is only \$1.91 in the multiple regression.[4] Suppose you are the manager of meals for CC Catering and are concerned that it will subcontract meal preparation to the local sandwich shop. Therefore, you want Cohen and Chun to believe you prepare meals at a lower cost than the sandwich shop. You would have incentives to choose cost drivers that make costs per meal appear low. In this case, you would choose the multiple regression over the simple regression.

You might even find ways to further reduce the cost-driver rate below \$1.91 by creatively selecting which months to include in the cost estimation. For example, reviewing the data input to the regression equation, suppose you find that meal costs were highest in three particular months. By omitting those months from the data, you

---

4One expects the cost-driver rate for the only cost driver in the simple regression to be higher than the same cost-driver rate in a multiple regression. The one cost driver in the simple regression picks up variation in costs that are associated with the cost drivers that are present in the multiple regression but missing in the simple regression. For example, meals in the simple regression probably pick up some variation in costs that are associated with jobs in the multiple regression.

could report a lower estimated cost per meal in your analysis. Of course, you would have to find a plausible reason to omit those months.

Playing games with models and data to get desired results is not ethical unless two conditions are satisfied: (1) one fully discloses what one has done and (2) the user of the results completely understands the implications of what has been done. If both of those conditions are satisfied, the manipulation of the model or data to get desired results is pointless.

Choice of Estimation Method

Each cost-estimation method discussed has advantages and disadvantages. If one has the capability to work with statistical software packages, regression analysis is usually the least costly method. Account analysis requires breakdowns of cost data that are expensive to obtain. In particular, regression requires only total cost data for each observation (i.e., each month for CC Catering), whereas account analysis requires the cost data to be divided into categories that correspond to the cost drivers (e.g., units, jobs, new products, new customers, and facility-level costs for CC Catering). Engineering estimates are costly because they require identifying and assigning a cost to each activity required to produce a good or service.

Relevance of Data Inputs

Regression and account analysis have a disadvantage because they rely on past data. The past might not be a good prediction of the future. Engineering estimates, on the other hand, rely on the present and therefore are likely to provide more relevant information. Each cost-estimation method might yield a different estimate of the costs that are likely to result from a particular management decision. This underscores the advantages of using two or more methods to arrive at a final estimate. By observing the range of cost estimates from different methods, management might be better able to decide whether to gather more data.

Costs and Benefits of More Sophisticated and Detailed Methods

Cost-management analysts must decide when the use of a more sophisticated and, therefore, more costly, cost estimation method is important. As with other managerial decisions, they should evaluate the costs and benefits of various cost-estimation techniques. If different estimates give about the same cost estimates, cost-management analysts might conclude that additional information gathering is not warranted.

Although Cohen and Chun were pleased with their cost estimation work for CC Catering, they decided not to perform so much analysis next time. They decided that they should go through the exercise once per year. Next year they would use multiple regression to estimate costs for all cost drivers. In addition, they would do engineering analysis for meal costs because they wanted to keep continuous track of those costs. They believed this was a reasonable compromise between simple and complex data analysis that would be relatively inexpensive yet provide them with relevant information.

Choice of Cost Equation

Sometimes analysts prepare several alternative cost equations. These alternatives could result from the use of alternative cost estimation methods: regression, account analysis, or engineering. Or they could result from the choice of several cost equations from using one method. For example, analysts frequently prepare several alternative cost equations using regression analysis by using various sets of independent variables. Which should one select among several possible cost equations?

We recommend using the following criteria to select among alternative estimated cost equations.

- *Economic plausibility.* This is the most important criterion. The independent variables should be plausible. The cost equation should make sense. It is always possible to find some association among variables that are not logically related, enter data, and print out a sophisticated-looking result.[5] Be sure the cost drivers are reasonable causes of costs.
- *Goodness of fit.* All other things equal, how well the variation in the independent variables explains variation in the dependent variables is important. In regression analysis, R^2, or adjusted R^2, is one estimate of goodness of fit. For account analysis and engineering methods, which do not have an R^2, one typically uses good sense and judgment to assess goodness of fit.
- *Significance of the independent variables.* Are the independent variables significant? The Appendix to this chapter discusses a statistical test used in regression. For account analysis and engineering estimates, one uses good sense and judgment to assess the significance of independent variables. Good sense and good judgment are valuable characteristics of successful cost-management analysts (and other managers, for that matter).

---

[5]To make this point, we know of an analyst who performed a regression analysis with the telephone numbers of department heads as the independent variable and department costs as the dependent variable. This analyst reported the results, tongue-in-cheek, only to find that some managers took the results seriously.

Chapter Summary

Cost estimation is the process of estimating the relationship between costs and the cost drivers that cause those costs. Companies estimate costs for three purposes: to manage costs, to make decisions, and to plan and set standards. The simplest cost behavior pattern is the breakdown of costs into fixed and variable components. More complex cost patterns include step costs (also known as *semifixed costs*), semivariable costs, and learning curves.

The three major methods of cost estimation are as follows: statistical methods using regression analysis, account analysis, and engineering estimates. Regression analysis is a statistical method used to relate independent variables (known as *cost drivers* in our application) to dependent variables (known as *costs* in our application). Simple regression has one independent variable; multiple regression has more than one independent variable. Using the account analysis method, an analyst separates costs from the accounting records into categories that correspond to the cost drivers. In the chapter example, that means the analyst separates monthly costs for CC Catering into unit-level costs, job-level costs, new-product costs, new-customer costs, and facilities-level costs.

Whereas regression and account analysis rely on past data, engineering estimates use data from current practices. Analysts (who are usually engineers) make engineering estimates by first measuring the work involved in the activities that go into a product and by then assigning a cost to each of those activities. Regression analysis usually requires fewer data than account analysis because it does not require costs to be divided into categories that correspond to cost drivers. Engineering estimates are probably the most costly method because they require time-consuming effort to identify activities and assign costs to them. Probably the most informative estimate of cost behavior results from using more than one of the methods because each has the potential to provide information that the others do not.

Key Terms

For each term's definition, refer to the indicated page or turn to the glossary at the end of the text.

account analysis, 444
cost estimation, 426
dependent variables, 435
engineering estimate, 447
high-low method, 438
independent variables, 435
learning curve, 432
learning phenomenon, 431
multicollinearity*, 458
multiple regression, 440
***R*-square, 439**

*Terms appear in the chapter Appendix.

Meeting the Cost-Management Challenges

1. Why should CC Catering estimate costs?

Estimating the relationship between costs and activities will help Cohen and Chun (a) in cost management, (b) in decision making, and (c) in planning and standard setting. Cost estimation helps cost management by pinpointing activities that are costly. It helps with decision making by informing managers about the costs of alternative actions they might consider. In planning, cost estimation helps managers know the amount of costs to be expected for a given level of activities. In standard setting, it estimates what the costs should be for performing particular activities.

2. What cost patterns do the (a) food, (b) cellular telephone, and (c) delivery labor costs at CC Catering follow?

Food is a variable cost. Cellular telephone costs are semivariable costs. Delivery labor costs are step costs.

3. After doing the multiple regression analysis, what additional information did Leah Cohen require to estimate costs using account analysis?

Her account analysis required a breakdown of monthly costs into those related to each of the four cost drivers—units, jobs, new products, and new customers—and those related to facilities.

4. What are the advantages to using the engineering method at CC Catering?

The engineering method forced Chun to work through all activities. From that process, she learned how to do some things better, such as taking advantage of the learning curve by improving training and finding ways to reduce employee turnover.

5. Based on information from the cost estimates and considering CC Catering's new strategy, will the company be successful in the future?

Acknowledging that there is no objective answer to a question such as this, we believe they will be successful. They have survived the early difficult years of a new business and have developed a customer base in the process. They are thoughtful managers with a sensible strategy.

6. Should Cohen and Chun give up CC Catering and take jobs in consulting?

Good jobs in consulting are to be taken seriously, as are the opportunity costs of lost salary and lost development of personal human capital to be gained from consulting. But starting one's own business and making it work has a special kind of reward. At worst, Cohen and Chun can continue with CC Catering for a few more years, sell the business, go back to school for an MBA, and take an even better job in consulting. We recommend that they hang in there with CC Catering for a few more years.

Solutions to You're the Decision Maker

11.1 Using Learning Curves in Marketing Products p. 434

a. The following chart shows the average and total cost at 1, 2, 4, 8, and 16 units.

Cumulative Number of Units Produced	Average Manufacturing Cost per Unit		Total Manufacturing Costs
1	$1,333		$1,333
2	1,000	($1,333 × 75%)	2,000 (2 units × $1,000)
4	750	($1,000 × 75%)	3,000 (4 units × $750)
8	562.50	($750 × 75%)	4,500 (8 units × $562.50)
16	421.88	($562.50 × 75%)	6,750 (16 units × $421.88)

b. If the learning curve is 75 percent, you will be able to sell 4 units and have a margin exceeding 20 percent of revenue: 4 units × ($1,000 − $750) = $1,000 margin; $1,000 margin ÷ $4,000 revenue = 25%. You could even give CC Catering a good deal and still make a healthy margin if you could sell 8 or 16 units. For example, suppose you offered to sell 8 units for $800 each. What would be your margin expressed in dollars and as a percentage of revenues?

Answer: (8 units × \$800 sales price) − (8 units × \$562.50 cost) = \$6,400 revenue − \$4,500 costs = \$1,900 margin. \$1,900 margin ÷ \$6,400 revenue = 30%. You could give CC Catering a good deal and still earn a margin of 30 percent. This exercise demonstrates the power of understanding the learning phenomenon.

c. Product designers, production managers, and cost-management analysts must be involved to estimate the cost of custom products. Also, industrial engineers, perhaps as consultants, do the studies to estimate the cumulative learning curve (75 percent in this example; 80 percent for CC Catering in the text example). Finally, marketing employees should be involved, as this example demonstrates, because they can use their understanding of learning curves to make better deals both for their company and for the customer.

11.2 Using Regression p. 444

a. The major benefits of simple regression are that it requires fewer data and is less likely to overload decision makers with information. Its major weaknesses, compared to multiple regression, are that it does not provide estimates of the other three cost-driver rates that multiple regression provided. Furthermore, the cost function for simple regression does not estimate costs as accurately as the multiple regression cost function because it omits some variables that are cost drivers.

b. The estimated costs for December equal \$8,215.42, as shown in the following table.

A	B	C	D
Facility	1	\$2,177.00	\$2,177.00
Meals	1,800	1.91	3,438.00
Jobs	30	28.18	845.40
New products	2	160.03	320.06
New customers	12	119.58	1,434.96
Total costs			\$8,215.42

11.3 Using Account Analysis p. 446

a. Cohen had to obtain costs for each month for *each of the cost-driver categories* listed in columns C through G in Exhibit 11–11. The regression analysis required only total costs per month—the amounts shown in column B.

b. The estimated costs for December equal \$8,185.51, as shown in the following table.

A	B	C	D
Facility	1	\$2,064.19	\$2,064.19
Meals	1,800	1.90	3,420.00
Jobs	30	30.56	916.80
New products	2	165.00	330.00
New customers	12	121.21	1,454.52
Total costs			\$8,185.51

Appendix to Chapter Eleven

Technical Notes on Regression

LO 6 Identify potential statistical problems with regression analysis (Appendix).

This Appendix discusses technical issues that often arise when using regression analysis. You should not view the Appendix as a substitute for courses and books that deal with these issues in much more depth. The purpose here is to alert you to issues of concern. The old adage that a little knowledge is a dangerous thing applies in a big way to regression analysis. You should always consult an expert in statistics when using regression analysis (just as statisticians should consult cost experts when using costs in their statistical analyses). Teamwork pays.

Confidence in the Coefficients

The ***t*-statistic,** t, *is the value of* b, *the coefficient, divided by its standard error,* SE_b

It is reasonable for managers to ask whether the *b's* (that is, the coefficients of the independent variables) are significantly different from zero. That is, do changes in the independent variables result in significant changes in the dependent variable? The ***t*-statistic** is used to test for the significance of the *b's*. This *t* is simply the value of *b* divided by its standard error (SE_b). The standard error of *b* is a measure of the uncertainty about the *b*; the larger the standard error, the more the dispersion of *b* values and the more uncertainty about its value.

Recall that for CC Catering, we estimated the relationship between the variation in the number of meals and the variation in total monthly costs in the simple regression. The coefficient *b* was the cost-driver rate for meals. As you may recall, that cost-driver rate, or *b,* was \$2.7684 (not rounded). Although we did not report it in the text, the standard error of that coefficient was \$.1988. Therefore, the *t*-statistic for the coefficient *b* is:

$$t = b/SE_b$$
$$= \$2.7684 \div \$.1988$$
$$= 13.93$$

where both the *b* and the SE_b are given by the computer output of the regression. As a rule of thumb, a *t* of 2.0 or better is usually considered statistically significant. With $t > 2.0$, analysts generally assume that the regression results are not due to chance. Clearly, the cost driver rate, \$2.7684, is statistically significant.

To construct a 95 percent confidence interval around *b*, we add to or subtract from *b* the appropriate *t* value for the 95 percent confidence interval times the standard error of *b*, as follows:

$$b \pm (t \times SE_b)$$

Recall that for this example, $SE_b = \$0.1988$. The value of *t* for a 95 percent confidence interval may be obtained from a table of *t* values in a statistics book. From this table, we find:

$$t = 2.145$$

Hence, the confidence intervals are:

$$b \pm (2.145 \times \$.1988) = b \pm \$.426$$

With *b* equal to \$2.7684, the upper limit is:

$$\$3.194 \text{ (that is, } \$2.7684 + \$.426)$$

and the lower confidence limit is:

$$\$2.342 \text{ (that is, } \$2.7684 - \$.426)$$

We would be 95 percent confident that the variable cost of a meal is between \$2.342 and \$3.194.

Assumptions about the Residuals

The differences between the estimated *Y* values (found on the regression line) and the actual *Y*'s are called *residuals.* If a residual is random, its expected value is zero for any observation. The three important assumptions about the residuals are that (1) they are normally distributed, (2) they are independent of each other, and (3) their variance is constant over the range of independent variables. Violation of these assumptions makes certain inferences about regression estimates questionable.

We mention these assumptions because they are often violated for cost data. Consequently, one should be careful about the inferences drawn from regression analyses. You should consult statistics books for more information about how to deal with violations of these assumptions.

Residuals are normally distributed. Drawing inferences about the predicted value, *Y* (total costs in the text examples), or the *b's* (cost-driver rates in the text examples) requires the residuals to be normally distributed around the regression line. If residuals are normally distributed, the expected value for the residual is zero. If the residuals are not normally distributed, the residual for any observation may be statistically related to that for another observation.

Residuals are independent. A common condition in which residuals are not independent occurs when observations are related to each other over time. This is known as *serial correlation* or *autocorrelation.* Serial correlation does not affect the accuracy of the *b*'s in the regression equation, but it affects the standard errors of the coefficients (i.e., the SE_b's). This effect on the standard errors affects the *t*-statistics and confidence intervals discussed earlier. The presence of serial correlation might be tested using the Durbin-Watson statistic, which is provided by regression software packages such as SAS and SPSS.

Variance of residuals is constant. The assumption of constant variance implies that the residuals are not affected by the level of the independent variable. For example, this means that the residuals are not systematically higher if the cost-driver volume is higher. Constant variance is known as *homoscedasticity.* Nonconstant variance is known as *heteroscedasticity.* (Try these words in a spelling bee.) As with serial correlation, heteroscedasticity does not affect the accuracy of the *b*'s in the regression equation, but it affects the standard errors of the coefficients (i.e., the SE_b's), which affects the *t*-statistics and confidence intervals discussed earlier.

For simple regressions, one can ascertain whether heteroscedasticity is present by plotting the residuals over different values of *Y.* If the scatter of residuals is not constant over these *Y* values, the residuals are likely to be heteroscedastic. In some cases, the problem can be cured by transforming the variables (*X*'*s* and/or *Y*'*s*) to their logarithms or square roots or by constructing a regression with a new set of variables.

Multicollinearity

If more than one predictor variable is used, as in multiple regression, the interpretation of the *b*'*s* as variable costs is somewhat more hazardous. Assume that a regression of machine hours and direct materials costs gave the following correlation matrix. The matrix shows that the machine hours and direct material dollars are highly correlated with each other (that is, a correlation of .832).

Estimate of *b*	
Machine hours	4.359
Direct materials cost	.258

Correlation Matrix	**Machine Hours**	**Direct Materials Costs**
Machine hours	1.00	.832
Direct materials costs	.832	1.00

This means that there is overlapping explanatory power among the two predictors. This problem is referred to as **multicollinearity.** It does not affect the *Y* estimate, but it does affect the interpretation of the contribution that each of the *X*'*s* (that is, direct material dollars and machine hours) is making to the prediction of *Y.* With multicollinearity, one can still estimate total costs from the cost equation, but one must question the accuracy of the particular cost-driver rates.

multicollinearity *is the correlation between two or more independent variables in a multiple regression equation*

Review Questions

11.1 For what reasons do companies estimate the relationship between costs and cost drivers?

11.2 Which method of cost estimation is least based on company records?

11.3 True or false: The relevant range is usually the range of observations included in a data set for cost-estimation purposes.

11.4 Under what conditions is the engineering method preferred to other estimation methods?

11.5 What problems might you encounter if you simply enter data into a program to compute regression estimates?

11.6 When using cost-estimation methods based on past data, what are the trade-offs between gathering more and fewer data?

11.7 Give an example of a step cost other than the examples mentioned in the text.

11.8 (Appendix) What is the purpose of the *t*-statistic?

11.9 (Appendix) True or false: Violations of assumptions that residuals are independent and are homoscedastic means that the cost drivers are correlated.

Critical Analysis

11.10 The following costs are labeled fixed or variable according to a typical designation in accounting. Under which circumstances would any of these costs behave in a manner opposite to that listed?

a. Direct labor—variable.

b. Equipment depreciation—fixed.

c. Utilities—variable.

d. Supervisory salaries—fixed.

11.11 Your boss says, "I don't trust regression analysis with all that mumbo jumbo. Give me an account analysis any time." How would you respond?

11.12 An associate of yours states, "I would never use account analysis or regression because the past is a poor predictor of the future." How would you respond?

11.13 How can one compensate for the effects of inflation when preparing cost estimates using regression techniques?

11.14 The fast-food restaurant McDonald's is known for high employee turnover, high quality, and low costs. Using your knowledge of the learning phenomenon, how does McDonald's get high quality and low costs when it has so much employee turnover?

11.15 Your boss says, "People who use multiple regression are indecisive. They cannot figure out what cost driver to use, so they throw a bunch of them into the analysis. Give me a cost-management analyst who uses simple regression with just one cost driver. Now that is a decisive person." How would you respond to justify the use of multiple regression?

11.16 Search the Internet using the word "regression" in your search. For sites discussing statistical regression (as opposed to behavioral regression, for example), list at least five applications of regressions. (*Hint:* You almost certainly will encounter a discussion of the use of regression in economics.)

11.17 A friend comes to you with the following problem. "I provided my boss a cost equation based on account analysis. He was unhappy with the results. He told me to do more work and not return until I had a lower cost estimate for one of the cost drivers—number of setups. My analysis covered the last 12 months, January through December of last year. I found that by including the 12 months before that, January through December of the year before last, I was able to get a lower estimated cost-driver rate for number of setups. My boss was happy with my new results. Do you think that what I did was unethical?" How would you respond?

11.18 After performing a regression analysis and giving the results to your boss, you discover an error in the data. Because of keyboard errors, you understated costs by three digits. For example, you entered \$100 when you should have punched in \$100,000. When you told your boss about the error, your boss said that the analysis had already been passed on to a top executive who was going to use it in a presentation to the board of directors tomorrow. Your boss does not want to tell the top executive about the error. Should you?

11.19 In doing an account analysis, you realize that there could be errors in the accounting records. For example, maintenance costs were recorded as zero in December. However, you know that maintenance was performed in December. You find that maintenance costs were about double the normal monthly amount in the next month, January. You suspect that maintenance costs were not recorded in December, the last month of the year, so the department's costs would appear to be below budget. The apparent error has no effect on your analysis because you are using both December and January in your analysis. Should you report your concerns about the way maintenance costs were recorded? If so, to whom would you report your concerns?

11.20 Assume that you are performing multiple regression using data from several countries. What potential problems might you encounter when using data from multiple countries?

Exercises

Exercise 11.21
Cost-Behavior Patterns
(LO 2)

Label each of the following graphs as to cost pattern: variable, fixed, step, semivariable.

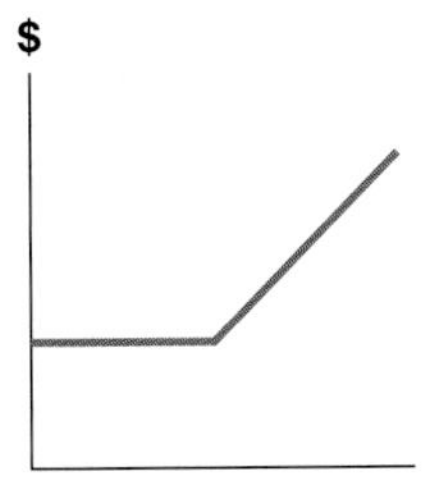

a.

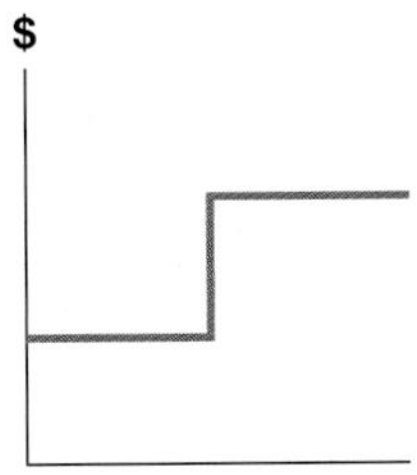

b.

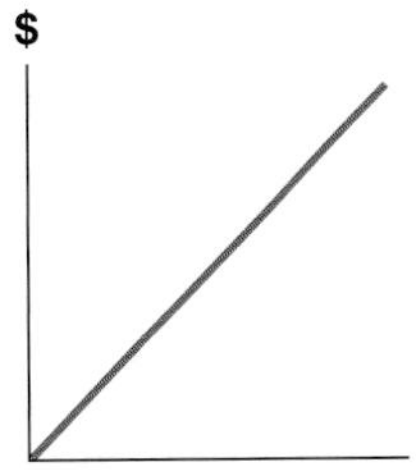

c.

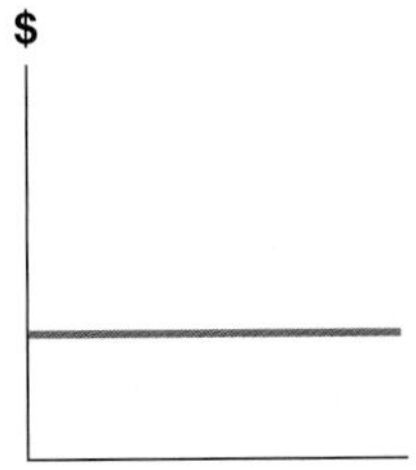

d.

Exercise 11.22
Cost-Behavior Patterns
(LO 2)

Select the following graph that best matches the description of each of the following cost items.

a. A telephone bill where the amount charged has two components: (1) a fixed amount for the first 60 minutes per month and (2) a variable cost for usage greater than 60 minutes per month. The horizontal axis is number of telephone minutes.

b. Insurance on an automobile for which the insured pays a fixed amount for the first 10,000 miles per year, and then the rate increases in a step as the car is driven more than 10,000 miles per year. The horizontal axis is the number of miles driven per year.

c. Wages paid to strawberry pickers paid $4 per crate picked. The horizontal axis is the number of crates of strawberries picked.

d. The salary of a college professor who is paid the same (low) salary regardless of the number of students taught. The horizontal axis is number of students taught.

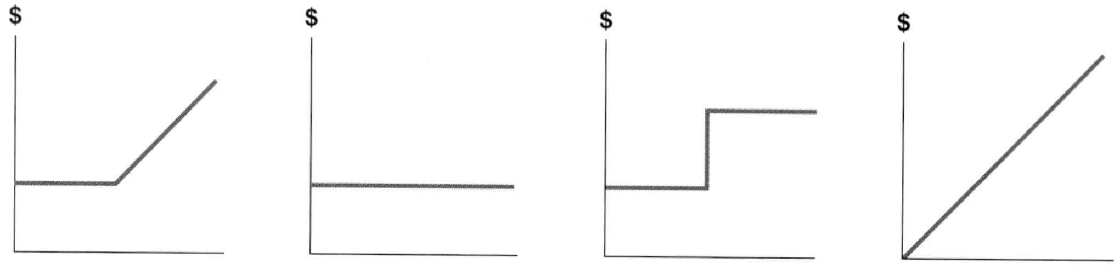

1. **2.** **3.** **4.**

Exercise 11.23
Learning Curves
(LO 2)

Assume that General Electric, which manufactures high-technology instruments for spacecraft, is considering the sale of a navigational unit to a government agency in India that wishes to launch its own communications satellite. The government agency plans to purchase eight units for a total of $2,500,000, although it would also consider buying 16 units for a total of $4,000,000. General Electric requires a margin of 40 percent of sales to cover administrative costs, contribute to basic research, and make a profit. For example, the sale of eight units must cost no more than $1,500,000 to produce [(1.00 − .40) × $2,500,000]. General Electric has started a chart for this product assuming the production costs are subject to a 75 percent cumulative learning curve.

Cumulative Number of Units Produced	Average Production Cost per Unit	Total Production Costs
1	$400,000	$400,000
2	300,000	600,000
4	?	?
8	?	?
16	?	?

Required

a. Complete the chart by filling in the cost amounts for volumes of 4, 8, and 16 units.

b. Should General Electric sell eight units? Should it sell 16 units?

Exercise 11.24
Learning Curves
(LO 2)

Assume that Whee, Cheatham, and Howe is an auditing firm that has found that its summer interns are subject to an 80 percent cumulative learning curve for one of its important tasks, proofreading financial statements. For one of its interns, Kim Down, the firm has started to analyze the relationship between costs and financial statement proofreading.

Cumulative Number of Financial Statements Proofread	Average Time Spent per Financial Statement	Total Time Spent
1	30 hours	30 hours
2	24 hours	48 hours
4	?	?
8	?	?
16	?	?

Required

a. Complete the chart by filling in the amounts for volumes of 4, 8, and 16 units.

b. If Down is paid $30 per hour, how much will it cost, in total, for Down to proofread 8 financial statements?

Exercise 11.25
Learning Curves
(LO 2)

Assume that the manager of a Ben and Jerry's ice cream shop uses the learning curve to estimate the cost of preparing a healthy product called carrot-tofu low-fat frozen yogurt in a whole wheat cone. The manager applies the learning curve to a new employee, Scoop Upf, assuming that preparation of this product is subject to a 75 percent cumulative learning curve.

Cumulative Number of Units Produced	Average Time Spent per Unit	Total Time Spent
1	8 minutes	8 minutes
2	6 minutes	12 minutes
4	?	?
8	?	?
16	?	?

Required

a. Complete the chart by filling in the amounts for volumes of 4, 8, and 16 units.

b. If Scoop is paid $12 per hour, how much will it cost, in total, for Scoop to produce 8 units?

Exercise 11.26
Simple Regression
(LO 3)

Aliens, Inc., has developed a regression equation to analyze the behavior of its maintenance costs (C) as a function of machine hours (MH). The following equation was developed using 30 months of data:

$$C = \$6{,}000 + \$5.25MH$$

Required

Using this cost equation, what are the total maintenance costs for 500 machine hours?

[CPA adapted]

Exercise 11.27
Simple Regression
(LO 3)

I. R. Esse Tax Consultants has developed a regression equation to analyze the behavior of its tax return preparation costs (C) as a function of the number of returns prepared (TR). The following equation was developed to estimate tax return preparation costs. Analysts used 24 observations of data for last year, one observation for each of its 24 offices:

$$C = \$112{,}000 + \$154TR$$

Required

What is the estimated tax return preparation cost for an office that prepares 1,000 tax returns?

[CPA adapted]

Exercise 11.28
Simple Regression
(LO 3)

The regression results for CC Catering in Exhibit 11–9 give the following equation:

$$\text{Total costs} = \$2{,}619 + \$2.77 \text{ meals}$$

Required

a. What are the estimated total costs for a month in which 3,000 meals will be sold?

b. What are the estimated fixed costs for a month in which 3,000 meals will be sold?

c. What are the estimated total variable costs for a month in which 3,000 meals will be sold?

d. What might be a problem with using the results in Exhibit 11–9 if CC Catering plans to sell 7,000 meals in a month?

Exercise 11.29
Simple Regression
(LO 3)

The regression results for CC Catering in Exhibit 11–9 give the following equation:

$$\text{Total costs} = \$2{,}619 + \$2.77 \text{ meals}$$

Required

a. What are the estimated total costs for a month in which 2,200 meals will be sold?

b. What are the estimated fixed costs for a month in which 2,200 meals will be sold?

c. What are the estimated total variable costs for a month in which 2,200 meals will be sold?

d. What might be a problem with using the results in Exhibit 11–9 if CC Catering plans to sell 400 meals in a month?

Exercise 11.30
Simple Regression
(LO 3)

The regression results for CC Catering in Exhibit 11–9 give the following results:

$$\text{Total costs} = \$2{,}619 + \$2.77 \text{ meals}$$

Required

a. What are the estimated total costs for a month in which 2,100 meals will be sold?

b. What are the estimated fixed costs for a month in which 2,100 meals will be sold?

c. What are the estimated total variable costs for a month in which 2,100 meals will be sold?

d. What might be a problem with using the results in Exhibit 11–9 if CC Catering plans to sell 8,000 meals in a month?

Exercise 11.31
Multiple Regression
(LO 3)

The regression results for CC Catering in Exhibit 11–10 give the following results:

$$\text{Total costs} = \$2{,}177 + \$1.91 \text{ meals} + \$28.18 \text{ jobs} + \$160.03 \text{ new products} + \$119.58 \text{ new customers}$$

Required

What are the estimated total costs in a month in which there are:

2,000 meals sold
30 jobs
1 new product
2 new customers

Exercise 11.32
Multiple Regression
(LO 3)

The regression results for CC Catering in Exhibit 11–10 give the following results:

$$\text{Total costs} = \$2{,}177 + \$1.91 \text{ meals} + \$28.18 \text{ jobs} + \$160.03 \text{ new products} + \$119.58 \text{ new customers}$$

Required

What are the estimated total costs in a month in which there are:

3,000 meals sold
40 jobs
4 new products
8 new customers

Exercise 11.33
High-Low and Simple Regression
(LO 3)

Fast Eddie's Limo Service operates a fleet of limousines. Management wants to estimate the fixed and variable costs per mile. A recent trade publication indicated that variable costs should be no more than $.25 per mile. To check his costs against those indicated in the trade journal, Fast Eddie collected the following data for his limousine fleet for last month:

Limousine Number	Costs	Miles
1	$3,500	12,400
2	3,400	11,800
3	3,200	10,600
4	3,800	11,500
5	3,500	11,800
6	4,000	13,200
7	3,200	9,800
8	3,000	9,200
9	4,200	11,700
10	3,900	12,300

Required

a. Use the high-low method to estimate the fixed and variable portions of overhead costs based on miles driven.

b. What is the estimated total variable cost of driving one limousine 10,000 miles?

c. Fast Eddie has heard that the high-low method has one major limitation compared to simple regression. What is it?

Exercise 11.34
High-Low Compared to Simple Regression
(LO 3)

(Computer required.) Refer to the data for Fast Eddie's Limousine Service in Exercise 11.33.

Required

Using miles as the cost driver, what are the simple regression results for Fast Eddie's Limousine Service?

Exercise 11.35
High-Low and Simple Regression
(LO3)

Spreadsheet

Feno Menn, the owner of Phenomeno's Pizza, wishes to estimate the fixed and variable costs per pizza to benchmark its costs against some data obtained from a competitor, Domino's Pizza. Feno collected the following data from the accounting records.

Month	Pizza Production Costs	Number of Pizzas Produced
1	$28,560	8,600
2	31,400	9,800
3	33,200	12,600
4	32,800	12,500
5	36,500	14,800
6	41,100	15,200
7	30,200	9,800
8	34,000	10,200
9	41,200	14,700
10	30,900	13,300

Required

a. Use the high-low method to estimate the fixed and variable portions of overhead costs based on number of pizzas produced.

b. What is the estimated total variable cost for a month in which 4,000 pizzas are produced?

c. Feno has heard that the high-low method has one major limitation compared to simple regression. What is it?

Exercise 11.36
High-Low Compared to Simple Regression
(LO 3)

Spreadsheet

(Computer required.) Refer to the data for Phenomeno's Pizza in Exercise 11.35.

Required

Using pizzas produced as the cost driver, what are the simple regression results for Phenomeno's Pizza?

Exercise 11.37
Interpretation of Regression Results
(LO 3)

Customers 'R First Bank is planning to offer a new debit card for which it expects to charge $1 per transaction. The following cost estimates have been made assuming 1 million transactions during the first month that the card is used.

Direct labor $500,000 (the labor rate is $25 an hour × 20,000 estimated direct-labor hours)

Overhead costs have not yet been estimated for the new product, but monthly data on total production and overhead costs have been analyzed for similar products using simple linear regression. The following results were derived from the simple regression and provide the basis for overhead cost estimates for the new product.

Simple regression analysis results based on the monthly data

Dependent variable—Overhead costs

Independent variable—Direct labor hours

Computed values

Intercept	$110,000
Coefficient of independent variable	$5.40
R^2	.908

Required

a. What percentage of the variation in overhead costs is explained by the independent variable?

b. What is the total overhead cost for an estimated activity level of 20,000 direct-labor hours per month?

c. Will the $1 per transaction charge cover the costs of direct labor and overhead, assuming one million transactions?

[CMA adapted]

Exercise 11.38
Interpretation of Regression Results
(LO 3)

The advertising manager of Leonine Company wants to know whether the company's advertising program is successful. The manager used a spreadsheet to estimate the relationship between number of advertisements (the independent variable) and sales dollars. Monthly data for the past two years were entered into the computer. The regression results indicated the following equation:

$$\text{Sales} = \$845{,}000 - (\$520 \times \text{Number of advertisements})$$
$$R^2 = .81$$

These results might imply that the advertising was reducing sales. The manager was about to conclude that statistical methods were so much nonsense when you walked into the room.

Required

Help the manager. What might cause the negative relationship between advertising and sales?

Exercise 11.39
Interpretation of Regression Results: Simple Regression
(LO 3)

Mimi's Dance Studio estimates costs based on student hours of instruction, where 1 student receiving a private lesson for 1 hour is "1 student hour." Data were gathered for the past 24 months and entered into a regression program. The following output was obtained:

Intercept	$ 1,450
Coefficient of the independent variable (student hours)	$33.150
R^2	.760

The company is planning to operate at a level of 250 student hours per month during the coming year.

Required

a. Use the regression output to write the cost equation.

b. Based on the cost equation, compute the estimated cost per month for the coming year.

Exercise 11.40
Account Analysis Method
(LO 4)

Farside Cards makes and produces greeting cards. Every month, it produces from 5 to 15 new products in batches. At the end of the month, the company destroys the master copy of all existing cards so that it produces new card products each month. The costs of designing the card, including design and art work, are product-level costs. The costs of materials, ink, and other printing costs are unit-level costs. The costs of setting up the production run are batch-level costs. All other costs are facility-level costs. Farside's accounting records report the following production costs for last December:

Unit-level costs	$24,000
Batch-level costs	8,000
Product-level costs	18,000
Facility-level costs	25,000

Production was 100,000 units for 10 different new products produced in 100 batches.

Costs for this coming December are expected to increase over last December's costs as follows: the unit-level costs, 20 percent per unit; the batch-level costs, increase 10 percent per batch; the product-level costs, 10 percent per product; and the facility-level costs, 10 percent for the month.

Required

a. What is the unit-level cost per unit for last December?

b. What is the estimated unit-level cost per unit for this coming December?

c. What are the estimated facility-level costs for this coming December?

d. If Farside expects to produce 120,000 units for 12 new products in 100 batches this coming December, what will be its estimated total costs for the month?

Exercise 11.41
Account Analysis Method
(LO 4)

Highland Music records and sells music. Every month, it produces several new products in batches. The costs of making the master CD, including hiring musicians and studio costs, are product-level costs. The costs of materials and packaging are unit-level costs. The costs of setting up the production run are batch-level costs. All other costs are facility-level costs. Highland Music's accounting records report the following production costs for January of this year:

Unit-level costs	$160,000
Batch-level costs	40,000
Product-level costs	180,000
Facility-level costs	50,000

Production was 50,000 units for eight new products, produced in 50 batches.

Costs for June of this year are expected to increase over the costs for January of this year as follows: the unit-level costs, 5 percent per unit; the batch-level costs, 4 percent per batch; the product-level costs, 4 percent per product; and the facility-level costs, 5 percent for the month.

Required

a. What is the unit-level cost per unit, the batch-level cost per batch and the product-level cost per product for January of this year?

b. What are the estimated facility-level costs for June of this year?

c. If in June of this year, Highland Music expects to produce 60,000 units for 12 new products in 100 batches, what will be its estimated total costs for the month?

Exercise 11.42
Account Analysis
(LO 4)

The account analysis results for CC Catering in Exhibit 11–11 give the following results:

Total costs = $2,064 for the facility + $1.90 per meal + $30.56 per job + $165.00 per new product + $121.21 per new customer

Required

What are the estimated total costs in a month in which there are:

3,000 meals sold
30 jobs
4 new products
10 new customers

(Don't forget the facility costs.)

Exercise 11.43
Engineering Estimates
(LO 5)

The engineering cost estimates for CC Catering presented in Exhibit 11–12 give the following results:

Total costs = $2,210 for the facility + $1.88 per meal + $35.50 per job + $168.00 per new product + $122.00 per new customer

Required

What are the estimated total costs in a month in which there are:

3,500 meals sold
50 jobs
5 new products
8 new customers

(Don't forget the facility costs.)

Unsafe Insurance Company needs to forecast its personnel department costs. The following output was obtained from a regression program used to estimate the department's costs as a function of the number of employees:

Exercise 11.44
Interpretation of Regression Data (Appendix)
(LO 6)

Equation

$$\text{Personnel costs} = \$8{,}420 + \$493.20 \text{ employees}$$

Statistical data

R^2	.852
SE_b	34.25
t-statistic for b	14.4

Monthly data for the past two years were used to construct these estimates. Cost relationships are expected to be the same for the coming period.

Required

a. What are the estimated personnel costs for 4,200 employees?

b. (Appendix) Construct a 95 percent confidence interval for the slope coefficient. (Use $t = 2.074$.)

Problems

Problem 11.45
Methods of Cost Estimation: Account Analysis, Simple and Multiple Regression
(LO 3, 4)

University Hospital has prepared a schedule of estimated overhead costs for its blood test unit for the coming year on the assumption that production will be 80,000 tests for the year. Costs have been classified as fixed or variable, according to the controller's judgment.

The following overhead items are classified as fixed or variable:

Item	Cost	
Supplies	$ 37,500	(all variable)
Indirect labor	194,200	($171,000 fixed)
Building occupancy	236,420	(all fixed)
Utilities	27,210	(all variable)
Equipment depreciation	181,000	(all fixed)
Equipment maintenance	24,330	($8,500 fixed)
Data processing	25,320	($15,820 fixed)
Technical support	16,940	(all fixed)
Total estimated overhead	$742,920	

In the past, the overhead costs have been related to the number of tests. Price instability has led management to suggest, however, that explicit consideration be given to including an appropriate price index that adjusts the historical data for inflation. Following management instructions, data were gathered on past costs, past production levels, and an appropriate price index for each period.

When these data were entered into a regression program using only the production level as the independent variable, the following results were obtained:

$$\text{Overhead} = \$626{,}547 + (\$1.504 \times \text{Number of tests})$$
$$R^2 = .976$$

When both independent variables were entered in the regression program, the following results were obtained:

$$\text{Overhead} = \$632{,}640 + (\$1.501 \times \text{Number of tests}) + (\$59.067 \times \text{Index})$$
$$\text{Adjusted } R^2 = .972$$

Required

a. Prepare a cost-estimation equation using the account analysis approach in which the only independent variable is the number of tests.

b. Prepare a cost estimate for 80,000 tests for the coming year using the simple regression results.

c. Use the multiple regression results to estimate overhead costs for 80,000 tests and a price index of 113 for the coming period.

Problem 11.46
Various Methods of Cost Estimation
(LO 3, 4)

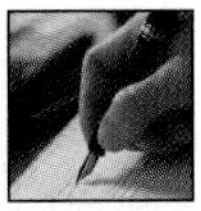

Team Communication

Refer to your results in Problem 11.45.

Required

As a group, decide which method you think is best to estimate costs: simple regression, multiple regression, or account analysis. Also recommend whether management should use just one method, any two of the methods, or all three methods. Consider both the costs and benefits of using multiple cost estimation methods in your recommendation. Have a member of your group write a short report to management that expresses your group's views.

Problem 11.47
Interpretation of Regression Results: Simple Regression
(LO 3, 4)

Communication Spreadsheet

(Computer recommended) Your company, Local Express Services, makes special deliveries to law firms. It is estimating its costs for the coming period.

The controller's office estimated overhead costs at $300 per day for fixed costs and $12 per delivery for variable costs. Your nemesis on the staff, Nick Witt, suggested that the company use the regression approach. Witt has already done the analysis on a home computer and reports the "correct" cost equation as:

Overhead = $883 + $10.70 per unit

When asked for the data used to generate the regression, Witt produces the following list:

Day	Costs	Number of Deliveries
1	$4,762	381
2	5,063	406
3	6,420	522
4	4,701	375
5	6,783	426
6	6,021	491
7	5,321	417
8	6,133	502
9	6,481	515
10	5,004	399
11	5,136	421
12	6,160	510
13	6,104	486

The company controller is somewhat surprised that the cost estimates are so different. You have therefore been assigned to check Witt's equation.

Required

Analyze Witt's results and state your reasons for supporting or rejecting his cost equation.

Problem 11.48
Interpretation of Regression Results
(LO 3)

Lerner, Inc., is accumulating data to prepare its annual profit plan for the coming year. The behavior pattern of the maintenance costs must be determined. The accounting staff has suggested that regression be employed to derive an equation in the form of $y = a + bx$ for maintenance costs. Monthly data regarding maintenance hours and costs for the preceding year were entered into the regression analysis.

Total hours of maintenance for the year:	4,800
Total costs for the year:	$43,200
Regression results:	
Intercept:	$684.65
b coefficient:	$7.2884
R^2:	.99724

Required

a. In a regression equation expressed as $y = a + bx$, what is the letter b best described as?

b. What is the letter y in the regression equation best described as?

c. What is the letter x in the regression equation best described as?

d. Based on the data derived from the regression analysis, what are the estimated costs for 360 maintenance hours in a month?

e. What is the percent of the total variance that can be explained by the regression equation?

[CMA adapted]

Problem 11.49
Multiple Regression, Activity-Based Costing
(LO 3)

(Computer required) The accounting department of Insecurity Protection Services, a company that provides security services for rich, famous, and insecure people (and anyone else who can afford them) is analyzing the costs of its accounting services. Analysts have selected the following cost drivers: number of paychecks processed, invoices processed, customer accounts maintained, responses to routine inquiries, and special analyses.

The cost data and level of cost-driver activity for the past 16 months follow:

Month	Costs	Paychecks Processed	Invoices Processed	Customer Accounts	Routine Inquiries	Special Analyses
1	$7,013.00	12,690	1,340	325	32	0
2	6,469.80	11,980	1,180	310	39	0
3	6,129.40	10,950	1,050	280	45	1
4	5,905.90	10,280	930	245	54	0
5	5,659.50	9,020	840	205	68	2
6	5,115.80	8,130	780	185	83	2
7	5,101.80	7,540	700	160	97	3
8	5,488.90	6,980	630	140	112	4
9	5,284.80	8,930	680	115	101	2
10	5,538.40	9,800	760	120	93	0
11	6,129.30	10,560	890	175	82	1
12	6,026.10	11,560	1,070	200	68	0
13	6,517.20	11,710	1,240	240	55	0
14	6,600.50	12,460	1,390	285	42	0
15	7,153.10	13,520	1,450	300	39	1
16	7,207.60	13,620	1,510	315	24	0
Totals	$97,341.10	169,730	16,440	3,600	1,034	16

Required

a. Using multiple regression, find the cost-driver rates for each cost driver.

b. Assuming the following level of cost-driver volume for a month, what is the accounting department's estimated costs of doing business based on the multiple regression results? (Don't forget to include the intercept of the regression in your estimate.)

8,000 paychecks processed
800 invoices processed
200 customer accounts maintained
50 routine inquiries
1 special analysis

c. Insecurity Protection Services is considering outsourcing the processing of all paychecks. Compared to your answer in requirement (b), how much would the accounting department save per month by outsourcing all paycheck processing (before considering the cost of outsourcing)?

Problem 11.50
Account Analysis
(LO 4)

Refer to problem 11.49.

Required

a. Before proceeding to requirement (b) of this problem, indicate the information required to perform account analysis for Insecurity Protection Services' accounting department cost estimation that is not in problem 11.49.

b. Now assume that Insecurity Protection Services' accounting department had the following total costs for each cost driver for the 16 months reported in Problem 11.49.

Total cost of paychecks processed	$55,782.12
Total cost of invoices processed	6,560.08
Total cost of maintaining customer accounts	17,380.68
Total cost of processing routine inquiries	12,693.45
Total cost of performing special analyses	1,744.50
Total facilities-level costs (total for 16 months)	3,180.27
Total costs	$97,341.10

What are the cost driver rates for (1) paychecks processed, (2) invoices processed, (3) customer accounts maintained, (4) routine inquiries processed, and (5) special analyses performed?

c. Assuming the following level of cost-driver volumes for a month, what is the accounting department's estimated costs of doing business using the account analysis approach? (Don't forget to include the facilities-level costs in your estimate.)

8,000	paychecks processed
800	invoices processed
200	customer accounts maintained
50	routine inquiries
1	special analysis

d. Insecurity Protection Services is considering outsourcing the processing of all paychecks. Compared to your answer in requirement (c), how much would the accounting department save by outsourcing payroll (before considering the cost of outsourcing)?

Problem 11.51
Engineering Estimates
(LO 5)

Refer to Problems 11.49 and 11.50. Insecurity Protection Services hired an engineering consulting firm to perform an engineering estimate of the accounting department's costs. The firm identified the following cost estimates based on information for the current period:

Facilities costs (per month)	$300.00	
Paycheck processing	.35	per paycheck
Invoice processing	.40	per invoice
Customer account maintenance	4.50	per account
Routine inquiries	12.00	per inquiry
Special analyses	110.00	per analysis

Required

a. Assuming the following level of cost-driver volume for a month, what is the accounting department's estimated costs of doing business? (Don't forget to include the facilities costs in your estimate.)

8,000	paychecks processed
800	invoices processed
200	customer accounts maintained
50	routine inquiries
1	special analysis

b. Insecurity Protection Services is considering outsourcing the processing of all paychecks. Compared to your answer in requirement (a), how much would the accounting department save by outsourcing payroll (before considering the cost of outsourcing)?

Problem 11.52
Multiple Regression, Activity-Based Costing
(LO 3)

(Computer required) Analysts for Sun Black, maker of fashionable sunglasses, have selected the following cost drivers: number of units produced, machine hours, batches of sunglasses, customer orders processed, new customers, and new products designed.

The cost data and levels of cost-driver activity for the past 18 months follows.

Month	Costs	Units	Machine Hours	Batches	Customer Orders	New Customers	New Products
1	$ 1,730,890	51,230	15,820	820	225	18	0
2	1,753,860	45,200	13,980	670	210	36	0
3	1,562,890	39,860	11,550	550	185	41	1
4	1,389,940	33,670	9,900	450	155	48	1
5	1,200,300	25,430	7,950	490	120	51	2
6	1,245,660	32,510	7,840	530	105	46	4
7	1,514,900	36,520	10,260	610	110	40	6
8	1,555,200	43,890	12,320	700	140	37	5
9	1,706,130	51,220	14,730	860	160	32	0
10	1,781,060	55,980	15,960	990	185	25	0
11	2,101,610	61,250	17,140	1,120	200	19	0
12	2,162,230	66,110	18,290	1,080	245	11	1
13	2,087,270	65,120	18,940	1,010	260	13	0
14	2,017,920	59,640	18,050	930	235	18	4
15	1,991,870	54,310	16,840	810	220	24	3
16	1,839,080	48,640	15,390	710	205	29	2
17	1,738,730	42,150	14,150	600	190	33	3
18	1,575,150	39,850	12,860	520	170	35	0
Totals	$30,954,690	852,580	251,970	13,450	3,320	556	32

Required

a. Using multiple regression, find the cost-driver rates for each cost driver.

b. Assuming the following level of cost-driver volume for a new plant for one month, what is the estimated cost using the multiple regression results? (Don't forget to include the intercept of the regression in your estimate.)

60,000 units produced
12,000 machine hours
1,000 batches
200 customer orders
10 new customers
2 new products

c. Sun Black is considering a plan to reduce the number of batches by 500 per factory per month. Compared to your answer in requirement (b), how much would *each factory save per month* by reducing the number of batches by 500 per month?

Problem 11.53
Account Analysis
(LO 4)

Refer to Problem 11.52.

Required

a. Before proceeding to requirement (b) of this problem, indicate the information in addition to that provided in Problem 11.52 required to perform account analysis.

b. Now assume that Sun Black had the following breakdown of costs:

Total costs of producing units	$ 8,420,100
Total costs of operating machines	12,510,080
Total batch-level costs	1,760,000
Total costs related to customer orders	4,100,300
Total costs of developing new customers	2,854,000
Total costs of developing new products	530,400
Total facilities-level costs (total for all 18 months)	779,810
Total costs	$30,954,690

What are the cost driver rates using account analysis?

c. What are the estimated costs for a month assuming the following level of cost-driver volumes using the account analysis approach? (Don't forget to include the facilities-level costs in your estimate.)

60,000	units produced
12,000	machine hours
1,000	batches
200	customer orders
10	new customers
2	new products

Problem 11.54
Engineering Estimates
(LO 5)

Refer to Problems 11.52 and 11.53. Sun Black hired an engineering consulting firm to perform an engineering estimate of sunglass production costs. The consulting firm identified the following monthly cost estimates based on information for the current period:

Facilities costs	$40,000	
Unit-level costs	9	per unit produced
Machine operating costs	60	per machine hour
Batch-level costs	120	per batch
Customer order costs	1,100	per customer order
New-customer costs	4,200	per new customer
New-product costs	14,000	per new product

Required

Assuming the following level of cost-driver volume for a month, what is the estimated cost using the engineering estimates? (Don't forget to include the facilities costs in your estimate.)

60,000	units produced
12,000	machine hours
1,000	batches
200	customer orders
10	new customers
2	new products

Problem 11.55
Learning Curves
(LO 3)

Jammin' Corporation plans to manufacture Inexcess, a product that requires a substantial amount of direct labor on each unit. Based on the company's experience with other products that required similar amounts of direct labor, management believes that a learning factor exists in the production process used to manufacture Inexcess.

Each unit of Inexcess requires 50 square feet of direct material at a cost of $30 per square foot, for a total material cost of $1,500. The standard direct-labor rate is $25 per direct-labor hour. Variable manufacturing overhead is assigned to products at a rate of $40 per direct-labor hour. In determining an initial bid price for all products, the company marks up variable manufacturing costs (= direct materials + direct labor + variable overhead) 30 percent. (That is, the bid = 130% of variable manufacturing costs.)

Data on the production of the first two lots (16 units) of Inexcess follow:

1. The first lot of eight units required a total of 3,200 direct-labor hours.
2. The second lot of eight units required a total of 2,240 direct-labor hours.

Based on prior production experience, Jammin' estimates that production time will show no significant improvement after the first 32 units. Therefore, a standard (for planning purposes) for direct-labor hours will be established based on the average number of hours per unit for units 17 through 32.

Required

a. What is the basic premise of the learning curve?

b. Based on the data presented for the first 16 units, what learning rate appears to be applicable to the direct labor required to produce Inexcess? Support your answer with appropriate calculations.

c. Calculate the standard for direct-labor hours that Jammin' should establish for each unit of Inexcess.

d. After the first 32 units have been manufactured, Jammin' was asked to submit a bid on an additional 96 units. What price should Jammin' bid on this order of 96 units? Explain your answer.

e. Knowledge of the learning curve can be a valuable management tool. Explain how management can apply this tool in planning and controlling business operations.

[CMA adapted]

Problem 11.56
Learning Curves
(LO 3)

Communication

Krylon Company has purchased 80,000 pressure gauges annually from CO2, Inc. The price of these gauges has increased each year, reaching $68 per unit last year. Because the purchase price has increased significantly, Krylon management has asked for a cost estimate of manufacturing gauges in its own facilities.

A team of employees from the engineering, manufacturing, and accounting departments have prepared a report for management that includes the following estimate for an assembly run of 10,000 units. Additional production employees will be hired to manufacture the pressure gauges. However, no additional equipment or space is needed.

The report states that total costs for 10,000 units are estimated at $957,000 as shown here, or $95.70 per unit.

Materials	$120,000
Direct labor consisting entirely of hourly production workers (varies with production volume)	300,000
Labor-related overhead that varies closely with direct labor (varies with production volume)	300,000
Overhead not related to labor (e.g., building rent)	150,000
General and administrative costs that are unrelated to production	87,000
Total costs	$957,000

The current purchase price is $68 a unit, so the report recommends a continued purchase of the product.

Required

a. Before considering the learning curve effects, was the recommendation to continue purchasing the gauges correct? Explain your answer and include any supportive calculations you consider necessary.

b. Assume that Krylon could experience labor-cost improvements on the pressure gauge assembly consistent with an 80 percent learning curve. An assembly run of 10,000 units represents the initial lot or batch for measurement purposes. Should Krylon produce 80,000 pressure gauges in this situation? Explain your answer.

[CMA adapted]

Cases

Case 11.57
Plausible Cost Drivers
(LO 1)

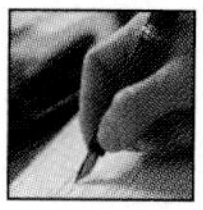
Communication

Team

Working in a group, identify plausible cost drivers for the cost of educating students at your college or university. Assume that these cost drivers would be entered into a regression to estimate a cost equation. (You do not have to perform the regression analysis.) The cost equation would have total costs of operating the college or university as the dependent variable and your list of cost drivers as the independent variables. The cost hierarchy can be a useful starting place for your work.

Keeping in mind the costs and benefits of collecting lots of data, prepare two lists of plausible cost drivers; an "A" list of no more than three cost drivers that everyone in your group thinks is important and a "B" list of additional cost drivers that at least some people in your group think are important.

Required

Prepare a report that lists your cost drivers and gives the rationale for including each in a regression to estimate the costs of operating your college or university.

Case 11.58
Regressions Run from Published Data
(LO 1, 3)

Communication

Internet

Obtain 11 years of data from the published financial statements of a company. For the first 10 years of data, perform a regression analysis in which the dependent variable is cost of goods sold and the independent variable is revenue (some companies call it *sales*). Now use the results from the regression on the first 10 years of data to estimate the cost of goods sold for the year 11. How far off were you in estimating cost of goods sold for the year 11? Estimate the cost of goods sold for year 5. How far off were you in estimating cost of goods sold for year 5?

Required

Prepare a report that describes your work and discusses reasons that your estimate of cost of goods sold is different than the actual cost of goods sold for year 11. (You may be able to find the data on the Internet. If not, libraries keep annual reports on file. Also, Moody's, Standard & Poor's and Value-Line are good sources of financial data.)

Case 11.59
Regressions Run from Published Data (Appendix)
(LO 6)

Communication

Refer to Case 11.58.

Required

a. What is the particular name of the difference between the actual cost of goods sold in year 5 and the estimated cost of goods sold in year 5 according to your regression?

b. Compute the t-statistic for the b. Is it greater than 2.0?

c. Is revenue a good predictor of cost of goods sold?

Case 11.60
Engineering Estimates
(LO 1, 5)

Communication

Go to a restaurant. For a given meal on the menu, prepare an engineering estimate of the cost of the food and of preparing the meal. Work only with the following costs: materials and labor required to prepare the meal. Do not be concerned with supervision, serving costs, and other costs that are not directly related to food and meal preparation labor. Many of your costs will be estimates. (That's why this topic is called cost *estimation*). Don't be bothered by that.

Required

Prepare a report that presents in detail your estimated food and meal preparation costs. Explain how you derived each component of the cost. (Grocery stores and cookbooks are good sources of data.)

CHAPTER

12

Financial and Cost-Volume-Profit Models

After completing this chapter, you should be able to:

1. Design financial models to match strategic and operational decisions, such as profit planning or optimal use of a scarce resource.
2. Build a basic cost-volume-profit (CVP) financial model.
3. Build a computerized financial planning model.
4. Build a financial model that reflects the effects of taxes, multiple products, and multiple cost drivers.
5. Manage scarce resources, and apply the Theory of Constraints to them.
6. Apply scenario and sensitivity analyses to model the risk of decisions (Appendix A).
7. Use linear programming to model decisions about the use of multiple scarce resources (Appendix B).

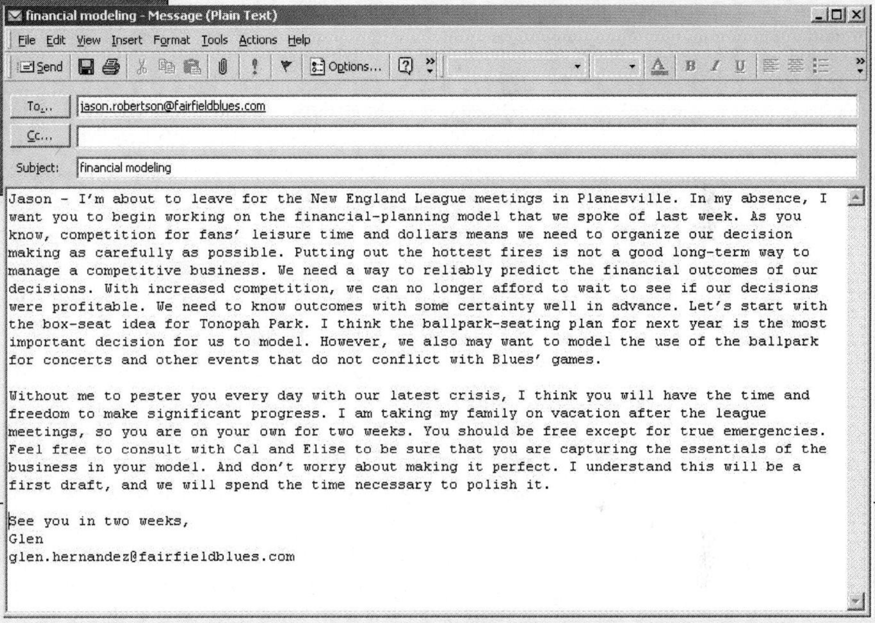

financial modeling - Message (Plain Text)

File Edit View Insert Format Tools Actions Help

To... jason.robertson@fairfieldblues.com

Cc...

Subject: financial modeling

Jason - I'm about to leave for the New England League meetings in Planesville. In my absence, I want you to begin working on the financial-planning model that we spoke of last week. As you know, competition for fans' leisure time and dollars means we need to organize our decision making as carefully as possible. Putting out the hottest fires is not a good long-term way to manage a competitive business. We need a way to reliably predict the financial outcomes of our decisions. With increased competition, we can no longer afford to wait to see if our decisions were profitable. We need to know outcomes with some certainty well in advance. Let's start with the box-seat idea for Tonopah Park. I think the ballpark-seating plan for next year is the most important decision for us to model. However, we also may want to model the use of the ballpark for concerts and other events that do not conflict with Blues' games.

Without me to pester you every day with our latest crisis, I think you will have the time and freedom to make significant progress. I am taking my family on vacation after the league meetings, so you are on your own for two weeks. You should be free except for true emergencies. Feel free to consult with Cal and Elise to be sure that you are capturing the essentials of the business in your model. And don't worry about making it perfect. I understand this will be a first draft, and we will spend the time necessary to polish it.

See you in two weeks,
Glen
glen.hernandez@fairfieldblues.com

Cost-Management Challenges

1. **What** does a cost-management analyst need to know to build useful financial planning models?

2. **Can** financial models help define future risks so that managers at least know what the uncertainties are?

3. **Should** organizations always try to maximize revenues or even the sales of products and services with the most throughput, contribution margin, or profit per unit? Are resource constraints an issue?

Introduction to Financial Modeling

Fairfield Blues, Inc., based in Fairfield, Massachusetts, owns a minor league baseball team of the same name and a ballpark, Tonopah Park. The team belongs to the independent New England League, which means that the 12 member teams are not affiliated with any major league team. The league's salary cap for a 24-person team is approximately $130,000 for the six-month season; players and coaches earn from $600 to $1,200 per month. The Fairfield Blues play all home games at Tonopah Park, which opened in 1919. The ballpark retains an old-time, family atmosphere and charm that continues to draw large crowds (4,000 seat capacity) regardless of the Blues' record. The Town of Fairfield runs a small concession stand outside the ballpark, which has always allowed ticket holders to bring in their own food and nonalcoholic drinks (no bottles or cans, however). The metropolitan area around Fairfield is experiencing significant growth as some Boston-area high-technology firms relocate seeking lower-cost housing and a more relaxed lifestyle. The growing population of people accustomed to many entertainment options also has created an opportunity for the company to promote outdoor concerts and other events at the ballpark on days or evenings without baseball games.

Four retired major-league players formed Fairfield Blues, Inc., and purchased Tonopah Park several years ago with funding from their retirement accounts, friends, family, a regional airline, and a local bank. In a short time, they have built the team and ballpark into a strong regional company. However, a neighboring city recently built a large amusement park and concert complex that threatens to drain attendance from Tonopah Park. Prior to leaving for two weeks for New England League meetings and a vacation, Fairfield Blues' chief operating officer and co-founder, Glen Hernandez, emailed his assistant, Jason Robertson, about several pressing issues that needed attention.

Hernandez's email raises several interesting issues in addition to the specific decisions facing the company. Many young firms, Fairfield Blues included, normally first devote efforts to developing an accounting system that concentrates on preparing financial reports. External parties such as stockholders, banks, and government agencies require financial reporting, and financial reports can be excellent for reviews of past operations. Young, successful companies typically outgrow their informal management styles and methods. As operations become larger and more complex, decisions become more difficult. Most firms develop financial *models* to help them organize and scrutinize their decision-making processes and options.

model *is a representation of reality*

A **model** is a representation of reality. You likely have had interactions with models over the years through role-playing computer games, architects' scale models of proposed real estate developments, and simulators used by driver education and pilot-training programs. These models represent realistic conditions and simulate actual outcomes, for example, given a pilot's decision to turn, land, or ascend to avoid a storm. Using models, gamers, architects, drivers, pilots, and managers can learn from their decisions quickly and without the possible adverse consequences of learning from mistakes made under actual conditions. Furthermore, these people can identify opportunities for success that they might not have seen otherwise.

LO 1 Design financial models to match strategic and operational decisions, such as profit planning or optimal use of a scarce resource.

Definition of Financial Models

financial model *is an accurate, reliable simulation of relations among relevant costs, benefits, value, and risk that is useful for supporting business decisions*

A **financial model** is an accurate, reliable simulation of relations among relevant costs, benefits, value, and risk that is useful for supporting business decisions. A good financial model works in much the same fashion as a flight simulator, allowing an organization to test the interactions of decisions and economic variables in a variety of settings. These models require analysts to develop a set of relations that represent a company's operating and financial activities, such as the ratio of variable costs to sales, inventory turnover ratios, and the relative proportions of various products sold. The financial model should allow a user to explore the effect of different situations on the business. For example, Fairfield Blues' managers might want to know the impact of a proposed ticket price increase on sales, cash flow, and profitability. For example, the following financial model predicts profits for different levels of sales, which in this simple model is the only driver of benefits and costs.

	Sales Levels		
Sales units	100	200	300
Sales revenue at $10 per unit	$1,000	$2,000	$3,000
Variable costs at $5 per unit	500	1,000	1,500
Contribution margin	$ 500	$1,000	$1,500
Committed costs	800	800	800
Operating income	($ 300)	$ 200	$ 700

Financial models offer several benefits to users. Once the model has been developed, users can spend significant time on business analysis without being overwhelmed by the related number crunching. In addition, like the simulators just discussed, many of these models allow an organization to study the impact of a possible business action by reviewing the potential results before that action occurs. In other words, it is possible to identify a good or bad project or decision prior to committing the organization's resources to a course of action.

The primary goal of this chapter is to explain and demonstrate methods of building, using, and interpreting financial models. To accomplish this goal, it presents specific decision contexts faced regularly by many organizations. These decision contexts include profit planning and the optimal use of scarce resources. Common examples of financial models used by organizations of all types and sizes include these:

- *Models of relations among an organization's costs, revenues, and income.* For example, a financial model of this type can compute product profitability given assumptions about quantity sold, sales price, activities, and variable and committed costs. This model also estimates the effects of adding or dropping a product or outsourcing a service or the effects of adding more scarce resources. Chapter 13 and a number of the earlier chapters of this text use this very broad class of financial model focused on financial planning. The present chapter also uses this model type to illustrate methods of building, using, and interpreting financial models.
- *Models of relations between current investments and long-term profitability or value.* Various types of investment models (e.g., discounted cash flow and payback models) are the focus of Chapter 14.
- *Models of pro forma (or budgeted) financial statements.* This type of model shows how a firm's financial position evolves from a beginning balance sheet, to a cash flow statement, to an income statement, and finally to an ending balance sheet. This important type of financial model is the topic of Chapter 15.
- *Specialized financial models for sophisticated decision making.* These include but certainly are not restricted to examples, such as the following:
  - Xcel Energy's models of consumer and industry demand for energy that contains hundreds of variables and simultaneous equations.
  - Econometric models of the economy that the Federal Reserve Board uses to estimate economic impacts of a possible change in interest rates.
  - Merck's R&D-impact model that incorporates the valuation of real options created by R&D projects.

These specialized models are beyond the scope of this text.

Objectives of Financial Modeling

Although financial models vary in complexity and purpose, they should be designed to have the following three common characteristics and objectives.

Usefulness for decision making. Decision makers must make better decisions using these models than they can without them, and the benefits of better decisions must exceed the costs of developing and using the models. Otherwise, the financial model is nothing but an elaborate (and probably expensive) toy. Unfortunately, anecdotes about resources wasted on complex, unused financial models or financial decision-support systems abound. The most common reasons for the failure of these models are (1) user lack of understanding of factors that are relevant to decisions and (2) excessive complexity.

Accurate and reliable simulation of relevant factors and relations. Decisions often hinge on the accuracy of measurements and the realism of the simulated relations among factors. The model should simulate the essential elements of business decisions, processes, and the environment. Clearly, models cannot capture all of the realism of the world (or the model would be the world!). However, a useful model must reflect the essential, relevant factors that drive decisions and relations among the factors. Furthermore, reliability requires that outcomes predicted by the model should closely approximate what is observed in the real world. If a model's predictions are not reliable, managers will not and should not use the model. The model builder must be able to demonstrate that decision makers can rely on a new model to be more reliable than earlier ones, past practice, or "gut feelings."

Flexible and responsive analyses. Financial models can be "back of the envelope" figures or more elaborate manual calculations. For example, your checkbook is a relatively simple, manual financial model of your cash position. Simple or not, an arithmetic error can cause you extensive grief and anxiety until you find and correct it. Think of the effort required to manually correct an arithmetic error or change a key factor in one of the Federal Reserve Board's complex economic models.

Complex financial modeling is not feasible today without taking advantage of the power of computer software (e.g., spreadsheets or specially designed modeling programs). Well-designed financial models allow decision makers to *easily* explore the predicted outcomes from varied decisions and assumptions about key factors. If the model is difficult to use or does not clearly show the effects of changes in decisions and key factors, decision makers probably will not use it. Before we explore building computer models, however, we first discuss some general principles of financial modeling in the context of manual profit-planning models.

Using Cost-Volume-Profit (CVP) Planning Models

LO 2 Build a basic cost-volume-profit (CVP) financial model.

cost-volume-profit (CVP) model *is a profit-planning model that reflects the effects of changes in an organization's sales volume, revenue, and costs on profit or income*

The most basic financial model, the **cost-volume-profit (CVP) model,** reflects the effects of changes in an organization's activities, such as sales volume, and of its prices and costs on profit or income. The simplest CVP model assumes that the only activity that drives profits is sales volume. The name of this basic model predates the popularity of activity-based costing, which recognizes many more potential drivers of profits than only sales volume. Nonetheless, the CVP name has stuck.[1] The basic model is worth learning and understanding because it can be extended to model the more complex profit impacts of changes in other revenue and cost drivers, demand, activity-based costs, taxation, and product or service mix. For example, basic or extended CVP models can help companies such as the following make decisions whether:

- Federal Express should add another cargo flight between San Francisco and Memphis.
- News Corp's profit will change if viewer ratings decline for *The Simpsons* program on Sunday evenings.

[1]A more general name for these financial planning models is CRD (cost and revenue driver) models, but CVP is widely used at this time. Besides, pronouncing this acronym might reduce confidence in the model.

- Kansas City Public Library can cover its costs for the year if it expands its current circulation capacity and replaces some librarians with computerized "help" and check-out functions.
- Boulder Community Hospital should enlarge its current laboratory or outsource some testing to independent laboratories.
- Fairfield Blues, this chapter's focus company, should convert some of its general admission seating to reserved box seating.

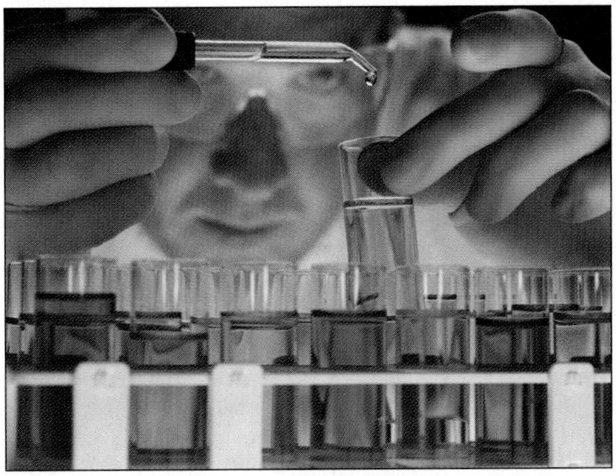

Laboratory testing is costly. If demand is growing, should a hospital enlarge its current laboratory or outsource some testing? Financial models can help managers estimate the impacts and risks of either alternative.

Each of these decisions concerns the effects of changing cost drivers or activities on costs, revenues, and profits. These decisions are candidates for CVP modeling.

Many nonprofit organizations also use forms of CVP modeling. Although legally they do not seek to generate profits, managers of nonprofit organizations must plan the effects of changing cost drivers and activities on their revenue and costs. For instance, commissioners of one of the fastest-growing counties in the United States, Douglas County, Colorado, must model the effects of rapid population growth on tax revenues and the cost of providing and maintaining infrastructure such as water, sewer system, schools, roads, and police protection. Pride Industries, a nonprofit employer of handicapped individuals in Sacramento, California, also uses financial modeling to determine whether revenues from its services and manufacturing operations will cover its costs.

Basic Cost-Volume-Profit Model

We apply the basic CVP model to the Fairfield Blues' seating plans for Tonopah Park.[2] Based on a review of past seasons' accounting records, Jason Robertson performed statistical analyses to estimate average committed (or fixed) facility costs per season, ticket prices, and unit-level variable costs per ticket sold.[3] He found that other cost and revenue drivers either might not be important factors for profitability or can be incorporated later into a more complex model.

Robertson then updated the historical amounts to reflect expected price and cost changes and developed the following cost and price estimates for the ballpark during the six-month baseball season:

Facility cost per season (mortgage, salaries, utilities, etc.)	$450,000
Variable cost per ticket sold (programs, custodians, etc.)	$2
Price per ticket	$7

He believed that these price and cost estimates are appropriate for typical seasonal operations for the coming year. He can easily adjust facility costs for more or fewer salaries or variable costs for more or less costly programs. Although he also can adjust ticket prices, doing so might not reflect the team's newly competitive situation. Robertson suspects that next year's attendance might be sensitive (i.e., elastic) to changes in ticket prices. Let's next discuss how he can use these factors in a simple, manual financial planning model. Later, we will transform this manual model into a more powerful computer model.

[2]Later in the chapter we also will model plans to promote concerts and other events at the ballpark.

[3]Chapter 11 presents detailed discussions of cost estimation.

Cost-Volume-Profit Model and the Break-Even Point

Suppose that the Fairfield Blues plans to sell 90,000 tickets during a season. The following income statement for the season shows that its estimated operating income is zero:

Volume, Revenues, and Costs	Estimated Amounts
Seasonal ticket volume	90,000 tickets
Sales revenue (90,000 × $7)	$630,000
Less variable costs (90,000 × $2)	180,000
Total contribution margin	$450,000
Less facility costs	450,000
Operating income	$ 0

Notice that the income statement (1) is a financial model of the key revenue and cost driver (ticket sales), (2) highlights the distinction between variable costs and committed facility costs, and (3) shows the outcome of the plan to sell 90,000 tickets, which is a profit of zero. The organization has no profit or loss at this activity level; it therefore *breaks even.* This ticket volume is the organization's **break-even point,** the volume of activity that produces equal revenues and costs. If no other activities drive costs and revenues except ticket sales, the team's break-even point is 90,000 tickets per season.[4]

break-even point *is the volume of activity that produces equal revenues and costs for the organization*

How can Robertson compute the Blues' break-even point if we did not already know that it is 90,000 tickets per month? He can use either a *contribution-margin* or an *equation* approach to the basic CVP model to find the break-even point.

Contribution-margin approach. Each ticket sells for $7, but $2 of this amount is used to cover variable costs. Thus, $5 per ticket is the *contribution margin* per ticket that in total covers the facility cost of $450,000. When enough tickets have been sold so that these $5 contributions add up to $450,000, the organization will break even. We can therefore compute the 90,000-ticket, break-even sales volume as follows:

$$\text{Break-even sales volume} = \text{Fixed costs per period} \div \text{Contribution margin per unit of volume}$$

$$\text{Fairfield Blues' break-even volume} = \$450{,}000 \text{ per month} \div \$5 \text{ per ticket} = 90{,}000 \text{ tickets per month}$$

Equation approach. An equivalent approach to finding the break-even point is based on this equation:

$$\text{Income (or profit)} = \text{Sales revenue} - \text{Costs}$$

If costs are separated into variable and committed (or fixed) components, the income calculation is captured by the following expression:

$$\text{Operating income} = \text{Sales revenue} - \text{Variable costs} - \text{Fixed costs}$$

This is also expressed as

$$\text{Operating income} = (\text{Selling price} \times \text{Sales volume}) - (\text{Variable cost per unit} \times \text{Sales volume}) - \text{Fixed costs}$$

This also equals

$$\text{Operating income} = [(\text{Selling price} - \text{Variable cost per unit}) \times \text{Sales volume}] - \text{Fixed costs}$$

[4]Recall from Chapter 4 that many organizations have a hierarchy of cost-driving activities. Our early examples consider only variable and facility-level activities. For convenience, some refer to all nonvariable costs as "fixed" costs, although this can be a dangerous practice because it can incorrectly imply to decision makers that these costs cannot be changed or do not change with respect to other activities. We address this in later sections.

Setting operating income equal to *zero* because we seek the break-even point, this becomes

[(Selling price − Variable cost per unit) × Break-even sales volume] − Fixed costs = 0

Moving fixed costs to the other side of the equal sign, the equation becomes

[(Selling price − Variable cost per unit) × Break-even sales volume] = Fixed costs

Now solving for sales volume, we have

Break-even sales volume = Fixed costs ÷ (Selling price − Variable cost per unit)

For Fairfield Blues this is

Break-even sales volume = \$450,000 ÷ (\$7 − \$2)
= \$450,000 ÷ \$5
= 90,000 tickets

Note that both the equation and contribution-margin approaches take us to the same place: dividing committed or fixed facility costs by the contribution margin per unit.

Basic CVP Model in Graphical Format

The contribution-margin and equation approaches are two equivalent techniques for finding the break-even point. Both methods reach the same conclusion, so personal preference dictates the approach to be used. The resulting figures for Fairfield Blues are graphed in Exhibit 12–1. Panel A shows a CVP graph, and panel B shows an alternative profit-volume graph, which condenses the revenue and cost information to a single line.

The graphs, which also are financial models, disclose more information than the break-even calculation and can be useful in presentations to illustrate the effects of changes in volume on profit. The vertical distance between the lines on the graph in panel A or the distance from the X-axis and the line in panel B reflects the profit or loss at a particular sales volume. If Fairfield Blues sells fewer than 90,000 tickets in a month, it will suffer a loss. The size of the loss increases as ticket sales decline. Conversely, the team enjoys a profit if sales exceed 90,000 tickets. For example, if the team sells 170,000 tickets in a season, its profit will be \$400,000.

Exhibit 12–1 CVP in Graphical Format

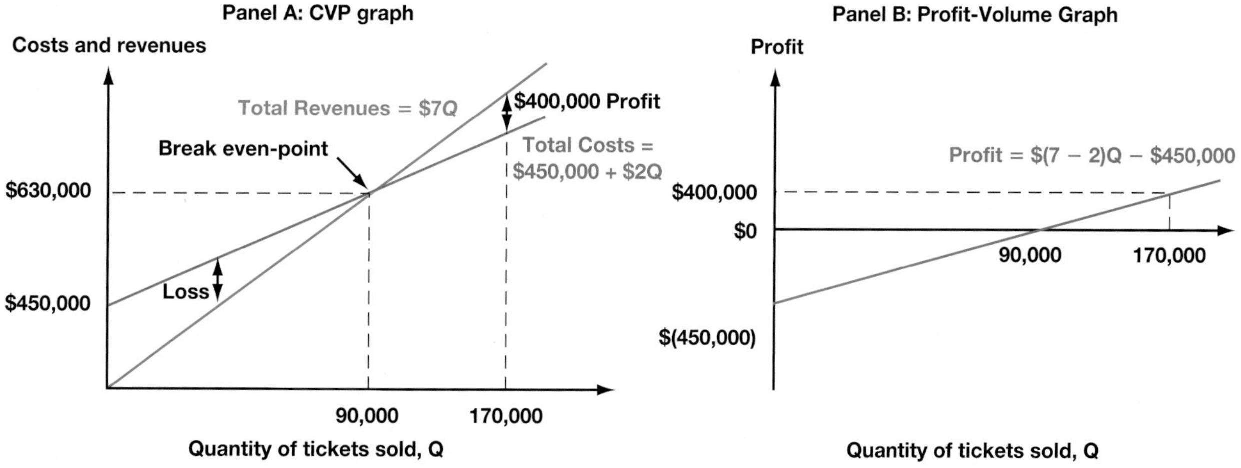

CVP and Target Income

The founders and other stockholders of the Fairfield Blues, like the owners of any other business, desire to earn a competitive return on their investment. The founders have invested some of their retirement funds in the team and ballpark, and other stockholders have contributed capital that they could invest elsewhere. In this case, the stockholders estimate that the value of the company is $4,000,000 and that they should receive a 10 percent return on that investment value. Therefore, they believe that the company should generate a target income of $400,000, which is a 10 percent return on their investment. The rationale is that the stockholders can sell the company, reinvest the proceeds, and earn a comparable return. To be a viable investment, the Fairfield Blues must meet stockholders' opportunity costs.

Integrating the target income into the CVP model is straightforward. In the previous case, the company had to sell 90,000 tickets to cover the fixed costs and break even. Now it must go one step further: Cover the fixed costs *and* earn $400,000 income. With each ticket continuing to contribute $5, the necessary calculation using either the contribution margin or equation method becomes

Target sales volume = (Fixed costs + Target income) ÷ Contribution margin per ticket
= ($450,000 + $400,000) ÷ $5
= $850,000 ÷ $5
= 170,000 tickets

Note that Exhibit 12–1 also shows the target break-even point, the quantity 170,000 that achieves the target income, to the right of the break-even point in both panels.

Operating Leverage

operating leverage *reflects the risk of missing sales targets and is measured by the ratio of contribution margin to operating income*

Most organizations, including the Fairfield Blues, commit to spending for resources such as salaries, rents, licenses, interest, and taxes, which can be very difficult to restructure in the short term. Large amounts of these committed costs expose an organization to the adverse effects of fluctuating sales because contribution margins are relatively small compared to committed costs. **Operating leverage** reflects the risk of missing sales targets and is measured by the ratio of the contribution margin to operating income. High levels of operating leverage reflect the risk that an organization faces from missing sales targets because committed costs are relatively high and small changes in sales can easily push the organization into a loss.[5] Conversely, low levels of operating leverage mean that committed costs are relatively low compared to the contribution margins. Consider the following example that contrasts the Fairfield Blues with a competitor that has relatively higher operating leverage.

	Fairfield Blues	Maxwell Espressos
Sales price per unit	$7.00	$9.00
Variable cost per unit	$2.00	$2.00
Contribution margin per unit	$5.00	$7.00
Expected sales quantity	170,000	170,000
Expected profitability:		
Sales revenue	$1,190,000	$1,530,000
Variable costs	340,000	340,000
Contribution margin	$ 850,000	$1,190,000
Committed costs	450,000	790,000
Operating income	$ 400,000	$ 400,000
Operating leverage	$850,000 ÷ $400,000 = 2.13	$1,190,000 ÷ $400,000 = 2.98

[5]Historically, one of the rationales behind the rate regulation of public utilities was to guarantee them an adequate return on very large committed costs in exchange for reliable public service. Guaranteed rates of return were compensation for assuming the risk associated with high operating leverage in the public interest.

These two companies have the same levels of expected sales and equal operating incomes; at this sales level, their difference in committed cost ($790,000 − $450,000) is covered by their difference in contribution margin ($1,190,000 − $850,000). Although one might be indifferent to the two companies at this level of sales, their exposure to changes in sales is different. Fairfield Blues' operating leverage, 2.13, is lower than that of Maxwell Espressos, which is 2.98. This reflects Espressos' higher exposure to the effects of lower than expected sales. What if each company's actual sales level declined by 10,000 units to 160,000? Which company's income is hurt more? Consider the following, which shows the effects of lower sales volume for both companies:

	Fairfield Blues	Maxwell Espressos
Sales price per unit	$7.00	$9.00
Variable cost per unit	$2.00	$2.00
Contribution margin per unit	$5.00	$7.00
Actual sales quantity	160,000	160,000
Actual profitability:		
Sales revenue	$1,120,000	$1,440,000
Variable costs	320,000	320,000
Contribution margin	$ 800,000	$1,120,000
Committed costs	450,000	790,000
Operating income	$ 350,000	$ 330,000
Operating leverage	2.29	3.39

Because sales are lower, both companies' operating incomes naturally are lower than expected, but Espressos has taken the larger hit because its committed costs are higher than that of the Blues. Note also that unless Espressos reduces committed costs, its situation becomes riskier as reflected by its still higher operating leverage. In contrast, if its sales were expected to be consistently above the indifference point of 170,000 tickets per season, Espressos' higher contribution margin per ticket makes it more profitable than the Fairfield Blues. Many aspects of financial models reflect this type of impact on profits. Appendix A to this chapter covers more general approaches to modeling variability and risk.

Identifying Elements of a Financial Model

Relations among Revenues and Costs

Revenue and cost drivers are the building blocks of financial models, and relations among them are the mortar that holds them together. A fundamental lesson of cost management is that many decisions drive costs; *costs do not just happen.* Decisions also drive revenues, but not all of them are at the discretion of managers. The previous example reflected an environment in which only unit-level activity (ticket sales) appeared to drive revenues and costs because the model builder considered all other driving activities to be fixed or committed. For now, we continue to model profits with a single, unit-level revenue and cost-driving activity, but we model the more general case later in the chapter.

Manual versus Computer Models

LO 3 Build a computerized financial planning model.

In concept, financial modeling does not require a computer. After all, organizations used manual financial models similar to our previous examples before computers were available. However, it is a fact of modern business that virtually all financial modeling is performed with computer spreadsheets or specialized modeling software. This software enables quicker, more flexible, and more complex modeling than was ever possible before. It is inconceivable that we should extend our discussion of financial modeling without recognizing the impact and value of computer software.

Set Up of Computer Spreadsheet Models

Computer spreadsheets such as Excel™ and Lotus 1-2-3™ are among the most powerful and most commonly used business tools. Mastery of the fundamentals of spreadsheets is essential for anyone who undertakes any cost-management analysis, particularly financial modeling. This discussion is not meant to substitute for either formal courses or diligent self-study, either of which can lead to mastery of spreadsheets. The purpose is to convey some fundamentals of building a flexible financial model.

Spreadsheets are ideally suited for financial modeling. One important key to unlocking the power of these spreadsheets is to use the spreadsheet *not* merely as a calculator but as a *model* of relations among financial and nonfinancial factors. Let's transform Fairfield Blues' manual profit-planning model into the computer model shown in Exhibit 12–2. The steps we perform can be extended to a more complex spreadsheet model and are outlined in the following sections.

Gathering information. First, gather all facts, assumptions, and estimates that underlie the model. These include estimates of sales prices, profit targets, and so forth. Some analysts call these the model's input data or *parameters.* They are the model's cost and revenue-driver building blocks. Fairfield Blues' profit-planning parameters include the ticket price, variable cost per ticket sold, facility costs per season, profit target, and percentage of seating capacity sold per game. Note that profit targets can be expressed as absolute dollar amounts or as returns on either sales or invested capital. To facilitate analysis with the model, these parameters should be located and clearly identified in a defined parameter or input-data area of the spreadsheet. Exhibit 12–2 clearly identifies the model's input-data cells. This is the only place that the parameters are located as numbers, but the analysis section of the model can use them throughout.

Modeling relations among parameters. Second, understand and describe the relations of the model's parameters. Changing a model's parameters should change its outcomes. This usually involves modeling how one parameter affects another with an algebraic relation or *formula.* For Fairfield Blues' profit-planning model, these formulas are the equations underlying the income statement and are located apart from the input data section. The model in Exhibit 12–2 has three types of CVP analyses below the data input section: break-even (cells A7 to B10), target profit (A11 to B16), and planned profit (C7 to D13). The last analysis shows expected profits at a planned

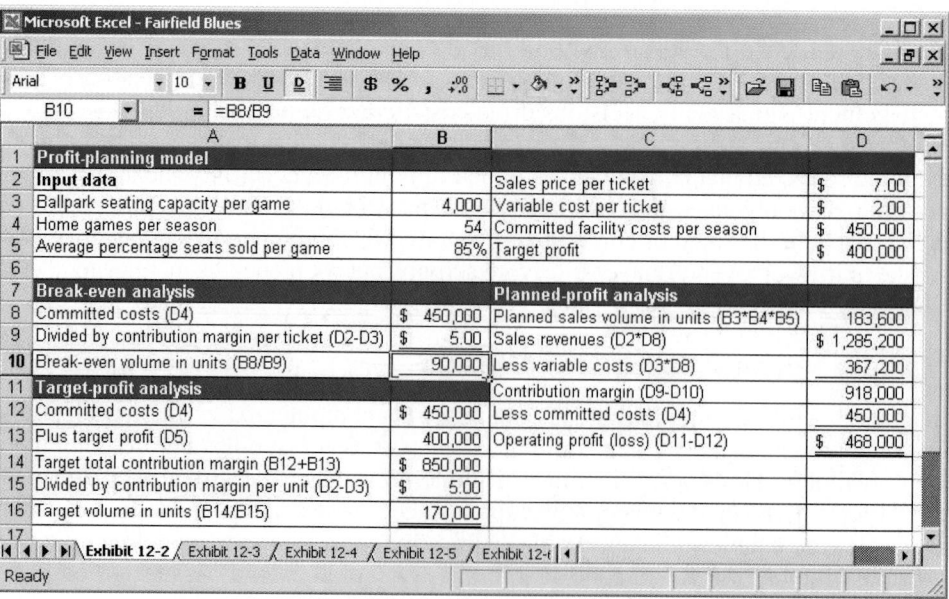

Exhibit 12–2

Computerized Profit-Planning Model

Fairfield BLUES INC.

Microsoft Excel - Fairfield Blues

B10 = =B8/B9

	A	B	C	D
1	**Profit-planning model**			
2	**Input data**		Sales price per ticket	$ 7.00
3	Ballpark seating capacity per game	4,000	Variable cost per ticket	$ 2.00
4	Home games per season	54	Committed facility costs per season	$ 450,000
5	Average percentage seats sold per game	85%	Target profit	$ 400,000
6				
7	**Break-even analysis**		**Planned-profit analysis**	
8	Committed costs (D4)	$ 450,000	Planned sales volume in units (B3*B4*B5)	183,600
9	Divided by contribution margin per ticket (D2-D3)	$ 5.00	Sales revenues (D2*D8)	$ 1,285,200
10	Break-even volume in units (B8/B9)	90,000	Less variable costs (D3*D8)	367,200
11	**Target-profit analysis**		Contribution margin (D9-D10)	918,000
12	Committed costs (D4)	$ 450,000	Less committed costs (D4)	450,000
13	Plus target profit (D5)	400,000	Operating profit (loss) (D11-D12)	$ 468,000
14	Target total contribution margin (B12+B13)	$ 850,000		
15	Divided by contribution margin per unit (D2-D3)	$ 5.00		
16	Target volume in units (B14/B15)	170,000		
17				

Exhibit 12-2 / Exhibit 12-3 / Exhibit 12-4 / Exhibit 12-5 / Exhibit 12-6

Ready

level of ticket sales (183,600 tickets = 4,000 seat capacity × 54 games × 85 percent seats sold, in this example) that might differ from either break-even volume or target volume.

Building models often is a group effort, requiring input from many perspectives and functions.

Separate parameters and formulas. Third, to facilitate the analysis of the model, the formulas in the analysis sections should *never* contain the actual numerical values of the parameters. Instead, use the parameters' cell locations in all formulas where they occur. Exhibit 12–2 models the financial relationships in column B, rows 8 to 16 and column D, rows 8 to 13. Placing the cursor on any of these cells shows that *none contain numbers.* Instead, the amounts displayed in the cells are the *computed effects of formulas* that combine the model's parameters and preceding calculations, as appropriate. For this exposition, columns A and C also show these formulas, although this usually is not done because some formulas are very complex. If you highlight the cell B10, you see in the formula bar at the top of the spreadsheet that it contains the formula "= B8/B9," which models the break-even relation. Likewise, cell B16 contains the formula, "= B14/B15," which computes the target unit volume. D13 contains the formula, "= D11 – D12," which completes the calculation of the operating profit or loss at the planned sales volume.

The major benefit to separating the model's parameters and relations follows:

> Making a change to a parameter in the one highly visible place where it occurs as a number causes the model to recalculate outcomes by incorporating the new parameter value everywhere it is used in formulas.

Otherwise, changing a parameter requires changing every formula that uses the parameter. For large models, this can be very difficult and wastes valuable analysis time. Furthermore, someone other than the model's creator who wishes to use it might not know where to find every occurrence of the parameter and might use the model to generate inaccurate information.

Following these guidelines for constructing financial models creates powerful and flexible decision-making aids. Analysts can extend simple models to include complications of taxes, multiple products, multiple revenue and cost drivers, scarce resources, and risk. You should consider replicating the model in Exhibit 12–2 on a computer so that you can better appreciate this and following sections of the chapter.

Modeling Taxes

LO 4 Build a financial model that reflects the effects of taxes, multiple products, and multiple cost drivers.

Profit-seeking firms pay taxes on their periodic profits, meaning that target income figures should be set high enough to meet profit requirements and cover the firm's tax obligations. The relationship between an organization's pretax income and after-tax income can be expressed in the following formula:

$$\begin{aligned}\text{After-tax income} &= \text{Before-tax income} - \text{Income taxes}\\ &= \text{Before-tax income} - (\text{Before-tax income} \times t)\\ &= \text{Before-tax income} \times (1 - t)\end{aligned}$$

where t is the average or *effective* income tax rate.

Dividing both sides by $(1 - t)$ gives

After-tax income/$(1 - t)$ = Before-tax income

Now we can find the desired before-tax income that will generate the desired after-tax income, given the company's effective tax rate, which will meet the profit target and cover the tax obligation.

To illustrate, we continue the previous Fairfield Blues example to show how the team can earn the desired $400,000 profit target *after-tax*. Assume that the company is subject to a 20 percent average or effective income tax rate. We first convert the after-tax target profit to a before-tax amount, as follows:

Before-tax income = After-tax income ÷ (1 − t)
= $400,000 ÷ (1 − .20)
= $500,000

The before-tax income of $500,000 is inserted as the target income in the following calculation, now requiring Fairfield Blues to sell 190,000 tickets to generate its after-tax profit target of $500,000:

Target sales volume = (Fixed cost + Target Before-tax income)
÷ Contribution margin per ticket
= ($450,000 + $500,000) ÷ $5 = 190,000 tickets

Exhibit 12–3 shows Fairfield Blues' profit-planning model that Robertson modified to include the tax obligation, modeled as the average tax rate in D6. Note that the break-even analysis in Exhibit 12–3 (A7 to B10) is unchanged because at zero profit, Fairfield Blues pays no taxes. Subsequent analyses differ because of the inclusion of the tax rate. The target-profit analysis (A11 to B16) uses the before-tax profit target, B13 = D5/(1-D6), to calculate the target volume of 190,000 tickets (B16). The planned profit analysis in cells C7 to D15 has been changed in this exhibit to reflect the effect of taxes. Note that because the average tax rate is included as an input parameter and in volume and profit analyses, Robertson also can model the company's operations given changes to its average tax rate that result from different tax-planning actions. More complexities of tax planning require a more complex profit-planning

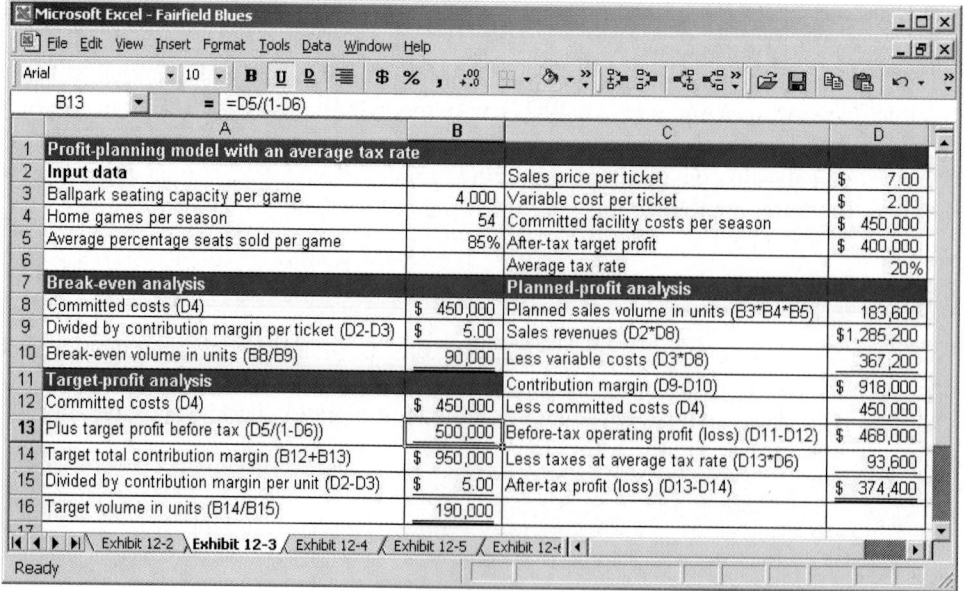

Exhibit 12–3

Profit-Planning Model with an Average, Effective Tax Rate

Microsoft Excel - Fairfield Blues

B13 = =D5/(1-D6)

	A	B	C	D
1	**Profit-planning model with an average tax rate**			
2	**Input data**		Sales price per ticket	$ 7.00
3	Ballpark seating capacity per game	4,000	Variable cost per ticket	$ 2.00
4	Home games per season	54	Committed facility costs per season	$ 450,000
5	Average percentage seats sold per game	85%	After-tax target profit	$ 400,000
6			Average tax rate	20%
7	**Break-even analysis**		**Planned-profit analysis**	
8	Committed costs (D4)	$ 450,000	Planned sales volume in units (B3*B4*B5)	183,600
9	Divided by contribution margin per ticket (D2-D3)	$ 5.00	Sales revenues (D2*D8)	$1,285,200
10	Break-even volume in units (B8/B9)	90,000	Less variable costs (D3*D8)	367,200
11	**Target-profit analysis**		Contribution margin (D9-D10)	$ 918,000
12	Committed costs (D4)	$ 450,000	Less committed costs (D4)	450,000
13	Plus target profit before tax (D5/(1-D6))	500,000	Before-tax operating profit (loss) (D11-D12)	$ 468,000
14	Target total contribution margin (B12+B13)	$ 950,000	Less taxes at average tax rate (D13*D6)	93,600
15	Divided by contribution margin per unit (D2-D3)	$ 5.00	After-tax profit (loss) (D13-D14)	$ 374,400
16	Target volume in units (B14/B15)	190,000		

Exhibit 12-2 | Exhibit 12-3 | Exhibit 12-4 | Exhibit 12-5 | Exhibit 12-

Ready

model.[6] Note also that this analysis shows that expected ticket sales will not meet the company's after-tax target (see the planned profit in D15). This shortfall is a motivation for modeling the possible impacts of altering the ballpark's seating.

Modeling Multiple Products

The previous Fairfield Blues' models assume that the company has only one product: a "general admission" seat. Most firms produce more than one product at their facilities, which adds some complexity to their profit-planning analyses.

Recall that Fairfield Blues' seasonal fixed costs total $450,000 and the variable cost per ticket is $2. Suppose that the company has decided to replace some of its 4,000 general admission seats with 800 reserved box seats. These 800 seats will be more comfortable and afford a better view of the field than the ballpark's remaining general admission seating, which will now have 3,200 seats. Management has decided to reduce its general admission price to $6 per ticket and charge $15 per ticket for box seats. The construction project will result in an increase in seasonal fixed costs of $100,000 because of added depreciation.[7] Variable costs per ticket are unchanged.

Notice that 80 percent of the available seats are general admission seats (3,200 ÷ 4,000) and 20 percent are box seats. Assume that ticket sales for each type of seat will be in the same proportion as the number of different seats available. Therefore, if it sells 100,000 tickets per season, for example, sales should be as follows:

General admission seat tickets	100,000 × .8 = 80,000 tickets
Box-seat tickets	100,000 × .2 = 20,000 tickets

For any organization that sells multiple products, the relative proportion of each type of product planned or actually sold is called the **sales mix** or **product mix.** It is an important assumption in multiproduct profit planning because it is used to compute a **weighted-average unit contribution margin (WAUCM),** a tool for finding the break-even point and performing other profit-planning exercises. WAUCM is the average of the various products' unit contribution margins *weighted* by the relative proportion of each product sold. Contribution margin for general admission seats is $4 per ticket ($4 = $6 − $2) and for box seats is $13 per ticket ($13 = $15 − $2). Fairfield Blues' weighted-average unit contribution margin for the sale of regular and box seats is:

sales mix or product mix *is the relative proportion of each type of product planned or actually sold*

weighted-average unit contribution margin (WAUCM) *is the average of the various products' unit contribution margins weighted by the relative proportion of each product sold*

Weighted-average unit contribution margin (WAUCM) = ($4 × .8) + ($13 × .2) = $5.80

The team's new break-even point in tickets is computed by replacing a single-product contribution margin with the multiproduct WAUCM in the break-even formula introduced earlier, namely:

Break-even sales volume = Fixed cost per period ÷ WAUCM per unit
= $550,000 ÷ $5.80
= 94,828 tickets (rounded)

(Recall that the construction of box seats increases fixed costs from $450,000 to $550,000.) This number of tickets, however, is a combination of regular and box seats and must be interpreted considering the sales mix. The team will break even for the month if it sells the following tickets:

General admission seat tickets	94,828 × .8 = 75,862 tickets
Box-seat tickets	94,828 × .2 = 18,966 tickets
Break-even sales volume	94,828 tickets

[6]The complexity of tax planning is beyond the scope of this text.

[7]Many organizations build financial models to reflect accounting accruals such as depreciation. However, financial models also can reflect cash flows, excluding depreciation and similar accruals.

One may convert these sales volume figures to sales dollar figures by multiplying each product sales volume by its sales price, as follows

Break-even sales dollars = ($6 × 75,862) + ($15 × 18,966) = $739,662

Observe that the break-even point of 94,828 tickets or $739,662 is valid only for the 80:20 sales mix assumed in computing the weighted-average unit contribution margin. A shift in sales mix generally results in a different WAUCM, which changes the break-even or target income figure. Thus, the sales mix is an important input parameter for the many organizations that provide multiple products or services from common facilities.

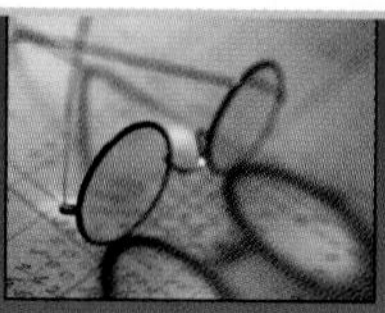

Cost Management in Practice 12.1

Sales Mix Concept in Action

You have no doubt seen the sales-mix concept in action by observing recent trends in gasoline sales. The old-fashioned gas station has rapidly given way to the convenience store that also sells gasoline. Or, in some cases, gas stations might be a partner with, say, Subway, BurgerKing, or McDonald's. In still other instances, the convenience store might also sell fresh produce and flowers, as well as provide services such as a post office, pharmacy, and laundry.

What's the reason behind the change? Although gas stations usually require expensive sites, gasoline retailing is a low-margin business—10 percent. Convenience-store items, on the other hand, have margins of around 30 percent. These latter goods now account for at least half of sales, and overall profitability has increased. The next step might be for the marketers to purposely take a loss on the gas just to attract customers who might also purchase food. This practice is already happening in some European markets. *Source: R. L. Sullivan, "Exxonsafeway." (Full citations to references are in the Bibliography.)*

Multiproduct Profit-Planning Model

Exhibit 12–4 shows Fairfield Blues' profit-planning model with the modification of two types of seating (A6 to B8) and the sales mix assumption (A9 to B11). The other addition to the model is the computation of the weighted-average unit contribution margin

Exhibit 12–4

Profit-Planning Model with Taxes and Multiple Products

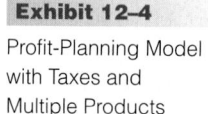

Microsoft Excel - Fairfield Blues

B14 = =B10*(B7-D3) + B11*(B8-D3)

	A	B	C	D
1	**Profit-planning model with multiple products**			
2	**Sales input data**		**Cost input data**	
3	Ballpark seating capacity per game	4,000	Variable cost per ticket	$ 2.00
4	Home games per season	54	Fixed facility costs per season	550,000
5	Average percentage seats sold per game	85%	After-tax target profit	400,000
6	Sales price per ticket		Average tax rate	20%
7	Box seating	$ 15.00		
8	General admission seating	6.00		
9	Sales mix assumption			
10	Box seating	20.0%		
11	General admission seating	80.0%		
12				
13	**Weighted average unit contribution margin**		**Planned-profit analysis**	
14	WAUCM (B10*(B7-D3) + B11*(B8-D3))	$ 5.80	Planned sales volume in units (B3*B4*B5)	183,600
15	**Break-even analysis**		Sales revenues	
16	Fixed costs (D4)	$ 550,000	Box seating (D14*B10*B7)	$ 550,800
17	Divided by WAUCM (B14)	5.80	General admission seating (D14*B11*B8)	881,280
18	Break-even volume in units (B16/B17)	94,828	Total revenues	$ 1,432,080
19	**Target-profit analysis**		Less variable costs (D14*D3)	367,200
20	Fixed costs (D4)	$ 550,000	Contribution margin (D18-D19)	$ 1,064,880
21	Before-tax target profit (D5/(1-D6))	500,000	Less fixed costs (D4)	550,000
22	Target contribution margin	$1,050,000	Before-tax profit (loss) (D20-D21)	$ 514,880
23	Divided by WAUCM (B14)	$ 5.80	Less taxes at average tax rate (D6*D22)	102,976
24	Target volume in units (B22/B23)	181,034	After-tax profit (loss) (D22-D23)	$ 411,904

Exhibit 12-2 / Exhibit 12-3 / **Exhibit 12-4** / Exhibit 12-5 / Exhibit 12-6

Ready

(WAUCM in cell B14), which is computed as explained earlier. Using the WAUCM value of $5.80 allows Robertson to compute the break-even volume of 94,828 tickets in cell B18. Why is the break-even ticket volume higher than before (recall that with only general admission seating, the breakeven was 90,000 tickets)? The break-even volume is higher now because, although Fairfield Blues has added a new product (box seating) with a higher unit contribution margin, it also has increased fixed costs per season by $100,000. Thus, the company must sell more tickets to break even. Notice, however, that the target sales to reach the desired after-tax profit is 181,034 tickets (B24). This is a lower ticket volume than before because the higher WAUCM ($5.80 versus $5.00) requires fewer tickets to be sold above the breakeven (after fixed costs are covered) to meet the same after-tax profit target.

Lower break-even and target volumes usually are desirable because they mean that committed costs are relatively low and the operation is less vulnerable to the effects of lower sales (recall the earlier discussion of operating leverage). Does this mean that the baseball team *will* be more profitable? It does only if customers are willing to pay the higher prices for box seats *and* if they purchase tickets in accordance with the planned sales mix. Achieving the planned sales volume (D14) of 183,600 tickets *and* the assumed sales mix should result in exceeding the after-tax profit target of $400,000 by $11,904 (see D24).

You're the Decision Maker 12.1

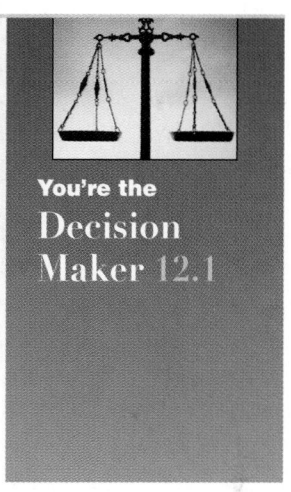

Effect of Sales Mix on Financial Performance

The sales mix is relevant not only for multiproduct profit planning but also for assessing an organization's actual sales and profit performance. Suppose that Fairfield Blues plans to sell 183,600 tickets next season (85 percent of seats sold) with the assumed 80:20 sales mix and expects to exceed its after-tax income target. Suppose also that during the next season, all ticket prices and costs occurred as planned. However, the team actually sold 185,760 tickets (86 percent of seats sold). One might expect that actual, after-tax profit should exceed the target even more because ticket volume exceeded the planned and target volumes. However, during this season when 185,760 tickets were sold, the actual sales mix was 84 percent general admission and 16 percent box seats, which is a departure from the 80:20 sales mix assumption.

a. What is the effect on break-even and target volumes and profit from the changes in sales volume and sales mix?

b. Explain how the changes in outcomes were caused by the actual inputs.

(Solutions begin on p. 499.)

Modeling Multiple Cost Drivers

LO 4 Build a financial model that reflects the effects of taxes, multiple products, and multiple cost drivers.

Drivers of Profits

A critique of the profit-planning model in Exhibit 12–4 reveals several limitations despite the addition of taxes and multiple products. As we just showed, for example, the sales mix must remain as predicted, or a change might influence the organization's profitability. Similarly, a company's technology, efficiency, and management must remain constant because these cost and revenue drivers also affect profit-planning relations. The model also is based on straight-line, linear relationships among revenues and costs, thus ignoring basic factors such as quantity discounts. Perhaps most troubling is the model's use of a single cost-driver activity, sales volume. Most organizations have multiple cost and revenue drivers that affect profits.

Cost-driver activities. Activity-based costing (Chapter 4) directs us to investigate decisions about activities performed at the unit, batch, product, customer, and facility levels to identify significant cost drivers. If these activities are relevant to profit planning, financial models should include them. Models should reflect the effects of all major cost-driving activities, some of which occur at other than the unit level. For example, the number of tickets sold drives some unit-level costs of the Fairfield Blues, but

Concessions and groundskeeping are examples of some activities that drive costs and revenues of organizations.

decisions about seating capacity, staffing, maintenance, and grounds keeping also drive the team's costs.

Revenue-driver activities. Revenues are the result of sales prices and sales volumes. Managers can set prices, but customers decide whether to pay them. In perfectly competitive markets, organizations are price takers, not price setters,[8] so modeling revenues is straightforward by multiplying the market price by the expected sales quantity, which is limited only by the organization's capacity. But if markets are less than perfect—and they often are—other factors also drive revenues. Ticket prices surely drive the team's revenues, but advertising, the quality (and cost) of the team and its competitors, and external competition for leisure time and dollars probably drive revenues, too. Because many factors driving revenues are external to the organization and because even internal ones are complex (e.g., the relation of advertising to revenues), many organizations understand revenue drivers less than they do their cost drivers. Because they represent half of the profit equation, understanding revenue drivers surely is as important as understanding cost drivers. However, an exploration of revenue drivers, except under conditions of perfect competition, is beyond the scope of this text.

Profit-Planning Models with Multiple Cost Drivers

Before we show the integration of multiple cost drivers into profit-planning models, we quickly review the nature of unit-, batch-, product-, customer-, and facility-level activities and costs. Recall the following:

- *Unit-level activities* are performed for each individual unit of product or service.
- *Batch-level activities* are performed to benefit multiple units of similar output equally and simultaneously (i.e., in batches). Batch-level activities include setting up machines to run a particular batch of units. Related costs are traced easily to specific batches but not to individual output units.
- *Product-level activities* are needed to support a specific product or service, that is, an entire product line. Such activities include new product designs, improved existing product quality and product function, product advertising, and production process monitoring.
- *Customer-level activities* are performed to meet the needs of specific customers. Examples of related costs include those attributable to unique packaging, shipping, and distribution needs, and to personnel assigned to handle specific customer accounts. (Chapter 6 discusses customer-level analysis in detail.)

---

[8]In a perfectly competitive market (an ideal situation), no single participant can affect prices, supply, or demand. Entry to the market has no restrictions, and prices reflect all relevant market knowledge.

- *Facility-level activities* are required for an organization to have the capacity to produce goods and services. These activities are at the highest level of the activity hierarchy and tend to support all organizational processes. Typical examples include physical plant operations and top management activities.

Including these cost-driving activities changes the nature of profit-planning models. The basic CVP model assumes that revenues and variable costs vary with sales activity while other costs remain constant. However, costs can vary because of drivers other than sales activity. The following is an example of a total cost expression reflecting multiple relevant activities (recall that we will model revenues assuming competitive markets):

Total cost = (Unit variable cost × Number of units) + (Batch cost × Batch activity)
+ (Product cost × Product activity) + (Customer cost × Customer activity)
+ (Facility cost × Facility activity)

Observe that this calculation no longer relies only on sales activity (e.g., the number of tickets sold) as the cost driver but introduces the impacts of multiple activities. As a result, some costs viewed as fixed under a traditional analysis are now considered variable with respect to appropriate cost-driving activities (batches, products, etc.).

Use of ABC in Financial Modeling

Using various statistical analyses and his own knowledge of cost behavior, Jason Robertson developed the following set of activities and costs to extend his previous financial model, now shown in Exhibit 12–5. In this more complex model, Robertson

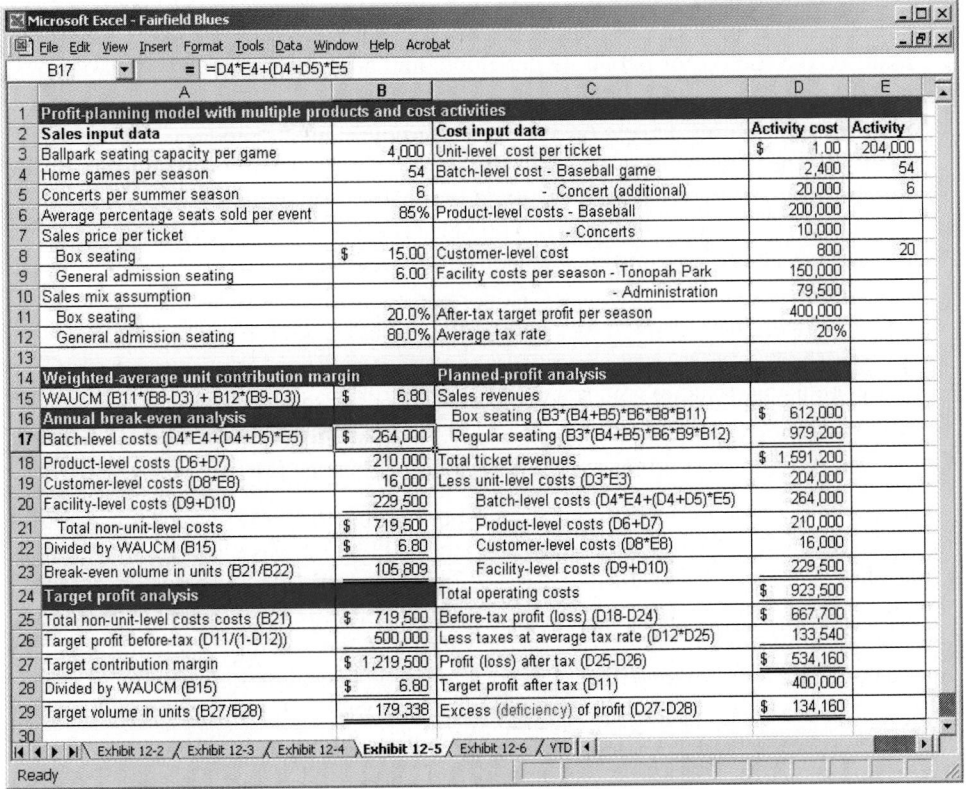

Exhibit 12–5

Profit-Planning Model with Multiple Cost Drivers

Microsoft Excel - Fairfield Blues

File Edit View Insert Format Tools Data Window Help Acrobat

B17 = =D4*E4+(D4+D5)*E5

	A	B	C	D	E
1	**Profit-planning model with multiple products and cost activities**				
2	**Sales input data**		**Cost input data**	**Activity cost**	**Activity**
3	Ballpark seating capacity per game	4,000	Unit-level cost per ticket	$ 1.00	204,000
4	Home games per season	54	Batch-level cost - Baseball game	2,400	54
5	Concerts per summer season	6	- Concert (additional)	20,000	6
6	Average percentage seats sold per event	85%	Product-level costs - Baseball	200,000	
7	Sales price per ticket		- Concerts	10,000	
8	Box seating	$ 15.00	Customer-level cost	800	20
9	General admission seating	6.00	Facility costs per season - Tonopah Park	150,000	
10	Sales mix assumption		- Administration	79,500	
11	Box seating	20.0%	After-tax target profit per season	400,000	
12	General admission seating	80.0%	Average tax rate	20%	
13					
14	**Weighted-average unit contribution margin**		**Planned-profit analysis**		
15	WAUCM (B11*(B8-D3) + B12*(B9-D3))	$ 6.80	Sales revenues		
16	**Annual break-even analysis**		Box seating (B3*(B4+B5)*B6*B8*B11)	$ 612,000	
17	Batch-level costs (D4*E4+(D4+D5)*E5)	$ 264,000	Regular seating (B3*(B4+B5)*B6*B9*B12)	979,200	
18	Product-level costs (D6+D7)	210,000	Total ticket revenues	$ 1,591,200	
19	Customer-level costs (D8*E8)	16,000	Less unit-level costs (D3*E3)	204,000	
20	Facility-level costs (D9+D10)	229,500	Batch-level costs (D4*E4+(D4+D5)*E5)	264,000	
21	Total non-unit-level costs	$ 719,500	Product-level costs (D6+D7)	210,000	
22	Divided by WAUCM (B15)	$ 6.80	Customer-level costs (D8*E8)	16,000	
23	Break-even volume in units (B21/B22)	105,809	Facility-level costs (D9+D10)	229,500	
24	**Target profit analysis**		Total operating costs	$ 923,500	
25	Total non-unit-level costs costs (B21)	$ 719,500	Before-tax profit (loss) (D18-D24)	$ 667,700	
26	Target profit before-tax (D11/(1-D12))	500,000	Less taxes at average tax rate (D12*D25)	133,540	
27	Target contribution margin	$ 1,219,500	Profit (loss) after tax (D25-D26)	$ 534,160	
28	Divided by WAUCM (B15)	$ 6.80	Target profit after tax (D11)	400,000	
29	Target volume in units (B27/B28)	179,338	Excess (deficiency) of profit (D27-D28)	$ 134,160	
30					

Exhibit 12-2 / Exhibit 12-3 / Exhibit 12-4 / **Exhibit 12-5** / Exhibit 12-6 / YTD

Ready

also has included costs and revenues related to offering another product at Tonopah Park: six summer concerts.

- *Unit-level activities and costs.* Robertson assumed that the ballpark can sell 85 percent of its seats for baseball games and concerts (total tickets computed in E3 = 204,000 = 4,000 × (54 + 6) × 85 percent). The only unit-level costs related to games or concerts are for printing tickets and preparing game or concert programs, which Robertson estimated per ticket to be $1 (in cell D3). He decided that the previously included variable custodial costs *used* were not supplied on a unit-level basis but were a game-level cost (see the next bullet point). Note that this lower per-unit cost increases the WAUCM of baseball games from $5.80 to $6.80 per average ticket (B15). This higher WAUCM does not magically make the team more profitable. Robertson's analysis has more accurately separated the costs that follow, which the simpler models had treated improperly as unit-level variable or fixed facility costs.
- *Batch-level activities and costs.* Each game or concert is like a batch of production. For example, if Fairfield Blues sells a total of 3,900 tickets for a Saturday game, this is a "batch" of 3,900 units. Robertson estimated the cost per game, or concert, to be $2,400 (D4), which includes wages paid to security, parking attendants, custodians, ticket takers, and ushers. This batch cost is the same even if the company sold only 3,000 tickets for a game or concert. The league schedule showed that the team will have 54 games per season next year (B4 and copied in E4). Robertson began the concert planning by assuming six summer concerts next year (B5 and E5). For top regional performers, the company additionally must pay approximately $20,000 per concert, which is another batch cost (D5).
- *Product-level activities and costs.* The baseball team and concert series hosted by the ballpark are separate product lines. Robertson identified the product-level costs to be the cost of acquiring the rights to the team, advertising, hiring the players and coaches, transporting the team to away games, and purchasing baseball equipment and uniforms. He estimated this cost to be $200,000 per season (D6). He estimated that managing the inaugural concert series costs an additional $10,000 for part-time personnel and advertising (D7).
- *Customer-level activities and costs.* As a community service, Fairfield Blues rents vans and hires drivers once per week to pick up customers who are unable to drive. The drivers bring these customers to games, usually on Saturday or Sunday afternoons, and then take them home after the games. Robertson estimated the cost of this service to be $800 (D8) every time the service is performed, about 20 games per season (E8).
- *Facility-level activities and costs.* Robertson identified facility-level activities and estimated their costs in two parts, the ballpark and administration.
  - *Tonopah Park.* Robertson estimated the ballpark, including depreciation, utilities, and maintenance, to cost $150,000 per season (D9).
  - *Administration.* Robertson estimated administrative activities, including payroll and marketing, to cost $79,500 per season (D10).

The results of Robertson's model and input parameters show estimated operating income to be $534,160 per season after taxes (cell D27). He was pleased to see that the initial plan exceeded the profit target by $134,160 (D29). By building this financial planning model, Robertson was able to anticipate this favorable outcome. He knew, however, that this outcome depended on the validity of the assumptions that formed the input data. Numerous alternative actual inputs must be considered. Possible variation in these parameters indicates the risk of decisions considered by the company. By focusing on the various cost-driving activities, Robertson now can identify different inputs that might be more likely to occur, producing different profit outcomes. Appendix A covers several types of risk analysis, sensitivity and scenario analyses, and shows the additional decision-making power of using financial planning models.

Modeling Scarce Resources

LO 5 Manage scarce resources, and apply the Theory of Constraints to them.

Choosing which goods and services to produce and sell is a basic managerial decision. For all organizations, the possible volume and mix of products is limited by available capacity (i.e., scarce resources). For instance, consider the following:

- A campus bookstore might decide to use its limited space to sell general merchandise or to increase textbook sales.
- Because of a personnel shortage, a small consulting firm must choose between working for client A or client B.
- A nonprofit health clinic must choose which patients it can serve and which it must turn away.
- Sales representatives, in their limited time, must call on customers that provide the greatest profit potential.

A manager must understand and analyze the factors that limit the organization's ability to achieve its objectives. Surprisingly, the solution to improvement usually is not to make each part of the operation as efficient as possible.

Profit from a Single Scarce Resource Maximization

As an introduction to modeling scarce resources, let's observe decision making in the television commercial division of Fairfield's Channel 2, which produces TV commercials for the Fairfield Blues and other regional companies. Manager Cerise Hamilton has built the division's reputation so that it has no shortage of work. The problem is deciding which jobs to accept. Demand exceeds the available time of her two skilled editors, which she has identified is the scarcest resource for completing commercials. To maintain quality (and to retain her skilled editors), she limits maximum editing time to 100 hours per week. The issue facing Hamilton is which jobs to accept to maximize weekly profits.[9]

When an organization has a scarce resource, it wants to make the best possible use of that resource. *In the short run, Hamilton can maximize her division's profit by processing jobs that generate the most throughput per unit of scarce resource,* in this case, editing hours. Recall from Chapter 2 that *throughput* is the sales price less unit-level spending for direct costs of products or services that can be readily sold.

In a typical week, Hamilton chooses among three types of jobs: short commercial advertising, long commercial advertising, and short public service announcements. The following job data are available:

	Short Commercials	Long Commercials	Short Public Service Announcements
Throughput value of each job	$2,500	$5,500	$1,800
Estimated editing hours per job	4	11	3

The following figures show that short commercial jobs have the highest throughput per editing hour, allowing Channel 2 to generate the highest profit for its scarce editing time.

[9]Hamilton may have other objectives, including diversity of creative work or maintaining a broad market presence, which might cause her to trade off some profit.

Short commercial: $2,500 ÷ 4 hours = $625 throughput per hour
Long commercials: $5,500 ÷ 11 hours = $500 throughput per hour
Short public service announcements: $1,800 ÷ 3 hours = $600 throughput per hour

Based on these figures, choosing to work on the short commercial jobs is the best use of the scarce editing time. Every hour spent on another job has an opportunity cost of the difference in throughput per hour compared to short commercials. For example, an editing hour spent on long commercials forgoes at least $125 in profit ($625 − $500). The total results for the week in the following table confirm the desirability of directing the use of scarce editing time to short commercials.

	Short Commercials	Long Commercials	Short Public Service Announcements
Throughput value of each job	$ 2,500	$ 5,500	$ 1,800
Estimated editing hours per job	4	11	3
Editing-hours capacity	100	100	100
Weekly jobs completed and sold	25	9	33
Weekly throughput	$62,500	$49,500	$59,400

Next, we extend the discussion of managing scarce resources to more complex situations.

Theory of Constraints

the Theory of Constraints *seeks to improve productive processes by focusing on constrained resources*

In the 1980s, Dr. Eliyahu Goldratt formalized an approach to management called the ***Theory of Constraints*** (**TOC**),[10] which seeks to improve productive processes by focusing on constrained resources. Theory of Constraints is a management method to improve productive processes by measuring process capacity, identifying process constraints, using process constraints effectively, and coordinating other processes to the needs of bottlenecks. It argues that improving the use of constrained resources involves six steps. We next summarize these steps, and then we apply them to the Fairfield Blues.

bottleneck *is the constraint or constraining factor limiting production or sales*

constraint *is a process or resource in a system that limits the capacity or throughput of the system*

1. *Identify the appropriate measure of value created.* In the short run, throughput is the measure appropriate for most profit-seeking firms. Other types of organizations should adopt measures of value appropriate for their goals; for example, the IRS might value the number of tax returns processed correctly the first time.
2. *Identify the organization's bottleneck.* A **bottleneck** is the *constraint* or constraining factor limiting production *or* sales. A **constraint** is a process or resource in a system that limits the capacity or throughput of the system. All productive processes have limited capacities, but most organizations have one or a few processes that limit throughput. Bottlenecks often are apparent because a backlog of parts, assemblies, casework, or paperwork builds up just before the bottleneck process.
3. *Use the bottleneck properly by using it to produce or sell only the most highly valued or profitable products or services.* With a single bottleneck, the most value can be generated by producing the product or service that creates the most value (e.g., throughput) per unit of constrained capacity. This is the simple case illustrated earlier. Multiple constraints require more complex tools, such as linear programming, which is described in Appendix B to this chapter.
4. *Synchronize all other processes to the bottleneck by producing no more of other intermediate outputs than the bottleneck can reasonably process.* Allowing all processes to produce up to their capacity wastes resources by creating unused

[10] Many books and articles discuss the Theory of Constraints. The most accessible and popular source is E. Goldratt and J. Cox, *The Goal;* it is highly recommended reading. A concise review that probably should be read after *The Goal* is J. Ruhl, "An Introduction to the Theory of Constraints." (Full citations to references are in the Bibliography.)

parts, assemblies, or partially completed services, which only add to inventory but do not create throughput. These excess inventories can become obsolete and usually obscure quality problems, as discussed in Chapter 7. Furthermore, some excess inventories might be defective inputs, which will waste the bottleneck capacity when processed.

5. *Increase the bottleneck's capacity or outsource the production of its output.* The only way to increase throughput is to relieve the bottleneck. In the long run, the organization can add capacity, but in the short run, outsourcing can be more profitable than forgone sales.
6. *Avoid inertia and return to step 1.* Relieving one bottleneck probably will create another one as production and sales grow. Managing by the Theory of Constraints involves always looking for ways to increase throughput. The Theory of Constraints can be applied to any productive process; it is by no means limited to manufacturing processes.

Research Insight 12.1

Theory of Constraints and Cost Management

The combination of the Theory of Constraints (TOC) with cost-management information in a complementary manner has been demonstrated. This combined information is modeled using mathematical programming methods, including linear programming (see Appendix B to this chapter) and integer programming. TOC plus mathematical programming enhances the identification of bottlenecks and their opportunity costs. This analysis has application in complex manufacturing and scheduling situations.

Researchers of one study surveyed and visited a number of companies that reported that they were implementing TOC principles. In general, these firms reported significant net benefits from doing so. The Boeing Co. has dramatically improved its management of bottleneck tool-manufacturing operations by applying the same process described in this chapter. Boeing's approach to managing the tooling area appears to be a resounding success and is being repeated in other areas of the company. Thus, although more research is needed, it seems likely that the logic and appeal of TOC management can generate significant improvements. *Sources: R. Kee, "Integrating Activity-Based Costing with the Theory of Constraints to Enhance Production-Related Decision Making"; and E. Noreen, D. Smith, and J. Mackey,* The Theory of Constraints and Its Implications for Management Accounting.

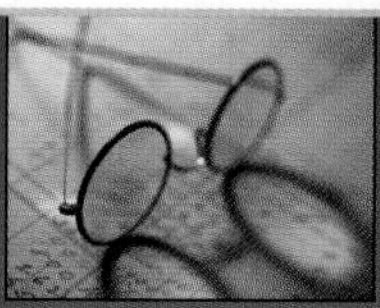

Cost Management in Practice 12.2

Benefits of Implementing the Theory of Constraints

Many descriptions of the benefits of implementing the Theory of Constraints (TOC) approach to process management are "self-reports"; that is, they are not objective, third-party evaluations of the benefits *and* costs, successes *and* failures. These reports abound on the Internet, usually attached to Web pages of consultants eager to sell their services. However, some verifiable applications are available. One report has demonstrated that coordinating the activities of purchasing, supply, and building subassemblies dramatically improved throughput, cycle times, and inventory levels at a mid-size British electrical manufacturer.

Square D, an electrical component manufacturer, integrated TOC elements with its cost-management information to improve scheduling, manufacturing, and customer service. In addition to improving throughput, this combination of TOC and cost management also generated valuable information about customers. Because combining this information required the cooperation of financial, manufacturing, and engineering personnel, this greatly improved communications among various departments at Square D, which further improved throughput and customer service. *Sources: B. Barker, "Development of Time Based Frameworks: Manufacturing System Analysis and Value Adding Performance"; R.C. Barker, "Production Systems without MRP: A Lean Time Based Design"; and R. Campbell, P. Brewer, and T. Mills, "Designing an Information System Using Activity-Based Costing and the Theory of Constraints."*

Application of the Theory of Constraints

Let's return to the management of Fairfield Blues to illustrate how Robertson can help management increase the company's profitability by modeling and interpreting its constrained resources. By following the steps outlined earlier for the Theory of

Constraints, Robertson can identify the company's bottleneck(s) and help develop strategies to improve profits.

Identify the appropriate measure of value created. From a seasonal perspective, ticket sales, baseball games, and concerts can be part of throughput. The spending for capacity to play baseball games, promote concerts, and provide facilities, however, appears to be committed for the longer term and, therefore, is not part of throughput, which is sales less spending for resources used (see Chapter 2). Ticket costs probably are directly related to the number of tickets sold, so ticket costs at $1 per ticket are part of throughput. If the team played one more game per season, however, do batch costs increase by $2,400 (the estimated batch cost per game), or is some part of that cost committed salary or depreciation that does not increase? Likewise, if Fairfield Blues decided to pick up nondriving customers for one additional game, do customer costs increase by $800, or is some of this cost committed too?

After investigating the differences between resource spending and usage and after subtracting portions of committed costs, Robertson measured the elements of monthly throughput as follows:

Throughput Element	Unit of Activity	Throughput Price or Cost per Unit of Activity	Capacity	Planned Usage
Box-seat price	Tickets sold, Q_B	$15	800 per event	680 per event
General admission price	Tickets sold, Q_{GA}	$6	3,200 per event	2,720 per event
Ticket cost	Tickets sold ($Q_B + Q_{GA}$)	$1	4,000 per event	3,400 per event
Game cost	Games, G	$2,400	54 per season	54 per season
Concert cost	Concerts, C	$22,400	6 per season	6 per season
Customer pickup	Pick-up games, G_P	$500	20 per season	20 per season

Total *periodic* throughput is the throughput per event multiplied by the number of events less other periodic throughput costs. The Fairfield Blues' seasonal throughput is measured by the following equation:

$$\text{Seasonal throughput} = (\$15 \times Q_B) + (\$6 \times Q_{GA}) - [\$1 \times (Q_B + Q_{GA})] \times (G + C) - [\$2{,}400 \times G] - [\$22{,}400 \times C] - [500 \times G_P]$$

Identify the organization's bottleneck(s). Unlike a manufacturing plant or a bank, Fairfield Blues has no stacks of excess inventory or stacks of loan applications to identify bottlenecks. What really limits the company's monthly throughput? The place to look is the company's capacity to perform major activities: ticket sales, number of events, customer pickups, and facilities.

The preceding table shows that the only *apparent* bottlenecks are the number of events, which the league has set at 54 home games per season and the company management has set at six concerts per season. By management policy, event capacity equals event usage. Other activities appear to have some excess capacity. Well, then, why not add to the number of seasonal events? First, if the number of concerts, for example, can be increased, what is the increase in throughput? The simplest answer is that each concert adds throughput equal to the following:

$$\begin{aligned}\text{Throughput from each concert} &= (\$15 \times Q_B) + (\$6 \times Q_{GA}) - [\$1 \times (Q_B + Q_{GA})] \times 1 - \$22{,}400 \\ &= (\$15 \times 680) + (\$6 \times 2{,}720) - [\$1 \times (680 + 2{,}720)] - \$22{,}400 \\ &= \underline{\underline{\$720}}\end{aligned}$$

Second, is this the correct answer? If Fairfield Blues added another concert (or 10) each season, does each really add $720 in throughput? If not, why not? The difficulty is that the number of concerts may not be the true bottleneck but only a visible symptom. If the number of concerts is not the constraining factor, what is? Perhaps we can understand the problem by looking at current operations a bit closer. Ticket sales do generate seasonal revenues and throughput for the company, but why is every event not a sellout? If the company does not sell out now, will adding events increase the number of tickets sold or merely cannibalize current performances?

The true bottleneck might be a marketing problem. Perhaps the events do not match the tastes of the majority of potential ticket buyers. Perhaps the local market is not large enough to support more baseball or concert fans. Perhaps the quality of the events is not sufficient to draw more customers at current prices. After applying the logic and analysis of the Theory of Constraints, many organizations are surprised to learn that their most significant bottleneck is not a production constraint but a marketing constraint—a failure to understand and meet market needs better.

Use the bottleneck(s) properly. By working with other members of the company's management team, Robertson began focusing on the company's marketing and learned the following about each marketing activity:

1. Improvements to facilities (ballpark and general management activities) and the quality of the team either were not feasible in the short run or would not increase ticket sales appreciably.
2. Advertising placed in club and company newsletters at a cost of $1,200 per season could increase box-seat sales by approximately 10 per event.
3. Advertising placed in neighborhood weekly papers at a cost of $600 per season might increase general admission seat sales by 10 per event.
4. Exhibition games between the Fairfield Blues and the four local high school teams would sell 50 percent of available seats, with net proceeds divided equally between the Fairfield Blues and the high school teams.
5. Increasing the number of concerts would not add appreciably to overall ticket sales. Six per summer season seems to be about the right number for the community.
6. Increasing the number of times that nondriving customers are picked up would not increase ticket sales appreciably at this time. Perhaps in 10 years when the population has aged, this might increase ticket sales or be necessary to maintain ticket sales.

Apply the Theory of Constraints

a. Evaluate the financial viability of each of the six proposed changes to Fairfield Blues' operations discussed. What would be the increase in monthly throughput from each action? Consider each change independently.

b. How would you assess the risk of each option? In your opinion, what is the most likely outcome of each?

c. What recommendations can you make to company management for choosing among the proposed changes?

(Solutions begin on p. 500.)

You're the Decision Maker 12.2

Synchronize all other processes to the bottleneck(s). Once company management decides on a course of action to manage a bottleneck, it must ensure the coordination of all activities; that is, no excess activity should exist in other areas. This might not be difficult for the Fairfield Blues, but it can be for manufacturing facilities. Historically, firms have evaluated their manufacturing departments on measures such as percentage of capacity used, unallocated overhead, percentage of downtime, or idle time. All of these measures provide the incentive to fully use productive capacity without regard to bottleneck constraints. Thus, before a firm can coordinate its manufacturing departments to bottleneck throughput, it should change its measures of manufacturing performance. Chapters 7, 20, and 21 discuss this important issue in more detail from quality or time, lead indicator, and compensation perspectives.

Increase the bottleneck's capacity or outsource the production of its output. In the short term, the Fairfield Blues can add a few more games and try to increase attendance at each performance. If the market can be developed to support even more ticket sales, Fairfield Blues might consider whether to increase its overall seating capacity. This is a longer-term decision that has investment implications. This type of strategic decision is covered in Chapter 14.

Avoid inertia and return to step 1. The Theory of Constraints warns that the elimination of a bottleneck, causes another to pop up elsewhere, so managers must be vigilant to continue to increase value created and throughput efficiently.

Chapter Summary

This chapter presents an overview of financial modeling and the management of scarce resources. An understanding of financial planning or cost-volume-profit (CVP) relationships is necessary for the successful management of any enterprise. Financial modeling provides a reliable overview of the effects on profit of changes in quantities, activity costs, sales mix, sales prices, and changes in bottlenecks. The basic CVP model is subject to several limitations, with one of the most troubling being the use of a single cost driver. The model can be expanded using activity-based costing to yield more realistic results. Any attempts to improve an organization's profitability must consider the effects of constrained resources. The Theory of Constraints offers an effective method for the short-term management of constraints. Spreadsheets used in conjunction with sensitivity and scenario analyses greatly facilitate risky decision making (Appendix A). Modeling multiple constraints is possible with linear programming (Appendix B).

Key Terms

For each term's definition, refer to the indicated page or turn to the glossary at the end of the text.

bottleneck, 494
break-even point, 480
constraint, 494
cost-volume-profit (CVP) model, 478
feasible solution space,* 504
financial model, 476
linear programming,* 504
model, 476
model elasticity,† 502
objective function,* 504
operating leverage, 482
optimum point,*504
product mix, 487
sales mix, 487
scenario analysis,† 503
Theory of Constraints (TOC), 494
weighted-average unit contribution margin (WAUCM), 487

†Term appears in the chapter Appendix A.
*Term appears in the chapter Appendix B.

Meeting the Cost-Management Challenges

1. What does a cost-management analyst need to know to build useful financial planning models? Is making good decisions the result of pure luck or good planning?

Managers make decisions all the time that affect future operations. Sometimes it is better to be lucky than good, but by nature, luck is random. A run of good luck is just as likely to be followed by one of bad luck unless managers take actions to make systematically good decisions. There might be intuitively brilliant managers who always make the right decisions. If they really exist, we can only envy them. Obviously, we believe that most of us can benefit from organizing decisions and building useful financial planning models. As the chapter explains, to build useful financial models, a cost-management analyst needs to know the following:

a. What is the manager is trying to manage (i.e., optimize)?
b. What are the parameters and relations among the parameters relevant to managers' decisions?
c. What are feasible ranges of parameters and realistic scenarios of combinations of parameters (Appendix A)?
d. How do constrained resources affect managers' ability to optimize operations? Can those constraints be relaxed? For example, can the organization obtain more capacity?

2. Can financial models help define future risks so that managers at least know where the uncertainties are?

Financial models can help define future risks and uncertainties. Unfortunately, some managers view the output of financial planning models as either gospel truth or fanciful dreaming. The key to building and using financial planning models successfully is to understand that as built, they represent only one of many tools available and that the numbers do not speak for themselves. In the hands of a questioning, skeptical user, a flexible financial planning model can be a wondrous time saver and realistic simulation of the organization's internal and external environments. The user can spin unlimited scenarios and try unlimited "what-if" analyses. If there is a method to this madness and a plan for testing the scenarios, the user can develop a good sense for where both opportunities and dangers exist.

3. Should organizations always try to maximize revenues or even the sales of products and services with the most throughput, contribution margin, or profit per unit? Are resource constraints an issue?

They should not. Focusing on the cost or revenues of products and services at the unit level can improve sales and production incentives, but that might not be enough to improve revenues. Some organizations do reward for maximizing sales growth, which can be an effective way to build market share but also can lead to suboptimal profits. Resource constraints are always an issue in some manner. The Theory of Constraints provides a good framework for managing constrained resources in any environment.

Solutions to You're the Decision Maker

12.1 Effect of Sales Mix on Financial Performance p. 489

a. Consider the following spreadsheet, which is identical to Exhibit 12–4 except for the changed and highlighted inputs of average percentage of seats sold (B5), which affects sales volume (D13), and sales mix (cells B10 and B11). This revised model shows that the change in actual sales mix has an adverse effect on after-tax profits despite a higher-than-planned ticket volume.

b. Actual sales emphasized lower contribution-margin general admission tickets at the expense of higher contribution-margin box-seat tickets. The sales-mix change lowered the WAUCM from $5.80 to $5.44 (B13) and consequently increased both the break-even volume (B17) and target volume (B23). Because the actual ticket volume was lower than the target volume required at the actual, lower WAUCM, Fairfield Blues did not reach its after-tax target of $400,000 (see D23). This type of adverse effect can occur whenever managers increase sales or market share without regard to the contribution margins of products. Motivating managers to increase sales or market share can be counterproductive to meeting an organization's goal of profitability. Designing incentive systems is the topic of chapter 21.

Microsoft Excel - Fairfield Blues

File Edit View Insert Format Tools Data Window Help Acrobat

B14 = =B10*(B7-D3) + B11*(B8-D3)

	A	B	C	D
1	**Profit-planning model with multiple products**			
2	**Sales input data**		**Cost input data**	
3	Ballpark seating capacity per game	4,000	Unit-level variable cost per ticket	$ 2.00
4	Home games per season	54	Fixed facility costs per season	550,000
5	Average percentage seats sold per game	86%	After-tax target profit	400,000
6	Sales price per ticket		Average tax rate	20%
7	Box seating	$ 15.00		
8	General admission seating	6.00		
9	Sales mix assumption			
10	Box seating	16.0%		
11	General admission seating	84.0%		
12				
13	**Weighted-average unit contribution margin**		**Planned-profit analysis**	
14	WAUCM (B10*(B7-D3) + B11*(B8-D3))	$ 5.44	Planned sales volume in units (B3*B4*B5)	185,760
15	**Break-even analysis**		Sales revenues	
16	Fixed costs (D4)	$ 550,000	Box seating (D14*B10*B7)	$ 445,824
17	Divided by WAUCM (B14)	5.44	General admission seating (D14*B11*B8)	936,230
18	Break-even volume in units (B16/B17)	101,103	Total revenues	$ 1,382,054
19	**Target-profit analysis**		Less variable costs (D14*D3)	371,520
20	Fixed costs (D4)	$ 550,000	Contribution margin (D18-D19)	$ 1,010,534
21	Before-tax parget profit (D5/(1-D6))	500,000	Less fixed costs (D4)	550,000
22	Target contribution margin	$1,050,000	Before-tax profit (loss) (D20-D21)	$ 460,534
23	Divided by WAUCM (B14)	$ 5.44	Less taxes at average tax rate (D6*D22)	92,107
24	Target volume in units (B22/B23)	193,015	After-tax profit (loss) (D22-D23)	$ 368,428
25				

YTDM 12.1 / YTDM 12.2 / Exhibit12-9 / operating leverage

Ready

12.2 Apply the Theory of Constraints p. 497

a. The following spreadsheet model computes the expected change in throughput (see column I) for each proposed resource and activity change as discussed in the chapter. Column G contains the added activities, and column H shows the costs to increase each activity by the proposed amounts. Column I contains the formulas for the increment in throughput expected from each change. Note that the formula in cell I2 (see the formula bar at the top) is the throughput from added box-seat sales at each event less the estimated advertising cost to increase demand (H2). Likewise, other formulas in column I are the changes in throughput and profit with respect to the proposed changes in activity in column G less added costs in column H. You should build a similar model or at least verify the calculations in column I.

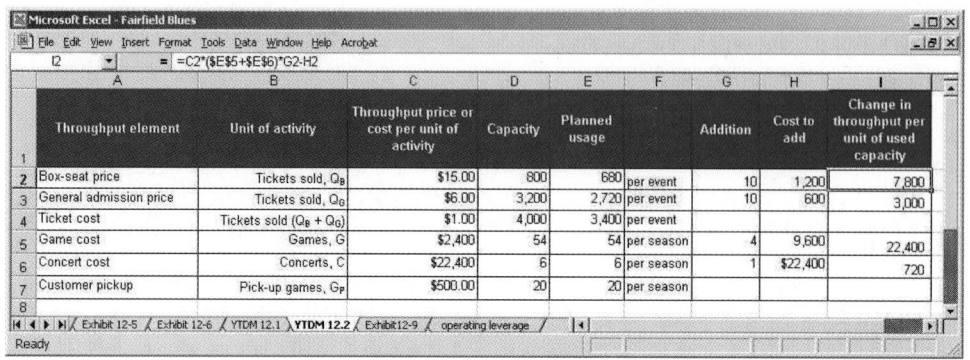

Microsoft Excel - Fairfield Blues

I2 = =C2*(E5+E6)*G2-H2

	A	B	C	D	E	F	G	H	I
1	Throughput element	Unit of activity	Throughput price or cost per unit of activity	Capacity	Planned usage		Addition	Cost to add	Change in throughput per unit of used capacity
2	Box-seat price	Tickets sold, Q_B	$15.00	800	680	per event	10	1,200	7,800
3	General admission price	Tickets sold, Q_G	$6.00	3,200	2,720	per event	10	600	3,000
4	Ticket cost	Tickets sold ($Q_B + Q_G$)	$1.00	4,000	3,400	per event			
5	Game cost	Games, G	$2,400	54	54	per season	4	9,600	22,400
6	Concert cost	Concerts, C	$22,400	6	6	per season	1	$22,400	720
7	Customer pickup	Pick-up games, G_P	$500.00	20	20	per season			
8									

Exhibit 12-5 / Exhibit 12-6 / YTDM 12.1 / **YTDM 12.2** / Exhibit12-9 / operating leverage

Ready

b. All of the proposed actions are risky because they assume known changes in ticket demand for the actions taken. Clearly, the proposal of exhibition games seems viable by estimating a gain of $22,400 per season; increased ticket sales do outweigh the increase in game and ticket costs. Sharing the net proceeds with high school teams also could increase goodwill in the community and lead to increases in normal attendance. Intuitively, the plan to increase advertising seems to be the riskiest of the other proposals because most of the cost must be incurred up front. It might be less risky to try one or both of the other advertising proposals to see whether ticket demand really can be influenced, even slightly, by increased advertising.

c. If management wants to try adding another concert, perhaps it is wise to do it on a trial basis, perhaps as a special event at a holiday without long-term commitments. At the same time, why not try the smaller advertising efforts? They seem to be low cost (too low?), and the benefits might increase over time.

Appendix A to Chapter Twelve

Sensitivity and Scenario Analyses

LO 6 Apply scenario and sensitivity analyses to model the risk of decisions.

All decisions about the future are made without knowing actual outcomes. Decisions might not translate into perfectly executed actions, and external factors might be different than those expected. This is the natural condition of risky decision making, which characterizes all business management. Financial planning models by themselves cannot reduce risks, but they can help managers understand the causes and extent of risk. They then can take actions that are most likely to result in favorable outcomes, for example by ruling out actions that are too risky or by hedging their bets.[11] In addition to operating leverage, discussed earlier, we consider two related sources of risk that can be modeled: parameter variability and alternative combinations of parameters. We present two common methods for modeling these risks more precisely: sensitivity analysis and scenario analysis.[12]

[11] A *hedging action* seeks to neutralize risks, for example, by simultaneously contracting to buy and sell a desired quantity of inputs at a fixed price; gains or losses on the two contracts may offset. The company's only cost could be the cost of the contract, which is similar to buying insurance. For example, General Mills might contract both to buy and sell grain for its cereals at a fixed price. If the eventual market price is higher (or lower) than the contract price, General Mills' gain on the "buy" contract matches the loss on the "sell" contract (or vice versa).

[12] *Monte Carlo simulation analysis* is another method used when sufficient data exist to estimate parameters' probability distributions.

Sensitivity Analysis: What If?

Previous analyses tentatively concluded that Fairfield Blues can exceed its monthly target profit. However, numerous assumptions about its financial variables formed this conclusion. Review the data input section of Exhibit 12–5. Any of these 19 data inputs (ticket prices, activity costs, activity levels, and so on) could be wrong. That is, actual values might be different from planned ones, and actual profits, therefore, also might differ. Jason Robertson and Fairfield Blues' management could wait to find out what will actually happen: whether they actually will have sufficient profit. Alternatively, they can use several methods to assess the risk of their decision-making problem and then take actions to manage their risks.

One of the most common methods of assessing risk is *sensitivity analysis,* introduced in an earlier chapter. It tests a financial planning model for changes in outcomes (e.g., profits) caused by changes in each of the model's parameters (e.g., ticket sales). Sensitivity analysis answers the question, What if this parameter is changed? The more sensitive the outcome is to a parameter change, the more risk the changes in that parameter pose. Obviously, manual sensitivity analysis is a tedious, error-prone task, and few organizations undertake it unless they use computerized financial models. This is where the power and ease of using a computerized model becomes apparent.

Robertson first determined the most likely value of each of the parameters ("base" values). Next, he determined the likely range of each parameter. An analyst can determine these values and ranges by considering historical data, or, in the case of new operations, similar experiences, test cases, or analysts' best estimates. Robertson then introduced a change to one of the parameters in Exhibit 12–5, first changing the parameter to the upper and then to the lower end of the range while keeping all other parameters in the exhibit at their most likely values. He then recorded the resulting profit caused by each change and repeated the analysis for all relevant parameters. Do analysts and managers always have the most reliable information they need to perform this detailed analysis? Unfortunately, no, but using informed estimates in most cases is better than performing no analysis at all. Exhibit 12–6 presents a summary of Robertson's sensitivity analysis of Fairfield Blues' financial model, which we now interpret.

Column A of Exhibit 12–6 identifies all parameters, and column B has the most likely or base parameter values. Robertson's estimates of the highest feasible parameter values are in column C, and the lowest feasible values are in column D. Using relations from Exhibit 12–5, column E computes the estimated base profit,[13] which is the same

[13]The formula in each cell of column E contains the revenue and cost relations from Exhibit 12–5 and the base parameters.

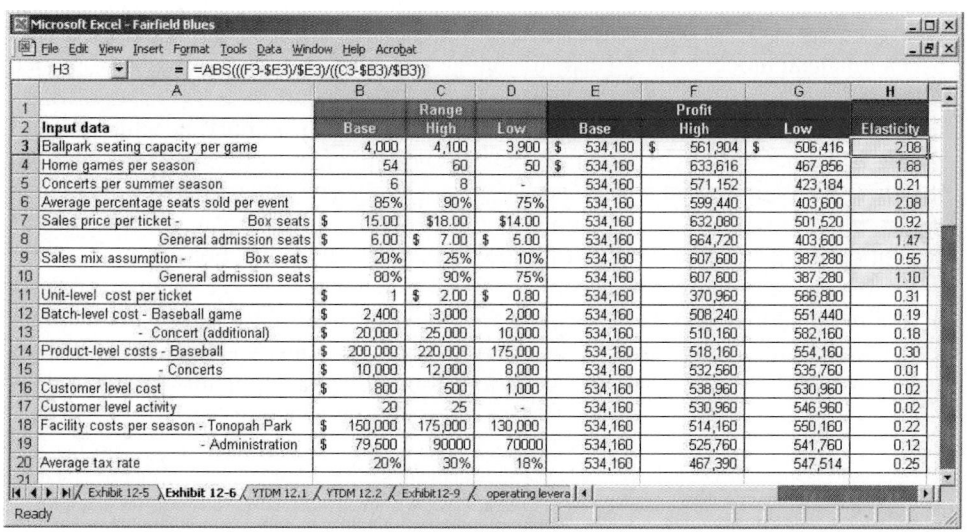

Exhibit 12–6

Summary of Sensitivity Analysis

Microsoft Excel - Fairfield Blues

File Edit View Insert Format Tools Data Window Help Acrobat

H3 = =ABS(((F3-$E3)/$E3)/((C3-$B3)/$B3))

	A	B	C	D	E	F	G	H
1			Range			Profit		
2	**Input data**	Base	High	Low	Base	High	Low	Elasticity
3	Ballpark seating capacity per game	4,000	4,100	3,900	$ 534,160	$ 561,904	$ 506,416	2.08
4	Home games per season	54	60	50	$ 534,160	633,616	467,856	1.68
5	Concerts per summer season	6	8	-	534,160	571,152	423,184	0.21
6	Average percentage seats sold per event	85%	90%	75%	534,160	599,440	403,600	2.08
7	Sales price per ticket - Box seats	$ 15.00	$18.00	$14.00	534,160	632,080	501,520	0.92
8	General admission seats	$ 6.00	$ 7.00	$ 5.00	534,160	664,720	403,600	1.47
9	Sales mix assumption - Box seats	20%	25%	10%	534,160	607,600	387,280	0.55
10	General admission seats	80%	90%	75%	534,160	607,600	387,280	1.10
11	Unit-level cost per ticket	$ 1	$ 2.00	$ 0.80	534,160	370,960	566,800	0.31
12	Batch-level cost - Baseball game	$ 2,400	3,000	2,000	534,160	508,240	551,440	0.19
13	- Concert (additional)	$ 20,000	25,000	10,000	534,160	510,160	582,160	0.18
14	Product-level costs - Baseball	$ 200,000	220,000	175,000	534,160	518,160	554,160	0.30
15	- Concerts	$ 10,000	12,000	8,000	534,160	532,560	535,760	0.01
16	Customer level cost	$ 800	500	1,000	534,160	538,960	530,960	0.02
17	Customer level activity	20	25	-	534,160	530,960	546,960	0.02
18	Facility costs per season - Tonopah Park	$ 150,000	175,000	130,000	534,160	514,160	550,160	0.22
19	- Administration	$ 79,500	90000	70000	534,160	525,760	541,760	0.12
20	Average tax rate	20%	30%	18%	534,160	467,390	547,514	0.25
21								

Exhibit 12-5 / **Exhibit 12-6** / YTDM 12.1 / YTDM 12.2 / Exhibit12-9 / operating levera

Ready

for all parameters because all are set at their most likely or base levels. Column F computes the estimated profit if each parameter in turn is set to its *highest* value while keeping all others at base levels. Similarly, Column G computes the estimated profit if each parameter is set in turn to its *lowest* value, again keeping all others at base levels. Monthly profits range between a high of $664,720 (F8), which reflects the highest price of general admission tickets, and a low of $370,960, which reflects the highest unit-level cost (F11). Clearly, profits are sensitive to ticket prices and unit-level costs, but sorting through the mass of numbers in this summary and comparing changes in profits with respect to such different changes in inputs can be difficult. We need a way to directly compare all of these profit and parameter changes.

model elasticity *is the ratio of the percentage change in profit divided by the percentage change of an input parameter*

We can compare outcome effects by computing the **model elasticity,** the ratio of the percentage change in profit divided by the percentage change in an input parameter. This calculation is analogous to the elasticity of demand, which economists use to compare reactions of demand to changes in prices of different goods. Because elasticity is a ratio of pure percentage numbers, it is independent of the units of measurement. Thus, we can compare the change in profit from a one-unit change in ticket sales to that from a one-unit change in the number of games. Column H shows the model elasticity for each of the parameters.

Model elasticity = Percentage change of profit ÷ Percentage change of input

For example, the model elasticity to general admission seat prices (H8) is computed as

General admission seat price elasticity = Percentage change of profit ÷ Percentage ÷ Percentage change of general admission seat price

$$H8 = [(F8 - E8) \div E8] \div [(C8 - B8) \div B8]$$
$$1.47 = [(664{,}720 - 534{,}160) \div 534{,}160] \div [(7 - 6) \div 6]$$

You may interpret this elasticity to indicate that a 1 percent change in general admission ticket price should cause a 1.47 percent change in profit.[14] An elasticity greater than 1.0 identifies a parameter with a disproportionate effect on profits (this column heading is highlighted in Exhibit 12–6). Actions to change parameters with the highest elasticity should have the greatest impacts on profits. The parameters with the greatest potential to affect profits, according to this model, are the ballpark seating capacity (row 3) and the average percentage of seats sold (row 6). With model elasticities of 2.08, the way to affect profits the most is to change either the seating capacity (temporarily or permanently) or the percentage of seats sold. Conversely, changes in parameters with low elasticity will have relatively small effects on profits. As informative as this analysis can be, it assumes that each parameter affects profits independently of the others. This is not the general case, but analysts should monitor and measure these elastic parameters carefully.

Scenario Analysis (Best, Worst, and Most Likely Cases)

scenario analysis *creates* realistic *combinations of changed parameters*

Robertson reasoned that some parameters should not be changed independently of others. His financial model makes it easy to change any combination of variables together, but the number of possible combinations of parameter changes is very large. Many managers assess the risk of their decision making by **scenario analysis,** which creates *realistic* combinations of changed parameters. Of all the many possible combinations, only a few are realistic; that is, they very well can happen or actually have happened in the past. By using the model to compute each scenario's profits, managers can see the different outcomes from a number of realistic sets of conditions. For example, an increase in ticket prices might be accompanied by a decrease in ticket volume. Analysts commonly prepare the *best-case, worst-case,* and *most likely case* for review by managers. The most likely case usually, but not necessarily, sets all parameters to their most likely or base values. The best-case scenario is the *realistic* combination of the highest

[14]Because the financial model contains only linear relations among the variables, using either the highest or lowest parameter value and corresponding profit results in the same estimated elasticity. This is not the general economic situation, but it could be a reasonable assumption in many situations.

Research Insight 12.2

Scenario Analysis

Researchers in many fields use scenario analysis to understand the dimensions of risky decision making. For example, weather researchers use complex computer models to predict the landfall of a hurricane several days in advance, given different ocean current, air, and water temperature scenarios. Research continues to improve the models' ability to predict hurricane intensity. Biologists use population dynamics models to predict the future of endangered species given alternative decisions to modify their environment. Recent modeling of Orca whales in Washington's Puget Sound examined seven likely scenarios including changes in (1) toxic chemicals, such as PCBs, (2) salmon populations, which are in decline forcing Orcas to eat contaminated bottom fish, (3) stress from whale-watching boats, and (4) effects of capturing young whales for marine parks 20 years ago. The results indicated that "even best-case scenarios do not look very good." *Sources: "Computer's View of a Hurricane,"* USA Today; *C. Dunagan, "Report: Washington Orcas Endangered," Scripps Howard News Service. November 18, 2000.*

prices, highest unit-volumes, and lowest costs and cost-driving activities. Conversely, the worst-case scenario is the *realistic* combination of lowest prices, lowest unit volumes, and highest costs and cost-driving activities. Describing these cases often requires the collective judgment of a cross-functional team because so many business interactions are involved. The range of outcomes resulting from the various cases shows how good or bad things might be, and the range of outcomes indicates the actual risks of the decision the manager faces.

Suppose that Robertson, without the help of other employees, identified best- and worst-case scenarios as shown in Exhibit 12–7 and set the model parameters to each case's values. The resulting profits are at the bottom of the exhibit. A careful look at the combinations might lead you to label them as "wildly optimistic" and "hopelessly catastrophic" cases! If these are realistic scenarios, one might characterize this company's management as "very risky." The best case seems extremely good, and the worst case seems just as extremely bad. If Robertson were to present these scenarios to Fairfield Blues' top management, he might receive many questions about their realism. Indeed,

Exhibit 12–7

Examples of Best, Worst, and Most Likely Cases

Input Data	Best Case	Worst Case	Most Likely
Ballpark seating capacity per game	4,100	3,900	4,000
Home games per season	60	50	54
Concerts per summer season	8	—	6
Average percentage seats sold per event	90%	75%	85%
Sales price per ticket—Box seats	$18.00	$14.00	$15.00
General admission seats	$7.00	$5.00	$6.00
Sales mix assumption—Box seats	25%	10%	20%
General admission seats	75%	90%	80%
Unit-level cost per ticket	$0.80	$2.00	$1.00
Batch-level cost—Baseball game	$2,000	$3,000	$2,400
—Concert (additional)	$10,000	$25,000	$20,000
Product-level costs—Baseball game	$175,000	$220,000	$200,000
—Concerts	$8,000	$12,000	$10,000
Customer-level cost	$500	$1,000	$800
Customer-level activity (games)	—	25	20
Facility costs per season—Tonopah Park	$130,000	$175,000	$150,000
—Administration	$70,000	$90,000	$79,500
Average tax rate	18%	30%	20%
Scenario profit	$ 1,350,322	$(71,138)	$534,160

before he considers presenting these scenarios, he should be confident that each tells a plausible story and that he can communicate this story to top management. He would be wise to consult others to develop realistic scenarios.

Appendix B to Chapter Twelve

Linear Programming

LO 7 Use linear programming to model decisions about the use of multiple scarce resources.

Many firms face the problem of how best to use multiple scarce resources. An example presented in the body of this chapter showed that when a single resource is constrained, management should produce the good or service that has the highest payoff per unit of scarce resource. However, the situation becomes more complicated if the organization faces decisions among multiple products with two or more scarce resources. Recall that we previously modeled multiproduct decision making by *assuming* a product mix. A quantitative tool called "linear programming" is designed to help find the product mix that maximizes profits when multiple constraints exist. Linear programming, as its name implies, assumes that all model relations are linear. Nonlinear methods are available when this assumption is not met.

Introduction to Linear Programming Models

linear programming *shows how best to allocate multiple scarce resources among alternative courses of action in the short run when capacity cannot be increased*

objective function *is a mathematical relation of inputs and outputs to be maximized or minimized*

feasible solution space *is the combination of input and output values that satisfy the constraints*

optimum point *is the set of inputs and outputs in the feasible solution space that maximizes or minimizes the objective function*

Linear programming shows how best to allocate multiple scarce resources among alternative courses of action in the short run when capacity cannot be increased. Linear programming finds the combination of products or services that maximizes throughput or contribution margin or minimizes cost within the limits of constrained resources. To illustrate how linear programming works, it is necessary first to describe its elements.

Objective function is a mathematical relation of inputs and outputs to be maximized or minimized. For example, the objective of the linear programming problem might be to maximize monthly throughput, revenues less throughput costs. The objective function is the equation that models throughput, for example. *Constraints* represent capacity limits of the various processes and resources. Linear programming constraints state algebraically that resources used must not exceed the resources available.

Feasible solution space is the combination of input and output values that satisfy the constraints. When more than one constraint is binding (i.e., acting as a bottleneck), maximizing the throughput per unit of constrained resource is not sufficient. Linear programming investigates the possibly numerous feasible combinations of inputs and outputs that satisfy the constraints to find the optimum point.

Optimum point is the set of inputs and outputs in the feasible solution space that maximizes or minimizes the objective function. In rare cases, multiple points are optimal.

For this discussion, we assume that linear programming problems are modeled on the computer. Our focus is on setting up the problems so they can be entered into the computer and on interpreting the output, not on the mathematical procedures used to derive the solutions. When reliable computer programs are used properly, the mathematical procedures are transparent. Of course, this also means that the user must know enough about linear programming and the decision context to recognize an improbable solution that is the result of improperly constructing the model.

Assume that a Fairfield company called Creative Constructs, Inc., makes the sets for television and theater productions. Over time it has developed an expertise in producing three standardized wood products from high-quality, recycled lumber (usually taken from demolished old houses and old farm buildings): armchairs (A), bookshelves

Exhibit 12–8 Creative Constructs' Model Parameters

	Armchairs (A) per Unit	Bookshelves (B) per Unit	Cabinets (C) per Unit
Selling price	\$14.00	\$18.00	\$24.00
Unit-level material cost (lumber)	6.00	7.20	10.80
Unit-level conversion cost (labor and overhead)	2.32	3.40	4.96
Contribution margins (also throughput)	5.68	7.40	8.24
Material requirements in board feet	4.00	7.00	6.00
Labor requirements in hours—Cutting department	0.30	0.30	0.40
Labor requirement in hours—Assembly and finishing department	0.50	0.20	0.50
Demand	At least 100 per week	No more than 100	No constraint

(B), and cabinets (C). The demand for its products is so high that it now markets these three products commercially.

Each product must be processed through two departments (1) cutting and (2) assembly and finishing before it is sold. Exhibit 12–8 presents data about product selling prices, costs, and the rate at which each product uses scarce resources. In addition to the information provided in Exhibit 12–8, we learn that the company can obtain only 2,000 board feet of high-quality, recycled lumber per week. The cutting department has a maximum of 180 hours of labor available each week, and the assembly and finishing department has a maximum of 240 hours of labor available each week. No overtime is allowed.

Only variable or unit-level costs, which primarily are the costs of materials and hourly labor, are affected by the choice of which product to make. Higher-level costs, such as batch-, product-, and facility-level costs, are the same regardless of which product Creative Constructs produces and sells. The production decision is to determine which product mix maximizes weekly profit.

Linear programming model formulation. Creative Construct's product mix decision can be solved using linear programming models. Building a linear programming model for it requires transforming the data (in this example, in Exhibit 12–8) into equation form. Maximize total contribution margin (higher-level costs are unaffected by short-run product mix):

$$\$5.68A + \$7.40B + \$8.24C$$

Subject to the following constraints:

Direct materials	$4A + 7B + 6C \leq 2{,}000$ **board feet**
Cutting	$.30A + .30B + .40C \leq 180$ **labor hours**
Assembly and finishing	$.50A + .20B + .50C \leq 240$ **labor hours**
Armchair sales	$A \geq 100$ **units sold**
Bookcase sales	$B \leq 100$ **units sold**

The direct materials constraint means that the number of board feet of lumber required for each armchair (product A) is 4, for each bookcase (product B) is 7, and for each cabinet (product C) is 6. The total of all the wood required cannot exceed the maximum of 2,000 board feet available per week. The cutting constraint similarly means that the total of all labor hours used to make A at .30 per unit, B at .30 per unit, and C at .40 per unit cannot exceed the maximum of 180 labor hours available per week. The assembly and finishing constraint likewise states that the total assembly and finishing labor

Exhibit 12–9
Spreadsheet Linear Programming Model

Microsoft Excel - Fairfield Blues

B14 = =B4*B12

	A	B	C	D	E	F
1	Data input	Armchairs	Bookcases	Cabinets		Constraint
2	Contribution margin per unit	$ 5.68	$ 7.40	$ 8.24		
3	Resource constraints					
4	Direct materials, board feet per unit	4.00	7.00	6.00	less than	2,000
5	Cutting, hours per unit	0.30	0.30	0.40	less than	180
6	Assembly and finishing, hours per unit	0.50	0.20	0.50	less than	240
7	Demand constraints					
8	Armchair sales, units				at least	100
9	Bookcase sales, units				no more than	100
10	Initial guess at sales levels	10	10	10		
11	Linear Program Model	Armchairs	Bookcases	Cabinets	Total	Constraint
12	Units sold (replaced by the optimal solution)	10	10	10	30	
13	Contribution margin (B2*B12,C2*C12,D2*D12)	$ 57	$ 74	$ 82	$ 213	
14	Board feet of material used (B4*B12, etc.)	40	70	60	170	2,000
15	Cutting hours used (B5*B12, etc.)	3	3	4	10	180
16	Assembly and finishing hours used (B6*B12, etc.)	5	2	5	12	240
17	Sales of Armchairs (B12)	10			10	100
18	Sales of Bookcases (C12)		10		10	100
19						

Exhibit 12-5 / Exhibit 12-6 / YTDM 12.1 / YTDM 12.2 / Exhibit12-9

Ready

hours used to complete products A, B, and C cannot exceed the 240 labor hours available per week. The sales constraints mean that the total units of A produced and sold must be at least 100 per week; sales and production of B cannot exceed 100 per week. Product C has no sales constraint.

Exhibit 12–9 displays the input of these parameters and relations into a spreadsheet model. Data inputs are in cells A1 to F9 and correspond to the preceding descriptions of the sales and production activities. An additional input is in row 10. This input, "initial guess at sales levels," is a beginning point for the model solution. To begin the solution, you can enter any feasible number of units, even zeros, into cells B10 to D10. We entered positive numbers so that the spreadsheet displays nonzero figures computed in the other cells.

Using the Excel spreadsheet, the model (rows 12 to 18) is entered in roughly the same format as our earlier financial planning models; each cell of the model is a formula of inputs and outputs. The number of units sold (row 12) initially is set equal to the number of guesses in row 10; these numbers can vary to create a more profitable solution. Contribution margins (CMs) in row 13 are computed by multiplying the CMs per unit in row 2 by the units sold in row 12. The sum of the product CMs is the current value of the objective function and is shown in E13.

Rows 4 through 9 display the data for the five constraints described previously. Row 14 computes the amount of lumber used for the number of units sold. Note that at the initial sales levels, the total amount of lumber used, 170 board feet (E14), is less than the constrained amount of 2,000 board feet, shown in F14. Cells E15 to E18 similarly compute the amounts of other scarce resources and of sales that are constrained for comparison with the constrained amounts in column F.

The Excel "Tools" menu has an option called "Solver," which is a powerful mathematical programming module (you might need to "add in" this module). Clicking on "Solver" generates the following window where you enter the linear programming elements as represented by the model. The "target cell" or objective function is E13, the sum of product contribution margins. Next you specify whether to maximize or minimize the value in this cell or to force it to meet a specific value. Then you show which cells to vary to find alternative solutions, the unit sales in row 12. By clicking on the "Add" button you can enter each of the constraints in equation form. Note the first three constraints (e.g., B12 > = 0). These equations state that each unit of sales cannot be negative, which makes eminent sense, but the program must be told this explicitly. Finally, clicking on the "Solve" button generates the optimal solution.

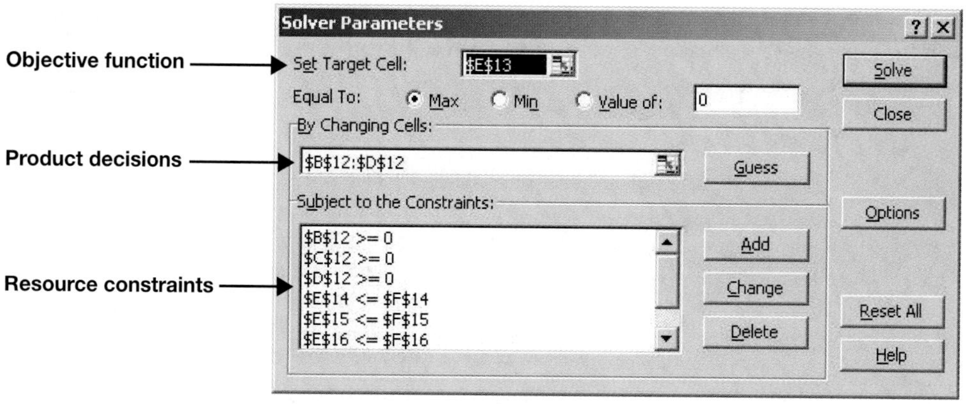

Linear programming model solution. Exhibit 12–10 is the revision of the model in Exhibit 12–9 after Solver has found the optimal solution and replaced the initial guesses in row 12 with the optimal sales levels. Note that you can produce other, more detailed reports on the properties of the solution (e.g., limits and sensitivity analyses) by clicking appropriate buttons after obtaining this solution. You should consult an appropriate linear programming text for the use of this additional information.

The linear programming model has replaced the initial guesses in row 12 with the optimal solution to produce and sell 440 armchairs (B12), no bookcases (C12), and 40 cabinets (D12). The weekly contribution margin generated by this solution is $2,829 (E13). Compare the total resources used by this solution (cells E14 to E18) to the corresponding constrained amounts (F14 to F18). This solution uses all lumber available (2,000 board feet, E14 = F14), and all assembly and finishing hours available (240 hours, E16 = F16). These appear to be the bottlenecks (or "binding" constraints) at this solution. We can compare the benefit of relaxing each of these constraints by some feasible amounts (i.e., change the constraint values by some feasible amounts and observe the increase in CM) to the costs of acquiring more capacity. Note, however, that the cutting department has excess capacity (or "slack") (E15 < F15) of 32 hours, nearly one full-time, hourly employee. Thus, the available cutting time is not a binding constraint. Maintaining this level or increasing capacity in this department might be a waste of resources in the long run if this solution represents future optimal operations. Creative Constructs also can consider dropping the bookcase product line if it appears

Exhibit 12–10

Linear Programming Solution

Microsoft Excel - Fairfield Blues

E13 = =SUM(B13:D13)

	A	B	C	D	E	F
1	Data input	Armchairs	Bookcases	Cabinets		Constraint
2	Contribution margin per unit	$ 5.68	$ 7.40	$ 8.24		
3	Resource constraints					
4	Direct materials, board feet per unit	4.00	7.00	6.00	less than	2,000
5	Cutting, hours per unit	0.30	0.30	0.40	less than	180
6	Assembly and finishing, hours per unit	0.50	0.20	0.50	less than	240
7	Demand constraints					
8	Armchair sales, units				at least	100
9	Bookcase sales, units				no more than	100
10	Initial guess at sales levels	10	10	10		
11	Linear Program Model	Armchairs	Bookcases	Cabinets	Total	Constraint
12	Units sold (replaced by the optimal solution)	440	-	40	480	
13	Contribution margin (B2*B12,C2*C12,D2*D12)	$ 2,499	$ -	$ 330	$ 2,829	
14	Board feet of material used (B4*B12, etc.)	1,760	-	240	2,000	2,000
15	Cutting hours used (B5*B12, etc.)	132	-	16	148	180
16	Assembly and finishing hours used (B6*B12, etc.)	220	-	20	240	240
17	Sales of Armchairs (B12)	440			440	100
18	Sales of Bookcases (C12)		-		-	100
19						

Exhibit 12-5 / Exhibit 12-6 / YTDM 12.1 / YTDM 12.2 / Exhibit12-9

Ready

that this solution will persist. The sales constraints also appear to have no effect on this solution because armchair sales easily exceed the minimum of 100 (E17 > F17) and bookcase sales are zero (shown by dashes in C12 to C19), well below the maximum (E18 < F18).

Review Questions

12.1 Review the chapter's key terms and define them.

12.2 What are the characteristics of a good financial planning model?

12.3 What benefits do financial models provide to users?

12.4 What are the objectives of financial modeling?

12.5 What are the elements of a cost-volume-profit (CVP) model? Is this the best name for this type of model?

12.6 Explain the difference between break-even point and target break-even point.

12.7 Explain how a cost-volume-profit (CVP) graph is also a financial model.

12.8 What are the advantages of computerized financial models compared to manual financial models?

12.9 Why should a financial model's parameters be located as numbers in only one place?

12.10 When is using the average tax rate desirable in modeling the effects of taxes in a financial model?

12.11 Explain the sales mix assumption in financial planning analysis. Why is this assumption made?

12.12 What is the meaning of the term "weighted-average unit contribution margin?" What does this amount contribute toward covering?

12.13 What is the difference between using throughput or contribution margin as the contribution toward profit in financial planning models?

12.14 Briefly explain how financial planning models benefit from activity-based costing (ABC).

12.15 What is sensitivity analysis? Scenario analysis? What are their purposes? (Appendix A)

12.16 Briefly describe the proper approach to making a production decision when a single limited resource is involved.

12.17 How is the Theory of Constraints as much a cost-management attitude as a modeling method?

Critical Analysis

12.18 In a strategy meeting, a manufacturing company's president said, "If we raise the price of our product, the company's break-even point will be lower." The financial vice president responded by saying, "Then we should raise our price. The company will be less likely to incur a loss." With whom do you agree and disagree? Why?

12.19 A company recently constructed a financial planning model to predict monthly cash inflows and outflows. The model is based on various financial relationships including collection patterns of receivables, inventory outflows, expense payments, and so forth, all obtained by analyzing monthly data of the past three years. Before the spreadsheet model is put into use, management insists that employees perform some validity testing to ensure that the model is working properly. Suggest how the model might be tested to ensure that it is, in fact, valid.

12.20 "Cost-volume-profit (CVP) analysis is an oversimplification of the real world. For this reason, it has little to offer a decision maker." Comment.

12.21 Picture the cost-volume-profit (CVP) model. Explain how the model can be used to evaluate the performance of an organization's (1) divisions and (2) divisional managers. The managers are evaluated annually for purposes of pay raises and promotions. What are the inherent dangers in using this model for evaluation purposes?

12.22 Management notes that the contribution from one product is higher than the contribution from a second product. Hence, management concludes that the company should concentrate on manufacturing the first product. Under what, if any, conditions will this approach result in maximum profits?

12.23 A sporting goods retailer is running a monthly special that prices tennis balls and golf balls to yield a negative contribution margin. What causes a negative contribution margin? What is the likely motive behind the retailer's actions?

12.24 You have built a fairly complex financial planning model for your organization. It contains many parameters and assumptions about how the parameters are related. When you presented the base-case results of the model to your planning committee, the general response was, "Well, I guess we need to drop product X from the product line and that probably will mean closing the manufacturing plant in Omaha." You were shocked by this reaction even though the model did show product X to be unprofitable. How should you have presented your model and the results?

12.25 You and your cost-management team spent months building and testing a financial planning model of your organization's operations. When you previewed the model to a long-time manager, her reaction was, "I don't trust computer models anymore than I trust manual election counts. Garbage in equals garbage out, as far as I am concerned." How should you use this reaction to prepare for presenting your model to the organization's chief executive?

12.26 Proponents of the Theory of Constraints approach to managing processes argue that managers should review every task or operation performed in an organization and ask, "Does completing this task help the organization achieve its goal?" If the answer is no, managers should find a way to eliminate the effort. Do you believe this test can be applied to every task in an organization? Should every task that fails the test be eliminated? Explain.

12.27 Respond to this comment: "We are unable to meet demand for our product, yet you refuse to let us operate all our processes at least at practical capacity. I think that is a waste of equipment and personnel. What am I supposed to do, have them sweep the floors and let this expensive equipment sit idle?"

12.28 One of your company's top salespersons approaches you and says, "I just heard that I am not allowed in the production area anymore because you have outlawed our efforts to push customers' orders through the process. Listen, my sales performance is the best in the company because my customers know that I will fight to get their orders through this labyrinth of a plant. You are threatening my ability to work effectively for this company. There is no way that you are going to keep me off the production floor without a huge fight. I'll see you at the executive committee meeting on Wednesday." Prepare your arguments to justify your decision to outlaw the expediting of customers' orders by sales personnel.

12.29 Provide possible reactions to recommendations to implement the Theory of Constraints from the perspective of an employee in a:

a. Bottleneck process.

b. Nonbottleneck process.

c. Sales organization.

d. Customer service organization.

Exercises

Exercise 12.30
Cost-Volume-Profit
(LO 2, 3)

Canyon Escape sells individual tickets for $60 for walking tours of the Grand Canyon. Unit-level costs, including lunch, are $12 per ticket; fixed costs total $240,000 per year.

Required

a. How many tickets must be sold to break even?

b. What level of revenue is needed to earn a target income of $36,000?

c. If unit-level costs increase to $20 per ticket, what decrease in annual fixed costs must be achieved to keep the same break-even point as calculated in requirement (a)?

d. (Optional) Prepare a computer spreadsheet to complete requirements (a)–(c) of this exercise.

Exercise 12.31
Cost-Volume-Profit
(LO 2, 3)

Delta Safety Systems manufactures a component used in aircraft radar systems. The firm's committed costs are $4,000,000 per year. Delta's variable cost of each component is $2,000, and it sells the components for $3,000 each. The company sold 5,000 components during the prior year.

Required

a. Compute the break-even point in units.

b. Suggest several possible actions that management can take if it wants to decrease the break-even point.

c. The sales manager believes that a reduction in sales price to $2,500 will result in orders for 1,200 more components each year. In comparison with last year's results, will the company benefit if it changes the price? Show calculations to support your answer.

d. (Optional) Prepare a computer spreadsheet to complete requirements (a)–(c) of this exercise.

Exercise 12.32
Cost-Volume-Profit and Capacity
(LO 2, 3)

Superior Manufacturing produced and sold 60,000 temperature gauges last year at $32 each. This level of activity amounted to 60 percent of the firm's total productive capacity. The costs related to this level of activity follow:

	Manufacturing	Selling	Administrative	Total
Unit level	$660,000	$180,000	$ 0	$840,000
Facility level	220,000	190,000	400,000	810,000

Required

a. How many gauges must it sell to break even?

b. Compute last year's income or loss from sales of temperature gauges.

c. Considering your answer in requirement (a), at what percentage of total productive capacity must Superior operate to achieve a break-even operation?

d. (Optional) Prepare a computer spreadsheet to complete requirements (a)–(c) of this exercise.

Exercise 12.33
Cost-Volume-Profit
(LO 2)

Choose the best answer for each of the following:

1. A firm has a negative contribution margin. To reach break-even, it must:
   a. Increase unit-selling price.
   b. Increase sales volume.
   c. Decrease sales volume.
   d. Decrease fixed cost.
   e. Increase fixed cost.
2. If the firm decreases total contribution margin by a given amount, operating profit:
   a. Remains unchanged.
   b. Decreases by the same amount.
   c. Decreases by more than the given amount.
   d. Increases by the same amount.
   e. Does none of the above.
3. The break-even point is increased by:
   a. A decrease in variable costs.
   b. A decrease in fixed costs.
   c. An increase in selling price.
   d. An increase in variable costs.
   e. None of the above.

[CPA adapted]

Exercise 12.34
Cost-Volume-Profit and Taxes
(LO 3, 4)

Aqua Systems Engineering provides consulting services to city water authorities. A recent income statement revealed variable costs of $640,000 on a sales level of $800,000. Annual committed expenses are $120,000, and the firm's income tax rate is 40 percent.

Required

a. Calculate the firm's break-even volume of service revenue.
b. How much before-tax income must the firm earn to make an after-tax net income of $48,000?
c. What level of revenue must the firm generate to earn an after-tax net income of $48,000?
d. Suppose the firm's income tax rate rises to 45 percent. What will happen to the break-even level of consulting revenue?
e. (Optional) Prepare a computer spreadsheet to complete requirements (a)–(d) of this exercise.

Exercise 12.35
Cost-Volume-Profit and Multiple Products
(LO 3, 4)

Ken's Bicycle Shop sells mountain bikes. For purposes of a cost-volume-profit analysis, the shop owner has divided sales into two categories, as follows:

Product Category	Sales Price	Invoice Cost	Sales Commissions
High quality	$500	$275	$25
Medium quality	300	135	15

The shop anticipates selling 480 bicycles, 360 of which will be medium quality. Annual fixed costs are $65,000. Ignore taxes.

Required

a. What is the shop's sales mix?
b. What is the shop's break-even sales volume in dollars? (*Hint:* Find the break-even sales volume first.)
c. How many bicycles of each type must the firm sell to earn a target net income of $48,750?
d. (Optional) Prepare a computer spreadsheet to complete requirements (a)–(c) of this exercise.

Exercise 12.36
Cost-Volume-Profit and ABC
(LO 3, 4)

Concord Manufacturing, which uses an activity-based costing system, sells 10,000 units per year of product 887 at $50 each. Unit-level activities cost $20 per unit; facilities costs total $81,000 per year. Additional data follow:

- Batch-level activities consist of 15 setups per year at a cost of $2,000 each.
- Product-level activities consist of 600 engineering hours per year at $40 per hour.

Required

a. From an activity-based costing perspective, identify one problem associated with the basic cost-volume-profit (CVP) model.

b. What is Concord's annual break-even point?

c. Compute Concord's expected operating income before tax, including the costs in the preceding bulleted list.

d. (Optional) Prepare a computer spreadsheet to complete requirements (a)–(c) of this exercise.

Exercise 12.37
Cost-Volume-Profit and Activity-Based Costing
(LO 3, 4)

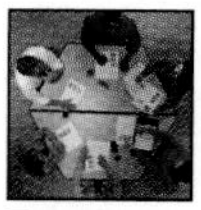

Team

Communication

Chicago Consulting Group, which uses an activity-based costing (ABC) system, offers a software-training seminar to companies for $10,000 per seminar. Unit-level activities cost $200 per student for 1,000 students per year; facility costs total $80,000 per year. Additional data follow:

- Batch-level activities consist of 50 seminars per year at a cost of $2,000 per seminar.
- Product-level activities consist of 2,000 product maintenance hours per year to keep the seminar up to date at $50 per hour.

Required

In small groups, complete the following:

a. From an ABC perspective, identify one problem associated with the basic cost-volume-profit model.

b. Compute Chicago Consulting Group's operating income before tax considering the costs in the preceding bulleted list.

c. (Optional) Prepare a computer spreadsheet to complete requirements (a) and (b) of this exercise. Be prepared to demonstrate this spreadsheet model to the class.

Exercise 12.38
Cost-Volume-Profit and Sensitivity Analysis (Appendix A)
(LO 3, 5)

Review the information in rows 1–5 of Exhibit 12–3. Assume that Fairfield Blues takes actions to decrease its average tax rate to 18 percent by outsourcing its tax planning. This increases facility-level costs by an average of $10,000 per season.

Required

a. Compute the new break-even volume.

b. Compute the new target profit volume.

c. Explain the changes in these volumes.

d. Compute the new profit (loss) after tax.

e. (Optional) Prepare a computer spreadsheet to complete requirements (a)–(d) of this exercise.

Exercise 12.39
Scarce Resource
(LO 5)

Quicksilver's management has been reviewing company profitability and is attempting to improve performance through better planning. The company manufactures three products in its jewelry line: necklaces, bracelets, and rings. Selected data follow.

	Necklaces	Bracelets	Rings
Selling price	$50.00	$37.50	$25.00
Contribution margin	$20.00	$15.00	$10.00
Machine time required	.5 hours	.25 hours	.30 hours

Machine time is limited to 120 hours per month, and demand for each product far exceeds the company's ability to produce. At the present time, Quicksilver manufactures an equal number of each product. The sales manager has urged the company to concentrate on necklace production because of its high selling price relative to bracelets and rings. Quicksilver will produce no bracelets or rings if it accepts this recommendation. Ignore taxes.

Required

a. If fixed costs are $2,500 per month, what profit will the company obtain by following the sales manager's recommendation?

b. What is the maximum profit obtainable and what product or product combination must be sold to obtain that maximum? (*Hint:* Compute the contribution margin of each product per unit of constrained resource.)

Exercise 12.40
Scarce Resource
(LO 5)

Manufacturing cost and other data for two components, 543 and 789, used by Baltimore Electronics follow.

	Component	
	543	**789**
Direct materials	$0.40	$8.00
Direct conversion cost	2.60	5.50
Sales price	5.00	15.00
Yearly demand (units)	6,000	8,000
Machine hours per unit	4	2

In past years, Baltimore has manufactured all of its components. However, during the coming year, the firm will have only 30,000 hours of machine time available. Ignore taxes.

Required

a. Can Baltimore fully satisfy demand? Show calculations to support your answer.

b. Determine the number of units of each component that Baltimore should make during the coming year.

[CPA adapted]

Exercise 12.41
Linear Programming
(Appendix B)
(LO 7)

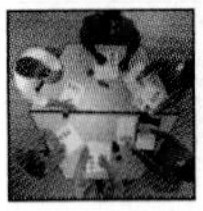
Team

Communication

Classic Corporation manufactures two models, small and large. Each model is processed as follows: The weekly time available for processing the two models is 100 hours in machining and 90 hours in polishing. The contribution margin is $3 for the small model and $4 for the large model.

	Machining	**Polishing**
Small	1 hour	2 hours
Large	4 hours	3 hours

Required

In small groups, complete the following:

a. Formulate the objective function and constraint equations necessary to solve for the optimum product mix.

b. Prepare a short memo explaining how the linear programming approach differs from profit planning with an assumed product mix.

[CPA adapted]

Exercise 12.42
Bottleneck Identification
(LO 5)

Spreadsheet

Identify which of the following insurance claim processes are most likely to be current and future bottleneck processes.

A Process	**B Available Hours per Week**	**C Value-Adding Time (hours per claim)**	**D Theoretical Capacity (claims per week) (D = B ÷ C)**	**E Practical Capacity (85%) (E = 0.85 × D)**	**F Average Demand**	**G Excess Capacity (G = E − F)**
Receive claim	40	.08 hr	?	?	400	?
Route claim to adjuster	80	.16 hr	?	?	400	?
Investigate and settle claim	400	1.20 hr	?	?	400	?
Issue payment and close claim	50	.12 hr	?	?	400	?

Exercise 12.43
Bottleneck Identification
(LO 5)

Spreadsheet

Identify which of the following business processes for a small (two-person) independent telephone company are most likely to be current and future bottleneck processes.

A Process	B Available Hours per Week	C Value-Adding Time (hours per claim)	D Theoretical Capacity (activity per week) (D = B ÷ C)	E Practical Capacity (85%) (E = 0.85 × D)	F Average Demand	G Excess Capacity (G = E − F)
Advertising (ads)	5	.50 hr	?	?	5	?
Bill collecting (bills)	10	.40 hr	?	?	50	?
Service installations	40	.25 hr	?	?	150	?
Credit analyses	10	.25 hr	?	?	150	?
Purchases of phone service I from Southwestern Bel	5	.15 hr	?	?	150	?
Invoicing and billing (bills)	10	.02 hr	?	?	1,000	?
Business planning and analysis (plans)	5	5.00 hr	?	?	2	?

Exercise 12.44
Theory of Constraints
(LO 5)

Internet Communication

Search the periodicals in your library or on the Internet for an article about or description of an organization that applied the principles of the Theory of Constraints to improve its productive processes. Prepare either a two-page written description or analysis of that organization's experience or a five-minute oral presentation (instructor's choice). You should cover the following points:

a. Description of the organization.
b. Description of the production problem.
c. Steps taken by the organization.
d. Results of the steps taken.
e. Credibility of the article or description.

Exercise 12.45
Theory of Constraints
(LO 5)

Communication Team

Prepare a group response either in favor of or against the following comment: "The greatest obstacle to improving the overall efficiency of an organization is the cost-accounting mentality that seeks to make each individual process as efficient as possible." Be prepared to debate your position.

Problems

Problem 12.46
Cost-Volume-Profit
(LO 2, 3)

DisKing is a retailer of high-tech recording disks. The current year's projected net income is $200,000 based on a sales volume of 200,000 units. The company has been selling the disks for $16 each; variable costs consist of the $10 purchase price and a $2 handling cost. DisKing's annual fixed costs are $600,000.

Required

a. Calculate DisKing's break-even point for the current year in units.
b. What will be the company's net income for the current year if projected unit sales volume increases by 10 percent?
c. Management is planning for the coming year when it expects the unit purchase price of the disks to increase by 30 percent. What volume of dollar sales must DisKing achieve in the coming year to maintain the current year's net income if its selling price remains at $16?
d. Is the use of a financial model helpful to the firm in addressing issues such as those raised in requirements (b) and (c)? Explain.
e. (Optional) Prepare a spreadsheet model of DisKing's retailing operation.

[CMA adapted]

Problem 12.47
Multiple Products and Scenario Analysis (Appendix A)
(LO 3, 4, 6)

Refer to the information presented in Exhibit 12–5, rows 1 to 12 for Fairfield Blues. Assume that you have some new information about costs and activities for next year. Namely, you learn that the cost per game should be $3,000 instead of $2,400, the cost per ticket should be $1.50 instead of $1.00, and the estimated number of tickets sold should be 200,000 instead of 204,000. Assume that all other information in rows 1–12 of Exhibit 12–5 is valid.

Required

a. Compute the new weighted-average unit contribution margin (WAUCM) considering this new information.

b. Compute the new break-even volume.

c. Compute the new target profit volume.

d. Compute the estimated operating income for next year for Fairfield Blues.

e. (Optional) Duplicate the spreadsheet model in Exhibit 12–5 to complete requirements (a)–(d) of this problem.

Problem 12.48
Cost-Volume-Profit
(LO 2, 3)

A financial analyst is studying two new conveyor systems, basic and deluxe. The basic system has variable operating costs of $8.00 per unit and annual committed costs of $520,000; in contrast, the deluxe system has variable costs of $6.40 and committed costs of $672,000. The company sells its products for $32 per unit, subject to a 10 percent sales commission. Ignore taxes.

Required

a. Which of the two systems will be more profitable for the firm if sales are expected to average 150,000 units per year?

b. How many units must the company sell to break even if it selects the deluxe system?

c. Suppose that the basic system requires the purchase of additional equipment that is not reflected in the preceding figures. The equipment will cost $224,000 and will be depreciated over a 10-year life using the straight-line method. How many units must the company sell to earn $40,000 of income if it selects the basic system?

d. Ignoring the information presented in requirement (c), at what volume level will management be indifferent to the basic system and the deluxe system?

e. (Optional) Prepare a spreadsheet model to analyze the choice between the two conveyor systems. Ignore part (c).

Problem 12.49
Cost-Volume-Profit
(LO 2, 3)

Communication

A financial analyst is studying the feasibility of two alternative assembly methods, manual and automated. The automated method has variable operating costs of $4 per unit and annual committed costs of $100,000; in contrast, the manual method has variable costs of $5 and committed costs of $75,000. The company sells its products for $20 per unit.

Required

a. Prepare a profit-volume graph displaying the profitability of each method.

b. What is the break-even point of each method?

c. At what volume level will management be indifferent to the manual method and the automated method?

d. Prepare a memo supported by a profit-volume graph that explains this level and the effects of volume levels above and below it.

e. (Optional) Prepare a spreadsheet model to analyze this choice of assembly methods.

Problem 12.50
Multiple Products
(LO 3, 4)

Kalifo Company manufactures a line of electric garden tools that hardware stores sell. The company's controller, Will Fulton, has just received the upcoming year's sales forecast for the firm's three products: weeders, hedge clippers, and leaf blowers. Kalifo has experienced considerable variations in sales volumes and variable costs over the past two years, and Fulton believes that the forecast should be carefully evaluated from a cost-volume-profit viewpoint. The preliminary budget information for next year follows.

	Weeders	Clippers	Blowers
Unit sales	50,000	50,000	100,000
Unit selling price	$28	$36	$48
Variable manufacturing cost per unit	$13	$12	$25
Variable selling cost per unit	$5	$4	$6

The fixed manufacturing overhead is budgeted at $2,000,000, and the company's fixed selling and administrative expenses are forecast to be $600,000. Kalifo has a tax rate of 40 percent.

Required

a. Estimate Kalifo Company's budgeted net income for next year.

b. Assuming that the sales mix remains as budgeted, determine how many units of each product Kalifo must sell to break even.

c. After preparing the original estimates, management determined that the variable manufacturing cost of leaf blowers will increase by 20 percent and the variable selling cost of hedge clippers will increase by $1. However, management has decided not to change the selling price of either product. In addition, management recently learned that the firm's leaf blower has been rated as the best value on the market, and the company now expects to sell three times as many leaf blowers as each of the other products. Under these circumstances, determine how many units of each product Kalifo must sell to break even.

d. (Optional) Prepare a spreadsheet model similar to Exhibit 12–5 to analyze the requirements of this problem.

[CMA adapted]

Problem 12.51
Financial Planning and Activity-Based Costing
(LO 3, 4)

Communication

GameCo, Inc., manufactures handheld electronic games. Last year the firm sold 25,000 games at $25 each. Total costs were $525,000, of which $150,000 were considered fixed. An ABC study recently revealed that GameCo's higher-level activities had the following costs:

Higher-Level Activity	Total Activity Cost
Setup (40 setups at $400 per setup)	$ 16,000
Engineering (500 hours at $25 per hour)	12,500
Inspection (1,000 inspections at $30 per inspection)	30,000
General factory overhead	61,500
Fixed selling and administrative costs	30,000
Total	$150,000

Management is considering both the installation of new, highly automated manufacturing equipment and the implementation of just-in-time (JIT) inventory and production management. If the new equipment is installed, setups will be quicker and less expensive. The proposed JIT approach will require 300 setups per year at $50 per setup. Since a total quality program will accompany JIT implementation, GameCo anticipates only 100 inspections at $45 each. After installation of the new equipment and system, 800 hours of engineering are required at $28 per hour. General factory overhead increases to $166,100; however, the automated equipment allows GameCo to cut its unit variable cost by 20 percent. Finally, the overall improvement in product quality supports a selling price of $26 per unit.

Required

a. Upon seeing the ABC analysis given in the problem, GameCo's vice president for manufacturing exclaimed to the controller, "I thought you told me this $150,000 cost was fixed. These don't look like fixed costs at all. What you're telling me now is that setup costs us $400 every time we start a production run. What gives?" As GameCo's controller, write a short memo to the vice president that clarifies the situation.

b. Compute GameCo's new break-even volume if the proposed automated equipment is installed.

c. Determine how many units GameCo must sell to show a profit of $140,000, assuming that the new technology is adopted (ignore taxes).

d. If GameCo adopts the new manufacturing approach, will its break-even point be higher or lower? Will the number of sales units required to earn a profit of $140,000 be higher or lower? Are the results in this case consistent with what you typically expect to find in a modern high-tech manufacturing facility? Explain.

e. (Optional) Prepare a spreadsheet model of GameCo's operations to complete requirements (a)–(d).

Problem 12.52
Financial Planning and Activity-Based Costing
(LO 3, 4)

Communication

Spreadsheet

Boing, Inc., operates a commuter airline. Last year the airline flew 10,000 flights and sold 400,000 one-way tickets at $60 per ticket. Total costs amounted to $21,600,000. An activity-based costing study recently revealed that Boing's costs include the following components:

Activity Cost Driver	**Activity Cost**
Miles flown (2,000,000 miles at $2 per mile)	$ 4,000,000
Number of passengers (400,000 passengers at $4 per passenger)	1,600,000
Number of flights (10,000 flights at $840 per flight)	8,400,000
Number of television promotions (20 at $60,000 each)	1,200,000
Airplane lease	4,200,000
Physical plant	1,600,000
Marketing and administrative	600,000
Total	$21,600,000

Required

Complete the following requirements; ignore taxes.

a. Assume that projections for next year are for 2,200,000 miles flown, 440,000 passengers, 11,000 flights, and 20 promotions. All cost-driver rates are projected to increase by 5 percent over the amounts listed. Cost for airplane leases will be $4,410,000, physical plant will be $1,680,000, and other marketing and administrative will be $630,000. With those projections, prepare a computerized financial model that has a ticket price of $65 per one-way ticket.

b. Assume that management wants to think about a new ticket-pricing method. Assume that it plans to sell 300,000 tickets for $70 per ticket. In addition, it proposes to sell discount tickets on less popular flights for $40 per ticket. Using the cost data in requirement (a), how many discount tickets must Boing sell to generate the same operating income as it did when it sold 440,000 tickets for $65 each?

c. For the analysis in this requirement, ignore requirement (b). Return to the model that you prepared in requirement (a). Management is considering implementing a new service that enables customers to purchase tickets and obtain seat assignments on the Internet either by accessing Boing's Web site or by linking to major carriers such as USAir or Delta. Although this service is available for major carriers, it is a first for Boing. Adding the new service drops the cost-driver rate per flight by $60 because of cost savings in ticketing and seat assignment. This new service adds $650,000 per year to other marketing and administrative costs. Management believes the new service will increase the number of passengers by 10 percent. All other costs, ticket prices, and volumes will be unaffected by adding the new service. Is this a financially viable service?

d. Write a report to management recommending whether to add the new service in part (c). Be sure to indicate the impact on Boing's operating income if the company adds the service. Also indicate any advantages and disadvantages that might not be captured in the preceding numbers (e.g., customer satisfaction).

Problem 12.53
Managing Scarce Resources
(LO 5)

Cerise Hamilton was having a conversation with her neighbor, a production supervisor for Avco Corporation, a metal products company. Avco's metal turning department has 90,000 machine hours to manufacture two products: S109 and T678. The following data are available:

	S109	**T678**
Unit contribution margin	$8	$6
Machine hours per unit	5 hours	3 hours
Maximum monthly sales	15,000 units	10,000 units

Required

Assume Cerise Hamilton's role in discussing the following issues with her neighbor.

a. Does Avco have sufficient machine time to fill all sales orders?

b. Should Avco focus on the manufacture of S109 or T678?

c. Set a production schedule for Avco that makes the most profitable use of its manufacturing time.

Problem 12.54
Scenario Analysis
(Appendix A)
(LO 3, 6)

Communication

Refer to the data in rows 1 to 12 of Exhibit 12–5 for Fairfield Blues. Assume that it is considering these alternative scenarios:

1. Increase the number of concerts to 10 per year. Average attendance at concerts will decline 10 percent per performance from the level planned, but all other data are the same as in rows 1 to 12 of Exhibit 12–5.
2. Decrease the number of concerts to four per year. Average concert attendance will increase 25 percent, but all other data are the same as in rows 1 to 12 of Exhibit 12–5.
3. Increase the box seating by 25 percent, maintain average attendance in each category of seating, and increase the number of concerts to 10 per year. All other data are the same as in rows 1 to 12 of Exhibit 12–5.

Required

a. Using a spreadsheet, duplicate the financial model in Exhibit 12–5 to project the operating income for each of the three scenarios.

b. Prepare a memo to management to recommend the scenario to choose from the three listed or the base-case scenario.

Problem 12.55
Theory of Constraints in a Nonprofit Organization
(LO 5)

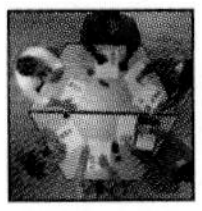

Team

Communication

University Bookstore is a nonprofit retail outlet for textbooks, computers, and general merchandise (including trade books, supplies, and university-licensed apparel and gifts). It is located near the main campus of State University and controls the majority of the local market share for new and used textbooks. Other retail outlets, such as Barnes & Noble, University Drugstore (a private company), and CompUSA, have larger shares of the local market for other items. Tammy Waialua is a full-time accounting student and part-time employee of University Bookstore who recently studied the current chapter on managing constrained resources. She observed that the bookstore's primary constraints are floor and shelf space for fast-selling items such as textbooks and market share for slow-selling items such as general merchandise.

Average inventory levels and the most recent year's cost of goods sold in the three departments follow.

Department	Average Inventory	Annual Cost of Goods Sold
New and used textbooks	$1,000,000	$4,000,000
Computers	400,000	1,500,000
General merchandise	1,200,000	1,400,000

Tammy approached her boss, the bookstore's general manager, and suggested that they try to improve its efficiency by managing its constraints more effectively. The general manager thanked Tammy for her concern but assured her that this manufacturing technique was neither needed by nor applicable to the nonprofit bookstore.

Required

In small groups, complete the following:

a. Explain how University Bookstore's constraints can be both floor space (internal) and market share (external).

b. Is Tammy or her boss correct about the relevance of the Theory of Constraints to the bookstore's operations? Explain.

c. Prepare a short report with recommendations for managing the bookstore more efficiently.

Problem 12.56
Financial Planning Software
(LO 1)

Internet

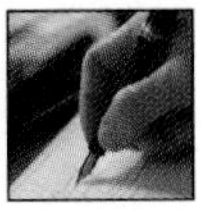

Communication

Many commercial companies offer computer software packages to build financial planning models. Managing complex operations can be very difficult without effective computer software. Selecting among the various available packages can be quite difficult, and many organizations rely on the advice and assistance of consultants to select and install the software. Nonetheless, anyone contemplating the purchase of such software is advised to become an informed consumer. The primary question is whether a software package generates the analysis and information needed to manage constrained resources. Beyond that general consideration are others:

1. *Design features.* How flexible or adaptable is the software?
2. *Thoroughness of analysis.* Does the software model all of the important processes? Does it allow tests of changes to conditions (what-if analysis)?

3. *Thoroughness of reports.* Does the software provide detailed but understandable effects of alternative process changes?
4. *Integration capability.* Does the software accept input from existing information systems or common software? Does it provide output that is compatible with existing systems and software?
5. *Technical elements.* Is the software compatible with existing hardware and operating systems?
6. *Customer service.* Is the supplier reputable? Does it provide full support for the software before and after the sale?
7. *Cost.* Is the cost of the software acceptable?

Required

a. Search the Internet for at least two commercial financial planning software packages (*Hint:* Search for the key words, "financial model software").

b. To the extent possible, contrast the two packages according to the preceding seven considerations.

c. Be prepared to present your analysis.

Problem 12.57
Theory of Constraints and Opportunity Costs
(LO 5)

Communication

The general manager of a machining company located in a southwestern US state described one of the company's production problems as follows:

"One of our problems was that we took on any and all work. If a farmer's plow broke, we'd fix it. After all, it was a neighborly thing to do, and those couple of bucks we'd make helped to pay the phone bill. Why not help the farmer and earn the contribution margin?

"Well, the reason is simple. Critical employees and equipment might be tied up on a small plow part while a five-figure oil field engine component is down. As the happy farmer hooks up his repaired plow, a very unhappy [oil] rig operator is screaming for his engine part. Yet, according to cost accounting, repairing the plow was good, extra money. We had the time to do it . . . the oil field part did get delivered and paid for . . . what's the problem? The problem is that farmers will definitely come back to us but that [oil] rig operator won't! Cost accounting doesn't measure lost business."

Required

a. Describe the nature and causes of the machining company's problem of using its constrained capacity. Is "cost accounting" at fault? Why or why not?

b. Write a memorandum to the general manager outlining recommendations for the company to improve its use of constrained capacity.

Problem 12.58
Financial Modeling, Theory of Constraints, and Accounting Education
(LO 1, 5)

Communication

Some critics of accounting education claim that the traditional ("cost-accounting") approach to managing resources emphasizes the measurement of costs or reported profits from each productive process within an organization. This focus on reported profits and individual processes, critics argue, causes students to ignore both opportunity costs and productive processes. Allegedly, when these students enter the workforce, their cost management-accounting mindset leads to improper decision making and lower long-term profits for their organizations.

Required

a. Compare the course offerings and requirements of your school and those of several competing schools (e.g., as described in catalogs or on Web sites).

b. Is there any evidence that accounting education narrowly focuses on traditional approaches to measuring resources? Do you agree that this might be a problem?

c. Write a memo to explain your conclusions.

Problem 12.59
Spreadsheet Model
(LO 2, 3)

Marie, your housemate and a young art student, plans to start a small T-shirt printing business to partially finance her education. A generous art teacher has donated old but serviceable equipment and the use of a heated garage. Marie will produce original and custom designs per customer requests. Relevant facts about the T-shirt printing operation follow:

- Jobs will be marked up 100 percent over the cost of materials to cover the cost of design and printing time.
- Plain, high-quality T-shirts cost $5 each.

- T-shirts can be printed with one or two colors, front and/or back, resulting from one to four different elements per shirt design.
- Each design element requires a separate silk screen, which costs $45.
- Each color application (i.e., up to four per shirt, one for each design element) uses heat-sensitive paint costing $0.20 per application.
- Orders must be placed in increments of 10 between a minimum of 30 and a maximum of 50.

Required

Marie has asked you to help build a spreadsheet model that will allow her to price jobs of different sizes and complexity.

Problem 12.60
Linear Programming
(Appendix B)
(LO 7)

A computer spreadsheet solution of a linear programming model follows:

Microsoft Excel - solch12-2e-excel

E226 = =SUM(B226:D226)

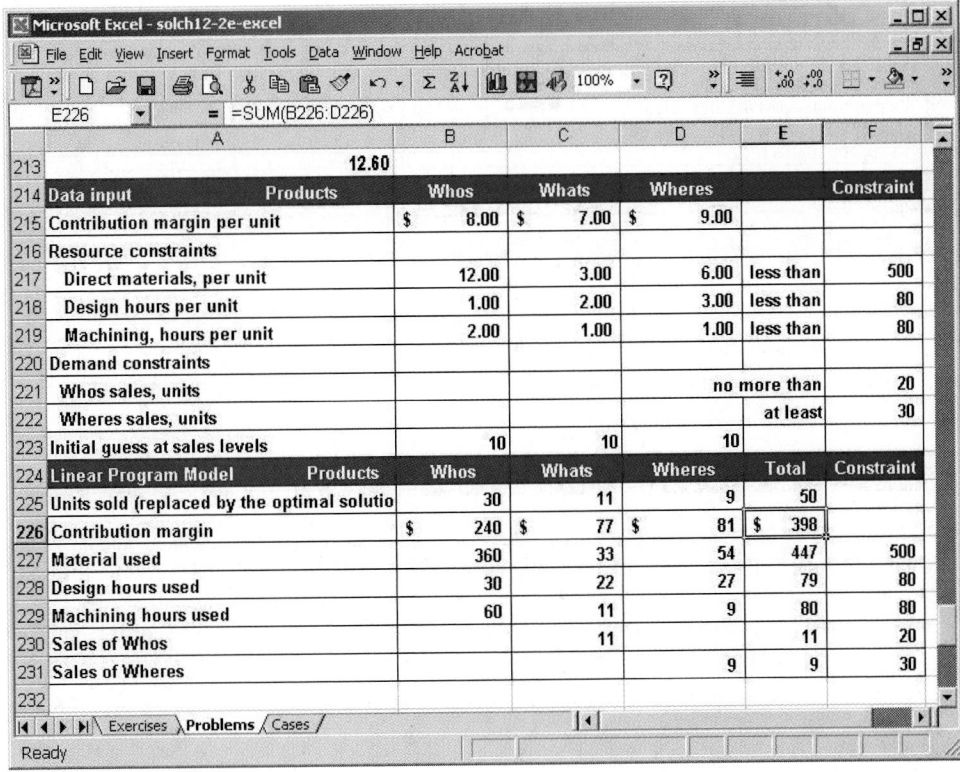

	A	B	C	D	E	F
213	12.60					
214	**Data input** Products	Whos	Whats	Wheres		Constraint
215	Contribution margin per unit	$ 8.00	$ 7.00	$ 9.00		
216	Resource constraints					
217	Direct materials, per unit	12.00	3.00	6.00	less than	500
218	Design hours per unit	1.00	2.00	3.00	less than	80
219	Machining, hours per unit	2.00	1.00	1.00	less than	80
220	Demand constraints					
221	Whos sales, units				no more than	20
222	Wheres sales, units				at least	30
223	Initial guess at sales levels	10	10	10		
224	**Linear Program Model** Products	Whos	Whats	Wheres	Total	Constraint
225	Units sold (replaced by the optimal solutio	30	11	9	50	
226	Contribution margin	$ 240	$ 77	$ 81	$ 398	
227	Material used	360	33	54	447	500
228	Design hours used	30	22	27	79	80
229	Machining hours used	60	11	9	80	80
230	Sales of Whos		11		11	20
231	Sales of Wheres			9	9	30
232						

Exercises | Problems | Cases

Ready

Required

a. Write the linear programming objective function and constraints in equation form.

b. Explain the meaning of each cell in the linear program model section of the spreadsheet.

Problem 12.61
CVP
(LO 1)

You are about to interview with Fairfield Blues for a Staff accountant's position. Upon arriving at the interview, a human resources specialist hands you a short examination that covers cost-volume-profit analysis.

Required

Briefly respond to the following questions.

a. Assume that Fairfield Blues has three full-time salaried employees. It is considering a proposal to reduce all salaries and replace them with a commission based on ticket revenue. What will be the effect of the new compensation plan on the company's fixed costs and variable costs? What might happen to total revenue if management compensation is based, in part, on a percentage of ticket revenue?

b. If the company experiences an increase in property taxes, will the firm's break-even point rise or fall?

c. If the costs for each ticket increase, what will be the effect on the company's unit contribution margin?

Problem 12.62
Linear Programming
(Appendix B)
(LO 7)

A computer spreadsheet solution of a linear programming model follows:

Microsoft Excel - chapter 12 solutions

E13 = =SUM(B13:D13)

	A		B	C	D	E	F
1	Data input	Products	Baubles	Bangles	Beads		Constraint
2	Contribution margin per unit		$ 12.00	$ 8.00	$ 14.00		
3	Resource constraints						
4	Direct materials, per unit		22.00	8.00	13.00	less than	800
5	Design hours per unit		4.00	1.00	5.00	less than	120
6	Machining, hours per unit		2.00	1.00	2.00	less than	80
7	Demand constraints						
8	Bangles sales, units					no more than	30
9	Beads sales, units					at least	10
10	Initial guess at sales levels		10	10	10		
11	Linear Program Model	Products	Baubles	Bangles	Beads	Total	Constraint
12	Units sold (replaced by the optimal solution)		10	30	10	50	
13	Contribution margin (B2*B12,C2*C12,D2*D12)		$ 120	$ 240	$ 140	$ 500	
14	Material used (B4*B12, etc.)		220	240	130	590	800
15	Design hours used (B5*B12, etc.)		40	30	50	120	120
16	Machining hours used (B6*B12, etc.)		20	30	20	70	80
17	Sales of Bangles (C12)			30		30	30
18	Sales of Beads (D12)				10	10	10
19							

12-62 / 12.60 / Sheet3 /
Ready

Required

a. Write the linear programming objective function and constraints in equation form.

b. Explain the meaning of each cell in the linear program model section of the spreadsheet.

Cases

Case 12.63
Cost-Volume-Profit
(LO 1, 2)

Internet

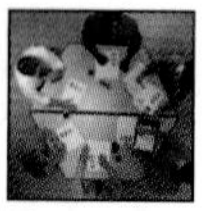
Team

Virtually no organization publicizes its break-even point to external parties. Airlines are a notable exception, but only a handful disclose this key operating statistic. Access the homepages of Continental Airlines and Comair Holdings, Inc. Continental is a global carrier and one of the largest in the industry. COMAIR, on the other hand, is a much smaller entity, operating regional jets and playing a major role in Delta Connection's program at its Cincinnati and Orlando hubs.

Required

In small groups, complete the following:

a. Learn more about these two firms by exploring their Web sites.

b. By reviewing key financial and operating statistics disclosed by the carriers, find the break-even load factor— the percentage of seats that must be occupied by paying passengers for the airline to break even. What break-even load factors have these carriers disclosed in recent periods?

c. Explain several underlying factors/characteristics of these carriers that likely cause their break-even points to differ.

Case 12.64
Managing Constraints—
Part 1
(LO 5)

The Tooling Business Unit (TBU) of the Huge Company manufactures tools, setup jigs, fixtures, and prototypes used throughout the company's operations. The market value of products produced at TBU is estimated to be $1 billion annually. These products are machined and/or welded from metal stock or are made from advanced composite materials. These products are used in turn to produce the company's ultimate products and must be manufactured to exceptionally close tolerances. TBU employs approximately 1,000 highly skilled machinists, operators, and toolmakers that take great pride in their skills and the high quality of their products (i.e., conformance to required tolerances).

For example, one of TBU's products is a jig that the aerospace division uses to manufacture aircraft wings. The jig has gross dimensions of 75 feet × 20 feet × 8 feet, which has elements (subassemblies) that are machined on a computer-numerically-controlled (CNC) machine to tolerances of one-thousandth of an inch. These are extremely close tolerances for such large fixtures.

Another critical feature of TBU's products is that they are made in very small numbers (e.g., almost never more than one or two of a kind). Because of the uniqueness of manufacturing at TBU, numerous manual and computer (i.e., software) setups are required during any month, and large production runs virtually are nonexistent.

The production of TBU's tools and fixtures precede the production of Huge's products. Any delays in delivering them to the manufacturing divisions set back delivery dates to customers. Furthermore, because of the complexities of manufacturing, any delays are often compounded with delays from other suppliers. An added complication for TBU is that tooling designs often arrive behind schedule from internal customers, who are the product divisions, and TBU is expected to make up as much lost time as possible.

Thus, TBU's objectives are to:

1. Manufacture complex parts to exacting tolerances.
2. Meet or improve scheduled delivery dates.

Dave Winfield, a young industrial engineer and recent MBA graduate, and his new management team inherited a chaotic manufacturing situation at TBU. Thousands of orders from dozens of manufacturing divisions were being shepherded through TBU by an extensive expediting system. Each customer division placed at least one expediter at TBU. This expediter's primary objective was to see that the division's jobs moved through TBU's machining or fabricating workstations as quickly as possible. It was common for a workstation operator to halt work on one order to begin work on another at the request of a favored or especially persuasive expediter. It also was common to find a behind-schedule order languishing at a workstation while the operator worked on another order that was not due for weeks. Because of the exacting tolerances required for most of TBU's products, these problems were most critical at its CNC workstations. The results were a large backlog of orders, many idle workstations, some overwhelmed workstations, and many unhappy customers who blamed TBU for their inability to meet their (external) customers' delivery dates.

Required

a. As Dave Winfield you have been charged with bringing order to TBU and improving the business unit's on-schedule performance. How do you proceed?

b. What do you recommend for managing TBU capacity?

Case 12.65
Managing Constraints — Part 2
(LO 5)

Dave Winfield and his team of analysts began to analyze TBU first by assessing the status of all orders currently in process. Toni Colovito, one of the analysts, literally walked the floor and itemized every order at TBU. Six months later, she had produced "before" charts like the one shown, which is for a representative workstation (of the 19) at TBU, A64. This figure shows that there was nearly as much *planned work* (dark-shaded bars) *behind schedule* (orders to the left of the current week) as was *planned for future delivery* from these workstations (orders to the right of "Current week"). Furthermore, operators then were working on some orders (light-shaded bars) that were not due for as many as 15 weeks (to the right of "Current week") while neglecting other orders that were behind schedule (to the left of "Current week").

The next step was to measure the capacity of each workstation. Winfield and his team decided to focus on the "order" as the unit of work to manage since nearly every order is unique. An "order" is defined as an agreement to make a specified tool, jig, fixture, or prototype. A single order can require multiple tasks (i.e., operations or processing at multiple workstations). Thus, one order can be counted multiple times internally at TBU because it is processed by multiple workstations. Colovito began to track the rate of order completion at each workstation. After gathering a time series of daily order completion data, she computed the capacity of each workstation as follows.

Capacity is a measure of the ability to do work within a particular time period (e.g., orders completed per week). To be realistic, she adjusted for unanticipated events (e.g., Murphy's Law) and historical rates of order completion. For each workstation she computed the weighted-average trend of order completion per day (approximately 19 orders per day for A64). She used a rule of thumb of 80 percent availability due to unanticipated events and computed each workstation's historical ratio of orders completed (e.g., 94 percent for A64). Thus, she computed a workstation's capacity as follows:

$$\text{Workstation capacity} = (\text{Historical orders completed per day}) \times (80\%) \times (\text{Historical ratio of orders completed}) \times (5 \text{ days per week})$$

$$\text{A64 capacity} = (19 \text{ orders per day}) \times (.80) \times (.94) \times (5 \text{ days per week}) = 71 \text{ orders per week}$$

The team set capacities and instituted procedures for accepting or outsourcing orders when bottleneck resources cannot process them on time. These resulted in a significantly reduced backlog, as shown in the "after" chart (again for workstation A64).

Required

a. What is your opinion of defining the unit of work in TBU as an "order"?

b. How do you identify bottleneck workstations?

c. Critique the approach to measuring workstation capacity.

d. Explain the differences between the "before" and "after" charts.

e. What measures of performance do you recommend to help Winfield and his team meet TBU's business objectives?

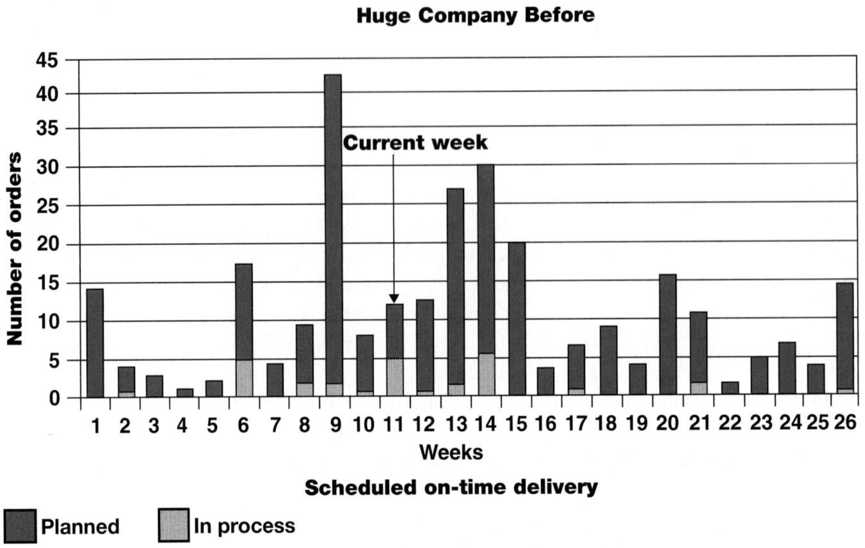

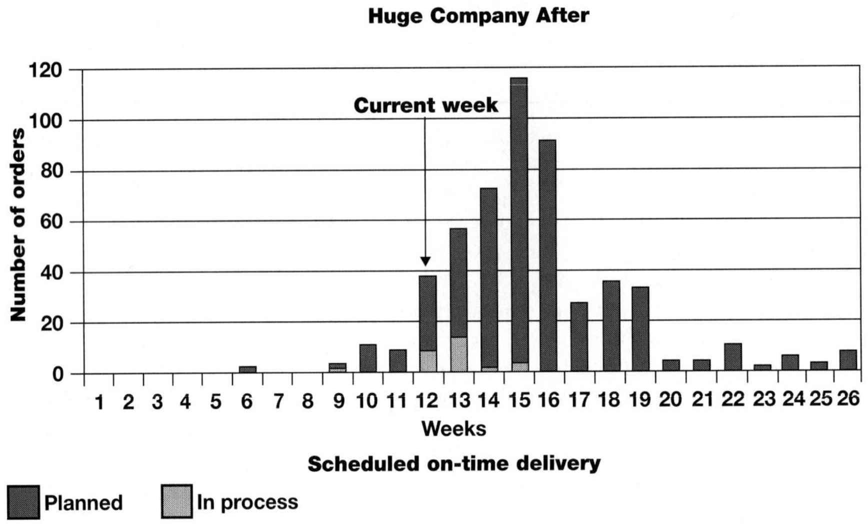

Case 12.66
Financial Modeling
(LO 1, 2, 3)

Consider the following newspaper article:

"Credit-card firms look for new penalties: GE Capital to charge $25 fee if cardholder pays off full balance" Patricia Lamiell.

NEW YORK — Caught between those who don't pay their credit-card bills and those who pay them before racking up interest charges, credit-card companies are looking for new penalties and fees to slip onto their statements.

One way is to begin charging customers who pay their balances in full or leave their cards in a sock drawer for emergencies.

About 20 percent of GE Capital Corp.'s GE Rewards MasterCard holders fit that description. GE Capital informed those card-holders by mail last week that it would begin charging them $25 per year if they don't carry a balance. The fee applies to customers who don't use the card at all. GE

Capital is the first major card issuer to assess such a fee. But other credit-card issuers have found other ways to collect more money from cardholders.

For example, AT&T has begun allowing less time to pay late bills before imposing a $15 fee. AT&T had waited 10 days to charge the fee but now gives customers as little as one day.

"I think it's inevitable that you're going to see a penalty fee arise" for those customers who do not incur interest charges, said Robert McKinley, president of RAM Research, a Frederick, Va., credit-card research company.

GE Capital, a subsidiary of General Electric Co., won't say how many accounts it has outstanding. RAM estimates it at 3.7 million, or around 5 million cards. Like others, GE doesn't charge an annual joining fee. In the days of heated competition in the industry in the early 1990s, many companies shunned annual fees and instituted elaborate incentives, such as cash rebates, to encourage use of their cards.

Many issuers gave out cards to people who turned out to be bad credit risks. But on the other end of the spectrum are people who paid off their balances, thus avoiding interest charges. The problem is, the issuers need the interest income to finance all of the incentives. So they have to begin charging all their customers, even those who don't pay interest.

"The big thing now is, how do you extract income from this group of people who basically freeload onto the system," McKinley said. "They'll bring the annual fee back disguised as a penalty."

GE says people who pay off their cards monthly—and thus don't pay interest—should still pay something for the convenience of a charge card and the benefits of GE's cash-back offers. GE Capital spokesman Neal McGarity said that the costs of running the program are covered largely by interest income.

"We chose a fee in this situation instead of cutting any of the rewards," he said.

GE cardholders who carry a balance for 25 days or more pay 17.1 percent in interest charges. GE uses the interest income to finance cash rebates to cardholders of up to $140 per year. To get the maximum rebate, customers have to charge $10,000 a year.

McKinley estimates that GE loses $65 a year for every customer who earns the maximum rebate but pays off the account. As an added incentive to cardholders to carry a balance, GE will lower the interest rate for those who pay off their balances to 11.9 percent. About 36 percent of all cardholders pay down their balances on any given month, McKinley said. That number has grown from 29 percent at the height of the recession in 1991, McKinley said.

Cardholders are also quite conscious of getting a good deal on their credit cards.

Required

In small groups, take the perspective of GE Capital Corp and prepare responses and a presentation that cover the following questions.

a. What are GE Capital's goals and tangible objectives? Do you consider them fair? Explain.

b. From the article, identify the likely drivers of revenue and costs.

c. Develop a spreadsheet model that allows GE Capital's managers to see the financial effects of alternative courses of action. Be prepared to demonstrate this model to the class.

CHAPTER

13

Cost Management and Decision Making

After completing this chapter, you should be able to:

1. Structure business decision-making problems into objectives, alternative actions, and expected outcomes.
2. Understand and use target costing.
3. Identify both quantitative and qualitative relevant costs and benefits of decision alternatives.
4. Use decision trees to describe business decisions.
5. Use a cost-benefit approach for common decisions such as obtaining new technology or capability; outsourcing (make versus buy); or modifying, adding, or dropping a product, service, or business unit; and pricing, including special orders.

Cost-Management
Challenges

1. **How** can cost management help organizations, including Bootstrap Industries, choose among competing alternative uses of the organizations' resources?

2. **Should** prices be based on costs or on what the market will pay?

Bootstrap Industries' mission is simple and unchanging: **to create jobs for people with disabilities**. We measure our success by the number of jobs created, the quality of those jobs, the environment we create within our organization, the service we deliver to our customers, and our impact in the community. We ended last year with 3,000 employees working in Washington and Oregon. Disabilities typically would have excluded more than half of them from employment. Our annual revenue grew 30% to almost $70 million as we continued to experience tremendous success in our businesses. That 99% of our total revenue last year came from service and product sales confirms Bootstrap's self-sufficiency. We are successful because of our commitment to core values:

Bootstrap's Core Values Are the Foundation of Our Success

Bootstrap
INDUSTRIES

Bootstrap Industries, based in Portland, Oregon, is a nonprofit organization that relies on careful business decision making to succeed in a competitive market. Note that its primary goal is to seek good jobs for otherwise unemployable people. It is able to do so on a long-term basis because it follows many of the decision-making practices of successful profit-seeking companies.

Bootstrap Industries provides outsourced services to customers such as federal and state governments, Intel Corporation, Boeing, Hewlett-Packard, NEC Electronics, Packard Bell, Wells Fargo Bank, Target, Blue Shield, *The Oregonian*, Kaiser Permanente, and Pasco Scientific. Bootstrap offers employment ranging from high-tech to low-tech jobs. It offers specialized services such as electronic circuit board assembly and clean room maintenance. It manages food-service operations at two major military bases in the State of Washington, preparing and serving more than 100,000 meals monthly. Additionally, Bootstrap Industries owns and operates Sasquatch Snowshoes, which manufactures snowshoes for recreational snowshoers and competitive racers. We use examples from this division of Bootstrap Industries to illustrate cost management and decision making.

Bootstrap's mission statement raises interesting trade-offs among possibly conflicting goals. Should managers make a decision that increases profits but requires the use of fewer disabled employees? Should managers decide to forgo an unprofitable opportunity that offers high-quality jobs? Should prices for services and products seek to generate profits or growth of sales and employment? Making these trade-offs is challenging but is easier when managers have good information about alternatives, their impacts, and the uses of resources.

The focus of this chapter is how cost-management information can support and improve the evaluation of trade-offs and alternatives. We begin with a discussion of the decision-making process, which leads us to consider important types and qualities of useful information for decision making. We also describe the use of several useful cost-management tools for evaluating profit-planning and cost-reduction decisions.

Decision-Making Process

LO 1 Structure business decision-making problems into objectives, alternate actions, and expected outcomes.

Understanding decision making and making recommendations for it have occupied philosophers and scientists for hundreds, if not thousands, of years. The literature is vast, and even a brief excursion into this field of human behavior can be both fascinating and confusing.[1] It is safe to say that great diversity of opinion exists about how humans *do* and *should* make decisions. We cannot hope to resolve all the unknowns and controversies here, but we can provide some guidance about systematic decision making. What follows is a cost-benefit framework of decision making with five stages within which we consider the role of cost management.[2] One objective of this framework is to demonstrate that cost management is a purposeful activity — more value creation at lower cost — and a proactive attitude — decisions drive costs; costs do not just happen.

Exhibit 13–1 presents the decision-making framework formally. Note that Chapters 1 and 2 of this book implicitly considered most of the stages of the framework. We will briefly discuss stage I: setting goals in this chapter. This chapter focuses more, however, on the role of cost management in stage II: gathering information and stage III: evaluating alternatives. Note that as shown in Exhibit 13–1, other parts of the text also consider types of information that support all five stages in more detail. One of the most important parts of this framework is the feedback to all other parts of the process. Feedback is critical to managers' and workers' sustained learning and retraining; it is the essence of a "learning

[1]A modern coverage of decision making is found in P. Kleindorfer, H. Kunreuther, and P. Schoemaker, *Decision Sciences: An Integrative Approach.* (Full citations to references are in the Bibliography.)

[2]This framework is adapted from Kleindorfer et al.; H. Simon, "Strategy and Organizational Evolution"; and J. Shank, "Strategic Cost Management: New Wine or Just New Bottles?"

organization" to learn from its successes and failures and improve future decisions.

Stage I: Setting Goals and Objectives

> **Alice:** Would you tell me, please, which way I ought to go from here?
> **Cheshire Cat:** That depends a good deal on where you want to get to.
> **Alice:** I don't much care where. . . .
> **Cheshire Cat:** Then it doesn't matter which way you go.
> **Alice:** . . . so long as I get somewhere.
> **Cheshire Cat:** Oh, you're sure to do that, if you only walk long enough.[3]

Do individuals or organizations succeed by luck alone? A critical assumption of professional management is that consistent organizational success is not the result of pure luck or random actions. Rather, long-term success is the result of carefully pursuing specific, attainable goals. Though Alice's adventures might have been dreams, she eventually navigated them by clarifying her goals and making the best decisions possible with available information. Organizations should do no less.

Exhibit 13–1

Decision-Making Framework (and links to the parts of this text)

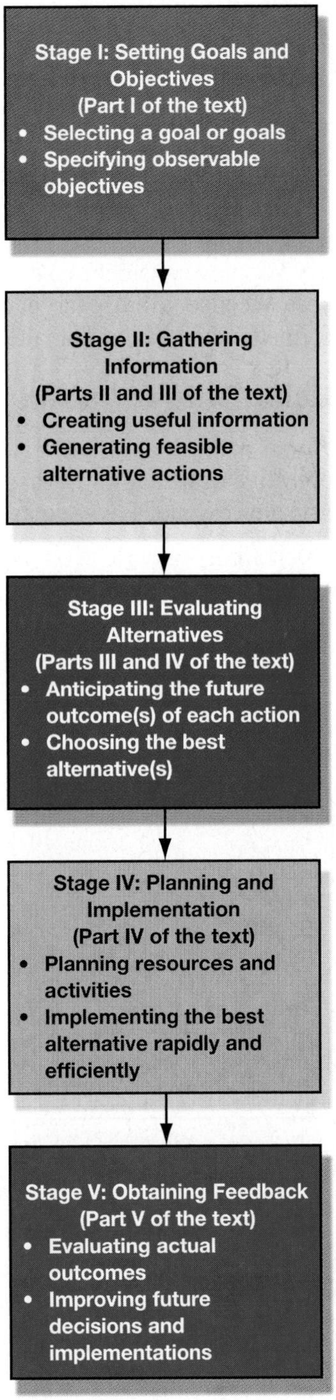
Stage I: Setting Goals and Objectives
(Part I of the text)
• Selecting a goal or goals
• Specifying observable objectives
Stage II: Gathering Information
(Parts II and III of the text)
• Creating useful information
• Generating feasible alternative actions
Stage III: Evaluating Alternatives
(Parts III and IV of the text)
• Anticipating the future outcome(s) of each action
• Choosing the best alternative(s)
Stage IV: Planning and Implementation
(Part IV of the text)
• Planning resources and activities
• Implementing the best alternative rapidly and efficiently
Stage V: Obtaining Feedback
(Part V of the text)
• Evaluating actual outcomes
• Improving future decisions and implementations

Selecting Goals

Organizations exist to achieve specific goals, such as generating superior returns to stockholders, offering the best customer service, providing meaningful employment, and eradicating hunger or disease. Without a clear set of goals, an organization's members have no clear guidance for their actions and decisions. Many organizational problems can be traced to the lack of either clear goals or clearly communicated goals. Bootstrap Industries, the focus organization of this chapter, clearly directs its activities and decisions to achieve the goal of meaningful employment for disabled persons.

As a nonprofit organization, generating an excess of revenues (profit) from operations means that Bootstrap can:

- Invest more in its programs and employees.
- Continue to improve the capabilities of its employees to deliver quality services.
- Continue to meet its specific employment goals.

Specifying Tangible Objectives

Most organizational goals are abstract in nature (achieving the "best customer service," for example). Although these goals provide essential guidance, successful organizations also provide tangible objectives or benchmarks by which to measure progress

[3] L. Carroll, *Alice's Adventures in Wonderland.*

tangible objectives *are benchmarks capable of being measured in some manner*

toward their goals. That is, **tangible objectives** are benchmarks capable of being measured in some manner. As shown in Exhibit 13–2, Bootstrap Industries provides specific guidance to its employees by translating its goal of meaningful employment for disabled persons into tangible objectives of annual increases in employment and acquisition of high-quality customers. For example, when making business decisions, Bootstrap managers ask themselves, Will this action lead to employment growth and improvement in the quality of jobs for our employees? Without tangible objectives, direction and progress toward goals is unclear.

We now consider two common types of tangible objectives: target profit and target cost. We also will use target cost objectives as motivation for gathering additional information and generating alternatives.

LO 2 Understand and use target costing.

Using Target Costing and Setting Tangible Objectives

target profit *is the desired excess of periodic or project sales revenues over costs*

Target profit. Nearly every organization that sells products or services has a tangible objective of generating a **target profit,** which is the desired excess of periodic or project sales revenues over costs. Nonprofit and most government organizations that sell

Exhibit 13–2

Bootstrap Industries' Mission, Goals, and Objectives

Bootstrap INDUSTRIES

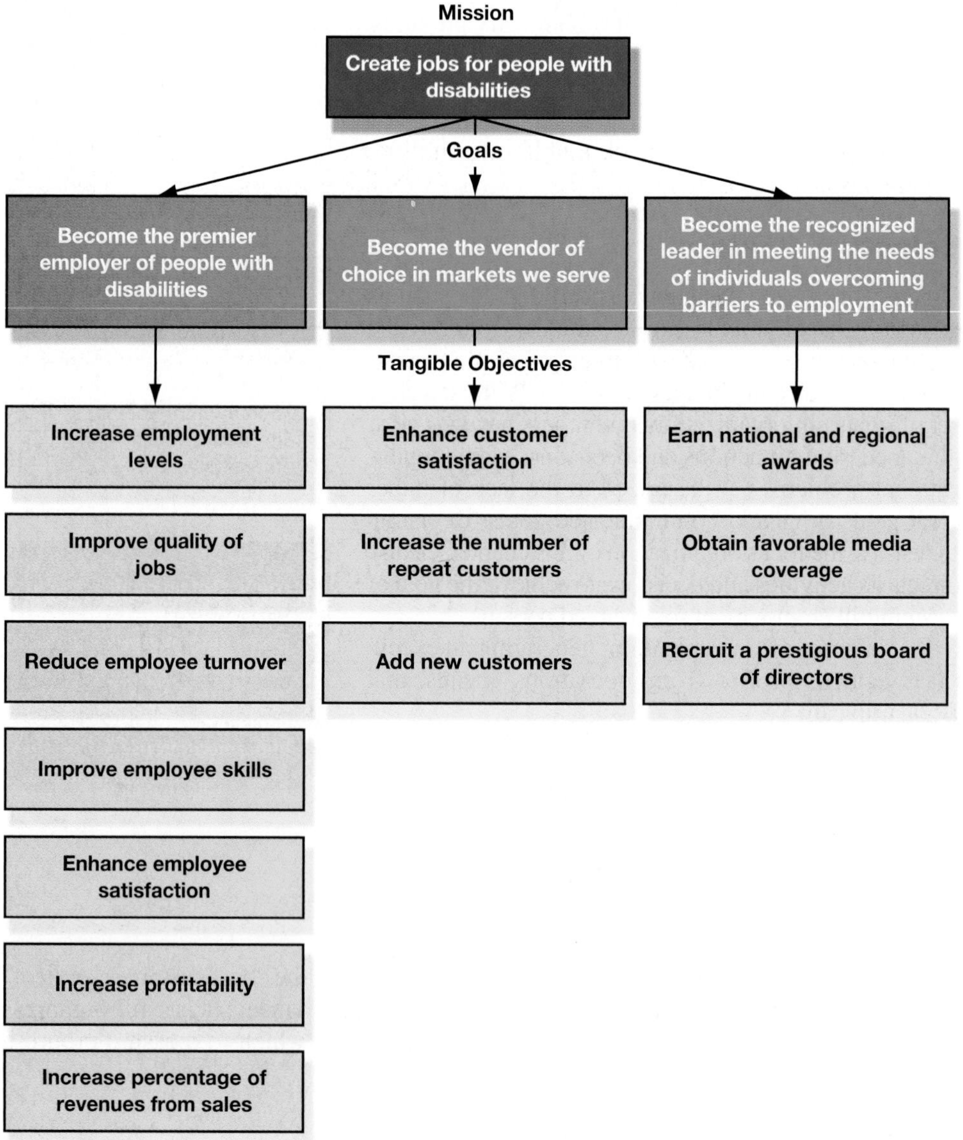

products or provide services have a target of zero profit, which means that they seek to recover the costs of operations from their activities. Profit-seeking organizations, including private companies and governmental enterprises, such as the postal service or railroads in some countries, seek a target profit sufficient to ensure survival or growth. These target profits might be the result of competitive market or governmental pressures and can be computed, for example, by applying a profit percentage to sales prices or invested assets. Target profits in turn generate plans for managing sales and costs.[4]

Bootstrap Industries computes a target profit for its Sasquatch Snowshoes division by multiplying a target profit percentage, 20 percent, by the market price, $100.[5]

$$\text{Target profit per unit} = \text{Target profit percentage} \times \text{Market price per unit}$$
$$= .20 \times \$100 = \$20 \text{ per unit}$$

Target cost. The *target cost* is the most that a good or service can cost and still meet both customer needs (e.g., quality and function) and company profit targets.[6] The target cost is a tangible objective that can be very difficult to meet without changes in organizations, processes, or designs. Bootstrap Industries' Sasquatch Snowshoe division competes with other manufacturers, such as Yuba, Tubbs, and Red Feather, and must meet market expectations for price and value. Bootstrap uses the process of target costing to manage the development of new snowshoe models to meet target costs. **Target costing** is a decision-making method that seeks to achieve products and services with specific features at target costs based on expected market prices and target profits. Target costing is not the only approach to setting goals, but its popularity is increasing because it focuses on a systematic process for creating products and services with features customers want at prices they are willing to pay.

target costing *is a decision-making method that seeks to achieve products and services with specific features at target costs based on expected market prices and target profits*

See Exhibit 13–3 for a simplified version of Bootstrap's target-costing spreadsheet that supports its decision to introduce this year's new recreation-level Rambler model snowshoe.[7]

In this analysis, the company's revenue and cost drivers are located in the "quantitative data" section. Note that different assumptions about the snowshoe market and Sasquatch's processes might cause managers to change these revenue and cost drivers. Target costing uses the following four steps.

1. Determine the target price per unit for the proposed product or service.
2. Set the target cost, per unit and in total.
3. Compare the total target cost to the currently feasible total cost to measure the cost-reduction target.
4. Redesign or concurrently design products and processes to achieve the cost-reduction target.

Step 1: Determine the target price per unit. The target price of $100 (cell B2) is what competitors are likely to charge and what customers are willing to pay for this product. This is the "expected market price."[8] The target profit percentage of

[4]Planning for sales and costs is the topic of Chapter 15.

[5]Many target-costing companies compute target profit as a percentage of the market price because other bases, such as invested assets, are too difficult to measure for individual products.

[6]Target costing is widely used by companies including DaimlerChrysler AG and Toyota in the automobile industry, Panasonic and Sharp in the electronics industry, and Apple and Toshiba in the personal computer industry. Generally speaking, the technique is popular with firms that develop new goods and services. Organizations commit to incurring the vast majority of costs that are related to new product lines (e.g., design, testing, manufacturing, marketing, distribution, and customer service obligations) long before the good or service is introduced to the marketplace. Many of these costs are not easily changed later in time.

[7]The decision making presented in this chapter is an application of financial modeling, as discussed in Chapter 12. Many organizations use spreadsheets to model their decisions and to perform sensitivity analysis on those decisions.

[8]Because target costing begins with the expected sales price of the product or service, it is an example of "price-led costing."

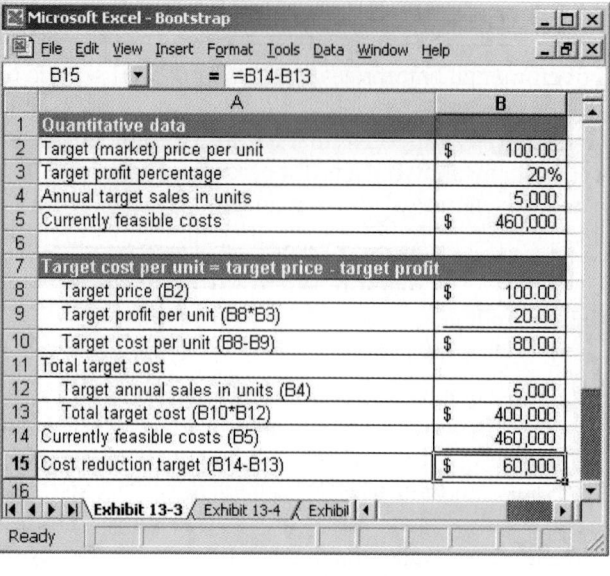

Exhibit 13-3

Spreadsheet for Bootstrap's Target-Costing Analysis

Microsoft Excel - Bootstrap

B15 = =B14-B13

	A		B
1	**Quantitative data**		
2	Target (market) price per unit	$	100.00
3	Target profit percentage		20%
4	Annual target sales in units		5,000
5	Currently feasible costs	$	460,000
6			
7	**Target cost per unit = target price - target profit**		
8	Target price (B2)	$	100.00
9	Target profit per unit (B8*B3)		20.00
10	Target cost per unit (B8-B9)	$	80.00
11	Total target cost		
12	Target annual sales in units (B4)		5,000
13	Total target cost (B10*B12)	$	400,000
14	Currently feasible costs (B5)		460,000
15	Cost reduction target (B14-B13)	$	60,000
16			

Exhibit 13-3 / Exhibit 13-4 / Exhibi

Ready

20 percent in cell B3 is the company's profit objective required for this type of product. The annual sales target of 5,000 units (B4) is the company's estimate of its share of this niche of the snowshoe market, given the sales price and characteristics of the product. The estimate of the *currently feasible cost* (B5) is what Sasquatch managers believe the cost will be to manufacture and distribute 5,000 pairs of Rambler snowshoes, given current manufacturing and distribution processes.[9]

Step 2: Set the target cost, per unit and in total. The target cost per unit is computed as the target price of the product *less* the target profit per unit. This calculation begins in row 7.

$$\text{Target cost per unit} = \text{Target price per unit} - \text{Target profit per unit}$$
$$= \$100 - [.20 \times \$100] = \underline{\underline{\$80}}$$

Target-costing firms compute the target cost by deducting the target profit per unit from the target price. If the snowshoe sells for $100, each unit sale must produce a 20 percent profit, or $20, which is computed in cell B9. Deducting the target profit ($20) from the target sales price ($100) yields the target cost of $80 per pair of snowshoes (B10).

$$\text{Total target cost} = \text{Target cost per unit} \times \text{Total unit sales}$$
$$= \$80 \text{ per unit} \times 5{,}000 \text{ units} = \underline{\underline{\$400{,}000}}$$

total target cost *is the target cost per unit multiplied by the total number of units to be sold over the product's life*

The **total target cost** is the target cost per unit multiplied by the total number of pairs of snowshoes that Bootstrap expects to sell over the product's one-year model life. This calculation is in rows 11–13 and identifies the tangible target cost objective of $400,000 that Bootstrap must meet. The cost-management task is to determine how Bootstrap can produce and deliver the snowshoes for $80 per pair and $400,000 overall while maintaining the market value of the product.

cost-reduction target *is the difference between the total target cost and the currently feasible cost*

Step 3: Compare the total target cost to the currently feasible total cost to measure the cost-reduction target. Comparing the total target cost ($400,000) to the currently feasible total cost ($460,000) is the final step. The **cost-reduction target** is the difference between the total target cost and the currently feasible cost, or the amount by which Bootstrap must reduce its overall costs to meet its profit objective.

$$\text{Cost reduction target} = \text{Currently feasible cost} - \text{Total target cost}$$
$$= \$460{,}000 - \$400{,}000 = \underline{\underline{\$60{,}000}}$$

Bootstrap must reduce the total, annual cost to make and deliver the snowshoe model by a total of $60,000, or it is not an economically feasible product. The value of target costing is its focus on a tangible, cost-reduction target rather than the more ambiguous objective to "reduce" costs.[10]

[9]See Chapter 11 for more information about estimating costs.

[10]Considerable goal-setting research has found that tangible, challenging objectives result in better performance than an ambiguous objective to "do your best." For example, see E.A. Locke and G.P. Latham, *A Theory of Goal Setting and Task Performance.*

Step 4: Redesign or concurrently design products and processes to achieve the cost-reduction target. Because all costs are driven by decisions, managers probably can find a way to reduce production costs by the target amount.[11] However, the decision problem often is not one-dimensional. Bootstrap's more complex problem is how to accomplish a cost-reduction target while meeting its other organizational goals. These other goals can conflict with simple cost reduction. After developing the cost-reduction target, the next decision-making step is gathering information useful to solving the decision problem.

You're the **Decision Maker 13.1**

Extended Target Costing Analysis

Prepare a computer spreadsheet that reflects the construction and analysis in Exhibit 13–3.

Consider the independent effects on the cost-reduction target of the following changes in spreadsheet inputs:

a. Target price = $130.

b. Target profit percentage = 15 percent.

c. Annual target sales = 4,000 units.

d. Currently feasible costs = $560,000.

(Solutions begin on page 551.)

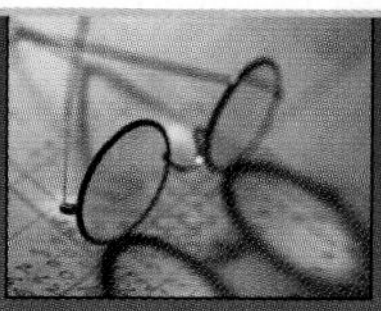

Cost Management in **Practice 13.1**

Target Costing and Some Adverse Effects

Target costing was pioneered in Japan. It is estimated that more than 80 percent of large Japanese manufacturing companies now use it to plan and control product development. The effects of target costing are pervasive in these companies since it affects budgeting, pricing, profit planning, organizational structures, and responsibilities and evaluations. Although target costing has had beneficial effects on costs and meeting customer needs, some Japanese researchers have observed adverse effects, including these:

- Longer development times because of numerous iterations of design and costing considerations.
- Employee burnout because of the immense pressure to meet targets.
- Extreme market segmentation that causes confusion.
- Organizational conflicts between designers who labor intensely to reduce costs only to see marketers give away promotional items costing even more. *Source: Y. Kato, G. Boer, and C. Chow,* "Target Costing: An Integrative Management Process." *(Full citations to references are in the Bibliography.)*

Stage II: Gathering Information

Cost-management information that supports management decision making often incorporates measures with varying **information quality,** the dimensions of which are decision usefulness, subjectivity, objectivity, accuracy, timeliness, cost, and relevance for current decisions. The overriding criterion of cost management information is **decision usefulness.** Does it help managers make sufficiently better decisions to justify the cost of the information?

information quality *has dimensions of usefulness, subjectivity, accuracy, timeliness, cost, and relevance*

decision usefulness *of information is whether managers make sufficiently better decisions to justify the cost of the information*

Objectivity versus Subjectivity

Cost management relies heavily on measurements of various kinds. All measurement inherently involves subjectivity and objectivity. **Subjectivity** describes the degree of disagreement about what to measure, how to measure it, what the observed measure is,

subjectivity *describes the degree of disagreement about what to measure, how to measure it, what the observed measure is, or whether the measurement is important*

[11] Methods to achieve target-cost reductions include activity-based management, value engineering, simultaneous engineering, and product or process redesign. Chapter 5 discusses these topics.

Choosing between automated and manual processes trades off costs, quality, and employment.

objectivity *is the degree of consensus about what to measure, how to measure it, what the observed measure is, or whether the measurement is important*

or whether the measurement is important. **Objectivity,** the degree of consensus about measurement, is the mirror image of subjectivity. Clearly, some measures are more subjective or objective than others; that is, all measures conceptually reside somewhere on a continuum from subjective to objective. For example, the numbers in the financial statements of Bootstrap Industries (and other companies) are considered to be *objective* measurements prepared with great care. Nonetheless, considerable judgment about financial statement measures and disclosures still exists. Closer to the subjectivity end of the spectrum is the measurement of Bootstrap's product or service quality perceptions, which reside in and vary among individuals. Even subjective measures can be useful, however. For example, perceptions of the quality of food or services can vary among Bootstrap's customers, but Bootstrap management believes that gathering these more subjective measures is essential because they can presage potential opportunities or problems. Similarly, many find value in the number of stars or "thumbs up" awarded to restaurants and movies.

Accuracy

accuracy *is precision in measurement*

Information pertinent to a decision problem must also be accurate or it will be of little use. **Accuracy** is precision in measurement. For example, the estimated cost Bootstrap incurred if it were to buy and maintain facilities for its snowshoe division, Sasquatch Snowshoes, is useful for decisions about whether to continue to rent or buy its own facilities. However, if the cost figures are inaccurate because of erroneous calculations or incomplete records, the usefulness of the figures is greatly diminished.

timeliness *means that information is available in time to fully consider it when making a decision*

Timeliness

Information is useful if it is timely; that is, **timeliness** means that information is available in time to fully consider it when making a decision. For example, information about alternative production processes is not very useful if it cannot be prepared before a deadline to decide which process Bootstrap should use.

relevance *of information refers to whether it is pertinent to a decision*

relevant costs and benefits *occur in the future* and *differ among feasible decision alternatives*

differential costs *are costs that differ between decision alternatives*

Relevance

The **relevance** of information refers to whether it is pertinent to a decision; that is, knowing the information or different values of the information can influence choice. Because different decisions typically require different information, an important issue is deciding what information is relevant to the specific situation. The most timely, accurate, objective information is useless if it is irrelevant to the decision. **Relevant costs and benefits** occur in the future *and* differ for feasible alternatives. Costs that differ for alternatives also are called **differential costs.** Some highly accurate information might not be useful to a decision maker. Suppose that Bootstrap will continue to operate manufacturing facilities in Oregon but is considering expanding the size of its rented facilities. Precise data about future rents in Colorado, where the company does not plan to locate, are irrelevant to the decision of whether to rent expanded facilities in Oregon. We elaborate on this important characteristic of cost-management information in the next section of the chapter

Identification of Relevant Costs and Benefits

LO 3 Identify both quantitative and qualitative relevant costs and benefits of decision alternatives.

A particular cost might or might not be relevant to the decision at hand. Some decisions involve many types of relevant, differential costs. For example, consider the problem of reducing the costs to produce Rambler snowshoes to meet the profit target. Suppose that the two alternatives to improving costs are to use either a robotic or an improved manual assembly process. All unit-, batch-, product-, customer-, and facility-level costs might differ for the robotic and manual assembly alternatives.[12] Therefore, this decision should consider all of these affected costs. However, if adding or replacing robotic machinery does not affect the manufacturing building itself, the decision process can ignore facility-related costs.

Now consider Exhibit 13–4, a preliminary analysis of costs and benefits of the two snowshoe production process alternatives considered by Bootstrap's managers: (1) installing robotic equipment or (2) improving the current manual process. Which benefits and costs are *relevant* to the choice in the alternatives to attempt the cost-reduction target?

[12]Recall that the activity cost hierarchy is discussed in Chapter 4.

Exhibit 13–4

Data Used for Preliminary Analysis of Two Snowshoe Production Process Alternatives

Bootstrap INDUSTRIES

Panel A

Quantitative Data	Alternative 1: Robotic Assembly	Alternative 2: Manual Assembly
Target (market) price (Ex. 13–3)	$ 100	$ 100
Sales and production in units (Ex. 13–3)	5,000	5,000
Unit-level cost per unit	$ 20	$ 40
Product-level costs:		
Equipment	$110,000	$ 40,000
Supervision	10,000	10,000
Training	5,000	20,000
Facility-level (building) costs	150,000	150,000

Panel B

Quantified Annual Benefit or Cost	Alternative 1: Robotic Assembly	Alternative 2: Manual Assembly	Difference in Alternatives
Sales revenue	$500,000	$500,000	$ 0
Unit-level costs	$100,000	$200,000	**$(100,000)**
Product-level costs:			
Equipment	110,000	40,000	**70,000**
Supervision	10,000	10,000	0
Training	5,000	20,000	**(15,000)**
Facility-level (building) costs	150,000	150,000	0
Total costs	375,000	420,000	**(45,000)**
Profit	$125,000	$ 80,000	$ 45,000
Return on sales	25%	16%	

Some quantitative data in panel A of Exhibit 13–4 came from Exhibit 13–3. The target price, sales and production volume[13] are the same. We have refined our estimates of alternative production costs to include unit-level costs per unit, product-level equipment and supervision costs, training, and facility-level or building costs. The analysis in panel B of Exhibit 13–4 uses these revenue and cost drivers to estimate the profitability of each alternative. Does the choice between the alternatives hinge on all of (or only) these factors?

Let's examine panel B of Exhibit 13–4. Observe that sales revenues of $500,000 are expected to be the same for each alternative. Therefore, although revenues are surely important to Bootstrap, they do not differ and, therefore, are not relevant to choosing one of the alternatives. Similarly, product-related supervision costs, $10,000, and facility-related building costs, $150,000, are irrelevant because they are the same for both alternatives. The decision hinges on other information.

Unit-level costs, product-level equipment, and training costs of the alternatives do differ, however, and therefore are relevant. Although it is important to list all benefits and costs (otherwise some might be omitted inadvertently), the decision clearly hinges on the three costs that differ for each alternatives: the annual unit-level cost and the product-level equipment and training costs. You can trace the total difference in cost and profit for the two alternatives, $45,000, to the net of the unit-level costs ($100,000 lower for robotic assembly), equipment costs ($70,000 higher for robotic assembly), and training costs ($15,000 lower for robotic assembly). In nearly all cases, you can make a choice between alternatives by identifying and comparing only their differential costs and benefits.

Cost difference for alternatives = $100,000 − 70,000 + 15,000
= $45,000 in favor of alternative 1

Observe that only alternative 1 meets the company's requirement for return on sales of at least 20 percent.

Impact on the Future

What time period is affected when a manager makes a decision? Possible answers to this question include tomorrow, next week, the next quarter, or the next two years. Notice that the past is not included in the response. Benefits and costs that have already occurred cannot be changed because they are history.

To be relevant to a decision, the cost or benefit must occur in the future. For example, Bootstrap Industries advertised last year's Rambler snowshoe for sale at prices below cost; you might wonder how the company can stay in business. Of course, its Sasquatch Snowshoe division cannot continue as an ongoing entity if it consistently follows this practice. Bootstrap recognizes that the original cost of last year's snowshoes is a *sunk cost,* which is a past payment for resources that cannot be changed by any current or future decision. For example, the purchase price paid in the past for equipment or merchandise or the past production cost of inventory is irrelevant to decisions about what to do with these assets in the future.

To illustrate, suppose that Sasquatch has 100 pairs of last year's Rambler snowshoes, which cost $92 per pair to manufacture.[14] This year's much improved model is now available, but competitive pressures are keeping sales prices constant. Bootstrap's management does not believe that it now can sell the old snowshoes at the current $100 price. Given the current market, management believes that the snowshoes must sell at a reduced price of $60. In this decision, Bootstrap's management disregards the original $92 cost; it is sunk, history. A number of future marketing and inventory control issues

[13] Sasquatch Snowshoes does not build products for inventory; thus, production equals sales. See Chapter 7 for a discussion of just-in-time production.

[14] Chapters 2 and 4 discuss measurements of production and service costs in more detail.

might arise, but the historical manufacturing cost is irrelevant to the decision of how to best dispose of the old-model snowshoes. Their cost might as well be considered to be zero when deciding how to dispose of them.

Managers are sometimes tempted to keep merchandise such as last year's snowshoes (or other assets, such as machines) rather than to sell them below cost. Losses have a negative connotation and depress a firm's financial performance for the period. In many cases, however, keeping the assets is the wrong decision. For example, if Bootstrap does not dispose of the old snowshoes immediately, even at an accounting loss, the company might have to sell them at a greater loss later or to write the inventory off entirely, with nothing to show in return. Under the circumstances, unless a higher price is likely in the future, the decision to sell now at a reduced price is probably preferred. The problem is that the old inventory already is devalued below production cost, but management just does not want to recognize this. Consider the following likely outcomes:

Alternative Decisions	Sell 100 Old Snowshoes Now	Write Off 100 Snowshoes Later	Difference
Revenue	100 × \$60 = \$6,000	\$ 0	\$6,000
Production (inventory) cost	100 × \$92 = 9,200	100 × \$92 = 9,200	0
Loss	\$(3,200)	\$(9,200)	\$6,000

Clearly, Bootstrap is better off by \$6,000 if it swallows a mild loss now to avoid a greater loss later. Sometimes managers want to avoid the loss now and hope that their successors will have to face the problem, but the company is better off if it ignores the sunk costs.

Trade-Off between Information Cost and Quality

In an ideal world, perhaps, the information of the highest quality possesses high levels of the characteristics of relevance, accuracy, and timeliness—all obtained at low cost. However, the most relevant, accurate, and timely information might be excessively expensive to create and maintain on an ongoing basis. Thus, cost management analysts often must make trade-offs between the cost and quality of information. At some point, managers should be unwilling to seek increased quality of information because its cost would exceed its benefit for making better decisions.

Feasible, alternative actions. Where do decision alternatives come from? (*Hint:* They do not magically appear like the Cheshire Cat.) One alternative, however, is always available: the status quo, which also is the "do nothing" or "do nothing differently" alternative. Organizations always should consider the status quo seriously, but its inertia should not be a deciding factor. Organizations often identify other alternatives by thoroughly seeking information from, among others:

- *Employees,* who know their work best and often have excellent suggestions for improvement.
- *Customers,* who can articulate their unmet needs and visions of the future.
- *Competitors,* which are seeking the same competitive edge and already have made changes that this organization can imitate or improve.
- *Noncompetitors,* which use "best practices" that might be transferrable to this organization.
- *Universities,* which seek to push beyond the boundaries of scientific, engineering, and social practices and exist to create and disseminate knowledge.
- *Consultants,* who observe best practices and can help adapt them to this organization.
- The *Internet,* which is a continually evolving repository of vast and growing knowledge.

Of course, managers could spend all of their time searching for and evaluating alternatives, which is a form of "analysis paralysis" and ignores the fact that information about decisions in a competitive world must be timely to be useful. Knowing when to cut off the search for more alternatives usually is a matter of management judgment, weighing the trade-off of the value of possibly finding a better alternative against the cost of delaying decisions.

Stage III: Evaluating Alternatives

qualitative factors *are the characteristics of a decision that cannot easily or should not be expressed in numerical terms*

Once alternatives have been identified, the next stage of decision making is to evaluate the quantitative and qualitative factors related to each alternative. **Qualitative factors** are the characteristics of a decision that cannot easily or should not be expressed in numerical terms. These include such things as employee morale, customers' perceptions of style of products or customization of services, control given up if certain processes currently performed internally are outsourced to external contractors, reputation that an organization develops if a manager emphasizes his or her own goals rather than those of the entire organization, and so on. Although we can never know for certain what all benefits and costs will be, the objective of careful evaluation is to significantly improve on the random choice of an alternative. Otherwise, why not just roll a die or flip a coin? If that were all there is to decision making, there would be far fewer interesting (and high-paying) management jobs.

Using the Decision Tree: A Helpful Decision Aid

LO 4 Use decision trees to describe business decisions.

decision tree *is a diagram of decisions and alternative outcomes expected from those decisions in a "tree, branch, and limb" format*

Since most decisions consider several alternatives or many alternatives with complex options, evaluating the alternatives systematically is advisable. A useful decision aid is a **decision tree,** which diagrams decisions and alternative outcomes expected from those decisions in a "tree, branch, and limb" format. The choice of the most desirable alternative is made after considering the benefits and costs of each "limb." Exhibit 13–5 is a decision tree of the two alternative choices for producing snowshoes that were discussed earlier. Although it might not be necessary for simple decisions, a decision tree can help identify and communicate the dimensions of complex decisions that managers face. Making complex decisions without such a decision aid can be confusing and prone to errors, particularly the omission of relevant factors.

To build the decision tree of Bootstrap's decision problem shown in Exhibit 13–5, follow these steps:

1. *Display the decision alternatives in the order the decisions must be made.* Bootstrap's cost-reduction alternatives shown in diamond shapes are *the status quo* or *change.* If the decision is to change, two alternatives exist: *automate the process* or *improve the manual process.* Complex situations can have multiple layers of decisions, and decision trees can be complicated.
2. *Trace the path of each decision to its ultimate outcomes and identify the set of outcomes that result from each decision path.* Exhibit 13–5 expresses outcomes in terms of Bootstrap's tangible objectives of the elements of profit, product quality, and employment.
3. *Measure the benefits and costs of each set of outcomes.* In this exhibit, we express the outcomes in qualitative terms, but we will quantify many of them in the next section.

Anticipating the Future Outcome(s) of Each Action

Predicting the future might be the most difficult aspect of decision making as well as the most important one. Managers choose among alternatives based on predicted costs and benefits, and the more reliable these estimates are, the more useful they are to sup-

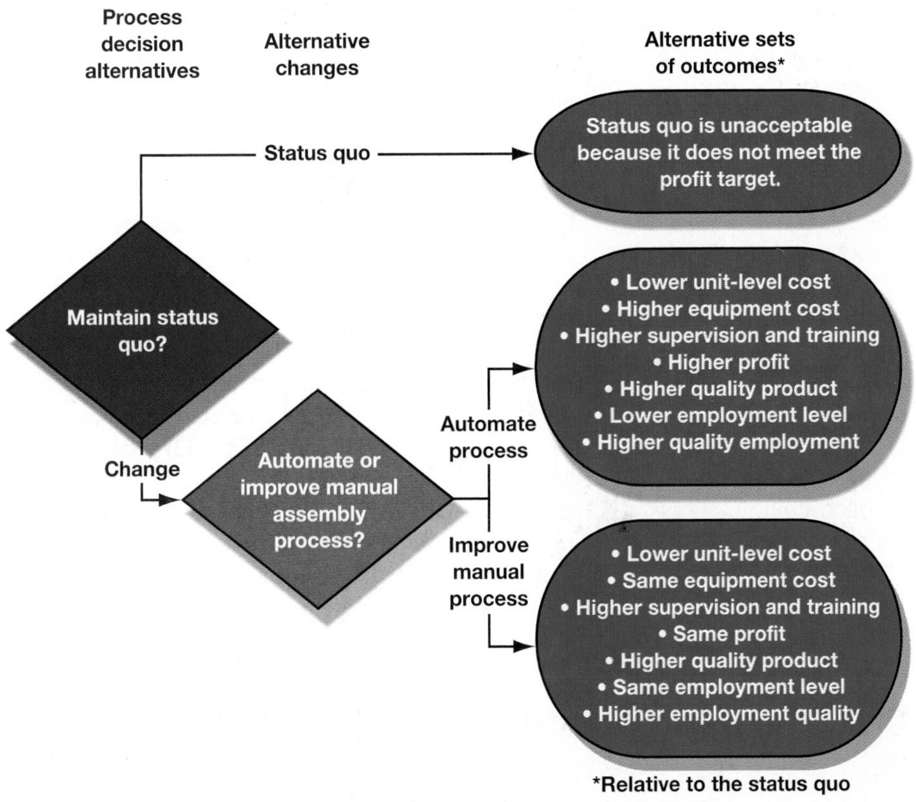

Exhibit 13–5

Bootstrap Industries Decision Tree: Rambler Model

Bootstrap INDUSTRIES

port decisions. The first task of anticipating future outcomes is to identify the types of relevant outcomes (costs and benefits). The second task is to estimate them quantitatively or qualitatively, as appropriate.

Considering the past. Relevant decision information must involve costs and benefits that will take place in the future. Although sunk costs are not directly relevant to a decision situation, a study of the past can prove beneficial for predicting the future. In our framework, the decision-making process requires various predictions—revenues, costs, cash flows, and the like—before making a decision. When making these predictions, the analyst considers past experience and historical data. Although this might seem contradictory to the earlier recommendation to ignore sunk costs, understanding the past can contribute reliable information about what the future will hold.[15] Although it is a subtle difference, sunk costs themselves are irrelevant to decisions, but analysts can use them to help estimate or predict future costs, which are relevant.

Predicting benefits and costs of completely new products. In new-product situations, the past might be of limited use to predicting benefits and costs. Before deciding to launch new products or services, many organizations produce prototype products or experiment with processes to learn what related future costs might be. After estimating the effects of learning to operate processes more efficiently, these prototype costs should be the bases for reliable estimates of future costs.

Organizations also can use the services of consultants who have experience in other organizations with similar products or services. Sometimes organizations hire employees from these organizations to acquire their knowledge of products, services, processes, and estimated costs and benefits.

[15]Chapter 11 covers the issue of cost estimation in detail.

Choosing the Best Alternative: Estimated Benefits and Costs

This section discusses the preparation of quantitative data that reflects the decision tree in Exhibit 13–5. This analysis using these data should faithfully represent the decision alternatives and each set of outcomes to clearly identify what can or cannot be measured quantitatively. The analysis also should clearly note any nonobvious assumptions so that managers can question and modify the analysis to reflect alternative assumptions. It should identify the net benefits (usually profits or cost reductions achieved) of each alternative.

Exhibit 13–6 shows an analysis of qualitative and quantitative benefits and costs of the alternatives shown graphically in Exhibit 13–5. Cost-management analysts have added quantitative and qualitative data relevant to Bootstrap's employment and quality goals (panel A) and costs related to the status quo. The quantitative data in panel B of Exhibit 13–6 are the same as those in Exhibit 13–4. Note that currently feasible costs ($460,000) are the sum of status-quo unit-level costs ($51 × 5,000) plus product- and facility-level costs ($40,000 + 10,000 + 5,000 + 150,000).

Each column shows a different alternative, including the status quo. Panel C of Exhibit 13–6 shows data regarding quantitative benefits and costs that differ for the alternatives. It is possible to create columns that show line-by-line differences for each alternative and the status quo. However, that creates a cluttered table that is difficult to read.

Exhibit 13–6

Data Regarding the Benefits and Costs of Process Alternatives: Bootstrap Industries' Rambler Model

Bootstrap INDUSTRIES

	1 Status Quo: Manual Assembly	2 Alternative 1: Robotic Assembly	3 Alternative 2: Improved Manual Assembly
Panel A: Qualitative Data			
Skill level	Medium	Higher	Higher
Product quality	Medium	Higher	Higher
Panel B: Quantitative Data			
Nonsupervisory employment level	50	20	50
Target (market) price	$ 100	$ 100	$ 100
Sales and production volume	5,000	5,000	5,000
Unit-level cost per unit	$ 51	$ 20	$ 40
Product-level costs:			
Equipment	40,000	110,000	40,000
Supervision	10,000	10,000	10,000
Training	5,000	5,000	20,000
Facility-level (building) costs	150,000	150,000	150,000
Currently feasible costs	460,000	—	—
Cost reduction target	60,000	—	—
Panel C: Quantified Annual Benefit or Cost			
Sales revenue	$500,000	$500,000	$500,000
Unit-level costs	$255,000	$100,000	$200,000
Product-level costs:			
Equipment	40,000	110,000	40,000
Supervision	10,000	10,000	10,000
Training	5,000	5,000	20,000
Facility-level (building) costs	150,000	150,000	150,000
Total costs	$460,000	$375,000	$420,000
Profit	$ 40,000	$125,000	$ 80,000
Return on sales	8.0%	25.0%	16.0%
Cost reduction achieved	**$ —**	**$ 85,000**	**$ 40,000**
Margin of safety	**$ (60,000)**	**$ 25,000**	**$ (20,000)**

Generally, keeping the presentation simple and directing attention to important outcomes is preferable. Because a desired cost reduction drove the decision-making problem, Exhibit 13–6 directs attention to the last two rows, which show that (1) the status quo achieves no cost reduction (of course), (2) the improved manual process does not achieve the desired cost-reduction, and (3) the robotic process does achieve the cost-reduction target with a cushion or **margin of safety** of $25,000, which is the amount by which a quantitative objective is exceeded. A quantitative margin of safety is not a sufficient guide to choose among alternatives if the qualitative factors also are important.

margin of safety *is the amount by which a quantitative objective is exceeded*

Choosing the Best Alternative Using Both Quantitative and Qualitative Information

A comparison of quantified factors that reduce to a single profit or cost-reduction number might not make the best alternative obvious. Other factors can be just as (or more) important to decision making. To clarify the importance of qualitative analyses, consider how quantitative analysis can allow managers to put a value on the sum total of the qualitative factors. For example, suppose that a cost-management analyst gives Bootstrap managers the numerical analysis of the Rambler-model process, provided in Exhibit 13–6. This analysis shows that robotics (alternative 1) will reduce annual costs by $25,000 more than the target and $45,000 more than improving the manual process by additional employee training (alternative 2). This seems to clearly favor the robotic process, but it conflicts with the organization's objectives of (1) employing persons with disabilities and (2) improving their skills, which favor alternative 1, improving the manual process through more training. How important are these qualitative factors to Bootstrap managers? If they decide to improve the manual process with more training, the qualitative considerations must be more important than the cost-reduction target and worth at least $45,000 to the organization and its stakeholders. The $45,000 given up by not selecting the robotic assembly process is the opportunity cost of the decision, or the amount forgone by choosing one mutually exclusive alternative or opportunity over another.[16]

Weighing trade-offs between quantitative and qualitative costs and benefits and considering opportunity costs in making decisions are hallmarks of management decision making. Managers' skill, experience, judgment, and ethical standards are crucial in making such difficult choices.

Examples of Common Decisions: Outsource, or Add or Drop a Product, or Service, or Business Unit

LO 5 Use a cost-benefit approach for common decisions such as obtaining new technology or capability; outsourcing (make versus buy); or modifying, adding, or dropping a product, service, or business unit; and pricing including special orders.

The decision-making framework and use of relevant information are applicable to many types of business decisions that involve identifying alternative courses of action and comparing alternative sets of relevant benefits and costs. Cost-management analysts can apply the framework in Exhibit 13–1 to virtually any business decision. We now consider several common business decisions.

Outsourcing or Make-or-Buy Decision

An **outsourcing** or make-or-buy decision is any decision an organization makes about acquiring goods or services internally or externally. A restaurant that uses its own ingredients to prepare meals from scratch has chosen the "make" alternative; one that serves meals from frozen entrees acquired from suppliers has chosen the "buy" alternative. An electronics firm that assembles its own circuit boards "makes," whereas one that contracts with Bootstrap Industries for the assembly of circuit boards "buys."

outsourcing *is acquiring goods or services from an outside provider*

[16]Sometimes organizations hedge their bets by adopting enough of an alternative to retain the *option* to fully adopt it in the future.

Credit card firms that process their own transactions with card holders "make"; those that turn over processing to outside entities that specialize in such work "buy."

The outsourcing or make-or-buy decision is part of a company's value-chain strategy. Some companies meet their goals by performing all processes of the value chain to control all activities that lead to the final product or service. Others prefer to rely on outsiders for some inputs and specialize in only certain steps of the total process (recall the example of Sara Lee Corporation from Chapter 1). Outsourcing is one of the fastest-growing business activities because many firms are choosing to concentrate on their core activities, leaving other peripheral tasks to organizations with expertise in performing them. An equipment manufacturer, for example, might outsource all printing activities to a Kinko's-type operation. Whether to rely on outsiders for a substantial amount of goods and services depends on relevant cost comparisons and other factors that are not so easily quantified, such as suppliers' dependability and quality.

Research Insight 13.1

Outsourcing and Business Partnerships

Eighty-eight percent of firms responding to a recent survey by KPMG Business Process Solutions found that outsourcing is a strategic tool that truly provides a competitive advantage. A KPMG spokesperson noted, "Companies are now looking beyond simply cutting costs and maintaining product quality. Companies are looking for business process partnerships that create real value and help them attain a global competitive edge." The areas with the most reengineering/outsourcing potential for an organization are legal (noted by approximately 71 percent of the responding firms), tax, information technology, and human resources, followed closely by finance/accounting, customer service, and administration.

Source: M. Ozanne, "Outsourcing: Managing Strategic Partnerships for the Virtual Enterprise."

Bootstrap Industries' Outsourcing. To analyze the outsourcing decision with our decision-making framework, let's look at Bootstrap Industries from the perspective of one of its customers, Hewlett-Packard (HP), which designs and manufactures computers, computer peripherals, and other electronics products. We focus on the part of HP's circuit-board function that it has outsourced to Bootstrap. HP certainly has the expertise to assemble (make) its own circuit boards, but this process is not how HP adds the most value to its products. HP has therefore outsourced much of the circuit-board assembly work to other organizations, such as Bootstrap, that have developed expertise in this area and that provide reliable, high-quality service. Outsourcing allows HP to

Exhibit 13–7

Data Regarding Circuit-Board Assembly Outsourcing

Monthly Costs Incurred by HP	1 Alternative 1: Status Quo: In House Assembly Costs	2 Alternative 2: Outsource Assembly to Bootstrap	3 Difference by Outsourcing
Unit-level costs	$ 35,000	$176,000	**$141,000** higher
Product-level costs	197,000	40,000	**($157,000)** lower
Facility-level costs	38,000	18,000	**($ 20,000)** lower
Total assembly costs	$270,000	$234,000	**($ 36,000) lower**

partner with Bootstrap in creating jobs for disabled persons and then to reassign its resources to higher-valued work elsewhere in the firm.

HP received a $176,000 bid from Bootstrap to perform the contracted assembly of circuit boards for a normal month of operations. The analysis in Exhibit 13–7 indicates why HP was inclined to outsource the work to Bootstrap.

The estimated monthly total assembly cost savings of $36,000 per month was enough to get HP's attention, but Bootstrap's reputation for quality, reliability, and just-in-time delivery convinced HP that it could safely outsource these assemblies to Bootstrap.[17]

Let's examine whether each part of the analysis appears to be relevant to the decision. (*Note:* Some people believe that the numbers "speak for themselves," but that is almost *never* true; judgment and analysis almost always are necessary.) Looking at the first row, outsourcing the assembly to Bootstrap increases HP's unit-level costs by $141,000. It saves $35,000 in-house (materials, testing, etc.) but spends $176,000 for the expected number of circuit boards it needs to support product manufacturing. This increase in unit-level costs must be made up in other cost areas. In return for the contract price, Bootstrap guarantees to provide defect-free circuit boards just in time to install in HP's products. Because Bootstrap is a certified supplier and regards certification seriously, HP can rely on this guarantee.

The second row of Exhibit 13–7 shows that outsourcing reduces HP's product-level costs by $157,000. Most of that cost reduction is the result of HP's sale of assembly equipment no longer needed to Bootstrap, which benefited both parties. HP still will incur some employee-related product-level costs because it prefers to not lay off its employees but will assign them to other work, so outsourcing will not cause HP's total product-level costs to decline to zero. HP will reduce facility-level costs by $20,000 by selling other unused equipment, for which neither HP nor Bootstrap has a use. Facility-level costs will not decline to zero because HP has created a new administrative function to administer, manage, and monitor its outsourcing contracts and activities, costing $18,000 per month to manage the Bootstrap contract. The net cost savings of $36,000 per month plus the virtual guarantee of high-quality service makes this outsourcing contract desirable; savings without the quality guarantee might not be sufficient.

Decision to Add or Drop a Product, Service, or Business Unit

One of the most difficult decisions managers make concerns adding or dropping a product, service, or business unit. These are difficult decisions because they usually have major effects on the organization's strategy and on its stakeholders. Consequently, managers do not make them lightly.

[17] Achieving ISO 9002 quality certification clearly has helped Bootstrap attract and retain demanding customers such as HP. ISO quality certification and just-in-time methods are discussed in Chapter 7.

The term "business unit" can refer to a product, a market territory, a department, a warehouse, or just about any other business segment imaginable (for example, HP's outsourced circuit-board assembly process). Products that were formerly profitable might be losing market share to newer goods and no longer adequately cover costs. On the other hand, a company can add a business unit to serve new product markets or geographic regions. In nearly all of these cases, managers must make difficult trade-offs among quantitative and qualitative costs and benefits.

Making these decisions is not easy, but managers can feel comfortable that they have made them correctly by following the decision-making framework. Note that no analysis of whether to drop or add a business unit is complete without considering the status quo: the current net benefits from the resources being used by the potentially dropped unit. For example, computing how much can be saved by dropping an unprofitable business unit is not adequate, managers also must consider whether the recovered resources can be used more profitably. At a minimum, for example, Bootstrap could sell its resources and invest the proceeds in low-risk, marketable securities, but this would not meet its organizational goals.

To illustrate the proper handling of these strategic decisions, let's analyze how Bootstrap decided whether to close a landscaping facility. The data considered in the initial analysis is shown in Exhibit 13–8. The status quo of this operation will generate an annual loss of $52,000, which indicates that, although the operation does employ 21 people, it does not meet the tangible objective of operating at a profit. A relevant issue is whether Bootstrap can improve overall profitability (eliminate the loss) by closing the operation.

The third column presents the benefits and costs that change by closing the facility but doing nothing else. Let's look at these items carefully because they are key to understanding what Bootstrap must do to improve its profitability.

Relevant benefits. The revenues in panel C of Exhibit 13–8 shows that for now Bootstrap does not have an alternative business use for the resources that can be recovered by closing the landscaping operation. Thus, it shows no revenues to replace the forgone $300,000 in sales that the operation generates. Let's leave this for now, but clearly we need to revisit this item.

Relevant costs. Unit-level costs will decline to zero by closing the landscaping facility, saving $30,000 annually because the landscaping materials and supplies will no longer be necessary. Service-level costs, the costs directly attributable to operating the service, also will decline to zero. Neither the landscaping equipment, which we assume will be sold, nor the building, whose rental agreement either has expired or can be canceled without penalty, will be necessary after closing the operation. This will save another $68,000 ($32,000 + $36,000) in service-level costs per year.

Perhaps surprisingly, Bootstrap expects no facility-level cost reductions attributable to closing the landscaping operation. The closed operation does not incur those costs, but Bootstrap's goals and commitments mean that the rest of the organization must bear them. It will not lay off the supervisor and 20 employees of the landscaping operation but will reassign them to other work. Many organizations, profit-seeking firms included, have similar employment commitments and lay off employees only as a last resort. Thus, employee wages and salaries of the operation are committed facility-level costs to the organization and closing it often will not result in these employee-related cost reductions. Similarly, although the closed operation will not use central office services, such as payroll or insurance services, closing it will not reduce Bootstrap's capability (e.g., administrative personnel) to provide those services. The rest of the organization will bear these costs also which will not be saved. Because of Bootstrap's goals and objectives to increase the skills of its employees, the organiza-

	Status Quo: Operate Landscaping Facility	Close Landscaping Facility	
Panel A: Qualitative Data			
Skill level	Low	Low	
Product quality	Low	NA	
Panel B: Quantitative Data			
Supervisory employment	1	1	
Nonsupervisory employment	20	20	
Service revenues per year	$300,000	$ 0	
Unit-level costs	30,000	0	
Service-level costs:			
Equipment	32,000	0	
Building rental	36,000	0	
Facility-level costs:			
Wages	200,000	200,000	
Supervision	24,000	24,000	
Central office services	20,000	20,000	
Training	10,000	10,000	
Panel C: Quantified Annual Benefit or Cost			**Difference if Closed**
Sales revenue	$300,000	$0	($300,000)
Unit-level costs	$ 30,000	$0	$ 30,000
Service-level costs:			
Equipment	32,000	0	32,000
Building rental	36,000	0	36,000
Facility-level costs:			
Wages	200,000	200,000	0
Supervision	24,000	24,000	0
Central office services	20,000	20,000	0
Training	10,000	10,000	0
Total costs	352,000	254,000	98,000
Profit (loss)	($ 52,000)	($254,000)	($202,000)

Exhibit 13–8

Data Regarding Dropping a Business Unit by Bootstrap Industries

Bootstrap INDUSTRIES

tion similarly does not expect to reduce annual training costs by closing the landscaping operation.

Unfinished business. Clearly, Exhibit 13–8 shows that the analysis of the decision to close the remote operation is not finished. Simply closing it (doing nothing else) would save $98,000 in annual costs but also would forgo $300,000 in revenues for a net reduction in profits of $202,000. Surely this do-nothing alternative does not advance Bootstrap's progress in meeting its goals of high-quality employment and profitable operations. What must Bootstrap's managers do, and what is the magnitude of the problem?

To complete the data needed for the analysis, Bootstrap must identify and analyze alternative uses of its recovered employee resources in a manner similar to that shown previously in Exhibit 13–6. The objectives of this analysis are to find the best alternative that generates quality employment and operates profitably. In fact, Bootstrap did find such an alternative (see You're the Decision Maker 13.2).

It is important to note that the presentation *form* of these data can be applied to any organization's decision making about adding or dropping a business unit, but the specifics of which benefits and costs might or might not be saved or avoided will differ across organizations.

You're the Decision Maker 13.2

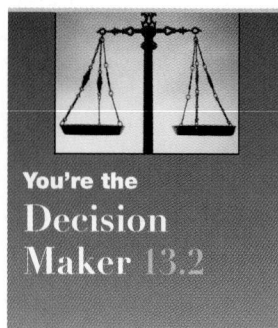

Further Analysis of Dropping a Business

Complete the analysis in Exhibit 13–8 by considering the changes predicted for the following two alternatives for fully employing the resources freed-up by closing the remote landscaping operation.

a. Increase in skill level to medium and product quality to high; realize service revenues of $400,000, unit-level costs of $40,000, equipment costs of $50,000, building rental of $40,000; and training costs of $40,000.

b. Increase product quality to medium; realize service revenues of $300,000, unit-level costs of $14,000, equipment costs of $20,000, building rental of $10,000.

(Solutions begin on page 551.)

Pricing Decisions

We conclude our overview of decision making with the topic of pricing. This is a troublesome area for many organizations; determining the "right" price for a good or service is important and can be very difficult. A company that sets its prices too high does not generate sales, resulting in total profitability below target. On the other hand, prices set too low might lead to an increase in sales activity, but the revenues might fail to cover costs. Both results miss the target profits.

Influences on Prices

Generally speaking, organizations consider several factors when determining prices: markets, customers, competitors, costs, life cycles, timing, and a variety of legal, political, and image-related issues.

Markets. Many products and services are offered in highly competitive markets (e.g., agricultural products, automobiles, personal desktop computers, cellular phones and service, small appliances) in which prices are readily observable. Deviating from market prices means either losing sales with prices that are too high or losing profits with prices that are too low. Setting prices in these markets requires understanding competitors' offerings and whether a product's or service's deviation from market norms (e.g., adding a higher or lower quality component) can support either higher or lower prices. In competitive markets, all producers must meet the market price; to make a profit, they must produce at a cost sufficiently below market price to survive.

Customers. An organization should consider pricing decisions for new products from the perspective of its customers. Prices that are too high will not generate the sales levels necessary to recover costs and target profits because customers will seek a less expensive or substitute product or service. They might wait for a competitor's offering. Conversely, setting prices too low could underestimate customers' willingness to pay for what might be a valuable innovation. Understanding customers' willingness to pay for the attributes and functions of a product or service is key to setting prices successfully.

Competitors. Competitors' reactions also influence pricing decisions. A competitor's aggressive pricing policy can force a business to lower its prices. On the other hand, a business without a competitor has some discretion and can set higher prices to take advantage of the lack of competition. Setting high prices for items that are unprotected by patents or copyrights will generate abnormally high profits and invite competition.

International borders frequently mean little to competitive firms. Firms with overcapacity in their domestic markets (i.e., domestic supply exceeds demand at desired prices) can price aggressively in export markets. For instance, software companies such as Microsoft with high development costs and low unit-level costs can seek foreign markets as an outlet for their goods. In a foreign market, a firm can exploit the high development costs that it has already incurred at home and therefore charge lower prices than local competition, which must incur these costs before introducing their own new products. Managers increasingly consider both their domestic and international competition when making pricing decisions. International firms that price aggressively in foreign markets must be careful to avoid charges of "dumping" their products at artificially low prices that discourage foreign competition. US manufacturers, for example, often complain that open markets allow foreign competitors to dump their products in the United States. Supporting those charges has been difficult because of the complexity of measuring costs and the values of other product features, such as postsale services, which might not be offered in all locations.[18]

Costs. The role of costs in price setting varies widely among organizations and industries. Managers of organizations that operate in less competitive markets might set prices at least partially on the basis of costs by adding a *markup* to production costs. While companies can price below cost as a promotion or "loss leader," no profit-seeking organization can price its goods and services on average below cost for an extended period.

Managers have some latitude in determining the markup, but market forces usually are influential here as well. No company's management can set prices blindly at cost plus a markup without considering the market. If, for example, a company has a markup policy of 40 percent and defines cost as $200, the target-selling price is $280 [$200 + $200 × .40]. Managers judge the marked-up $280 target price in light of what competitors are charging and the amount that customers are willing to pay.

Charging an excessive markup can increase profits in the short term, but it also invites competition to enter the market or customers to seek substitutes. If the price is deemed too high, management can lower its desired markup or redesign the product or service to achieve its target price. However, as Peter Drucker pointed out, cost-based pricing can be a dangerously expensive approach:

> Most American and practically all European companies arrive at their prices by adding up costs and then putting a profit margin on top. And then, as soon as they have introduced the product, they have to start cutting the price, have to redesign the product at enormous expense, have to take losses—and often have to drop a perfectly good product because it is priced incorrectly.[19]

Drucker argues that target or price-led costing is a much more effective approach to pricing for almost all companies because it requires up-front knowledge of the market and customers that is incorporated into products. Although market research is costly, Drucker argues cost-based pricing often requires much more costly fixing of pricing and product problems that never should have occurred. The analogy to managing quality is clear (see Chapter 7).

Some organizations, however, such as cable television or intrastate telecommunication in the United States, legally must base prices on costs. Managers propose prices based on marked-up costs that generally must be approved by a regulatory agency of the state or local government. Many government contracts are based on the recovery of costs, so measuring costs are of prime importance in pricing these contracts.

Many organizations consider only current production costs in production or pricing decisions when they should consider full life cycle costs. A **product's life cycle** is the time from its initial research and development to the point at which customer support is withdrawn. The specific phases of the cycle often include the following:

a **product life cycle** *is the time that elapses from its initial research and development to the point at which customer support is withdrawn*

1. Idea generation (early research and development).
2. Concept feasibility.
3. Product design and planning.

[18]An interesting twist to the practice of "dumping" is the domestic backlash that prescription drug companies received in 2001. Under pressure from the United Nations, they agreed to sell AIDS drugs in Africa at 10 percent or less of the domestic price only to receive scorn from domestic consumers who recoiled at the apparently high profits earned on domestic sales. See "AIDS Gaffes in Africa Come Back to Haunt Drug Industry in the United States," *The Wall Street Journal.*

[19]P. Drucker, "The Five Deadly Business Sins."

4. Prototype or working model.
5. Product launch or rollout.
6. Product manufacturing, delivery, and service to customers.
7. Product termination.

The cycle's duration varies considerably among industries, services, and products. For example, the life cycle of automobile models is 5 to 10 years; in contrast, it can be less than 1 year for fad toys and fashion clothing. The realization that the great majority of a product's cost is determined well before it is produced for customers is important. Thus, many organizations can use target costing to simultaneously manage both the development and cost of the product.

life cycle costing *tracks costs attributable to each product or service from start to finish*

Life cycle costing tracks costs attributable to each product or service from start to finish, from cradle to grave. It provides important information for cost management and pricing. Many organizations traditionally consider only future production, sales, and customer-service costs in pricing decisions. However, early activities such as research and development, product planning, and concept design for new products can consume significant resources, and sales prices must cover these costs if the firm is to operate profitably. In other words, sales revenues and, thus, prices must consider and eventually cover all life cycle costs, indeed, all value-chain costs, for the organization to meet target profits in the long term. Note that target costing explicitly considers life cycle costs in computing target costs.

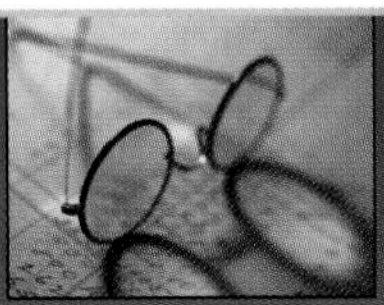

Cost Management in Practice 13.2

Pricing and the Internet

How does the Internet affect pricing? John Chambers of Cisco believes that because customers can quickly compare prices from many suppliers, "Everything gets cheaper forever." So the only survival techniques are to continuously manage costs and innovate to create new customer value. This access to multiple suppliers and lower costs is not restricted to large companies. Individuals increasingly turn to Internet-based retail outlets whose prices are constantly available to the market.

How do companies set prices on the Internet where the balance of pricing power is shifting to customers? The answer appears to be that companies are "price takers" when the products or services are commodities (similar, widely available products), and they must be very conscious of their costs to survive. On the other hand, innovative products and services can command premium prices until they, too, become commodities, which the Internet can cause to happen quickly. So companies charge high prices while they can, but they should have innovative replacements in process. Cisco itself is not immune to the power of the market to discipline a lack of innovation. The company has been criticized for outsourcing its new-product development and recently laid off thousands of employees and wrote off billions of dollars in restructuring and obsolete inventory in response to the bursting of the Internet bubble in 2001. *Sources:* "Letting the Masses Name Their Price," *Business Week;* "Cisco Revenue to Fall Well Short of Estimates amid Business Slowdown", *The Wall Street Journal.*

Pricing law in the United States. Organizations do not have complete freedom when they set prices for products and services. Legally, managers must adhere to laws that prohibit organizations from unfairly discriminating among their customers in setting prices. Law also prohibits collusion, the agreement of all major firms in an industry to set their prices at the same levels.

US antitrust laws, including the Robinson–Patman Act, the Clayton Act, and the Sherman Act, restrict certain types of pricing behaviors that often focus on deliberate attempts to reduce competition and ultimately charge higher prices. The Robinson–Patman Act in particular prohibits price discrimination, which refers to quoting different prices to different customers for the same products with the intent to harm competitors and consumers.[20] Such price differences are unlawful unless they can be clearly justified by variations in the costs incurred to produce, sell, or deliver goods. Managers must keep careful

[20]The Robinson–Patman Act covers products but not services.

records justifying these cost differences when they exist because the records can be vital to a legal defense in court challenges.

Law also prohibits **predatory pricing,** which involves temporarily setting a price below cost to injure competitors that cannot sustain losses and consequently must leave the market. Predatory pricing drives out competitors and allows the "predator" to earn abnormally high profits by charging higher prices after competitors have left the market. Note that the occasional sale or special price in a retail setting is not unlawful because the intent is to stimulate store traffic, not to drive out the competition. In determining whether a price is predatory, courts examine an organization's cost records.

predatory pricing *involves temporarily setting a price below cost to broaden demand for a product and injure competitors*

Cost determination is a troublesome area, especially for manufacturers, because cost can be calculated in a variety of ways, as covered in detail in Chapters 2 and 4. Cost determination also is a problem for warehouse-type retailers such as Wal-Mart, Home Depot, and Office Max, but in a different way. These large retailers have such significant influence on the market that they commonly are able to obtain price concessions from their suppliers. Low costs from suppliers coupled with their low overhead means that these large businesses can sell products to the public below the cost paid by, say, the local family-owned camera shop or hardware store and still earn a sizable profit margin. These large firms must be able to demonstrate that their low prices are justified by low costs that are themselves not the result of unfair business practices. This is one area in which a decision maker is well advised to have an accountant on the left and a lawyer on the right before setting very low prices that might be considered harmful to competition.[21]

Pricing politics and image. Political considerations can be relevant to price setting. For example, if consumers perceive that an industry reaps unfairly large profits, they might exert political pressure on legislators to tax those profits differentially or to intervene in some way to regulate prices.[22] For example, because it periodically raises retail prices, the oil and gas industry regularly attracts this type of attention, as it did during 2001.

Companies also consider their public image in the price-setting process. A firm with a reputation for top-quality goods usually sets the price of a new product high to be consistent with its image. As many have discovered, however, the same brand-name product might be available on the Internet or at a discount store or outlet mall at a fraction of the price charged by a more exclusive retailer. The wide availability of discounted merchandise prices is causing some high-end retailers, such as Nordstrom, to justify higher prices by offering ambience and services not offered elsewhere.

Special-Order Price Decisions

Occasionally companies receive requests from customers for either unexpected quantities of a product or service or one-time customized products or services. Because these are unusual occurrences, usual prices might not be appropriate. The decisions to accept these *special orders* and to price them obviously are tied together. One-time, **special orders** by definition are irregular and do not have lasting implications for other products or customers. For example, an athletic team's emergency order for replacement New Balance shoes that were lost enroute to a postseason tournament might occasion a short-term pricing decision by New Balance that would not affect the normal pricing of its shoes. We emphasize that deviations from normal pricing practices can have lasting effects if customers begin to expect the deviations to indicate changes in normal pricing.

special orders *are irregular and do not have lasting implications for other products or customers*

[21]For further information on predatory pricing, see P. Areeda and D. Turner, "Predatory Pricing and Related Practices under Section 2 of the Sherman Act." For recent case law, see the "Legal Developments" section of the *Journal of Marketing.* Also see B. Committee and D.J. Grinnell, "Predatory Pricing, the Price-Cost Test, and Activity-Based Costing"; and P. McLeod and M. Maher, "Analyzing Newspaper Costs in Predation Lawsuits" for a recent case study.

[22]See, for example, S. Cahan and W. H. Kaempfer. "Industry Income and Congressional Regulatory Legislation: Interest Groups vs. Median Voter."

Relevant costs of special orders. Special orders often affect only unit-level costs. Occasionally, however, a decision to accept a special order causes product-level or facility-level costs to change. For example, if to complete a one-time special order a company must purchase new equipment, secure additional supervisors, or lease more space, these costs should be considered as relevant parts of the order's total cost. The importance of identifying relevant, differential costs can be more important in pricing special orders than in regular pricing situations in which market forces provide a stronger guide to pricing.

The relevant costs required for producing and selling a good or service combine to form a firm's minimum selling price. In some cases, relevant costs might be very low, such as selling one additional seat on an already scheduled airline flight or allowing one more student to enroll in an already scheduled college course. The relevant costs in these cases are *only the differential costs incurred in the short term to fill the seat or enroll the student.* Prices often reflect this differential cost awareness (although college tuition does not, as far as we are aware). For example, a person making travel arrangements at the last minute can find steeply discounted airfares and hotel rooms on the Internet because airlines and hotels are eager to generate additional revenues that at least cover differential costs (fuel, food, cleaning, etc.) when they (1) have no prospects for charging normally higher prices and (2) can charge normal prices for most services. Obviously, they cannot afford to offer discounted prices to all customers all the time.

Bootstrap Industries normally prices its facility-support services to cover all costs plus a target profit but departs from that pricing practice in some special-order situations. For example, if it temporarily has unused resources (e.g., the employees from the closed landscaping operation discussed earlier), the opportunity cost at the moment is low. Bootstrap might try to obtain special-order business initially at a loss to impress the customer with the quality of its work in hopes of winning future, regular business. Bootstrap uses a target-costing approach to price special orders.

Exhibit 13–9 presents data for use in the analysis of a special-order request received by Bootstrap to clean up a state government building damaged by a severe storm. The first column of numbers in panels A, B, and C shows the normal elements of Bootstrap's service costs. Because of the nature of the special order, Bootstrap decided to make a few changes to its normal pricing (shown in italic in the following list). The elements of the decision, which are part of the input data of Exhibit 13–9, follow:

- Maximum crew size (6) and supervision cost ($84 per crew per day) are unchanged, and 12 employees are needed to do the work.
- Wage and benefit cost for employees is unchanged at $60 per day.
- Supplies and equipment cost is *increased by $2 per day* to reflect increased cleaning needs.
- Transportation cost is *zero* because the state will provide daily transportation.
- Central office services cost is *zero,* reflecting the facility-cost nature of this cost, which does not change as a result of this special order.
- Target profit as a percentage of sales is *reduced to 5 percent* from the normal 20 percent to increase chances of winning the bid in hopes of earning repeat business.

Exhibit 13–9 computes the special-order cost per unit, in this case the cost per employee, in the column Adjusted for Special Order.

Because Bootstrap will have a cost savings and will disregard irrelevant central office costs, the cost per employee per day is $12 lower than normal (the Adjustment for Special Order Column), which might justify a lower bid price than normal. Reducing the target profit from 20 percent to 5 percent also indicates that Bootstrap can charge a lower special-order price than normal.

Exhibit 13–9

Analysis of a Special Order

Bootstrap INDUSTRIES

	Normal Services	Adjustment for Special Order	Adjusted for Special Order
Panel A: Qualitative Data			
Employee skill level	Low	0	Low
Service quality	High	0	High
Panel B: Quantitative Data			
Number of employees	NA	NA	12
Number of days	NA	NA	8
Crew size	6	0	6
Supervision cost (per 6 person crew per day)	$ 84.00	$ 0.00	$84.00
Panel C: Costs per Employee per Day			
Wages and benefits	$ 60.00	$ 0.00	$60.00
Supplies and equipment	11.00	2.00	13.00
Supervision	14.00	0.00	14.00
Transportation (within city)	5.00	**(5.00)**	0.00
Central office services	9.00	**(9.00)**	0.00
Total cost per employee per day	$ 99.00	**(12.00)**	$87.00
Profit as a percent of sales	20%	(15.00)%	5%
Bid price per employee per day	$123.75	$(32.17)	$91.58*
Panel D: Special-Order Benefit or Cost			
Total bid price	$ 8,792		
Service costs:			
Wages and benefits	$ 5,760		
Supplies and equipment	1,248		
Supervision	1,344		
Transportation	0		
Facility costs:			
Central office services	0		
Total costs	8,352		
Profit	**$ 440**		
Return on bid	**5.00%**		

*$91.58 = $87.00 ÷ (1 − .05)

Note that the formula for the target price in panel D of Exhibit 13–9 is a variation of the target-cost formula presented earlier in the chapter. Bootstrap computes its target price for a special order as a target profit percentage markup over special-order costs. As in target costing, the percentage return defines the relation between price and cost, but, in the reverse of target costing, the cost now is given and the special order price is solved for.

Special-order price per unit = Special-order cost per unit + *Target profit per unit*

The required percentage return on the order price replaces the target profit per unit, as follows:

Special-order price = Special-order cost + *Target profit percentage × Special-order price*

Rearranging terms in three more steps yields:

Special-order cost = Special-order price − Target profit percentage × Special-order price
= Special-order price × (1 − Target profit percentage)
Special-order price = Special-order cost ÷ (1 − Target profit percentage)

Substituting the special-order cost ($87.00) and the target profit percentage (5 percent) into the last equation yields a special-order price of $91.58 per employee per day, which is $32.17 lower than normal.

Special-order price = $87.00 ÷ (1 − .05) = $91.58 per employee per day

Exhibit 13–9 computes the total bid price, $8,792, by multiplying the bid price per employee per day by 12 employees and 8 days. In a similar manner, service and facility costs of the total costs for the special order are shown. The expected profit from the special order, $440, is 5 percent of the total bid price, as expected.

If special orders indicate new, long-term business with the state, the relevant costs also should include costs to increase service or administrative capacity. Furthermore, long-term business should generate normal profits. Consider an airline example to add an additional base to serve growing demand; long-term differential costs include the costs to buy and maintain additional aircraft, pay salaries, and operate ground facilities, among others. These costs must be recovered by prices over the years that the airline will operate flights through this new base. Because of the need to consider the effects of interest costs, the decision-making framework varies slightly for long-term decision making.[23]

[23]Long-term decision making is the topic of Chapter 14.

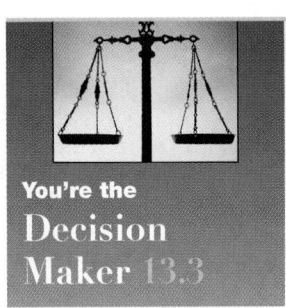

You're the Decision Maker 13.3

Alternative Analysis of Special Order

Consider that Bootstrap Industries did not have unemployed resources when the state made the special clean-up order.

a. Does this situation affect the pricing of the special order?

b. What bid price do you recommend in this situation?

(Solutions begin on page 551.)

Chapter Summary

This chapter provides a framework for decision making that explicitly describes the types of information necessary to make good business decisions. The decision-making framework was defined as follows:

Stage I. Setting goals and objectives.
Stage II. Gathering information.
Stage III. Evaluating alternatives.
Stage IV. Planning and implementing.
Stage V. Obtaining feedback.

This framework can be applied to nearly every type of business decision, as illustrated in this chapter by decisions involving target costing, cost reduction, process alternatives, make or buy, outsourcing, adding or dropping business, pricing, and special orders. In every case, managers should consider how alternative decisions affect estimated quantitative and qualitative benefits and costs.

In applying this framework, managers must consider the trade-offs involved between the cost and the quality of information, which is described by dimensions of subjectivity, accuracy, timeliness, and relevance. In many cases, qualitative information also is critical to making the best decisions.

Key Terms

For each term's definition, refer to the indicated page or turn to the glossary at the end of the text.

accuracy, p. 532
cost-reduction target, p. 530
decision tree, p. 536
decision usefulness, p. 531
differential costs, p. 532
information quality, p. 531
life cycle costing, p. 546
margin of safety, p. 539

objectivity, p. 532
outsourcing, p. 539
predatory pricing, p. 547
product life cycle, p. 545
qualitative factors, p. 536
relevance, p. 532
relevant costs and benefits, p. 532
special orders, p. 547
subjectivity, p. 531
tangible objectives, p. 528
target costing, p. 529
target profit, p. 528
timeliness, p. 532
total target cost, p. 530

Meeting the Cost-Management Challenges

1. How can cost management help organizations, including Bootstrap Industries, choose among competing, alternative uses of the organization's resources?

Organizations can never undertake all business alternatives available to them. Managers must have a straightforward, reliable decision-making approach that allows them to (a) set observable, tangible objectives, (b) gather useful information about opportunities to use resources, and (c) choose the best among the many alternatives. Cost-management information, including both quantitative and qualitative varieties, is critically important to nearly all business decisions. Managers must know where there are critical trade-offs and identify and understand the alternative benefits and costs that they must choose among. Furthermore, they must be confident that they have useful information that is accurate, timely, and relevant to their decisions.

Every decision can have some peculiarities that must be accommodated. As demonstrated in this chapter, carefully framing a decision to consider as many different, relevant benefits and costs as possible assures analysts that they will not overlook important decision features. That being said, numbers almost never speak for themselves. Professional judgment and analysis that are possible because of experience and knowledge will further enhance the decision-making framework.

2. Should prices be based on costs or on what the market will pay?

Eventually, prices received must cover all costs of operations for an organization to survive (unless it receives a subsidy from external parties). Therefore, prices can never be totally divorced from cost concerns. In competitive markets, however, firms do not have the ability to set prices based on their costs; they must make a profit given market prices. Thus, target-costing and cost-reduction exercises can be very important. In some situations, prices legally are based on costs, but often these situations involve competitive bidding that requires managers to anticipate prices that competitors are likely to offer. In other situations without ready market prices, managers must consider whether their pricing decisions will affect future business opportunities. Even if they are concerned with covering costs, they still must consider market impacts, including encouraging customers to seek lower cost solutions to their problems. This is the powerful message of market economics. Imagining a situation in which prices can be solely based on costs, without regard to eventual market effects is difficult. Even in former communist countries, where prices allegedly were based on costs, the inefficiencies caused by ignoring market forces encouraged black-market forces and eventually led to collapse of the non-market systems.

Solutions to You're the Decision Maker

13.1 Extended Target Costing Analysis p. 531

Constructing and manipulating the spreadsheet in Exhibit 13–3, as shown here, helps complete this exercise.

a. Increasing the target price to $130 (cell B2 in the spreadsheet, YTDM 13.1a) while maintaining target sales in units (B4), results in a higher unit and total target cost (B10 and B13), which is higher than currently feasible costs (B14). No cost reduction is required (B15 shows that the target cost exceeds currently feasible costs by $60,000), but the company is not likely to let currently feasible costs rise to the total target cost unless doing so achieves objectives that are more important than increased profitability. In this case, Bootstrap sees an opportunity to employ or train more disabled persons that increases costs by up to $60,000 but achieves other objectives.

Microsoft Excel - YTDM 13-1
File Edit View Insert Format Tools Data Window Help
B2 = 130

	A	B
1	**Input data**	
2	Target (market) price per unit	$ 130.00
3	Target profit percentage	20%
4	Annual target sales in units	5,000
5	Currently feasible costs	$ 460,000
6		
7	**Target cost per unit = target price - target profit**	
8	Target price (B2)	$ 130.00
9	Target profit per unit (B8*B3)	26.00
10	Target cost per unit (B8-B9)	$ 104.00
11	Total target cost	
12	Target annual sales (B4)	5,000
13	Total target cost (B10*B12)	$ 520,000
14	Currently feasible costs (B5)	460,000
15	Cost reduction target (B14-B13)	$ (60,000)

YTDM 13.1a / YTDM 13.1b / YTDM 1
Ready

b. Reducing the target profit percentage to 15 percent (B3 in YTDM 13.1b) has an effect similar to that of part (a). The lower target profit (B9) allows a somewhat higher unit and total target cost (B10 and B13). Nevertheless, a cost reduction of $35,000 is still needed to meet the target profit.

Microsoft Excel - YTDM 13-1

B3 = 15%

	A	B
1	**Input data**	
2	Target (market) price per unit	$ 100.00
3	Target profit percentage	15%
4	Annual target sales in units	5,000
5	Currently feasible costs	$ 460,000
6		
7	**Target cost per unit = target price - target profit**	
8	Target price (B2)	$ 100.00
9	Target profit per unit (B8*B3)	15.00
10	Target cost per unit (B8-B9)	$ 85.00
11	Total target cost	
12	Target annual sales (B4)	5,000
13	Total target cost (B10*B12)	$ 425,000
14	Currently feasible costs (B5)	460,000
15	Cost reduction target (B14-B13)	$ 35,000

YTDM 13.1a / YTDM 13.1b / YTDM 1

Ready

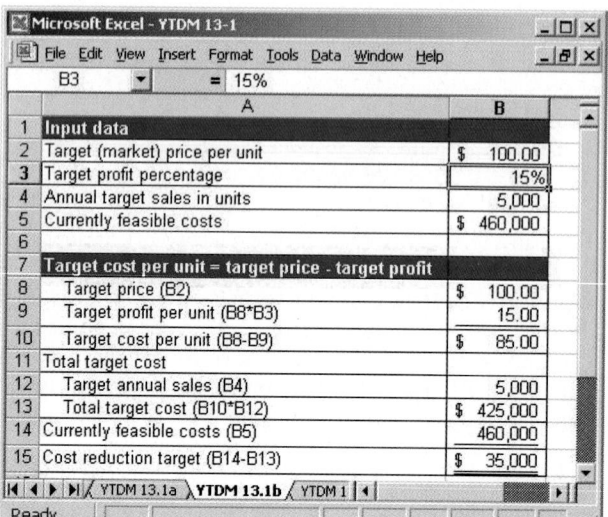

c. Reducing the target sales level to 4,000 units (B4 in YTDM 13.1c) means that fewer units must recover the target profit and currently feasible costs. This results in a much higher cost-reduction target of $140,000 (B15). Because this is nearly a 31 percent reduction from currently feasible cost, it is a very aggressive objective. At this new lower sales level, the product is not sufficiently profitable, and the firm might not be able to cut costs sufficiently. Not finding a solution, however, means dropping or revising the product or sacrificing the goal of profitable operations.

Microsoft Excel - YTDM 13-1

B4 = 4000

	A	B
1	**Input data**	
2	Target (market) price per unit	$ 100.00
3	Target profit percentage	20%
4	Annual target sales in units	4,000
5	Currently feasible costs	$ 460,000
6		
7	**Target cost per unit = target price - target profit**	
8	Target price (B2)	$ 100.00
9	Target profit per unit (B8*B3)	20.00
10	Target cost per unit (B8-B9)	$ 80.00
11	Total target cost	
12	Target annual sales (B4)	4,000
13	Total target cost (B10*B12)	$ 320,000
14	Currently feasible costs (B5)	460,000
15	Cost reduction target (B14-B13)	$ 140,000

YTDM 13.1b / YTDM 13.1c

Ready

d. Higher currently feasible costs (B5 in YTDM 13.1d) obviously mean that the cost-reduction target is higher than originally expected. This can be quite difficult to achieve.

Microsoft Excel - YTDM 13-1

B5 = 560000

	A	B
1	**Input data**	
2	Target (market) price per unit	$ 100.00
3	Target profit percentage	20%
4	Annual target sales in units	5,000
5	Currently feasible costs	$ 560,000
6		
7	**Target cost per unit = target price - target profit**	
8	Target price (B2)	$ 100.00
9	Target profit per unit (B8*B3)	20.00
10	Target cost per unit (B8-B9)	$ 80.00
11	Total target cost	
12	Target annual sales (B4)	5,000
13	Total target cost (B10*B12)	$ 400,000
14	Currently feasible costs (B5)	560,000
15	Cost reduction target (B14-B13)	$ 160,000

YTDM 13.1c / YTDM 13.1d

Ready

13.2 Further Analysis of Dropping a Business p. 544

Both alternatives promise improved profitability over the status quo, with alternative B showing the higher improvement of $54,000 compared to the status quo. However, several qualitiative features of both alternatives are worth additional scrutiny.

Alternative A appears to generate a loss (although much less than the status quo) but also promises improvements in both employee skill level and product quality. Are these qualitative improvements worth forgoing the increased profit ($16,000) of alternative B? Perhaps. Looking closer at alternative B reveals some possible additional risk. The work must achieve improved product quality with no additional training investment and the status quo skill level. Is that possible? Is the risk of failing to meet quality expectations warranted by possibly higher profits? Perhaps not. In either case, managers need to evaluate these trade-offs.

Microsoft Excel - YTDM 13-2

D30 = =D18-D29

	A	B	C	D
1	Input Data	Status quo: Operate remote facility	Alternative A	Alternative B
2	Supervisory employment	1	1	1
3	Nonsupervisory employment	20	20	20
4	Skill level	low	medium	low
5	Product quality	low	high	medium
6	Service revenues per year	$300,000	$400,000	$300,000
7	Unit-level costs	$30,000	$40,000	$14,000
8	Service-level costs			
9	Equipment	$32,000	$50,000	$20,000
10	Building rental	$36,000	$40,000	$10,000
11	Facility-level costs			
12	Wages	$200,000	$200,000	$200,000
13	Supervision	$24,000	$24,000	$24,000
14	Central office services	$20,000	$20,000	$20,000
15	Period costs			
16	Training	$10,000	$40,000	$10,000
17	Annual Benefit or Cost	Status quo: Operate remote facility	Alternative A	Alternative B
18	Sales revenue	$300,000	$400,000	$300,000
19	Unit-level costs	30,000	40,000	14,000
20	Service-level costs			
21	Equipment	32,000	50,000	20,000
22	Building rental	36,000	40,000	10,000
23	Facility-level costs			
24	Wages	200,000	200,000	200,000
25	Supervision	24,000	24,000	24,000
26	Central office services	20,000	20,000	20,000
27	Period costs			
28	Training	10,000	40,000	10,000
29	Total costs	352,000	414,000	298,000
30	Profit (Loss)	($52,000)	($14,000)	$2,000
31				

YTDM 13-2 / Sheet2 / Sheet3

Ready

13.3 Alternative Analysis of Special Order p. 550

a. If Bootstrap did not have unemployed resources, pricing the special order might be affected. Accepting the special order requires either additional capacity (hiring and training new employees) or deferring or canceling other work. The first alternative incurs additional costs that should be considered in pricing.

b. Bootstrap probably will price the special order to reflect at least normal cost levels, $123.75 per employee per day. Adding trained employees quickly might not be feasible in time to meet the special-order demands but can be attractive. If additional work with the state is likely, Bootstrap can discount its target profit as a way to win the work in the short run. If Bootstrap defers or cancels other work, it loses the net benefits of that other work and might harm its reputation. Bootstrap is unlikely to take actions that would harm its good reputation, but it requires covering at least normal costs and target profits (perhaps more to cushion losses from reduced reputation effects).

Review Questions

13.1 Review the chapter's key terms and define them.

13.2 List and briefly describe each of the five stages of the decision-making framework.

13.3 Distinguish between an organization's goals and tangible objectives.

13.4 What are the four major steps in target costing? Briefly describe them.

13.5 Describe a conflict that might occur between accuracy, timeliness, relevance, and cost of information.

13.6 What criteria must be satisfied for information to be relevant?

13.7 "A quantitative analysis allows a decision maker to put a price on the total value of qualitative characteristics in a decision situation." Explain this statement and give an example.

13.8 Give two examples of sunk costs and explain why these amounts might be both useful to and irrelevant in decision making.

13.9 Why might a manager inappropriately consider sunk costs when making a decision?

13.10 What considerations other than costs are relevant to outsourcing decisions?

13.11 Traditional accounting systems record only actual transactions. How can opportunity costs, which usually are not actual transactions, be important in decision making?

13.12 Explain several legal influences on pricing decisions.

13.13 Explain the following assertion: "Price setting generally requires a balance between market forces and cost considerations."

13.14 Explain how a company develops its target price and target cost.

13.15 Explain the relationship, if any, between life cycle costs and the pricing of goods and services.

13.16 Distinguish between *price discrimination* and *predatory pricing.*

Critical Analysis

13.17 Respond to the following statement: "Most measures of performance, such as profits and product costs, are useless for management decision making because they measure what has happened, not what will happen."

13.18 Peter Drucker argues that one of the seven deadly business sins is to base prices on costs, which means first measuring the current cost of a product or service and then "marking it up" by adding a profit margin. He blames the disappearance of the US consumer-electronics industry in part on its practice of basing prices on costs. Can a domestic industry disappear because of its pricing practice? What is an alternative to basing prices on costs? What does this alternative require that is different from basing prices on costs?

13.19 The manager of a telecommunications company once commented, "Not all future costs are relevant to business decisions, but costs are not relevant unless they occur in the future." Is the manager correct? Explain.

13.20 "In the long run, we need to achieve superior quantitative financial performance. But in the short run we need to achieve superior qualitative, nonfinancial performance." Is this correct? Explain.

13.21 CEO: "It's all well and good for you to say that I should disregard sunk costs when I consider whether to sell this unprofitable operation. After we report lower-than-expected profits, you won't have to answer the angry questions from stockholders and analysts because our share price has dropped or from employees who say this is just a way to keep from paying bonuses." Explain the CEO's rationale for not selling an unprofitable business unit. Do you agree? Why or why not?

13.22 Some skeptics suspect that continually upgrading an organization's information system has more to do with keeping up with appearances than with improving the accuracy, timeliness, relevance, and cost of information for decision making. How do you determine the accuracy of this suspicion?

13.23 Where to place the city's new shelter for homeless people has resulted in overwhelming recognition that a new shelter is needed but "not in my neighborhood." As winter approaches, the director of the shelter and the publisher of the local newspaper have accused the city of "analysis paralysis" as it continues meetings and hearings to find a suitable location. Can you suggest a feasible approach to making this difficult decision? Be as specific as you can.

13.24 "With our high fixed costs, high variable costs, and competitive markets, there really is little we can do to increase our profits." Should you accept this argument without question? Explain.

13.25 A medium-size retailer of upscale leather goods is considering outsourcing its data-processing, human resources, billing, and legal activities. Prepare a list of the benefits and costs of these considerations.

13.26 A manager in your organization has just received a special order at a price that is below cost. The manager points to the document and says, "These are the kinds of orders that will get you in trouble. Every sale must bear its share of the full costs of running the company. If we sell below our cost, we'll be out of business in no time." Comment on the manager's remark.

13.27 To go from Dallas to Los Angeles for a business meeting, Nancy Wilkinson booked a flight for $950 with a departure on Wednesday and a return on Friday of the same week. The reservation agent told Nancy that if she were to return on Sunday, the ticket price would fall to $288. What factor(s) did the airline appear to focus on when setting its ticket prices? Is it likely that the airline could have been accused of price discrimination and violating the Robinson–Patman Act? Explain.

Exercises

Exercise 13.28
Decision Making
(LO 1)

Consider the following decision-making problem and structure it using the framework presented in this chapter.

"I don't know where to begin. Right now, I feel that throwing a dart at a dartboard will give me just as much insight into how to make this decision as any other method. Can you help? I am paying my way through college using savings from my summer job. I get a small allowance from my parents, but they can't afford to send much. I find that I don't have enough money to pay my bills and have any left over for entertainment or new clothes. I am afraid that I will be broke before the year is over and have to drop out of school. I don't mind having to budget, but do I have to abandon any hope for a life, too?"

Exercise 13.29
Decision Making
(LO 1)

Consider the following decision-making problem and structure it using the framework presented in this chapter.

"We employ 20 full-time internal auditors who review internal operations for quality and efficiency and do much of the compliance work prior to our annual audit by a Big 5 firm. The auditors report directly to me as the CFO. I know that many similar firms have outsourced the internal audit function to Big 5 firms or others that specialize in internal auditing. They do so primarily for cost savings, but I am concerned about loss of control, quality, and sensitive information that might be leaked to competitors. We also use internal auditing as a management-training program, where fast-track managers get wide exposure to all parts of the company. How do we get that training if we outsource internal auditing?"

Exercise 13.30
Decision Making
(LO 1)

Consider the following decision-making problem and structure it using the framework presented in this chapter.

"We have a full-time staff who maintain and clean our buildings and facilities, but we are considering outsourcing that work to Bootstrap Industries. I think our own staff does a good job, but they really are not critical to the company's success. On the other hand, they are good people and have families to support. I also know that Bootstrap will do a good job, and, if we outsource, it will be cheaper and we won't have any paperwork or employment hassles. I'm having a hard time making this decision."

Exercise 13.31
Target Cost
(LO 2)

Compute the target costs and the total cost-reduction targets from the following information for each product, A, B, C.

	A	B	C
Expected market price per unit	$200	$850	$4,200
Required return on sales	37%	20%	25%
Currently feasible cost per unit	$150	$650	$3,500
Total expected sales	20,000 units	18,000 units	11,000 units

Exercise 13.32
Information dimensions
(LO 3)

Give an example of an information item at each extreme level for the following information dimensions.

	Example of Information at	
Information Dimensions	**Very High Level**	**Very Low Level**
Subjectivity	?	?
Accuracy	?	?
Timeliness	?	?
Cost	?	?
Relevance	?	?

Exercise 13.33
Information Dimensions
(LO 3)

You have a limited budget for obtaining information. Following are pairs of one information item and a decision to make. First, select the most important dimension for the information item for each decision. Set that dimension at "High." Then give your best estimate of an acceptable quality of the information, given a limited budget.

Information/Decision	Subjectivity	Accuracy	Timeliness	Relevance
Customer value/Pricing new product	High or low?	High or low?	High or low?	High or low?
Manufacturing cost/Make or buy	High or low?	High or low?	High or low?	High or low?
Employee satisfaction/Close a plant	High or low?	High or low?	High or low?	High or low?
Depreciation of plant and equipment/ Accept a special order	High or low?	High or low?	High or low?	High or low?

Exercise 13.34
Relevant Costs
(LO 3)

Match the cost(s) most likely to be relevant to each listed decision.

Decision	Cost
Accept a special order ________	a. Internal unit-level manufacturing cost
Close a plant ________	b. Cost to buy externally
Launch a new product ________	c. Opportunity cost of alternative use
Make or buy a product component ________	d. Cost paid for parts on hand
Outsource a business activity ________	e. Lease cost for facility
	f. Loss of quality reputation
	g. Loss of control
	h. Loss of employee trust

Exercise 13.35
Relevant Costs
(LO 3)

Match the cost(s) most likely to be relevant to each listed decision.

Decision	Cost
Accept a special order ________	a. $15 internal unit-level manufacturing cost
Close a plant ________	b. Increased employee turnover
Launch a new product ________	c. $20,000 opportunity cost of alternative use
Make or buy a product component ________	d. $20 cost paid for parts on hand
Outsource a business activity ________	e. Reduced ability to guarantee deliveries
	f. Increased warranty and repair expense
	g. $25 cost to buy externally
	h. $50,000 penalty to break annual lease for facility

Exercise 13.36
Decision Tree
(LO 4)

Prepare a decision tree to reflect the choice of living and eating on campus versus renting an apartment five miles from campus. The student living off campus can buy a meal ticket, but living off campus requires transportation costs (bicycle, walk, bus, or car). Identify quantitative and qualitative costs and benefits.

Exercise 13.37
Decision Tree
(LO 4)

Prepare a decision tree to reflect the choice between repairing an old car or buying a new or used car. Identify quantitative and qualitative costs and benefits.

Exercise 13.38
Quantitative and Qualitative Factors
(LO 3)

Consider the quantitative costs and benefits of two alternatives. What must be the value of the qualitative factors if the less profitable alternative is chosen?

Cost or Benefit	Status Quo	Alternative
Revenues	$50,000	$50,000
Costs	$30,000	$40,000
Quality	Medium	Very high
Meets production schedules	Medium	High

Exercise 13.39
Quantitative and Qualitative Factors
(LO 3)

Consider the quantitative costs and benefits of two alternatives. What must be the value of the qualitative factors if the less profitable alternative is chosen?

Cost or Benefit	Alternative 1	Alternative 2
Cost savings	$20,000	$30,000
Flexibility	High	Medium
Quality	Very high	Medium
Meets delivery schedules	High	Medium

Exercise 13.40
Pricing
(LO 5)

Write a short memo contrasting the "mark-up" and "target-costing" approaches to pricing.

Exercise 13.41
Pricing
(LO 5)

Replace the question marks with information based on markup over cost for A–E.

	A	B	C	D	E
Unit-level cost	$12	$20	$32	$8	$60
Product-level cost per unit	$ 6	$22	$12	?	$24
Facility-level cost per unit	$15	$16	?	$3	$16
Mark-up percentage	25%	?	40%	100%	75%
Price per unit	?	$87.00	$71.40	$54.00	?

Problems

Problem 13.42
Target Cost Reduction
(LO 2)

MicroStorage Technology (MST) is developing a high-speed modem to connect hand-held computers with a satellite-based data network.

Required

a. Given the following information, compute MST's cost-reduction target.

Expected market price	$150
Required return on sales	20%
Product life	3 years
Currently feasible cost	$50,000,000
Expected average annual sales, units	100,000

b. If MST believes it can reduce the cost of the modem by no more than 18 percent, is this a feasible product for MST? Why or why not?

Problem 13.43
Target Cost
(LO 2)
Spreadsheet

Mercy Hospital is a private hospital that serves an aging population. The hospital administrator, Donna Morgan, believes that insurance companies and Medicare will move to fixed payments for specific procedures, which will put increasing pressure on hospitals to control costs. A common procedure performed at Mercy Hospital is hip-replacement surgery. Morgan has asked the hospital's CFO to prepare information on the current costs of hip replacements at Mercy so that they can explore the application of target costing to this (and other) procedures. Consider the following information gathered by the CFO:

Expected charge reimbursement (sales price)	$21,000
Required return on charges (return on sales)*	40%
Current average cost per hip replacement	$18,800

*To cover profit goals and other support service costs

Required

a. Compute the target cost and cost-reduction target for hip-replacement surgeries.
b. A cross-functional team of administrators, surgeons, nurses, and support personnel analyzed the hospital's hip-replacement procedure and estimated that, through better scheduling and postoperative care, Mercy could reduce hospital stays from an average of nine days to five days with no loss of quality of care. In fact, because elderly patients would be hospitalized for shorter periods, they would be less likely to contract respiratory infections. Improvements in the procedure can result in a reduction of the average cost of a hip replacement by $9,000. If this were accomplished, what is the expected return on charges for a hip replacement?

[Adapted from J. H. Evans III, Y. C. Hwang, and N. Nagarajan, "Cost Reduction and Process Reengineering in Hospitals."]

Problem 13.44
Relevant Cost
(LO 3)

San Diego Construction (SDC) builds custom luxury homes along the coast of the Pacific Ocean. The company was nearing the completion of a home for Jan and Bill Kennedy when the couple suddenly declared bankruptcy. At that time, SDC had invested $1,525,000 in the project.

The firm can sell the uncompleted residence "as is" to a new buyer for $1,400,000, or it can invest another $160,000 to finish the project and sell it on the open market for $1,540,000.

Required

a. What is true about the original $1,525,000 investment from a decision-making perspective?

b. Which of the following options—do nothing, sell "as is" at $1,400,000, or sell "finished" at $1,540,000—should SDC pursue? Why?

Problem 13.45
Relevant Cost
(LO 3)

Chavez Digital Machining's performance for the first 11 months of the year has been a surprise with sales and profits somewhat above expectations. On December 20, just prior to the holiday break, Patrick Olmec faced the decision of scrapping some old equipment and replacing it. The old equipment had a book value of $340,000 but could be sold for only $250,000. The new machinery had a cost of $670,000 and was expected to produce net annual savings in cash operating costs of $150,000 over a 10-year life. The investment predicts returns higher than the minimum required by the company. Olmec's year-end bonus is computed on the basis of company profitability.

Required

a. Discuss the conflict that sometimes arises in business between decision making and performance evaluation.

b. Should Olmec acquire the new machinery? Why? Show computations to support your answer. Ignore the time-value of money.

Problem 13.46
Outsourcing
(LO 3, 5)

Black Diamond, Inc., has been manufacturing 5,000 units of part 10541 per month. At this level of production, the company's costs (expressed on a per-unit basis) follow.

Unit-level cost	$36
Facility-level cost	12
Total cost per unit	$48

Black Diamond can outsource the manufacture of 5,000 units of part 10541 to Mogul Company at a cost of $44 per unit to Black Diamond. If Black Diamond does outsource the part, it has determined that it can sell some facilities it presently uses to produce part 10541 and use the remaining facilities to manufacture a new product, RAC. Black Diamond also has determined that facility costs can drop by one-third if it outsources part 10541 to Mogul.

Required

a. How much profit must the new product RAC generate to justify the decision to outsource part 10541?

b. What other considerations are important to this outsourcing decision?

[CPA adapted]

Problem 13.47
Add/Drop Business Unit
(LO 3, 5)

Spreadsheet

Chapman & Tracy is a regional firm that offers audit, tax, and consulting services. The partners are concerned about the profitability of their audit business, and a closure decision might be forthcoming. If the firm drops the audit activities, it might do more tax work. Only 50 percent of the facility costs associated with auditing disappears by dropping the auditing function. More tax work can increase tax revenues by 45 percent, but tax service–level costs also increase by 45 percent. Total facility cost is unchanged whether or not tax work is increased. Segmented income statements for these three product lines follow.

	Auditing	**Tax**	**Consulting**
Sales	$300,000	$500,000	$600,000
Service-level cost	250,000	300,000	350,000
Shared facility cost	50,000	60,000	80,000
Operating income (loss)	$ 0	$140,000	$170,000

Required

a. Determine which alternative Chapman & Tracy should choose: (1) drop the auditing line without increasing tax work or (2) drop auditing and increase tax work.

b. What other considerations are important to the decision to drop auditing?

Problem 13.48
Add/Drop Business Unit
(LO 3, 5)

Buy-U Deli's owner is disturbed by the poor profit performance of her ice cream counter. She has prepared the following profit analysis for the year just ended:

Sales	$45,000
Less: Cost of food	20,000
Gross profit	$25,000
Less: Operating expenses:	
Wages of counter personnel	$12,000
Paper products (e.g., napkins)	4,000
Utilities (based on percent of sales)	2,900
Depreciation of counter equipment and furnishings	2,500
Depreciation of building (based on percentage of sales)	4,000
Deli manager's salary (based on percentage of time spent on ice cream)	3,000
Total operating expenses	28,400
Income (loss) on ice cream counter	$(3,400)

Required

a. Critique and revise the owner's analysis as you think appropriate. Justify your changes.

b. Should the owner close the counter? What other factors should she consider before closing it?

Problem 13.49
Opportunity Cost
(LO 3, 5)

Marlene Judd is a 55-year-old science teacher at Lamar Tech. She is considering leaving the teaching profession next year and going to graduate school to earn a master's degree in business administration (MBA). Judd plans to attend a prestigious university as a full-time student. The MBA takes two full years to complete with annual tuition of $25,000 and living costs of $10,000 (comparable to her current living costs).

Judd's annual salary upon graduation is anticipated to be $80,000 and likely will increase at 5 percent per year. This year she will earn $40,000 at Lamar Tech; expected pay raises in teaching are 3 percent annually.

Required

a. Is there an opportunity cost in this situation? If so, how much?

b. Calculate the real cost of attending school for two years and attaining the degree.

c. What options might Judd consider to reduce the degree's real cost?

d. What other factors should Judd consider in her decision to attend graduate school?

Problem 13.50
Special Order
(LO 5)

Intermountain Products Company is presently operating at 50 percent of capacity, producing 100,000 units of a patented electronic component. The firm recently received a special order from Scott Corporation for 60,000 components at $6 per unit. No other orders are expected from this firm. Unit-level costs and manufacturing facility costs will increase as a result of accepting this order. Planned production costs for 100,000 and 160,000 units of output follow.

	100,000	**160,000**
Unit-level costs	$300,000	$480,000
Facility costs	400,000	500,000
Total costs	$700,000	$980,000
Cost per unit	$ 7.00	$ 6.125

The sales manager believes that the firm should accept the order even if it results in a loss because the sale might build future markets. The production manager does not want it to be accepted primarily because it shows a loss of $.125 per unit when computed on the new average unit cost.

Required

a. Explain what caused the drop in cost from $7.00 per unit to $6.125 if production increases from 100,000 to 160,000 units. Show supporting computations.

b. Is the special order profitable? Show supporting computations.

c. What other factors should be considered before accepting this special order?

[CPA adapted]

Problem 13.51
Target Cost
(LO 2)

Modular TeleTechnologies uses target costing for selected reconditioning services that it performs. The following data relate to reconditioning a digital switch:

Current reconditioning cost	$28,900
Competitive prices for the same service	$35,000
Required profit margin (percent of sales)	25%

Required

a. How much is the company's target reconditioning cost?

b. Is the current reconditioning cost "on target"? Explain.

c. Assume that the current reconditioning cost is not "on target." Describe the process the company will likely perform to achieve its objective.

Problem 13.52
Target Cost/Cost Reduction
(LO 2)

Sayre Sewing Machine Company has been in operation for over 25 years. During this time, it has shown consistent growth and has developed a strong following of satisfied customers. Merlene Sayre, company president, states that her business philosophy is "a quality product at a competitive price." Until recently, this philosophy has carried the company to its current position. The company is planning for next year's operations, and Sayre is concerned about the projected increased foreign competition.

For the last three years, Sayre has been manufacturing as its only product a machine that has the characteristics of both a serger and a zigzag machine, called the Sergzig. During the current year, the company expects to sell 200,000 machines at an average price of $700. To remain competitive and continue to sell 200,000 machines, Sayre believes that the company will have to reduce the selling price to $600 for the next year.

At the current level of sales and production, Sayre earns 15 percent return on sales, as shown:

Sales price per unit		$700
Product costs per unit:		
Materials		
Computer chip	$77	
Motor	60	
Housing unit	50	
Mechanical parts	86	
Miscellaneous parts	22	
Assembly labor	90	
Testing labor	60	$445
Product-level equipment		70
General administrative cost		80
Total product costs		$595
Profit per unit		$105
Return on sales		15%

In planning for next year, the company wants to maintain the 15 percent return on sales by reducing costs as follows:

- Sayre can purchase the computer chip at $55 per unit by committing to a long-term purchase agreement for the year's needs with the supplier. The long-term agreement calls for the supplier to certify that all chips are defect-free.
- Sayre can reduce the number of housing units and miscellaneous parts by 20 percent by substituting equivalent but less expensive parts and by redesigning the housing to eliminate multiple parts.
- Because of these changes, the company can reduce assembly and testing labor and equipment and facility costs specific to the Sergzig by 20 percent.
- All other product costs will remain the same.

Required

a. List the advantages and disadvantages of Sayre's proposed changes. Explain the risks involved with the proposed changes.

b. Based on the new data for next year, can Sayre meet or exceed its target of 15 percent return on sales? Show calculations.

c. Assume that competition during the next year is stronger than Sayre anticipates and that the average selling price is only $580 per unit. Calculate the target cost reduction necessary to achieve the 15 percent return on sales. Show calculations.

[CMA adapted]

Problem 13.53
Target Cost
(LO 2)

Team

Review Exhibit 13–4.

Required

Compute the cost-reduction target under each of the following conditions. Make each calculation independently of the others, except for requirement (e). [*Hint:* These requirements are easier with a computer spreadsheet analysis. Set up Exhibit 13–4 as a spreadsheet and make individual changes, again except for requirement (e). If you are unfamiliar with how to set up computer spreadsheets, consult the Appendix to Chapter 2.]

a. Expected market price is raised to $120.

b. Unit-level costs: alternative 1 = $25, alternative 2 = $45.

c. Equipment costs: alternative 1 = $150,000, alternative 2 = $30,000.

d. Expected sales volume is increased by 20 percent.

e. Combine the conditions of (a) – (d) and compute the alternatives' cost reductions.

f. *Team Focus:* Assume that you are the cost-management member of the target-costing team. Your natural tendency is to be skeptical of expected increases in sales prices and reductions in costs, and the marketing member of the team has jokingly referred to you as the "grim reaper." (Accountants call this tendency "conservatism.") Learning how to temper marketing and engineering team members' natural optimism with "financial reality" without losing credibility and influence is an important lesson for cost-management analysts. What questions should you ask about the preceding alternatives for the target-costing analysis?

g. A friend of yours has a position similar to yours at Motorola's cellular phone division, which has used target costing for a number of years. In fact, your friend says, "It is common knowledge that at Motorola we require feasible costs of our phone products to decline by at least 25 percent each year from original target cost because we know that competitors will offer similar products within a year at 25 percent lower prices. We have to be able to lower prices to meet competition and still maintain our profit goals. We are constantly improving our processes to achieve these reductions in feasible costs." How can you use the approach illustrated in Exhibit 13–3 for the Rambler snowshoe to achieve similar cost reductions?

Problem 13.54
Target Cost/Cost Reduction
(LO 2)

SciFi Paperback Books is an internet retailer of science fiction paperback books. Based on a sales volume of 200,000 units, the projected net income for the current year is $700,000. The company has been selling the books for an average of $15 each; unit-level costs consist of the $8 purchase cost and a $1 handling cost. SciFi's annual committed facility and period costs are $500,000. SciFi's books generally have a one-year product life.

Required

a. If SciFi desires a 20 percent return on sales, what cost reduction is required at the current year's prices and costs?

b. What cost reduction is required if there are the following changes in next year's costs and prices that result from taking no management actions; that is, maintaining the status quo:

- 3 percent decrease in sales price
- 25 percent increase in purchase cost
- 50 percent increase in handling cost
- 10 percent increase in committed costs
- 5 percent decrease in sales quantity

c. Explain why maintaining the status quo often is a prescription for declining profitability.

[CMA adapted]

Problem 13.55
Alternative Processes
(LO 3, 5)

A financial analyst is studying two new distribution systems, basic and deluxe. The basic system has unit-level shipping costs of $8.00 per unit and annual facility costs of $500,000; in contrast, the deluxe system has unit-level costs of $4.00 per unit and annual facility costs of $1,100,000. The deluxe system promises greater customer service. The company sells its products for $25 per unit, less a 5 percent sales commission.

Required

a. Which of the two systems will be more profitable for the firm if sales are expected to average 125,000 units per year?

b. At what unit-volume level will management be indifferent as to the profit for the basic system and the deluxe system?

c. In requirement (a) by how much does the company value the promised greater customer service if it selects the deluxe system? How can the company verify this level of value?

Problem 13.56
Make or Buy
(LO 3, 5)

Communication

Xyon Company purchases 10,000 pumps annually from Kobec, Inc. Because the price keeps increasing and reached $68 per unit last year, Xyon's management has asked for a cost estimate to manufacture the pump internally. Xyon makes stampings and castings and has little experience with products that require assembly.

The engineering, manufacturing, and accounting departments have prepared a report for management that includes the following estimate for an assembly run of 10,000 pumps. To manufacture the pumps Xyon will hire additional production employees but will need no additional equipment, space, or supervision. The report estimates that total costs for 10,000 units are estimated at $957,000, or $95.70 a unit. The current purchase price is $68.00 a unit, so the report recommends the continued purchase of the product.

Components (outside purchases)	$120,000
Assembly labor*	300,000
Share of existing facility costs based on labor	537,000
Total costs	$957,000

*Assembly labor consists of hourly production workers.

Required

a. Was the analysis prepared by Xyon Company's engineering, manufacturing, and accounting departments and their recommendation to continue purchasing the pumps correct? Explain your answer and include any supporting calculations that you consider necessary.

b. Present several benefits and problems of dealing with outside suppliers such as Kobec, Inc.

[CMA adapted]

Problem 13.57
Drop a Service
(LO 3, 5)

Melville College is a small liberal arts school located in Massachusetts. It is evaluating its botany program because the program's tuition revenues and costs recently produced an $80,000 loss, which is typical of performance in the past few years. Tuition revenues earned totaled $320,000; operating expenses were faculty salaries, $215,000; supplies, $10,000; and other facility costs, $175,000. If the program is dropped, the following are expected:

- Some students will change majors, but overall college enrollment will decline as other students transfer to other universities. Total lost tuition revenue is estimated at $205,000.
- Untenured faculty members with combined salaries of $170,000 can be dismissed. The tenured faculty will transfer to the biology department. In addition, 60 percent of the program's supplies cost can be saved.
- Other facility costs include $98,000 of general college overhead costs that are assigned to the program and $77,000 of salaries earned by office and support personnel. One of these employees (annual salary, $22,000) will be transferred to the music school; other employees can be laid off.
- Equipment will be removed and transferred to the fine arts school at a cost of $1,100. The vacated space can be converted to a weight and physical conditioning facility for student athletes. This new facility likely will help attract better athletes and make the college's athletic programs more competitive.

The director of development reports that Florence Ficus, an alumna and supporter of the botany program, is now sole owner of the highly successful Ficus Scientific Corporation. Ficus has designated the college as a major beneficiary of her estate.

Required

a. Should Melville drop the botany program? Show calculations.

b. What other factors should be considered if the decision is made to drop the program?

c. What options might be open to Melville if it continues the program and the college's president mandates that "program losses must be eliminated within three years"?

Problem 13.58
Special Order
(LO 3, 5)

Communication

Cosmos Corporation manufactures unique toy cars in a plant that has theoretical capacity to produce 30,000 cars each month. Current monthly production is 80 percent of practical capacity. The normal selling price is $16; unit-level costs and facility costs for the current activity level are as follows:

Unit-level costs	$135,600
Facility-level costs:	
Manufacturing	96,000
Marketing	78,000
Total costs	$309,600

Cosmos has just received a special order from a Japanese company for 11,000 cars at $11 each, with a target completion date in three months. Cosmos has never competed in the global marketplace. The company has hired a consultant for $5,500 per month to obtain advice on conducting business in Japan.

Required

a. Does Cosmos have sufficient productive capacity to accept the order? Explain.

b. Is the order attractive from a financial perspective? Show computations to support your answer.

c. Discuss any other considerations that Cosmos should include in analyzing the order.

d. Is it beneficial for Cosmos to take a loss on this order if it desires to enter the Japanese market? Discuss briefly.

Problem 13.59
Special Order
(LO 3, 5)

Communication

Framar, Inc., manufactures automation machinery according to customer specifications. The company operated at 75 percent of practical capacity during the year just ended with the following results:

Sales revenue	$25,000,000
Less: Sales commissions (10%)	2,500,000
Net sales	$22,500,000
Expenses:	
Unit-level costs	$15,750,000
Facility-level costs	2,250,000
Total costs	$18,000,000
Income before taxes	4,500,000
Income taxes (40%)	$ 1,800,000
Net income	$ 2,700,000

Framar, which expects continued operations at 75 percent of capacity, recently submitted a bid of $135,238 on some custom-designed machinery to APA, Inc. To derive the bid amount, Framar used a pricing formula based on last year's operating results:

Estimated materials (unit level)	$ 29,200
Estimated labor (unit level)	56,000
Facility costs at 14.29% of unit-level costs	12,171
Estimated total costs excluding sales commissions	$ 97,371
Add 25% markup for profits and taxes	24,343
Suggested price (with profits) before sales commissions	$121,714
Suggested total price: $121,714 ÷ .9 to adjust for 10% commission	$135,238

Required

a. Calculate the impact the order will have on Framar's net income if APA accepts the $135,238 bid.

b. Assume that APA has rejected Framar's bid but has stated that it is willing to pay $127,000 for the machinery. Should Framar manufacture the machinery for the counteroffer of $127,000? Explain your answer, and show calculations.

c. At what bid price will Framar break even on the order?
d. Explain how the profit performance in the coming year is affected if Framar accepted all of its work at prices similar to APA's $127,000 counteroffer described in requirement (b).

[CMA adapted]

Problem 13.60
Special Order
(LO 3, 4, 5)

Hamilton Industries manufactures standard and custom-designed bottling equipment. Early in December, Lyan Company asked Hamilton to quote a price for a custom bottling machine to be delivered the following April. Lyan intends to make a decision on the purchase by January 1, so Hamilton has the entire first quarter of the year for construction if its bid is accepted.

Hamilton's pricing policy for custom-designed equipment is 50 percent markup on full manufacturing cost. Cost-management analysts have derived the following estimates for normal costs caused by the decision to accept the machine order:

Materials	$56,000
Labor (3,000 hours at $20 per hr.)	60,000

No new facilities are required, but because existing facility costs must be covered by work performed and delivered to customers, facility costs normally are added to cost estimates in direct proportion to labor hours used in the manufacturing effort. Hamilton typically employs 90 manufacturing workers equivalent to 180,000 labor hours per year (40 hours per week × 50 weeks = 2,000 per employee). Dividing the $2,448,000 expected facility cost for the year by the typical employment level of 180,000 hours provides the facility cost per labor hour rate of $13.60. Thus, an additional cost of $40,800 (= $13.60 per hour × 3,000 hours) normally would be added to the cost of the Lyan job.

Hamilton's current production schedule calls for the full use of its available direct-labor hours per month during the first quarter. If it is awarded the contract for the Lyan equipment, Hamilton must reduce production of one of its standard products or its employees must work overtime at 150 percent of their normal hourly rate. Because many workers have holiday bills to pay, enough employees might work overtime to complete both the Lyan order and Hamilton's standard products.

Should employees not work enough overtime hours, the company will lose sales of the standard product equal to the reduced production. Hamilton has maintained good relations with its normal customers. If Hamilton gives its normal customers sufficient notice, it is not likely to lose them permanently. The standard product that can be reduced has a unit sales price of $15,000 and the following costs:

Materials	$ 2,500
Labor (250 hours at $20)	5,000
Facility cost	3,400
Total	$10,900

Required

a. Construct a decision tree that represents Hamilton's business decision. For each alternative, identify both quantitative and qualitative benefits and costs.
b. Calculate the alternative bids that Hamilton would submit using its pricing policy for custom-designed equipment.
c. Calculate the minimum bids that Hamilton should be willing to submit on the equipment if management desired to generate the same total profit as currently planned for the year's first quarter.
d. Assume that Hamilton is prepared to submit a bid slightly above a minimum calculated in requirement (c). Prior to submitting a bid, one of Hamilton's design engineers got a call from an acquaintance at Tygar Corporation, one of Hamilton's chief competitors: "Hey, Joe, we've just prepared a bid for Lyan Company for some customized equipment. I want to come by the house this evening and show you our bid. You know I have always wanted to work for Hamilton." Should Joe accept his acquaintance's offer? Explain.
e. Contrast Hamilton's approach to pricing with the features of target costing.

[CMA adapted]

Cases

Case 13.61
Decision alternatives
(LO 1, 3, 4)

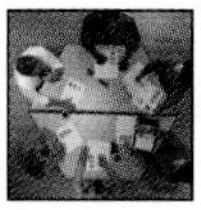
Team Internet

The small mountain town of **Telluride, Colorado,** is located in one of the most beautiful mountain valleys in the United States. The town's economy has evolved from mining activities to four-season tourism and recreation. The entry to the valley now is largely undeveloped rural land, which permits unrestricted views of the surrounding mountains and meadows. Consider the following local newspaper editorial.

> It seems only a few short weeks ago that some 1,500 Telluridians rallied to tell our local government, "Save the Valley Floor." What has happened since then? Well, to read about Telluride Town Hall activities since then, not much. Instead, the town is hemorrhaging money every which way for frills and goofy projects such as a Performing Arts Center and a $5 million parking lot.
>
> Now, no one, least of all me, expects the Telluride authorities to actually listen to the citizens. Not at this point, after fiascos like the repeated attempts to stick parking on the Pearl property [a sensitive location]. But somehow, one thought this might be different. After all, didn't Town Hall announce that the fate of the Valley Floor was absolutely vital to the future of Telluride, the Valley, and the whole east end of San Miguel County?
>
> Well, then, you'd think the Telluride government would be keeping the momentum going, full speed ahead . . . and, incidentally, marshaling its finite resources and concentrating their energies on nailing down the Valley Floor for good.
>
> Instead, we're being treated to the usual governing by fits and starts, herks and jerks, impulses and brainstorms. Whoopee! Let's commit a massive amount of money to adding yet another *building* to house arts in—a big, expensive building, of course.
>
> All we have now is the Sheridan Opera House, the huge theater facility in Mountain Village, another theater in town, and the Mason's and the Elk's lodges.
>
> What is this, Manhattan?
>
> And the parking lot scam, or scheme or dream, or whatever it is. Yeah, let's spend $50,000 per parking space for a chunk of land without a coherent parking plan to go with it.
>
> What's going to happen, of course, is the Valley Floor is going to be forgotten, ticking away like a time bomb, 'til some future date when it's up for development again. And then—whoops!—the Town is going to say, "Hey, our pockets are empty," like they never realized the Valley Floor was there all this time after all.
>
> Open Space remains the most important priority for our community, and the Valley Floor is the make-all, break-all heart of it all. Why doesn't our drunken sailor of a town government stop tossing money away like there's no tomorrow for white elephant edifices and addle-brained parking lot plans, and get to work doing what people here have been asking them to for years?
>
> Save our breathing room, our lines of sight, that really make Telluride what it is.

Required

As an individual or in a small group, assume the role of a consultant engaged by Telluride.

a. Using the preceding newspaper article as a starting point, describe the town's related decision alternatives using the framework of the chapter. Use a decision tree as part of a visual presentation of the town's choices.

b. Do organizations such as municipalities have decision-making difficulties that differ from those of profit-seeking organizations? Explain.

[Adapted from R. Shultheis, "Remember the Valley Floor." An Internet search on the keyword Telluride will initiate information that can be useful.]

Case 13.62
Decision alternatives and long-term decisions
(LO 5)

Liquid Chemical Company manufactures chemical products that require careful packing using a special patented container lining made from a material known as GHL. The company operates a department responsible for maintaining these containers in good condition and making new ones as needed.

Mr. Walsh, the general manager, believes the firm might save money and get equal service by buying its container lining from an outside source. He approached Packages, Inc., and asked for a quotation for making them. He also asked Ms. Dyer, his chief cost-management analyst, for a statement of the cost of operating the container department.

The quotation from Packages specified that it could supply 3,000 new container linings for $1,250,000 a year with a contract guaranteed for a term of five years and renewable from year to year thereafter. If the required quantity increases, the contract price will be increased proportionally. Additionally, and regardless of whether this contract is accepted, Packages offered to perform routine maintenance on containers for $375,000 a year on the same contract terms.

Walsh compared these figures with Dyer's cost figures for the container department's operations for one year. Those figures follow:

Materials		$ 700,000
Labor:		
Supervisor		50,000
Workers		450,000
Department overheads:		
Manager's salary (Duffy)	$ 80,000	
Rent on container department	45,000	
Depreciation on machinery	150,000	
Maintenance of machinery	36,000	
Other expenses	157,500	468,500
		$1,668,500
Proportion of general administrative overhead		225,000
Total cost of container department for year		$1,893,500

Walsh concluded that closing the department and entering into the contract offered by Packages was optimal. However, he gave the manager of the container department, Mr. Duffy, an opportunity to question this conclusion before he acted on it. Even if his department were closed, Duffy's own position was not in jeopardy. Transferring Duffy to another position would have no net cash consequences for the firm because he can fill a position that would otherwise be filled by a newly hired manager paid $80,000 per year.

Duffy thought the matter over. The next morning, he spoke to Walsh and said he thought Walsh should consider a number of factors before closing his department. "For instance," he said, "what will you do with the machinery? It cost $1,200,000 four years ago, but you'd be lucky if you got $200,000 for it now, even though it's good for another five years. And then there's the stock of GHL that cost us $1,000,000. At the rate we're using it now, it'll last us another four years. Dyer's figure of $700,000 includes $200,000 for GHL. We bought it for $5,000 per ton. Today's purchase price is still $5,000. But you won't have more than $4,000 a ton left if you sell it because of handling expenses."

Walsh presented Duffy's points to Dyer. She said, "I think my figures are pretty conclusive. We're paying $85,000 a year in rent for a warehouse we need for other corporate purposes. If we close Duffy's department, we'd have all the warehouse space we need without renting."

"That's a good point," said Walsh. "Moreover, I don't think we can find room for the supervisor or any of the workers elsewhere in the firm. We are bound to give some of them a pension; allow $30,000 a year for five years. We also should budget an additional $20,000 for severance pay to be paid in a lump sum when (if) we close the department."

Duffy added, "What about this $225,000 for general administrative overhead? You surely don't expect to sack anyone in the general office if my department is closed, do you?"

"Probably not," said Dyer, "but someone has to pay for these costs. We can't ignore them when we look at an individual department because if we do that with each department in turn, we shall finish up by convincing ourselves that word processing, accounting, administration, and the like don't have to be paid for."

"Well, I think we've thrashed this out pretty fully," said Walsh, "but I've been considering the possibility of keeping the maintenance work. What are your views on that, Duffy?"

"I don't know," said Duffy, "but it's worth looking into. We shouldn't need any machinery for that, and I can hand the supervision over to the current supervisior, who earns $50,000 per year. You'd only need about one-fifth of the workers. You can avoid the pension costs but probably still have the entire $20,000 severance pay. You won't save any space, so I suppose the rent will be the same. I shouldn't think the other expenses are more than $65,000 a year."

"What about materials?" asked Walsh.

"We use 10 percent of the total on maintenance," Duffy replied.

"Well, I've told Packages that I'd make my decision within a week," said Walsh. "I'll let you know what I decide to do before I contact people there."

Assume that the company has an after-tax cost of capital of 10 percent per year and uses an income tax rate of 40 percent for decisions such as these. Depreciation for book and tax purposes is based on the straight-line method over eight years. The machinery has a tax basis of $600,000. Any gain on the sale of machinery or loss on GHL sales is taxed at 40 percent. Any GHL needed for year 5 would be purchased in year 5. For ease of analysis, assume that all cash flows occur at the end of the year.

Required

a. What are the four alternative choices implied in the case?

b. What action should Walsh take? Support your conclusion with a net present value analysis of all the mutually exclusive alternatives. Assume a five-year time horizon.

c. What, if any, additional information do you think Walsh needs to make a sound decision? Explain.

[Adapted from a case by Professor David Solomons, Wharton School, University of Pennsylvania. Completing this case requires the use of discounted cash flow methods as discussed in Chapter 14.]

Case 13.63
Pricing methods
(LO 3, 5)

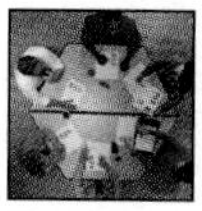
Team

Communication

Customers, costs, competitors, cost-plus formulas, and target-costing procedures all play a role in the pricing of goods and services. Sometimes the pricing process is relatively straightforward; on other occasions it is more complex. The preceding factors and the procedures followed often vary from one business to the next.

Required

Form a team with three other students in your class and visit the manager or sales manager of three distinctly different businesses: big, small, retailer, wholesaler, manufacturer, service business, and so forth—the more variety, the better. Determine the relative significance of customers, costs, competitors, cost-plus formulas, and target costing in each firms' pricing methods. What approach does each manager use when (1) the good or service is new, unique, and untested in the marketplace and (2) the manager has little knowledge on which to base a decision? What has been each manager's biggest success and failure in pricing? Submit your findings to your instructor in a memo or email with an attached table or diagram that summarizes your findings.

Case 13.64
Decision between leasing and buying
(LO 3, 5)

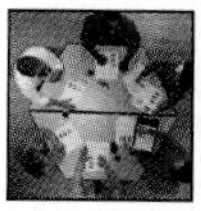
Team

Communication

In recent years, the number of new cars leased by individuals has increased significantly. Many consumers, dealers, and manufacturers find the leasing alternative preferable to bank financing or an outright purchase, especially when prices are high and vehicle sales are slow.

Required

Form small groups to visit a local automobile dealership. Talk to an employee in the financing area about the relative merits of leasing versus purchasing a new automobile. Obtain dollar amounts comparing leasing to purchasing. List the relevant costs and benefits associated with the two alternatives. Include any qualitative considerations as well. Summarize your findings in a decision-tree outline submitted to your instructor. (Do not lease or purchase an automobile as part of your assignment.)

Case 13.65
Outsourcing
(LO 3, 5)

Locate the article "Who Is Outsourcing and Why?" *Management Accounting,* July 1998, pp. 45–47. This article presents the results of an outsourcing survey noting that firms that use service providers report an average cost savings of 16 percent.

Required

a. What were the major underlying reasons for the survey respondents' decision to outsource?

b. What were the major concerns of the survey respondents to outsourcing?

c. Which business functions did the responding firms typically outsource?

Case 13.66
Pricing
(LO 3, 5)

Locate the article "Rattling Cages: Utilities' Quiet World Is Shaken Up as Enron Moves on Philadelphia," *The Wall Street Journal,* January 7, 1998, pp. A1, A14. This article looks at the 200 billion-dollar-a-year utility industry that is now being deregulated. As a result of the changing environment, firms are becoming serious price competitors. An example involves a Pennsylvania firm, Peco Energy, which offered its customers a 10 percent rate cut and Houston-based Enron, which doubled that offer.

Required

a. How were electric prices determined prior to deregulation?

b. What factors affect utility prices after deregulation? List some political, legal, and image-related issues.

Case 13.67
Forecasting
(LO 1)

Information about the future is critical to important decisions facing organizations, but this information can be quite subjective. Highly knowledgeable individuals can disagree about the future. Read the article "Visionary vs. Visionary," by J. A. Byrne in *Business Week,* August 28, 2000.

Required

Contrast the views of the two visionaries. Can they both be right? Explain.

CHAPTER

14

Strategic Issues in Making Long-Term Capital Investment Decisions

After completing this chapter, you should be able to:

1. Understand that capital investments have strategic importance.
2. Know the role of due diligence in investment decision-making.
3. Rank alternative sources of financial information based on usefulness for the particular investment decision being made.
4. Understand difficulties in investing in high technology projects.
5. Conduct sensitivity analyses of capital investment decisions based on nonfinancial and financial issues.
6. Know how audits contribute to the capital investment process.
7. Understand ethical issues in capital investment decisions.
8. Conduct discounted cash flow analysis (Appendix).

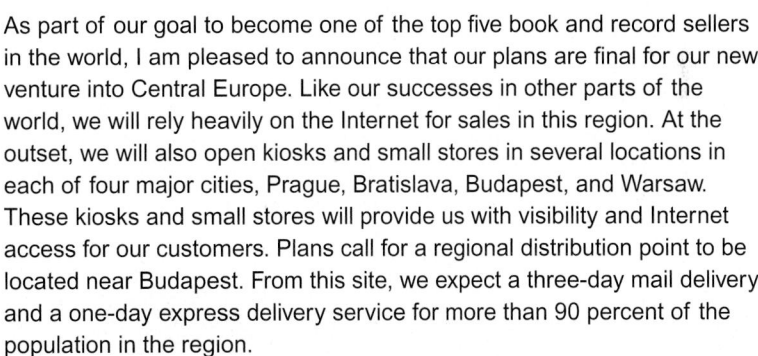

EMAIL MEMORANDUM

From: George Bailey, Chief Executive Officer
To: Senior Executives
Re: Announcement of new venture into Central Europe

Rascals inc.

As part of our goal to become one of the top five book and record sellers in the world, I am pleased to announce that our plans are final for our new venture into Central Europe. Like our successes in other parts of the world, we will rely heavily on the Internet for sales in this region. At the outset, we will also open kiosks and small stores in several locations in each of four major cities, Prague, Bratislava, Budapest, and Warsaw. These kiosks and small stores will provide us with visibility and Internet access for our customers. Plans call for a regional distribution point to be located near Budapest. From this site, we expect a three-day mail delivery and a one-day express delivery service for more than 90 percent of the population in the region.

This investment will require $200 million. Although this is a substantial sum, it is required for the infrastructure, stores, and delivery systems for Rascals, Inc., to be a major player in the area. We fully expect this investment to satisfy our after-tax hurdle rate of 15 percent.

Cost-Management Challenges

1. **Was** the proposed investment in Central Europe by Rascals, Inc., an example of an expansion, replacement, or strategic move investment?

2. **What** major areas should Rascals be concerned about in its due diligence review?

3. **What** would be the most useful source of information in considering whether to invest in Central Europe?

4. **Based** on sensitivity analysis, what was the downside risk of investing in the Central Europe project for George Bailey? For Rascals, Inc.?

This chapter focuses on long-term decisions that affect assets, revenues, and all of the costs in the cost hierarchy. The discussion in Chapter 13 focused on short-term decisions, many of which do not affect changes in facility-level costs. Long-term decisions affect everything, even the organization's strategy.

This chapter discusses the entire process of making capital investment decisions. We do not limit the discussion to financial aspects of the decision. In fact, we devote most of the chapter to issues that are not traditionally discussed in introductory managerial accounting and finance texts, such as the way organizations identify good investments and the role that nonfinancial factors play in the decision-making process. We assume that you have some background in the use of discounted cash-flow analysis. If that is not true, or if you want a refresher on the basic concepts, the appendix to this chapter presents the essential tools for understanding discounted cash-flow analysis.

Strategic Issues

LO 1 Understand that capital investments have strategic importance.

strategic planning *is the process of deciding on an organization's major programs and the approximate resources to be devoted to them*

Strategic planning is the process of deciding on an organization's major programs and the approximate resources to be devoted to them. Major programs are the principal products or product lines and major research and development projects. Strategic planning usually involves planning for several years into the future. Strategic planning by high-level executives and staff at Rascals, Inc., led to the decision to commit approximately $200 million to the Central Europe project.

You probably are aware of strategic decisions made by organizations without considering them as such. General Motors' decision to invest in Saturn Company committed the company to the technology and concepts involved in making the Saturn automobile for the foreseeable future. By deciding to expand outside of its home base in Arkansas, Wal-Mart made the commitment to change from a small, regional company to a large, national company. Southwest Airlines' emphasis on cost control committed it to a market niche. The US Postal Service changed itself from a bureaucratic to a market-oriented organization by committing to compete with Federal Express, Mail Boxes, Etc., and United Parcel Services, among others, in the market for mail and delivery services.

General Motors' decision to develop the Saturn automobile was a strategic investment.

Managers generally are aware of the financial benefits of making long-term investments, but they might not think about the strategic implications. Following are some common examples of strategic benefits that long-term investments might provide:

- Reducing the potential to make mistakes, thus improving the quality of the product (for instance, improving machine tolerances or reducing reliance on manual techniques).
- Making goods or delivering services that competitors cannot (for instance, developing a patented process to make a product that competitors cannot replicate).
- Reducing the cycle time to make the product (for instance, making a custom designed product on the spot).
- Permanently reducing costs to provide such an advantage that competitors cannot afford to enter the market.

Conversely, some companies have made strategic decisions unwittingly by failing to make long-term investments. US steel manufacturers fell far behind their Japanese counterparts when they failed to invest in new technology. Many retailers who were successful in the malls and Main Street stores are going by the wayside because they have not invested in Internet commerce.

Capital investment decisions should be made within the context of an organization's strategic plans. For example, Rascals, Inc., has a strategy of generating nearly all of its sales from customers using the Internet. Therefore, it would make little strategic sense to invest in large warehouse stores. When the president of Domino's Pizza decided to focus on delivery instead of in-store sales, it made little sense for Domino's Pizza to build stores in locations that were expensive because they had high levels of foot traffic.

Using the Rascals, Inc., example, the goal was to become one of the top five book and record sellers in the world. Top management believed the industry would eventually evolve to only about four other major players (e.g., Tower, Virgin, Barnes & Noble, Amazon.com) and numerous specialty stores. Top management also believed that Rascals could not survive unless it was at least fifth in size in the world, because name recognition of the high-volume companies would be required to attract Internet shoppers.

The winners among competitors for Internet customers would also need to be competitive on price and to offer excellent service. For example, if the company could not satisfy a customer's request for a rare book or record, it was not likely to see that customer hit the company's Web site again. Satisfying such customers would require large size. Furthermore, infrastructure costs to service Internet shoppers are largely facility costs that are approximately the same whether the company is large or small. Such a cost structure requires high sales volume for profitability.

Rascal's strategic plan for achieving its goal was to invest heavily in Internet commerce, starting in the United States where it was a small but growing player and moving to emerging markets where it hoped to become a major player. The decision to invest in Internet commerce in Central Europe fit this strategy. Rascals' top management viewed Central Europe as a profitable target market. Disposable income had been increasing there, as had ownership of personal computers.

The company intended to open kiosks that would carry a small selection of music and attract customers who would use the Internet to access Rascals' giant stock of inventory. Customers would come to the kiosks, listen to music, and then place orders, or they could place orders from their personal computers at home or at work.

Major capital investments start with strategic plans. If the investment does not fit the organization's strategic plan, it is probably not a good idea. If the investment appears sensible but does not fit the strategic plan, perhaps it is time to revise the strategic plan.

Identification of Good Investments

How do organizations come up with good ideas for capital investments? Some ideas come naturally. If a computer is too obsolete to run today's software, it is time to consider a replacement. If business is booming so that a company does not have sufficient space to produce goods and services, it is time to consider adding space. Managers might make investments in individual assets, such as one building or one piece of equipment. Or as discussed in Research Insight 14.1, managers might make investments in "bundles" of assets.

Organizations make three general types of long-term capital investments:

1. Replacements and minor improvements.
2. Expansion.
3. Strategic moves.

Replacements and Minor Improvements

Replacements and minor improvements are simply that—replacement of existing assets as they wear out or become obsolete. Simple examples are the replacement of automobiles as they wear out or of computers as they become obsolete. For Rascals, Inc.,

Research
Insight 14.1

Bundling Assets

In moving from traditional mass production to modern technology-based production methods, Caterpillar, Inc., the well-known producer of construction equipment, found that it needed to change its capital budgeting procedures. Historically, the company made incremental asset purchases for investing in mass production. For investing in high technology, the company found it more sensible to evaluate "bundles" of assets instead of one asset at a time.

Investing in bundles of assets forced managers to think about how assets created synergies. Sometimes, an investment that appeared only marginally profitable made good sense as part of a bundle of assets. For example, a machine that reduced labor cost might have a negative net present value when examined as a labor savings device. But when combined with other assets that together sped up the production process, the bundle of assets had a positive net present value.

This approach of investing in bundles is consistent with economic theory that recommends examining the complementarity of assets when making investment decisions.* *Source: P. Miller and T. O'Leary, "Capital Budgeting Practices and Complementarity Relations in the Transition to Modern Manufacture; A Field-Based Analysis." (Full citations to references are in the Bibliography.)*

*Milgrom and Roberts, "Complementarities and Fit: Strategies, Structure and Organizational Change in Manufacturing."

a replacement and minor improvement investment was the installation of a more sophisticated inventory control system that improved links among stores and its Internet marketing unit. In another example, a Federal Express driver demonstrated that with a smaller vehicle, she could more easily maneuver and park in the busy metropolitan area that was her route. Investing in the smaller vehicle is an example of a replacement and minor improvement investment.

The ideas for replacement and minor improvements generally come from the people who use the assets. There is rarely a shortage of ideas for replacing and making minor improvements; companies' suggestion boxes are full of such ideas.

Expansion

Expansion decisions come from desires for growth, either to meet the needs of an expanding market or to increase market share. Expansion decisions do not explore new ways of doing business; instead they expand existing businesses. Examples of expansion decisions are the addition of new stores by Wal-Mart, McDonald's, or Rascals, Inc. If American Airlines adds new routes, it is making an expansion decision.

Ideas for expansion decisions often come from marketing people or from top managers who keep an eye on market opportunities. If the market for the organization's products is growing, an almost obvious impetus for expansion exists. In cases such as when the market is mature, management might expand to take market share away from competitors as Wal-Mart has done in taking business from Kmart and small local retailers.

Strategic Moves

Strategic move investments reflect new initiatives for the company. General Motors' decision to start Saturn was a strategic move. Some observers might have viewed the Saturn investment as an expansion—after all, one might think the company was just opening another car division. In fact, General Motors' top management intended Saturn to be a major new way of doing business.

Rascals' decision to expand to Central Europe came from strategic decisions by top management that the company had to grow substantially and be a major player in Internet commerce to survive. The decision came after months of market research and consulting sessions with experts in business history who provided evidence about the successes and failures of US enterprises that have attempted to invest worldwide. Top management also consulted experts in Central European history and culture who provided insights into economic and cultural trends in that region and experts in other cultures around the world who provided similar advice. Next, top management called in experts in electronic commerce who provided advice about the feasibility of the investment in Central Europe using electronic commerce. Finally, top management and certain members of the staff, including experts in cost management, took a tour of likely regions for expansion.

The purpose of this information-gathering exercise was to get a sense of the wisdom and feasibility of a plan for worldwide investment, not to ascertain whether it was a sound financial decision. At least that was not the plan at this stage. Specific cost-benefit analysis would come later.

After the tour, and after discussing competitive threats from major players in the industry such as Tower, Virgin, Amazon.com, and Barnes & Noble, top management was convinced that the idea for expansion into several parts of the world should go to the next phase. Top management instructed the company's legal, operating, and financial staffs to perform detailed investigations of the costs and benefits of expanding into various regions of the world and eventually into worldwide Internet sales.

Ideas for strategic moves, such as the one General Motors made in starting Saturn and the one Rascals made in expanding into Central Europe, come from various sources. Some ideas come from visionary corporate leaders, such as Henry Ford, who decided to make a basic automobile affordable to working class families, or Herb Kelleher, who decided that Southwest Airlines would be a no-frills, low-cost (and therefore low ticket price) airline when the major airlines were competing on the basis of service instead of price.

Ideas also come from the marketplace. Although its historical success came from offering face-to-face service in large well-stocked stores, the management of Tower Records recognized that it had to move into Internet commerce if it was to continue competing in the retail music market. General Motors' move to invest in Saturn came largely from competition from high-quality, low-priced imports. Japanese industrial leaders recognized after World War II that they could not compete on the same scale as US steel, automobile, and other manufacturers, so they developed important market niches and focused on quality and efficiency.

Some companies have brainstorming groups that come up with ideas. One large forest products company that we visited uses a strategic planning group whose job it is to come up with new strategic moves for the company. During the course of a year, the group collects ideas and brainstorms until it has 400 ideas. Then the group analyzes each idea using nonfinancial criteria until the surviving number of ideas is approximately 40. Using discounted cash flow analysis, the group winnows the list to about four each year. Of these, an average of one idea per year is ultimately approved for implementation. The group's job appears to be a lot of fun and adds strategic value to the company.

Strategic Questions

a. You have been asked to provide consulting advice to the top management of Rascals, Inc. What questions might you ask at the beginning of your consulting engagement to help you understand whether Rascals is making the right strategic move by investing in Central Europe with a heavy reliance on electronic commerce?

b. One of Rascals' managers comments: "I don't think we should have invested in Central Europe. Nobody in the company knows the languages or the culture. I think we should have gone to Australia where we have more familiarity with the customs and we know the language." How would you respond to this manager's comments?

(Solutions begin on page 586.)

You're the Decision Maker 14.1

Due Diligence Investigations

LO 2 Know the role of due diligence in investment decision making.

due diligence *is the due process or appropriate steps in an investigation*

After the ideas have been developed and top management has given the green light for investigation, major projects are reviewed on three levels: due diligence, financial impact, and nonfinancial impact. We discuss due diligence in this section, leaving the financial and nonfinancial impact analyses to the following two sections.

Due diligence refers to the due process or appropriate steps in an investigation. During the due diligence investigation, people look for potential problems with the investment. The primary objective of the due diligence investigation is to prevent surprises from popping up after the investment has been made. Major areas for due diligence investigations follow:

- *Legal.* Does the project entail potential legal problems? One of the major problems that some companies have had in particular parts of the world is the payment of bribes to local officials. These bribes range from large payments to top government officials (which are illegal under US law) to small payments to government workers to get permits approved. Other problems for companies investing in a foreign country include restrictions on who is hired and how much of a company's profits can be taken out of the country.
- *Environmental.* Some companies have made investments only to learn to their chagrin that they have acquired a Superfund site.[1] Others have invested in production processes that created pollution. The book (and movie) *A Civil Action* eloquently explained how an investment in a tannery that dumped environmentally hazardous waste had a major negative effect on Beatrice Foods.[2] Of course, the major disaster was the effect of the tannery's waste on people's lives. Our point is that if the company had not purchased the tannery, Beatrice would not have experienced the nightmare that followed.

Utilities that invest in electricity generating facilities must perform substantial due diligence investigations.

- *Public relations.* Part of due diligence is using the company's public relations department to uncover potential public relations problems. Doing so can prevent what seems to be an economically sound investment from turning into a public relations nightmare, such as those experienced by executives at many companies after discovering that their plants in third world countries employed child labor or provided unsafe working conditions. Another problem for a company could be investing in a new product line only to be faced with unexpected criticism. Ford Motor Company's Excursion Sports Utility Vehicle was heavily criticized by environmentalists for its poor gas mileage, for example.
- *Employee relations.* Investments often upset previously stable working conditions. For example, investments in robotics might mean that employees will lose their jobs or at least must be retrained. A German company's opening of a pharmaceutical plant in Ireland could mean job losses in German plants.

Due diligence is most important in strategic move decisions because those decisions commit the organization's resources to new directions. Strategic moves require additional work because of the uncertainty.

---

[1]Superfund sites are hazardous waste sites targeted for cleanup by the US government.

[2]See J. Harr, *A Civil Action.* (Full citations to references are in the Bibliography.)

Rascals, Inc.'s legal staff discovered cases in which companies thought they had purchased property in Central Europe from local citizens only to have the sale voided because the property had historical significance. This finding alerted the company to do a thorough search of property records that were maintained by government agencies before finalizing the purchase or lease of property. In some cases, this search was made difficult by the lack of private property records from the 1940s through the 1980s because most property was taken over by the national governments. Although environmental issues are important in Central Europe, the Rascals investment did not appear to have much environmental impact (beyond creating some foot traffic in densely populated parts of Prague, Warsaw, Bratislava, and Budapest).

Rascals' public relations staff did a thorough job of surveying local residents and meeting with major political and business leaders to see if there would be opposition to the company's investment. They found some concerns that companies such as Rascals would control the music and book scene, displacing local talent with big-selling names from Western Europe, Australia, and the United States. Based on these findings, Rascals' management committed the company to marketing the music and books of local artists in each of the four countries. George Bailey, Rascals' CEO, made it clear to others in the company that he wanted Rascals to create a good impression with residents of the region.

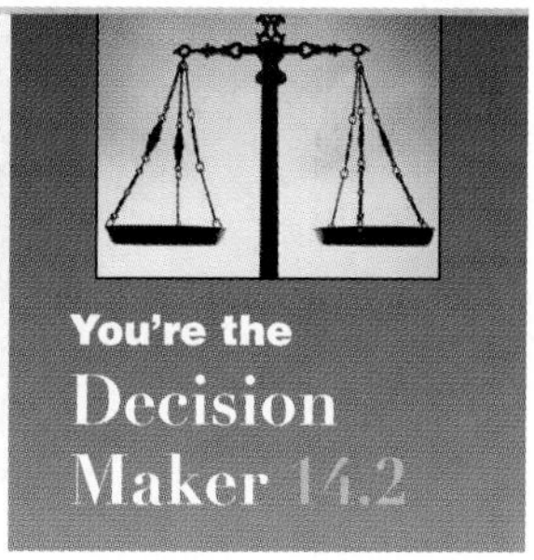

Due Diligence Investigations

Why is Rascals concerned about making a good impression in Central Europe?

(Solutions begin on page 586.)

Financial Analysis of Alternatives

LO 3 Rank alternative sources of financial information based on usefulness for the particular investment decision being made.

Cost-management analysts play a major role in obtaining financial information. The task is primarily to obtain good estimates of the cash flows for alternatives. These include the cash outlay for the investments, the cash inflows or cost savings from the investments, and the cash inflows or outflows for the end of project life or disinvestments. As you know, both the timing and the amount of cash flows are important: the amount for obvious reasons and the timing because of the time value of money. In addition to estimating cash flows, the use of the appropriate risk-adjusted discount rate is important. We leave finding the appropriate discount rate to finance texts and focus on the cash flow aspects of the analysis.

Three excellent sources of financial information follow:

1. Financial records, with adjustments for inflation since the data were recorded.
2. Interviews with operating and marketing personnel.
3. Industry data and competitor analysis.

Financial Records

If the investment is similar to past ones, records of actual cash flows from previous investments are useful. For example, assume that United Airlines is considering replacing six of its current aircraft with six new Boeing 757s on a particular set of routes. United's financial staff can easily obtain financial records that reveal useful information based on previous aircraft replacements.

Exhibit 14–1

Value of Alternative Sources of Financial Information

	Sources of Information		
	Financial Records	**Interviews with Operating and Marketing Personnel**	**Industry Data and Competitor Analysis**
Replacement decisions	Useful if modified to reflect new prices and other changes from past investments	The most useful of the three sources of information	Useful to learn competitors' experience
Expansion decisions	Useful as a starting point	Useful to learn how things may be different in the expansion compared to the present experience	Useful to learn competitors' experiences
Strategic moves	Not useful	Useful if operating and marketing people can think outside the box	The most useful of the three sources of information

Each capital investment is unique, of course, so one should modify the information from past records. Price-level changes create an obvious modification, but management should also consider other things that are different from the previous investment. For example, assume that Rascals, Inc., considers remodeling its Cleveland, Ohio, store. Rascals' financial records show the costs of remodeling other stores in Pittsburgh, Chicago, and Columbus. These are useful starting points, but suppose that Cleveland has unique regulations for energy savings and for providing wheelchair-accessible doors and aisles. Furthermore, prices of materials, labor, and permits are different in Cleveland than in the other cities, and prices have changed since the remodeling was done in the other cities. While past records are a good starting point, modifications will be needed to make the data more relevant for the current decision.

Financial records are most useful for replacement decisions and least useful for strategic moves, as shown in Exhibit 14–1, with expansion somewhere between the two. If strategic moves really reflect new directions for the organization, past records could be more of a hindrance than a help. For example, Rascals' financial staff found records of past investments in Western Europe and North America of little use in forecasting cash flows for the Central Europe investment because the former investments were for traditional large stores, not small stores, kiosks, and electronic commerce.

Interviews with Operating and Marketing Personnel

Some financial people are reluctant to go out of their offices to factory floors, sales offices, and the field to interview operating and marketing personnel who make and sell the product. But operating and marketing people are the ones who really know the business. They have a wealth of information that is useful in all decisions.

In considering the remodeling of the Cleveland store, financial people interviewed several employees at the store, from store manager to information technology specialists, to help understand how the Cleveland situation was different from other recent remodels. Financial people also interviewed several managers of other stores that had recently been remodeled to learn what problems the stores had encountered in the remodel that affected cash flows and what the managers would have done differently if they could do it over.

Interviews with operations and marketing personnel can be useful for strategic moves, as indicated in Exhibit 14–1, if these people can "think outside of the box"; that is, they can think of totally new ways to do business. For example, Rascals had creative people working in its information technology group who were able to think outside of the box to create ways to market the company's products using the Internet.

Industry Data and Competitor Analysis

Many industry publications, company and industry Web sites, company financial statements, and other publicly available data are potentially useful sources of information. Librarians are particularly helpful resources for accessing such information. Many companies hire people from competitors, use consultants, and otherwise obtain information about competitors' practices for making investment decisions. In considering its investment in Saturn, General Motors used a large amount of information about Japanese automobile companies, for example.

For strategic move investments, industry data and competitor analysis could be the only source of data. In evaluating the strategic move into Central Europe, financial staff at Rascals spent more time obtaining data about Amazon.com, Barnes & Noble, and other competitors than they spent obtaining data about Rascals' own operations because the competitor information was more useful for evaluating a strategic move.

Financial Analysis of Rascals, Inc.

Rascals, Inc., used the three sources of financial information previously discussed to estimate its after-tax cash inflows and outflows for the Central Europe operations. These cash flows are shown in Exhibit 14–2, line 2. An investment of $200 million is required at the beginning of the project, and the operations are expected to break even by the end of the third year. The present value factors are calculated using Rascals' discount rate of 15 percent. The $171 million cash inflow for year 10 assumes that Rascals, Inc. will sell the Central Europe operations to local investors.

As shown in Exhibit 14–2, the net present value totals $10 million. Recall that if a proposal has a net present value (NPV) greater than zero, the proposal exceeds the company's hurdle rate (assuming that the hurdle rate is used to calculate NPV). Thus, Rascals' Central Europe proposal exceeds the company's 15 percent hurdle rate. See the appendix to this chapter for a more detailed discussion of discounted cash flow analysis and calculating net present value.

Nonfinancial Analysis of Alternatives

Some important factors are difficult to financially quantify. Some examples from a very long list follow:

- *Impact on employee morale.* Most investments affect employees' job prospects, sometimes for the better, sometimes for the worse.

Exhibit 14–2 Rascals, Inc., Financial Analysis (Net Present Value)

	(dollar amounts in millions)										
	End of Year										
1.	0	1	2	3	4	5	6	7	8	9	10
2. After-tax cash flows	(200)	(10)	(5)	0	60	65	80	80	80	80	171
3. Present value factor at 15%	1.000	.870	.756	.658	.572	.497	.432	.376	.327	.284	.247
4. Present value for each period	(200.0)	(8.7)	(3.8)	0.0	34.3	32.3	34.6	30.1	26.2	22.7	42.3
5. Net present value of investment	10.0										

- *Impact on the community.* This is a particularly important consideration if the investment results in loss of jobs, addition of jobs, or elimination of small businesses. For example, critics have charged that replacing "mom-and-pop" businesses with large chains has reduced support for local community activities, educational activities, and the arts.
- *Impact on the environment.* Practices such as opening a mine, developing new pharmaceutical products that create environmentally harmful waste, putting waste products into streams or landfills, and developing products that are not biodegradable all have an impact on the environment. Some of these environmental effects feed back through estimated cash flows because companies expect to pay fines, incur litigation costs, and incur disposal and cleanup costs. This is particularly true for natural resource companies such as those engaged in mining. Companies might also consider environmental impacts from a social conscience perspective. Some people do not want their companies to have a reputation for being "dirty."
- *Ethical issues.* Some investments might be legal but might not be in line with management's ethics and code of conduct for the company. In many countries, payment of bribes to foreign government officials is legal.[3] Nevertheless, managers of many companies have refused to play the bribery game. We interviewed managers of a company that manufactures military equipment who said they would not sell arms to certain countries because those countries had military dictatorships that restricted free speech and democratic ideals. "There are some things we'll just not do, no matter how lucrative," is the attitude of many managers.
- *Learning.* Many investments, particularly those in advancing the organization's technology, provide opportunities for learning. For Rascals, Inc., management expects one of the major benefits from investing in the Central Europe project to be learning in two areas: (1) how to use the Internet to market products and (2) how to do business in countries that do not have mature market economies.

Nonfinancial factors often are uncovered in the due diligence process discussed earlier in this chapter. Often these nonfinancial factors tip the balance in favor of projects as described in the Cost Management in Practice 14.1.

[3]It is illegal for Swedish and US citizens or companies to pay bribes to foreign governmental officials. In 1999, many industrialized countries signed an agreement to stop paying bribes to foreign government officials. (See *www.oecd.org* for more information.) Nevertheless, bribery is still practiced in many countries.

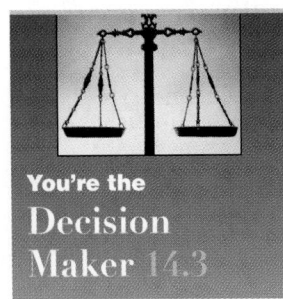

You're the Decision Maker 14.3

Sources of Information

Rascals is considering expanding into Austin, Texas, by opening a new store there. Identify three sources of information that should help estimate the financial and nonfinancial consequences of opening a store in Austin.

(Solutions begin on page 586.)

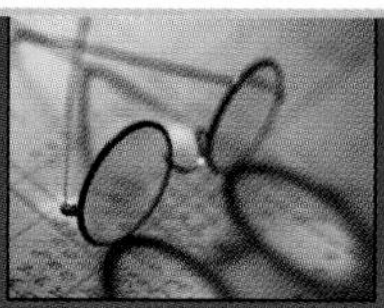

Cost Management in Practice 14.1

Nonfinancial Benefits of Investing in Improved Technology at Ford

Investments in improved technology frequently do not show a positive net present value when investment analysis is performed. Technological innovations usually have a high investment outlay and a long time period before the project returns cash flows. We observed this phenomena in capital investment decision making for technological improvements at Ford Motor Company.

Ford was considering investing in new computerized equipment that would revolutionize the company's production processes. With the new equipment, the company could change quickly from making one part to another, reduce batch-level costs, reduce inventory levels, and reduce production downtime, thereby freeing capacity for expansion. In addition to these explicit benefits, the engineers and production managers who supported the project saw it as a way to learn more about the use of computerized manufacturing processes, which could provide major benefits to the company in the future. These benefits were not quantifiable, however, so some analysts in the company argued against giving them explicit weight in the discounted cash flow analysis.

Ford initially rejected the project based on the discounted cash flow analysis. The chief executive officer of the company was convinced, however, that the project had additional benefits beyond those explicitly considered in the discounted cash flow analysis. He believed that the project was justified because it would help the company learn to better use highly technical production methods. Consequently, the investment was made despite the negative net present value analysis. By all reports, the investment has paid off in terms of both the financial and nonfinancial benefits. *Source: An author's interviews with executives and staff at Ford Motor Company.*

Justification of Investments in High-Tech Projects

LO 4 Understand difficulties in investing in high-technology projects.

Cost Management in Practice 14.1 discusses the problem of justifying investments when the benefits are difficult to quantify. This has been a major problem in high-tech investments to the extent that, in some companies, it has caused a rift between production and engineering people on one hand and finance and accounting people on the other hand. Some of the causes of the difficulties follow:

1. *Discount rate that is too high.* Sometimes managers set discount rates that are too high in an advanced technology investment analysis. The appropriate discount rate for any investment decision is the cost of capital adjusted for risk. Because of uncertainty about advanced manufacturing methods, managers might overstate this risk and, therefore, the discount rate.
2. *Time horizons that are too short.* The acquisition cost of an advanced technology system can be enormous, and the benefits can be realized over a lengthy period of time. If the discounted cash flow analysis does not include the benefits in later years, it is incomplete and could lead to an incorrect rejection decision.
3. *Exclusion of benefits that are difficult to quantify.* Many significant benefits from investing in high technology are difficult to quantify. Some of these benefits include greater flexibility in the production process, shorter cycle times, and reduced lead times.

Because benefits are difficult to quantify, they often are excluded from the discounted cash flow analysis. Excluding them from a discounted cash flow analysis means that they are being valued at zero, which is wrong. It is better to make some estimate of these benefits, no matter how rough an estimate it is, than to exclude them.

Managers sometimes assume that if they do not make the investment in high technology, the status quo will continue. In fact, competitors could make the investments and reduce costs, increase quality, or develop new products. If a high-technology investment opportunity exists, someone will likely make it. If so, companies that do not keep up face competitive pressure, perhaps even extinction.

If estimating the quantitative benefits of an investment is impossible, the investment analysis should include these intangible benefits along with a proposal's net present value. For example, if the net present value of a project is a negative $45 million, management can decide whether the intangible benefits are worth more than $45 million. If management judges that such intangible benefits are worth more than $45 million, the investment is justified. (Managers are paid well because they have the ability to make wise decisions without the benefit of totally quantifiable information.)

Because the estimation of cash flows for high-tech projects is difficult, some people have suggested that companies make these decisions without considering the usual capital investment criteria such as net present value. That would be a mistake. Companies should consider expected cash flows and net present values from such projects to the extent possible because the company is committing stockholders' funds and/or putting stockholders at risk in making these investments. Managers would fail in their role as stewards of stockholders' money if they did not consider the economic costs and benefits of investments.

Sensitivity Analysis

LO 5 Conduct sensitivity analyses of capital investment decisions based on nonfinancial and financial issues.

Having gone through the process of estimating financial and nonfinancial consequences of investments, management next faces making a decision under uncertainty. Although the present value analyses might appear to be sophisticated, they are based on estimates and, likely, some reasonable guesses about future cash flows. Furthermore, even the most careful analysts will overlook some factors. And nonfinancial factors exist.

sensitivity analysis *is the study of how the outcome of a decision-making process changes as one or more of the assumptions change*

In the face of this uncertainty about what will really happen if the investment is made, financial staff often perform sensitivity analyses on the proposed investment. To understand sensitivity analysis, we recall that decision making requires the use of assumptions. **Sensitivity analysis** is the study of how the outcome of a decision making process changes as one or more of the assumptions change. Sensitivity analysis results from a quantitative modeling process.

For example, what if the cash outlay for the investment is more than expected?[4] What if the timing of the cash inflows is later than expected? What if disposal of the assets is more costly than expected because it creates environmental hazards? All of these what-ifs lead analysts to perform sensitivity analysis, often called "what-if" analysis because it attempts to address what-if questions.

Financial staff at Rascals, Inc., performed sensitivity analysis for the investment in Central Europe. Based on this sensitivity analysis, the staff constructed four scenarios, summarized in Exhibit 14–3. The top row describes scenarios ranging from "disaster" to "optimistic." For each scenario, the staff thought about how the cash flows might differ from those expected. For example, for the disaster scenario, the staff thought about all of the things that might go wrong. One staff member called it the "Titanic" approach, saying, "We're looking at the case where we have more passengers than lifeboats, we hit an iceberg, the water is cold, no rescue ship is near, and so forth. We don't believe that would happen, but it could." In the disaster scenario, the net present value is negative. The project is a flop with insufficient cash inflows from operations to cover outflows from operations. And the company develops a bad reputation from the failed venture. In the optimistic scenario, all goes better than hoped. The disappointing and expected scenarios are between the two extremes.[5]

---

[4]Some managers adopt the "2 × approach." Accordingly, new projects cost 2 × as much as expected. And they take 2 × as long to install or complete as expected. We have observed many cases in which the 2 × approach appears to be correct.

[5]Analysts who perform sensitivity analysis generally observe what happens if they make small changes in the parameters or assumptions of their quantitative model. *Scenario analysis,* by contrast, generally examines various scenarios that result from a change in combinations of model parameters. Asking "What are the best, expected, and worst cases?" is scenario analysis. Asking "What is the effect on profits of a 1 percent increase in sales price?" is sensitivity analysis.

Exhibit 14–3

Four Scenarios: Rascals, Inc.

	Scenario			
	Disaster	**Disappointing**	**Expected**	**Optimistic**
What if	The project never generates a positive cash flow. We sell out after five years.	The project does not meet expectations; it has a negative net present value.	The project requires three years to break even but is profitable after that.	The project breaks even after two years and is more profitable than expected.
Net present value	($150 million)	($20 million)	$10 million	$40 million
Nonfinancial results	Company's reputation suffers substantially, which may preclude us from future ventures.	No negative impact on company's reputation. We learn how to do this right the next time.	Company develops strong brand reputation in Central Europe. We learn much.	Company has exceptional success that spills over into other prospective markets.

As shown in Exhibit 14–2, the net present value for this investment was $10 million, so the project was expected to earn more than the appropriate risk-adjusted rate of return (which was 15 percent). Management looked at the four scenarios to see how bad things could get on the down side for both financial and nonfinancial factors. Bailey, Rascals' CEO, remarked, "We are not exactly betting the company on this venture, but pretty close. The disaster would not only hurt us financially, but also would take a long time to overcome the bad reputation from failing at Internet marketing in this important part of the world. Nevertheless, I think the company would survive even a disaster. I take heart from how well Japanese companies did in US markets in the 1980s and 1990s after having to deal with a reputation for poor quality based on early ventures into the US markets in the 1950s and 1960s. A disaster will mean my job, of course, but I am sufficiently secure for that not to matter."

Approval Process

At some point, analysis ends and decisions are made. Who has the right to make the decision depends on the nature of the project and the size of the investment. Replacement and minor improvement decisions could be made at low levels of the organization, particularly if the investment is small. At Rascals, Inc., store managers are allowed to make decisions for replacement and minor improvements under $10,000. Regional managers, who oversee an average of 20 stores, have the authority to make decisions for replacement and minor improvements from $10,000 to $100,000. If the Cleveland store manager wants to remodel the store and if the investment outlay for the remodel is $10,000 or more but does not exceed $100,000, the store manager seeks authorization from the regional manager. If the investment exceeds $100,000, it must be approved by Rascals' board of directors.

The board of directors must nearly always approve investments in expansions and strategic moves. At Rascals, top executives were involved in the Central Europe investment from the beginning, and staff made monthly presentations to the board as members collected new information.

Biases in the Process

People who propose investments tend to become invested in the project's implementation. It is natural for them to put the best face on the investments they propose and to lose objectivity. Decision makers should cherish the enthusiasm of project proponents. Dampening enthusiasm for new investment ideas is a good way to reduce the number of good ideas. At the same time, it is important for decision makers to look past the enthusiasm for the objective information they can use to make wise decisions.

Top executives at Rascals, Inc., were initially skeptical about the notion of moving into Central Europe with a heavy reliance on the Internet for sales. Bailey commented, "People who buy books and records want personal service; they want face-to-face contact." Nevertheless, the people who brought forward the idea did their homework and convinced Bailey and the other top executives that the investment had merit. Throughout the process of developing the idea, performing due diligence, and forecasting financial and nonfinancial consequences of the investments, Bailey and the other executives worked hard to support the enthusiasm of the proponents of the idea while still asking tough questions and keeping their objectivity.

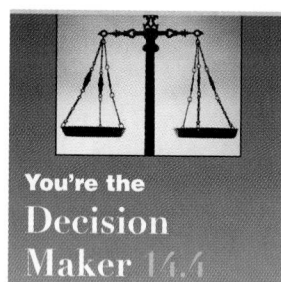

You're the Decision Maker 14.4

Nonfinancial Issues

Which of the following nonfinancial issues was likely a factor in Rascals' decision to open in Central Europe: impact on employee morale, impact on the community, impact on the environment, ethical issues, and learning?

(Solutions begin on page 586.)

Project Implementation and Control

In a sense, making the decision is the easy part. Implementation and control of the project so that it comes in on time and within budget are difficult. Implementation and control of replacement and minor improvement decisions are relatively easy. Much is known about the investment before the dollars are spent. That knowledge can be used to establish both time and cost controls to monitor how long it takes to complete the project and how much it costs.

Managers monitor a construction project's adherence to budget and schedule.

Management has greater difficulty with strategic moves and expansion investments that are dissimilar to past investments. In those cases, managers have less guidance from the past to develop schedules and budgets for cash outlays for the investment. Consequently, companies have more hands-on monitoring of the project.

Many companies have struggled with cost overruns and project delays for software development and other projects to automate processes, which are often new to them.[6] Consumers Power, a highly regarded public utility in Michigan, nearly went bankrupt in building its Midland nuclear power plant when nuclear power regulations were changing. The project was about $3 billion over budget and several years late when it was finally stopped before completion.[7] Cases such as this are scary to top management because nobody expects the project to be so far over budget. Each incremental expenditure seems appropriate to complete the project. Sometimes top management must recognize that past expenditures are sunk costs and pull the plug on the project.

---

[6]For example, the Department of Motor Vehicles in California incurred a $35 million cost overrun and numerous project delays when it tried to automate its automobile registration and driver-licensing process, according to M. McEnaney, "Cost Overruns Plague California DMV Automation Project."

[7]Based on the authors' interviews with Consumers Power executives and other research.

Managing and controlling projects is particularly difficult in foreign countries and even more so in developing countries. Research Insight 14.2 reports the results of a questionnaire survey of project managers in a developing country. These project managers report major causes of project costs and time overruns.

Cost and Time Overruns

Research Insight 14.2

The authors of a study on project cost and time overruns in developing countries sent questionnaires to the project managers of numerous investments in Indonesia to ascertain the causes of cost overruns and schedule delays. For cost overruns, they found the following:

Inflationary increases in material costs.

Inaccurate estimation of the materials required for the job.

Inaccurate estimates of the project complexity.

The predominant causes of schedule delays were:

Design changes.

Poor labor productivity.

Inadequate planning.

Although these results were based on construction projects in Indonesia, the results appear generalizable to other settings and projects. *Source: P. F. Kaming et al., "Factors Influencing Construction Time and Cost Overruns on High-Rise Projects in Indonesia."*

Audits

LO 6 Know how audits contribute to the capital investment process.

Audits of the decision and implementation of investment projects reveal how well the investment performed compared to expectations. The capital investment process is quite subjective and includes extensive forecasting. It is unlikely that the investment and its returns will turn out as planned. Audits can reveal problems and provide feedback for developing and implementing future projects.

- Audits identify what estimates were wrong so planners can incorporate that knowledge in future estimates to avoid making similar mistakes.
- Audits can identify and reward planners who are good at making capital budgeting decisions. Audits also provide information to decision makers so they can consider the skill of the planner in making the capital investment decision.
- Audits create an environment in which planners will not be tempted to inflate their estimates of the benefits associated with the project to get it approved.
- Audits provide an important discipline to a subjective judgmental process.

Ethical Issues

LO 7 Understand ethical issues in capital investment decisions.

Ethical problems in capital investment decisions generally fall into three categories:

1. Misstating information used for decision making.
2. Misstating results.
3. Investing in unethical projects.

Misstating Information

We have already commented that sometimes proponents of investment projects present biased information. Sometimes such biases come from excitement about the project. Other times project proponents intentionally leave out important information or otherwise intentionally misstate information. During your career, you could be pressured to omit certain data from capital investment proposals or to make inaccurate projections. Don't! We have seen plenty of evidence of such actions that came back to haunt the people misstating information. At a minimum, you will likely be discovered, and your credibility will be seriously damaged, even if you do not act on your own accord (e.g., a supervisor asks you to do it and threatens repercussions if you decline).

Misstating Results

Taking ownership of an investment project is a good thing. Becoming so invested in its success that you misstate progress toward implementation of the project or misstate the returns from the project is a bad thing. Many times top managers do not terminate a project soon enough because they were fed information that mislead them into thinking the project was doing well. Misstating results leads to inappropriate use of company resources and reduces the credibility (and prospects of keeping the job) of the people who provided the misleading results.

Investing in Unethical Projects

Managers turn down many opportunities for their companies to earn high returns on their investments. Why? Because the projects involve harming the environment, forming joint ventures with organizations of ill repute, or investing in activities to which top management simply will not agree. Some organizations, like Tom's of Maine and Ben and Jerry's Homemade, make ethical choices part of the company's strategy, and they do well from marketing that strategy. Cost Management in Practice 14.2 tells of other companies that are building a reputation for making environmentally friendly investments.

Cost Management in Practice 14.2

Environmental Friendly and Product Take-Back Decisions

Xerox, AT&T, IBM, and Hewlett-Packard, among other companies, are investing in ways to refurbish products at the end of their life cycles. This activity comes in the wake of product take-back regulations in Europe, Japan, and certain localities elsewhere. Product take-back is the idea that manufacturers are responsible for products after consumers are finished with them. This idea has created an extensive industry in refurbishing products. Xerox, for example, remanufactures copiers in Europe, often for sale in developing countries. Some computer companies refurbish their products for donation to schools. AT&T, Hewlett-Packard, and IBM have earned Germany's "Blue Angel" award for their product take-back efforts. *Sources: J. Ottman, "Product Take-Back Is a New Marketing Tool"; and M. J. Epstein, "'Greening' with EVA."*

Capital Budgeting in Nonprofit Organizations

Not-for-profit organizations, including government agencies, are subject to limitations on the availability of capital for investment purposes. These organizations should use capital investment analysis to allocate resources efficiently. Because not-for-profit organizations are exempt from income taxation, they experience no tax effects on the operating cash flows or on disinvestment flows. Likewise, they receive no tax shield from depreciation. The absence of tax issues makes the analysis simpler than it is for a taxpaying organization.

US federal government agencies generally use a discount rate of 10 percent, although the US Postal Service and some other agencies are exceptions. If inflation rates continue to range from 1 percent to 4 percent per year, a rate of 10 percent seems reasonable for governmental projects. If inflation increases, however, discount rates should increase as well.

Chapter Summary

This chapter focuses on long-term capital investment decisions. The body of the chapter addresses several strategic, conceptual, and behavioral issues. The Appendix to the chapter discusses the mechanics of discounted cash flow analysis.

Capital investment decisions are generally strategic decisions, so they should fit in the organization's strategic plan. Not making a decision can be strategic, also, such as when companies fail to make investments to keep themselves competitive.

Replacement, expansion, and strategic move investments have different sources of ideas, risks, and approval processes. Ideas for replacement decisions come from operating people, ideas for expansion generally come from marketing, whereas those for strategic moves often come from top management or strategic planning staff. Strategic moves commit the organization to a new course of action, usually requiring large sums of money, so they are approved at the highest levels of the organization and include extensive review by the board of directors.

Because they involve forecasts, capital investment decisions require assumptions. Sensitivity analysis enables top managers to see the effect of changing those assumptions. Discounted cash flow analysis may be biased against investing in advanced technology if the benefits of new technology are not quantifiable. Audits give important feedback by revealing how well projects did compared with expectations. Ethical issues arise when project proponents are tempted to bias the information used in decision making and when they misstate the results of the investment. Organizations differ in their consideration of ethical issues in making investments.

Key Terms

For each term's definition, refer to the indicated page or turn to the glossary at the end of the text.

discount rate*, 587
due diligence, 574
internal rate of return (IRR)*, 592
net present value (NPV)*, 587
present value*, 586
sensitivity analysis, 580
strategic planning, 570
tax credit*, 590
time value of money*, 586

*Term appears in the Chapter Appendix.

Meeting the Cost-Management Challenges

1. **Was** the proposed investment in Central Europe by Rascals, Inc., an example of an expansion, replacement, or strategic move investment?

The proposed investment was a major strategic move into a new part of the world and into Internet commerce.

2. **What** major areas should Rascals be concerned about in its due diligence review?

The legal status of its investment is important because the legal system in Central Europe is relatively new. In Central Europe, cases have been noted in which assets were reclaimed by pre-World War II owners, for example. Is there a chance of political reversal in which the Communist Party would control the executive branches of government? If so, would the state take over Rascals' assets and operations?

Many countries restrict the amount of profit that can be removed from them. This should be investigated and considered in the decision.

Companies investing overseas should always check for religious or cultural sensitivities. It is also wise to ascertain sources of good employees.

3. **What** would be the most useful source of information in considering whether to invest in Central Europe?

Good sources of information include business managers and consultants who have had considerable experience in the region. Also, Rascals should get advice from experts in Internet commerce, particularly those who have experience in Central Europe. Of course, the company should get information about disposable income, the current and future size of its projected major customer base (people ages 12–30), and information about the music and reading tastes of its projected customers.

4. **Based** on sensitivity analysis, what was the downside risk of investing in the Central Europe project for George Bailey? For Rascals, Inc.?

This project could have serious consequences for Bailey if it fails. It is a visible move that he champions. He probably would lose his job if the project is a disaster (using the scenario from Exhibit 14–3). He is less at risk of losing his job if the project is merely disappointing. On the other hand, not making the investment could also have negative consequences if the company slips behind its competitors. All things considered, this is a gutsy move by Bailey.

The downside risk is much less for the company. It would likely weather the disaster.

Solutions to You're the Decision Maker

14.1 Strategic Questions p. 573

a. You should ask whether Rascals has the expertise in electronic commerce and in Central Europe to make this move. If not, can the company acquire the expertise by, for example, using joint ventures or partnering with other companies that would have such expertise (e.g., Amazon.com for the electronic commerce expertise and a Central European retailer for expertise in retailing in the region).

b. The manager makes a good point. Managers sometimes act out of self-confidence, thinking because they have succeeded in one region of the world they can succeed in another. Furthermore, because "English is the language of commerce," many US managers do not appreciate the importance of doing business in local languages. Failure to understand language and local customs is a barrier to success. That barrier can be mitigated by training managers in local languages and in local customs. For Rascals, it would be wise to send teams of people into each of the four countries for at least six months to develop language skills and to learn about local customs before beginning the investment process.

14.2 Due Diligence Investigations p. 575

First, management might simply want the company to be a good citizen in the community. Second, having a good reputation can increase the demand for the organization's products and the supply of workers eager to work for the company. Third, having a good reputation could prevent undue regulatory interference or even government seizure of the company's assets.

14.3 Sources of Information p. 578

Rascals should get information from recent expansions, particularly from openings in college towns similar to Austin, and from new stores opened in the southwest region of the United States. It could survey target customers and competitors in Austin to get information about customer tastes. It could obtain economic and demographic data from the local Chamber of Commerce and government sources about population trends in the region.

14.4 Nonfinancial Information p. 582

Learning was undoubtedly important. This investment is like a pilot study providing a wealth of information that will be useful in subsequent similar investments. The impact on the community, (i.e., Central Europe) should also have been a factor. Will Rascals be welcomed as a good citizen that benefits the economy and the culture, or will it be viewed as a greedy foreigner trying to corrupt the youth of the region? The other nonfinancial issues were probably less important.

Appendix to Chapter Fourteen

Discounted Cash Flow Analysis

LO 8 Conduct discounted cash flow analysis.

The purpose of this appendix is to present the basic concepts in discounted cash flow analysis. It will serve as a review for readers who have learned discounted cash flow analysis but are rusty on the concepts or as an introduction for people who are unfamiliar with the topic. Textbooks in finance provide more extensive discussion.

Analyzing Cash Flows for Present Value Analysis

time value of money *is the concept that cash received earlier is worth more than cash received later*

present value *is the amount of future cash flows discounted to its equivalent worth today*

Capital investment models are based on the future cash flows expected from a particular asset investment opportunity. The amount and timing of the cash flows from a capital investment project determine its economic value. The timing of those flows is important because of the concept of the **time value of money,** which states that cash received earlier in time has greater economic value than cash received later. As soon as cash is received, it can be reinvested in an alternative profit-making opportunity. Thus, any particular investment project has an opportunity cost for cash committed to it. Because the horizon of capital investment decisions extends over many years, the time value of money is often a significant decision factor for managers.

To recognize the time value of money, the future cash flows associated with a project are adjusted to their present value using a discount rate. The **present value** of cash flows is the amount of future cash flows discounted to their equivalent worth today.

Summing the discounted values of the future cash flows and subtracting the initial investment yields a project's **net present value (NPV),** which represents the economic value of the project to the company at a given point in time.

net present value (NPV) *is the economic value of a project at a point in time*

The **discount rate** is the interest rate used to discount future cash flows to their present values. If the net present value of a project is positive, the project will earn a rate of return higher than its discount rate. The decision models used for capital investments attempt to optimize the economic value to the firm by maximizing the net present value of future cash flows. The discount rate takes risk and inflation into account as discussed in finance textbooks and courses.

discount rate *is an interest rate used to discount future cash flows to their present values*

Distinguishing between revenues, costs, and cash flows. A *timing difference* often exists between revenue recognition and cash inflow and between the recognition of an expense and the related cash outflow. When this occurs, *distinguishing cash flows from revenues and expenses* is important. Discounted cash flow analysis (as the term indicates) uses *cash flows,* not the revenues and expenses computed using accrual accounting. For example, revenue from a sale often is recognized on one date but the cash is not collected until a later date. The cash is not available for investment or consumption purposes until it is collected, so that is the point at which it is recognized as cash flow for purposes of discounted cash flow analysis.

Computing the net present value. The *net present value* of a project can be computed by using the following equation:

$$NPV = \sum_{n=0}^{N} [C_n \times (1 + d)^{-n}]$$

where

C_n = cash to be received or disbursed at the end of time period n
d = appropriate discount rate for the future cash flows
n = time period when the cash flow occurs
N = life of the investment, in years

Using calculators or computer spreadsheets is the most efficient approach to compute net present values. Tables of present value factors appear in Exhibit 14–4 and can be used to find present values.

We use the net present value equation in many Appendix illustrations, computations, and discussions, and we round all printed factors to three decimal places. Therefore, if we want to discount $20,000 to be received in two years, at 10 percent, we find the value of $(1.10)^{-2}$ by a power function in the calculator. In the calculator, the result of this computation is .826446281, which, multiplied by $20,000, yields the present value of $16,529. We show such computations as follows:

$$\$20{,}000 \times (1.10)^{-2} = \$20{,}000 \times .826$$
$$= \$16{,}529$$

We abbreviate the present value factor (.826) because it is simply an intermediate result. If you use the abbreviated factor or the factors from the present value tables, your answer will differ due to rounding, but this should not cause alarm. Capital investment decisions are yes or no decisions that are not affected by rounding.

If you use the table in Exhibit 14–4, simply look up the factor by referring to the appropriate year and discount rate. For a discount rate of 10 percent and a cash flow at the end of two years, Exhibit 14–4 shows the present value factor to be .826.

Now let's consider how present value analysis is used for capital investment decisions. As an example, consider two projects. Each project requires an immediate cash outlay of $10,000. Project 1 will return $14,000 at the end of two years; project 2 will

Exhibit 14–4 Present Value Tables

Present Value of $1

	Discount Rate																			
Year	**8%**	**10%**	**12%**	**14%**	**15%**	**16%**	**18%**	**20%**	**22%**	**24%**	**25%**	**26%**	**28%**	**30%**	**32%**	**34%**	**35%**	**36%**	**38%**	**40%**
1	0.926	0.909	0.893	0.877	0.870	0.862	0.847	0.833	0.820	0.806	0.800	0.794	0.781	0.769	0.758	0.746	0.741	0.735	0.725	0.714
2	0.857	0.826	0.797	0.769	0.756	0.743	0.718	0.694	0.672	0.650	0.640	0.630	0.610	0.592	0.574	0.557	0.549	0.541	0.525	0.510
3	0.794	0.751	0.712	0.675	0.658	0.641	0.609	0.579	0.551	0.524	0.512	0.500	0.477	0.455	0.435	0.416	0.406	0.398	0.381	0.364
4	0.735	0.683	0.636	0.592	0.572	0.552	0.516	0.482	0.451	0.423	0.410	0.397	0.373	0.350	0.329	0.310	0.301	0.292	0.276	0.260
5	0.681	0.621	0.567	0.519	0.497	0.476	0.437	0.402	0.370	0.341	0.328	0.315	0.291	0.269	0.250	0.231	0.223	0.215	0.200	0.186
6	0.630	0.564	0.507	0.456	0.432	0.410	0.370	0.335	0.303	0.275	0.262	0.250	0.227	0.207	0.189	0.173	0.165	0.158	0.145	0.133
7	0.583	0.513	0.452	0.400	0.376	0.354	0.314	0.279	0.249	0.222	0.210	0.198	0.178	0.159	0.143	0.129	0.122	0.116	0.105	0.095
8	0.540	0.467	0.404	0.351	0.327	0.305	0.266	0.233	0.204	0.179	0.168	0.157	0.139	0.123	0.108	0.096	0.091	0.085	0.076	0.068
9	0.500	0.424	0.361	0.308	0.284	0.263	0.225	0.194	0.167	0.144	0.134	0.125	0.108	0.094	0.082	0.072	0.067	0.063	0.055	0.048
10	0.463	0.386	0.322	0.270	0.247	0.227	0.191	0.162	0.137	0.116	0.107	0.099	0.085	0.073	0.062	0.054	0.050	0.046	0.040	0.035

return \$14,000 at the end of three years. If the appropriate discount rate is 15 percent, the net present value of each project can be computed as follows:

Project 1

Cash inflow $= \$14{,}000 \times (1 + .15)^{-2}$
$= \$14{,}000 \times .756$ (rounded)
$= \$10{,}586$
Cash outflow $= \$10{,}000$
Net present value $= \$586$

Project 2

Cash inflow $= \$14{,}000 \times (1 + .15)^{-3}$
$= \$14{,}000 \times .658$ (rounded)
$= \$9{,}205$
Cash outflow $= \$10{,}000$
Net present value $= \$(795)$

At a discount rate of 15 percent, project 1 is acceptable, but project 2 is not. This means that project 1 will earn more than the required 15 percent return; project 2 will earn less.

You should check for yourself to see that at a 20 percent discount rate, the present value of both projects is negative. Therefore, if our required rate of return were 20 percent, neither project meets the investment criterion. Alternatively, at 10 percent, both projects have positive net present values and are acceptable.

For both projects, assume that all of the cash outflows are made at the beginning of the project, which we call the end of year 0. The end of year 0 is the starting point of the project. Future cash inflows are discounted back to the end of year 0. This can be confusing. Think of the end of year 1 as one year later than the end of year 0, the end of year 2 as two years later than the end of year 0, and so forth. Discounted cash flow analyses generally assume that cash flows occur at some discrete point in time, say at the end of year 1, end of year 2, and so forth.

Visually, the cash flows are displayed along a time line as shown in Exhibit 14–5. The cash outflows are in parentheses ( ). Cash inflows are not in parentheses.

Understanding the categories of project cash flows. Projects can have as many as three major categories of cash flows:

1. Investment cash flows.
2. Periodic operating cash flows.
3. Disinvestment cash flows.

Each category of cash flows requires a separate treatment.

Investment cash flows. The three types of investment flows follow:

1. Asset acquisition, which includes
   a. New equipment costs, including installation (outflow).
   b. Proceeds of existing assets sold (inflow).
2. Tax effects arising from a loss or gain on the assets sold (inflow if a tax benefit or outflow if a tax increase, such as capital gains on the assets sold).
3. Tax credits (inflow).

	Year 0	End of Year 0	Year 1	End of Year 1	Year 2	End of Year 2	Year 3	End of Year 3	Year 4	End of Year 4
Project 1		**\$(10,000)**				**\$14,000**				
Project 2		**\$(10,000)**						**\$14,000**		

Exhibit 14–5
Display of Project Cash Flows along Time Line

For example, assume that Rascals, Inc., is considering replacing some of its computer equipment used for inventory management. The cash flow analysis is presented in Exhibit 14–6. The new hardware and installation costs would amount to $200,000 at time 0. Of the $200,000 investment, $180,000 is for hardware that will be depreciated for tax purposes in the following amounts:

End of Year	Amount of Tax Deduction
1	$30,000
2	60,000
3	30,000
4	30,000
5	30,000
Total	$180,000

The remaining $20,000 is for installation labor and training that is deductible for tax purposes in year 0.

We use a 40 percent tax rate for both ordinary income and for capital gains and losses in this example. This rate is assumed to cover federal, state (if any), and local (if any) corporate income taxes. Tax laws and tax rates change frequently, so we simplify the tax issues to focus on the discounting process. We advise you to check with tax experts for the latest word on tax regulations when you do these analyses in practice.

The $20,000 that is deductible in year 0 provides Rascals with a tax deduction of $20,000, which at a 40 percent tax rate reduces taxes by $8,000. This $8,000 appears in row 3 of Exhibit 14–6 as a benefit at the end of year 0. (To keep the example simple, we assume that all cash flows occur at the end of the year.)

Rascals has found a small independent record shop that is willing to pay the company $10,000 for its existing hardware. (See row 4, Exhibit 14–6.) The tax basis of the existing hardware is zero, so the entire salvage value is a capital gain taxed at the 40 percent rate, which increases taxes by $4,000. (See row 5.)

tax credit *A reduction in state and/or federal income taxes*

Particular types of investments could qualify for a **tax credit,** which reduces state and/or federal income taxes. For example, the investment tax credit, which has been in effect at various times, allows a credit against the federal income tax liability based on the cost of an acquired asset. Other examples include credits for providing particular types of employment training, credits for investing in low-income housing, and credits for investing in energy-efficient assets. These credits effectively reduce the cost of making investments by giving companies a credit against their corporate income taxes.

For illustrative purposes, assume that Rascals, Inc., would receive a tax credit equal to 5 percent of the cost of the new hardware for investing in high-technology equipment. The state in which Rascals is making this investment is attempting to attract high-technology business, so it offers a tax credit for high-tech investments. This tax credit, which is $9,000 (= .05 × $180,000 investment), appears in row 6, Exhibit 14–6.

Periodic operating cash flows. The primary reason for acquiring long-term assets is to generate positive periodic operating cash flows. These positive flows result from such revenue-generating activities as new products or from cost-saving programs.

For Rascals, Inc., the periodic cash flows are the savings in maintenance costs on the old hardware plus an estimate of the cost savings from better inventory management. Rascals' analysts estimated the before-tax cash savings shown in row 7 of Exhibit 14–6.

Row 8 of Exhibit 14–6 shows the tax effects of the combined cost savings and the depreciation on the hardware. For example, for year 1, the computations are as follows:

Periodic cash savings before tax	+$60,000	This savings reduces deductible expenses, so it increases taxes.
Depreciation deduction (see discussion above)	(30,000)	This deduction reduces taxes.
Net effect on taxable income	+$30,000	
Taxes (Cash outflow)	$12,000	$30,000 × .40 tax rate

Exhibit 14–6 Cash Flow Schedule with Present Value Computations, Rascals, Inc.

	End of Year					
1.	0	1	2	3	4	5
2. Equipment cost and installation	$(200,000)	—	—	—	—	—
3. Tax benefit from tax-deductible expenses in installation	8,000	—	—	—	—	—
4. Proceeds of old assets sold	10,000	—	—	—	—	—
5. Tax from gain on assets sold	(4,000)	—	—	—	—	—
6. Tax credit	9,000	—	—	—	—	—
7. Periodic operating flows before tax	—	$60,000	$60,000	$60,000	$60,000	$60,000
8. Taxes	—	(12,000)	0	(12,000)	(12,000)	(12,000)
9. Proceeds of assets sold	—	—	—	—	—	20,000
10. Tax from gain on assets sold	—	—	—	—	—	(8,000)
11. Cash flows for each period	$(177,000)	$48,000	$60,000	$48,000	$48,000	$60,000
12. Present value factor at 15%	1.000	.870	.756	.658	.572	.497
13. Present values	$(177,000)	$41,760	$45,360	$31,584	$27,456	$29,820
14. Net present value of the project	$(1,020)					

Explanation and computations for each row:

1. Time periods, where the end of year 0 is the start of the project and all cash flows occur at the end of each year.
2. Investment amounts given in the text.
3. Of the $200,000 investment, the $20,000 installation and training cost is a deductible expense for tax purposes. The tax rate is 40 percent. So, $8,000 = .40 × $20,000. This is a tax benefit, or reduction in taxes, so it is shown as a positive cash flow.
4. Proceeds of old hardware sold given in the text.
5. $4,000 = .40 × $10,000 proceeds from old hardware sold. The entire $10,000 is a taxable gain because the old hardware had been fully depreciated.
6. Tax credit (discussed in text) is .05 × $180,000 investment in hardware = $9,000.
7. Periodic cash savings from reduced hardware maintenance and better inventory management is estimated to be $60,000 per year.
8. The tax effects for years 1–5, excluding investment and disinvestment flows, are as follows:

   Year 1: (Periodic cash savings − Depreciation deduction) × Tax rate

   ($60,000 − $30,000) .40 = $12,000 outflow (that is, increase in taxes).

   Year 2: $60,000 periodic cash savings − $60,000 depreciation deduction (from discussion in text) × .40 tax rate = $0

   Years 3–5: Same as year 1.
9. Estimated proceeds of assets sold at end of year 5 = $20,000.
10. Assets are fully depreciated at the end of year 5, so the proceeds of assets sold are fully taxable: .40 × $20,000 = $8,000.
11. Sum of cash flows for each period.
12. PV factor shown is rounded to three places. Present value factors are shown in Exhibit 14–4.
13. Present value equals cash flows in row 11 × present value factors in row 12.
14. Net present value of the investment is the sum of the present values. In this case, the net present value is a small negative amount, meaning the project investment earns a little less than a 15% return.

Row 8 shows taxes as ($12,000). The negative term means an increase in taxes: $12,000 more taxes must be paid at the end of year 1 because of the investment cash savings from the new hardware. For each of the other years, subtract the depreciation deduction from the periodic cash savings to get the net increase in taxable income. Multiply the net increase in taxable income by the tax rate to compute the tax effect from operations in each year. Note that row 8 shows the tax effect only for the annual periodic cash flows and the depreciation deduction. The tax effects of the investment appear in rows 3, 5, and 6. The tax effects of the disinvestment appear in row 10, to be discussed next.

Rascals Inc.

Disinvestment cash flows. The end of a project's life usually results in some or all of the following cash flows:

1. Salvage of the long-term assets (usually a cash inflow unless there are substantial disposal costs).

2. Tax consequences for differences between salvage proceeds and the remaining depreciation tax basis of the asset.
3. Other cash flows, such as employee severance payments and restoration costs.

Ending a project usually requires the disposal of its assets. In some cases, more money is spent in disassembling the assets and disposing of them than is gained from their sale. Any net cash outflows from the disposal of a project's assets become tax deductions in the year of disposal. The net salvage value of an asset is listed as a cash inflow in the year that it is expected to be realized. For Rascals, analysts estimated the hardware to have a salvage value of $20,000, as shown in row 9 of Exhibit 14–6.

The difference between the net salvage value and the book value for tax purposes (that is, the tax basis) results in a taxable gain or loss. For Rascals, the hardware was totally depreciated, so the tax basis is $0. Therefore, the estimated proceeds of $20,000 at the end of year 5 results in a tax outflow of $8,000, assuming a 40 percent tax rate, as shown in row 10 of Exhibit 14–6.

The end of project operations also can generate costs not directly related to the sale of assets. It could be necessary to make severance payments to employees, for example. Sometimes payments are required to restore a project area to its original condition. Some projects incur regulatory costs when they are closed down. These expenditures are generally tax deductible in the year they are incurred.

Preparing the net present value analysis. Row 11 of Exhibit 14–6 shows the total cash flows for each period. Rascals, Inc., uses an after-tax discount rate of 15 percent for projects such as this one. The present value factors (rounded to three digits) appear in row 12. Row 13 shows the present value at the end of year 0 of the cash flows for each period. For example, $48,000 is the net cash inflow at the end of year 1. The present value of that $48,000 is $41,760.

Interpreting the net present value. Row 14 shows the project's net present value as the bottom line for which we have been striving. If it is positive, the investment earns more than a 15 percent return. On the other hand, if the net present value is negative, the investment earns less than a 15 percent return on investment. All other things set aside, positive net present value projects are generally accepted and negative net present value projects are generally rejected. Although the net present value is very important, it is not the only factor that managers consider in making decisions. Some of these nonfinancial factors are discussed in the chapter.

In this case, the net present value is negative but small. Note that a reduction in installation costs of only $2,000, or 1 percent of the investment, would have made the net present value positive. Analysts would likely conclude that, assuming the cash flow estimates are unbiased, the new installation is expected to generate just under a 15 percent return. If there are any intangible benefits, or if there are likely to be benefits that are not reflected in the cash flows, Rascals is likely to go ahead with the investment in new hardware.

internal rate of return (IRR) *is the interest rate that equates the present value of inflows and outflows from an investment project*

Understanding internal rate of return. The **internal rate of return (IRR)** is the interest rate that equates the present value of inflows and outflows from an investment project. If the internal rate of return (also known as the *time-adjusted rate of return*) were used as the cost of capital for discounting project cash flows, the net present value of the project would equal zero. Thus, the IRR is the rate that makes the present value of project cash outflows equal to the present value of project cash inflows. This contrasts with the net present value method, which employs a predetermined discount rate.

The internal rate of return can be calculated with many types of calculators or with the use of a spreadsheet by inputting the relevant cash flows and using the IRR function. We leave detailed discussions of internal rate of return computations to finance courses and textbooks.

The IRR is generally considered inferior to net present value because of its built-in assumption that net cash inflows are reinvested at the project's internal rate of return.

By contrast, the net present value method assumes that the net cash inflows are invested at the predetermined discount rate. If funds are reinvested at the cost of capital, the IRR method makes a project whose rate of return is higher than the cost of capital appear more attractive than a similar project using the net present value approach.

Review Questions

14.1 What is strategic planning?

14.2 What factors led the US Postal Service to become a market-oriented organization?

14.3 What is a good source of ideas for replacement decisions?

14.4 A few years ago, Daimler-Benz and Chrysler Corporation merged to form DaimlerChrysler. Was that an expansion decision or a strategic move?

14.5 Does the due diligence work come before, during, or after developing the financial projections for capital investment decisions?

14.6 Which type of decision is more likely to upset previously stable working conditions: replacement, expansion, or strategic moves? Why?

14.7 What are sources of information for estimating cash flows?

14.8 Why are financial records more useful for replacement decisions than for strategic moves?

14.9 Why are interviews with marketing and operating employees less useful for strategic capital investment decisions than for replacement or expansion decisions?

14.10 Capital investment decisions have an effect on the community in which the company operates. Give other examples of the impact of capital investment decisions.

14.11 When companies end investment projects, what termination costs are they likely to incur?

14.12 What is sensitivity analysis? Why is it wise to perform sensitivity analysis on capital investment decisions?

14.13 Why are replacement investments usually easier to manage than strategic move investments?

14.14 What are the major causes of cost overruns and schedule delays according to the survey of managers in Indonesia reported in Research Insight 14.2?

14.15 What do audits of capital investment projects reveal?

14.16 How are capital investment decisions similar and dissimilar for profit-seeking organizations and nonprofit organizations?

14.17 What are three categories of ethical problems in capital investment decisions?

14.18 (Appendix) How can tax policies provide an incentive for capital investment?

Critical Analysis

14.19 "The discounted cash flow method is too narrow and excludes important factors in decision making." How would you respond to that statement?

14.20 "If an investment does not fit with an organization's strategic plan, it is probably not a good idea, even if the net present value is positive." Under what conditions would this be a true statement? When would it be false?

14.21 The estimates in long-term decisions are subject to error. What type of projects are most subject to error in the estimated cash flows: replacement, expansion, or strategic moves? Why?

14.22 Of the numbers used in replacement decisions, which are most subject to error: amount of cash flows, timing of cash flows, or the cost of capital? Why? Would your answer change if you were dealing with strategic move decisions? Why or why not?

14.23 "I would get my information for making replacement decisions from operating employees (for example, production and sales personnel), my information for making expansion decisions from high-level marketing managers, and my information for making strategic moves from top executives in the firm." Do you agree with this statement? Why or why not?

14.24 Somebody said, "A vision without reality is just a hallucination." How might capital investment projects turn out to be hallucinations?

14.25 At what level in the organization are approvals for strategic move investment decisions made? Are approvals for replacement decisions usually made at the same level of the organization as strategic move investment decisions? Why or why not?

14.26 Southwest Airlines faces challenges from many of the larger carriers, yet it appears to retain its cost advantage. Why?

14.27 The chapter mentioned a strategic planning group at a large forest products company that started with 400 ideas for capital investment decisions and then winnowed the list to 40 before doing discounted cash flow analysis. Other than net present values, what criteria do you suppose this group used to winnow the list from 400 to 40?

14.28 When Rascals, Inc., started doing its due diligence work, it relied on its outside legal counsel who were part of a law firm, Dewey, Cheathem and Howe, located in Los Angeles, California. Dewey, Cheathem and Howe had offices in Chicago; New York; Cambridge, Massachusetts; and Washington, D.C., but none outside the United States. Do you think it was a mistake for Rascals to rely solely on Dewey, Cheathem and Howe for the legal part of its due diligence work?

14.29 Due diligence work includes studying the environmental impact of a capital investment decision. Name two industries in which environmental impact studies are likely to be very important and two industries in which they are likely to be relatively unimportant.

14.30 "All this due diligence is just a waste of time. All you need is a good old-fashioned discounted cash flow analysis to decide whether to make capital investment decisions." How would you respond?

14.31 What are the difficulties in using discounted cash flow analysis for investments in high-technology projects? Would one face similar problems in using discounted cash flow analysis to evaluate new-product decisions?

14.32 Sometimes capital investments with a positive net present value have a negative impact on earnings. For example, investing in certain types of research and development could result in a large expense at the time of investment with the benefits coming several years later. Suppose an executive tells you, "If our earnings go down, our stockholders are hurt because stock prices will fall and our managers are hurt because their bonuses are tied to earnings. Therefore, I will not approve any capital investment that decreases current earnings, no matter how high its net present value." What is wrong with the executive's statement?

14.33 How can audits of capital investment projects help managers construct better cash flow analyses?

14.34 (Appendix) Financial accounting writers emphasize that depreciation is not a source of funds, yet it appears in the discounted cash flow analysis. How would you reconcile those two facts?

14.35 (Appendix) Given two projects with equal cash flows but different timing, how can we determine which (if either) project should be selected for investment?

14.36 (Appendix) All other things equal, riskier projects are less likely to be accepted than less risky projects. True or False? Explain.

Exercises

Exercise 14.37
Present Value of Cash Flows (Appendix)
(LO 8)

New York Community Housing is considering investing in transition housing that will require outlays as follows:

End of Year	Item	Amount
0	Engineering studies	$ 50,000
1	Project construction	200,000
2	Project construction	900,000

Required

Compute the net present value of these cash outlays if the appropriate discount rate is 10 percent. The organization is tax exempt, so taxes are not applicable.

Exercise 14.38
Present Value of Cash Flows (Appendix)
(LO 8)

Spreadsheet

The City of Denver is considering an investment that would expand the community center. It is expected to return the following cash flows:

End of Year	Net Cash Flow
1	$ 80,000
2	100,000
3	160,000
4	160,000

This schedule includes all cash inflows from the project, which will also require an immediate $400,000 cash outlay (i.e., at the end of year 0). The city is tax exempt; therefore, taxes need not be considered.

Required

a. What is the net present value of the project if the appropriate discount rate is 10 percent?

b. What is the net present value of the project if the appropriate discount rate is 12 percent?

Exercise 14.39
Present Value of Cash Flows (Appendix)
(LO 8)

The US Postal Service is considering investing in automatic postal machines that use credit or debit cards to charge for the postage due on parcels. The following cash flow savings are expected:

End of Year	Net Cash Inflow (in millions)
1	$ 40
2	60
3	80
4	100
5	120

This schedule includes all cash inflows from the project, which will also require an immediate cash outlay of $200 million at the end of year 0. The US Postal Service is tax exempt.

Required

Compute the net present value of the project if the appropriate discount rate is 10 percent.

Problems

Problem 14.40
Discounted Cash Flows with Taxes (Appendix)
(LO 8)

Communication

Spreadsheet

Furby Manufacturing is considering investing in a robotics manufacturing line. Installation of the line will cost an estimated $3 million. This amount must be paid immediately. It will be depreciated at the rate of $500,000 in year 1, $1,000,000 in year 2, and $500,000 in each of years 3, 4, and 5. The cash operating benefits and costs are expected to just offset each other for three years, so no before-tax cash savings are expected for three years. Starting in year 4, the company expects to see a before-tax cash savings from quality improvements of $2.5 million per year in each of years 4 through 7. At the end of year 7, management expects to discontinue the manufacturing line and sell the robotic equipment for $100,000. The equipment will be fully depreciated when it is sold, so the entire sales price is a taxable gain.

Required

Compute the net present value of this investment using a discount rate of 20 percent and a tax rate of 40 percent for all taxable income and gains. What do you recommend that management do?

[CMA adapted]

Problem 14.41
Discounted Cash Flows with Taxes (Appendix)
(LO 8)

Neptune Company manufactures toys and gifts. Its research and development department developed a new toy. Neptune's sales personnel estimate that the new toy can be sold for the next three years but not after that.

To produce the amount demanded, Neptune needs to buy additional machinery and needs to provide about 25,000 square feet of space to produce this product. Neptune has 12,500 square feet of presently unused space available for the next three years. The company's present lease with 10 years to run costs $3 a square foot, including the 12,500 square feet of unused space that cannot be used for anything else. Neptune can rent another 12,500 square feet adjoining its facility for three years at $4 per square foot per year if it decides to make this product.

Year	1	2	3
Sales	$1,000,000	$1,600,000	$800,000
Material, labor, and other unit-level, batch-level, and product-level costs	400,000	750,000	350,000
Allocated administrative costs	40,000	75,000	35,000
Rent	87,500	87,500	87,500
Depreciation	300,000	300,000	300,000
Income before tax	$ 172,500	$ 387,500	$ 27,500
Income tax (40%)	69,000	155,000	11,000
Income after tax	$ 103,500	$ 232,500	$ 16,500

The equipment will be purchased for $900,000 and will have a salvage value of $180,000 at the end of the third year.

The above estimates of cash flows for this product for the three years have been developed:
The allocated administrative costs will not be affected by this product. Each product is allocated some administrative costs, however.

Required

Prepare a schedule to show the differential after-tax cash flows for this project. Assume that equipment must be depreciated on a three-year, straight-line basis, assuming no salvage value, for tax purposes. If the company sets a required discount rate of 20 percent after taxes, will this project be accepted?

[CMA adapted]

Problem 14.42
Evaluation of Rascals' Analyses
(LO 1, 2, 3, 4)

Form a team of students. Assume that George Bailey, the chief executive officer of Rascals, Inc., has just resigned to help form a rock group called "The Midlifers." Rascals' new chief executive officer has asked your team to evaluate the company's decision to open in Central Europe. At this time, the decision is reversible

 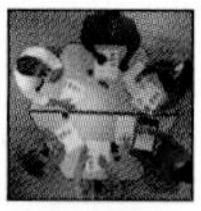

Communication Team

without any negative consequences to Rascals. You must do research on the industry and on Central Europe to respond to the chief executive officer's request.

Required

Given the information in the chapter, plus your research on the industry and on Central Europe, write a report that recommends whether Rascals, Inc., should continue with its investment plans to open in Central Europe. Be sure to state the reasons for your recommendation.

Problem 14.43
Critique of Rascals' Decision
(LO 1, 2, 3, 4)

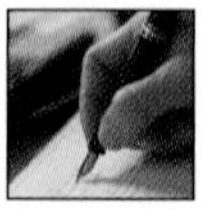 

Communication Team

Form a team of students. Assume that you are a group of loyal Rascals' managers concerned about the wisdom of opening in Central Europe as discussed in the chapter. You believe the financial numbers that generate a small positive net present value are unbiased. Despite that, you worry that top management is unaware of potential problems involved in going ahead with the investment.

Required

Based on your understanding of the investment from the chapter, your research into the industry, Internet commerce, and Central Europe, and any other things that you think are relevant, write a report to top management that critiques the investment. Be sure your criticism is founded and that your language is appropriate and professional. (For example, do not refer to those who support the plan as "idiots.")

Problem 14.44
Capital Investment Decisions
(LO 2, 3)

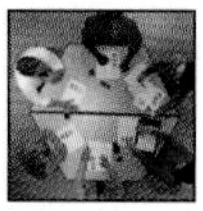 

Team Global

Investment analyses are prepared by teams of people. Assume that you, as a cost-management analyst, have been asked to put together a team to work on the following three investment decisions for Rascals, Inc.: (1) a proposed strategic move into Australia (much like the decision to open in Central Europe) that is estimated to cost \$150 million; (2) an expansion into the Southeast region of the United States by opening six new stores in that region that is estimated to cost \$60 million (Rascals currently operates in the Northeast and Midwest, but not the Southeast); and (3) an upgrade of the music systems in each store in Western Europe at an estimated cost of \$1 million.

Your team would perform the analyses, including discounted cash flow analysis and the analyses discussed in the chapter, and make a recommendation to management. Your team would be primarily responsible for the analyses and recommendations, but you could seek advice from other employees not on the team or from consultants. You do not have to use the same team for each investment decision. Management wants you to limit the team to four people, including yourself.

Required

Indicate whom you would want on each team and why. What would be your role as cost-management analyst? What additional expertise would you seek from employees or consultants who are not on the team?

Problem 14.45
Ethical Issues
(LO 7)

Ethics

Oakshade Corporation is considering expanding its manufacturing operations. It can either convert a warehouse that it currently owns in the suburbs, or it can expand its current manufacturing plant downtown. After the board of directors approved the expansion, George Watson, the controller, set about to determine which proposal had the higher net present value. He assigned this task to Helen Dodge, the assistant controller. She completed her task and discovered that the warehouse proposal had a negative net present value but the downtown expansion proposal was slightly positive. Watson was displeased with Dodge's report on the warehouse proposal. He returned it to her, stating, "You must have made an error. This proposal should look better." She suspected that Watson wanted the warehouse proposal to succeed so that he could avoid his daily commute to the city. She checked her figures and found nothing wrong. She made some slight revisions to her report, however, changing her estimates from those that were probable to those that were remotely possible.

Watson was quite angry and demanded a second revision. He told Dodge to start with a positive net present value of \$100,000 and work backward to compute supporting estimates and projections. She is quite upset and unsure what she should do!

Required

a. Was Helen Dodge's first revision on the proposal for the warehouse conversion unethical?

b. Was George Watson's conduct unethical when he gave Dodge specific instructions on preparing the second revision?

c. How should Dodge attempt to resolve this issue? Should she discuss this issue with those outside the organization?

[CMA adapted]

Problem 14.46
Sources of Information and Evaluation of Capital Investment Decisions
(LO 2, 3)

Communication

Montana Pharmaceuticals makes a variety of prescription drugs. Over the years, it has engaged in cost cutting that has made it a profitable company but one that does relatively little research and development. As a result, it lacks new products.

Taking its lead from Monsanto's purchase of Calgene, Montana Pharmaceuticals is considering investing in some small biotechnology companies to obtain new products and the intellectual capital that would create new biotech products.

Required

Write a report to the management of Montana Pharmaceuticals that recommends sources of financial information for a capital investment decision whether to purchase one or more small biotechnology companies. Also indicate particular areas of concern for a due diligence study. Finally, indicate what nonfinancial factors should be considered in the decision.

Problem 14.47
Due Diligence, Nonfinancial Information, and Sensitivity Analysis
(LO 2, 4)

Communication

Sandra Wells joined Ishima Corporation as a financial analyst three months ago. She is about to make her first presentation to the management committee responsible for selecting capital investments.

Wells has two proposals that require the same investment and have the same project life. Both involve an investment in new products. Project A would generate a net present value of $100,000; project B would generate a net present value of $150,000.

The management committee decided that taking on both projects at once would stretch managers' time beyond reasonable limits. The committee proposed going ahead with one project now and then starting the second project after the first one is going smoothly. The committee asks Wells which project she recommends. Based on its higher net present value, she is tempted to tell the committee to start with project B.

Required

Knowing that you are an expert in thinking beyond the net present value analysis, Wells asks your advice. Should she recommend project B? Write a report to her stating your recommendations.

Problem 14.48
Investments in New Technology, Audits
(LO 5, 6)

Communication

Using an after-tax discount rate of 30 percent, the financial staff of Admiral Motors Company sent an email to top management recommending rejection of a technological improvement that would have saved the company millions in quality control costs. Production managers believed that the new equipment was necessary to improve product quality. They argued that the reduction in quality control costs was only a small part of the benefits. The company's reputation would improve as the quality of its products improved.

Martha Adams, spokesperson for the financial staff, responded to the production and engineering people that "you have not quantified these so-called benefits from improved company reputation, so we are not going to consider them in the financial analysis. Based on our calculations, the net present value is negative, so the decision is 'no.' "

Production managers complained that the use of a 30 percent discount rate was too high. Speaking on behalf of his colleagues, Art Ritis said, "I don't know what thin air you've been breathing, but we almost never get a 30 percent return on investments."

Adams responded, "We have audited your past capital investments and found that they almost never perform as well as you say they will. Because of your unrealistic projections, we bumped up the discount rate."

After seeing these emails and a flurry of subsequent ones that went back and forth between Adams and Ritis, the president of the division took two aspirin and called you in for advice. "Make sense of this," she said. "Write a report that communicates what's really going on here. And tell me what to do about this project."

Required

Write the report requested by the division president.

Problem 14.49
New Machine Decision (Appendix)
(LO 8)

Assume that Starbucks is considering the purchase of newer, more efficient espresso machines for several of its stores. If it purchases them, it would acquire them on December 31, year 0, at a cost of $1,000,000. The old machines, which are fully depreciated for tax purposes, could be sold for $200,000 on December 31, year 0. Either set of machines could be used for three years, but the new machines would be faster and therefore create labor savings of $400,000 per year.

Communication

The tax depreciation schedule for the new set of machines follows:

Year	Tax Depreciation (Percent)
1	20%
2	40
3	40

If kept for three more years, the old machines would have no salvage value. However, the new machines would have a salvage value of $400,000 at the end of year 3.

Required

a. Use the net present value method to determine whether Starbucks should retain the old machines or acquire the new ones. Use an after-tax discount rate of 10 percent, a tax rate of 40 percent, and a three-year time horizon.

b. Assume that you work for the company that is attempting to sell the new espresso machines to Starbucks. The marketing group in your company has asked for your help. Write a short report to help the marketing group convince Starbucks to purchase your company's espresso machines.

Problem 14.50
Assessment of Net Present Value of Training Costs (Appendix)
(LO 8)

Communication

Management of PriceAndersonToucheErnst (PATE) Consultants is considering a proposal to offer employee training in several offices in Southeast Asia. The training would reduce labor and other operating costs.

The Southeast Asian income statement, with amounts (in thousands) converted to dollars, follows:

Revenues	$8,500
Costs:	
Direct labor	4,400
Supplies	200
Indirect labor	1,200
Utilities, taxes, etc.	600
Lease—office space	800
Computer hardware and software	600
Miscellaneous	120
Marketing	450
Administration	380

The costs are expected to continue in the future unless the training is obtained.

The training is expected to reduce direct labor by 25 percent and indirect labor by 20 percent. No other costs are expected to be affected by the training. The training will cost $4,000,000 and can be deducted for tax purposes in the year it is obtained. Assume a five-year time horizon.

Required

a. If the company's after-tax cost of capital is 12 percent and its marginal tax rate is 40 percent, determine whether the new training should be offered. Show supporting computations.

b. Assume you work for the company that provides the training program. Write a report to PATE's managers that would help convince them to buy your training program.

Cases

Case 14.51
Investment by amazon.com
(LO 5)

Internet

Obtain the financial statements for Amazon.com. One source is Amazon.com's Web site. Go to "about Amazon.com" and then to "investor relations." You should be linked to the company's financial statements. Another source is your library.

As an innovator, Amazon.com has been a great success. Some observers claim that the company has been less successful financially.

Required

Based on its financial statements, how well has Amazon.com performed from its origin through the most recent year for which you can obtain financial information? Assuming a 15 percent after-tax discount rate, if you had known in 1995 what you know now about Amazon.com, would you have considered the company to be a positive net present value investment?

Case 14.52
Characteristics of Strategic Leaders
(LO 1)

A strategic leader is an individual with vision who can lead people in new directions: As part of a team of students, study one person who you believe has been a strategic leader in business, government, public service, religion, or sports. Write a biographical report about this person that identifies the characteristics and behaviors that made her or him a strategic leader.

Case 14.53
Ethical Investments, Audits
(LO 6, 7)

Many companies provide information about the results of environmental audits. Search the Internet and/or your library for information about a company in the oil, chemicals, or pharmaceuticals industries, including the company's performance in making environmentally friendly investments and otherwise cleaning up the environment. Prepare a report for your instructor that summarizes the results of your research.

CHAPTER

15

Budgeting and Financial Planning

After completing this chapter, you should be able to:

1. Describe the key role that budgeting plays in the strategic planning process.
2. Explain five purposes of budgeting systems.
3. Describe and prepare a master budget, including each of its components.
4. Describe and evaluate a typical organization's process of budget administration.
5. Understand the behavioral implications of budgetary slack and participative budgeting.
6. Describe contemporary trends in the budgeting process as an element of a cost-management system.
7. Use the economic-order-quantity model to make inventory ordering decisions and discuss the implications of the JIT approach for inventory management (Appendix).

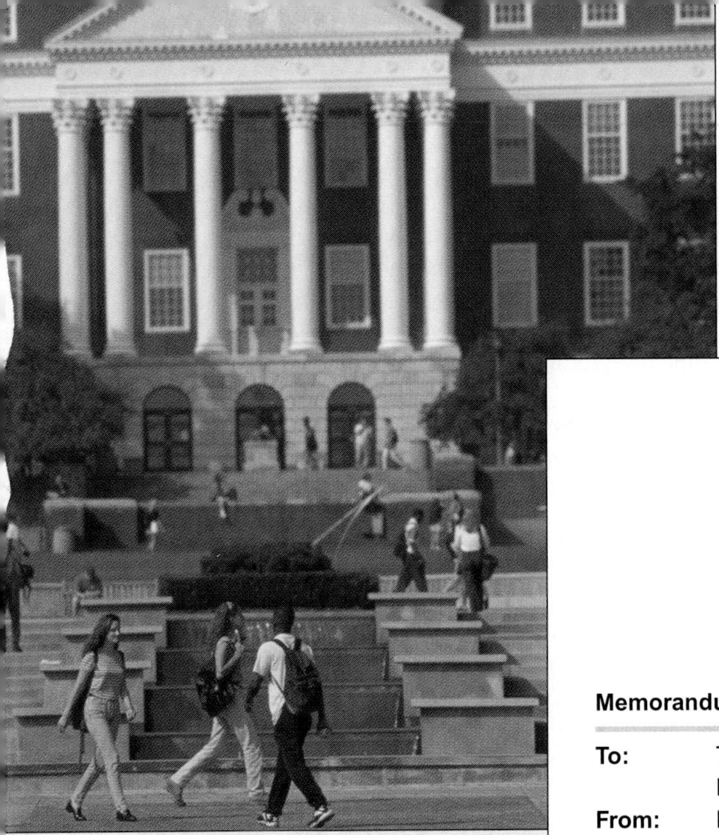

Cost-Management Challenges

1. **Why** does Collegiate Apparel need an annual budget? Specifically, what purposes would the budgeting process serve?

2. **How** could Collegiate Apparel's budget facilitate communication and coordination among the company's president, sales manager, and production supervisor?

3. **What** is a master budget? What are its main components for a manufacturer such as Collegiate Apparel?

4. **How** could Collegiate Apparel's president or a company's board of directors use the budget to influence the firm's future direction?

5. **Would** participative budgeting be effective for Collegiate Apparel Company?

COLLEGIATE • APPAREL • COMPANY

Collegiate Apparel Company
2150 Boundary Bay Road
Vancouver, British Columbia
Canada

Memorandum

To: Timothy Williams
President
From: Meg Johnston
Sales Manager
cc: Bradley Roaldsson
Production Supervisor
Subject: Sales forecast for the next four quarters

I have completed the sales forecast for the next four quarters for inclusion in the annual budget and anticipate unit sales as follows:

1st quarter	15,000 units
2nd quarter	5,000 units
3rd quarter	10,000 units
4th quarter	20,000 units
Total	50,000 units

As usual, the heaviest volume is expected to be in the first and fourth quarters. The first quarter sales reflect the return of students to campus for the spring semester (or winter quarter). The fourth quarter sales reflect not only heavy sales during the fall semester (or quarter) but also sales during the December holiday period. As you will notice, the forecast shows a slight increase over the current year's projected sales. (Next year's sales forecast of 50,000 units represents a 4.2 percent increase over the current year's projection of 48,000 units.) Interestingly, it appears that our volume at large universities will increase by about 5,000 units, but this is offset by an anticipated decline of 3,000 sales units at medium and small institutions. The reasons for this are not immediately clear, and I intend to explore this issue further. More targeted advertising at the small and medium school markets might be worth considering.

The assumptions on which the sales forecast is based include very little change in general economic conditions, a continued low rate of inflation, little change in the student populations at the institutions we serve, and no anticipated change in students' affinity for college logo apparel.

To support this forecast, I conducted telephone interviews with buyers from the campus book stores from a representative sample of institutions in the small, medium, and large college categories.

Please let me know if I can provide any further information at this time.

As the memo on the preceding page indicates, Collegiate Apparel Company is about to begin its annual budgeting, or financial planning, process. Developing a budget is a critical step in planning any economic activity. This is true for businesses, governmental agencies, and individuals. We all must budget our money to meet day-to-day expenses and to plan for major expenditures, such as buying a car or paying for college tuition. Similarly, businesses of all types and governmental units at every level must make financial plans to conduct routine operations, to plan for major expenditures, and to help make financing decisions.

Before exploring Collegiate Apparel Company's budgeting process in detail, let's step back and take a broader view of organizational planning and the role of budgeting in cost-management systems.

Auto manufacturers rely on district sales budgets in delivering new vehicles to their dealerships.

Class sizes and other activities in colleges are determined in part by budgetary considerations.

Strategic Planning: Achieving and Maintaining a Competitive Advantage

LO 1 Describe the key role that budgeting plays in the strategic-planning process.

critical success factors *are the key strengths that are most responsible for making the organization successful*

Every enterprise has a set of goals, such as profitability, growth, or public service. To achieve those goals, an organization's top management periodically (or even continuously) engages in strategic planning. Achieving and maintaining a competitive advantage usually are primary goals of this strategic-planning exercise. Management often outlines the organization's **critical success factors,** the key strengths that are most responsible for making the organization successful. Critical success factors enable a company to outperform its competitors. By identifying these factors and ensuring that they are incorporated into the strategic plan, companies are able to maintain an edge over competitors. In addition, important critical success factors can be exploited to improve the company's overall competitiveness.

For example, Southwest Airlines (*www.southwestair.com*) has relied on several factors to maintain its competitive edge. It keeps its prices consistently low and its routes in the short to medium range, and Southwest uses only one type of plane (keeping costs to a minimum). The company's management knows that these are among Southwest's critical success factors and has continued to increase the airline's competitiveness by building these factors into the strategic planning process.

Can you think of some critical success factors for a small manufacturer, such as Collegiate Apparel Company, whose target market consists of college students?

What Is a Strategic Long-Range Plan?

Although a statement of goals is necessary to guide an organization, it is important to detail the specific steps required to achieve them. A **strategic long-range plan** expresses these steps. Because the long-range plan considers the intermediate and distant future, it is usually stated in rather broad terms. Strategic plans discuss the major capital investments required to maintain present facilities, increase capacity, diversify products or processes, and develop particular markets. For example, a paper company's strategies included the following:[1]

strategic long-range plan *expresses the specific steps required to achieve an organization's goals*

- *Cost control.* Optimize the contribution from existing product lines by holding product cost increases to less than the general rate of inflation. This will involve acquiring new machinery proposed in the capital budget as well as replacing our five least efficient plants over the next five years.
- *Market share.* Maintain our market share by providing a level of service and quality comparable to our top competitors. This requires improving our quality control to reduce customer complaints and returned merchandise from a current level of 4 percent to 1 percent within two years.

Each strategy statement was supported by projected activity levels (sales volumes, aggregate costs, and cash flow projections) for each of the next five years. At this stage, management had not stated the plans in much detail, but the plans had been well thought out and provided a general framework for guiding management's operating decisions.

Long-range plans are achieved in year-by-year steps. The guidance is more specific for the coming year than it is for more distant years. The plan for the coming year is called the *master budget,* which we will explore in detail later in the chapter. First, however, let's look more closely at the purposes of budgeting systems and the various types of budgets.

What Are the Key Purposes of Budgeting Systems?

LO 2 Explain five purposes of budgeting systems.

A **budget** is a detailed plan, expressed in quantitative terms, that specifies how an organization will acquire and use resources during a particular period of time. The procedures used to develop a budget constitute a **budgeting system.** Budgeting systems have five primary purposes: planning, facilitating communication and coordination, allocating resources, managing financial and operational performance, and evaluating performance and providing incentives.

budget *is a detailed plan, expressed in quantitative terms, that specifies how an organization will acquire and use resources during a particular period of time*

budgeting system *comprises the procedures used to develop a budget*

Planning

The most obvious purpose of a budget is to quantify a plan of action. The budgeting process forces the individuals who constitute an organization to plan ahead. The development of a quarterly budget for a Westin Hotel, for example, forces the hotel manager, the reservation manager, and the food and beverage manager to plan for the staffing and supplies needed to meet anticipated demand for the hotel's services.

Facilitating Communication and Coordination

For any organization to be effective, each manager throughout the organization must be aware of the plans made by other managers. To plan reservations and ticket sales effectively, the reservations manager for American Airlines must know the flight schedules

[1]The source of these strategy statements was the company's internal documents, which the company provided to the authors.

developed by the airline's route manager. The budgeting process pulls together the plans of each manager in an organization.

Allocating Resources

Generally, an organization's resources are limited, and budgets provide one means to allocate resources among competing uses. The City of San Francisco, for example, must allocate its revenue among basic safety services (such as police and fire protection), maintenance of property and equipment (such as city streets, parks, and vehicles), and other community services (such as child care services and programs to prevent alcohol and drug abuse).

master budget, or profit plan, *is a comprehensive set of budgets covering all phases of an organization's operations for a specified period of time*

budgeted (or pro forma) financial statements *show how the organization's financial statements will appear at a specified time if operations proceed according to plan*

capital budget *is a plan for buying and selling capital assets*

financial budget *shows how the organization will acquire its financial resources*

rolling (or revolving or continuous) budget *is continually updated by periodically adding a new incremental time period*

Managing Financial and Operational Performance

A budget is a plan, and plans are subject to change. Nevertheless, a budget serves as a useful benchmark with which actual results can be compared. For example, Allstate Insurance Company can compare its actual sales of insurance policies for a year against its budgeted sales. Such a comparison can help managers evaluate the firm's effectiveness in selling insurance. (The next chapter examines the control purpose of a budget in more depth.)

Evaluating Performance and Providing Incentives

Comparing actual results with budgeted results also helps managers to evaluate the performance of individuals, departments, divisions, or entire companies. Since budgets are used to evaluate performance, they also can be used to provide incentives for people to perform well. For example, IBM Corporation, like many other companies, provides incentives for managers to improve profits by awarding bonuses to managers who meet or exceed their budgeted profit goals.

How would each of these five purposes of budgeting systems be relevant in managing a small manufacturing company such as Collegiate Apparel Company?

Organizations Use Many Types of Budgets

Different types of budgets serve different purposes. A **master budget,** or **profit plan,** is a comprehensive set of budgets covering all phases of an organization's operations for a specified period of time. We examine a master budget in detail later in this chapter.

Budgeted financial statements, often called **pro forma financial statements,** show how the organization's financial statements will appear at a specified time if operations proceed according to plan. Budgeted financial statements include a *budgeted income statement,* a *budgeted balance sheet,* and a *budgeted statement of cash flows.*

How would Universal Studios' Orlando theme park use budgeting for planning and resource allocation?

A **capital budget** is a plan for buying and selling capital assets, such as buildings and equipment. We cover capital budgeting in Chapter 14. A **financial budget** is a plan that shows how the organization will acquire its financial resources, such as issuing stock or incurring debt.

Budgets are developed for specific time periods. *Short-range budgets* cover a year, a quarter, or a month, whereas *long-range budgets* cover periods longer than a year. **Rolling** (or **revolving** or **continuous**) **budgets** are continually updated by periodically adding a new incremental time period, such as a quarter, and dropping the period just completed.

The Master Budget as a Planning Tool

The master budget, the principal output of a budgeting system, is a comprehensive profit plan that ties together all phases of an organization's operations. The master budget comprises many separate budgets, or schedules, that are interdependent. Exhibit 15–1 portrays these interrelationships in a flowchart, which shows the components of a master budget for a manufacturing firm. (Later in the chapter, we explore Collegiate Apparel Company's master budget in detail.)

Sales Budget: The Starting Point

The starting point for any master budget is a sales revenue budget based on forecasted sales of goods or services. Airlines forecast the number of passengers on each of their routes. Banks forecast the number and dollar amount of consumer loans and home mortgages to be provided. Hotels forecast the number of rooms that will be occupied

Exhibit 15–1 Components of a Master Budget for a Manufacturing Firm

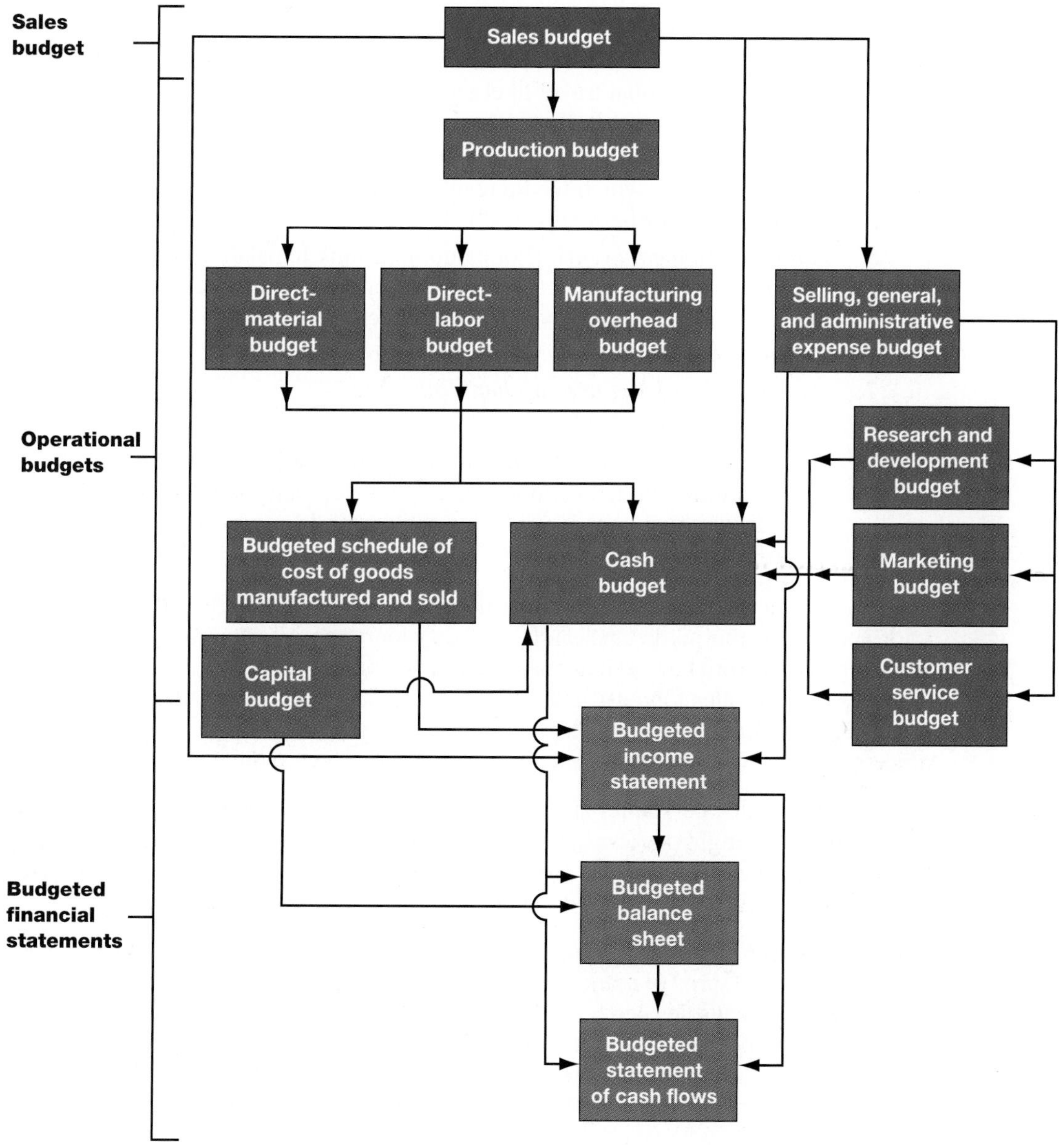

during various seasons. Manufacturing and merchandising companies forecast sales of their goods. Some companies sell both goods and services. For example, Kmart is a large merchandising company, but its automotive-service branch provides the firm with substantial service revenue.

LO 3 Describe and prepare a master budget, including each of its components.

sales forecasting *is the process of predicting sales of services or goods*

Sales forecasting. All companies have two things in common when it comes to forecasting sales of services or goods: Sales forecasting is a critical step in the budgeting process, and it is very difficult to do accurately. **Sales forecasting** is the process of predicting sales of services or goods. Various procedures are used in sales forecasting, and the final forecast usually combines information from many different sources. Many firms have a top-management-level market research staff whose job is to coordinate the company's sales forecasting efforts. Typically, everyone from key executives to the firm's sales personnel is asked to contribute sales projections. These are among the major factors considered when forecasting sales:

1. *Past sales levels and trends.*
   a. For the firm developing the forecast (for example, Exxon).
   b. For the entire industry (for example, the petroleum industry).
2. *General economic trends.* (Is the economy growing? How fast? Is a recession or an economic slowdown expected?)
3. *Economic trends in the company's industry.* (In the petroleum industry, for example, is personal travel likely to increase, thereby implying increased demand for gasoline?)
4. *Other factors expected to affect sales in the industry.* (Is an unusually cold winter expected, which would result in increased demand for home heating oil in northern climates?)
5. *Political and legal events.* (For example, is any legislation pending in Congress that would affect the demand for petroleum, such as tax incentives to use alternative energy sources?)
6. *The intended pricing policy of the company.*
7. *Planned advertising and product promotion.*
8. *Expected actions of competitors.*
9. *New products contemplated by the company or other firms.* (For example, has an automobile firm announced the development of a vehicle that runs on hydrogen fuel, thereby reducing the demand for gasoline?)
10. *Market research studies.*

The starting point in the sales forecasting process is generally the sales level of the prior year. Then the market research staff considers the information just discussed along with input from key executives and sales personnel. A great deal of effort generally goes into the sales forecast since it is such a critical step in the budgeting process. A slightly inaccurate sales forecast, coming at the very beginning of the budgeting process, will throw off all of the other schedules that make up the master budget.

Sales staff. Sales personnel are in the unique position of being close to the customers, and they might possess the best information in the company about customers' immediate and near-term needs. However, they might be tempted to bias their sales forecasts if such forecasts are used as the norm for performance evaluation.

Market researchers. To provide a check on forecasts from local sales personnel, management often turns to market researchers. This group probably does not have the same incentives that sales personnel have to bias the budget. Furthermore, researchers have a different perspective on the market. They might know little about customers' immediate needs, but they can predict long-term trends in attitudes and the effects of social and economic changes on the company's sales, potential markets, and products.

Delphi technique. The Delphi technique is another sales forecasting method used to enhance forecast accuracy and reduce bias in estimates. With this method, members of the forecasting group prepare individual forecasts and submit them anonymously. Each group member obtains a copy of all forecasts but is unaware of their sources. The group then discusses the results. In this way, group members address and reconcile differences among individual forecasts without involving the personality or position of individual forecasters. After discussing the differences, each group member prepares a new forecast and distributes it anonymously to the others. These forecasts are then discussed in the same manner as before. The process is repeated until the forecasts converge on a single best estimate of the coming year's sales level.

Econometric models. Another forecasting approach is to enter past sales data into a regression model to obtain a statistical estimate of factors affecting sales. For example, the predicted sales for the coming period could be related to factors such as economic indicators, consumer-confidence indexes, back-order volume, and other internal and external factors that the company deems relevant. Advocates of these econometric models contend that they can include many relevant predictors and manipulate the assumed values of the predictors to examine a variety of hypothetical conditions and then relate them to the sales forecast.

Sophisticated analytical models for forecasting are now widely available. Most companies' computers have software packages that allow economical use of these models. Nonetheless, it is important to remember that no model removes the uncertainty surrounding sales forecasts. Management often finds that the intuition of local sales personnel is a better predictor than sophisticated analysis and models. As in any decision, management should use cost-benefit tests to determine which methods are most appropriate.

Operational Budgets: Meeting the Demand for Goods and Services

Based on the sales budget, a company develops a set of **operational budgets,** which specify how its operations will be carried out to meet the demand for its goods or services. The budgets constituting this operational portion of the master budget are depicted in the middle portion of Exhibit 15–1, which portrays the master budget for a manufacturing firm.

operational budgets
specify how an organization's operations will be carried out to meet its demand for goods or services

Manufacturing firms. A manufacturing company develops a production budget, which shows the number of product units to be manufactured. From the production budget, a manufacturer develops budgets for the direct materials, direct labor, and overhead required in the production process. These budgets provide the basis for a budgeted schedule of cost of goods manufactured and sold. A budget for selling, general, and administrative (SG&A) expenses is also prepared. The SG&A budget includes budgets for research and development (R&D), design, marketing, distribution, and customer service.

Merchandising firms. The operational portion of a merchandising firm's master budget is similar to that of a manufacturer, but instead of a production budget for goods, a merchandiser develops a budget for merchandise purchases. A merchandiser does not have a budget for direct materials because it does not engage in production. However, the merchandiser develops budgets for labor (or personnel), overhead, and selling and administrative expenses.

Service-industry firms. Based on the sales budget for its services, a service-industry firm develops a set of budgets that show how it will meet the demand for those services. An airline, for example, prepares the following operational budgets: a budget of planned air miles to be flown; materials budgets for spare aircraft parts, aircraft fuel, and in-flight food; labor budgets for flight crews and maintenance personnel; and an overhead budget.

Cash budget. Every business prepares a cash budget. This budget shows expected cash receipts as a result of selling goods or services and planned cash disbursements to pay the bills incurred by the firm.

Capital budget. The capital budget, which is prepared in all types of organizations, details plans for major acquisitions and disposals of assets, such as plant and equipment, vehicles, and land.

Summary of operational budgets. Although operational budgets differ according to the operations of individual companies in various industries, they are also similar in important ways. In each firm, operational budgets encompass a detailed plan for using the basic factors of production (materials, labor, and overhead) to produce a product or provide a service.

Budgeted Financial Statements: Completing the Master Budget

The final portion of the master budget, depicted in Exhibit 15–1, includes a budgeted income statement, a budgeted balance sheet, and a budgeted statement of cash flows. These budgeted financial statements show the overall financial results of the organization's planned operations for the budget period.

Master Budget for Nonprofit Organizations

The master budget for a nonprofit organization includes many of the components shown in Exhibit 15–1. However, there are some important differences. Many nonprofit organizations provide services free of charge. Hence, they have no sales budget as shown in Exhibit 15–1. However, such organizations do begin their budgeting process with a budget that shows the level of services to be provided. For example, the budget for the City of Dallas would show the planned levels of various public services. Nonprofit organizations also prepare budgets showing their anticipated funding. The City of Dallas budgets for revenue sources such as city taxes, state and federal revenue sharing, and sale of municipal bonds.

In summary, all organizations begin the budgeting process with plans for (1) the goods or services to be provided and (2) the revenue to be available, whether from sales or from other funding sources.

International Aspects of Budgeting

As the economies and cultures of countries throughout the world become intertwined, more and more companies are becoming multinational in their operations. Firms with international operations face a variety of additional challenges in preparing their budgets. First, a US multinational firm's budget must reflect the translation of foreign currencies into US dollars. Since almost all the world's currencies fluctuate in their values relative to the dollar, this makes budgeting for those translations difficult. Although multinationals have sophisticated financial ways to hedge against such currency fluctuations, the budgeting task for these firms is still more challenging. Second, budget preparation is difficult when inflation (or deflation) is high or unpredictable. While the United States has experienced periods of high inflation, some foreign countries have experienced hyperinflation, sometimes with annual inflation rates well over 100 percent. Predicting such high inflation rates is difficult and further complicates a multinational's budgeting process. Finally, the economies of all countries fluctuate in terms of consumer demand, availability of skilled labor, laws

Multinational companies face special challenges in preparing their budgets. Cultural differences and currency fluctuations are among the issues to be considered. Pictured here is a Kentucky Fried Chicken restaurant in Bangkok, Thailand.

affecting commerce, and so forth. Companies with off-shore operations face the task of anticipating such changing conditions in their budgeting processes.

Research
Insight 15.1

Master Budgets Around the World

Surveys indicate that master budgets are used around the world in countries such as Australia, the United Kingdom, and Japan. In fact, more than 90 percent of all companies surveyed in these countries utilize a master budget. Differences arise, however, with respect to budget-planning participants and budget goals. Of Japanese firms, 67 percent request division managers' participation compared to 78 percent in the United States. Return on investment is the most important budget goal in the United States; the Japanese focus on sales revenue. (Both countries consider operating income to be the second most important budget goal.) Although different cultures focus on different elements of the budget, master budgets are common in business practice from one country to the next. *Source: T. Asada, J. Bailes, and M. Amano,* "An Empirical Study of Japanese and American Budget Planning and Control Systems." *(Full citations to references are in the Bibliography.)*

Activity-Based Budgeting

The process of constructing a master budget can be significantly enhanced if the concepts of activity-based costing are applied.[2] Activity-based costing uses a two-stage cost-assignment process. In stage I, overhead costs are assigned to cost pools that represent the most significant *activities* constituting the production process. The activities identified vary across manufacturers, but such activities as engineering design, materials handling, machine setup, production scheduling, inspection, quality control, and purchasing provide examples.

After assigning costs to the activity cost pools in stage I, cost drivers are identified that are appropriate for each cost pool. Then in stage II the overhead costs are allocated from each activity cost pool to cost objects (e.g., manufactured goods, services, and customers) in proportion to the amount of activity consumed.

activity-based budgeting (ABB) *is the process of developing a master budget using information obtained from an activity-based costing (ABC) analysis*

Applying ABC concepts to the budgeting process yields **activity-based budgeting (ABB)**,[3] which is the process of developing a master budget using information obtained from an activity-based costing (ABC) analysis. Under ABB, the first step is to specify the products or services to produce and the customers to serve. Then the activities that are necessary to produce these products and services are determined. Finally, the resources necessary to perform the specified activities are quantified. Conceptually, ABB takes the ABC model and reverses the flow of the analysis, as depicted in Exhibit 15–2. As portrayed in the diagram, ABC assigns resource costs to activities and then assigns activity costs to

[2]Activity-based costing (ABC) is covered in Chapter 4.

[3]This section is based on the following references: J. A. Brimson and J. Antos, *Driving Value Using Activity-Based Budgeting;* S. Borjesson, "A Case Study on Activity-Based Budgeting"; and R. S. Kaplan and R. Cooper, *Cost and Effect.*

Exhibit 15-2

Activity-Based Costing versus Activity-Based Budgeting*

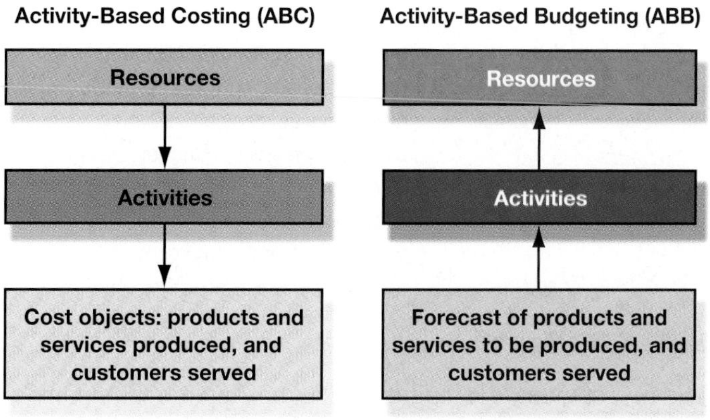

*Source: R. S. Kaplan and R. Cooper, *Cost and Effect.*

products and services produced and customers served. ABB, on the other hand, begins by forecasting the demand for products and services as well as the customers to serve. These forecasts then are used to plan the activities for the budget period and budget the resources necessary to carry out the activities.

In the next section of the chapter, we illustrate the process of constructing a master budget. Notice how the conceptual ABB model is employed in the budgeting process. After completing the master-budget illustration, we explore the benefits and implications of the ABB approach.

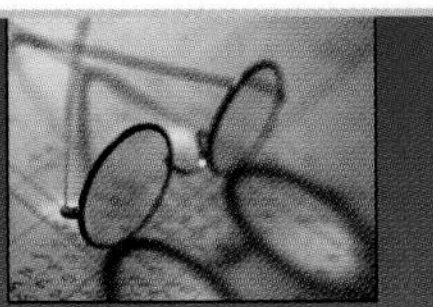

Cost Management in Practice 15.1

Benefits of ABB

American Express has successfully used ABB for its travel-related services in its New York operations. This relatively new system has been used to identify and implement cost reduction and process improvement initiatives. Then, an activity-by-activity analysis of each department has allowed process improvement savings to be factored into the forecasted costs for each department in the next budget cycle.

AT&T Paradyne designs and produces medium- and high-speed data communications equipment, which provides an interface between telephone networks and computers. The company's activity-based costing project ultimately led to activity-based budgeting. As ABM and ABB matured at AT&T Paradyne, the company began to experience a culture change. A key lesson learned in this case was that linking activity-based costing to the budgeting process and performance evaluation led to the integration of ABC into the management of the company. *Source: D. M. Aldea and D. E. Bullinger,* "Using ABC for Shared Services, Charge-Outs, Activity-Based Budgeting, and Benchmarking"; *and J. Collins,* "Advanced Use of ABM: Using ABC for Target Costing, Activity-Based Budgeting, and Benchmarking."

Illustrating the Master Budget

LO 3 Describe and prepare a master budget, including each of its components.

To illustrate the steps involved in developing a master budget, we focus on Collegiate Apparel Company, a small manufacturer of T-shirts bearing the names and logos of several major universities in Canada and the United States. Located in Vancouver, British Columbia, the company is wholly owned and managed by Timothy Williams, who started the firm four years ago. The entire business is operated in a single building. The manufacturing process is highly automated, using three machines to cut out pieces of fabric, stitch them together, and imprint the name and logo of one of several universities. The entire production cycle for a T-shirt requires just 12 minutes.

Collegiate Apparel Company's master budget for the year 20x1 has just been completed. It contains the following schedules, which are displayed and explained in the following pages.

Schedule	Title of Schedule
1	Sales Budget
2	Production Budget
3	Direct-Material Budget
4	Direct-Labor Budget
5	Manufacturing Overhead Budget
6	Selling, General, and Administrative Expense Budget
7	Cash Receipts Budget
8	Cash Disbursements Budget
9	Cash Budget
10	Budgeted Schedule of Cost of Goods Manufactured and Sold
11	Budgeted Income Statement
12	Budgeted Balance Sheet

Sales Budget

sales budget *displays the projected sales in units and the projected sales revenue*

The first step in developing Collegiate Apparel Company's 20x1 master budget is to prepare the **sales budget,** which is displayed in schedule 1. This budget displays the projected sales in units for each quarter, and then multiplies the unit sales by the sales price to determine sales revenue. Notice that there is a significant seasonal pattern in the sales forecast, with the bulk of the sales coming in the fall and winter. (This is the sales forecast to which Collegiate Apparel Company's sales manager, Meg Johnston, referred in the memo at the beginning of this chapter.)

Schedule 1

COLLEGIATE APPAREL COMPANY
Sales Budget
For the Year Ending December 31, 20x1

	Quarter				
	1st	**2nd**	**3rd**	**4th**	**Year**
Sales in units	15,000	5,000	10,000	20,000	50,000
Unit sales price	× $12	× $12	× $12	× $12	× $12
Total sales revenue	$180,000	$60,000	$120,000	$240,000	$600,000

Production Budget

The **production budget** shows the number of units of services or goods that are to be produced during a budget period. Collegiate Apparel's production budget, displayed in schedule 2, determines the number of T-shirts to be produced each quarter based on the quarterly sales projections in the sales budget (see schedule 2). Schedule 2 is based on the following formula.

production budget
shows the number of units of services or goods that are to be produced during a budget period

Sales in units + Desired ending inventory of finished goods = Total units required

Total units required − Expected beginning inventory of finished goods = Units to be produced

Focus on the second-quarter column in schedule 2, which is shaded. Expected sales are 5,000 T-shirts, and management desires to have 1,000 finished units on hand at the end of the quarter. This is 10 percent of the expected sales for the third quarter. However, 500 T-shirts are expected to be in inventory at the beginning of the second quarter. Thus, only 5,500 T-shirts need to be produced.

Schedule 2

COLLEGIATE APPAREL COMPANY
Production Budget
For the Year Ending December 31, 20x1

	Quarter				
	1st	**2nd**	**3rd**	**4th**	**Year**
Sales in units (from schedule 1)	15,000	5,000	10,000	20,000	50,000
Add desired ending inventory of finished goods*	500	1,000	2,000	1,500†	1,500
Total units required	15,500	6,000	12,000	21,500	51,500
Less expected beginning inventory of finished goods	1,500	500	1,000	2,000	1,500
Units to be produced	14,000	5,500	11,000	19,500	50,000

*10 percent of the next quarter's expected sales

†10 percent of the expected sales for the first quarter of the next year, 20x2, which is assumed to be 15,000 units

You're the Decision Maker 15.1

Revised Production Budget

Suppose you are in charge of Collegiate Apparel's budgeting process. The sales manager has just informed you that the sales forecast has been increased by 20 percent during each quarter of 20x1 and the first quarter of 20x2.

a. Revise Collegiate's production budget for 20x1. Assume that the expected finished-goods inventory on January 1, 20x1, is still 1,500 units.

b. Now put yourself in the position of Collegiate's production supervisor. If the sales manager said she was only somewhat confident in the increased sales forecast, would you recommend increasing production to the levels in your revised budget? Why?

(Solutions begin on page 630.)

Direct-Material Budget

direct-material budget
shows the number of units and the cost of material to be purchased and used during a budget period

The **direct-material budget** shows the number of units and the cost of material to be purchased and used during a budget period. As is true for almost all manufacturers, Collegiate Apparel's direct-material cost is a unit-level cost. Each shirt requires 1.5 yards of fabric. Collegiate Apparel's direct-material budget, displayed in schedule 3, shows the total amount of material needed to make T-shirts during each quarter. The shaded portion of schedule 3, which computes the amount of fabric to be purchased each quarter, is based on the following formula.

Raw material required for production + **Desired ending inventory of raw material** = **Total raw material required**

Total raw material required − **Expected beginning inventory of raw material** = **Raw material to be purchased**

The lower, unshaded portion of schedule 3 computes the cost of each quarter's raw-materials purchases. (This information also will be needed later in the budgeting process in schedule 10.)

Production and purchasing: An important link. Notice the important link between planned production and purchases of raw material. This link is apparent in schedule 3, and it is also emphasized in the formula preceding the schedule. Let's focus on the second quarter. Since 5,500 T-shirts are to be produced, 8,250 yards of material will be needed (5,500 units times 1.5 yards per unit). In addition, management desires to have 1,650 yards of material in inventory at the end of the quarter.[4] Thus, total needs are 9,900 yards. Does Collegiate Apparel Company need to purchase this much raw material? No, it does not, because 825 yards will be in inventory at the beginning of the quarter. Therefore, the firm needs to purchase only 9,075 yards of material during the quarter (9,900 yards less 825 yards in the beginning inventory).

Inventory management. Planned production and raw-material purchases is a particularly critical linkage in manufacturing firms. Thus, considerable effort is devoted to careful inventory planning and management. How did management decide how much raw material to have in inventory at the end of each quarter? Examination of schedule 3 reveals that each quarter's desired ending inventory of raw material is 10 percent of the *material needed for production* in the next quarter. For example, 1,650 yards of raw material (.10 × 16,500) will be in inventory at the end of the second quarter because 16,500 yards will be needed for production in the third quarter. The effect of this ap-

[4]It often is desirable to have a buffer inventory just before a bottleneck operation.

Schedule 3

COLLEGIATE APPAREL COMPANY
Direct-Material Budget
For the Year Ending December 31, 20x1

	Quarter				
	1st	2nd	3rd	4th	Year
Units to be produced (from schedule 2)	14,000	5,500	11,000	19,500	50,000
Raw material required per unit (yards of fabric)	× 1.5	× 1.5	× 1.5	× 1.5	× 1.5
Raw material required for production (yards)	21,000	8,250	16,500	29,250	75,000
Add desired ending inventory of raw material (yards)*	825	1,650	2,925	2,100†	2,100
Total raw material required	21,825	9,900	19,425	31,350	77,100
Less expected beginning inventory of raw material (yards)	2,100	825	1,650	2,925	2,100
Raw material to be purchased (yards)	19,725	9,075	17,775	28,425	75,000
Cost per yard	× $2	× $2	× $2	× $2	× $2
Total cost of raw material purchases	$39,450	$18,150	$35,550	$56,850	$150,000

*10 percent of the next quarter's expected raw material requirements.

†10 percent of the expected raw material requirements for the first quarter of the next year, 20x2, which is assumed to be 21,000 yards.

proach is to have a larger ending inventory when the next quarter's planned production is greater. Inventories are drawn down when the subsequent quarter's planned production is lower.

The Appendix to this chapter explores various other tools used in inventory management.

Direct-Labor Budget

The **direct-labor budget** shows the number of hours and the cost of the direct labor to be used during a budget period. Collegiate Apparel Company's direct-labor budget is displayed in schedule 4. Based on each quarter's planned production, this schedule computes the amount of direct-labor needed each quarter and the cost of the required labor. Collegiate Apparel is a small company, and owner Timothy Williams hires all of his direct-labor production employees from the Vancouver area collegiate community. College students are employed, on a part-time basis only, to meet the labor demands of a given time period. Thus, Collegiate Apparel's direct labor may be adjusted up or down to meet short-term needs. As a result, direct labor for this company is a unit-level cost. As schedule 4 shows, each T-shirt manufactured requires .2 hours (12 minutes) of direct labor.

direct-labor budget *shows the number of hours and the cost of direct labor to be used during a budget period*

A note on direct labor and the cost hierarchy. It is important to note that the position of direct labor in the cost hierarchy depends on management's ability to adjust the organization's labor force to match short-term requirements, as well as management's attitude about making such adjustments. For either strategic business reasons or ethical concerns, many companies strive to maintain a relatively stable labor force. If production employees are retained when production declines, direct labor will not be a unit-level cost. In the extreme case when employees are virtually never laid off, direct labor becomes a facility- or general-operations-level cost.

Collegiate Apparel's ability to easily adjust the total hours of its part-time workforce results in a unit-level designation for direct-labor cost in this situation.

Schedule 4

COLLEGIATE APPAREL COMPANY

COLLEGIATE APPAREL COMPANY
Direct-Labor Budget
For the Year Ending December 31, 20x1

	Quarter				
	1st	2nd	3rd	4th	Year
Units to be produced (from schedule 2)	14,000	5,500	11,000	19,500	50,000
Direct labor required per unit (hours)	× .2	× .2	× .2	× .2	× .2
Total direct-labor hours required	2,800	1,100	2,200	3,900	10,000
Direct-labor cost per hour	× $10	× $10	× $10	× $10	× $10
Total direct-labor cost	$28,000	$11,000	$22,000	$39,000	$100,000

Manufacturing-Overhead Budget

manufacturing-overhead budget *shows the cost of overhead expected to be incurred in the production process during the budget period*

The **manufacturing-overhead budget** shows the cost of overhead expected to be incurred in the production process during the budget period. Collegiate Apparel's manufacturing-overhead budget, displayed in schedule 5, lists the expected cost of each overhead item by quarter. At the bottom of the schedule, the total budgeted overhead for each quarter is shown. Then each quarter's depreciation is subtracted to determine the total cash disbursements to be expected for overhead during each quarter. This cash-disbursement information will be needed later in the budgeting process when the cash disbursements budget is constructed (schedule 8).

Activity-based budgeting and the cost hierarchy. Collegiate Apparel's unit-level costs include indirect material and electricity used to run the production machinery. Batch-level costs include machine setup, purchasing and material handling, and inspection. The cost driver for these costs is the number of production runs. A run typically produces 500 T-shirts. Collegiate Apparel's only product-level cost is design. The company typically commissions two new style designs each quarter from a local freelance textile designer. Each new design costs $500. The remaining overhead costs in schedule 5 include all costs at the facility or general-operations level.

Benefits of ABB. Proponents of ABB believe that real, sustainable payoffs from activity-based costing and activity-based management will not be forthcoming until an organization's budgeting process embraces the ABM approach. Utilizing ABC information in the budgeting process provides solid reasoning for budgeting costs at particular levels since the underlying ABC information is based explicitly on the relationships among cost drivers, activities, and resources consumed. Moreover, the resulting budget is more useful to management because it reveals how cost levels will change if the predicted quantities of the cost drivers change. For example, what will happen to Collegiate Apparel's setup costs in the first quarter if the quantity produced is 14,000 units as reflected in the budget (see schedule 5), but 35 production runs are used to produce these 14,000 units instead of 28 runs as specified in the budget? According to schedule 5, setup cost is $100 per production run ($2,800 ÷ 28 runs). Therefore, 35 runs would result in $3,500 of setup cost in the first quarter instead of $2,800 as forecast in the budget. This is true even if 14,000 units are produced as forecast in the budget.

Traditional budgeting processes, which do not embrace the ABB approach, often classify costs such as setup, purchasing and materials handling, quality control and in-

Schedule 5

COLLEGIATE APPAREL COMPANY
Manufacturing-Overhead Budget
For the Year Ending December 31, 20x1

	Quarter				
	1st	**2nd**	**3rd**	**4th**	**Year**
Unit-level costs					
Units	*14,000*	*5,500*	*11,000*	*19,500*	*50,000*
Indirect material	$ 3,500	$ 1,375	$ 2,750	$ 4,875	$ 12,500
Electricity (for machinery)	2,100	825	1,650	2,925	7,500
Total unit-level costs	$ 5,600	$ 2,200	$ 4,400	$ 7,800	$ 20,000
Batch-level costs					
Production runs	*28*	*11*	*22*	*39*	*100*
Setup	$ 2,800	$ 1,100	$ 2,200	$ 3,900	$ 10,000
Purchasing and material handling	3,360	1,320	2,640	4,680	12,000
Inspection	2,240	880	1,760	3,120	8,000
Total batch-level costs	$ 8,400	$ 3,300	$ 6,600	$11,700	$ 30,000
Product-level costs					
New style designs	*2*	*2*	*2*	*2*	*8*
Design	$ 1,000	$ 1,000	$ 1,000	$ 1,000	$ 4,000
Total product-level costs	$ 1,000	$ 1,000	$ 1,000	$ 1,000	$ 4,000
Facility- and general-operations-level costs					
Supervisory salaries	$14,000	$14,000	$14,000	$14,000	$ 56,000
Insurance and property taxes	2,400	2,400	2,400	2,400	9,600
Maintenance	2,600	2,600	2,600	2,600	10,400
Utilities	2,500	2,500	2,500	2,500	10,000
Depreciation	15,000	15,000	15,000	15,000	60,000
Total facility- and general-operations-level costs	$36,500	$36,500	$36,500	$36,500	$146,000
Total overhead	$51,500	$43,000	$48,500	$57,000	$200,000
Less depreciation	15,000	15,000	15,000	15,000	60,000
Total cash disbursements for overhead	$36,500	$28,000	$33,500	$42,000	$140,000

spection, or design engineering as *fixed costs* since they do not vary with the number of units produced. The ABB approach, however, recognizes that these costs are really *variable* if the budget analyst is careful to identify the appropriate cost driver with which each of these costs varies.

Revision of Manufacturing Overhead Budget

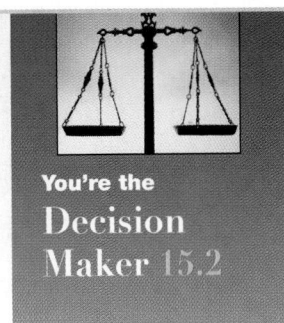

You're the **Decision Maker 15.2**

Suppose it is September 15, 20x1, and the production plan has been revised for the fourth quarter so that 24,000 units will be manufactured. The fourth quarter production runs will be 600 units each. Moreover, three new design styles will be commissioned instead of two.

a. Revise the *fourth quarter* manufacturing overhead budget to reflect the changed production plan.

b. Suppose a special adjustment will need to be made on the cutting machine at the midpoint of each production run at a cost of $150. Where will this cost appear in the overhead budget?

(Solutions begin on page 630.)

Selling, General, and Administrative (SG&A) Expense Budget

selling, general, and administrative (SG&A) expense budget *shows the planned amounts of expenditures for selling, general, and administrative expenses during a budget period*

The **selling, general, and administrative (SG&A) expense budget** shows the planned amounts of expenditures for selling, general, and administrative expenses during the budget period. Collegiate Apparel Company's selling, general, and administrative expense budget is displayed in schedule 6. This budget lists the expenses of administering the firm and selling its product.

Activity-based budgeting and the cost hierarchy. Sales commissions and freight-out (i.e., shipping) are unit-level expenses. The cost driver for these unit-level expenses is the number of units *sold* (not the number of units *produced*). Licensing fees paid to universities for permission to use their names and logos on Collegiate Apparel's T-shirts are customer-level costs. Each university typically charges a licensing fee, which is fixed within broad ranges of unit sales. As a small company, however, Collegiate generally pays the minimum fee at each university, since it sells a relatively small number of shirts at each college. Since Collegiate plans to sell to the same colleges during each quarter of 20x1, the licensing fees are the same each quarter. Collegiate sells its products to university bookstores.

The remainder of Collegiate Apparel's selling, general, and administrative expenses are incurred at the facility or general-operations level.

Schedule 6

COLLEGIATE APPAREL COMPANY
Selling, General, and Administrative Expense Budget
For the Year Ending December 31, 20x1

	Quarter				
	1st	**2nd**	**3rd**	**4th**	**Year**
Unit-level expenses					
Units	*15,000*	*5,000*	*10,000*	*20,000*	*50,000*
Sales commissions	$ 9,000	$ 3,000	$ 6,000	$12,000	$30,000
Freight-out	6,000	2,000	4,000	8,000	20,000
Total unit-level expenses	$15,000	$ 5,000	$10,000	$20,000	$50,000
Customer-level expenses					
Licensing fees for use of universities' names and logos	$ 1,500	$ 1,500	$ 1,500	$ 1,500	$ 6,000
Total customer-level expenses	$ 1,500	$ 1,500	$ 1,500	$ 1,500	$ 6,000
Facility- and general-operations-level expenses					
Sales salaries	$ 2,000	$ 2,000	$ 2,000	$ 2,000	$ 8,000
Advertising	250	250	250	250	1,000
Clerical wages	2,500	2,500	2,500	2,500	10,000
Total facility- and general-operations-level expenses	$ 4,750	$ 4,750	$ 4,750	$ 4,750	$19,000
Total expenses	$21,250	$11,250	$16,250	$26,250	$75,000

Cash Receipts Budget

cash receipts budget *details the expected cash collections during a budget period*

The **cash receipts budget** details the expected cash collections during a budget period. Collegiate Apparel Company's cash receipts budget is displayed in schedule 7. The firm collects 80 percent of its billings during the same quarter in which the sale is made and another 18 percent in the following quarter. Two percent of each quarter's sales are expected to be uncollectible accounts.

How to budget cash receipts. To understand how the cash receipts budget is prepared, let's focus again on the second quarter column, which is shaded. The $60,000 of

Schedule 7

COLLEGIATE APPAREL COMPANY
Cash Receipts Budget
For the Year Ending December 31, 20x1

	Quarter				
	1st	**2nd**	**3rd**	**4th**	**Year**
Sales revenue (from schedule 1)	$180,000	$60,000	$120,000	$240,000	$600,000
Collections in quarter of sale (80% of revenue)	$144,000	$48,000	$ 96,000	$192,000	$480,000
Collections in quarter following sale (18% of prior quarter's revenue)*	43,200†	32,400	10,800	21,600	108,000
Total cash receipts	$187,200	$80,400	$106,800	$213,600	$588,000

*Two percent of each quarter's sales are expected to be uncollectible, as follows:

	Quarter				
	1st	**2nd**	**3rd**	**4th**	**Year**
Uncollectible accounts	$3,600	$1,200	$2,400	$4,800	$12,000

†The revenue in the prior quarter (i.e., the 4th quarter of 20x0) is assumed to be $240,000. Therefore, the $43,200 is 18% × $240,000.

total revenue comes directly from schedule 1, the sales budget (second column, last row). Since most of Collegiate Apparel Company's sales are on account, not all of the second quarter's revenue will be collected during the second quarter. The cash that the firm will collect during the second quarter includes two components, as depicted in the following diagram.

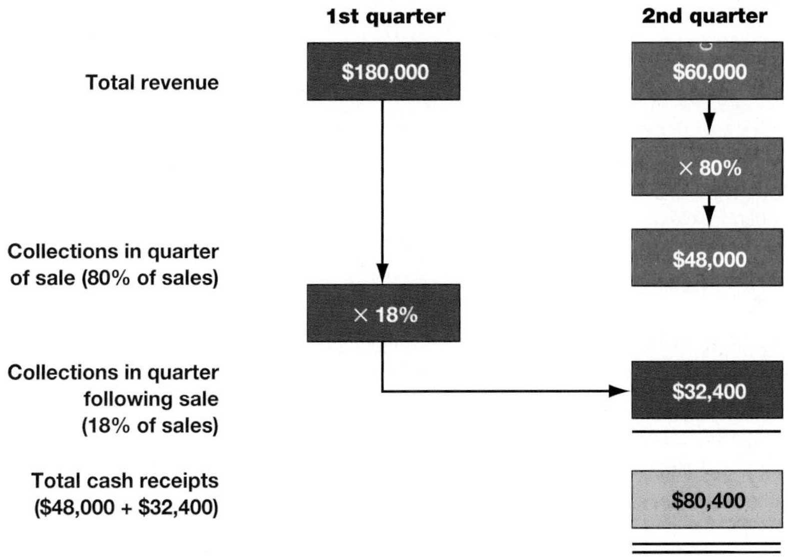

The second quarter's total cash receipts are the sum of $48,000 (which relates to second quarter sales) and $32,400 (which relates to first quarter sales).

One final point to notice is that 2 percent of each quarter's sales are not expected to be collected. Thus, the $1,200 of second quarter uncollectible accounts amounts to 2 percent of the second quarter's revenue (2% × $60,000).

Cash Disbursements Budget

cash disbursement budget *details the expected cash payments during a budget period*

The **cash disbursements budget** details the expected cash payments during a budget period. Schedule 8 displays Collegiate Apparel Company's cash disbursements budget. The shaded top portion shows the schedule of cash payments for raw material purchases, which are made on account. The company pays for 60 percent of its purchases on account during the quarter in which the purchase is made. The remaining 40 percent of each quarter's purchases are paid for during the quarter following the purchase.

The unshaded portion of schedule 8 shows all of the company's direct-labor, manufacturing overhead, and selling, general, and administrative expenditures.

Schedule 8

COLLEGIATE APPAREL COMPANY
Cash Disbursement Budget
For the Year Ending December 31, 20x1

	Quarter				
	1st	**2nd**	**3rd**	**4th**	**Year**
Cost of raw material purchases (from schedule 3)	$ 39,450	$18,150	$ 35,550	$ 56,850	$150,000
Cash payments for purchases made during the quarter (60% of current quarter's purchases)	$ 23,670	$10,890	$ 21,330	$ 34,110	$ 90,000
Cash payments for prior quarter's purchases (40% of prior quarter's purchases)	22,740*	15,780	7,260	14,220	60,000
Total cash payments for direct-material purchases	$ 46,410	$26,670	$ 28,590	$ 48,330	$150,000
Other cash disbursements:					
Direct labor (schedule 4)	$ 28,000	$11,000	$ 22,000	$ 39,000	$100,000
Indirect material (schedule 5)	3,500	1,375	2,750	4,875	12,500
Electricity (schedule 5)	2,100	825	1,650	2,925	7,500
Setup (schedule 5)	2,800	1,100	2,200	3,900	10,000
Purchasing and material handling (schedule 5)	3,360	1,320	2,640	4,680	12,000
Inspection (schedule 5)	2,240	880	1,760	3,120	8,000
Design (schedule 5)	1,000	1,000	1,000	1,000	4,000
Supervisory salaries (schedule 5)	14,000	14,000	14,000	14,000	56,000
Insurance and property taxes (schedule 5)	2,400	2,400	2,400	2,400	9,600
Maintenance (schedule 5)	2,600	2,600	2,600	2,600	10,400
Utilities (schedule 5)	2,500	2,500	2,500	2,500	10,000
Sales commissions (schedule 6)	9,000	3,000	6,000	12,000	30,000
Freight-out (schedule 6)	6,000	2,000	4,000	8,000	20,000
Licensing fees (schedule 6)	1,500	1,500	1,500	1,500	6,000
Sales salaries (schedule 6)	2,000	2,000	2,000	2,000	8,000
Advertising (schedule 6)	250	250	250	250	1,000
Clerical wages (schedule 6)	2,500	2,500	2,500	2,500	10,000
Total of other cash disbursements	$ 85,750	$50,250	$ 71,750	$107,250	$315,000
Total cash disbursements	$132,160	$76,920	$100,340	$155,580	$465,000

*40% of the purchases in the 4th quarter of the prior year, 20x0, which is assumed to be $56,850.

How to budget cash disbursements. Collegiate Apparel Company purchases raw material, direct labor, and various services. The raw material purchases are made on account, which means payment is not made in cash at the time of the purchase. The shaded top portion of schedule 8 shows the purchases on account. Let's focus on the second quarter column. The second quarter's raw material purchases on account amount to $18,150. Does the company pay for all of the $18,150 purchases on account during the same quarter? No, it does not. As the following diagram shows, the second quarter's actual cash payment for purchases made on account includes two components.

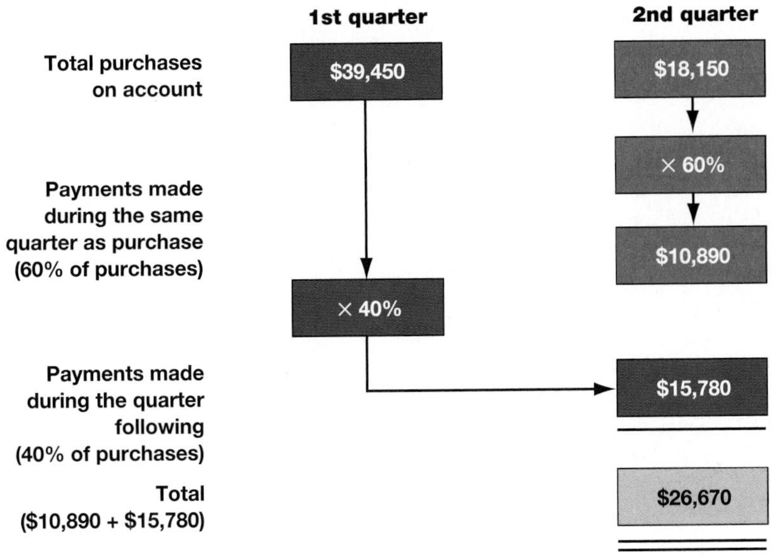

The second quarter's total cash payments *for purchases made on account* are the sum of $10,890 (which relates to second quarter purchases on account) and $15,780 (which relates to first quarter purchases on account).

We are not finished with the second quarter's cash disbursements yet, because Collegiate Apparel Company *also pays for some of its purchases in cash at the time of purchase.* These cash expenditures are detailed in the unshaded lower portion of schedule 8. The amounts are drawn from schedules 5 and 6, which detail expenditures for manufacturing overhead and selling, general, and administrative expenses, respectively. For example, schedule 5 lists $28,000 for cash expenditures on manufacturing overhead costs in the second quarter, and schedule 6 lists $11,250 for selling, general, and administrative expenditures.

Finally, the last row in the cash disbursements budget (schedule 8) shows the total cash disbursements during each quarter. Thus, the $76,920 total payment in the second quarter is the sum of $26,670 (for raw material purchases on account) and $50,250 for other purchases made in cash.

Cash Budget: Combining Receipts and Disbursements

The **cash budget** details the expected cash receipts and disbursements during a budget period. Collegiate Apparel's completed cash budget is displayed in schedule 9. The shaded top portion pulls together the cash receipts and cash disbursements detailed in schedules 7 and 8. The lower portion of schedule 9 discloses the company's plans to take out a short-term bank loan on January 2, 20x1, for the purpose of building an addition on to its production facility. The pattern of construction payments reflects high outlays early in the year as the major construction takes place. The high payment in the fourth quarter is due to the costs of reconfiguring the production line after the addition is finished. The company will repay the loan (with interest) in four installments on the last day of each quarter in 20x1. The funds for repayment will come from excess cash generated from operations during 20x1.

cash budget *details the expected cash receipts and disbursements during a budget period*

Also shown in schedule 9 are the interest payments on the short-term bank loan.

Schedule 9

COLLEGIATE APPAREL COMPANY
Cash Budget
For the Year Ending December 31, 20x1

	Quarter				
	1st	**2nd**	**3rd**	**4th**	**Year**
Cash receipts (from schedule 7)	$ 187,200	$ 80,400	$ 106,800	$ 213,600	$ 588,000
Less cash disbursements (from schedule 8)	(132,160)	(76,920)	(100,340)	(155,580)	(465,000)
Change in cash balance during quarter due to operations	$ 55,040	$ 3,480	$ 6,460	$ 58,020	$ 123,000
Proceeds from bank loan (1/2/x1)	100,000				100,000
Payments for construction of plant addition	(45,000)	(15,000)	(5,000)	(35,000)	(100,000)
Repayment of principal on bank loan (at the end of each quarter)	(25,000)	(25,000)	(25,000)	(25,000)	(100,000)
Interest on bank loan (at 10% per year)*	(2,500)	(1,875)	(1,250)	(625)	(6,250)
Change in cash balance during the period	$ 82,540	$(38,395)	$ (24,790)	$ (2,605)	$ 16,750
Cash balance, beginning of period	10,000	92,540	54,145	29,355	10,000
Cash balance, end of period	$ 92,540	$ 54,145	$ 29,355	$ 26,750	$ 26,750

*Interest computations:

Quarter	Unpaid Principal During the Quarter	Annual Interest Rate	Portion of Year	Interest Payment†
1st	$100,000	10%	1/4	$2,500‡
2nd	75,000	10	1/4	1,875
3rd	50,000	10	1/4	1,250
4th	25,000	10	1/4	625

†Unpaid principal × Annual interest rate × 1/4

‡$100,000 × .10 × 1/4 = $2,500

Budgeted Schedule of Cost of Goods Manufactured and Sold

budgeted schedule of cost of goods manufactured and sold *details the direct-material, direct-labor, and manufacturing overhead costs to be incurred and shows the cost of the goods to be sold during a budget period*

The **budgeted schedule of cost of goods manufactured and sold** details the direct-material, direct-labor, and manufacturing overhead costs to be incurred and shows the cost of the goods to be sold during a budget period. Schedule 10 shows Collegiate Apparel's budgeted schedule of cost of goods manufactured and sold. The following Excel spreadsheet shows how the cost of the beginning and ending inventories of finished goods in schedule 10 are determined. From schedule 2, we see that the expected beginning and ending inventories of finished goods for 20x1 consist of 1,500 units. The absorption manufacturing cost for one unit of product is $9. The direct-material cost per unit is $3 (schedule 3), and the unit direct-labor cost is $2 (schedule 4). Recall that the *absorption* cost includes the direct-materials and direct-labor costs and an allocation of *all* manufacturing overhead costs (i.e., overhead at the unit, batch, product, and facility or general operations levels). The overhead cost information comes from schedule 5.

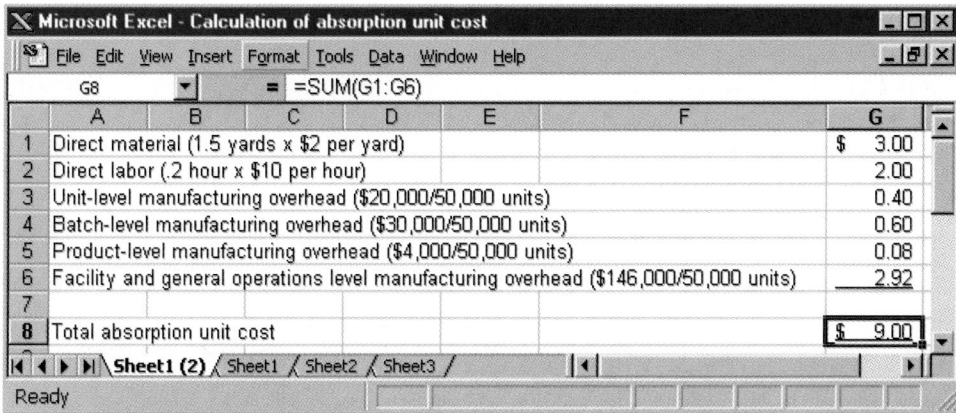

Microsoft Excel - Calculation of absorption unit cost

G8 = =SUM(G1:G6)

	A–F	G
1	Direct material (1.5 yards x $2 per yard)	$ 3.00
2	Direct labor (.2 hour x $10 per hour)	2.00
3	Unit-level manufacturing overhead ($20,000/50,000 units)	0.40
4	Batch-level manufacturing overhead ($30,000/50,000 units)	0.60
5	Product-level manufacturing overhead ($4,000/50,000 units)	0.08
6	Facility and general operations level manufacturing overhead ($146,000/50,000 units)	2.92
7		
8	Total absorption unit cost	$ 9.00

Sheet1 (2) / Sheet1 / Sheet2 / Sheet3

Ready

Schedule 10

COLLEGIATE APPAREL COMPANY
Budgeted Schedule of Cost of Goods Manufactured and Sold
For the Year Ending December 31, 20x1

Direct material (see schedule 3 for details):		
Raw-material inventory, January 1	$ 4,200*	
Add: Purchases of raw material	150,000	
Raw material available from use	$154,200	
Deduct: Raw-material inventory, December 31	4,200*	
Direct material used		$150,000
Direct labor (see schedule 4 for details)		100,000
Manufacturing overhead (see schedule 5 for details)		200,000
Total manufacturing costs		$450,000
Add: Work-in-process inventory, January 1		0†
Subtotal		$450,000
Deduct: Work-in-process inventory, December 31		0†
Cost of goods manufactured		$450,000
Add: Finished-goods inventory, January 1		13,500‡
Cost of goods available for sale		$463,500
Deduct: Finished-goods inventory, December 31		13,500‡
Cost of goods sold		$450,000

*From Schedule 3: 2,100 yards × $2 per yard.

†The company's production cycle is short enough that it has no work-in-process inventory at any time.

‡From Schedule 2: 1,500 units × $9 per unit, which is the absorption manufacturing cost per unit.

Budgeted Income Statement

The **budgeted income statement** shows the expected revenue and expenses for a budget period, assuming that planned operations are carried out. Collegiate Apparel Company's budgeted income statement is displayed in schedule 11.

budgeted income statement *shows the expected revenue and expenses for a budget period, assuming that planned operations are carried out*

Schedule 11

COLLEGIATE APPAREL COMPANY
Budgeted Income Statement
For the Year Ending December 31, 20x1

Sales revenue (from schedule 1)		$600,000
Less: Cost of goods sold (from schedule 10)		450,000
Gross margin		$150,000
Other expenses:		
Selling, general, and administrative expenses (from schedule 6)	$75,000	
Uncollectible accounts expense (from schedule 7: 2% × $600,000)*	12,000	
Interest expense (from schedule 9)*	6,250	
Total other expenses		93,250
Net income		$ 56,750

*Usually these two expenses are included in selling, general, and administrative expenses. They are listed separately in our illustration because they were determined after the selling, general, and administrative expense budget had already been explained.

Budgeted Balance Sheet

budgeted balance sheet *shows the expected end-of-period balances for the company's assets, liabilities, and owners' equity*

The **budgeted balance sheet** shows the expected end-of-period balances for the company's assets, liabilities, and owners' equity, assuming that planned operations are carried out. Collegiate Apparel Company's budgeted balance sheet for December 31, 20x1, is displayed in schedule 12. To construct this budgeted balance sheet, we start with the firm's balance sheet projected for the *beginning* of the budget year (Exhibit 15–3) and adjust each account balance for the changes expected during 20x1. These expected changes are reflected in the various 20x1 budget schedules.

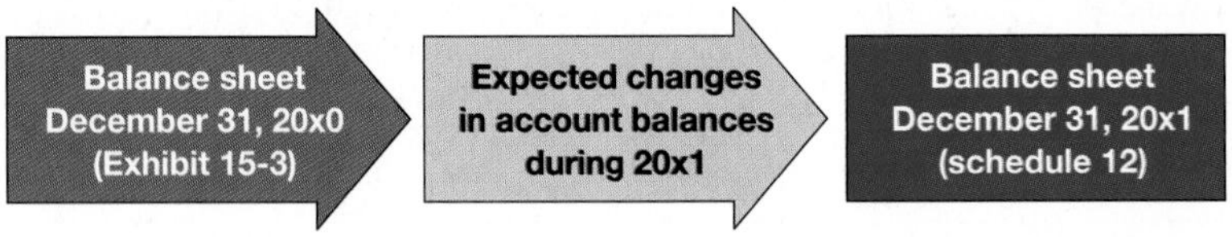

Explanations for the account balances on the budgeted balance sheet for December 31, 20x1, are given in the second half of schedule 12. Examine these explanations carefully. Notice how the budgeted balance sheet pulls together information from most of the schedules constituting the master budget.

Schedule 12

COLLEGIATE APPAREL COMPANY
Budgeted Balance Sheet
As of December 31, 20x1

Assets

Current assets:		
Cash (from schedule 9)		$ 26,750
Accounts receivable (net of allowance for uncollectible accounts)		43,200*
Inventory		
Raw material (from schedule 10)	$ 4,200	
Finished goods (from schedule 10)	13,500	
Supplies	2,000	
Total inventory		19,700
Total current assets		$ 89,650
Long-lived assets:		
Building	$ 500,000 †	
Equipment	320,000	
Less accumulated depreciation	(300,000)‡	
Building and equipment, net of accumulated depreciation		520,000
Total assets		$609,650

Schedule 12 (continued)

Liabilities and Owners' Equity

Current liabilities:	
Accounts payable	$ 22,740§
Total current liabilities	$ 22,740
Long-term liabilities:	
Note payable (noninterest bearing; due on December 31, 20x3)	200,000
Total liabilities	$222,740
Owner's equity	386,910#
Total liabilities and owner's equity	$609,650

Explanatory notes for schedule 12:

*From schedule 7: 4th quarter sales of $240,000 times 18% amounts to $43,200.

†Balance in the building account on the December 31, 20x0, balance sheet, plus the $100,000 cost of the building construction project in 20x1 (schedule 9).

‡Balance in the Accumulated Depreciation account on the December 31, 20x0, balance sheet, plus the $60,000 in depreciation during 20x1 (schedule 5).

§From schedule 8: 4th quarter raw material purchases of $56,850 times 40% amounts to $22,740.

#Balance in owner's equity on the December 31, 20x0, balance sheet, plus the 20x1 budgeted net income of $56,750 (schedule 11).

Assumptions and Predictions Underlying the Master Budget

A master budget is based on many assumptions and estimates of unknown parameters. What are some of the assumptions and estimates used in Collegiate Apparel Company's master budget? The professional sales budget was built on an assumption about the seasonal nature of demand for college T-shirts. The direct-material budget

Exhibit 15–3

Balance Sheet as of December 31, 20x0

COLLEGIATE APPAREL COMPANY
Balance Sheet
December 31, 20x0

Assets

Current assets:		
Cash		$ 10,000
Accounts receivable (net of allowance for uncollectible accounts)		43,200
Inventory		
Raw material	$ 4,200	
Finished goods	13,500	
Supplies	2,000	
Total inventory		19,700
Total current assets		$ 72,900
Long-lived assets:		
Building	$ 400,000	
Equipment	320,000	
Less accumulated depreciation	(240,000)	
Building and equipment, net of accumulated depreciation)		480,000
Total assets		$552,900

Liabilities and Owners' Equity

Current liabilities:	
Accounts payable	$ 22,740
Total current liabilities	$ 22,740
Long-term liabilities:	
Note payable (noninterest bearing; due on December 31, 20x3)	200,000
Total liabilities	$222,740
Owners' equity	330,160
Total liabilities and owner's equity	$552,900

uses an estimate of the direct-material price, $2 per yard, and the quantity of material required per T-shirt, 1.5 yards. An estimate of the direct labor required to make a T-shirt was used in the direct-labor budget.

These are only a few of the many assumptions and estimates used in Collegiate's master budget. Some of these estimates are much more likely to be accurate than others. For example, the amount of material required to make a T-shirt is not likely to differ from past experience unless the type of material or production process is changed. In contrast, estimates such as the price of material, the cost of utilities, and sales demand are much more difficult to predict.

Financial Planning Models

financial planning model *is a set of mathematical relationships that expresses the interactions among the various operational, financial, and environmental events that determine the overall results of an organization's activities*

Managers must make assumptions and predictions in preparing budgets because organizations operate in a world of uncertainty. One way to cope with that uncertainty is to supplement the budgeting process with a *financial planning model.* A **financial planning model** is a set of mathematical relationships that express the interactions among the various operational, financial, and environmental events that determine the overall results of an organization's activities. A financial planning model is a mathematical expression of all the relationships expressed in the flowchart of Exhibit 15–1.

To illustrate this concept, focus on the following equation, which was used to budget uncollectible accounts expense in schedule 7.

$$\begin{pmatrix}\text{Uncollectible}\\ \text{accounts expense}\end{pmatrix} = .02\ (\text{Sales revenue})$$

Suppose that Collegiate Apparel's management is uncertain about this 2 percent estimate. A financial planning model might include the following equation instead.

$$\begin{pmatrix}\text{Uncollectible}\\ \text{accounts expense}\end{pmatrix} = p\ (\text{Sales revenue})$$

where

$$0 \leq p \leq 1.0$$

The budget staff can run the financial planning model as many times as desired on a computer, using a different value for p each time. Perhaps the following values would be tried: .04, .045, .05, .055, and .06. Now management can answer the question, What if 4 percent of sales prove to be uncollectible? In a fully developed financial planning model, the key estimates and assumptions are expressed as general mathematical relationships. Then the model is run on a computer many times to determine the impact of different combinations of these unknown variables. "What-if" questions can be answered about unknown variables such as inflation, interest rates, the value of the dollar, demand, competitors' actions, production efficiency, union demands in forthcoming wage negotiations, and a host of other factors. The widespread availability of personal computers and electronic spreadsheet software has made financial planning models a more and more common management tool.

Chapter 12 includes a more thorough discussion of financial planning models.

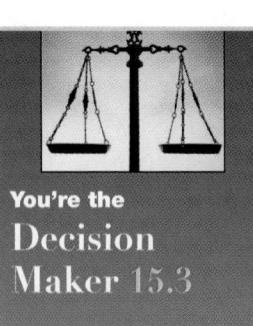

You're the Decision Maker 15.3

Financial Planning Model: Uncollectible Accounts Expense

Refer again to Collegiate's cash receipts budget in schedule 7. Apply the financial planning concept to perform sensitivity analysis on the implications of different estimates of the rate of uncollectible accounts expense.

a. Prepare a table with a row for each of the following estimates of the rate of uncollectible accounts: 1, 2, 3, and 4 percent. Also include a row for the budgeted sales revenue. Your table should have five columns, one for each quarter and one for the entire year. The entries in the table will be the budgeted uncollectible accounts expense. (If you have access to spreadsheet software, prepare the table as a spreadsheet.)

b. How could this financial planning model help Collegiate Apparel to manage its uncollectible accounts expense?

(Solutions begin on page 630.)

Responsibility for Budget Administration

LO 4 Describe and evaluate a typical organization's process of budget administration.

The procedures that small organizations use to gather information and construct a master budget are usually informal. At Collegiate Apparel Company, for example, the firm's owner, Tim Williams, coordinates the budgeting process. In contrast, larger organizations usually designate a **budget director** or **chief budget officer** who specifies the process by which budget data are gathered, collects the information, and prepares the master budget. This is often the organization's controller. To communicate budget procedures and deadlines to employees throughout the organization, the budget director often develops and disseminates a **budget manual.** The budget manual indicates who is responsible for providing various types of information, when the information is required, and what form the information is to take. For example, the budget manual for a large manufacturing firm might specify that each regional sales director is to send an estimate of the following year's sales, by product line, to the budget director by September 1. The budget manual also states who should receive each schedule when the master budget is complete.

A **budget committee,** consisting of key senior executives, often is appointed to advise the budget director during the preparation of the budget. The authority to give final approval to the master budget usually belongs to the board of directors, or the board of trustees in many nonprofit organizations. Usually the board has a subcommittee whose task is to examine the proposed budget carefully and recommend approval or any changes deemed necessary. By exercising its authority to make changes in the budget and grant final approval, the board of directors, or trustees, can wield considerable influence on the overall direction the organization takes.

budget director (or chief budget officer) *specifies the process by which budget data are gathered, collects the information, and prepares the master budget*

budget manual *indicates who is responsible for providing various types of budget information, when the information is required, and what form the information is to take*

budget committee *advises the budget director during the preparation of the budget*

Behavioral Implications of Budgets

LO 5 Understand the behavioral implications of budgetary slack and participative budgeting.

In perhaps no other area of management are behavioral implications more important than in budgeting. A budget affects virtually everyone in an organization: those who prepare the budget, those who use the budget to facilitate decision making, and those who are

Cost Management in Practice 15.2

E-Budgeting

E-budgeting is an increasingly popular, Web-based tool that can help streamline a company's budgeting process. The *E* in E-budgeting stands for both *electronic* and *enterprisewide.* Employees throughout an organization, at all levels and around the globe, can submit and retrieve budget-related information electronically via the World Wide Web. Among the organizations using E-budgeting is Toronto-Dominion Bank (*www.tdbank.com*). When the bank's executives were searching for a new solution capable of handling the bank's enterprisewide budgeting and planning function, they turned to the Internet. "In the past, we have compiled our business plan using hundreds of spreadsheets, and our analysts have spent a disproportionate amount of time compiling and verifying data from multiple sources," according to Toronto-Dominion's controller. "Implementing a Web-based, enterprisewide budgeting solution will help us develop business plans and allow our analysts to be proactive in monitoring quarterly results." *Source: S. Hornyak, "Budgeting Made Easy."*

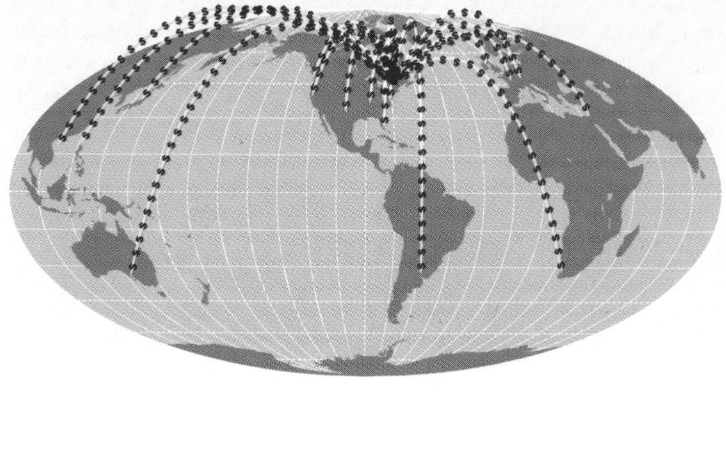

evaluated using the budget. The human reactions to the budgeting process can have considerable influence on an organization's overall effectiveness. A great deal of study has been devoted to the behavioral effects of budgets. This discussion barely scratches the surface by briefly considering two issues: budgetary slack and participative budgeting.

Budgetary Slack: Padding the Budget

The information on which a budget is based comes largely from people throughout an organization. For example, the sales forecast relies on market research and analysis by a market research staff but also incorporates the projections of sales personnel. If a territorial sales manager's performance is evaluated on the basis of whether the sales budget for the territory is exceeded, what is the incentive for the sales manager in projecting sales? The incentive is to give a conservative, or cautiously low, sales estimate. The sales manager's performance will look much better in the eyes of top management when a conservative estimate is exceeded than when an ambitious estimate is not met. At least that is the *perception* of many sales managers, and in the behavioral area, perceptions are what count most.

When a supervisor provides a departmental cost projection for budgetary purposes, there is an incentive to overestimate costs. When the actual cost incurred in the department proves to be less than the inflated cost projection, the supervisor appears to have managed in a cost-effective way.

padding the budget *means intentionally underestimating revenue or overestimating costs*

budgetary slack *is the difference between the revenue or cost projection that a person provides and a realistic estimate of the revenue or cost*

These illustrations are examples of **padding the budget,** which means intentionally underestimating revenue or overestimating costs. The difference between the revenue or cost projection that a person provides and a realistic estimate of the revenue or cost is called **budgetary slack.** For example, if a plant manager believes the annual utilities cost will be $23,000 but gives a budgetary projection of $25,000, the manager has built $2,000 of slack into the budget.

Why do people pad budgets with budgetary slack? There are three primary reasons. First, people often *perceive* that their performance will look better in their superiors' eyes if they can "beat the budget." Second, budgetary slack is often used to cope with uncertainty. A departmental supervisor might feel confident in the cost projections for 10 cost items. However, the supervisor also might believe that some unforeseen event during the budgetary period could result in unanticipated costs. For example, an unexpected machine breakdown could occur. One way to deal with that unforeseen event is to pad the budget. If nothing goes wrong, the supervisor can beat the cost budget. If some negative event does occur, the supervisor can use the budgetary slack to absorb the impact of the event and still meet the cost budget.

The third reason that people pad cost budgets is that budgetary cost projections are often cut in the resource-allocation process. Thus, a vicious circle exists. Budgetary projections are padded because they will likely be cut, and they are cut because they are likely to have been padded.

How does an organization solve the problem of budgetary slack? First, it can avoid relying on the budget as a negative evaluative tool. If a departmental supervisor is harassed by the budget director or some other top manager every time a budgetary cost projection is exceeded, the likely behavioral response will be to pad the budget. In contrast, if the supervisor is allowed some managerial discretion to exceed the budget when necessary, the tendency toward budgetary padding will decrease. Second, managers can be given incentives not only to achieve budgetary projections but also to *provide accurate projections.* This can be accomplished by asking managers to justify all or some of their projections and by rewarding managers who consistently provide accurate estimates.

participative budgeting *involves employees throughout an organization in the budgeting process*

Participative Budgeting

Most people will perform better and make greater attempts to achieve a goal if they have been consulted in setting that goal. The idea of **participative budgeting** is to involve employees throughout an organization in the budgetary process. Such participation can give employees the feeling that "this is our budget" rather than the all-too-common feeling that "this is the budget you imposed on us."

Although participative budgeting can be very effective, it can also have shortcomings. Too much participation and discussion can lead to vacillation and delay. Also, when those involved in the budgeting process disagree in significant and irreconcilable ways, the process of participation can accentuate those differences. Finally, the problem of budget padding can be severe unless incentives for accurate projections are provided.

Ethical Issues in Budgeting

A departmental or divisional budget often is the basis for evaluating a manager's performance. Actual results are compared with budgeted performance levels, and those who outperform the budget often are rewarded with promotions or salary increases. In many cases, bonuses are tied explicitly to performance relative to a budget. For example, the top-management personnel of a division might receive a bonus if divisional profit exceeds budgeted profit by a certain percentage.

Serious ethical issues can arise in situations when a budget is the basis for rewarding managers. For example, suppose a division's top-management personnel will split a bonus equal to 10 percent of the amount by which actual divisional profit exceeds the budget. This might create an incentive for the divisional budget officer, or other managers supplying data, to pad the divisional profit budget. Such padding would make the budget easier to achieve, thus increasing the chance of a bonus. Alternatively, there might be an incentive to manipulate the actual divisional results to maximize management's bonus. For example, year-end sales could be shifted between years to increase reported revenue in a particular year.

Budget personnel could have such incentives for either of two reasons: (1) they might share in the bonus or (2) they might feel pressure from the managers who would share in the bonus. Padding the budget or manipulating reported results to maximize one's personal gain or that of others is a serious ethical violation.

Zero-Base Budgeting for Discretionary Costs

Many organizations have attempted to measure discretionary costs through a budgeting method called zero-base budgeting. Numerous companies (e.g., Texas Instruments, Xerox, and Control Data) and governmental units (e.g., the State of Georgia) have implemented zero-base budgeting at one time or another. **Zero-base budgeting** initially sets the budget for virtually every activity in the organization to zero. To receive funding during the budgeting process, each activity must be justified in terms of its continued usefulness. The zero-base-budgeting approach forces management to rethink each phase of an organization's operations before allocating resources.

zero-base budgeting *initially sets the budget for virtually every activity in the organization to zero*

base budgeting *sets the initial budget for each organizational department in accordance with a base package, which includes the minimal resources required for the subunit to exist at an absolute minimal level*

base package *includes the minimal resources required for an organizational subunit to exist at an absolute minimal level*

incremental package *describes the resources needed to add various activities to the base package*

Base Budgeting

Some organizations use a base-budgeting approach without going to the extreme of zero-base budgeting. **Base-budgeting** sets the initial budget for each of the organization's departments in accordance with a **base package,** which includes the minimal resources required for the subunit to exist at an absolute minimal level. Below this level of funding, the subunit would not be a viable entity. Any increases above the base package would result from a decision to fund an **incremental package,** which describes the resources needed to add various activities to the base package. The decision to approve such an incremental budget package would have to be justified on the basis of the costs and benefits of the activities included. Base budgeting has been effective in many organizations because it forces managers to take an evaluative, questioning attitude toward each of the organization's programs.

Contemporary Trends in Budgeting and Financial Planning

LO 6 Describe contemporary trends in the budgeting process as an element of a cost-management system.

As with all aspects of the field of cost management, the area of budgeting is in transition. "When it comes to benchmarking and best practices, nothing is more in vogue than reengineering the financial planning process. 'This really is the number one topic in business right now,' " according to a partner with KPMG's World-Class Finance consulting division. "The emerging concept of financial planning is gradually replacing the traditional budgeting process, enabling controllers to become true business partners by focusing on value-added tasks."[5]

The whole concept of *cost management,* in which costs "don't just happen" but are actively managed, is key to the emerging philosophy of contemporary budgeting and financial planning. The use of activity-based costing concepts to construct a meaningful budget, coupled with the activity-based management objective of eliminating non-value-added costs, is key for improving the budgeting process.

In Collegiate Apparel's budgeting process, for example, a variety of cost drivers was recognized and costs were classified according to their level in the ABC cost hierarchy. By constructing the budget using ABC concepts, managers are better able to understand *why* costs are incurred, how to manage costs, and how to improve profitability.

Research Insight 15.2

Best Practices in Budgeting

According to research performed by The Hacket Group, an Ohio-based consulting firm, best practices in budgeting and financial planning include the following:

- Link the financial planning process to strategic planning through operational targets derived from strategic objectives.
- Integrate the forecasting process with the planning process.
- Make sure that users at all levels can retrieve and submit data electronically.
- Ensure that software and other financial modeling tools use multiple "what-if" scenarios.
- Focus budget reiterations on ways to meet operational targets not to process financials.
- Base line-item detail on materiality (substantially less detail than in the chart of accounts).

Source: I. McLemore, "Reinventing the Budget."

[5] I. McLemore, "Reinventing the Budget."

Chapter Summary

The *budget* is a key tool for planning, control, and decision making in virtually every organization. Budgeting systems are used to force planning, to facilitate communication and coordination, to allocate resources, to control profit and operations, and to evaluate performance and provide incentives. Various types of budgets are used to accomplish these objectives.

The comprehensive set of budgets that covers all phases of an organization's operations is called a "master budget." The first step in preparing a master budget is to forecast sales of the organization's services or goods. Based on the sales forecast, operational budgets are prepared to plan production of services or goods and to outline the acquisition and use of materials, labor, and other resources. Finally, a set of budgeted financial statements is prepared to show what the organization's overall financial condition will be if the organization carries out its planned operations.

Since budgets affect almost everyone in an organization, they can have significant behavioral implications. One common problem in budgeting is the tendency of people to *pad* budgets. The resulting *budgetary slack* makes the budget less useful because the padded budget does not present an accurate picture of expected revenue and expenses. Participative budgeting is the process of allowing employees throughout the organization to have a significant role in developing the budget. Participative budgeting can result in greater commitment to meet the budget by those who participated in the process.

Key Terms

For each term's definition, refer to the indicated page or turn to the glossary at the end of the text.

*Terms appear in the Appendix.

Meeting the Cost Management Challenges

1. **Why** does Collegiate Apparel need an annual budget? Specifically, what purposes would the budgeting process serve?

All organizations, including Collegiate Apparel Company, need to plan their operations. Budgeting is a crucial part of the planning process. The purposes of the budgeting process are planning, facilitating communication and coordination, allocating resources, managing financial and operational performance, and evaluating performance and providing incentives.

2. **How** could Collegiate Apparel's budget facilitate communication and coordination among the company's president, sales manager, and production supervisor?

A budget facilitates communication and coordination by making each manager throughout the organization aware of the plans made by other managers. The budgeting process pulls together the plans of each manager in the organization.

3. **What** is a master budget? What are its main components for a manufacturer, such as Collegiate Apparel?

A master budget, or financial plan, is a comprehensive set of budgets covering all phases of an organization's operations for a specified period of time. A manufacturer's master budget includes the following main components: sales budget, operational budgets (including a production budget, inventory budgets, a labor budget, an overhead budget, a selling and administrative expense budget, and a cash budget), and budgeted financial statements (including a budgeted income statement, budgeted balance sheet, and budgeted statement of cash flows).

4. **How** could Collegiate Apparel's president or a company's board of directors use the budget to influence the future direction of the firm?

A corporation's board of directors generally has final approval over the master budget. By exercising its authority to make changes in the budget and grant final approval, the board of directors can wield considerable influence on the overall direction the organization takes. Since the budget is used as a resource-allocation mechanism, the board of directors can emphasize some programs and curtail or eliminate others by allocating funds through the budgeting process.

In Collegiate Apparel's case, the company is wholly owned and managed by its president, who also has final approval over the firm's master budget.

5. **Would** participative budgeting be effective for Collegiate Apparel Company?

The idea of participative budgeting is to involve employees throughout an organization in the budgetary process. Such participation can give employees the feeling that "this is our budget," rather than the feeling that "this is the budget you imposed on us." When employees feel that they were part of the budgeting process, they are more likely to strive to achieve the budget. As in most organizations, participative budgeting would likely increase the effectiveness of Collegiate Apparel's budgeting process.

Solutions to You're the Decision Maker

15.1 Revised Production Budget for 20x1 p. 612

a. Revised budget:

	Quarter				
	1st	**2nd**	**3rd**	**4th**	**Year**
Sales in units (revised upward by 20%)	18,000	6,000	12,000	24,000	60,000
Add desired ending inventory of finished goods*	600	1,200	2,400	1,800†	1,800
Total units required	18,600	7,200	14,400	25,800	61,800
Less expected beginning inventory of finished goods	1,500	600	1,200	2,400	1,500
Units to be produced	17,100	6,600	13,200	23,400	60,300

*10 percent of the next quarter's expected sales

†10 percent of the expected sales for the 1st quarter of the next year, 20x2, which is now revised upward by 20% to 18,000 units

b. This is where the art of management comes into play. If the increase in sales is not very certain, management has a tough decision to make. One possible strategy is to increase production as indicated in the preceding table for the first quarter or two and to see whether the increased demand materializes and then cut back production if it does not. Another possibility is to produce quantities between those specified in the original and revised budgets.

15.2 Revision of Fourth Quarter Manufacturing Overhead Budget p. 615

a. Revised fourth quarter budget:

Unit-level costs	
Units	***24,000***
Indirect material	$ 6,000
Electricity	3,600
Total unit-level costs	$ 9,600
Batch-level costs	
Production runs (24,000 units ÷ 600 units)	***40***
Setup	$ 4,000
Purchasing and material handling	4,800
Inspection	3,200
Total batch-level costs	$12,000
Product-level costs	
New design styles	***3***
Design	$ 1,500
Total product-level costs	$ 1,500
Facility and general operations-level costs	
Supervisory salaries	$14,000
Insurance and property taxes	2,400
Maintenance	2,600
Utilities	2,500
Depreciation	15,000
Total facility and general-operations-level costs	$36,500
Total overhead	$59,600
Less depreciation	15,000
Total cash disbursements for overhead	$44,600

b. The special adjustment on the cutting machine will be a batch-level cost. The appropriate cost driver is production runs.

15.3 Financial Planning Model: Uncollectible Accounts Expense p. 624

a. This table shows the budgeted uncollectible accounts expense for different rates of uncollectible accounts.

Microsoft Excel - Uncollectible Accounts Expense

F5 = =+F1*A5

	A	B	C	D	E	F
1	Sales revenue	$180,000	$60,000	$120,000	$240,000	$600,000
2	0.01	1,800	600	1,200	2,400	6,000
3	0.02	3,600	1,200	2,400	4,800	12,000
4	0.03	5,400	1,800	3,600	7,200	18,000
5	0.04	7,200	2,400	4,800	9,600	24,000

b. Predictive information such as this is crucial for the management of uncollectible accounts expense. Management might decide, for example, to implement more restrictive credit and collection policies if the uncollectible accounts rate exceeds 2 percent.

Appendix to Chapter Fifteen

Inventory Management

A key decision in manufacturing, retail, and some service industry firms is how much inventory to keep on hand. Once inventory levels have been established, they become an important input to the budgeting system. Inventory decisions involve a delicate balance between three classes of costs: ordering costs, holding costs, and shortage costs. Examples of costs in each of these categories are given in Exhibit 15–4.

LO 7 Use the economic order quantity model to make inventory-ordering decisions and discuss the implications of the JIT approach for inventory management.

Economic Order Quantity

It is now 20x3 and Collegiate Apparel has expanded its production capability. Owner and president, Tim Williams, has signed a contract with a large US university to supply all its athletic T-shirts for use in its physical education program. Unlike the T-shirts in Collegiate's regular product line, which are 100 percent cotton, the athletic shirts for the contract are to be a cotton/polyester blend. The contract calls for 24,000 shirts to be delivered each year.

Collegiate Apparel's production supervisor, Brad Roaldsson, has decided to use an economic order quantity (EOQ) decision model to determine the size and frequency with which the fabric should be ordered. The **EOQ model** is a mathematical tool for determining the order quantity that minimizes the cost of ordering and holding inventory, which is called the **economic order quantity,** or **EOQ.**

EOQ model *is a mathematical tool for determining the order quantity that minimizes the cost of ordering and holding inventory*

economic order quantity (or EOQ) *is the order quantity that minimizes the cost of ordering and holding inventory*

Roaldsson has determined that Collegiate will need 1,200 bolts of cotton/polyester fabric per year to produce the shirts for the contract. Each bolt costs $110. He estimates that it costs $50 to place and receive a typical order, and that the annual cost of carrying fabric in inventory is $12 per bolt.

Tabular approach. Suppose that Roaldsson orders 150 bolts of fabric in each order placed during the year. The total annual cost of ordering and holding fabric in inventory is calculated as follows:

$$\frac{\text{Annual requirement}}{\text{Quantity per order}} = \frac{1{,}200}{150} = 8 = \text{Number of orders}$$

$$\text{Annual ordering cost} = 8 \text{ orders} \times \$50 \text{ per order} = \$400$$

Exhibit 15–4

Inventory Ordering, Holding, and Shortage Costs

Ordering costs
- Time spent in finding suppliers and expediting orders
- Clerical costs of preparing purchase orders
- Transportation costs
- Receiving costs (e.g., unloading and inspection)

Holding costs
- Costs of storage space (e.g., warehouse depreciation)
- Security
- Insurance
- Forgone interest on working capital tied up in inventory
- Deterioration, theft, spoilage, or obsolescence

Shortage costs
- Lost sales resulting in dissatisfied customers
- Loss of quantity discounts on purchases
- Disrupted production when raw materials are unavailable
  - Idle workers
  - Extra machinery setups

$$\text{Average quantity in inventory} = \frac{\text{Quantity per order}}{2} = \frac{150}{2} = 75 \text{ bolts}$$

$$\text{Annual holding cost} = \left(\begin{array}{c}\text{Average quantity}\\ \text{in inventory}\end{array}\right) \times \left(\begin{array}{c}\text{Average carrying}\\ \text{cost per bolt}\end{array}\right)$$

$$= 75 \times \$12 = \$900$$

$$\begin{array}{c}\text{Total annual cost}\\ \text{of inventory policy}\end{array} = \begin{array}{c}\text{Ordering}\\ \text{cost}\end{array} + \begin{array}{c}\text{Holding}\\ \text{cost}\end{array} = \$400 + \$900 = \$1{,}300$$

Notice that the \$1,300 cost does *not* include the purchase cost of the fabric at \$110 per bolt. We are focusing only on the costs of *ordering* and *holding* fabric inventory.

Can Roaldsson do any better than \$1,300 for the annual cost of the fabric inventory policy? Exhibit 15–5, which tabulates the inventory costs for various order quantities, indicates that Roaldsson can lower the costs of ordering and holding fabric inventory. Of the five order quantities listed, the 100-bolt order quantity yields the lowest total annual cost. Unfortunately, this tabular method for finding the least-cost order quantity is cumbersome. Moreover, it does not necessarily result in the optimal order quantity. It is possible that some order quantity other than those listed in Exhibit 15–5 is the least-cost order quantity.

Equation approach. The total annual cost of ordering and holding inventory is given by the following equation:

$$\begin{array}{c}\text{Total}\\ \text{annual}\\ \text{cost}\end{array} = \left(\frac{\text{Annual requirement}}{\text{Order quantity}}\right)\left(\begin{array}{c}\text{Cost per}\\ \text{order}\end{array}\right) + \left(\frac{\text{Order quantity}}{2}\right)\left(\begin{array}{c}\text{Annual}\\ \text{holding}\\ \text{cost per}\\ \text{unit}\end{array}\right)$$

The following formula for the least-cost order quantity, called the *economic order quantity* (or *EOQ*), has been developed using calculus:

$$\begin{array}{c}\text{Economic order}\\ \text{quantity}\end{array} = \sqrt{\frac{(2)(\text{Annual requirement})(\text{Cost per order})}{\text{Annual holding cost per unit}}}$$

Applying the EOQ formula in Collegiate Apparel's problem yields the following EOQ for fabric:

$$\text{EOQ} = \sqrt{\frac{(2)(1{,}200)(50)}{12}} = 100$$

Graphical approach. Another method for solving the EOQ problem is the graphical method, which is presented in Exhibit 15–6. Notice that the ordering-cost line slants down to the right. This indicates a decline in these costs as the order size increases and the order frequency decreases. However, as the order size increases, so does the average inventory on hand. This results in increased holding costs as indicated by the posi-

Exhibit 15–5

Tabulation of Inventory-Ordering and Holding Costs: Collegiate Apparel Company

Order size	50	80	100	120	150
Number of orders (1,200 ÷ order size)	24	15	12	10	8
Ordering costs (\$50 × number of orders)	\$1,200	\$ 750	\$ 600	\$ 500	\$ 400
Average inventory (order size ÷ 2)	25	40	50	60	75
Holding costs (\$12 × average inventory)	\$ 300	\$ 480	\$ 600	\$ 720	\$ 900
Total annual cost (ordering cost + holding cost)	\$1,500	\$1,230	\$1,200	\$1,220	\$1,300
			↑ Minimum		

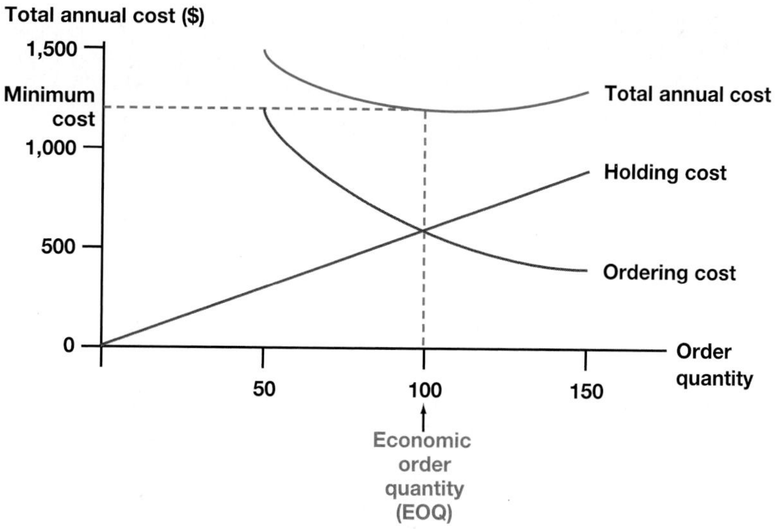

Exhibit 15–6

Graphical Solution to Economic Order Quantity Decision: Collegiate Apparel Company

tive slope of the holding-cost line. The EOQ falls at 100 units, where the best balance is struck between these two costs. Total costs are minimized at $1,200.

Timing of Orders

The EOQ model helps management decide how much each order will include. Another important decision is when to order. This decision depends on the **lead time,** which is the length of time it takes for the materials to be received after an order has been placed. Suppose that the lead time for fabric is 15 days (approximately one-half month). Collegiate Apparel's use of 1,200 bolts of fabric per year, with a constant production rate throughout the year, implies that it uses 100 bolts each month. Production manager Roaldsson should order fabric in the economic order quantity of 100 bolts when the inventory falls to 50 bolts. By the time the new order arrives one-half month later, the 50 bolts in inventory will have been used in production. Exhibit 15–7 depicts this pattern of ordering and using inventory. By placing an order early enough to avoid a stockout, management considers the potential costs of shortages.

lead time *is the time required for the material to be received after an order is placed*

Safety stock. Our example assumed that fabric usage is constant at 100 bolts per month. Suppose instead that monthly usage fluctuates between 80 and 120 bolts. Although average monthly usage still is 100 bolts, there is the potential for an excess

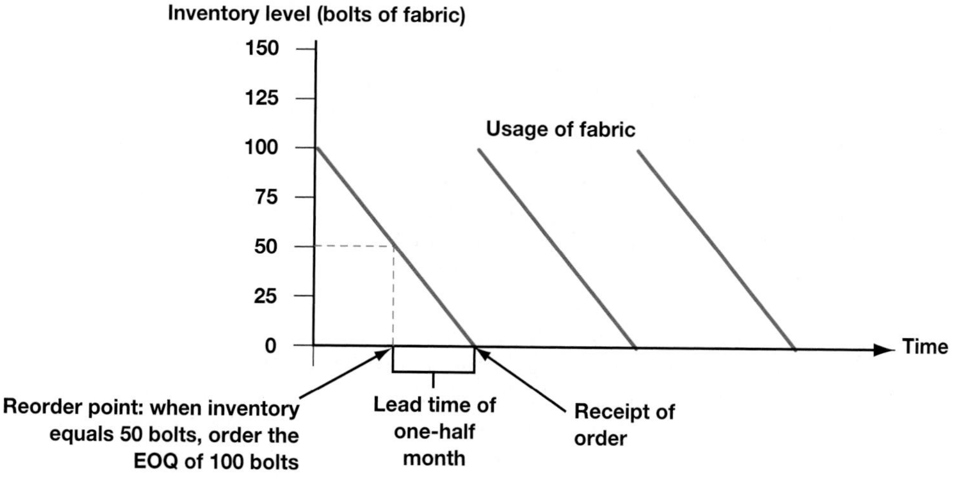

Exhibit 15–7

Ordering, Lead Time, and Usage of Inventory: Collegiate Apparel Company

Exhibit 15–8

Economic Order Quantity with Different Ordering and Holding Costs

Holding Costs per Unit	Ordering Costs per Order $50	$40	$30	$20	
$12	100	89	77	63	EOQ declines →
13	96	86	74	61	
14	93	83	72	59	
15	89	80	69	57	
	EOQ declines ↓				

Note: The annual requirement is assumed to be 1,200 units for each case in this table. This was the annual requirement for bolts of fabric in the Collegiate Apparel illustration. (Several of the EOQs in the table are rounded.)

safety stock *is the potential excess usage of material when material usage fluctuates during the lead time*

usage of 20 bolts in any particular month. This means that the usage during the half-month lead time required to receive an order fluctuates between 40 and 60 bolts, so there is the potential for excess usage of 10 bolts during the half-month lead time. In light of this uncertainty, management might wish to keep a **safety stock** of fabric equal to the potential excess usage of 10 bolts during the half-month lead time. With a safety stock of 10 bolts, the reorder point is 60 bolts. Thus, Roaldsson should order the EOQ of 100 bolts when fabric inventory falls to 60 bolts. During the half-month lead time, another 40 to 60 bolts of fabric will be consumed in production. Although a safety stock increases inventory holding costs, it minimizes the potential costs caused by shortages.

Inventory Management under JIT: Implications for EOQ

The EOQ model minimizes the total cost of ordering and holding purchased inventory. Thus, this inventory management approach seeks to balance the cost of ordering against the cost of storing inventory. Under the JIT philosophy, the goal is to keep *all* inventories as low as possible. *Any* inventory-holding costs are seen as inefficient and wasteful. Moreover, JIT purchasing minimizes ordering costs by reducing the number of vendors, negotiating long-term supply agreements, making less frequent payments, and eliminating inspections. The implication of the JIT philosophy is that inventories should be minimized by more frequent deliveries in smaller quantities. This result can be demonstrated using the EOQ formula, as shown in Exhibit 15–8. As the cost of holding inventory increases, the EOQ decreases. Moreover, as the cost of placing an order declines, the EOQ decreases.

The economics underlying the EOQ model supports the JIT viewpoint that inventory should be purchased or produced in small quantities and should be kept to the absolute minimum. However, the basic philosophies of JIT and EOQ are quite different. The EOQ approach takes the view that some inventory is necessary and the goal is to optimize the order quantity to balance the cost of ordering against the cost of holding inventory. Also implicit in this approach is the need to hold some buffer stock of inventory prior to bottleneck operations. (Review our discussion of this issue in Chapter 4.) In contrast, the JIT philosophy argues that holding costs tend to be higher than might be apparent because of the inefficiency and waste of storing inventory. Thus, inventory should be minimized, or even eliminated completely if possible. Moreover, under the JIT approach, orders typically vary in size, depending on needs. The EOQ model, in contrast, results in a constant order quantity.

The JIT approach to production and inventory management is much more than "just an inventory system." It has implications for many other issues in cost management. See Chapter 11 for additional discussion.

Review Questions

15.1 What are the relationships among organization goals, strategic plans, and a master budget for the coming period?

15.2 What is meant by the term *operational budgets?* List three operational budgets that a hospital would prepare.

15.3 Use an example to explain how a budget could be used to allocate resources in a university.

15.4 Give an example of the effect of general economic trends on sales forecasting in the airline industry.

15.5 What is the danger of relying entirely on middle-management estimates of sales, costs, and other data used in budget planning?

15.6 What is the purpose of a *budget manual?*

15.7 Describe the role of a *budget director.*

15.8 Discuss the importance of predictions and assumptions in the budgeting process.

15.9 What is the purpose of a financial planning model? Briefly describe how such a model is constructed.

15.10 Define the term *budgetary slack* and briefly describe a problem it can cause.

15.11 How can an organization help to reduce the problems caused by budgetary slack?

15.12 Explain the concept of *zero-base budgeting.*

15.13 (Appendix) Explain the differences in the basic philosophies underlying the JIT and EOQ approaches to inventory management.

Critical Analysis

15.14 Draw a flowchart similar to the one in Exhibit 15–1 for a service station. The service station provides automotive maintenance services in addition to selling gasoline and related products.

15.15 The chief executive officer of Home Workout Equipment Corporation remarked to a colleague, "I don't understand why other companies waste so much time in the budgeting process. I set our company goals, and everyone strives to meet them. What's wrong with that approach?" Comment on the executive's remarks.

15.16 Give three examples of how the City of San Diego could use a budget for planning purposes.

15.17 A budget is also a legal limitation on expenditures of governmental agencies. If governmental employees are asked about their agencies' needs for the coming fiscal period, what types of biases are they likely to incorporate in their estimates? Why?

15.18 If a company prepares budgeted income statements and balance sheets, why is a cash budget necessary?

15.19 List the steps you would go through in developing a budget to meet your college expenses.

15.20 Surveying the accounts payable records, a clerk in the controller's office noted that expenses appeared to rise significantly within a month of the close of the budget period. The organization did not have a seasonal product or service to explain this behavior. Can you suggest an explanation?

15.21 Briefly describe three issues that create special challenges for multinational firms in preparing their budgets.

15.22 Borealis Corporation has established a bonus plan for its employees. An employee receives a bonus if his or her subunit meets the cost levels specified in the annual budget plan. If the subunit's costs exceed the budget, its employees earn no bonus. What problems might arise with this bonus plan?

15.23 How would the use of a just-in-time inventory system affect a company's budget plans?

Exercises

Exercise 15.24
Estimate of Sales Revenue
(LO 2, 3)

Madison County Bank (MCB) has $30 million in commercial loans with an average interest rate of 11.5 percent. The bank also has $24 million in consumer loans with an average interest rate of 16 percent. Finally, the bank owns $4.5 million in government securities with an average rate of 9 percent.

MCB estimates that next year its commercial loan portfolio will fall to $29 million, and the interest rate will fall to 11 percent. Its consumer loans will expand to $25 million with an average interest rate of 16 percent, and its government securities portfolio will increase to $6 million with an average rate of 8 percent.

Required

Estimate MCB's revenues for the coming year.

Exercise 15.25
Estimate of Production Levels
(LO 3)

Pandora Pillow Corporation has just made its sales forecasts for the coming period. Its marketing department estimates that the company will sell 630,000 units during the coming year. In the past, management maintained inventories of finished goods at approximately two months' sales. The inventory at the start of the budget period is 48,000 units. Sales occur evenly throughout the year.

Required

Estimate the production level required for the coming year to meet these objectives.

Exercise 15.26
Estimate of Sales Revenue
(LO 2, 3)

Global

Ujvari & Zepf is a large securities dealer in Frankfurt, Germany. Last year, the company made 45,000 trades with an average commission of 220 euros. Small investors are abandoning the market, whose volume is expected to decline by 15 percent for the coming year. The firm's volume generally changes with the market. However, in addition to market factors, the firm expects an additional 10 percent decline in the number of trades due to unfavorable publicity.

Offsetting these factors is the observation that the average commission per trade is likely to increase by 20 percent because trades are expected to be large in the coming year.

Required

Estimate Ujvari & Zepf's commission revenue for the coming year. (Remember to express your answer in terms of euros.*)

Exercise 15.27
City or State Budget; Use of Internet
(LO 1, 2)

Global Internet

Choose a city or state in the United States (or a Canadian city or province), and use the Internet to explore the annual budget of the governmental unit you selected. For example, you could check out the budget for Los Angeles at *www.losangeles.com* or the Canadian regional budget at *www.rmoc.on.ca/finance/*. Alternatively, take a look at the US federal budget at *www.fms.treas.gov/annualreport/index.html*.

Required

List three items in the budget that you found surprising or particularly interesting, and explain why.

Exercise 15.28
Estimate of Production and Materials Requirements
(LO 3)

Plasto Tubing, Inc., makes a special line of plastic tubing items. During each of the next two years, it expects to sell 320,000 units. The beginning finished-goods inventory is 80,000 units. However, the target ending finished-goods inventory for each year is 40,000 units.

Each unit requires 5 feet of plastic tubing. At the beginning of the year, 200,000 feet of plastic tubing are in inventory. Management has set a target to have tubing materials on hand equal to three months of production requirements. Sales and production occur evenly throughout the year.

Required

Compute the total targeted production of the finished product for the coming year. Compute the required purchases of tubing materials for the coming year. (Note that production in the following year should be 320,000 units of finished product.)

Exercise 15.29
Estimate of Purchases and Cash Disbursements
(LO 3)

Interlaken Products' management wishes to purchase goods in one month for sale in the next. On January 31, the company has 8,000 digital tape players in stock, although sales for the next month (February) are estimated to total 8,600 players. Sales for March are expected to equal 7,000 players, and April sales are expected to total 7,400 players.

Tape players are purchased at a wholesale price of $290. The supplier has a financing arrangement by which Interlaken pays 60 percent of the purchase price in the month when the players are delivered and 40 percent in the following month. Interlaken purchased 10,000 players in January.

Required

a. Estimate purchases (in units) for February and March.

b. Estimate the cash required in February and March to pay for the company's first-quarter purchases.

Exercise 15.30
Impact of Major Unforeseen Events on the Airlines' Budgeting Processes
(LO 1, 2)

Team

Read these two articles: M.Mandel, P. Coy, and W. Symonds, "Rethinking the Economy," *Business Week*, October 1, 2001; and M. Arndt and L. Woellert, "What Kind of Rescue: Cash Won't Solve Air Carriers' Long-Term Woes," *Business Week,* October 1, 2001. These articles discuss the devastating impact of the terrorist attacks of September 11, 2001, on the US economy and the airlines in particular.

Required

As a group, discuss how an unforeseen event such as the September 11 attacks would affect the budgeting process of the airlines and the entertainment and travel industries.

Exercise 15.31
Estimate of Purchases and Cash Disbursements
(LO 3)

Special Times, Inc., buys plain mylar balloons and prints different designs on them for various occasions. It imports the balloons from Taiwan, so at all times it keeps on hand a stock equal to the balloons needed for two

*The Euro has been introduced in most European markets, and most day-to-day business will be conducted in euros after February 2002. On the day this exercise was written, the euro was equivalent in value to .8981 US dollars.

months' sales. The balloons cost $ .70 each and must be paid for in cash. The company has 14,000 balloons in stock. Sales estimates, based on contracts received, are as follows for the next six months:

Spreadsheet

June	6,200
July	8,900
August	6,600
September	7,100
October	4,800
November	3,600

Required

a. Estimate purchases (in units) for June, July, and August.

b. Estimate the cash required to make purchases in June, July, and August.

Exercise 15.32
Estimate of Cash Collections
(LO 3)

West Side Produce Company is preparing its cash budget for July. The following information is available concerning its accounts receivable:

Estimated credit sales for July	$380,000
Actual credit sales for June	250,000
Estimated collections in July for credit sales in July	25%
Estimated collections in July for credit sales in June	70%
Estimated collections in July for credit sales prior to June	$ 29,000
Estimated write-offs in July for uncollectible credit sales	16,000
Estimated provision for bad debts in July for credit sales in July	14,000

Required

What are the estimated cash receipts from accounts receivable collections in July?

[CPA adapted]

Exercise 15.33
Use of Budgets for Financial Planning
(LO 2, 3)

Serendipity Sound, Inc., is a large retailer of stereo equipment. The controller is about to prepare the budget for the first quarter of 20x1. Past experience has indicated that 75 percent of the store's sales are cash sales. The collection experience for the sales on account is as follows:

80 percent during month of sale
15 percent during month following sale
5 percent uncollectible

The total sales for December 20x0 are expected to be $190,000. The controller believes that sales in January 20x1 could range from $100,000 to $160,000.

Required

a. Demonstrate how financial planning can be used to project cash receipts in January 20x1 for three different levels of January sales. Use the following columnar format.

	Total Sales in January 20x1		
	$100,000	**$130,000**	**$160,000**
Cash receipts in January 20x1			
From December sales on account	$	$	$
From January cash sales			
From January sales on account			
Total cash receipts	$	$	$

b. How could the controller of Serendipity Sound, Inc., use this financial planning approach to help in planning operations for January?

Exercise 15.34
Estimate of Cash Receipts
(LO 3)

Bride to Be specializes in custom wedding attire. The average price of each of Bride's wedding ensembles is $3,200. For each wedding, Bride to Be receives a 20 percent deposit two months before the wedding, 50 percent the month before, and the remainder on the day the goods are delivered. Based on information at hand, Bride to Be expects to prepare outfits for the following number of weddings during the coming months:

January	5
February	3
March	2
April	4
May	5
June	11

Required

a. What are the expected revenues for Bride to Be for each month, January through June? Revenues are recorded in the month of the wedding.

b. What are the expected cash receipts for each month, January through April?

Exercise 15.35
Estimate of Cash Receipts
(LO 3)

Pool Pro, Inc., manages neighborhood pools in Oceanside. The company attempts to make service calls at least once a month to all homes that subscribe to its service. More frequent calls are made during the summer. The number of subscribers also varies with the season. The number of subscribers and the average number of calls to each subscriber for the months of interest follow:

	Subscribers	Service Calls
March	100	0.5
April	120	1.0
May	260	1.8
June	300	2.2
July	300	2.0
August	280	1.7

The average price charged for a service call is $50. Of the service calls, 20 percent are paid in the month the service is rendered, 60 percent in the month after the service is rendered, and 18 percent in the second month after. The remaining 2 percent is uncollectible.

Required

What are Pool Pro's expected cash receipts for May, June, July, and August?

Exercise 15.36
Preparation of Budgeted Financial Statements
(LO 2, 3)

Refer to the data in the preceding exercise. Pool Pro estimates that the number of subscribers in September should fall 10 percent below August levels, and the number of service calls should decrease by an estimated 20 percent. The following information is available for costs incurred in August. All costs except depreciation are paid in cash.

Service costs	
Variable costs	$ 4,720
Maintenance and repair	4,200
Depreciation (fixed)	2,200
Total	$11,120
Marketing and administrative costs:	
Marketing (variable)	$ 2,500
Administrative (fixed)	2,300
Total	$ 4,800
Total costs	$15,920

Variable cash and marketing costs change with volume. Fixed depreciation will remain the same, but fixed administrative costs will increase by 5 percent beginning September 1. Maintenance and repair are provided by contract, which calls for a 1 percent increase in September.

Required

Prepare a budgeted income statement for September.

Exercise 15.37
EOQ (Appendix)
(LO 7)

a. The following information relates to Mercer Industries:

Units required per year	240,000
Cost of placing an order	$300
Unit carrying cost per year	$400

Assuming that the units will be required evenly throughout the year, what is the EOQ?

b. Blairstown Company requires 160,000 units of product Q for the year. The units will be required evenly throughout the year. The cost to place an order is $54, and the cost to carry a unit in inventory for the year is $12. What is the EOQ?

[CPA adapted]

Exercise 15.38
Impact of Quantity Discounts on Order Quantity (Appendix)
(LO 7)

Aurora Company uses 810 tankloads a year of a specific input material. The tankloads are delivered by rail to a siding on the company property. The supplier is offering a special discount for buyers of large quantities. The schedule is as follows:

Quantity Ordered (tankloads)	Percentage Discount
1–19	0
20–79	2
80–149	5
150 and more	6

Ordering costs amount to $500, and carrying costs are $450 per tankload and are not affected by the discounts. Each tankload costs $1,500.

Required

Compute the optimal order quantity. (Round to the nearest whole number.)

Exercise 15.39
Impact of Constraints on Optimal Order (Appendix)
(LO 7)

Considering the situation in the preceding exercise, suppose that the maximum storage capacity for the company is 50 tankloads.

Required

What is the optimal order? Demonstrate why.

Problems

Problem 15.40
Budgeted Purchases and Cash Flows
(LO 3)

Delancey Corporation seeks your assistance in developing cash and other budget information for May, June, and July. On April 30, the company had cash of $5,500, accounts receivable of $437,000, inventories of $309,400, and accounts payable of $133,055. The budget is to be based on the following assumptions.

Sales

- Each month's sales are billed on the last day of the month.
- Customers are allowed a 3 percent discount if payment is made within 10 days after the billing date. Receivables are recorded in the accounts at their gross amounts (not net of discounts).
- The billings are collected as follows: 60 percent within the discount period, 25 percent by the end of the month, 9 percent by the end of the second month, and 6 percent are uncollectible.

Purchases

- Of all purchases of merchandise and selling, general, and administrative expenses, 54 percent is paid in the month purchased and the remainder in the following month.
- The number of units in each month's ending inventory equals 130 percent of the next month's units of sales.
- The cost of each unit of inventory is $20.
- Selling, general, and administrative expenses, of which $2,000 is depreciation, equal 15 percent of the current month's sales.

Actual and projected sales follow:

	Dollars	Units
March	$354,000	11,800
April	363,000	12,100
May	357,000	11,900
June	342,000	11,400
July	360,000	12,000
August	366,000	12,200

Required

Using the preceding information, compute the following amounts:

a. Budgeted purchases in dollars for May.
b. Budgeted purchases in dollars for June.
c. Budgeted cash collections during May.
d. Budgeted cash disbursements during June.
e. Budgeted number of units of inventory to be purchased during July.

[CPA adapted]

Problem 15.41
Preparation of a Production Budget
(LO 3)

Yolinda Garden Color, Inc., manufactures floral containers. The controller is preparing a budget for the coming year and asks for your assistance. The following costs and other data apply to container production:

Direct material per container:	
1 pound Z-A styrene at $.40 per pound	
2 pounds Vasa finish at $.80 per pound	
Direct labor per container:	
¼ hour at $8.60 per hour	
Overhead per container:	
Indirect labor	$ .11
Indirect material	.04
Power	.07
Equipment costs	.34
Building occupancy	.21
Total overhead per unit	$ .77

You learn that equipment costs and building occupancy are facility-level (fixed) costs and are based on a normal production of 20,000 units per year. Other overhead costs are unit-level (variable) costs. Plant capacity is sufficient to produce 25,000 units per year.

Labor costs per hour are not expected to change during the year. However, the Vasa finish supplier has informed Yolinda's management that it will impose a 10 percent price increase at the start of the coming budget period. No other costs are expected to change.

During the coming budget period, Yolinda expects to sell 18,000 units. Finished-goods inventory is targeted to increase from 4,000 units to 7,000 units to prepare for an expected sales increase the year after next. Production will occur evenly throughout the year. Inventory levels for Vasa finish and Z-A styrene are expected to remain unchanged throughout the year. There is no work-in-process inventory.

Required

Prepare a production budget and estimate the material, labor, and overhead costs for the coming year.

Problem 15.42
Preparation of Budgeted Financial Statements; Estimation of Cash Receipts
(LO 1, 2, 3)

The following information is available for 20x1 for Portsmouth Products:

Revenue (100,000 units)	$725,000
Manufacturing costs:	
Materials (unit level)	42,000
Unit-level (variable) overhead cash costs	35,600
Facility-level (fixed) overhead cash costs	81,900
Depreciation (facility level)	249,750

Marketing and administrative costs:	
Marketing (unit level, cash)	105,600
Marketing depreciation	37,400
Administrative (facility level, cash)	127,300
Administrative depreciation	18,700
Total costs	$698,250
Operating profit	$ 26,750

All depreciation charges are facility-level costs and are expected to remain the same for 20x2. Sales volume is expected to increase by 18 percent, but prices are expected to fall by 5 percent. Material costs are expected to decrease by 8 percent. Unit-level (variable) manufacturing overhead costs are expected to decrease by 2 percent per unit. Facility-level (fixed) manufacturing overhead costs are expected to increase by 5 percent.

Unit-level (variable) marketing costs change with volume. Administrative cash costs are expected to increase by 10 percent. Inventories are kept at zero.

Required

a. Prepare a budgeted income statement for 20x2.

b. Estimate the cash from operations expected in 20x2.

Problem 15.43
Activity-Based Overhead Budget; Sales, Production, and Purchases Budgets
(LO 3)

Global

Electromatics, Inc., based in Singapore, manufactures two different types of housings used for electric motors. In the fall of the current year, James Li, the controller, compiled the following data. (All monetary amounts are given in terms of the national currency of Singapore, the Singaporean *dollar.*) On the day this problem was written, the Singaporean dollar was equivalent in value to 0.5548 US dollars.

- Sales forecast for 20x0:

Product	Units	Price
Small housing	60,000	$65
Large housing	40,000	95

- Raw-material prices and inventory levels:

Raw Materials	Expected Inventories January 1, 20x0	Desired Inventories, December 31, 20x0	Anticipated Purchase Price
Sheet metal	32,000 lb.	36,000 lb.	$8
Bar stock	29,000 lb.	32,000 lb.	5
Base	6,000 units	7,000 units	3

- Use of raw material:

	Amount Used per Unit	
Raw Material	Small Housing	Large Housing
Sheet metal	4 lb.	5 lb.
Bar stock	2 lb.	3 lb.
Base		1 unit

- Direct-labor requirements and rates:

Product	Hours per Unit	Rate per Hour
Small housing	2	$15
Large housing	3	20

- Finished-goods inventories (in units):

Product	Expected January 1, 20x0	Desired December 31, 20x0
Small housing	20,000	25,000
Large housing	8,000	9,000

- Manufacturing overhead:

Overhead Cost Item	Activity-Based Budget Rate
Purchasing and material handling	$.25 per pound of sheet metal and bar stock purchased
Depreciation, utilities, and inspection	$4.00 per housing produced (either type)
Shipping	$1.00 per housing shipped (either type)
General manufacturing overhead	$3.00 per direct-labor hour

Required

Prepare the following budgets for 20x0:

a. Sales budget (in dollars).
b. Production budget (in units).
c. Raw-material purchases budget (in quantities).
d. Raw-material purchases budget (in dollars).
e. Direct-labor budget (in dollars).
f. Budgeted finished-goods inventory on December 31, 20x0 (in dollars).
g. Manufacturing overhead budget (in dollars).

[CPA adapted]

Problem 15.44
Sales Expense Budget
(LO 3)

Neptune Corporation has just received its sales expense report for January, which follows:

Item	Amount
Sales commissions	$141,000
Sales staff salaries	29,000
Telephone and mailing	16,200
Building lease payment	20,000
Heat, light, and water	4,100
Packaging and delivery	27,400
Depreciation	12,500
Marketing consultants	19,700

You have been asked to develop budgeted costs for the coming year. Since this month is typical, you decide to prepare an estimated budget for a typical month in the coming year, and you uncover the following additional data:

- Sales volume is expected to increase by 5 percent.
- Sales prices are expected to increase by 10 percent.
- Commissions are based on a percentage of selling price.
- Sales staff salaries will increase 4 percent next year regardless of sales volume.
- Building rent is based on a five-year lease that expires in three years.
- Telephone and mailing expenses are scheduled to increase by 8 percent even with no change in sales volume. However, these costs are variable with the number of units sold, as are packaging and delivery costs.
- Heat, light, and water are scheduled to increase by 12 percent regardless of sales volume.
- Depreciation includes furniture and fixtures used by the sales staff. The company has just acquired an additional $19,000 in furniture that will be received at the start of next year and will be depreciated over a 10-year life using the straight-line method.
- Marketing consultant expenses were for a special advertising campaign that runs from time to time. During the coming year, the costs are expected to average $35,000 per month.

Required

Prepare Neptune's budget for sales expenses for a typical month in the coming year.

Problem 15.45
Ethics; Budgetary Pressure; Management Bonuses; Budgetary Constraints
(LO 4, 5)

Ethics

Communication

Midwest Industries produces and distributes industrial chemicals in its Belco Division, which is located in Michigan's upper peninsula. Belco's earnings increased sharply in 20x0, and bonuses were paid to the management staff for the first time in several years. Bonuses are based in part on the amount by which reported income exceeds budgeted income.

Jim Kern, vice president of finance, was pleased with Belco's 20x0 earnings and thought that the pressure to show financial results would ease. However, Ellen North, Belco's division manager, told Kern that she saw no reason why the 20x1 bonuses should not be double those of 20x0. As a result, Kern felt pressure to increase reported income to exceed budgeted income by an even greater amount. This would ensure increased bonuses.

Kern met with Bill Keller of Pristeel, Inc., a primary vendor of Belco's manufacturing supplies and equipment. Kern and Keller have been close business contacts for many years. Kern asked Keller to identify all of Belco's purchases of perishable supplies as equipment on Pristeel's sales invoices. The reason Kern gave for his request was that Belco's division manager had imposed stringent budget constraints on operating expenses but not on capital expenditures. Kern planned to capitalize the purchase of perishable supplies and include them with the Equipment account on the balance sheet. In this way Kern could defer the expense recognition for these items to a later year. This procedure would increase reported earnings, leading to increased bonuses. Keller agreed to do as Kern had asked.

While analyzing the second quarter financial statements, Gary Wood, Belco's director of cost management, noticed a large decrease in supplies expense from one year ago. Wood reviewed the Supplies Expense account and noticed that only equipment but no supplies had been purchased from Pristeel, a major source for supplies. Wood, who reports to Kern, immediately brought this to Kern's attention.

Kern told Wood of North's high expectations and of the arrangement made with Keller of Pristeel. Wood told Kern that his action was an improper accounting treatment for the supplies purchased from Pristeel. Wood requested that he be allowed to correct the accounts and urged that the arrangement with Pristeel be discontinued. Kern refused the request and told Wood not to become involved in the arrangement with Pristeel.

After clarifying the situation in a confidential discussion with an objective and qualified peer within Belco, Wood arranged to meet with North, Belco's division manager. At the meeting, Wood disclosed the arrangement Kern had made with Pristeel.

Required

Prepare a presentation to the class covering the following issues:

a. Explain why the use of alternative accounting methods to manipulate reported earnings is unethical.

b. Is Gary Wood, Belco's director of cost management, correct in saying that the supplies purchased from Pristeel, Inc., were accounted for improperly? Explain your answer.

c. Assuming that Jim Kern's arrangement with Pristeel, Inc., was in violation of the Standards of Ethical Conduct for Management Accountants, discuss whether Wood's actions were appropriate or inappropriate. (The standards are given in the Appendix to Chapter 1).

[CMA adapted]

Problem 15.46
Comprehensive Budget Plan
(LO 1, 3)

Tipless Inc., a manufacturer of coffee cups, decided in October 20x0 that it needed cash to continue operations. It began negotiating for a one-month bank loan of $100,000 starting November 1, 20x0. The bank would charge interest at the rate of 1 percent per month and require the company to repay interest and principal on November 30, 20x0. In considering the loan, the bank requested a projected income statement and cash budget for November. The following information is available:

- The company budgeted sales at 120,000 units per month in October 20x0, December 20x0, and January 20x1, and at 90,000 units in November 20x0. The selling price is $2 per unit.
- The inventory of finished goods on October 1 was 24,000 units. The finished-goods inventory at the end of each month equals 20 percent of sales anticipated for the following month. There is no work-in-process inventory.
- The inventory of raw material on October 1 was 22,800 pounds. At the end of each month, the raw-material inventory equals no less than 40 percent of production requirements for the following month. The company purchases materials as needed in minimum quantities of 25,000 pounds per shipment.

- Selling expenses are 10 percent of gross sales. Administrative expenses, which include depreciation of $500 per month on office furniture and fixtures, total $33,000 per month.
- The manufacturing budget for coffee cups, based on normal production of 100,000 units per month, follows:

Material (½ pound per cup, 50,000 pounds, $1 per pound)	$ 50,000
Labor	40,000
Variable overhead	20,000
Fixed overhead (includes depreciation of $4,000)	10,000
Total	$120,000

- Tipless' customers are allowed a 1 percent discount if payment is made within 10 days, and these discounts are always taken. Bad debts are projected at ½ percent of gross sales.

Required

a. Prepare schedules computing inventory budgets by months for the following:

(1) Production in units for October, November, and December.

(2) Raw-material purchases in pounds for October and November.

b. Prepare a projected income statement for November. Cost of goods sold should equal the variable manufacturing cost per unit times the number of units sold plus the total fixed manufacturing cost budgeted for the period.

[CPA adapted]

Problem 15.47
Preparation of Budgeted Financial Statements; Estimation of Cash Receipts
(LO 1, 3)

Piedmont Plastics Company has the following data from 20x1 operations, which are to be used for developing 20x2 budget estimates:

Revenue (100,000)	$805,000
Manufacturing costs:	
Material (unit level)	133,000
Unit-level (variable) overhead cash costs	180,900
Facility-level (fixed) overhead cash costs	72,000
Depreciation (facility level)	89,000
Marketing and administrative costs:	
Marketing (unit level, cash)	95,000
Marketing depreciation	22,600
Administrative (facility level, cash)	90,110
Administrative depreciation	8,400
Total costs	691,010
Operating profits	$113,990

All depreciation charges are facility-level costs. Old manufacturing equipment with an annual depreciation charge of $9,700 will be replaced in 20x2 with new equipment that will incur an annual depreciation charge of $14,000. Sales volume and prices are expected to increase by 12 percent and 6 percent, respectively. On a per-unit basis, expectations are that material costs will increase by 10 percent and unit-level (variable) manufacturing overhead costs will decrease by 4 percent. Facility-level (fixed) overhead costs are expected to decrease by 7 percent.

Unit-level (variable) marketing costs will change with volume. Administrative cash costs are expected to increase by 8 percent. Inventories are kept near zero.

Required

a. Prepare Piedmont Plastics' budgeted income statement for 20x2.

b. Estimate the cash from operations expected in 20x2.

Problem 15.48
Production, Materials, Labor, and Overhead Budgets
(LO 3)

The Pittsburgh Division of Allegheny Corporation produces an intricate component used in the company's product line. The division manager has been concerned recently by a lack of coordination between purchasing and production personnel and believes that a monthly budgeting system would be better than the present system.

Pittsburgh's division manager has decided to develop budget information for the third quarter of the current year as an experiment before the budget system is implemented for an entire year. In response to the division manager's request, the divisional controller accumulated the following data.

- Sales through June 30, the first six months of the current year, are 24,000 units. Actual sales in units for May and June and estimated unit sales for the next four months are:

May (actual)	4,000
June (actual)	4,000
July (estimated)	5,000
August (estimated)	6,000
September (estimated)	7,000
October (estimated)	7,000

Pittsburgh Division expects to sell 60,000 units during the current year.

- Data regarding the materials used in the component are shown in the following schedule. The desired monthly ending inventory for all raw materials is an amount sufficient to produce the next month's estimated sales.

Raw Material	Units of Raw Material per Finished Component	Cost per Unit	Inventory Level June 30
B42	6	$2.40	35,000 units
F68	4	3.60	30,000 units
M03	2	1.20	14,000 units

- Each component must pass through three different processes to be completed. Data regarding direct labor follow:

Process	Direct-Labor Hours per Finished Component	Cost per Direct-Labor Hour
Forming	.400	$16.00
Assembly	1.000	11.00
Finishing	.125	12.00

- The division produced 27,000 components during the six-month period ending June 30. The actual unit-level (variable) overhead costs incurred during this six-month period are given in the following schedule. The divisional controller believes the unit-level (variable) overhead costs will be incurred at the same rate during the last six months of the current year.

Supplies	$ 59,400
Electricity	27,000
Indirect labor	54,000
Other	8,100
Total variable overhead	$148,500

The facility-level (fixed) overhead costs *actually incurred* during the first six months of the year amounted to $93,500. These facility-level overhead costs are *budgeted* for the full year as follows:

Supervision	$ 60,000
Taxes	7,200
Depreciation	86,400
Other	32,400
Total fixed overhead	$186,000

- The desired monthly ending inventory of completed components is 80 percent of the next month's estimated sales. There are 5,000 finished units in inventory on June 30.

Required

a. Prepare a production budget in units for Pittsburgh Division for the third quarter of the current year, ending September 30.

b. Independent of your answer to requirement (a), assume that Pittsburgh Division plans to produce 18,000 units during the third quarter ending September 30 and 60,000 units for the entire year ending December 31.
   (1) Prepare a raw-material purchases budget, in units and dollars, for the third quarter, ending September 30.
   (2) Prepare a direct-labor budget, in hours and dollars, for the third quarter, ending September 30.
   (3) Prepare a manufacturing-overhead budget for the six-month period ending December 31 of the current year.

[CMA adapted]

Problem 15.49
Production and Direct-Labor Budgets; Activity-Based Overhead Budget
(LO 2, 3, 4)

AccuSound Corporation manufactures stereo headphones. Brent Dean, controller, is responsible for preparing the company's master budget. In compiling the budget data for 20x1, Dean has learned that new automated production equipment will be installed on March 1. This will reduce the direct labor per set of headphones from 1 hour to .75 hours.

Labor-related costs include pension contributions of $.50 per hour, workers' compensation insurance of $.20 per hour, employee medical insurance of $.80 per hour, and employer contributions to Social Security equal to 7 percent of direct-labor wages. The cost of employee benefits paid by the company on its employees is treated as a direct-labor cost. AccuSound Corporation has a labor contract that calls for a wage increase to $18.00 per hour on April 1, 20x1. Management expects to have 16,000 headphone sets on hand at December 31, 20x0, and has a policy of carrying an end-of-month inventory of 100 percent of the following month's sales plus 50 percent of the second following month's sales.

These and other data compiled by Dean are summarized in the following table.

	January	February	March	April	May
Direct-labor hours per unit	1.0	1.0	.75	.75	.75
Wage per direct-labor hour	$16.00	$16.00	$16.00	$18.00	$18.00
Estimated unit sales	10,000	12,000	8,000	9,000	9,000
Sales price per unit	$50.00	$47.50	$47.50	$47.50	$47.50
Manufacturing overhead					
Shipping and handling (per unit sold)	$2.00	$2.00	$2.00	$2.00	$2.00
Purchasing, material handling, and inspection (per unit produced)	$3.00	$3.00	$3.00	$3.00	$3.00
Other manufacturing overhead (per direct-labor hour)	$7.00	$7.00	$7.00	$7.00	$7.00

Required

a. Prepare a production budget and a direct-labor budget for AccuSound Corporation by month and for the first quarter of 20x1. Both budgets can be combined in one schedule. The direct-labor budget should include direct-labor hours and show the detail for each direct-labor cost category.

b. For each item used in the firm's production budget and direct-labor budget, identify the other components of the master budget that also would use these data.

c. Prepare a manufacturing overhead budget for each month and for the first quarter.

[CMA adapted]

Problem 15.50
Economic Order Quantity; Equation Approach; JIT Purchasing (Appendix)
(LO 7)

Orbital Technology, Inc., manufactures specialized ceramic components used in the aerospace industry. The company's materials and parts manager is currently revising the inventory policy for XL-20, one of the chemicals used in the production process. The chemical is purchased in 10-pound canisters for $95 each. The firm uses 4,800 canisters per year. The controller estimates that to place and receive a typical order of XL-20 costs $150. The annual cost of storing XL-20 is $4 per canister.

Required

a. Write the formula for the total annual cost of ordering and storing XL-20.

b. Use the EOQ formula to determine the optimal order quantity.

Communication

c. What is the total annual cost of ordering and storing XL-20 at the economic order quantity?

d. How many orders will be placed per year?

e. Orbital Technology's controller, Jane Turnbull, recently attended a seminar on JIT purchasing. Afterwards she analyzed the cost of storing XL-20, including the costs of wasted space and inefficiency. She was shocked when she concluded that the real annual holding cost was $19.20 per canister. Turnbull then met with Doug Kaplan, Orbital Technology's purchasing manager. Together they contacted Reno Industries, the supplier of XL-20, about a JIT purchasing arrangement. After some discussion and negotiation, Kaplan concluded that the cost of placing an order for XL-20 could be reduced to just $20. Using these new cost estimates, Turnbull computed the new EOQ for XL-20.

(1) Use the equation approach to compute the new EOQ.

(2) How many orders will be placed per year?

Problem 15.51
Economic Order Quantity; Tabular Approach (Appendix)
(LO 7)

Refer to the *original* data given in the preceding problem for Orbital Technology, Inc.

Required

a. Prepare a table showing the total annual cost of ordering and storing XL-20 for each of the following order quantities: 400, 600, and 800 canisters.

b. What are the weaknesses in the tabular approach?

Problem 15.52
Economic Order Quantity; Graphical Approach (Appendix)
(LO 7)

Refer to the *original* data given in problem 15.50 for Orbital Technology, Inc.

Required

Prepare a graphical analysis of the economic order quantity decision for XL-20.

Problem 15.53
Economic Order Quantity; Lead Time and Safety Stock (Appendix)
(LO 7)

Refer to the *original* data given in problem 15.50 for Orbital Technology, Inc. The lead time required to receive an order of XL-20 is one month.

Required

a. Assuming stable usage of XL-20 each month, determine the reorder point for XL-20.

b. Suppose that the monthly usage of XL-20 fluctuates between 300 and 500 canisters, although annual demand remains constant at 4,800 canisters. What level of safety stock should the materials and parts manager keep on hand for XL-20? What is the new reorder point for the chemical?

Cases

Case 15.54*
Preparation and Interpretation of Cash Budget for Service Organization
(LO 1, 2, 3)

Communication

Triple-F Health Club (Family, Fitness, and Fun) is a nonprofit health club. Its board of directors is developing plans to acquire more equipment and expand club facilities. The board plans to purchase about $25,000 of new equipment each year and wants to begin a fund to purchase an adjoining property in four or five years when the expansion will need the space. The adjoining property has a market value of about $300,000.

The club manager is concerned that the board has unrealistic goals in light of its recent financial performance. She sought the help of a club member with an accounting background to assist her in preparing the club's records, including the cash-basis income statements that follow. The review and discussions with the manager disclosed the additional information that follows the statement.

**Note: Case 18.48 (River Beverages) in Chapter 18 includes significant managerial issues related to the budgeting process and may be assigned at this time.*

TRIPLE-F HEALTH CLUB Statement of Income (Cash Basis) For the Year Ended October 31 (in thousands)	20x7	20x6
Cash revenue:		
Annual membership fees	$355.0	$300.0
Lesson and class fees	234.0	180.0
Miscellaneous	2.0	1.5
Total cash received	$591.0	$481.5
Cash costs:		
Manager's salary and benefits	$ 36.0	$ 36.0
Regular employees' wages and benefits	190.0	190.0
Lesson and class employee wages and benefits	195.0	150.0
Towels and supplies	16.0	15.5
Utilities (heat and light)	22.0	15.0
Mortgage interest	35.1	37.8
Miscellaneous	2.0	1.5
Total cash costs	$496.1	$445.8
Cash income	$ 94.9	$ 35.7

Additional information follows:

1. Other financial information as of October 31, 20x7:
   a. Cash in checking account, $7,000.
   b. Petty cash, $300.
   c. Outstanding mortgage balance, $360,000.
   d. Accounts payable for supplies and utilities unpaid as of October 31, 20x7, and due in November 20x7, $2,500.
2. The club purchased $25,000 worth of exercise equipment during the current fiscal year. Cash of $10,000 was paid on delivery, with the balance due on October 1, which had not been paid as of October 31, 20x7.
3. The club began operations in 20x1 in rental quarters. In October 20x3, it purchased its current property (land and building) for $600,000, paying $120,000 down and agreeing to pay $30,000 plus 9 percent interest annually on the unpaid loan balance each November 1, starting November 1, 20x4.
4. Membership rose 3 percent during 20x7, approximately the same annual rate of increase the club has experienced since it opened and that is expected to continue in the future.
5. Membership fees were increased by 15 percent in 20x7. The board has tentative plans to increase them by 10 percent in 20x8.
6. Lesson and class fees have not been increased for three years. The number of classes and lessons has grown significantly each year, and the percentage growth experienced in 20x7 is expected to be repeated in 20x8.
7. Miscellaneous revenues are expected to grow in 20x8 (over 20x7) at the same percentage as experienced in 20x7 (over 20x6).
8. Lesson and class employees' wages and benefits will increase to $291,525. The wages and benefits of regular employees and the manager will increase 15 percent. Towels and supplies, utilities, and miscellaneous expenses are expected to increase 25 percent.

Required

a. Construct a cash budget for 20x8 for the Triple-F Health Club.

b. Write a memo to the health club's board of directors to accompany the budget. In the memo, identify any operating problem(s) that this budget discloses for the Triple-F Health Club.

c. Is the manager's concern that the board's goals are unrealistic justified? Explain your answer.

[CMA adapted]

Case 15.55
Comprehensive Master Budget; Acquisition of Automated Materials-Handling System
(LO 1, 2, 3)

Spreadsheet

Atlantico, Inc., is a small, rapidly growing wholesaler of consumer electronic products. The firm's main product lines are small kitchen appliances and power tools. Malinda Alexander, Atlantico's general manager of marketing, recently completed a sales forecast. She believes the company's sales during the first quarter of 20x1 will increase by 10 percent each month over the previous month's sales. Then Alexander expects sales to remain constant for several months. Atlantico's projected balance sheet as of December 31, 20x0, is as follows:

Cash	$ 29,000
Accounts receivable	276,000
Marketable securities	15,000
Inventory	154,000
Buildings and equipment (net of accumulated depreciation)	626,000
Total assets	$1,100,000
Accounts payable	$ 176,400
Bond interest payable	12,500
Property taxes payable	3,600
Bonds payable (10%; due in 20x6)	300,000
Common stock	500,000
Retained earnings	107,500
Total liabilities and stockholders' equity	$1,100,000

Shawn Garrity, the assistant controller, is now preparing a monthly budget for the first quarter of 20x1. In the process, the following information has been accumulated:

1. Projected sales for December 20x0 are $400,000. Credit sales typically are 75 percent of total sales. Atlantico's credit experience indicates that 10 percent of the credit sales is collected during the month of sale, and the remainder is collected during the following month.

2. Atlantico's cost of goods sold generally is 70 percent of sales. Inventory is purchased on account, and 40 percent of each month's purchases are paid during the month of purchase. The remainder is paid during the following month. To have adequate stocks of inventory on hand, the firm attempts to have inventory at the end of each month equal to half of the next month's projected cost of goods sold.

3. Garrity has estimated that Atlantico's other monthly expenses will be as follows:

Sales salaries	$21,000
Advertising and promotion	16,000
Administrative salaries	21,000
Depreciation	25,000
Interest on bonds	2,500
Property taxes	900

In addition, sales commissions run at the rate of 1 percent of sales.

4. Atlantico's president, Carrie Howland, has indicated that the firm should invest $125,000 in an automated inventory-handling system to control the movement of inventory in the firm's warehouse just after the new year begins. This equipment purchase will be financed primarily from the firm's cash and marketable securities. However, Howland believes that Atlantico needs to keep a minimum cash balance of $19,000. If necessary, the remainder of the equipment purchases will be financed using short-term credit from a local bank. The minimum period for such a loan is three months. Garrity believes that short-term interest rates will be 10 percent per year at the time of the equipment purchases. If a loan is necessary, Howland has decided it should be paid off by the end of the first quarter if possible.

5. Atlantico's board of directors has indicated its intention to declare and pay dividends of $50,000 on the last day of each quarter.
6. The interest on any short-term borrowing will be paid when the loan is repaid. Interest on Atlantico's bonds is paid semiannually on January 31 and July 31 for the preceding six-month period.
7. Property taxes are paid semiannually on February 28 and August 31 for the preceding six-month period.

Required

Prepare Atlantico's master budget for the first quarter of 20x1 by completing the following schedules and statements.

a. Sales budget:

	20x0	20x1			
	December	January	February	March	1st Quarter
Total sales					
Cash sales					
Sales on account					

b. Cash receipts budget:

	20x1			
	January	February	March	1st Quarter
Cash sales				
Cash collections from credit sales made during current month				
Cash collections from credit sales made during preceding month				
Total cash receipts				

c. Purchases budget:

	20x0	20x1			
	December	January	February	March	1st Quarter
Budgeted cost of goods sold					
Add: Desired ending inventory					
Total goods needed					
Less: Expected beginning inventory					
Purchases					

d. Cash disbursements budget:

	20x1			
	January	**February**	**March**	**1st Quarter**
Inventory purchases:				
Cash payments for purchases during the current month*				
Cash payments for purchases during the preceding month†				
Total cash payments for inventory purchases				
Other expenses:				
Sales salaries				
Advertising and promotion				
Administrative salaries				
Interest on bonds‡				
Property taxes‡				
Sales commissions				
Total cash payments for other expenses				
Total cash disbursements				

*40% of the month's purchases (schedule c).

†60% of the prior month's purchases (schedule c).

‡Bond interest is paid every six months, on January 31 and July 31. Property taxes also are paid every six months, on February 28 and August 31.

e. Complete the first three lines of the summary cash budget. Then do the analysis of short-term financing needs in requirement (f). Then finish requirement (e).

Summary cash budget:

	20x1			
	January	**February**	**March**	**1st Quarter**
Cash receipts (from schedule b)				
Less: Cash disbursements (from schedule d)				
Change in cash balance during period due to operations				
Sale of marketable securities (1/2/x1)				
Proceeds from bank loan (1/2/x1)				
Purchase of equipment				
Repayment of bank loan (3/31/x1)				
Interest on bank loan				
Payment of dividends				
Change in cash balance during first quarter				
Cash balance, 1/1/x1				
Cash balance, 3/31/x1				

f. Analysis of short-term financing needs:

Projected cash balance as of December 31, 20x0	$
Less: Minimum cash balance	____
Cash available for equipment purchases	$
Projected proceeds from sale of marketable securities	____
Cash available	$
Less: Cost of investment in equipment	____
Required short-term borrowing	$

g. Prepare Atlantico's budgeted income statement for the first quarter of 20x1. (Ignore income taxes.)

h. Prepare Atlantico's budgeted statement of retained earnings for the first quarter of 20x1.

i. Prepare Atlantico's budgeted balance sheet as of March 31, 20x1. (*Hint:* On March 31, 20x1, Bond Interest Payable is $5,000 and Property Taxes Payable is $900.)

PART

V

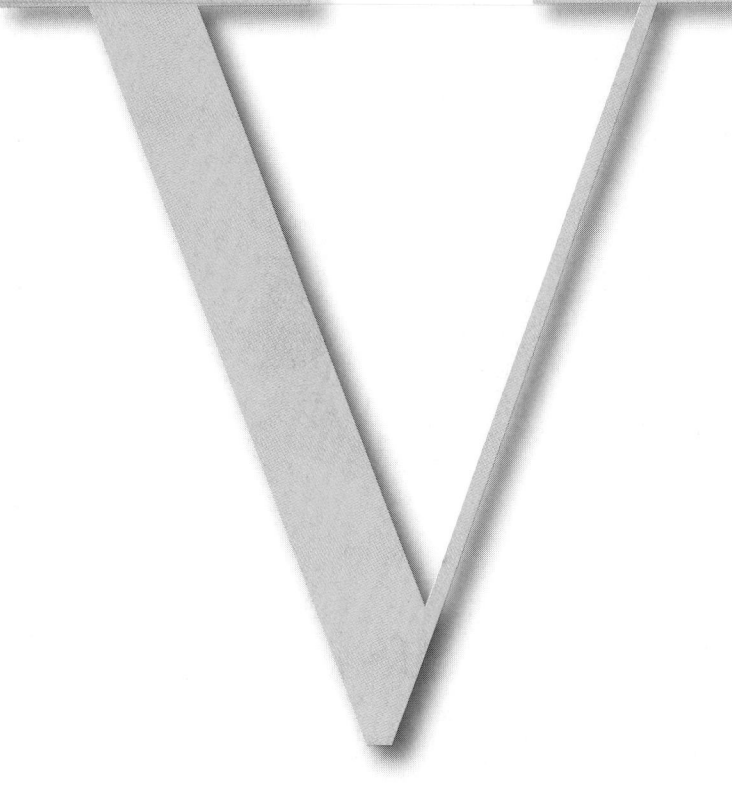

Evaluating and Managing Performance

Creating and Managing Value-Added Effort

A Look Back

The preceding part covered financial and operational budgeting, cost estimation, and decision making.

A Look at This Part

The first two chapters in Part V explore standard-costing systems and cost-variance analysis as a cost-management tool. The next chapter in this part covers organizational design issues, responsibility accounting, and various measures of investment center performance. The fourth chapter in Part V covers transfer pricing. The next chapter in this part explores the use of lead and lag measures to motivate, communicate, and evaluate. The final chapter of the part covers the relationship between incentive systems and performance measurements and includes a discussion of the balanced scorecard.

CHAPTER

16

Standard Costing, Variance Analysis, and Kaizen Costing

After completing this chapter, you should be able to:

1. Discuss how companies use standard-costing systems to manage costs, and describe two ways to set standards.
2. Distinguish between perfection and practical standards.
3. Compute and interpret the direct-material price and quantity variances and the direct-labor rate and efficiency variances.
4. Describe several methods used to determine the significance of cost variances.
5. Discuss some behavioral effects of standard costing and the controllability of variances.
6. Explain how companies use standard costs in product costing.
7. Summarize some advantages attributed to standard costing.
8. Describe the changing role of standard-costing systems in today's manufacturing environment.
9. Explain the concept of kaizen costing and its potential benefits.
10. Compute and interpret mix and yield variances (Appendix).

Cost-Management Challenges

1. **How** could Koala Camp Gear's controller set standards for the production of tents using the company's standard-costing system?
2. **What** is the appropriate interpretation of each variance detailed in Koala Camp Gear Company's cost-variance report?
3. **Who** is in the best position in the organization to influence each of these variances?
4. **What** criticisms are made of standard-costing systems as they are used in today's business environment?

EMAIL MEMORANDUM

Koala Camp Gear Company

2145 Yarra Drive
Melbourne, Victoria
Australia

To: Geoff Weatherby
Production Manager
From: Marc Wesley
Controller
cc: Margo Hastings
President and CEO
Subject: June cost-variance report

The cost-variance report for direct material and direct labor for the month of June appears below. I suggest that we add a discussion of the report to tomorrow morning's staff meeting. This report is based on June output of 3,000 Tree Line tents.

The unfavorable direct-material variances (both price and quantity), while cause for concern, are not nearly as high in percentage terms as the direct-labor rate variance. We need to get to the bottom of these variations from standard costs, and we can begin with tomorrow morning's meeting. Before then I will analyze the direct-labor costs in greater detail to see whether I can provide any insights into our June performance.

Cost Variance Report for June: Direct Material and Direct Labor

	Amount	Percentage of Standard Cost
Direct material:		
Standard cost, given actual output...	$288,000	
Direct-material price variance..........	6,000 U*	2.08%
Direct-material quantity variance.....	3,200 U*	1.11%
Direct labor:		
Standard cost, given actual output...	$108,000	
Direct-labor rate variance	5,900 U*	5.46%
Direct-labor efficiency variance........	1,800 F*	(1.67)%

*U denotes unfavorable; F denotes favorable

The memorandum on the preceding page includes a cost-variance report intended to help the management of Koala Camp Gear Company manage the company's production costs. How do small manufacturing companies such as Koala, or large companies such as Dell Computer or Daimler/Chrysler, manage and control the many costs they incur in their production process? As the preceding chapter explained, a budget provides a plan for managers to follow in making decisions and directing an organization's activities. At the end of a budget period, the budget serves another useful purpose. At that time, managers use it as a benchmark against which to compare the results of actual operations. Did the company make as much profit as anticipated in the budget? Were costs higher or lower than expected?

In addition to budgets, many companies use *standards* to help manage costs and profits. A *standard* is a benchmark performance level. For example, many manufacturing firms set standards for the amount and price of direct materials and for the amount and rate paid for direct labor used to produce their products. At the end of the period, management compares the standards with actual results. These comparisons help management gain insight into what went right and what went wrong in the production process.

General Motors uses standards to help manage direct material and direct labor costs. Pictured here is GM's Cadillac assembly line.

Service firms also use standards. McDonald's, for example, sets a standard for the quantity of meat in a Big Mac. This McDonald's restaurant is in Moscow, Russia.

Using Standard-Costing Systems for Control

LO 1 Discuss how companies use standard-costing systems to manage costs, and describe two ways to set standards.

Any control system has three basic parts: a predetermined or *standard* performance level, a measure of *actual* performance, and a *comparison* of standard and actual performances. A thermostat, a control system with which we are all familiar, has three parts. First, it has a predetermined or standard temperature, which you can set at any desired level. If you want the temperature in a room to be 70 degrees, you set the thermostat at the *standard* of 70 degrees. Second, the thermostat has a thermometer, which measures the *actual* temperature in the room. Third, the thermostat *compares* the preset or standard temperature with the actual room temperature. If the actual temperature differs from the preset or standard temperature, the thermostat activates a heating or cooling device.

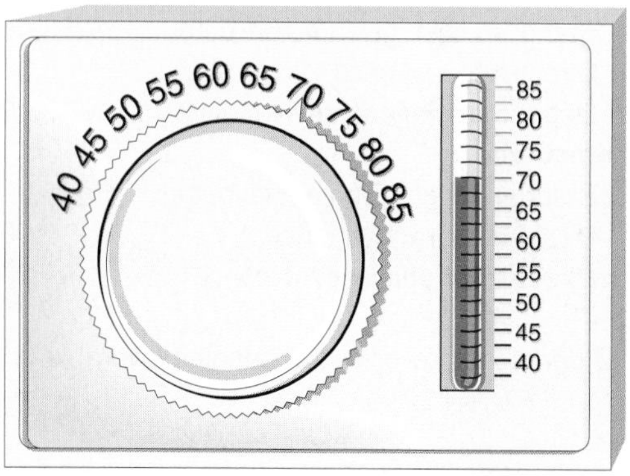

standard cost *is a budget for the production of one unit of product or service*

A cost manager's budgetary-control system works like a thermostat. First, a predetermined, or *standard cost* is set. In essence, a **standard cost** is a budget for the production of one unit of product or service. It is the cost chosen by the cost-management analyst to serve as the benchmark in the budgetary-control system. When the firm produces many units, the cost-management analyst uses the standard unit cost to determine the total standard or budgeted cost of production. For example, suppose that the standard direct-material cost for one of Koala Camp Gear's tent models is $96, and the firm manufactures 1,000 units. The total standard or budgeted direct-material cost, given actual output of 1,000 units, is $96,000 ($96 × 1,000).

Second, the cost-management analyst measures the actual cost incurred in the production process.

Third, the cost-management analyst compares the actual cost with the budgeted, or standard, cost. Any difference between the actual cost and the standard cost is called a **cost variance.** Cost-management analysts then use these cost variances to control costs.

cost variance *is the difference between the actual cost and the standard cost*

Widespread Use of Standard-Costing Systems

A recent survey of medium-size US manufacturers revealed that standard-costing systems remain in widespread use.* Although companies are increasingly implementing such cost-management practices as ABC, ABM, and target costing, these contemporary approaches are being used along side of standard-costing systems. A sampling of responses from the survey:

86% of the survey companies have a standard-costing system.

74% of the production managers surveyed reported satisfaction with the standards.

96% of the firms prepare periodic performance reports for management; these reports include variances from standard costs.

Similar results regarding the widespread use of standard costing were reported in two earlier surveys conducted in 1991 and 1988.†

*S. A. Moscove, "Enhancing Detective Controls through Performance Reporting." (Full citations to references are in the Bibliography.)

†B. R. Gaumnitz and F. P. Kollaritsch, "Manufacturing Variances: Current Practices and Trends"; and M. Cornick, W. Cooper, and S. Wilson, "How Do Companies Analyze Overhead?"

Research Insight 16.1

Management by Exception

Although managers do not have time to explore the causes of every variance between actual and standard costs, they do take the time to investigate the causes of significant cost variances. This process of following up only on significant cost variances is called **management by exception.** When operations are going along as planned, actual costs and profit are typically close to the budgeted amounts. However, significant departures from planned operations appear as significant cost variances. Managers investigate these variances to determine their cause, if possible, and take corrective action when indicated.

management by exception *is the process of following up only on significant cost variances*

What constitutes a significant variance? This question has no precise answer, since it depends on the size and type of the organization and its production process. We consider this issue later in the chapter when we discuss common methods for determining the significance of cost variances. First, however, we turn our attention to the process of setting standards.

Setting Standards

Cost-management analysts typically use two methods to set cost standards: analysis of historical data and task analysis.

Analysis of historical data. One indicator of future costs is historical cost data. In a mature production process, when the firm has considerable production experience, historical costs can provide a reliable basis for predicting future costs. The methods for analyzing cost behavior that we studied in Chapter 12 are used in making cost predictions. The cost analyst often needs to adjust these predictions to reflect movements in price levels or technological changes in the production process. For example, the amount of leather required to manufacture a pair of Dr Martens shoes is likely the same this year as last year unless a significant change in the process used to manufacture shoes has occurred. However, the price of leather is likely to be different this year than last, and this fact must be reflected in the new standard cost of a pair of shoes.

Despite the relevance of historical cost data in setting cost standards, cost-management analysts must guard against relying on these data excessively. Even a seemingly minor change in the way a product is manufactured could make historical data almost totally irrelevant. Moreover, new products also require new cost standards. For new products, such as genetically engineered vaccines, no historical cost data exist on which to base standards. In such cases, the cost analyst must turn to another approach.

task analysis *is the technique of setting standards by analyzing the production process*

Task analysis. Another way to set cost standards, called **task analysis,** is the technique of analyzing the process of manufacturing a product to determine what it *should* cost. The emphasis shifts from what the product *did* cost in the past to what it *should* cost in the future. In using this approach, the cost-management analyst typically works with engineers who are intimately familiar with the production process. Together they conduct studies to determine exactly the amount of direct material that should be required and the way that machinery should be used in the production process. Time-and-motion studies sometimes are conducted to determine how long each step performed by direct laborers should take. Storyboarding sessions sometimes are used to develop a detailed process map of all the activities in a work center.

A combined approach. Cost-management analysts often apply both historical cost analysis and task analysis in setting cost standards. It might be, for example, that the technology has changed for only one step in the production process. In such a case, the cost analyst works with engineers to set cost standards for the technologically changed part of the production process. However, the accountant likely relies on the less expensive method of analyzing historical cost data to update the cost standards for the remaining steps in the production process.

Participation in setting standards. Standards should not be determined by accounting staff alone. People generally are more committed to meeting standards if they are allowed to participate in setting them. For example, production supervisors should have a role in setting production cost standards, and sales managers should be involved in setting targets for sales prices and volume. In addition, knowledgeable staff personnel should participate in the standard-setting process—a team consisting of production engineers, production supervisors, and cost-management analysts should perform task analysis.

Research Insight 16.2

Collaboration in Developing Standards

According to a recent survey of US manufacturers, 74 percent of the respondents develop standards through the collaboration of accountants and production employees. Moreover, research suggests that production employees' participation "often contributes to better standards, as well as to buy into the standards by those employees." *Source: S. A. Moscove,* "Enhancing Detective Controls through Performance Reporting."

Employees Set Standards

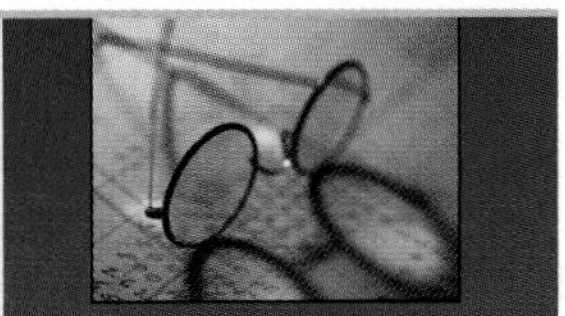

Cost Management in Practice 16.1

The Toyota–General Motors joint venture in Fremont, California, known as New United Motor Manufacturing, Inc. (NUMMI), allows employees to set their own work standards. The NUMMI plant had been a General Motors plant notorious for poor quality, low productivity, and morale problems.

At the old Fremont GM plant, industrial engineers who had little, if any, work experience making cars would shut themselves in a room and ponder how to set standards, ignoring the workers, who in turn ignored the standards. Now, at NUMMI, workers themselves hold the stopwatches and set the standards. Worker team members time each other, looking for the most efficient and safest way to do the work.

The workers standardize each task so that everyone in the team will do it the same way. They compare the standards across shifts and for different tasks and prepare detailed written specifications for each task. The workers are more informed about how to do the work right than industrial engineers are, and they are more motivated to meet the standards they set than those set by industrial engineers working in an ivory tower.

Involving the workers has had benefits in addition to improved motivation and standards. These include improved safety, higher quality, easier job rotation because tasks are standardized, and more flexibility because workers are both assembly line workers and industrial engineers. *Source: P. Adler, "Time-and-Motion Regained."*

Perfection versus Practical Standards: A Behavioral Issue

This Toyota–General Motors plant in Fremont, California, succeeded in letting employees set their own standards.

How difficult should it be to attain standard costs? Should cost-management analysts set standards so that actual costs rarely exceed standard costs? Or, should standards be so difficult to attain that actual costs frequently exceed them? The answers to these questions depend on the purpose for which standards are used and the way standards affect behavior.

LO 2 Distinguish between perfection and practical standards.

Perfection standards. A **perfection** (or **ideal**) **standard** is one that can be attained only under nearly perfect operating conditions. Such standards assume peak efficiency, the lowest possible input prices, the best-quality materials obtainable, and no disruptions in production due to causes such as machine breakdowns or power failures. Some managers believe that a perfection standard motivates employees to achieve the lowest cost possible. They claim that since the standard is theoretically attainable, employees have an incentive to come as close as possible to achieving it.

perfection (or **ideal**) **standard** *is one that can be attained only under nearly perfect operating conditions*

Other managers and many behavioral scientists disagree. They believe that perfection standards discourage employees, since such high standards are so unlikely to be attained. Moreover, setting unrealistically difficult standards could encourage employees to sacrifice product quality to achieve lower costs. By skimping on the quality of raw materials or the attention to manual production tasks, employees might be able to lower the production cost. However, this lower cost could come at the expense of a higher rate of defective units. Thus, the firm ultimately might incur higher costs than necessary if defective products are returned by customers or scrapped upon inspection.

Practical standards. Standards that are as tight as practical but still are expected to be attained are called **practical** (or **attainable**) **standards.** Such standards assume a production process that is as efficient as practical under normal operating conditions. Practical standards allow for events such as occasional machine breakdowns and normal amounts of raw-material waste. Attaining a practical standard keeps employees on their toes without demanding miracles. Most behavioral theorists believe that practical standards encourage more positive and productive employee attitudes than do perfection standards.

practical (or **attainable**) **standards** *are as tight as is practical but still are expected to be attained*

You're the **Decision Maker 16.1**

Setting Standards in the Service Industry

For what types of costs could standards be set in each of the following service businesses? Explain the reasoning behind your answers.

a. A Dominos pizza outlet.
b. An Avis car-rental agency.
c. A branch of Nation's Bank.
d. A county motor-vehicle department.

(Solutions begin on page 682.)

Use of Standards by Nonmanufacturing Organizations

Service-industry firms, nonprofit organizations, and governmental units also use standard costs. For example, airlines set standards for fuel and maintenance costs. A county motor-vehicle office might have a standard for the number of days required to process and return an application for vehicle registration. American Express (*www.americanexpress.com*) used standards to speed and improve service. According to *Business Week,* the company's financial service operations were broken into basic tasks. For each of these tasks, performance standards were set, and means were devised for achieving the standards.[1] Dutch Pantry, a restaurant chain in the eastern United States, established a standard-costing system in its centralized food-processing facility.[2] According to an article in *The Wall Street Journal,* the United Parcel Service (UPS) (*www.ups.com*) set standards for various delivery tasks. For example, a standard of 3 feet per second was established as the standard pace at which drivers should walk to a customer's door.[3] These and similar organizations use standards in budgeting and cost management in much the same way that manufacturers use standards.

American Express used standards to help management speed up and improve its customer service operations. This Amex express cash unit is in Singapore.

If you were managing an Avis car-rental agency, for what kinds of costs would you set standards?

Costs and Benefits of Standard-Costing Systems

Standard-costing systems provide information that can help managers control costs. However, implementing and maintaining cost standards is itself a costly endeavor. Establishing standards can be a time-consuming, labor-intensive, and expensive

[1] "Boosting Productivity at American Express," *Business Week.* (Full citations to references are in the Bibliography.)

[2] D. Boll, "How Dutch Pantry Accounts for Standard Costs."

[3] "Up to Speed: United Parcel Service Gets Deliveries Done by Driving Its Workers," *The Wall Street Journal.*

process. Moreover, standards must be updated periodically to reflect changes in the cost structure of a production process. As with any management-information system, each finer level of detail in a standard-costing system entails higher costs to generate and use the information. Deciding the appropriate level of standard-cost detail and the frequency with which reports should be generated is part of the cost analyst's information-system design problem. Ultimately, the benefits of the information, in terms of improved production cost control and decision making, must be weighed against the cost of generating the information.

Cost Variance Analysis

Koala Camp Gear Company

To illustrate the use of standards in controlling costs, we focus on Koala Camp Gear Company, a manufacturer of camping tents based in Melbourne, Australia. Although relatively small, Koala Camp Gear has established a reputation for excellence throughout Australia, Europe, and the United States. Most of the company's sales are domestic, but exports have been increasing to the United Kingdom, Germany, Switzerland, Italy, and the United States. Koala recently introduced its newest product, a lightweight but durable backpacking tent trade-named the Tree Line tent. Margo Hastings, Koala's founder and CEO, plans to market the Tree Line tent aggressively in Europe and the United States.

Koala Camp Gear plans to manufacture only the Tree Line tent itself. The company will purchase aluminum tent poles as finished components and package them with the tent. As detailed in the memorandum at the beginning of this chapter, Koala's controller, Marc Wesley, recently set standards for the direct materials and direct labor required to manufacture the Tree Line tent as follows.

Direct-Material Standards

The fabric in a tent is considered a direct material. The thread is inexpensive and is considered an indirect material, part of manufacturing overhead. The standard quantity and price of fabric for the production of one Tree Line tent are as follows:

Standard quantity:		
Fabric in finished product		11 sq. meters
Allowance for normal waste		1 sq. meter
Total standard quantity required per tent		12 sq. meters
Standard price:		
Purchase price per sq. meter of fabric (net of purchase discounts)	$7.75	
Transportation cost per sq. meter	.25	
Total standard price per sq. meter of fabric	$8.00	

The standard quantity of fabric needed to manufacture one Tree Line tent is 12 square meters, even though only 11 square meters actually remain in the finished product. One square meter of fabric is wasted as a normal result of the cutting and trimming that are part of the production process. Therefore, the entire amount of fabric needed to manufacture a tent is included in the standard quantity of material.

The standard price of fabric reflects all costs incurred to acquire the material and transport it to the plant. Notice that the cost of transportation is added to the purchase price. Any purchase discounts are subtracted out from the purchase price to obtain a net price.

To summarize, the **standard direct-material quantity** is the total amount of materials normally required to produce a finished product, including allowances for normal waste or inefficiency. The **standard direct-material price** is the total delivered cost after subtracting any purchase discounts.

standard direct-material quantity *is the total amount of material normally required to produce a finished product, including allowances for normal waste or inefficiency*

standard direct-material price *is the total delivered cost after subtracting any purchase discounts*

Direct-Labor Standards

The standard quantity and rate for direct labor for the production of one Tree Line tent are as follows:

Standard quantity:	
Direct labor required per tent	2 hours
Standard rate:	
Hourly wage rate	$15
Fringe benefits (20% of wages)	3
Total standard rate per hour	$18

standard direct-labor quantity *is the number of labor hours normally needed to manufacture one unit of product*

standard direct-labor rate *is the total hourly cost of compensation, including fringe benefits*

The **standard direct-labor quantity** is the number of labor hours normally needed to manufacture one unit of product. The **standard direct-labor rate** is the total hourly cost of compensation, including fringe benefits.

Standard Costs Given Actual Output

During June, Koala manufactured 3,000 Tree Line tents. The total standard or budgeted costs for direct material and direct labor are computed as follows:

Direct material:	
Standard direct-material cost per tent	
(12 sq. meters × $8 per sq. meter)	$ 96
Actual output	× 3,000
Total standard direct-material cost	$288,000
Direct labor:	
Direct labor cost per tent (2 hours × $18 per hour)	$ 36
Actual output	× 3,000
Total standard direct-labor cost	$108,000

Notice that the total standard cost for the direct-material and direct-labor inputs is based on Koala's *actual output.* The division should incur costs of $396,000 ($288,000 + $108,000) for direct material and direct labor, *given that it produced 3,000 tents.* The total standard costs for direct material and direct labor serve as the cost-management analyst's benchmarks against which to compare actual costs. This comparison then serves as the basis for controlling direct-material and direct-labor costs.

A note about manufacturing overhead. We focus in this chapter on the use of standard-costing systems to control direct-materials and direct-labor costs. In the next chapter, we extend our analysis to the control of overhead costs using a tool called *flexible budgeting.*

Analysis of Cost Variances

During June, Koala incurred the following actual costs for direct material and direct labor.

Direct-material purchases: actual cost	
40,000 sq. meters at $8.15 per sq. meter	$326,000
Direct material used: actual cost	
36,400 sq. meters at $8.15 per sq. meter	$296,660
Direct labor: actual cost	
5,900 hours at $19 per hour	$112,100

Compare these actual expenditures with the total standard costs for the production of 3,000 tents. Koala spent more than the budgeted amount for both direct material and direct labor. But why were these excess costs incurred? Could the cost-management analyst provide any other analysis to help answer this question?

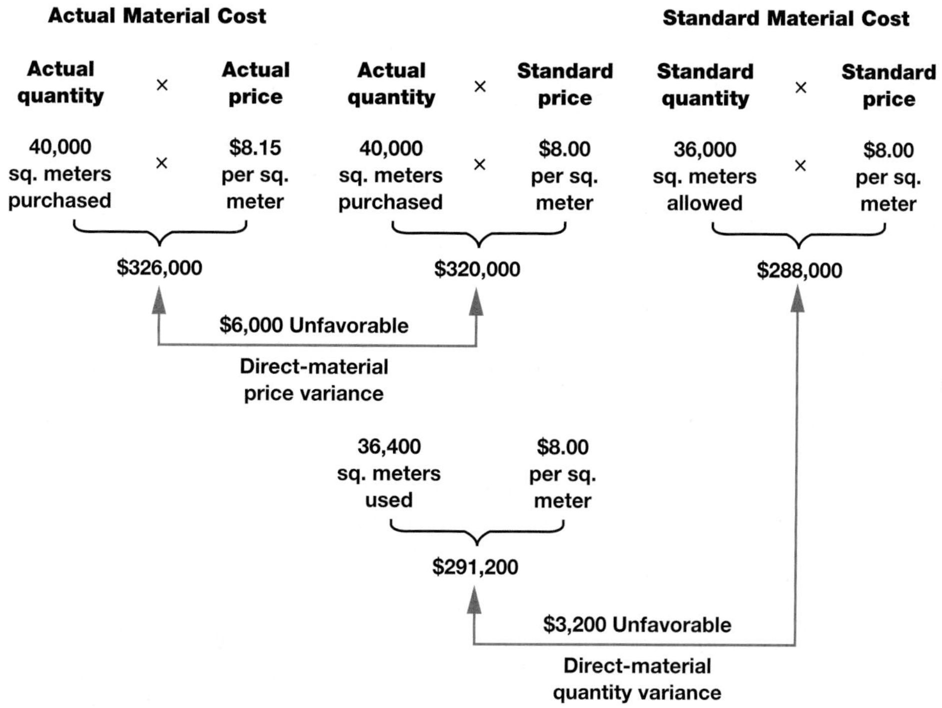

Exhibit 16–1

Direct-Material Price and Quantity Variances

Koala Camp Gear Company

Direct-Material Variances

What caused Koala to spend more than the anticipated amount on direct material? First, the company purchased fabric at a higher price ($8.15 per square meter) than the standard price ($8.00 per square meter). Second, the company used more fabric than the standard amount. The amount actually used was 36,400 square meters instead of the standard amount of 36,000 square meters, which is based on actual output of 3,000 tents. The cost-management analyst can show both of these deviations from standards by computing a **direct-material price variance** (or **purchase price variance**) and a direct-material quantity variance. The computations for these variances are displayed in Exhibit 16–1.

The formula for the direct-material price variance is as follows:

$$\text{Direct-material price variance} = (PQ \times AP) - (PQ \times SP)$$
$$= PQ(AP - SP)$$

where

$$PQ = \text{quantity purchased}$$
$$AP = \text{actual price}$$
$$SP = \text{standard price}$$

Koala's direct-material price variance for June is computed as follows:

$$\text{Direct-material price variance} = PQ(AP - SP)$$
$$= 40{,}000\ (\$8.15 - \$8.00)$$
$$= \$6{,}000\ \text{Unfavorable}$$

This variance is unfavorable because the actual purchase price exceeded the standard price. Notice that the price variance is based on the quantity of material *purchased* (*PQ*), not the quantity actually used in production.

As Exhibit 16–1 shows, the following formula defines the direct-materials quantity variance.

$$\text{Direct-material quantity variance} = (AQ \times SP) - (SQ \times SP)$$
$$= SP(AQ - SQ)$$

LO 3 Compute and interpret the direct-material price and quantity variances and the direct-labor rate and efficiency variances.

direct-material price variance (or **purchase price variance**) *is the difference between the actual and standard price multiplied by the actual quantity of material purchased*

direct-material quantity variance *is the difference between the actual quantity and the standard quantity of material allowed, given actual output, multiplied by the standard price* where

$$AQ = \text{actual quantity used}$$
$$SQ = \text{standard quantity allowed}$$

Koala's direct-material quantity variance for June is computed as follows:

$$\begin{aligned}\text{Direct-material quantity variance} &= SP(AQ - SQ)\\ &= \$8.00\ (36{,}400 - 36{,}000)\\ &= \$3{,}200\ \text{Unfavorable}\end{aligned}$$

This variance is unfavorable because the actual quantity of direct material used in June exceeded the standard quantity allowed, given actual June output of 3,000 tents. The quantity variance is based on the quantity of material actually *used* in production (*AQ*).

Identifying the quantity purchased versus quantity used. The direct-material price variance is based on the quantity purchased (*PQ*). This makes sense because deviations between the actual and standard price, which are highlighted by the price variance, relate to the *purchasing* function in the firm. Timely action to follow up a significant price variance will be facilitated by calculating this variance as soon as possible after the material is *purchased.*

In contrast, the direct-material quantity variance is based on the amount of material *used* in production (*AQ*). The quantity variance highlights the deviations between the quantity of material actually used (*AQ*) and the standard quantity allowed (*SQ*). Thus, it makes sense to compute this variance when the material is *used* in production.

Basing the quantity variance on actual output. Notice that the standard quantity of material must be based on the actual production output for the quantity variance to be meaningful. It makes no sense to compare standard or budgeted material usage at one level of output (say, 2,000 tents) with the actual material usage at a *different* level of output (say, 3,000 tents). Everyone would expect more direct material to be used in the production of 3,000 tents than of 2,000 tents. For the direct-material quantity variance to provide helpful information for management, the standard, or budgeted, quantity must be based on *actual output.* Then the quantity variance compares the following two quantities:

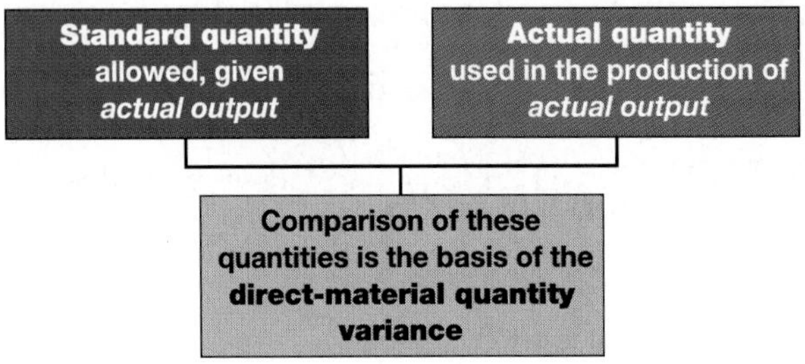

When we extend our analysis to the control of manufacturing overhead costs in the next chapter, you will see that a similar comment can apply to overhead cost control. Using a tool called *flexible budgeting,* we compare the overhead cost allowed, *given actual output,* with the actual overhead cost incurred.

direct-labor rate variance *is the difference between the actual and standard hourly labor rate multiplied by the actual quantity of direct labor used*

direct-labor efficiency variance *is the difference between the actual hours and the standard hours of direct labor allowed, given actual output, multiplied by the standard hourly labor rate*

Direct-Labor Variances

Why did Koala Camp Gear spend more than the anticipated amount on direct labor during June? First, the company incurred a cost of $19 per hour for direct labor instead of the standard amount of $18 per hour. Second, Koala used only 5,900 hours of direct labor, which is less than the standard quantity of 6,000 hours, given actual output of 3,000 tents. The cost-management analysts study direct-labor costs by computing a **direct-labor rate variance** and a **direct-labor efficiency variance.** Exhibit 16–2 displays the computations for these variances.

The formula for the direct-labor rate variance is as follows:

$$\begin{aligned}\text{Direct-labor rate variance} &= (AH \times AR) - (AH \times SR)\\ &= AH(AR - SR)\end{aligned}$$

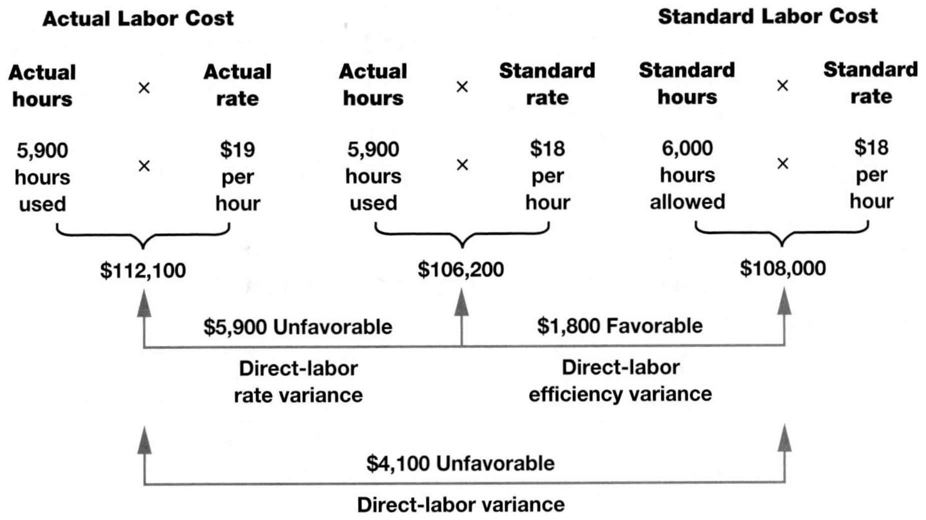

Exhibit 16–2

Direct-Labor Rate and Efficiency Variances

Koala Camp Gear Company

where

$$AH = \text{actual hours used}$$
$$AR = \text{actual rate per hour}$$
$$SR = \text{standard rate per hour}$$

Koala's direct-labor rate variance for June is computed as follows:

$$\begin{aligned}\text{Direct-labor rate variance} &= AH(AR - SR)\\ &= 5{,}900\ (\$19 - \$18)\\ &= \$5{,}900 \text{ Unfavorable}\end{aligned}$$

This variance is unfavorable because the actual rate exceeded the standard rate during June.

As Exhibit 16–2 shows, the formula for the direct-labor efficiency variance is as follows:

$$\begin{aligned}\text{Direct-labor efficiency variance} &= (AH \times SR) - (SH \times SR)\\ &= SR(AH - SH)\end{aligned}$$

where

$$SH = \text{standard hours allowed}$$

Koala's direct-labor efficiency variance for June is computed as follows:

$$\begin{aligned}\text{Direct-labor efficiency variance} &= SR(AH - SH)\\ &= \$18\ (5{,}900 - 6{,}000)\\ &= \$1{,}800 \text{ Favorable}\end{aligned}$$

This variance is favorable because the actual number of direct-labor hours used in June were less than the number of standard hours allowed, *given actual June output* of 3,000 tents.

Notice that the direct-labor rate and efficiency variances add up to the total direct-labor variance. However, the rate and efficiency variances have opposite signs since one variance is unfavorable and the other is favorable.

Direct-labor rate variance	$5,900 Unfavorable	Favorable and unfavorable variance designations cancel just as plus and minus signs cancel in arithmetic.
Direct-labor efficiency variance	1,800 Favorable	
Direct-labor variance	$4,100 Unfavorable	

Basing the efficiency variance on actual output. The number of standard hours of direct labor allowed is based on the *actual* production output. It is not meaningful to compare standard or budgeted labor usage at one level of output with the actual hours used at a different level of output.

Multiple Types of Direct Material and Direct Labor

Manufacturing processes usually involve several types of direct material. In such cases, direct-materials price and quantity variances are computed for each type of material. Then these variances are added to obtain a total price variance and a total quantity variance, as follows:

Direct material X	\$1,500 F*	\$1,900 U+
Direct material Y	2,400 U	300 U
Direct material Z	900 U	400 F
Total variance	\$1,800 U	\$1,800 U

*F denotes a favorable variance. +U denotes an unfavorable variance.

Similarly, if a production process involves several types of direct labor, rate and efficiency variances are computed for each labor type. Then they are added to obtain a total rate variance and a total efficiency variance.

When a manufacturing process involves multiple types of direct material or direct labor, additional variance analysis can be conducted to analyze the proportions with which the multiple inputs are used. This analysis is covered in the Appendix to this chapter.

Allowance for Defects or Spoilage

In some manufacturing processes, a certain amount of defective production or spoilage is normal. This must be considered when the standard quantity of material is computed. To illustrate, suppose that 1,000 liters of chemicals are normally required in a chemical process to obtain 800 liters of good output. If total good output in February is 5,000 liters, what is the standard allowed quantity of input?

$$\text{Good output quantity} = 80\% \times \text{Input quantity}$$

Dividing both sides of the equation by 80%

$$\frac{\text{Good output quantity}}{80\%} = \text{Input quantity allowed}$$

Using the numbers in the illustration

$$\frac{\text{5,000 liters of good output}}{80\%} = \text{6,250 liters of input allowed}$$

The total standard allowed input is 6,250 liters, given 5,000 liters of good output.

Research Insight 16.3

Global Use of Standard-Costing Systems

Standard-costing systems are common throughout the world. Research has shown, for example, that standard costing is widely used in Japan, the United Kingdom, and Germany, as well as in the United States. In Germany, *grenzplankostenrechnung,* which means "flexible standard costing," is used for cost planning and control. "Reporting systems based on *grenzplankostenrechnung* consist of monthly statements of each cost center's actual and planned demand for resources, actual costs, standard costs, and different types of variances." *Source: B. Gaiser,* "German Cost Management Systems."

Significance of Cost Variances: When to Follow Up

LO 4 Describe several methods used to determine the significance of cost variances.

Managers are busy people. They do not have time to investigate the causes of every cost variance. *Management by exception* enables managers explore the causes of only significant variances. But what constitutes an exception? How does the manager know when to follow up on a cost variance and when to ignore it?

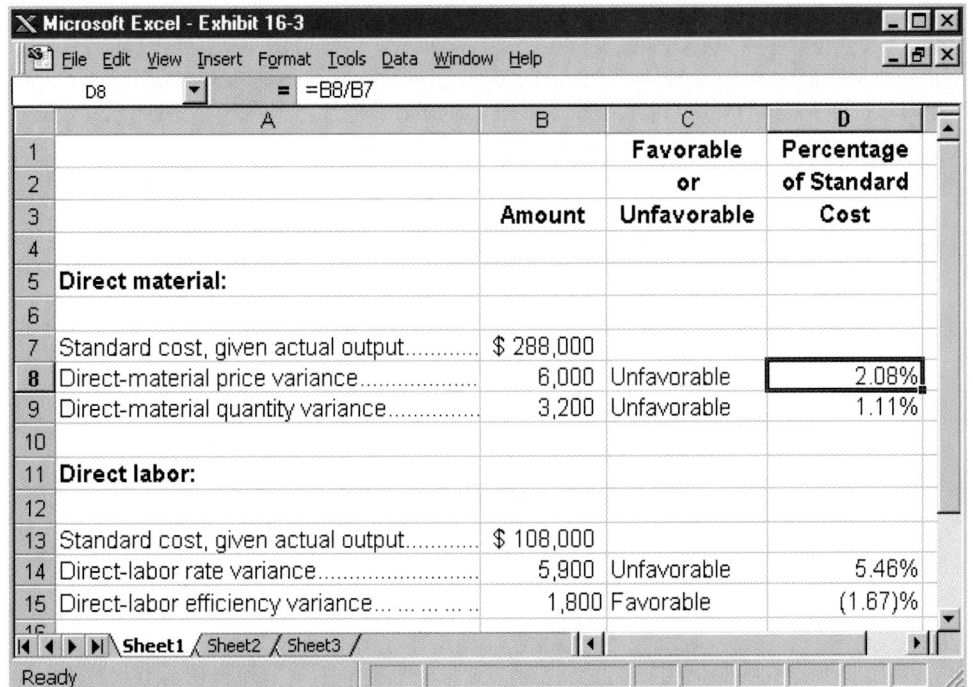

Exhibit 16–3

Cost-Variance Report for June. Koala Camp Gear

Microsoft Excel - Exhibit 16-3

D8 = =B8/B7

	A	B	C	D
1			Favorable	Percentage
2			or	of Standard
3		Amount	Unfavorable	Cost
4				
5	**Direct material:**			
6				
7	Standard cost, given actual output	$ 288,000		
8	Direct-material price variance	6,000	Unfavorable	2.08%
9	Direct-material quantity variance	3,200	Unfavorable	1.11%
10				
11	**Direct labor:**			
12				
13	Standard cost, given actual output	$ 108,000		
14	Direct-labor rate variance	5,900	Unfavorable	5.46%
15	Direct-labor efficiency variance	1,800	Favorable	(1.67)%

Sheet1 / Sheet2 / Sheet3

Ready

These questions are difficult to answer because to some extent the answers are part of the art of management. A manager applies judgment and experience in making guesses, pursuing hunches, and relying on intuition to determine when to investigate a variance. Nevertheless, there are guidelines and rules of thumb that managers often apply.

Size of Variances

The absolute size of a variance is one consideration. Managers are more likely to follow up on large variances than on small ones. The relative size of the variance is probably even more important. A manager is more likely to investigate a $40,000 material quantity variance that is 20 percent of the standard direct-material cost of $200,000 than a $60,000 labor efficiency variance that is only 2 percent of the standard direct-labor cost of $3,000,000. The *relative* magnitude of the $40,000 material quantity variance (20 percent) is greater than the *relative* magnitude of the $60,000 labor efficiency variance (2 percent). For this reason, cost-management analysts often show the relative magnitude of variances in their cost-variance reports. For example, Koala's June cost-variance report is shown in the spreadsheet in Exhibit 16–3.

Managers often apply a rule of thumb that considers both the absolute and the relative magnitude of a variance. An example of such a rule is the following: Investigate variances that are either more than $10,000 or more than 10 percent of standard cost.

Recurring Variances

Another consideration in deciding when to investigate a variance is whether the variance occurs repeatedly or only infrequently. Suppose that a manager uses the rule of thumb just stated and the following direct-materials quantity variances occur.

Month	Variance	Percentage of Standard Cost*
September	$6,000 F	6.0%
October	6,400 F	6.4%
November	3,200 F	3.2%
December	6,200 F	6.2%

*The standard direct-material cost is $100,000.

Strict adherence to the rule of thumb indicates no investigation since none of the monthly variances is more than $10,000 or 10 percent of standard cost. Nevertheless, the manager might investigate this variance in December, since it has *recurred* at a reasonably high level for several consecutive months. In this case, the consistency of the variance triggers an investigation, not its absolute or relative magnitude.

Trends

A trend in a variance also might call for investigation. Suppose that a manager observes the following direct-labor efficiency variances.

Month	Variance	Percentage of Standard Cost*
September	$ 250 U	.25%
October	840 U	.84%
November	4,000 U	4.00%
December	9,300 U	9.30%

*The standard direct-labor cost is $100,000.

None of these variances is large enough to trigger an investigation if the manager uses the "$10,000 or 10 percent" rule of thumb. However, the four-month *trend* is worrisome. An alert manager will likely follow up on this unfavorable trend to determine its causes before costs get out of hand.

Controllability

Another important consideration in deciding when to investigate the causes of a variance is the manager's view of the controllability of the cost item. A manager is more likely to investigate a variance for a cost that someone in the organization can control than a variance for a cost that cannot be controlled. For example, there might be little point to investigating a materials-price variance if the organization has no control over the price. This could happen, for example, if the firm has a long-term contract with a supplier of the material at a price determined on the international market. In contrast, the manager is likely to follow up on a variance that should be controllable, such as a direct-labor efficiency variance or a direct-materials quantity variance.

Favorable Variances

Investigation of significant favorable variances is just as important as of significant unfavorable variances. For example, a favorable direct-labor efficiency variance could indicate that employees have developed a more efficient way to perform a production task. By investigating the variance, management can learn about the improved method. A similar approach might be used elsewhere in the organization.

Costs and Benefits of Investigation

The decision to investigate a cost variance is a cost-benefit decision. The costs of investigation include the time spent by the investigating manager and the employees in the department where the investigation occurs. Other potential costs include the disruption of the production process to conduct the investigation and to take corrective actions to eliminate the cause of a variance. The benefits of a variance investigation include reduced future production costs if the cause of an unfavorable variance can be eliminated. Another potential benefit is the cost savings associated with lowering the cost standards when the cause of a favorable variance is discovered. Weighing these considerations takes the judgment of skillful and experienced managers. Key to this judgment is an intimate understanding of the organization's production process and day-to-day contact with its operations.

Computerized databases of cost information facilitate statistical analysis of cost performance.

Statistical Analysis

Cost variances are caused by many factors. For example, a direct-labor efficiency variance could be caused by inexperienced employees, employee inefficiency, poor-quality raw materials, poorly maintained machinery, or an intentional work slowdown due to employee grievances. In addition to these substantive reasons, there are purely random causes of variances. People are not robots, and they are not perfectly consistent in their work habits. Random fluctuations in direct-labor efficiency variances can be caused by factors such as employee illnesses, sleep deprivation, workers experimenting with different production methods, or simply random fatigue. Ideally, managers are able to sort out the randomly caused variances from those with substantive and controllable underlying causes. Although accomplishing this with 100 percent accuracy is impossible, a *statistical control chart* can help.

A **statistical control chart** plots cost variances across time and compares them with a statistically determined *critical value* that triggers an investigation. Determination of this critical value usually involves assuming that cost variances have a normal probability distribution with a mean of zero. The critical value is set at some multiple of the distribution's standard deviation. Variances greater than the critical value are investigated. (Chapter 7 discusses the use of statistical control charts for quality control.)

statistical control chart *plots cost variances across time and compares them with a statistically determined critical value that triggers an investigation*

Exhibit 16–4 shows a statistical control chart with a critical value of 1 standard deviation. The manager would investigate the variance observed in April since it falls

Exhibit 16–4

Statistical Control Chart

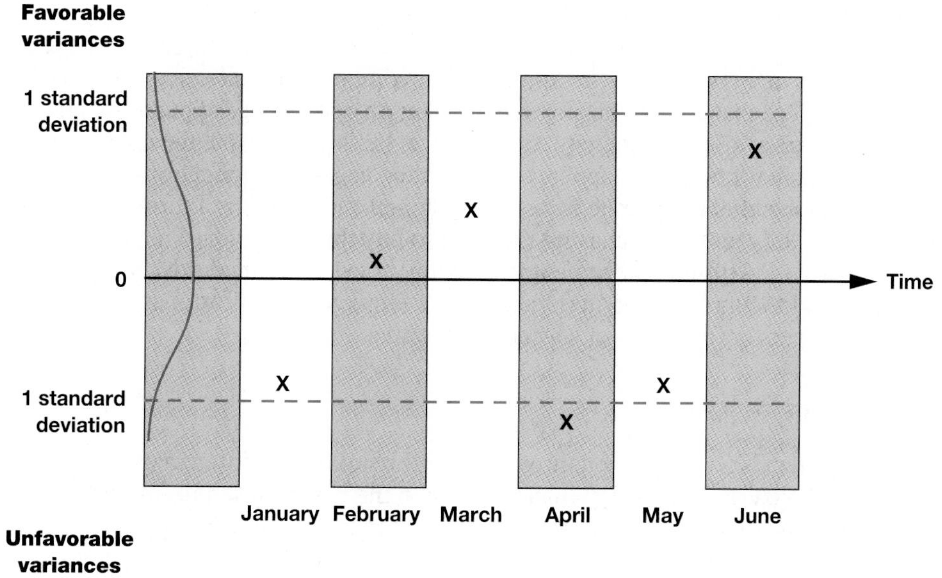

further than 1 standard deviation from the mean (zero). The variances for the remaining five months would not be investigated. The presumption is that these minor variances are due to random causes and are not worth the cost of investigating.

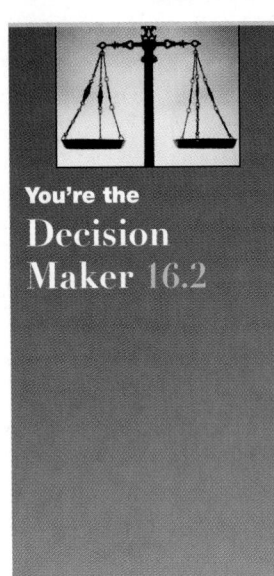

You're the Decision Maker 16.2

Direct-Material and Direct-Labor Variances

In December, Koala Camp Gear Company produced 2,000 Tree Line tents and incurred the following actual costs for direct material and direct labor:

Purchased 25,000 sq. meters of tent fabric at $8.25 per sq. meter.

Used 24,500 sq. meters at $8.25 per sq. meter.

Used 4,200 hours of direct labor at $16.75 per hour.

The standard costs for tent production were the same in December as those given earlier in the chapter for June.

a. Compute Koala's direct-material and direct-labor variances for December using the format shown in Exhibits 16–1 and 16–2.

b. Suppose that Koala's management uses a statistical control chart to plot cost variances and help management decide which variances to investigate. Let's assume that the cost-management team has estimated that all of Koala's variances exhibit a normal probability distribution with a mean of zero and a standard deviation of $4,800. The critical value is 1 standard deviation. Which of Koala's December cost variances would you investigate? Explain.

(Solutions begin on page 682.)

Behavioral Effects of Standard Costing

LO 5 Discuss some behavioral effects of standard costing and the controllability of variances.

Standard costs and variance analysis help managers discern "the story behind the story"—the details of operations that underlie reported cost and profit numbers. Standard costs, budgets, and variances also are used to evaluate the performance of individuals and departments. The performance of individuals, relative to standards or budgets, often is used to help determine salary increases, bonuses, and promotions. When standards and variances affect employee reward structures, they can profoundly influence behavior.

For example, suppose that the manager of a hotel's Food and Beverage Department earns a bonus when food and beverage costs are below the budgeted amount, given actual sales. This reward structure will provide a concrete incentive for the manager to control food and beverage costs. But such an incentive can have either positive or negative effects. The bonus might induce the manager to seek the most economical food suppliers and to watch more carefully for employee theft and waste. However, the bonus also might persuade the manager to buy cheaper but less tender steaks for the restaurant. This could ultimately result in lost patronage for the restaurant and the hotel.

Ethical issues also might arise when employees' performance relative to standards affects their reward system. Assume, for example, that a manufacturer's purchasing manager earns a bonus when a significant favorable material-price variance is recorded. Suppose that the purchasing manager has an opportunity to purchase below-standard material at a significant reduction in price. Let's assume that the inferior quality of the material is not readily apparent and that the negative implications will not be realized until long after the products are manufactured and sold. It is a serious violation of ethical standards for the purchasing manager to buy the off-standard material.

One aspect of skillful management is knowing how to use standards, budgets, and variances to get the most out of an organization's employees. Unfortunately, there are no simple answers or formulas for success in this area.

Controllability of Variances

Cost management is accomplished through the efforts of individual managers in an organization. By determining which managers are in the best position to influence each cost variance, the managerial accountant can assist managers in deriving the greatest benefit from cost variance analysis.

Which Managers Influence Cost Variances?

Who is responsible for the direct-materials price and quantity variances? The direct-labor rate and efficiency variances? Answering these questions is often difficult because any one person rarely has complete control of any event. Nevertheless, it often is possible to identify the manager who is *most able to influence* a particular variance even if he or she does not exercise complete control over the outcome.

Direct-material price variance. The purchasing manager generally is in the best position to influence material price variances. Through skillful purchasing practices, an expert purchasing manager can get the best prices available for purchased goods and services. To achieve this goal, the purchasing manager uses practices such as buying in quantity, negotiating purchase contracts, comparing prices among vendors, and global sourcing.

Despite these purchasing skills, the purchasing manager is not in complete control of prices. The need to purchase component parts with precise engineering specifications, the all-too-frequent rush requests from the production department, and world-wide shortages of critical materials all contribute to the challenges that the purchasing manager faces.

Direct-material quantity variance. The production supervisor is usually in the best position to influence material quantity variances. Skillful supervision and motivation of production employees, coupled with the careful use and handling of materials, contribute to minimal waste. Production engineers also are partially responsible for material quantity variances since they determine the grade and technical specifications of materials and component parts. In some cases, using a low-grade material results in more waste than using a high-grade material.

Direct-labor rate variance. Direct-labor rate variances generally result from using a different mix of employees than that anticipated when the standards were set. Wage rates differ among employees due to their skill levels and their seniority with the organization. Using a higher proportion of more senior or more highly skilled employees than a task requires can result in unfavorable direct-labor rate variances. The production supervisor is generally in the best position to influence the employee work schedules.

Direct-labor efficiency variance. The production supervisor is usually most responsible for the efficient use of employee time. Through motivation toward production goals and effective work schedules, employee efficiency can be maximized.

Interaction among Variances

Interactions among variances often occur, making the determination of the responsibility for a particular variance even more difficult. To illustrate, consider the following incident, which occurred at Koala Camp Gear Company during March. The purchasing manager obtained a special price on tent fabric from a new supplier. When the material was placed into production, it turned out to be a lower grade of material than the production employees were used to. The fabric was of a slightly different composition, which made the material tear easily during cutting. Koala could have returned the material to the supplier, but doing so would have interrupted production and kept the company from filling its orders on time. Since using the off-standard material would not affect the quality of the company's finished products, the production manager decided to keep the material and make the best of the situation.

The ultimate result was that Koala incurred four interrelated variances during March. The material was less expensive than normal, so the direct-material price variance was favorable. However, the employees had difficulty using the material, which resulted in more waste than expected. Hence, the division incurred an unfavorable direct-material quantity variance.

What were the labor implications of the off-standard material? Due to the difficulty in working with the fabric, the employees required more than the standard amount of time. This resulted in an unfavorable direct-labor efficiency variance. Finally, the production supervisor had to use his most senior employees to work with the off-standard material. Since these people earn relatively high wages, the direct-labor rate variance was also unfavorable.

To summarize, the purchase of off-standard material resulted in the following interrelated variances:

Purchase of off-standard material ⇒
- **Favorable direct-material price variance**
- **Unfavorable direct-material quantity variance**
- **Unfavorable direct-labor rate variance**
- **Unfavorable direct-labor efficiency variance**

Such interactions of variances make the assignment of responsibility more difficult for any particular variance.

Trade-offs among variances. Does the preceding incident mean that the decision to buy and use the off-standard material was a poor one? Not necessarily. Perhaps these variances were anticipated, and a conscious decision was made to buy the material anyway. How could this be a wise decision? Suppose the amounts of the variances were as follows:

$(7,900)	Favorable direct-material price variance
1,100	Unfavorable direct-material quantity variance
1,900	Unfavorable direct-labor rate variance
2,100	Unfavorable direct-labor efficiency variance
$(2,800)	Favorable net overall variance

Koala saved money overall on the decision to use a different grade of fabric. Given that the quality of the final product was not affected, the company's management acted wisely.

A value-chain perspective. Think back to our discussions of the value chain in earlier chapters. Recall that the *value chain* is the set of linked operations or processes that begins by obtaining resources and ends with providing products or services that customers value. Exhibit 16–5 depicts Koala Camp Gear Company's value chain.

The preceding discussion regarding interactions and trade-offs among variances emphasizes that variances in one part of the value chain can result from root causes in another part of the chain. For example, when Koala Camp Gear's purchasing manager bought tent fabric at a special price, and the material turned out to be below standard, several direct-material and direct-labor variances resulted in the production process. Thus, an incident in the supply component of Koala's value chain resulted in cost variances in the production component of the chain.

Think about other possible interactions in Koala's value chain. Could production cost variances be caused by events in Koala's design process? How about its downstream processes, such as marketing or distribution?

Exhibit 16–5

Koala Camp Gear Company's Value Chain

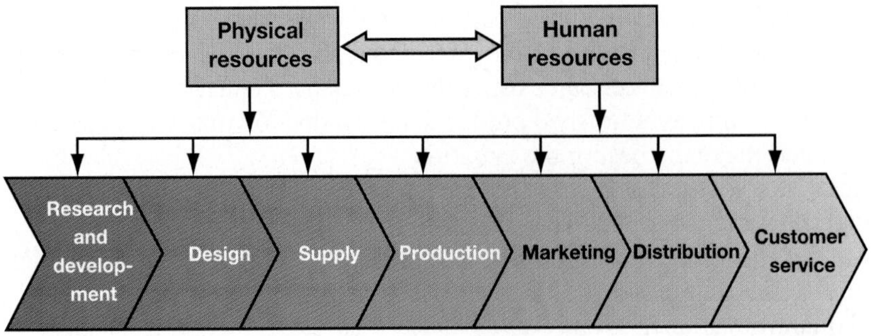

Using Standard Costs for Product Costing

LO 6 Explain how companies use standard costs in product costing.

Our discussion of standard costing has focused on its use in controlling costs. Firms that employ standard-costing systems also use standards for product costing. As production takes place, product costs are added to the Work-in-Process Inventory account. The flow of product costs through a firm's manufacturing accounts is depicted in Exhibit 16–6. In a **standard-costing system** the *standard* costs of direct material and direct labor are entered into Work-in-Process Inventory.

standard-costing system *enters the standard costs of direct material and direct labor into the Work-In-Process Inventory account*

Journal Entries under Standard Costing

Direct material. During June, Koala purchased 40,000 square meters of direct material for $326,000. It actually used 36,400 square meters in production. However, the standard cost of direct material, given June's actual output of 3,000 Tree Line tents, was only $288,000. The following journal entries record these facts and isolate the direct-material price and quantity variances.

Raw-Material Inventory	320,000	
Direct-Material Price Variance	6,000	
Accounts Payable		326,000

To record the purchase of raw material and the incurrence of an unfavorable price variance.

Work-in-Process Inventory	288,000	
Direct-Material Quantity Variance	3,200	
Raw-Material Inventory		291,200

To record the use of direct material in production and the incurrence of an unfavorable quantity variance.

Notice that the material purchase recorded in the Raw-Material Inventory account appears at its standard price ($320,000 = 40,000 square meters purchased × $8 per square meter). The $288,000 debit entry to Work-in-Process Inventory adds only the standard cost of the material to Work-in-Process Inventory as a product cost ($288,000 = 36,000 square meters allowed × $8 per square meter). The two variances are isolated in their own variance accounts. Since both are unfavorable, they are represented by debit entries.

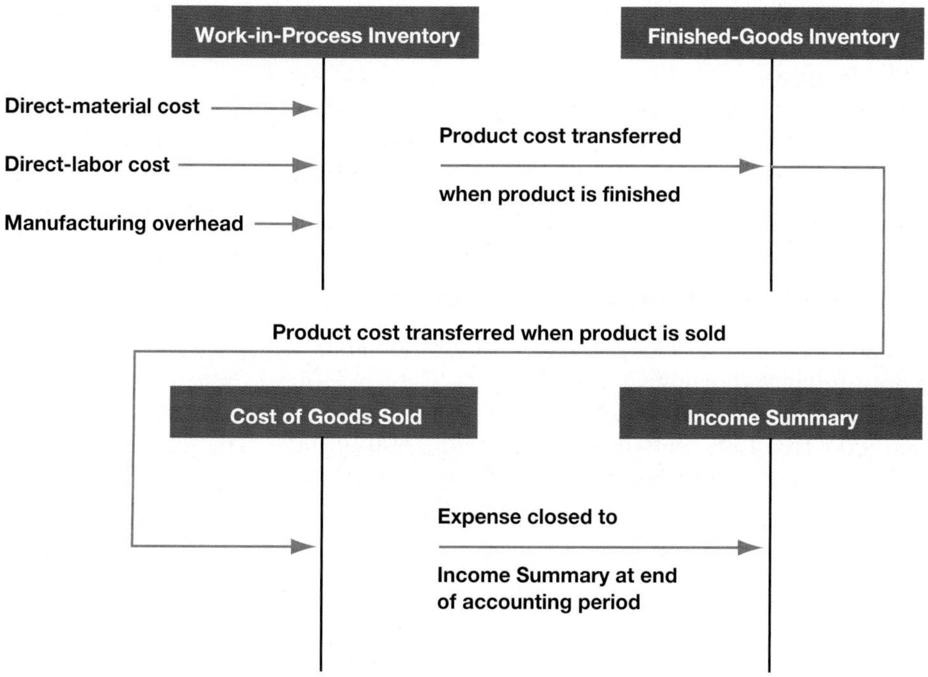

Exhibit 16–6
Flow of Product Costs through Manufacturing Accounts

Direct labor. The following journal entry records the actual June cost of direct labor as an addition to Wages Payable. The entry also adds the standard cost of direct labor to Work-in-Process Inventory and isolates the direct-labor variances.

Work-in-Process Inventory	108,000	
Direct-Labor Rate Variance	5,900	
Direct-Labor Efficiency Variance		1,800
Wages Payable		112,100

To record the usage of direct labor and the direct-labor variances for June.

Since the direct-labor efficiency variance is favorable, it is recorded as a credit entry.

Disposition of variances. Variance accounts are temporary accounts as are revenue and expense accounts, and they are closed at the end of each accounting period. Most companies close their variance accounts directly into Cost of Goods Sold. The journal entry required to close Koala's June variance accounts follows:

Cost of Goods Sold	13,300	
Direct-Labor Efficiency Variance	1,800	
Direct-Labor Rate Variance		5,900
Direct-Material Price Variance		6,000
Direct-Material Quantity Variance		3,200

The increase of $13,300 in Cost of Goods Sold is explained as follows:

	Unfavorable Variances Increase Cost of Goods Sold		Favorable Variance Decreases Cost of Goods Sold		Net Increase in Cost of Goods Sold
Direct-labor efficiency variance			$1,800		
Direct-labor rate variance	$ 5,900				
Direct-material price variance	6,000				
Direct-material quantity variance	3,200				
Total	$15,100	−	$1,800	=	$13,300

The unfavorable variances represent costs of operating inefficiently, relative to the standards, and thus cause Cost of Goods Sold to be higher. The opposite is true for favorable variances.

An alternative method of variance disposition is to apportion all variances among Work-in-Process Inventory, Finished-Goods Inventory, and Cost of Goods Sold. This accounting treatment reflects the effects of unusual inefficiency or efficiency in all accounts through which the manufacturing costs flow. This method, called *variance proration,* is covered in Appendix A to Chapter 17.

Cost Flows under Standard Costing

In a standard-costing system, standard costs are entered in Work-in-Process Inventory and flow through all manufacturing accounts. Thus, in Exhibit 16–6, all product costs flowing through the accounts are standard costs. To illustrate, suppose that Koala finished 3,000 Tree Line tents in June and sold 2,500 of them. The journal entries to record the flow of standard direct-material and direct-labor costs are as follows:

Finished-Goods Inventory	396,000*	
Work-in-Process Inventory		396,000

*Total standard cost of direct material and direct labor: $396,000 = $288,000 + $108,000.

Cost of Goods Sold	330,000*	
Finished-Goods Inventory		330,000

*2,500 of 3,000 tents sold; five-sixths of $396,000 is $330,000.

Our Koala Camp Gear illustration is not really complete yet because we have not discussed manufacturing overhead costs. This topic is covered in the next chapter. The important point at this juncture is that in a standard-costing system, *standard costs flow through the manufacturing accounts rather than actual costs.*

Impact of Information Technology on Standard Costing

Standard-costing systems can facilitate the use of information technology to link together several business processes. When a manufacturer uses standard costing for product costing and cost management, the standard costs of materials and labor are loaded into the computer. When raw materials or purchased components are requisitioned for production, the standard cost of the materials or components used is automatically recorded by accessing the computer database where the standard quantities and prices of the materials are stored. Similarly, when production employees work on a production job, their time on the job is recorded and the standard labor cost is automatically determined by accessing the standard labor times and rates in the computer database.

Use of Bar Codes

Bar codes are now widely used to capture important events in manufacturing processes. In *real-time shop floor data-collection systems,* production employees can record the time they begin working on a particular job order by scanning the bar code on their employee ID badge and a bar code assigned to the production job order. The standard direct-labor cost is assigned to the production job.

When raw materials arrive at the production facility, their bar code is scanned and the event is recorded. Inventory records are updated automatically. Raw materials and partially completed components are assigned bar codes, and their movement through the production process is efficiently recorded. For example, raw materials might be requisitioned by a production employee simply by scanning the bar code assigned to the needed raw materials. When the materials are sent from the warehouse to the requisitioning production department, the bar code is scanned again. Inventory records are updated instantly, and the standard cost of the materials is recorded as a product cost.

Computer-Aided Design

Standard-costing systems also can be integrated with a computer-aided design (CAD) system to assist design engineers in the product design process. The standard costs of material and labor are stored in the computer database where the product design team can access them easily. This information enables a product design engineer to get a quick answer to the question, What will be the new product cost if certain design

Many companies use computer-aided design (CAD) systems, which make standard cost information available to the design engineers.

changes are made to the product? If, for example, the engineer wants to know the cost of changing the exterior case on a particular computer model, this information is easily determined by accessing the cost data base.[4]

In other applications, cost data from target-costing or value engineering approaches are used in new product design. At Boeing, for example, "firm-specific cost and productivity data are used to improve traditional engineering cost estimates in the early, system design stage of product development."

Standard Costing: Its Traditional Advantages

LO 7 Summarize some advantages attributed to standard costing.

Standard costing has been a widely used accounting system in manufacturing companies for both cost control and product-costing purposes for several decades. This remains true today, and the use of standard costing is spreading to nonmanufacturing firms as well. The widespread use of standard costing over such a long time period suggests that it has traditionally been perceived as advantageous. However, today's manufacturing environment is changing dramatically. Some managers are calling into question the usefulness of the traditional standard-costing approach. They argue that the role of standard-costing systems must change.

In this section, we will list some advantages traditionally attributed to standard-costing systems. In the next section, we will discuss some of the contemporary criticisms of the standard-costing approach and suggest several ways in which the role of standard costing is beginning to change.

Some advantages traditionally attributed to standard costing include these:

- Computation of standard costs and cost variances enables managers to employ *management by exception.* This approach conserves valuable management time.
- Standard costs provide a basis for *sensible cost comparisons.* As we discussed earlier, comparing budgeted costs at one (planned) activity level with actual costs incurred at a different (actual) activity level makes no sense. Standard costs enable the cost manager to compute the standard allowed cost, given actual output, which then serves as a sensible benchmark to compare with the actual cost.
- Variances provide a means of *performance evaluation* and rewards for employees.
- Since the variances are used in performance evaluation, they provide *motivation* for employees to adhere to standards.
- Use of standard costs in product costing results in *more stable product costs* than the use of actual production costs. Actual costs often fluctuate erratically, whereas standard costs change only periodically.
- A standard-costing system is usually *less expensive* than an actual or normal costing system. (In actual and normal costing systems, the *actual* cost of direct material and direct labor is accumulated as product costs. See Chapter 3 for further discussion.)

Like any tool, a standard-costing system can be misused. When employees are criticized for every cost variance, the positive motivational effects will quickly vanish. Moreover, if standards are not revised often enough, they will become outdated. Then the benefits of cost benchmarks and product costing will disappear.

Changing Role of Standard-Costing Systems in Today's Manufacturing Environment

LO 8 Describe the changing role of standard-costing systems in today's manufacturing environment.

The rise of global competition, the introduction of JIT production methods and flexible manufacturing systems, the goal of continuous process improvement, and the empha-

[4]S. W. Anderson and K. Sedatole, "Designing Quality into Products: The Use of Accounting Data in New Product Development." J. M. Patell, "Cost Accounting, Process Control, and Product Design: A Case Study of the Hewlett-Packard Personal Office Computer Division."

sis on product quality are dramatically changing the manufacturing environment. What are the implications of these changes for the role of standard-costing systems? We begin by listing some contemporary criticisms of standard costing.

Criticisms of Standard Costing in Today's Manufacturing Environment

Listed here are several drawbacks attributed to standard costing in an advanced manufacturing setting.[5]

- The variances calculated under standard costing are too aggregated and come too late to be useful. Some accountants argue that traditional standard costing is out of step with the philosophy of *cost-management systems* and *activity-based management*. A production process comprises many activities, and these activities result in costs. By focusing on the activities that incur costs, by eliminating non-value-added activities, and by continually improving performance in value-added activities, an organization can minimize costs and maximize profit. What is needed are performance measures that focus directly on performance issues that management wants to improve. For example, such issues could include product quality, processing time, and delivery performance.
- Traditional cost variances also are too aggregated in the sense that they are not tied to specific product lines, production batches, or flexible-manufacturing-system (FMS) cells. The aggregate nature of the variances makes determining their cause difficult.
- Traditional standard-costing systems focus too much on the cost and efficiency of direct labor, which is rapidly becoming a relatively unimportant factor of production.
- One of the most important conditions for the successful use of standard costing is a stable production process. However, the introduction of flexible manufacturing systems has reduced this stability, with frequent switching among a variety of products on the same production line.
- Shorter product life cycles mean that standards are relevant for only a short time. When new products are introduced, new standards must be developed.
- Traditional standard-costing systems tend to focus too much on cost minimization, rather than increasing product quality or customer service. Indeed, standard-costing systems can cause dysfunctional behavior in a JIT/FMS environment. For example, buying the least expensive materials of a given quality to avoid a material price variance could result in using a vendor whose delivery capabilities are not consistent with JIT requirements.
- Automated manufacturing processes tend to be more consistent in meeting production specifications. As a result, variances from standards tend to be very small or nonexistent.
- Traditional standard costs are not defined broadly enough to capture various important aspects of performance. For example, the standard direct-materials price does not capture all *costs of ownership*. In addition to the purchase price and transportation costs, the *total cost of ownership (TCO)* includes the costs of ordering, paying bills, scheduling delivery, receiving, inspecting, handling, and storing, as well as any production-line disruptions resulting from untimely or incorrect delivery.[6]

---

[5]The sources for this material are R. S. Kaplan, "Limitations of Cost Accounting in Advanced Manufacturing Environments"; H. T. Johnson, "Performance Measurement for Competitive Excellence"; R. A. Bonsack, "Does Activity-Based Costing Replace Standard Costing?"; and M. Sukurai, "The Influence of Factory Automation on Management Accounting Practices: A Study of Japanese Companies."

[6]Some companies are developing cost-of-ownership reporting systems. Among them are Northrop Aircraft Division, McDonnell Douglas, Texas Instruments, and Black & Decker. See L. Carr and C. Ittner, "Measuring the Cost of Ownership"; and L. M. Ellram, "Activity-Based Costing and Total Cost of Ownership: A Critical Linkage."

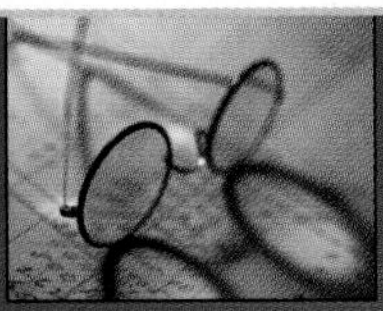

Cost Management in Practice 16.2

Cost of Ownership

Northrop Aircraft Division (*www.northgrum.com*) tracks various elements of the total cost of ownership (TCO)* through its cost-based Supplier Performance Rating System (SPRS). Among the cost factors that SPRS measures are the costs Northrop incurs due to suppliers' hardware, paperwork, or delivery deficiencies. Any "nonconformance event is assigned a standard cost based on industrial engineering studies of the hours required to resolve the problem."

Texas Instruments (*www.ti.com*) has developed a supplier rating system that "incorporates quality and delivery factors." The company computes a Supplier Performance Index (SPI) "based on studies of the additional costs incurred in dealing with supplier deficiencies."

At a Spennymore, England, plant owned by Black & Decker (*www.blackanddecker.com*), the company "has integrated the cost-of-ownership concept into its activity-based costing system." Among the TOC issues included are quality, delivery, flexibility, and customer service. Also considered is a suppliers' billing reliability. "As one Spennymore manager noted, 'You can be dealing with the best company in the world in terms of quality, but if they can't get their invoices right, you're going to have trouble doing business with them.'" *Source: L. Carr and C. Ittner,* "Measuring the Cost of Ownership."

*The *total cost of ownership* includes all costs incurred to have materials in place and ready for use in production, including the purchase price; the transportation cost; and the costs of ordering, receiving, inspecting, and storing the materials.

Adaptation of Standard-Costing Systems

As a result of these criticisms of standard-costing systems, some highly automated manufacturers have deemphasized standard costing in their control systems. Most manufacturing firms continue to use standard costing to some extent, however, even after adopting advanced manufacturing methods.[7] Such firms make changes in their use of standard costing to reflect various features of advanced manufacturing technology.

Reduced importance of labor standards and variances. As direct labor has come to occupy an ever-diminishing role in the manufacturing environment, the standards and variances used to control labor costs also have declined in importance. The heavy emphasis of traditional standard-costing systems on labor efficiency variances is giving way to variances that focus on the more critical inputs to the production process. Machine hours, materials and support-department costs, product quality, and manufacturing cycle times have assumed greater importance as the objects of managerial control.

Emphasis on material and overhead costs. As labor continues to diminish in importance, materials and support-department costs also have assumed greater significance. Controlling the costs of materials and quality and controlling non-unit-level costs through cost-driver analysis become key aspects of the cost-management system.

Cost drivers. Identification of the factors that drive production costs becomes more important in the cost-management system. Cost drivers such as machine hours, number of parts, engineering change orders, and production runs become the focus of the cost-management system.

Shifting cost structures. Advanced manufacturing systems require large outlays for production equipment, which entail a shift in the cost structure from unit-level costs toward non-unit-level costs. Overhead cost control becomes especially critical. The next chapter explores the role of standard-costing systems in controlling overhead costs.

High quality and zero defects. Total quality management (TQM) programs that typically accompany a JIT approach strive for very high quality levels for both raw ma-

[7]For example, see J. M. Patell, "Cost Accounting, Process Control, and Product Design: A Case Study of the Hewlett-Packard Personal Office Computer Division"; J. B. Schiff, "ABC at Lederle"; and R. A. Bonsack, "Does Activity-Based Costing Replace Standard Costing?"

terials and finished products. One result should be very low materials price and quantity variances and low costs of rework.

Non-value-added costs. A key objective of a cost-management system is to eliminate non-value-added costs. As these costs are reduced or eliminated, standards must be revised frequently to provide accurate benchmarks for cost control.

Shorter product life cycles. As product life cycles shorten, developing standards and revising them more frequently became necessary.

Nonfinancial measures for operational control. Managerial accountants traditionally have focused on financial measures of performance such as deviations from budgeted costs. Financial measures still are very important, but to an ever-greater extent, financial performance criteria are being augmented by nonfinancial measures. In today's advanced manufacturing environment, operational measures are being developed to control key aspects of the production process.

Benchmarking. One widely used method to control costs and improve operational efficiency is *benchmarking*—the continual search for the most effective method of accomplishing a task by comparing existing methods and performance levels with those of other organizations or other subunits within the same organization. For example, hospitals routinely benchmark their costs of patient care by diagnostic-related groups (such as circulatory disorders) with the costs of other hospitals.

Real-time information systems. A computer-integrated manufacturing (CIM) system enables the cost-management analyst to collect operating data as production occurs and to report relevant performance measures to management on a real-time basis. This enables managers to eliminate the causes of unfavorable variances more quickly.

Kaizen Costing

LO 9 Explain the concept of kaizen costing and its potential benefits.

kaizen costing *is the process of cost reduction during the manufacturing phase of a product*

In today's global business environment, for some companies to survive, they must continually seek to reduce production costs. If a standard-costing system is used in such a competitive environment, the standards must be reduced every year or even every month. **Kaizen costing** is the process of cost reduction during the manufacturing phase of a product.[8] The Japanese word *kaizen* refers to continual and gradual improvement through small betterment activities rather than large or radical improvement made through innovation or large investments in technology. The idea is simple. Improvement is the goal and responsibility of every worker, from the CEO to the manual laborers, in every activity, every day, all the time! Through the small but continual efforts of everyone, significant reductions in costs can be attained over time.

To help achieve the continuous cost reduction implied by the kaizen costing concept, an annual (or monthly) *kaizen cost goal* is established. Then actual costs are tracked over time and compared to the kaizen goal. Depending on the nature of the production process and the competitive environment, a company could focus its kaizen costing efforts on a particular segment of its cost structure. For example, Sumitomo Electric Industries (*www.sei.com.jp*), a Japanese company that is the world's third largest manufacturer of electrical wire and cable, concentrates its kaizen cost-reduction program on material costs.[9] In contrast, "at the Kyoto brewery of Kirin beer (*www.kirin.com*), cost reduction programs typically identified four or five targets for improvement each year. This continuous change of focus helped keep the programs active."[10]

Citizen Watch Company (*www.citizenwatch.com*) focuses its kaizen costing efforts on direct labor. "The major way to reduce labor is to alter the time required to operate

[8]Y. Monden and K. Hamada, "Target Costing and Kaizen Costing in Japanese Automobile Companies."

[9]R. Cooper, *When Lean Enterprises Collide.*

[10]Ibid., p. 251.

Exhibit 16–7
Typical Kaizen Costing Chart

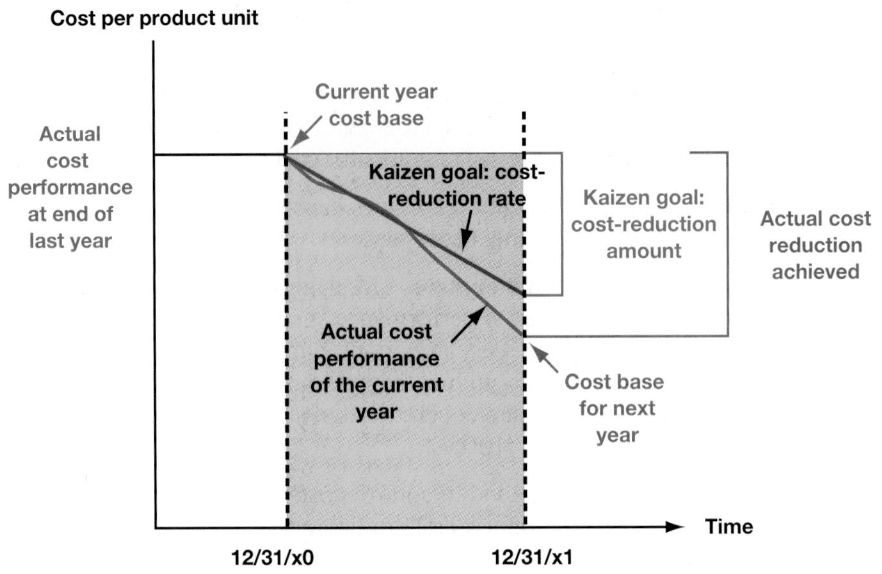

or support the production machines. Alterations can be achieved in two ways. First, the running speed of the machines can be increased so that more parts per hour can be produced. Second, a single employee can be used to operate more machines."[11]

We present a typical kaizen costing chart in Exhibit 16–7.[12] Notice that the cost base, or reference point, is the actual cost performance at the end of the prior year. A kaizen goal is established for the cost-reduction rate and amount during the current year. Actual cost performance throughout the year is compared with the kaizen goal. At the end of the current year, the current actual cost becomes the cost base, or reference point, for the next year. Then, a new (lower) kaizen goal is established, and the cost-reduction effort continues.

How are kaizen costing goals met? The continual and relentless reduction of non-value-added activities and costs, the elimination of waste, and improvements in manufacturing cycle time all contribute to the effort. In addition, management takes seriously the improvement suggestions and kaizen efforts of all employees and implements them when appropriate. The result is a continually more efficient and cost-effective production process.

Cost Management in Practice 16.3

Cost Reduction at Ford Motor Company

Ford Motor Company (*www.ford.com/us*) is asking the people who build its popular Taurus to find ways to build the car at a lower cost. According to *The Wall Street Journal,* "During a three-week campaign, workers and engineers at factories in Chicago and Atlanta came up with ideas to trim $1 here and 50 cents there, totaling $180 in cost reductions." For a car with a sticker price over $18,000, that might sound like a trivial amount, but it could save Ford over $73 million in just one year. Such savings would allow the company to "hold down sticker prices or offer bigger discounts helping the top-selling Taurus stay competitive in the cutthroat market for midsize sedans. In fact, no savings are too small given the competition Ford is facing. Prices for Japanese cars are dropping." This is in part due to aggressive cost cutting by Japanese automakers. "Most of the cost cutting is meant to be invisible to Taurus customers." The cost-reduction efforts at Ford are an example of the fact that a manufacturer must meet the market price for its product, but the price must also cover the product's production costs. In the globally competitive automobile industry, often the only way to be competitive and still price a product sufficiently above its production cost is to lower that cost. *Source: O. Suris,* "How Ford Cut Costs on Its Taurus, Little by Little."

[11] Ibid., pp. 240, 241.

[12] The kaizen costing chart depicted is based on one used at Daihatsu, a Japanese auto manufacturer owned in part by Toyota. See Y. Monden and J. Lee, "How a Japanese Auto Maker Reduced Costs."

Chapter Summary

A standard-costing system is a traditional cost-management technique with two purposes: cost control and product costing. Accountants work with others in the organization to set standard costs for direct material, direct labor, and manufacturing overhead through either historical cost analysis or task analysis. The cost-management analyst uses the standard cost as a benchmark against which to compare actual costs incurred. Managers then use management by exception to determine the causes of significant cost variances. This cost-management purpose of the standard-costing system is accomplished by computing a direct-materials price variance, a direct-materials quantity variance, a direct-labor rate variance, and a direct-labor efficiency variance.

Managers determine the significance of cost variances through judgment and rules of thumb. The absolute and relative size of variances, recurrence of variances, variance trends, and controllability of variances are all considered in deciding whether variances warrant investigation. The product-costing purpose of the standard-costing system is achieved by entering the standard cost of production in Work-in-Process Inventory as a product cost. Standard-costing systems offer an organization many benefits, but these benefits will be obtained only if the standard-costing system is used properly.

Today's manufacturing environment is changing rapidly due to the influences of worldwide competition, JIT, flexible manufacturing systems, and an emphasis on product quality and customer service. As a result, many manufacturers are adapting their standard-costing systems to reflect these aspects of the contemporary manufacturing environment.

Kaizen costing is the process of cost reduction during the manufacturing phase of a product. *Kaizen* refers to continual and gradual improvement through small betterment activities. Many companies facing global competition find that continual cost reduction is crucial to their survival.

Key Terms

For each term's definition refer to the indicated page, or turn to the glossary at the end of the text.

cost variance, 657
direct-labor efficiency variance, 664
direct-labor mix variance,* 686
direct-labor rate variance, 664
direct-labor yield variance,* 686
direct-material mix variance,* 685
direct-material price variance (or purchase price variance), 663
direct-material quantity variance, 663
direct-material yield variance,* 685
kaizen costing, 679
management by exception, 657
perfection (or ideal standard), 659
practical (or attainable) standard, 659
standard cost, 656
standard-costing system, 673
standard direct-labor quantity, 662
standard direct-labor rate, 662
standard direct-material price, 661
standard direct-material quantity, 661
statistical control chart, 669
task analysis, 658

*Term appears in the chapter Appendix.

Meeting the Cost-Management Challenges

1. **How** could Koala Camp Gear's controller set standards for the production of tents using the company's standard-costing system?

Koala Camp Gear's controller could use several approaches to set standards. One method of setting standards is the analysis of historical cost data, which provide an indicator of future costs. The methods for analyzing cost behavior described in Chapter 11 are used to predict future costs on the basis of historical costs. These predictions then form the basis for setting standards. Another standard-setting method is task analysis, which analyzes a production process to determine what the cost to produce a product or service should be. The emphasis shifts from what the product did cost in the past to what it should cost in the future.

A perfection (or ideal) standard is the cost expected under perfect or ideal operating conditions. A practical (or attainable) standard is the cost expected under normal operating conditions.

2. **What** is the appropriate interpretation of each variance detailed in Koala Camp Gear Company's cost-variance report?

Koala Camp Gear's unfavorable direct-material price variance means that it paid a higher price for the material than was expected when the standard was set. (A favorable variance has the opposite interpretation.)

Koala's unfavorable direct-material quantity variance means that a larger amount of material was used in the production process than should have been used in accordance with the standard. (A favorable variance has the opposite interpretation.)

The unfavorable direct-labor rate variance experienced by Koala Camp Gear Company means that it paid a higher labor rate than was anticipated when the standard was set. One possible cause is that labor rate raises granted were higher than those anticipated in setting the standards. Another possibility is that more highly skilled workers were used to perform tasks than were required or anticipated when the standards were set. (A favorable variance has the opposite interpretation.)

Koala Camp Gear's favorable direct-labor efficiency variance means that it used less labor to accomplish a given task than was required in accordance with the standards. (An unfavorable variance has the opposite interpretation.)

3. **Who** is in the best position in the organization to influence each of these variances?

The purchasing manager is in the best position to influence the direct-material price variance.

The production manager is usually in the best position to influence the direct-material quantity variance.

In some cases, the production manager is in the best position to influence the direct-labor rate variance. In other cases, the personnel manager or union negotiator has more influence.

The production manager is usually in the best position to influence the direct-labor efficiency variance.

4. **What** criticisms are made of standard-costing systems as they are used in today's business environment?

Eight criticisms of standard costing in an advanced manufacturing setting are the following:

- Variances are too aggregate and too late to be useful.
- Variances are not tied to specific product lines, production batches, or flexible manufacturing system (FMS) cells.
- Standard-costing systems focus too much on direct labor.
- Frequent switching among products in an FMS cell makes cost standards less appropriate.
- Shorter product life cycles mean that individual standards are soon outmoded.
- Traditional standard-costing systems tend to focus too much on cost minimization rather than on increasing product quality or customer service.
- Automated manufacturing processes are highly reliable in meeting production specifications. As a result, variances from standards tend to be very small or nonexistent.
- Traditional standard costs are not defined broadly enough to include important costs, such as the total cost of ownership.

Solutions to You're the Decision Maker

16.1 Setting Standards in the Service Industry p. 660

a. **Dominos pizza outlet** The amount of dough for each size of pizza, the quantity of sauce and other toppings, and the quantity of paper products (e.g., napkins) are likely candidates for setting materials standards.

Labor standards could be set for the wage rates for employees doing various jobs (e.g., making pizzas, taking phone orders, operating the cash register, delivering pizzas, or managing the outlet).

b. **Avis car-rental agency** Standards could be set for the routine maintenance required for each vehicle (e.g., lubrication, oil, oil filters, and tires).

Labor standards could be set for wage rates for employees performing different tasks (e.g., cleaning and gassing up vehicles, providing customer service at the sales counter, and taking phone reservations).

c. **Nation's Bank branch** Standards could be set for the time required to process a personal loan application, a home mortgage, or a customer credit check. Quality-control standards could be set for check-processing errors.

d. **County motor-vehicle department** Standards could be set for the amount of time it takes to serve a customer for each of several services, such as obtaining a new driver's license; renewing a driver's license; administering eye exams, written tests, and road tests; and licensing a vehicle.

16.2 Direct-Material and Direct-Labor Variances p. 670

a. The direct-material and direct-labor variances are computed in Exhibits 16–8 and 16–9, respectively.

b. The direct-material price variance and the direct-labor rate variance should be investigated since they exceed 1 standard deviation. The direct-material price variance is $6,250 unfavorable, and the direct-labor rate variance is $5,250 favorable.

Exhibit 16–8

Direct-Material Price and Quantity Variances: You're the Decision Maker

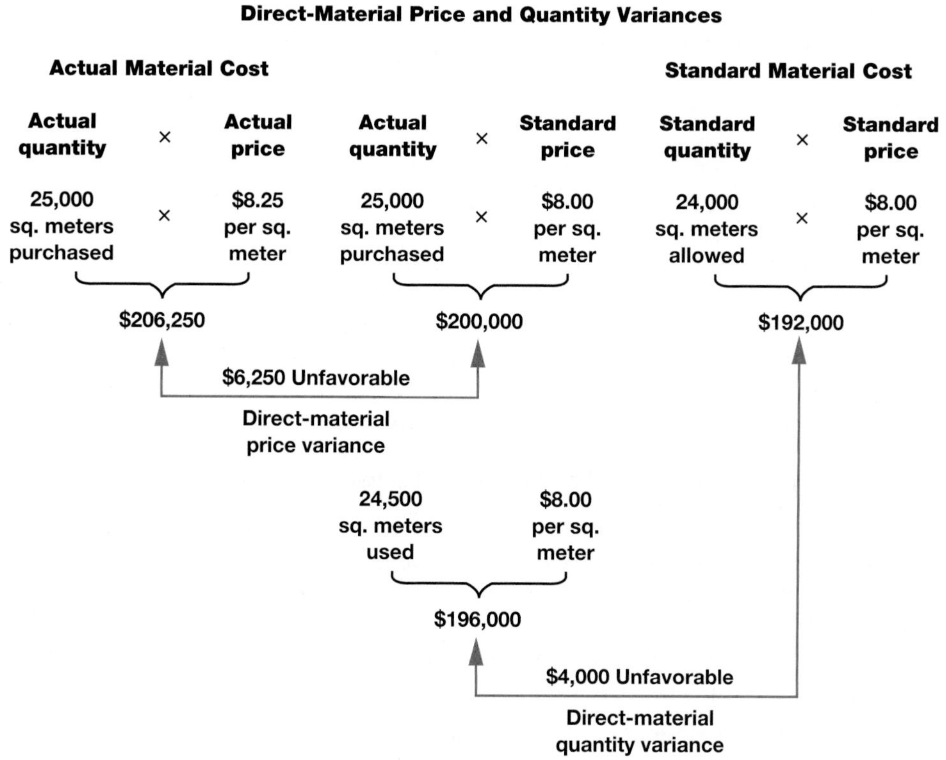

Using Formulas

Direct-material price variance = $PQ(AP - SP)$

= 25,000 ($8.25 − $8.00) = $6,250 Unfavorable

Direct-material quantity variance = $SP(AQ - SQ)$

= $8.00 (24,500 − 24,000) = $4,000 Unfavorable

Exhibit 16–9

Direct-Labor Rate and Efficiency Variances: You're the Decision Maker

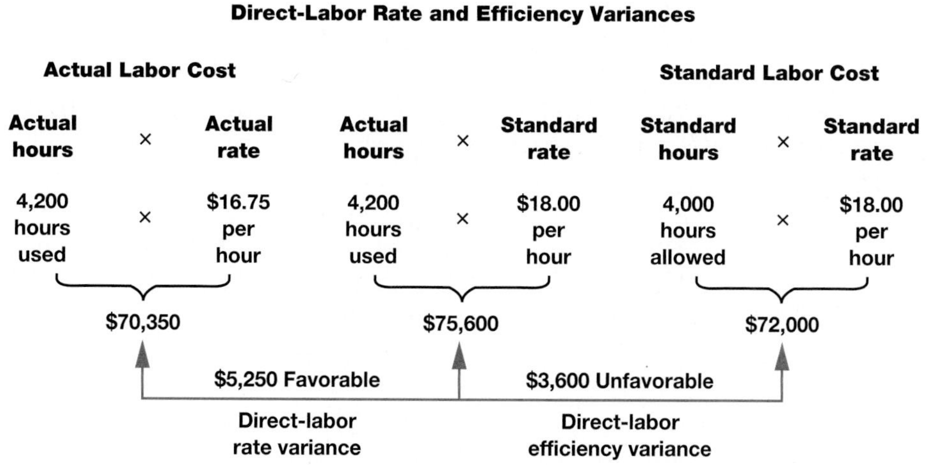

Using Formulas:

Direct-labor rate variance = $AH(AR - SR)$

= 4,200 ($16.75 − $18.00) = $5,250 Favorable

Direct-labor efficiency variance = $SR(AH - SH)$

= $18.00 (4,200 − 4,000) = $3,600 Unfavorable

Appendix to Chapter Sixteen

Production Mix and Yield Variances

LO 10 Compute and interpret mix and yield variances.

Manufacturing processes typically involve multiple direct-material inputs. Food, chemical, steel, fabric, plastic, and many other products require a mix of direct materials, some of which can be substituted for each other without greatly affecting product quality. Moreover, multiple types of direct labor often are required (e.g., machinists and assembly employees). When a manufacturing process involves multiple types of direct material or direct labor, additional variance analysis can be conducted to analyze the proportions with which the multiple inputs are used. Such an analysis assumes that some degree of substitutability exists among the inputs to the production process.

Production Mix and Yield Variances Illustrated

Koala Camp Gear Company

Let's return to Koala Camp Gear Company. Margo Hastings's nephew has convinced her that Koala should expand its product line to include certain camp foods. For its initial entry into this market, Koala has begun to produce trail mix. Variously known to outdoor enthusiasts as trail mix or gorp (for "good ole' raisins and peanuts"), this venerable food has sustained many a hiker. Koala has introduced its trail mix product under the brand name Crocodile Chomp.

Multiple direct-material inputs. The three inputs to Crocodile Chomp are raisins (R), peanuts (P), and sunflower seeds (S). The standard costs and quantities for Crocodile Chomp are given in the following table. The trail mix is produced in 10-kilogram units; subsequently, each unit is divided into 20 half-kilo packages (a little over a pound).

(a) Direct Material	(b) Standard Price per Kilogram	(c) Standard Number of Kilograms per Unit of Finished Product	(d) Standard Proportion (Col c ÷ 10)
R	$2.00	4	.4
P	1.60	4	.4
S	1.50	2	.2
Total		10	

During September, Koala produced 1,000 units of Crocodile Chomp (i.e., 10,000 kilograms of trail mix). However, it purchased and consumed 10,800 kilograms of inputs, as the following table shows.

(a) Direct Material	(b) Actual Price	(c) Actual Amount Used	(d) Actual Proportion Used (Col. c ÷ 10,800)
R	$2.00	3,780 kilograms	.35
P	1.80	5,400 kilograms	.50
S	1.45	1,620 kilograms	.15
Total		10,800 kilograms	

First, let's compute the direct-material price and quantity variances for September. Notice that the quantity purchased (*PQ*) and the actual quantity used (*AQ*) are the same, due to the perishability of the inputs.

Direct Material	PQ (AP − SP)	Price Variance	SP (AQ − SQ*)	Quantity Variance
R	3,780 ($2.00 − $2.00)	0	$2.00 (3,780 − 4,000)	$ 440 F
P	5,400 ($1.80 − $1.60)	$1,080 U	$1.60 (5,400 − 4,000)	2,240 U
S	1,620 ($1.45 − $1.50)	81 F	$1.50 (1,620 − 2,000)	570 F
Total		$ 999 U		$1,230 U

*SQ, the standard quantity allowed given actual output, is equal to the standard input proportion multiplied by 10,000 kilograms (the actual output produced).

As the variance analysis shows, the total price variance is $999 unfavorable, and the total quantity variance is $1,230 unfavorable. Now we divide the quantity variance into a *direct-material mix variance* and a *direct-materials yield variance.* The **direct-material mix variance** is defined as follows. Notice that the total direct-material mix variance is defined as the sum of the direct-material mix variances for each input.

direct-material mix variance *for a particular direct material is the difference between the actual and standard input proportions for that direct material multiplied by that material's standard price and multiplied by the actual total quantity of all direct materials used*

$$\text{Direct-material mix variance} = \text{Sum of direct material mix variances for each direct material used}$$

$$\begin{pmatrix}\text{Direct-material mix}\\ \text{variance for direct}\\ \text{material } i\end{pmatrix} = \begin{pmatrix}\text{Standard price of}\\ \text{direct material } i\end{pmatrix} \times \begin{pmatrix}\text{Actual input proportion}\\ \text{for direct material } i\end{pmatrix} - \begin{pmatrix}\text{Standard input proportion}\\ \text{for direct material } i\end{pmatrix} \times \begin{pmatrix}\text{Actual total quantity of}\\ \text{all direct materials used}\end{pmatrix}$$

Using this formula, Koala's September direct-material mix variances are computed as follows:

R mix variance = $2.00 × (.35 − .40) × 10,800 =	$1,080 F
P mix variance = $1.60 × (.50 − .40) × 10,800 =	1,728 U
S mix variance = $1.50 × (.15 − .20) × 10,800 =	810 F
Total mix variance	$ 162 F

Koala's September direct-material mix variance is $162 favorable, which means that the mix of inputs was altered in such a way that it had a favorable impact on the total production cost. Notice that signs (F or U) are assigned to the individual input components of the mix variance in accordance with this rule: F if the actual input proportion is lower than the standard input proportion and U otherwise. During September, the actual input proportions for raisins and sunflower seeds were lower than their standard input proportions; the actual proportion for peanuts was higher than its standard. It is important to note, however, that *it is the total direct-material mix variance of $162 F that is a meaningful measure for management's analysis, not the individual mix variance components.*

Now we define the **direct-material yield variance.** Again, the total direct-material yield variance is defined as the sum of the individual yield variance components for the several inputs.

direct-material yield variance *for a particular direct material is the difference between the actual quantity of all direct materials used and the standard quantity of all direct materials, given actual output, multiplied by that particular direct material's standard price and multiplied by that direct material's standard input proportion*

$$\text{Direct-material yield variance} = \text{Sum of direct-material yield variances for each direct material used}$$

$$\begin{pmatrix}\text{Direct-material yield}\\ \text{variance for direct}\\ \text{material } i\end{pmatrix} = \begin{pmatrix}\text{Standard price of}\\ \text{direct material } i\end{pmatrix} \times \begin{pmatrix}\text{Actual quantity of}\\ \text{all direct materials used}\end{pmatrix} - \begin{pmatrix}\text{Standard allowed total quantity of}\\ \text{all direct materials given actual output}\end{pmatrix} \times \begin{pmatrix}\text{Standard input proportion}\\ \text{for direct material } i\end{pmatrix}$$

Using this formula, Koala's September direct-material yield variances are computed as follows:

R yield variance = $2.00 × (10,800 − 10,000) × .40 =	$ 640 U
P yield variance = $1.60 × (10,800 − 10,000) × .40 =	512 U
S yield variance = $1.50 × (10,800 − 10,000) × .20 =	240 U
Total yield variance	$1,392 U

Koala's September direct-material yield variance is $1,392 unfavorable. The interpretation is that the total inputs used (10,800 kilograms) exceeded the standard quantity allowed given actual output (10,000 kilograms of input allowed for 10,000 kilograms of output). As with the mix variance, the most meaningful interpretation applies to the *total yield variance* rather than its individual components.

Exhibit 16–10

September Direct-Material Variances in the Production of Crocodile Chomp Trail Mix

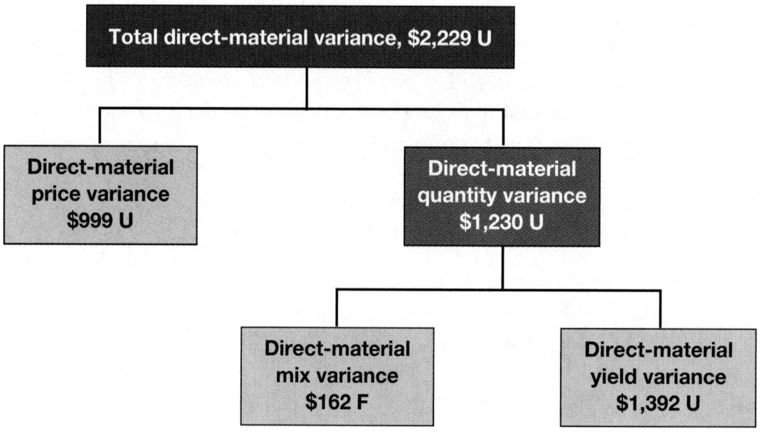

Notice that Koala's direct-material mix variance ($162 F) and yield variance ($1,392 U) add up to the direct-material quantity variance ($1,230 U). Koala's September direct-material variances in the production of Crocodile Chomp are summarized in Exhibit 16–10.

Multiple direct-labor inputs. The same analysis for direct material can be applied to direct labor if a company has multiple types of direct-labor input. Suppose, for example, that Koala's direct-labor employees in the Crocodile Mix line include inspectors, mixers, and packers, each with a different standard pay rate. Moreover, assume that there is a standard or expected input proportion for each type of direct labor. Then we can apply the same analysis to direct labor as we used for direct material. Just substitute the words "direct labor" for "direct material" in all of the formulas given in the preceding section. Now the total direct-labor variance consists of the direct-labor rate and efficiency variances, and the direct-labor efficiency variance is decomposed into a **direct-labor mix variance** and a **direct-labor yield variance.** As with direct materials, this analysis makes sense only if some degree of substitutability exists among the various types of direct labor.

direct-labor mix variance *for a particular type of direct labor is the difference between the actual and standard input proportions for that type of direct labor multiplied by that labor type's standard rate and multiplied by the actual total quantity of all direct labor used*

direct-labor yield variance *for a particular type of direct labor is the difference between the actual quantity of all direct labor used and the standard quantity of all direct labor, given actual output, multiplied by the standard rate for that particular type of direct labor and multiplied by the standard input proportion for that type of direct labor*

Mix and Yield Variances in Service Organizations

The concepts underlying production mix and yield variances can be applied to service organizations also. Service organizations often make substitutions among different types of labor. Ernst & Young, for example, might substitute partner time for staff time on a particular audit job.

Consider the well-known consulting firm of Kirk, Spock and McCoy, which has bid a job for 1,000 hours: 300 hours of partner time at a cost of $60 per hour and 700 hours of staff time at a cost of $20 per hour. Due to scheduling problems, the partner spends 500 hours, and the staff member spends 500 hours. If the actual costs are $60 for partner time and $20 for staff time, no labor rate variance exists. However, even though the 1,000 hours required were exactly what was bid, the job cost is $8,000 over budget, as shown here:

$$\begin{aligned}\text{Actual cost} &= (500\text{ hours} \times \$60) + (500\text{ hours} \times \$20)\\ &= \$30{,}000 + \$10{,}000\\ &= \$40{,}000\\ \text{Budgeted cost} &= (300\text{ hours} \times \$60) + (700\text{ hours} \times \$20)\\ &= \$18{,}000 + \$14{,}000\\ &= \$32{,}000\\ \text{Cost overrun} &= \$8{,}000\end{aligned}$$

We can apply the mix and yield variance analysis to help us understand this cost overrun. First, there is no yield variance because the total number of actual hours and total budgeted hours are the same. (Review the formula for the yield variance.)

However, there is an unfavorable mix variance of $8,000, which is calculated as follows by applying the mix variance formula given earlier in the appendix.

Partner labor mix variance	= $60 × (.5* − .3†) × 1,000 =	$12,000 U
Staff labor mix variance	= $20 × (.5* − .7†) × 1,000 =	4,000 F
Total mix variance		$ 8,000 U

*The actual input proportions were .5 for both partner and staff time (500 ÷ 1,000).

†The budgeted (standard) input proportions were .3 for partner time (300 ÷ 1,000) and .7 for staff time (700 ÷ 1,000).

Thus, the entire budget overrun of $8,000 is due to the unfavorable mix effect of substituting expensive partner time for less expensive staff time. This scenario had no rate (price) or yield effects at all.

Review Questions

16.1 One of the principles espoused by management is that one should manage by exception. How can responsibility reporting systems and/or analysis of variances assist in that process?

16.2 Explain how standard material prices and quantities are set.

16.3 What is the interpretation of the *direct-material price variance?*

16.4 What manager usually is in the best position to influence the direct-material price variance?

16.5 What is the interpretation of the *direct-material quantity variance?*

16.6 What manager usually is in the best position to influence the direct-material quantity variance?

16.7 Describe the factors that managers often consider when determining the significance of a variance.

16.8 What is the interpretation of the *direct-labor rate variance?* What are some possible causes?

16.9 What manager generally is in the best position to influence the direct-labor rate variance?

16.10 What is the interpretation of the *direct-labor efficiency variance?*

16.11 What manager generally is in the best position to influence the direct-labor efficiency variance?

16.12 Describe how standard costs are used for product costing.

16.13 What is meant by the term *kaizen costing?*

16.14 (Appendix) List four companies that probably use direct-material mix and yield variances.

Critical Analysis

16.15 Distinguish between *perfection* and *practical* standards. Which type of standard is likely to produce the best motivational effects?

16.16 In a service environment with no inventories, is variance analysis useful? Why or why not?

16.17 Why should management want to divide production cost variances into price and efficiency variances?

16.18 Explain why the quantity purchased (*PQ*) is used in computing the direct-material price variance, but the actual quantity consumed (*AQ*) is used in computing the direct-material quantity variance.

16.19 Refer to question 16.18. Why does an analogous question *not* arise in the context of the direct-labor variances?

16.20 Many companies set wage rates through union negotiations. Under these circumstances, how could a labor price variance arise that is the responsibility of a line manager?

16.21 Discuss several ways in which standard-costing systems should be adapted in today's advanced manufacturing environment.

16.22 Which of the following terms is most consistent with the old saying, "Slow and steady wins the race": advanced manufacturing system, product innovation, kaizen costing, or investment in high technology? Explain.

Exercises

Exercise 16.23
Direct-Material Variances: Material Purchased and Material Used Are Not Equal
(LO 3)

Global

Yamaguchi Company manufactures laboratory glassware in its plant near Osaka, Japan. The controller recently reported the following information concerning direct-material requirements in department 8.

Actual production	28,000 units
Standard direct-material cost per unit produced	1.31 *yen*
Direct material purchased (actual)	58,158 *yen*
Standard cost of material purchased	57,510 *yen*
Standard price times actual amount of material used	38,340 *yen*

Required

Compute the direct-material cost variances for department 8. Prepare an analysis for management like the one in Exhibit 16–1. (Remember to express your analysis in terms of *yen,* the Japanese national currency.)

Exercise 16.24
Direct-Labor Variances
(LO 3)

The standard direct-labor cost per unit for Korosa Company was $10 ($5 per hour times 2 hours per unit). During the period, actual direct-labor costs amounted to $18,800, 3,900 direct-labor hours were worked, and 1,900 units were produced.

Required

Compute the direct-labor rate and efficiency variances for the period. (Refer to Exhibit 16–2 for the format.)

Exercise 16.25
Direct-Labor Variances
(LO 3)

The standard direct-labor cost per reservation for Eagle Air Charters is $ .65 ($6.50 per hour divided by 10 reservations per hour). During the period, actual direct-labor costs totaled $44,500, 6,800 direct-labor hours were worked, and 72,000 reservations were made.

Required

Compute the direct-labor rate and efficiency variances for the period. (Refer to Exhibit 16–2 for the format.)

Exercise 16.26
Standard Costs; Ethics
(LO 1, 5)

Ethics

Jamestown Joe's produces items made from local farm products that it distributes to supermarkets. Because price competition has become increasingly important over the years, Abby Tyler, the company's controller, is planning to implement a standard-costing system for Joe's. She asked her cost-management analyst, Larry Madison, to gather cost information on the production of strawberry jam (Jamestown Joe's most popular product). Madison reported that strawberries cost $ .90 per quart, the price he intends to pay to his good friend who has been operating a strawberry farm in the red for the last few years. Due to an oversupply in the market, the prices for strawberries have dropped to $ .65 per quart. Madison is sure that the $ .90 price will be enough to pull his friend's strawberry farm out of the red and into the black.

Required

Is Madison's behavior regarding the cost information he provided to Tyler unethical? Explain your answer.

[CMA adapted]

Exercise 16.27
Standards for a New High-Tech Product
(LO 1, 2)

Read "U.S. Auto Makers to Rev Up Output of 'Hybrid' Vehicles," *The Wall Street Journal,* October 24, 2000, by Jeffrey Ball. The article discusses how DaimlerChrysler has pledged to build a "hybrid" version of one of its popular light truck models.

Required

What is a "hybrid" vehicle? How would you go about developing standard costs for a radical new product like the hybrid vehicles discussed in the article?

Exercise 16.28
Straightforward Computation of Variances
(LO 3)

Cato Container Company manufactures recyclable soft-drink cans. A unit of production is a case of 12 dozen cans. The following standards have been set by the production-engineering staff and the controller.

Direct material:	Direct labor:
Quantity, 4 kilograms	Quantity, .25 hour
Price, $ .79 per kilogram	Rate, $16 per hour

Actual material purchases amounted to 240,000 kilograms at $ .81 per kilogram. Actual costs incurred in the production of 50,000 units follow:

Direct labor	$211,900 for 13,000 hours
Direct material	$170,100 for 210,000 kilograms

Required

Use the variance formulas to compute the direct-material price and quantity variances and the direct-labor rate and efficiency variances. Indicate whether each variance is favorable or unfavorable.

Exercise 16.29
Determination of Variances Using Diagrams
(LO 3)

Spreadsheet

Refer to the data in the preceding exercise.

Required

Use diagrams similar to those in Exhibits 16–1 and 16–2 to determine the direct material and direct-labor variances. Indicate whether each variance is favorable or unfavorable.

Exercise 16.30
Preparation of Journal Entries under Standard Costing; Posting Journal Entries for Variances
(LO 6)

Refer to the data in Exercise 16.28 for Cato Container Company.

Required

a. Prepare journal entries to:

   (1) Record the purchase of direct material on account.

   (2) Add direct-material and direct-labor cost to Work-in-Process Inventory.

   (3) Record the direct-material and direct-labor variances.

   (4) Close these variances to Cost of Goods Sold.

b. Set up T-accounts, and post the journal entries to the general ledger.

Exercise 16.31
Development of Standards for New Products; Internet Use
(LO 1, 2, 8)

Internet

Choose one of the following manufacturers (or any manufacturer of your choosing), and use the Internet to gather information about any new products the company has recently introduced or plans to introduce.

Kodak (*www.kodak.com*)	Boeing (*www.boeing.com*)
Pfizer (*www.pfizer.com*)	Caterpillar (*www.caterpillar.com*)
Xerox (*www.xerox.com*)	Ford (*www.ford.com/us*)

Required

Discuss the steps you think the company took in establishing standard costs for its new product.

Exercise 16.32
Standard Allowed Input
(LO 1)

Due to evaporation during production, Plattsburg Plastics Company requires 8 pounds of material input for every 7 pounds of good plastic sheets manufactured. During May, the company produced 4,550 pounds of good sheets.

Required

Compute the total standard allowed input quantity given the good output produced.

Exercise 16.33
Determination of Standard Material Cost
(LO 1)

Ozark Chemical Company manufactures industrial chemicals. The company plans to introduce a new chemical solution and needs to develop a standard product cost. The new chemical solution is made by combining a chemical compound (nyclyn) and a solution (salex), heating the mixture, adding a second compound (protet), and bottling the resulting solution in 10-liter containers. The initial mix, which is 11 liters in volume, consists of 12 kilograms of nyclyn and 9.6 liters of salex. A 1-liter reduction in volume occurs during the boiling process. The solution is cooled slightly before 5 kilograms of protet are added. The addition of protet does not affect the total liquid volume.

The purchase price of the direct materials used in the manufacture of this new chemical solution follow:

Nyclyn	$1.60 per kilogram
Salex	1.80 per liter
Protet	2.40 per kilogram

Required

Determine the standard direct-material cost of a 10-liter container of the new product.

[CMA adapted]

Exercise 16.34
Cost Variance Investigation
(LO 4)

The controller for Midtown Caterers', Inc., uses a statistical control chart to help management determine when to investigate variances. The critical value is 1 standard deviation. The company incurred the following direct-labor efficiency variances during the first six months of the current year.

January	$250 F	April	$ 900 U
February	800 U	May	1,050 U
March	700 U	June	1,200 U

The standard direct-labor cost during each of these months was $19,000. The controller has estimated that the firm's monthly direct-labor variances have a standard deviation of $950.

Required

a. Draw a statistical control chart and plot the preceding variance data. Which variances should be investigated?

b. Suppose that the controller's rule of thumb is to investigate all variances equal to or greater than 6 percent of standard cost. Which variances will be investigated?

c. Would you investigate any of the variances listed other than those indicated by the rules discussed in requirements (a) and (b)? Why?

Exercise 16.35
Labor Mix and Yield Variances (Appendix)
(LO 10)

Speedy Burrito has two categories of direct labor, unskilled, which costs $6.50 per hour, and skilled, which costs $10.30 per hour. Management has established standards per "equivalent meal," which has been defined as a typical meal consisting of a burrito, a drink, and a side order. Standards have been set as follows:

Skilled labor	4 minutes per equivalent meal
Unskilled labor	10 minutes per equivalent meal

During May, Speedy Burrito sold 30,000 equivalent meals and incurred the following labor costs:

Skilled labor	1,800 hours	$17,500
Unskilled labor	4,600 hours	33,000

Required

a. Compute the direct-labor rate and efficiency variances.

b. Compute the direct-labor mix and yield variances.

Exercise 16.36
Direct-Material Mix and Yield Variances (Appendix)
(LO 10)

Spreadsheet

Solar Industries has set the following direct-material standards for its product, the cosmic gismo.

Standard costs for one unit of output:
Material A, 10 units of input at $100 per unit
Material B, 20 units of input at $150 per unit

During August, the company had the following results:

Cosmic gismos produced	2,000 units
Materials purchased and used:	
Material A	22,000 units at $94
Material B	38,000 units at $152

Required

a. Compute the direct-material price and quantity variances.

b. Compute the direct-material mix and yield variances.

Problems

Problem 16.37
Direct-Material and Direct-Labor Variances
(LO 3)

Andromeda Corporation has established the following standards for the prime costs of one unit of its chief product, dartboards.

	Standard Quantity	Standard Price or Rate	Standard Cost
Direct material	8.5 pounds	$1.80 per pound	$15.30
Direct labor	.25 hour	$8.00 per hour	2.00
Total			$17.30

During May, Andromeda purchased 160,000 pounds of direct material at a total cost of $312,000. The total wages for May were $42,000, 90 percent of which were for direct labor. Andromeda manufactured 19,000 dartboards during May, using 142,500 pounds of direct material and 5,000 direct-labor hours.

Required

Compute the following variances for May, and indicate whether each is favorable or unfavorable.

a. Direct-material price variance.

b. Direct-material quantity variance.

c. Direct-labor rate variance.

d. Direct-labor efficiency variance.

[CMA adapted]

Problem 16.38
Direct-Material and Direct-Labor Variances; Missing Data
(LO 3)

Analyze each of the following scenarios independently.

a. Information about Arbosheski Company's direct-material cost follows:

Standard price per direct-material ounce	$ 345
Actual quantity purchased and used	420 ounces
Standard quantity allowed for production	435 ounces
Price variance	$2,950 F

What was the actual purchase price per ounce, rounded to the nearest cent?

b. Maxey Company reports the following direct-labor information for its primary product for October:

Standard rate	$ 7.00 per hour
Actual rate paid	$ 7.20 per hour
Standard hours allowed for actual production	1,400 hours
Direct-labor efficiency variance	$ 500 U

What were the actual hours worked, and what was the direct-labor rate variance?

Problem 16.39
Direct-Material and Direct-Labor Variances
(LO 3)

Adelphi Fabrics Corporation manufactured 500 units of a special multilayer fabric with the trade name Stylex during July. The following information from the Stylex production department pertains to July:

Direct material purchased: 18,000 yards at $1.38 per yard	$24,840
Direct material used: 9,500 yards at $1.38 per yard	13,110
Direct labor used: 2,100 hours at $9.15 per hour	19,215

The standard prime costs for one unit of Stylex are:

Direct material: 20 yards at $1.35 per yard	$27
Direct labor: 4 hours at $9.00 per hour	36
Total standard prime cost per unit of output	$63

Required

Compute the following variances for the month of July, indicating whether each variance is favorable or unfavorable.

a. Direct-material price variance.

b. Direct-material quantity variance.

c. Direct-labor rate variance.

d. Direct-labor efficiency variance.

[CPA adapted]

Problem 16.40
Behavioral Impact of Implementing a Standard-Costing System
(LO 1, 5)

Cumberland Corporation, a manufacturer of custom-designed home health care equipment, has been in business for 15 years. Last year, to better control the costs of its products, the controller implemented a standard-costing system. Reports for tracking performance are issued monthly, and any unfavorable variances are investigated further.

The production manager complained that the standards are unrealistic, stifle motivation by concentrating only on unfavorable variances, and are out of date too quickly. He noted that his recent switch to titanium for the wheelchairs has resulted in higher material costs but decreased labor hours. The net result was no increase in the total cost to produce the wheelchair. The monthly reports continue to show an unfavorable material variance and a favorable labor variance despite indications that the workers are slowing down.

Required

a. Describe several ways that a standard-costing system strengthens management cost control.

b. Give at least two reasons to explain why a standard-costing system could negatively impact the motivation of production employees.

[CMA adapted]

Problem 16.41
Development of Standard Costs; Causes of Variances; Ethics
(LO 1, 5, 7)

Ethics

Communication

TasteeFruit Company is a small producer of fruit-flavored frozen desserts. For many years, its products have had strong regional sales on the basis of brand recognition. However, other companies have begun marketing similar products in the area, and price competition has become increasingly important. John Wakefield, the company's controller, is planning to implement a standard-costing system and has gathered considerable information on production and materials requirements for TasteeFruit's products. He believes that the use of standard costing will allow the company to make better pricing decisions.

TasteeFruit's most popular product is raspberry sherbet. The sherbet is produced in 10-gallon batches, and each batch requires six quarts of good raspberries. The fresh raspberries are sorted by hand before entering the production process. Because of imperfections in the raspberries and normal spoilage, one quart of berries is discarded for every four quarts accepted. Three minutes is the standard direct-labor time for the sorting required to obtain one quart of acceptable raspberries. The acceptable raspberries are then blended with the other ingredients; blending requires 12 minutes of direct-labor time per batch. After blending, the sherbet is packaged in quart containers. Wakefield has gathered the following information from Teresa Adams, TasteeFruit's cost accountant.

- TasteeFruit purchases raspberries at a cost of $ .80 per quart. All other ingredients cost a total of $ .45 per gallon.
- Direct labor is paid at the rate of $9 per hour.
- The total cost of material and labor required to package the sherbet is $ .41 per quart.

Adams has a friend who owns a berry farm that has been losing money in recent years. Because of good crops, an oversupply of raspberries has been available, and prices have dropped to $ .50 per quart. Adams has arranged for TasteeFruit to purchase raspberries from her friend and hopes that $ .80 per quart will help her friend's farm become profitable again.

Required

a. Develop the standard cost of direct material, direct labor, and packaging for a 10-gallon batch of raspberry sherbet.

b. As part of the implementation of a standard-costing system, Wakefield plans to train those responsible for maintaining the standards in the use of variance analysis. He is particularly concerned with the causes of unfavorable variances. As his assistant, prepare a page for a company training document that discusses the following:

(1) The possible causes of unfavorable material price variances and identifies the individual(s) who should be held responsible for these variances.

(2) The possible causes of unfavorable labor efficiency variances and identifies the individual(s) who should be held responsible for these variances.

c. Citing the specific ethical standards of competence, confidentiality, integrity, and objectivity for management accountants, explain why Adams's behavior regarding the cost information provided to Wakefield is unethical. (See the Appendix to Chapter 1 for these ethical standards.)

[CMA adapted]

Problem 16.42
Variances; Journal Entries; Missing Data
(LO 3, 6)

Sand Dune Company manufactures fiberglass boards used for riding the waves at the beach. The products are sold under the brand name Crazy Board. The standard cost for material and labor is $89.20 per board. This includes 8 kilograms of direct material at a standard cost of $5.00 per kilogram and 6 hours of direct labor at $8.20 per hour. The following data pertain to November:

- Work-in-process inventory on November 1: none.
- Work-in-process inventory on November 30: 800 units (75 percent complete as to labor; material is issued at the beginning of processing).
- Units completed: 5,600 units.
- Purchases of material: 50,000 kilograms for $249,250.
- Total actual labor costs: $300,760.
- Actual hours of labor: 36,500 hours.
- Direct-material quantity variance: $1,500 unfavorable.

Required

a. Compute the following amounts. Indicate whether each variance is favorable or unfavorable.

(1) Direct-labor rate variance for November.

(2) Direct-labor efficiency variance for November.

(3) Actual kilograms of material used in the production process during November.

(4) Actual price paid per kilogram of direct material in November.

(5) Total amounts of direct-material and direct-labor cost transferred to Finished-Goods Inventory during November.

(6) Total amount of direct-material and direct-labor cost in the balance of Work-in-Process Inventory at the end of November.

b. Prepare journal entries to record the following:

- Purchasing raw material.
- Adding direct material to Work-in-Process Inventory.
- Adding direct labor to Work-in-Process Inventory.
- Recording variances.

[CMA adapted]

Problem 16.43
Cost-Variance Investigation
(LO 4)

Global

British Isles Agribusiness, Ltd. (BIA), manufactures agricultural machinery in its London, England, plant. At a recent staff meeting the controller presented the following direct-labor variance report for the year just ended.

BRITISH ISLES AGRIBUSINESS, LTD.
Direct-Labor Variance Report
(all variances in British pounds sterling)

	Direct-Labor Rate Variance		Direct-Labor Efficiency Variance	
	Amount	**Standard Cost, %**	**Amount**	**Standard Cost, %**
January	£ 800 F	.16%	£ 5,000 U	1.00%
February	4,900 F	.98	7,500 U	1.50
March	100 U	.02	9,700 U	1.94
April	2,000 U	.40	12,800 U	2.56
May	3,800 F	.76	20,100 U	4.02
June	3,900 F	.78	17,000 U	3.40
July	4,200 F	.84	28,500 U	5.70
August	5,100 F	1.02	38,000 U	7.60
September	4,800 F	.96	37,000 U	7.40
October	5,700 F	1.14	42,000 U	8.40
November	4,200 F	.84	60,000 U	12.00
December	4,300 F	.86	52,000 U	10.40

BIA's controller uses the following rule of thumb: Investigate all variances equal to or greater than £30,000, which is 6 percent of standard cost.

Required

a. Which variances would have been investigated during the year? (Indicate month and type of variance.)

b. What characteristics of the variance pattern shown in the report should draw the controller's attention regardless of the usual investigation rule? Explain. Given these considerations, which variances would you have investigated? Why?

c. Is it important to follow up on favorable variances, such as those shown in the report? Why?

d. The controller believes that the firm's direct-labor rate variance has a normal probability distribution with a mean of zero and a standard deviation of £5,000. Prepare a statistical control chart and plot the company's direct-labor rate variances for each month. The critical value is 1 standard deviation. Which variances would have been investigated under this approach?

Problem 16.44
Kaizen Costing Chart
(LO 8, 9)

Brisbane Television Corporation manufactures TV sets in Australia, largely for the domestic market. The company recently implemented a kaizen costing program with the goal of reducing the manufacturing cost per television set by 10 percent during 20x1, the first year of the kaizen effort. The cost per TV set at the end of 20x0

Global

was $500. The following table shows the average cost per television set estimated during each month of 20x1. (On the day this problem was written, the Australian dollar was equivalent in value to .5153 US dollars.)

Month	Cost per Set	Month	Cost per Set
January	$500	July	$485
February	500	August	470
March	495	September	460
April	492	October	460
May	490	November	450
June	485	December	440

Required

Prepare a kaizen costing chart for 20x1 to show the results of Brisbane Television Corporation's first year of kaizen costing. In developing the chart, use the following steps:

a. Draw and label the axes of the kaizen costing chart.

b. Indicate the current year cost base and the kaizen goal (cost-reduction rate) on the chart.

c. Label the horizontal axis with the months of 20x1. Label the vertical axis with dollar amounts in the appropriate range.

d. Plot the 12 monthly estimates of the average cost per TV set. Then draw a line connecting the cost points that were plotted.

e. Complete the chart with any other labels necessary.

f. Briefly explain the purpose of kaizen costing. How could a continuous quality-improvement program, coupled with the kaizen costing effort implemented by Brisbane Television Corporation, help the firm begin competing in the worldwide market?

Problem 16.45
Direct-Labor Mix and Yield Variances (Appendix)
(LO 10)

Franconia Insurance Company compares actual results with standard costs. The standard direct-labor rates are established each year when the annual plan is formulated and held constant for the entire year. The standard direct-labor rates in effect for the current fiscal year and the standard hours allowed for the actual output of insurance claims for April in the claims department are shown in the following schedule:

	Standard Direct-Labor Rate per Hour	Standard Direct-Labor Hours Allowed for Actual Output
Labor class III	$8	500
Labor class II	7	500
Labor class I	5	500

The wage rates for each labor class increased under the terms of a new contract. The standard wage rates were not revised to reflect the new contract.

The actual direct-labor hours worked and the actual direct-labor rates per hour experienced for the month of April were as follows:

	Actual Direct-Labor Rate per Hour	Actual Direct-Labor Hours
Labor class III	$8.50	550
Labor class II	7.50	650
Labor class I	5.40	375

Required

a. Calculate the dollar amount of the total direct-labor variance for April for Franconia Insurance Company, and break the total variance into the following components:

(1) Direct-labor rate and efficiency variances.

(2) Direct-labor mix and yield variances.

b. Prepare a variance chart similar to Exhibit 16–10.

[CMA adapted]

Problem 16.46
Direct-Material Mix and Yield Variances (Appendix)
(LO 10)

Birmingham Chemical Company manufactures a wide variety of chemical compounds and liquids for industrial uses. The standard mix for producing a single batch of 500 gallons of doroxaline follows:

Input Chemical	Quantity (in gallons)	Cost (per gallon)	Total Cost
Maxan	100	$2.00	$200
Salex	300	.75	225
Cralyn	225	1.00	225
Total	625		$650

A 20 percent loss in the doroxaline's liquid volume occurs during processing due to evaporation. The finished liquid is sold in 10-gallon bottles. Thus, the standard material cost for a 10-gallon bottle is $13.

The actual quantities and the cost of direct materials placed in production during November were as follows. (All materials purchased are immediately placed into production during the same period.)

Input Chemical	Quantity (in gallons)	Total Cost
Maxan	8,480	$17,384
Salex	25,200	17,640
Cralyn	18,540	16,686
Total	52,220	$51,710

A total of 4,000 bottles (40,000 gallons) of doroxaline were produced during November.

Required

a. Calculate the total direct-material variance for doroxaline for the month of November, and then further analyze the total variance by computing these variances:

(1) Direct-material price and quantity variances.

(2) Direct-material mix and yield variances.

b. Prepare a variance chart similar to Exhibit 16–10.

Cases

Case 16.47*
Direct-Material and Direct-Labor Variances; Job-Order Costing; Journal Entries
(LO 3, 6)

Metro Fashions, Inc., manufactures inexpensive men's dress shirts, which are produced in lots to fill each special order. Its customers are department stores in various cities. Metro Fashions sews the particular store's labels on the shirts. During November the company worked on three orders, for which the month's job-cost records disclose the following data.

Lot Number	Boxes in Lot	Material Used (yards)	Hours Worked
63	1,000	24,100	2,980
64	1,700	40,440	5,130
65	1,200	28,825	2,890

The following additional information is available:

1. The firm purchased 95,000 yards of material during November at a cost of $106,400.
2. Direct labor during November amounted to $165,000. According to payroll records, production employees were paid $15 per hour.
3. There was no work in process on November 1. During November, lots 63 and 64 were completed. All material was issued for lot 65, which was 80 percent completed as to labor.
4. The standard costs for a box of six shirts are as follows:

Direct material	24 yards at $1.10	$ 26.40
Direct labor	3 hours at $14.70	44.10
Manufacturing overhead	3 hours at $12.00	36.00
Standard cost per box		$106.50

*Note: Cases 17.67 and 17.68 in Chapter 17 include more integrative cost-variance analyses as well as more significant managerial implications.

Required

a. Prepare a schedule computing the standard cost of lots 63, 64, and 65 for November.

b. For each lot produced during November, prepare a schedule showing the following:

(1) Direct-material price variance.

(2) Direct-material quantity variance.

(3) Direct-labor efficiency variance.

(4) Direct-labor rate variance.

Indicate whether each variance is favorable or unfavorable.

c. Prepare journal entries to record each of the following events for Metro Fashions.

- Purchase of material.
- Incurrence of direct-labor cost.
- Addition of direct-material and direct-labor cost to Work-in-Process Inventory.
- Recording of direct-material and direct-labor variances.

[CPA adapted]

Case 16.48
Comprehensive Problem on Variance Analysis
(LO 3, 5, 7)

Lyric Guitar Company manufactures acoustic guitars. The company uses a standard, job-order cost-accounting system in two production departments. Highly skilled artisans build the wooden guitars in the construction department and coat them with several layers of lacquer. Then the units are transferred to the finishing department, where the bridge of the guitar is attached and the strings are installed. The guitars also are tuned and inspected in the finishing department. The following diagram depicts the production process:

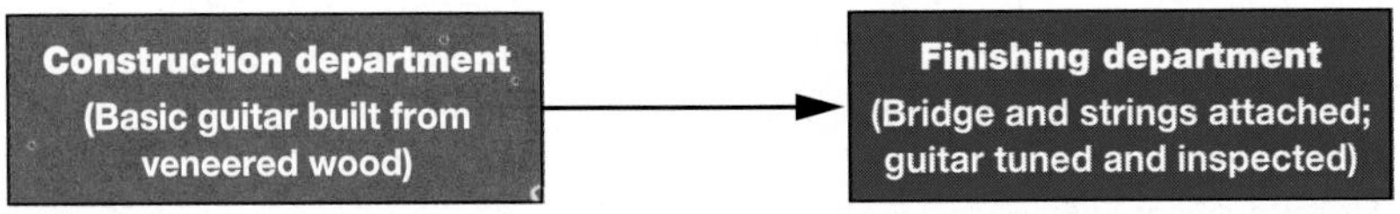

Each finished guitar contains seven pounds of veneered wood. In addition, one pound of wood is typically wasted in the production process. The veneered wood used in the guitars has a standard price of $12 per pound. The other parts needed to complete each guitar, such as the bridge and strings, cost $15 per guitar. The labor standards for Lyric's two production departments follow:

Construction department: 6 hours of direct labor at $20 per hour
Finishing department: 3 hours of direct labor at $15 per hour

The following additional information pertains to the month of July:

1. Neither production department had any beginning or ending work-in-process inventories.
2. The company had no beginning finished-goods inventory.
3. The company actually produced 500 guitars and sold 300 guitars on account for $400 each.
4. The company purchased 6,000 pounds of veneered wood at a price of $12.50 per pound.
5. Actual usage of veneered wood was 4,500 pounds.
6. Enough parts (bridges and strings) to finish 600 guitars were purchased at a cost of $9,000.
7. The construction department used 2,850 direct-labor hours. The total direct-labor cost in the construction department was $54,150.
8. The finishing department used 1,570 direct-labor hours. The total direct-labor cost in that department was $25,120.
9. The finishing department had no direct-material variances.

Required

a. Prepare a schedule that computes the standard costs of direct material and direct labor in each production department.

b. Prepare three exhibits that compute the July direct-material and direct-labor variances in the construction department and the July direct-labor variances in the finishing department. (Refer to Exhibits 16–1 and 16–2 for guidance.)

c. Prepare a cost variance report for July similar to that shown in Exhibit 16–3.

Case 16.49
Journal Entries under Standard Costing; Continuation of Case 16.48
(LO 6)

Refer to the preceding case.

Required

a. Prepare journal entries to record all events listed for Lyric Guitar Company during July. Specifically, the journal entries should reflect the following events.

(1) Purchase of direct material.

(2) Use of direct material.

(3) Incurrence of direct-labor costs.

(4) Addition of production costs to the Work-in-Process Inventory account for each department.

(5) Incurrence of all variances.

(6) Completion of 500 guitars.

(7) Sale of 300 guitars.

(8) Closing all variance accounts to Cost of Goods Sold.

b. Draw T-accounts and post the journal entries prepared in requirement (a). Assume that the beginning balance in all accounts is zero.

CHAPTER 17

Flexible Budgets, Overhead Cost Management, and Activity-Based Budgeting

After completing this chapter, you should be able to:

1. Explain how cost-management analysts use flexible budgets to control overhead.
2. Prepare and interpret a flexible overhead budget using formula and columnar formats.
3. Explain how overhead is applied to Work-in-Process Inventory under standard costing.
4. Discuss some important issues in choosing an activity measure for budgeting overhead.
5. Compute and interpret the variable-overhead spending and efficiency variances and the fixed-overhead budget and volume variances.
6. Prepare and interpret an overhead cost performance report.
7. Record manufacturing overhead under standard costing by preparing journal entries.
8. Explain why an activity-based flexible budget can provide more useful cost-management information than a conventional flexible budget.
9. Prorate variances among the relevant accounts (Appendix A).
10. Explain and illustrate backflush costing in a just-in-time environment (Appendix B).
11. Compute and interpret sales variances (Appendix C).

Cost-Management
Challenges

1. **How** can Koala Camp Gear's management use a flexible budget to manage overhead costs?

2. **How** would you respond to the concerns raised by Koala Camp Gear's production manager in his memo to the controller?

3. **How** could Koala's managers improve the management of overhead costs?

EMAIL MEMORANDUM

Koala
Camp
Gear
Company

2145 Yarra Drive
Melbourne, Victoria
Australia

To: Marc Wesley
Controller

From: Geoff Weatherby
Production Manager

Subject: Flexible budget and overhead-variance report for June

Since joining Koala Camp Gear Company in May, I have appreciated the information provided by your department in support of production operations. I was a bit surprised, however, upon receiving the overhead-variance report for June. Having carefully examined the flexible budget and the June overhead-variance report, and having followed up on several of the more significant variances, several questions remain.

First, the $1,680 variable-overhead spending variance is of concern. Does this mean that the company is paying excessive prices for overhead items, such as electrical power or heat?

Second, the $1,800 variable-overhead efficiency variance seems out of line. In the production area, we have paid particular attention lately to controlling our usage of overhead types of items, such as the various indirect materials and indirect labor. I do not believe we have been inefficient in their usage.

Third, the $7,500 fixed-overhead volume variance seems to be totally beyond our control. How is this variance computed, and what does it mean?

I would appreciate an opportunity to discuss these issues at your earliest convenience.

Geoff Weatherby's questions, expressed in the memo to Marc Wesley, Koala Camp Gear's controller, reflect concern about how Weatherby and his department are performing in their management of overhead costs. Also apparent in the memo is some uncertainty about how the variances on which he and his department are evaluated in part are determined and interpreted. This Koala Camp Gear Company memo raises the issue as to how companies manage and control overhead costs.

How do manufacturing firms, such as Nike and General Electric, control the many overhead costs incurred in their production processes? Unlike direct material and direct labor, manufacturing-overhead costs are not traceable to individual products. Moreover, manufacturing overhead is a pool of many different types of costs. Indirect material, indirect labor, and other indirect production costs often exhibit different relationships to productive activity. Moreover, different individuals in an organization are responsible for different types of overhead costs. Considering all of these issues together, controlling manufacturing overhead presents a challenge for cost-management analysts. This chapter presents a traditional cost-management system that is widely used to control overhead costs. We begin with flexible budgets.

Definition of Flexible-Overhead Budgets

LO 1 Explain how cost-management analysts use flexible budgets to control overhead costs.

Direct material and direct labor are traceable to products, and the determination of standard costs for these inputs is straightforward. If a surfboard requires 9.1 kilograms of fiberglass at $10 per kilogram, the standard direct-material cost for the surfboard is $91. But how much electricity does it take to produce a surfboard? How much supervisory time, equipment depreciation, or machinery repair services does the board require? Since all of these overhead costs are indirect costs of production, we cannot set overhead cost standards for the surfboard. If this approach does not provide the answer to managing overhead costs, what does?

flexible budget *is a budget that is valid for a range of activity*

relevant range *is the range of activity levels within which management expects the organization to operate and within which cost behavior patterns remain relatively stable*

static budget *is valid for only one planned activity level*

The cost-management tool that most companies use to control overhead costs is called a **flexible budget.** A flexible budget resembles the budgets we studied in Chapter 15, with one important difference: A *flexible budget is not based on only one level of activity.* Instead, a flexible budget covers a range of activity within which the firm operates. This range of activity often is referred to as the **relevant range.** A *flexible overhead budget* is defined as a detailed plan for controlling overhead costs that is valid in the firm's *relevant range* of activity.[1] In contrast, a **static budget** is based on a particular planned level of activity.

Flexible budgets and the overhead-control techniques based on them traditionally are based on a simplified view of a firm's overhead cost structure. Overhead costs are classified as variable or fixed. Variable costs change in total in proportion to changes in the company's activity, as expressed in terms of a single, volume-based measure such as machine hours, labor hours, or throughput. Fixed costs do not change in total as the organization's activity changes. Chapter 11, which covers cost estimation, presents various methods for classifying costs as variable or fixed.

Koala Camp Gear Company

To illustrate, suppose that the cost-management analyst for Koala Camp Gear Company determines that electricity is a variable cost, incurred at the rate of $ .20 per machine hour. Examine the two different budgets for electricity costs in Exhibit 17–1. The static budget is based on management's predicted level of activity for June, 6,000 machine hours. This estimate is based on *planned* production of 4,000 Tree Line tents, each of which requires 1.5 machine hours. The flexible budget includes three different production activity levels within the relevant range: 4,500, 6,000, and 7,500 machine hours.

[1]See Chapter 11, which covers cost estimation, for a discussion of the relevant range concept.

Exhibit 17–1

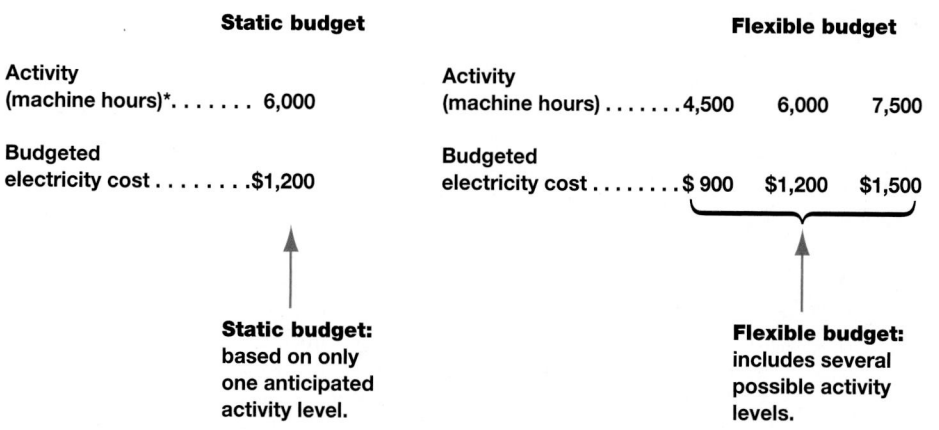

Static Budget versus Flexible Budget

Koala Camp Gear Company

Static budget

Activity (machine hours)*	**6,000**
Budgeted electricity cost	**$1,200**

Static budget: based on only one anticipated activity level.

Flexible budget

Activity (machine hours)	**4,500**	**6,000**	**7,500**
Budgeted electricity cost	**$ 900**	**$1,200**	**$1,500**

Flexible budget: includes several possible activity levels.

*Based on *planned* June production of 4,000 tents, at 1.5 machine hours per tent.

Advantages of Flexible Budgets

Why is the distinction between static and flexible budgets so important? Suppose that Koala produced 3,000 Tree Line tents during June, used 4,500 machine hours, and incurred electricity costs of $1,050. Does this constitute effective or ineffective control of electricity costs? Which budget in Exhibit 17–1 is more useful in answering this question?

A manager using the static budget makes the following comparison:

Actual Electricity Cost	Budgeted Electricity Cost (static budget)	Cost Variance
$1,050	$1,200	$150 Favorable

This comparison suggests that operating personnel maintained excellent control over electricity costs during June, generating a favorable variance of $150. Is this a valid analysis and conclusion?

The fault with this analysis is that the manager is comparing the electricity cost incurred at the *actual* activity level, 3,000 tents, with the budgeted electricity cost at the *planned* activity level, 4,000 tents. Since these activity levels are different, we should expect the electricity cost to be different.

A more sensible approach is to compare the actual electricity cost incurred with the cost that should be incurred when 3,000 tents are manufactured. At this production level, 4,500 machine hours should be used (1.5 per tent). The flexible budget in Exhibit 17–1 shows that the manager should expect $900 of electricity cost at the 4,500 machine-hour level of activity. Therefore, an analysis based on the flexible budget gives the following comparison:

Actual Electricity Cost	Budgeted Electricity Cost (flexible budget)	Cost Variance
$1,050	$900	$150 Unfavorable

Now the manager's conclusion is different; the revised analysis indicates an unfavorable variance. Electricity cost was higher than it should have been, given the actual level of output. The flexible budget provides the correct basis for comparison between actual and expected costs, given actual activity.

Activity Measure: Based on Input or Output?

Notice that the flexible budget for electricity cost in Exhibit 17–1 is based on machine hours, which is an **input** in the production process. The machine-hour activity levels shown in the flexible budget are the standard allowed machine hours given various levels

Managing overhead costs in this manufacturing operation is crucial if this company is to be profitable in its production of tents. The flexible budget is an important tool in cost management.

of output. If 3,000 tents are produced, and the standard allowance per tent is 1.5 machine hours, the standard allowed number of machine hours is 4,500.

Why are the activity levels in the flexible budget based on machine hours, an *input* measure, instead of the number of tents produced, an *output* measure? When only a single product is manufactured, it makes no difference whether the flexible budget was based on input or output. In our illustration, either of the flexible budgets shown in Exhibit 17–2 could be used.

Now suppose that during July, Koala Camp Gear Company manufactured three different tent model products: 1,000 Tree Line, 1,500 River's Edge, and 600 Valley. The controller has assigned the following standards to these products.

Product Model	Standard Machine Hours per Unit
Tree Line	1.5
River's Edge	1.8
Valley	2.0

During July, Koala's production output was 2,800 tents. Is 2,800 tents a meaningful output measure? Adding numbers of Tree Line, River's Edge, and Valley model tents, which require different amounts of productive inputs, is like adding apples and oranges. It is not sensible to base a flexible budget for electricity cost on units of output when the output consists of different products with different electricity requirements. In this case, the flexible budget must be based on an *input* measure. The standard allowed number of machine hours for the July production is computed as follows:

Product Model	Units Produced	Standard Machine Hours per Unit	Total Standard Allowed Machine Hours
Tree Line	1,200	1.5	1,800
River's Edge	900	1.8	1,620
Valley	700	2.0	1,400
Total			4,820

Exhibit 17–2

Flexible Budgets: Input versus Output

1.5 standard machine hours allowed per tent

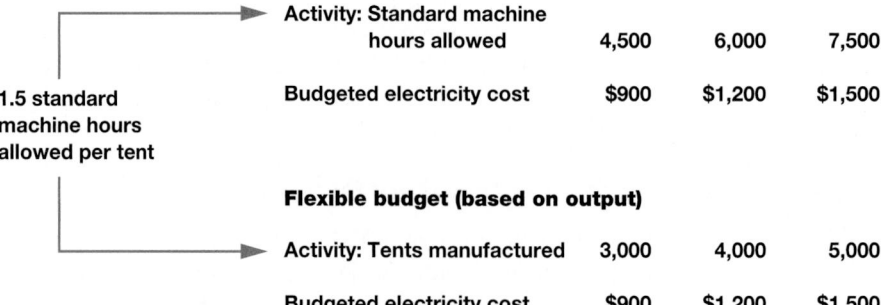

Flexible budget (based on input)

Activity: Standard machine hours allowed	**4,500**	**6,000**	**7,500**
Budgeted electricity cost	**$900**	**$1,200**	**$1,500**

Flexible budget (based on output)

Activity: Tents manufactured	**3,000**	**4,000**	**5,000**
Budgeted electricity cost	**$900**	**$1,200**	**$1,500**

Recall that Koala's cost-management analyst estimates electricity cost at $ .20 per machine hour. Thus, the flexible budget cost of electricity during July is computed as follows:

Standard allowed machine hours given July output	4,820
Electricity cost per machine hour	×$ .20
Flexible budget for electricity cost	$ 964

The important point here is that the number of *units of output* usually is not a meaningful measure in a multiproduct firm because it requires the addition of numbers of dissimilar products. To avoid this problem, output is measured in terms of the standard input allowed *given actual output.* Then it is possible to base the flexible overhead budget on this standard input measure.

In a multiproduct company, flexible budgets usually are based on standard inputs allowed (such as machine hours) rather than outputs (such as the number of tents manufactured).

Flexible Overhead Budget Illustrated

LO 2 Prepare and interpret a flexible overhead budget using formula and columnar formats.

Koala's monthly flexible-overhead budget appears in Exhibit 17–3. The overhead costs in the flexible budget are divided into variable and fixed costs. The total budgeted variable cost increases proportionately with increases in the activity. Thus, when the number of machine hours increases by 25 percent, from 6,000 hours to 7,500 hours, the total budgeted variable-overhead cost also increases by 25 percent, from $36,000 to $45,000. In contrast, the total budgeted fixed overhead does not change with increases in activity; it remains constant at $30,000 per month.

Formula flexible budget. When overhead costs can be divided into variable and fixed categories, we can express the flexible overhead budget differently. The format used in Exhibit 17–3 is called a *columnar flexible budget.* The budgeted overhead cost for each overhead item is listed in a column under a particular activity level. Notice that the columnar format allows for only a limited number of activity levels. Koala's flexible budget shows only three.

A more general format for expressing a flexible budget is called a *formula flexible budget.* In this format, the cost-management analyst expresses the relationship between activity and total budgeted overhead cost with the following formula.

$$\text{Total budgeted monthly overhead cost} = \left(\text{Budgeted variable-overhead cost per activity unit} \times \text{Total activity units}\right) + \text{Budgeted fixed-overhead cost per month}$$

To use this formula for Koala, we first compute the budgeted variable-overhead cost per machine hour. Dividing total budgeted variable-overhead cost by the associated activity level yields a budgeted variable-overhead rate of $6 per machine hour. Notice that we can use any activity level in Exhibit 17–3 to compute this rate.

$$\frac{\$27{,}000}{4{,}500} = \frac{\$36{,}000}{6{,}000} = \frac{\$45{,}000}{7{,}500} = \$6 \text{ per machine hour}$$

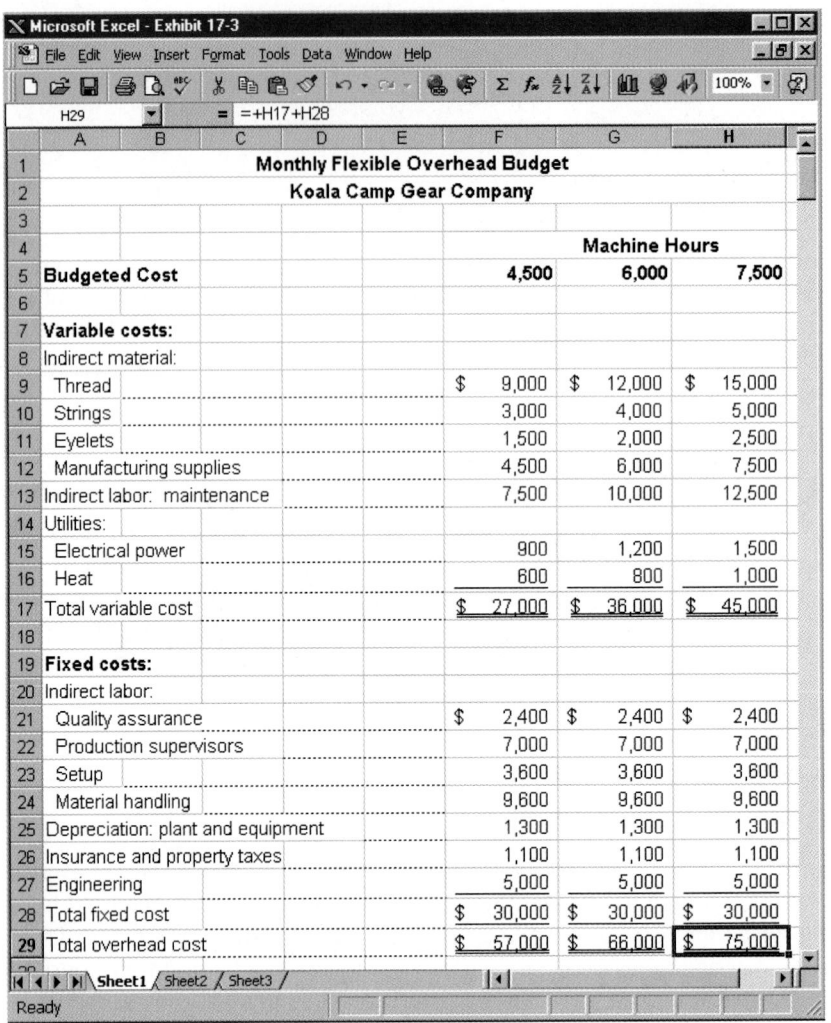

Exhibit 17–3

Flexible-Overhead Budget

Koala Camp Gear Company

Microsoft Excel - Exhibit 17-3

H29 = =+H17+H28

Monthly Flexible Overhead Budget			
Koala Camp Gear Company			
	Machine Hours		
Budgeted Cost	**4,500**	**6,000**	**7,500**
Variable costs:			
Indirect material:			
Thread	$ 9,000	$ 12,000	$ 15,000
Strings	3,000	4,000	5,000
Eyelets	1,500	2,000	2,500
Manufacturing supplies	4,500	6,000	7,500
Indirect labor: maintenance	7,500	10,000	12,500
Utilities:			
Electrical power	900	1,200	1,500
Heat	600	800	1,000
Total variable cost	$ 27,000	$ 36,000	$ 45,000
Fixed costs:			
Indirect labor:			
Quality assurance	$ 2,400	$ 2,400	$ 2,400
Production supervisors	7,000	7,000	7,000
Setup	3,600	3,600	3,600
Material handling	9,600	9,600	9,600
Depreciation: plant and equipment	1,300	1,300	1,300
Insurance and property taxes	1,100	1,100	1,100
Engineering	5,000	5,000	5,000
Total fixed cost	$ 30,000	$ 30,000	$ 30,000
Total overhead cost	$ 57,000	$ 66,000	$ 75,000

Sheet1 Sheet2 Sheet3

Ready

Koala's formula flexible-overhead budget is as follows:

$$\text{Total budgeted monthly overhead cost} = (\$6 \times \text{Total machine hours}) + \$30{,}000$$

To check the accuracy of the formula, compute the total budgeted overhead cost at each activity level shown in Exhibit 17–3.

Activity (machine hours)	Formula Flexible Overhead Budget	Budgeted Monthly Overhead Cost
4,500	\$6 × 4,500 + \$30,000 =	\$57,000
6,000	\$6 × 6,000 + \$30,000 =	\$66,000
7,500	\$6 × 7,500 + \$30,000 =	\$75,000

The budgeted monthly overhead cost computed here is the same as that shown in Exhibit 17–3 for each activity level.

The formula flexible budget is more general than the columnar flexible budget because the formula allows the cost-management analyst to compute budgeted overhead costs at any activity level. Then the flexible-budgeted overhead cost can be used at the end of the period as a benchmark against which to compare the actual overhead costs incurred.

Exhibit 17–4

Overhead Application

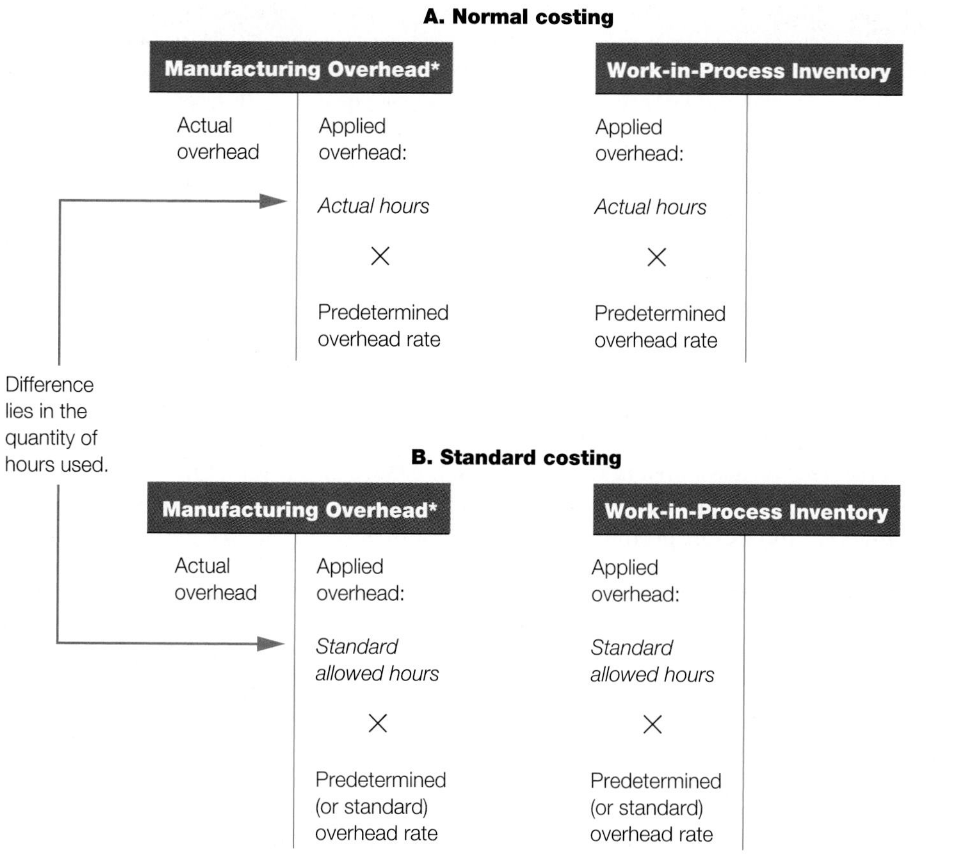

*Many companies have only one Manufacturing Overhead account. Actual overhead is accumulated on the left-hand (debit) side of the account. Applied overhead is accumulated on the right-hand (credit) side of the account.

Overhead Application in a Standard-Costing System

LO 3 Explain how overhead is applied to Work-in-Process Inventory under standard costing.

Recall that *overhead application* refers to the addition of overhead cost to the Work-in-Process Inventory account as a product cost. In a normal-costing system, as described in Chapter 3, overhead is applied as shown in panel A of Exhibit 17–4. Overhead application is based on *actual* hours. In a standard-costing system, overhead application is based on *standard* hours allowed given actual output (panel B of Exhibit 17–4). Notice that the difference between normal costing and standard costing, insofar as overhead is concerned, lies in the quantity of hours used.

Both normal-costing and standard-costing systems use a predetermined overhead rate (i.e., an overhead rate computed at the beginning of the accounting period). In a standard-costing system, the predetermined overhead rate is also referred to as the *standard overhead rate.* Koala Camp Gear Company calculates its predetermined or standard overhead rate annually. The rate for the current year, computed in Exhibit 17–5, is based on *planned* activity of 6,000 machine hours per month. Notice that Koala breaks its predetermined overhead rate into a variable rate and a fixed rate.

We continue the discussion of the use of standard costs for product costing later in this chapter.

Choice of Activity Measure

LO 4 Discuss some important issues in choosing an activity measure for budgeting overhead.

Koala Camp Gear Company bases its flexible overhead budget on machine hours. Different companies use a variety of activity measures in practice. Machine hours, direct-labor hours, direct-labor cost, total process time, and direct-materials cost are among the most common measures.

Exhibit 17-5

Predetermined Overhead Rate: Koala Camp Gear Company

	Budgeted Overhead	Planned Monthly Activity	Predetermined Overhead Rate
Variable	$36,000*	6,000 machine hours	$ 6.00 per machine hour
Fixed	30,000*	6,000 machine hours	5.00 per machine hour
Total	$66,000	6,000 machine hours	$11.00 per machine hour

*From the flexible budget (Exhibit 17–3) for planned monthly activity of 6,000 machine hours.

Criteria for choosing the activity measure. How should the cost-management analyst select the activity measure for the flexible budget? The activity measure should be one that varies in a similar pattern to the way that variable overhead varies. As productive activity increases, both variable-overhead cost and the activity measure should increase in roughly the same proportion. As productive activity declines, both variable-overhead cost and the activity measure should decline in roughly the same proportion. In short, variable-overhead cost and the activity measure should *move together* as overall productive activity changes.

Impact of changing manufacturing technology. Direct-labor time has traditionally been the most popular activity measure for manufacturing firms. However, as automation increases, more and more firms are switching to measures such as machine hours or process time for their flexible overhead budgets. Machine hours and process time are linked more closely than direct-labor hours to the robotic technology and computer-integrated manufacturing (CIM) systems common in today's manufacturing environment.

Dollar measures can be misleading. Companies sometimes use dollar measures, such as direct-labor or raw-materials costs, as the basis for flexible-overhead budgeting. However, such measures have significant drawbacks. Dollar measures are subject to price-level changes and fluctuate more than physical measures. For example, the direct-labor *hours* required to manufacture a tent are relatively stable over time. However, the direct-labor *cost* varies as wage levels and fringe-benefit costs change with price-level changes in the economy.

Increasing automation in manufacturing has resulted in direct labor becoming a less appropriate activity measure in flexible budgeting. Advanced manufacturing environments, such as flexible manufacturing systems (FMS) and computer-integrated manufacturing (CIM), have caused a shift in many companies' cost structures away from direct-labor cost and toward overhead costs. Pictured here are the labor-intensive Emyco shoe factory in Guanajuata State, Mexico, and a high-tech circuit-board manufacturing robot in Seoul, South Korea.

The choice of an activity measure on which to base the flexible budget for variable overhead is really a problem in cost estimation, which Chapter 11 addresses.

Impact of Information Technology

Spreadsheet programs such as Excel® make flexible budgeting easier than traditional computing methods.[2] Once the variable cost rates have been determined, generating a flexible budget for any activity level is a simple exercise. (Refer to the Excel® spreadsheet in Exhibit 17–3, which displays Koala Camp Gear's columnar flexible budget.)

Many businesses are adopting integrated business software packages that handle a broad range of computing needs such as customer and supplier databases, personnel and payroll functions, production scheduling and management, inventory records, financial accounting, and cost-management functions. Flexible budgeting typically is included in such software packages. Among the integrated software packages in wide use are PeopleSoft (*www.peoplesoft.com*) and the German product SAP, which stands for Systems Applications and Products in Data Processing (*www.sap.com*).

Overhead Cost Variances

LO 5 Compute and interpret the variable-overhead spending and efficiency variances and the fixed-overhead budget and volume variances.

The flexible-overhead budget is the cost-management analyst's primary tool for controlling manufacturing-overhead costs using this traditional cost-management technique. At the end of each accounting period, the cost-management analyst uses the flexible-overhead budget to determine the level of overhead cost that should have been incurred, given the actual level of activity. Then the cost-management analyst compares the overhead cost in the flexible budget with the actual overhead cost incurred. The analyst then computes four separate overhead variances, each of which conveys information useful in managing overhead costs.

To illustrate overhead variance analysis, we continue our illustration of Koala Camp Gear Company.

Flexible Budget: Basis for Management of Overhead Cost

Koala's monthly flexible-overhead budget, displayed in Exhibit 17–3, shows budgeted variable and fixed manufacturing-overhead costs at three levels of production activity. During June, Koala manufactured 3,000 Tree Line tents. Since production standards allow 1.5 machine hours per tent, the total standard number of machine hours allowed is 4,500 hours, computed as follows.

Actual production output	3,000	Tree Line tents
Standard machine hours allowed per tent	× 1.5	
Total standard machine hours allowed	4,500	machine hours

From the 4,500 machine-hours column in Exhibit 17–3, the budgeted overhead cost for June follows:

	Budgeted Overhead Cost for June
Variable overhead	$27,000
Fixed overhead	30,000

From the cost-accounting records, the controller determined that the following overhead costs were actually incurred during June:

	Actual Cost for June
Variable overhead	$30,480
Fixed overhead	32,500
Total overhead	$62,980

[2]EXCEL® is a registered trademark of Microsoft Corporation (*www.microsoft.com*).

variable-overhead spending variance *is the difference between the actual variable-overhead cost and the product of the standard variable-overhead rate and the actual quantity of an activity base (or cost driver).*

variable-overhead efficiency variance *is the difference between the actual and standard quantity of an activity base (or cost driver) multiplied by the standard variable-overhead rate.*

The production supervisor's records indicate that actual machine usage in June was:

Actual machine hours for June	4,800

Notice that the actual number of machine hours used (4,800) exceeds the standard number of machine hours allowed given actual production output (4,500).

We now have assembled all of the information necessary to compute Koala's overhead variances for June.

Variable-Overhead Variances

Koala's total variable-overhead variance for June is computed as follows:

Actual variable overhead	$30,480	
Budgeted variable overhead	27,000	
Total variable-overhead variance	$ 3,480	Unfavorable

What caused the company to spend $3,480 more than the budgeted amount on variable overhead? To discover the reasons behind this performance, the cost-management analyst computes a **variable-overhead spending variance** and a **variable-overhead efficiency variance.** Exhibit 17–6 depicts the computation of these variances.

Two equivalent formulas for the variable-overhead spending variance follow.

1. Variable-overhead spending variance $= \text{Actual variable overhead} - (AH \times SVR)$

or

2. Variable-overhead spending variance $= (AH \times AVR) - (AH \times SVR)$

Exhibit 17–6

Variable-Overhead Spending and Efficiency Variances

Koala Camp Gear Company

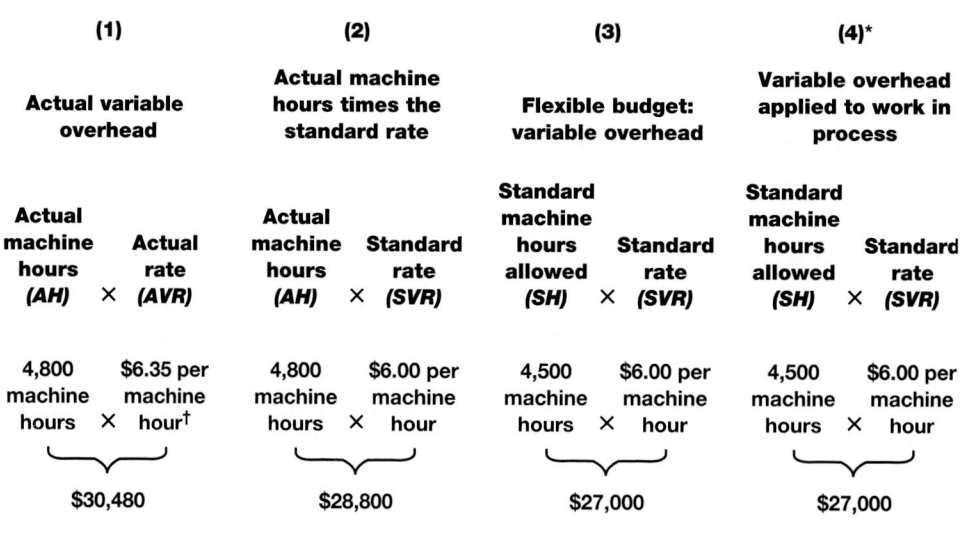

(1)	(2)	(3)	(4)*
Actual variable overhead	**Actual machine hours times the standard rate**	**Flexible budget: variable overhead**	**Variable overhead applied to work in process**
Actual machine hours (*AH*) × Actual rate (*AVR*)	Actual machine hours (*AH*) × Standard rate (*SVR*)	Standard machine hours allowed (*SH*) × Standard rate (*SVR*)	Standard machine hours allowed (*SH*) × Standard rate (*SVR*)
4,800 machine hours × $6.35 per machine hour†	4,800 machine hours × $6.00 per machine hour	4,500 machine hours × $6.00 per machine hour	4,500 machine hours × $6.00 per machine hour
$30,480	$28,800	$27,000	$27,000

(1) to (2)	(2) to (3)	(3) to (4)
$1,680 Unfavorable	$1,800 Unfavorable	
Variable-overhead spending variance	Variable-overhead efficiency variance	No difference

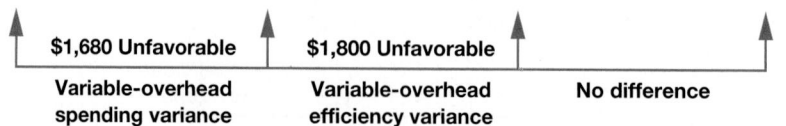

*Column (4) is not used to compute the variances. It is included to point out that the flexible-budget amount for variable overhead, $27,000, is the amount that will be applied to Work-in-Process Inventory for product-costing purposes.

†Actual variable-overhead rate $(AVR) = \dfrac{\text{Actual variable-overhead cost}}{\text{Actual machine hours}} = \dfrac{\$30{,}480}{4{,}800} = \$6.35$

where

AH = Actual machine hours

AVR = Actual variable-overhead rate (actual variable overhead ÷ AH)

SVR = Standard variable-overhead rate

These two formulas are equivalent because actual variable overhead is equal to actual hours times the actual variable-overhead rate ($AH \times AVR$). Formula 2 can be simplified:

3. Variable-overhead spending variance = $AH(AVR - SVR)$

Koala's variable-overhead spending variance for June is computed as follows (using formula 1):

Variable-overhead spending variance	=	Actual variable overhead	−	$(AH \times SVR)$
	=	\$30,480	−	(4,800 × \$6.00)
	=	\$1,680 Unfavorable		

This variance is unfavorable because the actual variable-overhead cost exceeded the expected amount after adjusting that expectation for the actual number of machine hours used.

As Exhibit 17–6 shows, the following formula defines the variable-overhead efficiency variance.

Variable-overhead efficiency variance = $(AH \times SVR) - (SH \times SVR)$

where

SH = Standard machine hours

Writing this formula more simply, we have the following expression:

Variable-overhead efficiency variance = $SVR(AH - SH)$

Koala's variable-overhead efficiency variance for June is computed as follows:

Variable-overhead efficiency variance	=	$SVR(AH - SH)$
	=	\$6.00 (4,800 − 4,500)
	=	\$1,800 Unfavorable

This variance is unfavorable because actual machine hours exceeded the standard machine hours allowed given actual output.

Cost-management versus product costing. Columns (1), (2), and (3) in Exhibit 17–6 are used to compute the variances for *cost-management purposes.* Column (4) is not needed to compute the variances, but it is included in the exhibit to show the variable overhead applied to work in process for the *product-costing purpose.* Notice that the variable-overhead cost on the flexible budget, \$27,000, is the same as the amount applied to work-in-process.

Graph of variable-overhead variances. Exhibit 17–7 provides a graphical analysis of Koala's variable-overhead variances for June. The graph shows the variable-overhead rate per machine hour on the vertical axis. The standard rate is \$6.00 per machine hour; the actual rate is \$6.35 per machine hour (actual variable-overhead cost of \$30,480 divided by 4,800 actual machine hours). Machine hours are shown on the horizontal axis.

The medium-shaded blue area on the graph represents the flexible-budget amount for variable overhead given actual June output of 3,000 Tree Line tents. The large area on the graph enclosed by colored lines on the top and right sides represents actual

Exhibit 17–7

Graphical Analysis of Variable-Overhead Variances

Koala Camp Gear Company

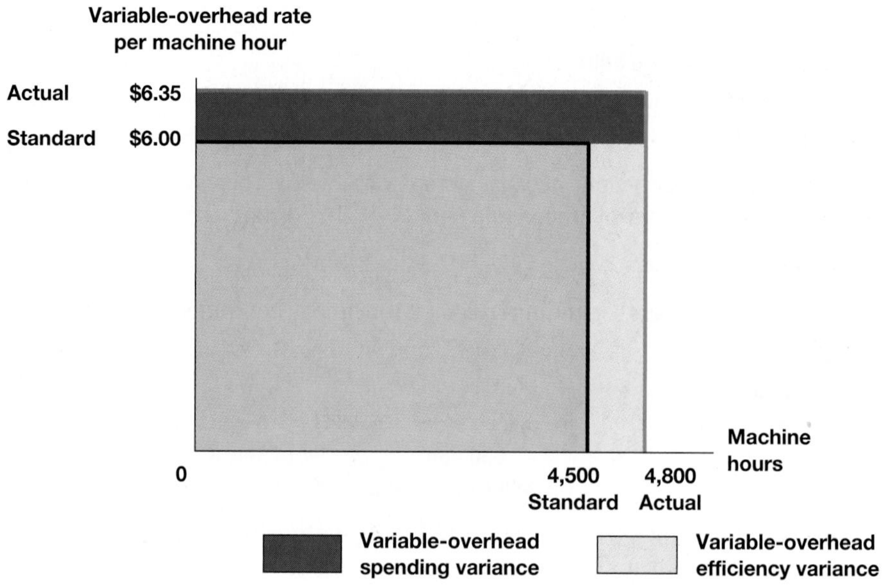

variable-overhead cost. The colored area between, representing the total variable-overhead variance, is divided into the spending and efficiency variances.

Managerial interpretation of variable-overhead variances. What do the variable-overhead variances mean? What information do they convey to management? The formulas for computing the variable-overhead variances resemble those used to compute the direct-labor variances. To see this, compare Exhibit 17–6 (variable overhead) with Exhibit 16–2 (direct labor).

Despite the similar formulas, the interpretation of the variable-overhead variances is quite different from that of the direct-labor variances.

How to interpret the efficiency variance. Recall that an unfavorable direct-labor efficiency variance results when more direct labor is used than the standard allowed quantity. Thus, direct labor has been used inefficiently relative to the standard. However, that is not the proper interpretation of an unfavorable variable-overhead efficiency variance. Koala's variable-overhead efficiency variance did *not* result from using more of the variable-overhead items, such as electricity and indirect materials, than the standard allowed amount. Instead, this variance resulted when Koala used *more machine hours* than the standard quantity given actual output. Recall that the cost-management analyst had found that variable-overhead cost varies in a pattern similar to the way machine hours vary. Since 300 more machine hours were used than the standard quantity allowed, the division's management should expect that variable-overhead costs will be higher. Thus, the variable-overhead efficiency variance has nothing to do with efficient or inefficient usage of electricity, indirect material, and other variable-overhead items. This variance simply reflects an adjustment in the cost-management analyst's expectation about total variable-overhead cost because the company used more than the standard quantity of machine hours.

What is the important difference between direct labor and variable overhead that causes this different interpretation of the efficiency variance? Direct labor is a traceable cost and is budgeted on the basis of direct-labor hours. Variable overhead, on the other hand, is a pool of *indirect* costs that are budgeted on the basis of *machine hours.* The indirect nature of variable-overhead costs causes the different interpretation.

What does the spending variance reveal? An unfavorable direct-labor rate variance is straightforward to interpret; the actual labor rate *per hour* exceeds the standard rate. Although the formula for computing the variable-overhead spending variance is similar to that for the direct-labor rate variance, its interpretation is quite different.

An unfavorable spending variance simply means that the total actual cost of variable overhead is higher than expected after adjusting for the actual quantity of machine hours used. An unfavorable spending variance could result from paying a higher than expected price per unit for variable-overhead items. The variance also could result from using more of the variable-overhead items than expected based on the flexible budget.

Suppose, for example, that electricity was the only variable-overhead cost item. An unfavorable variable-overhead spending variance could result from paying a higher than expected price per kilowatt-hour for electricity or from using more than the expected amount of electricity (based on the flexible budget), or both.

Variable-overhead cost management. Since the variable-overhead efficiency variance indicates nothing about efficient or inefficient usage of variable overhead, the spending variance is the real control variance for variable overhead. Managers can use the spending variance to alert them if variable-overhead costs are out of line with expectations.

Fixed-Overhead Variances

To analyze performance with regard to fixed overhead, the cost-management analyst calculates two fixed-overhead variances: the fixed-overhead budget variance and the fixed-overhead volume variance.

Fixed-overhead budget variance. The variance that managers use to control fixed overhead is called the **fixed-overhead budget variance.** It is defined as:

fixed-overhead budget variance *is the difference between actual fixed overhead and budgeted fixed overhead*

Fixed-overhead budget variance = Actual fixed overhead − Budgeted fixed overhead

Koala's fixed-overhead budget variance for June is computed as follows:

Fixed-overhead budget variance = Actual fixed overhead − Budgeted fixed overhead
= \$32,500 − \$30,000*
= \$2,500 Unfavorable

*From the flexible budget (Exhibit 17–3).

The fixed-overhead budget variance is unfavorable because Koala spent more than the budgeted amount on fixed overhead. Notice that we need not specify an activity level to determine budgeted fixed overhead. All three columns in the flexible budget (Exhibit 17–3) specify \$30,000 as budgeted fixed overhead.

Fixed-overhead volume variance. The **fixed-overhead volume variance** is defined as:

fixed-overhead volume variance *is the difference between budgeted fixed overhead and applied fixed overhead*

Fixed-overhead volume variance = Budgeted fixed overhead − Applied fixed overhead

Koala's applied fixed overhead for June is \$22,500, which is computed as follows:

Applied fixed overhead = Predetermined fixed-overhead rate × Standard hours allowed
\$22,500 = \$5 per machine hour × 4,500 machine hours

The \$5 predetermined fixed-overhead rate was calculated in Exhibit 17–5. The 4,500 standard machine hours allowed is based on actual June production of 3,000 tents, each with a standard allowance of 1.5 machine hours.

Koala's fixed-overhead volume variance is calculated as follows:

Fixed-overhead volume variance = Budgeted fixed overhead − Applied fixed overhead
= \$30,000 − \$22,500
= \$7,500 Unfavorable

Exhibit 17–8

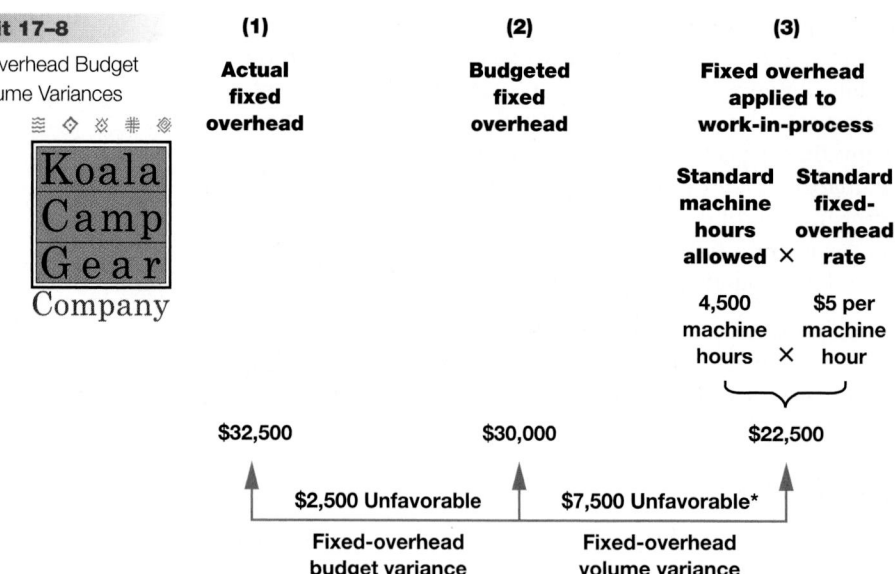

Fixed-Overhead Budget and Volume Variances

(1)	(2)	(3)
Actual fixed overhead	**Budgeted fixed overhead**	**Fixed overhead applied to work-in-process**
		Standard machine hours allowed × Standard fixed-overhead rate
		4,500 machine hours × $5 per machine hour
$32,500	**$30,000**	**$22,500**

$2,500 Unfavorable — Fixed-overhead budget variance (between (1) and (2))

$7,500 Unfavorable* — Fixed-overhead volume variance (between (2) and (3))

*Consistent with our discussion of the fixed-overhead volume variance, some accountants would designate a positive variance as unfavorable.

Managerial interpretation of fixed-overhead variances. Exhibit 17–8 shows Koala's two fixed-overhead variances for June. The budget variance is the real control variance for fixed overhead because it compares actual expenditures with budgeted fixed-overhead costs.

The volume variance provides a way to reconcile two different purposes of the cost-accounting system. For the *cost-management purpose,* the cost-accounting system recognizes that fixed overhead does not change as production activity varies. Hence, budgeted fixed overhead is the same at all activity levels in the flexible budget. (Review Exhibit 17–3 to verify this.) Budgeted fixed overhead is the basis for controlling fixed overhead because it provides the benchmark against which actual expenditures are compared.

For the *product-costing purpose* of the cost-accounting system, budgeted fixed overhead is divided by planned activity to obtain a predetermined (or standard) fixed-overhead rate. For Koala, this rate is $5 per machine hour (budgeted fixed overhead of $30,000 divided by *planned* activity of 6,000 machine hours). This predetermined rate is then used to apply fixed overhead to Work-in-Process Inventory. During any period in which the standard number of machine hours allowed, given actual output, differs from the planned level of machine hours, budgeted fixed overhead will differ from applied fixed overhead.

Exhibit 17–9 illustrates this point graphically. Budgeted fixed overhead is constant at $30,000 for all levels of activity. However, applied fixed overhead increases with activity since fixed overhead is applied to Work-in-Process Inventory at the rate of $5 per standard machine hour allowed. Notice that budgeted and applied fixed overhead are equal *only* if the number of standard hours allowed equals the planned activity level of 6,000 machine hours. When this happens, no fixed-overhead volume variance exists. Koala has a $7,500 volume variance in June because the standard hours allowed and planned hours are different.

Capacity utilization. A common, but faulty, interpretation of a positive volume variance is that it measures the cost of underutilizing productive capacity. The reasoning behind this view is that the planned activity level used to compute the predetermined fixed-overhead rate is a measure of normal capacity utilization. Moreover, fixed-overhead costs such as depreciation and property taxes are costs incurred to create productive capacity. Therefore, the predetermined fixed-overhead rate measures the cost to provide an hour of productive capacity. If 6,000 machine hours are planned, but output is such that only 4,500 standard machine hours are allowed, capacity has been underutilized by 1,500 hours. Since each hour costs $5 (Koala's predetermined fixed-overhead rate), the cost of underutilization is $22,500 (4,500 × $5), which is Koala's volume variance.

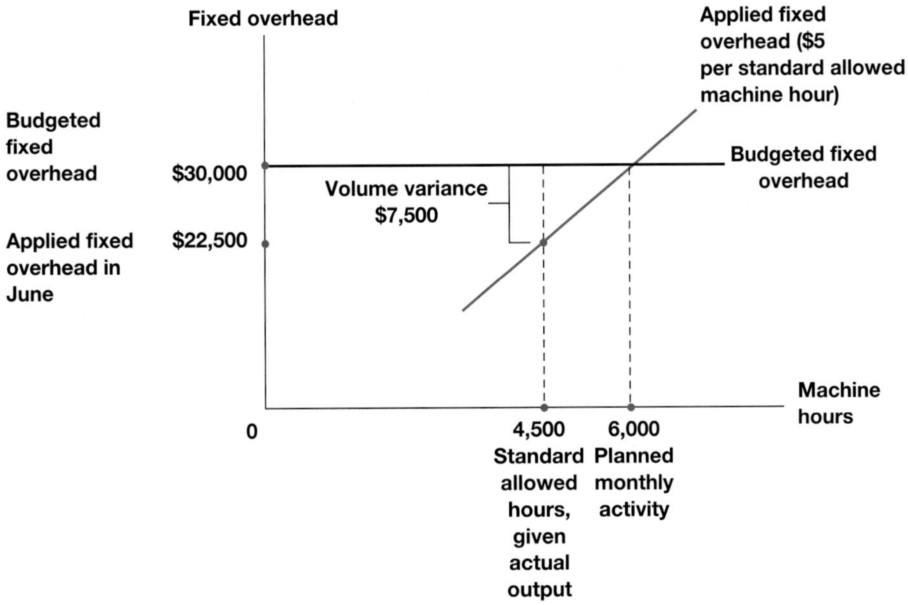

Exhibit 17-9

Budgeted versus Applied Fixed Overhead

Koala Camp Gear Company

Research Insight 17.1

International Use of Flexible Budgeting to Control Costs

Flexible budgeting as a means of controlling overhead costs is found in cost-management systems worldwide. In Germany, for example, *grenzplankostenrechnung* (or "flexible standard costing") exhibits many of the features illustrated in this chapter. Under the German approach "each cost center distinguishes between variable costs (e.g., energy) and fixed costs (e.g., a manager's salary)." The number of machine hours is a common activity measure. "For purposes of cost planning and control, companies budget each cost center's expenses and then distribute the expenses to each month of the budgeted year. The budgeted costs are standards for efficient resource consumption. . . ." The cost and performance information "allows for effective discussions about productivity improvement" among department managers, management accountants, and plant managers. (Refer to Research Insight 16.3 for more information on *grenzplankostenrechnung*.) *Source: B. Gaiser,* "German Cost Management Systems." *(Full citations to references are in the Bibliography.)*

The fault with this interpretation of the volume variance is that it ignores the real cost of underutilizing productive capacity. The real cost results from the lost contribution margins of the products *not* produced when capacity is underutilized. Moreover, this interpretation fails to recognize that underutilizing capacity and reducing inventory could be a wise managerial response to slackening demand.

For this reason, we interpret the volume variance merely as a way to reconcile the two purposes of the cost-accounting system. Some accountants designate a positive volume variance as *unfavorable.* Their reasoning is that when the volume variance is closed to Cost of Goods Sold expense at the end of the accounting period (as explained later in the chapter), the effect is to increase cost of goods sold, which in turn has an unfavorable effect on income. In contrast, other accountants argue that no sign (favorable or unfavorable) should be assigned to the volume variance.

What Do Four-Way, Three-Way, and Two-Way Variance Analyses Tell the Cost Manager?

Four variances were discussed in the preceding two sections: the variable-overhead spending and efficiency variances and the fixed-overhead budget and volume variances. Some managers prefer to combine the variable-overhead spending and fixed-overhead budget variances into a single *combined spending variance.* Since this presentation leaves only three separate variances, it is called a *three-way analysis.* Other managers prefer to

Exhibit 17–10

Four-Way, Three-Way, and Two-Way Variance Analyses: Koala Camp Gear Company

	Variable-overhead spending variance	Fixed-overhead budget variance	Variable-overhead efficiency variance	Fixed-overhead volume variance
Four-way analysis	$1,680 U	$2,500 U	$1,800 U	$7,500 U*
	Combined spending variance			
Three-way analysis	$4,180 U		$1,800 U	$7,500 U*
		Combined budget variance		
Two-way analysis		$5,980 U		$7,500 U*
			Underapplied overhead $13,480†	

*The volume variance is positive since budgeted fixed overhead is higher than applied fixed overhead. Consistent with the discussion in the preceding section, some accountants would designate it as unfavorable.

†The underapplied overhead is the difference between actual overhead, $62,980, and overhead applied to Work-in-Process Inventory, $49,500 ($27,000 variable + $22,500 fixed).

overhead cost performance report *shows the actual and flexible-budget cost levels for each overhead item, together with the variable-overhead spending and efficiency variances and the fixed-overhead budget variance*

combine the variable-overhead spending, variable-overhead efficiency, and fixed-overhead budget variances into a single *combined budget variance.* Since this presentation leaves only two separate variances, it is called a *two-way analysis.* Exhibit 17–10 displays the four-way, three-way, and two-way variance analyses for Koala's June performance.

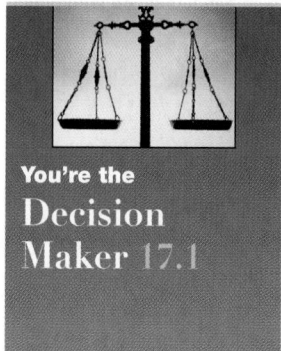

You're the Decision Maker 17.1

Overhead Variances

In December, Koala Camp Gear Company produced 3,600 Tree Line tents, used 5,700 machine hours, and incurred the following manufacturing-overhead costs:

Variable overhead	$37,050
Fixed overhead	29,000

Koala's monthly flexible overhead budget for December is the same as that given in Exhibit 17–3.

a. Compute Koala's variable-overhead variances using the format shown in Exhibit 17–6. Compute the company's fixed-overhead variances using the format shown in Exhibit 17–8.

b. How should Koala's management interpret the fixed-overhead budget variance?

c. Under what circumstances would there have been no fixed-overhead volume variance for Koala Camp Gear's December operations?

(Solutions begin on page 722.)

Using the Overhead Cost Performance Report in Cost Management

LO 6 Prepare and interpret an overhead cost performance report.

The variable-overhead spending and efficiency variances and the fixed-overhead budget variance can be computed for each overhead cost item in the flexible budget. When these itemized variances are presented along with actual and budgeted costs for each overhead item, the result is an **overhead cost performance report.** Koala's performance report is displayed in Exhibit 17–11. Management would use this report to exercise control over each of the division's overhead costs.

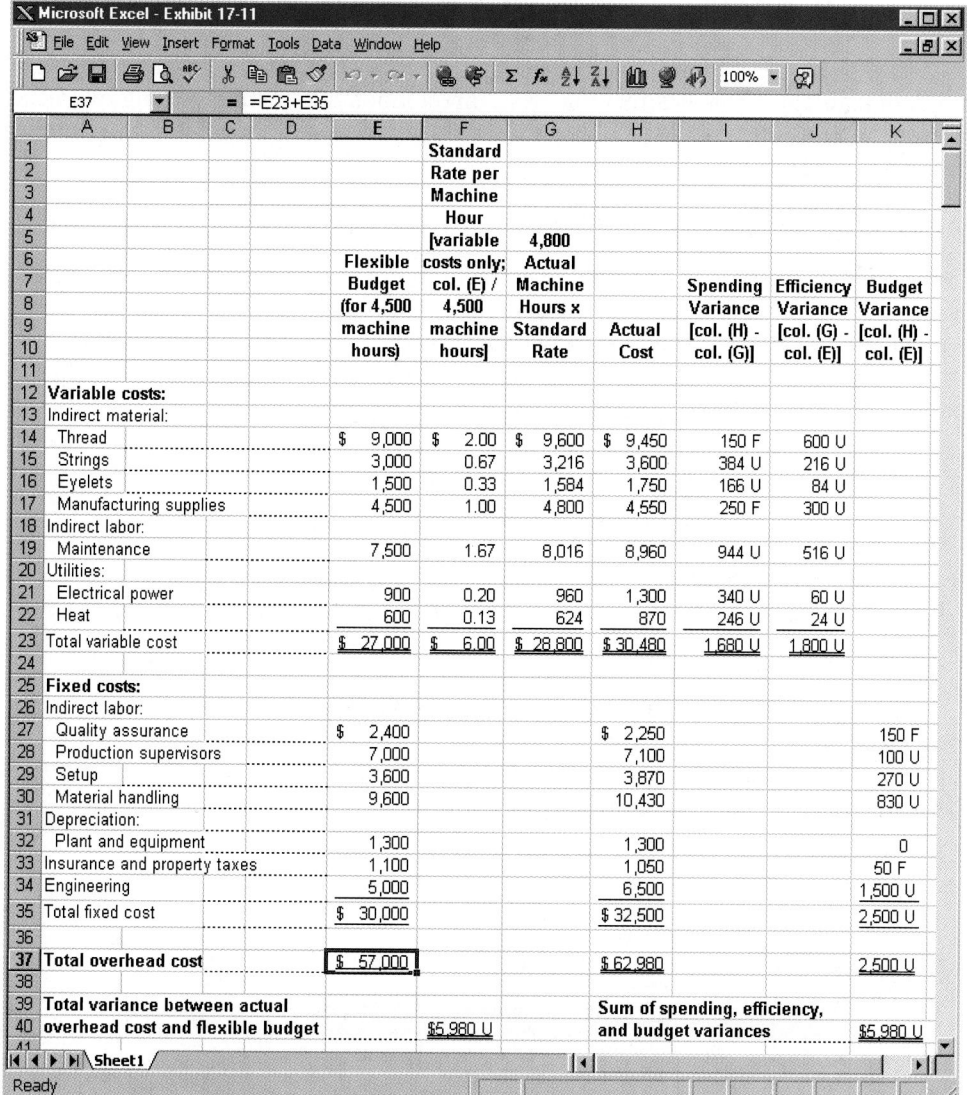

Microsoft Excel - Exhibit 17-11

E37 = =E23+E35

	Flexible Budget (for 4,500 machine hours)	Standard Rate per Machine Hour [variable costs only; col. (E) / 4,500 machine hours]	4,800 Actual Machine Hours x Standard Rate	Actual Cost	Spending Variance [col. (H) - col. (G)]	Efficiency Variance [col. (G) - col. (E)]	Budget Variance [col. (H) - col. (E)]
Variable costs:							
Indirect material:							
Thread	$ 9,000	$ 2.00	$ 9,600	$ 9,450	150 F	600 U	
Strings	3,000	0.67	3,216	3,600	384 U	216 U	
Eyelets	1,500	0.33	1,584	1,750	166 U	84 U	
Manufacturing supplies	4,500	1.00	4,800	4,550	250 F	300 U	
Indirect labor:							
Maintenance	7,500	1.67	8,016	8,960	944 U	516 U	
Utilities:							
Electrical power	900	0.20	960	1,300	340 U	60 U	
Heat	600	0.13	624	870	246 U	24 U	
Total variable cost	$ 27,000	$ 6.00	$ 28,800	$ 30,480	1,680 U	1,800 U	
Fixed costs:							
Indirect labor:							
Quality assurance	$ 2,400			$ 2,250			150 F
Production supervisors	7,000			7,100			100 U
Setup	3,600			3,870			270 U
Material handling	9,600			10,430			830 U
Depreciation:							
Plant and equipment	1,300			1,300			0
Insurance and property taxes	1,100			1,050			50 F
Engineering	5,000			6,500			1,500 U
Total fixed cost	$ 30,000			$ 32,500			2,500 U
Total overhead cost	$ 57,000			$ 62,980			2,500 U
Total variance between actual overhead cost and flexible budget		$5,980 U		**Sum of spending, efficiency, and budget variances**			$5,980 U

Sheet1

Ready

Exhibit 17-11

Overhead Cost Performance Report: Koala Camp Gear Company

Koala Camp Gear Company

Notice that the performance report includes only spending and efficiency variances for the variable items and only a budget variance for the fixed items. Upon receiving this report, a manager might investigate the relatively large variances for indirect material (thread), indirect labor (maintenance), and engineering.

Performance Reports

A recent survey of US manufacturers found that 96 percent of the responding companies' prepare periodic performance reports including variances from standard costs for management. However, 62 percent of the respondents believed that the reports contained too much detail, and only 41 percent of the responding production managers believed their reports to be timely. Just 37 percent of the survey respondents believed that their performance reports enabled them to assign responsibility for the variances. A need for improvement in the performance reporting system was suggested by 71 percent of the surveyed managers. *Source: S. A. Moscove,* "Enhancing Detective Controls through Performance Reporting."

Research Insight 17.2

Using Standard Costs in Product Costing

LO 7 Record manufacturing overhead under standard costing by preparing journal entries.

A standard-costing system uses the standard costs for product costing as well as for cost control. The costs of direct material, direct labor, and manufacturing overhead are all entered into Work-in-Process Inventory at their standard costs. (Review Exhibit 17–4.)

Journal Entries under Standard Costing

During June, Koala incurred actual manufacturing-overhead costs of $62,980, which include $30,480 of variable overhead and $32,500 of fixed overhead. A summary journal entry to record these actual expenditures follows:

Manufacturing Overhead	62,980	
Indirect-Material Inventory		19,350*
Wages Payable		32,610*
Utilities Payable		2,170
Accumulated Depreciation		1,300
Prepaid Insurance and Property Taxes		1,050
Engineering Salaries Payable		6,500

*The credit amounts can be verified in column H of Exhibit 17–11. For example, indirect-material costs amounted to $19,350 ($9,450 + $3,600 + $1,750 + $4,550). The credit to Wages Payable is for indirect-labor costs, which amounted to $32,610 ($8,960 + $2,250 + $7,100 + $3,870 + $10,430).

The application of manufacturing overhead to Work-in-Process Inventory is based on a predetermined overhead rate of $11 per machine hour (the total of the variable and the fixed rates) and 4,500 standard machine hours allowed given an actual output of 3,000 tents. The summary journal entry is:

Work-in-Process Inventory	49,500	
Manufacturing Overhead		49,500*

*Applied overhead = $11.00 × 4,500 = $49,500

Now the Manufacturing Overhead account appears as follows:

Manufacturing Overhead			
Actual	62,980	49,500	Applied

The *underapplied overhead* for June is $13,480 ($62,980 − $49,500). This means that the overhead applied to Work-in-Process Inventory in June was $13,480 less than the actual overhead cost incurred. Notice that the underapplied overhead equals the sum of the four overhead variances for June. The total of the four overhead variances always equal the overapplied or underapplied overhead for the accounting period.

Disposition of Variances

As explained in Chapter 16, variances are temporary accounts, and most companies close them directly to Cost of Goods Sold at the end of each accounting period. The journal entry required to close out Koala's underapplied overhead for June is:

Cost of Goods Sold	13,480	
Manufacturing Overhead		13,480

The journal entry to close underapplied or overapplied overhead typically is made annually rather than monthly.

An alternative accounting treatment is to prorate (or allocate) underapplied or overapplied overhead among Work-in-Process Inventory, Finished-Goods Inventory, and Cost of Goods Sold, as explained in Appendix A to this chapter.

Activity-Based Flexible Budget

LO 8 Explain why an activity-based flexible budget can provide more useful cost-management information than a conventional flexible budget.

The flexible budget shown in Exhibit 17–3, which underlies our variance analysis for Koala Camp Gear Company, is based on a single cost driver. Overhead costs that vary with respect to *machine hours* are categorized as variable; all other overhead costs are treated as fixed. This approach is consistent with traditional, volume-based product-costing systems.

Under the more accurate product-costing method called *activity-based costing* (ABC), several cost drivers are identified.[3] Costs that could appear fixed with respect to a single volume-based cost driver, such as machine hours, can be variable with respect to other appropriate cost drivers. The activity-based costing approach also can be used as the basis for a flexible budget for planning and cost-management purposes. Exhibit 17–12 displays an **activity-based flexible budget** for Koala, using the same data as Exhibit 17–3.

activity-based flexible budget *is based on several cost drivers rather than a single, volume-based cost driver*

Compare the conventional flexible budget (Exhibit 17–3) and the activity-based flexible budget (Exhibit 17–12). The key difference lies in the costs that were

[3]Activity-based costing is covered in Chapter 4.

Exhibit 17–12

Activity-Based Flexible Budget

Koala Camp Gear Company

Microsoft Excel - Exhibit 17-12

H38 = =+H16+H22+H26+H30+H36

Monthly Flexible Overhead Budget
Koala Camp Gear Company

Budgeted Cost	**Level of Activity**		
Cost Pool I (cost driver: machine hours)	**$ 4,500**	**$ 6,000**	**$ 7,500**
Indirect material:			
Thread	$ 9,000	$ 12,000	$ 15,000
Strings	$ 3,000	$ 4,000	$ 5,000
Eyelets	$ 1,500	$ 2,000	$ 2,500
Manufacturing supplies	$ 4,500	$ 6,000	$ 7,500
Indirect labor: maintenance	$ 7,500	$ 10,000	$ 12,500
Utilities:			
Electrical power	$ 900	$ 1,200	$ 1,500
Heat	$ 600	$ 800	$ 1,000
Total of cost pool I	$ 27,000	$ 36,000	$ 45,000
Cost Pool II (cost driver: production runs)	**10**	**12**	**14**
Indirect labor:			
Quality assurance	$ 2,000	$ 2,400	$ 2,800
Setup	$ 3,000	$ 3,600	$ 4,200
Total of cost pool II	$ 5,000	$ 6,000	$ 7,000
Cost Pool III (cost driver: engineering design specs)	**12**	**15**	**18**
Engineering	$ 4,000	$ 5,000	$ 6,000
Total of cost pool III	$ 4,000	$ 5,000	$ 6,000
Cost Pool IV (cost driver: sq. meters of material handled)	**$ 36,000**	**$ 48,000**	**$ 90,000**
Material handling	$ 7,200	$ 9,600	$ 18,000
Total of cost pool IV	$ 7,200	$ 9,600	$ 18,000
Cost Pool V (facility level costs)			
Indirect labor: production supervisors	$ 7,000	$ 7,000	$ 7,000
Depreciation: plant and equipment	$ 1,300	$ 1,300	$ 1,300
Insurance and property taxes	$ 1,100	$ 1,100	$ 1,100
Total of cost pool V	$ 9,400	$ 9,400	$ 9,400
Total overhead cost	$ 52,600	$ 66,000	$ 85,400

Sheet1

Ready

categorized as fixed on the conventional flexible budget. These costs *are* fixed with respect to machine hours but are *not* fixed with respect to other more appropriate cost drivers. For example, cost pool II includes quality assurance and setup costs, which vary with respect to the number of production runs.

An activity-based flexible budget uses a variety of cost drivers. For example, the cost driver used for material handling often is the number of setups or batches produced. Machine hours might be an appropriate cost driver for equipment maintenance. Purchasing costs should be driven by the number of part numbers stocked. Shown here is a material-handling operation in the automobile industry.

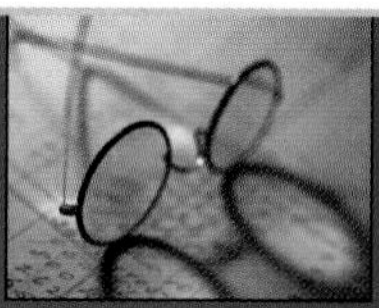

Cost Management in
Practice 17.1

Activity-Based Budgeting at Whirlpool

When managers at Whirlpool Corporation's (*www.whirlpool.com*) Evansville, Indiana, plant developed their activity-based costing system, more accurate information for budgeting was high on the list of priorities. The Evansville plant's product lines included 333 different refrigerator and vertical freezer models. These products exhibited a wide range of complexity, and the annual production volume ranged from a single unit to 12,000 units. The ABC cost hierarchy in Whirlpool's system designated costs at the following five levels: unit, batch, product, process, and plant. Among the cost drivers used were the following:

- Setups
- Purchase orders
- Assembly complexity
- Engineering change orders
- Receipts
- Design complexity
- Machine hours
- Inspections
- Scrap dollars
- Direct-labor hours

One of the main objectives of a flexible budgeting system is to enable management to predict cost incurrence at different levels of production for each type of product. At Whirlpool, management found that its traditional accounting system significantly distorted product costs. The traditional system, which budgeted overhead costs on the basis of either machine hours or direct-labor hours, undercosted low-volume products and overcosted high-volume products. "An interesting but extreme example of this phenomenon involved the overhead comparison for a product with an annual production rate of one unit. Under the traditional system, this product carried an overhead burden of $64.48, whereas the overhead assigned by the ABC system was a whopping $25,447.11." More typical of the results, though, is the following comparison among three of Whirlpool's product lines.

Production Volume Class	Annual Production Volume	Traditional Overhead Assigned	ABC Overhead Assigned	Percentage Change in Assigned Overhead
Low	292	$66.23	$132.55	100.0%
Medium	2,959	67.91	56.46	(16.9)
High..............................	12,000	64.17	42.92	(33.1)

The main cause of such cost distortion is that many of Whirlpool's production costs are not unit-level costs. Thus, the traditional system, which budgets overhead on the basis of a unit-level cost driver (either machine hours or direct-labor hours), cannot possibly capture the consumption of (support department) overhead costs by product lines with widely differing production volumes. An ABC system enables management to budget production costs much more accurately by accounting for the many overhead costs that are batch-, product-, process-, or plant-level costs. "In the past decade, Whirlpool has faced increasing competition, higher overhead, and greater product diversity. Managers initiated and supported the ABC pilot program to obtain accurate information for dealing with these challenges." *Source: C. B. Greeson and M. C. Kocakulah,* "Implementing an ABC Pilot at Whirlpool."

How Does ABC Affect Performance Reporting?

The activity-based flexible budget provides a more accurate prediction (and benchmark) of overhead costs. For example, suppose that activity in August is as follows:

Machine hours	7,500
Production runs	14
Engineering design specs	12
Direct material handled (sq. meters)	90,000

The following table compares the budgeted cost levels for several overhead items on the conventional and activity-based flexible budgets.

Overhead Cost Item	Conventional Flexible Budget (Exhibit 17–3)	Activity-Based Flexible Budget (Exhibit 17–12)
Electrical power	$1,500	$1,500
Quality assurance	2,400	2,800
Setup	3,600	4,200
Material handling	9,600	18,000
Engineering	5,000	4,000
Insurance and property taxes	1,100	1,100

The budgeted electrical power is the same on both budgets because both use the same cost driver (machine hours). Insurance and property taxes are also the same because both budgets recognize them as facility-level fixed costs. However, the other overhead costs are budgeted at different levels because the conventional and activity-based flexible budgets use *different cost drivers* for these items. The conventional budget treats quality assurance, setup, materials-handling, and engineering costs as fixed, but the activity-based flexible budget shows that they are all variable with respect to the appropriate cost driver.

These differences are important for performance reporting. The activity-based flexible budget provides a more accurate benchmark against which to compare actual costs. Suppose that the actual quality assurance cost in August is $2,700. Using the conventional flexible budget would result in an unfavorable variance of $300 ($2,700 − $2,400). However, the activity-based flexible budget yields a favorable variance of $100 ($2,800 − $2,700).[4]

How would you design an activity-based flexible budget for American Airlines' commuter operations?

Activity-Based Flexible Budget

Suppose that you are developing an activity-based flexible budget for a small commuter airline. Give an example of a cost item in each of the following categories of the ABC cost hierarchy.

a. Unit level (What is a *unit* for the airline?)
b. Batch level (What is a *batch* for the airline?)
c. Product-line level
d. Customer level
e. Facility or general-operations level

(Solutions begin on page 722.)

You're the Decision Maker 17.2

[4] For further reading on this topic, see R. E. Malcolm, "Overhead Control Implications of Activity Costing"; Y. T. Mak and M. L. Roush, "Flexible Budgeting and Variance Analysis in an Activity-Based Costing Environment"; and R. S. Kaplan, "Flexible Budgeting in an Activity-Based Costing Framework."

Research
Insight 17.3

Cost Hierarchy and Overhead Variances

The overhead variance analysis presented in this chapter is based on the traditional approach to flexible budgeting, which classifies overhead costs as variable or fixed. The variable-fixed model of cost structure is based on a single, volume-based measure of activity, such as machine hours or throughput. When an organization implements activity-based costing, however, this simplified variable-fixed model of cost structure gives way to a more elaborate ABC cost hierarchy. Here we designate costs as unit level, batch level, product-line level, customer level, or facility level. Appropriate cost drivers then are chosen for costs in each level of the hierarchy. A cost that might have been classified as fixed under the traditional approach (e.g., inspection) might now be classified as a batch-level cost, which is *variable* with respect to a batch-level cost driver (e.g., number of setups).

This more elaborate cost-hierarchy view gives rise to the activity-based flexible budget. However, this approach raises a question as to how to devise a system of overhead cost variances that is based on the ABC cost hierarchy as opposed to the traditional variable-fixed cost model. Researchers are addressing this problem, and a few proposals have been made. In one such proposed approach, variances are computed for costs at each level in the ABC hierarchy (e.g., unit-level).[*] Under another proposal, costs at each level in the ABC hierarchy are categorized as variable or fixed, and then a variance analysis is conducted. So, for example, batch-level setup costs are categorized as variable setup costs and fixed setup costs.[†]

The authors are not aware of any such ABC variance analysis scheme currently used in practice. The oft-stated conclusion here seems to be "more research is needed."

*J. M. Ruhl, "Activity-Based Variance Analysis."

†Y. T. Mak and M. L. Roush, "Flexible Budgeting and Variance Analysis in an Activity-Based Costing Environment."

Other Issues in Variance Analysis

We conclude the chapter with a brief mention of two other issues in variance analysis, which we explore in detail in Appendices B and C.

Standard Costing in a Just-in-Time Environment

A just-in-time manufacturing setting, with demand-pull of products through the manufacturing process, minimizes inventories. As a result, some companies have simplified their accounting system by charging all manufacturing costs directly to Cost of Goods Sold. This method of accounting, known as *backflush costing,* is explained in detail in Appendix B to this chapter. [Also, see Chapter 7 for a discussion of just-in-time (JIT) production and inventory management systems.]

Sales-Variance Analysis

We have concentrated in this chapter on *cost* variance analysis as a tool for cost management. Equally important in affecting a company's bottom line, though, is its *sales* performance. The sales price and the sales volume of each product have a significant impact on a company's revenue, contribution margin, and profit. Appendix C to this chapter covers *sales variance analysis,* a technique used to help management understand and manage the effects of the company's sales performance on its profitability.

Chapter Summary

Overhead is a heterogeneous pool of indirect costs. Since it is not easy to trace overhead costs to products or services, a flexible budget specifies budgeted overhead costs at various levels of activity. A columnar flexible budget is based on several distinct activity levels, and a formula flexible budget is valid for a continuous range of activity. A conventional flexible overhead budget is based on some activity measure, or cost driver, that varies in a pattern similar to that of variable overhead. Machine hours, process time, and direct-labor hours are common cost drivers.

In a standard-costing system, the flexible budget is used to manage overhead costs. The cost-management analyst uses the amount of overhead cost specified by the flexible budget as a benchmark against which to compare actual overhead costs. The analyst computes four overhead variances: the variable-overhead spending and efficiency variances and the fixed-overhead budget and volume variances. These variances help management to control overhead costs.

The standard or predetermined overhead rate also is used as the basis for product costing in a standard-costing system. The amount of overhead cost entered into Work-in-Process Inventory equals the standard overhead rate multiplied by the standard amount of the cost driver allowed, or activity base, given actual output.

With an activity-based costing system, the development of an activity-based flexible budget is possible. Such a flexible budget is more accurate than conventional flexible budgets because multiple cost drivers are identified to explain the behavior of overhead costs.

Key Terms

For each term's definition, refer to the indicated page or turn to the glossary at the end of the text.

*Appears in Appendix A.
†Appears in Appendix B.
‡Appears in Appendix C.

Meeting the Cost-Management Challenges

1. **How** can Koala Camp Gear's management use a flexible budget to manage overhead costs?

A static budget is based on only one level of activity. In contrast, Koala Camp Gear's flexible budget allows for several different levels of activity. The advantage of a flexible budget is that it responds to changes in the activity level. It enables a comparison between actual costs incurred at the actual level of activity and the standard costs allowed that should have been incurred at the actual level of activity. Flexible-overhead budgets are based on an input activity measure, such as machine hours or direct-labor hours, to provide a meaningful measure of production activity. An output measure, such as the number of units produced, could be used effectively only in a single-product enterprise. If multiple, heterogeneous products are produced, basing the flexible budget on an output measure aggregated across highly different types of products would not be meaningful.

2. **How** would you respond to the concerns raised by Koala Camp Gear's production manager in his memo to the controller?

The following explanation regarding the interpretation of the overhead variances would be an appropriate response to the concerns raised by Koala Camp Gear's production manager.

The interpretation of the variable-overhead spending variance is that a different total amount was spent on variable overhead than should have been spent in accordance with the variable-overhead rate, given the actual level of the cost driver on which the variable-overhead budget is based. For example, if machine hours are used to budget variable overhead, an unfavorable spending variance means that a higher total amount was spent on variable overhead than should have been spent, after adjusting for the actual machine time used. The spending variance is the control variance for variable overhead.

Suppose, for example, that electricity is the only variable-overhead cost item. An unfavorable variable-overhead spending variance does not imply that the company paid more than the anticipated rate per kilowatt-hour for electricity. An unfavorable spending variance could result from spending more per kilowatt-hour for electricity or from using more electricity than anticipated, or some combination of these two causes.

The interpretation of the variable-overhead efficiency variance is related to the efficiency of activity use on which variable overhead is budgeted. For example, if the basis for the variable-overhead budget is machine hours, an unfavorable variable-overhead efficiency variance results when the actual machine hours exceed the standard machine hours allowed. Thus, the variable-overhead efficiency variance will disclose no information about the efficiency with which variable-overhead items are used. Rather, it results from inefficiency or efficiency, relative to the standards, in the usage of the cost driver (such as machine hours).

The interpretations of the direct-labor and variable-overhead efficiency variances are very different. The direct-labor efficiency variance conveys information about the efficiency with which direct labor was used, relative to the standards. In contrast, the variable-overhead efficiency variance conveys no information about the efficiency with which variable-overhead items were used.

The fixed-overhead volume variance is the difference between budgeted fixed overhead and applied fixed overhead. The best interpretation for this variance is that it is a means of reconciling two disparate purposes of the standard-costing system: the control purpose and the product-costing purpose. For the control purpose, budgeted fixed overhead recognizes the fixed nature of this cost. Budgeted fixed overhead does not change as activity changes. For product-costing purposes, budgeted fixed overhead is divided by an activity measure (or cost driver) and applied to products on the basis of a fixed-overhead rate. The result of this dual purpose for the standard-costing system is that budgeted fixed overhead and applied fixed overhead will differ when the actual production activity differs from the budgeted production activity.

A common but misleading interpretation of the fixed-overhead volume variance is that it is a measure of the cost of underutilizing or overutilizing production capacity. For example, when budgeted fixed overhead exceeds applied fixed overhead, the fixed-overhead volume variance is positive. (Some accountants designate a positive fixed-overhead volume variance as unfavorable.) Some people claim that it is a measure of the cost of not having utilized production capacity to the anticipated level. However, this interpretation is misleading because the real cost of underutilizing capacity lies in the forgone contribution margins from the products that were not produced and sold.

3. **How** could Koala's managers improve the management of overhead costs?

An activity-based flexible budget would give Koala Camp Gear's management team a richer, more detailed perspective on the behavior and control of the company's overhead costs.

Conventional flexible budgets typically are based on a single cost driver, such as direct-labor hours or machine hours. Costs are categorized as variable or fixed. The fixed costs do not vary with respect to the single cost driver on which the flexible budget is based. An activity-based flexible budget is based on multiple cost drivers. Cost drivers are selected on the basis of how well they explain the behavior of the costs in the flexible budget. Costs that are treated as fixed in a conventional flexible budget can vary with respect to an appropriate cost driver in an activity-based flexible budget.

Solutions to You're the Decision Maker

17.1 Overhead Variances p. 714

a. The solution is given in Exhibits 17–13 and 17–14.

b. The fixed-overhead budget variance is the difference between actual fixed overhead and budgeted fixed overhead. During December, Koala Camp Gear simply spent less for these cost items than anticipated in the budget.

c. There will be no fixed-overhead volume variance during a period in which budgeted and applied fixed overhead are equal. This will happen only if the number of standard allowed hours equals the planned monthly activity level of 6,000 machine hours.

17.2 Activity-Based Flexible Budget for a Commuter Airline p. 719

a. Unit level: A *unit* for the airline could be defined in several ways, including one passenger transported from point A to point B, or one passenger-mile flown, or one mile flown. Most airlines use passenger-miles as the most basic measure of activity. An example of a unit-level cost, then, is airplane fuel.

b. Batch level: A *batch* might be considered a flight from point A to point B. The *batch,* then, consists of the people and cargo transported on the flight. An example of a batch-level cost is take-off and landing fees assessed on a per-flight basis.

Exhibit 17–13

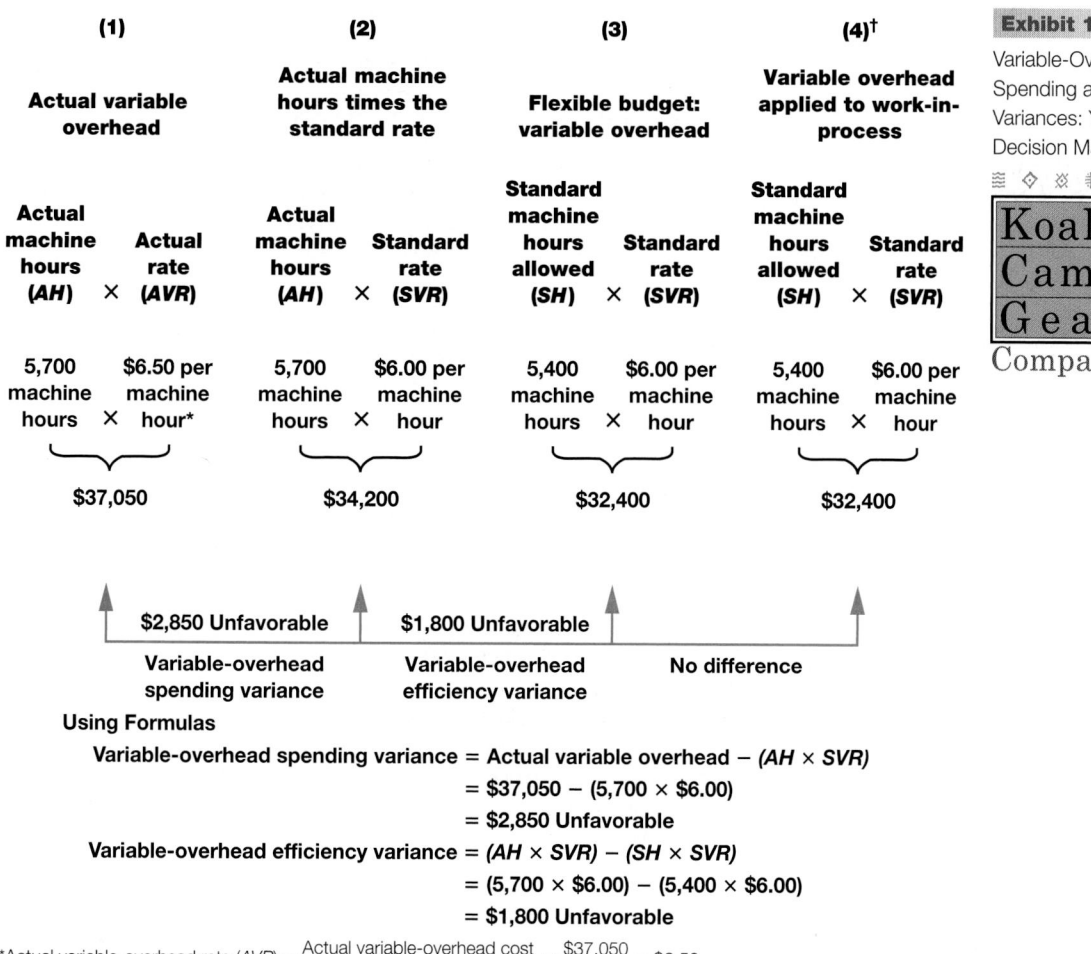

Variable-Overhead Spending and Efficiency Variances: You're the Decision Maker

Koala Camp Gear Company

(1)	(2)	(3)	(4)†
Actual variable overhead	**Actual machine hours times the standard rate**	**Flexible budget: variable overhead**	**Variable overhead applied to work-in-process**
Actual machine hours *(AH)* × Actual rate *(AVR)*	**Actual machine hours *(AH)* × Standard rate *(SVR)***	**Standard machine hours allowed *(SH)* × Standard rate *(SVR)***	**Standard machine hours allowed *(SH)* × Standard rate *(SVR)***
5,700 machine hours × $6.50 per machine hour*	5,700 machine hours × $6.00 per machine hour	5,400 machine hours × $6.00 per machine hour	5,400 machine hours × $6.00 per machine hour
$37,050	$34,200	$32,400	$32,400

(1) to (2)	(2) to (3)	(3) to (4)
$2,850 Unfavorable	$1,800 Unfavorable	
Variable-overhead spending variance	Variable-overhead efficiency variance	No difference

Using Formulas

Variable-overhead spending variance = Actual variable overhead − *(AH × SVR)*
= $37,050 − (5,700 × $6.00)
= $2,850 Unfavorable

Variable-overhead efficiency variance = *(AH × SVR)* − *(SH × SVR)*
= (5,700 × $6.00) − (5,400 × $6.00)
= $1,800 Unfavorable

*Actual variable-overhead rate *(AVR)* $= \dfrac{\text{Actual variable-overhead cost}}{\text{Actual machine hours}} = \dfrac{\$37{,}050}{5{,}700} = \$6.50$

†Column (4) is not used to compute the variances. It is included to point out that the flexible-budget amount for variable overhead, $32,400, is the amount that will be applied to Work-in-Process Inventory for product-costing purposes.

c. Product-line level: A *product line* might be considered to be a particular market (e.g., all flights to or from Spokane, Washington). An example of a product-line cost is rental of jetways at the Spokane airport.

d. Customer level: There are various ways to view the *customer level.* One possibility is a particular class of airplane seats: coach class, business class, or first class. Another is a particular type of flight (e.g., the *shuttles* run hourly between Boston and New York City or between Washington, D.C., and New York City.) Examples of customer-level costs are amenities reserved to a particular class of flights (e.g., breakfast served only in business or first class, or gate-area snacks served for shuttle passengers only).

e. Facility level or general-operations level: Examples of these costs include the airline president's salary and the airline's main maintenance facility.

Exhibit 17–14

Fixed-Overhead Budget and Volume Variances: You're the Decision Maker

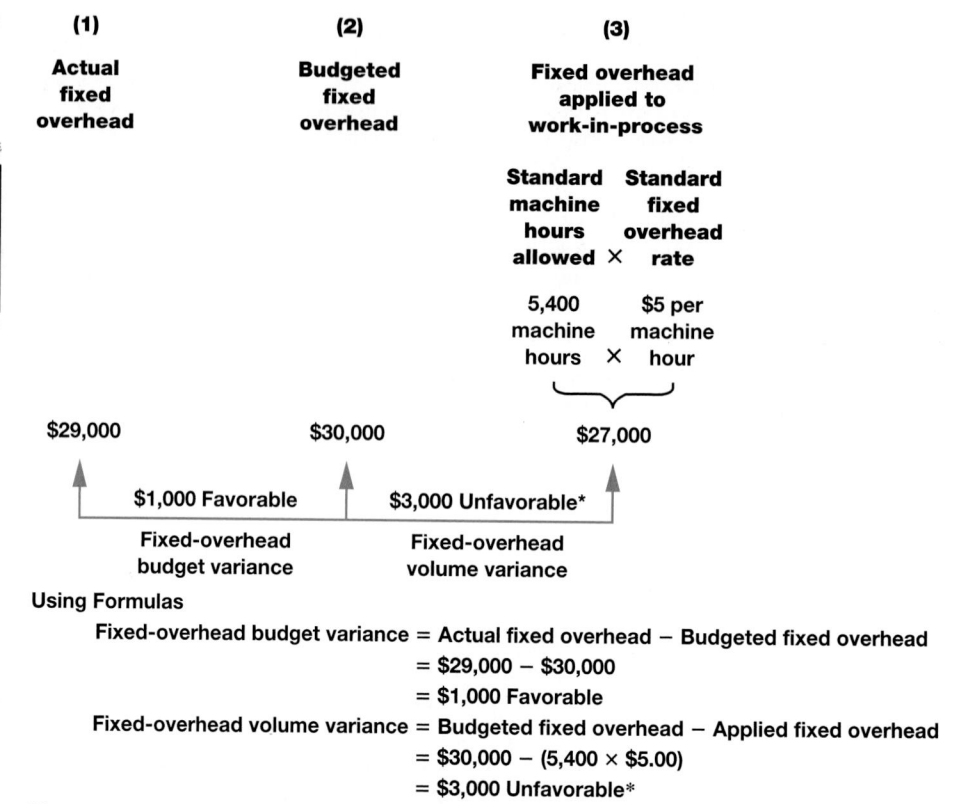

Koala Camp Gear Company

(1) Actual fixed overhead	(2) Budgeted fixed overhead	(3) Fixed overhead applied to work-in-process
		Standard machine hours allowed × Standard fixed overhead rate
		5,400 machine hours × $5 per machine hour
$29,000	$30,000	$27,000

$1,000 Favorable — Fixed-overhead budget variance (between (1) and (2))

$3,000 Unfavorable* — Fixed-overhead volume variance (between (2) and (3))

Using Formulas

Fixed-overhead budget variance = Actual fixed overhead − Budgeted fixed overhead
= $29,000 − $30,000
= $1,000 Favorable

Fixed-overhead volume variance = Budgeted fixed overhead − Applied fixed overhead
= $30,000 − (5,400 × $5.00)
= $3,000 Unfavorable*

*Some accountants designate a positive fixed-overhead volume variance as unfavorable. Others choose not to designate a fixed-overhead volume variance as either favorable or unfavorable.

Appendix A to Chapter Seventeen

Proration of Cost Variances

LO 9 Prorate variances among the relevant accounts.

The direct-materials, direct-labor, and manufacturing overhead variances computed in this and the preceding chapter are *temporary accounts.* They are computed as a cost-management tool to direct management's attention to situations that could require their intervention. At the end of an accounting period, most companies close all of the variances to Cost of Goods Sold. This approach was demonstrated in the Koala Camp Gear illustration.

Some companies use a more accurate procedure to dispose of variances. This approach recognizes that underestimation or overestimation of the production costs affects not only Cost of Goods Sold but also Work-in-Process Inventory and Finished- Goods Inventory. As the following display shows, direct materials, direct labor, and applied overhead pass through all three of these accounts. Therefore, all three accounts are affected by any deviation from the standards.

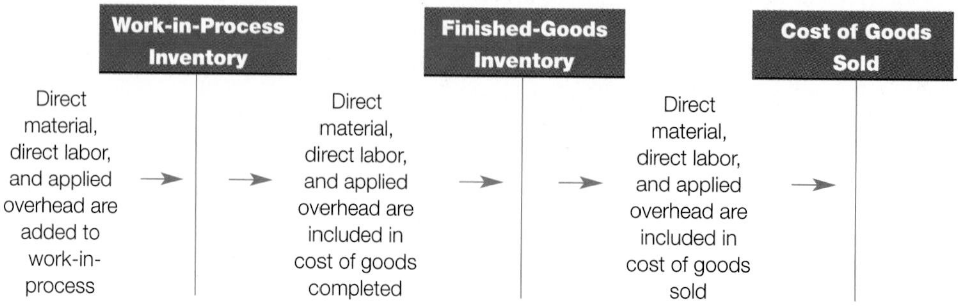
Work-in-Process Inventory
Finished-Goods Inventory
Cost of Goods Sold
Direct material, direct labor, and applied overhead are added to work-in-process
Direct material, direct labor, and applied overhead are included in cost of goods completed
Direct material, direct labor, and applied overhead are included in cost of goods sold

When cost variances are allocated among the three accounts shown, the process is called **proration.** The amount of the current period's standard cost remaining in each account is the basis for the proration procedure.

Among the companies that prorate cost variances are those required to do so under the rules specified by the **Cost Accounting Standards Board (CASB).** This US federal agency was chartered by Congress in 1970 to develop cost-accounting standards for large US government contractors. Congress discontinued the agency in 1980 but recreated it in 1990. The standards set forth by the agency apply to significant government contracts and have the force of federal law in the United States.

proration *is the process of allocating cost variances to Work-in-Process Inventory, Finished-Goods Inventory, and Cost of Goods Sold*

Cost Accounting Standards Board (CASB) *is a federal agency chartered by Congress in 1970 to develop cost-accounting standards for large government contractors*

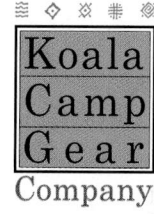

Illustration of Variance Proration

Koala Camp Gear Company recently added a second product to its Camp Foods product line. In addition to trail mix, sold under the name Crocodile Chomp, Koala now produces an instant-drink powder brand-named Kiwi Boost. The instant drink is a mix of dried fruit powders, sugar, and vitamins designed to provide quick energy and essential nutrients on the trail.

During September, Koala purchased 5,000 kilograms of the raw materials used to make Kiwi Boost. The following table shows what happened to the purchased materials during the month. As the table indicates, 1,500 kilograms of the materials remained in raw-materials inventory on September 30, and the remaining 3,500 kilograms were consumed in production.

Koala Camp Gear Company

Remaining in Raw-Material Inventory on 9/30	1,500 kilograms
Standard quantity allowed in Work-in-Process Inventory on 9/30	500 kilograms
Standard quantity allowed in Finished-Goods Inventory on 9/30	750 kilograms
Standard quantity allowed in Cost of Goods Sold for September	1,250 kilograms
Amount consumed in production in excess of standard quantity allowed during September	1,000 kilograms
Total quantity purchased in September	5,000 kilograms

The standard costs to produce Kiwi Boost are given in Exhibit 17–15. The exhibit also includes the variances computed for September. Notice that 1,000 of the 5,000 kilograms of raw materials purchased were consumed by inefficiency and are reflected in the unfavorable direct-materials quantity variance. Therefore, we can account for the 5,000 kilograms of material purchased as follows:

Remaining in Raw-Material Inventory (1,500 kilograms)	30%
In the unfavorable quantity variance (1,000 kilograms)	20
In Work-in-Process Inventory (500 kilograms)	10
In Finished-Goods Inventory (750 kilograms)	15
In Cost of Goods Sold (1,250 kilograms)	25
Total purchased amount accounted for (5,000 kilograms)	100%

An analysis of the labor records shows that 20 percent of the standard direct-labor hours allowed for September were related to the units remaining in Work-in-Process Inventory on September 30; 30 percent of the standard direct-labor hours allowed were related to Finished-Goods Inventory; and 50 percent of the hours were related to Cost of Goods Sold.

The proration of variances is illustrated in Exhibit 17–16. The eight variances are prorated to each manufacturing account in proportion to the standard amount of the period's inputs remaining in that account at the end of the period. For example, 30 percent of the 5,000 kilograms of materials purchased remained in the Raw-Materials Inventory account. Therefore, 30 percent of the unfavorable direct-materials price variance is prorated to the Raw-Materials Inventory account. The

Exhibit 17–15

Standard Costs and September Variances in the Production of Kiwi Boost

Koala Camp Gear Company

Direct material:		
Purchases (added to Raw-Material Inventory at standard price): 5,000 kilograms × $1.00 per kilogram	$5,000	
Standard cost: 2,500 kilograms × $1.00 per kilogram	2,500	
(1) Price variance: $PQ(AP - SP)$ = 5,000($1.30 − $1.00)		1,500 U
(2) Quantity variance: $SP(AQ - SQ)$ = $1.00(3,500 − 2,500)		1,000 U
Direct labor:		
Standard cost: 500 hours × $25.00 per hour	12,500	
(3) Rate variance: $AH(AR - SR)$ = 600($25.50 − $25.00)		300 U
(4) Efficiency variance: $SR(AH - SH)$ = $25.00(600 − 500)		2,500 U
Variable overhead (applied based on direct-labor hours):		
Standard cost: 500 hours × $10.00 per hour	5,000	
(5) Spending variance: Actual variable overhead − (AH) (SVR) = $5,400 − (600) ($10.00)		600 F
(6) Efficiency variance: $SVR(AH - SH)$ = $10.00(600 − 500)		1,000 U
Fixed overhead (applied based on direct-labor hours):		
Budgeted cost: 700 hours × $20.00 per hour	14,000	
(7) Budget variance: Actual fixed overhead − Budgeted fixed overhead = $12,800 − $14,000		1,200 F
(8) Volume variance: Budgeted fixed overhead − Applied fixed overhead = $14,000 − (500 hours) ($20.00 per hour)		4,000 U
Total of all variances		$8,500 U

balance in the account will be increased by $450 (.30 × $1,500). Since the direct-materials quantity variance is calculated using the standard price, the quantity variance is adjusted to reflect the actual price of the materials before the quantity variance is prorated. Thus, the actual cost of inefficiently consuming 1,000 kilograms of material is not $1,000 but is $1,300 (1,000 kilograms consumed inefficiently × $1.30 per kilogram). The adjusted quantity variance then is prorated to the accounts affected by efficiency (i.e., the Work-in-Process Inventory, Finished-Goods Inventory, and Cost of Goods Sold accounts). The adjusted quantity variance is not prorated to the Raw-Material Inventory account because efficiency is a concept that applies only to the production process, not to materials that remain in raw-materials inventory.

The following journal entry is required to prorate the variances, as computed in Exhibit 17–16.

Raw-Material Inventory	450	
Work-in-Process Inventory	1,610	
Finished-Goods Inventory	2,415	
Cost of Goods Sold	4,025	
Variable-Overhead Spending Variance	600	
Fixed-Overhead Budget Variance	1,200	
Direct-Material Price Variance		1,500
Direct-Material Quantity Variance		1,000
Direct-Labor Rate Variance		300
Direct-Labor Efficiency Variance		2,500
Variable-Overhead Efficiency Variance		1,000
Fixed-Overhead Volume Variance		4,000

Now all of the variance accounts have been closed out to zero to begin the next period. The inventory and cost of goods sold accounts have been adjusted to reflect the deviations from standard costs as reflected in the variances.

Exhibit 17–16

Proration of September Variances in the Production of Kiwi Boost

Koala Camp Gear Company

Microsoft Excel - Exhibit 17-16

F18 = =+F10+F14

	Name of Variance	Amount of Variance	Raw-Material Inventory	Direct-Material Quantity Variance	Work-in-Process Inventory	Finished-Goods Inventory	Cost of Goods Sold
	Proportion of the quantity of materials purchased		***30%***	***20%***	***10%***	***15%***	***25%***
(1)	Direct-material price	$1,500 U	$ 450	$ 300	$ 150	$ 225	$ 375
(2)	Direct material quantity (unadjusted)	1,000 U		1,000			
	Direct material quantity (adjusted)			$ 1,300	260	390	650
	Proportion of standard allowed direct-labor hours				***20%***	***30%***	***50%***
(3)	Direct-labor rate	300 U			$ 60	$ 90	$ 150
(4)	Direct-labor efficiency	2,500 U			500	750	1,250
(5)	Variable-overhead spending	600 F			(120)	(180)	(300)
(6)	Variable-overhead efficiency	1,000 U			200	300	500
(7)	Fixed-overhead budget	1,200 F			(240)	(360)	(600)
(8)	Fixed-overhead volume	4,000 U			800	1,200	2,000
	Total proration	$8,500 U	$ 450		$ 1,610	$ 2,415	$ 4,025

Appendix B to Chapter Seventeen

Standard Costing in a Just-in-Time Environment

LO 10 Explain and illustrate backflush costing in a just-in-time environment.

Just-in-time manufacturing settings with a demand-pull of products through manufacturing minimize inventories. As a result, the accounting system can be simplified by charging all costs directly to Cost of Goods Sold (CGS). If inventories exist at the end of the period, a portion of the current period costs originally charged to Cost of Goods Sold is credited to Cost of Goods Sold and debited back to the respective inventory account as an end-of-period adjustment. This method of accounting is known as **backflush costing.**

backflush costing *is a simplified system in which all manufacturing costs are charged to CGS, and then end-of-period adjustments are made to credit CGS and debit the inventory accounts*

Using backflush standard costing, costs are charged to Cost of Goods Sold at standard. Variances are charged to a separate account. If there are no inventories at the end of the period, the variance account is expensed or combined with Cost of Goods Sold at standard. The latter result is Cost of Goods Sold *at actual.*

If inventories exist at the end of the period, and if the difference between the standard cost of inventories and actual cost is immaterial, the inventories can be stated at standard cost. In this situation, variances need not be prorated. (Appendix A covers proration.)

If prorating variances makes a material difference in the financial statements or is required by contract, the variance is prorated from the variance account to the respective inventory accounts based on the proportions of the current period costs in each of the inventory accounts and Cost of Goods Sold, as described in Appendix A. The results should be the same as if the variances had been accounted for in the traditional manner discussed earlier in this chapter.

Koala Camp Gear Company

To illustrate, suppose that during the next year, Koala Camp Gear Company switched to demand-pull accounting. Assume that the Cost of Goods Sold and related variance account appear as follows before adjustment:

Cost of Goods Sold (at Standard Cost)

Direct material	60,000		
Direct labor	30,000		
Manufacturing overhead	70,000		

Cost Variances

Direct-material price	3,500		
Direct-material quantity	2,500		
		6,600	Direct-labor and manufacturing overhead

The debits to Cost of Goods Sold are at standard price (*SP*) multiplied by the standard quantity of input per unit of output (*SQ*) multiplied by the actual units produced. If inventories are minimal, the balance in the variance account is expensed.

If the company has substantial ending inventories, the costs in Cost of Goods Sold are transferred to the inventory accounts. Assume that no beginning inventories exist and that $42,000 of the $60,000 standard cost of materials is traced to the inventory accounts:

Direct-material Inventory	$35,000
Work-in-Process Inventory	5,000
Finished-Goods Inventory	2,000
Total	$42,000

The total amount is credited to Cost of Goods Sold with debits to each inventory account, as shown in Exhibit 17–17.

A similar adjustment is made for direct labor and manufacturing overhead. Suppose that 20 percent of the labor and overhead amounts are still in Work-in-Process Inventory and 8 percent are in Finished-Goods Inventory. The dollar amounts to be transferred from Cost of Goods Sold to the inventory accounts are as follows:

	Direct Labor	Manufacturing Overhead
Work-in-Process Inventory	$6,000	$14,000
Finished-Goods Inventory	2,400	5,600
Total	$8,400	$19,600

The resulting inventory and Cost of Goods Sold accounts appear in Exhibit 17–17 after the adjustments.

Exhibit 17–17

Backflush Standard Costing

Koala Camp Gear Company

Direct-Material Inventory

	0	
	35,000	

Work-in-Process Inventory

	0	
Direct material	5,000	
Direct labor	6,000	
Manufacturing overhead	14,000	
Balance	25,000	

Finished-Goods Inventory

	0	
Direct material	2,000	
Direct labor	2,400	
Manufacturing overhead	5,600	
Balance	10,000	

Cost of Goods Sold (at Standard Cost)

Direct material	60,000	42,000
Direct labor	30,000	8,400
Manufacturing overhead	70,000	19,600

Variances

Direct-material price	3,500		
Direct-material quantity	2,500		
		6,600	Direct labor and manufacturing overhead

Appendix C to Chapter Seventeen

Sales Variance Analysis

LO 11 Compute, and interpret sales variances.

In this and the preceding chapter, we explored cost-variance analysis as a tool for cost management. In this appendix we turn our attention to assessing a company's overall sales performance. One common method for analyzing sales performance is *sales variance analysis.* This approach examines the difference (variance) between actual sales performance and budgeted sales performance by computing a set of variances, with each variance focusing on some underlying aspect of sales performance. Sales variance analysis can be carried out in either of two alternative ways:

1. *Focus on sales revenue.* The first approach to sales variance analysis analyzes the difference (variance) between actual and budgeted *sales revenue.*
2. *Focus on contribution margin.* The second approach to sales-variance analysis analyzes the difference (variance) between actual and budgeted *contribution*

margin. Under this approach we are implicitly assuming that the organization's cost structure can be represented by the traditional (and relatively simple) cost-behavior pattern that includes only variable costs and fixed costs. *Variable costs* are those that vary in proportion to the level of a single, unit-level cost driver. A product's *unit contribution margin,* then, is the product's sales price minus its variable cost (including both variable manufacturing costs and variable selling costs). (See Chapter 2 for further discussion of fixed and variable costs.)

The next section discusses the revenue approach to sales variance analysis in more detail. After computing and interpreting all of the revenue sales variances, we conclude the section with a general discussion of the contribution-margin approach to sales-variance analysis.

Illustration of Sales-Variance Analysis

Koala Camp Gear Company

To illustrate sales variance analysis, let's focus again on Koala Camp Gear Company, the small Australian manufacturer of camping equipment. To keep the illustration relatively simple, we focus on the company's early years when it manufactured only tents. This occurred before Koala added other product lines, such as camp foods and other camping equipment. During these early years, Koala Camp Gear Company manufactured three models of camping tents: the Tree Line (T), the River's Edge (R), and the Valley (V). Data from the year on which our illustration is based appear in Exhibit 17–18. The exhibit presents both budget data and actual data for the year of the analysis. Notice that the budgeted total sales revenue for the year was \$9,950,000, but the actual total sales revenue achieved was \$11,110,000. What was behind this difference (variance) of \$1,160,000 in sales revenue?

Notice also that Koala's budgeted total contribution margin for the year was \$1,750,000, but the company's actual total contribution margin was \$2,227,500. This actual total contribution-margin result was \$477,500 higher than expected. How did this come about?

To help Koala's management gain insight into the answers to these questions, we now consider the sales-variance analysis for the year summarized in Exhibit 17–18.

Focus on revenue. First we present Koala's sales-variance analysis from a sales-revenue perspective. The analysis to be conducted is summarized in Exhibit 17–19. Notice that the terms *revenue* or *sales price* preface the name of each variance to make it clear that these variances focus on *sales revenue.*

revenue budget variance *is the difference between the actual total sales revenue and the budgeted total sales revenue*

The **revenue budget variance** is defined by the following formula.[5] This variance is simply the difference between the actual total sales revenue and the budgeted total sales revenue.

$$\text{Revenue budget variance} = \text{Sum of revenue budget variances for each product}$$

$$\text{Revenue budget variance for product } i = \left(\text{Actual sales revenue for product } i - \text{Budgeted sales revenue for product } i\right)$$

Applying the formula yields the following results for Koala Camp Gear Company.

T revenue budget variance	=	(\$190) (30,250) − (\$180) (30,000)	=	\$ 347,500 F
R revenue budget variance	=	(\$215) (22,000) − (\$220) (15,000)	=	1,430,000 F
V revenue budget variance	=	(\$230) (2,750) − (\$250) (5,000)	=	617,500 U
Revenue budget variance		....		\$1,160,000 F

[5]Some accountants refer to this variance as a *static-budget variance in revenues.*

Exhibit 17–18

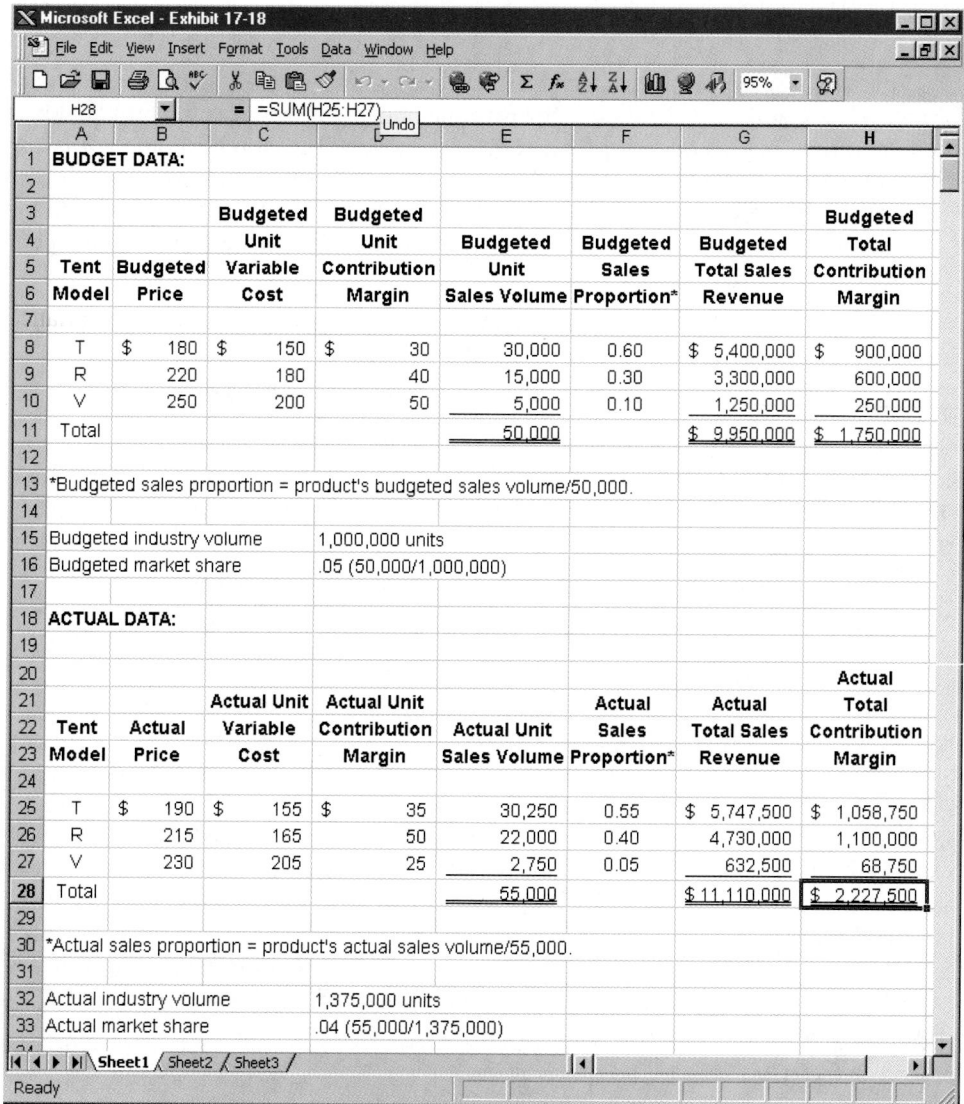

Data for Illustration of Sales Variance Analysis: Koala Camp Gear Company

Koala Camp Gear Company

Microsoft Excel - Exhibit 17-18

H28 = =SUM(H25:H27)

BUDGET DATA:

Tent Model	Budgeted Price	Budgeted Unit Variable Cost	Budgeted Unit Contribution Margin	Budgeted Unit Sales Volume	Budgeted Sales Proportion*	Budgeted Total Sales Revenue	Budgeted Total Contribution Margin
T	$ 180	$ 150	$ 30	30,000	0.60	$ 5,400,000	$ 900,000
R	220	180	40	15,000	0.30	3,300,000	600,000
V	250	200	50	5,000	0.10	1,250,000	250,000
Total				50,000		$ 9,950,000	$ 1,750,000

*Budgeted sales proportion = product's budgeted sales volume/50,000.

Budgeted industry volume	1,000,000 units
Budgeted market share	.05 (50,000/1,000,000)

ACTUAL DATA:

Tent Model	Actual Price	Actual Unit Variable Cost	Actual Unit Contribution Margin	Actual Unit Sales Volume	Actual Sales Proportion*	Actual Total Sales Revenue	Actual Total Contribution Margin
T	$ 190	$ 155	$ 35	30,250	0.55	$ 5,747,500	$ 1,058,750
R	215	165	50	22,000	0.40	4,730,000	1,100,000
V	230	205	25	2,750	0.05	632,500	68,750
Total				55,000		$ 11,110,000	$ 2,227,500

*Actual sales proportion = product's actual sales volume/55,000.

Actual industry volume	1,375,000 units
Actual market share	.04 (55,000/1,375,000)

Sheet1 Sheet2 Sheet3

Ready

Exhibit 17–19

Revenue Sales-Variance Analysis

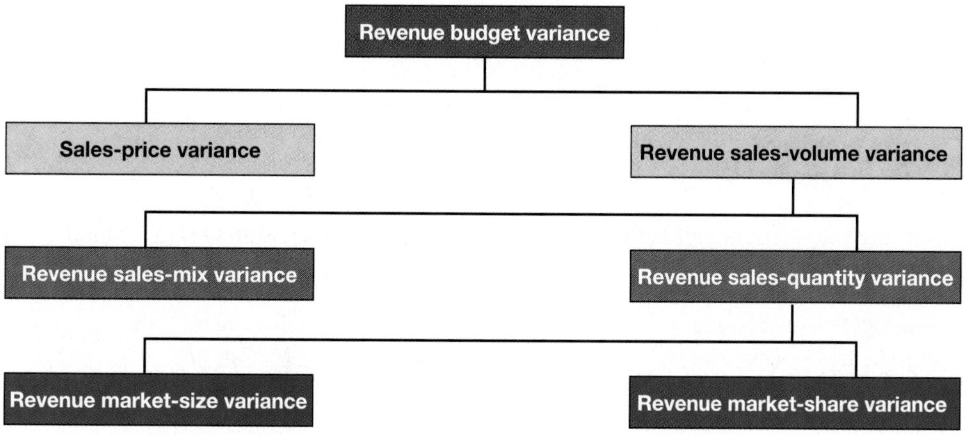

An individual component of the revenue budget variance is favorable if the product's actual revenue exceeds its budgeted revenue but is unfavorable if it is less than the budgeted amount. Although Koala's revenue budget variance for Valley model tents is unfavorable, the company's revenue budget variance is favorable overall, $1,160,000 F. This result also is apparent from the information given in Exhibit 17–18, since it reveals that Koala's actual total sales revenue of $11,110,000 exceeded budgeted sales revenue of $9,950,000.

What additional insight can management learn about Koala's sales-revenue performance? As Exhibit 17–19 shows, the revenue budget variance can be broken down into two variances: *the sales-price variance* and the *revenue sales-volume variance.* We next turn our attention to these variances and their interpretations.

sales-price variance *focuses on the differences between actual and budgeted sales prices while holding constant the sales volume at its actual level*

The **sales-price variance** is defined in the following formula.[6] This holds constant the effect of sales volume and focuses on the differences between actual and budgeted sales prices.

$$\text{Sales-price variance} = \text{Sum of sales-price variances for each product}$$

$$\text{Sales-price variance for product } i = \left(\text{Actual sales price for product } i - \text{Budgeted sales price for product } i\right) \times \text{Actual sales volume for product } i$$

Using this formula, Koala's sales price variance is computed as follows:

T sales price variance	= ($190 − $180) × 30,250 =	$302,500	F
R sales price variance	= ($215 − $220) × 22,000 =	110,000	U
V sales price variance	= ($230 − $250) × 2,750 =	55,000	U
Sales price variance	....	$137,500	F

Each individual component of the sales-price variance is favorable if the product's actual sales price exceeds its budgeted sales price (and unfavorable otherwise). Koala's overall sales-price variance is favorable, because of the Tree Line tent's higher than expected sales price, even though the sales price of the other two tent models was lower than expected.

revenue sales-volume variance *holds constant the products' sales prices at their budgeted levels and focuses on deviations between actual and budgeted sales volumes*

The **revenue sales-volume variance,** which is defined in the following formula, holds constant the effects of the products' sales prices and focuses on deviations between actual and budgeted sales volumes.[7]

$$\text{Revenue sales-volume variance} = \text{Sum of revenue sales-volume variances for each product}$$

$$\text{Revenue sales-volume variance for product } i = \left(\text{Actual unit sales volume for product } i - \text{Budgeted unit sales volume for product } i\right) \times \text{Budgeted sales price for product } i$$

Applying the formula yields the following results for Koala Camp Gear Company.

T revenue sales-volume variance	= (30,250 − 30,000) × $180 =	$ 45,000	F
R revenue sales-volume variance	= (22,000 − 15,000) × $220 =	1,540,000	F
V revenue sales-volume variance	= (2,750 − 5,000) × $250 =	562,500	U
Revenue sales-volume variance	....	$1,022,500	F

Each individual component of the revenue sales-volume variance is favorable if the product's actual sales volume exceeds its budgeted sales volume but unfavorable if

[6]Some accountants refer to this variance as a *flexible-budget variance in revenues.*

[7]Some accountants refer to this variance as a *revenue sales-activity variance.*

it is lower than the budgeted amount. Notice that the higher than expected sales volume for Tree Line tents and River's Edge tents were sufficient to make Koala's overall revenue sales-volume variance favorable ($1,022,500 F) even though the Valley model tent experienced disappointing sales-volume results.

We can derive more insight into the revenue implications of the sales-volume results by breaking down the revenue sales-volume variance into two variances: the *revenue sales-mix variance* and the *revenue sales-quantity variance.*[8] Let's now turn our attention to those variances and their interpretation.

The **revenue sales-mix variance,** defined in the following formula, focuses on the effects of changes in the sales mix among the products sold.

revenue sales-mix variance *focuses on the effects of changes in the sales mix while holding constant the effects of the products' sales prices and the total sales volume*

$$\text{Revenue sales-mix variance} = \text{Sum of revenue sales-mix variances for each product}$$

$$\begin{matrix}\text{Revenue sales-mix} \\ \text{variance for product } i\end{matrix} = \begin{matrix}\text{Budgeted sales price} \\ \text{for product } i\end{matrix} \times \left(\begin{matrix}\text{Actual sales proportion} \\ \text{for product } i\end{matrix} - \begin{matrix}\text{Budgeted sales proportion} \\ \text{for product } i\end{matrix}\right) \times \begin{matrix}\text{Actual total unit sales} \\ \text{volume for all products}\end{matrix}$$

Using this formula, Koala's revenue sales-mix variance is computed as follows:

T	revenue sales-mix variance	= $180 × (.55 − .60) × 55,000 =	$ 495,000	U
R	revenue sales-mix variance	= $220 × (.40 − .30) × 55,000 =	1,210,000	F
V	revenue sales-mix variance	= $250 × (.05 − .10) × 55,000 =	687,500	U
	Revenue sales-mix variance		$ 27,500	F

Each individual component of the revenue sales-mix variance is favorable if the product's actual sales proportion exceeds its budgeted sales proportion but unfavorable if it is lower than the budgeted proportion. Koala's overall favorable revenue sales-mix variance ($27,500 F) tells us that Koala's actual sales mix differed from its budgeted sales mix in such a way that the effect on overall sales revenue was positive. The higher than expected proportion of sales for the River's Edge tent was sufficiently favorable to overcome the lower proportions of sales for the other two tent models. Note that *it is the overall revenue sales-mix variance that conveys a meaningful interpretation for management's analysis, not the individual products' mix-variance components.*[9]

Next we compute the **revenue sales-quantity variance,** which is defined by the following formula. The revenue sales-quantity variance holds constant the sales-price and sales-mix effects and focuses on the implications of overall unit sales volume.

revenue sales-quantity variance *holds constant the sales-price and sales-mix effects and focuses on the effect of the overall unit sales volume*

$$\text{Revenue sales-quantity variance} = \text{Sum of revenue sales-quantity variances for each product}$$

$$\begin{matrix}\text{Revenue sales-quantity} \\ \text{variance for product } i\end{matrix} = \begin{matrix}\text{Budgeted sales price} \\ \text{for product } i\end{matrix} \times \left(\begin{matrix}\text{Actual total unit sales} \\ \text{volume for all products}\end{matrix} - \begin{matrix}\text{Budgeted total unit sales} \\ \text{volume for all products}\end{matrix}\right) \times \begin{matrix}\text{Budgeted sales proportion} \\ \text{for product } i\end{matrix}$$

[8] Review Exhibit 17–19.

[9] Students who completed the Appendix to Chapter 16, which covers production mix and yield variances, might notice a conceptual and computational similarity between the revenue sales-mix variance and the production mix variance.

The formula yields the following calculation of Koala's revenue sales-quantity variance:

T	revenue sales-quantity variance	= $180 × (55,000 − 50,000) × .60 =	$540,000	F
R	revenue sales-quantity variance	= $220 × (55,000 − 50,000) × .30 =	330,000	F
V	revenue sales-quantity variance	= $250 × (55,000 − 50,000) × .10 =	125,000	F
	Revenue sales-quantity variance	....	$995,000	F

The revenue sales-quantity variance is favorable if actual total sales volume exceeds budgeted total sales volume but is unfavorable if it is lower. Since Koala's actual sales volume, 55,000 units, exceeded the budgeted level of 50,000 units, the company's revenue sales-quantity variance is favorable.[10]

Although Koala's actual total sales volume exceeded the budget, did the company maintain its market share? Was the increase in Koala's sales volume due to an industry wide increase in sales, or did Koala increase its share of a constant or declining market? We can address these questions by decomposing the revenue sales-quantity variance into two variances: the *revenue market-size variance* and the *revenue market-share variance.*[11]

revenue market-size variance *holds constant the company's market share at its budgeted level and focuses on changes in total industry volume*

The **revenue market-size variance,** defined by the following formula, holds constant the company's market share at its budgeted level and focuses on changes in total industry volume (i.e., market size).[12]

$$\text{Revenue market-size variance} = \text{Budgeted weighted-average unit sales price} \times \left(\text{Actual total market-unit sales volume} - \text{Budgeted total market-unit sales volume}\right) \times \text{Budgeted market-share proportion}$$

To apply the formula, we first need to compute Koala's budgeted weighted-average unit sales price.

T	($180) (30,000)	=	$5,400,000
R	($220) (15,000)	=	3,300,000
V	($250) (5,000)	=	1,250,000
	Total budgeted revenue		$9,950,000

$$\text{Budgeted weighted-average unit sales price} = \$9{,}950{,}000 \div 50{,}000 \text{ units} = \$199$$

Another way to compute the budgeted weighted-average unit sales price is to weight the three products' budgeted sales prices by their budgeted sales proportions as follows:

$$(\$180)(.60) + (\$220)(.30) + (\$250)(.10) = \$199$$

Applying the formula yields the following result for Koala Camp Gear Company.

$$\text{Revenue market-size variance} = \$199 \times (1{,}375{,}000 - 1{,}000{,}000) \times .05 = \$3{,}731{,}250 \text{ F}$$

Koala's revenue market-size variance is favorable simply because the actual total industry sales volume of 1,375,000 units exceeded the expected total industry volume

[10]Students who completed the Appendix to Chapter 16 might notice a conceptual and computational similarity between the revenue sales-quantity variance and the production yield variance.

[11]Review Exhibit 17–19.

[12]Some accountants refer to this variance as a *revenue industry-volume variance.*

of 1,000,000 units (see Exhibit 17–18). However, did Koala maintain its expected market share in the face of this overall industry expansion?

The **revenue market-share variance,** which is defined by the following formula, holds constant the total industry volume at the actual sales level and focuses on the company's market share.

revenue market-share variance *holds constant the total industry volume at its actual sales level and focuses on the company's market share*

$$\text{Revenue market-share variance} = \text{Budgeted weighted-average unit sales price} \times \left(\text{Actual market-share proportion} - \text{Budgeted market-share proportion}\right) \times \text{Actual total market-unit sales volume}$$

Using this formula, Koala's revenue market-share variance is computed as follows:

$$\text{Revenue market-share variance} = \$199 \times (.04 - .05) \times 1{,}375{,}000 = \$2{,}736{,}250 \text{ U}$$

Although the total industry sales volume was higher than expected, Koala Camp Gear Company's share of the market was lower than expected. Koala garnered only 4 percent of overall industry volume instead of the anticipated 5 percent share. This decline in market share is likely of considerable concern to Koala's management.

We have completed the revenue sales-variance analysis for Koala Camp Gear Company, and our results are summarized in Exhibit 17–20. The exhibit highlights the hierarchical design of the sales-variance analysis for which some variances are decomposed into others to gain additional insight into the phenomena underlying Koala's overall sales revenue performance.

Focus on contribution margin. Now we will briefly discuss Koala's sales variance analysis from the contribution-margin perspective. The analysis is summarized in Exhibit 17–21 (using the data from Exhibit 17–18, as in the preceding section). Notice that the name of each variance is prefaced by the term *contribution margin* to make clear that the analysis has a contribution-margin focus rather than a sales-revenue focus. Each variance is analogous to its counterpart in the revenue sales variance analysis. For example, the contribution-margin budget variance is calculated in exactly the same way as the revenue budget variance except for the fact that the products' contribution margins are used instead of their sales prices. Moreover, the interpretations of the contribution-margin budget variance and the revenue budget variance are analogous. It simply comes down to whether management wants to focus its analysis on sales revenue or contribution margin.

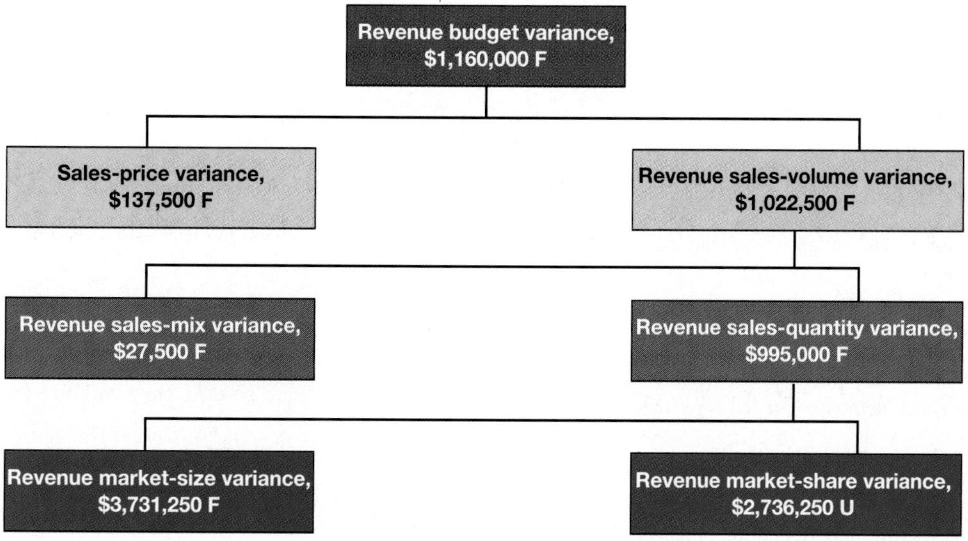

Exhibit 17–20

Revenue Sales-Variance Analysis: Koala Camp Gear Company

Exhibit 17–21

Contribution-Margin-Sales Variance Analysis

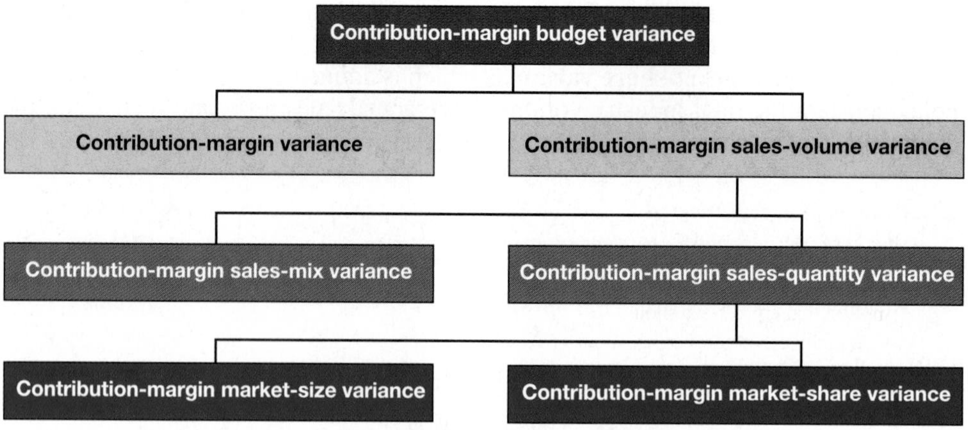

Exhibit 17–22

Contribution-Margin Sales-Variance Analysis: Koala Camp Gear Company

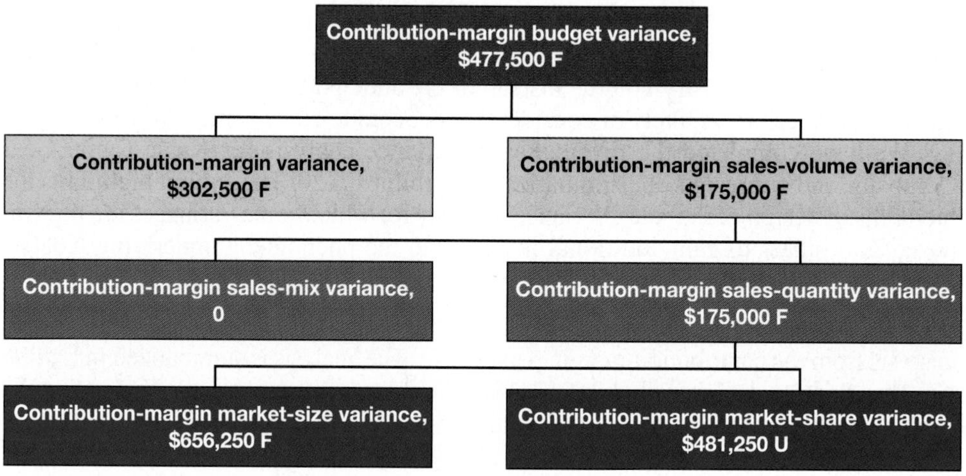

The results of Koala Camp Gear's contribution-margin sales-variance analysis is shown in Exhibit 17–22. Once again, the exhibit highlights the hierarchical nature of the variance analysis for which certain variances comprise other variances to gain insight into the phenomena underlying a company's sales performance.

Review Questions

17.1 What types of organizations use flexible budgets?

17.2 Distinguish between a columnar and a formula flexible budget.

17.3 What is the interpretation of the variable-overhead spending variance?

17.4 What is the interpretation of the variable-overhead efficiency variance?

17.5 Distinguish between the interpretations of the direct-labor and variable-overhead efficiency variances.

17.6 What is the fixed-overhead budget variance?

17.7 Why are fixed-overhead costs sometimes called *capacity-producing costs?*

17.8 Draw a graph showing budgeted and applied fixed overhead with a positive (or *unfavorable*) volume variance.

17.9 Distinguish between the control purpose and the product-costing purpose of standard costing and flexible budgeting.

17.10 Show, using T-accounts, how manufacturing overhead is added to Work-in-Process Inventory when standard costing is used.

17.11 (Appendix A) Explain two ways to dispose of variances at the end of the year.

17.12 (Appendix B) Briefly describe the procedure known as *backflush costing.*

17.13 (Appendix C) Into what two variances is a revenue sales-volume variance decomposed? What is the purpose of computing these two variances?

17.14 (Appendix C) Why is there no efficiency variance for revenue?

17.15 (Appendix C) What information does the computation of a market-size variance provide?

17.16 (Appendix C) If the sales-volume variance is zero, is there any reason to compute a sales mix variance?

Critical Analysis

17.17 "I don't understand why you accountants want to prepare a budget for a period that is already over. We know the actual results by then—all that flexible budgeting does is increase the controller's staff and add to our overhead." Comment on this remark.

17.18 Why are flexible overhead budgets based on an activity measure such as machine hours or direct-labor hours?

17.19 How does the concept of flexible budgeting reinforce the notion that employees should be held responsible only for what they can control or heavily influence?

17.20 How has computer-integrated-manufacturing (CIM) technology affected overhead application?

17.21 Give one example of a plausible activity base to use in flexible budgeting for each of the following organizations: an insurance company, an express delivery service, a restaurant, and a state tax-collection agency.

17.22 Budgets for government units are usually prepared one year in advance of the budget period. Expenditures are limited to the budgeted amount. At the end of the period, performance is evaluated by comparing budget authorizations with actual receipts and outlays. What management-control problems are likely to arise from such a system?

17.23 Bodin Company's only variable-overhead cost is electricity. Does an unfavorable variable-overhead spending variance imply that the company paid more than the anticipated rate per kilowatt hour?

17.24 Describe a common but misleading interpretation of the fixed-overhead volume variance. Why is this interpretation misleading?

17.25 Does the fixed-overhead volume variance represent a difference in the cash outflows for the company when compared to budgeted cash outflows?

17.26 What is the conceptual problem of applying fixed-manufacturing overhead as a product cost?

17.27 (Appendix C) The marketing manager of a company noted, "We had a favorable revenue budget variance of $391,000, yet company profit went up by only $98,000. Some part of the organization has dropped the ball; let's find out where the problem is and straighten it out." Comment on this remark.

17.28 (Appendix C) A company sells three products that must be purchased in a single package. Does computing a sales-mix variance provide any benefit under these circumstances?

17.29 (Appendix C) How could a CPA firm use a sales-mix variance to analyze its revenue?

Exercises

Exercise 17.30
Construction of a Flexible-Overhead Budget; Hospital
(LO 1, 2)

Pocono Community Hospital's controller estimates that the hospital uses 30 kilowatt-hours of electricity per patient-day, and that the electric rate will be $ .10 per kilowatt-hour. The hospital also pays a fixed monthly charge of $1,000 to the electric utility to rent emergency backup electric generators.

Required

Construct a flexible budget for the hospital's electricity costs using each of the following techniques.

a. Formula flexible budget.

b. Columnar flexible budget for 30,000, 40,000, and 50,000 patient-days of activity. List variable and fixed electricity costs separately.

Exercise 17.31
Cost-Cutting Programs
(LO 1)

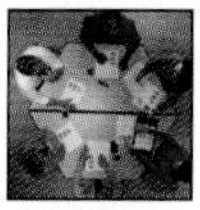

Team

Read these two articles: "Xerox Pledges to Cut $1 Billion in Costs, Reports a Quarterly Loss of $167 Million," *The Wall Street Journal,* October 25, 2000, by J. Hechinger and L. Johannes; and "GE Says Earnings Rose 20% in 3rd Period: Results Reflect Net Growth in Every Major Unit, the Fruit of Cost Cuts," *The Wall Street Journal,* October 12, 2000, by M. Murray. According to these articles, Xerox and GE both reported major cost-cutting programs to bolster the companies' profits.

Required

How did each company implement its cost-cutting program? Could standard costing have an important role to play in cutting costs?

Exercise 17.32
Straightforward Computation of Overhead Variances
(LO 5)

Saturn Glassware Company has the following standards and flexible-budget data.

Standard variable-overhead rate	$6.00 per direct-labor hour
Standard quantity of direct labor	2 hours per unit of output
Budgeted fixed overhead	$100,000
Budgeted output	25,000 units

Actual results for April follow:

Actual output	20,000 units
Actual variable overhead	$320,000
Actual fixed overhead	$97,000
Actual direct labor	50,000 hours

Required

Use the variance formulas to compute the following variances. Indicate whether each variance is favorable or unfavorable where appropriate.

a. Variable-overhead spending variance.
b. Variable-overhead efficiency variance.
c. Fixed-overhead budget variance.
d. Fixed-overhead volume variance.

Exercise 17.33
Diagram of Overhead Variances
(LO 5)

Refer to the data in the preceding exercise.

Required

Use diagrams similar to those in Exhibits 17–6 and 17–8 to compute the variable-overhead spending and efficiency variances and the fixed-overhead budget and volume variances.

Exercise 17.34
Graph of Overhead Variances
(LO 5)

Refer to the data in Exercise 17.32.

Required

Draw graphs similar to those in Exhibit 17–7 (variable overhead) and Exhibit 17–9 (fixed overhead) to depict the overhead variances.

Exercise 17.35
Interpretation of Variable-Overhead Efficiency Variance
(LO 1, 5)

Communication

You recently received the following note from the production supervisor of the company where you serve as controller. "I don't understand these crazy variable-overhead efficiency variances. My employees are very careful in their use of electricity and manufacturing supplies, and we use very little indirect labor. What are we supposed to do?"

Required

Write a brief memo responding to the production supervisor's concern.

Exercise 17.36
Nonmanufacturing Cost Variances
(LO 4, 5)

Philadelphia Financial originates mortgage loans for residential housing. The company charges a service fee for processing loan applications that is set twice a year based on the cost of processing a loan application. For the first half of this year, Philadelphia Financial estimated that it would process 75 loans. Correspondence, credit reports, supplies, and other materials that vary with each loan are estimated to cost $45 per loan. The company hires a loan processor at an estimated cost of $27,000 per year and an assistant at an estimated cost of $20,000 per year. The cost to lease office space and pay utilities and other related costs are estimated at $58,000 per year.

During the first six months of this year, Philadelphia Financial processed 79 loans. Cost of materials, credit reports, and other items related to loan processing were 8 percent higher than expected for the volume of loans processed.

The loan processor and her assistant cost $23,800 for the six months. Leasing and related office costs were $28,100.

Required

Analyze the variances for Philadelphia Financial. (*Hint:* Loans are the output.)

Exercise 17.37
Activity-Based Flexible Budget; Ethics
(LO 8)

Ethics

Refer to Koala Camp Gear's activity-based flexible budget in Exhibit 17–12. Suppose that the company's activity in February is described as follows:

Machine hours	7,500
Production runs	16
Engineering design specs	12
Direct material (sq. meters)	40,000

Required

a. Determine the flexible budgeted cost for each of the following:
  (1) Indirect material (thread)
  (2) Utilities (heat)

(3) Quality assurance

(4) Engineering

(5) Material handling

(6) Insurance and property taxes

b. Compute the variance for setup cost during the month assuming that the actual setup cost was $4,540.

(1) Using the activity-based flexible budget.

(2) Using Koala's conventional flexible budget (Exhibit 17–3).

c. Compute the variance for engineering cost during the month assuming the actual engineering cost was $4,750.

(1) Using the activity-based flexible budget.

(2) Using Koala's conventional flexible budget (Exhibit 17–3).

d. Comment on the ethical issues in the following scenario: When Koala's director of engineering, John Margrove, was shown a preliminary copy of the February cost-variance report, which was based on the activity-based flexible budget, he was dismayed at the unfavorable variance. Refer to your answer to requirement (c).

The next day, during an afternoon golf outing with his friend Marc Wesley, Koala's controller, Margrove learned that the reported unfavorable engineering cost variance would have been favorable if the report had been based on the traditional flexible budget instead of the activity-based flexible budget. Margrove was quite annoyed about this, and he began to pressure his friend to use the traditional flexible budget as the basis for the variance report. "What's the big deal?" pressed Margrove. "Who's going to know anyway? Just bury that ABC stuff, and use the tried and true method. Nobody will question your methods, and my report will look better."

(1) Comment on John Margrove's behavior.

(2) How should Marc Wesley respond? What standards of ethical behavior for management accountants are involved here? (See the Appendix to Chapter 1.)

Exercise 17.38
City or State Budget; Activity-Based Flexible Budget; Cost Drivers; Use of Internet
(LO 4, 8)

Global

Internet

Choose a city or state in the United States (or a Canadian city or province), and use the Internet to explore the annual budget for the governmental unit you selected. For example, you could check out the annual budget for Los Angeles at *www.losangeles.com,* or the Canadian regional budget at *www.rmoc.on.ca/finance/.*

Required

a. Select three items in the budget and explain how these items would be treated if the budget were converted to an activity-based flexible budget.

b. What would be appropriate cost drivers for the budgetary items you selected?

Exercise 17.39
Standard Material Costs; Proration of Variances (Appendix A)
(LO 9)

Tonawanda Corporation acquired 50,000 units of direct material for $70,000 last year. The standard price paid for the material was $1.30 per unit. During last year, 45,000 units of material were used in the production process. Materials are entered into production at the beginning of the process. The standard allowed quantity for the amount of output that was actually produced is 48,000 units. Eighty percent of the units that used these materials were completed and transferred to Finished-Goods Inventory. Sixty percent of these units that had been transferred to Finished-Goods Inventory were sold this period. There were no beginning inventories.

Required

a. Prepare journal entries, and show the flow of costs through T-accounts.

b. Prorate the direct-materials price variance to the appropriate accounts.

Exercise 17.40
Standard Costing in a Just-in-Time Environment (Appendix B)
(LO 10)

Refer to the data for Tonowanda Corporation in the preceding exercise. If the company were operating in a just-in-time environment and charging its standard costs directly to Cost of Goods Sold (at standard cost), show the flow of costs through the T-accounts required to adjust Cost of Goods Sold (at standard cost), to reflect end-of-period inventories. Variances are expensed.

Exercise 17.41
Standard Costing in a Just-in-Time Environment (Appendix B)
(LO 10)

During the current period, Punxatawny Pipe Company paid $38,000 for 30,000 units of material, all of which was immediately put into process. During the period, 14,800 units of output were produced, and 14,500 units were sold. Three hundred units remain in finished-goods inventory. Each unit of output requires two units of material, which has a standard cost of $1.35 per unit of material. Standard variable overhead is $69,600 for

15,000 units of production. The variable-overhead efficiency variance was $1,800 U, and actual variable overhead was $69,341.

Fixed overhead, which includes all labor costs, is budgeted at $146,000. Actual fixed overhead for the period was $143,200. Fixed overhead is applied to production at $10 per unit of output. All variances are expensed.

Required

a. Show the flow of these costs if the company initially charges all manufacturing costs to Cost of Goods Sold (at standard cost), that is, using backflush standard costing.

b. Show the adjustment that would be made to reflect the ending inventory balances.

Exercise 17.42
Sales Variances (Appendix C)
(LO 11)

Surf's Up Beach Wear, Inc., manufactures and sells beach T-shirts. The business is very competitive. The budget for last year called for sales of 200,000 units at $9 each. However, as the summer season approached, management realized that the company could not sell 200,000 units at the $9 price but would have to offer price concessions. Budgeted variable cost is $3.65 per unit. Actual results showed sales of 190,000 units at an average price of $8.50 each. The actual variable cost was $3.65 per unit.

Required

Compute the following variances for Surf's Up Beach Wear: revenue budget variance, sales-price variance, and revenue sales-volume variance.

Exercise 17.43
Sales-Mix and Sales-Quantity Variances (Appendix C)
(LO 11)
Spreadsheet

Tiger Corporation sells two models of golfing gloves. The budgeted per-unit price is $10.95 for Basic and $24.95 for Ultra. The budget called for sales of 400,000 Basics and 180,000 Ultras during the current year. Actual results showed sales of 300,000 Basics, with a price of $11.29 per unit, and 200,000 Ultras, with a price of $25.39 per unit. The standard variable cost is $5 per unit for a Basic and $10 per unit for Ultras.

Required

Compute each of the following variances from a contribution-margin perspective: (*Hint:* Use the formulas given in Appendix C but substitute each product's contribution margin for its sales price.)

a. Sales-volume variance.

b. Sales-mix and sales-quantity variances.

Exercise 17.44
Market-Size and Market-Share Variances (Appendix C)
(LO 11)
Global

Cabrerra Company manufactures valves in its plant outside Rio de Janeiro, Brazil. For the most recent year, the company budgeted sales of 20,000 units of its sole product, assuming that the company would have 20 percent of 100,000 units sold in a particular market. The actual results were 18,000 units, based on a 15 percent share of a total market of 120,000 units. The budgeted contribution margin is 3 *real* per unit. (The *real* is Brazil's national monetary unit.)

Required

Compute the sales-quantity variance and break it down into the market-size and market-share variances. Cabrerra's cost-management team takes a contribution-margin perspective when doing sales variance analysis. (*Hint:* Use the same formulas given in Appendix C but substitute the contribution margin for the sales price. Remember to express your analysis in terms of the *real,* Brazil's national currency.)

Exercise 17.45
Market-Share Analysis; Use of Internet (Appendix C)
(LO 11)
Internet

One aspect of sales-variance analysis involves helping management gain insight into the company's market share. Select one of the following companies (or any company you choose) and use the Internet to gather information about that company's share of a particular market. You also might need to use the Internet to access economic data about the overall industry volume for the type of product you selected (e.g., *www.ia-online.com/stats/index.htm).*

DaimlerChrysler (*www.daimlerchrysler.com*)
Ford (*www.ford.com/us*)
General Motors (*www.gm.com*)
Toyota (*www.toyota.com*)

Required

Estimate the market share in a particular product area (e.g., minivans or sport utility vehicles) for the company you selected.

Exercise 17.46
Sales-Price, Sales-Volume, Market-Size, and Market-Share Variances (Appendix C)
(LO 11)

San Joaquin Condiments, Inc., makes bulk artificial seasonings for use in processed foods. A seasoning was budgeted to sell in 20-liter drums at a price of $48 per drum. The company expected to sell 150,000 drums. Budgeted variable costs are $10 per drum. During the year, San Joaquin Condiments sold 125,000 drums at a price of $47.

Required

San Joaquin Condiments' cost-management staff computes sales variances from a revenue perspective.

a. Compute the sales-price and sales-volume variances.

b. Assume that the budgeted sales volume was based on an expected 10 percent share of a total market volume of 1.5 million drums, but the actual results were based on a 12.5 percent share of a total market of 1 million drums. Compute the market-size and market-share variances.

Problems

Problem 17.47
Overhead Cost and Variance Relationships
(LO 5)

Across the Miles Greeting Cards, Inc., reported a $50 unfavorable spending variance for variable overhead and a $500 unfavorable budget variance for fixed overhead. The flexible budget had $32,100 variable overhead based on 10,700 direct-labor hours; only 10,600 hours were worked. Total actual overhead was $54,350. Estimated number of hours for computing the fixed-overhead application rate was 11,000.

Required

a. Prepare a variable-overhead variance analysis.
b. Prepare a fixed-overhead variance analysis.

Problem 17.48
Manufacturing Variances for Variable Costs; Review of Chapters 16 and 17
(LO 5)

Global

Blair and Thatcher, Ltd., manufactures a special type of brass fitting in its plant in Manchester, England. The company prepares its budgets on the basis of standard costs. A monthly responsibility report shows the differences between budgeted and actual costs. Variances are analyzed and reported separately. Material price variances are computed at the time of purchase.

The following information relates to the current period. [All monetary amounts are given in British pounds (£) sterling.]

Standard costs (per unit of output)	
Direct material, 1 kilogram @ £1 per kilogram	£ 1
Direct labor, 2 hours @ £4 per hour	8
Manufacturing overhead	
Variable (25% of direct-labor cost)	2
Total standard cost per unit	£11

Actual costs for the month follow:

Material purchased	3,000 kilograms at £.9 per kilogram
Output	1,900 units using 2,100 kilograms of material
Actual direct-labor cost	3,200 hours at £5 per hour
Actual variable overhead	£4,500

Required

Prepare a cost-variance analysis for the variable costs (i.e., direct material, direct labor, and variable overhead). Remember to express your analysis in terms of the British monetary unit, pounds.

Problem 17.49
Overhead Variances; Journal Entries
(LO 3, 5, 7)

Manitoba Apparel Company, located in Winnipeg, uses a standard-costing system. The firm estimates that it will operate its manufacturing facilities at 800,000 machine hours for the year. The estimate for total budgeted overhead is $2,000,000. The standard variable-overhead rate is estimated to be $2 per machine hour or $6 per unit. The actual data for the year follow.

Actual variable overhead	$1,690,000
Actual fixed overhead	$ 389,000
Actual finished units	250,000
Actual machine hours	764,000

Required

a. Compute the following variances. Indicate whether each is favorable or unfavorable where appropriate.
   (1) Variable-overhead spending variance.
   (2) Variable-overhead efficiency variance.
   (3) Fixed-overhead budget variance.
   (4) Fixed-overhead volume variance.

b. Prepare journal entries to do the following:
   - Record the incurrence of actual variable overhead and actual fixed overhead.
   - Add variable and fixed overhead to Work-in-Process Inventory.
   - Close underapplied or overapplied overhead to Cost of Goods Sold.

[CMA adapted]

Problem 17.50
Overhead Variances
(LO 5)

Superior Metal Stamping, Inc., shows the following overhead information for the current period:

Actual overhead incurred	$14,700, of which $9,800 is variable
Budgeted fixed overhead	$4,320
Standard variable-overhead rate per direct-labor hour	$3
Standard direct-labor hours allowed for actual production	3,500 hours
Actual direct-labor hours used	3,300 hours

Required

a. Compute the variable-overhead spending and efficiency variances and the fixed-overhead budget variance.

b. Interpret each variance.

Problem 17.51
Standard Hours Allowed; Flexible Budget; Multiple Products; Insurance Company
(LO 1, 2, 4)

Four Corners Insurance Company insures clients in Colorado, New Mexico, Arizona, and Utah. The company uses a flexible overhead budget for its application-processing department. The firm offers five types of policies, with the following number of standard hours allowed for clerical processing.

Automobile	1.5 hour
Renter's	1.0 hour
Homeowner's	2.0 hours
Health	2.0 hours
Life	5.0 hours

The company processed the following number of insurance applications during July:

Automobile	250
Renter's	200
Homeowner's	100
Health	400
Life	200

Four Corners' controller estimates that the variable-overhead rate in the application-processing department is $4 per hour and that fixed-overhead costs will amount to $2,000 per month.

Required

a. How many standard clerical hours are allowed in July given actual application activity?

b. Why is it not sensible to base the company's flexible budget on the number of applications processed instead of the number of clerical hours allowed?

c. Construct a formula flexible overhead budget for the company.

d. What is the flexible budget for total overhead cost in July?

Problem 17.52
Graph of Budgeted and Applied Overhead; Recording Studio
(LO 1, 2, 3)

Communication

Countrytime Studios is a recording studio in Nashville. The studio budgets and applies overhead costs on the basis of production time. Its controller anticipates 10,000 hours of production time to be available during the year. The following overhead amounts have been budgeted for the year.

Variable overhead	$40,000
Fixed overhead	90,000

Required

a. Draw two graphs, one for variable overhead and one for fixed overhead. The variable on the horizontal axis of each graph should be production time, in hours, ranging from 5,000 to 15,000 hours. The variable on the vertical axis of each graph should be overhead cost (variable or fixed). Each graph should include two lines, one for the flexible-budget amount of overhead and one for applied overhead.

b. Write a brief memo to Countrytime Studio's general manager explaining the graphs so that she will understand the concepts of budgeted and applied overhead.

Problem 17.53
Variance Computations with Missing Data; Review of Chapters 16 and 17
(LO 5, 6)

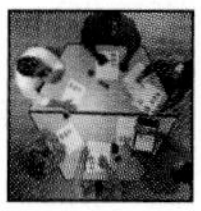
Team

Communication

The following information is provided to assist you in evaluating the performance of the production operations of Cyclops Company:

Units produced (actual)	21,000
Master production budget:	
Direct material	$165,000
Direct labor	140,000
Manufacturing overhead	199,000
Standard costs per unit:	
Direct material	$ 1.65 × 5 pounds per unit of output
Direct labor	14.00 per hour × ½ hour per unit
Variable overhead	11.90 per direct-labor hour
Actual costs:	
Direct material purchased and used	$188,700 (102,000 pounds)
Direct labor	140,000 (10,700 hours)
Manufacturing overhead	204,000 (61% is variable)

Variable overhead is applied on the basis of direct-labor hours.

Required

As a group, prepare a complete cost-variance report suitable for presentation to the class. Include the following in your report:

- Direct-materials price and quantity variances.
- Direct-labor rate and efficiency variances.
- Variable-overhead spending and efficiency variances.
- Fixed-overhead budget and volume variances.

Problem 17.54
Analysis of Cost Reports
(LO 6)

Communication

Bo Vonderweidt is the production manager of Cyclaris Plant, a division of the large corporation, Plantimum, Inc. He has complained several times to the corporate office that the cost reports used to evaluate his plant are misleading. Vonderweidt states, "I know how to get good quality product out. Over a number of years, I've even cut materials used to do it. The cost reports don't show any of this; they're always negative, no matter what I do. There's no way I can win with accounting or the people at headquarters who use these reports."

A copy of the latest report is shown here.

CYCLARIS PLANT
Cost Report
For the Month of October
(in thousands)

	Budgeted Cost	Actual Cost	Excess Cost
Direct material	$ 390	$ 437	$47
Direct labor	560	540	(20)
Overhead	100	134	34
Total	$1,050	$1,111	$61

Required

Write a brief report to management that identifies and explains at least three changes to the report that would make the cost information more meaningful and less threatening to the production manager.

[CMA adapted]

Problem 17.55
Flexible Budget; Performance Report
(LO 1, 2, 6)

Communication

EduSoft, Inc., distributes educational software packages used in the public schools nationwide. Mark Fletcher, president of EduSoft, was looking forward to seeing the performance reports for November because he knew the company's sales for the month had exceeded budget by a considerable margin. The company had been growing steadily for approximately two years. Fletcher's biggest challenge at this point was to ensure that the company did not lose control of expenses during this growth period. When Fletcher received the November reports, he was dismayed to see the large unfavorable variance in the company's Monthly Selling Expense Report that follows.

EDUSOFT, INC.
Monthly Selling Expense Report
For the Month of November

	Annual Budget	November Budget	November Actual	November Variance
Unit sales	2,000,000	280,000	310,000	30,000
Dollar sales	$80,000,000	$11,200,000	$12,400,000	$1,200,000
Orders processed	54,000	6,500	5,800	(700)
Sales personnel per month	90	90	96	(6)
Advertising	$19,800,000	$ 1,650,000	$ 1,660,000	$ 10,000 U
Staff salaries	1,500,000	125,000	125,000	—
Sales salaries	1,296,000	108,000	115,400	7,400 U
Commissions	3,200,000	448,000	496,000	48,000 U
Per-diem expense	1,782,000	148,500	162,600	14,100 U
Office expenses	4,080,000	340,000	358,400	18,400 U
Shipping expenses	6,750,000	902,500	976,500	74,000 U
Total expenses	$38,408,000	$ 3,722,000	$ 3,893,900	$ 171,900 U

Fletcher called in the company's new controller, Susan Porter, to discuss the implications of the variances reported for November and to plan a strategy for improving performance. Porter suggested that the company's reporting format might not be giving Fletcher a true picture of the company's operations. She proposed that EduSoft implement flexible budgeting. Porter offered to redo the Monthly Selling Expense Report for November using flexible budgeting so that Fletcher could compare the two reports and see the advantages of flexible budgeting.

Porter discovered the following information about the behavior of EduSoft's selling expenses:

- The total compensation paid to the sales force consists of a monthly base salary and a commission, which varies with sales dollars.
- Sales office expense is a semivariable cost with the variable portion related to the number of orders processed. The fixed portion of office expense is $3,000,000 annually and is incurred uniformly throughout the year.
- Subsequent to the adoption of the annual budget for the current year, EduSoft decided to open a new sales territory. As a consequence, the company hired six additional salespeople effective November 1. Porter decided that these additional six people should be recognized in her revised report.
- Per-diem reimbursement to the sales force, while a fixed amount per day, is variable with the number of sales personnel and the number of days spent traveling. EduSoft's original budget was based on an average sales force of 90 people throughout the year with each salesperson traveling 15 days per month.
- The company's shipping expense is a semivariable cost with the variable portion, $3 per unit, dependent on the number of units sold. The fixed portion is incurred uniformly throughout the year.

Required

a. As Porter's assistant, draft a memo for her to send to Fletcher citing the benefits of flexible budgeting. Explain why EduSoft should use flexible budgeting in this situation.

b. Prepare a revised Monthly Selling Expense Report for November that would permit Fletcher to more clearly evaluate EduSoft's control over selling expenses. The report should have a line for each selling expense item showing the appropriate budgeted amount, the actual selling expense, and the monthly dollar variance.

[CMA adapted]

Problem 17.56
Comprehensive Variance Problem; Review of Chapters 16 and 17
(LO 5)

Constellation, Inc., manufactures a special fabric used in space suits. The standard costs are detailed as follows:

Direct material, 20 meters at $ .90 per meter	$18
Direct labor, 4 hours at $6 per hour	24
Manufacturing overhead applied at five-sixths of direct-labor cost (variable costs = $15; fixed costs = $5)	20
Variable selling and administrative cost	12
Fixed selling and administrative cost	7
Total unit cost	$81

Standards have been computed based on a budgeted activity level of 2,400 direct-labor hours per month. Actual activity for the past month follows:

Material purchased	18,000 meters at $ .92 per meter
Material used	9,500 meters
Direct labor	2,100 hours at $6.10 per hour
Total manufacturing overhead	$11,100
Production	500 units

Required

Prepare variance analyses for the variable and fixed costs. Indicate which variances, if any, cannot be computed.

Problem 17.57
Overhead Variances
(LO 5)

Blankenship Corporation developed its overhead application rate from the annual budget, which is based on an expected total output of 720,000 units requiring 3,600,000 machine hours. The company is able to schedule production uniformly throughout the year.

A total of 66,000 units requiring 315,000 machine hours were produced during May. Actual overhead costs for May amounted to $375,000. The actual costs, as compared to the annual budget and to one-twelfth of the annual budget, are as follows:

BLANKENSHIP CORPORATION
Annual Budget

	Total Amount	Per Unit	Per Machine Hour	Monthly Budget	Actual Costs for May
Variable overhead:					
Indirect material	$1,224,000	$1.70	$ .34	$102,000	$111,000
Indirect labor	900,000	1.25	.25	75,000	75,000
Fixed overhead:					
Supervision	648,000	.90	.18	54,000	51,000
Utilities	540,000	.75	.15	45,000	54,000
Depreciation	1,008,000	1.40	.28	84,000	84,000
Total	$4,320,000	$6.00	$1.20	$360,000	$375,000

Required

a. Prepare a schedule showing the following amounts for Blankenship Corporation for May.
   (1) Applied overhead costs.
   (2) Variable-overhead spending variance.
   (3) Fixed-overhead budget variance.
   (4) Variable-overhead efficiency variance.
   (5) Fixed-overhead volume variance.
   Where appropriate, be sure to indicate whether each variance is favorable or unfavorable.

b. Draw a graph similar to Exhibit 17–7 to depict the variable-overhead variances.

c. Why does your graph differ from Exhibit 17–7 other than the fact that the numbers differ?

[CMA adapted]

Problem 17.58
Sales-Price, Sales-Volume, Sales-Mix, and Sales-Quantity Variances (Appendix C)
(LO 11)

Christo, Egner, and Vinocour, is a law firm with partners and staff members. Each billable hour of partner time has a $275 budgeted price and $130 budgeted variable cost. Each billable hour of staff time has a budgeted price of $65 and budgeted variable cost of $35. This month, the partnership budget called for 8,500 billable partner hours and 34,650 staff hours. Actual results follow:

	Revenue	Billable Hours	Variable Cost
Partner	$2,150,000	8,000 hours	$1,040,000
Staff	2,225,000	34,000 hours	1,190,000

Required

Compute the following variances from a revenue perspective:

a. Sales-price and sales-volume variances.

b. Sales-mix and sales-quantity variances.

Problem 17.59
Contribution-Margin, Sales-Mix, and Sales-Quantity Variances (Appendix C)
(LO 11)

The following information has been prepared by Alexis Wells, a member of the cost-management staff of Brain Teaser Puzzles, Inc.:

BRAIN TEASER PUZZLES
Income Statement
For the Year Ended December 31, 20x0
(dollar amounts in thousands)

	Product AR-10		Product ZR-7		Total	
	Budget	Actual	Budget	Actual	Budget	Actual
Unit sales	2,000	2,800	6,000	5,600	8,000	8,400
Sales	$6,000	$7,560	$12,000	$11,760	$18,000	$19,320
Variable costs	$2,400	$2,800	$ 6,000	$ 5,880	$ 8,400	$ 8,680
Fixed costs	1,800	1,900	2,400	2,400	4,200	4,300
Total costs	$4,200	$4,700	$ 8,400	$ 8,280	$12,600	$12,980
Operating profit	$1,800	$2,860	$ 3,600	$ 3,480	$ 5,400	$ 6,340

Required

Analyze the preceding data to show the impact of sales volume, contribution margin, sales quantity, and sales mix on operating profit. Brain Teaser Puzzles' cost-management staff analyzes sales variances from a contribution-margin perspective. (*Hint:* Use the formulas given in Appendix C, but substitute each product's contribution margin for its sales price.)

[CMA adapted]

Problem 17.60
Contribution-Margin Sales-Variance Analysis (Appendix C)
(LO 11)

SeaAir Airlines plans its budget and subsequently evaluates sales performance based on passenger miles. A passenger mile is one paying passenger flying one mile. For this month, the company estimated that its contribution margin would amount to 20 cents per passenger mile and that 40 million passenger miles would be flown.

As a result of improvement in the economy, 43 million passenger miles were flown this month. The price per passenger mile averaged 32 cents. The budgeted variable cost per mile was 10 cents. Management's subsequent analysis indicated that the industry flew 107 million passenger miles this month, which was 7 percent more passenger miles than expected. The actual variable cost per passenger mile was 10 cents.

Required

Taking a contribution-margin perspective, do as complete a sales variance analysis as possible. (*Hint:* Use the formulas given in Appendix C, but substitute the contribution margin for the sales price.)

Problem 17.61
Revenue Sales-Variance Analysis Using Industry Data and Multiple Product Lines (Appendix C)
(LO 11)

Cleveland Carpet Company makes three grades of indoor-outdoor carpets. Sales volume for the annual budget is determined by estimating the total market volume for indoor-outdoor carpet and then applying the company's prior year market share, adjusted for planned changes due to company programs for the coming year. Volume is apportioned for the three grades based on the prior year's product mix, again adjusted for planned changes due to company programs for the coming year.

The following are the budgeted and the actual results of operations for March (dollar amounts in thousands).

Budget	**Grade 1**	**Grade 2**	**Grade 3**	**Total**
Sales, units	1,000 rolls	1,000 rolls	2,000 rolls	4,000 rolls
Sales, dollars	$1,000	$2,000	$3,000	$6,000
Variable costs	700	1,600	2,300	4,600
Contribution margin	$ 300	$ 400	$ 700	$1,400
Manufacturing fixed cost	200	200	300	700
Product margin	$ 100	$ 200	$ 400	$ 700
Marketing and administrative costs (all fixed)				250
Operating profit				$ 450
Actual				
Sales, units	800 rolls	1,000 rolls	2,100 rolls	3,900 rolls
Sales, dollars	$ 810	$2,000	$3,000	$5,810
Variable costs	560	1,610	2,320	4,490
Contribution margin	$ 250	$ 390	$ 680	$1,320
Manufacturing fixed cost	210	220	315	745
Product margin	$ 40	$ 170	$ 365	$ 575
Marketing and administrative costs (all fixed)				275
Operating profit				$ 300

Industry volume was estimated at 40,000 rolls for budgeting purposes. Actual industry volume for March was 38,000 rolls.

Required

From a revenue perspective:

a. Prepare an analysis to disaggregate the revenue budget variance into the sales price and sales-volume variances.

b. Break down the sales-volume variance into the parts caused by sales mix and sales quantity.

c. Break down the sales-quantity variance into its market-size and market-share components.

[CMA adapted]

Problem 17.62
Commentary on Sales-Variance Analysis; Continuation of Problem 17.61 (Appendix C)
(LO 11)

Communication

Refer to your solution to the preceding problem for Cleveland Carpet Company.

Required

Write a memo to the company president that summarizes and comments on the sales variance analysis.

Problem 17.63
Sales-Variance Analysis; Continuation of Problem 17.61 (Appendix C)
(LO 11)

Refer to your solution for Problem 17.61.

Required

Prepare a sales variance-chart similar to Exhibit 17–20 to summarize the sales variance analysis for Cleveland Carpet Company.

Problem 17.64
Comprehensive Variance Analysis; Review of Chapters 16 and 17
(LO 5)

Toledo Chemical Company manufactures two products, Florimene and Glyoxide, used in the plastics industry. The company prepares its budget on the basis of standard costs. The following data are for August:

	Florimene	Glyoxide
Standards:		
Direct material	3 kilograms at $1 per kilogram	4 kilograms at $1.10 per kilogram
Direct labor	5 hours at $14 per hour	6 hours at $15 per hour
Variable overhead (per direct-labor hour)	$3.20	$3.50
Fixed overhead (per month)	$22,356	$26,520
Expected activity (direct-labor hours)	5,750	7,800
Actual data:		
Direct material	3,100 kilograms at $ .90 per kilogram	4,700 kilograms at $1.15 per kilogram
Direct labor	4,900 hours at $14.05 per hour	7,400 hours at $15.10 per hour
Variable overhead	$16,170	$25,234
Fixed overhead	$20,930	$26,400
Units produced	1,000 units	1,200 units

Required

a. Prepare a complete variance analysis for each variable cost for each product.

b. Prepare a complete fixed-overhead variance analysis for each product.

c. Now assume that the fixed-overhead costs are applied to units produced using the following standard rate per direct-labor hour:

$$\text{Florimene: \$3.888 per hour} = \frac{\$22{,}356}{5{,}750 \text{ expected direct-labor hours}}$$

$$\text{Glyoxide: \$3.40 per hour} = \frac{\$26{,}520}{7{,}800 \text{ expected direct-labor hours}}$$

Prepare two-way, three-way, and four-way analyses of overhead variances for each product.

Problem 17.65
Use of a Flexible Budget; Review of Chapters 16 and 17
(LO 1, 2, 5)

Dayton Machine Tool Company has an automated production process, and production activity is quantified in terms of machine hours. It uses a standard-costing system. The annual static budget for 20x1 called for 6,000 units to be produced, requiring 30,000 machine hours. The standard-overhead rate for the year was computed using this planned level of production. The 20x1 manufacturing cost report follows.

DAYTON MACHINE TOOL COMPANY
Manufacturing Cost Report
For the Year 20x1
(in thousands of dollars)

	Static Budget	Flexible Budget		
Cost Item	30,000 Machine Hours	31,000 Machine Hours	32,000 Machine Hours	Actual Cost
Direct material:				
G27 aluminum	$ 252.0	$ 260.4	$ 268.8	$ 270.0
M14 steel alloy	78.0	80.6	83.2	83.0

Direct labor:				
Assembler	273.0	282.1	291.2	287.0
Grinder	234.0	241.8	249.6	250.0
Manufacturing overhead:				
Maintenance	24.0	24.8	25.6	25.0
Supplies	129.0	133.3	137.6	130.0
Supervision	80.0	82.0	84.0	81.0
Inspection	144.0	147.0	150.0	147.0
Insurance	50.0	50.0	50.0	50.0
Depreciation	200.0	200.0	200.0	200.0
Total cost	$1,464.0	$1,502.0	$1,540.0	$1,523.0

Dayton Machine Tool Company develops flexible budgets for different levels of activity for use in evaluating performance. It produced a total of 6,200 units during 20x1, requiring 32,000 machine hours. The preceding manufacturing cost report compares the company's actual cost for the year with the static budget and the flexible budget for two different activity levels.

Required

Compute the following amounts. For variances, indicate favorable or unfavorable where appropriate. Answers should be rounded to two decimal places when necessary.

a. The standard number of machine hours allowed to produce one unit of product.

b. The actual cost of direct material used in one unit of product.

c. The cost of material that should be processed per machine hour.

d. The standard direct-labor cost for each unit produced.

e. The variable-overhead rate per machine hour in a flexible-budget formula. (*Hint:* Use the high-low method to estimate cost behavior. In the high-low method of cost estimation, the difference between the cost levels at the high and low *activity* levels is divided by the difference between the high and low *activity* levels. This quotient provides a simple estimate of the *variable* cost rate per unit of activity.)

f. The standard fixed-overhead rate per machine hour used for product costing.

g. The variable-overhead spending variance. (Assume that management has determined that the actual fixed overhead cost in 20x1 amounted to $324,000.)

h. The variable-overhead efficiency variance.

i. The fixed-overhead budget variance.

j. The fixed-overhead volume variance. [Make the same assumption as in requirement (g).]

k. The total budgeted manufacturing cost (in thousands of dollars) for an output of 6,050 units. (*Hint:* Use the flexible-budget formula.)

[CMA adapted]

Problem 17.66
Comprehensive Sales-Variance Analysis; Revenue Perspective and Contribution Margin Perspective (Appendix C)
(LO 11)

The Louisville plant of TimeCo manufactures three styles of clock radio. The economy model (E) targets the teenage market. The standard model (S) is popular with college students. TimeCo's newest product, the deluxe model (D), is designed for home and office use.

For the most recent year, TimeCo's sales manager predicted a total annual industry volume for clock radios of 200,000 units, and the following budget data were compiled by the controller for TimeCo's three products.

Model	Budgeted Price	Budgeted Unit Variable Cost	Budgeted Unit Sales Volume
Economy	$30	$20	4,000
Standard	50	30	5,000
Deluxe	90	50	1,000

When actual results for the year were recorded, the actual industry volume for clock radios was much higher than anticipated, 250,000 units. TimeCo's actual results for the year follow:

Model	Actual Price	Actual Unit Variable Cost	Actual Unit Sales Volume
Economy	$32	$17	6,000
Standard	55	30	5,400
Deluxe	85	50	600

To help top management understand the year's sales results, TimeCo's controller has asked you, his assistant, to prepare a complete sales-variable analysis.

Required

a. Summarize the preceding information for TimeCo by preparing a table similar to Exhibit 17–18.

b. Prepare a complete sales-variance analysis from a revenue perspective.

c. Prepare a complete sales-variance analysis from a contribution-margin perspective.

Cases

Case 17.67
Comprehensive Review of Variances; Behavioral Effects (Appendix C)
(LO 5, 11)*

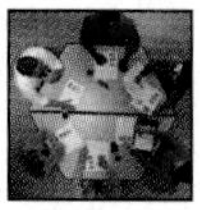

Communication Team

Ace Arcade, Inc. manufactures video game machines. Market saturation and technological innovations have caused pricing pressures that have resulted in declining profits. To stem the slide in profits until new products can be introduced, top management has turned its attention to both manufacturing economies and increased production. To realize these objectives, an incentive program has been developed to reward production managers who contribute to an increase in the number of units produced and achieve cost reductions. In addition, a just-in-time purchasing program has been implemented, and raw materials are purchased on an as-needed basis.

The production managers have responded to the pressure to improve manufacturing performance in several ways that have resulted in an increased number of completed units over normal production levels. The video game machines put together by the Assembly Group require parts from both the Printed Circuit Boards (PCB) and the Reading Heads (RH) groups. To attain increased production levels, the PCB and RH groups started rejecting parts that previously would have been tested and modified to meet manufacturing standards. Preventive maintenance on machines used in the production of these parts has been postponed with only emergency repair work being performed to keep production lines moving. The Maintenance Department is concerned that there will be serious breakdowns and unsafe operating conditions.

The more aggressive Assembly Group production supervisors have pressured maintenance personnel to attend to their machines at the expense of other groups. This has resulted in machine downtime in the PCB and RH groups which, when coupled with demands for accelerated parts delivery by the Assembly Group, has led to more frequent part rejections and increased friction among departments. Ace Arcade operates under a standard-costing system. The standard costs are as follows:

	Standard Cost per Unit		
	Quantity	**Cost**	**Total**
Direct material:			
Housing unit	1 unit	$20	$ 20
Printed circuit boards	2 boards	15	30
Reading heads	4 heads	10	40
Direct labor:			
Assembly group	2.0 hours	8	16
PCB group	1.0 hour	9	9
RH group	1.5 hours	10	15
Total	4.5 hours		
Variable overhead*		2	9
Total standard cost per unit			$139

*Applied on the basis of direct labor: 4.5 direct-labor hours at $2 per hour.

*This case integrates material from Chapters 15, 16, and 17 and relates to learning objectives from all three chapters.

Ace Arcade prepares monthly performance reports based on standard costs. The following table shows the contribution report for May, when production and sales both reached 2,200 units. The budgeted and actual unit sales price in May were the same at $200.

ACE ARCADE,INC.
Contribution Report
For the Month of May

	Budgeted	Actual	Variance
Units	2,000	2,200	200 F
Revenue	$400,000	$440,000	$40,000 F
Variable costs:			
Direct material	$180,000	$220,400	$40,400 U
Direct labor	80,000	93,460	13,460 U
Variable overhead	18,000	18,800	800 U
Total variable costs	$278,000	$332,660	$54,660 U
Contribution margin	$122,000	$107,340	$14,660 U

Ace Arcade's top management was surprised by the unfavorable contribution-margin variance in spite of the increased sales in May. Jack Rath, director of cost management, was assigned to report on the reasons for the unfavorable contribution results as well as the individuals or groups responsible. After a thorough review of the data, Rath prepared the following usage report.

ACE ARCADE, INC.
Usage Report
For the Month of May

Cost Item	Actual Quantity	Actual Cost
Direct material:		
Housing units	2,200 units	$ 44,000
Printed circuit boards	4,700 boards	75,200
Reading heads	9,200 heads	101,200
Direct labor:		
Assembly	3,900 hours	31,200
Printed circuit boards	2,400 hours	23,760
Reading heads	3,500 hours	38,500
Total	9,800 hours	
Variable overhead		18,800
Total variable cost		$332,660

Rath reported that the PCB and RH groups supported the increased production levels but experienced abnormal machine downtime, causing idle personnel. This required the use of overtime to keep up with the accelerated demand for parts. The idle time was charged to direct labor. Rath also reported that the production managers of these two groups resorted to parts rejections as opposed to testing and modifying procedures formerly applied. Rath determined that the Assembly Group met management's objectives by increasing production while utilizing lower than standard hours.

Required

As a group, prepare a presentation to the class addressing the following requirements.

a. Calculate the following variances, and explain the $14,660 unfavorable variance between the budgeted and actual contribution margin during May. Assume that all raw material purchased during May was placed into production.

(1) Direct-labor rate variance.
(2) Direct-labor efficiency variance.
(3) Direct-material price variance.
(4) Direct-material quantity variance.
(5) Variable-overhead spending variance.
(6) Variable-overhead efficiency variance.
(7) Sales-price variance.
(8) Contribution-margin sales-volume variance.

b. (1) Identify and briefly explain the behavioral factors that could promote friction among the production managers and between the production managers and the maintenance manager.

(2) Evaluate Rath's analysis of the unfavorable contribution results in terms of its completeness and its effect on the behavior of the production groups.

[CMA adapted]

Case 17.68
Comprehensive Overview of Budgets and Variance Analysis*†
(LO 5)

Communication

"I just don't understand these financial statements at all!" exclaimed Elmo Knapp. Knapp explained that he had turned over management of Racketeer, Inc., a division of American Recreation Equipment, Inc., to his son, Otto, the previous month. Racketeer, Inc., manufactures tennis rackets.

"I was really proud of Otto," he beamed. "He was showing us all the tricks he learned in business school, and if I say so myself, I think he was doing a rather good job for us. For example, he put together this budget for Racketeer, which makes it very easy to see how much profit we'll make at any sales volume. (See Exhibit A.) As best as I can figure it, in March we expected to have a volume of 8,000 units and a profit of $14,500 on our rackets. But we did much better than that! We sold 10,000 rackets, so we should have made almost $21,000 on them."

"Another one of Otto's innovations is this standard-costing system," said Knapp proudly. "He sat down with our production people and came up with a standard production cost per unit. (See Exhibit B.) He tells me this will let us know how well our production people are performing. Also, he claims it will cut down on our clerical work."

Knapp continued, "But one thing puzzles me. My calculations show that we should have earned profit of nearly $21,000 in March. However, our accountants came up with less than $19,000 in the monthly income statement. (See Exhibit C.) This bothers me a great deal. Now, I'm sure our accountants are doing their job properly. But still, it appears to me that they're about $2,200 short."

"As you can probably guess," Knapp concluded, "we are one big happy family around here. I just wish I knew what those accountants are up to . . . coming in with a low net income like that."

*© Michael W. Maher.

†This case integrates material from Chapters 15, 16, and 17 and relates to learning objectives from all three chapters. Students might wish to review the discussion in Chapter 2 on absorption and variable costing before beginning this case.

Exhibit A
Profit Graph, Racketeer, Inc.

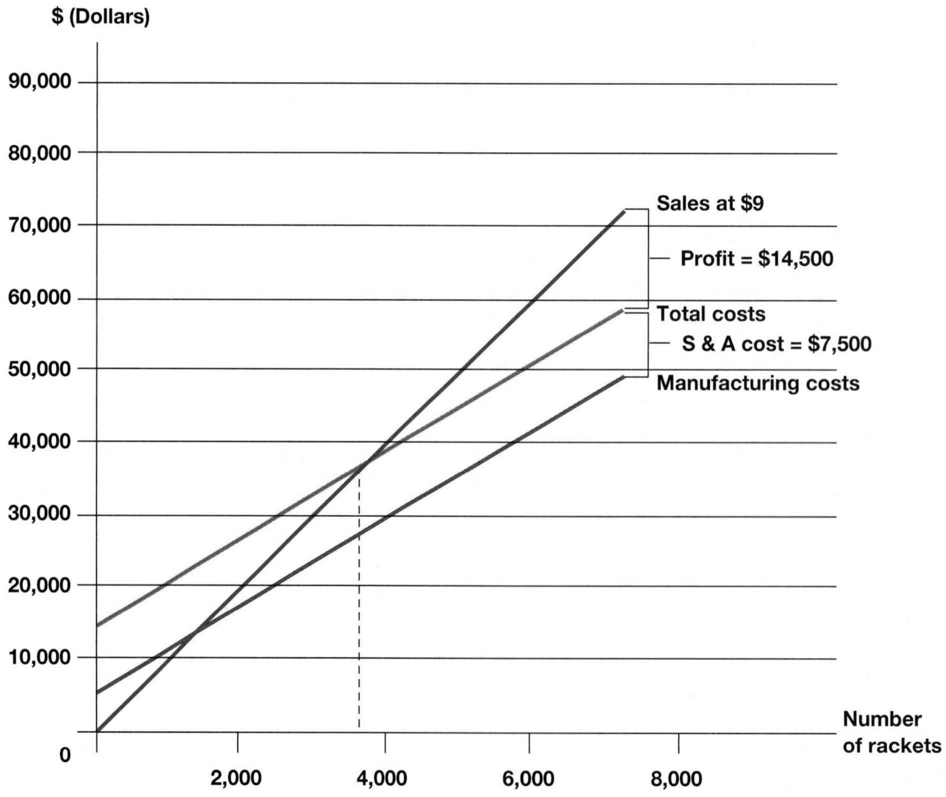

Required

Prepare a report for Elmo Knapp and Otto Knapp that reconciles the profit graph with the actual results for March. (See Exhibit D.) Show the source of each variance from the original plan (8,000 rackets) in as much detail as you can, and evaluate Racketeer's performance in March. Recommend improvements in Racketeer's profit-planning and control methods.

Exhibit B

Standard Costs, Racketeer, Inc.*

	Per Racket
Raw material:	
Frame (one frame per racket)	$3.15
Stringing materials: 20 feet at $.03 per foot	.60
Direct labor:	
Skilled: 1/8 hour at $9.60 per hour	1.20
Unskilled: 1/8 hour at $5.60 per hour	.70
Manufacturing overhead:	
Indirect labor	.10
Power	.03
Supervision†	.12
Depreciation†	.20
Other†	.15
Total standard cost per frame	$6.25

*Standard costs are calculated for an estimated production volume of 8,000 units each month.

†Fixed costs.

Exhibit C

Income Statement for March, Racketeer, Inc.

RACKETEER, INC.
Income Statement for March
Actual

Sales:	
10,000 rackets at $9	$90,000
Standard cost of goods sold:	
10,000 rackets at $6.25	62,500
Gross profit after standard costs	$27,500
Variances:	
Material variance	(490)
Labor variance	(392)
Overhead variance	(660)
Gross profit	$25,958
Selling and administrative expense	$ 7,200
Operating profit	$18,758

Exhibit D

Actual Production Data for March, Racketeer, Inc.

Direct material purchased and used:	
Stringing materials	175,000 feet at $.025 per foot
Frames (Note: some frames were ruined during production)	7,100 at $3.15 per frame
Direct labor:	
Skilled ($9.80 per hour)	900 hours
Unskilled ($5.80 per hour)	840 hours
Overhead:	
Indirect labor	$ 800
Power	250
Depreciation	1,600
Supervision	960
Other	1,250
Production	7,000 rackets

CHAPTER

18

Organizational Design, Responsibility Accounting, and Evaluation of Divisional Performance

After completing this chapter, you should be able to:

1. Understand the role of responsibility accounting in fostering goal or behavioral congruence.
2. List several benefits and costs of decentralization.
3. Describe the distinguishing characteristics of a cost center, a discretionary cost center, a revenue center, a profit center, and an investment center.
4. Prepare a performance report and explain the relationships between the reports for various responsibility centers.
5. Compute an investment center's return on investment, residual income, and economic value added.
6. Explain how a manager can improve return on investment by increasing either the sales margin or capital turnover.
7. Describe some advantages and disadvantages of return on investment and residual income as performance measures.
8. Explain various approaches for measuring a division's income and invested capital.

EMAIL MEMORANDUM

Outback Outfitters, Ltd.
10 Woolloomooloo Place
Sydney, New South Wales
AUSTRALIA

OUTBACK OUTFITTERS

PRESS RELEASE

For immediate release; no restrictions.
Contact: Talia Demarest, Media Relations

Outback Outfitters, Ltd., announces its acquisition of Koala Camp Gear Company. One of Australia's largest retailers of camping equipment and outdoor apparel, Outback Outfitters operates retail outlets throughout Australia, New Zealand, and the United Kingdom. Outback also operates a mail-order business from its headquarters in Sydney. Outback's president and CEO, Jack Darwin, made this comment on the acquisition: "For some time we have been looking to acquire a manufacturing company that could supply us with our own private-label merchandise. In Koala Camp Gear Company, we have found just the right firm. Koala has achieved a reputation around the world for the quality of its product. The Koala Camp Gear and Wallaby Wear product lines are well known from Melbourne to San Francisco to London. With this acquisition, Outback Outfitters will be poised to extend its reach throughout Europe and the United States. We couldn't ask for a better fit between Koala Camp Gear Company and Outback Outfitters. We welcome the folks from Koala into our corporate family, and we look forward to a very prosperous future."

Cost-Management Challenges

1. **When** companies grow larger, as typified by the acquisition described in Outback Outfitters' press release, how should they manage operations? What are some benefits and costs of decentralization?
2. **How** could a responsibility accounting system foster goal or behavioral congruence for Outback Outfitters?
3. **What** are the major types of responsibility accounting centers?
4. **What** is the key feature of activity-based responsibility accounting?
5. **How** is investment center performance typically measured?

When an organization begins its operations, it is usually small, and its decision making generally is centralized. It is relatively easy in a small organization for managers to keep in touch with routine operations through face-to-face contact with employees. A manager's task is increasingly difficult as an organization becomes larger and more complex. For example, as Outback Outfitters grows through the acquisition of Koala Camp Gear Company, as described in the press release on the preceding page, the new company's operations will be more complicated. Managers must make more decisions and manage more employees. A common rule of thumb is that one supervisor usually can manage about 10 subordinates. Consequently, all but very small organizations delegate managerial duties.

Decentralized Organizations and Responsibility Accounting

LO 1 Understand the role of responsibility accounting in fostering goal or behavioral congruence.

goal congruence *results when managers of subunits throughout an organization have a common set of objectives*

Most large organizations are divided into smaller units, each of which is assigned particular responsibilities. These units are called by various names, including *divisions, segments, business units, work centers, and departments.* Each department comprises individuals who are responsible for particular tasks or managerial functions. The managers of an organization should ensure that the people in each department are striving toward the same overall goals. **Goal congruence** results when the managers of subunits throughout an organization have a common set of objectives. This occurs when the group acts as a team in pursuit of a mutually agreed upon goal. Individual goal congruence occurs when an individual's personal goals are consistent with organizational goals.

Although complete congruence is rare, in some cases, a strong team spirit suppresses individual desires to act differently. Examples include some military units and some athletic teams. Many companies attempt to achieve this esprit de corps. Japanese companies have worked particularly hard to create a strong team orientation among workers that has resulted in considerable goal congruence.

behavioral congruence *occurs when an individual behaves in the best interests of the organization regardless of his or her own goals*

responsibility accounting *refers to the various concepts and tools used to measure the performance of people and departments in order to foster goal or behavioral congruence*

centralization *places the responsibility for decisons with the top echelon of management*

decentralization *places decision-making responsibility at divisional and departmental levels*

In most business settings, however, personal goals and organization goals differ. Performance evaluation and incentive systems are designed to encourage employees to behave as if their goals were congruent with organization goals. This results in **behavioral congruence;** that is, an individual behaves in the best interests of the organization regardless of his or her own goals.

How can an organization's cost-management system promote goal, or at least behavioral, congruence? **Responsibility accounting** refers to the various concepts and tools used to measure the performance of people and departments in order to foster goal or behavioral congruence.

Centralization versus Decentralization

Some organizations are very **centralized;** decisions are handed down from the top echelon of management and subordinates carry them out. The military is a good example of centralized authority. At the other extreme are highly **decentralized** companies in which decisions are made at divisional and departmental levels. In many conglomerates, operating decisions are made in the field; corporate headquarters is, in effect, a holding company. The majority of companies fall between these two extremes. At General Motors, for example, operating units are decentralized, and the research and development and finance functions are centralized.

Many companies begin with a centralized structure but become more and more decentralized as they grow. Consider the following example of a fast-food franchise that started with one hamburger stand.

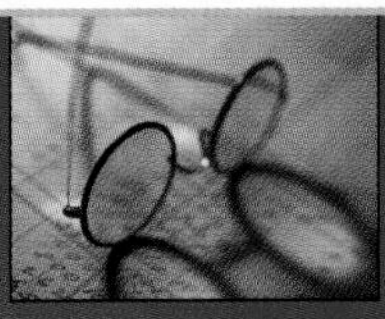

Cost Management in Practice 18.1

Benefits of Decentralization

We had a counter and 10 stools when we started. When winter came, we had to take out two stools to put in a heating furnace and almost went broke from the loss of revenue! But during the following year, I obtained the statewide franchise for a nationally known barbecue chain, and I expanded my menu.

At first, I did a little of everything—cooking, serving, bookkeeping, and advertising. I hired one full-time employee. There was little need for any formal management control system—I made all important decisions, and they were carried out. Soon we had eight outlets. I was still trying to manage everything personally. Decisions were delayed. A particular outlet would receive food shipments, but no one was authorized to accept delivery. If an outlet ran out of supplies or change, its employees had to wait until I arrived to authorize whatever needed to be done. With only one outlet, I was able to spend a reasonable amount of time on what I call high-level decision making—planning for expansion, arranging financing, developing new marketing strategies, and so forth. But with eight outlets, all of my time was consumed with day-to-day operating decisions.

Finally, I realized that the company had grown too big for me to manage alone. So I decentralized, setting up each outlet just like it was an independent operation. Now each outlet manager takes care of day-to-day operating decisions. This not only frees my time for more high-level decision making but also provides a better opportunity for the managers to learn about management, and it gives me a chance to evaluate their performance for promotion to higher management positions, which I intend to create soon. *Source: This example, based on the actual experience of a small company, came to light during an author's research.*

Benefits and Costs of a Decentralized Organization Structure

LO 2 List several benefits and costs of decentralization.

Most large organizations are decentralized. To better understand the purpose of a responsibility accounting system, it is helpful first to consider the benefits and costs associated with decentralization.

Benefits of decentralization. Decentralization has several positive effects:

- Managers of the organization's subunits are specialists. They have *specialized information and skills* that enable them to manage their departments most effectively.
- Allowing managers some autonomy in decision making provides *managerial training* for future higher-level managers. For example, the manager of a company-owned McDonald's restaurant might eventually be promoted to regional supervisor in the company.
- Managers with some decision-making authority usually exhibit more positive *motivation* than those who merely execute the decisions of others.
- Delegating some decisions to lower-level managers provides *time relief to upper-level managers,* enabling them to devote time to strategic planning.
- *Empowering* employees to make decisions draws on the knowledge and expertise of those closest to day-to-day operations.
- Delegating decision making to the lowest level possible enables an organization to give a *timely response* to opportunities and problems as they arise.

Costs of decentralization. Decentralization also has potential negative consequences:

- Managers in a decentralized organization sometimes have a *narrow focus* on their own subunit's performance rather than on the attainment of their organization's overall goals.
- As a result of this narrow focus, managers might tend to *ignore the consequences of their actions on the organization's other subunits.*

- In a decentralized organization, some tasks or *services might be duplicated* unnecessarily. For example, two departments in a decentralized university might both have a computer system (e.g., server and networked personal computers), when one might serve both departments at a lower cost.

The fundamental purpose of a responsibility accounting system is to help an organization reap the benefits of decentralization, while minimizing the costs. To this end, responsibility accounting systems are designed to foster goal or behavioral congruence throughout an organization.

Responsibility Accounting

LO 3 Describe the distinguishing characteristics of a cost center, a discretionary cost center, a revenue center, a profit center, and an investment center.

The purpose of a responsibility accounting system is to ensure that each manager and employee in an organization is striving to meet the overall goals set by top management. The basis of a responsibility accounting system is the designation of each subunit in the organization as a particular type of *responsibility center.* A **responsibility center** is a subunit in an organization whose manager is held accountable for specified financial (and nonfinancial) results of the subunit's activities. Five common types of responsibility centers are (1) cost, (2) discretionary cost, (3) revenue, (4) profit, and (5) investment.

responsibility center *is a subunit in an organization whose manager is held accountable for specified results of the subunit's activities*

cost center *is an organizational subunit whose manager is responsible for the cost of an activity for which a well-defined relationship exists between inputs and outputs*

discretionary cost center *is an organizational subunit whose manager is held accountable for costs, but the subunit's input-output relationship is not well specified*

Cost Center

A **cost center** is an organizational subunit, such as a work center or department, whose manager is responsible for the cost of an activity for which a well-defined relationship exists between inputs and outputs. Cost centers often are found in manufacturing operations where inputs, such as direct materials and direct labor, can be specified for each output. The production departments of manufacturing plants are usually cost centers. The concept has been applied in nonmanufacturing settings as well. In banks, for example, standards can be established for check processing, so check-processing departments might be cost centers. In hospitals, food-service departments, laundries, and laboratories often are set up as cost centers.

Discretionary Cost Center

The cost centers just described require a well-specified relationship between inputs and outputs for performance evaluation. A **discretionary cost center** is an organizational subunit whose manager is held accountable for costs, but the subunit's input-output relationship is not well specified. Examples of discretionary cost centers include legal, accounting, research and development, advertising, marketing, and numerous other administrative departments. Discretionary cost centers also are common in government and other nonprofit organizations whose budgets are used as a ceiling on expenditures. Managers typically are evaluated on bases other than costs. However, there usually are penalties for exceeding the budget ceiling.

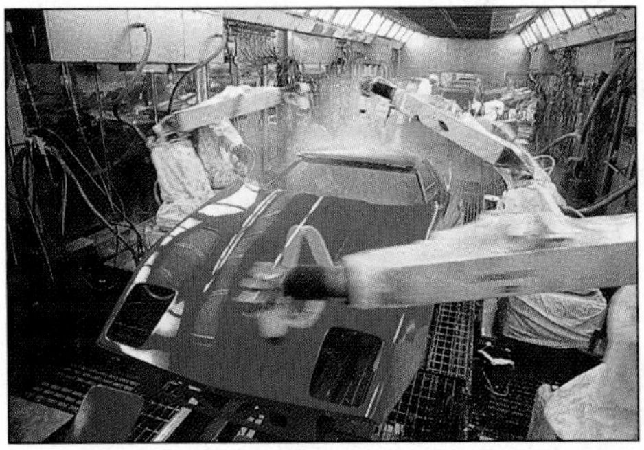

The painting department in this automobile factory is a cost center.

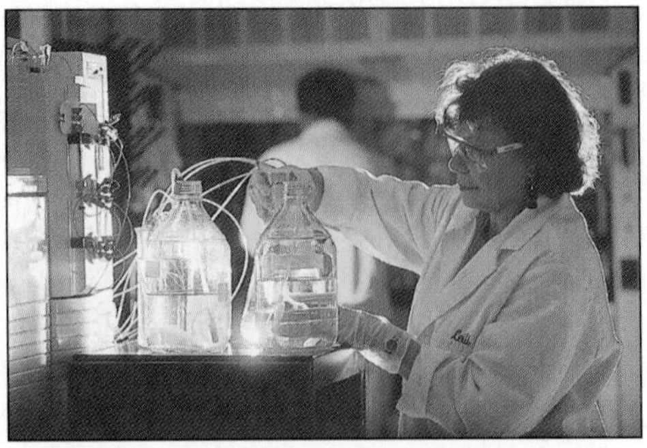

Research and development departments typically are discretionary cost centers. An example is this biotechnology R&D department.

American Airlines' reservations center in Tucson, Arizona, is a revenue center.

Fast-food restaurants, such as this Burger King in Ukiah, California, are profit centers.

This airplane assembly plant is an investment center.

Revenue Center

The manager of a **revenue center** is held accountable for the revenue attributed to the subunit. For example, the reservations department of an airline and the sales department of a manufacturer are revenue centers.

revenue center *is an organizational subunit whose manager is held accountable for the revenue attributed to the subunit*

Profit Center

A **profit center** is an organizational subunit whose manager is held accountable for profit. Since profit is equal to revenue minus expenses, profit-center managers are held accountable for both the revenue and expenses attributed to their subunits. An example of a profit center is a company-owned restaurant in a fast-food chain.

profit center *is an organizational subunit whose manager is held accountable for profit*

Investment Center

The manager of an **investment center** is held accountable for the subunit's profit *and the invested capital* used by the subunit to generate its profit. A division of a large corporation is typically designed as an investment center.[1]

investment center *is an organizational subunit whose manager is held accountable for the subunit's profit and the invested capital used by the subunit to generate its profit*

Illustration of Responsibility Accounting

Koala Camp Gear Company

OUTBACK OUTFITTERS

To illustrate the concepts used in responsibility accounting, we refer again to Koala Camp Gear Company. Margo Hastings' company prospered through its first decade. Hastings added additional products, and the firm grew rapidly. Then Hastings sold her company to Outback Outfitters, Ltd., a large Australian retailer specializing in outdoor apparel, camping gear, and other outdoor equipment. Hastings retired and now is basking in the sun in Fiji.

Outback Outfitters is a household name throughout Australia, New Zealand, and the United Kingdom. The retailer is known for its high-quality outdoor apparel and equipment and its experienced and helpful sales personnel. Outback Outfitters owns retail stores in all the major cities in Australia and New Zealand, as well as in London and Manchester in England, and Glasgow in Scotland. In addition to its retail outlets throughout the world, Outback operates a large mail-order sales operation based in Sydney. Outback's mail-order operation was modeled after the operation of L. L. Bean, the highly successful U.S. mail-order company based in Freeport, Maine.

[1]Although an important conceptual difference exists between profit centers and investment centers, the latter term is not always used in practice. Some managers use the term "profit center" to refer to both types of responsibility centers. Hence, when businesspeople use the term "profit center," they may be referring to a true profit center (as defined in this chapter) or to an investment center.

Exhibit 18–1

Organization Chart: Outback Outfitters, Ltd.

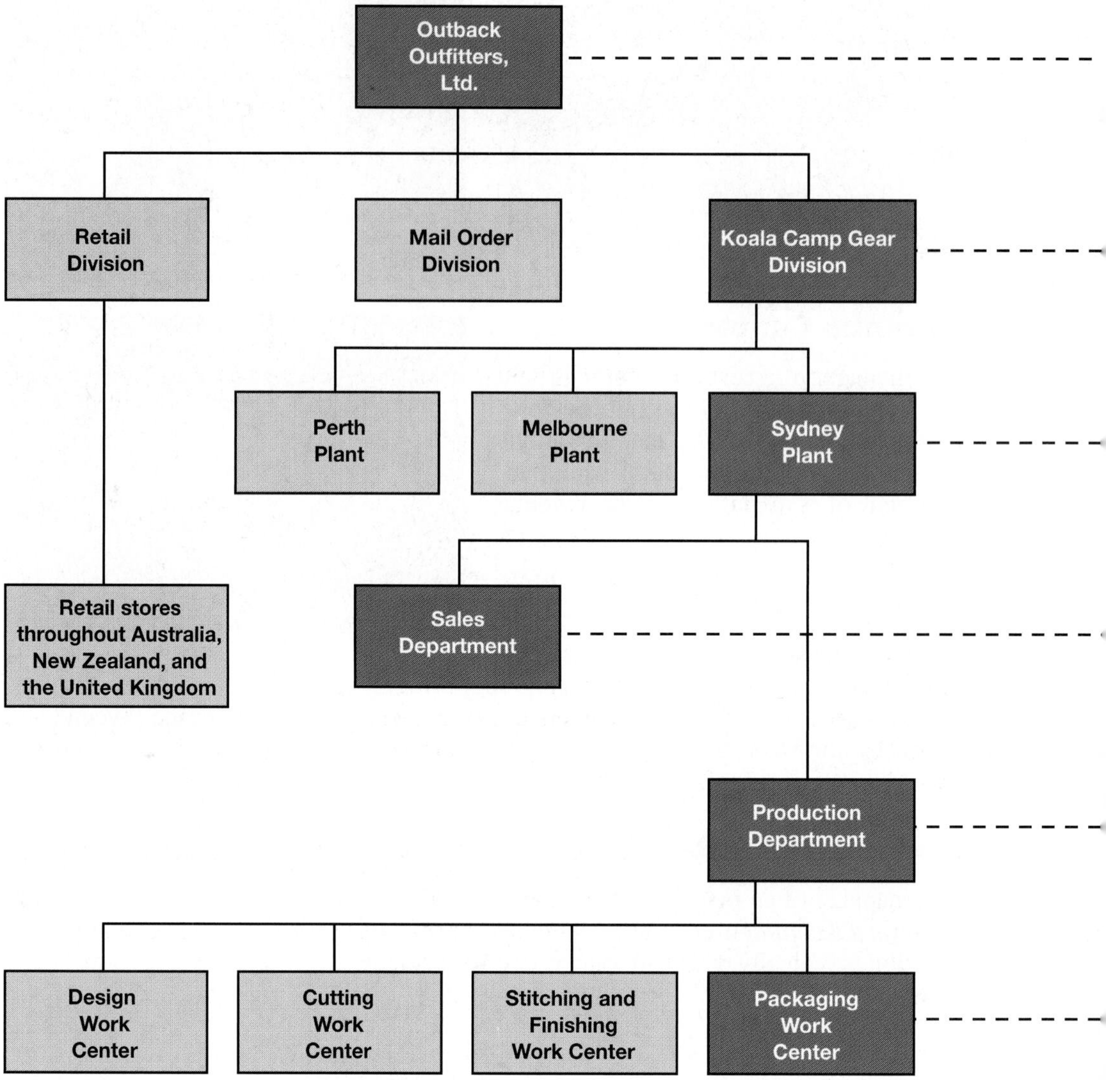

Jack Darwin, Outback's founder and CEO, had long thought that Outback should acquire a high-quality manufacturing company to provide Outback with its own private-label line of outdoor merchandise. Darwin had kept an eye on Koala Camp Gear Company for several years and, when the time seemed right, entered into negotiations with Hastings for the acquisition of the company she founded.

Outback Outfitters is now organized into three divisions. The Retail Division operates the company's sales outlets in Australia, New Zealand, and the United Kingdom. The Mail-Order Division, based in Sydney, is responsible for Outback's mail-order sales operation. The Koala Camp Gear Division manufactures a wide variety of camping gear and outdoor apparel. The camping gear retains the successful trade name Koala Camp Gear, and the division's outdoor apparel carries the trade name Wallaby Wear.

The Koala Camp Gear Division operates three manufacturing plants, and each plant has a sales department and a production department. The production department in each plant is organized into several work centers.

Exhibit 18–1 shows Outback Outfitter's organization chart, and Exhibit 18–2 depicts the firm's responsibility accounting system. As depicted in Exhibit 18–1, Outback has five levels in its organization chart: corporate, division, plant, department, and work center.

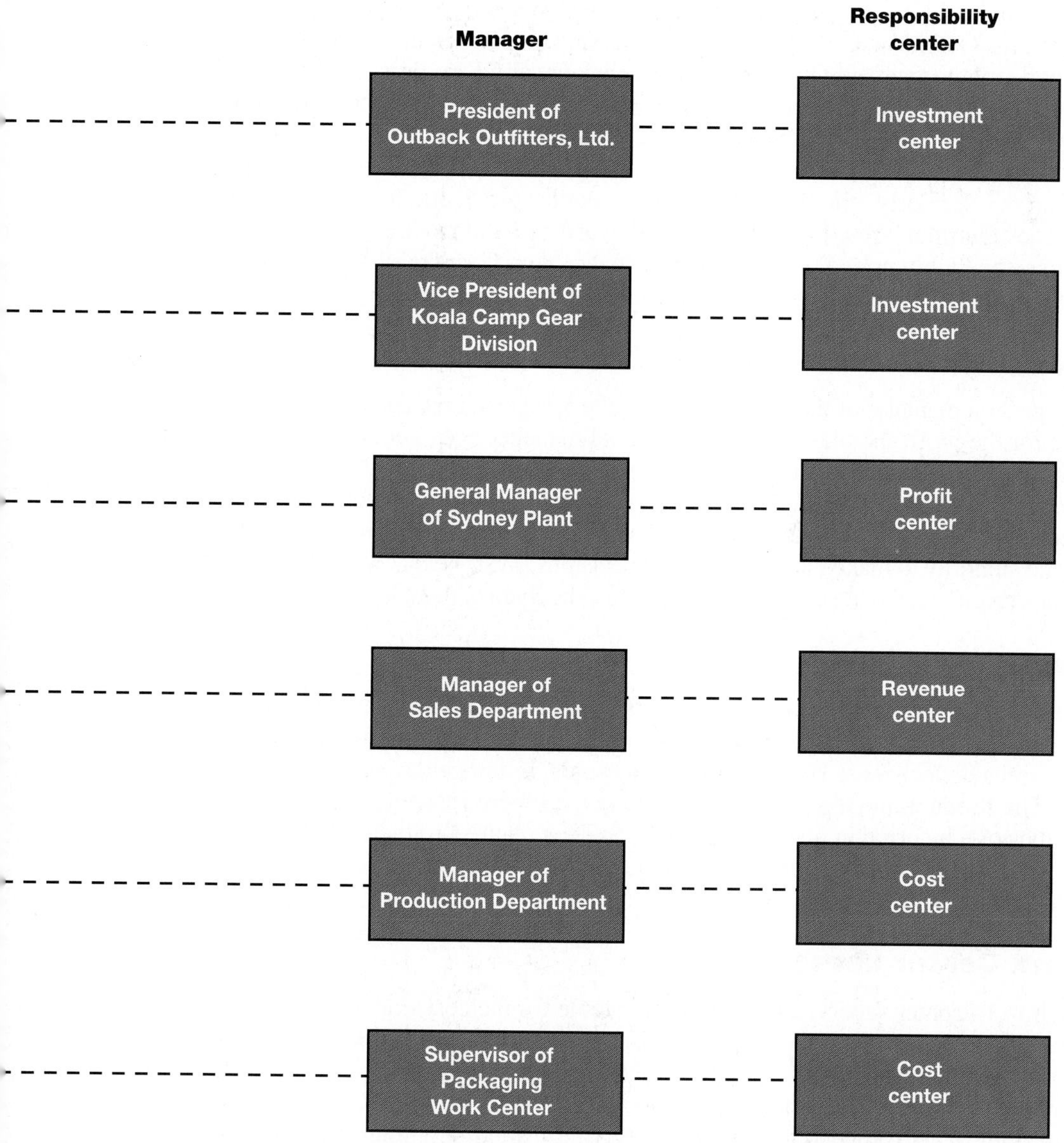

Exhibit 18-2

Responsibility Accounting System: Outback Outfitters, Ltd.

Corporate Level

The chief executive officer of Outback Outfitters, Ltd., is the company's president. The president, who is responsible to the company's stockholders, is accountable for corporate profit in relation to the capital (assets) invested in the company. Therefore, the entire company is an *investment center.* The president has the autonomy to make significant decisions that affect the company's profit and invested capital. For example, the president would make the final decision to build a new plant for the Koala Camp Gear Division.

Division Level

The vice president of Koala Camp Gear Division is accountable for the profit it earns in relation to the capital invested in this division. Hence, the Koala Division is an *investment center.* Its vice president has the authority to make significant investment decisions regarding the division, up to a monetary limit specified by Outback Outfitters' CEO. For example, the vice president could decide to buy new production equipment but could not buy a new plant.

All three division managers enjoy a great deal of autonomy in managing their business units. Outback's CEO, Jack Darwin, has said on more than one occasion, "I hired good people to manage Outback's three divisions, and I'm going to stay out of their way and let them do it." In keeping with Darwin's philosophy of decentralization for Outback Outfitters, the Retail Division and the Mail-Order Division are free to buy merchandise not only from the Koala Camp Gear Division but also from other manufacturers. Similarly, the Koala Division's goods are marketed not only through Outback Outfitter's retail sales operations but also to retailers throughout the world. Of course, the highly prized brand names of Koala Camp Gear and Wallaby Wear are imprinted only on the merchandise sold through Outback Outfitters.

Plant Level

The general manager of the Sydney plant in the Koala Camp Gear Division is accountable for the profit the plant earns. The general manager does not have the authority to make major investment decisions but is responsible for operational decisions. For example, the general manager hires the managers and supervisors in the plant, approves salary increases, and generally oversees the plant's operation. Since the plant's general manager has no authority to make major investment decisions, she is held accountable only for the plant's profit, not for the capital invested. Thus, the Sydney plant is a *profit center.*

Department Level

The Sales Department manager is held accountable for the sales made from the Sydney plant. He has the authority to set sales prices, hire sales personnel, and make other sales-related decisions. Thus, the sales department is a *revenue center.*

The Production Department is a *cost center,* whose manager is held accountable for the costs incurred in manufacturing the Sydney plant's products. He has the authority to make decisions about purchasing raw materials, hiring production employees, and so forth.

Work Center Level

LO 4 Prepare a performance report and explain the relationships between the reports for various responsibility centers.

Each work center supervisor is held accountable for the costs incurred in that particular work center. For example, the supervisor of the Packaging Work Center has the authority to make decisions about the choice of packaging materials, the scheduling of employees involved in packaging, and the packaging process itself. Hence, the Packaging Work Center is a *cost center.* The Cutting and Stitching and Finishing Work Centers are also cost centers. The Design Work Center, however, is a *discretionary cost center.* In the Design Work Center, the relationship between inputs and outputs is less definitive than in the other two work centers.

Performance Reports

performance report *shows the budgeted and actual amounts of key financial (or nonfinancial) results appropriate for the type of responsibility center involved*

management by exception *means that managers follow up on only the most significant variances between budgeted and actual results*

Each responsibility center's performance is summarized periodically on a **performance report,** which shows the budgeted and actual amounts of key financial results appropriate for the type of responsibility center involved. For example, a cost center's performance report concentrates on budgeted and actual amounts for various cost items attributable to the cost center. Performance reports also typically show the variance between budgeted and actual amounts for the financial results conveyed in the report. The data in a performance report help managers use *management by exception* to control an organization's operations effectively. **Management by exception** means that managers follow up on only the most significant variances between budgeted and actual results. This allows the managers to use their limited time most effectively.[2] The per-

[2]See the preceding two chapters for discussion of cost-management systems designed to facilitate management by exception.

Exhibit 18–3

Performance Report for Second Quarter: Cutting Work Center, Sydney Plant

Microsoft Excel - Exhibit 18-3

C12 = =+SUM(C6:C11)

	Budget 2nd Quarter	Budget Year to Date	Actual 2nd Quarter	Actual Year to Date	Variance* 2nd Quarter	Variance* Year to Date
Wages	$ 79,000	$ 167,000	$ 77,000	$ 168,000	$ 2,000 F	$ 1,000 U
Fabric	795,000	1,670,000	793,000	1,669,000	2,000 F	1,000 F
Manufacturing overhead:						
Unit level	60,000	140,000	61,000	144,000	1,000 U	4,000 U
Batch level	65,000	104,000	59,000	120,000	6,000 F	16,000 U
Product-sustaining level	31,000	87,000	35,000	72,000	4,000 U	15,000 F
Total expense	$ 1,030,000	$ 2,168,000	$ 1,025,000	$ 2,173,000	$ 5,000 F	$ 5,000 U

Sheet1 / Sheet2 / Sheet3

Ready

*F denotes favorable variance: U denotes unfavorable variance.

formance report for the Sydney plant's Cutting Work Center is displayed as the spreadsheet in Exhibit 18–3.

As the organization chart in Exhibit 18–1 shows, Outback Outfitters, Ltd., is a *hierarchy.* This means that each subunit manager reports to one higher-level manager, from the work center supervisor all the way up to the president and chief executive officer. Such an organization also has a hierarchy of performance reports since the performance of each subunit constitutes part of the performance of the next higher-level subunit. For example, the cost performance in the Sydney plant's Cutting Work Center constitutes part of the cost performance of the plant's production department.

Exhibit 18–4 shows the relationships between the March performance reports for several subunits of Outback Outfitters. The Cutting Work Center is the lowest-level subunit shown, and its performance report is the same as that displayed in Exhibit 18–3. The *total cost* line from the Cutting Work Center's performance report is included as one line in the performance report of the Production Department. Also included are the total cost figures for the department's other work centers. How is the *total cost* line for the Production Department used in the performance report for the Sydney plant? Follow the relationships in Exhibit 18–4, which are emphasized with arrows.

The hierarchy of performance reports starts at the bottom and builds toward the top, just as the organization structure depicted in Exhibit 18–1 builds from the bottom upward. Each manager in the organization receives the performance report for his or her own subunit in addition to the performance reports for the major subunits in the next lower level. For example, the general manager of the Sydney plant receives the reports for each of its departments, sales and production. With these reports, the plant's general manager can evaluate her subordinates as well as her own performance. This will help the general manager to improve the plant's performance, motivate employees, and plan future operations.

In addition to the financial information in the performance reports, managers at all levels in the organization make significant use of nonfinancial performance data. See Chapters 1 and 21 for discussions of such nonfinancial information and the balanced scorecard perspective on performance evaluation.

Budgets, Variance Analysis, and Responsibility Accounting

Notice that the performance reports in Exhibit 18–4 make significant use of budgets and variance analysis. Thus, the topics of budgeting, variance analysis, and responsibility accounting are closely interrelated. The flexible budget provides the benchmark against which actual revenues, expenses, and profits are compared. As you learned in

Exhibit 18–4 Performance Reports for Second Quarter: Selected Subunits of Outback Outfitters, Ltd. (all numbers in thousands)

	Budget*		Actual*		Variance†	
	Second Quarter	Year to Date	Second Quarter	Year to Date	Second Quarter	Year to Date
Company	$29,655	$63,562	$29,711	$63,565	$ 56 F	$ 3 F
Retail Division	$12,395	$26,415	$12,365	$26,325	$ 30 U	$ 90 U
Mail Order Division	5,000	11,200	5,100	11,300	100 F	100 F
Koala Camp Gear Division	12,260	25,947	12,246	25,940	14 U	7 U
Total profit	$29,655	$63,562	$29,711	$63,565	$ 56 F	$ 3 F
Koala Camp Gear Division						
Perth Plant	$ 6,050	$12,700	$ 6,060	$12,740	$ 10 F	$ 40 F
Melbourne Plant	2,100	4,500	2,050	4,430	50 U	70 U
Sydney Plant	4,110	8,747	4,136	8,770	26 F	23 F
Total profit	$12,260	$25,947	$12,246	$25,940	$ 14 U	$ 7 U
Sydney Plant						
Sales Department	$ 5,570	$11,780	$ 5,590	$11,815	20 F	35 F
Production Department	(1,460)	(3,033)	(1,454)	(3,045)	6 F	12 U
Total profit	$ 4,110	$ 8,747	$ 4,136	$ 8,770	$ 26 F	$ 23 F
Production Department						
Design Work Center	$ (20)	$ (40)	$ (22)	$ (39)	$ 2 U	$ 1 F
Cutting Work Center	(1,030)	(2,168)	(1,025)	(2,173)	5 F	5 U
Stitching and Finishing Work Center	(300)	(600)	(295)	(603)	5 F	3 U
Packaging Work Center	(110)	(225)	(112)	(230)	2 U	5 U
Total cost	$ (1,460)	$ (3,033)	$ (1,454)	$ (3,045)	$ 6 F	$ 12 U
Cutting Work Center						
Wages	$ (79)	$ (167)	$ (77)	$ (168)	$ 2 F	$ 1 U
Fabric	(795)	(1,670)	(793)	(1,669)	2 F	1 F
Manufacturing overhead:						
Unit level	(60)	(140)	(61)	(144)	1 U	4 U
Batch level	(65)	(104)	(59)	(120)	6 F	16 U
Product-sustaining level	(31)	(87)	(35)	(72)	4 U	15 F
Total cost	$ (1,030)	$ (2,168)	$ (1,025)	$ (2,173)	$ 5 F	$ 5 U

*Numbers without parentheses denote profit; numbers with parentheses denote expenses.

†F denotes favorable variance; U denotes unfavorable variance. For comparisons between budgeted and actual *profit* amounts, a favorable variance results when actual profit *exceeds* budgeted profit. For comparisons between budgeted and actual *cost* amounts, a favorable variance results when the actual cost is *lower than* the budgeted amount.

the preceding chapters, the use of a flexible budget is important so that appropriate comparisons can be made. Comparing the actual costs incurred in the Sydney plant's Cutting Department, for example, with the budgeted costs established for a different level of activity makes no sense.

The performance reports in Exhibit 18–4 also show variances between budgeted and actual performance. These variances often are broken down into smaller components to help management pinpoint responsibility and diagnose performance. Variance analysis, which was discussed in detail in the preceding two chapters, is an important tool in a responsibility accounting system.

Activity-Based Responsibility Accounting

Traditional responsibility accounting systems tend to focus on the financial performance measures of cost, revenue, and profit for the *subunits* of an organization. Contemporary cost-management systems, however, are beginning to focus more and more on *activities.* Costs are incurred in organizations and their subunits because of activities. *Activity-based costing (ABC)* systems associate costs with the activities that drive those costs. The database created by an ABC system, coupled with nonfinancial measures of operational performance for each activity, enables management to employ **activity-based responsibility accounting.**[3] Under this approach management's attention is directed not only to the cost incurred in an activity, but also to the activity itself. Is the activity necessary? Does it add value to the organization's product or service? Can the activity be improved? By seeking answers to these questions, managers can eliminate non-value-added activities and increase the cost effectiveness of the activities that do add value.

activity-based responsibility accounting *is a system for measuring the performance of an organization's employees and subunits, which focuses not only on the cost of performing activities but on the activities themselves*

Global Use of Responsibility Accounting

Research Insight 18.1

Responsibility accounting concepts are widely used in cost-management systems around the world. In Japan, for example, many firms emphasize the creation of profit centers (or pseudomicroprofit centers). "Treating work groups as profit centers as opposed to cost centers affects how workers view themselves and the pressure they place on themselves to perform. . . . Since a profit center manager is interested in both increasing revenues and decreasing costs, he or she is willing to take actions that could increase both costs and revenues or decrease costs and revenues, if the overall effect is to increase profits. . . . This shift in mind-set from reducing costs to increasing profits encourages workers to identify new ways to reduce costs, and thus revitalizes cost-management systems." Among the Japanese companies employing this approach are Kirin Breweries, Olympus Optical (a manufacturer of optoelectronic equipment, e.g., cameras, camcorders, microscopes), and Higashimaru Shoyu (a manufacturer of soy sauce).*

In Germany, "responsibility centers are the focal point of cost planning, cost control, and product costing. . . . German companies typically use more cost centers than U.S. companies. For example, Marquardt GmbH is a $150 million German company that manufactures electric and electronic switches. Although Marquardt has only three essential manufacturing stages, it uses about 100 cost centers. . . . Big plants of other companies can have 1,000 to 2,000 cost centers."†

In recent years, many companies in Germany, Austria, and Switzerland have adopted activity-based costing (or *prozesskostenrechnung*), and this has resulted in a move toward activity-based responsibility accounting.‡

*R. Cooper, *When Lean Enterprises Collide.* (Full citations to references are in the Bibliography.)

†B. Gaiser, "German Cost Management Systems."

‡Ibid.

How Does Responsibility Accounting Affect Behavior?

Responsibility accounting systems can influence employee behavior significantly. Whether the behavioral effects are positive or negative, however, depends on how an organization implements responsibility accounting.

Information or Blame?

The proper focus of a responsibility accounting system is *information.* The system should identify the individual in the organization who is in the best position to explain each particular event or financial result. The emphasis should be on providing that individual and higher-level managers with information to help them understand the reasons behind the organization's performance. When properly used, a responsibility accounting system *does not emphasize blame.* If managers believe they are beaten over the head with criticism and rebukes when unfavorable variances occur, they are unlikely to respond in a positive way. Instead, they will tend to undermine the system and view it with skepticism. But when the responsibility accounting system emphasizes its informational role, managers tend to react constructively and strive for improved performance.

[3]See C. J. McNair, "Interdependence and Control: Traditional vs. Activity-Based Responsibility Accounting." (Full citations to references are in the Bibliography.)

Is There Really Cost or Revenue Controllability?

Some organizations use performance reports that distinguish between controllable and uncontrollable costs or revenues. For example, the supervisor of the Cutting Work Center influences the hours and efficiency of the work center employees, but this manager probably cannot change the wage rates. A performance report that distinguishes between the financial results influenced by the supervisor and those the supervisor does not influence has the advantage of providing complete information to the supervisor, but the report recognizes that certain results are beyond his or her control.

Identifying costs as controllable or uncontrollable is not always easy. Many cost items are influenced by more than one person. The time frame also can be important in determining controllability. Some costs are controllable over a long time frame, but not within a short time period. To illustrate, suppose that the Cutting Work Center supervisor has signed a one-year contract with a local fabric supplier. The supervisor can influence the cost of fabric if the time period is a year or more but cannot control the cost on a weekly basis.

Motivating Desired Behavior

Organizations often use the responsibility accounting system to motivate actions that upper-level management considers desirable. Sometimes the responsibility accounting system can solve behavioral problems and promote teamwork. The real-world illustration in Cost Management in Practice 18.2 provides a case in point.

Cost Management in Practice 18.2

Teamwork and Responsibility Accounting System

The production scheduler in a manufacturing firm was frequently asked to interrupt production of one product with a rush order for another product. Rush orders typically resulted in higher costs because more production setups were required. Since the production scheduler was evaluated on the basis of costs, he was reluctant to accept rush orders. The sales manager, on the other hand, was evaluated on the basis of sales revenue. By agreeing to customers' demands for rush orders, the sales manager satisfied his customers. This resulted in more future sales and favorable performance ratings for the sales manager.

As the rush orders became more and more frequent, the production manager began to object. The sales manager responded by asking whether the production scheduler wanted to take the responsibility for losing a customer by refusing a rush order. The production scheduler did not want to be blamed for lost sales, so he grudgingly accepted the rush orders. However, considerable ill will developed between the sales manager and production scheduler.

The company's managerial accountants came to the rescue by redesigning the responsibility accounting system. The system was modified to accumulate the extra costs associated with rush orders and charge them to the sales manager's responsibility center rather than the production scheduler's center. The ultimate result was that the sales manager chose more carefully which rush-order requests to make, and the production manager accepted them gracefully. *Source: R. R. Villers, "Control and Freedom in a Decentralized Company."*

The responsibility accounting system can facilitate cooperation between different subunits in the organization, such as the production and sales departments.

Acceptance or rejection of a rush order is a cost-benefit decision.

Potential Costs of Accepting Rush Order	Potential Benefits of Accepting Rush Order
Disrupted production	Satisfied customers
More setups	Increased future sales
Higher costs	
Need to outsource*	

*See Chapter 7 for a discussion of issues pertaining to the effects of binding capacity constraints.

The problem described in the Cost Management in Practice 18.2 illustration developed because two different managers were considering the costs and benefits of the rush-order decision. The production manager was looking only at the costs while the sales manager was looking only at the benefits. The modified responsibility accounting system made the sales manager look at *both the costs and the benefits* associated with each rush order. Then the sales manager could make the necessary trade-off between costs and benefits in considering each rush order. Some rush orders were rejected because the sales manager decided that the costs exceeded the benefits. Other rush orders were accepted when the importance of the customer and potential future sales justified it.[4]

This example in Cost Management in Practice 18.2 illustrates how a well-designed responsibility accounting system can make an organization run more smoothly and achieve higher performance.

Modifying the Responsibility Accounting System

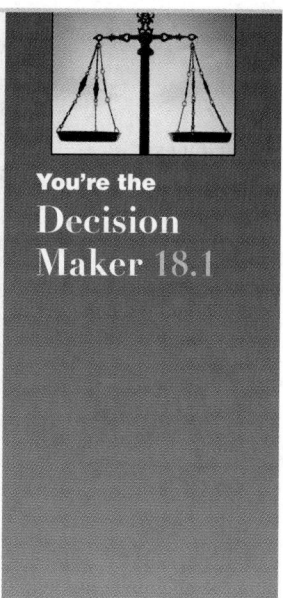

You're the **Decision Maker 18.1**

Consider the following scenario, which occurred in the Perth plant of Koala Camp Gear Company during the past year. Demand for the products made at the Perth plant had fallen in recent months, and the plant cut its production significantly. Many unskilled workers were temporarily laid off. Top management made a decision, however, not to lay off any highly skilled employees, such as inspectors and machinery operators. Management was concerned that these highly skilled employees could easily find new jobs elsewhere and not return when production returned to normal levels.

To occupy the skilled employees during the production cutback, they were reassigned temporarily to the maintenance department. Here they were performing general maintenance tasks, such as repainting the interior of the factory, repairing the loading dock, and building wooden storage racks for the warehouse. The skilled employees continued to receive their normal wages, which average $19 per hour. However, the normal wages for maintenance department employees average $12 per hour.

The supervisor of the maintenance department recently received a performance report indicating that his department's labor cost exceeded the budget by $19,130. The department's actual labor cost was approximately 70 percent over the budget. The department supervisor complained to the plant controller.

As the controller, how would you respond? Would you make any modification in the Perth plant's responsibility accounting system? If so, list the changes you would make. Explain your reasoning.

(Solutions begin on page 782.)

Performance Measurement in Investment Centers

LO 5 Compute an investment center's return on investment, residual income, and economic value added.

How do the top managers of large companies such as Microsoft and Exxon evaluate their divisions and other major subunits? The largest subunits within these and similar organizations usually are designated as *investment centers.* The manager of this type of

[4]Customer profitability analysis, which was covered in Chapter 6, can help in making a rush-order acceptance decision when key customers are involved. Also critical to the decision about accepting a rush order are considerations of the impact of accepting the order on production capacity. If accepting the rush order does not affect bottleneck processes, the organization will not incur an opportunity cost by producing the order.

responsibility center is held accountable not only for the investment center's *profit* but also for the *capital invested* to earn that profit. Invested capital refers to assets, such as buildings and equipment, used in a subunit's operations. In this section, we study the methods used to evaluate investment centers and the performance of their managers.[5]

OUTBACK OUTFITTERS

Refer again to Outback Outfitters' organization chart (Exhibit 18–1). The Mail-Order Division, Koala Camp Gear Division, and the Retail Division are investment centers. This responsibility center designation is appropriate because each division manager has the authority to make decisions that affect both profit and invested capital. For example, the Retail Division manager approves the overall pricing policies in the Retail Division's stores and has the autonomy to sign contracts to buy merchandise for resale. These actions influence the division's profit. In addition, the Retail Division manager has the authority to build new Outback Outfitters stores, rent space in shopping centers, or close existing stores. These decisions affect the amount of capital invested in the division.

The primary goals of any profit-making enterprise include maximizing its profitability and using its invested capital as effectively as possible. Cost managers use three different measures to evaluate the performance of investment centers: return on investment, residual income, and economic value added (EVA®, a registered trademark of Stern Stewart.) We illustrate each of these measures for Outback Outfitters, Ltd., using the following data from the most recent year.

	Mail-Order Division	Koala Camp Gear Division	Retail Division
Sales revenue	$350,000,000	$405,000,000	$960,000,000
Income	14,000,000	45,000,000	48,000,000
Invested capital	70,000,000	300,000,000	480,000,000

Return on Investment as a Performance Measure

return on investment (ROI) *for an investment center is its income divided by its invested capital*

Traditionally, the most common investment-center performance measure is **return on investment (ROI),** which is defined as follows:

$$\text{Return on investment (ROI)} = \frac{\text{Income}}{\text{Invested capital}}$$

The ROI calculations for Outback Outfitters' three divisions for the most recent year are:

	Income / Invested Capital	=	Return on Investment (ROI)
Mail-Order Division	$\frac{\$14,000,000}{\$70,000,000}$	=	20%
Koala Camp Gear Division	$\frac{\$45,000,000}{\$300,000,000}$	=	15%
Retail Division	$\frac{\$48,000,000}{\$480,000,000}$	=	10%

Note that the ROI calculation for each division considers *both divisional income and the capital invested* in the division. Why is this important? Suppose that each division were evaluated only on the basis of its divisional profit. The Retail Division reported a higher divisional profit than the Mail-Order Division. Does this mean that the Retail Division performed better than the Mail-Order Division? The answer is no; al-

[5]Recall that in practice the term *profit center* sometimes is used interchangeably with the term *investment center.* To be precise, however, the term *profit center* should be reserved for a subunit whose manager is held accountable for profit but not for invested capital.

though the retail division's profit exceeded the Mail-Order Division's profit, the Retail Division used much more invested capital to earn its profit. The Retail Division's assets are almost seven times the assets of the Mail-Order Division.

Considering the relative size of the two divisions, we would expect the Retail Division to earn a higher profit than the Mail-Order Division. The important question is not how much profit each division earned but how effectively each division used its invested capital to earn a profit.

Factors underlying ROI. We can rewrite the ROI formula as follows:

$$\text{Return on investment} = \frac{\text{Income}}{\text{Invested capital}} = \frac{\text{Income}}{\text{Sales revenue}} \times \frac{\text{Sales revenue}}{\text{Invested capital}}$$

Notice that the *sales revenue* term cancels out in the denominator and numerator when the two right-hand fractions are multiplied.

Writing the ROI formula in this way highlights the factors that determine a division's return on investment. Income divided by sales revenue is called the **sales margin,** a measure of the percentage of each sales dollar that remains as profit after all expenses are covered. Sales revenue divided by invested capital is called the **capital turnover;** it focuses on the number of sales dollars generated by every dollar of invested capital. The sales margin and capital turnover for Outback Outfitters' three divisions are calculated as follows:

sales margin *is income divided by sales revenue*

capital turnover *is sales revenue divided by invested capital*

	Sales margin	×	Capital turnover	= ROI
	$\frac{\text{Income}}{\text{Sales revenue}}$	×	$\frac{\text{Sales revenue}}{\text{Invested capital}}$	= ROI
Mail-Order Division	$\frac{\$14,000,000}{\$350,000,000}$	×	$\frac{\$350,000,000}{\$70,000,000}$	= 20%
Koala Camp Gear Division	$\frac{\$45,000,000}{\$405,000,000}$	×	$\frac{\$405,000,000}{\$300,000,000}$	= 15%
Retail Division	$\frac{\$48,000,000}{\$960,000,000}$	×	$\frac{\$960,000,000}{\$480,000,000}$	= 10%

The Retail Division's sales margin is 5 percent ($48,000,000 profit ÷ $960,000,000 sales revenue). Thus, each dollar of divisional sales resulted in a 5 cent profit. The division's capital turnover was 2 ($960,000,000 sales revenue ÷ $480,000,000 invested capital). Thus, each dollar of capital invested in the division's assets, such as store buildings, display shelves, checkout equipment, and inventory, generated $2 of sales revenue.

Improving a division's ROI. How could the Retail Division manager improve the division's return on investment? Since ROI is the product of the sales margin and the capital turnover, ROI can be improved by increasing either or both of its components. For example, if the Retail Division manager increases the division's sales margin to 7 percent while holding the capital turnover constant at 2, the division's ROI would climb from 10 percent to 14 percent, as follows:

LO 6 Explain how a manager can improve return on investment by increasing either the sales margin or capital turnover.

$$\text{Retail Division's improved ROI} = \text{Improved sales margin} \times \text{Same capital turnover}$$

$$14\% = 7\% \times 2$$

To bring about the improved sales margin, the Retail Division manager would need to increase divisional profit to $67,200,000 on sales of $960,000,000 ($67,200,000 ÷ $960,000,000 = .07). How could profit be increased without changing total sales revenue? There are two possibilities: (a) increase sales prices while selling less quantity, and thereby incurring lower cost of goods sold expense, or (b) decrease operating expenses. Neither of these is necessarily easy to do. In increasing sales prices, the division manager must be careful not to lose sales to the extent that total sales revenue declines. Similarly, reducing the expenses must not diminish product quality, customer service, or overall store atmosphere. Any of these changes could also result in lost sales revenue.

An alternative way to increase the Retail Division's ROI is to increase its capital turnover. Suppose that the Retail Division manager increased the division's capital turnover to 3 while holding the sales margin constant at 5 percent. The division's ROI would climb from 10 percent to 15 percent:

Retail Division's improved ROI	=	Same sales margin	×	Improved capital turnover
15%	=	5%	×	3

To obtain the improved capital turnover, the Retail Division manager would need to either increase sales revenue or reduce the division's invested capital. For example, the improved ROI could be achieved by reducing invested capital to $320,000,000 while maintaining sales revenue of $960,000,000—a very tall order. The division manager can lower invested capital somewhat by reducing inventories and can increase sales revenue by using store space more effectively. Reducing inventories might lead, however, to stockouts and lost sales, and crowded aisles could drive customers away.

Improving ROI is a difficult challenge, and it requires the expertise and constant attention of a skilled management team.

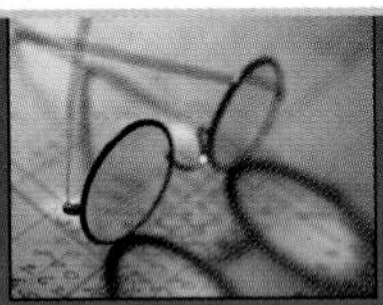

Cost Management in Practice 18.3

Electronic Data Interchange and Return on Investment

Many retailers and other companies have improved their return on investment through the use of *electronic data interchange (EDI)* and *Web-based shopping.* EDI is the direct exchange of data between organizations via a computer-to-computer interface. EDI is used to transmit such documents as purchase orders, shipping notices, receiving notices, invoices, and a host of other production-related data. This eliminates the need for paperwork, speeding up the flow of information and substantially reducing errors. Retailers have found EDI especially beneficial because it allows them to relay inventory restocking orders electronically to their suppliers instantaneously. Wal-Mart (*www.walmart.com*) was one of the first large retailers to install EDI capabilities. In fact, Wal-Mart gave deadlines to its suppliers for the switch to EDI. The suppliers had to either comply or lose the giant retailer's business. According to a senior Wal-Mart executive, "Our technology helps us buy the right merchandise at the right time, and have it in the right place at the right price."

Web-based shopping uses the Internet to enable customers to access a company's product information, make inquiries, and place orders 24 hours a day without requiring attention from a sales person. This technology allows the retailer to increase customer service while maintaining, or cutting, selling expenses.*Sources: F. Borthick and H. P. Roth, "EDI for Re-engineering Business Processes", and a Wal-Mart annual report.*

Residual Income as a Performance Measure

Although ROI has traditionally been the most popular investment-center performance measure, it has one major drawback. To illustrate, suppose that Outback's Koala Camp Gear Division manager is considering a major investment in computer-integrated manufacturing (CIM) equipment for all three of Koala's plants. The equipment will cost

$50 million. The investment in the CIM system is expected to result in annual operating savings of $5.5 million and will therefore increase divisional income by $5.5 million. Thus, the return on this new investment is 11 percent:

$$\frac{\text{Return on investment}}{\text{in new equipment}} = \frac{\text{Increase in divisional profit}}{\text{Increase in invested capital}} = \frac{\$5{,}500{,}000}{\$50{,}000{,}000} = 11\%$$

Now suppose that it costs Outback Outfitters 10 cents for each dollar of capital to invest in operational assets. What is the optimal decision for the Koala Camp Gear Division manager to make, *viewed from the perspective of the company as a whole?* Since it costs Outback Outfitters 10 percent for every dollar of capital, and the return on the investment in new equipment is 11 percent, an autonomous division manager should decide to buy the new equipment.

Now consider what is likely to happen. The Koala Camp Gear Division manager's performance is evaluated on the basis of his division's ROI. Without the new equipment, the divisional ROI is 15 percent ($45,000,000 divisional profit ÷ $300,000,000 invested capital). If he purchases the new equipment, his divisional ROI will decline:

Koala Camp Gear Division's Return on Investment

Without Investment in New CIM Equipment	With Investment in New CIM Equipment
$\frac{\$45{,}000{,}000}{\$300{,}000{,}000} = 15\%$	$\frac{\$45{,}000{,}000 + \$5{,}500{,}000}{\$300{,}000{,}000 + \$50{,}000{,}000} < 15\%$

Why did this happen? Although the investment in new equipment earns a return of 11 percent, which is higher than the company's cost of raising capital (10 percent), the return is less than the division's ROI without the equipment (15 percent). Averaging the new investment with that already in place in the Koala Camp Gear Division merely reduces the division's ROI. Since the division manager is evaluated using ROI, he will be reluctant to decide to acquire the new equipment.

The problem is that the ROI measure omits an important piece of information: It ignores the firm's cost of raising investment capital. For this reason, many managers prefer to use a different investment-center performance measure called *residual income* instead of ROI. Before turning our attention to residual income, however, let's consider the ethical issues involved in the scenario just described.

Ethical considerations. The Koala Camp Gear Division manager faces a tough decision regarding the purchase of the new equipment. The equipment will earn a return greater than Outback Outfitters' cost of acquiring investment capital. Thus, the purchase is in the best interest of the company as a whole. However, purchasing the equipment will lower Koala Camp Gear Division's ROI, and the division manager is evaluated on the basis of divisional ROI. Perhaps his promotion potential, salary increases, and bonuses are affected by the division's ROI, to say nothing of similar opportunities for his fellow managers in the Koala Camp Gear Division.

What should the division manager do? Ethical considerations suggest that the division manager should go ahead and purchase the CIM equipment, even though this decision could potentially jeopardize his prospects with the company, along with those of his divisional colleagues. The division manager, like all managers and employees, is supposed to be looking out for the best interests of the company and its owners. Nevertheless, anecdotal evidence, along with considerations of basic human nature, suggest that it might be unrealistic to expect such a manager to put the interests of corporate shareholders ahead of his own perceived interests, those of his family, and those of his colleagues and their families. What would you do?

Regardless of how you answer this rhetorical question, a very important point for our study of cost-management systems is just this: To the extent possible, it is best for all concerned if the performance evaluation system results in goal or (at least behavioral) congruence so that managers have an incentive to make decisions consistent with corporate goals.

residual income (RI) *of an investment center is its profit minus its invested capital times an imputed interest rate*

Computing residual income. An investment center's **residual income (RI)** is defined as follows:

$$\text{Residual income} = \text{Investment center's profit} - \left(\text{Investment center's invested capital} \times \text{Imputed interest rate} \right)$$

where the imputed interest rate is the firm's cost of acquiring investment capital.

Residual income is a dollar amount, not a ratio like ROI. It is the amount of an investment center's profit that remains (as a residual) after subtracting an imputed interest charge. The imputed interest charge is estimated and reflects the organization's minimum required rate of return on invested capital. The imputed interest rate should be the rate of return on investments of similar risk that is being forgone by Outback Outfitters, Ltd., as a result of tying up invested capital in the investment center being evaluated. In some firms, the imputed interest rate depends on the risk of the investment for which the funds will be used. Thus, divisions that have different levels of risk sometimes are assigned different imputed interest rates.

The residual income of Outback's Koala Camp Gear Division is computed here, both with and without the investment in the new CIM system. The imputed interest rate is 10 percent.

Koala Camp Gear Division's Residual Income

	Without Investment in New CIM Equipment		With Investment in New CIM Equipment	
Divisional profit		$45,000,000		$50,500,000
Less imputed interest charge:				
Invested capital	$300,000,000		$350,000,000	
× Imputed interest rate	× .10		× .10	
Imputed interest charge	→	30,000,000	→	35,000,000
Residual income		$15,000,000		$15,500,000

Investment in new equipment raises residual income by $500,000

Notice that the Koala Camp Gear Division's residual income will *increase* if the new equipment is purchased. What will be the division manager's incentive if he is evaluated on the basis of residual income instead of ROI? He will want to make the investment because that decision will increase his division's residual income. Thus, goal congruence is achieved when divisional performance is evaluated using residual income.

LO 7 Describe some advantages and disadvantages of return on investment and residual income as divisional performance measures.

Why does residual income facilitate goal congruence while ROI does not? Because the residual-income formula incorporates an important piece of data that is excluded from the ROI formula: the firm's minimum required rate of return on invested capital. To summarize, ROI and RI are compared as follows:

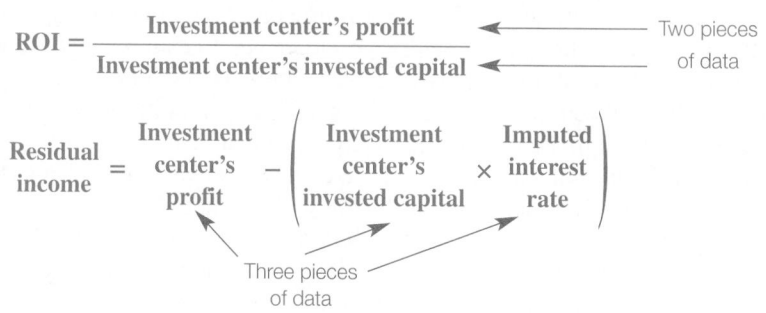

$$\text{ROI} = \frac{\text{Investment center's profit}}{\text{Investment center's invested capital}}$$

← Two pieces of data

$$\text{Residual income} = \text{Investment center's profit} - \left(\text{Investment center's invested capital} \times \text{Imputed interest rate} \right)$$

↑ Three pieces of data

Unfortunately, residual income also has a serious drawback: It should not be used to compare the performance of different-sized investment centers because it incorporates a bias in favor of the larger investment center. To illustrate, the following table compares the residual income of Outback's Mail-Order and Koala Camp Gear Divisions. Notice that the Koala Camp Gear Division's RI is considerably higher than that of the Mail-Order Division. This is entirely due to the much larger size of the Koala Division, as evidenced by its far higher invested capital amount.

Comparison of Residual Income: Two Divisions

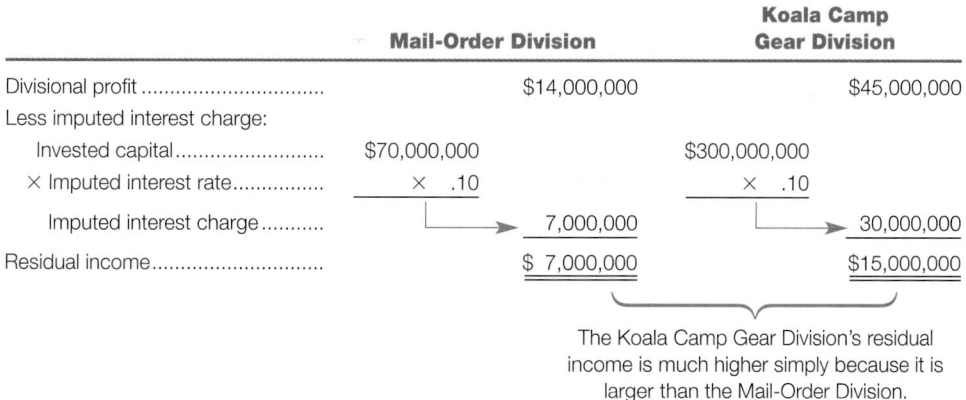

	Mail-Order Division		Koala Camp Gear Division	
Divisional profit		$14,000,000		$45,000,000
Less imputed interest charge:				
Invested capital	$70,000,000		$300,000,000	
× Imputed interest rate	× .10		× .10	
Imputed interest charge	→	7,000,000	→	30,000,000
Residual income		$ 7,000,000		$15,000,000

The Koala Camp Gear Division's residual income is much higher simply because it is larger than the Mail-Order Division.

In short, neither ROI nor RI provides a perfect measure of investment-center performance. ROI can undermine goal congruence. Residual income distorts comparisons between investment centers of different sizes. As a result, some companies routinely use both measures for divisional performance evaluation.

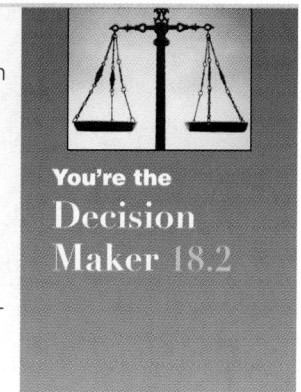

Evaluating the Success of a Division

One of Koala Camp Gear Division's suppliers, Queensland Fabrics Company, has two divisions, which reported the following results for the most recent year:

	Brisbane Division	Cairns Division
Income	$ 900,000	$ 200,000
Invested capital	6,000,000	1,000,000
ROI	15%	20%

Which was the most successful division for the year? Think carefully about this and back up your answer with a quantitative analysis.

(Solutions begin on page 782.)

You're the Decision Maker 18.2

Economic Value Added (EVA) as a Performance Measure

The most contemporary measure of investment center performance is **economic value added (EVA),** which is defined as follows:

$$\text{Economic value added} = \text{Investment center's after-tax operating profit} - \left[\left(\text{Investment center's total assets} - \text{Investment center's current liabilities}\right) \times \text{Weighted-average cost of capital}\right]$$

economic value added (EVA) *is an investment center's after-tax operating income minus its total assets (net of its current liabilities) times the company's weighted-average cost of capital*

Like residual income, the economic value added is a dollar amount. It differs from residual income in two important ways. First, an investment center's current liabilities are subtracted from its total assets. Second, the weighted-average cost of capital is used in the calculation.

Weighted-average cost of capital. Outback Outfitters, Ltd., has two sources of long-term capital: debt and equity. The cost of issuing debt to Outback Outfitters is the after-tax cost of the interest payments on the debt, considering the fact that the interest payments are tax deductible. The cost of Outback's equity capital is the investment opportunity rate of its investors, that is, the rate they could earn on investments of similar risk to that of investing in Outback Outfitters. The **weighted-average cost of capital (WACC)** is defined as follows:

weighted-average cost of capital (WACC) *is the average of the after-tax cost of debt capital and the cost of equity capital, weighted by the relative proportions of the firm's capital provided by debt and equity*

$$\text{Weighted-average cost of capital} = \frac{\begin{pmatrix}\text{After-tax}\\\text{cost of}\\\text{debt}\\\text{capital}\end{pmatrix}\begin{pmatrix}\text{Market}\\\text{value}\\\text{of debt}\end{pmatrix} + \begin{pmatrix}\text{Cost of}\\\text{equity}\\\text{capital}\end{pmatrix}\begin{pmatrix}\text{Market}\\\text{value of}\\\text{equity}\end{pmatrix}}{\text{Market value of debt} + \text{Market value of equity}}$$

The interest rate on Outback Outfitters' \$400 million debt is 9 percent, and the company's tax rate is 30 percent. Therefore, Outback's after-tax cost of debt is 6.3 percent [9% × (1–30%)]. Let's assume that the cost of Outback's equity capital is 12 percent. Moreover, the market value of the company's equity is \$600 million.[6] The following calculation shows that Outback Outfitters' WACC is 9.72 percent.

$$\text{Weighted-average cost of capital} = \frac{(.063)(\$400{,}000{,}000) + (.12)(\$600{,}000{,}000)}{\$400{,}000{,}000 + \$600{,}000{,}000} = .0972$$

Finally, Outback Outfitters has \$20 million in current liabilities, distributed as follows:

Division	Current Liabilities
Mail Order	$6,000,000
Koala Camp Gear	5,000,000
Retail	9,000,000

Now we can compute the economic value added (or EVA) for each of Outback's three divisions.

Division	After-Tax Operating Income (in millions)	–	[(Total Assets (in millions)	–	Current Liabilities (in millions))	× WACC]	=	Economic Value Added
Mail-Order	$14 × (1 – .30)	–	[($ 70	–	$6)	× .0972]	=	$ 3,579,200
Koala Camp Gear	$45 × (1 – .30)	–	[($300	–	$5)	× .0972]	=	$ 2,826,000
Retail	$48 × (1 – .30)	–	[($480	–	$9)	× .0972]	=	$(12,181,200)

The EVA analysis reveals that Outback's Retail Division is in trouble. Its substantial negative EVA merits the immediate attention of the management team. It could be that Outback should focus more of its resources on the mail-order and manufacturing businesses.

We return to the EVA measure in Chapter 21, which explores its relationship to managerial incentives and the balanced scorecard.

Measuring Income and Invested Capital

LO 8 Explain various approaches for measuring a division's income and invested capital.

The return-on-investment, residual-income, and economic-value-added (EVA) measures of investment-center performance all use profit and invested capital in their formulas. This raises the question of how to measure divisional profit and invested capital. This section illustrates various approaches to resolving these measurement issues.

[6]The *book value* of Outback Outfitters' equity is \$430 million, but that amount does not reflect the current value of the company's assets or the value of intangible assets such as the Koala Camp Gear and Wallaby Wear brand names.

Exhibit 18–5

Assets and Liabilities Associated with Koala Camp Gear Division

Assets*		
Current assets (cash, accounts receivable, inventories, etc.)		$ 34,000,000
Long-lived assets (land, buildings, equipment, vehicles, etc.):		
Gross book value (acquisition cost)	$304,000,000	
Less: Accumulated depreciation	64,000,000	
Net book value		240,000,000
Plant under construction		26,000,000
Total assets		$300,000,000
Liabilities*		
Current liabilities (accounts payable, salaries payable, etc.)		$ 5,000,000

*This is not a balance sheet, but a list of the average balances of certain assets and liabilities associated with the Koala Camp Gear Division during the year.

Invested Capital

We focus on Outback's Koala Camp Gear Division to illustrate several alternative approaches to measuring an investment center's capital. Exhibit 18–5 lists the assets and liabilities associated with the Koala Camp Gear Division. Notice that Exhibit 18–5 does not constitute a complete balance sheet. First, there are no long-term liabilities, such as bonds payable, associated with the Koala Camp Gear Division. Although Outback Outfitters has long-term debt, assigning portions of that debt to the company's individual divisions is not meaningful. Second, it has no stockholders' equity associated with the Koala Camp Gear Division. The owners of the company own stock in Outback Outfitters, not in its individual divisions.

Average balances. ROI, residual income, and EVA are computed for a period of time, such as a year or a month. Asset balances, on the other hand, are measured at a point in time, such as December 31. Since divisional asset balances generally change over time, we use average balances in calculating ROI, residual income, and EVA. For example, if the Koala Camp Gear Division's balance in invested capital was $290 million on January 1, and $310 million on December 31, we would use the average invested capital of $300 million in the ROI, residual income, and EVA calculations.

Should total assets be used? Exhibit 18–5 shows that during the most recent year the Koala Camp Gear Division had *average balances* of $34 million in current assets, $240 million in net long-lived assets, and $26 million tied up in a plant under construction. (Outback Outfitters is building a new high-tech plant in Brisbane to manufacture its new line of diving equipment.) In addition, Exhibit 18–5 discloses that the Koala Camp Gear Division's average balance of current liabilities was $5 million.

What is the division's invested capital? Consider several possibilities here:

- *Total assets.* The management of Outback Outfitters has decided to use *average total assets* for the year in measuring each division's invested capital. Thus, $300 million is the amount used in the ROI, residual income, and EVA calculations discussed earlier in this chapter. This measure of invested capital is appropriate if the division manager has considerable authority in making decisions about *all* of the division's assets, *including nonproductive assets.* In this case, the Koala Division's partially completed plant is a nonproductive asset. Since the division manager had considerable influence in deciding to build the new plant and is responsible for overseeing the project, average total assets provides an appropriate measure.
- *Total productive assets.* In other companies, top management direct division managers to keep nonproductive assets, such as vacant land or construction in progress. In such cases, the exclusion of nonproductive assets from the measure of invested capital is appropriate. Then *average total productive assets* are used to

measure invested capital. If Outback Outfitters had chosen this alternative, $274 million would have been used in the ROI, residual income, and EVA calculations (total assets of $300 million less $26 million for the plant under construction).

- *Total assets less current liabilities.* Some companies allow division managers to secure short-term bank loans and other short-term credit. In such cases, invested capital often is measured by *average total assets less average current liabilities.* This approach encourages investment-center managers to minimize resources tied up in assets and maximize the use of short-term credit to finance operations. If Outback Outfitters had used this approach, the Koala Camp Gear Division's invested capital would have been $295 million, total assets of $300 million less current liabilities of $5 million. (*Note:* Current liabilities are always subtracted from total assets for the measure of invested capital used in the EVA measure.)

Gross or net book value. Another decision to make in choosing a measure of invested capital is whether to use the *gross book value (acquisition cost)* or the *net book value* of long-lived assets. (Net book value is the acquisition cost less accumulated depreciation.) Outback Outfitters' management has decided to use the average net book value of $240 million to value the Koala Camp Gear Division's long-lived assets. If gross book value had been used instead, the division's measure of invested capital would have been $364 million, as the following calculation shows.

Current assets	$ 34,000,000
Long-lived assets (at gross book value)	304,000,000
Plant under construction	26,000,000
Total assets (at gross book value)	$364,000,000

Advantages are associated with both gross and net book value as a measure of invested capital.

Advantages of Net Book Value

- Using net book value maintains consistency with the balance sheet prepared for external reporting purposes. This allows for more meaningful comparisons of ROI measures across different companies.
- Using net book value to measure invested capital is also more consistent with the definition of income, which is the numerator in ROI calculations. In computing income, the current period depreciation on long-lived assets is deducted as an expense.

Advantages of Gross Book Value

- The usual methods of computing depreciation, such as the straight-line and the declining-balance methods, are arbitrary. Hence, they should not be allowed to affect ROI, residual-income, or EVA calculations.
- When long-lived assets are depreciated, their net book value declines over time. This results in a misleading increase in ROI, residual income, and EVA across time. The spreadsheet in Exhibit 18–6 illustrates this phenomenon for the ROI calculated on an equipment purchase under consideration by the Koala Camp Gear Division manager. Notice that the ROI rises steadily across the five-year horizon if invested capital is measured by net book value. However, using gross book value eliminates this problem. The use of an accelerated depreciation method instead of the straight-line method is even more pronounced in the increasing trend in ROI.

Dysfunctional behavioral effects. The tendency for net book value to produce a misleading increase in ROI over time can seriously affect the incentives of investment-center managers. Investment centers with old assets show much higher ROIs than investment centers with relatively new assets. This can discourage investment-center

Acquisition cost of equipment	$10,000,000
Useful life	5 years
Salvage value at end of useful life	0
Annual straight-line depreciation	$2,000,000
Annual income generated by asset (before deducting depreciation)	$3,000,000

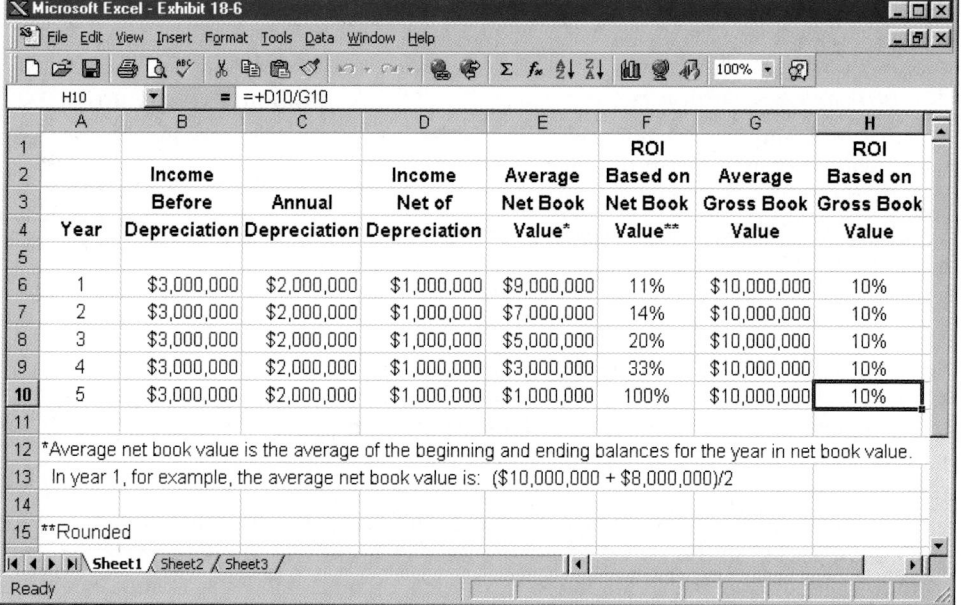

Exhibit 18–6

Increase in ROI over time (when net book value is used)

Microsoft Excel - Exhibit 18-6

H10 = =+D10/G10

Year	Income Before Depreciation	Annual Depreciation	Income Net of Depreciation	Average Net Book Value*	ROI Based on Net Book Value**	Average Gross Book Value	ROI Based on Gross Book Value
1	$3,000,000	$2,000,000	$1,000,000	$9,000,000	11%	$10,000,000	10%
2	$3,000,000	$2,000,000	$1,000,000	$7,000,000	14%	$10,000,000	10%
3	$3,000,000	$2,000,000	$1,000,000	$5,000,000	20%	$10,000,000	10%
4	$3,000,000	$2,000,000	$1,000,000	$3,000,000	33%	$10,000,000	10%
5	$3,000,000	$2,000,000	$1,000,000	$1,000,000	100%	$10,000,000	10%

*Average net book value is the average of the beginning and ending balances for the year in net book value.
In year 1, for example, the average net book value is: ($10,000,000 + $8,000,000)/2

**Rounded

Sheet1 / Sheet2 / Sheet3

Ready

managers from investing in new equipment. If this behavioral tendency persists, a division's assets can become obsolete, making the division uncompetitive.

Allocating assets to investment centers. Some companies control certain assets centrally, although these assets are needed to operate the divisions. Common examples are cash and accounts receivable. Divisions need cash to operate, but many companies control cash balances centrally to minimize their total cash holdings. Some large retail firms manage accounts receivable centrally. A credit customer of Outback Outfitters, for example, can make a payment at the local store, mail the payment to corporate headquarters, or use a credit card.

When certain assets are controlled centrally, some basis generally is chosen to allocate these asset balances to investment centers for measuring invested capital. For example, cash could be allocated based on the budgeted cash needs in each division or on the basis of divisional sales. Accounts receivable usually are allocated on the basis of divisional sales. Divisions with less stringent credit terms are allocated proportionately larger balances of accounts receivable.

Measuring Investment-Center Income

In addition to choosing a measure of investment-center capital, management must also decide how to measure an investment center's income. The key issue is controllability; the choice involves the extent to which uncontrollable items are allowed to influence the income measure. Exhibit 18–7 illustrates six different possibilities for measuring the income of Outback's Koala Camp Gear Division, using the division's revenue and expense data for the most recent year. All of the information in Exhibit 18–7 is derived from data

Exhibit 18–7

Divisional Income Statement: Koala Camp Gear Division

	Sales revenue	$405,000,000
	Unit-level, batch-level, product-line-level, and customer-level expenses	273,000,000
(1)	Divisional contribution margin	$132,000,000
	General and facility-level expenses controllable by division manager	87,000,000
(2)	Profit margin controllable by division manager	$ 45,000,000
	General and facility-level expenses traceable to division but controlled by others	15,000,000
(3)	Profit margin traceable to division	$ 30,000,000
	Common general and facility-level expenses, allocated from company headquarters	5,000,000
(4)	Divisional income before interest and taxes	$ 25,000,000
	Interest expense allocated from company headquarters	13,000,000
(5)	Divisional income before taxes	$ 12,000,000
	Income taxes allocated from company headquarters	3,600,000
(6)	Divisional net income	$ 8,400,000

collected by the division's cost-accounting system, but notice that some of the numbers require making judgments about controllability, which would be made by the corporate-level cost-management staff. For example, the corporate cost-management staff makes a judgment regarding how much of the division's general and facility-level expenses is controllable by the division manager and how much of these expenses is controllable by others.

Outback Outfitters' top management uses the *profit margin controllable by division manager,* $45 million, to evaluate the Koala Camp Gear Division manager. This profit measure is used in calculating ROI, residual income, and EVA. Some fixed costs traceable to the division have not been deducted from this $45 million amount, but the division manager cannot control or significantly influence these costs. Hence, they are excluded from the ROI calculation in evaluating the division manager. In calculating economic value added (EVA), the $45 million profit-margin amount is converted to an after-tax basis by multiplying by 1 minus the tax rate of 30 percent.

Managers versus investment centers. A distinction between an investment center and its manager is important. In evaluating the *manager's* performance, only revenues and costs that the manager can control or significantly influence should be included in the profit measure. The performance measure's overall objective is to provide incentives for goal-congruent behavior. No performance measure can motivate a manager to make decisions about the costs he or she cannot control. This explains the reliance of Outback Outfitters' top management on the profit margin controllable by the division manager to compute the manager's performance measure.

Evaluating the Koala Camp Gear Division as a viable economic investment is a different matter altogether. In this evaluation, traceability of costs rather than controllability is the issue. For this purpose, Outback's top management uses the profit margin traceable to the division to compute the divisional ROI, residual income, or EVA. As Exhibit 18–7 shows, this amount is $30 million.

Other profit measures. Some companies also use the other measures of divisional profit shown in Exhibit 18–7 (lines 4, 5, and 6). The rationale behind these divisional income measures is that all corporate costs must be covered by the operations of the divisions. Allocating corporate costs, interest, and income taxes to the divisions makes division managers aware of these costs.

Inflation and Deflation: Current Value versus Historical-Cost Accounting

Whether measuring investment-center income or invested capital, the impact of price-level changes should not be forgotten. During periods of inflation, historical-cost asset values soon cease to reflect the cost of replacing those assets. Therefore, some managers argue that investment-center performance measures based on historical-cost accounting are misleading. Yet surveys of corporate managers indicate that an accounting system based on current values would not alter their decisions. Most managers believe that measures based on historical-cost accounting are adequate when used in conjunction with budgets and performance targets. As managers prepare those budgets, they build their expectations about inflation (or deflation) into the budgets and performance targets.

Another reason for using historical-cost accounting for internal purposes is that it is required for external reporting. Thus, historical-cost data already are available, while installing current-value accounting would add substantial incremental costs to the organization's information system.

Measuring Income and Invested Capital: Summary

To summarize, the primary objective in choosing measures for the evaluation of investment centers and their managers is goal (or at least behavioral) congruence. Cost managers should design investment-center performance measures that reward managers for pursuing the goals of the overall organization.

You're the Decision Maker 18.3

Deciding between Alternative Merchandise Inventory Plans

The manager of the Outback Outfitters store in Adelaide is evaluated using ROI. Corporate headquarters requires an ROI of 10 percent of assets. The manager estimates that for the coming year revenue will be $260,000, and cost of goods sold will be $163,000. Operating expenses for this level of sales will be $26,000. Investment in the store assets throughout the year is $187,500 before considering the following proposal.

A representative of Tasmania Trading Company approached the Outback Outfitters manager about carrying its line of camp cookware. This line is expected to generate $75,000 in sales in the coming year at the Adelaide store with a cost of merchandise sold of $57,000. Annual operating expenses for this additional merchandise line are $8,500. To carry the line of goods, an inventory investment of $55,000 throughout the year is required.

As an alternative, Tasmania is willing to "floor plan" the merchandise so that the Adelaide store will not have to invest in any additional inventory. Tasmania's charge for floor planning would be $6,750 per year. The floor-planning arrangement with Tasmania would offer two advantages to Outback's Adelaide store. First, Tasmania rather than Outback Outfitters would maintain the $55,000 investment in the inventory. Outback would still incur the $57,000 annual cost-of-merchandise-sold expense and the $8,500 in additional operating expenses, plus the $6,750 charge for floor planning. Second, Tasmania would take charge of maintaining floor displays for its merchandise in the Adelaide store, as well as giving Outback's management advice on optimal merchandise placement within the store.

Assume that Outback's cost of capital is 10 percent.

a. What is the Adelaide store's expected ROI for the coming year if it does not carry Tasmania's cookware in the store?

b. What is the store's expected ROI if the manager invests in the Tasmania inventory and carries the cookware line?

c. What is the store's expected ROI if the manager elects to take the floor-plan option?

d. Would the manager prefer (a), (b), or (c)? Why?

(Solutions begin on page 782.)

Other Issues in Divisional Performance Evaluation

Alternatives to Return on Investment, Residual Income, and Economic Value Added

ROI, residual income, and EVA are short-run performance measures. They focus on only one period of time, yet an investment center is really a collection of assets (investments), each of which has a multiperiod life. To evaluate any one of these individual investments correctly requires a multiperiod viewpoint, which considers the timing of the cash flows from the investment. For example, an investment could start out slowly in its early years but could be economically justified by its expected high performance in later years. Any evaluation of the investment center in one particular year that ignores the long-term performance of its various investments can result in a misleading conclusion. Thus, single-period performance measures suffer from myopia; they focus on only a short time segment that slices across the division's collection of investments.

To avoid this short-term focus, some organizations downplay such measures as ROI, residual income, and EVA in favor of an alternative approach. Instead of relating profit to invested capital in a single measure, these characteristics of investment-center performance are evaluated separately. Actual divisional profit for a time period is compared to a flexible budget, and variances are used to analyze performance. The division's major investments are evaluated through a *postaudit* of the investment decisions.[7] For example, a particular investment could have been undertaken because of expected high performance several years into the future. When that time comes, a review will determine whether the project lived up to expectations.

Evaluating periodic profit through flexible budgeting and variance analysis, coupled with postaudits of major investment decisions, is a more complicated approach to evaluating investment centers. However, it does help management avoid the myopia of single-period measures such as ROI, RI, and EVA.

Importance of Nonfinancial Information

Although financial measures such as segment profit, ROI, RI, and EVA are widely used in performance evaluation, nonfinancial measures also are important. Manufacturers collect data on rates of defective products, airlines record information on lost bags and aircraft delays, and hotels track occupancy rates. The proper evaluation of an organization and its segments requires the definition and use of multiple performance measures. The balanced scorecard approach to performance evaluation is covered in Chapters 1 and 21. Moreover, Chapter 20 also discusses nonfinancial performance measures.

Performance Measurement in Nonprofit Organizations

Management control in a nonprofit organization presents a special challenge. These organizations are often managed by professionals, such as physicians in a hospital. Moreover, many people participate in a nonprofit organization at some personal sacrifice, motivated by humanitarian or public service ideals. Often, such people are less receptive to formal control procedures than their counterparts in business.

The goals of nonprofit organizations often are less clear-cut than those of businesses. Public service objectives can be difficult to specify with precision and even more difficult to measure in terms of achievement. For example, one community health center was established in an economically depressed area with three stated goals:

1. To reduce costs in a nearby hospital by providing a clinic for people to use instead of the hospital emergency room.
2. To provide preventive as well as therapeutic care and establish outreach programs in the community.
3. To become financially self-sufficient.

These objectives conflict somewhat since goal 2 does not provide revenue to the center but goals 1 and 3 focus on financial efficiency. Moreover, the health center was staffed with physicians who could have achieved much higher incomes in private practice. The management control tools described in this and the preceding two chapters can be used in nonprofit organizations. However, the challenges in doing so effectively often are greater.

---

[7]The evaluation of long-term investment decisions is covered in Chapter 14.

Need for New Performance Measures in a Changing Business Environment

Today's business environment is changing at a breakneck pace. The rampant pace of global competition, the speed of technological development, the rapidly changing demographics, and the incredible increase in information technology have resulted in a business environment that changes day to day, hour to hour. To remain competitive in such a dynamic environment, businesses must continually improve their management-information systems in general and their cost-management systems in particular. Managers must continually look for ways to improve all aspects of the cost-management system, including the performance measures used to evaluate organizational subunits and provide goal-congruent incentives to managers at all levels in the enterprise.

Research Insight 18.2

When New Performance Measures are Needed

Research suggests that the following warning signals often indicate the need for new performance measures in an organization.

- Organizational strategy has changed.
- Nonfinancial measures are nonexistent.
- No measures are associated with a critical process or success factor.
- A new technology, process, or organization structure has been adopted.
- Market share drops.
- Financial crisis occurs.
- Managers ignore or avoid reports.
- Managers are motivated to do non-value-added tasks.
- Performance measures monitor only costs.
- Measures are short-term in nature.
- Product has moved into new life cycle phase.
- Measures tell only "how we are doing," not "how we can do better."
- Functional groups are not working well together.
- Measures are extremely precise.
- Measures are only internally focused.
- Managers and employees cannot articulate critical success factors for the organization.

Source: P. McMann, "You May Need New Performance Measures When . . ."

Chapter Summary

Responsibility accounting systems are designed to foster *goal* or *behavioral congruence* among the managers in decentralized organizations. Each subunit in an organization is designated as a cost center, discretionary cost center, revenue center, profit center, or investment center. The cost-management team prepares a performance report for each responsibility center. These reports show the performance of the responsibility center and its manager for a specified time period. The most effective performance reports include both financial and nonfinancial information pertaining to performance.

To use responsibility accounting effectively, the emphasis must be on information rather than blame. The intent should be to provide managers with information to help them better manage their subunits. Responsibility accounting systems can bring about desired behavior, such as reducing the number of rush orders in a manufacturing company.

The three most common measures of investment-center performance are return on investment (ROI), residual income (RI), and economic value added (EVA). Each of these performance measures relates an investment center's income to the capital invested to earn it. Residual income and EVA have the additional advantage of incorporating the organization's cost of acquiring capital in the performance measure. An investment center's ROI may be improved by increasing either the sales margin or capital turnover. ROI, residual income, and EVA all require the measurement of a division's income and invested capital, and the methods for making these measurements vary in practice.

The primary criterion for judging the effectiveness of performance measures for responsibility-center managers is the extent to which the measures promote goal or behavioral congruence.

Key Terms

For each term's definition, refer to the indicated page or turn to the glossary at the end of the text.

activity-based responsibility accounting, 765
behavioral congruence, 756
capital turnover, 769
centralization, 756
cost center, 758
decentralization, 756
discretionary cost center, 758
economic value added (EVA), 773
goal congruence, 756
investment center, 759
management by exception, 762
performance report, 762
profit center, 759
residual income (RI), 772
responsibility accounting, 756
responsibility center, 758
return on investment (ROI), 768
revenue center, 759
sales margin, 769
weighted-average cost of capital (WACC), 774

Meeting the Cost-Management Challenges

1. When companies grow larger, as typified by the acquisition described in Outback Outfitters' press release, how should they manage operations? What are the benefits and costs of decentralization?

Several benefits of decentralization follow:

- The managers of an organization's subunits have specialized information and skills that enable them to manage their departments most effectively.
- Allowing managers autonomy in decision making provides managerial training for future higher-level managers.
- Managers with some decision-making authority usually exhibit more positive motivation than those who merely execute the decisions of others.
- Delegating some decisions to lower-level managers provides time relief to upper-level managers.
- Delegating decision making to the lowest level possible enables an organization to give a timely response to opportunities and problems.

Several costs of decentralization are as follows:

- Managers in a decentralized organization might have a narrow focus on their own unit's performance.
- Managers might tend to ignore the consequences of their actions on the organization's other subunits.
- In a decentralized organization, some tasks or services might be duplicated unnecessarily.

2. How could a responsibility accounting system foster goal or behavioral congruence for Outback Outfitters?

A responsibility accounting system fosters goal or behavioral congruence by establishing the performance criteria by which to evaluate each manager. Development of performance measures and standards for those measures can help to ensure that managers are striving to meet goals that support the organization's overall objectives.

3. What are the major types of responsibility accounting centers?

The major types of responsibility accounting centers are cost centers, discretionary cost centers, revenue centers, profit centers, and investment centers.

4. What is the key feature of activity-based responsibility accounting?

Under activity-based responsibility accounting, management's attention is directed to activities rather than focused primarily on cost, revenue, and profit measures of subunit performance. Activity-based responsibility accounting uses the database generated by an activity-based costing system coupled with nonfinancial measures of operational performance for key activities. This approach can help management eliminate non-value-added activities and improve the cost effectiveness of activities that do add value to the organization's product or service.

5. How is investment center performance typically measured?

The three commonly used measures of investment center performance are return on investment (ROI), residual income (RI), and economic value added (EVA).

Solutions to You're the Decision Maker

18.1 Modifying the Responsibility Accounting System p. 767

The maintenance department should not be charged for the excess wages of the skilled employees who are temporarily assigned to it. Modifications should be made in the responsibility accounting system as follows: (1) The maintenance department should be charged only the normal wages for maintenance employees, $12 per hour. (2) The additional $7 per hour ($19 − $12) should be charged to a top-management-level account since top management made the decision to keep these employees on the payroll.

18.2 Evaluating the Success of a Division p. 773

The answer to the question as to which division is the most successful depends on the firm's cost of capital. To see this relationship, compute the residual income (RI) for each division using various imputed interest rates.

a. Imputed interest rate of 10%:

	Brisbane Division	Cairns Division
Divisional profit	$900,000	$200,000
Less: Imputed interest charge:		
$6,000,000 × 10%	600,000	
$1,000,000 × 10%		100,000
Residual income	$300,000	$100,000

b. Imputed interest rate of 14%:

	Brisbane Division	Cairns Division
Divisional profit	$900,000	$200,000
Less: Imputed interest charge:		
$6,000,000 × 14%	840,000	
$1,000,000 × 14%		140,000
Residual income	$ 60,000	$ 60,000

c. Imputed interest rate of 15%:

	Brisbane Division	Cairns Division
Divisional profit	$900,000	$200,000
Less: Imputed interest charge:		
$6,000,000 × 15%	900,000	
$1,000,000 × 15%		150,000
Residual income	$ 0	$ 50,000

If the firm's cost of capital is 10 percent, the Brisbane division has a higher residual income than the Cairns division. With a cost of capital of 15 percent, the Cairns division has a higher residual income. At a 14 percent cost of capital, the divisions have the same residual income. This scenario illustrates one of the advantages of RI over ROI. Since the RI calculation includes an imputed interest charge reflecting the firm's cost of capital, it gives a more complete picture of divisional performance.

18.3 Deciding between Alternative Merchandise Inventory Plans p. 779

a. and b. Income statements summarizing the alternatives are as follows:

	Regular Merchandise	Camp Cookware	Total
Revenue	$260,000	$75,000	$335,000
Cost of goods sold	163,000	57,000	220,000
Gross margin	$ 97,000	$18,000	$115,000
Operating expenses	26,000	8,500	34,500
Operating profit	$ 71,000	$ 9,500	$ 80,500
Investment	$187,500	$55,000	$242,500
ROI	37.87%	17.27%	33.20%

Although the camp cookware provides a higher return than the cost of capital, it lowers the status quo ROI.

c. If the floor plan is used, the investment base will remain at $187,500 because Outback will not have to carry the additional $55,000 inventory investment for the Tasmania product line. Operating profits will equal $80,500 minus the floor-plan charge of $6,750 for a net profit of $73,750. The ROI will be 39.33 percent ($73,750 ÷ $187,500).

d. The manager would prefer the floor plan because it would raise the store's ROI above the current ROI of 37.87 percent.

Review Questions

18.1 Why is goal congruence important to an organization's success?

18.2 Could the type of budget items for which some responsibility centers are accountable differ? That is, might some responsibility centers be responsible only for costs, some only for revenues, and some for both? Give examples.

18.3 Accounting is supposed to provide a neutral, relevant, and objective measure of performance. Why would problems arise when applying accounting measures in the context of performance evaluation?

18.4 Suppose you overheard this comment, "This whole problem of measuring performance for segment managers using accounting numbers is so much hogwash. We pay our managers a good salary and expect them to do the best possible job. At least with our system, there is no incentive to play with the accounting data." Does the comment make sense?

18.5 Define and give examples of the following terms: *cost center, discretionary cost center, revenue center, profit center,* and *investment center.*

18.6 What are the advantages of using an ROI-type measure rather than a division's profit as a performance evaluation technique?

18.7 The production department manager has just received a responsibility report showing a substantial unfavorable variance for overtime premium. The manager objects to the inclusion of this variance because the acceptance of a large rush order by the sales department caused the overtime. To whom should this variance be charged?

18.8 Under what conditions does the use of ROI measures inhibit a division manager's goal-congruent decision making?

18.9 Create an example showing the calculation of residual income. What information is used in computing residual income that is not used in computing ROI?

18.10 Why do some companies use gross book value instead of net book value to measure a division's invested capital?

18.11 Define the term *economic value added (EVA).* How does it differ from residual income?

18.12 Describe an alternative to using ROI, residual income, or EVA to measure investment-center performance.

Critical Analysis

18.13 Under what circumstances is it appropriate to change Outback Outfitters' Sydney plant from a profit center to an investment center?

18.14 "Performance reports based on controllability are impossible. Nobody really *controls* anything in an organization!" Do you agree or disagree? Explain your answer.

18.15 Central management of Adler, Inc., evaluated divisional performance using residual income (RI) measures. The division managers were ranked according to the RI in each division. All division managers with residual income in the upper half of the ranking received a bonus. The bonus amount was in proportion to the RI amount. No bonus was paid to managers in the lower half of the ranking. What biases might arise in this system?

18.16 Explain why distinguishing between investment centers and their managers is important in performance evaluation.

18.17 Explain how the manager of the automobile division of an insurance company could improve her division's ROI.

18.18 Management of division A is evaluated based on residual income measures. The division can either rent or buy a certain asset. Might the performance evaluation technique have an impact on the rent-or-buy decision? Why or why not?

18.19 What is the chief disadvantage of ROI as an investment-center performance measure? How does the residual-income measure eliminate this disadvantage?

18.20 Distinguish between the following measures of invested capital and briefly explain when each should be used: (1) total assets, (2) total productive assets, and (3) total assets less current liabilities.

18.21 Bleak Prospects, Inc., found that its market share was slipping. Bleak encouraged division managers to maximize ROI and make decisions consistent with that goal. Nonetheless, frequent customer complaints resulted in lost business. Moreover, Bleak depended on an established product line and was unable to find new products for expansion while its competitors seemed to be able to generate new products almost yearly. What would you suggest Bleak Products' management do to improve its situation?

18.22 Why does ROI or residual income typically rise across time in a division? What undesirable behavioral implications could this phenomenon have?

Exercises

Exercise 18.23
Designating Responsibility Centers
(LO 1, 3)

For each of the following organizational subunits, indicate the type of responsibility center that is most appropriate.

a. An orange juice factory operated by a large orange grower.
b. The College of Engineering at a large state university.
c. The European Division of a multinational manufacturing company.
d. The outpatient clinic in a profit-oriented hospital.
e. The Mayor's Office in a large city.
f. A movie theater in a company that operates a chain of theaters.
g. A radio station owned by a large broadcasting network.
h. The claims department in an insurance company.
i. The ticket sales division of a major airline.
j. A bottling plant of a soft-drink company.

Exercise 18.24
Return on Investment
(LO 7, 8)

Read "What's a New Economy without Research?" *Fortune,* May 15, 2000, by Stewart Alsop. The author reviews corporate projects that have given rise to such items as the laser printer, the graphical word processor, the computer mouse, and the main protocol for the World Wide Web. Much research was done under conditions that did not demand an intermediate return on investment. Corporations today are interested in developing new products for which technology is already understood, thus avoiding research and development expenses. The corporate interest in research has waned.

Required

Why would capital investment on research and development activities tend to provide a lower return on investment than other activities?

Exercise 18.25
Performance Report; Hotel
(LO 4)

The following data pertain to the Nantucket Inn for the month of July. The inn's organization chart shows that the food and beverage department has the following subunits: banquets and catering, restaurants, and kitchen.

	Flexible Budget: July (in thousands)*	Actual Results: July (in thousands)*
Banquets and catering	$ 650	$ 658
Restaurants	1,800	1,794
Kitchen staff wages	(85)	(86)
Food	(690)	(690)
Paper products	(125)	(122)
Unit-level (variable) overhead in kitchen	(75)	(78)
Facility-level (fixed) overhead in kitchen	(90)	(93)

*Numbers without parentheses denote profit; numbers with parentheses denote expenses.

Required

Prepare a July performance report for Nantucket Inn's food and beverage department similar to the lower portion of Exhibit 18–4, which relates to Koala's Production Department and Cutting Work Center. The report should have three numerical columns instead of six with headings analogous to those in Exhibit 18–4. (Your report will not have any year-to-date columns.) Your performance report should cover only the food and beverage department and the kitchen. Draw arrows to show the relationships among the numbers in the report. Refer to Exhibit 18–4 for guidance.

Exercise 18.26
Responsibility Accounting; Equipment Breakdown
(LO 1)

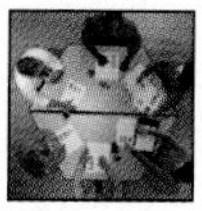
Team

Communication

As a group, prepare a report to the class regarding how a responsibility accounting system should handle each of the following scenarios.

a. Department A manufactures a component, which Department B then uses. Department A recently experienced a machine breakdown that held up production of the component. As a result, Department B was forced to curtail its own production, thereby incurring large costs of idle time. An investigation revealed that Department A's machinery had not been properly maintained.

b. Refer to the scenario in requirement (a), but suppose that the investigation revealed that the machinery in Department A had been properly maintained.

Exercise 18.27
ROI versus Residual Income
(LO 5, 7)

Global

Spreadsheet

Rosario Company manufactures clothing in Buenos Aires, Argentina. The company's outer wear division is considering the acquisition of a new asset that will cost 360,000 pesos and have a cash flow of 140,000 pesos per year for each of the five years of its life. Depreciation is computed on a straight-line basis with no salvage value.*

*Several countries call their currency the *peso*. On the day this exercise was written, Argentina's peso was worth 1.0002 U.S. dollars.

Required

a. What is the ROI for each year of the asset's life if the division uses beginning-of-year asset balances and net book value for the computation?

b. What is the residual income each year if the imputed interest rate is 25 percent?

Exercise 18.28
Impact of New Project on Performance Measures
(LO 5)

A division manager is considering the acquisition of a new asset that will increase the division's profit. The division already earns $390,000 on assets of $1.3 million. The company's cost of capital is 20 percent. The new investment has a cost of $225,000 and will have a yearly cash flow of $84,000. The asset will be depreciated using the straight-line method over a six-year life and is expected to have no salvage value. Division performance is measured using ROI with beginning-of-year net book values in the denominator.

Required

a. What is the division ROI before acquisition of the new asset?

b. What is the division ROI in the first year after acquisition of the new asset?

Exercise 18.29
Impact of Purchasing versus Leasing on Performance Measures
(LO 5, 7)

The division manager in the preceding exercise has the option to lease the asset on a year-to-year lease for $74,000 per year. All depreciation and other tax benefits would accrue to the lessor.

Required

a. What is the division ROI if it leases the asset?

b. What is the division's residual income before considering the project?

c. What is the division's residual income if the asset is purchased?

d. What is the division's residual income if the asset is leased?

Exercise 18.30
Alternative Measures of Division Performance
(LO 5, 7)

Team

The following data are available for the two divisions of National Products, Inc.

	East Division	West Division
Division operating profit	$ 35,000	$195,000
Division investment	100,000	750,000

The cost of capital for the company is 20 percent.

Required

a. As a group, determine which division had the better performance. Explain your answer.

b. Would your evaluation change if the company's cost of capital were 25 percent? Why?

Exercise 18.31
ROI and Residual Income; Annual Reports; Use of Internet
(LO 5, 7)

Internet

Select one of the following companies (or any company of your choosing), and use the Internet to explore its most recent annual report.

American Airlines (*www.americanair.com*)
Deere and Company (*www.deere.com*)
Firestone Tire & Rubber (*www.firestone.com*)
IBM (*www.ibm.com*)
Pizza Hut (*www.pizzahut.com*)
Ramada Inn (*www.ramada.com*)
Wal-Mart (*www.wal-mart.com*)

Required

a. Calculate the company's overall return on investment (ROI). Also, calculate the company's overall residual income. (Assume an imputed interest rate of 10 percent.) List and explain any assumptions you make.

b. Does the company include a calculation of ROI in its on-line annual report? If it does, do your calculations agree with those of the company? If not, what are some possible explanations?

Exercise 18.32
Compare ROI Using Historical Cost Net Book Value versus Gross Book Value
(LO 5, 8)

Aries Division of California Metals Corporation just started operations. It purchased depreciable assets costing $2 million and having an expected life of four years, after which the assets can be salvaged for $400,000. In addition, the division has $2 million in assets that are not depreciable. After four years, the division will have $2 million available from these nondepreciable assets. In short, the division has invested $4 million in assets that will last four years, after which it will salvage $2.4 million, so annual depreciation is $400,000. Annual cash-operating flows are $1,000,000. In computing ROI, this division uses end-of-year asset values in the denominator. Depreciation is computed on a straight-line basis, recognizing the salvage values noted.

Required

a. Compute ROI using net book value for each year.

b. Compute ROI using gross book value for each year.

c. Assume the same data except that the division uses beginning-of-year asset values in the denominator for computing ROI.

   (1) Compute ROI using net book value.

   (2) Compute ROI using gross book value.

   (3) How different is the ROI computed using end-of-year asset values from the ROI using beginning-of-year values?

Exercise 18.33
Calculation of Weighted-Average Cost of Capital for EVA
(LO 5)

Tribeca Construction Associates, a real estate developer and building contractor in Manhattan, has two sources of long-term capital: debt and equity. Tribeca's cost of issuing debt is the after-tax cost of the interest payments on the debt, considering the fact that the interest payments are tax deductible. Tribeca's cost of equity capital is the investment opportunity rate of Tribeca's investors, that is, the rate they could earn on investments of similar risk to that of investing in Tribeca Construction Associates. The interest rate on Tribeca's $60 million of long-term debt is 10 percent, and the company's tax rate is 40 percent. Tribeca's cost of equity capital is 15 percent. Moreover, its market value (and book value) of equity is $90 million.

Required

Calculate Tribeca Construction Associates' weighted-average cost of capital.

Exercise 18.34
Economic Value Added; Continuation of Preceding Exercise
(LO 5)

Refer to the data in the preceding exercise for Tribeca Construction Associates. The company has two divisions, real estate and construction. The divisions' total assets, current liabilities, and before-tax operating income for the most recent year follow:

Division	Total Assets	Current Liabilities	Before-Tax Operating Income
Real estate	$100,000,000	$6,000,000	$20,000,000
Construction	60,000,000	4,000,000	18,000,000

Required

Calculate the economic value added for each of Tribeca Construction Associates' divisions. (You will need to use the weighted-average cost of capital, which was computed in the preceding exercise.)

Problems

Problem 18.35
Responsibility Centers Designation; Hotel
(LO 1, 2, 3)

Communication

The following partial organization chart pertains to the Martha's Vineyard Hotel and Resort.

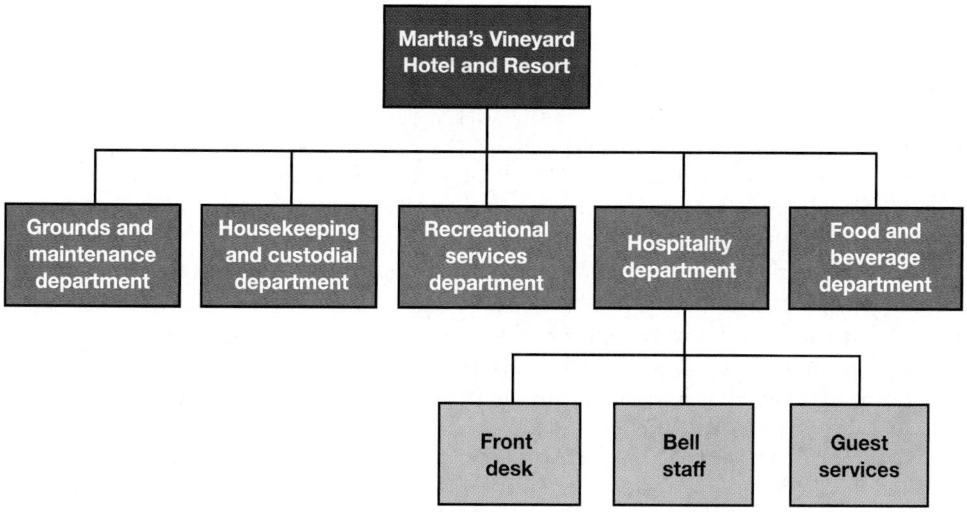

Each of the hotel's main departments is managed by a director (e.g., director of hospitality). The front desk subunit, which is supervised by the front desk manager, handles the hotel's reservations, room assignments, guest payments, and key control. The bell staff, managed by the bell captain, is responsible for greeting guests, front-door service, assisting guests with their luggage, and delivering room-service orders. The guest services subunit, supervised by the manager of guest services, is responsible for assisting guests with local transportation arrangements, advising guests on tourist attractions, and conveniences such as valet and floral services.

Required

As an outside consultant, write a memo to the hotel's general manager suggesting a responsibility-center designation for each of the subunits shown in the organization chart. Justify your choices.

Problem 18.36
Design of a Responsibility Accounting System
(LO 1, 2, 3)

Communication

Los Angeles Medical Equipment Company manufactures a variety of equipment used in hospitals. The company operates in a very price-competitive industry, so it has little control over the price of its products. It *must* meet the market price. To do so, the firm must keep production costs in check by operating as efficiently as possible. Sandra Jefferson, the company's president, has stated that to be successful, the company must provide a very high-quality product and meet its delivery commitments to customers on time. Los Angeles Medical Equipment Company is organized as shown below.

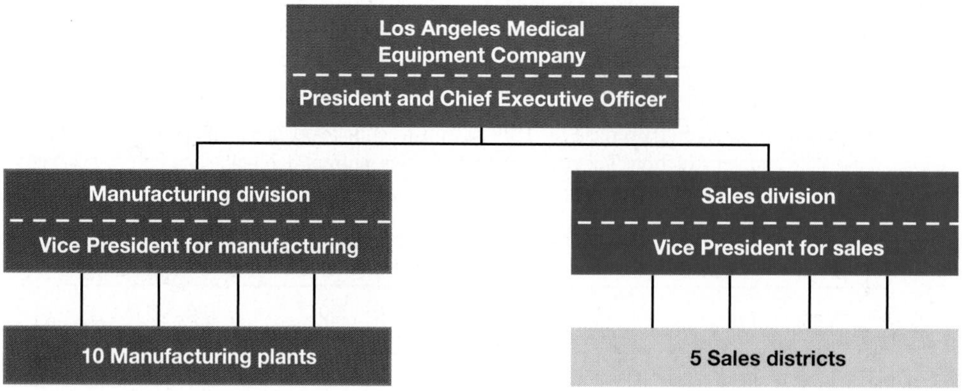

The company's two vice presidents currently disagree regarding the responsibility-accounting system. The vice president for manufacturing claims that the 10 plants should be cost centers. He recently expressed the following sentiment: "The plants should be cost centers because the plant managers do not control the sales of our products. Designating the plants as profit centers would result in holding the plant managers responsible for something they can't control." The vice president for marketing holds a contrary view. He recently made the following remarks: "The plants should be profit centers. The plant managers are in the best position to affect the company's overall profit."

Required

As the company's new controller, you have been asked to make a recommendation to Sandra Jefferson regarding the responsibility-center issue. Write a memo to her making a recommendation and explaining the reasoning behind it. In your memo address the following points.

a. Assuming that Los Angeles Medical Equipment Company's overall goal is profitability, what are the company's critical success factors? A *critical success factor* is a variable that meets these two criteria: It is largely under the company's control, and the company must succeed in this area to reach its overall goal of profitability.

b. Which responsibility-accounting arrangement for the plants is most consistent with achieving success on the company's critical success factors?

c. What responsibility-center designation is most appropriate for the company's sales districts?

d. As a specific example, consider the rush-order problem illustrated in the chapter. Suppose that Los Angeles Medical Equipment Company often receives rush orders from its customers. Which of the two proposed responsibility-accounting arrangements is best suited to making good decisions about accepting or rejecting rush orders? Specifically, should the plants be cost centers or profit centers?

Problem 18.37
Performance Report Analysis for a Decentralized Organization
(LO 1, 4)

Old Century Products manufactures antique reproduction furniture. The need for a widely based manufacturing and distribution system has led to a highly decentralized management structure. Each division manager is responsible for producing and distributing corporate products in one of eight geographical areas of the country.

Residual income is used to evaluate division managers. The residual income for each division equals its contribution to corporate profits before taxes less a 20 percent investment charge on a division's investment base. Each division's investment is the sum of its year-end balances of accounts receivable, inventories, and net plant fixed assets (cost less accumulated depreciation). Corporate policies dictate that divisions minimize their investments in receivables and inventories. Investments in plant fixed assets are a joint division/corporate decision based on proposals made by division managers, available corporate funds, and general corporate policy.

Patrick Anderson, division manager for the southeastern sector, prepared the year 2 and preliminary year 3 budgets for his division late in year 1. Final approval of the year 3 budget took place in late year 2 after adjustments for trends and other information developed during year 2. Preliminary work on the year 4 budget also took place at that time. In early October of year 3, Anderson asked the division controller to prepare the following report, which presents performance for the first nine months of year 3.

OLD CENTURY PRODUCTS
Southeastern Sector
(in thousands)

	Year 3			Year 2	
	Annual Budget	Nine-Month Budget*	Nine-Month Actual	Annual Budget	Actual Results
Sales revenue	$2,800	$2,100	$2,200	$2,500	$2,430
Divisional costs and expenses:					
Direct material and labor	$1,064	$ 798	$ 995	$ 900	$ 890
Supplies	44	33	35	35	43
Maintenance and repairs	200	150	60	175	160
Plant depreciation	120	90	90	110	110
Administration	120	90	90	90	100
Total divisional costs: and expenses	$1,548	$1,161	$1,270	$1,310	$1,303
Divisional margin	$1,252	$ 939	$ 930	$1,190	$1,127
Allocated corporate fixed costs	360	270	240	340	320
Divisional profits	$ 892	$ 669	$ 690	$ 850	$ 807

	Budgeted Balance 12/31/Year 3	Budgeted Balance 9/30/Year 3	Actual Balance 9/30/Year 3	Budgeted Balance 12/31/Year 2	Actual Balance 12/31/Year 2
Divisional investment:					
Accounts receivable	$ 280	$ 290	$ 250	$ 250	$ 250
Inventories	500	500	650	450	475
Plant fixed assets (net)	1,320	1,350	1,100	1,150	1,100
Total	$2,100	$2,140	$2,000	$1,850	$1,825

*Old Century's sales occur uniformly throughout the year.

Required

a. Evaluate Patrick Anderson's performance for the nine months ending September 30 of year 3. Support your evaluation with pertinent facts from the problem.

b. Identify the features of Old Century Products' division performance-measurement reporting and evaluation system that need to be revised if it is to be effective.

[CMA adapted]

Problem 18.38
Preparation of Performance Reports; Hospital
(LO 1, 4)

LaJolla General Hospital serves three counties in southern California. The hospital is a nonprofit organization supported by patient billings, county and state funds, and private donations. An organization chart and cost information for August follow.

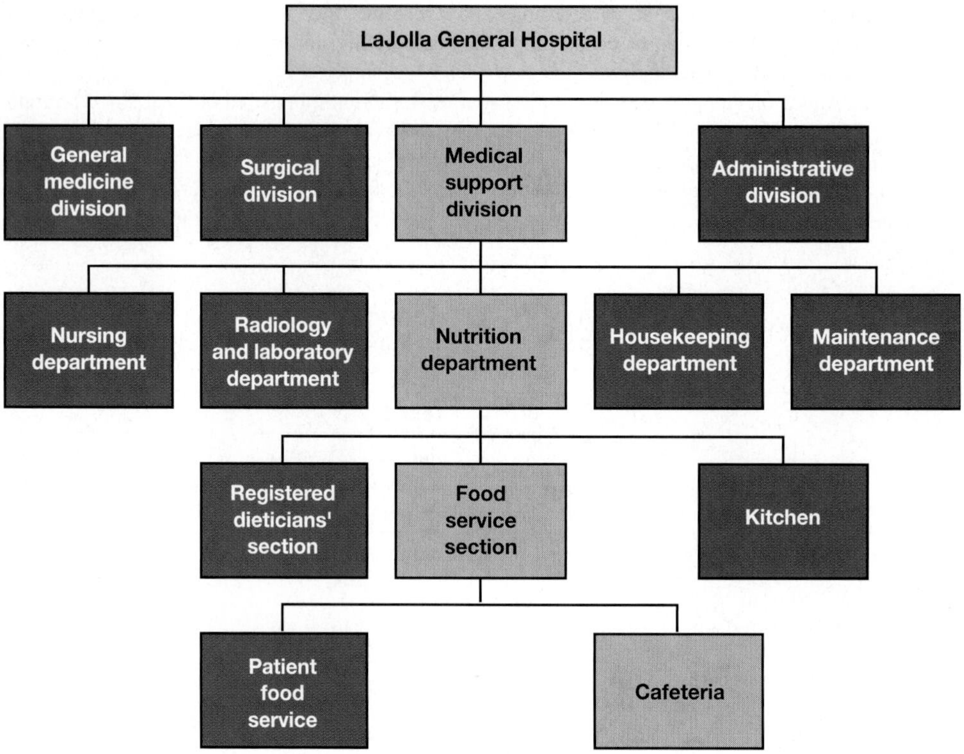

	Budget		Actual	
	August	**Year to Date**	**August**	**Year to Date**
Cafeteria:				
Food servers' wages	$ 8,000	$ 64,000	$ 9,000	$ 72,000
Paper products	4,500	36,000	4,400	36,200
Utilities	1,000	8,000	1,050	8,100
Maintenance	400	3,200	100	1,100
Custodial	1,100	8,800	1,100	8,600
Supplies	1,200	9,600	900	9,600
Patient food service	17,000	136,000	18,500	137,000
Registered dieticians' section	7,500	60,000	7,500	60,000
Kitchen	31,000	248,000	29,400	246,000
Nursing department	70,000	560,000	75,000	580,000
Radiology and laboratory department	18,000	144,000	18,100	144,000
Housekeeping department	10,000	80,000	11,600	86,000
Maintenance department	13,000	104,000	6,000	77,000
General medicine division	210,000	1,680,000	204,000	1,670,900
Surgical division	140,000	1,120,000	141,000	1,115,800
Administrative division	50,000	400,000	53,500	406,000

Required

a. Prepare a set of cost-performance reports similar to Exhibit 18–4 with six columns. The first four columns will have the same headings as those in the preceding table. The last two columns will have the following headings: Variance—August, and Variance—Year to Date.

Since all information in the performance reports for LaJolla General Hospital is cost information, you do not need to show these data in parentheses. Use F or U to denote whether each variance in the reports is favorable or unfavorable.

b. Using arrows, show the relationships between the numbers in your performance reports for LaJolla General Hospital. Refer to Exhibit 18–4 for guidance.

c. As the hospital's administrator, which variances in the performance reports would you want to investigate further? Why?

Problem 18.39
ROI and Residual Income; Missing Data; Improving ROI
(LO 5, 6)

The following data pertain to two divisions of Ohio Pipe Fittings Corporation. The company's required rate of return on invested capital is 8 percent.

	Cleveland Division	Toledo Division
Sales revenue	$10,000,000	?
Income	$ 2,000,000	$400,000
Average investment	$ 2,500,000	?
Sales margin	?	20%
Capital turnover	?	1
ROI	?	?
Residual income	?	?

Required

a. Fill in the blanks in the preceding table.

b. Explain three ways the Cleveland Division manager could improve her division's ROI. Use numbers to illustrate these possibilities.

c. Suppose the Toledo Division's sales margin increased to 25 percent while its capital turnover remained constant. Compute the division's new ROI.

Problem 18.40
Equipment Replacement and Performance Measures; Ethics
(LO 5, 7)

Ethics

You have been appointed manager of an operating division of MicroTech, Inc., a manufacturer of products using the latest microprocessor technology. Your division has $800,000 in assets and manufactures a special chip assembly. On January 2 of the current year, you invested $1 million in automated equipment for chip assembly. At that time, your expected income statement was as follows:

Sales revenue	$3,200,000
Operating costs:	
Unit level (variable)	400,000
Facility level (fixed, all cash)	1,500,000
Depreciation:	
New equipment	300,000
Other	250,000
Division operating profit	$ 750,000

On October 25 a sales representative from Klondike Machine Company approached you. For $1.3 million, Klondike offers a new assembly machine with significant improvements over the equipment you bought on January 2. The new equipment would expand department output by 10 percent while reducing cash fixed costs by 5 percent. The new equipment would be depreciated for accounting purposes over a three-year life. Depreciation would be net of the new machine's $100,000 salvage value. The new equipment meets your company's 20 percent cost of capital criterion. If you purchase the new machine, it must be installed prior to the end of the year. For practical purposes, though, you can ignore depreciation on the new machine because it will not go into operation until the start of the next year.

The old machine, which has no salvage value, must be disposed of to make room for the new machine.

Your company has a performance evaluation and bonus plan based on ROI. The return includes any losses on disposals of equipment. Investment is computed based on the end-of-year balance of assets, net book value.

Required

a. What is your division's ROI this year if it does not acquire the new machine?

b. What is your division's ROI this year if it does acquire the new machine?

c. If the new machine is acquired and operates according to specifications, what ROI is expected for next year?

d. Is it ethical to decline to purchase the new machine? Explain.

Problem 18.41
Evaluation of Trade-Offs in Return Measurement; Continuation of Preceding Problem
(LO 5, 7)

Refer to the information given in the preceding problem. As a division manager of MicroTech, you are still assessing the problem of whether to acquire Klondike Machine Company's machine. You learn that the new machine could be acquired next year, but it will cost 15 percent more then. Its salvage value would still be $100,000. Other costs or revenue estimates would be apportioned on a month-by-month basis for the time each machine is in use. (Ignore fractions of months.)

Required

a. When would you want to purchase the new machine if you wait until next year?

b. What are the costs that must be considered in making this decision?

Problem 18.42
ROI Increases over Time; Accelerated Depreciation; Increasing Residual Income Over Time
(LO 5, 7)

Refer to Exhibit 18–6. Prepare a similar table of the changing ROI assuming the following accelerated depreciation schedule. Assume income before depreciation of $150,000 per year. (If there is a loss, leave the ROI column blank.)

Year	Depreciation
1	$200,000
2	120,000
3	72,000
4	54,000
5	54,000
Total	$500,000

Required

a. How does your table differ from the one in Exhibit 18–6? Why?

b. What are the implications of the ROI pattern in your table?

c. Prepare a table similar to Exhibit 18–6, which focuses on residual income. Use a 10 percent rate to compute the imputed interest charge. The table should show the residual income on the investment during each year in its five-year life. Assume income before depreciation of $150,000 per year and straight-line depreciation with no salvage value.

Problem 18.43
Impact of Decisions to Capitalize or Expense on Performance Measurement
(LO 5, 7)

Aberdeen Drilling Company is an oil and gas exploration and drilling company operating off the coast of Scotland. Oil and gas companies inevitably incur costs on unsuccessful exploration ventures called *dry holes.* A debate continues over whether those costs should be written off as period expenses or capitalized as part of the full cost of finding profitable oil and gas ventures. Aberdeen has been writing these costs off to expense as incurred. However, this year a new management team was hired to improve the profit picture of the firm's Oil and Gas Exploration Division with the provision that it would receive a bonus equal to 10 percent of any profits in excess of the division's base-year profits. However, no bonus would be paid if profits were less than 20 percent of end-of-year investment. The following information was included in the division's performance report.

	This Year	Base Year	Increase over Base Year
Sales revenue	$4,100,000	$4,000,000	
Costs incurred:			
Dry holes	0	800,000	
Depreciation and other amortization	780,000	750,000	
Other costs	1,600,000	1,550,000	
Division profit	$1,720,000	$ 900,000	$820,000
End-of-year investment	$8,100,000*	$6,900,000	

*Includes other investments not at issue here.

During the year, the new team spent $1 million on exploratory activities, of which $900,000 was for unsuccessful ventures. The new management team has included the $900,000 in the current end-of-year investment base because, it states, "You can't find the good ones without hitting a few bad ones."

Required

a. What is the ROI for the base year and the current year?

b. What is the amount of the bonus that the new management team is likely to claim?

c. If you were on Aberdeen's board of directors, how would you respond to the new management's claim for the bonus?

Problem 18.44
Divisional Performance Measurement; Behavioral Issues
(LO 1, 5, 7)

Division managers of Galaxy Corporation have been expressing growing dissatisfaction with the methods Galaxy uses to measure division performance. Division operations are evaluated every quarter by comparison with the master budget prepared during the prior year. Division managers claim that many factors are completely out of their control but are included in this comparison, resulting in an unfair and misleading performance evaluation.

The managers have been particularly critical of the process used to establish standards and budgets. The annual budget, stated by quarters, is prepared six months prior to the beginning of the operating year. Pressure by top management to reflect increased earnings has often caused divisional managers to overstate revenues and/or understate expenses. In addition, once the budget is established, divisions must "live with the budget." Frequently, external factors such as the state of the economy, changes in consumer preferences, and actions of competitors have not been recognized in the budgets that top management supplied to the divisions. The credibility of the performance review is curtailed when the budget cannot be adjusted to incorporate these changes.

Recognizing these problems, top management agreed to establish a committee to review the situation and to make recommendations for a new performance evaluation system. The committee consists of each division manager, the corporate controller, and the executive vice president. At the first meeting, one division manager outlined an achievement of objectives system (AOS). In this performance evaluation system, division managers are evaluated according to three criteria:

- *Doing better than last year.* Various measures are compared to the same measures of the prior year.
- *Planning realistically.* Actual performance for the current year is compared to realistic plans and/or goals.
- *Managing current assets.* Various measures are used to evaluate division management's achievements and reactions to changing business and economic conditions.

One division manager believed that this system would overcome many of the current system's inconsistencies because divisions could be evaluated from three different viewpoints. In addition, managers would have the opportunity to show how they would react and account for changes in uncontrollable external factors.

Another manager cautioned that the success of a new performance evaluation system would be limited unless it had the complete support of top management.

Required

a. Explain whether the proposed AOS would improve Galaxy Corporation's evaluation of division performance.

b. Develop specific performance measures for each of the three criteria in the proposed AOS that could be used to evaluate division managers.

c. Discuss the motivational and behavioral aspects of the proposed performance measurement system. Also recommend specific programs that could be instituted to promote morale and give incentives to divisional management.

[CMA adapted]

Problem 18.45
ROI and Management Behavior
(LO 1, 5, 7)

Global

Vancouver Industrial Tool Corporation (VITC) is a highly diversified and decentralized company. Each division is responsible for its own sales, pricing, production, and costs of operations; management of accounts receivable, inventories, and accounts payable; and use of existing facilities. Corporate headquarters manages cash.

Division executives present investment proposals to corporate management, who analyze and document them as well as make the final decision to commit funds for investment purposes.

The corporation evaluates divisional executive performance using the ROI measure. The asset base is composed of fixed assets employed plus working capital, exclusive of cash. The ROI performance of a division executive is the most important appraisal factor for salary changes. In addition, each executive's annual performance bonus is based on ROI results, with increases in ROI having a significant impact on the amount of the bonus.

VITC adopted the ROI performance measure and related compensation procedures about 10 years ago and seems to have benefited from the program. The corporation's ROI increased during the first years of the program. Although each division's ROI continued to grow, corporate ROI declined in recent years. The corporation has accumulated a sizable amount of short-term marketable securities in the past three years.

Corporate management is concerned about the increase in the short-term marketable securities. A recent article in a financial publication suggested that some companies had overemphasized the use of ROI with results similar to those experienced by VITC.

Required

a. Describe the specific actions that division managers might have taken to cause the ROI to increase in each division but decline for the corporation. Illustrate your explanation with appropriate examples.

b. Using the concepts of goal congruence and motivation of division executives, explain how VITC's overemphasis on the use of the ROI measure might result in the recent decline in the corporation's ROI and the increase in cash and short-term marketable securities.

c. What changes could be made in VITC's compensation policy to avoid this problem? Explain your answer.

[CMA adapted]

Problem 18.46
Weighted-Average Cost of Capital; Economic Value Added
(LO 5)

Spreadsheet

Louisiana Shrimp Boats, Inc., (LSB) is a seafood restaurant chain operating throughout the south. The company has two sources of long-term capital: debt and equity. LSB's cost of issuing debt is the after-tax cost of the interest payments on the debt, considering the fact that the interest payments are tax deductible. LSB's cost of equity capital is the investment opportunity rate of LSB's investors, that is, the rate they could earn on investments of risk similar to that of investing in Louisiana Shrimp Boats, Inc. The interest rate on LSB's $80 million of long-term debt is 9 percent, and the company's tax rate is 40 percent. LSB's cost of equity capital is 14 percent. Moreover, the market value (and book value) of LSB's equity is $120 million.

Louisiana Shrimp Boats, Inc., consists of two divisions: properties division and food service division. The divisions' total assets, current liabilities, and before-tax operating income for the most recent year are as follows:

Division	Total Assets	Current Liabilities	Before-Tax Operating Income
Properties	$145,000,000	$3,000,000	$29,000,000
Food Service	64,000,000	6,000,000	15,000,000

Required

a. Calculate the weighted-average cost of capital for Louisiana Shrimp Boats, Inc.

b. Calculate the economic value added (EVA) for each of LSB's divisions.

Cases

Case 18.47
Evaluation of Performance Evaluation System; Behavioral Issues
(LO 1, 5, 8)

Communication

Team

Drawem Company purchased Bildem Company three years ago. Prior to the acquisition, Bildem manufactured and sold electronic products to third-party customers. Since becoming a division of Drawem, Bildem now manufactures electronic components only for products made by Drawem's Macon Division.

Drawem's corporate management gives the Bildem Division management considerable latitude in running the division's operations. However, corporate management retains authority for decisions regarding capital investments, product pricing, and production quantities.

Drawem has a formal performance evaluation program for all divisional management teams that relies substantially on each division's ROI. Bildem Division's income statement provides the basis for the evaluation of its divisional management. (See the following income statement.)

The corporate accounting staff prepares the division's financial statements. Corporate general services costs are allocated on the basis of sales dollars, and the computer department's actual costs are apportioned among the divisions on the basis of use. The net division investment includes division fixed assets at net book value (cost less depreciation), division inventory, and corporate working capital apportioned to the divisions on the basis of sales dollars.

DRAWEM COMPANY
Bildem Division
Income Statement
For the Year Ended October 31
(in thousands)

Sales revenue		$4,000
Costs and expenses:		
Product costs:		
Direct material	$ 500	
Direct labor	1,100	
Manufacturing overhead	1,300	
Total	$2,900	
Less: Increase in inventory	350	2,550
Engineering and research		120
Shipping and receiving		240
Division administration:		
Manager's office	$ 210	
Cost management	40	
Human services	82	332
Corporate cost:		
General services	$ 230	
Computer	48	278
Total costs and expenses		$3,520
Divisional operating profit		$ 480
Net plant investment		$1,600
Return on investment		30%

Required

a. As a group, discuss Drawem Company's financial reporting and performance evaluation program as it relates to the responsibilities of Bildem Division.

b. Based on your response to requirement (a), write a memo to management recommending appropriate revisions of the financial information and reports used to evaluate the performance of Bildem's divisional management. If revisions are not necessary, explain why.

[CMA adapted]

Case 18.48
Budgeting and Responsibility Accounting
(LO 1, 2, 3)*†

Communication

Global

Overview

River Beverages is a food and soft-drink company with worldwide operations. The company is organized into five regional divisions with each vice president reporting directly to the CEO, Cindy Wilkins. Each vice president has an R&D department, controller, and three divisions; carbonated drinks, juices and water, and food products. Management believes that the structure works well for River Beverages because different regions have different tastes and the division's products complement each other. River Beverages' companywide and divisional organization charts are shown here.

*©Michael W. Maher.

†This integrative case relates to issues from Chapters 15 and 18, and it relates to learning objectives from both chapters.

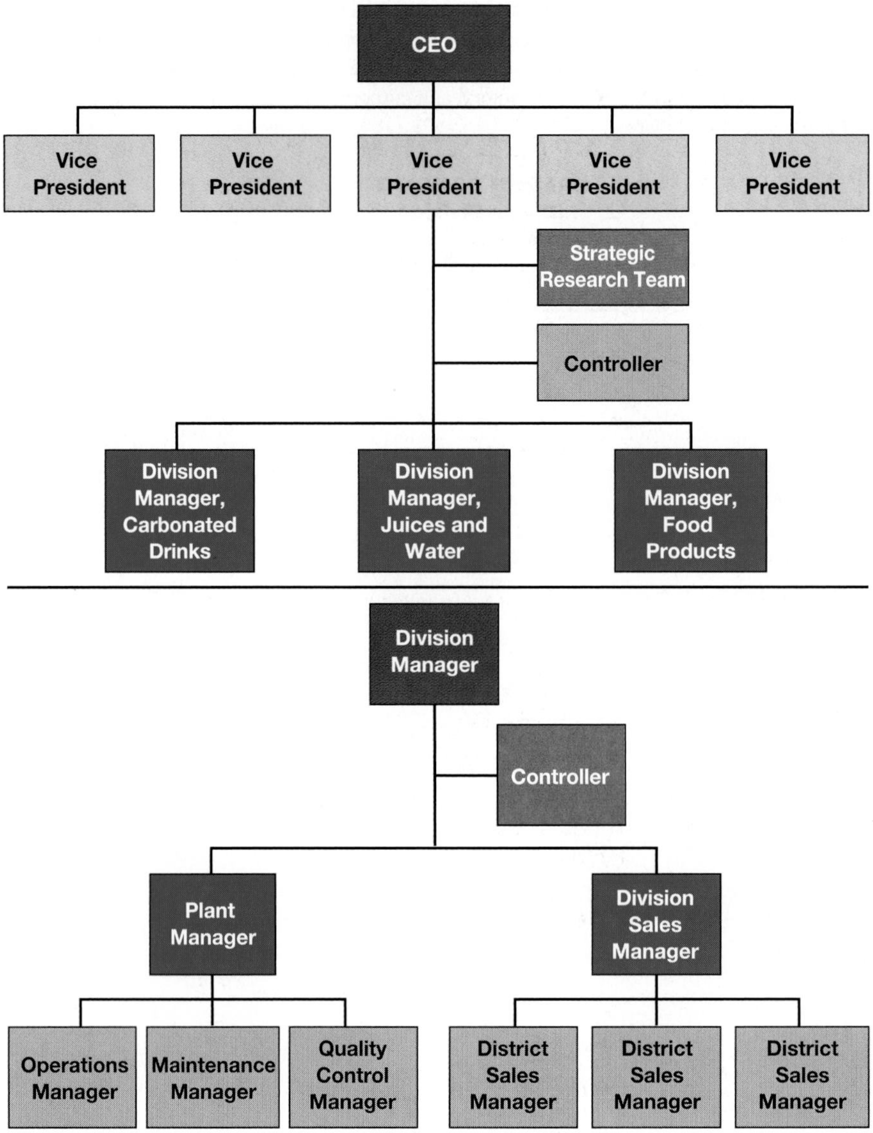

Industry

The US beverage industry has become mature with its growth matching population growth. In one recent year alone, consumers drank about 50 billion gallons of fluids. Most of the industry growth has come from the nonalcoholic beverage market, which is growing by about 1.1 percent annually. In the nonalcoholic arena, soft drinks are the largest segment, accounting for 53.4 percent of the beverages consumed. Americans consume about 26 billion gallons of soft drinks, ringing up retail sales of $50 billion every year. Water (bottled and tap) is the next largest segment, representing 23.7 percent of the market. Juices represent about 12 percent of the beverages consumed. The smallest but fastest-growing segment is ready-to-drink teas, which is growing by more than 91 percent in volume but accounts for less than 1 percent of the beverages consumed.

Sales Budgets

Susan Johnson, plant manager at River Beverages' noncarbonated drink plant in St. Louis, recently completed the annual budgeting process. According to Johnson, division managers have decision-making authority in their business units except for capital financing activities. Budgets keep the division managers focused on corporate goals.

At the beginning of December, division managers submit a report to the vice president for the region summarizing capital, sales, and income forecasts for the upcoming fiscal year beginning July 1. Although the initial report is not prepared with much detail, it is prepared carefully because it is used in the strategic planning process.

Next, the strategic research team begins a formal assessment of each market segment in its region. The team develops sales forecasts for each division and compiles them into a company forecast. The team considers economic conditions and current market share in each region. Management believes the strategic research team is effective because it is able to integrate division products and more accurately forecast demand for complementary products. In addition, the team ensures continuity of assumptions and achievable sales goals.

Once the corporate forecast has been completed, the district sales managers estimate sales for the upcoming budget year. The district sales managers are ultimately responsible for the forecasts they prepare. The district sales forecasts are then compiled and returned to the division manager. The division manager reviews the forecast but cannot make any revisions without discussing the changes with the district sales managers. Next, the district sales forecasts are reviewed by the strategic research team and the division controller. Finally, top management reviews each division's competitive position, including plans to increase market share, capital spending, and quality improvement plans.

Plant Budgets

After top management approves the sales budget, it is separated into a sales budget for each plant. Plant location is determined by product type and where the product needs to be distributed. The budget is broken down further by price, volume, and product type. Plant managers budget contribution margins, fixed costs, and pretax income using information from the plant sales budget.

Budgeted profit is determined by subtracting budgeted variable costs and budgeted fixed costs from the sales forecast. If actual sales fall below forecasts, the plant manager is still responsible for achieving the budgeted profit. One of the most important aspects of the plant budgeting process is that plant managers break the plant budget down into various plant departments.

Operations and maintenance managers work together to develop cost standards and cost-reduction targets for all departments. Budgeted cost reductions from productivity improvements, unfavorable variances, and facility-level costs are developed for each department, operation, and cost center in the plant.

Before plant managers submit their budgets, a member of the strategy team and the regional controller visit the plant to keep corporate management in touch with what is happening at the plant level and to help corporate management understand how plant managers determine their budgets. The visits also allow corporate management to provide budget preparation guidance if necessary. The visits are especially important because they force plant management to keep in touch with corporate-level managers.

The final budgets are submitted and consolidated by April 1. The vice president reviews them to ensure that they are in line with corporate objectives. After all changes have been made by the vice presidents and the chief executive officer (CEO), the budgets are submitted to the board of directors for approval. The board votes on the final budget in early June.

Performance Measurement

The corporate office generates variance reports monthly. River Beverages has a sophisticated information system that automatically generates reports based on input downloaded daily from each plant. Managers in the organization also can manually generate the reports. Most managers generate variance reports several times during the month, allowing them to solve problems before the problems get out of control.

Corporate management reviews the variance reports, looking closely at overbudget variance problems. Plant managers are questioned only about overbudget items. Management believes that this ensures that the plant managers are staying on top of problem areas, and that this keeps the plants operating as efficiently as possible. One week after the variance reports are generated, plant managers are required to submit a response outlining the causes of any variances and how they plan to prevent the problems in the future. If a plant manager has repeated problems, corporate management might send a specialist to the plant to work with the plant manager to solve the problems.

Sales and Manufacturing Relations

"We are expected to meet our approved budget," remarked Kevin Greely, a division controller at River Beverages. "A couple years ago, one of our major restaurant customers switched to another brand. Even though the restaurant sold over one million cases of our product annually, we were not allowed to make revisions to our budget."

Budgets are rarely adjusted after approval. However, if sales decline early in the year, plant managers might file an appeal to revise the budgeted profit for the year. If sales decline late in the year, management usually does not revise the budgeted amounts but asks plant managers to cut costs wherever possible and delay any unnecessary expenditures until the following year. Remember that River Beverages sets budgets so it is able to see where to make cuts or where it can find any operating inefficiencies. Plant managers are not forced to meet their goals, but they are encouraged to cut costs below budget.

The sales department is primarily responsible for product price, sales volume, and delivery timing while plant managers are responsible for plant operations. As you might imagine, problems occur between plant and regional sales managers from time to time. For example, rush orders could cause production costs to be higher than normal for some production runs. Another problem could occur when a sales manager runs a promotional campaign that causes margins to shrink. In both instances, a plant manager's profit will be affected negatively while a sales manager's sales will be affected positively. Such situations are often passed up to the division level for resolution; however, the customer is always the primary concern.

Incentives

River Beverages' management has devised what it thinks is an effective system to motivate plant managers. First, plant managers are promoted only when they have displayed outstanding performance in their current position. Second, monetary incentives reward plant managers for reaching profit goals. Finally, charts produced monthly display budgeted items versus actual results. Although not required to do so, most plant managers publicize the charts and use them as a motivational tool. The charts allow department supervisors and staff to compare activities in their department to similar activities in other plants around the world.

CEO's Message

Cindy Wilkins, CEO of River Beverages, looks to the future and comments, "Planning is an important aspect of budget preparation for every level of our organization. I would like to decrease the time spent on preparing the budget, but I believe that it keeps people thinking about the future. The negative aspect of the budgeting process is that sometimes it overcontrols our managers. We need to stay nimble enough to react to customer demands while staying structured enough to achieve corporate objectives. For the most part, our budget process keeps our managers aware of sales goals and alerts them when sales or expenses are off track."

Required

a. Discuss each step in River Beverages' budgeting process. Begin with the division manager's initial reports and end with the board of directors' approval. Is each step necessary? Explain.

b. Evaluate River Beverages' responsibility-accounting system. Specifically, should the plant managers be held responsible for costs or profits? Why?

c. Write a report to River Beverages' management stating the advantages and disadvantages of the company's budgeting process. Start your report by stating your assumption(s) about what River Beverages' management wants the budgeting process to accomplish.

CHAPTER

19

Transfer Pricing

After completing this chapter, you should be able to:

1. Explain the purpose and role of transfer pricing.
2. Use the general economic rule to set an optimal transfer price.
3. Explain how to base a transfer price on market prices, costs, or negotiations.
4. Discuss the implications of transfer pricing in a multinational company.
5. Discuss the effects of transfer pricing on segment reporting.

Cost-Management
Challenges

1. **What** is the primary objective of Outback Outfitters' cost-management team in determining a transfer-pricing policy?

2. **Describe** four methods by which Outback Outfitters can set transfer prices.

3. **Explain** the significance of excess capacity in the transferring division.

4. **Why** might income tax laws affect the transfer-pricing policies of multinational companies?

EMAIL MEMORANDUM

Outback Outfitters, Ltd.
Retail Division
212 Rushcutters Bay Road
Sydney, New South Wales
AUSTRALIA

Memorandum

To: Eric Devon
Vice President, Koala Camp Gear Division

From: Marie Waters
Vice President, Retail Division

Subject: Transfer price for 'RooPacks

I have received an inquiry from a local civic organization regarding the purchase of 800 'RooPacks to be distributed in conjunction with the Australia Day celebration coming up on January 26. My contact has offered the Retail Division a price of $55 per backpack. This price is substantially below our usual retail price of $70, so I am requesting a transfer price from the Koala Camp Gear Division to enable each of our divisions to make a profit on the transfer.

Please advise me at your earliest convenience as to the transfer price that Koala would need in this special situation. I have promised a response to our potential customer by the end of business on Tuesday next.

The memo from Marie Waters of Outback Outfitters' Retail Division to Eric Devon of Koala Camp Gear Division (Koala Division) indicates that in this company, as in many others, divisions often exchange products. Internal transfers of products create the need for some pricing mechanism between divisions to accurately reflect the costs and revenues of doing business. The pricing mechanism commonly used to reflect transfers, called a **transfer price,** is the amount charged when one division of an organization sells goods or services to another division. In this example, Outback Outfitters' Retail Division is requesting a transfer price from the company's Koala Division for a special order of 'RooPacks, one of Outback's most popular items.

transfer price *is the amount charged when one division of an organization sells goods or services to another division*

Although transfer prices commonly are used in today's organizations, they present some challenges for cost-management analysts. For example, when a division of General Electric Corporation buys parts for the kitchen appliances it manufactures from another GE division, how does GE record this exchange in its accounting records for the two divisions? When an engineering student at Cornell University takes an accounting course in the school of management, how does the university record this event? Both of these situations require the transfer of goods or services from one subunit of the organization to another.

Let's explore some of the challenges that cost-management analysts face in determining how to establish transfer prices to represent the substance of the transactions that occur between divisions.

Impact of Transfer Pricing on Organizations

LO 1 Explain the purpose and role of transfer pricing.

The transfer price charged when one division of an organization sells goods or services to another division does not affect the overall organization's total profit, *assuming that a transfer is made.* However, the transfer price does affect the profit measurement for both the selling and buying divisions because, in effect, the divisions are completing sales transactions with each other. A high transfer price results in high profit for the selling division but low profit for the buying division. A low transfer price has the opposite effect. Consequently, the transfer-pricing policy *can* affect the *incentives* of autonomous division managers as they decide whether to make the transfer. Exhibit 19–1 depicts this scenario.

Exhibit 19–1 The Transfer-Pricing Scenario

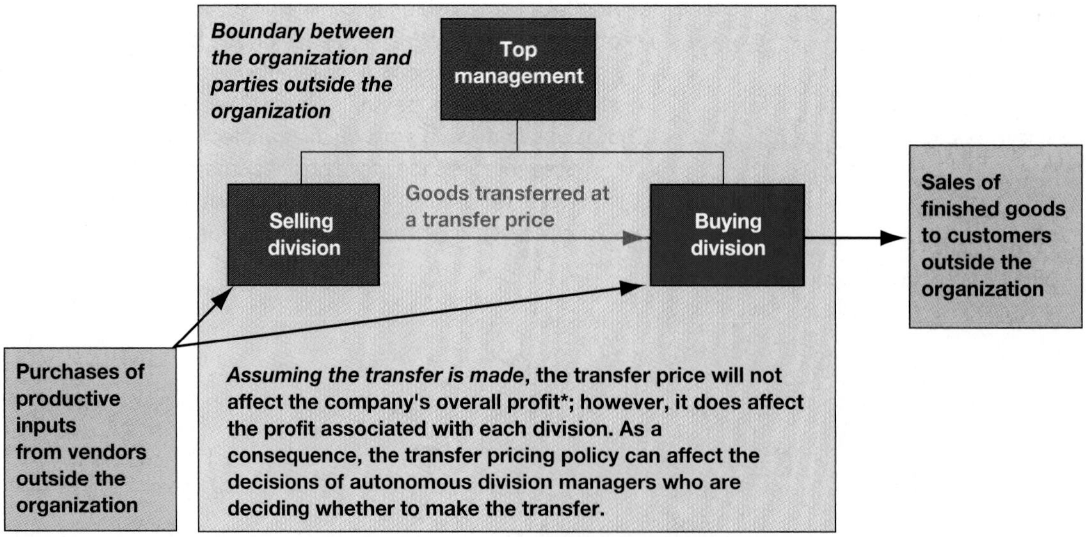

• Assumes no tax complexities involving multinational companies. This issue is addressed later in the chapter.

This General Motors assembly division in Baltimore, Maryland, buys parts from several other GM divisions.

Companies such as Sega of America and Nintendo, which buy video games from their Japanese parent companies, and Honda, which buys motorcycles from its Japanese parent company, make international transfers of goods and, therefore, require transfer prices to reflect these transactions. The transfer price becomes a cost to the buying division and revenue to the selling division, which has important implications for both divisions.

If the divisions are evaluated using some investment-center performance measure, such as return on investment (ROI), residual income (RI), or economic value added (EVA), the transfer price can affect each division's reported performance. The higher the transfer price, the more favorable is the performance measure for the selling division and the less favorable is the comparable performance measure for the buying division, all other things being equal.

Goal and Behavioral Congruence

What should be management's goal in setting transfer prices for internally transferred goods or services? In a decentralized organization, the managers of profit centers and investment centers often have considerable autonomy in deciding whether to accept or reject orders and whether to buy from inside or outside the organization. For example, a large manufacturer of farm equipment allows its assembly division managers to buy parts either from another division of the company or from independent manufacturers. The goal in setting transfer prices is to establish incentives for autonomous division managers to make decisions that support the organization's overall goals.

Suppose that it is in the best interests of Outback Outfitters for the camping equipment manufactured by the Koala Camp Gear Division to be transferred to the Retail Division's stores throughout Australia and the United Kingdom, as well as to Outback's Mail-Order Division. In other words, if Outback Outfitters were centralized, manufactured products would be transferred from the Koala Camp Gear Division to the Retail and Mail-Order Divisions. However, Outback is a decentralized company, and the Retail and Mail-Order Division managers are free to buy goods from either the Koala Camp Gear Division or an outside company. Similarly, the Koala Camp Gear Division manager is free to accept or reject an order for products, at any given price, from the Retail or Mail-Order Divisions. The goal in setting the transfer price is to provide incentives for each of these division managers to act in the company's best interests. The transfer price should be chosen so that each division manager, when striving to maximize his or her own division's profit, makes the decision that maximizes the company's profit.

General Transfer-Pricing Rule

LO 2 Use the general economic rule to set an optimal transfer price.

Management's objective in setting a transfer price is to encourage goal, or at least behavioral, congruence among the division managers involved in the transfer. A general rule to ensure goal congruence follows.

$$\text{Transfer price} = \begin{array}{c}\text{Additional } \textit{outlay} \\ \textit{cost} \text{ per unit} \\ \text{incurred because} \\ \text{goods are transferred}\end{array} + \begin{array}{c}\textit{Opportunity cost} \\ \text{per unit to the} \\ \text{organization} \\ \text{because of the transfer}\end{array}$$

The general rule specifies the transfer price as the sum of two cost components. The first component is the *outlay cost* incurred by the division that produces the goods or services to be transferred. Outlay costs include the direct unit-level costs of the product or service and any other outlay costs incurred as a result of the transfer. The second component in the general transfer-pricing rule is the opportunity cost incurred by the organization as a whole because of the transfer. Recall that an *opportunity cost* is a benefit that is forgone as a result of taking a particular action.

We illustrate the general transfer-pricing rule for Outback Outfitters. Its Koala Camp Gear Division manufactures backpacks in its Melbourne plant. The division transfers some of its products to the company's Retail and Mail-Order Divisions. These backpacks carry the brand name 'RooPack and are imprinted with the Koala Camp Gear label. The Koala Camp Gear Division also sells some of its backpacks to other companies in the *external market* under different labels.

The Melbourne plant incurs the following costs to manufacture a backpack and transport it to a buyer.

Production:	
Standard unit-level cost (including packaging)	$39
Transportation:	
Standard unit-level transportation cost	1

In applying the general transfer-pricing rule, we distinguish between two different scenarios.

Scenario 1: No excess capacity. Suppose that the Koala Camp Gear Division can sell all backpacks it can produce to outside buyers at a market price of $60 each. Since the division can sell all of its production, it has *no excess capacity. Excess capacity* exists only when more goods can be produced than the producer is able to sell because of low demand for the product.

What transfer price does the general rule yield under this scenario of no excess capacity? The transfer price is determined as follows:

Outlay cost per backpack:	
Standard unit-level cost of production	$39
Standard unit-level cost of transportation	1
Total outlay cost	$40
Opportunity cost per backpack:	
Wholesale selling price in external market	$60
Unit-level cost of production and transportation	40
Opportunity cost (forgone contribution margin)	$20

The general transfer-pricing rule yields the following transfer price.

$$\text{Transfer price} = \text{Outlay cost} + \text{Opportunity cost}$$
$$\$60 = \$40 + \$20$$

The *outlay cost* that the Koala Camp Gear Division incurs to transfer a backpack includes the standard unit-level production cost of $39 and the standard unit-level transportation cost of $1. The *opportunity cost* incurred by Outback Outfitters when its Koala Division transfers a backpack to the Retail or Mail-Order Division *instead of* selling it in the external market is the forgone contribution margin from the lost sale, equal to $20. The company loses a sale in the external market for every backpack transferred to the Retail or Mail-Order Division because the Koala Camp Gear Division has *no excess capacity.* Every backpack transferred to another company division results in one less backpack sold in the external market.

Goal or behavioral congruence. How does the general transfer-pricing rule promote goal or behavioral congruence? Suppose the Retail Division's stores can sell a 'RooPack for $70. What is the best way for Outback Outfitters to use the limited production capacity in the Koala Camp Gear Division's Melbourne plant? The answer is determined as follows:

Contribution to Outback Outfitters from Sale in External Market		**Contribution to Outback Outfitters from Transfer to Retail Division**	
Wholesale selling price per backpack	$60	Retail selling price per backpack	$70
Standard unit-level cost	40	Standard unit-level cost	40
Contribution margin	$20	Contribution margin	$30

The best use of the Melbourne plant's limited production capacity is to produce 'RooPacks for transfer to the Retail Division. If the transfer price is set at $60, as the general rule specifies, goal congruence is maintained. The Koala Camp Gear Division manager is willing to transfer 'RooPacks to the Retail Division because the transfer price of $60 equals the external wholesale market price. The Retail Division manager is willing to buy the 'RooPacks because her division will have a contribution margin of $10 on each 'RooPack transferred ($70 retail sales price minus the $60 transfer price).

Now consider a different situation. A local organization has made a special offer to the Retail Division manager to buy several hundred 'RooPacks to sell in a promotional campaign associated with the annual Australia Day celebration. The organization has offered to pay $55 per backpack. What will the Retail Division manager do? She must pay a transfer price of $60 per backpack, so the Retail Division would lose $5 per unit if the special offer were accepted ($60 − $55). The Retail Division manager will decline the special offer. Is this decision in the best interests of Outback Outfitters as a whole? If she accepts the offer, the positive contribution to the company as a whole would be $15 per backpack as shown in the following table:

Contribution to Outback Outfitters If Special Offer Is Accepted	
Special price per backpack	$55
Standard unit-level cost to company	40
Contribution to company per backpack	$15

However, the company can make even more if its Koala Camp Gear Division sells 'RooPacks directly in its external market. Then the contribution to the company is $20, as we have just seen. (The external market price of $60 per backpack minus a standard unit-level cost of $40 per backpack equals $20 per unit.) Thus, Outback Outfitters is better off, as a whole, if the Retail Division's special offer is rejected. Once again, the general transfer-pricing rule results in goal-congruent decision making.

Scenario II: Excess capacity. Now let's change our basic assumption and suppose that the Koala Division's Melbourne plant has excess production capacity. This means that the total demand for its products from all sources, including the Retail and Mail-Order Divisions and the external market, is less than the plant's production capacity. Under this scenario of excess capacity, what does the general rule specify for a transfer price?

$$\text{Transfer price} = \text{Outlay cost} + \text{Opportunity cost}$$
$$\$40 \quad = \quad \$40 \quad + \quad 0$$

The *outlay cost* in the Koala Camp Gear Division's Melbourne plant is still $40, since it does not depend on whether there is idle capacity or not. The *opportunity cost,* however, is now zero. There is no opportunity cost to the company when a backpack is transferred to the Retail Division because the Koala Camp Gear Division can still satisfy all of its external demand for backpacks. Thus, the general rule specifies a transfer price of $40, the total standard unit-level cost of production and transportation.

Goal or behavioral congruence. Let's reconsider what will happen when the Retail Division manager receives the local organization's special offer to buy backpacks at

$55 per unit. The Retail Division will now show a positive contribution of $15 per backpack on the special order:

Special price per backpack	$55
Transfer price paid by Retail Division	40
Contribution to Retail Division	$15

The Retail Division manager will accept the special offer. This decision is also in the best interests of Outback Outfitters. The contribution to the company, as a whole, will be $15 per unit on every backpack transferred to the Retail Division to satisfy the special order. Once again, the general transfer-pricing rule maintains goal-congruent decision-making behavior.

Notice that the general rule yields a transfer price that leaves the Koala Camp Gear Division manager indifferent to making the transfer. At a transfer price of $40, the contribution to the Koala Camp Gear Division is zero (transfer price of $40 less outlay cost of $40). To avoid this problem, we can view the general rule as providing a lower bound on the transfer price. Some companies allow the producing division to add a markup to this lower bound in order to provide a positive contribution margin. This in turn provides a positive incentive to make the transfer.

Difficulty in implementing the general rule. The general transfer-pricing rule always promotes goal-congruent decision making *if the rule can be implemented.* However, the rule is often difficult or impossible to implement due to the difficulty of measuring opportunity costs. Such a cost-measurement problem can arise for a number of reasons. One reason is that the external market might not be perfectly competitive. Under **perfect competition,** the market price does not depend on the quantity sold by any one producer. Under **imperfect competition,** a single producer can affect the market price by varying the amount of product available in the market. In such cases, the external market price depends on the producer's production decisions. This in turn means that the opportunity cost the company incurs as a result of internal transfers depends on the quantity sold externally. These interactions could make accurately measuring the opportunity cost caused by a product transfer impossible.

perfect competition *describes the situation when the market price does not depend on the quantity sold by any one producer*

imperfect competition *describes the situation when a single producer can affect the market price by varying the amount of product available in the market*

Transfer pricing can be quite complex when selling and buying divisions cannot sell and buy all they want in perfectly competitive markets. In some cases, no outside market exists at all. Companies often find that not all transactions between divisions occur as top management prefers. In extreme cases, the transfer-pricing problem is so complex that top management reorganizes the company so that buying and selling divisions report to one manager who oversees the transfers.

Other reasons for difficulty in measuring the opportunity cost associated with a product transfer include uniqueness of the transferred goods or services, a need for the producing division to invest in special equipment to produce the transferred goods, and interdependencies among several transferred products or services. For example, the producing division might provide design services as well as production of the goods for a buying division. What is the opportunity cost associated with each of these related outputs of the producing division? In many such cases, sorting out the opportunity costs is difficult.

The general transfer-pricing rule provides a good conceptual model to use in setting transfer prices. Moreover, in many cases it can be implemented. When the general rule cannot be implemented, organizations turn to other transfer-pricing methods, as we shall see next.

Transfers Based on the External Market Price

LO 3 Explain how to base a transfer price on market prices, costs, or negotiations.

A common approach is to set the transfer price equal to the price in the external market. In the Outback Outfitters illustration, the Koala Camp Gear Division would set the transfer price for a 'RooPack at $60 per unit since that is the price the division can obtain in its external market. When the producing division has no excess capacity and perfect competition prevails, when no single producer can affect the market price, the general transfer-pricing rule and the external market price yield the same transfer price. This fact is illustrated for Outback Outfitters as follows:

General Transfer-Pricing Rule

Transfer price	=	**Outlay cost**	+	**Opportunity cost**		
	=	**Unit-level cost of production and transportation**	+	**Forgone contribution margin on an external sale**		
	=	**$40**	+	**($60 − $40)**	=	**$60**

Market Price

Transfer price = External market price = $60

In more complicated situations in which the producing division has excess capacity or the external market is imperfectly competitive, the general rule and the external market price do not yield the same transfer price.

If the transfer price is set at the market price, the producing division should have the option to either produce goods for internal transfer or sell them in the external market. The buying division should be required to purchase goods from inside its organization if the producing division's goods meet the product specifications. Otherwise, the buying division should have the autonomy to buy from a supplier outside its own organization. The company should establish an arbitration process to handle pricing disputes that may arise.

Transfer prices based on market prices are consistent with the responsibility-accounting concepts of profit centers and investment centers. In addition to encouraging division managers to focus on divisional profitability, market-based transfer prices help to show each division's contribution to the company's overall profit. Suppose that the Koala Camp Gear Division of Outback Outfitters transfers backpacks to the Retail Division at a market-based transfer price of $60 per unit. The following contribution margins will be earned by the two divisions and the company as a whole.

Koala Camp Gear Division		Retail Division	
Transfer price	$60	Retail sales price	$70
Standard unit-level cost	40	Transfer price	60
Contribution margin	$20	Contribution margin	$10

Outback Outfitters	
Retail sales price	$70
Standard unit-level cost	40
Contribution margin	$30

When aggregate divisional profits are determined for the year, and ROI, residual income, and EVA are computed, the use of a market-based transfer price helps to assess each division's contributions to overall corporate profits.

Distress market prices. Occasionally an industry experiences a period of significant excess capacity and extremely low prices. For example, when gasoline prices soared due to a foreign oil embargo, the market prices for recreational vehicles and power boats fell temporarily to very low levels.

Under such extreme conditions, basing transfer prices on market prices can lead to decisions that are not in the best interests of the overall company. Basing transfer prices on artificially low *distress market prices* could lead the producing division to sell or close the productive resources devoted to producing the product for transfer. Under distress market prices, the producing division manager might prefer to move the division into a more profitable product line. Although such a decision might improve the division's profit in the short run, it could be contrary to the best interests of the company overall. It might be better for the company as a whole to avoid divesting itself of any productive resources and to ride out the period of market distress. To encourage an autonomous division manager to act in this fashion, some companies set the transfer price equal to the long-run *average external market price* rather than the current (possibly depressed) market price.

You're the Decision Maker 19.1

Setting a Transfer Price

Fast Track Shoe Company has two divisions, production and marketing. Production manufactures Fast Track shoes, which it sells to both the marketing division and to other retailers (the latter under a different brand name). Marketing operates several small shoe stores in shopping centers that sell both Fast Track and other brands.

Relevant facts for production, which is operating far below its capacity, follow:

Sales price to outsiders	$28.50 per pair
Unit-level cost to produce	$18.00 per pair
Facility-level costs	$100,000 per month

The following data pertain to the sale of Fast Track shoes by marketing, which is operating far below its capacity:

Sales price	$40 per pair
Unit-level marketing costs	$1 per pair

The company's unit-level manufacturing and marketing costs are differential costs in this decision, but the facility-level manufacturing and marketing costs are not.

a. What is the minimum price that the marketing division can charge for the shoes and still cover the company's differential manufacturing and marketing costs?

b. What is the appropriate transfer price for this situation?

c. What effect would a transfer price set at $28.50 have on the minimum price set by the marketing manager?

d. How would your answer to (b) change if the production division were operating at full capacity?

(Solutions begin on page 817.)

Negotiated Transfer Prices

LO 3 Explain how to base a transfer price on market prices, costs, or negotiations.

Many companies use negotiated transfer prices. Division managers or their representatives actually negotiate the price at which transfers will be made. Sometimes they start with the external market price and then make adjustments for various reasons. For example, the producing division could enjoy some cost savings on internal transfers that are not obtained on external sales. Commissions might not have to be paid to sales personnel on internally transferred products. In such cases, a negotiated transfer price could split the cost savings between the producing and buying divisions. In other instances, a negotiated transfer price could be used because no external market exists for the transferred product.

Two drawbacks sometimes characterize negotiated transfer prices. First, negotiations can lead to divisiveness and competition between participating division managers. This can undermine the spirit of cooperation and unity that is desirable throughout an organization. Second, although negotiating skill is a valuable managerial talent, it should not be the sole or dominant factor in evaluating a division manager. If, for example, the producing division's manager is a better negotiator than the buying division's manager, the producing division's profit might look better than it should simply because of its manager's superior negotiating ability.

Cost-Based Transfer Prices

cost-based transfer pricing *sets the transfer price on the basis of the cost of the product or service transferred*

Organizations that do not base transfer prices on market prices or negotiations often turn to **cost-based transfer-pricing,** which sets the transfer price on the basis of the cost of the product or service transferred.

Unit-level cost. One cost-based approach is to set the transfer price equal to the standard unit-level cost. The problem with this approach is that even when the producing division has excess capacity, it is not allowed to show any contribution margin on the transferred products or services. To illustrate, suppose that the Koala Camp Gear Division has excess capacity and the transfer price is set at the standard unit-level cost of $40 per backpack. The division has no positive incentive to produce and transfer backpacks to the Retail Division. The Koala Division's contribution margin from a transfer will be zero (transfer price of $40 minus unit-level costs of $40 equals zero). Some companies avoid this problem by setting the transfer price at standard unit-level cost plus a markup to allow the producing division a positive contribution margin.

Absorption or full cost. An alternative cost-based approach is to set the transfer price equal to the absorption, *or* full, cost of the transferred product or service. *Absorption* (or *full*) *cost* equals the product's unit-level cost plus an assigned portion of the higher-level costs (batch-level, product-line-level, customer-level, and general or facility-level costs).

Suppose that for the current year, the Koala Camp Gear Division's Melbourne plant has budgeted higher-level costs totaling $1.8 million and production of 100,000 backpacks. The full cost per backpack is calculated as follows:

$$\text{Full cost} = \begin{array}{c}\text{Standard}\\ \text{unit-level}\\ \text{cost}\end{array} + \text{Assigned higher-level costs}$$

$$= \$40 + \frac{\$1{,}800{,}000 \text{ budgeted higher-level costs}}{100{,}000 \text{ budgeted units of production}}$$

$$= \$40 + \$18$$

$$= \$58$$

Under this full-cost-based approach, the transfer price is set at $58 per backpack.

Possible dysfunctional decision-making behavior. Basing transfer prices on full cost entails a serious risk of causing dysfunctional decision-making behavior. Full-cost-based transfer prices lead the buying division to view those costs that are non-unit-level costs for the entire company as unit-level costs to the buying division. This can cause faulty decision making.

To illustrate, suppose that the Koala Camp Gear Division has excess capacity, and the transfer price of backpacks equals the full cost of $58 per pack. What happens if the Retail Division receives the special offer discussed previously, to sell backpacks to a local organization at a special price of $55 per unit? The Retail Division manager will reject the special order since her division would incur a loss of $3 per backpack.

Special price per backpack	$55
Transfer price based on full cost	58
Loss	$ 3

What is in the best interests of the company as a whole? Outback Outfitters would realize a positive contribution of $15 per backpack on those sold in the special order:

Special price per backpack	$55
Standard unit-level cost in Koala Camp Gear Division	40
Contribution to company as a whole	$15

What has happened here? Setting the transfer price equal to the full cost of $58 has turned a non-unit-level cost in the Koala Camp Gear Division and, hence, a non-unit-level cost for the company as a whole into a unit-level cost from the viewpoint of the Retail Division manager. The manager would tend to reject the special offer, even though accepting it would benefit the company as a whole.

Although the practice is common, transfer prices should not be based on full cost. The risk is too high that the cost behavior in the producing division will be obscured. This can all too easily result in dysfunctional decisions in the buying division.

A note on ethics. What are the ethical implications in the situation just discussed? If the retail division manager realizes that buying the backpacks from the Koala Division is in the best interests of Outback Outfitters, shouldn't she buy from Koala, even if it hurts her division's performance? Strict adherence to ethical standards suggest that she should. Realistically, however, human nature suggests that we cannot always count on such behavior to take place. Moreover, most transfer-pricing scenarios are much more complicated than the Outback Outfitters situation. More often than not, a buying division manager does not have enough information to clearly conclude what is in the overall company's best interests. It is important, therefore, to strive to set transfer pricing policies so that goal or behavioral congruence will be maintained.

Standard versus Actual Costs

Throughout our discussion of transfer prices, we have used *standard costs* rather than *actual costs.* This was true in our discussion of the general transfer-pricing rule as well as for cost-based transfer prices. Transfer prices should not be based on actual costs because such a practice would allow an inefficient producing division to pass its excess production costs on to the buying division via the transfer price. When standard costs are used in transfer-pricing formulas, the selling division is not forced to pick up the tab for the producer's inefficiency. Moreover, the producing division is given an incentive to control its costs since any costs of inefficiency cannot be passed on.

Deere and Co. was one of the pioneers in developing activity-based costing. One of the company's objectives for the ABC system was more accurate transfer prices.

Activity-Based Costing

Many companies are implementing activity-based costing to improve the accuracy of costs in cost-based transfer pricing. One of the primary motives for Deere and Co. to develop its activity-based costing system, for example, was to improve the accuracy of cost numbers in its internal transfers of parts.

Remedying Motivational Problems of Transfer-Pricing Policies

When the transfer-pricing policy does not give a supplier a profit on the transaction, motivational problems can arise. For example, if transfers are made at differential unit-level costs, the supplier earns no contribution toward profit on the transferred goods. Then the transfer-pricing policy does not motivate the supplier to transfer internally because internal transfers have no likely profit. This situation can be remedied in several ways.

A supplier whose transfers are almost all internal usually is organized as a cost center. The cost center manager is normally held responsible for costs, not for revenues. Hence, the transfer price does not affect the manager's performance measures. In companies in which such a supplier is a profit center, the artificial nature of the transfer price should be considered when evaluating the results of that profit center's operations.

A supplying center that does business with both internal and external customers could be set up as a profit center for external business when the manager has price-setting power and as a cost center for internal transfers when the manager does not have such power. Performance on external business could be measured as if the responsibility center were a profit center; performance on internal business could be measured as if the responsibility center were a cost center.

Undermining Divisional Autonomy

Suppose the manager of Outback's Koala Camp Gear Division has excess capacity but insists on a transfer price of $58 based on full cost. The Retail Division manager is faced with the special offer for backpacks at $55 per unit. She regrets that she must decline the offer because it would cause her division's profit to decline although the company's interests would be best served by accepting it. The Retail Division manager calls the company president and explains the situation. She asks the president to intervene and force the Koala Camp Gear Division manager to lower his transfer price.

As the company president, what would you do? If you stay out of the controversy, your company will lose the contribution on the special order. If you intervene, you will run the risk of undermining the autonomy of your division managers. You established a decentralized organization structure for Outback Outfitters and hired competent managers because you believed in the benefits of decentralized decision making.[1]

There is no obvious answer to this dilemma. In practice, central managers are reluctant to intervene in such disputes unless the negative financial consequences to the organization are quite large. Most managers believe that decentralized decision making has benefits that are important to protect even if it results in an occasional dysfunctional decision.

Dysfunctional Decisions and Transfer-Pricing Policy

You're the **Decision Maker 19.2**

Meridian Electronics Company's production division was operating below capacity. Its assembly division received a contract to assemble 10,000 units of a final product, XX-1. Each unit of XX-1 required one part, A-16, which the production division makes. Both divisions are decentralized, autonomous investment centers and are evaluated based on operating profits and ROI.

The vice president of the assembly division called the vice president of the production division and made a proposal:

Megan (Assembly VP): Look, Joe, I know you're running below capacity out there in your division. I'd like to buy 10,000 units of A-16 at $30 per unit. That will enable you to keep your production lines busy.

Joe (Production VP): Are you kidding, Megan? I happen to know that it would cost you a lot more if you had to buy A-16s from an outside supplier. We refuse to accept less than $40 per unit, which gives us our usual markup and covers our costs.

Megan: Joe, we both know that your unit-level costs for each unit of A-16 are only $22. I realize I'd be getting a good deal at $30, but so would you. You should treat this as a special order. Anything over your differential costs on the order is pure profit. Look, Joe, if you can't do better than $40, I'll have to go elsewhere. I have to keep my costs down, too, you know.

Joe: The $40 per unit is firm. Take it or leave it!

The assembly division subsequently sought bids on the part and was able to obtain its requirements from an outside supplier for $40 per unit. The production division continued to operate below capacity. The actions of the two divisions cost the company $180,000.

a. Show how the $180,000 cost to Meridian Electronics Company was calculated.

b. Put yourself in the place of Meridian's CEO. If you were approached by the assembly division VP to intervene in this situation, what would you do? Explain.

(Solutions begin on page 817.)

Dual Transfer Prices

A *dual transfer-pricing system* could be installed to provide the selling division a profit but charge the buying division with costs only. A **dual transfer-pricing system** charges the buying division for the cost of the transferred product, however the cost might be determined, and credits the selling division with the cost plus some profit

dual transfer-pricing *charges the buying division for the cost of the transferred product and credits the selling division with the cost plus some profit allowance*

[1]See the discussion of the costs and benefits of decentralization at the beginning of the preceding chapter.

allowance. The difference is accounted for in a special centralized account. This system would preserve cost data for subsequent buyer divisions and would encourage internal transfers by providing a profit on such transfers for the selling divisions.

Some companies use dual transfer prices to encourage internal transfers; however, other methods can also encourage internal transfers. For example, many companies recognize internal transfers and incorporate them explicitly in their reward systems. Other companies base part of a supplying manager's bonus on the purchasing center's profits.

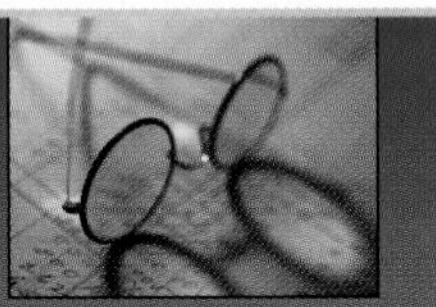

Cost Management in Practice 19.1

Transfer Pricing and Taxes

According to a survey reported by Ernst & Young, LLP in April 2000, transfer pricing is the top tax issue facing multinational corporations. Of the international tax directors at 582 multinational organizations polled in the survey, 75 percent expect their company to face a transfer-pricing audit within the next two years. Respondents cited related-party transactions (including the intercompany transfer of goods, services, properties, loans, and leases) involving administrative and management services as the most likely to be audited. *Source:* Current Practices, Perceptions and Trends: Transfer Pricing—1997 Global Survey *(Full citations to references are in the Bibliography.)*

Global Transfer-Pricing Practices

The authors of surveys of corporate practices summarized in Research Insight 19.1 reported that nearly half of the US companies surveyed used a cost-based transfer-pricing system: 33 percent used a market-price-based system, and 20 percent used a negotiated system. Similar results have been found for companies in Canada and Japan. Generally, we find that when negotiated prices are used, the prices negotiated are between the market price at the upper limit and some measure of cost at the lower limit.[2]

No optimal transfer-pricing policy dominates all others. An established policy most likely is imperfect in the sense that it does not always lead to the economically optimal outcome. As with other management decisions, however, the cost of any system must be weighed against its benefits. Improving a transfer-pricing policy beyond some point (for example, to obtain better measures of unit-level costs and market prices) results in the system's costs exceeding its benefits. As a result, management tends to settle for a system that seems to work reasonably well rather than to devise a "textbook-perfect" system.

Research Insight 19.1

International Transfer-Pricing Practices

Surveys of transfer-pricing practices in three countries yielded the following results.

Method used	United States	Canada	Japan
Cost based	45%	47%	47%
Market based	33	35	34
Negotiated transfer prices	22	18	19
Total	100%	100%	100%

Sources: S. Borkowski, "Environmental and Organizational Factors Affecting Transfer Pricing: A Survey"; *R. Tang,* "Canadian Transfer Pricing Practices"; *R. Tang, C. Walter, and R. Raymond,* "Transfer Pricing—Japanese vs. American Style." *(Full citations to references are in the Bibliography.)*

[2] R. Benke and J. Edwards, *Transfer Pricing: Techniques and Uses.*

Multinational Transfer Pricing

LO 4 Discuss the implications of transfer pricing in a multinational company.

In international transactions, transfer prices could affect tax liabilities, royalties, and other payments because laws vary in different countries (or states). Because tax rates vary among countries, companies have incentives to set transfer prices that will increase revenues (and profits) in low-tax countries and increase costs (thereby reducing profits) in high-tax countries.

Tax avoidance by foreign companies using inflated transfer prices has been a controversial issue in recent years. Foreign companies that sell goods to their US subsidiaries at inflated transfer prices artificially reduce the profit of the US subsidiaries. According to some reports, the United States could collect billions per year in additional taxes if transfer pricing was calculated according to US tax laws. (Many foreign companies dispute this claim.)

Transfer prices and tax effects: An illustration. To understand the effects of transfer pricing on taxes, consider the case of Nehru Jacket Corporation. Its facility in Country B imports materials from the company's Country S facility.[3] The tax rate in Country B is 70 percent and in Country S is 40 percent.

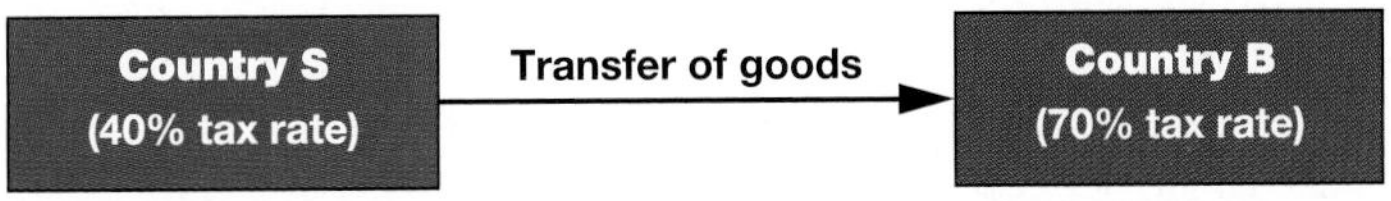

During the current year, Nehru incurred production costs of $2 million in Country S. Costs incurred in Country B, aside from the cost of the jackets, amounted to $6 million. (We call these "third-party costs.") Sales revenues in Country B were $24 million. Similar goods imported by other companies in Country B would have cost an equivalent of $3 million. However, Nehru points out that because of its special control over its operations in Country S and the special approach it uses to manufacture its goods, the appropriate transfer price is $10 million. What would Nehru's total tax liability in both jurisdictions be if it used the $3 million transfer price? What would the liability be if it used the $10 million transfer price?

Assuming that the $3 million transfer price is used, the tax liability is computed in Exhibit 19–2. In contrast, Exhibit 19–3 computes the tax liability assuming the $10 million transfer price. Nehru Jacket Corporation can save $2,100,000 in taxes simply by changing its transfer price!

To say the least, international taxing authorities look closely at transfer prices when they examine the tax returns of companies engaged in related-party transactions that cross national boundaries. Companies frequently must provide adequate support for the use of the transfer price that they have chosen for such a situation. Transfer-pricing disputes also occur at the state and province levels because of different tax rates.

[3] B denotes country with buying division; S denotes country with selling division.

Exhibit 19–2

Tax Liability for Corporation Assuming a $3 Million Transfer Price

	Country S		Country B
Revenue	$ 3,000,000		$24,000,000
Third-party costs	(2,000,000)		(6,000,000)
Transferred goods costs			(3,000,000)
Taxable income	$ 1,000,000		$15,000,000
Tax rate	× .40		× .70
Tax liability	$ 400,000		$10,500,000
Total tax liability		$10,900,000	

Exhibit 19–3

Tax Liability for Corporation Assuming a $10 Million Transfer Price

	Country S		Country B
Revenue	$10,000,000		$24,000,000
Third-party costs	(2,000,000)		(6,000,000)
Transferred goods costs			(10,000,000)
Taxable income	$ 8,000,000		$ 8,000,000
Tax rate	× .40		× .70
Tax liability	$ 3,200,000		$ 5,600,000
Total tax liability		$8,800,000	

You're the Decision Maker 19.3

Transfer Pricing for Multinational Companies

Refer to the preceding information for Nehru Jacket Corporation. Assume that the tax rate for both countries is 40 percent.

What would be the tax liability for Nehru if the transfer were set at $3 million? At $10 million? (Solutions begin on page 817.)

Import duties. Another international issue that can affect a firm's transfer-pricing policy is the imposition of import duties, or tariffs. These are fees a government charges an importer, generally on the basis of the reported value of the goods being imported. Consider as an example a firm with divisions in Europe and Asia. If the Asian country im-

Research Insight 19.2

Variables Affecting International Transfer-Pricing Policies

Many variables come into play when multinational companies determine their international transfer-pricing policies. A survey of US Fortune 500 firms revealed the following ranking of variables affecting international transfer-pricing policies.

Ranking of Average Importance Score	Variable
1	Overall profit to the company.
2	Differentials in income tax rates and income tax legislation among countries.
3	Restrictions imposed by foreign countries on repatriation of profits or dividends.
4	The competitive position of subsidiaries in foreign countries.
5	Rate of customs duties and customs legislation where the company has operations.
6, 7, 8	Restrictions imposed by foreign countries on the amount of royalty management fees that can be charged against foreign subsidiaries.
6, 7, 8	Maintaining good relationships with host governments.
6, 7, 8	The need to maintain adequate cash flows in foreign subsidiaries.
9	Import restrictions imposed by foreign countries.
10	Performance evaluation of foreign subsidiaries.
11	The need of subsidiaries in foreign countries to seek local funds.
12	Devaluation and revaluation in countries where the company has operations.
13, 14	Antidumping legislation of foreign countries.
13, 14	Antitrust legislation of foreign countries.
15	The interests of local partners in foreign subsidiaries.
16	Rules and requirements of financial reporting for subsidiaries in foreign countries.
17	Volume of interdivisional transfers.
18	Rates of inflation in foreign countries.
19	Risk of expropriation in foreign countries where the company has operations.
20	U.S. government requirements on direct foreign investments.

Source: R. Tang, "Transfer Pricing in the 1990s."

poses an import duty on goods transferred in from the European division, the company has an incentive to set a relatively low transfer price on the transferred goods. This minimizes the duty to be paid and maximizes the overall profit for the company as a whole. As in the case of taxation, countries sometimes pass laws to limit a multinational firm's flexibility in setting transfer prices for the purpose of minimizing import duties.

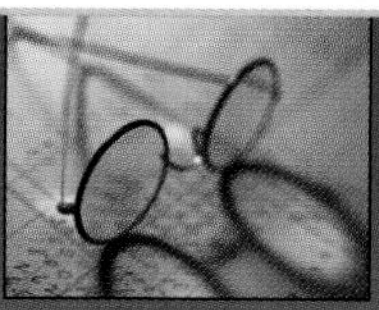

Cost Management in Practice 19.2

International Implications of Transfer Pricing

A Japanese motorcycle manufacturer uses just-in-time production for its manufacturing facility in Japan. Its US subsidiary is a distribution company that sells to dealers in the United States. Both the Japanese manufacturing facility and the US distribution subsidiary were profitable as long as demand for the product in the United States remained high.

Eventually, demand in the United States for motorcycles declined. The US subsidiary found itself with lots of inventory, so much that it had more than a year's supply of the product on hand. Meanwhile, the Japanese manufacturing plant was reluctant to reduce production below its efficient operating level and, because it followed the just-in-time philosophy, did not stockpile finished-goods inventory in Japan.

As inventories increased at the US subsidiary, so did expenses to store and sell them. The US subsidiary showed declining profits and eventually incurred losses. The US Internal Revenue Service claimed that the low profits and losses were the result of the transfer price set by the Japanese manufacturer (which was based on full-absorption manufacturing costs) and the fact that the Japanese manufacturer continued to ship products that the US subsidiary had difficulty selling. Consequently, according to the IRS, the Japanese manufacturer should bear some of the costs of the US subsidiary's high inventory levels. *Source: Based on an author's research.*

Segment Reporting and Transfer Pricing

LO 5 Discuss the effects of transfer pricing on segment reporting.

The Financial Accounting Standards Board (FASB) requires companies engaged in different lines of business to report certain information about their segments that meet its technical requirements.[4] This reporting requirement is intended to provide a measure of the performance of those segments of a business that are significant to the company as a whole.

The following are the principal items that must be disclosed about each segment:

- Revenue
- Operating profits or loss
- Identifiable assets
- Depreciation and amortization
- Capital expenditures
- Certain specialized items

In addition, if a company has significant foreign operations, it must disclose revenues, operating profits or losses, and identifiable assets by geographic region.

Negotiated transfer prices, which could be useful for internal purposes, are not generally acceptable for external segment reporting. In general, the accounting profession has indicated a preference for market-based transfer prices.[5] This preference arises because the purpose of the segment disclosure is to enable an investor to evaluate a company's divisions as though they were free-standing enterprises. Presumably, sales would be based on market transactions, not on managers' ability to negotiate prices.

Although the conceptual basis for market-based transfer prices is sound in this setting, the practical application can be difficult. Frequently, the segments are really interdependent, so market prices might not really reflect the same risk in an intracompany sale that they do in third-party sales.

---

[4]The requirements, which are too detailed to cover here, are specified in FASB, *Statement of Financial Accounting Standards No. 14,* "Financial Reporting for Segments of a Business Enterprise."

[5]See, for example, FASB, *Statement of Financial Accounting Standards No. 69,* which specifies the use of market-based transfer prices when calculating the results of operations for an oil and gas exploration and production operation.

In addition, in many situations, market prices either are not readily available or might exist for only some products. When these problems arise, management usually attempts to estimate the market price by obtaining market prices for similar goods and adjusting the price to reflect the characteristics of the goods transferred within the company. An alternative is to take the cost of the item transferred and add an allowance to represent the normal profit for the item.

Transfer Pricing in the Service Industry

When students in one university department take courses in another department, many colleges use a transfer price to account for these credit hours. How is this situation handled at the college you attend?

Service industry firms and nonprofit organizations also use transfer pricing when services are transferred between responsibility centers. For example, the interest rate at which banks transfer depositors' funds to the loan department is a form of transfer price. At Cornell University, if a student in the law school takes a course in the school of management, a transfer price is charged to the law school for the credit hours of instruction provided to the law student. At Cornell, the transfer price is called an *accessory instruction fee.* Since the transfer price is based on tuition charges, it is a market-price-based transfer price.

Chapter Summary

When products or services are transferred between divisions in the same organization, divisional performance is affected by the *transfer price.* A general rule states that the transfer price should equal the outlay cost incurred to make the transfer plus the organization's opportunity cost associated with the transfer. Due to difficulties in implementing the rule, most companies base transfer prices on external market prices, costs, or negotiations. In some cases, these practical transfer-pricing methods could result in dysfunctional decisions. Top management then must weigh the benefits of intervening to prevent suboptimal decisions against the costs of undermining divisional autonomy.

Since tax rates vary in different countries, companies have incentives to set transfer prices to increase revenues (and profits) in low-tax countries and increase costs (thereby reducing profits) in high-tax countries.

Companies with significant segments are required to report on those segments separately in the financial statements. The accounting profession has indicated a preference for market-based transfer prices when reporting on a segment of a business.

Key Terms

For each term's definition, refer to the indicated page or turn to the glossary at the end of the text.

cost-based transfer pricing, 808
dual transfer pricing, 811
imperfect competition, 806
perfect competition, 806
transfer price, 802

Meeting the Cost-Management Challenges

1. **What** is the primary objective of Outback Outfitters' cost-management team in determining a transfer-pricing policy?

The goal of Outback Outfitters' cost-management team in setting transfer prices is to establish incentives for autonomous division managers to make decisions that support the organization's overall goals. Transfer prices should be chosen so that each division manager, when striving to maximize his or her own division's profit, makes the decision that maximizes the company's profit.

2. **Describe** four methods by which Outback Outfitters can set transfer prices.

Outback Outfitters could set transfer prices using four methods as follows:

1. Transfer price is equal to additional outlay costs because goods are transferred plus opportunity costs to the organization because of the transfer.
2. Transfer price is the external market price.
3. Transfer prices can be set on the basis of negotiations among the division managers.
4. Transfer prices can be based on the cost of producing the goods or services to be transferred.

3. **Explain** the significance of excess capacity in the transferring division.

When the transferring division has excess capacity, the opportunity cost to produce a unit for transfer is zero.

4. **Why** might income tax laws affect the transfer-pricing policies of multinational companies?

The management of a multinational company has an incentive to set transfer prices to minimize the income reported for divisions in countries with relatively high income tax rates and to shift this income to divisions in countries with relatively low income tax rates. Some countries' tax laws prohibit this practice; other countries' laws permit it.

Solutions to You're the Decision Maker

19.1 Setting a Transfer Price p. 808

a. From a company's perspective, the minimum price is the unit-level cost to produce and market the goods, $19. If the company were centralized, we would expect this information to be conveyed to the marketing manager, who would be instructed not to set a price below $19.

b. The transfer price per pair that correctly informs the marketing manager about the differential costs of manufacturing is $18.

c. If the production manager set the price at $28.50, the marketing manager would set the minimum price at $29.50 ($28.50 + $1.00). So the marketing manager sets the price in excess of $29.50 per pair. In fact, prices of $28, $25, or anything higher than $19 would have generated a positive contribution margin from the production and sale of shoes.

d. If the production division had been operating at capacity, an implicit opportunity cost of internal transfers to the company is the lost contribution margin ($28.50 − $19.00 = $9.50) from not selling in the wholesale market.

The transfer price should have been as follows:

Outlay cost of production	+	Opportunity cost to company if goods are transferred internally
	=	$19.00 + $9.50
	=	$28.50

Marketing would have appropriately treated the $28.50 as part of its differential cost to buy and sell the shoes.

19.2 Dysfunctional Decisions and Transfer-Pricing Policies p. 811

a. The two divisions' actions cost Meridian $180,000. This amount is the difference between the price paid for part A-16 from the outside supplier ($40) and the differential unit-level cost to produce one unit of A-16 in the production division ($22) times the 10,000 units in the order.

b. This is a tough call with no clearly correct answer. If the CEO does not intervene, it will cost Meridian $180,000. The cost of intervention, however, is undermining the autonomy of the production and assembly division managers.

19.3 Transfer Pricing for Multinational Companies p. 814

For the $3 million transfer, the total tax is (.40 × $1,000,000) + (.40 × $15,000,000) = $6,400,000

For $10 million, the total tax is (.40 × $8,000,000) + (.40 × $8,000,000) = $6,400,000.

With equal tax rates, inflating the transfer price has no advantage.

Review Questions

19.1 Why do transfer prices exist even in highly centralized organizations?

19.2 Describe four methods by which transfer prices can be set.

19.3 Why are market-based transfer prices considered optimal under many circumstances?

19.4 What are the limitations to market-based transfer prices?

19.5 What are the advantages and disadvantages of top management's direct intervention in a transfer-pricing dispute?

19.6 Why do companies often use prices other than market prices for interdivisional transfers?

19.7 What is the basis for choosing between actual and standard costs for cost-based transfer pricing?

19.8 Some have suggested that managers should negotiate transfer prices. What are the disadvantages of a negotiated transfer-pricing system?

19.9 What is the general transfer-pricing rule?

19.10 Explain the effect of import duties, or tariffs, on the transfer-pricing policies of multinational companies.

Critical Analysis

19.11 How does the choice of a transfer price affect the operating profits of both segments involved in an intracompany transfer?

19.12 What are some goals of a transfer-pricing system in a decentralized organization?

19.13 Division A has no external markets. It produces monofilament used by division B, which cannot purchase this particular type of monofilament from any other source. What transfer-pricing system would you recommend for the interdivisional sales of monofilament? Why?

19.14 Refer to Cost Management in Practice 19.2 on page 815. Why did the Internal Revenue Service dispute the US subsidiary's reported profits and losses?

19.15 When setting a transfer price for goods sold across international boundaries, what factors should management consider?

19.16 "Setting transfer prices by negotiation is detrimental to the company." Do you agree or disagree with this statement by the CEO of a midsize manufacturing company? Why?

19.17 "Basing transfer prices on full absorption costs can really screw up decision making in a company!" Explain this remark by a manufacturing vice president, and construct a simple numerical example to make the point.

19.18 "In setting transfer prices for multinationals, tax considerations can be the tail that wags the dog." Explain.

Exercises

Exercise 19.19
Application of Transfer Pricing Rules
(LO 1, 2)

Cayuga Associates is a real estate company operating in the Finger Lakes region of central New York. Its leasing division rents and manages properties for others, and its maintenance division performs services such as carpentry, painting, plumbing, and electrical work. The maintenance division, which has an estimated variable cost of $34 per labor hour, works for both Cayuga and other companies. It could spend 100 percent of its time working for outsiders. Maintenance division charges $68 per hour for labor performed for outsiders, the same rate that other maintenance companies charge. The leasing division complained that it could hire its own maintenance staff at an estimated variable cost of $39 per hour.

Required

a. What is the minimum transfer price that the maintenance division should obtain for its services, assuming that it is operating at capacity?

b. What is the maximum price that the leasing division should pay?

c. Would your answers in requirements (a) or (b) change if the maintenance division had idle capacity? If so, which answer would change, and what would the new amount be?

Exercise 19.20
Transfer-Pricing System Evaluation
(LO 1, 2)

The selling division, which offers its product to outside markets for $150, incurs variable costs of $55 per unit and fixed costs of $37,500 per month based on monthly production of 1,000 units.

The buying division can acquire the product from an alternate supplier for $157.50 per unit or from the selling division for $150 plus $10 per unit in transportation costs.

Required

a. What are the costs and benefits of the alternatives available to the selling and buying divisions with respect to the transfer of the selling division's product? Assume that the selling division can market all that it can produce.

b. How would your answer change if the selling division had idle capacity sufficient to cover all of the buying division's needs?

Exercise 19.21
General Transfer-Pricing Rule
(LO 1, 2)

Three Rivers Fabrication Corporation has two divisions. The fabrication division transfers partially completed components to the assembly division at a predetermined transfer price. The fabrication division, which has a standard variable production cost per unit of $300, has no excess capacity and could sell all of its components to outside buyers at $380 per unit in a perfectly competitive market.

Required

a. Determine a transfer price using the general rule.

b. How would the transfer price change if the fabrication division had excess capacity?

Exercise 19.22
Cost-Based Transfer Pricing; Ethics
(LO 1, 3)

Refer to the preceding exercise. The fabrication division's full (absorption) cost of a component is $340, which includes $40 of applied fixed-overhead costs. The transfer price has been set at $374, which is the fabrication division's full cost plus a 10 percent markup.

The assembly division has a special offer of $465 for its product. The assembly division incurs variable costs of $100 in addition to the transfer price for the fabrication division's components. Both divisions currently have excess production capacity.

Ethics

Required

a. Is the assembly division's manager likely to accept or reject the special offer? Why?

b. Is this decision in the best interests of Three Rivers Fabrication Corporation as a whole? Why?

c. Suppose that the assembly division manager decides to reject the special offer. Is the manager acting ethically? Explain.

d. How could the situation be remedied using the transfer price?

Exercise 19.23
Transfer-Pricing System Evaluation
(LO 1, 2, 3)

Pandora Box Company has two decentralized divisions, X and Y. Division X always has purchased certain units from division Y at $150 per unit. Because division Y plans to raise the price to $200 per unit, division X desires to purchase these units from outside suppliers for $150 per unit. Division Y's costs follow:

Variable costs per unit	$140
Annual fixed costs	$30,000
Annual production of these units for X	1,000 units

Required

If division X buys from an outside supplier, the facilities that division Y uses to manufacture these units would remain idle. What would be the result if Pandora enforces a transfer price of $200 per unit between divisions X and Y?

[CPA adapted]

Exercise 19.24
International Transfer-Pricing Policy: Use of Internet
(LO 4)

Communication Internet

Use the Internet to explore international transfer-pricing policies by going to the Web site for the OECD (Organization for Economic Cooperation and Development) at *www.oecd.org.* Use the *Search OECD Online* function and enter *transfer pricing* when prompted for a word or phrase for which to search. Then click on one of the following OECD on-line documents: *OECD Transfer Pricing Guidelines* or *Transfer Pricing Guidelines for Multinational Enterprises and Tax Administrations.*

Required

Peruse the OECD transfer-pricing guidelines. Choose an issue that interests you and report on it to the class.

Exercise 19.25
Transfer-Pricing System Evaluation
(LO 1, 2, 3)

Seattle Transit, Ltd., operates a local mass transit system. The transit authority is a governmental agency related to the state government. It has an agreement with the state government to provide rides to senior citizens for 10 cents per trip. The government reimburses Seattle Transit for the "cost" of each trip taken by a senior citizen.

The regular fare is 80 cents per trip. After analyzing its costs, Seattle Transit figured that with its operating deficit, the full cost of each ride on the transit system is $2.00. The number of senior citizens on any route does not affect routes, capacity, or operating costs.

Required

a. What alternative prices could be used to determine the governmental reimbursement to Seattle Transit?

b. Which price would Seattle Transit prefer? Why?

c. Which price would the state government prefer? Why?

d. If Seattle Transit provides an average of 200,000 trips for senior citizens in a given month, what is the monthly value of the difference between the prices in requirements (b) and (c)?

Exercise 19.26
Transfer-Pricing System Evaluation
(LO 1, 2, 3)

Team

A company permits its decentralized units to "lease" space to one another. Division X has leased some idle warehouse space to division Y for $1.50 per square foot per month. Recently, division X obtained a new five-year contract, which will increase its production sufficiently so that the warehouse space is more valuable to it. Division X has notified division Y that it will increase the rental price to $5.30 per square foot per month. Division Y can lease space at $2.90 per square foot in another warehouse from an outside company but prefers to stay in the shared facilities. Division Y's management states that it prefers not to move. If division X cannot use the space now being leased to division Y, it will have to rent other space for $4.45

per square foot per month. (The difference in rental prices occurs because division X requires a more substantial warehouse building than division Y.)

Required

As a group, recommend a transfer price and explain your reasons for choosing that price.

Exercise 19.27
Transfer Pricing
(LO 4)

Team

Global

Read "Harvard University–Soros Suit Brings Russian Bankruptcy Fight to U.S. Court," *The Wall Street Journal,* November 23, 1999, by Steve Liesman. The bankruptcy of AO Sidanco, a Russian oil company, has been filed in a New York state court. The Harvard University endowment owns an interest in AO Sidanco. Tyumen Oil Company, a smaller Russian oil company, has been accused of tampering with the bankruptcy process to gain control of Sidanco's subsidiaries. The Harvard group of investors owns the interest in Sidanco through TPT Ltd., a Cayman Islands company. TPT Ltd. claims that Tyumen Oil used transfer pricing methods to steal oil revenues from the subsidiaries.

Required

According to the allegations made by TPT Ltd., how did Tyumen Oil use transfer pricing to its advantage?

Exercise 19.28
Transfer-Pricing System Evaluation
(LO 1, 2, 3)

Outdoor Greenery, owned 60 percent by Kwasi Peterson and 40 percent by Maya Jefferies, grows specimen plants for landscape contractors. The wholesale price of each plant is $15. During the past year, Outdoor sold 5,000 specimen plants.

Of the plants sold last year, 1,000 were sold to Lively Landscape Co. Peterson has a 20 percent interest in Lively Landscape Co., and Jefferies has a 60 percent interest in Lively Landscape Co. At the end of the year, Jefferies noted that Lively was the largest buyer of Outdoor Greenery's plants. She suggested that the plant company give Lively Landscape a 10 percent reduction in prices for the coming year in recognition of its position as a preferred customer.

Required

Assuming that Lively Landscape purchases the same number of plants at the same prices in the coming year, what effect would the price reduction have on the operating profits that accrue to Peterson and to Jefferies for the coming year?

Exercise 19.29
Segment Reporting and Transfer Pricing
(LO 1, 5)

Bay Area Homes, Inc., has two divisions, building and financing. The building division oversees construction of single-family homes in "economically efficient" subdivisions. The financing division takes loan applications and packages mortgages into pools and sells them in the loan markets. It also services the mortgages. Both divisions meet the requirements for segment disclosures under accounting rules.

The building division had $68 million in sales last year. Costs, other than those charged by the financing division, totaled $52 million. The financing division obtained revenues of $16 million from servicing mortgages and incurred outside costs of $14 million. In addition, the financing division charged the building division $8 million for loan-related fees. The building division's manager complained to Bay Area's CEO that the financing division was charging twice the commercial rate for loan-related fees and that the building division would be better off sending its buyers to an outside lender.

The financing division's manager stated that although commercial rates might be lower, it was more difficult to service Bay Area mortgages, and therefore, the higher fees were justified.

Required

a. What are the reported segment operating profits for each division, ignoring income taxes and using the $8 million transfer price for the loan-related fees?

b. What are the reported segment operating profits for each division, ignoring income taxes and using a $4 million commercial rate as the transfer price for the loan-related fees?

Exercise 19.30
International Transfer Prices
(LO 4)

Global

North American Building Products, Inc., has two operating divisions. Its logging operation in Canada mills and ships logs to the United States where the company's building supplies division uses them. Operating expenses amount to $2 million in Canada and $6 million in the United States exclusive of the costs of any goods transferred from Canada. Revenues in the United States are $15 million.

If the lumber were purchased from one of the company's U.S. lumber divisions, the costs would be $3 million. However, if the lumber had been purchased from an independent Canadian supplier, the cost would be $4 million. Assume that the marginal income tax rate is 60 percent in Canada and 40 percent in the United States.

Required

What is the company's total tax liability to both jurisdictions for each of the two alternative transfer-pricing scenarios ($3 million and $4 million)? Explain.

Exercise 19.31
Segment Reporting and Transfer Pricing
(LO 1, 5)

Global

Down Under Corporation, based in Melbourne, Australia, has two operating divisions, an amusement park in Sydney and a hotel in Brisbane. The two divisions meet the Australian requirements for segment disclosures. Before transactions between the two divisions are considered, revenues and costs were as follows (in thousands of *Australian dollars*):

	Amusement Park	Hotel
Revenue	$11,200	$7,400
Costs	6,200	5,000

The amusement park and the hotel had a joint marketing arrangement by which the hotel gave free passes to the amusement park and the amusement park gave discount coupons good for stays at the hotel. The value of the free passes to the amusement park redeemed during the past year totaled $1,600,000. The discount coupons redeemed at the hotel resulted in a $600,000 decrease in hotel revenues. As of the end of the year, all current year coupons have expired.

Required

a. What are the operating profits for each division, considering the effects of the costs arising from the joint marketing agreement?

b. Is there a transfer-pricing issue in this exercise? Explain.

Problems

Problem 19.32
Basic Transfer Pricing
(LO 1, 2, 3)

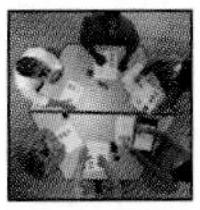

Communication Team

Tampa division of Carlyle Corporation produces electric motors, 20 percent of which Tampa sells to Carlyle's Redstone division. It sells the remainder to outside customers. Carlyle treats its divisions as profit centers and allows division managers to choose their sources of sale and supply. Corporate policy requires that all interdivisional sales and purchases be recorded at variable cost as a transfer price. Tampa division's budgeted sales and standard-cost data for the current year, based on capacity of 100,000 units, are as follows:

	Outside Companies	Redstone Division
Sales	$8,000,000	$ 900,000
Unit-level (variable) costs	(3,600,000)	(900,000)
Facility-level (fixed) costs	(1,200,000)	(300,000)
Gross margin	$3,200,000	$(300,000)
Unit sales	80,000	20,000

Tampa has an opportunity to sell the 20,000 units shown in the table to an outside customer at a price of $75 per unit. Redstone can purchase its requirements from an outside supplier for $85 per unit.

Required

As a group, make a presentation to your class addressing the following questions.

a. Assuming that Tampa division desires to maximize its gross margin, should it sell to the new customer and drop its sales to Redstone during the current year? Why?

b. Assume, instead, that Carlyle permits division managers to negotiate the transfer price. The managers agree on a tentative transfer price of $75 per unit, to be reduced based on an equal sharing of the additional gross margin to Tampa resulting from the sale of 20,000 motors to Redstone at $75 per unit. What is the actual transfer price?

c. Assume now that Tampa division has an opportunity to sell the 20,000 motors that Redstone division would buy to the same customers that are buying the other 80,000 motors produced by Tampa. Tampa could sell all 100,000 motors to outside customers for $100. What actions by each division manager are in the best interests of Carlyle Corporation?

d. Under the scenario described in requirement (c), use the general transfer-pricing rule to compute the transfer price that Tampa should charge Redstone for motors.

e. Will the transfer price computed in requirement (d) result in the most desirable outcome from the standpoint of Carlyle Corporation? Explain your answer.

[CPA adapted]

Problem 19.33
Analysis of Transfer-Pricing Data
(LO 1, 2, 3)

Spreadsheet

Global Electronics, Inc., is a decentralized organization that evaluates division management based on measures of division contribution margin. Divisions L and N operate in similar product markets. Division L produces a sophisticated electronic assembly that it can sell up to 140,000 units to the outside market for $16 per unit per year. These units require 2 direct-labor hours each.

If L modifies the units with an additional one-half hour of labor time, it can sell them for $18 per unit to N, which will accept up to 120,000 of these units per year.

If N does not obtain 120,000 units from L, it purchases them for $18.50 each from the outside. Division N incurs $8 of additional labor and other out-of-pocket costs to convert the assemblies into a home digital electronic radio, calculator, telephone monitor, and clock unit. The units can be sold to the outside market for $45 each.

Division L estimates that its total costs are $925,000 for fixed costs and $6 per direct-labor hour. Its capacity is limited to 400,000 direct-labor hours per year.

Required

Determine the following:

a. Total contribution margin to L if it sells 140,000 units to the outside.

b. Total contribution margin to L if it sells 120,000 units to N.

c. The costs to be considered in determining the optimal company policy for sales by division L.

d. The annual contributions and costs for L and N under the optimal policy.

Problem 19.34
Transfer Pricing with Imperfect Markets; ROI Evaluation; Normal Costing
(LO 1, 2, 3)

Spreadsheet

Aquarius Corporation's division S has an investment base of $600,000. The division produces and sells 90,000 units of a product at a market price of $10 per unit. Its variable costs total $3 per unit. The division also charges each unit with a share of fixed costs. The fixed cost is computed as $5 per unit, based on planned production of 100,000 units. The budgeted and actual fixed overhead are equal, and any volume variances are closed to Cost of Goods Sold.

Division T wants to purchase 20,000 units from division S but is willing to pay only $6.20 per unit because it has an opportunity to accept a special order at a reduced price. The order is economically justifiable only if division T can acquire the division S output at a reduced price.

Required

a. What is the ROI for division S without the transfer to division T?

b. What is division S's ROI if it transfers 20,000 units to division T at $6.20 each?

c. What is the minimum transfer price for the 20,000-unit order that S would accept if it were willing to maintain the same ROI with the transfer as it would accept by selling its 90,000 units to the outside market?

Problem 19.35
Transfer Pricing: Performance Evaluation Issues
(LO 1, 2, 3)

The Kansas City (KC) division of Great Plains Corporation, operating at capacity, has been asked by Jaydee division to supply it with electrical fitting no. 1726. KC sells this part to its regular customers for $7.50 each. Jaydee, which is operating at 50 percent capacity, is willing to pay $5 each for the fitting. It will put the fitting into a brake unit that it is manufacturing on a cost-plus basis for a commercial airplane manufacturer.

KC has a $4.25 variable cost of producing fitting no. 1726. The cost of the brake unit as built by Jaydee follows:

Purchased parts—outside vendors	$22.50
KC fitting no. 1726	5.00
Other variable costs	14.00
Fixed overhead and administration	8.00
Total	$49.50

Jaydee believes that the price concession is necessary to get the job. The company uses ROI and dollar profits to measure divisional and division manager performance.

Required

a. If you were KC's division controller, would you recommend that it supply fitting no. 1726 to Jaydee? Why or why not? (Ignore any income tax issues.)

b. Is it to the short-run economic advantage of Great Plains Corporation for KC to supply Jaydee with fitting no. 1726 at $5 each? Explain your answer. (Ignore any income tax issues.)

c. Discuss the organizational and managerial behavior difficulties, if any, inherent in this situation. As Great Plains Corporation's controller, what would you advise the corporation's president to do in this situation?

[CMA adapted]

Problem 19.36
Comprehensive Transfer-Pricing Problem
(LO 1, 2, 3)

Ozark Mountain Industries, Inc., manufactures windows for the home-building industry. The frame division produces the window frames. It then transfers the frames to the glass division, which installs the glass and hardware. The company's best-selling product is a three-by-four-foot, double-paned operable window.

The frame division also can sell frames directly to custom home builders, which install the glass and hardware. The sales price for a frame is $80. The glass division sells its finished windows for $190. The markets for both frames and finished windows exhibit perfect competition.

The standard cost of the window is detailed as follows:

	Frame Division	Glass Division
Direct material	$15	$30*
Direct labor	20	15
Variable overhead	30	30
Total	$65	$75

*Not including the transfer price for the frame.

Required

a. Assume that the frame division has no excess capacity.

(1) Use the general rule to compute the transfer price for window frames.

(2) Calculate the transfer price if it is based on standard variable cost with a 10 percent markup.

b. Assume that the frame division has excess capacity.

(1) Use the general rule to compute the transfer price for window frames.

(2) Explain why your answers to requirements (a1) and (b1) differ.

(3) Suppose that the predetermined fixed-overhead rate in the frame division is 125 percent of direct-labor cost. Calculate the transfer price if it is based on standard full cost plus a 10 percent markup.

(4) Assume that the transfer price established in requirement (b3) is used. The glass division has been approached by the U.S. Army with a special order for 1,000 windows at $155. From the perspective of Ozark Mountain Industries as a whole, should the glass division accept or reject the special order? Why?

(5) Assume the same facts as in requirement (b4). Will an autonomous glass division manager accept or reject the special order? Why?

c. Comment on the use of full cost as the basis for setting transfer prices.

Problem 19.37
International Transfer Prices
(LO 1, 4)

Global

Interglobal Merchants Co-op (IMC) operates a fleet of container ships in international trade between Great Britain and Thailand. All of the shipping income (that is, that related to IMC's ships) is deemed as earned in Great Britain. IMC also owns a dock facility in Thailand that services IMC's fleet. Income from the dock facility is deemed earned in Thailand, however. IMC's income attributable to Great Britain is taxed at a 75 percent rate. Its income attributable to Thailand is taxed at a 20 percent rate. Last year, the dock facility had operating revenues of $4 million, excluding services performed for IMC's ships. IMC's shipping revenues for last year were $26 million.

Costs to operate the dock facility were $5 million last year; costs to operate the shipping operation, before deduction of dock facility costs, were $17 million. No similar dock facilities in Thailand are available to IMC.

However, a facility in Malaysia would have charged IMC an estimated $3 million for the services that IMC's Thailand dock provided its ships. IMC management noted that if the services had been provided in Great Britain, the costs for the year would have totaled $8 million. IMC argued to the British tax officials that the appropriate transfer price is the price that would have been charged in Great Britain. British tax officials suggest that the Malaysian price is the appropriate one.

Required

What is the difference in tax costs to IMC for the alternate transfer prices for dock services, that is, its price in Great Britain versus that in Malaysia?

Problem 19.38
Transfer Prices and Tax Regulations
(LO 1, 4)

Global

Two Continents, Inc., has two operating divisions in a semiautonomous organization structure. Division X, located in the United States, produces part XZ-1, which is an input to division Y, located in the south of France. Division X uses idle capacity to produce XZ-1, which has a domestic market price of $60. Its variable costs are $25 per unit. The company's U.S. tax rate is 40 percent of income.

In addition to the transfer price for each XZ-1 received from division X, division Y pays a $15 shipping fee per unit. Part XZ-1 becomes a part of division Y's output product. The output product costs an additional $10 to produce and sells for an equivalent $115. Division Y could purchase part XZ-1 for $50 per unit from a Paris supplier. The company's French tax rate is 70 percent of income. Assume that French tax laws permit transferring at either variable cost or market price.

Required

What transfer price is economically optimal for Two Continents, Inc.? Support your answer with an appropriate analysis.

Problem 19.39
Transfer-Pricing System Evaluation
(LO 1, 2, 3)

Communication

Tri-City, Inc., consists of three divisions—Boston Corporation, Raleigh Company, and Memphis Company—that operate as if they were independent companies. Each division has its own sales force and production facilities. Each division management is responsible for sales, cost of operations, acquiring and financing divisional assets, and working capital management. Tri-City corporate management evaluates the performance of the divisions and division managements on the basis of ROI.

Memphis Company has just been awarded a contract for a product that uses a component manufactured by outside suppliers and by Raleigh Company, which is operating well below capacity. Memphis used a cost figure of $3.80 for the component in preparing its bid for the new product. Raleigh supplied this cost figure in response to Memphis's request for the average variable cost of the component; it represents the standard variable manufacturing cost and variable marketing costs.

Raleigh's regular selling price for the component that Memphis needs is $6.50. Raleigh management indicated that it could supply Memphis the required quantities of the component at the regular selling price less variable selling and distribution expenses. Memphis management responded by offering to pay standard variable manufacturing cost plus 20 percent.

The two divisions have been unable to agree on a transfer price. Corporate management has never established a transfer price policy. The corporate vice president of finance suggested a price equal to the standard full manufacturing cost (that is, no selling and distribution expenses) plus a 15 percent markup. The two division managers rejected this price because each considered it grossly unfair.

The unit cost structure for the Raleigh component and the suggested prices follow.

Costs:	
Standard variable manufacturing cost	$3.20
Standard fixed manufacturing cost	1.20
Variable selling and distribution expenses	.60
Total	$5.00
Prices:	
Regular selling price	$6.50
Regular selling price less variable selling and distribution expenses ($6.50 − $ .60)	$5.90
Variable manufacturing plus 20% ($3.20 × 1.20)	$3.84
Standard full manufacturing cost plus 15% ($4.40 × 1.15)	$5.06

Required

a. Discuss the effect that each proposed price might have on the attitude of Raleigh's management toward intracompany business.

b. Is the negotiation of a price between the Memphis and Raleigh divisions a satisfactory method to solve the transfer price problem? Explain your answer.

c. As an outside consultant, write a letter to Tri-City's corporate management recommending whether it should become involved in this transfer-pricing controversy.

[CMA adapted]

Problem 19.40
Segment Reporting and Transfer Pricing
(LO 1, 5)

Gulliver's Travel, Ltd., has four operating divisions: airline, hotel, auto rental, and travel services. Each division is a separate segment for financial reporting purposes. Revenues and costs for the past year related to outside transactions were as follows (dollars in millions):

	Airline	Hotel	Auto Rental	Travel Services
Revenue	$245	$106	$89	$32
Costs	157	71	66	30

The airline participated in a frequent stayer program with the hotel chain. The airline reported that it had traded hotel award coupons during the past year for travel that had a $26 million retail value, assuming that the travel was redeemed at full airline fares. Auto rental division offered 20 percent discounts to Gulliver's Travel's airline passengers and hotel guests. These discounts to airline passengers were estimated to have a $7 million retail value. Gulliver's Travels hotel guests redeemed $3 million in auto rental discount coupons. Gullivers' Travels hotels also provided rooms for flight crews of the airline division, a $13 million value for the year.

Travel services division booked flights on Gulliver's Travels' airline valued at $4 million for the year. This service for intracompany hotel bookings was valued at $2 million and for intracompany auto rentals at $1 million.

While preparing these data for financial statement presentation, the hotel division's controller stated that the value of the airline coupons should be based on the differential and opportunity costs of the travel awards, not on the full fare for the tickets issued. The fact that a travel award is usually allocated to seats that would otherwise be empty or that are restricted similar to those on discount tickets supported this argument. If the differential and opportunity costs were used for this transfer price, the value would be $5 million instead of $26 million. The airline controller made a similar argument concerning the auto rental discount coupons. If the differential cost basis were used for the auto rental coupons, the transfer price would be $1 million instead of the $7 million.

Gulliver's Travels, Ltd., reports assets in each segment as follows:

Airline	$955 million
Hotel	385 million
Car rental	321 million
Travel services	65 million

Required

a. Using the retail values for transfer pricing for segment-reporting purposes, what are the operating profits for each of Gulliver's Travels' divisions?

b. What are the operating profits for each division using the differential cost basis for pricing transfers?

c. Rank each division by ROI using the transfer pricing method in (a), as well as using the transfer pricing method in (b). What effect does the transfer-pricing system have on the rankings?

Problem 19.41
Evaluation of the Profit Impact of Alternative Transfer Decisions
(LO 1, 2, 3)

Seneca Company manufactures a line of fingernail polish. The manufacturing process entails adding and mixing coloring ingredients; the finished product is packaged in a company-produced glass bottle and packed in cases containing six bottles each. Because the appearance of the bottle highly influences sales volume, the company developed an unusual bottle production process.

The polish manufacturing plant uses all bottle production. Each division is considered a separate profit center and is evaluated as such. As the new corporate controller, you are responsible for determining the proper transfer price to use for the bottles produced for the polish division.

Bottle division's cost analysis indicates that it can produce bottles at these costs:

Volume (cases)	Total Cost	Cost per Case
2,000,000	$3,200,000	$1.60
4,000,000	5,200,000	1.30
6,000,000	7,200,000	1.20

These costs include fixed costs of $1.2 million and variable costs of $1 per equivalent case. These data have caused considerable corporate discussion as to the proper price to use in the transfer of bottles to the polish division. This interest is heightened because a significant portion of a division manager's income is an incentive bonus based on profit center results.

The polish division has the following costs in addition to the bottle costs:

Volume (cases)	Total Cost	Cost per Case
2,000,000	$16,400,000	$8.20
4,000,000	32,400,000	8.10
6,000,000	48,400,000	8.07

At your request, bottle division's general manager asked other bottle manufacturers to quote a price for the number and sizes that the polish division demands. These competitive prices follow:

Volume (equivalent cases)	Total Price	Price per Case
2,000,000	$ 4,000,000	$2.00
4,000,000	7,000,000	1.75
6,000,000	10,000,000	1.67

The marketing department provided the following price-demand relationship for the finished product:

Sales Volume (cases)	Total Sales Revenue	Sales Price per Case
2,000,000	$25,000,000	$12.50
4,000,000	45,600,000	11.40
6,000,000	63,900,000	10.65

Required

a. Seneca Company has used market-price transfer prices in the past. Using the current market prices and costs and assuming a volume of 6 million cases, calculate operating profits for the:

(1) Bottle division.

(2) Polish division.

(3) Corporation.

b. Is this production and sales level the most profitable volume for the:

(1) Bottle division?

(2) Polish division?

(3) Corporation?

[CMA adapted]

Cases

Case 19.42
Transfer Pricing; Incentive Issues*
(LO 1, 2, 3)

Global

"We can't drop our prices below $210 per hundred pounds," exclaimed Greg Berman, manager of Forwarders, a division of Custom Freight Systems. "Our margins are already razor thin. Our costs just won't allow us to go any lower. Corporate rewards our division based on our profitability, and I won't lower my prices below $210."

Custom Freight Systems is organized into three divisions: Air Cargo provides air cargo services; Logistics Services operates distribution centers and provides truck cargo services; and Forwarders provides international freight-forwarding services. Freight forwarders typically buy space on planes from international air cargo companies. This is analogous to a charter company that books seats on passenger planes and resells them to passengers. In many cases, freight forwarders hire trucking companies to transport the cargo from the plane to the domestic destination. The following diagram depicts Custom Freight Systems' operations.

*Prepared by Thomas B. Rumzie under the direction of Michael W. Maher. © Copyright Michael W. Maher.

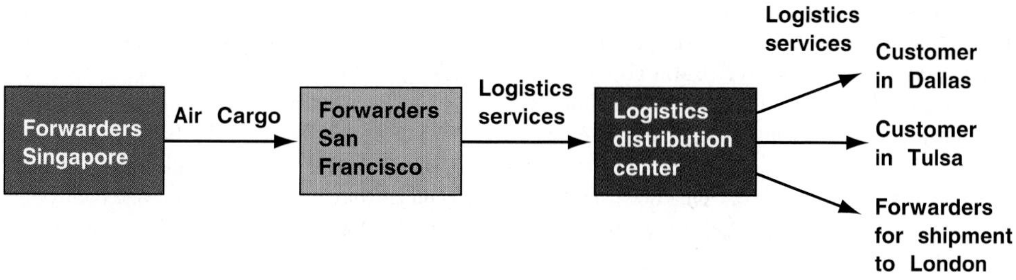

Management believes that the three divisions integrate together well and are able to provide one-stop transportation services to customers. For example, a Forwarders branch in Singapore receives cargo from a shipper, prepares the necessary documentation, and then ships the cargo on Air Cargo to a domestic Forwarders station. The domestic Forwarders station ensures that the cargo passes through customs and ships it to the final destination with Logistics Services as shown in the preceding diagram.

Management evaluates each division separately and rewards division managers based on profit and return on investment. Responsibility and decision-making authority are decentralized. Similarly, each division has a sales and marketing organization. Division salespeople report to the vice president of sales for Custom Freight Systems as well as a division sales manager as depicted in the following organization chart. Custom Freight Systems believes that it has successfully motivated division managers by paying bonuses for high division profits.

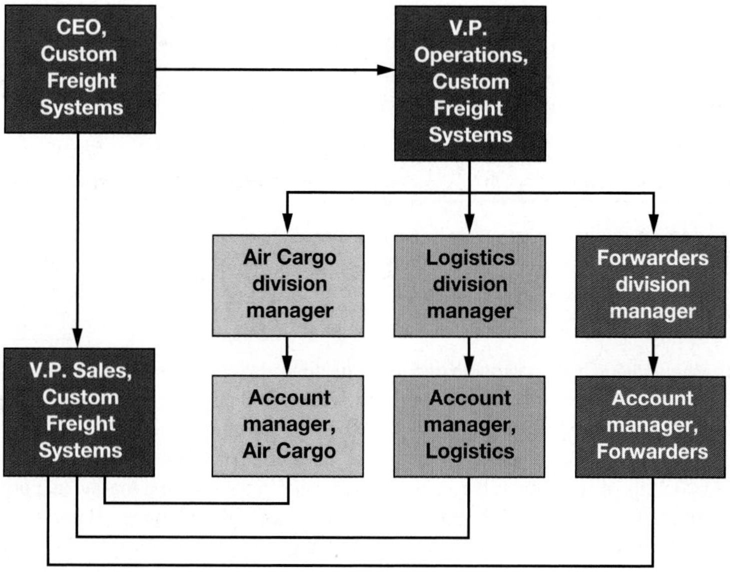

Recently, Logistics Services was preparing a bid for a customer. The customer had freight to import from an overseas supplier and wanted Logistics Services to submit a bid for a distribution package that included providing air freight from the supplier, receiving the freight and providing customs clearance services at the airport, warehousing the shipment, and distributing it to customers.

Because this was a contract for international shipping, Logistics Services needed to contact different freight forwarders for shipping quotes. Logistics Services requested quotes from the Forwarders division and United Systems, a competing freight forwarder. Divisions of Custom Freight Systems are free to use the most appropriate and cost-effective suppliers.

Logistics Services received bids of $210 per hundred pounds from Forwarders and $185 per hundred pounds from United Systems. Forwarders specified in its bid that it will use Air Cargo, a division of Custom Freight Systems. Forwarder's variable costs were $175 per hundred pounds, which included the cost of subcontracting air transportation. Air Cargo, which was experiencing a period of excess capacity, quoted Forwarders the market rate of $155; its variable costs typically are 60 percent of the market rate.

The price difference between the two different bids alarmed Susan Burns, a contract manager at Logistics Services. Burns knows this is a competitive business and is concerned because the difference between the high and low bids was at least $1,000,000 (current projections for the contract estimated

4,160,000 pounds during the first year). Burns contacted Greg Berman, the manager of Forwarders, and discussed the quote. "Don't you think full markup is unwarranted due to the fact that you and the airlines have so much excess capacity?" Burns complained.

She soon realized that Berman was not going to drop the price quote. "You know how small margins are in this business. Why should I cut my margins even smaller just to make you look good?" Berman asked.

Burns went to Bennie Espinosa, vice president of Custom Freight Systems and chairperson for the corporate strategy committee. "That does sound strange," said Espinosa, "I need to examine the overall cost structure and talk to Berman. I'll get back to you by noon Monday."

Required

a. Which bid should Logistics Services accept: the internal bid from Forwarders or the external bid from United Systems?

b. What should the transfer price be on this transaction?

c. What should Bennie Espinosa do?

d. Do the reward systems for the division managers support the best interests of Forwarders and of Custom Freight Systems? Give examples that support your conclusion.

e. Assume the same information as given in the case, but instead of receiving one outside bid, Logistics Services receives two. The new bid is from World Services for $195 per hundred pounds. It offered to use Air Cargo for air cargo. Air Cargo will charge World $155 per hundred pounds. The bids from Forwarders and United Systems remain the same as before (i.e., $210 and $185, respectively). Which bid should the Logistics Services take? Explain.

Case 19.43
Minimum and Maximum Acceptable Transfer Prices*†
(LO 1, 2)

Oakland Gauge Company manufactures small gauges for use in household appliances and industrial machinery. The firm has two divisions: appliance and industrial. The company is decentralized, and each division is completely autonomous in its decision making.

The appliance division produces two instruments, A and B. Cost information about these products follows.

Appliance Division	Instrument A	Instrument B
Direct material	$ 5.00	$ 4.00
Direct labor	10.00	20.00
Fixed overhead	20.00	40.00
Full cost	$35.00	$64.00

The appliance division has no variable overhead. Its direct-labor rate is $10 per hour, and a maximum of 10,000 hours is available per year. Fixed overhead is $200,000 per year and is applied on the basis of direct-labor hours. The planned activity level is 10,000 direct-labor hours per year.

The demand in the external market for instrument A at a price of $45 per unit is unlimited. Anywhere from zero to 3,000 units of instrument B can be sold annually in the external market at a price of $94 per unit. The external market has demand for no more than 3,000 units of instrument B per year.

The industrial division also has two products, type Y gauges and type Z gauges. Cost information about these products follows.

Industrial Division	Type Y Gauges	Type Z Gauges
Direct material	$12.00	$ 7.00
Direct labor	10.00	20.00
Fixed overhead	10.00	20.00
Full cost	$32.00	$47.00

In addition to the costs listed in the preceding table, each type Z gauge unit uses one unit of instrument B, which is produced in the appliance division and transferred to the industrial division. The costs in the preceding table for type Z gauge are the *only* costs incurred in the industrial division to transform a B instrument into a type Z gauge. They do *not* include the transfer price of instrument B or the costs of manufacturing instrument B.

*This is a very challenging case.

The industrial division has no variable overhead. The direct-labor rate is $10 per hour, and a maximum of 10,000 hours is available per year. Fixed overhead of $100,000 per year is applied on the basis of direct-labor hours. The planned activity level is 10,000 hours per year.

The demand for type Z gauges at a fixed price of $257 is unlimited. Anywhere from zero to 6,000 units of type Y gauges can be sold annually at a fixed price of $92 per unit. Demand for type Y gauges is no more than 6,000 per year.

The labor used in the two divisions is different and is *not* transferable between them. The situation is summarized in the following diagram.

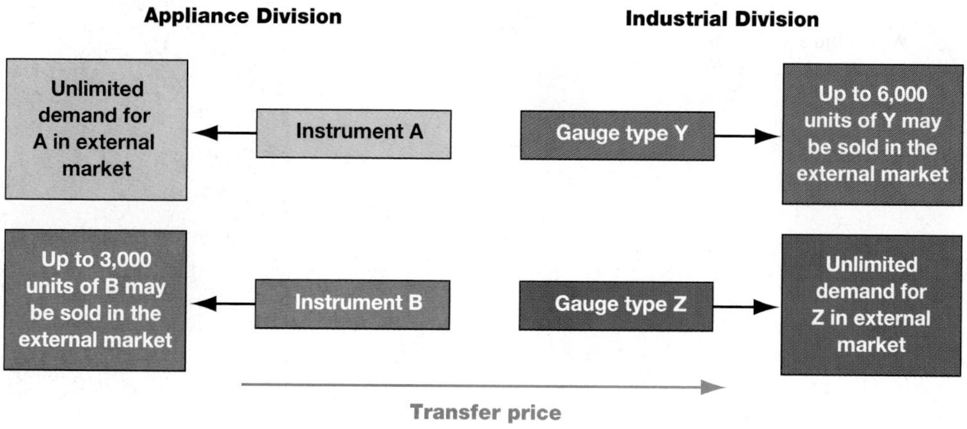

Required

The first four questions refer to the transfer price *per unit of instrument B* for units transferred. Show calculations. Ignore any long-term or qualitative factors.

a. What is the minimum unit transfer price acceptable to the appliance division for any number of units of instrument B transferred in the range zero to 2,000 units?

b. What is the minimum unit transfer price acceptable to the appliance division for any number of B units transferred in the range 2,001 to 5,000 units?

c. What is the maximum unit transfer price acceptable to the industrial division for any number of B units transferred in the range zero to 2,000 units?

d. What is the maximum unit transfer price acceptable to the industrial division for any number of B units transferred in the range 2,001 to 5,000 units?

e. Suppose that appliance division sets the transfer price at its minimum acceptable level in each of the ranges zero to 2,000 units, and 2,001 to 5,000 units. How many units will be transferred? Remember that each division manager has the authority to accept or reject a transfer between the two divisions.

CHAPTER

20

Using Lead and Lag Measures to Communicate, Motivate, and Evaluate

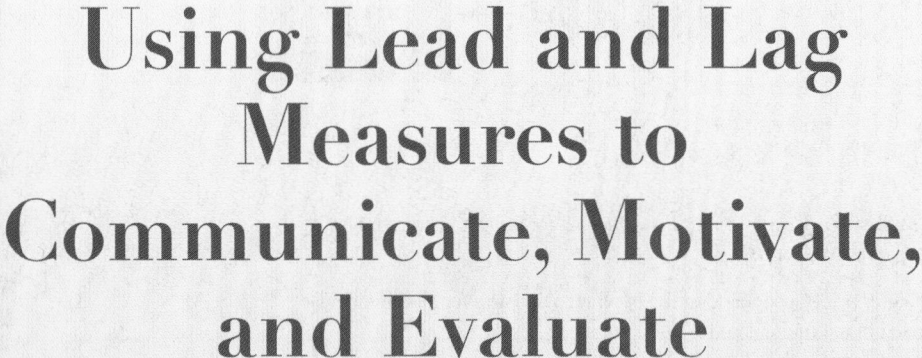

After completing this chapter, you should be able to:

1. Recognize and recommend lead indicators in the areas of organizational learning and growth, business production process efficiency, and customer value.
2. Explain the importance of lead indicators in building a balanced scorecard for communication, motivation, and evaluation.
3. Understand how organizations implement a balanced scorecard of performance measures.
4. Use quantified lead and lag relations to predict the effects of changes in performance measures (Appendix).

Cost-Management
Challenges

1. **How** do analysts use their understanding of current operations to help predict future outcomes?
2. **How** does the use of the balanced scorecard at Valley Commercial Bank show each employee how her or his performance affects the bank's financial success?
3. **How** does the balanced scorecard differ from the measures of organizational cost and performance, which have been used for as long as organized companies have existed? What does it add that previous measures do not?

Valley
COMMERCIAL BANK

What do busy professionals and business owners want from a bank? Vision? Spirit?

Or service and lots of money immediately?

Busy professional business owners aren't hard to please. They simply want service and money when they need them. You'll be glad Valley Commercial Bank is there 24–7 whether you need financing for equipment, want to consolidate loans, or need a responsive line of credit. We can develop a plan to meet your individual business needs. Is this what you're looking for? Then stop in, call, or email Dave Frederick.

555-234-5678

dave.frederick@valleycommercialbank.com

www.valleycommercialbank.com

Valley Commercial Bank: Ahead of the Competition

Valley COMMERCIAL BANK

The financial services market has become increasingly competitive as banks, insurance companies, stock brokerages, and hybrids compete to manage retirement funds, provide access to securities markets, and meet the banking needs of individuals and growing entrepreneurial businesses. The need to provide these services quickly, cheaply, accurately, and innovatively has transformed the once stodgy, conservative financial services industry. Banks, in particular, have become more aggressive in designing and marketing innovative services in response to other organizations that now are able to offer competitive services, in some cases without the same level of regulatory requirements that banks face.

Since its founding 10 years ago, Valley Commercial Bank (VCB) has managed to stay ahead of its competition by consistently creating and designing innovative, reliable services that are first to market. VCB offers commercial-customer services in traditional branch banks but to a greater extent via its e-banking Website and round-the-clock customer service that is available by telephone or the Internet.

"Anyone who can predict the future of financial services and technology has identified lucrative opportunities. We have wonderfully visionary employees whose value I cannot overestimate. Capitalizing on these opportunities, though, requires knowledge, effort, and a bit of luck—but we work at making our own luck, too," acknowledged Valley Commercial Bank's vice president of marketing. "We regard our accounting staff as valuable analysts and business partners who help us anticipate and measure the effects of service and market changes. Without their help, we can design superior services and grow revenues, but we would be guessing about whether we can earn a profit. This industry is too competitive to allow any bad guesses."

Using Lead and Lag Indicators: Signals of Performance

LO 1 Recognize and recommend lead indicators in the areas of organizational learning and growth, business production process efficiency, and customer value.

lead indicators *are measures that identify future nonfinancial and financial outcomes to guide management decision making*

Valley Commercial Bank identifies and uses lead indicators of organizational performance to motivate and evaluate its employees, communicate plans and results to employees, and evaluate its success at meeting its financial goals. **Lead indicators** are measures that identify future nonfinancial and financial outcomes to guide management decision making. VCB accomplishes these tasks by combining relevant lead indicators into a balanced scorecard. This chapter focuses on how VCB identified balanced-scorecard elements and how it uses the balanced scorecard to manage its operations.

Valley Commercial Bank uses several lead indicators of performance to help decision makers predict future problems, identify opportunities for improvement, and prevent costly mistakes. For example, lead indicators of success in retaining current customers can predict subsequent levels of sales and profitability.

Identifying and measuring reliable lead indicators of performance is an important part of modern cost management because these measures allow employees to plan or gauge their progress toward meeting performance objectives. Employees know, for example, that certain levels of these lead indicators signal desired future cost or profit performance. If, as plans are implemented, the measured lead indicators show that the organization is likely to miss its performance target, employees can take corrective actions in time to get back on course.

lag indicators *are measures of the final outcomes of earlier management plans and their execution*

In contrast to using lead indicators, when analysts at Valley Commercial Bank and other companies report the profits from the services or products that they have sold in the market, they are reporting **lag indicators,** which are measures of the final outcomes of earlier management plans and their execution. Financial performance measures are lag indicators and in many cases measure results too late to significantly affect future products and services. The lag indicators of financial performance are important, however, and ignoring them is neither wise nor even possible in the increasingly competitive, global economic environment.

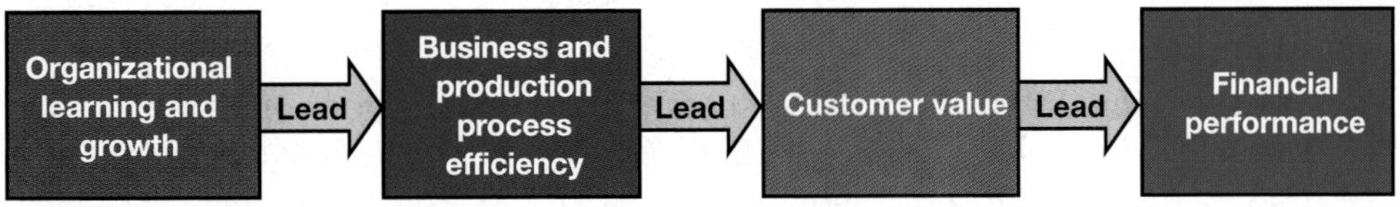

Exhibit 20–1
Lead and Lag Relations among Indicators of Performance

The major types of lead indicators of performance are often nonfinancial in nature and include the following measures:

- *Organizational learning and growth measures,* which describe the way employees and organizations increase their capabilities to develop new products and services and provide existing products and services more efficiently.
- *Business and production process efficiency measures,* which describe how efficiently the organization actually transforms resources into products and services. (*Note:* This can include outsourced processes and processes in the extended value chain.)
- *Customer value measures,* which describe how the organization creates customer satisfaction and loyalty.

These lead indicators are performance measures at different stages of an organization's value chain. Therefore, a lead indicator at one stage could be a lag indicator of a preceding stage, as shown in Exhibit 20–1. Process efficiency can lag organizational learning and growth, customer satisfaction and loyalty can lag changes in process efficiency, and financial outcomes of profit and cash flow can lag changes in the preceding measures. Organizations that monitor and effectively communicate these lead indicators are more likely to consistently and efficiently create valued services and products and generate competitive profit and cash flow. Another valued contribution that analysts can provide is to develop reliable measures of these types of lead indicators.

Communicating Strategy to Employees

Many employees of an organization do not understand the impacts of their activities on customer value and profitability because their jobs are narrow or they do not interact directly with customers. Communicating lead indicators can make the effects of employees more visible. Once they realize how they affect customer value, all employees are more likely to find and support ways to improve activities and processes. A comprehensive and reliable set of lead indicators can tell employees a credible story about how the organization can meet its strategic goals. This credible story can be a powerful communication device to overcome the natural skepticism many people have about why certain measures are gathered, reported, and monitored. Designing a set of lead indicators to communicate strategy is a primary focus of this chapter.

Motivating Employees and Evaluating Performance

Visible lead indicators can contribute to employees' improved motivation and commitment. Simply posting weekly sales or quality charts on the team bulletin board, as many companies do, probably is not enough. Even awarding bonuses for improving lead indicators can backfire if this practice reduces cooperation among individuals or teams in competition for the bonuses. Unless employees know how their efforts to improve processes actually result in improved organizational performance—better customer satisfaction, for example—charts and reports of these lead indicators can recede into background noise. The important issue of incorporating diverse performance measures into a successful incentive system is deferred until Chapter 21. Briefly, many organizations are finding benefits from basing evaluations in part on lead indicators of financial performance, but designing and implementing a diverse incentive system is not a trivial exercise.

Balanced Scorecard

balanced scorecard *is a strategy formulation and communication device as well as a causal model of lead and lag indicators of performance*

Robert Kaplan and David Norton have combined the dimensions of lead indicators of performance into what they call a *balanced scorecard.*[1] The **balanced scorecard** is a strategy formulation and communication device as well as a model of lead and lag indicators of performance. Although the concept of using lead and lag indicators is not new, the balanced scorecard is a new way to package and present them that appears to be more successful than previous, less organized methods. The balanced scorecard's structure and intuitive appeal appear to add value to strategic management.

If the balanced scorecard is a valid model of how the organization can achieve success, showing every person in the organization how her or his job contributes to its ultimate goal should be possible. If the ultimate goal is financial, as in the example for Valley Commercial Bank, the balanced scorecard should tell all employees from janitor to teller to branch manager how their work leads to VCB's financial success. This approach represents a fundamental change in management style for most companies that previously focused just on achieving the financial objectives that lag the activities of most of the organization's employees.

Research Insight 20.1

Small Companies and the Balanced Scorecard

Many large, international firms, including Bank of Montreal, KPMG, Tenneco, Allstate, AT&T, and Elf Atochem, are reporting the adoption of the balanced scorecard approach. It is less well known that many small companies, government, and nonprofit organizations also are adopting it. This is not a trivial undertaking for any company, and small companies often do not have sufficient staff to develop the balanced scorecard on their own. Many companies rely on experienced consultants to guide the development of a balanced scorecard. *Sources: C. Chow et al.,* "Applying the Balanced Scorecard to Smaller Companies." *For a description of a European model that predates the balanced scorecard by nearly 50 years, see M. Epstein and J.-F. Manzoni,* "The Balanced Scorecard and Tableau de Bord: Translating Strategy into Action." *See also C. Ittner and D. Larcker,* "Are Non-financial Measures Leading Indicators of Financial Performance?" *for an investigation of statistical relations among lead and lag indicators of performance. (Full citations to references are in the Bibliography).*

Several years ago, VCB used its balanced scorecard's lead indicators to identify a large gap between the capabilities of some people working in the bank and the capabilities required for significantly improved performance. Although management knew that the short-term costs were high, it nevertheless developed an extensive training program to educate employees about the business practices of their customers. As a result, employees were able to devise creative ways to anticipate the business' short-term loan needs based on regional economic forecasts from a local university. For example, when the president of a software engineering company called in a panic to say that he needed funds to recruit additional engineers because of an unexpected increase in business, he was told that the bank was extending his business line-of-credit account as he spoke. To be sure, he was a loyal customer after that.

Exhibit 20–2 shows the link from increased employee training to speeding up the loan approval process to increased customer satisfaction to better financial results. The rationale is that if VCB improves customer satisfaction, it is more likely to retain a loyal customer base. A loyal customer base will provide word-of-mouth promotion that will lead to a larger customer base. A larger base of the right customers (see Chapter 6) means more revenue, which should lead to better financial performance.

---

[1]See Kaplan and Norton's books, *The Balanced Scorecard* and *The Strategy-Focused Organization. (Full citations to references are in the Bibliography.)*

Exhibit 20–2 Sequence of Performance from Employee Training to Financial Results

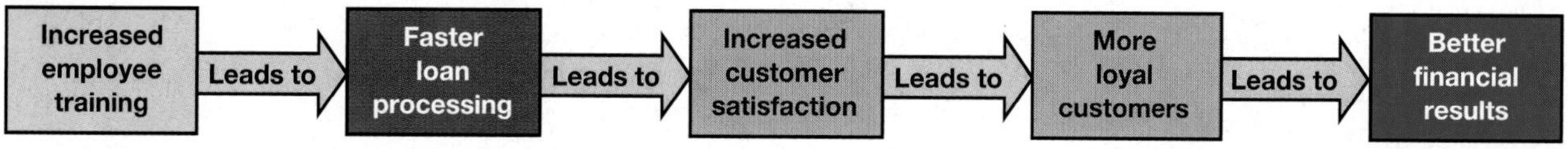

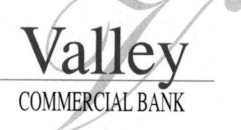

Balanced Scorecard's Four Areas of Strategic Performance

The balanced scorecard expresses an organization's mission and strategy in four activity areas, reflecting the major areas of lead and lag performance. Exhibit 20–3 shows that all four of these areas of performance can interact and reflect the organization's strategy in a more complex way than previously shown in Exhibits 20–1 and 20–2. Every area can affect every other area. A successful balanced scorecard is not a random selection of readily available measures of performance. These carefully designed and selected measures reflect the tangible objectives that are consistent with meeting the organization's goals.

The learning and growth area indicates how the infrastructure for innovation and long-term growth should contribute to strategic goals. In many ways, this is the most exciting perspective because it is the source of the organization's future value. The business and production process area indicates how these processes should work to add value to customers. The customer area indicates how the company's customer-oriented strategy and operations adds financial value. Finally, the financial area measures the company's success in adding value to shareholders (or other stakeholders). For organizations that do not have shareholders, the financial area indicates how well the strategy and operations contribute to improving the organization's financial health. We now examine how to use the four perspectives of the balanced scorecard.

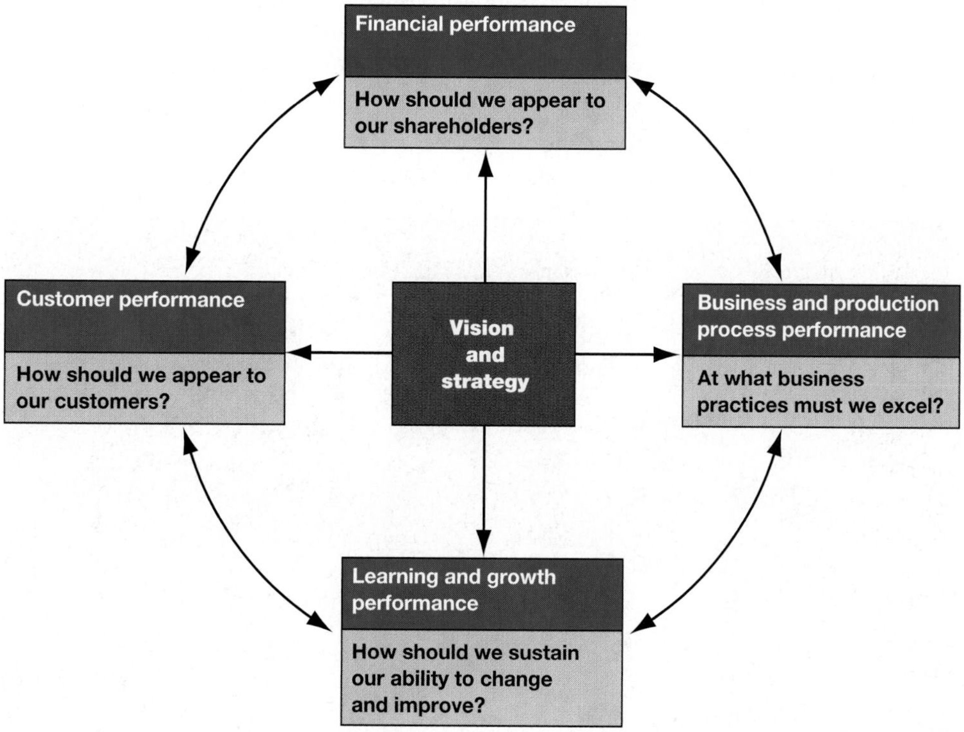

Exhibit 20–3

The Balanced Scorecard: Four Areas of Strategic Action (adapted from R. Kaplan and D. Norton, *The Balanced Scorecard*)

You're the Decision Maker 20.1

Designing the Balanced Scorecard

Consider the following independent questions.

a. Virtually all companies use financial performance measures to evaluate division and department managers. What are the advantages of focusing on nonfinancial performance?

b. You are interviewing for a job. The interviewer says, "Historically, we have relied just on financial performance measures to evaluate division managers. We know the limitations of relying solely on financial performance measures, but we see the balanced scorecard as being too costly to implement. What do you think we should do?"

c. Team Focus: You work for an internationally known consulting firm that has been asked by Singapore Airways to design and install a balanced scorecard system. You are starting to assemble a team of airline consultants and employees to work on the project. What characteristics should team members have? What airline departments or segments do you want on the team?

(Solutions begin on page 852.)

Organizational Learning and Growth

employee capabilities *are employees' knowledge and skills that indicate the organization's ability to meet future customer needs and generate new sales*

Improvements in operating performance result largely from enhancing the capabilities of the organization's employees and motivating them to use those capabilities for the good of the organization. **Employee capabilities** are employees' knowledge and skills that indicate the organization's ability to meet future customer needs and generate new sales. Organizational learning involves the use of employees' capabilities to create new or improved business and production processes, procedures, products and services, customer databases, and proprietary, copyrighted, or patented intellectual property.

Different organizations might require different levels of some employee capabilities, such as education, to prosper. However, all organizations can expect better operating results when employees are well trained, motivated, committed, and encouraged to improve processes.

Valley Commercial Bank developed strategic objectives to improve its organizational learning. The bank believes that its investments in employee education have caused increases in the percentage of sales from new services, numbers of suggestions, and time to develop new services. For example, designing and delivering a complex service such as its new e-banking site in less than one year would not have been possible without highly capable and motivated employees.

Educating employees is a major determinant of the success of new strategies and performance measurement. Here General Electric conducts the successful Workout program.

Valley Commercial Bank sets objectives for a number of measures of employee capabilities, and it regularly monitors employees to encourage improvement. The areas of performance include the following:

1. Employee training and education.
2. Employee satisfaction.
3. Employee turnover.
4. Innovativeness.
5. Opportunities for improvement.

These are shown in the following expansion of Exhibit 20–1 to reflect effects of investments in organizational learning and growth.

Employee Training and Education

Valley Commercial Bank has always paid for employee education programs, but several years ago, to motivate employees to improve their individual and team capabilities, it began paying an annual bonus to employees who successfully complete approved educational or training courses. Hiring and promotions also depend, in part, on the educational levels achieved by potential or current employees.

One top manager stated the rationale for measuring employee training, "Yes, we want long-term loyal employees, but we don't want people who have become uncreative or who lack the drive for constant improvement. By giving managers incentives to send their people to training programs, the bank should have people who are really up to date with the latest ideas. And, frankly, I don't care whether they take classes in virtual banking or foreign language or communications skills, as long as it's expanding their minds and keeping them creative."

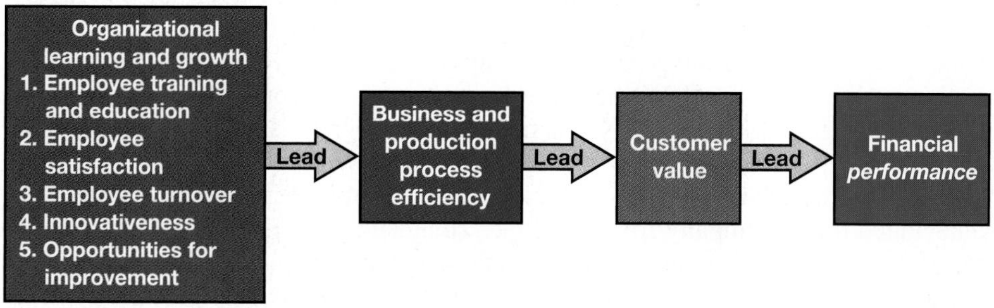

VCB trusts its managers and employees to take appropriate training and educational courses. Because measuring knowledge or specific skills obtained can be quite difficult, the company measures a broader outcome, the percentage of employees who are involved in approved training, education, and team-building courses. VCB is approaching its objective of having 100 percent of its employees complete such courses.

Employee Satisfaction

Managing employee satisfaction recognizes that employee morale is important for improving retention, productivity, quality, customer satisfaction, and responsiveness to situations. Managers can measure employee satisfaction by taking surveys, interviewing employees, or observing employees at work. VCB employs an external consultant to measure employee satisfaction twice a year. Its objective is at least to maintain its current level of employee satisfaction.

Employee Turnover

Managing employee turnover recognizes that employees develop organization-specific intellectual capital and are a valuable nonfinancial asset to the company. Finding and hiring good talent to replace people who leave are costly. A common measure of employee turnover is the percentage of people who leave voluntarily each year. VCB's objective is to have below average turnover for the industry, nationally and regionally.

Innovativeness

Competition in Valley Commercial Bank's industry requires continuous innovation and attention to customer needs. New products and services or improvements to current offerings depend on the ability of an organization's employees to be innovative and to translate innovations into new offerings. VCB measures its innovativeness by the percentage of sales generated by new services, which it considers as those developed in the past two years. Tracking this percentage industrywide and over time indicates that the trend is for new services to contribute an increasing percentage of sales. The bank's objective, which it has not reached, is to have new services generate 50 percent of its sales.

Knowledge developed by key individuals to benefit the organization is of no benefit unless it is shared. Furthermore, a key individual can leave the organization and take his or her knowledge, which can be doubly costly if the employee joins a competitor. To encourage employees to share their capabilities and thus transform individual knowledge into organizational knowledge, VCB uses teams to manage nearly every decision and process. It formerly measured the percentage of team decisions, but since that percentage has stabilized at nearly 100 percent, this measure is no longer necessary.

Opportunities for Improvement

Organizations can encounter new opportunities to improve processes, products, and services. Proactive organizations, however, work to create these opportunities. Valley Commercial Bank encourages all employees to make suggestions for innovations and improvements. The bank's president recently visited a Japanese bank and was astounded by the average number of suggestions each employee made per year—96 and increasing! On the president's return, VCB began its own suggestion program, and although the number of suggestions per employee is modest, the program is gaining wide visibility and acceptance—particularly since many suggestions have been implemented.

The performance measure of estimating value of employee suggestions reflects the value added to the company from employee suggestions. This measure reflects estimates of cost savings or revenue enhancements. A top manager who proposed the measure stated, "We'd rather have employees come up with one excellent idea a year that had a large impact rather than a hundred trivial ideas that did not amount to much in the end."

Do investments in organizational learning and growth pay off? Most organizations intuitively believe that they do; however, predicting and measuring the impacts of these investments is particularly difficult. As noted earlier, one complication is that investments in employees can walk out the door if these employees leave. Another complication is that investments in employees might not result in tangible outcomes for years, and, by then, many other events could have occurred to obscure the impacts of training and education.

Evaluation of Measures of Organizational Learning and Growth

In concept, evaluation of these investments can use concepts in previous chapters: modeling of Chapter 12, decision making of Chapter 13, and discounted cash-flow techniques of Chapter 14. Consider the following example of VCB's decision to spend $80,000 annually for the next three years on training for its branch-bank employees. If the effects of each year's training are expected to lag one year and persist for three years, what annual benefit (X) can justify this training investment?

First, ignore the time value of money, and then consider the following pattern of expenditures and benefits:

Investments in Learning and Growth	**Year 0**	**Year 1**	**Year 2**	**Year 3**	**Year 4**	**Year 5**	**Total**
Training cost	($80,000)	($80,000)	($80,000)				($240,000)
First year's training benefits		*X*	*X*	*X*			
Second year's training benefits			*X*	*X*	*X*		
Third year's training benefits				*X*	*X*	*X*	
Total training benefits		*X*	2*X*	3*X*	2*X*	*X*	9*X*

The break-even benefit level equates the total benefits to total costs as follows:

$$\text{Incremental profit} = \text{Total benefits} - \text{Total costs}$$
$$\text{Break-even profit} = 0 = 9X - \$240{,}000$$
$$9X = \$240{,}000$$
$$\text{Break-even benefit level, } X = \underline{\underline{\$26{,}667 \text{ per year}}}$$

The preceding analysis ignores the time value of money. Now assume that VCB's cost of capital is 10 percent. The break-even analysis becomes a bit more complex because of the need to discount each of the future expenditures and unknown annual benefits by the appropriate factors.

Investments in Learning and Growth	**Year 0**	**Year 1**	**Year 2**	**Year 3**	**Year 4**	**Year 5**
Training cost	($80,000)	($80,000)	($80,000)			
First year's training benefits		X	X	X		
Second year's training benefits			X	X	X	
Third year's training benefits				X	X	X
Total benefits		X	2X	3X	2X	X
10% discount factors	1.000	0.909	0.826	0.751	0.683	0.621

$$\text{Break-even profit} = 0 = .909X + .826(2X) + .751(3X) + .683(2X) + .621(X)$$
$$- 1.000(80{,}000) - .909(80{,}000) - .826(80{,}000)$$
$$0 = 6.803X - 2.736(80{,}000)$$
$$\text{Break-even benefit level, } X = \underline{\underline{\$32{,}170 \text{ per year (rounded)}}}$$

Should VCB invest in this customer-satisfaction training? The answer is, yes, if the bank believes that the benefits occur in the expected pattern and (including the effects of the time value of money) equal at least $32,170 annually. This analysis contains many assumptions about an uncertain future, which can be modeled using sensitivity and scenario analyses (see Chapter 12). Perhaps the biggest assumption is that the benefits of investments in learning and growth can be quantified in dollar terms. VCB might accomplish this by using a quantified balanced scorecard, which is discussed later in this chapter.

Business and Production Processes Efficiency

Logically, a cause-and-effect relation exists between improvements in organizational learning and growth and improvements in internal business and production processes. Ideally, a well-trained workforce has the capability to improve internal business processes. Valley Commercial Bank has learned what its most important areas of process performance are:

1. New service development.
2. Employee productivity and error rates.
3. Service costs.

4. Process improvements.
5. Supplier relations.

The following diagram extends Exhibit 20–1 to show effects of these measures.

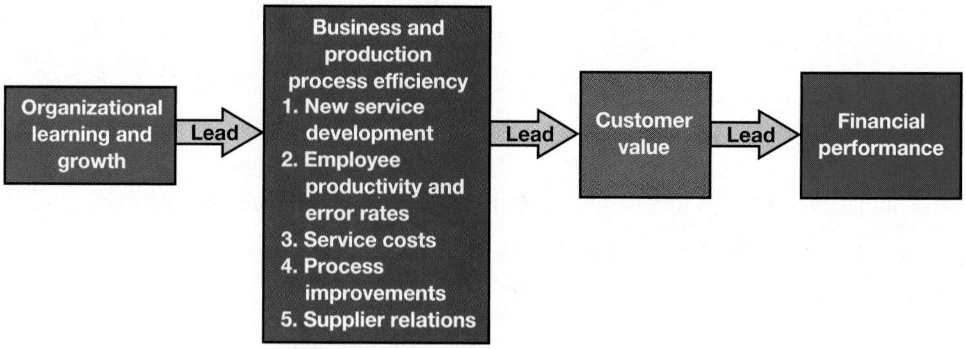

New Service Development

Beating the competition with new products or services means anticipating customer needs and then meeting them before competitors do so. Companies that consistently can meet new customer needs first (and well) can attract and keep customers and can earn higher profits than can slower competitors. One of Valley Commercial Bank's most important lead indicators of the capability to beat the competition is the average time to develop a new service (from the first team meeting to the delivery of the first service). In part because of innovative suggestions from employees, VCB has reduced the average new-service development time by more than 50 percent in the past five years. This allows the bank to consistently be early to the market with innovative services. It also has led to VCB's reputation and stature as the premiere supplier of financial services to emerging high-technology businesses. While the bank cannot expect this rate of improvement to continue indefinitely, it does expect continuous improvement.

Employee Productivity and Error Rates

Managing productivity recognizes the importance of output per employee. Output can be measured in terms of a physical measure, such as miles driven, pages produced, or lawns mowed, or as a financial measure, such as revenue per employee or profits per employee. One simple measure of productivity at VCB is the number of loans processed without error per loan officer each month. The bank's objective is to reduce the error rate to zero while maintaining or improving its rate of loan processing. The bank has similar productivity measures for the other major parts of its business.

Service Costs

Like many manufacturing and service organizations, VCB has used activity-based costing for a number of years to better measure and manage its costs. The bank regularly computes costs per loan, checking account, and other services. The bank uses the ABC information to effect continuous improvements in these costs without losses of quality or customer service.

Process Improvements

Employees who do the work are the best source of new ideas for better processes. For example, at Saturn, workers have demonstrated that increasing the height of an automobile assembly line made it easier for them to screw on the lug nuts for wheels and

Saturn's production process reflects numerous employee-led improvements.

assemble other parts. Raising the height of the assembly line improved productivity and reduced back injuries.

Customers value receiving goods and services reliably and on time. Manufacturing suppliers can satisfy customers if they hold large amounts of inventory to ensure that goods are on hand. Holding large inventory leads, however, to high inventory carrying and storage costs, inventory obsolescence, and a host of other problems that we have documented in earlier chapters. Suppliers can avoid excessive inventory buildup by reducing cycle-time. Thus, cycle-time measures are often used as indicators of process improvement.

Several years ago, Valley Commercial Bank had a problem with the cycle time for processing many loans. Customers complained, and the bank believed that it was about to lose existing and future customers. Loan-application cycle time was not a visible measure, so loans were sometimes taking more than a month to process. To remedy this situation, the bank increased the importance of cycle-time management. Performance measures were average cycle time (from application to provision of funds) and percentage of loans completed within one month. The long-term objectives were to decrease the cycle time to one week without an increase in loan processing errors or the default rate (the percentage of loans not repaid according to loan terms).

As a result of the focus on loan-cycle time, the bank's employees developed permanent loan application files on the bank's Web site for repeat customers. With a few keystrokes, customers can update their files and usually complete their self-correcting loan applications within a few minutes. These innovations in service were possible because the workers were trained, experienced, and sufficiently motivated that they wanted to help their companies.

Supplier Relations

Supplier relations are becoming increasingly important as companies outsource more business or production activities that the companies once performed internally. Obviously, even though a company has outsourced an internal process, it still must ensure the quality of that process. Many manufacturing and retail companies develop supplier rating systems to indicate which suppliers are certified for delivery of product without inspection and which are not. If not certified, suppliers' goods must be inspected on receipt, which increases the cost of goods from these suppliers. Service firms also outsource activities; successful service outsourcing requires careful attention to the capabilities and current performance of the supplier. Customers usually notice any errors first.

Valley Commercial Bank outsourced its statement preparation for bank accounts and billing for loan payments. Any errors made by the companies performing those services reflected badly on the bank, as if its own employees had performed the services themselves. Therefore, the bank appointed a manager to be in charge of each outsourced service. The outsourcing contract required the supplier to provide auditable performance statistics, including cycle times and internal error rates, which the bank's manager reviewed daily. The bank's objective was to drive these statistics to below the industry averages.

Evaluation of Measures of Business and Production Process Efficiency

VCB can evaluate investments in its process efficiency in much the same way as it evaluates learning and growth improvements: Estimate future relevant costs and benefits, and evaluate process-efficiency decisions as break-even or investment decisions using the methods of Chapters 12, 13, and 14. Again, having a quantified balanced scorecard, or at least the portion that models the costs and benefits of changes to business and production process efficiency might be of great help.

Customer Value

customer value *reflects the degree to which products and services satisfy customers' expectations about price, function, and quality*

Successful organizations satisfy customers' expectations. **Customer value** reflects the degree to which products and services satisfy customers' expectations about price, function, and quality. To meet strategic goals of improving customer value, an organization must first define its customers and second know its customers' expectations.[2]

Southwest Airlines, for instance, focuses on nonbusiness travelers who want low price and are not bothered by the inconvenience of having to line up to obtain their seats. Knowing those customers are willing to drive or take the train as an alternative to flying, Southwest Airlines recognizes that it must compete on price to make air travel competitive with auto or train travel. Its methods most likely do not appeal to business travelers who do not want to wait in line at the airport to get a good seat and who are willing to pay more for the convenience of an assigned seat. However, business travelers are not Southwest's primary customers.

As another example, Federal Express developed successfully by knowing its customers and their expectations. It knew that its customers wanted an overnight delivery service with defect-free quality. It also found that its particular customers were willing to pay a premium for that service and quality compared with those of competitors such as the US Postal Service.

Valley Commercial Bank knows that its customers are business owners and professionals who want considerable personal attention and 24-hour service, and they are willing to pay higher fees to get that service. The bank knows that it cannot compete with large interstate banks on price and breadth of services, but it can compete on the basis of the personal attention and availability of service to its customers. The bank uses the following performance measures, among others, to manage customer value:

1. Customer satisfaction.
2. Customer retention and loyalty.
3. Sales growth.
4. Market share.
5. Customer risk.

The following figure illustrates how these measures can affect financial performance.

Valley COMMERCIAL BANK

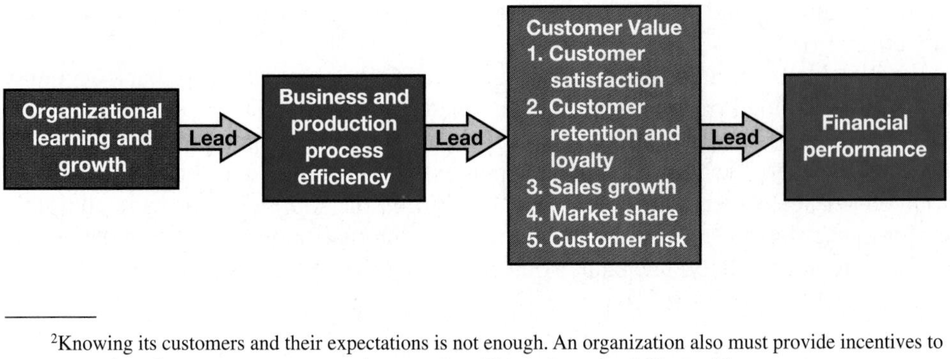

[2]Knowing its customers and their expectations is not enough. An organization also must provide incentives to managers and employees to meet customers' expectations. This is the topic of Chapter 21.

Feedback from customers is valuable in helping a company evaluate itself and is a lead indicator of future success.

Customer Satisfaction

Customer-satisfaction measures indicate whether the company is meeting customers' expectations or even delighting them. You have probably completed customer-satisfaction forms for restaurants, hotels, or automobile repair shops. Customer satisfaction with current products and services is a lead indicator of future sales. If a company knows that customers are becoming dissatisfied, its alert and well-trained employees are able to take corrective actions in time to prevent loss of future sales. Usually, a combination of several attributes of products and services, in addition to sales price, determine customer satisfaction.

Improvements in customer satisfaction on these attributes usually lag organizational capabilities and process efficiency. In addition, customer measures can give advance notice about changing customer perceptions, influencing future sales and indicating needs for improvements in capabilities and efficiency. Some companies wait to see whether customers buy their products and services. Others, like Valley Commercial Bank, are more aggressive and obtain lead indicators of customer satisfaction to help them keep ahead of the competition.

VCB regularly surveys random samples of customers to measure their satisfaction with current services. In addition, the bank regularly meets with groups of customers to discuss their future needs. At these meetings, customers also express what they value about the bank's services relative to those provided by competitors. This is valuable benchmarking information that can help Valley Commercial Bank position its current services and design future ones to gain a competitive advantage over its competitors from achieving customer satisfaction measures.

Innovative Lead Indicators of Customer Value

Many organizations benefit from timely information about how customers' needs are being met. For example, the CFO of 20th Century Fox measures daily box-office ticket sales to monitor the success of new movie releases. If ticket sales are much less than the expected pattern over time, managers can decide whether to pull the movie from theaters or immediately begin advertising and promotion campaigns to boost sales. Every morning the CFO of Current, Inc., a mail-order greeting card company, measures the day's volume of mail (actually, the linear feet of mail) to estimate the day's cash receipts and sales orders and to gauge the success of recent catalog mailings. He is confident that feet-of-mail is a reliable lead indicator because of his careful observations over a number of years. He can begin financial planning and provide feedback to catalog sales managers even before the mail is opened and analyzed.

Cost Management in Practice 20.1

Customer Retention and Loyalty

customer retention or loyalty *measures how well a company is doing in keeping its customers*

Customer retention or **loyalty** measures how well a company is doing in keeping its customers. A rule of thumb is that obtaining a new customer costs at least five times as much as keeping an existing one. We might quibble with the number 'five,' but the point is well taken. Once a firm has a customer, keeping that customer is much easier than convincing a new one to do business with it. Satisfied customers, whose needs are met, tend to be loyal customers who continue to buy existing and probably new products and services from reliable providers. Customer loyalty is the tendency for existing customers to continue to obtain products and services from the same organization. The strength of that tendency, sometimes measured by the percentage of sales to repeat customers, or customer retention, is a measure of customer loyalty.

Some industries have higher customer retention than others, and a higher than average retention rate can be counted as a key lead indicator of future sales from new products. Valley Commercial Bank measures its average customer retention rate and seeks to beat the industry average.

Sales Growth

Many organizations improve profits by minimizing costs. However, half of the profit equation is sales revenue; to increase profits, organizations must manage both halves. Thus, most profit-seeking firms, like VCB, have sales-growth objectives that encourage employees to find new customers and extend additional services to existing customers. The bank seeks to increase its customer base and revenues by 10 percent annually. Recall from Chapter 6 that selecting and attracting the right customers is equally important to growth in profitability.

Market Share

Market share measures a company's proportion of the total business in a particular market. Companies typically measure market share in terms of dollar sales, unit volume, or number of customers. For example, VCB management determined that 22 percent of the small businesses and professionals in the region had accounts and/or loans with it. Its goal was to become the dominant bank in that market segment, with "dominant" defined as securing more than 30 percent of the small business and professional accounts and loans. Having the largest share of this market would indicate that VCB is the bank of choice for new business and professional customers moving into the region, which should ensure continued sales growth.

Customer Risk

Many organizations implicitly loan money to customers by allowing them to buy products and services on credit. Banks such as Valley Commercial do this explicitly and are exposed to more risk (i.e., loan default) because the amounts are larger and terms of the loans usually are longer than the typical 30- or 60-day-credit sales terms. To moderate the incentives created by desires for sales growth and market share, VCB also monitors the risk profiles of its customers, from information in new loan applications. Risk information is a lead indicator of future default rates. Although a default rate of zero is undesirable because it implies taking no risks and missing sales opportunities, the bank cannot let the default rate increase to an excessive level without affecting its profitability and its regulatory status. Monitoring the default rate, however, is an important source of feedback on the effectiveness of screening its customers' risk profiles.

Evaluation of Measures of Customer Value

Ideally, improvements in measures of customer value are lead indicators of improvements in financial performance. VCB and other organizations can apply the decision-making and modeling methods described in earlier chapters. Certainly, this application

Exhibit 20–4 Valley Commercial Bank's Customer Satisfaction

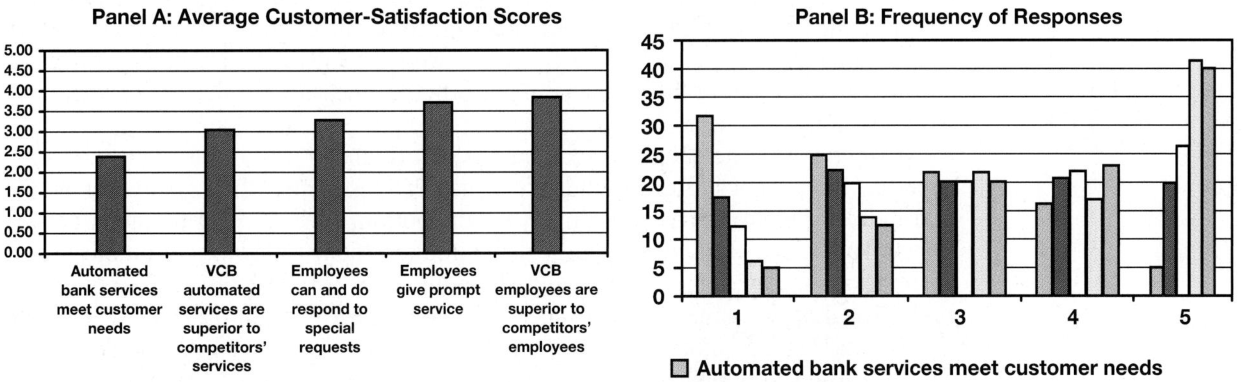

requires valid customer-related measures, which can be difficult to obtain at reasonable cost. Many organizations use customer-satisfaction surveys, which—if administered carefully—can illuminate customer problems and opportunities. Consider the following survey results (1 = a very unfavorable evaluation and 5 = a highly favorable evaluation).

	Number of Customer Responses						
VCB Customer Satisfaction Variable	**1**	**2**	**3**	**4**	**5**	**Total**	**Ave.**
Automated bank services meet customer needs	32	25	22	16	5	100	2.37
Automated services are superior to competitors' services	17	22	20	21	20	100	3.05
Employees can and do respond to special requests	12	20	20	22	26	100	3.30
Employees give prompt service	6	14	22	17	41	100	3.73
Employees are superior to competitors' employees	5	12	20	23	40	100	3.81

What can you infer from these data? If the survey respondents are representative of VCB's preferred customers, the survey data reveal both inferior and superior services.

Review the charts in Exhibit 20–4. Panel A of Exhibit 20–4 shows that customers on average have low regard for the bank's automated services but consider them to be comparable to its competitors' automated services. This seems to be an opportunity for VCB to improve its automated bank services and, perhaps, create a competitive advantage. Conversely, the bank appears to have a competitive advantage because of customers' high regard for its employees. The bank should exploit this advantage, perhaps by advertising that features its employees. Panel B, which shows the frequency of responses, reinforces these conclusions. Note that the unfavorable pattern of responses on the first question regarding VCB's automated services is nearly a mirror image of employee-related responses. VCB should improve its automated services and exploit the favorable view of its employees. Of course, VCB should consider the costs and benefits of these alternatives.

Financial Performance

The relations among the lead indicators in the areas of organizational learning and growth, business and production process efficiency, and customer value logically result in financial outcomes. This is the compelling "story" of the balanced scorecard. As Chapters 6, 18, and 21 demonstrate, different measures of financial performance suit the strategic goals and incentive structures of different organizations and their subunits. When organizations use the balanced scorecard as an overall picture of themselves, for example, financial performance might mean customer profitability, net income, return on investment, EVA, or stock price gains—all of these and others are commonly used. Because this text covers these financial performance measures in detail elsewhere, we do not explore them here.

A key point of the balanced scorecard is that financial performance measures are important but are not sufficient guides for organizations to meet their goals. Nor are the lead-indicator measures a replacement for the bottom-line score of financial performance. The balanced scorecard, as the name implies, looks for a *balance* among multiple performance measures, both lead and lag indicators of perfor-mance, to guide organizational performance toward success. Lead indicators point the way to financial success, and lag indicators, including actual financial performance, provide opportunities for learning about what worked, what did not, and what should be improved.

Like most banks, Valley Commercial had relied almost exclusively on overall financial measures before implementing its balanced scorecard. The bank used and continues to use four financial performance measures:

1. Net interest margin.
2. Revenue growth.
3. Customer profitability (see Chapter 6).
4. Overall return on assets (see Chapter 18).

The following figure illustrates how other areas of performance affect financial performance.

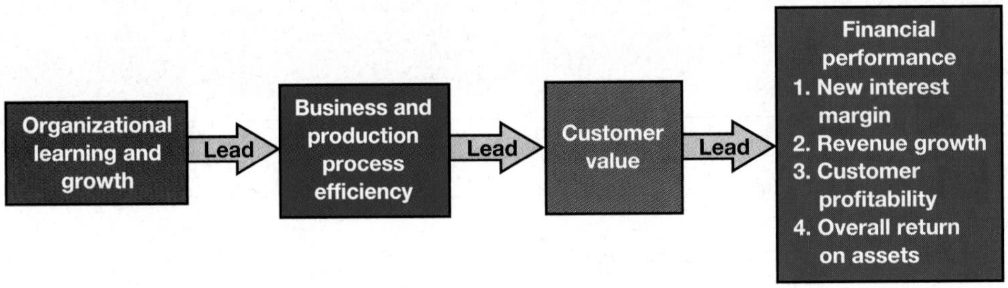

Net interest margin is the difference between the bank's cost of funds and its average earnings from the use of those funds. For example, the cost of funds paid to owners of checking accounts averaged about 3 percent. The average interest that VCB charged for commercial loans was about 8 percent, creating a net interest margin of 5 percent. Banks adjust the rates they charge for loans based on competitive pressures and expectations of the probability of loan default.

Revenue growth is the percentage change in revenue from one period to the next. It is a measure of how an organization is responding to economic conditions and opportunities. An organization can compare its revenue growth to percentage changes in general business activity, revenue growth goals, or revenue growth of comparable organizations. VCB's objective is above-average revenue growth compared to other banks in its region.

Managers had difficulty explaining financial performance, good or bad, with only these measures because they did not fully understand their causes. However, they now understand that financial success follows good lead indicator performance. Poor financial performance can be traced to lapses in lead indicator performance; more important, managing those lead indicators can prevent poor financial performance. Explaining financial performance provides important feedback, but bank employees know that monitoring and correcting lead indicator performance is an effective way to ensure future financial success—and avoid unpleasant explanations of financial shortfalls.

Evaluation of Measures of Financial Performance

LO 2 Explain the importance of lead indicators in building a balanced scorecard for communication, motivation, and growth.

Financial measures of performance tend to be the most objective measures because most organizations have dedicated significant resources (e.g., auditing and internal controls) to ensure the validity of their financial performance measures. Even so, incidents of financial fraud or earnings manipulation are not rare, necessitating continual reliance on monitoring activities (see Chapter 21). If the organization has valid measures of financial performance, it can use them to rate or rank performance fairly objectively. See Chapter 18 for extensive coverage of evaluating measures of financial performance.

Linked Performance Measures = Balanced Scorecard

We have presented four areas of performance and have discussed VCB's 19 related perfor-mance measures. There is nothing magic about having four areas of performance; companies have used more or fewer. Organizations should use the performance measures that reflect their critical processes and the links between them. Linking these performance measures distinguishes a balanced scorecard from a list of important or key performance indicators, also known as "critical success factors."

Values of the Balanced Scorecard

The balanced scorecard's greatest value is that it encourages all employees to consider the impact of their decisions on profitability. The balanced scorecard can be a reliable guide because of its modeled cause-and-effect relationships. An example of a cause-and-effect relationship included in a balanced scorecard is this: "Reducing the number of defective products decreases the average production cycle time because there are fewer products to rework." This clearly demonstrates the importance of controlling the number of defects. A reasonable question is whether the label, format, and method of the balanced scorecard are essential to achieving the benefits of modeling cause-and-effect relations among key performance indicators. Can other formulations of cause and effect achieve these benefits? Probably, but little objective research currently exists in this area. Early studies attribute some effects to the balanced scorecard, both favorable and unfavorable. This is an important area of research that will receive increased attention in coming years.[3]

Another important value of the balanced scorecard is that it appears to work in various types of organizations. Cost Management in Practice 20.2 describes the process and result at Sears, the large retailing organization. Other types of organizations also report successful applications, including small companies, government, universities, and nonprofit hospitals (see cases 20.58, 20.59, and 20.62 at the end of the chapter). At least two key differences between commercial and nonprofit organizations exist. First, many employees in the noncommercial sector are unaccustomed to thinking about the users of their services (e.g., students or taxpayers) as "customers." Employees might not perceive that they must compete for customers by providing quality services at a reasonable price. Universities and government organizations must stress the customer area of performance much more than must a typical private-sector company, whose employees readily understand that customers are important to the company. The second difference is the measurement of financial performance. In the private sector, financial performance measures typically revolve around profitability. Nonprofit organizations do not have a profit-oriented bottom line. Instead, they focus on their service mission, cost efficiency, and accountability (being sure that their assets are not stolen or embezzled). These differences mean that the development of a balanced scorecard

[3]For example, see M. Lipe and S. Salterio, "The Balanced Scorecard: Judgmental Effects of Information Organization and Diversity"; M. Malina and F. Selto, "Communicating and Controlling Strategy: An Empirical Study of the Effectiveness of the Balanced Scorecard"; and C. D. Ittner, D. F. Larcker, and M. W. Meyer, "The Use of Subjectivity in Multi-Criteria Bonus Plans."

(or its equivalent) of linked performance measures can be more challenging in non-profit organizations but just as valuable.

Cost Management in Practice 20.2

Sears' Employee-Customer-Profit Chain

Managers at Sears, one of the largest US retailers, credit its return to profitability to the development and use of its own balanced scorecard, which it calls the "employee-customer-profit chain." This scorecard, which took nearly three years to develop, enables Sears to measure and manage the drivers of employee and customer satisfaction. Equally important was Sears' ability to integrate its scorecard into its incentive system (see Chapter 21) and communicate its underlying strategy to all employees. The best set of measures does little to improve the interaction of employees and customers unless the employees believe the scorecard's "story" of successful retailing. Key to telling the story was Sears' ability to demonstrate the causal links among its scorecard measures; the story sounded plausible and hard data supported it.

The Sears scorecard has three areas of performance, which the company labels as (1) a compelling place to work (corresponds to organizational learning and growth), (2) a compelling place to shop (corresponds to business and production process efficiency and customer value, and (3) a compelling place to invest (corresponds to financial performance). Exhibit 20–5 illustrates the cause-and-effect relations among Sears' measures of performance, which the retailer claims are statistically valid. This is one of the few published accounts of the causal properties of the balanced scorecard. *Source: A. Rucci, S. Kirn, and R. Quinn,* "The Employee-Customer-Profit Chain at Sears."

Costs of the Balanced Scorecard

The value of the balanced scorecard comes with costs. Presently, no studies of the costs to design and implement the balanced scorecard have been published, but these costs surely exist. They include the costs of mea-surement, education, and use. Some reported and unreported balanced scorecard failures might be attributed to the failure to anticipate these costs. We do know that developing and implementing a balanced scorecard is not an overnight endeavor. Many organizations have spent several years on the process from concept to general use. Furthermore, a balanced scorecard is never completed; it continuously evolves as the organization learns and evolves, so many costs are ongoing.

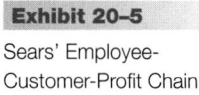

Exhibit 20–5

Sears' Employee-Customer-Profit Chain

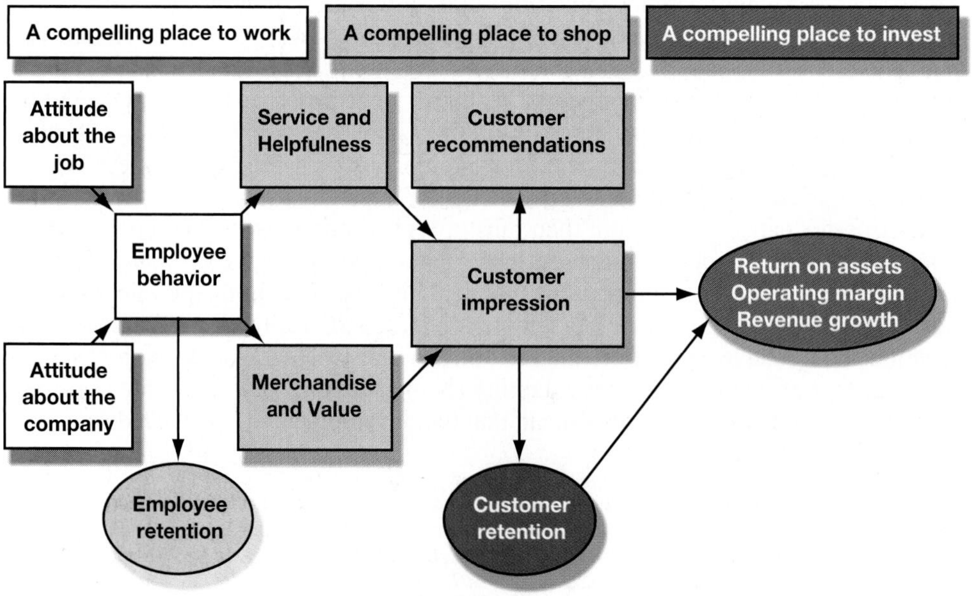

Source: A. Rucci, S. Kirn, R. Quinn, "The Employee-Customer-Profit Chain at Sears"

Measurement costs. Because of the urgency of creating a balanced scorecard, some organizations try to reuse existing measures and piece together a balanced scorecard. Picking and choosing from an inventory of existing measures can be a good first step, but new measures inevitably are necessary. Each performance measure has a cost of design, data collection, maintenance, and revision, which can be significant. Establishing credible links between measures or areas of performance is not a trivial task. Anticipating the full costs of additional performance measures is more an art than an exact science, but that does not justify ignoring these costs.

Education costs. Just as numbers almost never speak for themselves, creating a balanced scorecard does not ensure that members of the organization understand it or how to use it. Organizations should plan for and not underestimate the education, training, coaching, and interpretation activities needed to integrate the balanced scorecard.

Use costs. The costs of using a balanced scorecard also might be significant. Although early studies indicate that information overload is not a problem, assuming that individuals can manage many performance measures simultaneously is unwise, particularly if some conflict and require trade-offs. Organizations are learning to assign responsibility or "ownership" to balanced scorecard measures just as they did for responsibility accounting in the past (see Chapter 18).

Balanced Scorecard Implementation at Valley Commercial Bank

LO 3 Understand how organizations implement a balanced scorecard of performance measures.

Valley
COMMERCIAL BANK

Some organizations develop a balanced scorecard at top levels of management and impose it. This approach can be successful, just as top-down management succeeds in some situations, but most observers believe that a participative, bottom-up approach to designing a balanced scorecard improves its acceptance and use by the organization's members. After all, the foundation of the balanced scorecard is learning and growth, reflecting employee capabilities to gain, transfer, and apply knowledge. It makes sense to involve them in the balanced scorecard design.

Valley Commercial Bank's cost-management team sketched the initial balanced scorecard based on its understanding of the bank's strategy and processes and input from key employees. The team then spent more than a year working with employees representing all levels, functions, and major activities of the bank to design the scorecard. After more than a year of interaction with other employees, the team unveiled a balanced scorecard using the 19 performance measures previously discussed. Exhibit 20–6 displays Valley Commercial Bank's scorecard areas and measures.

Exhibit 20–7 is a graphical representation of part of VCB's balanced scorecard model. The cost-management team used this simplified chart to explain several cause-and-effect relationships among the four areas of performance. In this simplified model, profitability—VCB's ultimate goal—is achieved, in part, by retaining existing customers through improving loan processing. These links tell the story of VCB's success in its competitive market for banking services. This graphical representation of the bank's strategy was an effective communication and education tool. You should "walk through" this model carefully, beginning with the hours of job-related training, following the direction of the arrows from one box to the next. The Appendix to this chapter shows how a quantified balanced scorecard can measure whether the net effect of changes is beneficial.

Balanced Scorecard Incentives

Because the balanced scorecard had no major surprises and most employees can see the rationale behind each scorecard area and its measures, almost no debate about the scorecard itself occurred. Employees at all levels understood that the scorecard is a balanced set of measures that reflects the bank's strategy to grow and prosper. Bank employees reported that they understood why and how their efforts can improve the bank's financial performance. This was a major improvement in the communication of the bank's strategy and led employees to focus on improving the measures that they can influence.

Exhibit 20-6 Valley Commercial Bank's Balanced Scorecard Areas and Measures

Scorecard Areas	Scorecard Performance	Scorecard Measures	Performance Targets
Organizational learning and growth	Employee training and education	Percentage of employees involved in approved training and education	100 percent
	Employee satisfaction	Employee satisfaction index	Maintain current level
	Employee turnover	Voluntary turnover percentage	Below industry average
	Innovativeness	Percentage of sales from new services	50 percent
	Opportunities for improvement	Employee suggestions	Estimated value of employee suggestions
Business and production process efficency	New service development	Average new service development time	Continuous improvement
	Productivity (loans)	Error-free loans processed per employee	Continuous improvement
	Defective service (loans)	Errors per loan officer	Zero
	Service costs	Cost per loan, checking account, and other services	Continuous improvement
	Process improvements	Average process (e.g., loan) cycle time	One week
	Supplier relations	Supplier cycle time, error rates	Below industry averages
Customer value	Customer satisfaction	Customer satisfaction index	Above competitors' average
	Customer retention and loyalty	Customer retention rate	Above industry average
	Sales growth	Account and revenue growth	10 percent per year
	Market share	Professional and business market share	30 percent
	Customer risk	Customer risk profiles and loan default rate	Maintain current levels
Financial performance	Service profitability	Net interest margin	5 percent
	Growth	Revenue growth	Above industry average
	Customer profitability	Percentage of loss customers	Zero
	Competitive return	Return on assets	Above industry average

Although none of the performance measures was perfect, top management believed that using them for performance assessment can reinforce the desired behavior and generate superior profitability. However, many employees expressed concern about the use of the scorecard as an evaluation and incentive system because they believed that some measures were too subjective or capable of manipulation. They wondered how they should act when faced with trade-offs between measures that might conflict (e.g., reducing costs or improving customer satisfaction) and whether they will be penalized for making trade-offs.

As discussed in more detail in Chapter 21, extending the balanced scorecard to an evaluation and incentive system involves two additional developments: weighting the performance measures and tying explicit incentives to measures (individually or in total). Effective incentive systems usually require reliable, objective, and verifiable performance measures and clear guidance for evaluating trade-offs. Because the primary purpose of the balanced scorecard is to communicate and implement strategy, many organizations have not resolved these incentive issues. Partly as a result, some companies have experienced significant internal conflict when they began to use the balanced scorecard as an incentive device. In certain cases, these companies have dispensed with

Exhibit 20-7 Portion of Valley Commercial Bank's Balanced Scorecard

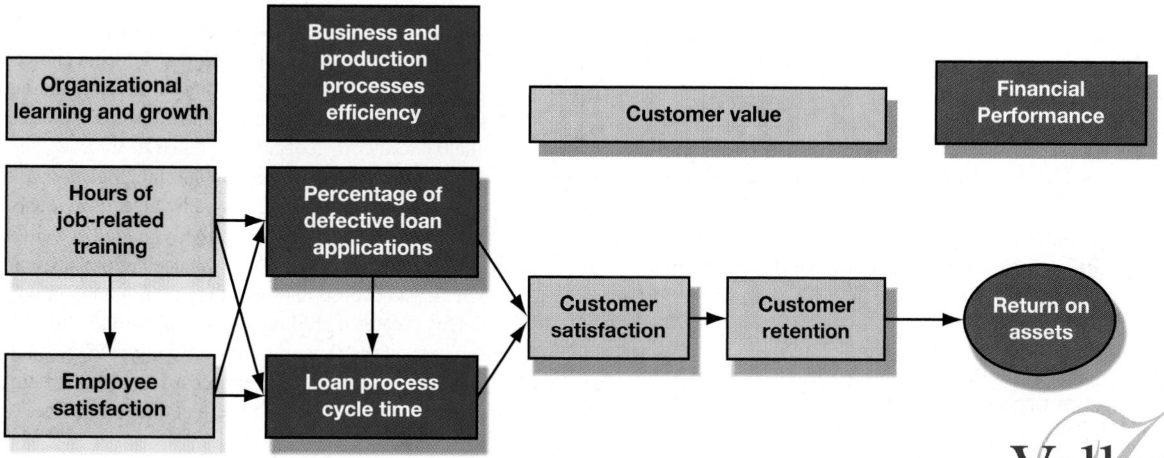

Valley COMMERCIAL BANK

the balanced scorecard altogether, but in others the conflict has led to compromises and improvements in performance measures and internal auditing procedures. Chapter 21 discusses incentive systems in general and how Valley Commercial Bank developed an incentive system consistent with its balanced scorecard.

Chapter Summary

Lead indicators of performance are early measures of outcomes of activities that allow organizations to predict problems, identify opportunities, and prevent mistakes. Lead indicators predict organizational outcomes such as customer satisfaction and future sales. Employees use lead indicators to manage activities and processes to ensure favorable final outcomes. Employees act to make improvements based on signals from lead indicators rather than wait to see whether final outcomes are favorable or unfavorable before making improvements or corrections.

Organizations use measures of (1) organizational learning and growth, (2) business and production process efficiency, and (3) customer value as lead indicators of (4) financial performance.

The balanced scorecard is a model of cause-and-effect relations among lead and lag indicators of performance. It is useful for measuring and communicating the effects of activities on organizational performance. The balanced scorecard shows the cause and effect among these four areas of performance. One can think logically of performing well on learning and growth as leading to improved business processes and improved customer satisfaction, which leads to improved financial performance. Various linkages exist among the four areas, but the point is that performing well on the three leading (usually nonfinancial) areas should lead to improved financial performance and that financial performance lags nonfinancial performance. If it is possible to quantify these cause-and-effect relationships, the balanced scorecard can be a valuable financial planning model.

Key Terms

For each term's definition, refer to the indicated page or turn to the glossary at the end of the text.

balanced scorecard, 834
customer retention or loyalty, 844
customer value, 842
employee capabilities, 836
lag indicator, 832
lead indicator, 832

Meeting the Cost-Management Challenges

1. How do analysts use their understanding of current operations to help predict future outcomes?

By understanding how current operations can be lead indicators of future performance, analysts are able to build reliable lead and lag relationships to help employees predict the effects of their current actions on future performance.

2. How does the use of the balanced scorecard at Valley Commercial Bank show each employee how her or his performance affects the bank's financial success?

Each employee should be able to see how her or his work contributes to at least one of the four balanced scorecard performance areas. Maintenance workers keep the building clean, which increases customer satisfaction. Employee trainers contribute to the learning and growth perspective, which helps employees do their jobs better, which increases customer satisfaction, and which ultimately links to financial success. Ideally, each individual has objectives consistent with the portions of the balanced scorecard that he or she influences. Tying individuals' objectives to the organization's balanced scorecard can greatly increase the effectiveness and acceptance of the balanced scorecard.

3. **How** does the balanced scorecard differ from the measures of organizational cost and performance, which have been used for as long as organized companies have existed? What does it add that previous measures do not?

The balanced scorecard is a cost-management tool that is gaining in popularity. Its validity as a guide for managers' strategic choices and operating actions depends on the validity of the lead and lag relationships that are built into this tool. A valid balanced scorecard predicts the financial outcomes of actions taken to improve performance in organizational capabilities and learning, business and production process efficiency, and customer value. Previously, managers and employees understood intuitively that all activities affect bottom-line profitability, but the balanced scorecard can both display and measure cause-and-effect relations among important activities. This creates a credible "story" about the way that the organization can succeed that perhaps only top managers understood before. Use of the balanced scorecard can help all employees to appreciate how their activities affect the bottom line.

Solutions to You're the Decision Maker

20.1 Designing the Balanced Scorecard p. 836

a. Financial measures indicate how well the organization has done in the past whereas nonfinancial measures indicate future success. Organizations that perform well on the nonfinancial performance measures should have financial success in the future. Therefore, directing employee attention to nonfinancial areas, such as improving business efficiency, should result in future financial success. In addition to these advantages, most employees can relate better to nonfinancial performance measures. For example, it is easier for a supervisor to think about training employees well and reducing employee turnover than to think about increasing return on investment.

b. The company will incur considerable costs to design and implement the balanced scorecard. The company should specify its vision and strategy (if not already done), develop nonfinancial performance measures, design an information system to collect the nonfinancial performance data, collect data, use the data to evaluate performance, and provide rewards and penalties based on such performance evaluation. The benefits are improved organizational performance, which might be difficult to measure. Management will have to decide whether the benefits outweigh the costs, which are easier to measure. Note that there is a high start-up cost; the benefits generally come later.

c. You want somebody on the team who is well respected by top management because its buy-in is important. This would be someone who has "the ear of top management," so to speak. The team should include someone who understands each of the four perspectives; someone with financial expertise; someone who knows what is needed to generate customer satisfaction; someone who understands the operations of the airline who can improve business processes; and someone who knows how to link learning and growth to the other perspectives. That team should presumably include people who know both marketing and operations very well. Inclusion of someone who knows the industry to help benchmark Singapore Airways with competitors will be helpful. The team should include employees who are respected by their peers and who are creative and willing to take risks.

Appendix to Chapter Twenty

Quantifying Causal Relations

LO 4 Use quantified lead and lag relations to predict the effects of changes in performance measures.

Quantifying the relations among performance measures transforms the balanced scorecard from a strategy-communication device to a financial planning model that allows managers to estimate the effects on profitability from changes in activities in general or changes in scorecard elements that are "upstream."[4] Consider the following diagram, which is the customer value section of Exhibit 20–5.

[4]Chapter 11 presents an introduction to measuring these relations.

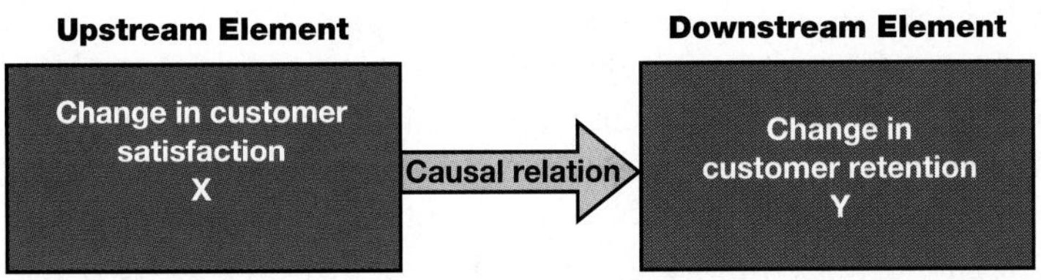

The quantified financial planning model expresses the causal relationships between the upstream and downstream elements as algebraic equations in the form, $\delta Y = b \times \delta X$, where δ is the Greek letter delta and signifies a change. In this simple example, δY is the estimated increase (or decrease) in customer retention from an increase (decrease) in customer satisfaction. The term *b* measures the proportional relation between a change in *X* (or δX) and the resulting change in *Y* (or δY). Methods for estimating these proportional effects are covered in Chapter 11. In the complete model, δX itself is influenced by balanced scorecard elements that are upstream of it.

Numerical Example

Consider that a 1.0 percentage point increase in customer satisfaction is estimated to cause the organization's retained customers to increase by 1.1 percentage points. What if customer satisfaction increased by 2.0 percentage points? What is the estimated increase in retained customers? The increase can be found by using the following relation:

$$\delta Y = b \times \delta X$$

where

δY (delta *Y*) = estimated increase in retained customers (to be computed)
b = measured impact on the change in retained customers of a change in customer satisfaction, 1.1
δX (delta *X*) = increase in customer satisfaction, 2 percentage points

Therefore, the estimated increase in retained customers is

$$\delta Y = (1.1) \times (2.0) = 2.2 \text{ percentage points}$$

If the company's retained customers had been 40 percent, the increase in customer satisfaction should increase customer retention to 42.2 percent.

Estimating these relationships (that is, the *b* terms) can be very difficult because processes and conditions can change frequently, rendering some historical data obsolete.[5] If feasible, a quantified financial planning model can be an extremely valuable source of competitive advantage. For example, Sears, the large retail company discussed in Cost Management in Practice 20.2, reportedly uses its scorecard model to estimate the profitability effects of alternative projects. By letting managers estimate the revenues, costs, and risks associated with each project, this model helps the company choose among the many alternative uses of its resources.

Quantified Balanced Scorecard

Exhibit 20–8 shows Valley Commercial Bank's simplified balanced scorecard with quantified relationships. Trace each relationship described in the following list through this balanced scorecard. The following numbered list corresponds to the numbered boxes, and the letters in parentheses correspond to the lettered arrows in Exhibit 20–8. A VCB cost-management team estimated the following:

1. A 1,000-hour increase in job-related training will (a) increase the average employee satisfaction level by 2.0 points (on a 100-point scale), (b) reduce

[5] For example, see M. Malina, "An Empirical Test of a Causal Balanced Scorecard."

average loan-processing cycle time by 1.2 hours, and (c) decrease loan application errors by .4 percentage points.

2. A 1.0 point increase in average employee satisfaction (on a 100-point scale) will (d) decrease average loan-processing cycle time by .5 hours and (e) decrease loan application errors by .2 percentage points.
3. A 1.0 percent decrease in loan application errors will (f) decrease average loan-processing cycle time by 1.3 hours and (g) increase the customer satisfaction level by .4 percentage points.
4. A 1.0 hour decrease in average loan process cycle time will (h) increase customer satisfaction by .2 percentage points.
5. A 1.0 percentage point increase in customer satisfaction will (i) increase retained customers by 1.1 percentage points.
6. A 1.0 percentage point increase in retained customers will (j) increase return on assets by .5 percentage points.

The quantity next to each arrow of Exhibit 20–8 (the *b* term in the proceding numerical example) measures how much a one-unit increase in the respective upstream element changes the downstream element. Consider the following example:

- A 1,000-hour increase in job-related training is expected to directly increase the average employee satisfaction level by 2.0 scale points, decrease the percentage of the loan applications with errors by .4 percentage points, and decrease the average loan-processing cycle time by 1.2 hours. An important part of these causal relations to remember is that each upstream element can have indirect effects on other downstream elements because the effects are expected to flow through the organization.
- An increase in hours of job-related training also indirectly increases the customer satisfaction level through its impacts (decreases) on defects and cycle time.

Valley COMMERCIAL BANK

Exhibit 20–8 Valley Commercial Bank's Quantified (Partial) Balanced Scorecard

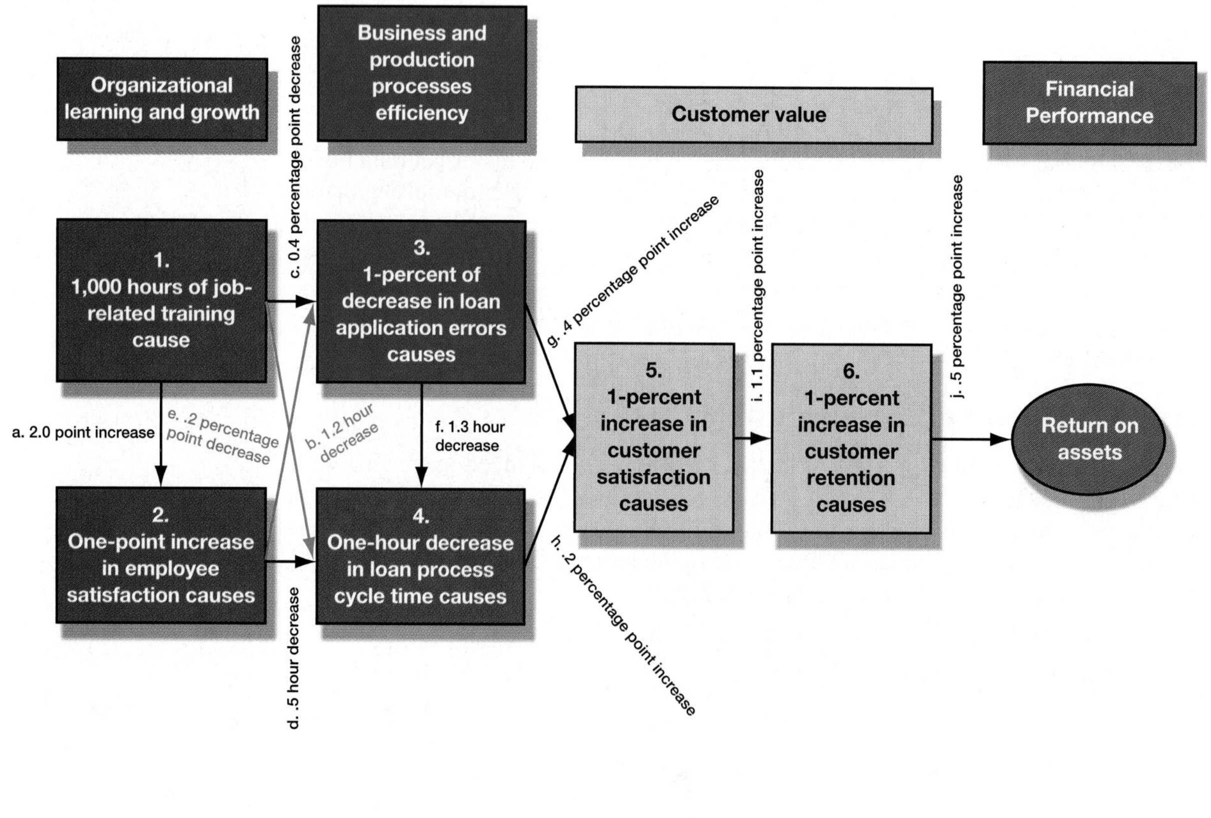

If the relationships are measured accurately, we can trace the estimated effects from an increase in employee job-related training, through the other elements, to changes in return on assets.

Managers can use the model to estimate the effects of changes in other elements in the balanced scorecard. For example, Valley Commercial Bank might purchase new software that reduces loan-processing errors. The effects of the new software flow downstream in the directions of the arrows.

Review Questions

20.1 Review and define each of the chapter's key terms.

20.2 What is the difference between a *lead* and a *lag* indicator of performance?

20.3 How can employee capabilities be measured? Why is this important for improving efficiency, identifying opportunities, and preventing mistakes?

20.4 Describe how improvements in employee capabilities can affect process efficiency.

20.5 What are some useful indicators of process efficiency? How are they measured?

20.6 Describe how improvements in process efficiency can affect customer value.

20.7 Explain how concern for supplier relations is part of managing internal processes.

20.8 What is customer value and how is it measured?

20.9 Briefly describe the elements of customer value.

20.10 Describe how improvements in customer value can affect financial performance.

20.11 How can knowledge of cultural differences lead to improvements in customer value and financial performance?

20.12 Is financial performance important to all types of organizations, even nonprofits? Explain.

20.13 What are the elements of a balanced scorecard?

20.14 What is the difference between a set of lead and lag indicators and a balanced scorecard?

20.15 In what ways can a balanced scorecard be useful?

20.16 Explain how the four areas of balanced scorecard performance might interact.

20.17 Explain why it can take months or years to develop a balanced scorecard. How do you know whether the effort is worthwhile?

20.18 Explain differences in balanced scorecards for profit-seeking and nonprofit organizations.

20.19 Explain how an increase in employee capabilities can flow through an organization and how the effects are reflected in the balanced scorecard.

20.20 Explain how the balanced scorecard can be used as a financial planning model.

Critical Analysis

20.21 The chief operating officer of a nonprofit organization states, "It's all very well for a company like Sears to implement a balanced scorecard. It has measures in all four areas of the scorecard and has to satisfy stockholders. Without a profit measure or motive in the last area of the scorecard, I just don't see how or why we should expend the effort to build a partial balanced scorecard." (Refer to Cost Management in Practice 20.2.) How do you answer this observation?

20.22 A business executive says, "The financial perspective of the balanced scorecard indicates how the organization adds value to shareholders. I am involved with two organizations; a small business that is a partnership, so it has no shareholders, and a church that has no shareholders. The balanced scorecard makes a lot of sense to me, but the financial perspective is clearly irrelevant for these two organizations." How do you respond to this statement?

20.23 Respond to the following statement: "Most measures of performance, such as profits and product costs, are useless for management decision making because they measure what has happened, not what will happen."

20.24 Until recently the CEO of Xerox Corporation prominently stated in his letter to the company's annual reports that Xerox always strives to improve customer satisfaction. Xerox no longer makes this claim so prominently. Is it possible to create too much customer satisfaction? Explain.

20.25 Customers' perceptions of value can differ across cultures. Many people believe that US–based companies are ignorant or arrogant when it comes to appreciating other cultures. Do you think this is true? What are the possible costs of lack of appreciation of other cultures? How can you prepare yourself to contribute value to an organization by appreciating other cultures?

20.26 Westinghouse Corporation formerly advertised that its employees are its most important assets. If that is true for Westinghouse (and presumably for other organizations, too), why does its balance sheet (and presumably those of other organizations) not have a category of assets for employees?

20.27 Do you believe that improved employee capabilities always lead to process improvements or improvements in customer value and profitability? If not, what else is necessary to transform improved employee capabilities into other improvements?

20.28 If a company measures cycle time for only the products that pass through its processes without defects, is this necessarily a bad practice? What incentives might motivate such a practice?

20.29 Is it possible to increase the throughput efficiency of one process in a company to the point at which an additional increase in efficiency can reduce the company's overall profitability? If so, give an example.

20.30 Explain this comment from a sales manager: "The most expensive product we make is a defective one that ends up in the hands of a long-term customer."

20.31 "It is a bigger mistake to develop an unreliable balanced scorecard than to never build one at all." Do you agree with this statement? Why or why not?

Exercises

Exercise 20.32
Balanced Scorecard Perspectives
(LO 1)

Match each of the following performance measures to one or more of the four perspectives of the balanced scorecard. Note that a performance measure can relate to more than one perspective.

Performance Measures	Balanced Scorecard Perspectives
Employee productivity	Organizational learning and growth
Employee satisfaction	Business and production process efficiency
Return on assets	Customer value
Customer satisfaction	Financial performance
Employee turnover	
On-time delivery performance from suppliers	
Percent of customers who are repeat customers	
On-time delivery performance to customers	
Product quality	

Exercise 20.33
Balanced Scorecard Perspectives
(LO 1)

Match each of the following performance measures to one or more of the four perspectives of the balanced scorecard. Note that a performance measure can relate to more than one perspective.

Performance Measures	Balanced Scorecard Perspectives
Throughput time	Organizational learning and growth
Return on sales	Business and production process efficiency
Customer satisfaction	Customer value
Percent of sales dollars invested in employee training	Financial performance
Ratings of supplier performance	
Increase in market share	
Employee retention	
On-time delivery performance to customers	
Product quality	

Exercise 20.34
Lead and Lag Indicators
(LO 2)

Arrange the following measures in an order that reflects their possible use as lead or lag indicators of performance. Note that a measure of performance can itself be a lead indicator of later performance.

Customer satisfaction	Anticipation of customer needs
Acquisition of new customers	Product quality
On-time deliveries	Process efficiency
Customer retention	Employee satisfaction
Customer profitability	Employee skills
Product innovations	Compliance with environmental regulations
Market share	Supplier reliability and quality
Overall profitability	

Exercise 20.35
Learning and Growth
(LO 1)

Perform a library or Internet search for a comprehensive article on an actual organization's management of organizational learning and growth. Prepare a five-minute presentation (with transparencies or PowerPoint slides) of your findings and how they relate to the chapter's coverage of this topic.

Exercise 20.36
Customer Satisfaction
(LO 1)

State three customer-satisfaction performance measures for each of the following organizations:

McDonald's, a fast-food franchise
Nordstrom's, an upscale retailer
United Airlines, an airline company

Exercise 20.37
Customer Satisfaction
(LO 1)

State three customer-satisfaction performance measures for each of the following organizations:

The school of business and management in Hong Kong University of Science and Technology
The United Nations
The New York Stock Exchange

Exercise 20.38
Customer Satisfaction
(LO 1)

Perform a library or Internet search for a comprehensive article on an actual organization's management of customer satisfaction or cultural differences. Prepare a five-minute presentation (with transparencies or PowerPoint slides) of your findings and how they relate to the chapter's coverage of this topic.

Exercise 20.39
Customer Satisfaction
(LO 1)

FirstBank conducts regular customer surveys to assess its customer satisfaction, which is measured by averaging responses (from 1 = highly unfavorable to 5 = highly favorable) on five variables that measure customers' satisfaction with the bank's services. Quantify FirstBank's recent customer satisfaction from the following information. Do you see a pattern in the scores? If so, what does it tell FirstBank about its customer satisfaction?

	Number of Customer Responses				
Customer Satisfaction Variable	**1**	**2**	**3**	**4**	**5**
Automated bank services meet customer needs	16	25	22	22	15
FirstBank services are superior to competitors' services	8	17	24	36	15
Employees give prompt service	6	14	22	41	17
Employees are courteous and friendly	7	12	20	38	23
Employees can and do respond to special requests	12	26	20	21	21

Exercise 20.40
Customer Satisfaction
(LO 1)

PMI conducts regular customer surveys to assess customer satisfaction with its products and postsale services, which is measured by averaging responses (from 1 = highly unfavorable to 5 = highly favorable) on five variables that measure customer satisfaction with the company's products. Quantify PMI's recent customer satisfaction from the following information. Do you see a pattern in the scores? If so, what does it tell PMI about its customer satisfaction?

	Number of Customer Responses				
Customer Satisfaction Variable	**1**	**2**	**3**	**4**	**5**
PMI's products are defect-free	20	21	22	22	15
PMI's products are superior to competitors' products	8	17	24	36	15
PMI's products perform reliably	6	14	22	41	17
PMI's repair services are prompt	7	12	20	38	23
PMI's warranty is superior to competitors' warranty	12	21	20	26	21

Exercise 20.41
Balanced Scorecard Implementation
(LO 3)

In a small group, conduct a library or Internet search for an article that describes how an organization successfully designed and implemented its balanced scorecard. Prepare a five-minute presentation (with transparencies or PowerPoint slides) of your findings and how they relate to the chapter's coverage of this topic.

Exercise 20.42
Balanced Scorecard Implementation
(LO 3)

In a small group, conduct a library or Internet search for an article that describes how an organization *unsuccessfully* designed or implemented its balanced scorecard. Prepare a five-minute presentation (with transparencies or PowerPoint slides) of your findings and how they relate to the chapter's coverage of this topic.

Exercise 20.43
Quantified Balanced Scorecard (Appendix)
(LO 4)

Compute the downstream effects of each of the following *independent* changes in upstream balanced scorecard measures (similar to those in Exhibit 20–8):

Upstream Element	Change	Effects on Downstream Element(s) per Unit of Change in Upstream Element	Amount of Change(s) Caused by Upstream Element(s)
a. Hours of job-related training	+ 100 hours	Increases employee satisfaction by 1 scale point per 100 hours	?
		Decreases service errors by .3 percentage point per 100 hours	?
b. Employee satisfaction	+ 3 scale points	Decreases service errors by .2 percentage points per scale point	?
		Decreases service cycle time by .8 hour per scale point	?
c. Percentage defective services	− 2 percentage points	Decreases service cycle time by .5 hour per point	?
		Increases customer satisfaction by 1.5% per point	?
d. Service cycle time	− 2 hours	Increases customer satisfaction by 2% per hour	?
e. Customer satisfaction	+ 3 percentage points	Increases customer retention by .4% per point	?
f. Customer retention	+ 2 percentage points	Increases return on assets by .03% per point	?

Problems

Problem 20.44
Organizational Learning and Growth
(LO 1)

Communication

eToys, Inc., has been one of the leading Internet-based retailers of children's toys. However, in 2000 eToys generated a large loss, and its stock price plummeted from $86 to $5. The following table summarizes the causes of its unprofitability and near disaster that eToys identified.

Problem	Solution	Lesson
Loss of control over shipping and late shipments resulting from outsourcing some order fulfillment	Opened two additional warehouses, staffed entirely by eToys employees	Provide the best service to customers by keeping the work in-house
Severe seasonal peaks and drops in revenue	Expanded into baby supplies, party goods, and hobbies	Diversify while staying true to the target market
Serious doubts on Wall Street that the company can turn a profit and survive	Held first-ever analysts' conference, committed to profitability by a specific target date	Communicate with the people who hold the purse strings even when the news is not positive

Required

a. In your opinion, what types of employees and what specific skills should eToys develop and maintain to successfully solve its problems?

b. Write a memo outlining the steps you think eToys should take, including the development of lead indicators of employee capabilities.

[Adapted from A. Weintraub, "He's Not Playing."]

Problem 20.45
Evaluation of Customer Service
(LO 1)

Communication

Spreadsheet

As prices for many items have stabilized because of competition, some Internet-based retailers (only 1 percent of "e-tailers" in 2000) now are competing on the basis of real-time customer service provided by live company representatives. These e-tailers report improved customer satisfaction, traffic, and sales growth that they attribute to real-time customer service. Whether this improved customer satisfaction and sales growth has led to improved profitability is unclear. Consider the following actual and predicted data for HomeMarket.com, which is contemplating adding real-time customer service, through online chat technology

Current data:	
Annual sales	$11,500,000
Average cost of sales as percent of sales	60%
Sales growth percent	3%
Predictions related to new customer service:	
Increase in customer satisfaction percents	5%
Software and training costs for new customer service	$ 300,000
Ongoing operating costs for new customer service	$ 2,500,000
Cost savings from reduction of email response service	$ 100,000
Additional sales growth	20%

Required

a. Identify the costs and benefits of HomeMarket.com's proposed customer service operation. (Ignore taxes.)

b. Use a spreadsheet to thoroughly analyze the profitability of the proposed customer service operation. Be prepared to present your analysis.

[Adapted from T. Mullaney, "Needed: The Human Touch."]

Problem 20.46
Evaluation of Customer Satisfaction
(LO 1)

Communication

Paragon Sports, a major sporting goods retailer, is considering upgrading its customer-support activities by improving online databases and training of customer-service personnel. Consider the following data:

Current data:	
Annual sales	$20,000,000
Average cost of sales as percent of sales	60%
Sales growth	4%
Predictions related to new-customer service:	
Increase in customer satisfaction	10%
Software and training costs for new customer service	$ 400,000
Ongoing operating costs for new customer service	$ 500,000
Cost savings from reduction of email response service	$ 100,000
Additional sales growth	6%

Required

a. Prepare an analysis of the costs and benefits of Paragon Sports' proposed customer-service improvements. (Ignore taxes.)

b. Use a spreadsheet to thoroughly analyze the profitability of the proposed customer-service operation. Be prepared to present your analysis.

Problem 20.47
Evaluation of Learning and Growth
(LO 1)

Communication

Paragon Sports is considering enrolling in ConditCorp's Customer Value Seminar, a $2,500 per-person, week-long intensive seminar that teaches sales people to build customer satisfaction and loyalty and to sell products and services more effectively by understanding customers' needs. ConditCorp advertises a money-back guarantee if its sales seminars do not pay for themselves in increased profits so long as new employees also are trained. Paragon Sports will send its entire sales force of 100 to the seminar in the current year and its new employees each year thereafter for five years. The company normally experiences annual turnover in sales personnel of 20 percent; its annual cost of capital is 10 percent.

Required

What equal, annual net benefit must Paragon Sports experience to validate ConditCorp's money-back guarantee over this six-year period? (Ignore taxes.) Prepare a spreadsheet analysis of the costs and benefits of Paragon Sports' proposed customer service improvements. Be prepared to present your analysis.

Problem 20.48
Evaluation of Process Improvements
(LO 1)

Spreadsheet

Paragon Sports is considering improvements to its warehousing and distribution operations including a $500,000 purchase of robotic machinery with a useful life of five years. Other improvements entail the installation of new computing equipment and software at a start-up cost of $350,000 and $75,000 per year for the next five years. Employee training costs will increase by $40,000 this year and remain at that level for the next five years. The firm's annual cost of capital is 10 percent.

Required

What equal, annual net benefit must Paragon Sports experience over the current and next five years to justify the process improvements? (Ignore taxes.) Prepare a spreadsheet analysis of the costs and benefits of Paragon Sports' proposed process improvements. Be prepared to present your analysis.

Problem 20.49
Performance Measurement
(LO 2, 3)

Communication

Ruth Chambers, an executive in a large bank, recently attended a conference on management in the banking industry. At the conference, a Citibank manager presented a diagram similar to the one in Exhibit 20–2. Chambers is intrigued by the performance measurement problems posed by the diagram. She asks, "How do you measure the performance of each step in the sequence from increased employee training to better financial results?"

Required

Using the balanced scorecard as a reference point, write a report to Chambers that explains how to measure performance for each step in the sequence from increased employee training to better financial results.

Problem 20.50
Performance Measurement
(LO 2, 3)

Branford San Miguel, the managing partner of the Melbourne office of the consulting firm of PriceAndersonCoopersErnst (PACE) developed a diagram similar to the one in Exhibit 20–2 for a client who owns a small manufacturing company. The diagram had the following links:

Afterward, San Miguel commented to his fellow consultants, "I wish I could apply this model to our consulting business. But what we produce is advice, which is not very tangible."

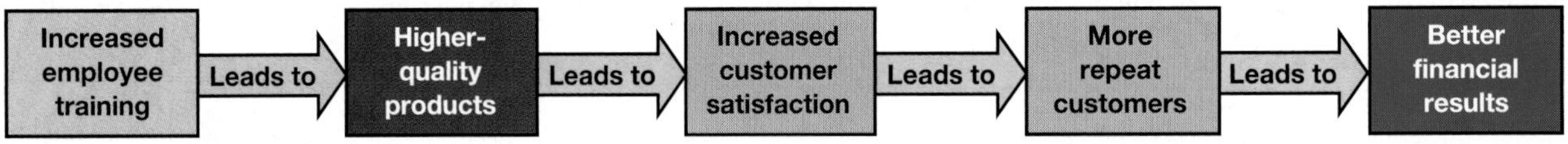

Communication Team

Required

In a small group and using the balanced scorecard as a reference point, write a report to San Miguel that explains how to implement the model shown in the problem to the consulting business. Be specific in stating how to measure the performance of each step in the sequence from increased employee training to better financial results.

Problem 20.51
Balanced Scorecard
(LO 2, 3)

Communication

Sheila Mack, an owner of 42 fast-food franchises, has come to you for advice. She wants to try the balanced scorecard in her stores. She is concerned because some attempts to implement improvements in the past have not been successful. "I've heard store managers say, 'Somebody must have gone to a conference or read some book, because here comes another crackpot idea for us to implement. If we just play along for a while, this too will pass. Then we can get back to business as usual.' I don't want store managers to think the balanced scorecard is just another fad. I want them to take it seriously. I want them to give it a fair trial."

Required

Write a short report to Mack that advises her how to implement the balanced scorecard in a way that her store managers will give it a fair trial.

Problem 20.52
Balanced Scorecard
(LO 2)

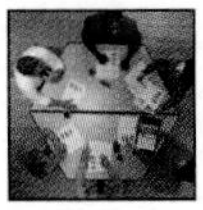

Team Communication

Work in a small group.

Required

Select an organization for study. For each of the four balanced scorecard perspectives, identify no more than four performance measures. Write a report that states specifically how you plan to measure performance. How might you validate these measures? If possible, you might find it useful to interview a manager in the company that you pick.

Problem 20.53
Predicting Performance (Appendix)
(LO 4)

Compute the downstream effects from the following upstream elements, or lead indicators, in a balanced scorecard similar to the one in Exhibit 20–8.

Upstream Element	**Cumulative Change (from prior causes)**	**Effects on Downstream Element(s) per Unit of Change of Upstream Element**	**Amount of Change(s) Caused by Upstream Element(s)**
Hours of job-related training	+100 hours	Increases employee satisfaction by 1 scale point per 100 hours	?
		Decreases service errors by .3 percentage point per 100 hours	?
Employee satisfaction	?	Decreases service errors by .2 percentage point per scale point	?
		Decreases service cycle time by .8 hour per scale point	?
Percentage service errors	?	Decreases service cycle time by .5 hour per percentage point	?
Service cycle time	?		

Problem 20.54
Predicting Performance (Appendix)
(LO 4)

Compute the downstream effects from the following upstream elements, or lead indicators, in a balanced scorecard similar to the one in Exhibit 20–8.

Upstream Element	**Cumulative Change (from prior causes)**	**Effects on Downstream Element(s) per Unit of Change of Upstream Element**	**Amount of Change(s) Caused by Upstream Element(s)**
Hours of job-related training	+100 hours	Increases employee education level by 2 scale points per 100 hours	?
		Decreases defective products by .4 percentage point per 100 hours	?
Employee education level	?	Decreases defective products by .3 percentage point per scale point	?
		Decreases process cycle time by .9 hour per scale point	?
Percentage defective products	?	Decreases process cycle time by .4 hour per percentage point	?
Process cycle time	?		

Problem 20.55
Supplier Relations
(LO 1)

Communication

One of your suppliers comes to your next meeting in a new Ferrari, mentions new membership to an exclusive country club, and has started to build a lake house.

Required

a. Obtain and read the article, Strand et al., "Are Your Vendors Stealing from You?" (See Bibliography for full reference.)

b. Write a memo that explains how the information in the article can be used to develop lead indicators of problematic supplier relations.

Problem 20.56
Customer Value
(LO 1)

Global

Some argue that the only obligation of a business is to earn a competitive profit. Market forces, so the argument goes, reward good behavior and punish bad. However, in recent years, global companies such as Shell, Boeing, BP Amoco, and Nike have sought to blunt criticisms and protests against their so-called unethical global business practices.

Required

a. Obtain and read the article, "Doing Well by Doing Good," *The Economist,* 65–67. (See Bibliography for full reference.)

b. Explain how the information in the article can be used to develop lead indicators of problematic customer relations and costly criticisms and protests.

Cases

Case 20.57
Lead Indicators and Corporate Intelligence
(LO 1)

Internet Communication

"All this talk about developing lead indicators of our process performance and customer needs is really missing the mark," argued Ronald Melcher, the executive vice president of marketing for Industrial Foods, Inc. (IFI), which provides food items for airline kitchens. "What we need most are lead indicators of what Fulsome Foods, our chief competitor, will do. I know a very capable corporate intelligence [CI] firm that will find out pretty much everything we need to know and do it very discreetly."

Harold Baum, IFI's CEO, agreed, "I don't ever want to be in a fair fight. I want an edge everyplace I go. What type of information do you have in mind?"

"Well, how about how Fulsome makes decisions on pricing? I'm thinking that if we knew who has to approve price cuts and how long it takes them to make those approvals, we can find the right time, say when those people are out of town, and ambush them by offering serious discounts to their customers. We can have the price cuts in place before they can respond. We can snare some serious market share."

"Wait just a minute, fellows," cautioned Kerry Kahaner, IFI's chief financial officer. "I assume you know that industrial espionage is now a federal crime, and we can land in jail for 15 years and pay $10 million in fines for spying on our competitors."

"Calm down, Kerry, nobody's talking about doing anything illegal here, and besides, we won't be doing it. That's what consultants are for," explained Melcher. "The CI firm I am talking about, New World Intelligence, assures me that what they do is legal, although some of their tactics stray into gray areas. But it's their necks on the line, not ours. We just tell them what we want to know, and they generate the report."

"And send us a hefty bill for their efforts," retorted Kahaner. "Still, I want a better idea of their methods and possible results before I sign on. Do you have any examples, Ron?"

"As a matter of fact, I read about one recent example in *Business Week.* New World Intelligence saved Monsanto over $80 million in advertising planned to combat sucralose, Johnson & Johnson's new competitor to Monsanto's artificial sweetener, Nutrasweet. NWI got information from inside the FDA [US Food & Drug Administration] that, even though Canada approved sucralose, it was unlikely that the FDA ever would. And you know what? The FDA still hasn't approved sucralose. Monsanto would have wasted $80 million without NWI. Wouldn't you buy information that can save $80 million? That's what I call a useful lead indicator."

Required

a. Search your library or the Internet to find information on the practice, ethics, and legality of corporate intelligence.

b. Based on your research, how do you advise the management team of Industrial Foods regarding its plans to use corporate intelligence? In particular, what is your opinion of Ronald Melcher's plan?

c. Some argue that the use of corporate intelligence is common practice in Asia and Europe and that US firms are foolish not to use it and use it as thoroughly as their international competitors. Others, including E. A. Kampouris, CEO of $5.2 billion American Standard, Inc., disagree. He stated, "This is not warfare. I don't consider our competitors as communists or Hitler." Prepare a memo to IFI management explaining your stand on the use of corporate intelligence.

[Adapted from "How Corporations Snoop to Conquer," *Business Week.*]

Case 20.58
Balanced Scorecard Design
(LO 1, 2 ,3)

Internet Communication

"I am really confused," sighed Brian Allen, the CFO of a newly formed biotechnology firm. "I think we need to build a balanced scorecard to guide our decision making and to help us see whether we are meeting our goals, but everything I have read about balanced scorecards makes me wonder whether we, as a small company, can really succeed. I don't think we can afford to waste the time if we don't succeed.

"Here's an article in *Fortune* that implies that the balanced scorecard is essential, but professors and businesses using scorecards can't agree whether the relationships must be quantified or not. Professor Shank said great companies 'don't talk profits, they talk key drivers [lead indicators].' He seems to be saying that managing the lead indicators will lead to improved profits but that you don't necessarily need a quantified relationship to know that. On the other hand, Professor Selden says in the article that you have to begin with financial measurements; otherwise, how can you be sure that doing more of something really will add value? And the example companies are all large and well established, like Shell Oil, Motorola, and Analog Devices. If everything has to be quantified, we won't be able to build a useful balanced scorecard. After all, we have existed as a company for only two years, and how much data can we have?"

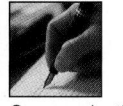

You reply, "I've just seen another article by Professor Chow that indicates even small companies can use a balanced scorecard. From the examples in this article, I'm not sure that you have to be able to quantify scorecard relationships to build a useful scorecard. Look at this scorecard for another biotechnology company. I imagine that its information needs must be similar to yours, Brian."

Refer to the goals and objectives in the following example scorecard.

Example Scorecard	
Objectives	**Measures**
Goal: Increase Customer Value	
New products	Percent of sales from new products
Early purchase of seasonal products	Percent of sales that are early purchases
Accurate invoices	Percent of error-free invoices
Early payment	Percent of customers that pay early
Product quality	Product performance vs. industry standards
Customer satisfaction	Customer-satisfaction surveys
Goal: Improve Business and Production Process Efficiency	
Low-cost producer	Product cost vs. competitors' product cost
Inventory reduction	Inventory as a percent of sales
New products	Number of new product introductions
Goal: Lead by Innovation	
New active ingredients	Number of new ingredients
Proprietary products and processes	Number of patents
Goal: Financial Performance	
Growth	Percent increase in revenue
Profitability	Return on equity; earnings per share
Industry leadership	Market share

Required

Write a report in which you do the following:

a. Expand on "your" comment; do balanced scorecard relationships need to be quantified to be useful? Explain.

b. Comment on the completeness of the example scorecard. Can you suggest additions and/or deletions from the objectives and measures? If possible, review Web sites or annual reports of several biotechnology companies (e.g., Amgen, Genentech, or other companies that you might find from an Internet search of the keyword "biotechnology"), and read the letter from the president or the management discussion and analysis to help you. Annual reports or 10-K reports are available for publicly traded US companies on the Security and Exchange Commission's EDGAR database (*http://www.sec.gov/edaux/searches.htm*).

c. Explain how a balanced scorecard similar to the preceding one can help Allen and his management team to achieve the following objectives:

(1) Develop cost-management information to help meet strategic goals.

(2) Analyze and evaluate organizational change.

(3) Evaluate the effects of alternative uses of resources on performance.

(4) Implement and manage change.

Case 20.59
Balanced Scorecard Design
(LO 1, 2, 3)

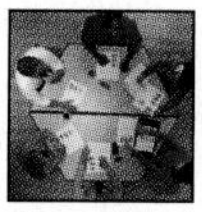
Team

Communication

A recent survey of accounting faculty and representatives of business advisory firms by two accounting professors identified performance measures for university accounting programs that can be incorporated into a balanced scorecard. These measures include the following:

Customer	Effective student placement
	Student success on professional examinations
	Quality instruction
	Quality advising
	External ranking of program

Adapted from C. Chow, K. Haddad, and J. Williamson, "Applying the Balanced Scorecard to Small Companies" Management Accounting, August 1997, 21–27, and J. Kurtzman, "Is Your Company Off Course? Now You Can Find Out Why," *Fortune,* February 17, 1997, 128–30.

Process	Quality assurance
	Cost of instruction
	Optimal class size
Faculty	Faculty professional growth
	Use of technology in teaching
	Innovation in teaching
	Curriculum innovation
Financial	Annual gifts to department by alumni and friends
	Annual gifts by employers of students
	Enrollment level and trend
	University funding per student

Required

In a small group, address the following:

a. Prepare a graphical display of the preceding measures of performance similar to the one in Exhibit 20–5.

b. Classify each performance measure according to whether you believe that the difficulty in the measurement itself (not the strength or direction of the linkages among measures) is "easy" or "difficult," or if you are "unsure" about the difficulty of measurement.

c. What factors influence whether academic accounting departments will use your balanced scorecard?

Case 20.60
Balanced Scorecard Implementation
(LO 2)

FMC Corporation is a highly diversified company based in Chicago, Illinois. In the 1990s, the company performed a comprehensive strategic review to ascertain how best to increase shareholder value. Over the next several years, it developed and implemented a balanced scorecard to give the company a greater external focus.

The process of developing the balanced scorecard started with top management developing strategic objectives for the company. The balanced scorecard implementation team, with the help of numerous middle managers, developed performance measures and targets for the lithium division, which was the site of the pilot implementation. In total, the team developed four performance measures for each of the four balanced scorecard perspectives, or 16 performance measures in total. Of those 16, management believed that four were particularly important for the lithium division:

1. On-time delivery.
2. Cost control.
3. Developing sources of raw materials.
4. Developing new products.

Management communicated the measures, which included both objective "hard" and subjective "soft" measures, to employees in terms of what performance on these measures meant to the employees' jobs. For example, managers explained how meeting on-time delivery targets improved customer relations, repeat business, job security, and prospects for pay increases and promotions. This communication step was critical for ensuring that the performance measures were not just a management and staff idea but were being implemented by the people doing the work.

In setting targets for the measures, the balanced scorecard implementation team looked at how FMC's best competitors were doing and what customers would demand in the future. For example, if 10 percent of FMC's deliveries were late while the best competitor's deliveries were only 5 percent late and future customers expect 99 percent on-time delivery, FMC should substantially improve its on-time deliveries to be competitive.

The implementation at FMC's lithium division appears to have gone well and is now used by other parts of the company.

[Adapted from R. Kaplan, "Measuring Corporate Performance: The Balanced Scorecard."]

Required

a. In developing its balanced scorecard, why did FMC Corporation pick these four measures as particularly important for the company?

b. How did managers communicate the importance of meeting on-time delivery targets to employees?

c. What can other organizations learn from FMC's experience?

Case 20.61
Predicting Financial Performance
(LO 3)

Communication

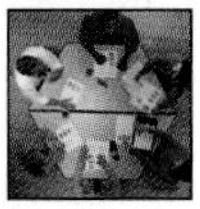
Team

Obtain and read the article by A. Rucci, S. Kirn, and R. Quinn, "The Employee-Customer-Profit Chain at Sears."

Required

In a small group, prepare a written or visual report that addresses the following questions.

a. Is this article an objective report of a design and an implementation of a balanced scorecard performance-measurement system? Explain.

b. What additional information do you want about Sears' employee-customer-profit chain? How can you use that information to guide the design and implementation of a similar system in another organization?

c. How has Sears performed financially over time and relative to its competitors since its reported use of the employee-customer-profit chain? Can you attribute any differences to its employee-customer-profit chain? Why or why not?

Case 20.62
Cal-Davis' Balanced Scorecard
(LO 2)

Following several years of budget cuts, administrators at the University of California, Davis, sought ways to make the university more efficient, "to do more with less." Janet Hamilton, vice chancellor of administration, searched books and articles, contacted consulting firms, and talked to her counterparts at universities across the United States looking for new management methods that could change the university from a bureaucratic to a customer-oriented organization. After reading about reengineering, total quality initiatives, and a variety of other management techniques, she came across the balanced scorecard. She believed that it was the right tool for the campus and set about implementing it.

At first, she did not call the balanced scorecard by name, fearing that employees would think of it as just another management fad to endure until the administration tired of it and went on to something new. Instead, Hamilton pilot tested the balanced scorecard ideas in one support department, environmental health and safety (EHS), until it worked. With the success at EHS behind her, she moved to implement it across the board in other support departments, such as police, fire, and printing services.

Each department developed its own particular performance measures to achieve the following objectives (the list has been shortened to save space):

Organizational Learning and Growth

- Create a workplace that fosters teamwork, pride, and integrity.
- Attract and retain a highly skilled workforce.
- Encourage and reward enterprising behaviors.

Business and Production Process Efficiency

- Develop clear policies, simple procedures, and efficient work processes.
- Anticipate the future, and design programs and services to ensure future success.

Customer Value

- Consistently satisfy customers.

Financial Performance

- Ensure financial integrity for capital and financial assets throughout the campus.
- Deliver services in a cost-effective manner.

[Adapted from interviews with university administrative staff.]

Required

a. Was the vice chancellor overly cautious in not calling this a "balanced scorecard"?

b. Comment on the wisdom of beginning a balanced scorecard with a pilot project. How can you extrapolate the experience of a support-service department, such as environmental health and safety, to an academic unit, such as a college of business?

c. What opportunities and difficulties do you see in applying the balanced scorecard to a university setting?

Case 20.63
Considering Customers' Tastes and Preferences as Lead Indicators of Sales
(LO 1)

Communication

Global

Although the revolutions in telecommunications and the Internet have made the world seem smaller, tremendous differences in cultures still exist around the world. Organizations seeking to operate globally must be aware of the fact that customer preferences differ greatly across cultures. Respecting and understanding these differences can lead companies to provide products and services that appeal to many different customers. Some of these cultural differences, such as language and arts, seem obvious, but there are numerous examples of companies that have introduced products to different markets without advance knowledge of social and cultural differences.

Fortunately, successful uses of advance knowledge of social and cultural differences are becoming more common, allowing firms to design and provide products and services to broader markets. A US entrepreneur, for example, founded Automotive Resources Asia, Ltd., to serve the growing Southeast Asian automobile market. It has succeeded in providing services to Asian auto manufacturers and suppliers, when larger, less-sensitive US firms have failed. Its success is based on its understanding of how to initiate and negotiate contracts in different Asian cultures.

More established companies also use cross-cultural as well as cross-functional teams to capture cultural differences at the design stage of products and services. China, for example, represents one of the largest potential markets in the developing world, prompting many Western companies to recognize the importance of learning and being sensitive to cultural differences between Western and Chinese cultures. The following are examples of companies' experiences in foreign countries.

- Since Coca-Cola completely has localized its operations and advertising in China, it has experienced 25 percent annual sales growth.
- Hasbro, Inc., the US toy maker, introduced versions of its popular GI Joe toys to China after redesigning them to achieve an "international" appearance and packaging them in the colors of China's People's Liberation Army.
- Also in China, Nestle SA packaged its Nescafe instant coffee in red and gold gift boxes to connote prosperity and happiness. As a result, a majority of its increasing Nescafe sales in China are for gifts.
- In the late 1980s, IBM failed to design its PS/2 personal computer to accommodate hardware add-ons necessary to process Chinese characters. This design lapse cost IBM its once-dominant market share in China.
- AT&T failed to recognize that Chinese telephone habits were much different than those in the United States and installed improperly designed switching equipment that cannot handle the demand caused by the lengthier calls that the Chinese commonly prefer. Only recently has AT&T regained a foothold in China with new digital switching equipment designed for that market.
- The Chevrolet division of General Motors failed to generate significant sales of its economical and domestically popular Nova automobile in Mexico, which might not be surprising once one realizes that "no va" means "does not go" in Spanish.
- EuroDisney near Paris almost failed, in part because when it enforced its customary bans against bringing food into the park and serving alcoholic beverages, it ignored the French custom of picnicking and drinking wine with meals.

Required

In a small group, find two examples of organizations that have successfully integrated knowledge of cultural values into their management of customer value. Prepare a five-minute visual presentation that clearly illustrates the cultural difference and the product or service response. Evaluate the possible effectiveness of these efforts.

Case 20.64
Quantified Balanced Scorecard
(LO 4)

Communication

Part 1. SecondData Corporation provides outsourced data-processing services for large banks, insurance companies, and credit-card companies. The president and CEO of SecondData, Christine Howard, recently attended a conference at which Professor Robert Kaplan of the Harvard Business School delivered the keynote address. His speech covered recent innovations in management techniques that, in his opinion, are revolutionizing modern organizations. He spent most of his time explaining the concept of the balanced scorecard, but he also analyzed several successful applications of the balanced scorecard for which he had first-hand knowledge.

Howard came away from the conference convinced that the balance scorecard is a powerful concept, but she was skeptical that organizations really can build models of its uses of resources and important outcomes. She wondered whether other respected management "gurus" were as enthusiastic about the balanced scorecard.

Requirement 1

Write a memorandum (two pages, double-spaced maximum) to Howard describing the concept of the balanced scorecard as explained by Kaplan and Norton and several other authors. Provide references.

Part 2. Howard invited you to attend her next executive committee meeting (attended by senior officers in the firm) to discuss the concept of the balanced scorecard and to generate discussion about whether SecondData Corporation should consider implementing the concept. Following is a partial transcript of that meeting.

Howard: I'm pleased to welcome one of our bright young staff members, who is going to briefly explain the balanced scorecard I told you about last week. I want us to begin discussions about the concept and move toward deciding whether to implement it.

You: I'm delighted to be here, and I'm eager to present this exciting concept to you. I hope you will ask lots of questions and all contribute answers. If you think there is more information I should develop, I'll be happy to do so and report back to you as soon as possible.

Marketing VP: I've heard of this so-called balanced scorecard, and I must say that it sounds like nothing more than the latest management fad. Of course, we should pay attention to our critical variables, inputs and outputs, but do you really think it is possible to build these models? I remember a little of my college statistics, and I particularly remember that statistical modeling is very complex. I suspect that by the time you collected enough data to analyze, it would be obsolete.

CFO: I'm not sure that statistical analysis is what is called for anyway. Aren't these balanced scorecards just someone's best guess about what variables are important and how they might be connected? I think it's meant to be a way to communicate strategy, not actually manage it. Even then, I worry about whose "guesses" we will use.

Human Resources Director: I know that whatever we choose to measure will be the focus of all our division managers' attention. We have 18 divisions that are directly responsible for generating our profits. We had better be careful about what we measure and how we get everyone to buy in. Any suggestions?

Requirement 2

Compose a brief reply (two pages, double-spaced maximum) to these executives' concerns about the balanced scorecard.

Part 3. You decide to talk to several division managers and their key staff members to get their beliefs about key scorecard variables and possible linkages. A transcript of several of these interviews that you believe are representative follows.

Division Manager 1: I'm glad you are taking the time to talk to me and other managers out here on the front lines. I think there has been too much "top-down" management lately, and I hate to see the executive committee impose a balanced scorecard on us. They don't always know what is happening out here. Fire away with your questions; I'll help as much as I can.

You: Can you tell me what you pay most attention to as you manage this division?

DM 1: Well, as one of the oldest and largest divisions in SecondData, I'm very concerned about labor costs and a market that seems more competitive. We also have one of the oldest labor forces, so I am concerned about their skills and education level. I think there is a strong relation between the quality of employees and errors and the time it takes to complete orders. I want to hire some younger employees with more current skills, but I have to wait for attrition.

You: What do you think your customers most want from you?

DM 1: Obviously, they want our service at the lowest price, but they are willing to pay for high quality and orders completed on time. The marketing department developed a customer-satisfaction survey that I have never understood. I suppose it is trying to measure something related to our ability to meet customers' needs.

Division Controller 11:	You can talk all you want about fancy new concepts of measurement, but the only measurement that really counts at SecondData is return on assets. (I've learned this the hard way!) I understand that there is talk about using economic value added rather than ROA, but I'm not sure what that will add. It's just a variation on the same theme.
You:	Are there process measures that you worry about, too?
DC 11:	Yes, we do monitor the number of defects, you know, incorrect billings and such. They really drive up our cycle time, and I am sure our customers are not happy if some of those errors slip by. I also monitor our employee voluntary turnover rate, which is one of the lowest in the company. I think that this reflects good management and our ability to control the quality of our processes.
Division Manager 17:	Unfortunately, we have the special difficulty of being in one of the regions with the smallest population. We have to pay higher wages for employees, and we don't have the revenue potential of some of the other divisions. I tell you, it's difficult to meet corporate's profit goals under these conditions. I'll tell you another thing: I think there is a lot of randomness in our environment. I don't think we understand how factors affect each other. Sorting that out will be quite a challenge. Good luck.

Requirement 3

From this interview and your own reasoning, develop a possible balanced scorecard model. Explain how the interview has influenced your model. Describe each of the measures you have included in your model and explain how they should be causally linked. Prepare a graphical representation of your scorecard model.

Part 4. You have collected the following data on each of the 18 business units of SecondData Corporation.

Requirement 4

To the extent possible, use these data to test the validity of your proposed balanced scorecard model. Describe which aspects of the model that the analysis supports and which it refutes. Briefly discuss the advantages and disadvantages of using these data to verify the model. What additional data would you like to have? Make recommendations to Howard and the executive committee about whether they should proceed to develop and implement a balanced scorecard. What opportunities and difficulties do you foresee?

SECOND DATA CORPORATION
Various Statistics Collected for Domestic Business Units

Division	Age of Division (years)	Number of Employees	Voluntary Turnover Rate	Average Grade Level Completed	Average Hourly Wage	Average Defects per Month	Cycle Time per Order (hours)	Percentage On-Time Deliveries	Customer Satisfaction Score	Regional Population (thousands)	($ millions) Throughput	($ millions) Operating Expense	($ millions) Assets Employed
1	10.1	1,709	4.5%	10.71	$11.11	149.24	61.11	80.6%	78.3	973.0	$3,081	$3,197	$6,690
2	7.4	1,220	5.1	11.93	9.49	140.71	55.84	84.5	89.9	872.0	3,073	2,340	11,856
3	7.2	1,169	6.2	11.95	10.11	123.94	57.22	82.1	68.5	556.0	2,952	2,043	8,236
4	11.0	1,726	6.4	10.15	10.13	143.49	51.92	85.2	83.4	760.0	3,140	2,435	7,158
5	7.1	1,567	5.4	11.62	9.89	123.70	53.53	81.6	82.7	676.0	3,259	2,971	5,126
6	6.1	1,314	5.6	10.31	9.59	158.26	69.98	79.1	71.0	862.0	2,920	2,485	10,315
7	10.2	1,136	8.6	11.14	7.59	169.65	76.23	78.9	83.0	618.0	2,778	1,873	8,034
8	8.4	1,108	4.3	11.97	8.35	141.68	50.83	82.2	84.7	593.0	3,383	2,335	10,945
9	7.9	1,815	5.1	10.47	8.02	183.40	67.36	78.3	73.0	539.0	2,762	2,291	7,274
10	9.9	1,655	4.9	11.02	8.65	151.12	58.15	84.8	81.2	946.0	3,108	2,492	3,991
11	10.0	1,076	4.4	10.65	8.66	151.87	55.79	82.2	86.6	731.0	3,409	1,677	4,623
12	9.6	1,248	6.2	10.96	6.42	131.04	61.12	78.9	79.1	814.0	3,291	1,783	9,445
13	8.4	1,563	8.3	10.14	10.13	164.41	55.67	82.2	84.8	831.0	3,392	2,703	5,676
14	10.4	1,210	8.0	10.73	8.71	143.53	52.36	84.9	92.4	517.0	2,647	1,718	4,382
15	8.0	1,133	6.0	10.75	8.09	160.04	54.21	86.1	84.4	598.0	2,431	1,823	7,524
16	11.1	1,954	8.9	10.36	5.72	157.51	62.19	83.8	87.4	948.0	3,215	2,115	4,520
17	6.6	1,401	4.5	11.34	10.59	148.51	72.26	77.0	72.7	515.0	2,825	2,816	12,030
18	10.8	1,141	5.1	10.65	10.31	171.69	59.69	81.6	82.6	507.0	2,427	2,240	8,854

CHAPTER

21

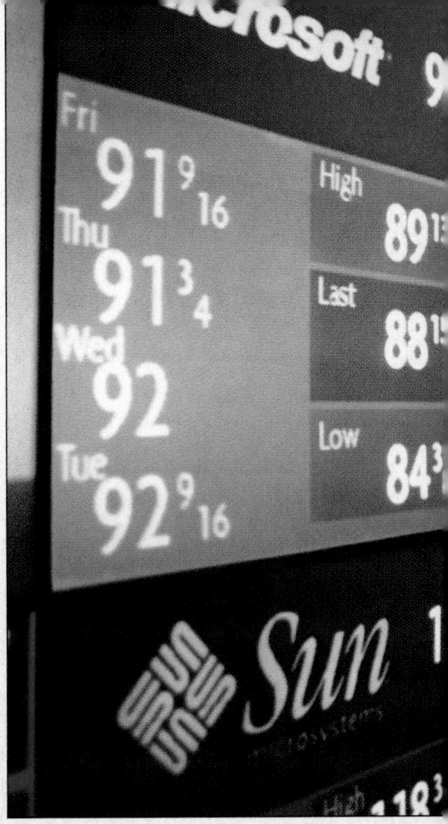

Incentive Systems and Performance Evaluation

After completing this chapter, you should be able to:

1. Apply basic knowledge of expectancy and agency approaches to motivation to the evaluation of incentive plans.

2. Use various nonfinancial and financial performance measures to evaluate performance.

3. Evaluate the advantages and disadvantages of alternative features of incentive compensation plans.

Cost-Management Challenges

1. **Should** Valley Commercial Bank design its incentive system to increase customer satisfaction? Is it possible to overstress customer satisfaction?

2. **Is** it possible to balance concerns for nonfinancial and financial performance in an effective incentive and performance evaluation system for Valley Commercial Bank? If so, how?

3. **How** can Valley Commercial Bank or any organization weigh the trade-offs of various incentives for improving financial performance?

Valley Commercial Bank IPO Exceeds Expectations
By Dissociated Press financial reporter, Graham Crystal

Valley
COMMERCIAL BANK

BOSTON: Valley Commercial Bank (VCB) President and CEO William Grom announced an initial public offering (IPO) of shares of that generated $25 million, which was more than the bank and its underwriters expected.

Speaking to the state's financial press online from bank headquarters, Grom remarked, "This shows that the market values a successful track record and a bright future. There is abundant capital for good business plans and capable management, and ours are second to none. Valley Commercial Bank has served an important market niche by providing financial services for fast-growing, well-managed, high-technology firms. They see us as valuable partners, and it definitely helps that we have experienced and overcome the same growing pains that they face."

Twenty-three investors founded VCB 10 years ago to serve the hot local economy. The founders, some of whom are officers of the bank, now have gained expansion capital and many new stockholders.

The independent five-branch bank specializes in banking with high-technology businesses and professionals such as public accountants, architects, and dentists. VCB has dominated its niche based on personal relations and customer service.

VCB's prospectus shows that its management compensation plan resembles those found at many of its high-tech customers. CEO Grom emphasized that although unusual for a bank, this performance-based incentive plan is necessary to attract, motivate, and retain its highly competent and sought-after employees.

The bank's design of its incentive system to align the bank employees' fortunes with those of its new stockholders might be another reason for the success of its IPO.

Valley COMMERCIAL BANK

The news report of its initial public offering (IPO) followed intensive efforts by Valley Commercial Bank's board of directors, officers, and key executives and was the occasion of a well-deserved celebration. The bank had positioned itself for the successful IPO of shares in part by structuring its performance-based, incentive compensation plans to (1) attract, motivate, and retain excellent employees and (2) align their interests with the long-term interests of external stockholders. Accomplishing these objectives is both extremely important and challenging for all types of organizations, even those without stockholders per se. Furthermore, one can regard the design of incentive systems as a "capstone" topic of cost management because it brings together concerns about costs, revenues, value, and their drivers to create information that guides and motivates individuals to create long-term value at lowest cost.

This chapter focuses on the philosophy and elements of incentive or performance-based incentive compensation. This topic, particularly as it applies to top-management compensation, is the subject of continual comment, consulting, and academic research including criticism (especially in the United States where CEOs are the highest paid). For example, the press and academic research have made much of the strength of the relation between CEO compensation and company performance. The press each year wonders how US CEOs on average can make more than 200 times their lowest paid employees while the ratio in Brazil is 49 times, and in Great Britain is only 24 times, for example. Not all of this discussion is motivated by fairness or jealousy because compensation represents the majority of many firms' costs, and it is natural (especially from a cost-management perspective) to want this cost to create value efficiently.

Fundamental Principles of Incentive Compensation Plans

Alfred Sloan, famous chief executive officer of General Motors, instituted one of the first incentive compensation plans. A strong advocate of using incentives, he started a bonus plan in 1918 at General Motors to better motivate division managers to act in the best interests of the company and its shareholders. This bonus plan stressed the achievement of desired levels of performance.

Today, virtually all large companies, many small companies, and an increasing number of nonprofit organizations use incentive compensation plans. These plans have a substantial impact on managers' pay. For example, CEOs in the United States are paid millions of dollars per year on average, and much of this pay is based on incentives related to performance. The highest paid executive in the United States, according to a recent *Business Week* survey, was Charles Wang of Computer Associates International. His annual salary was $5 million, but his total compensation that year was $655 million; the remainder was mostly stock grants paid according to the company's incentive plan.[1]

Pay for Performance

The driving concept of performance-based, incentive compensation plans is to pay individuals for performance. Pay for performance means that at least some portion of a manager's income is not guaranteed but depends on measure(s) of organizational performance. Thus, these are the two key elements of an incentive compensation plan.

1. Measure(s) of performance.
2. Method(s) of compensation.

[1]J. Reingold and F. Jespersen, "Executive Pay." Wang's compensation was labeled the bonus "that launched a dozen lawsuits" by angry stockholders. The courts forced Wang to return some of the stock. (Full citations to references are in the Bibliography.)

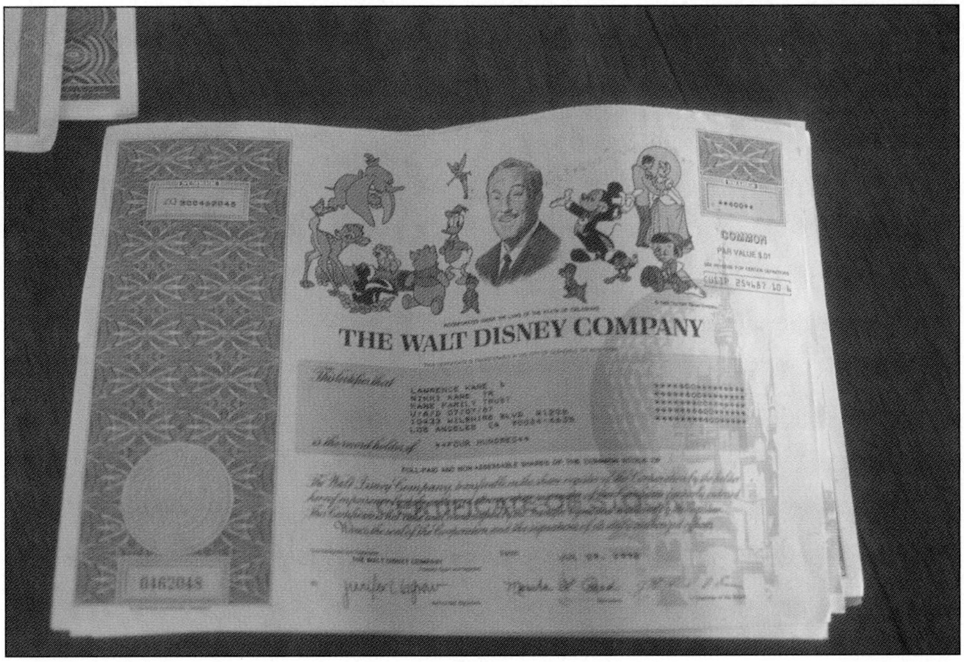

Walt Disney Co. regularly compensates key executives with stock grants and stock options based on meeting annual objectives.

For example, VCB annually evaluates its branch bank managers in part on their achievement of environmental recycling standards. International Telephone and Telegraph (ITT) has historically paid a substantial cash bonus to division managers based on the return on divisional assets. Caterpillar has used a profit-sharing plan that pays cash based on the company's profitability. Johnson & Johnson gives company stock to key employees based on supervisors' evaluations of them.

How common are incentive plans? Incentive plans apply to most executives and as much as one-quarter of the workforce at large firms and are used widely by small companies, particularly in high-technology fields. Many nonprofit organizations also have incentive plans for their executives. You could easily find yourself eligible to participate in incentive compensation plans soon after completing your studies. You might have a choice among employment opportunities with greatly different compensation packages. For example, employment with a business advisory or consulting firm might offer mostly salary with a long-term opportunity of a partnership. A high-technology company, on the other hand, might offer a relatively low initial salary with an early opportunity for stock options. What do these alternatives mean? How do you choose? Conversely, once you are with an organization, whom do you attract and retain with different plans?

Is the "real world" different? If you are currently a student, you already work within a performance-based incentive plan; grades in courses are based on performance. You can easily imagine how differences in the rewards or incentives might alter your motivation and behavior. Do you study as hard for a course that you take pass-fail as for one you take for a grade? Do you concentrate on the same parts of the course if the grade is based on a comprehensive paper versus a single, problem-oriented final exam? Variations in incentives and rewards affect student behavior as they do employees who work for pay. The key to designing incentive systems is to understand as well as possible which behaviors are desired and how incentives and rewards are likely to influence behaviors. In nearly every case, you get what you measure and reward—even if it is not what you intended.

Folly of Rewarding A When You Want B

A classic article titled "On the Folly of Rewarding A While Hoping for B" speaks to fundamental problems with many incentive plans.[2] The title of the article conveys the idea that designers of incentive plans are often surprised to find that these plans motivate unintended behavior or create disincentives to desired behavior. A classic example is the disincentive a company causes by emphasizing the achievement of current performance targets at the expense of long-term benefits. For example, after being added to a list of major polluters, Polaroid Corp. in the 1990s realized that focusing primarily on current financial performance was leading managers to dispose of waste cheaply and to ignore the significant long-term costs and the impairment of the company's reputation caused by its pollution. Polaroid now has broadened its evaluation criteria to include environmental performance and has improved its reputation and lowered costs related to pollution.

To see how disincentives might work in your life, imagine that a consulting firm wants to hire the best students from your college. Consequently, it interviews only students who have at least a 3.5 (out of 4.0) grade-point average and then ranks interviewees based on their grade-point average. Assuming that the firm can hire whomever it wishes, will it get the best students? What incentives does this hiring plan provide? The answer to the first question is that the firm will get students with the highest GPAs but not necessarily with the most relevant knowledge or talent to be successful consultants. The answer to the second question is that it gives incentives for students to take easy courses to pad their GPAs. It is doubtful that this is the talent the company wants to reward and hire.

Early on, Valley Commercial Bank (VCB) also had a problem of rewarding A when top management really wanted B. As a small service-oriented bank, VCB realized the importance of customer relations and relied on satisfying its customers to keep them coming back for more loans and services. The incentive plan, however, emphasized short-term profits and cost minimization, which gave branch managers the incentive to reduce staff, which resulted in spending less time with customers and lower customer satisfaction. The bank began to lose some of its vital customers because of its incentive plan, which it soon revised, as we shall see.

Where to Begin

The starting point of designing an effective incentive compensation plan is to know the desired behavior that the organization wants to motivate. The organization cannot motivate people to "do the right thing" if it does not know what the right thing is. An effective incentive system should motivate managers to achieve the organization's goals and objectives and reward them if they do. In this chapter, we assume that the organization can articulate its goals and objectives clearly and even decide the order of their importance if they conflict at all.

Reality intrudes. Unfortunately, translating goals into tangible objectives is not always as easy as it might seem because sometimes the desired outcome is not easily observed. Here is a seemingly easy question: What is the right thing for a profit-seeking corporation? The standard answer in a market economy is a long-term competitive return for stockholders. The reality is that translating even this standard statement into an incentive plan might be a challenge. One comforting aspect of this reality is that the challenge of designing incentive systems creates interesting and well-paying jobs for human resource and financial executives and compensation consultants.

What's so hard about creating an incentive system that promotes a "long-term competitive return for stockholders"? For one thing, the "long-term" might be 5 or 10 years from now. A company might wait that long to reward or penalize managers, but what if it needs to reward good managers now or risk losing them to competitors? What is the "com-

---

[2] S. Kerr, "On the Folly of Rewarding A While Hoping for B."

petitive" benchmark? What is the proper measure of "return?" And are "stockholders" the only *stakeholders* in the company (that is, those that have an interest in its actions)?

Add to the basic design problem of defining desired behavior the fact that a surprising number of organizations have plans that give rewards (or penalties) but do not indicate explicitly the basis for them. Furthermore, some organizations that do have explicit elements in their incentive plans often appear to weigh other factors more heavily. Poorly designed, communicated, or implemented incentive plans almost guarantee morale problems, excessive office politics, and lost opportunities for the organization to excel. All in all, designing incentive systems is a challenge that must begin somewhere.

As stated earlier, the first step is to identify the organization's goal(s). Why was it created? What is its desired purpose? What must it achieve to survive or thrive? Articulating whatever these goals are (profits, employment, eradication of disease, etc.) is the starting point for the design of a performance-based incentive compensation plan. Not surprisingly, this also is the starting point for the formulation of an effective organizational strategy—everything really is connected.

Not for corporations only. An increasing number of nonprofit and governmental organizations are copying features of corporate incentive plans to improve their effectiveness, but their design problems can be even greater. Without a "bottom line" measure of profit, these organizations must rely more on nonfinancial measures to reflect the achievement of their goals, which can be even more difficult to measure reliably. So, the "right thing" for short-run incentives and performance evaluation (in many organizations) might be a *leading indicator* of the truly desired behavior, which either is far in the future or not readily observable anytime.

A role for theories of incentives and behavior. A company could develop incentive plans by trial and error, trying alternatives until an incentive plan appears to generate the desired behavior. Although it might succeed eventually, using trial and error is not the most efficient way to proceed. Fortunately, a number of theories are well grounded in observations of individuals and organizations and can provide reliable advice. Not surprisingly because incentives are so important, researchers have studied the psychology and economics of incentives for many years. We now present an overview of the theoretical drivers of motivation, the roots of individual motivation. What makes people respond to incentives and why? Relying on this guidance is an efficient way to begin to design an incentive plan.

Theories of Incentives and Behavior

We discuss two views of incentives and human behavior that address key parts of incentive compensation plans, the expectancy and the agency theories of motivation and incentives. These are not opposing views, but they stress different aspects of motivation and behavior. Together, they provide a relatively complete picture of the nature of incentives that motivate behavior.

Expectancy Theory of Motivation and Incentives

Expectancy theory has its roots in organizational psychology. It explains that people are motivated by monetary or nonmonetary incentives to act in ways that they expect to provide them the rewards that they desire and to prevent the penalties that they wish to avoid.[3] Therefore, to motivate people to behave in a particular way, incentive plans must do two things:

expectancy theory *explains that people are motivated to act in ways that they expect to provide them the rewards that they desire and to prevent the penalties that they wish to avoid*

1. Provide desirable rewards or undesirable penalties.
2. Provide a high probability that behaving as the organization desires will lead to those rewards or penalties.

[3] T. B. Green, *Performance and Motivation Strategies for Today's Workforce: A Guide to Expectancy Theory Applications.*

That is, the incentive plan provides *expectancy* that desired behavior leads to desired rewards. For example, the goal of a course of study is to disseminate or acquire knowledge. The incentive system to motivate achievement of that goal is a system of grades awarded for examination performance. It is fair to assume that high grades are desirable, so the reward itself is in place. What if the instructor's exams, the measures of performance, are so unrelated to the material being studied that there is a low probability that studying will improve exam scores? Expectancy theory predicts that students will not be motivated to study by this incentive system because they believe that studying has a low probability of improving test scores. Thus, neither the instructor nor the students will achieve the goal of learning, acquiring knowledge through study, because the incentive plan does not provide sufficient expectancy that rewards will be related to studying.

Expectancy success and failure. Exhibit 21–1 reflects the basic elements of expectancy theory. Panel A shows the ideal incentive system: Effort is high when employees have a high expectancy that their efforts affect performance *and* that the performance will be rewarded appropriately. The feedback arrows in panel A reflect that both of the high expectancies reinforce the motivation to exert effort. Panel B, however, shows a breakdown in the incentive system. This is the situation describing students exerting low study effort if they have a low expectancy that studying will affect exam performance. The promise of a high grade based on high performance has no effect because the link in the expectancy chain between studying and exam performance has broken. Some incen-

Exhibit 21–1 Expectancy Theory, Incentives, and Motivation

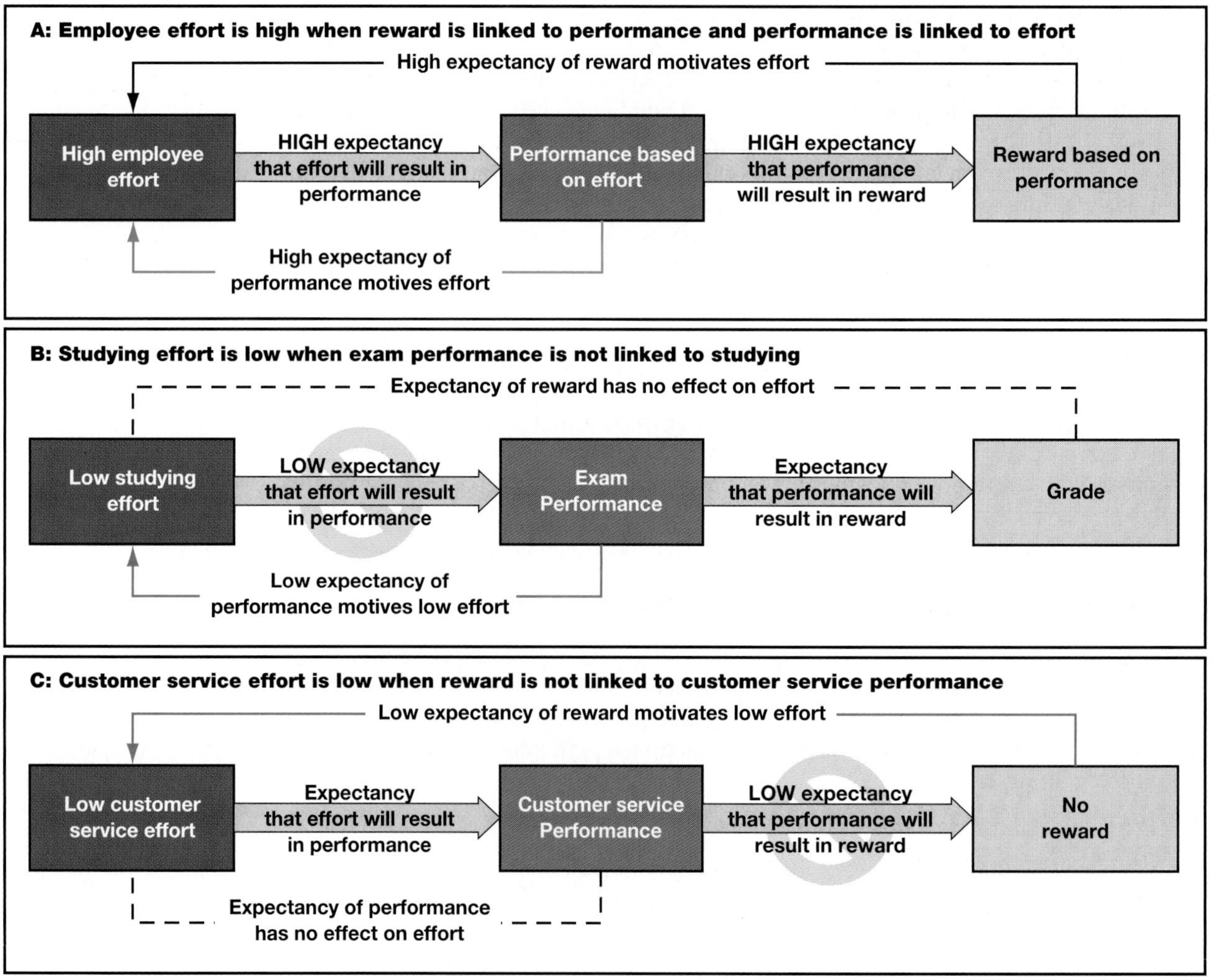
A: Employee effort is high when reward is linked to performance and performance is linked to effort
High expectancy of reward motivates effort
High employee effort
HIGH expectancy that effort will result in performance
Performance based on effort
HIGH expectancy that performance will result in reward
Reward based on performance
High expectancy of performance motives effort
B: Studying effort is low when exam performance is not linked to studying
Expectancy of reward has no effect on effort
Low studying effort
LOW expectancy that effort will result in performance
Exam Performance
Expectancy that performance will result in reward
Grade
Low expectancy of performance motives low effort
C: Customer service effort is low when reward is not linked to customer service performance
Low expectancy of reward motivates low effort
Low customer service effort
Expectancy that effort will result in performance
Customer service Performance
LOW expectancy that performance will result in reward
No reward
Expectancy of performance has no effect on effort

tive systems' expectancy chains are broken at the link between performance and reward; still others are broken at both links.

Expectancy theory and VCB's old incentives. Panel C of Exhibit 21–1 applies expectancy theory to customer service activities at VCB before improving the incentive system. Top management wants to improve customer relations and for several years has gathered measures of customer satisfaction using customer-satisfaction questionnaires about the bank's services. (You might have completed these concerning restaurant or hotel quality and service and in evaluating your instructors.) At one time the bank provided no rewards to employees for efforts that build customer satisfaction. As shown in panel C of Exhibit 21–1, expectancy theory explains why VCB's employees were not motivated to build customer satisfaction—they were not rewarded for it. (This does not consider personal rewards that might have come from employees' interactions with the customers.) Consequently, VCB probably did not have as many satisfied customers as it might have had with a better incentive plan.

Recently, to promote customer satisfaction, the bank began to reward employees if customers are satisfied with the services they receive. This makes the incentive system more like Panel A of Exhibit 21–1. Because VCB management and employees believe that good service is likely to build customer satisfaction and customer satisfaction predictably leads to rewards, this incentive system promotes the desired behavior.

Extrinsic and intrinsic rewards. **Extrinsic rewards** come from outside the individual from teachers, parents, organizations, or partners and include grades, money, praise, and prizes. **Intrinsic rewards,** on the other hand, come from within the individual, such as the satisfaction from studying hard, the feeling of well-being from physical exercise, the pleasure from helping someone in need, or the satisfaction of doing a good job. Getting an A on an exam is an extrinsic reward; satisfaction with your performance is an intrinsic reward.

extrinsic rewards *including grades, money, praise, and prizes come from outside the individual*

intrinsic rewards *come from within the individual, including the satisfaction from studying hard, the feeling of well-being from physical exercise, the pleasure from helping someone in need, or the satisfaction of doing a good job*

Although VCB originally did not reward its employees for building customer satisfaction, the employees might have received an intrinsic reward, such as internal satisfaction from providing good service. They also might have been rewarded with thanks and affection from loyal customers, which are also extrinsic rewards, but not from the bank. By adding extrinsic rewards to the incentive plan, VCB reinforced existing rewards and increased the likelihood that employees would work to improve customer satisfaction by increasing the expectancy of rewards from desired behavior.

People receive many intrinsic and extrinsic rewards. Teachers and caregivers, such as nurses, often work for wages less than their ability and effort can command because they receive intrinsic rewards from the work. In addition, many people volunteer their services not only because of the intrinsic rewards but also for the extrinsic rewards—praise and gratitude—they receive. These are factors to consider in designing incentive systems. Some jobs inherently have more rewards than others do, and what people consider to be rewards differs. Some are motivated mostly by money; others are more motivated by public praise.

One size does not fit all. Creating incentives tailored to each individual is difficult for most organizations. However, improving everyone's opportunities for intrinsic rewards from desired behavior by making work interesting might be possible. To ensure that extrinsic rewards are distributed fairly and based on the terms of the incentive plan is also important. To augment rewards from the job, many organizations encourage employees to seek intrinsic (satisfaction) and extrinsic ("volunteer of the month") rewards by donating their time to charitable work; some companies even allow employees to take some time from their jobs for charitable work.

An effective incentive plan considers opportunities for both intrinsic and extrinsic rewards and penalties and allows opportunities for variations, particularly of intrinsic rewards. Effective motivation usually requires a balance between extrinsic and intrinsic rewards, but the balance point varies with the organization and the people it attracts and retains.

Agency Theory of Incentives and Behavior

agency theory is an economic theory of incentives and behavior based on the relationship between a principal who offers an incentive plan and an agent who accepts the plan to work on behalf of the principal

Agency theory is an economic theory of incentives and behavior based on the relationship between a principal (e.g., employer) who offers an incentive plan (or contract) and an agent (e.g., employee) who accepts the contract to work on behalf of the principal. In agency theory, incentive plans serve four purposes: they (1) improve organizational success by (2) motivating the employee to work, (3) by aligning the employee's goals with the employer's goals, and (4) allocating decision authority. A corporation such as VCB, for example, exhibits multiple principal-agent relationships, which include the following:

Principals	Contract	Agents
VCB shareholders	Rewards ↔ Oversight of management	VCB board of directors
VCB board of directors	Rewards ↔ Strategic management of VCB	VCB top management
VCB top management	Rewards ↔ Operational management of branch banks	VCB branch managers
VCB branch managers	Rewards ↔ Performance of branch-bank activities	VCB branch employees

VCB employees are agents of branch managers, who are agents of top managers at bank headquarters, who are agents of the board of directors and shareholders who own the company. Note that most employees have both a principal role and an agent role. What binds them together is an enforceable incentive plan or contract; principals offer rewards in exchange for making specific decisions.

The focus of expectancy theory and agency theory differs, but they complement each other. *Expectancy theory* focuses on the characteristics of the incentive plans that motivate people whereas *agency theory* focuses on the contracting behavior between principal and agent. In a sense, they are two sides of the same coin. Applied to organizational settings, expectancy theory seeks to understand the types of performance measures and rewards that motivate employees. Agency theory, on the other hand, reflects the nature of economic agents. Agency theory assumes that both principals and agents want to maximize their rewards at minimum cost, but they need each other.

The principal provides the work and the rewards, which the agent does not, but the agent has the ability to do the work, which the principal does not. However, each has an opportunity cost in most cases: the agent can work elsewhere, and the principal can put her money in the bank and earn interest. The principal wants to maximize her profits, which includes minimizing incentive costs, and the agent wants to minimize his effort to earn a market wage. The incentive plan needed to bring them together at least meets both parties' opportunity costs, aligns both parties' goals, and clearly describes the decisions to be made.

Improper incentives can cause misbehavior. Agency theory is complicated by the reality that once employed, employees do not necessarily behave in the ways that their employers desire. Furthermore, because any measure of performance is imperfect, neither party can regard the incentive system as entirely fair. Employers might suspect undetected manipulation of performance measures, and employees might resent the risk imposed on them by imperfect measures. The employer could respond with other constraints on or monitoring of behavior at work. Employees might believe that working at a more leisurely pace, surfing the Web instead of working on company projects, or loafing with their friends at work are fair. Some employees even have incentives to steal more than time from the company. Furthermore, some employees might not have the skills or knowledge that they professed when they were hired or that they should maintain to stay employable at their current pay. All of these result in costs—lost opportunities to create value—for the employer and the employee. The incentive system not only must motivate employees to work but also must be designed so that employees' rewards are fair and contingent on the organization's meeting its goals.

Minimizing agency costs with incentives and monitoring. The principal seeks to minimize total **agency costs,** which are the sum of opportunity costs of misbehavior and out-of-pocket costs for incentives and monitoring performance. The incentive plan must attract and motivate qualified employees to behave according to the organization's goals, but doing this costs money for paying employees and for monitoring to ensure that performance measures are valid. These payments reduce the value left for principals, so they seek to minimize them. A company might spend so much money on incentives and reporting (e.g., bonuses, accounting reports, internal audits) that no employee will ever do something that is not in shareholders' interests—or no qualified employee will submit to the working conditions. However, such actions are unlikely to be economical given the high costs of the incentives and reporting compared to the opportunity costs of misbehavior. As Exhibit 21–2 shows, the best incentive plan trades off the costs of administering alternative incentive plans against the costs of misbehavior. The best incentive plan is not the one that drives the costs of misbehavior to zero (far right), nor is it the one that spends the least on incentives and reporting (far left). The best plan is located between these extremes, reflected by a "level" of incentives and monitoring on the X-axis. In theory, this is the mix of incentives and monitoring mechanisms that minimizes total agency costs. Agency theory shows that the "perfect" incentive system is too expensive and that some level of employee misbehavior is desirable; the overall best system is a result of evaluating trade-offs.

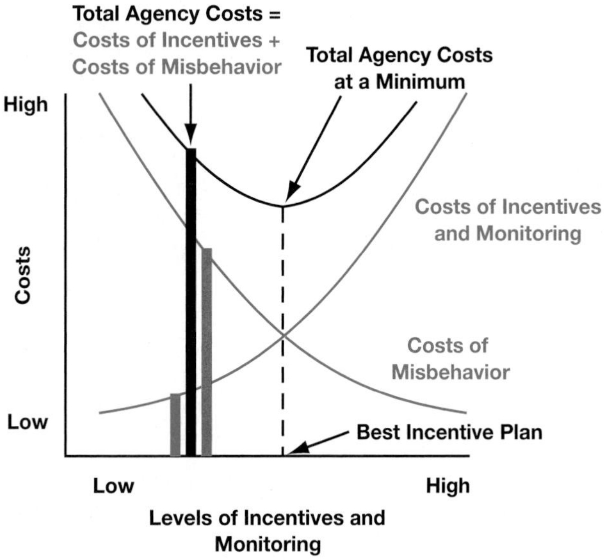

Exhibit 21–2

Best Incentive Plans Minimize Total Agency Costs

agency costs *are the sum of opportunity costs of misbehavior and out-of-pocket costs for incentives and monitoring performance*

Changes to reduce agency costs. All organizations experience some agency costs. According to agency theory, organizations change their incentive plans when they perceive an opportunity to reduce total agency costs. For example, VCB's board of directors realized that the bank's incentive system motivated managers to minimize current spending and cut staff rather than to build customer satisfaction. Bank managers were "playing by the rules," but the incentive plan directed them to act in a way that was not in the long-term interests of the bank's shareholders. One agency cost identified was a loss of profits because the bank was losing dissatisfied customers. Note that this also hurt employees because the bank was less profitable. As described earlier, VCB changed the incentive system to include rewards for improved customer satisfaction because the bank believed the cost of the new incentive system was less than the lost profit from losing dissatisfied customers.

Integration of Expectancy and Agency Theories' Views of Incentives

Are these theories of incentives too abstract, conflicting, or can they be combined to guide incentive plan designers? Our interpretation of these theories and observations of successful practice generate the following guidelines for designing effective incentive plans.

Observation	Guideline
Most individuals are motivated by self-interest	Performance-based rewards must be greater than alternative rewards from nonperformance
Companies get the behavior they reward	Performance measures and related rewards must reflect organizational goals
Effort follows rewards	Employees must believe that their efforts influence performance
Fairness is a basis for sustained motivation	Rewards must be linked to desired performance in a fair manner
Manipulation undermines fairness and effort	Performance measures must be observable and verifiable
Both extrinsic and intrinsic rewards can motivate effort	Extrinsic rewards must meet market conditions, and intrinsic rewards must be available
Every realistic incentive system involves trade-offs	Minimizing the overall costs of aligning goals and monitoring behavior is a goal

As we have seen, incentive systems can include many alternative features. We now turn to a number of specific choices that designers of incentive compensation plans must make.

Performance-Based Incentive Systems

The preceding discussions indicate that designing an efficient incentive system is a challenging, evolving task. Identifying the required trade-offs between effective rewards, goal alignment, monitoring, and cost necessitates choosing among many alternative incentive-system configurations and reviewing systems in place to be sure they are still effective.

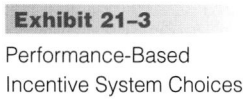

Exhibit 21–3 displays the many choices that accumulate to create the elements of an effective performance-based incentive system. Designers of incentive systems should consider all of these choices because ignoring any of them can lead to a less-effective system. All of the decisions in Exhibit 21–3 speak to this question: *Given the goal(s) of the organization, which alternative(s) will motivate the desired behavior most effectively?* The answer to that question must be placed in context: *The situation faced by each company determines the answer.* There are no universally right or wrong answers, but there are better or worse answers in a particular situation. Furthermore, many equally effective combinations of incentive plan elements might exist in similar situations. Clearly, the design of an incentive plan is a very complex topic. Our aim is to provide an overview of the choices, not to suggest which are the correct choices for any situation.[4] We discuss each of the boxed alternatives in Exhibit 21–3 in turn.

[4]For a more extensive discussion of the components of incentive compensation plans and descriptions of companies using them, see S. Butler and M. Maher, *Management Incentive Compensation Plans.*

Exhibit 21–3

Performance-Based Incentive System Choices

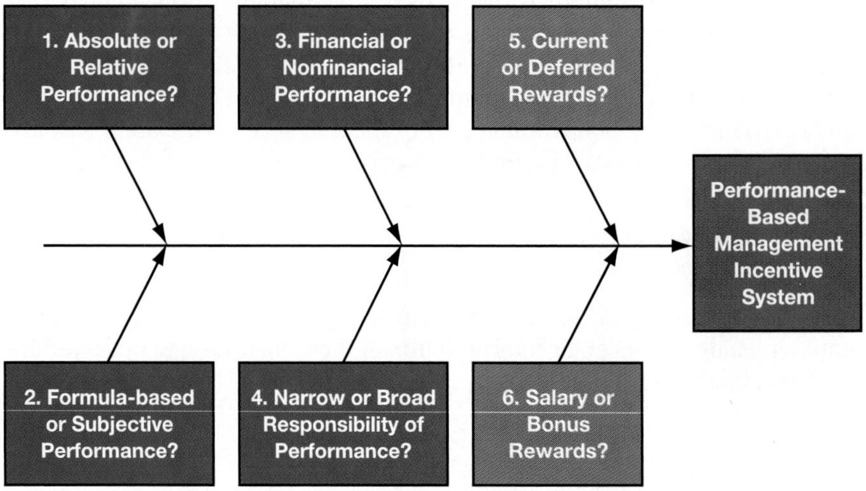

Absolute or Relative Performance

One may evaluate performance against absolute objectives or relative to others' performance. Undoubtedly, you have taken some classes that use absolute performance evaluation and others that use relative performance evaluation. **Absolute performance evaluation** compares individual performance to set objectives or expectations. In classes that use absolute performance evaluation, the instructor grades on an absolute scale, and how well others perform does not affect your grade. For example, panel A of Exhibit 21–4 illustrates a grade distribution that uses absolute cutoffs (100 percent $\geq$ A $\geq$ 90 percent; 90 percent $\geq$ B $\geq$ 80 percent, etc.). **Relative performance evaluation** compares an individual's performance to that of others. In classes that use relative performance evaluation, the instructor grades on the curve; that is, your grade depends on how you perform relative to everyone else. For example, panel B of Exhibit 21–4 reflects a grade distribution relative to an instructor's desired curve of 12.5 percent As, 50 percent Bs, 25 percent Cs, and 12.5 percent Ds and Fs. Both approaches can be effective, but the situation determines the effectiveness. For example, grading on an absolute basis, when exams are extremely difficult, can lower the expectancy that studying can lead to a high grade. Thus, studying effort might be less in this situation than if the instructor graded on a relative basis, where final grades reflect relative performance on difficult exams.

absolute performance evaluation *compares individual performance to set standards or expectations*

relative performance evaluation *is based on comparing an individual's performance to that of others*

Like other companies that use relative performance evaluation, VCB compares business-unit performance with that of other business units in the same industry.[5] Thus, a branch that generated 3 percent revenue growth in a market where the average revenue growth was 4.5 percent might receive a lower evaluation than a VCB branch that earned 3 percent in a market with 2 percent average revenue growth. Just as grading on the curve shields students from the risk of an extremely difficult test, relative performance evaluation shields a manager from the risk of managing a division in a market that performs poorly. On the other hand, relative performance evaluation requires very high performance if the manager's division is in a market that performs well.

Valley COMMERCIAL BANK

[5]For a field study of companies using relative performance evaluation, see M. Maher, "The Use of Relative Performance Evaluation in Organizations."

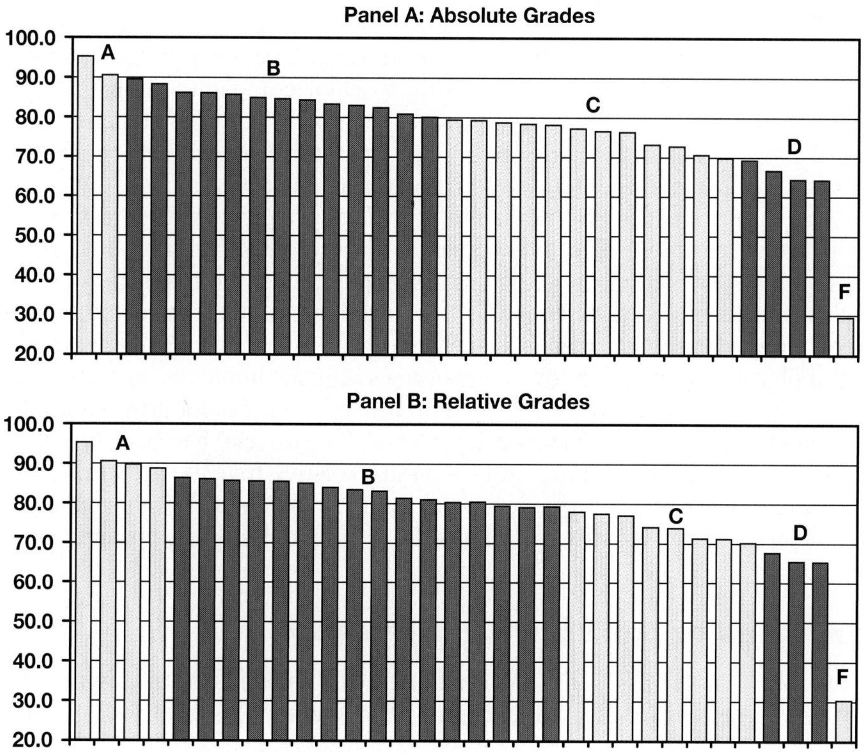

Exhibit 21–4
Absolute versus Relative Grading

Exhibit 21–5
Relative Revenue Growth

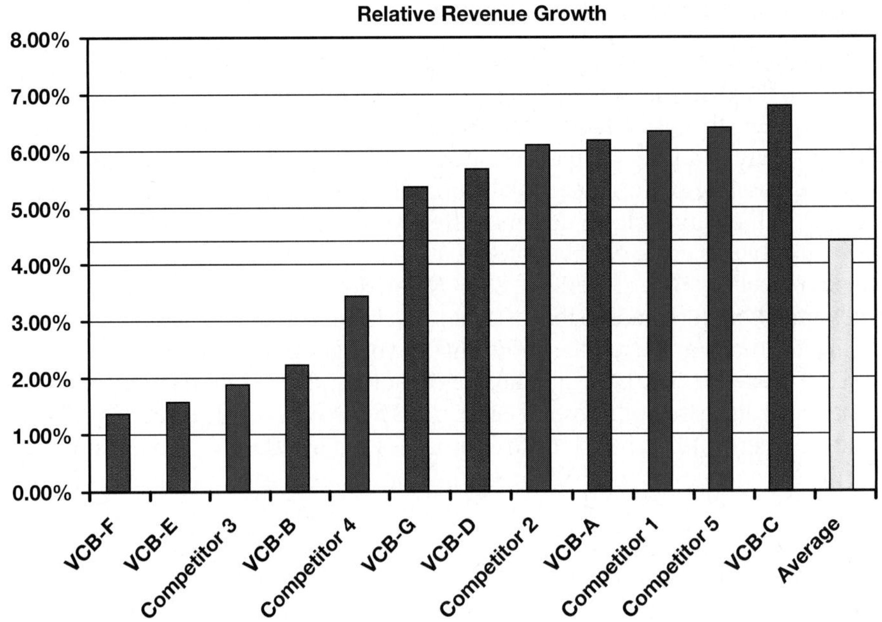

The disadvantage of relative performance evaluation is that it does not provide incentives for managers to move out of poorly performing markets into those that perform well. Why would successful managers in a poor market move to a more competitive market where relative performance evaluation makes the expectancy of rewards low? Furthermore, if good managers decide to move, they might have to work much harder for the same relative performance. Because most companies want these managers to seek new, better opportunities, the companies need to design incentives compatible with its objectives and those of its managers.

At VCB, top management believes that relative performance evaluation of some aspects of performance is effective. Using relative performance evaluation, top management assesses each branch bank's revenue growth performance relative to each other and to similar banks in the same market. The bank rewards the managers of branches with the highest relative revenue growth. This controls for unforeseen changes in business conditions that might affect all banks' revenue growth. Consider the relative evaluations in Exhibit 21–5. Using a set of comparative banks, VCB branches B, E, and F achieved below-average revenue growth, but VCB branches A, C, D, and G had above-average revenue growth. Thus, under the same conditions that all faced, branches A, C, D, and G outperformed the average.

Using relative performance evaluation allows VCB to avoid the difficult task of setting appropriate revenue growth objectives necessary for absolute performance evaluation. Unless the objectives are sufficiently high and accurately reflect future business conditions, the absolute objectives might be ineffective motivators. If they are set too high or business conditions deteriorate, managers perceive little chance of earning rewards. Conversely, if objectives are set too low or the business climate improves, managers can easily earn their rewards. In the first case, VCB misses opportunities for growth because managers do not try, and in the second case, it pays too much for less than best efforts.

VCB uses more performance measures than just relative revenue growth; it also evaluates executives and branch managers on absolute achievement of other financial and nonfinancial measures for which the bank finds it possible to set appropriate absolute objectives.

Formula-Based or Subjective Performance

performance evaluation formula *describes rewards earned for specific achievements*

Some companies base rewards on a **performance evaluation formula,** which describes rewards earned for specific achievements. For example, VCB rewards revenue growth by paying branch managers a bonus based on the following explicit formula: For each percentage point by which revenue growth exceeds the market average, say 5 percent, the manager receives a bonus of 4 percent of his or her base salary. Thus, a manager knows, for example, that if her branch's revenue growth was 8 percent for a particular year (that is, three percentage points above the 5 percent threshold percent) and her base salary is $100,000 per year, her bonus is $12,000 (three percentage points times 4 percent per point times $100,000). A manager who did not meet the market average revenue growth rate receives no bonus.

Valley COMMERCIAL BANK

Target revenue growth for bonus = 5 percent per year
Actual branch revenue growth = 8 percent per year
Branch manager base salary = $100,000 per year
Branch manager bonus = (8 − 5) growth points × (.04) × $100,000 = $12,000

This bonus is in addition to the manager's base salary. VCB included this incentive as part of its formula but rejected a formula-*only* approach to performance evaluation for branch managers as too restrictive to its culture and business climate. One consideration was that using only a formula penalizes managers assigned to problem branches, which VCB management believed is demoralizing and leads to unwanted loss of talented managers. Another factor that limited VCB's enthusiasm for using only an incentive formula was concern about setting the right formula parameters (e.g., average market growth and bonus percentage). Different parameters generate different incentives and might lead to different actions. Having diverse sources of compensation minimizes the risk of incentive-formula mistakes and allows for some experimentation with different formula parameters.

Formula-based evaluations importantly require measures that are accurate, reliable, and verifiable. Inaccurate, unreliable, or manipulated measures can create the opportunity for conflict over measured performance and incentives to cheat. Conflict and cheating might encourage eventual measurement improvements but can seriously impair the organization's performance while the inadequate measures are in place.[6] Sometimes taking actions that improve the evaluation numbers but that are detrimental to the organization in the long run is possible (e.g., branch managers can add riskier customers to increase recorded revenues without adjusting for expected future losses.) Organizations also can measure some areas of formula-based nonfinancial performance as reliably as financial performance, but most organizations historically have had more ability and need to measure and verify financial performance because of financial and tax reporting requirements.

Many companies also (or exclusively) use **subjective performance evaluation** by providing compensation above the base salary based on nonquantified criteria. The advantage of subjective evaluation is that it considers factors that a formula does not explicitly capture. For example, suppose that the sales growth of one of VCB's branches was below target because it serves a declining market but that the bank wants to maintain a presence there because the market area will be the focus of economic redevelopment activities by local and federal governments. Matching the future benefits and opportunity costs of this management decision in an explicit formula can be difficult. Subjective performance evaluation also can eliminate opportunities for "gaming" that exist when formula-based evaluations are used. Subjective evaluation can counter the tendency to manipulate the numbers in the formula, which can be more severe when the incentive plan includes multiple measures of performance.

subjective performance evaluation *is based on nonquantified criteria*

The advantage of a formula-based plan is that managers know precisely what is expected of them and what reward they will receive relative to expectations. The subjective approach is a less certain form of incentive plan and can be susceptible to favoritism, political maneuvering, and even a "good-old-boys" approach to incentive compensation. Incentive compensation might become a function more of how well

[6]This is a major reason that proponents of the balanced scorecard caution against using it in a formula-based incentive system.

superiors like managers than of performance, thus reducing the expectancy between effort and reward. Employees often are comfortable with a subjective approach when they believe in upper management's ability, are willing to take some risks, and trust upper management. Otherwise, employees tend to prefer a formula approach.

An increasing number of organizations use elements of both subjective and formula-based incentives. For example, VCB rewards branch managers based on a formula that includes revenue growth, net interest margin, and return on net assets as well as subjective evaluation based on a manager's level of responsibility and the judged value of a manager's contributions plus the industry norms.

Financial or Nonfinancial Performance

Financial performance reflects the achievement of financial goals, such as cost control, revenue growth, earnings, and residual income. Nonfinancial performance usually is not measured in monetary terms and often reflects the drivers of financial performance, such as measures of organizational learning and growth, business production process efficiency, and customer value (see Chapter 20 for a discussion of a balanced scorecard of performance measures). Organizations that ostensibly measure performance with only financial or only nonfinancial performance measures could be found. Some profit-seeking firms apparently base rewards only on "bottom-line" financial performance. Some nonprofit organizations overtly reward only on the basis of meeting nonfinancial goals. However, nearly every organization really uses both financial and nonfinancial measures of performance. For example, in the most bottom-line-oriented corporation, an executive who exceeds financial goals will not last long after being convicted of a serious crime. Furthermore, the most altruistic, nonfinancial, nonprofit organization cannot tolerate an executive who repeatedly fails to operate within the organization's financial means or diverts the organization's funds for personal use. Financial and nonfinancial performance measurement is not an either-or issue but involves identifying which measures and what balance to use. We next discuss financial performance measures.

Financial performance: earnings or stock. Chapter 18 describes a multitude of financial performance measures, so we will not repeat those discussions here. Most financial performance measures are based on periodic earnings (quarterly or annual), components of earnings, or a variation of earnings. Remember that although components of earnings used in external reports must comply with GAAP, those in incentive compensation plans need not. Designers of incentive plans should match incentives from earnings numbers to desired behavior. For example, some incentive plans in the United States omit or capitalize R&D expenses from earnings to counter any disincentives to conduct research caused by required expensing of R&D for GAAP.

Financial performance measures commonly include levels or *changes* of the following:

- Revenues.
- Costs.
- Cash flow.
- Operating income (before or after extraordinary items, taxes).
- Return on investment (total assets, net assets, or equity).
- Residual income or EVA®.[7]
- Stock price.

All of these measures except stock price are explicitly based on earnings-related numbers. The last three items are most commonly used to evaluate business-unit performance and provide interesting opportunities for the discussion of incentives and motivation. Let's briefly discuss them in this context.

---

[7]EVA is a registered trademark of Stern Stewart & Company, but most agree that it is a variation of residual income. See Chapter 18.

Return on investment (ROI). Allowing for the many possible variations of its components (i.e., alternative measures of return and investment), ROI is the most commonly used measure of business-unit performance for several reasons. First, measuring the components of ROI causes no additional costs because they are part of periodic financial reporting. Second, ROI components are among the most reliable, verifiable, and objective numbers the company prepares, and using them leads to few disputes. Third, as a percentage return, ROI is easy to understand and compare across similar business units. These benefits, in fact, have caused some companies that jumped on the EVA "bandwagon" to return to using ROI as the predominant financial performance measure.[8]

Residual income or economic value added. Residual income (and its more recent variation EVA) has been recommended as a measure of business-unit performance since at least the 1920s when General Motors adopted it.[9] Residual income (RI) is a desirable performance measure in corporate incentive plans because it increases when investments generate earnings in excess of the cost of capital. RI also increases when companies eliminate investments that earn less than the cost of capital. Thus, residual income should reflect changes in the firm's value.[10]

One of the selling points for EVA is that it permits multiple adjustments to reported earnings to adjust for "accounting distortions," but adjusting earnings to align incentives with desired behavior is not new. For many years, companies have adjusted reported earnings in the following ways:

- Capitalize expenditures on research and development (in the United States).
- Capitalize expenditures on customer development, advertising, and promotion if these expenditures will benefit future years.
- Capitalize expenditures on employee training that will benefit future years.
- Make price-level adjustments so assets, revenues, and expenses are stated in current year currency values.
- Use gross book values or restated net book values to reflect the assets' actual economic value.
- Restate inventories to replacement cost.
- Do not amortize goodwill.

Note that this list is neither a recommended guideline nor a complete list of adjustments (one consulting company advertises more than 160 adjustments to reported earnings). Each situation is unique and could require its own set of adjustments (or none at all).

Another selling point of EVA is that allegedly it more closely reflects (e.g., is a lead indicator of) stock price performance than do reported earnings.[11] Thus, using EVA as the performance measure for incentive plans should more closely align managers' and stockholders' interests. Recent research partially supports this claim, but at

---

[8]See C. Ittner and D. Larcker, "Innovations in Performance Measurement: Trends and Research Implications" for an extensive discussion.

[9]General Electric apparently coined the actual term "residual income" in the 1950s. See M. Bromwich and M. Walker, "Residual Income Past and Future."

[10]A number of technical issues must be met to guarantee this relation (e.g., NPV-based depreciation), but most RI and EVA users appear to treat these as minor issues.

[11]Both TIAA-CREF, the teacher's retirement system and CALPERS, the public employees retirement system in California have used EVA to evaluate how well corporate managers are using resources. In some cases, these giant retirement systems have taken corporate managers to task for failing to create sufficient value for shareholders. Valley Commercial Bank also uses EVA to evaluate its investments. Each of its major loan customers annually provides a set of financial statements to the bank. Using these financial statements and an industry cost of capital provided by Ibbotson and Associates as well as making a few accounting adjustments, VCB's employees compute the EVA for each major loan customer. The file of any customer for which EVA was less than zero was flagged to indicate a high-risk loan. Computing these figures for its customers both assessed the customer's financial performance for bank lending decisions and gave added incentives to its customers to generate earnings in excess of the cost of capital. See valuation.ibbotson.com.

this time the superiority of EVA or RI over reported earnings is open to question (see Research Insight 21.1 for a discussion). This might be another reason that some companies continue to use or are returning to more conventional financial measures of performance, such as ROI. Residual income, in some form, however, is unlikely to be only a passing fad because it is based on a fundamental concept of economic profit generated after considering all costs, including the opportunity cost of capital. The notion that companies earning an economic profit will add wealth to their owners is well grounded in economic theory and in practice.

Research Insight 21.1

Does EVA Pay?

Residual income (RI) and economic value added (EVA) have a long history as prescriptions for better performance evaluations. Economic researchers have been interested in finding the conditions when RI or EVA will reflect changes in firm value: If RI or EVA go up, stock prices should go up, and vice versa (yes, these conditions might exist). Current accounting and finance research indicates that division managers evaluated using residual income make investing, financing, and operating decisions that should increase stock prices. Thus, residual income/EVA might be an effective incentive device. However, the stock market does not appear to increase prices of shares of companies when they *adopt* EVA-based incentive plans, but if managers make better decisions, stock prices should increase. Perhaps the value of EVA-based plans does not exceed their cost. Furthermore, some research indicates that stock-price returns are more closely correlated with net income than with EVA. Perhaps net income is a better reflection of changes in firm value than EVA. At this time, we cannot establish a clear link between EVA-based incentives and increased stockholder value. More research is needed in this area. *Sources: M. Bromwich and M. Walker, "Residual Income Past and Future"; G. Biddle, R. Bowen, and J. Wallace, "Economic Value Added: Some Empirical EVAdence"; J. S. Wallace, "Adopting Residual Income-Based Compensation Plans: Do You Get What You Pay For?"; G. C. Biddle, R. M. Bowen, and J. S. Wallace, "Does EVA® Beat Earnings? Evidence on Associations with Stock Returns and Firm Values." For alternative points of view, see P. A. Dierks and A. Patel, "What Is EVA® and How Can It Help Your Company?."; and J. Freedman, "New Research Red Flags EVA® for Stock Picks." (Full citations to references are in the Bibliography.)*

Stock-price performance. If an objective is to align managers' interests to those of stockholders, why not use stock-price performance as the performance evaluation measure? When stock price rises, both managers and stockholders are better off and vice versa. However, business-unit managers in large companies might see little connection between their actions and the performance of the company's stock. Furthermore, a company's stock can fluctuate widely based on factors over which the manager has no control, including economic and industry trends, interest rates, politics, technology, and customer tastes and preferences.

Therefore, tying managers' compensation to stock-price performance places a good deal of risk on them. Furthermore, this type of risk is not easy for managers to diversify because the performance measure is based on just one stock—that of their company.

Tying managers' incentive compensation to the company's stock performance has the obvious benefit of aligning managers' incentives with those of shareholders.

Despite these problems with stock price as a measure of performance, many companies generally provide at least some incentive for managers to be concerned about stock performance by rewarding with stock awards. Some companies go beyond stock awards. Polaroid, for example, requires its executives to own stock valued at a multiple of their base pay (one, three, or five times, depending on the position). Extensive stock ownership gives executives an interest in how well their company's stock is doing even if stock price is not an explicit performance measure.

VCB uses a mix of financial performance measures in its performance evaluations. Executives are evaluated on residual income, and branch managers are evaluated on net interest margin, return on assets, and revenue growth.

You're the Decision Maker 21.1

Return on Investment and Economic Value Added

Recall the following formulas from Chapter 18:

Return on investment = Net income ÷ Invested capital

Economic value added or Residual income = Net income − Weighted-average cost of capital × Invested capital

Assume the following data for a business unit:

- *Net income* is measured as operating income *before* interest and R&D and *after* tax.
- *Invested capital* is measured as total assets less current liabilities.
- *Operating income before tax* equals $500,000 for the year.
- The *effective tax rate* equals 40 percent.
- *Interest expense* equals $90,000.
- *R&D expense* equals $150,000.
- The *weighted-average cost of capital* appropriate for the business unit equals 10 percent.
- The *total assets* in the business unit equal $5,500,000.
- The business unit's *current liabilities* equal $500,000.

a. What are possible reasons for the adjustments to measures of earnings and invested capital used in this situation? What are the likely incentive effects?

b. Compute both return on investment and residual income (or economic value added) for this business unit. (*Hint:* Your solution will be more flexible if you use a spreadsheet to model this financial performance.)

c. What do these measures say or not say about the financial performance of the business?

(Solutions begin on page 898.)

Source: Organizations frequently use the information published by Ibbotson and Associates, Cost of Capital Quarterly, *as a starting point for their cost of capital computations. See valuation.ibbotson.com.*

Nonfinancial performance: operations and organizational social and environmental factors. Evidence indicates that the use of nonfinancial measures of performance in incentive plans is increasing. Of course, organizations have used nonfinancial measures for managing operations for many years,[12] but including them in incentive plans is an important development.[13] Recall from Chapter 20 that carefully selected nonfinancial measures can be reliable lead indicators of financial performance. For example, at VCB, measures of loan application quality indicate problems that, left unchecked, significantly can affect future customer satisfaction, revenues, and profits adversely. By the time top managers observe poor financial performance, however, a problem already has occurred and caused damage. To manage the drivers of profits than to correct problems later can be better for all concerned. Because of the time lags between the observation of nonfinancial performance (e.g., in the balanced scorecard areas of organizational learning and growth, business production process efficiency, and customer value) and their effects on financial performance,

[12] See Chapter 7 of this text for examples of commonly used quality, time, and productivity measures and Chapter 20 for examples of nonfinancial performance measures included in performance measurement.

[13] See R. Banker, G. Potter, and D. Srinivasan, "An Empirical Investigation of an Incentive Plan That Includes Nonfinancial Performance Measures," for an example.

the number of companies using nonfinancial measures of performance in their incentive plans to reinforce their importance is increasing.

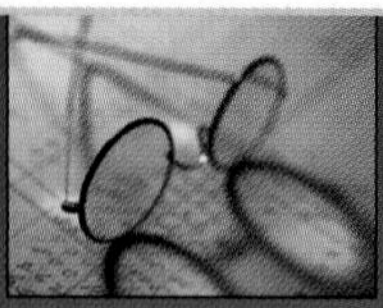

Cost Management in Practice 21.1

Use of Nonfinancial Measures of Performance

Professors Ittner and Larcker of the Wharton School of Business have reviewed the findings of many surveys, cases, and field studies investigating firms' uses of nonfinancial measures of performance for both management and incentive compensation. They report that as many as 36 percent of firms explicitly include nonfinancial measures in executive incentive plans. On average, 37 percent of the total evaluation was based on these nonfinancial measures. Firms that use nonfinancial measures in their incentive plans tend to be more innovative, to have adopted TQM, to have long product-development cycles, to have been more subject to regulation, and to have had "noisier" financial performance. Thus, factors, such as innovativeness and adoption of TQM, apparently affect the use of nonfinancial measures of performance in incentive plans.

Nonfinancial measures of performance used most commonly in incentive plans include customer satisfaction, productivity, employee performance, community/environmental performance, and innovation. But Ittner and Larcker point out that very little objective research reflects whether using these measures in incentive plans results in better *long-term* financial performance. At this point, firms might be reluctant to disclose that they have found successful packages of measures alternatively, they might include these measures based on the logic of linkages among lead and lag indicators of performance rather than hard evidence.

Ittner and Larcker found in a different study that perceived subjectivity of nonfinancial performance measures led to the abandonment of the balanced scorecard as the basis for incentive compensation in a large bank. The bank's incentive system returned its primary focus to financial performance despite the validity of nonfinancial measures as lead indicators of financial performance. As mentioned earlier, perceived subjectivity of some measures could impair their usefulness as incentive devices.

Sources: C. Ittner and D. Larcker, "Innovations in Performance Measurement: Trends and Research Implications" and "The Use of Subjectivity in Multi-Criteria Bonus Plans."

Perhaps the greatest advantages of adding nonfinancial measures to the incentive system are (1) focus on the drivers of profit and (2) recognition of the time lags between nonfinancial and financial performance. Recall that expectancy theory leads us to expect that incentives based on nonfinancial performance direct employees' attention to leading activities more effectively than do indirect incentives based on financial performance alone. Although employees might know that poor quality can surface later as lower profits, for example, the time lag and lack of direct effect can lower the expectancy that their quality-related actions affect performance. Thus, adding an explicit incentive related to managing quality can improve that aspect immediately and financial performance subsequently. Value Commercial Bank evaluates nonfinancial performance for compensation, although it does so subjectively.

As with all aspects of incentive plans, however, nonfinancial performance measures have costs as well as benefits. Difficulties of including nonfinancial measures in incentive plans include these:

- Increased cost of performance measurement and supporting information systems.
- Increased cost of reporting and verifying the validity of performance measures.
- Difficulty in determining the proper balance between financial and nonfinancial measures.
- Danger of "information overload" from too many measures causing lack of focus on overall performance.
- Increased opportunities for disputes over the validity of performance measures.
- Increased opportunities for manipulating formula-based incentive plans that include multiple measures.

If adding nonfinancial measures adds problems, why not use financial performance over a period of time long enough to capture the effects of nonfinancial performance?[14] One answer might be that nonfinancial measures can add value in excess of their costs. Another might be that although competition for managerial talent requires frequent evaluation and payment of compensation, financial performance cannot be matched to efforts in a timely manner. These answers might explain why many organizations have added problematic nonfinancial performance measures to their incentive systems. The measures to use and how to include them in performance-based incentive plans are some of the greatest challenges of incentive plan design, and more research is needed in this area.

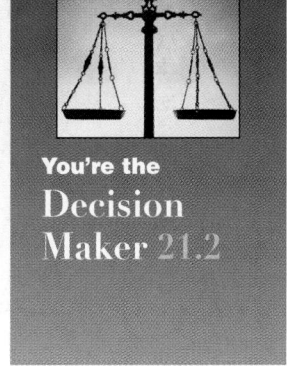

You're the Decision Maker 21.2

Integrating the Balanced Scorecard and Incentive Plans

Review Valley Commercial Bank's balanced scorecard in Exhibit 20–6 of Chapter 20 (page 850). Most of the performance measures in this scorecard are nonfinancial.

a. Do you think VCB should or should not try to include all of its balanced scorecard measures in its incentive plans? Explain.

b. If you decide to include those measures shown in Exhibit 20–6 in the bank's incentive plans, how can you do it?

c. If you do not include those measures in the bank's incentive plans, how can you motivate employees to manage those areas of performance?

(Solutions begin on page 898.)

Narrow or Broad Responsibility of Performance

An organization can define performance narrowly or broadly. Should a manager's rewards depend on the performance of that individual, of the manager's division, or of the company as a whole? For example, should VCB evaluate its branch managers based their performance on a set of personal goals, the performance of the manager's branch bank, or the performance of the bank as a whole? Basing compensation on only the performance of the company as a whole gives managers incentives to consider the impact of their actions on the entire organization. This is especially important in large companies whose managers might not see much of a relationship between their actions and the company's performance.

Expectancy theory reminds us that incentives work best when individuals see a strong link between their actions and performance results. Moving from incentives based on individual performance to bankwide performance lessens an individual's influence on the performance measure. Thus, companywide incentives are expected to be less effective motivators than are incentives based on individual performance. For example, Honeywell has hundreds of divisions. One particular division's performance has very little impact on that of the company as a whole. Thus, Honeywell and many other large companies base much of a division's manager's compensation on the performance of that manager's division.

Other considerations make broader performance measures desirable. First, narrowly focused incentives reduce the motivation for broad cooperation and information sharing. This is true particularly if the organization uses relative performance evaluation, causing managers to compete among themselves for rewards. Organizations are reluctant to set up disincentives to cooperation and conversion of individual knowledge into organizational knowledge because these are key competitive factors.

Second, the development of a valid measure of financial performance at narrow levels of responsibility is difficult. For example, although the measurement of operating income for the bank might be easy, the measurement of each branch's contribution can be more difficult and the measurement of each individual manager's contribution to bank

[14]A. Rappaport articulates this question in his book *Creating Shareholder Value.*

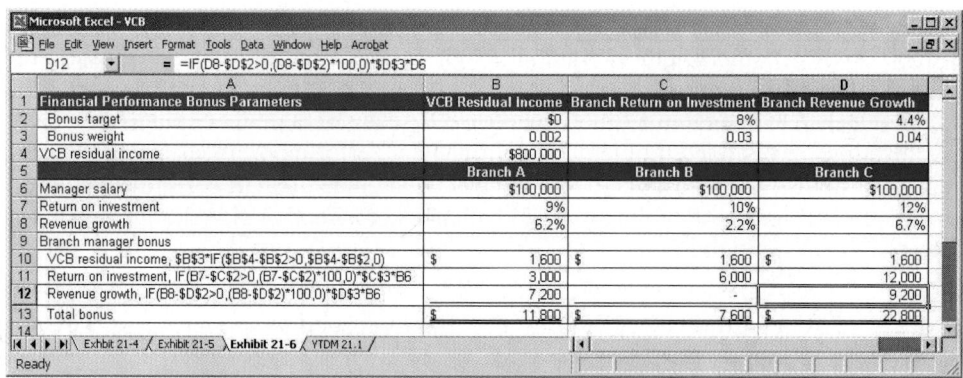

Exhibit 21–6

Bonuses Based on Bank and Branch Financial Performance

Valley COMMERCIAL BANK

Microsoft Excel - VCB

D12 = =IF(D8-D2>0,(D8-D2)*100,0)*D3*D6

	A	B	C	D
1	Financial Performance Bonus Parameters	VCB Residual Income	Branch Return on Investment	Branch Revenue Growth
2	Bonus target	$0	8%	4.4%
3	Bonus weight	0.002	0.03	0.04
4	VCB residual income	$800,000		
5		Branch A	Branch B	Branch C
6	Manager salary	$100,000	$100,000	$100,000
7	Return on investment	9%	10%	12%
8	Revenue growth	6.2%	2.2%	6.7%
9	Branch manager bonus			
10	VCB residual income, B3*IF(B4-B2>0,B4-B2,0)	$ 1,600	$ 1,600	$ 1,600
11	Return on investment, IF(B7-C2>0,(B7-C2)*100,0)*C3*B6	3,000	6,000	12,000
12	Revenue growth, IF(B8-D2>0,(B8-D2)*100,0)*D3*B6	7,200	-	9,200
13	Total bonus	$ 11,800	$ 7,600	$ 22,800
14				

Exhbit 21-4 / Exhibit 21-5 / Exhibit 21-6 / YTDM 21.1

Ready

income could be impossible. The problem is that drivers of both revenues and costs often are higher-level activities, which are not influenced by an individual or a business subunit. Thus, any attempt to measure individual profit (or the profit of "micro-profit centers"—a current development[15]) can be either too restricted to be informative or mired in arbitrary revenue and cost allocations.

Most companies reward division managers for both business-unit and companywide performance, seeking a balance that is appropriate for their situations. Companies that are decentralized and have numerous divisions with diverse activities tend to base incentives more on the performance of the division and less on that of the company. ITT, for example, is a decentralized and diverse company that bases nearly all of the compensation of its business-unit managers on the performance of each manager's business unit. Caterpillar, another large company, is highly integrated and much more centralized than ITT. Caterpillar ties more of the compensation of its business-unit managers to companywide performance.

VCB rewards executives based on overall bank performance. The bank also strives to create incentives for cooperation by linking some of branch managers' rewards to the bank's overall economic performance. Because interactions among branches are minimal, VCB primarily evaluates branch managers on their branch's revenue growth, net asset margin, and return on assets. These provide incentives to improve individual branch performance and inject some competition among branches. The trick for VCB is to balance these incentives so that managers will strive to improve the performance of their branches but still have a significant stake in the bank's overall performance.

Consider the partial bonuses based on individual branch and overall bank financial performance shown in Exhibit 21–6. Note that each branch manager receives a $1,600 bonus based on VCB's overall residual income performance (row 10) computed as follows:

$$\begin{aligned}\textbf{Residual income bonus} &= \textbf{Residual income bonus weight} \\ &\quad \times \textbf{VCB residual income in excess of target} \\ &= \textbf{B3* IF(B4} - \textbf{B2}>\textbf{0,B4} - \textbf{B2,0)}^{16} \\ &= \textbf{.002} \times \textbf{(\$800,000} - \textbf{\$0)} = \underline{\underline{\textbf{\$1,600}}}\end{aligned}$$

Other bonus components also reflect branch financial performance compared to targets.

Current or Deferred Rewards

Expectancy theory says that it is better to offer rewards sooner than later, but agency theory suggests some value from waiting. Rewards for performance can be given now

---

[15]See R. Cooper and R. Slagmulder, "Micro Profit Centers."

[16]Note that the use of the "IF" function ensures a bonus *only if* residual income (B4) exceeds the target (B2). Other formulas compute bonuses based on branch performance in excess of targets in similar ways.

based on current performance or later on sustained performance. Current compensation rewards can be in the form of cash or stock that can be cashed immediately or soon after the award. For example, a manager might be rewarded quickly with a cash bonus if the stock price increases 10 percent by the end of the year or later on a deferred basis if the stock price increases by an average of 10 percent per year over the next three years. Thus, the company defers any rewards for the first and second years' performance until after the third year. These deferred rewards can be cash or stock as well as stock options. We defer coverage of stock options rewards to the next section.

Current rewards. Current rewards have the obvious advantage of being closely linked to current performance. Because uncertainty related to current rewards is low, the high expectancy associated with current rewards should provide strong motivation to improve current performance. The disadvantage of current rewards is that they can induce employees to manipulate the performance measures without concern for future performance or with the expectation of "cashing out" and leaving the organization.

Deferred rewards. Advantages of deferred rewards based on sustained performance are that (1) good managers might have incentives to stay with the company (e.g., "golden handcuffs") and (2) managers have incentives to focus attention on long-term performance. Many commentators argue that managers, particularly in the United States, are too short-term oriented. They take actions now that look good in the short term but are detrimental in the long term. A good example is the failure of some companies to invest in new technology. This "myopic" view of performance keeps earnings high in the short term by avoiding write-offs or high depreciation expenses but is detrimental in the long term. Switching to deferred rewards based on sustained financial performance can capture the lagged effects of good or poor nonfinancial performance and avoid disincentives to make costly improvements.

A disadvantage of a deferred reward is that managers might view it as coming too far in the future to be motivational. Recall from expectancy theory that the reward should be attractive to be motivational. Giving a manager a reward in stock to be paid five years from now is less attractive than giving a payment at the end of the current year.

VCB uses a combination of current and deferred awards for top managers but primarily pays current awards for lower-level managers and their subordinates. When making deferred awards to executives, the bank defers the award for three to five years. This time appears to be sufficiently long (1) to capture lagged effects of actions and (2) to motivate the managers to think about the future but (3) is not so far in the future that incentive effects or the managers themselves are lost.

Valley COMMERCIAL BANK

Salary, Bonus, or Stock Rewards

Most management incentive plans include multiple forms of reward, including salary, bonus, stock, and stock options. Organizations design the reward package to address the motivational issues raised earlier within stockholder and taxation guidelines, and many have found that a combination of rewards is more effective than a single form of reward.[17] Most large organizations have compensation committees that design the mix of rewards to reflect the company's compensation philosophy. Some organizations stress salary; others stress performance-based compensation to provide more motivation. For example, VCB states the following:

> One of the essential elements of the Bank's compensation policy is to align the interests of the CEO, executive officers, and key employees with the interests of stockholders. . . . The total compensation package is designed to provide a significant percentage of executive compensation from programs such as the bonus plan and stock based long-term incentive programs, which link executive rewards to long-term shareholder rewards.

---

[17]Personal and corporate income tax regulations have major effects on the design of incentive compensation plans. These issues are beyond the scope of this text.

The financial press often portrays large grants of stock options as not in the best interest of other stockholders.

Salary. Nearly all management employees work in exchange for some salary that is more or less guaranteed. Occasionally, an executive works without salary, but this usually is in exchange for stock or other deferred rewards or is a charitable contribution to a nonprofit organization. The typical salary issues are (1) the level of salary and (2) the proportion of compensation that is salary versus performance-based reward. Salary levels often are benchmarked with the organization's industry and the level of responsibility within the organization. Most organizations operate within industry norms. At extremes, a manager receives 100 percent of his compensation from salary, or another manager receives 100 percent of her compensation based on performance. What difference does the proportion of salary make?

At 100 percent of compensation, a salary insulates an employee from most risks so the employee might be inclined to make risky decisions. In reality, however, such compensation is more likely to attract employees who are not inclined to take risk. Furthermore, set salaries can turn away employees who recognize that their compensation has no upside potential, regardless of their effort or ability to manage. Because most stockholders can diversify their investments, they prefer that managers take some risks, but they must compensate managers for doing so.

One way to motivate risk taking is to shift some compensation from salary and make it depend on performance that managers' risky decisions can improve. Making all compensation based on performance might not be desirable, however, because, as mentioned earlier, this places all of the risk on managers. The organization might attract only extreme risk takers or those who demand a large stake in the organization in exchange for the risk they must bear. Most organizations find a balance between guaranteed salary and performance-based compensation that attracts, retains, and motivates employees to make good decisions.

Cash bonuses. Cash bonus awards have the advantage of being liquid and highly attractive because the reward is immediate and unconstrained. Companies usually make cash bonus awards based on the achievement of financial performance objectives. Often these bonuses have a floor or lower threshold of performance (e.g., a minimum return on investment) before the employee earns any bonus. Many cash bonus incentives also have a ceiling or an upper threshold beyond which no more bonuses will be earned. Much interesting research[18] has focused on the motivational

[18]The classic article is by P. Healy, "The Effect of Bonus Schemes on Accounting Procedure and Accrual Decisions."

properties of these plans and the incentives they generate to manipulate financial measures of performance.[19]

Stock awards. Stock awards, in contrast to cash bonuses, might not be redeemable for cash until some time in the future. Some companies have an unwritten rule that managers cannot sell company stock until they leave the firms or retire. Stock awards that cannot be immediately sold, while perhaps not as attractive as an equivalent amount of cash, align the interests of managers with those of shareholders better than cash awards do. For this reason, top-executive compensation commonly is composed more heavily of stock than of cash bonus or salary. Stock might not align managers' interests, however, as well as stock options do.

Stock options. **Stock options,** which give an individual the right to purchase a certain number of shares at a specified price over a specified time period, provide strong incentives for managers to increase stock value over the long run.[20] The use of stock-option rewards has increased dramatically over the past decade. A stock option has a lower monetary value than a share of stock, so a company can create more incentive to increase share prices by awarding stock options than simply awarding the same value and fewer shares of stock. Managers who receive large awards of stock options have much to gain from increases in share prices. This does not mean that managers lose nothing if the stock price declines, however, because the value of the options decline and managers suffer the opportunity cost of not increasing stock value (or earning an alternative cash bonus). Awards of stock options, therefore, have the motivational impact of stock grants but at a lower cost to the company.

***stock options** give an individual the right to purchase a certain number of shares at a specified price over a specified time period*

The popular press portrays many executives who have worked for relatively small salaries to be eager to cash in their stock options after years of hard work and "relative poverty." Nonetheless, current estimates are that US executives hold billions of dollars of unexercised stock options, even after the Internet bubble burst in 2000–2001. These options continue to align their incentives with those of stockholders. Although some concern exists that stock-option awards give managers incentives to manipulate stock prices in the short run rather than build the company for the long term, most of this concern appears to be misguided. Although agency theory predicts that managers will manipulate if the benefits of higher stock prices exceed the costs of being caught, available evidence from the United States indicates a high correspondence between executive wealth (largely from stock options) and company value. Designing stock option plans to properly align pay with performance is quite complicated, however, and the choice of the wrong type of plan can create disincentives.

Valley
COMMERCIAL BANK

VCB rewards its branch managers with cash bonuses for meeting revenue growth, net interest margin, and return on net asset objectives. Executives also earn stock options that are exercisable over a four-year period based on meeting overall residual income objectives. The proportions of executive compensation value have averaged 30 percent salary, 30 percent cash bonus, and 40 percent stock options. At present, VCB does not extend significant performance-based compensation to lower-level managers. Most of their compensation is salary and bonus based.

---

[19]Some companies give prizes instead of cash, stock, or stock options, particularly to lower-level employees. One small company that we studied awarded managers points for performing well. The managers could trade in the points for automotive accessories or sporting goods such as golf clubs or fishing rods. Managers who received these awards told us this was a highly motivational reward. One of them said, "A cash bonus would be eaten up paying the bills and soon forgotten. Every time I use my new fishing rod I remember the work I put in to earn it." Applying expectancy theory, these prizes were more attractive and, therefore, more motivational than are cash awards.

[20]A readable article on stock options is B. Hall, "What You Need to Know About Stock Options."

You're the Decision Maker 21.3

Designing Incentive Compensation Plans

You are a consultant advising Valley Commercial Bank about its incentive compensation plans for lower-level managers and employees. Your interviews with branch and department managers inform you that they are satisfied with the new balanced scorecard performance measurement system (see Exhibit 20–6) but believe that they are not rewarded for performing well. Nonmanagement employees likewise enjoy their jobs but do not believe that they have real incentives to work harder or better. At the end of each year, most branch and department managers and employees receive annual salary increases between 4 percent and 6 percent. Branch managers also earn bonuses up to 10 percent of their salary for meeting sales growth and return on asset objectives. Promotions appear to be based on seniority; the longer a person is in a job, the better the person's chances for promotion.

a. Do the interview responses signal a potential problem? If so, what do you think that VCB should do?

(Solution begins on page 898.)

Summary of Valley Commercial Bank's Incentive Plan

Valley COMMERCIAL BANK

Review Exhibit 21–3 (p. 880), which is the framework of this chapter's discussion of performance-based incentive plans. As mentioned, plan designers should consider each element of this diagram to ensure that the incentive plan addresses all alternative choices. To sum, VCB seeks to attract, motivate, and retain competent employees and to align their interests with shareholders' long-term interests. The bank's incentive plan has the following features.

1. *Absolute or relative performance.* VCB uses both forms of performance: Residual income and environmental performance are compared to absolute objectives; evaluations of revenue growth, net interest margin, and return on assets are based on relative performance.
2. *Formula-based or subjective performance.* VCB also uses both formula and subjective evaluations. Residual income, net interest margin, and return-on-asset incentives for branch managers are formula based, but the bank subjectively evaluates other areas of performance that are important to its balanced scorecard (see Exhibit 20–6) but are measured less reliably (e.g., value of employee suggestions).
3. *Financial or nonfinancial performance.* As mentioned, VCB uses only financial measures of performance in its formula-based incentive plans. The bank understands the value of its nonfinancial performance for long-term success, but quality of measurement is an issue. If the bank could reliably measure key nonfinancial measures from its balanced scorecard (see You're the Decision Maker 21.2), it would formally include some of them in its formula-based incentives. Until then, VCB will continue to evaluate nonfinancial performance subjectively. Top candidates for inclusion in the incentive formula include employee satisfaction, productivity, and customer satisfaction because they are based on reliable instruments and can be audited.
4. *Narrow or broad responsibility of performance.* VCB evaluates its executives on bankwide performance but its branch managers primarily on branch performance, with a relatively small emphasis on bankwide performance.
5. *Current or deferred rewards.* VCB executives receive both current and deferred rewards; lower-level managers receive mostly current rewards.
6. *Salary or bonus rewards.* All VCB employees receive a salary, but executives receive most of their compensation from bonus or stock option rewards. Currently, lower-level managers receive most compensation from salaries, and lower-level employees receive all compensation from salaries (see You're the Decision Maker 21.3).

Although VCB has put much effort into designing its incentive plans, every plan can be improved. The bank's board of directors annually reviews it in light of recent developments and changes in competitive pressures and recommends improvement. Current recommendations include refining some nonfinancial performance measures for inclusion in the bank's incentive formulas. The bank's president and CEO also serves on the boards of directors of several charitable, nonprofit organizations and has been urging their boards to adopt features of the incentive plans of VCB and other successful companies.

Incentive Plans in Nonprofit Organizations

Nonprofit organizations range from small, informal organizations such as sports clubs, student organizations, and parent groups supporting sports and music activities to large well-established organizations such as the United Way, the American Red Cross, most universities, and government departments and agencies, such as the US Postal Service, the Department of Transportation, and the Environmental Protection Agency. Many of these nonprofit organizations apply the concepts in this chapter, with some modifications, for the same reasons that profit-seeking firms do: to attract, motivate, and retain competent employees and to align their interests with those of the organizations. By definition, a nonprofit organization has something other than earning a profit as its primary goal. Thus, effective nonprofit incentive plans primarily should create incentives for managers to perform well on nonfinancial dimensions.[21]

Key Nonfinancial Performance

This focus on nonfinancial performance largely is due to the absence of prices or objective values for the outputs of nonprofit organizations. For example, although most agree that helping victims of natural disasters is a valuable activity, there is not a ready market value for American Red Cross services. Indeed, the lack of formal markets is one of the major reasons for the existence on nonprofit organizations; they fill needs not addressed by markets. When markets do exist for government services, in particular, increasing privatization of government activities is occurring.

Because they are not seeking to earn profits, nonprofit organizations do not manage themselves by the numbers to the same extent as for-profit companies do. Whereas a company can evaluate a business unit manager's performance by measures such as return on investment or economic value added, these comparisons usually are not available or relevant for nonprofit organizations. Although many large charitable organizations publicize financial performance measures such as the percentage of revenues directly devoted to providing services, most nonprofits do not and perhaps should not manage themselves primarily by financial numbers.

Some nonprofit organizations operate more by culture or shared values than for-profits do. For example, the parents in a school-support organization share the value of providing support for their children's educational activities. Likewise, the culture of religious organizations binds members and provides a powerful force for acting to achieve common goals.[22] None of this means that financial performance is unimportant at a nonprofit organization, however.

Importance of Financial Performance

Although nonprofits do not try to maximize profits, they have strong needs to provide services in a cost-effective manner. Nonprofits compete for scarce funds and nonmonetary

---

[21]For a comprehensive treatment of management control in nonprofit organizations, see R. N. Anthony and D. W. Young, *Management Control in Nonprofit Organizations.*

[22]For an excellent discussion of markets, bureaucracies, and culture as alternative means of management control, see W. Ouchi, "A Conceptual Framework for the Design of Organizational Control Mechanisms."

support and must be able to show donors and supporters that their contributions are being used effectively. *Smart Money* magazine, for example, annually analyzes the efficiency of charitable organizations.[23] Thus, a nonprofit's concern for creating value at lowest cost can be similar to that of a profit-seeking firm. Nonprofit organizations also must demonstrate proper accountability for the use of funds and manage their operations and revenues to ensure that they break even.

For example, the US Postal Service is under a mandate to break even financially and to manage itself more like a for-profit enterprise. It controls billions of dollars of assets in buildings, vehicles, and sorting equipment, so management adopted economic value-added policies to help control its capital costs.[24] Management evaluated its performance by applying a cost of capital to the assets for each responsibility center using its borrowing rate that Congress mandated: one-eighth of a percent over the three-month Treasury Bill rate.

With stiff competition from the private sector, such as United Parcel Service and Federal Express, the US Postal Service also must concentrate on customer service. To see it and other government agencies adopt a balanced scorecard with economic value added as one of the financial measures will not be surprising.

Increasing the Use of Private-Sector-Developed Incentive Plans

In some voluntary and charitable organizations, incentive compensation plans rely heavily on intrinsic rewards. Most employees generally earn a lower salary than they do in the private sector. Furthermore, nonprofits do not offer opportunities for large financial payoffs for excellent performance. However, these voluntary and charitable organizations attract people for whom the intrinsic reward from doing good work compensates for the lost financial compensation available in the private sector. Government agencies also attract people who obtain intrinsic rewards from the work and/or people who prefer the security and benefit packages that are often available in government organizations.

Despite differences between for-profit and nonprofit organizations, nonprofit organizations increasingly use features of executive incentive plans developed in the private sector. These organizations also compete for top management talent and must align executive's interests with those of the organizations. Expectancy and agency theories do not disappear in nonprofit organizations. *The NonProfit Times* reported a recent salary survey, which indicated that "nonprofits are faced with greater competition [for executive talent] with the private sector that's unparalleled to anything they've seen before."[25] Furthermore, 20 percent of responding organizations reported awarding performance bonuses up to 10 percent of salary. Some nonprofit hospitals offer performance bonuses based on cost savings, health care improvements, and other factors. Many organizations, however, decline to develop incentives to retain management talent only to find that they must pay much more to replace talent lost to the private sector or more aggressive nonprofits.

Some nonprofit organizations even have developed stock-option plans to compete with for-profit firms. How can that be when nonprofits have no shares to option? Clever compensation consultants have found tax loopholes that allow nonprofit organizations to award options for mutual fund or corporate shares. One Big-5 consultant stated, "The tax-exempt organization is going to have to compete with taxable corporations for talent, and this gives them more flexibility."[26] Such plans are controversial because nonprofits fear turning off donors who expect their executives not to be so concerned with personal wealth and who are skeptical that awarding options in stock

[23]A. Kadet, "Put Your Money Where Our Math Is."

[24]K. Spinner, "Signed and Sealed—But Can EVA® Deliver?"

[25]P. Clolrery, "NPT Salary Survey."

[26]T. Billitteri, "Seeking an Option on Pay."

of for-profit firms can align managers' goals with those of the nonprofit. Still, stock options can be a way to attract and retain management talent.

Incentive plans also can create other difficulties for nonprofits. For example, Harrisburg Hospital in Pennsylvania lost its nonprofit, tax-exempt status in part because the state's courts ruled that its executive compensation plan, which gave cash bonuses for return on equity and revenue performance, clearly was designed to promote the hospital's bottom line. The court observed that, although incentive plans were not contrary to the notion of a nonprofit organization, this incentive plan aligned managers' interests more with earning profits than providing charitable health care services. The incentive plan was convincing evidence that the hospital had a strong profit motive.[27]

Despite controversy and difficulties, we expect incentive plans to become more common (but perhaps more sensitive to the organization's mission) in nonprofit organizations.

[27] *Harrisburg Hospital v. Dauphin County Board of Assessment Appeals.*

Chapter Summary

This chapter discussed motivating employees to take actions that benefit the organization. The two key elements of an incentive compensation plan are the *measure(s) of performance* and the *method(s) of compensation.* The expectancy view of motivation recommends two things: providing desirable rewards and providing a high probability that behaving as the organization wishes will lead to the rewards. The agency view focuses on the relations between principals and agents and develops incentives to encourage agents (e.g., employees) to act in the interests of principals (e.g., managers).

Managers make many choices regarding incentive compensation plans. Regarding performance evaluation, these choices include whether to rely on measures of current or future performance, whether to use division or companywide performance measures, whether to base performance on accounting results or stock performance, and whether to use absolute or relative performance evaluation. Furthermore, these choices include whether to base rewards on a subjective evaluation or a fixed formula and whether to reward good performance with cash, stock, or prizes. The objective of designing incentive plans is to select a package of performance measures and rewards that will attract, motivate, and retain good employees and align their interests with those of the organization.

Key Terms

For each term's definition, refer to the indicated page or turn to the glossary at the end of the text.

absolute performance evaluation, 891
agency costs, 879
agency theory, 878
expectancy theory, 875
extrinsic rewards, 877
intrinsic rewards, 877
performance evaluation formula, 882
relative performance evaluation, 881
stock options, 893
subjective performance evaluation, 883

Meeting the Cost-Management Challenges

1. **Should** Valley Commercial Bank design its incentive system to increase customer satisfaction? Is it possible to overstress customer satisfaction?

VCB should measure customer satisfaction and reward employees who enhance it. There is a saying that "what gets measured gets noticed." Measurement by itself is a strong motivator. Having customers complete satisfaction surveys and tracking complaints are ways to measure customer satisfaction. It is important for bank employees to see how effort leads to performance and how performance leads to rewards. The bank should reward performance that leads to customer satisfaction, including the performance of employees who do not have direct contact with customers. For example, maintenance employees keep the place clean, which enhances customer satisfaction. Bank management should note that rewards are not necessarily limited to pay and promotions. Praise is an excellent reward.

It is possible to overstress customer satisfaction by losing sight of the costs to provide it. Therefore, any incentive plan should include incentives for customer satisfaction and other drivers of bank profits. The trick is to balance these incentives so that the overall result is improved long-term profitability.

2. **Is** it possible to balance concerns for nonfinancial and financial performance in an effective incentive and performance evaluation system for Valley Commercial Bank? If so, how?

It is possible but not easy to balance these concerns. Using the balanced scorecard is one approach to identifying appropriate financial and nonfinancial measures. The advantage of the balanced scorecard is that each employee should be able to see how her or his work contributes to at least one of the three lead indicator areas of performance, which ultimately link to financial success. Doing so increases the expectancy of the incentive system. Balance means, however, that performance in each of these areas must be weighted appropriately so that employees both understand the relative importance of each area and are rewarded appropriately for related performance. Developing the appropriate weights can be quite difficult, and little research or developed body of practice exists to guide designers of incentive plans. Our research indicates that companies go through several iterations of measures and weights before finding the combination that seems to generate the right incentives. For example, see M. Malina and F. Selto, "Communicating and Controlling Strategy: An Empirical Investigation of the Effectiveness of the Balanced Scorecard."

3. **How** can Valley Commercial Bank or any organization weigh the trade-offs of various incentives for improving financial performance?

This obviously is a key issue. Why develop a performance-based incentive plan unless it is going to improve financial performance (assuming a profit-seeking firm)? Otherwise, this is just another non-value-added activity that should be eliminated. Managers can never know in advance whether a package of incentives will be worthwhile, but several sources of information can help. First, a manager's own knowledge of the organization and the drivers of its success can lead her to identify the most important measures of performance. Second, benchmarking current incentive plans against those of the competition or of "world-class" organizations might show opportunities for adopting new measures and rewards that will be successful. Reputable consultants also have a wealth of knowledge about the determinants of successful incentive plans their clients use and might be able to predict how different features are likely to work with or against each other to affect financial performance in your situation. Many organizations treat new incentive plans, such as new products or services and test them on subunits as prototypes for the rest of the organizations. That way, management can learn how the measures and rewards work, what trade-offs they require, and how they affect financial performance without risking mistakes that affect the whole organization.

Solutions to You're the Decision Maker

21.1 Return on Investment and Economic Value Added, p. 887

a. Computations of earnings and invested capital used for performance evaluation need not correspond to the figures reported under GAAP. Many organizations modify these figures to better measure relevant performance and align managers' actions with desired behavior. The specific adjustments made in this example appear to reflect a desire to measure performance in a way that eliminates disincentives to perform R&D by eliminating it from earnings. The earnings measure is taken after tax, perhaps to remind managers that the company has tax liabilities that reduce the ability of the company to make payouts to owners and managers. Eliminating interest expense from earnings used in economic value added reflects the fact that the performance measure will levy an interest charge as part of the cost of capital. This avoids double-counting interest on debt. The exclusion of current liabilities from the measurement of invested capital gives an incentive to manage working capital (current assets — current liabilities) to the company's advantage (e.g., let suppliers finance as much of the business unit's current assets as possible.)

b. Return on investment and economic value added for the business unit follow:

Microsoft Excel - VCB.xls

File Edit View Insert Format Tools Data Window Help

D19 = =D13-D18

	A	B	C	D
1	**Computations of Return on investment and Economic value added**			
2	**Income before tax**	**$ 500,000**	**Total assets**	**5,500,000**
3	**Interest expense**	**90,000**	**Current liabilities**	**500,000**
4	**R&D expense**	**150,000**	**Effective tax rate**	**40%**
5			**Weighted average cost of capital**	**10%**
6	**Return on Investment**		**Economic Value Added**	
7	Calculation of income		Calculation of income	
8	Income before tax (B2)	$ 500,000	Income before tax (B2)	$ 500,000
9	Plus: Interest expense (B3)	90,000	Plus: Interest expense (B3)	90,000
10	Plus: R&D expense (B4)	150,000	Plus: R&D expense (B4)	150,000
11	Income before tax & R&D	740,000	Income before tax, interest, R&D	740,000
12	Tax (D4*B11)	296,000	Tax (D4*D11)	296,000
13	Revised income after tax	$ 444,000	Revised income after tax	$ 444,000
14	Invested capital		Cost of invested capital	
15	Total assets (D2)	5,500,000	Total assets (D2)	5,500,000
16	Less: current liabilities (D3)	500,000	Less: Current liabilities (D3)	500,000
17	Invested capital	5,000,000	Invested capital	5,000,000
18			Cost of invested capital (D5*D17)	500,000
19	**Return on investment (B13/B17)**	**8.9%**	**Economic value added (D13-D18)**	**$ (56,000)**
20				

Exhbit 21-4 / Exhibit 21-5 / Exhibit 21-6 / YTDM 21.1

Ready NUM

$$\begin{aligned}\text{Income before tax, interest, and R\&D} &= \text{Income before tax} + \text{Interest expense} + \text{R\&D expense}\\ &= \$500{,}000 + 90{,}000 + 150{,}000 = \$740{,}000\\ \text{Revised income after tax} &= \$740{,}000 \times (1 - .40) = \$444{,}000\\ \text{Invested capital} &= \text{Total assets} - \text{current liabilities}\\ &= \$5{,}500{,}000 - 500{,}000 = \$5{,}000{,}000\\ \text{Return on investment} &= \$444{,}000 \div \$5{,}000{,}000 = \underline{\underline{8.9\%}}\\ \text{Economic value added} &= \$444{,}000 - .10 \times \$5{,}000{,}000 = \underline{\underline{\$(56{,}000)}}\end{aligned}$$

c. These figures show that the business unit is profitable (ROI = 8.9 percent) but not sufficiently so to cover the cost of invested capital [economic value added = $(56,000)]. Comparing the business unit's 8.9 percent ROI to the cost of capital (10 percent) tells much the same story, but the negative economic value added tells the shortfall in dollar terms. This shortfall of $56,000 can be interpreted as the profit or revenue enhancement target or the cost-reduction target necessary for the business unit at least to breakeven in economic terms.

21.2 Integrating the Balanced Scorecard and Incentive Plans, p. 889

a. If these performance measures are important to VCB's success, employees should take actions to improve each of them and the measures should be in the scorecard. The issue is whether they will do that without explicit incentives attached to each measure? Perhaps, if employees believe the story that the balanced scorecard tells, as discussed in Chapter 20, they will manage their activities to improve the measures with or without explicit incentives. However, VCB can increase the expectancy associated with each measure by attaching rewards.

b. Performance on each measure should have rewards. It does seem likely that no one person or management level should be evaluated on all of the measures, however. That can lead to information overload. A more reasonable approach is to assign responsibility and incentives for the various measures to persons who can best affect or control outcomes. Some organizations also assign incentives to managers at higher levels to reinforce the goal to ensure that subordinates are working to improve the measures they directly control. The nature of the incentive system (measures and rewards) will differ according to the organization. The bank appears progressive and wants to instill an entrepreneurial attitude in its employees. It might want to make a large percentage of employee compensation contingent on appropriate measures of performance. The bank also can consider other options discussed in this chapter.

c. Without explicit incentives, the bank must be sure that employees understand how performance on these measures affects the bank's financial performance and that rewards and penalties will result from successful financial performance. Removing rewards one or more levels of activity away from individuals' actions can reduce their effectiveness, however. As a result, the success story told by the balanced scorecard measures must be repeated again and again until it is part of the organization's culture. In some organizations this can be as effective as explicit incentives. However, organizational culture is difficult to change, so an organization might find it difficult to revise the story of success if needed.

21.3 Designing Incentive Compensation Plans, p. 894

a. There does appear to be a problem with the incentive system. The bank seems to have convinced these employees that the balanced scorecard measures are appropriate for their activities. This is an important step in instituting any performance-measurement system. The bank appears not to do well, however, in linking rewards to performance at all levels. Executives can be motivated by overall bank performance and the attendant bonus and stock awards, but lower-level employees do not have the same reward system or motivation; the expectancy chain is broken at the link between performance and reward. This can create a problem causing lower-level employees to seek their own rewards in ways that are detrimental to the bank. For example, they might spend excessive time on personal business or surfing the Web when they should be working to improve their knowledge, internal processes, or customer satisfaction. They might understand that their actions are detrimental, but they also might believe that out of a sense of fairness they have a right to steal time and effort from the bank. As long as they do not shirk so much that they get fired, their salaries and annual raises appear to be secure.

You might recommend setting up an incentive plan that provides bonuses for performance on each of the balanced scorecard measures for lower-level employees who can affect those measures (if appropriate). The bonuses can be cash, prizes, or stock (depending on the management level of the individual and the interests of the particular employees). Lower-level employees might be more motivated by prizes; branch and department managers might be more motivated by cash and stock. The bank should include incentives to focus on the future, especially for managers, so at least some of the rewards should be deferred and based on future performance. Performance should be measured combining individual and organizational performance so employees see the payoff of their own individual actions as well as take actions that benefit the organization as a whole.

Review Questions

21.1 Review and define each of the chapter's key terms.

21.2 Why is "pay for performance" the basic idea behind incentive compensation plans?

21.3 What are the key elements of an incentive compensation plan?

21.4 Explain how an incentive systems' design might create disincentives to desired behavior.

21.5 What is the starting point in designing an effective incentive compensation plan?

21.6 What are the two ingredients of a successful incentive system according to expectancy theory?

21.7 Explain how the expectancy chain can be broken, which reduces the effectiveness of an incentive system.

21.8 What is an intrinsic reward? How is an intrinsic reward different than an extrinsic reward? Are both necessary?

21.9 What are the roles of an incentive system according to agency theory?

21.10 According to agency theory, what is the best incentive system?

21.11 Expectancy theory deals with the motivation of individuals; agency theory deals with the relationship between superiors and subordinates. Is this statement true or false? Explain.

21.12 Give an example of the way an individual can have both principal and agent roles in a job.

21.13 What are the six choices involved in designing a performance-based incentive plan?

21.14 Contrast absolute and relative performance evaluations.

21.15 What are the advantages and disadvantages of formula-based versus subjective performance evaluations?

21.16 What is the possible relation between the balanced scorecard and the use of financial and non-financial measures of performance?

21.17 What are the advantages and disadvantages of narrowly defining performance for evaluations? Of broadly defining performance?

21.18 What are the advantages and disadvantages of making all rewards immediate and of deferring them?

21.19 What are the incentive effects of salary, cash bonus, stock, and stock options?

21.20 Nonprofit organizations generally do not have net income or return on investment targets. Are financial incentives irrelevant to the management of these organizations?

21.21 What are the advantages and disadvantages of using financial performance measures in an incentive system for a nonprofit organization?

Critical Analysis

21.22 A consulting firm interviews only undergraduate students who are accounting majors and whose grade-point average exceeds 3.5 on a 4.0 scale. Partners in the firm complain that the firm is not hiring people with diverse interests—physics, music, art history—that help the firm to relate to a variety of clients, many of whom have science or humanities backgrounds. Does the firm's hiring policy have anything to do with creating this situation?

21.23 College Town has two competing bookstores; Avid Reader is a local bookstore, and Barnum and Mobile is part of a national chain. Avid Reader rewards its employees by giving them a small bonus at the end of each month based on the bookstore's total revenues. Barnum and Mobile also rewards its employees by giving them a small bonus at the end of each month, but its bonus is based on the store's operating income. Why might the two bookstores have different bonus plans? Is the manager of one of the bookstores mistaken about the appropriate basis for incentives?

21.24 The manager of an organization is having trouble getting employees to perform adequate work for the organization's benefit. "I pay them a good salary," says the manager, "and I give them big pay increases when I feel generous. I just can't figure out why they won't work harder. Maybe it's this generation of people. You know, when I was a young worker. . . ." At this point, your brain shuts down. Using the principles of expectancy and agency theories, explain why the employees might not be working as desired.

21.25 How can different parameters of a formula-based incentive plan create different incentives and lead to different levels of effort and different decisions? Use an example to illustrate.

21.26 Shauna Dormino is taking a job in a nonprofit organization, Freedom from Hunger. Anisa Morenez is taking a job at IBM. The women are equally qualified, each will do the same type of work, and each will put in the same number of hours each week, yet Dormino's job pays $10,000 less than Morenez's job, has fewer benefits, and offers less opportunity for advancement. Why might Dormino take such a job?

21.27 Give two examples of principal-agent relationships that you have experienced or observed. Identify who the principal and the agent in each relationship. What brought them together?

21.28 Most students fill out instructor evaluation forms at the end of a course. What role does this information play in the context of agency theory? What role does it play in the context of expectancy theory?

21.29 Why are financial performance measures by themselves insufficient to provide incentives for financial success?

21.30 The president of a large company says, "I want my managers to focus on their own responsibility centers. If they take care of their responsibility centers, the overall business will take care of itself." Evaluate and comment on the president's statement.

21.31 You are offered the CEO position of a small high-technology company. The salary is considerably lower than your current salary, but after one year, you will be eligible for many stock options. Your only performance measure will be the company's stock price. What are the advantages and disadvantages of this incentive plan to you and to the company?

21.32 You are offered the general manager position of a large, mostly autonomous division of a very large company. The company is market driven and has 20 similar divisions in different industries. The division you are offered has performed poorly in the past, but it is in an industry with high profit potential. Describe elements of an incentive plan that induces you to take this job and that the company might accept.

21.33 You are the chair of the board of directors of a large regional charitable organization that has been recognized nationally for outstanding public service. It has just lost its CEO to a profit-seeking firm poised for its initial public offering of shares. You must convene the board to recruit a new CEO and are concerned about attracting, motivating, and retaining a highly competent executive. What major factors should you consider when designing an incentive plan for this executive?

21.34 What are the major barriers to instituting performance-based incentive plans in governmental agencies? What are the potential benefits and costs of using these plans in government agencies?

Exercises

Exercise 21.35
Performance Evaluation
(LO 2)

The managers of Biogenetics, a company that clones various living things, have provided you the following information about its new division:

- Operating income before tax equals $2,000,000 for the year.
- The tax rate equals 30 percent.
- The appropriate weighted-average cost of capital equals 15 percent.
- The total assets equal $9,000,000.
- The current liabilities equal $1,000,000.

Required

a. Compute the return on investment and economic value added based on operating income after tax and total assets less current liabilities. Did this company meet its performance objectives?

b. Is it a good idea for Biogenetics to make an additional investment of $1,000,000, which adds $100,000 to current liabilities and increases before-tax operating income by $200,000?

Exercise 21.36
Performance Evaluation
(LO 2)

The managers of Fieflish, a company that makes fishing equipment, have provided you the following information about the fly division:

- Operating income before tax equals $500,000 for the year.
- The tax rate equals 40 percent.
- The appropriate weighted-average cost of capital equals 12 percent.
- The total assets equal $1,300,000.
- The current liabilities equal $100,000.

Required

a. Compute the return on investment and economic value added based on operating income after tax and total assets less current liabilities. Did this company meet its performance objectives?

b. Is it a good idea for Fieflish to eliminate $200,000 of assets and decrease before-tax operating income by $50,000? Everything else is the same as before.

Exercise 21.37
Performance Evaluation
(LO 2)
Spreadsheet

The managers of Liu Ltd. have provided the following information about a division:

- Operating income before tax equals $10,000,000 for the year.
- The tax rate equals 10 percent.
- The appropriate weighted-average cost of capital equals 10 percent.
- The total assets equal $85,000,000.
- The current liabilities equal $5,000,000.

Required

a. Compute the return on investment and economic value added based on operating income after tax and total assets less current liabilities. Did this company meet its performance objectives?

b. Is it a good idea for Liu Ltd., make an additional $10,000,000 investment, which adds $500,000 to current liabilities and increases before-tax operating income by $1,000,000?

Exercise 21.38
Evaluation of Incentive Plans
(LO 3)

International Electronics, Inc. (IEI), a large, multidivision maker of industrial and consumer electrical products is organized into various division investment centers. The company rewards each division manager with a bonus based on the division's operating income and return on investment.

Communication

Each division has its own controller, who reports directly to the central corporate controller. Central corporate management wants division controllers to be responsible primarily to it and to be independent of division managers. Despite this organizational design, the controllers' bonus depends on the same formula as that used to evaluate division managers; it uses division operating income and division return on investment.

Required

Write a brief report to central corporate management of this company that explains potential conflicting incentives the division controllers face.

Exercise 21.39
Motivation and Behavior
(LO 1)

Communication Team

Wannabe University (WU) is a medium-size public university with 15,000 students and 1,000 faculty members. The university built its national reputation on the excellence of its teaching and interactions with undergraduate students. Because government support of the university has dropped dramatically, the administration has decided that it must now build the university's reputation on research, which will require obtaining research grants to replace the lost government funding. The university proposes to reward each faculty member with a salary increase that is primarily based on the annual number of articles they publish in high-quality journals.

Most faculty members and students were attracted to WU because of its focus on teaching and faculty/student interaction.

Required

In a small group, prepare a brief report or visual presentation to WU's central administration that explains the advantages and disadvantages of its incentive plan proposal.

Exercise 20.40
Motivation and Behavior
(LO 1)

Communication Team

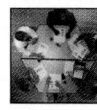

Magnum Aerospace rewards its key executives exclusively on return on investment (ROI). The vice president of administration suggests to the CEO that Magnum can increase its ROI by outsourcing most of its support and operating activities to business partners and suppliers, thereby greatly reducing its asset base. The CFO/treasurer cautions that although this would reduce the company's asset base, such extensive outsourcing would reduce the company's earnings, cash flow, and flexibility. The vice president of marketing also warns that the company might outsource its competitive advantage as well.

Required

In a small group, prepare a brief report or visual presentation to Magnum Aerospace's CEO that evaluates the impact of the company's incentive plan on the recommendation to outsource most activities. What trade-offs should the company's executives consider?

Exercise 21.41
Motivation and Behavior
(LO 1, 3)

Communication

Fundamental Supply, Inc. (FSI), is a large international supplier of office products to businesses, charitable organizations, and government agencies. The company is organized into business units by customer type, and business units obtain products from centrally located regional supply centers. The company rewards each division manager with a bonus based on the division's revenue growth (50 percent) and return on investment (50 percent).

Required

Write a brief report to the central corporate management of this company to explain potential problems that its incentive plan has for business-unit managers.

Problems

Problem 21.42
Alternative Incentive Formula Parameters
(LO 1,3)

Valley Commercial Bank wants to reward its branch bank managers for exceeding revenue growth targets and is considering two alternative incentive formulas that award bonuses as a percentage of salary for each percentage point that actual revenue growth exceeds the target as follows.

Formula Parameter	Alternative 1	Alternative 2
Revenue growth target	5 percent	10 percent
Bonus percentage	4 percentage points	8 percentage points

Required

a. Compute and then contrast the bonus earned by a branch bank manager with an average salary of $50,000 per year and branch revenue growth of 8 percent with each of the four combinations of formula parameters.

b. What are the motivational advantages and disadvantages of each of the four incentive formulas?

c. What are the advantages and disadvantages of the incentive formula approach to motivating revenue growth?

Problem 21.43
Alternative Incentive Formula Parameters
(LO 1, 3)

PMI wants to reward its operations managers for reducing the number of defects below target rates. It is considering two alternative incentive formulas that award bonuses as a percentage of salary for each percentage point that actual defect rates are under the target as follows.

Formula Parameter	Alternative 1	Alternative 2
Defect rate target	1 percent	4 percent
Bonus percentage	5 percentage points	8 percentage points

Required

a. Compute and contrast the bonus earned by a branch bank manager with an average salary of $70,000 per year and a defect rate of 2 percent with each of the four combinations of formula parameters.

b. What are the motivational advantages and disadvantages of each of the four incentive formulas?

c. What are the advantages and disadvantages of the incentive formula approach to motivating reduction of defects?

Problem 21.44
Evaluation Performance
(LO 2)

Valley Commercial Bank has a criterion to loan only to companies that have an economic value added greater than zero for the past year and for the past three years, on average. Answer the following questions.

a. The bank is considering loaning money to a small company that has the following economic characteristics. Does this company meet the bank's criterion for a positive economic value added?
   - Average operating income before tax for the last three years equals $2,000,000 per year.
   - The tax rate equals 35 percent for all three years.
   - The appropriate weighted-average cost of capital equals 15 percent, which is applicable to all three years.
   - The average total assets over the past three years equal $7,000,000.
   - The average current liabilities over the past three years equal $1,000,000.

b. You work as a loan officer for VCB. A prospective borrower who just graduated from college has come to you for advice. Because her father had been seriously injured in an automobile accident, she is now running the family business, which is a small winery. She wants to borrow money from VCB to buy some wine-processing equipment that will make the company more efficient. The winery had been profitable in the past, but at this point, its economic value added, according to VCB's calculations, is $(100,000) for a company that has revenue of $6,000,000 and total assets of $5,000,000. Ordinarily, the bank will not loan her the money to buy the new equipment. What do you advise?

Problem 21.45
Effects of Incentives
(LO 2, 3)

Spreadsheet

The following pertains to the current year. On January 1, you were appointed manager of a new operating division of Olympics, Inc., a manufacturer of products using the latest microprocessor technology. Also on January 1, your division had $1,500,000 assets, all in cash. On January 2, you invested $900,000 of the cash in equipment. On January 3, your expected income items for this year were as follows:

Sales revenue	$1,200,000
Operating costs	
Cash costs	
Unit level	400,000
Batch level	200,000
Product level	100,000
Facility level	100,000
Depreciation on new equipment	300,000
Other information	
Tax rate	40%
After-tax cost of capital used for EVA computations	12%
Current liabilities	0

On January 4, a sales representative from Interesting Biostatic Machines (IBM) approached you, offering to sell you a machine that offers significant improvements over the equipment you bought on January 2. The machine can expand department sales revenue and unit-level costs by 50 percent while reducing cash facility costs by 10 percent. The purchase would affect no batch-level or product-level costs.

The new machine costs $1,200,000 and will be depreciated for accounting purposes over a three-year life, with no salvage value at the end of the third year. It has a positive net present value. If you purchase it, it must be installed immediately so that one year of depreciation can be expensed this year.

The machine purchased on January 2 has dropped in value to $800,000. It must be disposed of to make room for the new machine. Financial staff at corporate headquarters informs you that you will not be charged any depreciation on the old machine if you sell it now, but you will be charged the $100,000 loss as an expense in your EVA computations.

Required

a. What is your division's estimated residual income (economic value added) if it does *not* acquire the new IBM machine?

b. What is your division's residual income this year if it does acquire the new IBM machine?

c. Is the use of residual income giving you, as a division manager, incentives to make decisions that are in the best interest of the company?

Problem 21.46
EVA Evaluations
(LO 2)

Communication

Yonkers Consulting Group (YCG) purchased the law firm of Max R. Prophet, LLP two years ago. Prior to the acquisition, Prophet did legal work for a variety of clients. Since becoming a division of YCG, it now does legal work only for YCG and YCG' s consulting clients.

YCG's management gives Prophet division management little latitude in running the division's operations and retains authority for choosing clients and jobs, pricing, investing in the division's assets, hiring legal staff, and determining salaries paid to legal staff.

When YCG purchased Max R. Prophet, LLP, its analysts performed an EVA calculation and computed the EVA to be $200,000. YCG management is concerned that Prophet's EVA has deteriorated and wonders if it should find somebody other than Max Prophet to manage the firm.

Yonkers Consulting Group
Prophet Division
Income Analysis
For the Year Ended December 31

Sales revenue	$4,000,000
Costs and expenses	3,800,000
Total assets, net of current liabilities	$1,000,000
After-tax cost of capital to be used for EVA	15%
Tax rate	40%

Required

a. Using the preceding income information, calculate the Prophet division's EVA.

b. Write a report to YCG management indicating whether EVA is the appropriate performance measure for the Prophet division. If you recommend against using EVA, what do you recommend as a replacement? Give reasons for all of your recommendations.

[CMA adapted]

Problem 21.47
Effects of Incentives
(LO 3)

Communication

Division managers of Atlantis, Ltd., have expressed dissatisfaction with the company's division performance measurement system. Division operations are evaluated every quarter by comparing their EVA with the expected EVA identified in the prior year. Division managers claim that many factors are completely out of their control but are included in this comparison, which they say results in an unfair and misleading performance evaluation.

Pressure by top management to reflect increased earnings has often caused division managers to overstate operating income before taxes. In addition, once the EVA target has been set, divisions must live with it; no adjustments for unforeseen events are possible. Frequently, external factors (the economy, competitors' actions, and changes in consumer tastes) have not been recognized in the EVA targets that top management supplied to the divisions.

Recognizing these problems, top management agreed to review its procedures. Based on this review, it proposed to change its procedures so division managers have the opportunity to show how they deal with unforeseen events. Top management also agreed to use relative performance evaluation by comparing each division's performance to the performance of other divisions in the same industry and to the performance of outside companies in the same industry.

Required

Write a report to Atlantis top management that explains whether the proposed changes are an improvement over the evaluation of division performance that it now uses. Be sure to address how the company proposes to implement relative performance evaluation.

[CMA adapted]

Problem 21.48
Motivation and Incentives
(LO 1, 3)

Communication Internet

Many critics of business executives complain that they focus on short-term financial results at the expense of investing in the long-term success of their companies. Executives themselves comment that they are constantly pressured to meet annual or even quarterly earnings targets. One executive said, "If I don't perform well in the short term, I won't be around in the long term." The critics argue that focusing on the short term means that companies do not invest in research and development or new technology, things that might have a negative short-term impact on earnings but might benefit the company in the long run. For purposes of answering these questions, assume that the short term is one year or less, the middle term is one to five years, and the long term is more than five years.

Required

Prepare a written report that addresses the following:

a. Why might a high-tech company focus on the short term? Why might it focus on the long term?

b. Why might an apparel company focus on the short term? Why might it focus on the long term?

c. Based on library and/or Internet research, indicate whether the following organizations appear to be focusing on the short, middle, or the long term?

Toys R'Us (toys)

Cisco (Internet hardware and software)

United Way (charitable nonprofit)

d. Give examples of decisions that you would want the top executives in each of the three organizations in requirement (c) to make if they were to focus on the organization's long-term success.

e. What is your recommendation for the design of an incentive plan that helps the top executives in requirement (c) to make the decisions that you gave in (d)?

Problem 21.49
Motivation and Incentives
(LO 1, 3)

Leslie Fay, the dressmaker, had a compensation plan that offered the chief operating officer and the chief financial officer bonuses if the company's net income reached $16 million (approximately 2 percent of sales). The company reported a net income of $23 million, and the two executives received bonuses. However, much of the net income was fraudulent, resulting from recording sales that had not occurred. The fraud occurred away from corporate headquarters in New York at the company's Wilkes-Barre, Pennsylvania, office where the company's finances were handled. Leslie Fay's chief financial officer set up an autocratic rule in Wilkes-Barre. The chairman and chief executive officer of the company, who was paid $3.6 million, mostly in the form of a bonus, said he was bewildered by the accounting scandal.

Required

a. What effect might the bonus plan for the chief operating officer and chief financial officer have had on the fraud, if any?

b. How might the location of financial operations in Wilkes-Barre, Pennsylvania, instead of at corporate headquarters in New York have made it easier for someone to commit fraud?

[Adapted from "Loose Threads: Dressmaker Leslie Fay Is an Old-Style Firm That's in a Modern Fix,"] *The Wall Street Journal,* February 23, 1993: A1, A20.

Problem 21.50
Alternative Incentives
(LO 3)

Communication Internet

Perform an Internet search to investigate the goals, objectives, and incentive systems used by

Patagonia

CitySoft

Working Assets

Pride Industries

Write a short report that list the organizational goals, objectives, and any disclosed information on incentive systems for each.

Problem 21.51
Motivation and Incentives
(LO 1, 3)

Obtain a copy of the article, "Accounting Sleuths," *Strategic Finance,* October 2000, pp. 55–64. Prepare a short report that discusses the linkage between executive compensation plans and financial fraud.

Problem 21.52
Motivation and Incentives
(LO 1, 3)

Obtain a copy of the articles, "Blind Ambition," *Business Week,* October 23, 1995, and "Judgment Day at Bausch & Lomb," *Business Week,* December 25, 1995. Write a short report that outlines allegations of financial fraud caused by financial performance pressures at Bausch & Lomb, Inc.[28]

Problem 21.53
Alternative Incentives
(LO 3)

Review Polaroid's Environmental Report, particularly section 2 (*www.polaroid.com/polinfo/environment/*). Identify and critique the incentive system that Polaroid reports that it uses to motivate improved environmental performance.[29]

Problem 21.54
Motivation and Incentives
(LO 1, 3)

M. Payne reports that employee theft costs US businesses billions of dollars per year and is growing at 2 percent per year.[30] Obtain a copy of the article "Are You Teaching Your Employees to Steal?" *Strategic Finance,* August 2000, pp. 34–39. Prepare a short report that identifies common organizational practices that often lead to employee theft.

Problem 21.55
Alternative Incentive Formula Parameters
(LO 1, 3)

Communication

Nantucket Market wants to reward revenue growth by paying its 50 store managers a bonus based on an explicit formula: For each percentage point by which revenue growth exceeds target growth, the manager receives a bonus of 1 percent of his or her base salary. Nantucket Market's corporate annual revenue growth target is 30 percent, but half of that is expected from acquiring or opening new stores. Store managers' salaries average $40,000 per year but range from $30,000 to $60,000. In the prior year, existing stores' revenue growth averaged 12 percent but ranged from −2 percent to +18 percent.

Required

a. At the average store manager salary and average store revenue growth levels, what is the expected individual and total bonus earned with a 10 percent growth target and a 6 percent bonus percentage?

b. If Nantucket Market's average gross margin percentage is 20 percent, by how much must corporate sales increase to at least pay for the revenue growth bonus incentive computed in requirement (a)?

c. Compute the individual and total bonus earned and required revenue increase for each of the 16 combinations of incentive formula parameters: 10 or 15 percent growth targets, 12 or 18 percent actual store growth, 2 or 6 percent bonus, and $30,000 or $60,000 salary. Note that the number of possible parameters and combinations is nearly unlimited. (*Hint:* Use a spreadsheet to compute these bonuses.)

d. Make a recommendation to Nantucket Market about how to design its revenue growth incentive formula. How should the company create incentives for managers whose stores do not qualify for the revenue growth bonus?

Problem 21.56
Alternative Incentive Formula Parameters
(LO 1, 3)

Communication

Contaminant Measuring Devices (CMD) wants to reward on-time deliveries to customers by paying its 10 department managers a bonus based on an explicit formula: For each percentage point by which on-time deliveries exceed the target, the manager receives a bonus of 1 percent of his or her base salary. CMD's corporate annual on-time delivery target is 85 percent. Store managers' salaries average $60,000 per year but range from $50,000 to $80,000. In the prior year, the company's on-time delivery rate averaged 90 percent but ranged from 75 percent to 98 percent across departments.

Required

a. At the average store manager salary and average department on-time delivery rate, what is the expected individual and total bonus earned with a 85 percent on-time delivery rate target and a 10 percent bonus percentage?

---

[28]Bausch & Lomb's troubles also are the focus of Harvard Business School case 9-198-009.

[29]A history of Polaroid's polluting activities and management initiatives can be found in Harvard Business School case 9-194-052.

[30]M. Payne, "Employee Theft a Rising Concern," *Sacramento Bee,* December 3, 2000.

b. CMD's average gross margin percentage is 65 percent. If a 1 percent annual increase in on-time deliveries is expected to increase revenues by $100,000, by how much must the corporate on-time delivery rate increase to at least pay for the on-time delivery rate bonus incentive computed in requirement (a)?

c. Compute the individual and total bonus earned and required on-time delivery rate increase for each of the 16 combinations of incentive formula parameters: 85 or 95 percent on-time delivery rate targets, 92 or 98 percent actual on-time deliveries, 5 or 10 percent bonus, and $50,000 or $80,000 salary. Note that the number of possible parameters and combinations is nearly unlimited. (*Hint:* Use a spreadsheet to compute these bonuses.)

d. Make a recommendation to CMD about how to design its on-time delivery rate incentive formula. Include in your recommendation how the company should create incentives for managers whose stores do not qualify for the revenue growth bonus. Approximately 3 percent of late deliveries have been attributed to failures by the delivery company used by CMD.

Cases

Case 21.57
Design of Incentive Systems
(LO 1, 2, 3)

In a small group, conduct an Internet search to find a company that discloses its incentive formula for top executives in its proxy statement. Prepare a visual presentation that describes, explains, and critiques this company's incentive formula.

Case 21.58
Performance Evaluation
(LO 2)

Communication

Team

Establishing the relationship between customer satisfaction and companies' financial performance is important to including customer satisfaction in an incentive plan. In a small group, select an organization to study and determine how to answer this question: Is there a reliable relationship between customer satisfaction and company profitability that can support an incentive system?

Required

Write a report that describes the organization that you want to study, the study you want to conduct, and the criteria you want to apply to answer the question.

Case 21.59
Design of Nonprofit Incentive System
(LO 1, 2, 3)

In a group, select a specific nonprofit organization for study. For each of the four balanced scorecard perspectives, identify two or three performance measures that appear to be appropriate for that organization. Write a report that states specifically how to measure performance and link rewards to it. If possible, you might find it useful to investigate the organization's homepage or interview a manager in the organization that you pick.

Case 21.60
Executive Compensation
(LO 3)

Internet

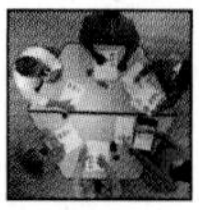
Team

Communication

Top executives of US companies receive 10s of millions of dollars per year in compensation. Many observers think their pay is too high. Some observers point out that US executives receive extraordinary compensation regardless of the performance of their company. Others also observe that US executives are paid much more than their counterparts in other countries.

Required

In a small group, prepare a visual presentation that addresses the following:

a. Research the library and/or the Internet to obtain information about the determinants and levels of top executive pay for a *pair* of US and foreign companies in each of two industries (e.g., oil and gas, telecommunication).

b. Does it appear that US companies pay more than their foreign counterparts? Do the US companies perform better than their foreign counterparts?

c. In general, have the companies that paid more performed better?

Case 21.61
Motivation and Incentives
(LO 1, 3)

Communication

Ethics

Advocates for workers and critics of business argue that executives should not receive pay increases when employees do not. According to a labor union official, "I don't know what's fair, but they (executives) shouldn't be making 200 times more than their average employee." This official continued to state that 20 years ago, the average CEO pay was 42 times more than that of lowest-paid worker but now it is more than 200 times more. In contrast, executive pay in Europe and Japan is about 50 times more than that of the lowest paid worker.

The union official went on to say, "It's unthinkable that workers at the bottom of the ladder have either stagnant wages or are being laid off while executives receive exorbitant salaries."

Required

Work in groups, fulfill these requirements.

a. Discuss the ethical and political issues involved in giving executives large pay increases (for example 30 percent increases) during a period of layoffs and stagnant wages for workers.

b. Prepare a short report to a government representative that indicates whether companies should be allowed a tax deduction for executive salaries. If so, if you believe they should, do you believe that the deduction for the salary be capped at some amount (for example, 50 times the lowest full-time worker's pay)?

[Adapted from statement by Bob Carson, executive secretary of the Hawkeye (Iowa) Labor Council, www.gazetteonline.com/money/mon207.htm]

Case 21.62
Motivation and Incentives
(LO 1, 3)

Ethics

Global

Ben and Jerry's Homemade, Inc., is a US company with a long history of charitable giving, reliance on local suppliers, and support of activist causes. Its products include ice cream flavors such as Rainforest Crunch, made with natural rainforest ingredients, and Cherry Garcia, in honor of the late leader of the Grateful Dead. As the company grew, the founders, Ben and Jerry, found it difficult to manage in the "laid-back" style of the company's early years.

a. Ben and Jerry, the company's largest stockholders, admitted that the company had grown too large for their style and attempted to hire a proven chief executive officer for pay that was seven times the amount paid to the lowest paid worker (plus unlimited ice cream). Do you think a competitive company can be successful in hiring a proven CEO for seven times the pay of its lowest paid worker? Why or why not?

b. Under pressure from stockholders, Ben and Jerry recently sold the company to the giant European food company, Unilever, with the agreement that it will support the company's activist goals and stress their importance. Ben recently complained that the company's name was being transformed into just another "soulless, heartless, spiritless brand." Do you think it is possible to operate a laid-back, activist company in a competitive market? What trade-offs are involved? What incentives are necessary to succeed in maintaining an activist agenda?

[Adapted from G. Smith, "Life Won't Be Just a Bowl of Jerry Garcia"; and "A Famous Brand on a Rocky Road."]

Case 21.63
Performance Manipulation
(LO)

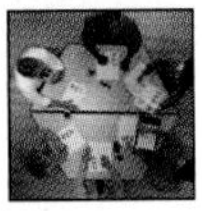

Team

Ethics

A report on "income transferal" activities at the H. J. Heinz Company stated that decentralized authority was the central principle of the company's operations, that the company expected its divisions to generate an annual growth in profits of approximately 10 to 12 percent per year, and that third, it was not unusual or undesirable for management to put pressure on the division managers and employees to produce improved results.

The report also noted that pressuring the divisions to produce improved results coupled with the company's philosophy of autonomy, which it extended to financial and accounting controls, provided both an incentive and an opportunity for division managers to misstate financial results. The report stated, "The autonomous nature of the [divisions] combined with the relatively small World Headquarters financial staff permitted the conception of what at best can be described as a communications gap. . . . In its simplest form, there seems to have been a tendency to issue an order or set a standard with respect to achieving a financial result without regard to whether complete attainment was possible." It continued, "In the managements of certain of the [divisions], there was a feeling of 'us versus them' towards World Headquarters."[30]

The report indicated an effort in certain divisions to transfer income from one fiscal period to another to provide a "financial cushion" for achieving the goal for the succeeding year. For example, divisions might overpay expenses to get a credit or refund in a subsequent year, or they might pay an expense such as insurance or advertising early, but instead of charging the amount to a prepaid expense account, they might charge it to expense. In good years, this practice keeps profits down and provides a cushion to meet the company headquarters' requirement that divisions constantly increase their profits.

---

[30]"Report of the Audit Committee to the Board of Directors, Income Transferal and Other Practices," H. J. Heinz Company, p. 9.

Required

In a small group, complete the following requirements.

a. Comment on how the communications gap and the "us-versus-them" attitude contributed to the fraud.

b. Refer to requirement (a). Have you seen communications gaps in organizations that have resulted in an this attitude on the part of employees? If so, briefly describe the circumstances and the cause of this attitude. Discuss in your example what might have been or could be done to change it.

Glossary

A

ABC full costing assigns as many costs to products as possible

ABC unit costing assigns only the costs of unit-level resources to products

abnormal spoilage is due to reasons other than the usual course of operations of a process

absolute performance evaluation compares individual performance to set standards or expectations

absorption or **full costing** applies all manufacturing-overhead costs to (or absorbs) manufactured goods

account analysis is the cost-estimation method based on the past costs associated with each cost driver

accuracy is precision in measurement

activity refers to a description of the organization's use of resources

activity-based budgeting (ABB) is the process of developing a master budget using information obtained from an activity-based (ABC) analysis

activity-based costing (ABC) is a costing method that first assigns costs to activities and then to goods and services based on how much each good or service uses the activities

activity-based flexible budget is based on several cost drivers rather than a single, volume-based cost driver

activity-based management (ABM) is used by management to evaluate the costs and values of process activities to identify opportunities for improved efficiency

activity-based responsibility accounting is a system for measuring the performance of an organization's employees and subunits, which focuses not only on the cost of performing activities but on the activities themselves

activity dictionary lists activities performed by an organization to produce its products

actual costing assigns only actual costs of both direct and indirect resources (i.e., direct materials, direct labor, and manufacturing overhead) to products

actual overhead is the amount of manufacturing overhead actually incurred during an accounting period

administrative costs are incurred to manage the organization and provide staff support

agency costs are the sum of opportunity costs of misbehavior and out-of-pocket costs for incentives and monitoring performance

agency theory is an economic theory of incentives and behavior based on the relationship between a principal who offers an incentive plan and an agent who accepts the plan to work on behalf of the principal

applied overhead calculated by multiplying the predetermined overhead rate by the actual amount of the cost driver, is the amount of manufacturing overhead assigned to Work-in-Process Inventory as a product cost

appraisal activities (also called *detection* or *inspection activities*) inspect inputs and attributes of individual units of product or service to detect whether they conform to specifications or customer expectations

attributes of a product or service are its tangible and intangible features

average cycle time equals total processing time for all units divided by good units produced

B

backflush costing is a simplified cost-accounting system in which all manufacturing costs are charged directly to Cost of Goods Sold, and then end-of-period adjustments are made to credit Cost of Goods Sold and debit the respective inventory accounts

balanced scorecard is a strategy formulation and communication device and a causal model of lead and lag indicators of performance

bar-coding systems create a unique bar code for each order and allow companies to mark and track all orders electronically

base budgeting the initial budget for each organizational department, is set in accordance with a base package, which includes the minimal resources required for the subunit to exist at an absolute minimal level

base package includes the minimal resources required for the subunit to exist at an absolute minimal level

batch-level costs are incurred for every batch of product or service produced

batch-level resources and activities are acquired and performed to make a group, or batch, of similar products

behavioral congruence occurs when an individual behaves in the best interests of the organization regardless of his or her own goals

benchmarking is a technique for determining an organization's competitive advantage by learning about its own products, services, and operations and comparing them against the best performers

benchmarks are important competitive features that form the bases of comparison and exist either inside or outside one's own organization, or in other industries

bottleneck is the *constraint* or constraining factor limiting production *or* sales

break-even point is the volume of activity that produces equal revenues and costs for the organization

budget is a detailed plan, expressed in quantitative terms, that specifies how an organization will acquire and use resources during a particular period of time

budget committee advises the budget director during the preparation of the budget

budget director (or **chief budget officer**) specifies the process by which budget data are gathered, collects the information, and prepares the master budget

budget manual indicates who is responsible for providing various types of budget information, when the information is required, and what form the information is to take

budgetary slack is the difference between the revenue or cost projection that a person provides and a realistic estimate of the revenue or cost

budgeted (or **pro forma**) **financial statements** show how the organization's financial statements will appear at a specified time if operations proceed according to plan

budgeted balance sheet shows the expected end-of-period balances for the company's assets, liabilities, and owners' equity

budgeted income statement shows the expected revenue and expenses for a budget period, assuming that planned operations are carried out

budgeted schedule of cost of goods manufactured and sold details the direct-materials, direct-labor, and manufacturing overhead costs to be incurred and shows the cost of the goods to be sold during a budget period

budgeting system comprises the procedures used to develop a budget

business processes support or enable production processes

by-product is the output from a joint-production process that is minor in quantity and/or NRV when compared to the main products

C

capacity is a measure of a process's ability to transform resources into valued products and services

capital budget is a plan for buying and selling capital assets

capital turnover is sales revenue divided by invested capital

cash budget details the expected cash receipts and disbursements during a budget period

cash disbursement budget details the expected cash payments during a budget period

cash receipts budget details the expected cash collections during a budget period

cause-and-effect analysis involves formulating diagnostic signals that identify potential causes of product or service defects

centralization places the responsibility for decisions with the top echelon of management

committed costs are not intended to vary with production or sales volume

common-size statements express items as percentages of revenue

constant gross margin percentage method allocates joint costs to products in a way that the gross margin percentages as a percent of revenue are the same for each product

constraint is a process or resource in a system that limits the throughput of the system

contribution margin is the amount of sales revenue remaining, after covering all variable costs, to contribute to covering fixed cost and profit

control chart describes variation in product or service attributes over time by measuring important quality features but additionally compares them to maximum- and minimum-desired levels

conversion costs include direct labor and manufacturing overhead

cost is the sacrifice made, usually measured by the resources given up, to achieve a particular purpose

cost-accounting systems measure the use of resources in production

Cost Accounting Standards Board (CASB) is a federal agency chartered by Congress in 1970 to develop cost-accounting standards for large government contractors

cost allocation assigns indirect costs to products or organizational units (e.g., departments)

cost allocation bases are factors used to assign indirect costs to cost objects

cost center is an organizational subunit whose manager is responsible for the cost of an activity for which a well-defined relationship exists between inputs and outputs

cost driver is a characteristic of an activity or event that causes costs to be incurred by that activity or event

cost estimation is the process of estimating the relationship between costs and the cost drivers that cause those costs

cost object is any end to which a cost is assigned

cost of goods sold is the expense measured by the cost of the units sold during a specific period of time

cost of quality (COQ) is the cost of activities to *control quality* and costs of activities to correct *failure to control quality*

cost pools are groups or categories of individual cost items

cost-reduction target is the difference between the total target cost and the currently feasible total cost

cost variance is the difference between the actual cost and the standard cost

cost-based transfer pricing sets the transfer price on the basis of the cost of the product or service transferred

cost-benefit analysis is a method of measuring the effects of proposed improvements by comparing both the costs and benefits of a proposal

cost-driver base is the base used to trace or assign costs to activities

cost-driver rate is the estimated cost of resource consumption per unit of cost-driver base for each activity

cost-management systems a set of cost-management techniques that function together to support the organization's goals and activities

cost-volume-profit (CVP) model is a profit-planning model that reflects the effects of changes in an organization's sales volume, revenue, and costs on profit or income

critical success factors are the key strengths that are most responsible for making the organization successful

currently feasible cost is the cost of all current operations necessary to produce and deliver a product

customer costing analyzes the costs of activities devoted to serving specific customers at each level

customer-level costs are incurred for specific customers

customer-level resources and activities are acquired and performed to serve specific customers

customer profile categorizes individual or types of customers according to the major activities that drive revenues and costs

customer profitability analysis identifies the costs and benefits of serving specific customers or customer types to improve an organization's overall profitability

customer retention or **loyalty** measures indicate how well a company is doing in keeping its customers

customer satisfaction is the degree to which expectations of attributes, customer service, and *price* have been or are expected to be met

customer value reflects the degree to which products and services satisfy customers' expectations about price, function, and quality

customer-focused quality is a broad focus on meeting or exceeding customer expectations

customer-response time is the amount of time between a customer's placing an order for a product or requesting service and the delivery of the product or service to the customer

D

decentralization places decision-making responsibility at divisional and departmental levels

decision tree is a diagram of decisions and alternative outcomes expected from those decisions in a "tree, branch, and limb" format

decision usefulness of information is whether managers make sufficiently better decisions to justify the cost of the information

defect is an attribute (tangible or intangible) that falls short of customer expectations

Deming Prize, created in Japan by the Japanese Union of Scientists and Engineers, is awarded to companies around the world that excel in quality improvement

dependent variables are caused by, or at least correlated with, independent variables

differential costs are costs that differ between decision alternatives

direct costs of a cost object are traceable to that cost object

direct materials are resources such as raw materials, parts, and components that one can feasibly observe being used to make a specific product

direct method of cost allocation charges the costs of support-service departments to internal customers without making allocations among support-service departments

direct labor is the effort of employees who transform direct materials into a finished product

direct-labor budget shows the number of hours and the cost of direct labor to be used during a budget period

direct-labor efficiency variance is the difference between the actual hours and the standard hours of direct labor allowed, given actual output, multiplied by the standard hourly labor rate

direct-labor mix variance for a particular type of direct labor is the difference between the actual and standard input proportions for that type of direct labor multiplied by that labor type's standard rate and multiplied by the actual total quantity of all direct labor used

direct-labor rate variance is the difference between the actual and standard hourly labor rate multiplied by the actual quantity of direct labor used

direct-labor yield variance for a particular type of direct labor is the difference between the actual quantity of all direct labor used and the standard quantity of all direct labor, given actual output, multiplied by the standard rate for that particular type of direct labor and multiplied by the standard input proportion for that type of direct labor

direct-material budget shows the number of units and the cost of materials to be purchased and used during a budget period

direct-material mix variance for a particular direct material is the difference between the actual and standard input proportions for that direct material multiplied by that material's standard price and multiplied by the actual total quantity of all direct materials used

direct-materials price variance (or **purchase price variance**) is the difference between the actual and standard price multiplied by the actual quantity of material purchased

direct-materials quantity variance is the difference between the actual quantity and the standard quantity of material allowed, given actual output, multiplied by the standard price

direct-material yield variance for a particular direct material is the difference between the actual quantity of all direct materials used and the standard quantity of all direct materials, given actual output, multiplied by that particular direct material's standard price and multiplied by that direct material's standard input proportion

direct-service (or **line**) **departments** provide services directly to external customers

discount rate is an interest rate used to discount future cash flows to their net present values

discretionary cost center is an organizational subunit whose manager is held accountable for costs, but the subunit's input-output relationship is not well specified

distribution costs include the costs of packing, shipping, and delivering products or services to customers

dual transfer-pricing system charges the buying division for the cost of the transferred product and credits the selling division with the cost plus some profit allowance

due diligence is the due process or appropriate steps in an investigation

E

economic order quantity (or **EOQ**) is the order quantity that minimizes the cost of ordering and holding inventory

economic value added (EVA®) is an investment center's after-tax operating income minus its total assets (net of its current liabilities) times the company's weighted-average cost of capital

employee capabilities are employees' knowledge and skills that indicate the organization's ability to meet future customer needs and generate new sales

engineering estimates are cost estimates based on measuring and pricing the work involved in the activities that go into a product

EOQ model is a mathematical tool for determining the order quantity that minimizes the cost of ordering and holding inventory

equivalent units represent the amount of work actually performed on products not yet complete translated to the work required to complete an equal number of whole units

excess capacity is the amount (if any) by which practical capacity exceeds the demand for the output of the process

expectancy theory explains that people are motivated to act in ways that they expect to provide them the rewards that they desire and to prevent the penalties that they wish to avoid

expense is defined as the cost incurred when an asset is used up or sold for the purpose of generating revenue

extended value chain encompasses the ways companies obtain their resources and distribute their products and services, possibly using the services of other organizations

external failure activities are required when defective products or services are detected after being delivered to customers

extrinsic rewards including grades, money, praise, and prizes come from outside the individual

F

facility (or **general-operations**) **level** costs are incurred to maintain the overall facility and infrastructure of the organization

facility-level resources and activities are acquired and performed to provide the general capacity to produce goods and services

feasible solution space is the combination of input and output values that satisfy the constraints

final product is one that is ready for sale without further processing

financial budget shows how the organization will acquire its financial resources

financial model is an accurate, reliable simulation of relations among relevant costs, benefits, value, and risk that is useful for supporting business decisions

financial planning model is a set of mathematical relationships that expresses the interactions among the various operational, financial, and environmental events that determine the overall results of an organization's activities

finished goods are products ready for sale

first-in, first-out (FIFO) costing is an inventory method that identifies the first units completed as the first ones sold or transferred out

fixed costs remain unchanged in total as the volume of activity changes

fixed-overhead budget variance is the difference between actual fixed overhead and budgeted fixed overhead

fixed-overhead volume variance is the difference between budgeted fixed overhead and applied fixed overhead

flexible budget is a budget that is valid for a range of activity

flowchart reflects cause-and-effect and sequential linkages among process activities

G

Gantt chart depicts the stages required to complete a project and the sequence in which the stages are to performed

goal congruence results when managers of subunits throughout an organization have a common set of objectives

H

high-low method estimates a cost function using only the costs and the level of cost-driver activity from the highest and lowest levels of cost-driver activity

histogram is a chart that displays the *frequency distribution* of an attribute's measures—its range and degree of concentration around an average attribute value

I

idle time is time not spent productively by an employee

imperfect competition describes the situation when a single producer can affect the market price by varying the amount of product available in the market

incremental package describes the resources needed to add various activities to the base package

independent variables are the cost drivers that the analyst believes cause, or at least are correlated with, the dependent variable costs

indirect costs of a cost object are not feasibly traceable to that cost object

indirect labor cost consists of the wages of production employees who do not work directly on the product but are required for the manufacturing facility to operate

indirect materials cost relates to materials that either (1) are not a part of the finished product but are necessary to manufacture it or (2) are part of the finished product but are insignificant in cost

information quality has dimensions of usefulness, subjectivity, accuracy, timeliness, cost, and relevance

intangible features of products and services include reputation, taste, appearance, style, and appeal

intermediate product is a product that might require further processing before it is salable to the ultimate consumer

internal failure activities are required to correct defective processes, products, and services that are detected before delivering them to customers

internal rate of return (IRR) is the interest rate that equates the present value of inflows and outflows from an investment project

intrinsic rewards come from within the individual including the satisfaction from studying hard, the feeling of well-being from physical exercise, the pleasure from helping someone in need, or the satisfaction of doing a good job

inventoriable cost is another term for *product cost*

inventory carrying costs are costs of receiving, handling, storing, insuring, and becoming obsolete

investment center is an organizational subunit whose manager is held accountable for the subunit's profit and the invested capital used by the subunit to generate its profit

ISO 9000 is a set of international standards for quality management

J

job-cost record (or **file, card** or **sheet**) reports the costs of all production-related resources used on the job to date

job-order costing treats each individual job as the unit of output and assigns costs to each job as resources are used

joint products are the products that jointly result from processing a common input

joint costs are costs to operate joint processes, including the disposal of waste

joint process simultaneously converts a common input into several outputs

just-in-time (JIT) processes purchase, make, and deliver services and products just when needed

K

kaizen costing the process of cost reduction during the manufacturing phase of a product

L

lag indicators are measures of the final outcomes of earlier management plans and their execution

lead indicators are measures that signal future outcome of later operations

lead time is the time required for the material to be received after an order is placed

learning curve is the mathematical or graphic representation of the systematic relationship between the amount of experience in performing a task and the time required to perform it

learning phenomenon is a systematic relationship between the amount of experience in performing a task and the time required to perform it

life cycle costing tracks costs attributable to each product or service from start to finish

linear programming shows how best to allocate multiple scarce resources among alternative courses of action in the short run when capacity cannot be increased

lost units are goods that evaporate or otherwise disappear during a production process

lower control limit is the minimum-desired levels of product or service feature

M

main product is a joint output that generates a significant portion of the net realizable value from the process

Malcolm Baldrige Quality Award created by the US Congress in 1987, recognizes U.S. firms with outstanding records of quality improvement and quality management

management by exception is the process of following up only on significant cost variances

manufacturing overhead includes all costs of transforming material into a finished product other than direct material and direct labor

manufacturing-overhead budget shows the cost of overhead expected to be incurred in the production process during the budget period

margin of safety is the amount by which a quantitative objective is exceeded

marketing costs include the costs of personnel, databases, equipment, and facilities dedicated to providing market research, marketing strategy, and marketing plans

master budget, or **profit plan** is a comprehensive set of budgets covering all phases of an organization's operations for a specified period of time

material requisition form is the source document for the transfer of raw material from Raw-Material Inventory to Work-in-Process Inventory and to the job-cost record for the production job

maximum quality level is total delight of the customer or zero defects, depending on one's definition of quality

model is a representation of reality

model elasticity is the ratio of the percentage change in profit divided by the percentage change of an input parameter

multicollinearity is the correlation between two or more independent variables in a multiple regression equation

multiple regression is a regression equation with more than one independent variable

N

net present value (NPV) is the economic value of a project at a point in time

net realizable value (NRV) is the measure of a product's contribution to profit after the split-off point and is computed as sales revenue minus additional processing costs

net realizable value (NRV) method allocates joint costs based on the NRV of each *main product* at the split-off point

new product (or **service**) **development time** is the period between the first consideration of a product and its initial sale to the customer

non-value-added activities do not contribute to customer-perceived value

normal costing system assigns to production jobs the cost of actual direct materials, actual direct labor, and applied manufacturing overhead, which are calculated by multiplying the predetermined overhead rate by the actual amount of the cost driver

normal spoilage is a result of the regular operation of the production process

O

objective function is a mathematical relation of inputs and outputs to be maximized or minimized

objectivity describes the degree of consensus about what to measure, how to measure it, what the observed measure is, or whether the measurement is important

operating leverage reflects the risk of missing sales targets and is measured by the ratio of contribution margin to operating income

operation is a standardized method of making a product that is repeatedly performed

operation costing is a hybrid of job-order and process costing, which is used when companies produce batches of similar products with significantly different types of material

operational budgets specify how an organization's operations will be carried out to meet its demand for goods or services

opportunity cost is the largest net benefit given up by choosing one action that precludes taking other actions

optimum point is the set of inputs and outputs in the feasible solution space that maximizes or minimizes the objective function

optimum quality level of products and services maximizes profits rather than quality

outsourcing is acquiring goods or services from an outside provider

overapplied overhead refers to actual overhead that is less than applied overhead

overhead cost performance report shows the actual and flexible-budget cost levels for each overhead item, together with the variable-overhead spending and efficiency variances and the fixed-overhead budget variance

overhead variance is the difference between the actual and the applied manufacturing overhead amounts

overtime premium is the extra hourly compensation paid to an employee who works beyond the time normally allowed by regulation or labor contracts

P

padding the budget means intentionally underestimating revenue or overestimating costs

Pareto chart prioritizes the causes of problems or defects as bars of varying height, in order of frequency or size

participative budgeting involves employees throughout an organization in the budgeting process

perfect competition describes the situation when the market price does not depend on the quantity sold by any one producer

perfection (or **ideal**) **standard** is one that can be attained only under nearly perfect operating conditions

performance evaluation formula describes rewards earned for specific achievements

performance report shows the budgeted and actual amounts of key financial (or nonfinancial) results appropriate for the type of responsibility center involved

period costs are identified with the time period in which they are incurred rather than with units of purchased or produced goods

physical-measures (or **quantities**) **method** is a joint-cost allocation based on the relative volume, weight, energy content, or other physical measure of each joint product at the split-off point

pilot project is a limited-scope project intended to be a small-scale model of a larger, possibly systemwide, project

practical (or **attainable**) **standards** are as tight as practical but still are expected to be attained

practical capacity of a process is its *theoretical capacity* less planned downtime for scheduled maintenance or improvements

predatory pricing involves temporarily setting a price below cost to broaden demand for a product and injure competitors

predetermined overhead rate is the budgeted manufacturing overhead divided by the budgeted level of the cost driver

present value is the amount of future cash flows discounted to its equivalent worth today

prevention activities seek to prevent defects in the products or services being produced

price discrimination is the quoting of different prices to different customers for the same products, with an intent to harm competitors

prime costs include direct materials and direct labor

prior department costs are manufacturing costs incurred in another department and transferred to a subsequent department in the manufacturing process

process is a related set of tasks, manual or automated, that transforms inputs into identifiable outputs

process costing treats all units processed during a time period as the output to be costed and does not separate and record costs for each unit produced

process efficiency is the ability to transform inputs into outputs at lowest cost

product cost is a cost assigned to goods that were either purchased or manufactured for resale

product life cycle is the time that elapses from its initial research and development to the point at which customer support is withdrawn

product mix is the relative proportion of each type of product planned or actually sold

production budget shows the number of units of services or goods that are to be produced during a budget period

production cost reports summarize production and cost results for a period

production cycle time is the time between starting and finishing a production process, including time to correct mistakes

production (or line) departments provide goods and services directly to external customers

production processes directly result in the production of products or services provided to external customers

productivity is the ratio of outcomes of a process divided by the amount of resources necessary to complete the process

product-costing system accumulates the costs of a production process and assigns them to the products that constitute the organization's output

product-level costs are incurred for each line of product or service

product-level resources and activities are acquired and performed to produce and sell a specific good or service

profit center is an organizational subunit whose manager is held accountable for profit

prorated overhead variance assigns proportionate amounts of it to Work-in-Process Inventory, Finished-Goods Inventory, and Cost of Goods Sold

proration is the process of allocating cost variances to Work-in-Process Inventory, Finished-Goods Inventory, and Cost of Goods Sold

Q

qualitative factors are the characteristics of a decision that cannot easily or should not be expressed in numerical terms

qualitative information is descriptive and based on characteristics or perceptions, such as relative desirability, rather than quantities

quality dimensions are (1) product or service attributes and (2) customer service before and after the sale

quantitative information is expressed in dollars or other quantities relating to size, frequency, and so on

R

raw material refers to material that has not yet been entered into production

reciprocal method recognizes and allocates costs of all services provided by any support-service department, including those provided to other support-service departments

reciprocal services are services provided among multiple support-service departments

regression analysis is a statistical method used to create an equation relating independent (or X) variables to dependent (or Y) variables

relative performance evaluation is based on comparing an individual's performance to that of others

relative sales value at split-off method allocates joint costs based on the relative sales values of the joint products at their split-off point

relevant costs and benefits occur in the future *and* differ among feasible decision alternatives

relevant range the range of activity within which the organization usually operates

residual income of an investment center is its profit minus its invested capital times an inputted interest rate

resources supplied refer to the capacity that the organization makes available for use

resources used refer to the resources actually used for productive purposes

responsibility accounting refers to the various concepts and tools used to measure the performance of people and departments in order to foster goal or behavioral congruence

responsibility center is a subunit in an organization whose manager is held accountable for specified results of the subunit's activities

return on investment (ROI) for an investment center is its income divided by its invested capital

return on quality (ROQ) is the view that assumes there is a trade-off between the costs and benefits of improving quality

revenue budget variance is the difference between the actual total sales revenue and the budgeted total sales revenue

revenue center is an organizational subunit whose manager is held accountable for the revenue attributed to the subunit

revenue market-share variance holds constant the total industry volume at its actual sales level and focuses on the company's market share

revenue market-size variance holds constant the company's market share at its budgeted level and focuses on changes in total industry volume

revenue sales-mix variance focuses on the effects of changes in the sales mix while holding constant the effects of the products' sales prices and the total sales volume

revenue sales-quantity variance holds constant the sales-price and sales-mix effects and focuses on the effect of the overall unit sales volume

revenue sales-volume variance holds constant the products' sales prices at their budgeted levels and focuses on deviations between actual and budgeted sales volumes

revolving (or **continuous) budget** is another name for a rolling budget

rolling (or **revolving or continuous**) **budget** is continually updated by periodically adding a new incremental time period

R-square (R^2) is the proportion of the variation in the dependent variable explained by the *X*, or independent, variables

run is sequential values above or below the mean or values sequentially increasing or decreasing

run chart shows trends in variation in product or service attributes over time by reflecting measures of important quality features taken at defined points in time

S

safety stock is the potential excess usage of material when material usage fluctuates during the lead time

sales budget displays the projected sales in units and the projected sales revenue

sales forecasting is the process of predicting sales of services or goods

sales margin is income divided by sales revenue

sales mix is the relative proportion of each type of product planned or actually sold

sales-price variance focuses on the differences between actual and budgeted sales prices while holding constant the sales volume at its actual level

sales value at split-off method allocates joint costs based on the relative sales values of the joint products at their split-off point

scatter diagram is a plot of two measures that could be related

scattergraph plots costs against activity levels

scenarios are *realistic* combinations of changed parameters

selling costs are the costs of sales personnel, databases, equipment, and facilities devoted to sales activities

selling, general, and administrative (SG&A) expense budget shows the planned amounts of expenditures for selling, general, and administrative expenses during a budget period

semivariable costs have both a fixed and a variable component

sensitivity analysis is the study of how the outcome of a decision-making process changes as one or more of the assumptions change

simple regression is a type of statistical analysis in which the regression equation has only one independent variable

special orders are irregular and do not have lasting implications for other products or customers

split-off point is the point at which joint products appear in the production process

spoilage represents goods that are damaged, do not meet specifications, or are otherwise not suitable for further processing or sale as good output

standard cost is a budget for the production of one unit of product or service

standard costing uses a predetermined (or standard) rate for both direct and indirect costs (i.e., direct material, direct labor, and manufacturing overhead) to assign manufacturing costs to products

standard direct-labor quantity is the number of labor hours normally needed to manufacture one unit of product

standard direct-labor rate is the total hourly cost of compensation, including fringe benefits

standard direct-material price is the total delivered cost after subtracting any purchase discounts

standard direct-material quantity is the total amount of materials normally required to produce a finished product, including allowances for normal waste or inefficiency

standard-costing system enters the *standard* costs of direct materials and direct labor into the Work-in-Process Inventory account

static budget is valid for only one planned activity level

statistical control chart plots cost variances across time and compares them with a statistically determined *critical value* that triggers an investigation

step (semifixed) costs increase in steps as the amount of the cost-driver volume increases

step method of cost allocation allocates costs first from the support-service department with the largest proportion of its total allocation base in other support-service departments to other support-services or support- and direct-service or production departments, then allocates costs from less general support-service departments

stock options give an individual the right to purchase a certain number of shares at a specified price over a specified time period

strategic long-range plan expresses the specific steps required to achieve an organization's goals

strategic planning is the process of deciding on an organization's major programs and the approximate resources to be devoted to them

subjective performance evaluation is based on nonquantified criteria

subjectivity describes the degree of disagreement about what to measure, how to measure it, what the observed measure is, or whether the measurement is important

sunk costs are past payments for resources that cannot be changed by any current or future decision

support (or **service**) **departments** do not work directly on a product but are necessary for the production process to operate

support-service costs are the costs of resources supplied by an organization to provide the support services

support-service (or **indirect**) **departments** provide support services to each other and to the production departments

T

tangible features include performance, adherence to specifications, and functionality

tangible objectives are benchmarks capable of being measured in some manner

target cost is the highest cost of a good or service that meets both customer needs and company profit goals

target costing is a decision-making method that seeks to achieve products and services with specific features at target costs based on expected market prices and target profits

target profit is the desired excess of periodic or project sales revenues over costs

task analysis is the technique of setting standards by analyzing the production process

tax credit is a reduction in state and/or federal income taxes

theoretical capacity of a process is the maximum possible rate of transformation of inputs into outputs if the process were fully used, with no downtime or unused capacity

throughput costing assigns only the unit-level spending for direct costs as the cost of products or services

throughput (cycle) time ratio is the ratio of time spent adding customer value to products and services divided by total cycle time

throughput efficiency is the relation of throughput achieved to resources used

throughput time ratio is the ratio of the time spent adding customer value to products and services divided by total cycle time (also known as the "ratio of work content to lead time")

time value of money is the concept that cash received earlier is worth more than cash received later

timeliness means that information is available in time to fully consider it when making a decision

total delight occurs when a customer receives a product or service that far exceeds his or her expectations of quality

total factor productivity is the value of goods and services divided by the total cost of providing them

total quality management (TQM) is the view that improvements in quality, as defined by customers, will always result in improved organizational performance because improving quality will improve efficiency as problems are identified and eliminated

total target cost is the target cost per unit multiplied by the total number of units to be sold over the product's life

transfer price is the amount charged when one division of an organization sells goods or services to another division

***t*-statistic,** *t*, is the value of *b*, the coefficient, divided by its standard error, SE_b

U

underapplied overhead refers to actual overhead that exceeds applied overhead

unit-level costs are incurred for every unit of product manufactured or service produced

unit-level resources and activities are acquired and performed specifically for individual units of product or service

unused capacity is the difference between the resources supplied and the resources used. Unused capacity is the amount of capacity that the organization has supplied that is not being used for productive purposes

upper control limits are maximum-desired levels of product or service features

V

value chain is a set of linked operations or processes that begins with obtaining resources and ends with providing products or services that customers value

value-added activities enhance the value of products and services in the eyes of the organization's customer while meeting its own goals

variable (or **direct**) **costing** applies only variable manufacturing overhead to manufactured goods as a product cost along with direct materials and direct labor

variable costs change in total in direct proportion with a change in the activity volume

variable-overhead efficiency variance is the difference between the actual and standard hours of an activity base (or cost driver) multiplied by the standard variable-overhead rate

variable-overhead spending variance is the difference between the actual variable-overhead cost and the product of the standard variable-overhead rate and the actual hours of an activity base (or cost driver).

virtual organizations maintain only the most important operations of the value chain and outsource everything else

W

weighted-average cost of capital (WACC) is the average of the after-tax cost of debt capital and the cost of equity capital, weighted by the relative proportions of the firm's capital provided by debt and equity

weighted-average costing is an inventory method that for product-costing purposes combines costs and equivalent units of a period with the costs and the equivalent units in beginning inventory

work in process refers to partially completed products

Z

zero-base budgeting initially sets the budget for virtually every activity in the organization to zero

Photo Credits

p. 2: © Bob Rowan; Progressive Image/CORBIS
p. 6: © Dick Luria/FPG International LLC
p. 12: © Michael L. Abramson/Woodfin Camp & Associates
p. 14: Photo courtesy of Hewlett-Packard Company
p. 34: © Cindy Charles/PhotoEdit
p. 41 (top): © Museum of Flight/CORBIS
p. 41 (left): © Vincent Dewitt/Stock, Boston
p. 41 (right): Courtesy of Dell Computer Corp.
p. 53 (left): Courtesy Toyota Motor Manufacturing, Kentucky, Inc.
p. 53 (right): © 2001 Corbis. All rights reserved.
p. 53 (middle): © Kevin Horan/Stone
p. 53 (bottom left): © Corbis Stock Market/William Taufic, 1995
p. 53 (bottom right): Digital Imagery © copyright 2001 PhotoDisc, Inc. Photographer: Joshua Ets-Hokin
p. 88: © James L. Amos/CORBIS
p. 93: © Daniel Sheehan/Liaison Agency
p. 97: NASA
p. 100: © Peter Aprahamian/CORBIS
p. 114 (left): © Michael L.Abramson/Woodfin Camp & Associates
p. 114 (right): © Charles Thatcher/Stone
p. 115: © Phil Degginger/Stone
p. 140: © Index Stock Imagery/Grayce Roessler
p. 142: © 2001 Corbis. All rights reserved.
p.147: © David Joel/Stone
p. 154: © Kathy McLaughlin/The Image Works
p. 184: © Index Stock Imagery/James Smalley
p. 191: © Spencer Grant/PhotoEdit, Inc.
p. 195: Digital Imagery © copyright 2001 PhotoDisc, Inc. Photographer: Ryan McVay
p. 200: © John Chiasson/Liasion Agency
p. 218: © Joseph Nettis/Stock, Boston
p. 222: Digital Imagery © copyright 2001 PhotoDisc, Inc. Photographer: Ryan McVay
p. 230: © 2001 Bob Sacha
p. 237: © 2001 Corbis. All rights reserved.
p. 252: © 2001 Corbis. All rights reserved.
p. 255: AP Photo/Richard Drew
p. 261: © Steve Rubin/The Image Works
p. 267: Courtesy TRW
p. 278: Courtesy of Dell Computer Corp.
p. 304: Digital Imagery © copyright 2001 PhotoDisc, Inc. Photographer: David Buffington
p. 307: © Mark Joseph/Stone
p. 319: AP Photo/Yves Logghe
p. 322: Digital Imagery © copyright 2001 PhotoDisc, Inc. Photographer: Skip Nall
p. 346: © 2001 Corbis. All rights reserved.
p. 348: © Richard A.Cooke/CORBIS
p. 356: © 2001 Corbis. All rights reserved.
p. 361: © D Cavagnaro/Visuals Unlimited
p. 376: © Index Stock Imagery/Scott J. Witte
p. 383: © Index Stock Imagery/Matthew Borkoski
p. 424: © Index Stock Imagery/Great American Stock
p. 430: © Paul Solomon/Woodfin Camp & Associates
p. 436: © Michael A. Schwarz/The Image Works
p. 442: © Michael Newman/ PhotoEdit
p. 474: © John McAnulty/CORBIS
p. 479: Digital Imagery © copyright 2001 PhotoDisc, Inc. Photographer: Ryan McVay.
p. 485: Digital Imagery © copyright 2001 PhotoDisc, Inc. Photographer: Ryan McVay
p. 490 (left): © Denise Marcotte/Stock, Boston
p. 490 (right): © David H. Wells/CORBIS
p. 524: © Billy Hustace/Stone
p. 532 (left): © Matthew Borkoski/Stock,Boston
p. 532 (right): © Jeffrey Muir Hamilton/Stock,Boston
p. 540: © 2001 Corbis. All rights reserved.
p. 568: © Corbis Stock Market/Chuck Savage
p. 570: AP Photo/HO
p. 574: © Premium Stock/CORBIS
p.582: © Jon Riley/Stone
p. 600: © Paul A. Souder/CORBIS
p. 602 (left): © Mark E.Gibson/Visuals Unlimited
p. 602 (right): Digital Imagery © copyright 2001 PhotoDisc, Inc. Photographer: Scott T. Baxter
p. 604: © Index Stock Imagery/Timothy O'Keefe
p. 608: © Bonnie Kamin/PhotoEdit
p. 654: © 2001 Corbis. All rights reserved.
p 656 (left): © Spencer Grant/PhotoEdit
p. 656 (right): © Kevin R. Morris/CORBIS
p. 659: © Lawrence Migdale/Stone
p. 660 (left): © Joe Lynch/Liaison Agency
p. 660 (right): © Jose Carrillo/PhotoEdit
p. 669: © Mark Richards/PhotoEdit
p. 675: © Michael Rosenfeld/Stone
p. 698: © Index Stock Imagery/Don B. Stevenson
p. 702: © Bob Mahoney/The Image Works
p. 706 (left): © Jeff Greenberg/Visuals Unlimited
p. 706 (right): © Mark Segal/Stone
p. 718 © Rob Johns/Liaison Agency
p. 719: © E de Malaive/Liaison Agency
p. 754: © Index Stock Imagery/Matthew Borkoski
p. 758 (left): © Andrew Sacks/Stone
p. 758 (right): © Seth Resnick/Liaison Agency
p. 759 (left): © Jeffrey Muir Hamilton/Liaison Agency
p. 759 (top right): © AFP/CORBIS

p. 759 (bottom): © 2001 Corbis. All rights reserved.
p. 770: © Charlie Westerman/Stone
p. 800: © Spencer Grant/PhotoEdit
p. 803: © Frank Fisher/Liaison Agency
p. 810: © David Young-Wolff/PhotoEdit
p. 816: © David H. Wells/CORBIS
p. 830: © Corbis Stock Market/William Taufic
p. 836: Photo Courtesy of GE
p. 841: © Corbis Stock Market/John Madere
p. 843: © John Thoeming
p. 870: © AFP/CORBIS
p. 873: © Amy Etra/PhotoEdit
p. 886: © 2001 Corbis. All rights reserved.
p. 892: © 2001 Time Inc. All rights reserved.

Bibliography

Chapter 1

Coburn, S., et al. "Benchmarking with ABCM." *Management Accounting,* January 1995: 56–60.

Cooper, R., and R. Slagmulder. "Strategic Cost Management." *Management Accounting,* February 1998: 16.

Drucker, P. *Managing in a Time of Great Change.* New York: Dutton, 1995.

Edwards, J. B., editor. *Emerging Practices in Cost Management.* Boston: Warren Gorham & Lamont: 1997.

Freeman, T. "Transforming Cost Management into a Strategic Weapon. *Journal of Cost Management,* November/December 1998: 13–26.

Hollander, D., and J. Cherrington. *Accounting Information Technology, and Business Solutions.* New York: McGraw-Hill, 2000.

Kotter, J. P. "Why Transformation Efforts Fail." *Harvard Business Review* (March–April 1995): 61.

Leonhardt, L. "Sara Lee: Playing with the Recipes." *Business Week,* April 27, 1998.

National Association of Accountants. *Standard No. 1B.* "Statement on Management Accounting: Objectives of Management Accounting." New York: MAA; 1982, *www.imanet.org.*

Spicer, B., et al. *Transforming Government Enterprises.* St. Leonards, Australia: The Centre for Independent Studies, 1996.

Walther, T., H. Johansson, J. Dunleavy, and E. Hjelm. *Reinventing the CFO: Moving from Financial Management to Strategic Management.* New York: McGraw-Hill, 1997.

Widener, S., and F. Selto. "Management Control Systems and Boundaries of the Firm." *Journal of Management Accounting Research,* 1999: 45–74.

Chapter 2

Drucker, P. "The Information Executives Truly Need." *Harvard Business Review,* January–February 1995: 54–62.

Drury, C., and M. Tayles. "Product Costing in UK Manufacturing Organisations." *The European Accounting Review,* 3, no. 3 (1994): 443–69.

Hanks, G., M. Freid, and J. Huber. "Shifting Gears at Borg-Warner." *Management Accounting,* February 1994: 25–29.

Shim, E., and E. Sudit. "How Manufacturers Price Products." *Management Accounting,* 76 no. 8, February 1995: 37–39.

Chapter 3

Business Week. "Earth to Congress: Scrap the Space Station," May 20, 1991; "The Super Collider Is Science. The Space Station Is Pork," September 13, 1993; "2002, a Space Odyssey—or Just Pork in the Sky?" August 15, 1994; "Curse of the Chunnel," December 9, 1996 (international edition); "A Money Pit Called the Chunnel," December 22, 1997; "Virgin vs. British Airways: The Great Train Rivalry," March 30, 1998 (international edition).

Drucker, P. "The Next Information Revolution." Forbes ASAP (*www.forbes.com/asap*), August 24, 1998.

Jacobs, K. "Costing Health Care: A Study of the Introduction of Cost and Budget Reports into a GP Association." *Management Accounting Research,* 1998: 55–70.

Pfeiffer, G., R. Capettini, and G. Whittenburg. "Gump, Forest—Accountant: A Study of Accounting In The Motion Picture Industry," *Journal of Accounting Education,* 1997, v15 (3, Summer): 319–344.

Chapter 4

Banker, R., and H. Johnson. "An Empirical Study of Cost Drivers in the U.S. Airline Industry." *The Accounting Review,* July 1993: 576–601.

Boyd, L. "Cost Information: The Use of Cost Information for Making Operating Decisions." *Journal of Cost Management,* May/June 1997: 42–47.

Campbell, R., P. Brewer, and T. Mills. "Designing an Information System Using Activity-Based Costing and the Theory of Constraints." *Journal of Cost Management,* January/February 1997: 16–25.

Carlson, D., and S. M. Young. "Activity-Based Total Quality Management at American Express." *Journal of Cost Management,* Spring 1993: 48–58.

Foster, G., and M. Gupta. "Manufacturing Overhead Cost Driver Analysis." *Journal of Accounting and Economics,* 1989: 309–37.

Gurowka, J. "ABC, ABM, and the Volkswagen Saga." *CMA Magazine,* May 1996: 30–33.

Johnson, H. T. "It's Time to Stop Overselling Activity-Based Concepts: Start Focusing on Total Customer Satisfaction Instead." *Management Accounting,* September 1992: 26–35.

Innes, J., F. Mitchell, and D. Sinclair. "Activity-Based Costing in the U.K.'s Largest Companies: A Comparison of 1994 and 1999 Survey Results." *Management Accounting Research* 11: 349–62.

Kee, R. "Integrating Activity-Based Costing with the Theory of Constraints to Enhance Production-Related Decision Making." *Accounting Horizons,* December 1995: 48–61.

Novin, A. M. "Applying Overhead: How to Find the Right Bases and Rates." *Management Accounting,* 1992.

Porter, M. *Competitive Advantage.* New York: Free Press, 1985.

Selto, F. "Implementing Activity-Based Management," *Journal of Cost Management,* Summer 1995: 36–49.

Chapter 5

Brewer, P. "National Culture and Activity-Based Costing Systems: A Note." *Management Accounting Research,* June 1998: 241–60.

"Call It Dumbsizing: Why Some Companies Regret Cost-Cutting." *The Wall Street Journal,* May 14, 1996: A1.

Compton, T., L. Hoshower, and W. Draeger. "Reengineering Transaction Processing Systems at Cummins Engine." *Journal of Cost Management,* May/June 1998: 6–12.

Convey, S. "Eliminating Unproductive Activities and Processes." *CMA Magazine,* 1991: 20–24.

Cooper, R., and R. Kaplan. "Activity-Based Systems: Measuring the Costs of Resource Usage." *Accounting Horizons,* September 1992: 1–13.

Maher, M., and M. L. Marais. "A Field Study on the Limitations of Activity-Based Costing When Resources Are Provided on a Joint and Indivisible Basis." *Journal of Accounting Research* 36, no. 1: 136–42.

Noreen, E. "Conditions under Which Activity-Based Costing Systems Provide Relevant Costs." *Journal of Management Accounting Research,* 3: 159–68.

Palmer, C. "Dial Tones for Deadbeats." *Forbes,* November 3, 1997: 81–82.

Pederson, R. B. "Weyerhaeuser: Streamlining Payroll." *Management Accounting* (US), October 1991: 38–41.

Selto, F. "Implementing Activity-Based Management." *Journal of Cost Management,* Summer 1995: 36–49.

Shields, M., and M. McEwen. "Implementing Activity-Based Costing Systems Successfully." *Journal of Cost Management,* Winter 1996: 13–22.

Silver & Gold Record, University of Colorado at Boulder, March 12, 1998.

Spicer, B., D. Emanuel, and M. Powell. *Transforming Government Enterprises: Managing Radical Change in Deregulated Environments,* St. Leonards, Australia: Centre for Independent Studies, 1996.

Stiles, R., and S. Mick. "What Is the Cost of Controlling Quality? Activity-Based Accounting Offers an Answer." *Hospital & Health Services Administration,* Summer 1997: 193.

Turney, P. "Activity-Based Management." *Management Accounting,* January 1992: 20–25.

Chapter 6

Anderson, E. W., C. Fornell, and D. R. Lehmann. "Customer Satisfaction, Market Share and Profitability: Findings from Sweden." *Journal of Marketing* 58, no. 3 (1994) 53–66.

Banker, R. D., G. Potter, and D. Srinivasan. "An Empirical Investigation of an Incentive Plan That Includes Nonfinancial Performance Measures." *The Accounting Review* 75, no. 1 (2000) 65–92.

Bose, G., and E. Haskell. "Keeping the Ones with the 'Right Stuff.'" *Journal of Lending & Credit Risk Management,"* April 1999: 59–62.

Boston Consulting Group. "Naturix-Bowen Case Study-MEL-Training-1st Yr Finance-1999." Melbourne, Aus.

Brady, D. "Why Service Stinks." *Business Week,* October 23, 2000.

Burrows, P. "Sun's Bid to Rule the Web." *Business Week,* July 24, 2000.

Carroll, P., and M. Tadikonda. "Customer Profitability: Irrelevant for Decisions?" *Banking Strategies,* November/December 1997: 76–82.

Foster, G., M. Gupta, and L. Sjoblom. "Customer Profitability Analysis: Challenges and New Directions." *Journal of Cost Management,* Spring 1996: 5–17.

Foster, G., and M. Gupta. "The Customer Profitability Implications of Customer Satisfaction." Working paper, Stanford University and Washington University in St. Louis, 1999.

Green, C. "Profitability Measurement for Small-Business Banking: A Strategic View." *Commercial Lending Review,* Fall 1997.

Ittner, C. D., and D. F. Larcker. "Measuring the Impact of Quality Initiatives on Firm Financial Performance." In *Advances in the Management of Organizational Quality,* vol. 1. S. Ghosh and D. Fedor, eds. Greenwich, CT: JAI, 1996, 1–37.

Ittner, C. D., and D. F. Larcker. "Are Non-Financial Measures Leading Indicators of Financial Performance? An Analysis of Customer Satisfaction." *Journal of Accounting Research,* 36 (1998 supplement): 1–35.

Johnson, H. T. "It's Time to Stop Overselling Activity-Based Concepts." *Management Accounting,* September 1992: 26–35.

Judge, P. C. "Do You Know Who Your Most Profitable Customers Are?" *Business Week,* September 14, 1998.

Kaplan, R. S. "In Defense of Activity-Based Cost Management." *Management Accounting,* November 1992: 58–63.

Nelson, E., R. T. Rust, A. Zahorik, R. L. Rose, P. Batalden, and B. Siemanski. "Do Patient Perceptions of Quality Relate to Hospital Financial Performance?" *Journal of Healthcare Marketing,* December 1992: 1–13.

Rucci, A. T., S. P. Kim, and R. T. Quinn. "The Employee-Customer-Profit Chain at Sears." *Harvard Business Review* 76, no. 1 (1998): 82–97.

Rust, R. T., and A. J. Zahorik. "Customer Satisfaction, Customer Retention, and Market Share." *Journal of Retailing* 69, no. 2 (1993): 193–215.

Smith, M., and S. Dikoli. "Customer Profitability Analysis: An Activity-Based Costing Approach." *Managerial Auditing Journal* 10, no. 7 (1995).

Chapter 7

Balakrishnan, R., T. Linsmeier, and M. Venkatachalam. "Financial Benefits from JIT Adoption: Effects of Customer Concentration and Cost Structure." *The Accounting Review,* April 1996: 183–205.

Barker, R. C. "Production Systems without MRP: A Lean Time-Based Design." *Omega International Journal of Management Science* 22, no. 4 (1994): 394–60.

Billesbach, T., and R. Hayen. "Long-Term Impact of Just-in-Time on Inventory Performance Measures." *Production and Inventory Management Journal,* 1st Quarter 1994: 62–67.

Brinkman, S., and M. Appelbaum. "The Quality Cost Report: It's Alive and Well at Gilroy Foods." *Management Accounting* (U.S.), September 1994: 61–65.

Burkins, G., and F. R. Bleakley. "UAW Strike Hits GM 'Just in Time' to Cripple Firm." *The Wall Street Journal,* March 14, 1996: p. A3.

Burrows, P. "Health Care: The Quest for Quality." *Business Week,* April 8, 1996.

Carr, L. "Quality: Cost of Quality—Making It Work." *Journal of Cost Management,* Spring 1995: 61–65.

Clark, K., and T. Fujimoto. *Product Development Performance: Strategy, Organization, and Management in the World Auto Industry.* Boston: Harvard Business School Press, 1991.

Clayman, M. "Excellence Revisited." *Financial Analysts Journal,* May/June 1994: 61–65.

Deming, W. E. "A Seminal Thinker Takes a Detailed Look at the Quality of Quality." *Automobile Magazine,* October 1991: 106–11.

Dugan, I. J. "If They Can Make It There . . ." *Business Week,* September 16, 1996.

Echikson, E. "How Iomega Lost Its Zip." *Business Week,* April 13, 1998.

Hof, R. D. "The Sad Saga of Silicon Graphics." *Business Week,* August 4, 1997.

Ittner, C., and D. Larcker. "Product Development Cycle Time and Organizational Performance." *Journal of Marketing Research* 34 (1997): 13–23.

Ittner, C., and D. Larcker. "Quality Strategy, Strategic Control Systems, and Organizational Performance." *Accounting, Organizations and Society* 22, no. 3/4 (1997): 293–314.

Kalagnanam, S., and E. M. Matsumura. "Quality: Costs of Quality in an Order Entry Department." *Journal of Cost Management,* Fall 1995: 68–74.

Magnuson, P. "GM's German Lessons." *Business Week,* December 20, 1993.

Miller, K. "The Virtual Corporation." *Business Week,* February 8, 1993.

Procter, S. "The Extent of JIT Manufacturing in the UK: Evidence from Aggregate Economic Data." *Integrated Manufacturing Systems* 6, no. 4 (1995): 16–25.

Coy, P. "Researching the Nitty-Gritty of Quality Control," *Business Week.* May 29, 1995.

Rust, R., A. Zahorik, and T. Keiningham. "Return on Quality (ROQ): Making Service Financially Accountable." *Journal of Marketing,* April 1995: 58–70.

Selto, F., C. Renner, and S. M. Young. "Assessing the Organizational Fit of a JIT Manufacturing System." *Accounting, Organizations and Society* 20 (1995): 665–84.

Simpson, P. "As Workers Turn Into Risk-Takers . . . One Plant Really Turns on the Steam." *Business Week,* December 15, 1997 (international edition).

Templin, N. "GM Walkout Hits Production at Mexican Sites." *The Wall Street Journal,* March 20, 1996: A3.

White, R. "An Empirical Assessment of JIT in U.S. Manufacturers." *Production and Inventory Management Journal* 34 no. 2 (1993): 38–42.

Youssef, M. "Measuring the Intensity Level of JIT Activities and Its Impact on Quality." *International Journal of Quality & Reliability Management,* 1995: 59–80.

Chapter 8

Joshi, S., R. Krishnan, and L. Lave. "Estimating the Hidden Costs of Environmental Regulation," *The Accounting Review,* vol. 76, no. 2, p. 171–198.

Kunes, T. "A Green and Lean Workplace?" *Strategic Finance,* February 2001, p. 71–83; reprinted in Edwards, J., ed., *Emerging Practices in Cost Management,* Women, Gorham & Lamont: Valhalla, NY: 2001.

"Splinters Everywhere," *Business Week,* January 10, 1994.

"Targeting Costs in Process and Service Industries," *Harvard Business Review,* January–February 1996: 93.

Timian, K. A., and M. Fleming, "Toward Diversified Cost Accounting Systems," *National Public Accountant,* vol. 45, no. 1, p. 24–26.

Chapter 9

"The First Report and Order Re Local Competition." FCC Common Carrier Docket 96–98, Part Two. Deposition by Mr. Dennis L. Rica (MCI, Inc.) for the Ohio Public Utilities Commission. United States Court of Appeals for the Eighth Circuit Opinion No. 96-3321.

North American Recycled Rubber Association, "Tire Recycling in Europe," and "Synopsis of Scrap Rubber Reclamation in Canada." (*www.recycle.net/recycle/assn/narra*).

"A Power Pinching Way to Recycle Rust-Proof Steel." *Business Week,* November 11, 1991.

Slater, K. and C. Wootton, *A Study of Joint and By-Product Costing in the U.K.* London: The Chartered Institute of Management Accountants, U.K., 1988.

Chapter 10

Dean, G. W., M. P. Moye, and P. J. Blayney. *Overhead Cost Allocation and Performance Evaluation Practices of Australian Manufacturers.* Sydney, Australia: The Accounting and Finance Foundation, 1991.

Fremgren, J. M., and S. S. Liao. *The Allocation of Corporate Indirect Costs.* New York: National Association of Accountants, 1981.

Johnson, H. T., and D. Loewe. "How Weyerhaeuser Manages Corporate Overhead Costs." *Management Accounting,* August 1987: 20–26.

Spicer, B., D. Emmanuel, and M. Powell. *Transforming Government Enterprises.* St. Leonards, Australia: Centre for Independent Studies, 1996.

Wolfson, M. "Empirical Evidence of Incentive Problems and Their Mitigation in Oil and Gas Tax Shelter Programs." In *Principals and Agents,* J. Pratt and R. Zeckhauser, eds. Boston: Harvard Business School Press, 1985.

Zimmerman, J. L. "The Costs and Benefits of Cost Allocations." *The Accounting Review* 54, no. 3: 510–11.

Chapter 11

Anderson, S. W. "Measuring the Impact of Product Mix Heterogeneity on Manufacturing Overhead Cost." *The Accounting Review* 70, no. 3: 363–387.

Banker R. J., G. Potter, and R. G. Schroeder. "An Empirical Analysis of Manufacturing Overhead Cost Drivers." *Journal of Accounting and Economics* 19, no. 1: 115–37.

Ittner, C., D. F. Larcker, and T. Randall. "The Activity-Based Cost Hierarchy, Production Policies and Firm Profitability." *Journal of Management Accounting Research* 9: 143–62.

Maher, M. W., and M. L. Marais. "A Field Study on the Limitations of Activity-Based Costing When Resources Are Provided on a Joint and Indivisible Basis." *Journal of Accounting Research* 36, no. 1: 129–42.

Noreen, E., and N. Soderstrom. "Are Overhead Costs Strictly Proportional to Activity? Evidence from Hospital Service Departments." *Journal of Accounting and Economics* 17, no. 1/2: 255–78.

Chapter 12

Barker, B. "Development of Time Based Frameworks: Manufacturing System Analysis and Value Adding Performance." *Omega International Journal of Management Science* 25, no. 2 (1977): 171–79.

Barker, R. C. "Production Systems without MRP: A Lean Time-Based Design." *Omega International Journal of Management Science* 22, no. 4 (1994): 349–60.

Campbell, R., P. Brewer, and T. Mills. "Designing an Information System Using Activity-Based Costing and the Theory of Constraints." *Journal of Cost Management,* January/February 1997: 16–25.

"Computer's View of a Hurricane." *USA Today* (*www.usatoday.com/weather/whurl15.htm*).

Dunagan, C. "Report: Washington Orcas Endangered." Scripps Howard News Service, November 18, 2000.

Goldratt, E., and J. Cox. *The Goal.* Great Barrington, MA: North River Press, 1984.

Kee, R. "Integrating Activity-Based Costing with the Theory of Constraints to Enhance Production-Related Decision Making." *Accounting Horizons,* December 1995: 46–61.

Lamiell, P. "Credit Card Firms Look for New Penalties: G. E. Capital to Charge $25 Fee if Cardholder Pays Off Full Balance." *Boulder Daily Camera,* September 11, 1996.

Noreen, E., D. Smith, and J. Mackey, *The Theory of Constraints and Its Implications for Management Accounting.* Montvale, NJ: IMA Foundation for Applied Research, 1995.

Ruhl, J. "An Introduction to the Theory of Constraints." *Journal of Cost Management,* Summer 1996: 43–48.

Sullivan, R. L. "Exxonsafeway." *Forbes* 157, no. 5: 106.

Chapter 13

"AIDS Gaffes in Africa Come Back to Haunt Drug Industry in the US." *The Wall Street Journal,* April 22, 2001.

Areeda, P., and D. Turner, "Predatory Pricing and Related Practices under Section 2 of the Sherman Act." *Harvard Law Review* 88, no. 4: 697–733.

Byrne, J. A. "Visionary vs. Visionary." *Business Week,* August 28, 2000.

Cahan, S., and W. H. Kaempfer, "Industry Income and Congressional Regulatory Legislation: Interest Groups vs. Median Voter." *Economic Inquiry* 3, no. 1 (1992): 47–56.

Carroll, L. *Alice's Adventures in Wonderland,* Chapter 6.

"Cisco Revenue to Fall Well Short of Estimates Amid Business Slowdown." *The Wall Street Journal,* April 12, 2001.

Committee, B., and D. J. Grinnell, "Predatory Pricing, the Price-Cost Test, and Activity-Based Costing." *Journal of Cost Management* 6, no. 3: 52–58.

Drucker, P. "The Five Deadly Business Sins." *The Wall Street Journal* CXXII, no. 79: 18.

Evans, J. III, Y. C. Hwang, and N. Nagarajan, "Cost Reduction and Process Reengineering in Hospitals." *Journal of Cost Management,* May–June 1997: 20–27.

Kato, Y., G. Boer, and C. Chow, "Target Costing: An Integrative Management Process." *Journal of Cost Management,* Spring 1995: 39–51.

Kleindorfer, P., H. Kunreuther, and P. Schoemaker. *Decision Sciences: An Integrative Approach.* Cambridge University Press, 1993.

"Letting the Masses Name Their Price." *Business Week,* September 18, 2000.

Locke, E. A., and G. P. Latham, *A Theory of Goal Setting and Task Performance.* Englewood Cliffs, NJ: Prentice Hall, 1990.

McLeod, P., and M. Maher. "Analyzing Newspaper Costs in Predation Lawsuits" *Newspaper Research Journal* 19, no. 4: 58–70.

Ozanne, M. "Outsourcing: Managing Strategic Partnerships for the Virtual Enterprise." *Fortune* 72, no. 3: S21–22.

"Rattling Cages: Utilities' Quiet World Is Shaken Up as Enron Moves on Philadelphia." *The Wall Street Journal,* January 7, 1998: A1, A14.

Shank, J. "Strategic Cost Management: New Wine or Just New Bottles?" *Journal of Management Accounting Research,* Fall 1989: 47–65.

Simon, H. "Strategy and Organizational Evolution." *Strategic Management Journal,* 14: (1993) 131–42.

Shultheis, R. "Remember the Valley Floor." *Telluride Daily Planet,* September 25, 2000: 2.

"The 21st Century Corporation." *Business Week,* August 28, 2000.

"Who Is Outsourcing and Why?" *Management Accounting,* July 1998: 45–47.

Chapter 14

Epstein, M. J. "'Greening' with EVA." *Management Accounting,* January 1999: 45–49.

Harr, J. *A Civil Action,* New York: Vintage Books, 1996.

Kaming, P. F., P. O. Olomalaiye, G. D. Holt, and F. C. Harris, "Factors Influencing Construction Time and Cost Overruns on High-Rise Projects in Indonesia." *Construction Management & Economics,* January 1997: 83–94.

McEnaney, M. "Cost Overruns Plague California DMV Automation Project." *Computerworld,* January 20, 1986: 15.

Milgrom, P., and J. Roberts, "Complementarities and Fit: Strategies, Structure and Organizational Change in Manufacturing." *Journal of Accounting and Economics,* 19, no. 2–3, 179–208.

Miller, P., and T. O'Leary, "Capital Budgeting Practices and Complementarity Relations in the Transition to Modern Manufacture: A Field-Based Analysis." *Journal of Accounting Research,* 35, no. 2, 257–271.

Ottman, J. "Product Take-Back Is a New Marketing Tool." *Marketing News,* January 20, 1997: 8.

Chapter 15

Aldea, D. M., and Bullinger, D. E. "Using ABC for Shared Services, Charge-Outs, Activity-Based Budgeting, and Benchmarking." In *Activity-Based Management: Arthur Andersen's Lessons from the ABM Battlefield.* S. Player and D. E. Keys, eds. New York: John Wiley & Sons, 1999: 152–58.

Asada, T., J. Bailes, and M. Amano. "An Empirical Study of Japanese and American Budget Planning and Control Systems." Working paper, Tsu Kuba University and Oregon State University, 1989.

Borjesson, S. "A Case Study on Activity-Based Budgeting," *Journal of Cost Management* 10, no. 4: 7–18.

Brimson, J., and J. Antos. *Driving Value Using Activity Based Budgeting.* New York: John Wiley & Sons, 1999.

Collins, J. "Advanced Use of ABM: Using ABC for Target Costing, Activity-Based Budgeting, and Benchmarking." In *Activity-Based Management: Arthur Andersen's Lessons from the ABM Battlefield.* S. Player and D. E. Keys, eds. New York: John Wiley & Sons, 1999: 152–58.

Hornyak, S. "Budgeting Made Easy." *Management Accounting,* October 1998: 18–23.

Kaplan, R. S., and R. Cooper. *Cost and Effect.* Boston: Harvard Business School Press, 1998: 301–15.

McLemore, I. "Reinventing the Budget." *Controller,* August 1998: 87–90.

Chapter 16

Adler, P. "Time and Motion Regained." *Harvard Business Review,* January/February 1993: 97–108.

Anderson, S. W., and K. Sedatole. "Designing Quality into Products: "The Use of Accounting Data in New Product Development." *Accounting Horizons,* September 1998: 213–233.

Boll, D. "How Dutch Pantry Accounts for Standard Costs." *Management Accounting,* October 1982: 32.

Bonsack, A. "Does Activity-Based Costing Replace Standard Costing?" *Journal of Cost Management,* Winter 1990: 46–47.

"Boosting Productivity at American Express." *Business Week,* October 5, 1981.

Carr, L., and C. Ittner. "Measuring the Cost of Ownership." *Journal of Cost Management,* Fall 1992: 42–51.

Cooper, R. *When Lean Enterprises Collide.* Boston: Harvard Business School Press, 1995: 241–42.

Cornick, M., W. Cooper, and S. Wilson. "How Do Companies Analyze Overhead?" *Management Accounting,* June 1997.

Ellram, L. M. "Activity-Based Costing and Total Cost of Ownership: A Critical Linkage." *Journal of Cost Management,* Winter 1994: 22–30.

Gaiser, B. "German Cost Management Systems." *Journal of Cost Management,* September/October 1997: 35–41.

Gaumnitz, B. R., and F. P. Kollaritsch. "Manufacturing Variances: Current Practices and Trends." *Journal of Cost Management,* Spring 1991: 58–64.

Johnson, H. T. "Performance Measurement for Competitive Excellence." In *Measures for Manufacturing Excellence.* R. S. Kaplan, ed. Boston: Harvard Business School Press, 1990: 63–90.

Kaplan, R. S. "Limitations of Cost Accounting in Advanced Manufacturing Environments." In *Measures for Manufacturing Excellence.* Robert S. Kaplan, ed. Boston: Harvard Business School Press, 1990: 1–14.

Monden, Y., and K. Hamada. "Target Costing and Kaizen Costing in Japanese Automobile Companies." *Journal of Management Accounting Research* 3 (1991): 16–17.

Monden, Y., and J. Lee. "How a Japanese Auto Maker Reduces Costs." *Management Accounting,* August 1993: 24.

Moscove, S. A. "Enhancing Detective Controls through Performance Reporting." *Journal of Cost Management,* Summer 1988: 4–14.

Patell, J. M. "Cost Accounting, Process Control, and Product Design: A Case Study of the Hewlett-Packard Personal Office Computer Division." *The Accounting Review,* October 1987: 808–37.

Schiff, J. B. "ABC at Lederle." *Management Accounting,* August 1993: 58.

Sukurai, M. "The Influence of Factory Automation on Management Accounting Practices: A Study of Japanese Companies." In *Measures for Manufacturing Excellence,* Robert S. Kaplan, ed. Boston: Harvard Business School Press, 1990: 39–62.

Suris, O. "How Ford Cut Costs on Its Taurus, Little by Little." *The Wall Street Journal,* B1 and B8.

"Up to Speed: United Parcel Service Gets Deliveries Done by Driving Its Workers." *The Wall Street Journal.*

Chapter 17

Gaiser, B. "German Cost Management Systems." *Journal of Cost Management,* September/October 1997: 35–41.

Greeson, C. B., and M. C. Kocakulah. "Implementing an ABC Pilot at Whirlpool." *Journal of Cost Management,* March/April 1997: 16–21.

Kaplan, R. S. "Flexible Budgeting in an Activity-Based Costing Framework." *Accounting Horizons,* June 1994: 104–9.

Mak, Y. T., and M. L. Roush. "Flexible Budgeting and Variance Analysis in an Activity-Based Costing Environment." *Accounting Horizons,* June 1994: 93–103.

Malcolm, R. E. "Overhead Control Implications of Activity Costing." *Accounting Horizons,* December 1991: 69–78.

Moscove, S. A. "Enhancing Detective Controls through Performance Reporting." *Journal of Cost Management,* March/April 1998: 28.

Ruhl, J. M. "Activity-Based Variance Analysis." *Journal of Cost Management,* July/August 1994: 38–47.

Chapter 18

Borthick, F., and H. P. Roth. "EDI for Re-engineering Business Processes." *Management Accounting,* October 1993: 32–37.

Cooper, R. *When Lean Enterprises Collide.* Boston: Harvard Business School Press, 1995: 106–7.

Gaiser, B. "German Cost Management Systems." *Journal of Cost Management,* September/October 1997: 35, 38–40.

McMann, P. "You May Need New Performance Measures When . . ." *Journal of Strategic Performance Measurement,* February/March 1998: 13.

McNair, C. J. "Interdependence and Control: Traditional vs. Activity-Based Responsibility Accounting." *Journal of Cost Management,* Summer 1990: 15–23.

Villers, R. R. "Control and Freedom in a Decentralized Company." *Harvard Business Review,* July/August 1954: 817–96.

Chapter 19

Benke, R., and J. Edwards. *Transfer Pricing: Techniques and Uses.* New York: National Association of Accountants, 1980.

Borkowski, S. "Environmental and Organizational Factors Affecting Transfer Pricing: A Survey." *Journal of Management Accounting Research* 2 (1990): 1–15.

Current Practices, Perceptions and Trends: Transfer Pricing — 1997. Global Survey (Chicago: Ernst & Young, 1997).

FASB. *Statement of Financial Accounting Standards No. 14.* "Financial Reporting for Segments of a Business Enterprise." Stamford, CT: FASB, 1976.

FASB. *Statement of Financial Accounting Standards No. 69.* "Disclosures About Oil and Gas Producing Activities." Stamford, CT: FASB, 1982.

Tang, R. "Canadian Transfer Pricing Practices." *CA Magazine,* March 1980.

Tang, R. "Transfer Pricing in the 1990s." *Management Accounting,* February 1991: 25.

Tang, R., C. Walter, and R. Raymond. "Transfer Pricing—Japanese vs. American Style." *Management Accounting,* January 1978.

Chapter 20

Chow, C., et al. "Applying the Balanced Scorecard to Smaller Companies." *Management Accounting,* August 1997: 21–27.

Chow, C., K. Haddad, and J. Williamson. "Applying the Balanced Scorecard to Small Companies." *Management Accounting,* August 1997: 21–27.

"Doing Well by Doing Good." *The Economist,* April 22, 2000: 65–67.

Epstein, M., and J. F. Manzoni. "The Balanced Scorecard and Tableau de Board: Translating Strategy into Action." *Management Accounting,* August 1997: 28–36.

"How Corporations Snoop to Conquer." *Business Week,* October 28, 1996.

Ittner, C. D., D. F. Larcker, and M. W. Meyer. 2000. "The Use of Subjectivity in Multi-Criteria Bonus Plans." Working paper, The Wharton School, 2000.

Ittner, C., and D. Larcker. "Are Non-financial Measures Leading Indicators of Financial Performance?" *Journal of Accounting Research* 36 (supplement): 1–35.

Kaplan, R. S. "Measuring Corporate Performance: The Balanced Scorecard," Harvard Business School Publishing, VHS/NTSC Video, 1993.

Kaplan, R. S., and D. P. Norton. *The Balanced Scorecard.* Boston, MA: Harvard Business School Press, 1996.

Kaplan, R. S., and D. P. Norton. *The Strategy-Focused Organization.* Boston, MA: Harvard Business School Press, 2000.

Kurtzman, J. "Is Your Company Off Course? Now You Can Find Out Why." *Fortune,* February 17, 1997: 128–30.

Lipe, M. G., and S. Salterio. "The Balanced Scorecard: Judgmental Effects of Information Organization and Diversity." *The Accounting Review* 75, July: 283–298.

Malina, M. "An Empirical Test of a Causal Balanced Scorecard." Working paper, University of Colorado at Boulder, 2001.

Malina, M., and F. Selto. "Communicating and Controlling Strategy: An Empirical Study of the Effectiveness of the Balanced Scorecard" *Journal of Management Accounting Research,* 2001.

Mullaney, T. "Needed: The Human Touch," *Business Week,* Dec. 13, 1999.

Rucci, A., S. Kirn, and R. Quinn. "The Employee-Customer-Profit Chain at Sears." *Harvard Business Review,* January–February, 1998: 83–97.

Strand, C., et al. "Are Your Vendors Stealing from You?" *Strategic Finance,* October 2000: 66–71.

Weintraub, A. "He's Not Playing," *Business Week,* July 24, 2000.

Chapter 21

Anthony, R. N., and D. W. Young. *Management Control in Nonprofit Organizations.*

Banker, R., G. Potter, and D. Srinivasan. "An Empirical Investigation of an Incentive Plan that Includes Nonfinancial Performance Measures." *The Accounting Review* 75: 65–92.

Biddle, G., R. Bowen, and J. Wallace. "Economic Value Added: Some Empirical EVAdence."

Biddle, G. C., R. M. Bowen, and J. S. Wallace. "Does EVA® Beat Earnings? Evidence on Associations with Stock Returns and Firm Values." *Journal of Accounting and Economics,* 1997, v24 (3, Dec.), 301–336.

Billitteri, T. "Seeking an Option on Pay," *The Chronicle of Philanthropy,* March 25, 1999.

Bromwich, M., and M. Walker. "Residual Income Past and Future." *Management Accounting Research* 5, no. 9: 391–419.

Butter, S., and M. Maher. Management Compensation Plans.

Carson, B. executive secretary of the Hawkeye (Iowa) Labor Council. (*www.gazetteonline.com/monev/mon207.htm*)

Clolrery, P. "NPT Salary Survey." *The NonProfit Times,* February 1, 2000.

Cooper, R., and R. Slagmulder. "Micro Profit Centers." *Management Accounting,* June 1998.

Dierks, P. A., and A. Patel. "What Is EVA® and How Can It Help Your Company?"

Freedman, J. "New Research Red Flags EVA® for Stock Picks."

Green, T. B. *Performance and Motivation Strategies for Today's Workforce: A Guide to Expectancy Theory Applications.*

Hall, B. "What You Need to Know about Stock Options." *Harvard Business Review,* March–April 2000: 121–200.

Harrisburg Hospital v. Dauphin County Board of Assessment Appeals. Commonwealth Court of Pennsylvania 708 A.2d 1284 (1998).

Healy, P. "The Effect of Bonus Schemes on Accounting Procedure and Accrual Decisions." *Journal of Accounting and Economics* 7, no. 1: 85–107.

Ibbotson and Associates, *Cost of Capital Quarterly. www.valuation.ibbotson.com.*

Ittner, C., and D. Larcker. "Innovations in Performance Measurement: Trends and Research Implications." *Journal of Management Accounting Research* 1998: 205–38.

Ittner, C., and D. Larcker. "The Use of Subjectivity in Multi-Criteria Bonus Plans." Working paper, The Wharton School, 1999.

Kadet, A. "Put Your Money Where Our Math Is." *Smart Money,* November 10, 2000.

Kerr, S. "On the Folly of Rewarding A While Hoping for B."

Maher, M. "The Use of Relative Performance Evaluation in Organizations."

Malina, M., and F. Selto, "Communicating and Controlling Strategy: An Empirical Investigation of the Effectiveness of the Balanced Scorecard." *Journal of Management Accounting Research,* 2001.

Maremont, M. "Blind Ambition," *Business Week,* October 23, 1995.

Maremont, M. "Judgment Day at Bausch & Lomb," *Business Week,* December 25, 1995.

Ouchi, W. "A Conceptual Framework for the Design of Organizational Control Mechanisms."

Payne, M. "Employee Theft a Rising Concern." *Sacramento Bee,* December 3, 2000.

Quinn, L. "Accounting Sleuths," *Strategic Finance,* October 2000: 55–64.

Rappaport, A. *Creating Shareholder Value: A Guide for Managers and Investors.* Free Press, 1997.

Reingold, J., and F. Jespersen. "Executive Pay." *Business Week.*

"Report of the Audit Committee to the Board of Directors, Income Transferal and Other Practices," H. J. Heinz Company, p. 9.

Sapir, A., and I. Reinbergs, "Bausch & Lomb, Inc.: Pressure to Perform." Harvard Business School Case 9-198-009.

Smith, G. "A Famous Brand on a Rocky Road," *Business Week,* December 1, 2000.

Smith, G. "Life Won't Be Just a Bowl of Jerry Garcia." *Business Week,* July 18, 1994.

Spinner, K. "Signed and Sealed—But Can EVA® Deliver?"

Stark, R. "Polaroid: Managing Environmental Responsibilities and Their Costs," Harvard Business School Case 9-194-052.

Wallace, J. S. "Adopting Residual Income-Based Compensation Plans: Do You Get What You Pay For?"

Zeune, G. "Are You Teaching Your Employees to Steal?" *Strategic Finance,* August 2000: 34–39.

Company Name Index

Subject Index

You're the Decision Maker Boxes